BIRDS TO WATCH 2
The World List of Threatened Birds

The Official Source for Birds on the IUCN Red List

N. J. Collar, M. J. Crosby and A. J. Stattersfield

BirdLife®
INTERNATIONAL

Distributed in the Americas by Smithsonian Institution Press, Washington, DC

ISBN 1 56098 528 3

Series editor   Duncan Brooks
Design   CBA (Cambridge) and Duncan Brooks
Layout and indexing   Duncan Brooks, Regina Pfaff

Text set in Times (9/11 pt), Optima and Delphin

Imageset by Spire Origination (Norwich)
Printed and bound in Great Britain by Page Bros (Norwich) Ltd

Cover illustration   Two species from the forests of the Hawaiian Islands, drawn by Norman Arlott: Nukupuu *Hemignathus lucidus* (upper, p. 195) and Akialoa *H. obscurus* (lower, p. 212). The latter is probably already extinct.

DEDICATED TO

HRH Prince Bernhard of the Netherlands

BY THE *Rare Bird Club*

BIRDS TO WATCH 2 IS SPECIALLY SPONSORED BY
THE FOLLOWING MEMBERS

CONTENTS

ACKNOWLEDGEMENTS

HIS ROYAL HIGHNESS Prince Bernhard of the Netherlands receives the dedication of this book from the members of the Rare Bird Club, which was established by BirdLife International in 1988, the year of the first *Birds to watch*, to help save the thousand bird species which that book had identified as in danger of extinction. On behalf of the entire BirdLife Partnership we add a ringing endorsement of that dedication to someone whose long years of service to the cause of conservation around the world represent a record of inspirational leadership and incalculable achievement. His honorary presidency of the Rare Bird Club has given it focus and force, and everyone associated with it knows how powerful an influence he has been in its growth and direction. We salute him.

Also on behalf of the BirdLife Partnership, we express our enormous gratitude to the **Rare Bird Club** itself for six years of solid support, and for the collective contribution that made this book possible. To be able to set and pursue long-term targets with confidence, and to respond to short-term demands with speed, every organization needs the strength and flexibility that comes from security: the Rare Bird Club has brought that security to BirdLife International, and we are delighted to be able to pay this public tribute to the vital role which the Club continues to play.

This book is authored by three people serving as a conduit and filter of information provided, in many and various forms, by hundreds. Many are identified in the text against the data which they have contributed, but it should not be forgotten that negative evidence is no less helpful in the process of species status evaluation: a book like this depends so heavily on material that does *not* get published that it is actually very hard to keep track of all the sources that have helped decide its final content, so if we cause offence to any of BirdLife's many friends and supporters by the omission of their name, we apologize most sincerely.

It should also not be forgotten that this book's predecessors, *Threatened birds of Africa and related islands* (1985), *Birds to watch* (1988) and *Threatened birds of the Americas* (1992), themselves drew on the knowledge and experience of hundreds of informants, and that this material is the foundation for the present study. Particularly because *Threatened birds of the Americas* is so recent, relatively little new input was sought from the New World beyond what was available through the literature or the unprompted contributions of our network, so the 550 people acknowledged in that book are owed a second round of thanks for their part in the shaping of this new study. In a similar vein, the many contributors to BirdLife's *Putting biodiversity on the map* (1992) helped to generate the BirdLife Biodiversity Project Database on which *Birds to watch 2* has drawn substantially, and they too deserve double thanks. Then we must also express our gratitude to the constituency of European conservationists who supplied the data in BirdLife's *Birds in Europe: their conservation status* (1994), another major source of information for this study.

In a real sense, then, these acknowledgements are but the tip of the iceberg that makes up both the formal and informal BirdLife network. The following are, for this particular exercise, its visible parts, and we thank them all: A. Adhikerana, W. J. Adsett, P. D. Alexander-Marrack, D. G. Allan, D. Allen, P. Alström, P. Andrew, G. W. Archibald, T. Arndt, J. S. Ash, D. R. Aspinwall, J. D. Atkins, P. Atkinson, M. Aurivillius, C. Attié, M. Aviss, S. Baha El Din, A. J. Baker, N. E. Baker, D. Baker-Gabb, C. S. Balchin, M. I. Bampi, A. J. Bartle, T. Beai, M. A. S. Beaman, R. E. Beck, B. M. Beehler, V. Belik, P. Bennett, L. A. Bennun, A. Berruti, B. J. Best, J. M. Black, A. Blade, R. van Bocxstaele, G. Boere, P. Boesman, N. Bostock, M. Boulet, C. G. R. Bowden, J. Bowler, H. L. Bregulla, V. Bretagnolle, N. Brickle, M. de L. Brooke, R. K. Brooke, T. M. Brooks, D. F. Bruning, J. Bryden, P. Bulens, A. Burbidge, N. D. Burgess, T. Burr, S. H. M. Butchart, Y. Cahyadin, C. A. R. Carvalho, M. C. Catsis, P. Christy, J. Clay, N. Cleere, S. Clegg, B. J. Coates, J. Cooper, P. Coopmans, N. J. Cordeiro, A. J. Crivelli, A. J. Cruikshank, D. Cunningham, R. L. Curry, J. Curson, T. Dahmer, M. Dakki, A. Danks, P. Davidson, S. Davies, A. Davis, G. W. H. Davison, W. R. J. Dean, P. A. Dejaifve, R. W. R. J. Dekker, J. M. Diamond, R. J. Dowsett, J. W. Duckworth, A. Duncan, J. C. Durbin, J. C. Eames, A. Elliott, E. C. Enkerlin, K. R. Ennis, S. Ericsson, P. Escalante, C. F. Estades, J. Estudillo López, O. Evans, T. D. Evans, W. T.

Everett, P. Feldmann, M. Felley, T. H. Fisher, B. W. Finch, D. Finch, T. H. Fisher, J. Fjeldså, T. Flannery, B. Flint, A. D. Forbes-Watson, B. C. Forrester, R. C. Fotso, M. Fowler, D. Franklin, C. Frith, D. Frith, M. D. Gallagher, I. Gardner, S. Garnett, P. J. Garson, A. J. Gaston, R. Gnam, A. Grajal, L. P. Gonzaga, P. C. Gonzales, S. M. Goodman, P. D. Goriup, A. Green, A. Gretton, T. M. Gullick, H. Hafner, Han Lianxian, F. Hannecart, L. A. Hansen, G. N. Harrington, J. A. Hart, S. Hatch, A. F. A. Hawkins, P. V. Hayman, C. J. Hazevoet, He Fen-Qi, C. J. Heij, S. van Helvoort, H. Higuchi, R. Hill, R. Hills, T. W. Hoffmann, D. A. Holmes, J. Hornbuckle, S. N. G. Howell, J. del Hoyo, S. A. Hussain, N. Ichida, M. B. Iles, M. J. Imber, J. Innes, C. Inskipp, T. P. Inskipp, M. P. S. Irwin, M. Jäderblad, D. F. Jeggo, A. Jensen, C. G. Jones, M. J. Jones, P. J. Jones, P. M. B. Kasoma, G. Kattan, M. Katti, R. Kaul, R. S. Kennedy, V. V. Khrokov, W. B. King, K. M. Kisokau, J. Kiure, J. Komen, S. W. Kotagama, G. R. Kula, C. Lalas, F. R. Lambert, C. Landa, O. Langrand, M. Languy, A. Ledru, A. Lees, T. Lehmberg, Y. Létocart, A. Lewis, J. Lewis, A. Lieberman, Lim Kim Keang, G. Loh, R. H. Loyn, A. Luy, S. C. Madge, A. Madroño Nieto, P. Magsalay, K. Martin, J. E. Martínez Gómez, P. Martuscelli, S. Maturin, S. Mayer, I. McAllan, M. N. McCulloch, K. McDermond, M. A. McDonald, P. J. K. McGowan, J. McKean, D. McNiven, D. S. Melville, D. V. Merton, J. E. Miskell, C. M. Miskelly, C. O. F. Mlingwa, C. W. Moeliker, J. Molloy, P. J. Moore, K. Morgan, P. Morris, D. C. Moyer, Rishad Naoroji, A. J. Negret, D. N. Nettleship, J. Neville, P. Njoroge, R. Noske, E. Nowak, C. J. R. O'Donnell, L. G. Olarte, Y. Oniki, P. Osborne, J. F. Pacheco, T. Palliser, Park Jin-Young, V. Parker, B. Patton, M. Pearman, A. Perry, S. L. Pimm, C. Poole, V. Prakesh, R. Pyle, A. R. Rahmani, R. K. Ramunujam, M. Rank, S. M. A. Rashid, P. Raust, R. H. Raza, N. J. Redman, L. M. Renjifo, D. Rinke, H. Robertson, I. S. Robertson, O. Robinet, C. R. Robson, D. D. Roby, D. Rockingham-Gill, W. Rodenburg, P. Rodewald, P. D. Round, D. Rounsevell, R. A. Rowlett, F. G. Rozendaal, H. Rumpff, Y. Rusila Noor, B. L. Rusk, P. Salaman, G. Sangster, R. Sankaran, R. J. Safford, D. E. Sargeant, S. Sawyer, T. S. Schulenberg, P. Scofield, D. A. Scott, T. Searock, J. Seitre, R. Seitre, L. Liu Severinghaus, F. H. Sheldon, T. W. Sherry, M. Silvius, J. C. Sinclair, P. Singh, S. Sirgouant, N. F. R. Snyder, T. Soehartono, G. Speight, A. Shull, J.-C. Stahl, N. Stead, J. Stevenson, T. Stevenson, F. G. Stiles, D. W. Stinson, D. F. Stotz, F. C. Straube, N. Stronach, S. N. Stuart, A. Studer, K. Sugimura, J. O. Svendsen, P. O. Syvertsen, Tan Yao-Kuang, W. R. Tarboton, G. A. Taylor, P. B. Taylor, P. M. Taylor, K. Teeb'ai, S. A. Temple, J.-C. Thibault, H. S. S. Thompson, R. J. Timmins, J. Tobias, W. D.

Toone, D. B. Trent, R. Trevelyan, D. M. Tully, D. A. Turner, A. Tye, A. Varney, F. J. Vilella, P. Villard, M. Z. A. Virani, Vo Quy, K. Walker, J. G. Walmsley, D. Watling, J. Watson, H. P. Webb, G. R. Welch, H. J. Welch, D. R. Wells, A. Whittaker, R. S. R. Williams, D. Willis, J. R. Wilson, J. Wind, D. B. Wingate, J. A. Wolstencroft, Won Pyong-Oh, P. Wood, C. A. Woods, Wu Zhikang, the late Y. Yamashina, C. Yamashita, D. Yong, H. G. Young, Zhang Zheng-Wang, Zheng Guang-Mei, B. Zhou, Zhou Fang, F. Zino.

A special vote of thanks, for assistance on a major scale over the length of this project, either with the direct provision of information or with arranging for such provision, goes to Brian D. Bell, K. D. Bishop, D. Buckingham, I. Burrows, R. F. Burrows, J. P. Croxall, G. C. L. Dutson, K. Fitzherbert, D. Gibbs, P. Gregory, G. McCormack, T. Mundkur, H. D. Pratt, R. S. Ridgely, A. J. Tennyson and other colleagues at the Department of Conservation in New Zealand, and B. M. Whitney.

Several names above are of chairmen or members of BirdLife specialist groups (some of which are run in association with the International Waterfowl and Wetlands Research Bureau and the World Pheasant Association, and all of which are affiliated to IUCN's Species Survival Commission), and we express our gratitude to all groups (and to IWRB and WPA) for their help. We particularly thank the BirdLife/WPA Pheasant Specialist Group Core Committee for access to unpublished material and the draft Pheasant Action Plan, and for commenting on the draft pheasant texts.

I. Dawson of the library at the Royal Society for the Protection of Birds, and L. Birch at the Alexander Library, Edward Grey Institute, were as obliging and understanding as ever during our literature searches. G. M. Mace worked with us on categorization problems, and kindly reviewed the second chapter, on the new IUCN criteria. We take this opportunity to emphasize the exceptional importance of museum material in generating high-resolution data, and of BirdLife's special indebtedness to the many institutions that allow us access to their collections.

The entire staff at the BirdLife Secretariat in Cambridge, U.K., has helped with this book, if only by contributing to the remarkable community feeling that makes work there so enjoyable, whatever the hour. Among them we must identify for their special help: J. Barnes, C. J. Bibby, N. D. Coulthard, A. C. Dunn, M. I. Evans, J. H. Fanshawe, J. Fenton, R. F. A. Grimmett, M. F. Heath, B. Heredia, M. L. Hines, Ch. Imboden, M. G. Kelsey, J. S. Loughlin, N. Parker, M. R. Parnwell, R. Phillips Farfán, R. F. Porter, M. K. Poulsen, M. R. W. Rands, S. Squire, L. Stanton,

R. Wirth and D. B. Sinclair. We particularly thank G. A. Allport, L. D. C. Fishpool, A. J. Long, G. M. Tucker and D. C. Wege for their major contributions of support over many months, and four volunteer workers, R. P. Clay, D. Gandy, J. C. Lowen and A. Saltmarsh, for their enthusiastic assistance. We register—as much in awe as in gratitude—the professionalism, dedication and skill of D. J. Brooks and R. Pfaff in preparing the text for publication, and the former's formidable editorial authority and sheer work-station stamina.

The BirdLife Indonesia Programme coordinated data-gathering for Indonesia, and provided much new information itself. We especially thank S. van Balen, who had lead responsibility for compiling the data, and P. Jepson for their crucial help in this work. Full acknowledgement of all contributors will be given in the Indonesian translation of the relevant parts of *Birds to watch 2* in 1995, but we must also here register our gratitude to the Asian Wetlands Bureau Indonesia Programme for its participation in the work.

The Asian Continental Section of ICBP, now the BirdLife Asian Partnership, through the work of its Chairman, N. Ichida, and Vice-Chairman, S. A. Hussain, advised us over the integration of our data-gathering activities with those planned for *Threatened birds of Asia*. We are most grateful for their counsel.

Continuing support for BirdLife's Red Data Book programme is provided by the Bromley Trust, to which we offer our warmest thanks.

Finally here we remember with deep affection and sorrow Ted Parker, who was a co-author of *Threatened birds of the Americas*, on which this book draws so heavily, and whose death in 1993 was a catastrophic blow to the cause of wildlife conservation in the Western Hemisphere. This happened before work on *Birds to watch 2* had begun, but we have so much information from him on file that he still played a major part in the shaping of the book. A special issue of BirdLife's journal *Bird Conservation International* will appear next year in his memory.

BIRDS TO WATCH IN CONTEXT

AT THE 1992 Earth Summit in Rio de Janeiro biological diversity rose from its humble origins in the recondite vocabulary of tropical ecologists to become a new influence in the social, economic and political thinking of late twentieth century man. The coming into force of the Convention on Biological Diversity, on 29 December 1993, was perhaps final confirmation that the conservation of nature has attained an appropriate level on the global agenda of the community of nations.

The community of conservationists accordingly rejoiced, but not for long; there is not the time. After years of struggling to find a voice, to find a *message*, with which to articulate the truth about the fate of the planet's wildlife, the winning formula proved to be one in which generality was crucial. Tales of the plight of tigers, dolphins, beetles and even the rosy periwinkle—that hardy perennial of the utilitarian dreamscape—had ultimately failed; yet, as virtual stowaways in the ark called biodiversity, all these things have suddenly found a possible future. So now the urgent challenge to conservation is to be specific once more, but this time in an orderly, rational manner that optimizes the integration of its aspirations with those of wider human development.

Part of the challenge lies in simply defining biodiversity, deciding what strategies are most appropriate to which of its components, and setting priorities in terms of relative values and time limits. Information is of course the fuel that drives this process but, like fuel, its value depends on its refinement and on its adaptability to different needs. Since it is, after all, those elements of biodiversity which the planet is likely to lose that should be the prime target of conservation (Collar 1994a), there are two plain steps to be taken: identify and document the potential losses from the global stock of biodiversity, and identify and document the sites on the planet where those potential losses can be saved in the most cost-effective aggregations.

BirdLife International (formerly the International Council for Bird Preservation, ICBP), has consist-

ently practised and pioneered both these activities over the past decade. It has focused on those elements of the global avifauna that are most fragile: threatened and near-threatened species, species with restricted ranges, species exposed to danger by their dependence on vulnerable habitats, species beyond the reach of protected-area networks. The conversion of the resulting mass of data into user-friendly packages that make sites rather than species the units of concern (since 1989 under the label of 'Important Bird Areas') has merely been the logical extension of the refinement process, and will serve as the central plank of BirdLife policy and programme for the remainder of the millenium.

This is not to pretend that the goals of biodiversity conservation can be met simply through a series of species-driven but site-oriented initiatives to create a network of variously protected areas. As Imboden (1994) has pointed out, the problem with a *net*work is that it is full of holes. The impact of human development on our planet is incurring virtually unquantifiable but assuredly massive losses of biodiversity through the steady, undramatic erosion of populations of thousands of species of animals and plants which, *as species*, are currently regarded as secure. The challenge here is one that only a collective acceptance of responsibility and a broad commitment of resources can overcome: Imboden's concept of an 'ecoblanket', to catch and hold the diversity of nature through the assignation of purposely defined functions to all parts of the landscape, sketches out the basis for a new kind of thinking and planning that will help to harmonize the integration of conservation and development in the twenty-first century.

BIRDS TO WATCH AND THE RED DATA BOOK

The most basic of all BirdLife's commitments remains, however, the prevention of global extinction through the identification and documentation of threatened species. Red Data Books (RDBs) were instituted 30 years ago, in 1964, for this precise purpose, and their compilation has been a part of the BirdLife programme ever since. The first *Birds to watch* came into being in response to calls for an annotated list of all globally threatened birds, to fill the information gap that was arising as parts of the international bird Red Data Book were being prepared. After two early versions (Vincent 1966–1971, King 1978–1979), the third 'edition' of the RDB was initiated in 1981 and has been anticipated to take the form of four parts, for Africa (Collar and Stuart 1985), the Americas (Collar *et al.* 1992), Asia (volume now being planned; see below) and Australasia and the Pacific, possibly with the inclusion of the (non-Asian) Holarctic. The delay between parts has not, it should be stressed, reflected the time it takes to compile them—rather the availability of manpower and money (Collar 1994b); but irrespective of this issue, it was still clear that a single volume, serving as an abbreviated RDB, would keep track of the plight of species already treated in past RDBs, and highlight the plight of many others due for full treatment in future RDBs.

This, then, is a replacement volume of a book first published six years ago (Collar and Andrew 1988). Bearing almost the same title, and dealing in the same basic manner with the same subject, this new work has the character of a second edition; nevertheless, it represents an entirely new evaluation of the world's threatened bird species, using new criteria, a more standardized presentation of the texts, and some overview analysis of the data.

One obvious difficulty with the *Birds to watch* approach is the difference in data quality influencing the evaluation of species' status. Those that have not yet been fully investigated or treated by the RDB process cannot be judged with the same degree of confidence as many of those that have. It is particularly difficult to be confident of the appropriate categorization of species (the first *Birds to watch* did not even attempt this; merely identifying threatened species was challenge enough). We must stress that considerable effort and thought (outlined below) have been invested in our reviews of Asia, Australasia and the Pacific (and, in the case of Australia, we were able to draw directly on an independently produced analysis of threatened birds by Garnett 1992, 1993). However, because the consultation process was necessarily constrained by considerations of time and budget, the listings of species from these regions should be regarded as candidate lists for *Threatened birds of Asia*, a project of the BirdLife Asian Partnership (supported by the Environmental Agency of Japan through the Wild Bird Society of Japan) beginning in 1994, and, in due course, for the fourth

volume that will complete the third edition of the RDB.

Birds to watch 2 was begun in the third quarter of 1993, with the target of completion by the time of the BirdLife World Conference in Rosenheim, Germany, in August 1994, and with the intention that this second edition should use the new criteria for evaluating threatened species being developed (with BirdLife's participation) for IUCN. As it happened, the finalization of the IUCN committee's proposals took until November 1993, but even as we worked on the book we identified certain problems and actually caused a few minor adjustments to be made to the criteria as late as May 1994; so the book and the criteria have developed together.

Finally here it should be noted that BirdLife's Red Data Book programme is the source of birds treated on the 'IUCN Red List' series. However, the most recent Red List (Groombridge 1993a) was revised at a stage when work on *Birds to watch 2* was only just beginning, and it was agreed that the 1994 Red List would conflate species from its 1990 list (derived from the first *Birds to watch*) with those from *Threatened birds of the Americas*. In other words, the 1994 Red List has a very different composition of bird species from *Birds to watch 2*. Nevertheless, *Birds to watch 2* is the official source for birds for the IUCN Red List, so the list of threatened birds it contains replaces the list in Groombridge (1993a).

DATA-GATHERING

Candidate lists for the project existed in the form of species listed as threatened and near-threatened in Collar and Stuart (1985), Collar and Andrew (1988) and Collar *et al.* (1992), species identified in Stattersfield *et al.* (in prep.) as being of restricted range (<50,000 km²; see ICBP 1992), and species characterized as having unfavourable conservation status in Europe (Tucker and Heath 1994). The BirdLife Secretariat library holdings (which includes correspondence files for hundreds of fieldworkers and observers) are constantly extended and updated with material on all such species and the topics relating to their conservation, and these, together with the distributional database compiled during BirdLife's Biodiversity Project (see ICBP 1992, Crosby 1994), provided the bulk of further material. However, recent literature was also surveyed in the Zoology Library, Scientific Periodicals Library and University Library, Cambridge, the RSPB Library, Sandy, and the Alexander (Edward Grey Institute) Library, Oxford, U.K.

From these sources draft texts were prepared and sent for review. The list for Europe had the benefit of input from the many sources brought together in Tucker and Heath (1994). For Africa, the review was fairly extensive, since the African RDB has now been in print for nine years. For the Americas, the review was much more limited, since the Americas RDB is only two years old. For Australasia and the Pacific, the target was to have each species text reviewed at least once. For Asia, the review was confined to a small number of experts, since the full RDB programme is shortly to begin, and there was concern not to cause confusion by a major review at this stage; for this reason, the Asian species list remains provisional and awaits fuller evaluation in the impending RDB programme. The Australasia and Pacific lists are also essentially provisional (except for Australia, for which a recent formal in-country assessment has been used).

Data for the Indonesian species texts were compiled with the full participation of the BirdLife Indonesia Programme, chiefly by S. van Balen and P. Jepson, who organized the review of draft texts by a small number of experts in-country.

Contributions from users of this book—corrections, commentary, updates—are always welcome and will be stored for future reference and/or passed to the relevant BirdLife Partner organizations. Information concerning Asian species will be particularly timely, and be used in *Threatened birds of Asia*.

TAXONOMY, NAMES AND TERMS

The collision between the phylogenetic and biological species concepts has deprived the world of a broadly accepted list of bird species. Previously the bird RDB, like CITES, used Morony *et al.* (1975) as the basic list, but the publication of Sibley and Monroe (1990, 1993), for all the controversy surrounding this work, could not long be ignored. In March 1992 CITES officially adopted this new list as its taxonomic guide, and it was also adopted by ICBP in its study of global centres of endemism (ICBP 1992). We do likewise, but not without points of divergence (see below), and like CITES we retain the sequence of families as in Morony *et al.* (1975), accepting the need for stability in macrosystematics until judgements on avian relationships are more widely and confidently agreed (see Mayr and Bock 1994). This arrangement has, however, led to certain sequential anomalies in the large subfamilies of thrushes (Turdinae) and babblers (Timaliinae).

The points of divergence on species limits particularly refer to Africa, where some of the judgements in Sibley and Monroe (1990) have been subject to review and rejection by Dowsett and Forbes-Watson (1993) and Dowsett and Dowsett-Lemaire (1993). We have largely followed the opinions of

these latter authors, although in a number of cases we have retained or advanced specific status based on earlier RDB listing or else on the recent evidence of fieldworkers. Elsewhere in the world we have sometimes accepted forms elevated to species status in evaluations too recent to be in Sibley and Monroe (1990, 1993); all cases where our own judgements have prevailed are explicit in the species texts and listed here in Box 1. Some other potential splits were brought to our attention by reviewers (Box 2), but we were unable to research their taxonomic and conservation status in the time available. What certainly emerges here is the considerable discrepancy between the recent levels of taxonomic scrutiny in the Americas and those elsewhere in the world, suggesting that many more forms are liable for future elevation to species level in the Old World.

> **Box 1. Species additional to Sibley and Monroe (1990, 1993).**
>
> Any species recognized by us but not by Sibley and Monroe (1990, 1993) has a comment indicating this in the text. In addition, we list these birds here.
>
> Newell's Shearwater *Puffinus newelli*
> Dwarf Olive Ibis *Bostrychia bocagei*
> Udzungwa Forest-partridge *Xenoperdix udzungwensis*
> Chatham Islands Oystercatcher *Haematopus chathamensis*
> Veracruz Quail-dove *Geotrygon carrikeri*
> Seychelles Scops-owl *Otus insularis*
> Anjouan Scops-owl *Otus capnodes*
> Bogotá Sunangel *Heliangelus zusii*
> White-chested Tinkerbird *Pogoniulus makawai*
> Atlantic Royal Flycatcher *Onychorhynchus swainsoni*
> Pacific Royal Flycatcher *Onychorhynchus occidentalis*
> Chestnut-bellied Cotinga *Doliornis remseni*
> Mauritius Bulbul *Hypsipetes olivaceus*
> Nava's Wren *Hylorchilus navai*
> Cobb's Wren *Troglodytes cobbi*
> Somali Thrush *Turdus ludoviciae*
> Taita Thrush *Turdus helleri*
> Taita Apalis *Apalis fuscigularis*
> Namuli Apalis *Apalis lynesi*
> Hainan Leaf-warbler *Phylloscopus hainanus*
> Biak Gerygone *Gerygone hypoxantha*
> Furtive Flycatcher *Ficedula disposita*
> Annobon Paradise-flycatcher *Terpsiphone smithii*
> Visayan Flowerpecker *Dicaeum haematostictum*
> Kulal White-eye *Zosterops kulalensis*
> South Pare White-eye *Zosterops winifredae*
> Taita White-eye *Zosterops silvanus*
> Rota White-eye *Zosterops rotensis*
> Black-eared Miner *Manorina melanotis*
> Chocó Vireo *Vireo* sp.
> Salvadori's Serin *Serinus xantholaema*
> Sillem's Mountain-finch *Leucosticte sillemi*

Box 2. Some threatened subspecies which may be valid species.

We have attempted to be responsive to views and judgements on species limits, but after considerable deliberation concluded that the following may require wider endorsement as full species. Nevertheless, we strongly urge recognition of their plight, as some of them are highly threatened forms (all would qualify as globally threatened), and at the national level deserve high priority.

Chatham Islands Albatross *Diomedea* (*cauta*) *eremita*: New Zealand.

Heard Island Shag *Phalacrocorax* (*atriceps*) *nivalis*: Australia.

Macquarie Island Shag *Phalacrocorax* (*atriceps*) *purpurascens*: Australia.

Mauritanian Heron *Ardea* (*cinerea*) *monicae*: Mauritania.

Cape Verde Heron *Ardea* (*purpurea*) *bournei*: Cape Verde.

Cape Verde Kite *Milvus* (*milvus*) *fasciicauda*: Cape Verde.

Cape Verde Buzzard *Buteo* (*buteo*) *bannermani*: Cape Verde.

Ryukyu Hawk-eagle *Spilornis* (*cheela*) *perplexus*: Japan.

Cape Verde Falcon *Falco* (*peregrinus*) *madens*: Cape Verde.

Hawaiian Stilt *Himantopus* (*mexicanus*) *knudseni*: Hawaiian Islands (U.S.A.).

Chatham Islands Parakeet *Cyanoramphus* (*auriceps*) *forbesi*: Chatham Islands (New Zealand).

Orange-fronted Parakeet *Cyanoramphus auriceps* (= *C. malherbi*): New Zealand.

Caatinga Black-tyrant *Knipolegus* (*aterrimus*) *franciscanus*: Brazil.

Pohnpei Cicadabird *Coracina* (*tenuirostris*) *insperatum*: Micronesia.

Yap Cicadabird *Coracina* (*tenuirostris*) *nesiotis*: Micronesia.

Kadavu Island Thrush *Turdus* (*poliocephalus*) *ruficeps*: Fiji.

Guadalcanal Thrush *Zoothera* (*margaretae*) *turipavae*: Solomon Islands.

Cinnamon Quail-thrush *Cinclosoma* (*cinnamomeum*) *alisteri*: Australia.

Manua Fiji Shrikebill *Clytorhynchus* (*vitiensis*) *powelli*: American Samoa.

Vella Lavella Monarch *Monarcha* (*browni*) *nigrotectus*: Solomon Islands.

Biak Golden Monarch *Monarcha* (*chrysomela*) *kordensis*: Indonesia.

Ugi Monarch *Monarcha* (*castaneiventris*) *ugiensis*: Solomon Islands.

Kosrae White-eye *Zosterops* (*cinerea*) *cinerea*: Micronesia.

Oahu Elepaio *Chasiempis* (*sandwichensis*) *ibidis*: Hawaiian Islands (U.S.A.).

Oahu Amakihi *Viridonia* (*virens*) *chloris*: Hawaiian Islands (U.S.A.).

English names are based as far as possible on Sibley and Monroe (1990, 1993), but again there are points of divergence, again with Africa being an area of resistance to apparently undebated alterations to long-standing names. Names of birds are an abiding cause of discussion among ornithologists, and it is clearly impossible for workers producing international lists to satisfy both the interests of uniformity and the expectations of tradition, and we would plead with all parties to see the virtues of each other's position, and to work steadily towards compromise. Meanwhile, where alternatives present themselves we continue to apply one principle first expressed in Collar and Stuart (1985, p. xix), which is to prefer places to people in the names of birds, thereby perhaps enhancing the local or national motivation to conserve the species in question.

Place names are spelt, as far as it has been possible to check, in accordance with *The Times atlas of the world: comprehensive edition* (1993). Geopolitical units are recognized according to the latest lists produced by the International Standards Organization (ISO) and the United Nations (but we separate the islands of Ascension, Gough and the Tristan da Cunha group from St Helena, which otherwise subsumes them in these lists); political association and

dependency are indicated by placing the appropriate nation in brackets. There is an unresolved—and probably unresolvable—problem over the global standardization of habitat and vegetation descriptions; we have used local names where these have been considered the most appropriate.

ORGANIZATION OF TEXT

The text entry for each species is intended to reveal four key items of information: distribution at least by country, population status or trend, habitat(s), and threat(s). All these elements are necessary for the sound application of the criteria we have adopted in order to evaluate the candidacy of species (see next chapter). However, the order in which these data appear depends on how the entry was constructed, and this in turn has depended on a variety of factors, notably the quantity and type of material available.

Geopolitical units in **bold type** are range states, that is to say those in which the species breeds or otherwise occurs with regularity. These range states are listed with the species they hold in Appendix 1 (p. 243). Geopolitical units for which a species is mentioned as of likely occurrence, to which it is vagrant, or from which it has died out, are treated in normal type (if mentioned at all) and excluded from Appendix 1.

Standard conventions and methods of organization, such as referencing, follow those explained in the introductions to the third edition RDBs and the first *Birds to watch*. In some cases information was conflated from a set of references in such a way that the only sensible option was to group the sources at the end of a full sentence; in others it was possible to locate references adjacent to the information they impart. It should be noted that data summarized in previous RDBs, particularly *Threatened birds of the Americas*, are usually referred to these sources only (this sometimes may appear unfair on major sources of information on which the RDB has drawn, but it remains the simplest and most even-handed method); other references added to such entries usually represent updating sources, or else have been found to contain information that modifies what appears in the RDB entry in question. In general, species which have been treated fully in RDBs have slightly shorter entries. Abbreviations have been used for some sources, as follows.

A.J.S.	A. J. Stattersfield
AMNH	American Museum of Natural History
AWB IP	Asian Wetlands Bureau Indonesia Programme
BirdLife BPD	BirdLife Biodiversity Project Database
BirdLife IP	BirdLife Indonesia Programme
CITES	Convention on International Trade in Endangered Species
CM	Carnegie Museum of Natural History
CVRD	Companhia Vale do Rio Doce
FMNH	Field Museum of Natural History
ICBP	International Council for Bird Preservation
IUCN	International Union for Conservation of Nature and Natural Resources (the World Conservation Union)
M.J.C.	M. J. Crosby
N.J.C.	N. J. Collar
PHPA	Directorate General of Forest Protection and Nature Conservation, Indonesia
RSNC	Royal Society for Nature Conservation
UFPE	Universidade Federal de Pernambuco
UMMZ	University of Michigan Museum of Zoology
USFWS	United States Fish and Wildlife Service
UV	Universidad del Valle
WWF	World Wide Fund for Nature
YPM	Peabody Museum, Yale University

At the end of each species entry is the category of threat in which it has been placed (see next chapter), followed by the criterion or criteria that cause that category to apply. Where a species meets one or

more criteria for Vulnerable and one or more criteria for a higher category, we have placed in **bold type** those criteria that cause the highest category to apply; in other words, if a species is Critical by one criterion, Endangered by another, and Vulnerable by a third, we highlight the criterion triggering Critical, and do not distinguish Endangered from Vulnerable.

DATA STORAGE, OUTPUT AND ANALYSIS

The text of this book is largely an output from a simple database that contains a single record for each of the species covered (Box 3). This was developed from one of the databases used during the BirdLife Biodiversity Project and described in ICBP (1992) and Crosby (1994).

Species may be output from the database in taxonomic sequence using two fields, 'Family' and 'Se-

---

Box 3. The *Birds to watch* database.

The names of fields in the database, with a description of the contents of each.

Species
Scientific name.

English
Vernacular name.

Family
Sequential family codes based on Morony *et al.* (1975).

Sequence
Sequential species codes based on Sibley and Monroe (1990, 1993).

Category
Threatened, Data Deficient and non-threatened categories.

Species text
Text on distribution, population status and trends, habitat and threats (free-text field).

IUCN codes
IUCN criteria codes allocated.

Breeding range
ISO codes of range states where a species is known or believed to breed.

Non-breeding range
ISO codes of the range states where a species regularly occurs but does not breed or is not believed to do so.

Habitats
Codes for habitats which the species regularly uses (see p. 243).

Threats
Codes for threats which are believed to be affecting the species (see p. 243).

Previous threat status
Status of the species in Collar and Andrew (1988).

quence'. By indexing on both of these fields we have output species in the family sequence of Morony *et al.* (1975), and the within-family species sequence of Sibley and Monroe (1990, 1993).

The IUCN threat categories are stored in the 'Category' field, which permits the output of data on all species within a particular category or group of categories (e.g. Appendix 3). The 'Globally Threatened Species' section of the book (p. 28) was produced by outputting to a text file the 'Species text' field for those species in the categories Critical, Endangered, Vulnerable and Extinct in the Wild, together with the category of threat and the IUCN codes allocated to them. The species texts for 'Extinct Species' (p. 210), 'Conservation Dependent Species' (p. 213) and 'Data Deficient Species' (p. 215) were output in a similar manner. It is not possible to use text-formatting commands (e.g. italics or bold) within database fields in the package used, so such commands were included as text codes and subsequently converted into the required formats using word-processor macros.

The 'Breeding range' and 'Non-breeding range' fields were used to store the ISO codes of all geopolitical units within each species' range. These were used to generate the range state lists given for Near-threatened Species (p. 222). They were also used, together with several other fields, to generate Appendix 1 (p. 243), which summarizes and lists the occurrence of species by category within each geopolitical unit.

All threatened species were coded according to the broad habitats which they regularly use and the threats which are currently affecting them (the simple classification system employed is shown on p. 243), and these codings were stored in the 'Habitats' and 'Threats' fields. These codings have been used to perform the analyses which are described under 'Trends and Factors in the Global Endangerment of Birds' (see Figures 5 and 6 on p. 25). Further codes record each species' status in the previous edition of *Birds to watch*.

■

THE NEW IUCN CRITERIA

THE IUCN CRITERIA for assigning threat status and category, in use in various forms ever since the RDB programme began in the 1960s, have been a source of recurrent uncertainty and dissatisfaction, and moves have been made since the mid-1980s to replace them with a less subjective and more accountable system, using numerical criteria that reflect stepwise increases in the risk of extinction (Figure 1) based on measured or reasoned rates of decline, population levels, and range sizes (for a brief history of this development, see Collar and Stattersfield 1994, Mace and Collar 1994).

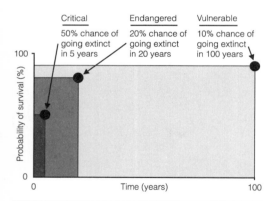

Figure 1. Extinction probabilities and the IUCN threat categories. This representation indicates the relative difficulty (represented by the relatively small, dark rectangles enclosed by their threshold lines) of qualifying as Endangered and, especially, Critical, compared with Vulnerable (large, pale rectangle).

The first outline of the new system was in Mace and Lande (1991). Although their proposals were explicitly declared provisional, they were rapidly adopted by the Captive Breeding Specialist Group of IUCN and widely deployed in its joint workshops (with taxon-specific groups) to develop Conservation Action and Management Plans (CAMPs) for particular families. This has meant that several such CAMPs for birds, on (e.g.) penguins, waterfowl,

Galliformes, parrots and pigeons, have taken place using this prototype system, and their results are in some cases about to be published. We have sought to achieve consistency between these documents and ours, particularly as our work, extending into August 1994, has produced important updated status assessments of many species that were the subject of CAMPs. However, we cannot guarantee precise alignment of judgements.

Mace and Lande (1991) was replaced by Mace *et al*. (1992), which was in turn upgraded by the proposals that went before the IUCN General Assembly in January 1994 and which are summarized in Collar and Stattersfield (1994); and these were themselves refined (basically through the absorption of the problematic 'Susceptible' category into 'Vulnerable') in a final review made by G. M. Mace for IUCN's Species Survival Commission in late May 1994. Our categorizations and codings make use of this last version of the proposals (Mace and Stuart 1994). The definitions of the categories are given in Box 1 and their relationship to the criteria is shown in Figure 2, with their relationship to one another in Figure 3; the criteria and codings for the threatened categories are summarized in Table 1, with rather more detail given in Tables 2–5. We must emphasize, however, the importance of referring to the original document (Mace and Stuart 1994), as it

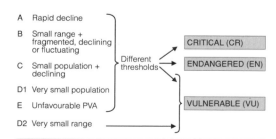

Figure 2. Relationship of criteria to threatened categories. The categories are decided by different thresholds in five main criteria, with Vulnerable additionally being decided by a range-size stand-alone.

Box 1. Definitions of proposed IUCN categories (as given in Mace and Stuart 1994).

EXTINCT (EX) A taxon is Extinct when there is no reasonable doubt that its last individual has died.

EXTINCT IN THE WILD (EW) A taxon is Extinct in the Wild when it is known only to survive in cultivation, in captivity, or as a naturalized population (or populations) well outside the past range. A taxon is presumed extinct in the wild when exhaustive surveys in known and/or expected habitat, at appropriate times (diurnal, seasonal, annual), throughout its historic range, have failed to record an individual. Surveys should be over a time frame appropriate to the taxon's life cycle and life form.

CRITICALLY ENDANGERED (CR) A taxon is Critically Endangered[1] when it is facing an extremely high risk of extinction in the wild in the immediate future, as defined in any of the criteria (A–E)[2].

ENDANGERED (EN) A taxon is Endangered when it is not Critical but is facing a very high risk of extinction in the wild in the near future, as defined in any of the criteria (A–E)[2].

VULNERABLE (VU) A taxon is Vulnerable when it is not Critical or Endangered but is facing a high risk of extinction in the wild in the medium-term future, as defined in any of the criteria (A–E)[2].

CONSERVATION DEPENDENT (CD) Taxa which do not currently qualify as Critical, Endangered or Vulnerable may be classified as Conservation Dependent. To be considered Conservation Dependent, a taxon must be the focus of a continuing taxon-specific or habitat-specific conservation programme which directly affects the taxon in question. The cessation of this conservation programme would result in the taxon qualifying for one of the threatened categories above.

LOW RISK (LR) A taxon is Low Risk when it has been evaluated and does not qualify for any of the categories Critical, Endangered, Vulnerable, Conservation Dependent or Data Deficient. It is clear that a range of forms will be included in this category, including: (i) those that are close to qualify-

ing for the threatened categories[3], (ii) those that are of less concern, and (iii) those that are presently abundant and unlikely to face extinction in the foreseeable future. It may be appropriate to indicate into which of these three classes taxa in Low Risk seem to fall. It is especially recommended to indicate an appropriate interval, or circumstance, before re-evaluation is necessary for taxa in the Low Risk class, especially for those indicated in (i) above.

DATA DEFICIENT (DD) A taxon is Data Deficient when there is inadequate information to make a direct, or indirect, assessment of its risk of extinction based on its distribution and/or population status. A taxon in this category may be well studied, and its biology well known, but appropriate data on abundance and/or distribution are lacking. DD is therefore not a category of threat or Low Risk. Listing of taxa in this category indicates that more information is required. Listing a taxon as DD acknowledges the possibility that future research will show that threatened classification is appropriate. It is important to make positive use of whatever data are available. In many cases great care should be exercised in choosing between DD and threatened status. If the range of a taxon is suspected to be relatively circumscribed, if a considerable period of time has elapsed since the last record of a taxon, or if there are reasonable chances of unreported surveys in which the taxon has not been found, or that habitat loss has had an unfavourable impact, threatened status may well be justified.

NOT EVALUATED (NE) A taxon is Not Evaluated when it has not yet been assessed against the criteria.

[1] 'Critically Endangered' is the formal term under consideration; it is referred to throughout this book as 'Critical'.

[2] See Tables 1–5.

[3] This is the distinction which in this book bears the title 'Near-threatened'.

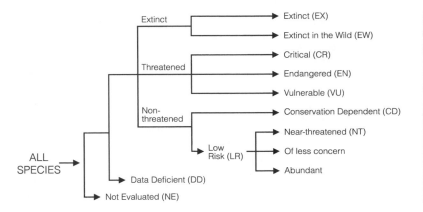

Figure 3. Relationships between the IUCN categories. The dendrogram shows the path down which a species travels to arrive at a particular categorization. The line-up of categories on the right reflects the way in which the new system attempts to rank species in categories that are almost, but not entirely, nested.

Table 1. The new IUCN threatened category thresholds at a glance. 'Extent of occurrence' and 'area of occupancy' are defined in the caption to Table 3.

Criteria	Main numerical thresholds		
	Critical	**Endangered**	**Vulnerable**
A RAPID DECLINE	>80% over 10 years or 3 generations	>50% over 10 years or 3 generations	>50% over 20 years or 5 generations
B SMALL RANGE fragmented, declining or fluctuating	Extent of occurrence <100 km^2 or area of occupancy <10 km^2	Extent of occurrence <5,000 km^2 or area of occupancy <500 km^2	Extent of occurrence <20,000 km^2 or area of occupancy <2,000 km^2
C SMALL POPULATION declining	<250 mature individuals	<2,500 mature individuals	<10,000 mature individuals
D1 VERY SMALL POPULATION	<50 mature individuals	<250 mature individuals	<1,000 mature individuals
D2 VERY SMALL RANGE	—	—	<100 km^2 or <5 locations
E UNFAVOURABLE PVA	Probability of extinction >50% within 5 years	Probability of extinction >20% within 20 years	Probability of extinction >10% within 100 years

contains many important qualifying remarks and points of clarification that cannot be reproduced in this outline of the system.

Our only departure from the system is to retain (from previous BirdLife RDBs) the unofficial category of 'Near-threatened' which, although not used as such in the newest proposals, covers what those proposals refer to as 'Low Risk (type i)' taxa (see Box 1). It should be noted that in the case of Asia the Near-threatened list is disproportionately large, reflecting our wish to establish a comprehensive list of candidates for evaluation in the forthcoming *Threatened birds of Asia*. Moreover, the category Extinct has been used here only for species that had been included as possibly extant in the first *Birds to watch*

but which we now feel are more appropriately placed apart from the main list, plus a few species that, since 1988, are thought to have become extinct.

PROBLEMS IN THE APPLICATION OF THE NEW CRITERIA

For the most part we have found it relatively straightforward to apply the new criteria, so our judgement is that they appear to work well with birds (further commentary on this is provided in the next chapter). Here we simply wish to outline certain problems that we encountered when applying them, and in some cases the decisions we took to overcome these difficulties.

Table 2. Criteria for the IUCN threatened categories: species undergoing rapid decline. 'Extent of occurrence' and 'area of occupancy' are defined in the caption to Table 3.

Rapid decline			
Main criteria	Sub-criteria	Qualifiers	Codes
A. Decline of:	**1.** Decline which has happened observed, estimated, inferred or suspected, based on:	**a.** Direct observation	**A1a**
>80% over 10 years or 3 generations **(CR)**		**b.** Decline in area of occupancy, extent of occurrence, and/or quality of habitat	**A1b**
>50% over 10 years or 3 generations **(EN)**		**c.** Actual or potential levels of exploitation	**A1c**
>50% over 20 years or 5 generations **(VU)**		**d.** Effects of introduced taxa, hybridization, pathogens, pollutants, competitors or parasites	**A1d**
involving *either*:	**2.** Decline likely in near future based on:	**b.** As above	**A2b**
		c. As above	**A2c**
		d. As above	**A2d**

Small range, plus any two of: fragmented, declining, fluctuating

Main criteria	Sub-criteria	Qualifiers	Codes
B. Extent of occurrence estimated: <100 km^2 (**CR**) <5,000 km^2 (**EN**) <20,000 km^2 (**VU**) *or* Area of occupancy estimated: <10 km^2 (**CR**) <500 km^2 (**EN**) <2,000 km^2 (**VU**) in *either* case with *any two of*:	**1.** Severe fragmentation *or* At 1 location (**CR**) <5 locations (**EN**) <10 locations (**VU**)	None	**B1**
	2. Continuing decline observed, inferred or projected in any of:	a. Extent of occurrence	**B2a**
		b. Area of occupancy	**B2b**
		c. Area, extent and/or quality of habitat	**B2c**
		d. Number of locations or subpopulations	**B2d**
		e. Number of mature individuals	**B2e**
	3. Extreme fluctuations in any of:	a. Extent of occurrence	**B3a**
		b. Area of occupancy	**B3b**
		c. Number of locations or subpopulations	**B3c**
		d. Number of mature individuals	**B3d**

Table 3. Criteria for the IUCN threatened categories: species with a small range and declining. 'Extent of occurrence' is the area contained within the shortest continuous imaginary boundary which encompasses all known, inferred or projected sites of present occurrence. 'Area of occupancy' is the area within the extent of occurrence which is occupied by a taxon (this measure is often applicable to species with highly specific habitats).

Two points to emphasize are that the guidelines to the new criteria insist on the use of the *precautionary principle*, and the criteria themselves explicitly require the use of numbers of *mature individuals*, when assessing a species for categorization. Any apparently inappropriate listing of criteria, in relation to the range or level of figures we cite, will in most cases be attributable to these two latent factors.

The precautionary principle is the arbiter in borderline cases, chiefly between threatened and non-threatened status. It simply requires the use of the lowest figures on range or population and of the

Small population and declining

Main criteria	Sub-criteria	Qualifiers	Codes
C. Population: <250 (**CR**) <2,500 (**EN**) <10,000 (**VU**) mature individuals and *either*:	**1.** Continuing decline >25% within 3 years or 1 generation (**CR**) >20% within 5 years or 2 generations (**EN**) >20% within 10 years or 3 generations (**VU**)	None	**C1**
	2. Continuing decline in numbers of mature individuals *and* population structure . observed, inferred or projected in form of *either*:	a. Severe fragmentation no population >50 (**CR**) >250 (**EN**) >1,000 (**VU**) mature individuals	**C2a**
		b. All breeding individuals in single subpopulation	**C2b**

Table 4. Criteria for the IUCN threatened categories: species with a small population and declining.

Table 5. Criteria for the IUCN threatened categories: species with a very small population and/or a very small range.

Very small or restricted population

Main criteria	Sub-criteria	Qualifiers	Codes
D. Population:	None	None	
<50 (**CR**)			D1
<250 (**EN**)			D1
<1,000 (**VU**)			D1
mature individuals			
and/or			
Area of occupancy <100 km²			D2
or			
at <5 locations (**VU** only)			

worst circumstance in terms of decline and threats that can *reasonably* be accepted. It therefore disallows 'worst-case scenarios', but urges caution (what one might call responsible pessimism) in accordance with the evidence.

The number of mature individuals is regarded as a better guide to the conservation status of a species than is a simple total of all individuals (in the case of many invertebrates and fish the importance of this distinction is much easier to appreciate). In many cases where a species has qualified under the C criterion (<10,000 and declining) we acknowledge that the total population may be several thousand higher than 10,000, but with immature birds making up the difference.

A further point to register is the difficulty surrounding the concepts of 'location' and '(sub)-population'. The guidelines for the new criteria attempt definitions (Box 2), but these are by no means comprehensive and probably never can be. The problem affects many of the criteria and technically destabilizes them.

Box 2. Definitions of 'Location', 'Population' and 'Subpopulation' in the proposed IUCN criteria.

Location A geographically or ecologically distinct area in which a single event (e.g. pollution) will soon affect all individuals of the taxon present. A location usually, but not always, contains all or part of a subpopulation of the taxon, and is typically a small proportion of the taxon's total distribution.

Population The total number of individuals of the taxon.

Subpopulation Geographically or otherwise distinct groups in the population between which there is little exchange (typically one successful migrant individual or gamete per year or less).

In the following paragraphs we describe various difficulties (some of which are very closely related), and in some cases how we have responded to them. While we have attempted to group them in a sequence that reflects this relatedness, and while some may be more important than others, we have given each a separate heading for the sake of clarity.

Data Deficient, inference and appropriate categorization

Despite the intended shift in the new criteria towards greater objectivity and accountability, the classification of species for which information is sparse remains largely intractable and hence liable to great variation between users of the system. In the guidelines to the criteria, emphasis is laid on the importance of attempting to classify poorly known species, and on allowing them threatened status (on the precautionary principle) if there are any signs from which this could be inferred. The category Data Deficient exists to accommodate only those species which cannot reasonably be assessed from the assembled evidence (see pp. 15 and 215). Typical Data Deficient species are known from one or very few specimens or sites within a habitat that remains largely intact and where no other threats (such as introduced predators) are expected; many are highly cryptic (the list includes nine nightbirds and four rails). However, when long-term absence of a species combines with suspected habitat loss, it is more or less obligatory to assign threatened status, although the role played by assumption is still enormous: Archer's Lark *Heteromirafra archeri* (Endangered, being the chosen precautionary compromise between the plain possibilities that it might be extinct and that it might conceivably prove locally common) is an example. Clearly there is considerable scope for variation in the categorization of such species, which in other reviewers' hands might, with some justification, appear as anything from Extinct to Data Deficient.

Suitability and use of Conservation Dependent

Conservation Dependent exists for species that would very rapidly qualify as threatened if they were not under management; it is not for species which are under management but have already met the criteria (these are threatened species, irrespective of their management). It has been applied very infrequently (11 species in total: p. 213), partly because so few species are genuinely under conservation management, and partly because so little conservation management can confidently be judged effective. This is especially true for protected areas which, despite covering most of a species' range, may suffer external pressure, or be managed inappropriately, or provide protection for only part of a life-cycle (as is the case with seabirds, where factors in the wider marine environment may be of greater conservation concern). In many cases, further research and consultation are needed to ascertain whether CD is indeed the most suitable category (e.g. some of the Australian species allocated this status). In some developed countries, e.g. New Zealand, it could be argued that all Low Risk species are to a large extent CD and will remain so forever, but, for simplicity's sake, the category has been assigned to Saddleback *Philesturnus carunculatus* only, a species which was in the recent past listed as threatened. The same is true for species on predator-free islands where measures to prevent the introduction of exotics render all their endemics potentially CD; we opted for threatened status in such cases only when an introduction is thought very likely to happen, using criterion A2d (i.e. future rapid decline).

Intensively managed species in Vulnerable

Species that satisfy the numerical criteria must be treated as threatened, irrespective of the intensity and effectiveness of the management they receive; they are not Conservation Dependent. However, the situation arises in which a bird like Kirtland's Warbler *Dendroica kirtlandii*, which intuitively appears 'critical', being very intensively managed both to prevent breeding success dropping to zero and to maintain its highly specific breeding habitat, can only qualify as Vulnerable, precisely because that management is currently preventing any decline. There may be some merit in coding to promote an otherwise Vulnerable (and perhaps Endangered) species to a higher category, for example by a new criterion that predicts a decline in the near future based on abandonment of current conservation programmes. For Vulnerable, this could express either of the two higher degrees of threat according to the reviewer's perception of the situation, but the criterion would have to be formulated in such a way that Conservation Dependent species did not then all qualify as Vulnerable.

Thresholds for Critical

The thresholds for the different threat categories have been set to try and reflect probabilities of extinction (see Figure 1, p. 14). However, the discovery that as many as 100 species are thereby expected to become Extinct within the next five years (see p. 22) suggests that the probability level at least for Critical is too high; it does not necessarily imply that the thresholds are set at the wrong levels. However, we certainly find that a species can move too easily from Vulnerable (under D2) to Critical (under B1+2c) as a result of any comment reflecting loss of habitat.

Species with naturally small ranges, especially when their habitat is for the most part under protection, can consequently appear mistakenly classified: Ascension Frigatebird *Fregata aquila*, Grand Comoro Scops-owl *Otus pauliani*, Seychelles Scops-owl *O. insularis*, Puerto Rican Nightjar *Caprimulgus noctitherus*, Mount Karthala White-eye *Zosterops mouroniensis* and San Andrés Vireo *Vireo caribeus* are all clearly threatened, but intuitively not such that one fears for them in the short term (equivalent to a 50% chance of extinction in five years); several others, including the three Cocos (Costa Rica) and two Annobon (Equatorial Guinea) endemics, could also all instantly transfer to Critical on the slightest evidence of loss of habitat. The problem lies in the interpretation of 'continuing decline': in many cases information is poor, and thus, under the precautionary principle, the mention of the loss or deterioration of any small quantity of habitat may be enough to trigger this shift. An additional qualifying clause for the B1+2c criterion (for Critical and Endangered) indicating a rate or extent of decline may be appropriate.

Small stable versus larger declining ranges and populations

The new system can theoretically disqualify species that are stable in their small ranges while accepting species with larger ranges that also occupy these areas and are stable within them, but which are suffering declines elsewhere. The equivalent problem arises with population thresholds, where a species with (say) a stable population of 1,500 mature individuals fails to be listed while one with six times as many qualifies because of a decline affecting even a small subset of its total numbers. Almost exemplifying this problem is the recently discovered Udzungwa Forest-partridge *Xenoperdix udzungwensis*, which (until hunting was assumed to be extensive) had proved difficult to list, since it had been found in two intact forest patches totalling almost 300 km^2, although several already known species (Swynnerton's Robin *Swynnertonia swynnertoni*, Dappled Mountain-robin *Modulatrix orostruthus*, White-winged Apalis *Apalis chariessa*), also then encountered in these previously unexplored patches, continued to qualify on the grounds of their declines elsewhere.

Another case is the Brown Teal *Anas aucklandica*, which in its three races, *chlorotis* (2,100 birds and declining), nominate *aucklandica* (1,500 birds and stable), and *nesiotis* (60–100 birds and stable), qualifies under criterion B. However if, as is currently being proposed, these three races are treated as good species, the resulting 'new' *A. aucklandica* would probably lose its threatened status, since neither a decline in its numbers nor a contraction in its range

19

(genuine influences while it remained a member of the 'old' *A. aucklandica*) exists, and both its population and range size are just too large to trigger a stand-alone criterion (D1 or D2). (Of course, splitting of species will tend to result in more taxa in higher categories, since they will inevitably have smaller range sizes and populations; in this case both *chlorotis* and *nesiotis* would be likely to emerge with a higher categorization than they currently do as members of *A. aucklandica*.)

Rapid declines and islands

The rapid decline criterion exists to record seemingly uncontrolled and catastrophic circumstances affecting a species. Its application becomes problematic when these circumstances are contained as a result of geographical isolation. For example, two Marianas pigeons, White-throated Ground-dove *Gallicolumba xanthonura* and Mariana Fruit-dove *Ptilinopus roseicapilla*, both went extinct on Guam, but survive in fair numbers (higher than the population criteria) on several other islands. However, the total area of these other islands is roughly the size of Guam, so that a 50% decline in 20 years has technically been registered. Nevertheless, as the decline was finite it was felt that both these species would better be placed as Near-threatened for the moment.

Definitions of subpopulation and location

The choice between criteria C2a (population fragmented) and C2b (one single subpopulation) is often difficult owing to the emphasis in the proposed definition of subpopulation (Box 2, above) falling on the issue of gene-exchange rather than on the impact of discontinuity in food availability or in other resources. Although theoretically there may be genetic interchange between fragmented populations such that they can be regarded as a single population, in practice the massive fragmentation of habitats, leaving many small populations stranded, seems far more logical to register as C2a, whether genes continue to be exchanged or not. In the case of locations, scale was a problem as no size limits are given in the proposed IUCN system, so criteria relying on number of locations (B and D2) are open to application in an inconsistent way; our guiding (practical conservation) principle was to regard 'small' areas as single locations where threats (e.g. introduced predators) could have a rapid effect throughout.

Discretionary use of the range-size stand-alone (D2)

The criterion D2, which at one stage in the formulation of the new criteria was the category Susceptible (see Collar and Stattersfield 1994), was intended to indicate the risk of extinction inherent in species

with highly restricted ranges, such that they can easily disappear before a threat to them has even been recorded. We use D2 with some discretion: with seasonally gregarious species, such as geese and seabirds, we have tended to take number of flock areas or colonies to equal locations (bearing in mind the point above); but with species which do not congregate we have allocated this criterion to those which have a range of less than 100 km^2.

Population viability analysis (PVA)

No E coding (whose criteria correspond to the probabilities of extinction depicted in Figure 1, p. 14) was attempted because the formally published record of the results of population viability analyses is virtually non-existent. Moreover, there is real difficulty both in interpreting these analyses (since they provide a variety of results depending on combinations of anticipated futures) and even simply in knowing the status of the exercises (since to date most appear entirely informal and provisional). This is not, of course, to deny the value of such simulations; the entry for Nene *Branta sandvicensis* cites an interesting multiple-outcome PVA (which nevertheless illustrates the point that these outcomes are not easy to match to the new criteria).

The importance of background data

The new system has been developed to minimize subjectivity, so that as far as possible assessments of risk are comparable between taxa. However, considerable emphasis is laid in the criteria on future prospects, and the future is an area where speculation and assumption inevitably play major roles. Moreover, the distribution of knowledge concerning broader types of key information such as on habitat destruction is inevitably very patchy. This means that while a specialist can be expected to assemble all the relevant species-specific material for an assessment (distribution, population, ecology), he or she cannot be expected to have access to general data relevant to a species' environment. Thus future (as well as present) assessments can be seriously influenced by knowledge or ignorance of key pieces of information. For the process of assessment to approach comparability between assessors, the distribution of knowledge on habitat loss and general conservation measures (e.g. the existence, condition and precise location of protected areas within a species' range) has to be as even as possible. This is one very good reason for publishing findings in detail, for example in Red Data Books and species action plans, as it discloses what knowledge has informed the judgements made and renders that knowledge accessible to other assessors of species with similar ranges and problems.

Predictable finality

One problem in risk assessment is that the probability of a particular event may be very low while the probability of its outcome, unless immediately countered, is very high. Hybridization with vigorous invasive species is a threat that perhaps can only be neutralized at the moment the invader establishes itself in or near the range of the invaded (as in the case of the White-headed Duck *Oxyura leucocephala* and the Ruddy Duck *O. jamaicensis*). The introduction to or escape onto islands of certain predators or competitors is another predictably 'final' event, although the time it may take to have an impact (and indeed which taxa it may affect) may be impossible to predict. After the unforeseen but astonishingly rapid loss of the Guam avifauna to the brown tree snake *Boiga irregularis* it has been tempting to code as A2d every bird species on every island, irrespective of its size, wherever ships from Guam commonly dock. The establishment of primates on an island even as large as New Guinea—let alone Halmahera and other parts of the Moluccan archipelago—could, unless remedied by action within a few months, seal the fate of an unknown number of avian (and other) frugivores—pigeons, parrots, birds of paradise—that have speciated in the absence of competition from such a source.

It is impossible to devise a set of criteria that respond helpfully and consistently to this problem. The D2 criterion exists to highlight a particular condition under which the process of extinction can occur very rapidly and often without detection until after its completion; yet, as the examples above show, highly restricted range is only one of several evolutionary circumstances that permanently expose certain species to seemingly irreversible events. Understanding all such circumstances and guarding against all such events is a hydra-headed challenge in biodiversity conservation, connected ultimately to wider problems in the realm of global environmental management (such as carbon emission, global warming and sea-level rise) with which conservation biologists have had, to date, relatively little practical involvement.

TRENDS AND FACTORS IN THE GLOBAL ENDANGERMENT OF BIRDS

A TOTAL of 1,111 bird species (11% of the world's avifauna) have been identified as threatened, with a further 11 (0.1%) being allocated to the category of Conservation Dependent, 66 (1%) to Data Deficient and 875 (9%) to Near-threatened (Figure 1). In other words, over a fifth of all bird species give some cause for concern in terms of global extinction risk. If to this we add the consideration that high levels of the remaining 80% are declining in overall numbers—in Europe 25% of species have experienced a decline of more than 20% in over one-third of their populations in the past 20 years (Tucker and Heath 1994), which intimates the likely situation in many other regions—and, further, that these levels will almost certainly be reflected in all other terrestrial life-form groups (for evidence of which see Groombridge 1993b), then the future of the planet's biological diversity is nothing if not bleak.

Of the 1,111 threatened bird species, four (0.4%) are identified as Extinct in the Wild, 168 (15%) as Critical, 235 (21%) as Endangered and 704 (63%) as Vulnerable (Figure 2). The Extinct in the Wild, Critical and Endangered species form the subject of Appendix 3 and of a species-by-country review (Box 1).

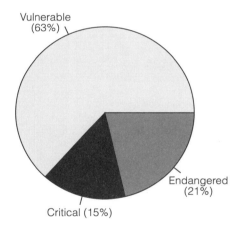

Figure 2. Proportions of the world's threatened bird species in the different threatened categories.

Given that the threat categories are characterized by different probabilities of extinction (50% chance in five years for Critical, 20% in 20 years for Endangered, 10% in 100 years for Vulnerable; see Figure 1 on p. 14), it is possible to calculate the number and rate of avian species extinctions over the next 100 years, assuming no action is taken on their behalf, and making no allowance for new species entering the lists (Figure 3). From this it emerges that over 400 bird species are likely to die out in the next hundred years; but far more disturbing is the anticipation that 200 will disappear in the next 20 years, 100 of them in the next 5–10. Intuitively, however, this scenario appears too extreme: as we have al-

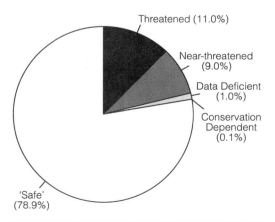

Figure 1. Proportions of the world's bird species in the different categories of risk.

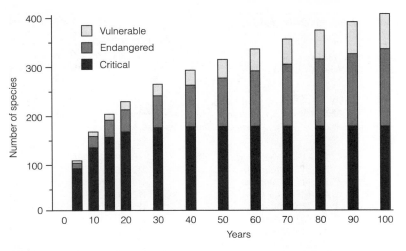

Figure 3. Future extinction trajectory of threatened birds as predicted by the population viability criteria (see Figure 1 on p. 14). This analysis does not factor in species entering the list over time, or the categories into which they will fall.

ready pointed out under 'Thresholds for Critical' (p. 19), there is a condition which satisfies a criterion for this category which does not truly reflect a 50% chance of extinction in five years. Nevertheless, the basic point cannot be sidestepped: only concerted action at key points across the globe is now going to prevent a major wave of species losses.

USE OF CRITERIA

Apart from the population viability analysis criterion (code E; not used at all, as explained on p. 20), the other criteria (codes A–D) were all used extensively in the triggering of threatened status, most usually in combination rather than singly (Figure 4). The commonest way in which bird species have been judged to be at risk is by their possessing a declining popu-

lation numbering less than 10,000 mature individuals (code C). No fewer than 764 species out of 1,111 (almost 70%) are believed to exhibit this characteristic, and over 100 of them qualify on this criterion alone. This does not mean that good population data are available, rather that reasonable inference from the evidence often allows a judgement against the threshold in question.

The other notable feature of Figure 4 is the influence exerted by the population and range-size standalone criteria, both of which reflect the view that a species is inherently at risk, irrespective of any threat (actual or potential), if it falls below a certain level in terms of either numbers of individuals or the area it occupies. Eighty-six species (c.8%) qualify on the range-size criterion (D2) alone.

DISTRIBUTION

An analysis of species by geopolitical unit (Appendix 1) and subsequent ranking (Box 1 and Appendix 2, p. 342) places Indonesia, Brazil and the Philippines in the top three countries for total numbers of threatened species (all categories), with China, India, Colombia, Peru and Ecuador in the next five positions. It is notable that the great majority of the land surface of the New World and Asia features in the first 25 geopolitical units (together contributing 19 units), whereas only a small proportion of Africa is registered through three countries, none of them in the top 20 (Box 1, column A). This reflects the relative species-richness and higher levels of local endemism in the Oriental and particularly the Neotropical regions when compared with the Afrotropical, and perhaps also indicates the fragility of the situation in Asia, where roughly 60% of the human population of the planet is concentrated.

When only the higher categories of threat (i.e. Extinct in the Wild, Critical, Endangered) are con-

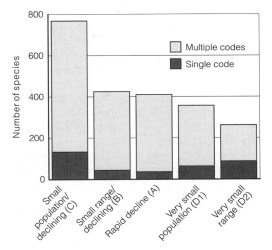

Figure 4. Distribution of criteria amongst the threatened species.

Box 1. Geopolitical units ranked by their numbers of threatened species.

A   By total number of threatened bird species.

B   By total number of threatened bird species categorized as Extinct in the Wild, Critical and Endangered.

C   By total number of species covered by B that are also endemic to the unit in question.

Numbers of species are given in brackets.

Under A and B, where units are ranked above others with the same score, this is because weighting has been given either to the threatened species total (in B) or to the degree of endangerment within the species total (in A). Under C, priority where scores are tied has been given to units with higher numbers of endemic species categorized as Vulnerable or as Near-threatened. See also Appendix 2 (p. 342).

A	B	C
1. (104) Indonesia	1. (47) Brazil	1. (40) Philippines
2. (103) Brazil	2. (45) Philippines	2. (32) Brazil
3. (86) Philippines	3. (31) Colombia	3. (24) Colombia
4. (86) China	4. (25) U.S.A.	4. (17) U.S.A.
5. (71) India	5. (20) Indonesia	5. (13) Mexico
6. (62) Colombia	6. (20) Mexico	6. (12) Indonesia
7. (60) Peru	7. (18) Peru	7. (12) New Zealand
8. (50) Ecuador	8. (16) Vietnam	8. (11) Australia
9. (46) U.S.A.	9. (16) Ecuador	9. (10) Madagascar
10. (45) Vietnam	10. (16) Argentina	10. (9) Peru
11. (45) New Zealand	11. (13) China	11. (7) French Polynesia
12. (44) Thailand	12. (13) India	12. (7) Venezuela
13. (44) Australia	13. (13) New Zealand	13. (6) Ecuador
14. (43) Myanmar	14. (12) Australia	14. (6) Mauritius
15. (40) Argentina	15. (11) Thailand	15. (6) Cuba
16. (35) Russia	16. (11) Japan	16. (5) Vietnam
17. (34) Mexico	17. (11) Venezuela	17. (5) Angola
18. (31) Japan	18. (10) Madagascar	18. (5) Kenya
19. (31) Malaysia	19. (10) Cuba	19. (5) Somalia
20. (31) Papua New Guinea	20. (10) Paraguay	20. (4) India
21. (30) Tanzania	21. (9) Solomon Islands	21. (4) Ethiopia
22. (28) Madagascar	22. (9) French Polynesia	22. (4) Seychelles
23. (28) Bangladesh	23. (8) Myanmar	23. (4) New Caledonia
24. (27) Bolivia	24. (8) Malaysia	24. (4) Micronesia
25. (26) Zaïre	25. (8) Bolivia	25. (4) Comoros

sidered (Box 1, column B), the dominance of the New World and Asia is further increased (20 units), with only Madagascar remaining from Africa among the top 25. The high degree of vulnerability of island avifaunas also emerges in the upward progress of the U.S.A. (which includes Hawaii), Mexico (which includes the Revillagigedos and Guadalupe), French Polynesia and the Solomons.

If these latter figures are yet further refined to score for national endemics only (Box 1, column C), the order changes more dramatically, again with many small island units (French Polynesia, Mauritius, Cuba, Seychelles, New Caledonia, Micronesia, Comoros) pushing higher upwards and several previously leading countries (China, India, Ecuador) dropping sharply. Most notable is the emergence of the Philippines as of exceptional significance, followed by Brazil and Colombia, and it is fairly startling to see that four of the five top places in this list are occupied by nations of the New World.

It may not always be appropriate to use levels of national endemism as a measure of priority, but the global conservation community needs to know where

unique assemblages of biological diversity lie (as indeed do the parties to the Convention on Biological Diversity, which commits them to the preparation of national conservation strategies). Moreover, weighting for complementarity certainly revives the challenge inherent in the concept of 'ultimate responsibility'. For example, analysis of *Threatened birds of the Americas* reveals the almost total absence of overlap in threatened species complement between Brazil, Peru, Colombia and Mexico, the first two accounting for 50%, the first three for 66% and all four for 75% of the threatened birds of the New World (Collar *et al.* in press).

Differences between insular and continental areas were to be expected, with much higher total proportions of avifaunas being at risk on islands, through the influence of introduced predators and competitors. The elevated importance of islands for threatened birds, long recognized (King 1978, 1985, Temple 1986), is certainly reaffirmed here; however, the issue is relatively complex for a variety of reasons, and an analysis of globally threatened island birds will have to be undertaken elsewhere.

HABITATS AND THREATS

The simple system of coding species for broad habitat types and threats, giving these habitats and threats equal weight where multiple types are allocated (see Appendix 1, p. 243, for classification), reveals similar results to previous analyses (e.g. King 1978, Temple 1986), reinforcing forest as the most important habitat (well over 50%) for threatened birds (Figure

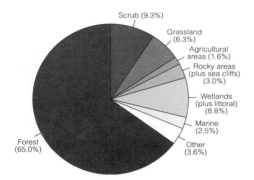

Scrub (9.3%)
Grassland (6.3%)
Agricultural areas (1.6%)
Rocky areas (plus sea cliffs) (3.0%)
Wetlands (plus littoral) (8.8%)
Marine (2.5%)
Other (3.6%)
Forest (65.0%)

Figure 5. Habitats of threatened bird species (see text for explanation of analysis). 'Other' habitats comprise savanna (1.1%), introduced/exotic vegetation (1.0%), deserts (0.5%), urban (0.1%) and unknown (0.9%).

5), and habitat loss and degradation as the most significant threat (almost exactly 50%) worldwide (Figure 6). The importance of forest is probably slightly downplayed in this analysis, as it is likely to be the more significant habitat for many species that range through several types. The seemingly rather

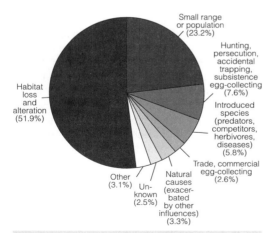

Small range or population (23.2%)
Hunting, persecution, accidental trapping, subsistence egg-collecting (7.6%)
Introduced species (predators, competitors, herbivores, diseases) (5.8%)
Habitat loss and alteration (51.9%)
Trade, commercial egg-collecting (2.6%)
Other (3.1%)
Unknown (2.5%)
Natural causes (exacerbated by other influences) (3.3%)

Figure 6. Threats affecting threatened bird species (see text for explanation of analysis). 'Other' threats comprise disturbance by humans and livestock (1.5%), pollution, pesticides and accidental poisoning (1.3%) and fisheries (0.3%).

strong presence of scrub in the habitat breakdown probably reflects the use of this descriptor to cover a wide variety of dryland and secondary habitats, and in many cases the species involved are likely to use forest as well.

Given this, it is perhaps surprising that as *little* as 50% of the threat burden derives from habitat destruction. This may reflect the weighting procedure described above, when in many cases habitat loss may be by far the most important threat but has been allocated equal status with all other threats. This effect will have been compounded by the influence in the criteria of small ranges and small populations, the stand-alones that can trigger threatened status even if no actual or potential threat has been identified (see 'Use of Criteria', above); Figure 6 shows that these two contribute about a quarter of the burden of threats to all threatened birds.

The general habitat classification and analysis detailed above could be refined by subdividing several of the categories, notably forest, to take into account variations in habitat type related to altitude, climate, soil and other environmental variables. Such a review was not attempted here because of the difficulties inherent in devising a detailed habitat classification at the global level and because of time constraints. Further analysis of the data in Appendix 1 will, of course, be possible, for example by making comparisons between families, or (with a little further work) between guilds or size-classes of species. A review of the parrots (Wirth *et al.* in press), requested several months before the finalization of the book, confirmed the prominence of trade amongst the threats to the family, although even then habitat destruction affects twice as many members of the family.

CHANGES BETWEEN 1988 AND 1994

A total of 1,030 bird species was considered threatened with global extinction in 1988 (Collar and Andrew 1988). This figure has increased to 1,111 in the present study, a rise of only 81 (c.8%), much of which might appear attributable to taxonomic changes. However, the new list does not simply consist of the old list with 81 additions. As Table 1 indicates, the similarities between the two lists are far greater than the differences, but the differences

Table 1. Changes in the numbers of threatened bird species between 1988 and 1994.

	Common	Unique	Total
1988	816	214	1,030
1994		295	1,111

require consideration. Analysis (Tables 2 and 3) shows the crucial role played by improved knowledge of the status of the many species under review in these works (a point already brought out in a comparison of the first *Birds to watch* and *Threatened birds of the Americas* by Bibby 1994). Thus, of the 214 species unique to the 1988 list, 140 became Near-threatened (mainly—although this is not stated—through improved information) and a further 13 disappeared altogether from consideration as at risk; this accounts for over 70% of the species in question. Similarly, of the 295 species unique to the 1994 list, 93 have moved up from Near-threatened (again, mainly through improved information), 85 are elevated from their previous but erroneous position in Low Risk (these are species for which there had been no easily accessible evidence of threat before, but which we now know were then at risk), and 10 have genuinely deteriorated from what is now called Low Risk status six years ago; this accounts for 64% of the species in question.

Table 2. Numbers of species downgraded from threatened status between 1988 and 1994, with reasons.

Reason	No. of species
Now Extinct	16
Now Near-threatened	140
Now Data Deficient	25
Now Conservation Dependent	7
Invalid taxon	12
Status based on better knowledge	13
Status genuinely improved	0
Change in criteria	1
Total	214

Table 3. Numbers of species upgraded to threatened status between 1988 and 1994, with reasons.

Reason	No. of species
From Near-threatened	93
Taxonomic factors	80
Status based on better knowledge	85
Status genuinely worse	10
Change in criteria	27
Total	295

The impression from Table 2 that 16 species have become extinct during the last six years is, of course, misleading; there was no separate Extinct Species list in the 1988 edition of *Birds to watch* and all 16 were retained as threatened in that book in the hope that they might yet be found to persist; in fact only one, the Ivory-billed Woodpecker *Campephilus principalis*, at that stage appeared likely to be extant. Essentially, therefore, these 16 should be discounted

as a source of difference in the two lists. The same is true of the 25 species which have transferred to Data Deficient, since their presence in the first *Birds to watch* resulted from qualifying—although individual categories were not explicit in that book—under the old IUCN category Insufficiently Known (which, under an earlier version of the precautionary principle, was interpreted as denoting threatened status); so they are all products of a particular change in the criteria.

Two important influences behind the changes between lists derive from taxonomic developments and from the range-size stand-alone (D2). The importation of 80 species into the 1994 list on taxonomic grounds (which includes a number of newly described birds) indicates the abiding need for conservation to keep in close contact with systematics. The addition of 27 species through changes in the criteria certainly stems in large part from the requirement to list species whose ranges are less than 100 km^2 in extent, where before this was a matter of discretion (which is not to say that we find this criterion problematic).

One of the most disheartening features of the table is the fact that active intervention has caused not a single species to move from threatened status into Low Risk (beyond that part of Low Risk we have labelled Near-threatened). It is, of course, true that any threatened species under active management is far more likely to move out of threatened status only as far as Conservation Dependent, yet there are only seven such species, and even in those cases perhaps only three have earnt their new status as a result of active management instituted in the past six years.

A seemingly more optimistic interpretation, based on this comparison between studies (and indeed on broader experience gained in researching this and other books), is that the earth tends to be more resourceful than we are able to judge it: if 153 of 1988's threatened species have been shown by improved knowledge not to be so, then many others may also be faring better than was once believed. It is certainly true that bird populations tend to prove larger than the educated guesses of desk-bound researchers reviewing what little evidence they can muster. All the same, such findings are no cause for complacency, and indeed the hope they may engender is largely illusory: the earth *is* finite, and the upgrading of species, often to just beyond a threshold they were once thought to have passed, is no more than to find them the smallest of spaces in which, unless the category Near-threatened is taken seriously, they will quite probably be ignored until they are once more deemed to have reached the level at which emergency responses are required.

CONCLUSIONS

This is the first time the new IUCN criteria have been used on a complete class of animals. They bring rigour, objectivity and accountability to the difficult process of threatened species analysis. However, the relatively high proportion of species shared between *Birds to watch* in 1988 and 1994 prompts the unorthodox consideration that the old IUCN criteria were, in fact, capable of working efficiently, just so long as they were applied reasonably and responsibly; moreover, they were short and simple. The problem with them was that their vagueness was an invitation to misuse, and this (in our view) allowed the distortion of the red-listing process through the undue influence of flagship species, 'sacred cows' and other inappropriate elements. The new criteria, unwieldy though they are, with their various thresholds, qualifiers, definitions and explanations, greatly reduce the opportunities for such misuse; they, too, have necessarily vague areas and require assumption and inference, often on a very informal basis, but they establish a framework which tends to contain and reduce subjectivity and renders the whole process of assessment more accountable. We therefore warmly commend them to IUCN and other potential users, and encourage the Species Survival Commission specialist groups to adopt them when reviewing the taxa in their charge.

Despite this, and indeed despite our emphasis above on the relative insignificance of the disparity between the 1988 and 1994 listings, it is a certain conclusion of this entire exercise that assessment of status becomes both more accurate and more feasible in proportion not only to the quality but also to the applicability of available data. Put more simply, solid information makes for sound judgement. In this sense, the changes that have occurred since 1988 may in many cases be linked to advances in the Red Data Book and associated BirdLife research programmes: work on *Threatened birds of the Americas*, *Putting biodiversity on the map* and the forthcoming *Global directory of endemic bird areas* (Stattersfield *et al.* in prep.) have between them pulled together high-resolution data on 2,759 species of bird around the world (28% of all bird species). Moreover, the African and American RDBs precipitated fieldwork on rare species (in many cases even before the books were published), and of course the first *Birds to watch*

played a key role in highlighting many other cases (the BirdLife Indonesia Programme, a major contributor to this its replacement, actually grew out of its findings). The result of all these exercises has been a constant stream of new information on birds in what are biologically the lesser known parts of the world, feeding in from and back out to the networks of BirdLife contacts in an ever-strengthening loop of understanding and commitment.

Birds to watch 2 has, we hope, continued the process. The preservation of the species in this book (including those that are Data Deficient and Near-threatened) is a major challenge to the great body of ornithologists and conservationists that lies both within and beyond the formal BirdLife network. Part of that challenge can be met, as we indicated at the start of this introduction (under '*Birds to watch* in Context'), by the strategic use of areas of overlap between the species. BirdLife has already identified 'Endemic Bird Areas' through its Biodiversity Project (ICBP 1992, Stattersfield *et al.* in prep.), key forests for threatened Afrotropical birds (Collar and Stuart 1988), key sites for threatened Neotropical birds (Wege and Long in prep.), 'Important Bird Areas' in both Europe (Grimmett and Jones 1989) and the Middle East (Evans 1994), and there is now a commitment to identify all the planet's IBAs, according to standard criteria, by the year 2000. There will always, however, be bird species beyond easy reach of the area-based approach, and their conservation by other means (species-specific intervention, policy implementation, legal enforcement) forms the other main part of the challenge. In many cases, the framework for such action is already in place, so that what is needed is mainly direction and motivation, through advocacy and example.

The ideal is that nothing should slip through the net. Red Data Books exist to prevent this from happening. This is their central and abiding contribution to the biodiversity initiative of the late twentieth century. All the same, as we noted at the outset (p. 8), the best guarantee against slipping the net is the use of a *blanket*. Stewardship of this planet—its ecologically sound management and development—requires very much more from us than the cradling of the most vulnerable of its life-forms (vital though this be); and that requirement, and all that it entails, is the strongest challenge of them all.

GLOBALLY THREATENED SPECIES

Family CASUARIIDAE

CASSOWARIES

Southern Cassowary *Casuarius casuarius* inhabits primary lowland forest, gallery forest and swamp forest to 500 m in the Aru Islands and most of the lowlands of New Guinea (Irian Jaya, **Indonesia**, and **Papua New Guinea**), except for the northwest, the Sepik–Ramu region, and some of the hilly coastal areas bordering the Vitiaz Strait and Huon Gulf (Beehler *et al.* 1986). It is also found on Seram in Indonesia (although there is reason to believe that the population there has descended from escaped birds brought from the Aru Islands: White and Bruce 1986) and in two, or possibly three, isolated populations in northern Queensland, **Australia**; there is no information on numbers in the Cape York peninsula but the more southern Australian population is estimated to total 1,500–3,000 individuals, and it has declined in most areas where habitat has been cleared or fragmented, as well as being vulnerable to dogs, shooting, traffic accidents when crossing roads, starvation and possibly also disease and but nest predation and competition from feral pigs (Garnett 1992). In New Guinea it is a species reported only infrequently by birdwatchers (and may be overlooked because of its retiring behaviour) but it is vulnerable to hunting wherever access to its habitat is increased by logging activites (K. D. Bishop *in litt.* 1994): adults are usually shot, and chicks are reared in villages to be killed for meat, creating the illusion that they have been domesticated (I. Burrows *in litt.* 1994). **VULNERABLE:** A1a,b,c,d; A2b,c,d.

Northern Cassowary *Casuarius unappendiculatus* inhabits primary lowland forest and swamp forest at altitudes of up to 700 m in the northern lowlands of New Guinea (Irian Jaya, **Indonesia**, and **Papua New Guinea**), from the Vogelkop east to the Ramu River, and including Yapen, Batanta and Salawati islands (Beehler *et al.* 1986). As with Southern Cassowary *C. casuarius* (see above) it is reported only infrequently by birdwatchers (although it may be under-recorded, as its range is little visited). It is vulnerable to hunting wherever access to its habitat is increased through logging activities (K. D. Bishop *in litt.* 1994): adults are usually shot, and chicks are reared in villages to be killed for meat, creating the illusion that they have been domesticated (I. Burrows *in litt.* 1994). **VULNERABLE:** A1a,b,c; A2b,c.

Family APTERYGIDAE

KIWIS

Brown Kiwi *Apteryx australis* (possibly comprising four species, but its taxonomy requires further clarification: A. J. Baker *per* H. Robertson *in litt.* 1994) was probably found originally throughout forest and scrub on North Island (race *mantelli*), forests and subalpine–alpine zones on South Island (nominate *australis*), and forests and scrub on Stewart Island (race *lawryi*), **New Zealand**, but has been restricted since the time of European settlement to residual forests, adjacent semi-cleared scrub, rough farmland and non-native forests (Turbott 1990). It is declining owing to predation by introduced mammals (and in some areas through being caught in poorly set gin-traps intended for possums *Trichosurus vulpecula*), but it persists in four main disjunct areas on North Island (only two of which have good numbers and long-term viability), on the west coast of South Island, and in Fiordland and Stewart Island (the only good population being on Stewart Island where there are no mustelids or pigs and few dogs) (Butler and McLennan 1990, H. Robertson *in litt.* 1994). **VULNERABLE:** A1d.

Little Spotted Kiwi *Apteryx owenii* originally
(i.e. during pre-European times) occurred in forested areas throughout **New Zealand** (H. Robertson *in litt.* 1994), but it is today known to survive only on Kapiti Island (20 km², where the population is believed to have been derived from introduced stock), Red Mercury and Hen Islands (to which translocations took place in 1983 and 1989), and Long Island (also as the result of translocation) (Turbott 1990, B. D. Bell *in litt.* 1994), and one bird has recently been found at Franz Josef on the west coast of South Island (Anon. 1993a). Total numbers have diminished to a little over 1,000 birds, of which

c.95% are on Kapiti, with the population on Red Mercury an estimated 11 pairs in 1992, although expected to grow as a result of an apparently successful rat eradication operation (Robertson *et al.* 1993); breeding has been reported on Long Island (B. D. Bell *in litt.* 1994). Productivity on Kapiti appears to vary: annual nest failure rates of 87%, 89% and 100% have been recorded in some areas, with 67% of egg losses being attributable to predation by Weka *Gallirallus australis* (Jolly 1989). On the other hand, populations comprising up to 35% juveniles have also been recorded, suggesting a high level of productivity, at least in some seasons (Colbourne 1992). **VULNERABLE:** D2.

Great Spotted Kiwi *Apteryx haastii* may have
been distributed originally throughout Westland and north-west Nelson on South Island, **New Zealand**, but it is now common and widespread only in the forests of north-west Nelson, the Paparoa Range and near Arthur's Pass in the southern Alps (Turbott 1990, H. Robertson *in litt.* 1994). Habitat destruction does not threaten the species today as it is now found mostly within protected areas, but numbers are nevertheless declining in some areas as a result of predation by feral dogs and possibly by pigs and stoats, which may take the chicks, while some birds are caught in gin-traps intended for possums *Trichosurus vulpecula* (Butler and McLennan 1990). **VULNERABLE:** B1+2e.

Family TINAMIDAE
TINAMOUS

Tepuí Tinamou *Crypturellus ptaritepui* is known only from cerros Ptari-tepuí and Sororopán-tepuí, south-east Bolívar, **Venezuela**, where it inhabits cloud-forests between 1,350 and 1,800 m; the combined area of the summit and talus at these two sites is only 28 km², and fire has been shown to be a threat to the slope vegetation in the past (Mayr and Phelps 1967, Meyer de Schauensee and Phelps 1978). **VULNERABLE:** D2.

Chocó Tinamou *Crypturellus kerriae* is a poorly known endemic species of the humid primary forest of foothills (at altitudes of 300–760 m) in the border region of Darién province, **Panama**, and Chocó department, **Colombia**, where it has been recorded

on just a small number of occasions. It has been judged fairly common or uncommon to rare. Although it may be safe within the Darién National Park of Panama, habitat in Colombia is disappearing through road construction, settlement and timber extraction (Collar *et al.* 1992). **VULNERABLE:** B1+2c; C2a.

Magdalena Tinamou *Crypturellus saltuarius*, still of some taxonomic uncertainty, remains known from only the type-specimen collected in 1943 at Ayacucho, Cesar, in the Río Magdalena valley, **Colombia**, where if it is not already extinct it will be at risk probably from hunting and certainly from clearance of the dry deciduous forest that grows (or grew) in the area, most of which is now converted to cattle-ranches (Collar *et al.* 1992). **CRITICAL: B1+2c; C2b; D1; D2**.

Taczanowski's Tinamou *Nothoprocta taczanowskii* inhabits grassland and semi-humid montane scrub at the edge of fields near the treeline (2,700–4,000 m) in southern **Peru** (Junín, Apurímac, Cuzco and Puno), where it is uncommon and perhaps local, being affected by human pressures such as hunting, frequent burning of grassland and the exploitation and diminution of high-elevation copses and shrubby patches for firewood (Collar *et al.* 1992). **VULNERABLE: C2a**.

Kalinowski's Tinamou *Nothoprocta kalinowskii*, endemic to **Peru**, remains known from only two old specimens: one collected in 1894, apparently at 4,575 m south of and near Cuzco town, Cuzco, and the second taken in 1900 at c.3,000 m on the Pacific slope east of Santiago de Chuco, western La Libertad; its habitat may have been montane scrub (which is correct for the latter altitude) or else grassland or conceivably *Polylepis* woodland, although long-term occupancy of the Andes by man may have altered its original habitat and been the cause of its evident rarity and possible extinction (Collar *et al.* 1992). **CRITICAL: D1**.

Lesser Nothura *Nothura minor* appears (like the virtually sympatric Dwarf Tinamou *Taoniscus nanus*) to be at risk from the rapid and extensive conversion of its grassland and cerrado habitat to agriculture in central and south-east **Brazil** (Federal District, Goiás, Minas Gerais, Mato Grosso, Mato Grosso do Sul, São Paulo), there being few recent records, the majority of which are from three protected areas that retain original habitat in pristine condition (Collar *et al.* 1992). **VULNERABLE: A1b; C2a**.

Dwarf Tinamou *Taoniscus nanus* appears (like the virtually sympatric Lesser Nothura *Nothura minor*, see above) to be at considerable risk from the rapid and extensive conversion of its grassland and cerrado habitat to agriculture in central and south-east **Brazil** (Federal District, Goiás, Minas Gerais, Mato Grosso do Sul, São Paulo, Paraná in 1820; pre-1900 records also from the Río Bermejo, **Argentina**), there being few recent records from very scattered areas that retain original habitat (Collar *et al.* 1992). **VULNERABLE: A1b; C2a**.

Family SPHENISCIDAE
PENGUINS

Fiordland Penguin *Eudyptes pachyrhynchus* nests only in dense coastal forest on Stewart Island and several offshore islands, Solander Island and on the south-west coast of South Island, **New Zealand**, where an estimated 1,000–2,000 breeding pairs remain, mostly nesting on predator-free islands, e.g. Codfish Island; in isolated mainland colonies it is threatened by stoats, rats and the native Weka *Gallirallus australis* (McLean *et al.* 1993, Maloney *et al.* 1993, Studholme *et al.* 1994, G. A. Taylor *in litt.* 1994). **VULNERABLE: C2a**.

Snares Islands Penguin *Eudyptes robustus* breeds in forest (or other vegetation for shade), usually at 70–600 m, in the Snares Islands (3 km^2), **New Zealand** (population estimated at 23,250 pairs in 1985–1986), and has an unknown wintering range, although seven records from the waters off Tasmania and South Australia suggest a movement to-wards Australia; it is currently under no threat on shore as there are no introduced predators on the breeding islands and landing by people is strictly controlled by permit (Marchant and Higgins 1990), but the accidental introduction of rats, especially *Rattus norvegicus*, could be a problem (B. D. Bell verbally 1993). **VULNERABLE: D2**.

Erect-crested Penguin *Eudyptes sclateri* breeds on rocky terrain, primarily on the Antipodes and Bounty Islands (20 km^2 and 1 km^2 respectively) and formerly in small numbers also on Campbell Island, **New Zealand**, with a total population of probably about 200,000 breeding pairs; one pair has been found breeding on the Auckland Islands, and breeding has been attempted on the Otago peninsula of South Island (Marchant and Higgins 1990). The breeding grounds of the species lie within protected reserves but the pelagic distribution and population trends are largely unknown (A. J. Tennyson *in litt.* 1994). **VULNERABLE:** D2.

Yellow-eyed Penguin *Megadyptes antipodes* occurs on South, Stewart, Auckland and Campbell Islands, **New Zealand**, and is vulnerable when breeding (at least on South Island) to farm development, disturbance by humans and predation by introduced mammals (Robertson and Bell 1984). Nesting usually takes place within dense vegetation (this was formerly forest but scrubland, open woodland and remnant vegetation amongst pasture are now used), from near sea-level up to 250 m. The total breeding population, estimated at 1,410–1,770 pairs, has fluctuated historically, but such changes are poorly documented and are not well understood, although on South Island there appears to have been an overall downward trend (and a population decrease was also recently documented at Campbell Island), but breeding numbers have been recovering on the mainland after a crash in 1990 (Marchant and Higgins 1990, Moore 1992, Gill and Darby 1993). **VULNERABLE:** C2a.

Galápagos Penguin *Spheniscus mendiculus* nests in cracks or caves in lava at sea-level, feeding in inshore waters, in the Galápagos Islands, **Ecuador**, where a population of 6,000–15,000 birds in 1977 fell to 463 in 1984 following an El Niño event in 1982/1983, with numbers now apparently restored (minimum 3,000 pairs) but still susceptible to further perturbations (del Hoyo *et al.* 1992, Cepeda and Cruz 1994). **VULNERABLE:** A1a; C2b.

Family PODICIPEDIDAE

GREBES

Alaotra Grebe *Tachybaptus rufolavatus* is endemic to **Madagascar** and is known chiefly from Lake Alaotra, where it is now extremely rare, with the population guessed to be no more than 20 pairs, and the species is in the irreversible process of disappearing through hybridization with the Little Grebe *T. ruficollis*, hunting and trapping, the conversion of Lake Alaotra to rice production, and the various impacts of introduced fish (Collar and Stuart 1985, Young and Smith 1989, Langrand 1990, Wilmé 1994). There have been no direct observations in recent years other than 12 seen at Lake Alaotra in December 1982 (Wilmé 1994) and two seen (in addition to several apparent hybrids) near Andreba on Lake Alaotra in September 1985 (Thompson *et al.* 1987). **CRITICAL:** A1d; B1+2a,b,c,d,e; C1; C2b; **D1**.

Madagascar Grebe *Tachybaptus pelzelnii* is endemic to **Madagascar**, where in the recent past (up to the 1960s) it was common and widespread on lakes, pools and rivers at altitudes from sea-level up to 2,000 m. It has suffered a considerable decline in certain areas and the total population is now judged to number between 5,000 and 10,000 birds, facing threats from reduction of habitat (areas of lilypad may be important, and are much reduced by rice cultivation), introduction of exotic fish, and competition with the Little Grebe *T. ruficollis* (Collar and Stuart 1985; also Dee 1986, Langrand 1990, Rose and Scott 1994), by far the greatest of these threats being the loss of habitat (A. F. A. Hawkins *in litt.* 1994, O. Langrand *in litt.* 1994, T. S. Schulenberg *in litt.* 1994). It is recorded from six protected areas (Nicoll and Langrand 1989). **VULNERABLE:** A1a,b,d; A2b,d; C1; C2b.

New Zealand Dabchick *Poliocephalus rufopectus* is endemic to **New Zealand**, where it formerly occurred on South Island (last proved breeding in the early 1940s), but is today confined to North Island (with gaps in its distribution) and has a total population of perhaps 600–700 pairs (Turbott 1990). It inhabits small bodies of fresh water such as sanddune lakes and lagoons, larger inland lakes with shallow, sheltered inlets, and artificial farm dams (Robertson 1985). It is now at risk from changes in water quality, the destruction of nesting habitat, increased human activity on waterways, and predation by introduced rats and mustelids, especially when nesting (G. A. Taylor *in litt.* 1994). **ENDANGERED:** C2a.

Junín Grebe *Podiceps taczanowskii* is confined (it is flightless) to Lago de Junín in the highlands of west-central **Peru**, where in the absence of major intervention it faces immediate extinction through the effects of pollution from mining activities, regulation of the water level for a hydroelectric plant supplying the mines, and by plans to divert water to supply Lima. In the early and mid-1980s there were c.250 birds surviving, but in 1992 only 100 could be counted (Collar *et al.* 1992). This figure fell to c.50 in 1993 (Valqui 1994). **CRITICAL:** A1a,b,d; A2b,d; **B1+2c,d,e; C1; C2b**; D1; D2.

Family DIOMEDEIDAE
ALBATROSSES

Wandering Albatross *Diomedea exulans* nests on open or patchy vegetation (tussock, fern or shrubs) near exposed ridges or hillocks (for take-off) on several subantarctic islands in the Southern Ocean, including Bird Island, **South Georgia (to U.K.)**, Crozet and Kerguelen Islands (**French Southern Territories**), Prince Edward Islands (**South Africa**), Macquarie Island (**Australia**), Auckland, Antipodes and Campbell islands (**New Zealand**) and Gough Island, **Tristan da Cunha group (to U.K.)**. The total annual breeding population is estimated at less than 20,000 pairs (Marchant and Higgins 1990). Where populations have been monitored numbers have fallen by c.50% in the last 20–30 years and, although some colonies have been reduced by introduced animals (such as pigs) in historical times, the primary cause for its continuing decline today appears to be the drowning of birds on tuna longlines (Tomkins 1985, Weimerskirch and Jouventin 1987, Croxall *et al.* 1990, A. J. Tennyson *in litt.* 1994). **VULNERABLE:** A1a,c; A2c.

Amsterdam Albatross *Diomedea amsterdamensis* breeds on the Plateau des Tourbières at 500–600 m on Amsterdam Island, southern Indian Ocean (part of the **French Southern Territories**), an original total population estimate of 30–50 birds (Roux *et al.* 1983) being revised upwards in 1990 to 70, composed of 15 pairs, of which only 10 breed annually; cattle appear to have displaced the species from a wide area of the island, so in 1987 their numbers were reduced and a fence was erected to seal off part of the island, but there may yet be mortality at sea and any decrease in survival rate (94%) would be catastrophic (Jouventin *et al.* 1989, Jouventin 1994b). **CRITICAL: D1**; D2.

Short-tailed Albatross *Diomedea albatrus* once bred in huge numbers on at least 11 islands in the Izu–Bonin island chains and in the Ryukyu Islands in **Japan**, and in Taiwan and probably also on several islands off China, but exploitation for their feathers from the late nineteenth century onwards almost wiped out most populations by 1930, and the only places where breeding has recently been confirmed are the volcanic ash slopes of Torishima in the Izu Islands, on a cliff on Minami-kojima in the Senkaku Islands (King 1978–1979, Hasegawa 1984, 1991) and on Midway Atoll, Northwestern Hawaiian Islands (**U.S.A.**) (Richardson 1994). The population on Torishima increased from perhaps less than 50 birds in 1951 to approximately 500 birds in 1991 (breeding success having improved with grass transplantation to stabilize the nesting areas), but this population, while increasing at about 7% per year, remains vulnerable to volcanic eruptions, and efforts are being made to create a new colony at a stable site on the other side of the island (Hasegawa 1984, 1991). On Minami-kojima, 12 adults were observed in 1971, but breeding was not confirmed until 1988 when chicks were seen; a population of 75 was estimated in 1991, with 15 breeding pairs (Hasegawa 1991). On Midway Atoll, one or two birds have been present for the past two decades, with a single incubating bird found in November 1993, but the egg was abandoned (Richardson 1994). It is likely that there is some mortality at sea caused by driftnet and longline fisheries, it is possible that the abundant rats on Torishima predate eggs and newly hatched young, and plastic debris inadvertently fed to chicks by their parents may also be a problem (Gales 1993). **ENDANGERED: C1**; D1; D2.

Family PROCELLARIIDAE
PETRELS, SHEARWATERS

Mascarene Black Petrel *Pterodroma aterrima* is known only from **Réunion (to France)** in the Indian Ocean by four specimens collected during the nineteenth century, by two birds found dead in the 1970s, by subfossil remains on Rodrigues (Mauritius), and by rare observations of birds in the waters south of Réunion since 1964, notably in October–March (Collar and Stuart 1985, Barré 1988, Sargeant 1992, A. J. Bartle, V. Bretagnolle and J.-C. Stahl *in litt.* 1994), and with 3–5 seen off the St Etienne estuary on 30 October 1989 (R. A. Rowlett *in litt.* 1990). Threats are unknown, but must include the illegal hunting known to afflict Barau's Petrel *P. baraui* (see next page). **CRITICAL: D1**; D2.

Beck's Petrel *Pterodroma becki* (sometimes regarded as a subspecies of Tahiti Petrel *P. rostrata*: Jouanin and Mougin 1979) is known from two specimens taken at sea in 1928, one east of New Ireland and north of Buka, **Papua New Guinea**, the other north-east of Rendova Island, **Solomon Islands** (King 1978–1979). If it survives at all (and the 65-year absence of records suggests that it has either been overlooked or that numbers are very low), Bougainville Island, Papua New Guinea, is a likely place for it to breed (Hadden 1981) and, like many *Pterodroma* species, it will almost certainly be threatened by introduced predators. There have been possible sightings at sea off Wuvula, north-east New Guinea (Bourne and Dixon 1973) and in the Admiralty Islands (I. McAllan and T. Palliser *per* D. Buckingham *in litt.* 1994). **CRITICAL: D1**; D2.

Fiji Petrel *Pterodroma macgillivrayi* was known from one specimen collected on Gau Island, **Fiji**, in 1855 (King 1978–1979), until in 1984 an adult was captured there and released (Watling and Lewanavanua 1985). In 1985 a fledgling (which later died) was found (D. Watling *in litt.* 1986) and, as a result of the increased awareness among villagers and visiting ornithologists, the number of observations on Gau (mostly of juveniles) has risen to eight; although nests have still not been located (despite many hundreds of hours of searching), breeding conditions appear favourable with sufficient undisturbed mature forest, but predation by feral cats is a potential threat (Watling 1986, Watling and Gillison 1993). **CRITICAL: C2b**; **D1**; D2.

Chatham Islands Petrel *Pterodroma axillaris* breeds on South East Island (= Rangatira, c.2 km²) in the Chatham Islands, **New Zealand**, where it burrows amongst the roots of the forest floor on lowland flats and low coastal slopes (Marchant and Higgins 1990). The island has been managed as a reserve since 1954, resulting in the recovery of vegetation, but the population has remained small, recently estimated at c.800 birds, and research has shown that competition for burrows from the abundant Broad-billed Prion *Pachyptila vittata* (including lethal attacks on adults, chicks and eggs) is the main threat, whilst exploitation by man for food, and predation by introduced cats, pigs, rats and dogs probably contributed to its disappearance from Chatham and Mangere islands (Marchant and Higgins 1990, G. A. Taylor *in litt.* 1994). **CRITICAL: B1+2e**; C2b; D1; D2.

White-necked Petrel *Pterodroma cervicalis* breeds on gently sloping areas with sedges and low scrubs, over most of Macauley Island (c.2 km²) in the Kermadec Islands, **New Zealand**, and formerly bred on nearby Raoul Island (whose population was probably destoyed by feral cats); numbers were estimated at 50,000 pairs in 1988 and are possibly increasing following the removal of goats, but, despite the island being a nature reserve with access by permit only (Marchant and Higgins 1990, B. D. Bell *in litt.* 1994, A. J. Tennyson *in litt.* 1994), it remains vulnerable to the introduction of predators. A small colony (c.10 breeding pairs) has been recently reported from Philip Island, off **Norfolk Island (to Australia)** (O. Evans *per* B. D. Bell *in litt.* 1994). **VULNERABLE:** D2.

Cook's Petrel *Pterodroma cookii* is a **New Zealand** breeding species nesting in burrows on forested ridges and steep upper slopes (Marchant and Higgins 1990) on Little Barrier Island (10,000–50,000 pairs: Robertson and Bell 1984), with small colonies on Great Barrier Island (less than 20 pairs: Robertson 1985, Scofield 1990) and on Codfish Island (c.100 pairs: Robertson 1985). Introduced predators on its breeding islands have been the main threats (King 1978–1979) but eradication programmes have removed cats from Little Barrier Island (Veitch 1985) and Wekas *Gallirallus australis* from Codfish Island (Veitch and Bell 1990), and the species is now recovering (M. J. Imber *per* G. A. Taylor *in. litt.* 1994). **VULNERABLE:** D2.

Pycroft's Petrel *Pterodroma pycrofti* breeds on coastal slopes up to 140 m, burrowing under forest on 11 offshore islands along the east coast of **New Zealand** and formerly Norfolk Island (to Australia), and has an estimated population of c.2,000–2,500 breeding pairs out of a total population of c.10,000 birds; it is predated by rats *Rattus exulans* and (less seriously) by tuataras *Sphenodon punctatus* on some islands (Marchant and Higgins 1990, G. A. Taylor and A. J. Tennyson *in litt.* 1994), although rats have been eliminated from its main colony on Red Mercury Island (B. D. Bell *in litt.* 1994). **VULNERABLE:** C2a.

Defilippe's Petrel *Pterodroma defilippiana* is an eastern Pacific seabird that breeds, in burrows in grassy slopes, only on the Desventurada Islands (San Ambrosio, 10,000 or more birds in 1970; San Félix, 150–200 pairs in 1970) and Juan Fernández Islands (Robinson Crusoe or Más á Tierra, very few if any birds now; Santa Clara, hundreds, possibly thousands, in 1986, but only considered capable of holding 100–200 in 1991), **Chile**. Feral cats and coatis are blamed for the near-extinction on Robinson Crusoe, and cats are also present and causing heavy damage on San Félix, but the other two islands appear to be predator-free, although rats have been named as present at an unspecified site (Collar *et al.* 1992). **VULNERABLE:** D2.

Hawaiian Petrel *Pterodroma sandwichensis* nests in the Hawaiian Islands (**U.S.A.**) and ranges throughout the central Pacific, having once been common with large colonies on all the main islands, but numbers are today reduced to c.900 pairs in the Haleakala National Park on Maui (in shrubby vegetation between 2,500 and 3,000 m); the most serious threat is predation by introduced mammals including feral cats and mongooses (control efforts are under way), whilst fledglings occasionally become grounded after colliding with lights, a problem likely to increase with growing urbanization (Simons 1985). Records of fledglings (c.30 birds have been collected on beaches) and observations on Kauai suggest that there may be several nesting sites on that island (Gon 1988), and it may also occur on Molokai (S. L. Pimm *in litt.* 1994) and possibly Lanai (H. D. Pratt *in litt.* 1994). **VULNERABLE:** D2.

Galápagos Petrel *Pterodroma phaeopygia* is a Pacific Ocean seabird that breeds, in burrows on grassy slopes, in the highlands of the Galápagos Islands, **Ecuador** (9,000 pairs on Santa Cruz and 1,000 pairs on Floreana, but declining at around 30% per year in the five years 1978–1982, with no data for Santiago and San Cristóbal, where breeding

also occurs); introduced predators (dogs, cats, pigs, rats) and nest-site destruction (by goats, donkeys, cattle and horses) have been the chief threats, continuing in various mixes in the remaining breeding areas (Collar *et al.* 1992). A recent assessment indicates 10,000–50,000 pairs in four colonies (Cepeda and Cruz 1994). **CRITICAL: A1a,b,d; A2b,d;** B1+2b,c,e.

Barau's Petrel *Pterodroma baraui* breeds at high altitudes (c.2,700 m), probably in burrows in cinder soils under sparse vegetation on **Réunion (to France)** in the western Indian Ocean, where its estimated population of 3,000 pairs (Bretagnolle and Attié 1991) has in recent years been subjected to illegal but persistently unpoliced inshore shooting by the local citizenry, such that numbers are already believed to have been halved (C. Attié and V. Bretagnolle *in litt.* 1994). **CRITICAL: A1c;** A2c; C1; C2b.

Providence Petrel *Pterodroma solandri* nests in burrows or rock crevices on the (protected) forested upper slopes (up to 600 m) of Mounts Lidgbird and Gower on Lord Howe Island (**Australia**) (96,000 birds in 1975) and Philip Island near **Norfolk Island (to Australia)** (at least 20 birds discovered breeding in 1985), having been exterminated on Norfolk Island itself between 1790 and 1800 by hunting and by introduced pests such as pigs and goats (Marchant and Higgins 1990). **VULNERABLE:** D2.

Magenta Petrel *Pterodroma magentae* was recently rediscovered on the Chatham Islands, **New Zealand**, two birds being located in 1978, 111 years after the type-specimen was collected at sea in the southern Pacific Ocean (King 1978–1979, Crockett 1979, Williams and Given 1981). Since 1978, 64 adults have been ringed (G. A. Taylor *per* A. J. Tennyson *in litt.* 1994) and in 1993 a total population of 45–70 (M. J. Imber *per* A. J. Tennyson *in litt.* 1994) or 100–150 (D. Crockett *per* A. J. Tennyson *in litt.* 1994) individuals was postulated, but only four pairs in burrows (in forest) are known with a maximum of two chicks being produced in any one season, with none detected in 1994 (A. J. Tennyson *in litt.* 1994). The main threat is predation by cats, rats, possums and Wekas *Gallirallus australis* (B. D. Bell *in litt.* 1994). **CRITICAL: A1d; B1+2e; C2b;** D1; D2.

Zino's Petrel *Pterodroma madeira* remains known from only a few localities high in the mountains of Madeira (**Portugal**), where two small colonies held 11 occupied burrows on sheer grassy cliffs in 1969 and 20 pairs in 1981 (Collar and Stuart 1985). Recent fieldwork, undertaken as part of the Freira Conservation Project operated by the BirdLife representative in Madeira, has indicated an estimated 20–30 pairs with breeding grounds restricted to a relatively small area at c.1,600 m, where earlier threats posed by egg and specimen collectors have been replaced by predation by rats and cats (countered by project initiatives) and the degradation of the habitat by rabbits, goats, sheep and shepherds, who set fire to the area to create grazing (Zino and Zino 1986b, Zino and Biscoito 1994). **CRITICAL: D1**; D2.

Fea's Petrel *Pterodroma feae* has been recorded breeding (in burrows on grassy and rocky slopes) on four islands in the **Cape Verde Islands** and on Bugio in the Desertas off Madeira (**Portugal**), with reports in the mid-1980s suggesting a total population, under considerable human exploitation, of several hundred pairs (Collar and Stuart 1985). Fieldwork, 1986–1992, confirmed its presence on Fogo, Santo Antão, São Nicolau (several hundred pairs inferred present on Monte Cintenha, 1989) but not on Santiago, where numbers will at best be small, and altogether as many as 500 pairs may perhaps be present in the Cape Verdes, albeit hunted for food and pseudo-medicinal purposes (Hazevoet 1994). On Bugio in the mid-1980s there were judged to be about 75 pairs (Zino and Zino 1986b), but ongoing fieldwork has suggested that as many as 150–200 pairs may be present in what is now the Desertas Special Protection Area (Zino and Biscoito 1994). **VULNERABLE: D1**; D2.

Atlantic Petrel *Pterodroma incerta* occupies subtropical waters of the Atlantic Ocean between Argentina and South Africa, breeding in burrows on grassy slopes only on the **Tristan da Cunha group (to U.K.)** ('some hundreds' of pairs) and Gough Island ('some thousands' of pairs), with introduced predators present on the main island of the former (del Hoyo *et al*. 1992). **VULNERABLE: D2**.

Bermuda Petrel *Pterodroma cahow*, once an abundant nesting seabird throughout **Bermuda (to U.K.)**, was thought extinct (from habitat loss, exploitation and predation) for three centuries before 18 pairs were found breeding on tiny suboptimal rocky islets (total area 1 ha) in Castle Harbour during 1951, and since 1961 intensive management (including the creation of artificial burrows and the elimination of nest-site competition by the White-tailed Tropicbird *Phaethon lepturus*) has wrought a slow but steady increase to over 40 pairs in the 1990s (Collar *et al*. 1992). Recent numbers of breeding pairs have been 44 (with 21 young fledged) in 1993 and 45 (21 young fledged) in 1994, but with a worrying decline in hatching rate (D. B Wingate *in litt*. 1994). **ENDANGERED: D1**; D2.

Black-capped Petrel *Pterodroma hasitata* survives in small colonies in cliffs and montane forests on **Haiti** (where nests are burrowed in cliffs at 1,500–2,000 m), **Dominican Republic**, **Cuba** and probably Dominica (in that order of known importance). Records at sea both in the Caribbean and off the North American Atlantic seaboard indicate a greater numerical strength than reflected at the known or suspected sites, but predation by introduced mammals is likely to remain a serious threat, compounded in one case by a recent earthquake and possibly by human exploitation for food (Collar *et al*. 1992). **ENDANGERED: C2a**; D1; D2.

Jamaica Petrel *Pterodroma caribbaea*, a plentiful seabird two centuries ago, was killed off by introduced mongooses and human exploitation in the forests of the Blue and John Crow mountains of eastern **Jamaica**, the only certain area in which it is known to have nested (in holes under trees at 1,800–2,100 m) and where conceivably it may still survive (Collar *et al*. 1992), there having been a report of 'noisy birds flying overhead from the ocean to the high mountains' in 1965 (Gochfeld *et al*. 1994). **CRITICAL: C2b**; D1; D2.

Black Petrel *Procellaria parkinsoni* breeds in forested mountains above 300 m on Little and Great Barrier Islands, **New Zealand**, where the populations are estimated to be c.2,000 and 200 birds respectively (Marchant and Higgins 1990). Predation by cats appears to have been the biggest threat, with 100% of fledglings killed on Little Barrier Island in 1974 and 1975 (King 1978–1979), but cats have now been eradicated (Veitch 1985) and the population is increasing slowly (although birds are killed in unknown numbers on tuna longlines: A. J. Tennyson *in litt*. 1994). Populations on Great Barrier Island survive with little interference from rats and cats, but birds may still occasionally be killed for food by Maori residents (Marchant and Higgins 1990). **VULNERABLE: D2**.

Westland Petrel *Procellaria westlandica* nests only on densely forested hills near the coast at Punakaiki, South Island, **New Zealand**, where the population was estimated at 1,000–5,000 breeding pairs in 1982 (having increased since 1958 possibly because of increased amounts of offal available from fishing trawlers), with current population estimates up to 20,000 birds (Marchant and Higgins 1990). It remains vulnerable owing to predation by introduced mammals (such as dogs) and from the native Weka *Gallirallus australis* (A. J. Tennyson *in litt*. 1994). **VULNERABLE: D2**.

Pink-footed Shearwater *Puffinus creatopus* is an eastern Pacific seabird that breeds, in burrows on grassy slopes, only on Robinson Crusoe (= Más á Tierra) and Santa Clara in the Juan Fernández Islands, plus Isla Mocha off Arauco province, **Chile**, wintering in waters off western North America from April to November. A few thousand pairs exist in the main colony on Robinson Crusoe (where threats include predation by feral cats and coatis and soil erosion by goats and rabbits), up to 3,000 pairs are present on Santa Clara (where no threats are known), and the numbers and situation on Isla Mocha remain unknown (Collar *et al.* 1992). **VULNERABLE:** D2.

Townsend's Shearwater *Puffinus auricularis* (excluding race *newelli*, which is treated here as specifically distinct) is an eastern Pacific seabird that only breeds, in rocky burrows, on the three Revillagigedo Islands, **Mexico**, 650 km west of the Mexican state of Colima; the population on Clarión has been almost wiped out by feral pigs, that on San Benedicto was obliterated in a volcanic eruption in 1952 with only recent evidence of recolonization, and that on Socorro divides into at least three colonies and was in 1981 estimated at 1,000 pairs, with feral cats now known to be causing substantial losses (Collar *et al.* 1992, R. L. Curry verbally 1994). **VULNERABLE:** A1d; A2d; B1+2e; C1; C2b.

Newell's Shearwater *Puffinus newelli* (here split from Townsend's Shearwater *P. auricularis*) has a breeding population estimated at c.8,000 adults (total population probably c.10,000, perhaps more) and nests only in burrows on grassy slopes on the mountains of (mongoose-free) Kauai (but formerly bred on Maui and Molokai) in the Hawaiian Islands (**U.S.A.**); it suffers from predation (e.g. by cats, rats, dogs and pigs), destruction of some colonies by fire, possibly avian malaria and mortality of fledglings attracted to street lights (exacerbated by the fact that developing areas of Kauai are located between the colonies and the sea), and each year some 1,500 disoriented fledglings are recovered and released (Harrison *et al.* 1984, Harrison 1990, Rauzon 1991). There is now an active programme to control lights (S. L. Pimm *in litt.* 1994) and the population is probably no longer declining (H. D. Pratt *in litt.* 1994). **VULNERABLE:** D2.

Black-vented Shearwater *Puffinus opisthomelas* is restricted as a breeding bird (in burrows on grassy and rocky slopes) to the islands of Guadalupe (2,500 breeding pairs), San Benito (250–500 pairs) and Natividad (5,000–10,000 pairs, all these figures being described as rough, non-quantitative estimates) off the Pacific coast of **Mexico**, where, however, substantial predation by cats occurs, at least on Natividad, with possible mortality from gill-net fisheries (Everett and Anderson 1991, del Hoyo *et al.* 1992). **VULNERABLE:** D2.

Hutton's Shearwater *Puffinus huttoni* breeds in two colonies (c.160,000 and less than 10,000 breeding pairs, with major declines in colony size and numbers of birds) in the coastal watersheds of the Kaikoura Range, north-east South Island, **New Zealand**, from 1,200 to 1,800 m and 12–18 km inland, nesting on gentle or steep mountain slopes under tussock grass or low alpine scrubland (Marchant and Higgins 1990). Introduced stoats *Mustela erminea* prey on both adults and chicks, and this is perhaps the primary cause of declines; red deer *Cervus elaphus* and chamois *Rupicapra rupicapra* trample burrows and graze vegetation, but both these species have been reduced since 1970 and the tussock grass has regenerated (Marchant and Higgins 1990, B. D. Bell *in litt.* 1994, B. Patton *per* G. A. Taylor *in litt.* 1994). **ENDANGERED:** B1+2b,c,e; D2.

Heinroth's Shearwater *Puffinus heinrothi* is known only from a small number of specimens from the northern coast of New Britain, **Papua New Guinea** (King 1978–1979). The discovery of two individuals (one recently fledged) on eastern Bougainville suggests that it probably breeds in the Crown Prince Range (Hadden 1981), this being supported by several further records from around the island and in the Bismarck Sea (Coates 1985, K. D. Bishop *in litt.* 1987, Gardner 1987, Simpson 1990, Bailey 1992), including one flock totalling 250 birds between Buka and Kieta (Coates 1990). Observations near Kolombangara, **Solomon Islands** (Lees 1991, D. Gibbs *in litt.* 1994, M. B. Iles *in litt.* 1994, Buckingham *et al.* in prep.), suggest that it could (also) breed in the mountain forests there. Loss of breeding sites, or excessive predation on breeding colonies by feral mammals, could lead to rapid extinction (Schodde 1978) and on Kolombangara pigs are a pest with dogs becoming increasingly common (M. B. Iles *in litt.* 1994). **ENDANGERED:** C2b.

Family HYDROBATIDAE

STORM-PETRELS

Guadalupe Storm-petrel *Oceanodroma macrodactyla* was an eastern Pacific seabird only known from Guadalupe Island, **Mexico**, 280 km west of Baja California, where it nested in forested areas of the island, abundant there in 1906 but gone by 1922, apparently in reaction to predation by cats and the degradation of nesting habitat by goats; yet even now not every wooded part of the island has been checked (at least at the appropriate season), and there remains the remote possibility that small numbers survive (Collar *et al.* 1992). **CRITICAL: D1**; D2.

Family PELECANOIDIDAE

DIVING-PETRELS

Peruvian Diving-petrel *Pelecanoides garnotii* is a species endemic to the Humboldt Current, breeding in deep burrows (in rocky ground or in guano) on offshore islands along the western coast of South America from Isla Lobos de Tierra (6°27′S) in **Peru** to Isla Chiloé (42°30′S) in **Chile**. Although once abundant, its population has crashed (c.1,500 birds in Peru and an unknown number in Chile, although the largest of the two known colonies was recently only 220 pairs) under the combined strain of guano extraction (destroying nesting areas), direct exploitation by man for food, predation by introduced mammals, and loss of food supply owing to commercial fisheries (Collar *et al.* 1992). **ENDANGERED: A1a**; C2a.

Family PELECANIDAE

PELICANS

Dalmatian Pelican *Pelecanus crispus* breeds colonially within a highly fragmented range (between 30° and 50°N) from eastern Europe into east-central Asia (former **Yugoslavia** in Montenegro, **Albania, Greece, Romania, Bulgaria, Russia, Ukraine, Azerbaijan, Armenia, Turkey, Iran, Turkmenistan, Uzbekistan, Kazakhstan, Mongolia** and **China**), the European populations dispersing in winter, while those north and east of the Black Sea migrate south to **Egypt, Lebanon, Syria, Iraq, Afghanistan, Pakistan, India, Bangladesh** and **Hong Kong** (records of vagrancy from up to 14 countries) (del Hoyo *et al.* 1992, Inskipp and Collins 1993). Drainage of wetlands throughout the range (compounded by shooting, persecution by fishermen who regard the species as a competitor, collision with power lines, pesticides and disturbance at colonies) has caused a massive decline in numbers, such that, where once millions were reported from Romania alone in the past century, the total global breeding population is now 3,200–4,300 pairs (most in Kazakhstan; maximum 1,200 pairs in Europe west of the Urals) and, since many existing or proposed conservation measures cannot be assured, the prospect of further decline is real (King 1978–1979, Tucker and Heath 1994, Heredia in prep., A. J. Crivelli verbally 1994). **VULNERABLE:** C2a.

Spot-billed Pelican *Pelecanus philippensis* was once a widespread species in Asia, breeding in colonies near natural lakes and reservoirs and in tree clumps in villages, and feeding in shallow wetlands, but it has suffered a considerable decline in the past few decades, probably owing to the combination of human disturbance, hunting, destruction of nesting and roosting/loafing areas, declines in fish availability and increased pesticide usage, such that the total world population is now estimated at 11,500 individuals (not necessarily mature) (Crivelli and Schreiber 1984, Rose and Scott 1994). Breeding is currently confirmed only in **India**, **Sri Lanka** and **Cambodia**, and suspected in Sumatra, **Indonesia** (recent sightings throughout the year, including ju-

veniles, but may now be down to only a few birds: AWB IP, D. A. Holmes *in litt.* 1994), with recent non-breeding records from **Bangladesh**, **Nepal**, the **Philippines**, **Thailand** and **Vietnam**, and the status is poorly known in **China** (largely because of confusion with Dalmatian Pelican *P. crispus*), **Laos** (formerly present, but not observed during recent surveys: Salter 1993) and **Myanmar** (millions of birds until the early 1900s) (Crivelli and Schreiber 1984, Johnson *et al.* 1993; see van Marle and Voous 1988, Harvey 1990, Inskipp and Inskipp 1991, Boonsong and Round 1991, Lu 1993b, MacKinnon and Phillipps 1993, *Oriental Bird Club Bull.* 1993, 18: 67–70). **VULNERABLE:** A1a,b,c,d; C1.

Family SULIDAE

BOOBIES, GANNETS

Abbott's Booby *Papasula abbotti*, with an estimated total breeding population of 1,900 pairs in 1989 and c.3,000 pairs in 1991 (Yorkston and Green 1992), breeds only on **Christmas Island (to Australia)** (135 km²), having become extinct on Rodrigues Island, Mauritius, during the eighteenth century and on Assumption Island, Seychelles, by 1916; it perhaps bred formerly also in the Chagos group, British Indian Ocean Territory (Marchant and Higgins 1990). The birds disperse when not breeding to the nearby Indian Ocean (Diamond 1994), including waters off the south coast of Java, **Indonesia**, with one record from the east Banda Sea in May 1994 representing a major eastward extension of its known range (Becking 1976, S. van Balen *in litt.* 1994). It nests in the tops of forest trees on the island plateau and upper terraces between 100 and 260 m, where one-third of the known nesting areas were cleared for open-cut phosphate mining before

1987 (when such clearance ceased), with further damage occurring in 1988 following a cyclone (killing approximately one-third of fledglings and an unknown number of adults) (Nelson and Powell 1986, Yorkston and Green 1992). Although the estimated total population size is now greater than any previous estimate, this is probably due to the discovery of hitherto unknown nesting sites or to the colonization of new nesting areas (R. Hill *in litt.* 1994); nevertheless the population continues to decline overall because air turbulence downwind of clearings kills adults and young, and crowding by displaced breeders also reduces productivity of pairs breeding elsewhere in the forest (Garnett 1992, Reville and Stokes 1994). Since 1984 about 20% of mined areas adjacent to nesting areas have been planted in an ongoing restoration programme (R. Hill *in litt.* 1994). **VULNERABLE:** C2b; D2.

Family PHALACROCORACIDAE
CORMORANTS

Galápagos Cormorant *Phalacrocorax harrisi* is restricted to 370 km of coastline on Fernandina and Isabela in the Galápagos Islands, **Ecuador**, where it numbers around 1,000 individuals, dipping in El Niño years (a 50% decline occurred in 1983) but seeming to recover within a few seasons (some pairs may nest twice a year). It is a flightless species and shows no dispersal tendencies, rendering it extremely vulnerable to events such as human disturbance or oil pollution (Collar *et al.* 1992) and, currently, Japanese sea-cucumber fisheries (A.J.S.). Recently there were 700–800 pairs in 112+ colonies (Cepeda and Cruz 1994). **VULNERABLE:** B1+3c; D1; D2.

Campbell Island Shag *Phalacrocorax campbelli* is endemic to Campbell Island (114 km²), **New Zealand**, and adjacent waters, nesting on exposed rocky ledges or in sea caves. The population was estimated at 8,000 individuals in 1975 (Marchant and Higgins 1990). The effect of introduced rats and cats is apparently small (G. A. Taylor *in litt.* 1994). **VULNERABLE:** D2.

New Zealand King Shag *Phalacrocorax carunculatus* is a species endemic to **New Zealand**, and in 1992 it was breeding on only four rock stacks in the Marlborough Sounds of the Cook Strait, with the possibility of one further very small colony (one nest was seen at this additional site in 1981). The population has probably always been small (524 birds in the most recent count) and has been stable for the last 45 years, but early collecting by ornithologists, hunting for the fashion trade and, more recently, illegal shooting to protect fisheries are judged to have affected numbers, whilst disturbance from 'nature' tourists may be a threat today, as well as the activities of scuba divers, which can result in eggs being spilled from nests in panic departures when boats come too close, permitting subsequent predation by Kelp Gull *Larus dominicanus* and Silver Gull *L. novaehollandiae* (Schuckard 1994). **VULNERABLE:** D1; D2.

Stewart Island Shag *Phalacrocorax chalconotus* is endemic to **New Zealand**, ranging around Stewart Island and south-eastern South Island, and nesting on rocky headlands and islands (there are 11 known localities), population estimates date from the 1950s–1970s and indicate a total of c.3,000 birds (but more likely to be 5,000–8,000, perhaps 10,000, with the trend unclear: C. Lalas *in litt.* 1994) (Marchant and Higgins 1990). Most colonies are located on isolated islands and are threatened by disturbance from visitors and possibly invasion by predators (B. D. Bell *in litt.* 1994), and some birds are drowned in gill nets (A. J. Tennyson *in litt.* 1994). **VULNERABLE:** C2a.

Chatham Islands Shag *Phalacrocorax onslowi* is restricted to the Chatham Islands, **New Zealand**, with a population estimated to be less than 1,000 birds; colonies on the main Chatham Island have been disturbed by humans and farm stock, and only a single small colony now remains there, with others on offshore islands (three) and rock stacks (four) (Marchant and Higgins 1990). On one of these islands fur seals *Arctocephalus forsteri* are expanding and overwhelming the colony, which was once one of the largest (B. D. Bell *in litt.* 1994). **VULNERABLE:** B1+2d; D1.

Auckland Islands Shag *Phalacrocorax colensoi* is restricted to the Auckland Islands (62 km²) and adjacent waters, **New Zealand**, breeding on ledges and the tops of very steep cliffs on Auckland Island (less than 2,000 birds) and Enderby Island (also 2,000: G. A. Taylor *in litt.* 1994); sites are abandoned when sheltering plants are killed by guano deposition, and nests may be destroyed by sea action (Marchant and Higgins 1990). The major threat on Auckland Island is from feral pigs which destroy any colony they can reach, and thus most, if not all, colonies are now in inaccessible places (B. D. Bell *in litt.* 1994); cats are also potential predators (G. A. Taylor *in litt.* 1994). **VULNERABLE:** D2.

Bounty Islands Shag *Phalacrocorax ranfurlyi* occurs only on the Bounty Islands (1 km²), **New Zealand**, nesting there on ledges and alcoves of coastal cliffs (where it is restricted owing to the large numbers of fur seals *Arctocephalus forsteri*, White-capped Albatrosses *Diomedea cauta* and Erect-crested Penguins *Eudyptes sclateri*) (Marchant and Higgins 1990). Fewer than 1,200 individuals are estimated present in the 12 known colonies, but numbers are likely to fluctuate as a result of weather affecting feeding; the islands are free of introduced predators and protected as nature reserves (Robertson and van Tets 1982, B. D. Bell *in litt.* 1994, A. J. Tennyson *in litt.* 1994). **VULNERABLE:** D2.

Pitt Island Shag *Phalacrocorax featherstoni* is found only on the Chatham Islands, **New Zealand**, where it nests on rocky shores, headlands and cliffs on Chatham, Pitt, Mangere, Little Mangere and South East (= Rangatira) Islands, Star Keys, Pyramid Rock and Rabbit Island (Marchant and Higgins 1990).

The population is estimated to comprise fewer than 1,000 breeding pairs (Robertson and Bell 1984), and there is little information available on population trends or possible threats (A. J. Tennyson *in litt.* 1994). **VULNERABLE: D2.**

Family FREGATIDAE

FRIGATEBIRDS

Ascension Frigatebird *Fregata aquila* now has its entire breeding population confined to the 3 ha of Boatswainbird Islet, which lies 250 m off the northeast coast of **Ascension Island (to U.K.)** in the Atlantic Ocean, and since 1982 the species has been at considerably increased risk of serious disturbance. Numbers have declined from being 'huge' when breeding occurred on Ascension itself, to (up to) 10,000 breeding adults in the late 1950s, to 5,000 birds visible in 1976 (Collar and Stuart 1985), to 2,500 birds and 1,000 nests in 1988 (Blair 1989), although it is possible that recent counts reflect less a population decline than differences in counting efficiency (Ashmole *et al.* 1994). **CRITICAL: A1a; B1+2e; C2b; D2.**

Christmas Island Frigatebird *Fregata andrewsi* breeds in a small area of forest on **Christmas Island (to Australia)** (135 km^2), where the current population is estimated to be fewer than 1,600 breeding pairs (Stokes 1988). There is no information on survival rates, recruitment or trends, but pairs require 17 months to raise their single chick successfully and hence the potential of the species to recover

from population losses is low (Garnett 1992, R. Hill *in litt.* 1994). Non-breeding birds disperse northwards to **Indonesia** (Sumatra, Java, Bali, also Lombok and East Timor: MacKean 1987, Johnstone *et al.* 1993), Borneo (Indonesia, **Malaysia** and **Brunei**), **Myanmar** and **Thailand**, with isolated adults seen in the **Cocos (Keeling) Islands (to Australia)**, and as far north as the South China Sea near Guangdong (**China**) and **Hong Kong (to U.K.)** (Marchant and Higgins 1990), and also on Rennell (**Solomon Islands**) (Buckingham *et al.* in prep.). Poaching and the destruction and degradation of habitat (associated with municipal development and mining activities) on Christmas Island have probably caused a moderate reduction in the size of the population, but two of the three remaining breeding colonies are now protected within the Christmas Island National Park and hunting no longer appears to be a significant threat; the colony outside the park has, however, declined, almost certainly because of dust fallout associated with mining (Stokes 1988) and it may now be abandoned (G. Beech *per* R. Hills *in litt.* 1994). **VULNERABLE: D2.**

Family ARDEIDAE

HERONS, EGRETS, BITTERNS

Slaty Egret *Egretta vinaceigula*, with a total population now judged to number 5,000–10,000 individuals (although this may have been before the recent disclosure of its occurrence, in unstated num-

bers, in the Zambezi delta, **Mozambique**: Ginn *et al.* 1989), occurs in the Okavango delta in northern **Botswana** (breeding has been recorded), the Caprivi Strip and other parts of northern **Namibia** (breeding recorded), and the Kafue Flats, Liuwa Plain and Bangweulu Swamp in **Zambia**, wandering occasionally into Zimbabwe when not breeding (it shows some movements in response to rains, and will also breed at temporary wetlands) and probably also occurring in Shaba province, Zaïre, and adjacent eastern Angola, but it is nowhere common. Flood regulation has caused it to disappear from one part of the Kafue Flats, and there are development plans that may seriously affect the ecology of the Okavango delta, while in Namibia rice cultivation in the Caprivi Strip and developments taking place in the tourist and livestock industries are likely to have a negative impact (Collar and Stuart 1985; also Clancey 1985, Fry *et al.* 1986, MacCallum 1990, Hines 1992, Rose and Scott 1994). **VULNERABLE: C2a.**

Chinese Egret *Egretta eulophotes* formerly ranged widely in eastern Asia, but was almost eradicated by the trade in plumes which was prominent at the end of the nineteenth century and never fully recovered from this (King 1978–1979, Hancock and Kushlan 1984). The current world population is estimated to number approximately 2,500 individuals (Rose and Scott 1994), with known breeding colonies on rocky islets off the west coast of **North Korea** (200–250 birds estimated on Tegam, Sogam and Sorap islands: Scott 1989; see map in Sonobe and Izawa 1987), **South Korea** (429 nests on Shin Island in 1988, 385 in 1991: Long *et al.* 1988, Swennen and Won 1993) and **China** (60 pairs off Jiangsu, a small colony off Shandong, and a colony reported on an island in a reservoir in Henan, of 18 pairs in 1990 and five in 1991: Lansdown 1990, Wen and Sun 1993, B. Zhou *per* D. S. Melville 1994, C. Poole *in litt.* 1994) and formerly Hong Kong (to U.K.) (where there were small numbers breeding until the early 1980s: Chalmers 1986). The species winters on intertidal mudflats and in coastal marshes in the **Philippines** (probably the most important wintering area, with counts of 1,600 on Leyte, 600+ off Bohol, up to 164 on Palawan and 80+ on Olango Island near Cebu: Redman 1993, P. Magsalay *per* N. Bostock 1994, C. Poole *in litt.* 1994), **Vietnam** (up to 10: Eames *et al.* 1992, T. Mundkur *in litt.* 1994), **Thailand** (Boonsong and Round 1991), peninsular and East **Malaysia** (Lansdown 1990, D. R. Wells *in litt.* 1994), **Singapore** (rare but annual: K. K. Lim *in litt.* 1994), **Indonesia** (Sumatra, Java, Kalimantan and Sulawesi: Andrew 1992) and **Brunei** (Mann 1987), and occurs on passage in **Japan** (Brazil 1991), China (Lu 1993b), **Taiwan** (Wang *et al.* 1991a) and **Hong Kong (to U.K.)** (Chalmers 1986). The main threats are wetland reclamation and coastal development at many important breeding and wintering sites; for example, an airport being built on Yongjong island

will destroy the most important feeding area for the South Korean breeding population (Anon. 1993b). **ENDANGERED: C1**; C2a.

Madagascar Heron *Ardea humbloti*, a large but very little known waterbird breeding only in **Madagascar** though recorded also on the **Comoro Islands** (where it possibly breeds) and **Mayotte (to France)**, was reported in 1973 to have declined alarmingly and to be facing extinction unless given complete protection—although it is recorded from four protected wetland areas (Collar and Stuart 1985; also Dee 1986, Draulans 1986, Nicoll and Langrand 1989). Its relatively strong numbers in parts of northwest Madagascar (Langrand 1990, Safford 1993b, Taylor 1993b) are very patchy, and the total numbers may be well below 5,000 individuals (although this is considered unlikely by O. Langrand *in litt.* 1994), and are certainly likely to fall with persecution at breeding sites as the human population of the region increases (A. F. A. Hawkins *in litt.* 1994). **VULNERABLE: C2a.**

White-bellied Heron *Ardea insignis* is known historically from the foothills of the eastern Himalayas from **Nepal**, through north-east **India** and **Bhutan** to northern **Myanmar** (and probably south-east Tibet, China: Meyer de Schauensee 1984), and south to the hills of eastern **Bangladesh** and western and southern Myanmar; it is found along rivers in forest and in wetlands, and is apparently rare and seen singly or in small parties of four or five (Ali and Ripley 1987). It has not been recorded in Nepal during the twentieth century (Inskipp and Inskipp 1991), and the few recent records are from northeast India (Choudhury 1992, M. Jäderblad *in litt.* 1994), Bangladesh (Thompson *et al.* 1993) and Bhutan (Inskipp and Inskipp 1993a,b). It is presumably threatened by the destruction and fragmentation of its habitat (see Collins *et al.* 1991). **ENDANGERED: A1a,b; C1; C2a.**

White-eared Night-heron *Gorsachius magnificus* appears to be a bird of well-watered and densely forested habitats, including bamboo, in the foothills of mountainous areas (Hancock and Kushlan 1984). It is known from just a small number of records, in southern **China**, in Anhui, Zhejiang, Fujian, Hainan Island and Guangxi (Cheng 1987), and by one record from northern **Vietnam** (Vo Quy 1983). The only known occurrences since 1950 are in Hainan, where there were two sightings during surveys carried out in the 1960s, and Guangxi, where individuals were seen at three localities during the period 1990–1992 (F. Zhou *in litt.* 1993). The habitat of the species has been much reduced and fragmented by the extensive deforestation which has taken place within its range (see Collins *et al.* 1991). **CRITICAL:** A1b; **C1**; **C2a**; D1.

Japanese Night-heron *Gorsachius goisagi* breeds in heavily forested areas in low mountains, preferring broadleaf evergreen forest with watercourses and damp areas, on Honshu, Shikoku, Kyushu and associated islands in **Japan** (Sonobe 1982, Brazil 1991) and in small numbers on **Taiwan** (Severinghaus 1989, L. L. Severinghaus *in litt.* 1994), and has occurred on passage, in winter or as a vagrant in southern Japan, Taiwan, the **Philippines** (uncommon in winter in dense forest near water up to 1,200 m: Dickinson *et al.* 1991), eastern **Russia** (recorded in southern Ussuriland and Sakhalin: Hancock and Kushlan 1984, Knystautas 1993), **South Korea** (four records: J. Y. Park verbally 1992), south-east **China** (extremely rare: Cheng 1987), **Hong Kong (to U.K.)** (five records: Chalmers and Kennerley 1989), the Volcano Islands (Japan), **Indonesia** (three records on Sulawesi and one on the Moluccas: Andrew 1992, K. D. Bishop *in litt.* 1994), **Brunei** (one record: Elkin 1993) and **Palau (to U.S.A.)** (Hancock and Kushlan 1984). In the past 30 years it

has declined in Japan, where it appears to have become uncommon or rare throughout its former range (Brazil 1991), and its habitat is being converted to plantations (Collar and Andrew 1988). **VULNERABLE:** C1; C2a.

Australasian Bittern *Botaurus poiciloptilus* occurs in the wetlands of southern **Australia**, **New Caledonia (to France)** and **New Zealand**. There is a population probably numbering fewer than 100 pairs in south-west Australia, no overall estimate for south-east Australia (though there are only small numbers at any one site), fewer than 725 individuals in New Zealand in 1985, and in New Caledonia and the Loyalty Islands the population is likely to be small; in Australia it has probably suffered from the drainage of its habitat for agriculture, as well as from changes brought about by overgrazing and the salinization of swamps (Garnett 1992), whilst in New Zealand, swamp drainage and the grazing of wetland margins have been major factors in its decline, with shooting and collisions with powerlines being further contributory causes (B. D. Bell *in litt.* 1994). **ENDANGERED:** C2a.

Family CICONIIDAE
STORKS

Milky Stork *Mycteria cinerea* is known from southern **Vietnam**, **Cambodia**, peninsular **Malaysia** and **Indonesia** (Sumatra, Java, Bali, Sumbawa and Sulawesi) (with a single old record from peninsular Thailand: Boonsong and Round 1991), where it nests in coastal mangroves, and feeds on wetlands, tidal mudflats and saline pools, and visits fishponds and ricefields (Hancock *et al.* 1992). The bulk of the world population breeds in Indonesia, with c.5,000 individuals on Sumatra (Silvius and Verheugt 1989), birds quite widespread along the north and central-southern coasts of Java, with an estimate of 400 for West Java alone (Allport and Wilson 1986) but only one known breeding colony (AWB IP), and smaller numbers observed recently on Sulawesi (seen at several localities with a maximum count of 73: S. van Balen *in litt.* 1994) and western Sumbawa (17 birds: Silvius and Verheugt 1989), where its status is unclear. Elsewhere, 100–150 individuals form the esti-

mated population for peninsular Malaysia, with c.20 nests located at Kuala Gula in 1989 (Hancock *et al.* 1992); it is probably rare in Cambodia, where 15 individuals were observed in a stork colony at Tonle Sap in 1994 (T. Mundkur *in litt.* 1994), and it is perhaps only a vagrant in Vietnam (J. C. Eames *in litt.* 1994). The principal threats are the destruction of mangroves and wetlands for tidal rice cultivation and aquaculture, and timber exploitation, hunting and human disturbance at nesting colonies (Luthin 1987, Verheugt 1987). Several Indonesian colonies have been lost in recent years (AWB IP). **VULNERABLE:** C1.

Storm's Stork *Ciconia stormi* is known from Kalimantan and Sumatra (including the Mentawai Islands), **Indonesia**, both peninsular and East **Malaysia**, **Brunei** and peninsular **Thailand**, where it is recorded from lowland forest, including peat-swamp forest, usually along rivers or streams, or near ponds or freshwater swamps (Hancock *et al.* 1992; see Mann 1987), the optimal habitat being extreme lowland river flood-plain forest (D. R. Wells *in litt.* 1994). The species occurs widely through the Indonesian part of its range, but at only low densities, and with possibly under 300 individuals there (Silvius and Verheugt 1989), of which fewer than 150 are in southern Sumatra (Verheugt *et al.* 1993). In peninsular Malaysia the last significant (but now tiny) population is being eliminated by the clearance of riverine forest patches along the lower Perak (D. R. Wells *in litt.* 1994), and the only record in Thailand was of a nesting pair found in 1986 in an area which is now flooded by the construction of a dam (Hancock *et al.* 1992). The species is threatened by lowland deforestation, development along rivers (which are the main transport routes) in Kalimantan, and perhaps by hunting and capture for the international zoo trade; swamp forests in Indonesia are under pressure from logging activities, although it is not clear how tolerant this species is of the consequent habitat degradation (AWB IP, S. van Balen *in litt.* 1994, D. R. Wells *in litt.* 1994). **ENDANGERED:** A1b,c; **C1**; C2a; D1.

Oriental Stork

Oriental Stork *Ciconia boyciana* breeds in river valleys, wet meadows and marshes with scattered clumps of trees in the Amur and Ussuri River regions of south-east Siberia, **Russia** (a total of 700–800 pairs was found in the mid-1970s), and Heilongjiang, Jilin and eastern Inner Mongolia, north-east **China**, but it is extinct as a breeding bird in Japan (by the start of the twentieth century: King 1978–1979), South Korea (where the only post-war breeding record was in 1971: Gore and Won 1971) and North Korea (Sonobe and Izawa 1987), countries where it was formerly common. The main wintering grounds are the wetlands in the lower Chang Jiang (= Yangtze) valley, but there have also been large winter counts in **Hong Kong (to U.K.)** since 1990, and smaller numbers occur in winter (and on passage) elsewhere in China, in **Japan**, **South Korea**, **North Korea** and **Taiwan**, and at least formerly in north-east **India**, **Bangladesh** and **Myanmar** (Chan 1991, Hancock *et al.* 1992; see Scott 1989). The world population has recently been estimated at 2,500 individuals (Rose and Scott 1994), although this is perhaps too low as 2,729 were counted on autumn passage in 1986 at Beihaihe in eastern China (Williams *et al.* 1992). Threats include hunting and human disturbance, habitat destruction (draining of wetlands for agriculture and disease control, burning and cutting of nesting trees) and pesticides and other pollution (Chan 1991, Hancock *et al.* 1992, Lu 1993b), while the proposed Three Gorges Dam

Project would alter seasonal water levels of the Chang Jiang River and would put many of the major wintering grounds at risk (see Zhu *et al.* 1987). **ENDANGERED:** A2b; **C1**.

Lesser Adjutant

Lesser Adjutant *Leptoptilos javanicus* has an extensive range through southern and south-east Asia, where it is found in wetlands, pools in forest and rice-paddies, sometimes moving to agricultural fields and grasslands, and particularly in south-east Asia and the Greater Sundas it is a bird of mangroves and coastal mudflats, but its numbers appear to be much reduced throughout and it is extinct as a breeding bird in several of its range states, as a result of habitat loss (both the cutting of nesting trees and the draining of feeding areas), hunting and human disturbance (Luthin 1987, Hancock *et al.* 1992). The total world population is now estimated to be below 10,000 individuals and still declining (Rose and Scott 1994). Recent reports are from **Sri Lanka** (c.100 pairs: Hancock *et al.* 1992), **India** (135 nests located by a survey in Assam, and also nesting in Madhya Pradesh and the Sundarbans: Hancock *et al.* 1992), **Nepal** (breeds in two areas: Inskipp and Inskipp 1991), **Bangladesh** (widespread but fast disappearing: Collar and Andrew 1988), **Laos** (small numbers recorded recently in the south: Salter 1993, Duckworth *et al.* 1993a), **Cambodia** (quite numerous and widespread throughout the country, with evidence of breeding from at least three sites: T. Mundkur *in litt.* 1994), **Vietnam** (small numbers may breed in one or two protected areas, but this has not been confirmed: J. C. Eames *in litt.* 1994), **Thailand** (rare resident and occasional visitor: Boonsong and Round 1991), **Malaysia** (national total of perhaps 250–300 individuals, mostly old birds, with no proven breeding success in the peninsula for a long time: D. R. Wells *in litt.* 1994), **Brunei** (Mann 1987) and **Indonesia** (under 2,000 birds, the majority nesting in southern and eastern Sumatra with one colony known in Kalimantan, another presumed present on Bali, and occurrence on Java: Silvius and Verheugt 1989, Galdikas and King 1989, Andrew 1992, S. van Balen *in litt.* 1994). The species is known historically from southern **China** (Cheng 1987) and from **Myanmar** (Smythies 1986), but there appears to be no recent information available from these countries. **VULNERABLE:** C1.

Greater Adjutant

Greater Adjutant *Leptoptilos dubius* formerly ranged widely in northern **India**, Pakistan (vagrant only: Roberts 1991), **Nepal**, **Bangladesh**, **Myanmar** (large colonies once existed, but now believed extinct, possibly as a result of the cutting of nest trees: Hancock *et al.* 1992), **Thailand**, southern **Laos**, **Cambodia** and **Vietnam**, and was a common scavenger in the city of Calcutta and elsewhere (King *et al*. 1975, Ali and Ripley 1987). However, the only recent breeding records are from north-east India and Cambodia: in India, up to 126 nests have been located in six colonies in the 1990s around the floodplain of the Brahmaputra River in Assam, and non-breeding counts of up to 455 individuals have been made, the birds nesting in groups of trees and feeding mainly in wetlands, but seasonally moving into towns to scavenge, the main threats being the cutting of nesting trees and some hunting (Bhattacharjee 1993). In Cambodia, a population of less than 100 birds is estimated at Tonle Sap and one or two other localities, where they nest in freshwater flooded forest, and feed on inland and coastal marshes and intertidal mudflats, the main threat being considered the taking of eggs and chicks for food (Mundkur 1994). Recent records of small numbers in Nepal (Inskipp and Inskipp 1991), Thailand (Boonsong and Round 1991), Vietnam (J. C. Eames *in litt*. 1994) and an unconfirmed sighting from southern Laos (Salter 1993) presumably involve birds from these two populations. **ENDANGERED:** A1b,c; **C1**; C2a; D1.

Family THRESKIORNITHIDAE
IBISES, SPOONBILLS

Dwarf Olive Ibis *Bostrychia bocagei* is confined to primary rainforest in southern São Tomé, **São Tomé e Príncipe**, where, following an absence of records dating back to 1928 (Collar and Stuart 1985), its survival was affirmed by evidence from a hunter in 1988 (Jones and Tye in press) and confirmed by the sighting of one bird along a river in primary forest in August 1990 (Atkinson *et al*. 1991) and of four birds—whose voice and size supported the view that they belong to a distinct species (*contra* Sibley and Monroe 1990)—on flat ridges where soil had been rootled by pigs in August 1991, these latter records suggesting that the population could be small but reasonably widespread in the south of the island (T. M. Gullick *in litt*. 1994; see also Sargeant 1994). However, the future of the island's forests remains uncertain (Jones *et al*. 1992). **CRITICAL: D1**.

Northern Bald Ibis *Geronticus eremita* is in long-term decline throughout its range for reasons which are only partly attributable to habitat loss, persecution and pesticides, suggesting the possibility of some obscure natural cause (Collar and Stuart 1985). It has now lost its tiny relict breeding population at Birecik in southern Turkey, which had been supported by a local captive breeding operation, and whence the wild birds migrated through the intervening Middle East to Sudan and Eritrea (no recent records) and Ethiopia, and (presumably) to **Yemen** and **Saudi Arabia** (birds still being seen in these latter two countries, suggesting either that some Birecik birds remain on the winter quarters over several years, or that an undiscovered breeding area in Turkey, Syria or Iraq exists, or that there are undiscovered breeding areas locally in the southwest of the Arabian peninsula) (Nikolaus and Hamed 1984, Collar and Stuart 1985, Brooks *et al*. 1987, Brooks 1987a, Akçakaya 1990, Bezzel and Wartmann 1990, Schulz and Schulz 1992). The species otherwise survives only at a few dwindling colonies in **Morocco**, and hope for its long-term conservation rests with the population which is protected there in the Souss–Massa National Park, where three colonies containing a total of some 50 pairs remain stable; a colony in Algeria is now apparently extinct or almost extinct (Collar and Stuart 1985, Arhzaf 1993). The species breeds well in captivity and there are plans for re-introduction to Italy and Spain (del Hoyo Calduch 1989, Thaler *et al*. 1992, *Re-introduction News* 1993, 5: 8). **CRITICAL:** A1a; C1; **C2a**; D1.

Southern Bald Ibis *Geronticus calvus* has a population judged in the mid-1980s to be in the range 5,000–8,000 individuals, though by the end of that decade it was considered to be around 10,000, restricted to the highlands of **South Africa, Lesotho** and **Swaziland** (between 1,525 and 1,830 m in Transvaal), where it requires safe, undisturbed nesting cliffs and areas of short-grazed and recently burnt grassland in a moist environment, with a rainfall level of more than 700 mm per year (Collar and Stuart 1985; also Brooke 1984, Clancey 1985, Manry 1985a,b, Allan 1989, W. R. Tarboton *in litt*. 1994). There are only around 100 birds (breeding at several localities in the highveld) in Swaziland (Parker in press), numbers are possibly decreasing in Lesotho

(Bonde 1993), and commercial afforestation (affecting tens of thousands of hectares of habitat), coal extraction activities and human population pressures are starting to destroy habitat in one of its strongholds, Transvaal (Allan 1989, D. G. Allan *in litt.* 1994, W. R. Tarboton *in litt.* 1994). **VULNERABLE:** C2b.

White-shouldered Ibis *Pseudibis davisoni* is

known from **Myanmar** (no recent records), southwest Yunnan, **China** (no recent records), **Thailand** (once common, but now believed extinct: Boonsong and Round 1991, Hancock *et al.* 1992), **Cambodia** (none observed during surveys in 1994, but reported to be present though rare around Tonle Sap by local people: T. Mundkur *in litt.* 1994), southern **Laos** (one seen in an extension to Xe Piane protected area in 1993: Duckworth *et al.* 1993a), southern **Vietnam** (three seen and up to six reported by local people in Nam Cat Tien National Park in 1991: Robson *et al.* 1993a), East **Malaysia** (no recent records) and Kalimantan, **Indonesia** (confirmed records in the Mahakam region of flocks of seven and two at Long Iram in 1983, and a flock of 12 and a single bird between Long Wae and Tukon in 1989, plus several unconfirmed sightings: Holmes and Burton 1987, Silvius and Verheugt 1989, Petersen 1991). In Vietnam, the species occurs in narrow marshy valleys and grassy ponds in clearings within flat, forested country, and in Laos near small seasonal pools in dry woodland on level plains; widespread deforestation in the lowlands is reducing the suitable breeding habitat, hunting is considered a threat in Laos, and disturbance by fishermen is a problem in Nam Cat Tien National Park (Eames *et al.* 1992, Duckworth *et al.* 1993a, Salter 1993). **ENDANGERED:** A1b; A2b; C1; C2a; D1.

Giant Ibis *Pseudibis gigantea* formerly occurred

in central and peninsular Thailand, central and northern **Cambodia**, southern and central **Laos** and southern **Vietnam** (King *et al.* 1975, King 1978–1979), but it is believed now to be extinct in Thailand (Boonsong and Round 1991) and possibly Vietnam (J. C. Eames *in litt.* 1994), and the only definite recent records are the sightings of two individuals along rivers in an extension to the Xe Piane protected area in southern Laos in 1993 (Duckworth *et al.* 1993a). It is a lowland bird, found in both open and forested wetland habitats, and it is threatened by habitat destruction, disturbance and hunting (Hancock *et al.* 1992, T. D. Evans and R. J. Timmins verbally 1994). It was locally common in the Mekong watershed in Cambodia in the 1920s, and although none was observed during surveys in 1994 it was reported to be present but rare around Tonle Sap by local

people (T. Mundkur *in litt.* 1994), and the extensive wetlands which remain in lowland Cambodia are probably crucial to for the survival of the species (see Archibald 1992). **CRITICAL:** A1b; A2b,c; B1+2c; C1; C2a; D1.

Crested Ibis *Nipponia nippon* formerly bred in

south-east Siberia, Russia (a sighting in 1983 suggested a possible remnant population), in north-east **China**, from Zhejiang and south Shaanxi north to North Korea (with a sighting in South Korea in 1981), and in Japan, but it declined from the middle of the nineteenth century onwards—apparently because of shooting, habitat loss and, more recently, pesticides—to the point where the only known wild breeding population is in what is now a small reserve on the edge of its former range in the Qinling Mountains of southern Shaanxi, China, in forest patches at c.1,200 m and adjacent rice-paddies, ponds and rivers (King 1978–1979, Hancock *et al.* 1992). Despite the fact that 50 young birds have fledged over the past 10 years, a maximum of only 22 individuals has been counted, and the continued use of chemical fertilizers and pesticides, plus the effects of possible inbreeding, are considered to be threats to the remaining population (Zhang 1992). There are several birds in captivity in China, which have hatched several young since 1989 (see Li 1991), and two on Sado Island in Japan (N. Ichida *in litt.* 1994). **CRITICAL:** B1+2e; C1; **C2b**; **D1**; D2.

Black-faced Spoonbill *Platalea minor* is known

to breed only on four small rocky islands off the west coast of **North Korea**, where about 30 birds have been recorded in the breeding season, and in **South Korea** (a colony of 10–20 pairs discovered on an islet in the Han estuary in 1994: P. O. Won *in litt.* 1994), where it was said to be common earlier in the twentieth century, but as the world population is estimated to be 323 individuals (based on passage and winter counts), there must be undiscovered breeding sites, possibly on islands off the east coast of China (Kennerley 1990, Hancock *et al.* 1992, Dahmer and Felley in prep.). Major wintering sites listed by Dahmer and Felley (in prep.), all coastal/estuarine wetlands, are the Tsen-Wen River estuary in **Taiwan** (206 birds in 1993/1994), Mai Po and inner Deep Bay marshes, **Hong Kong (to U.K.)** (70 in 1993/1994) and the Red River and Day River estuaries in **Vietnam** (only 25 in total in 1993/1994, but counts of 68 and 27 respectively in 1992/1993: Duc *et al.* 1993), with smaller numbers in **China** (recent records from the Hong Kong area, Poyang Lake in Jiangxi, the Jiangsu coast and Hainan: see Kennerley 1987a, 1990, Wang 1993), **Japan**, South Korea, the **Philippines** (though there have been no records since

1914: Dickinson *et al.* 1991), **Thailand**, southern Vietnam (J. C. Eames *in litt.* 1994), and possibly Brunei (Mann 1987). Threats include the reclamation of intertidal mudflats for agriculture, conversion to aquaculture or industrial uses, increased disturbance, hunting and pollution, the largest known wintering concentration (in Taiwan) being immediately threatened by industrial development (Kennerley 1990, Hancock *et al.* 1992, J. C. Eames *in litt.* 1994, Dahmer and Felley in prep.). **CRITICAL: A2b**; C1; C2a; D1; D2.

Family PHOENICOPTERIDAE

FLAMINGOS

Andean Flamingo *Phoenicopterus andinus* occurs on high mountain lakes in the puna zone of south-west **Peru**, northern **Chile**, south-west **Bolivia** and north-west **Argentina**, at altitudes which are mainly between 2,300 and 4,000 m, breeding having been recorded at only a few localities: Laguna Vilama (Argentina), Laguna Colorada (Bolivia: 1,000 breeding pairs in 1992–1993, although human predation of eggs caused 100% failure) and five sites in Chile, of which Salar de Atacama is the bird's main and perhaps only regular breeding location, with a total population judged well under 50,000 birds (Blake 1977, Hurlbert and Keith 1979, Scott and Carbonell 1986, Maier and Kelly 1994). Egg-harvesting and mining activities may be to blame for consistently low breeding success (Johnson 1965, Glade 1988, Maier and Kelly 1994, J. Fjeldså *in litt.* 1986), and the species may in any case be nomadic in search of temporally patchy food, rendering it particularly susceptible to man-induced perturbations to its natural cycle (see Bucher 1992). **VULNERABLE:** A2b,c.

Puna Flamingo *Phoenicopterus jamesi* occurs at a large number of scattered brackish and salty lakes in the high mountains of the puna zone of south-western **Peru**, northern **Chile**, south-western **Bolivia** and north-western **Argentina**, at altitudes mainly between 2,300 and 4,500 m, with most (and the only regular) breeding taking place at Laguna Colorada (Bolivia), where up to 30,000 birds (including 9,000 breeding pairs) have been present, although a second colony has flourished under protection at Salar de Tara (Chile) (Blake 1977, Hurlbert and Keith 1979, Scott and Carbonell 1986, Glade 1988, Maier and Kelly 1994); egg-collecting and disturbance cause considerable problems (Flores 1988, Maier and Kelly 1994), and the species may in any case be nomadic in search of temporally patchy food, rendering it particularly susceptible to man-induced perturbations to its natural cycle (see Bucher 1992). **VULNERABLE:** A2b,c.

Family ANATIDAE

DUCKS, GEESE, SWANS

West Indian Whistling-duck *Dendrocygna arborea*, despite its large range in fresh- and saltwater marshes through the **Bahamas, Turks and Caicos (to U.K.), Cuba, Cayman Islands (to U.K.), Jamaica, Haiti, Dominican Republic, Puerto Rico (to U.K.), Virgin Islands (to U.K.), Virgin Islands (to U.S.A.), St Kitts and Nevis** and **Antigua and Barbuda**, has suffered everywhere from wetland drainage and relentless but continuing illegal hunting pressure, so that today its status is precarious (no clear population estimates even at the national or island level, but overwhelming qualitative evidence of massive declines in the past), with serious needs for law enforcement, key-site conservation, and much more detailed survey work (Collar *et al*. 1992). The 200–300 birds that feed overnight on Hog Cay, Bahamas, are now the subject of a radio-tracking study of habitat use and breeding biology (Staus 1994). **VULNERABLE:** C2a.

White-headed Duck *Oxyura leucocephala*

breeds on small, shallow, brackish or freshwater lakes, marshes and lagoons (often endorreic, i.e. with a closed-basin hydrology) with dense fringing vegetation in arid regions in **Spain**, **Algeria**, **Tunisia**, **Romania** (now irregularly), **Turkey** (in small numbers, but Burdur Gölü hosts the largest known wintering population: 11,000 birds), **Iran**, **Afghanistan**, **Uzbekistan**, **Kazakhstan** (major breeding country) and **Russia** (with breeding records also from **Mongolia** and **China**, where current status is unclear), having become extinct as a breeding bird this century in Morocco, France (Corsica only), Italy (also Sardinia and probably Sicily), Hungary, former Yugoslavia (Serbia), Albania, Israel and Azerbaijan, although still dispersing on passage and in winter to similar (though sometimes entirely saline) habitats in the countries above plus **Morocco**, **Italy**, **Albania**, **Bulgaria**, **Greece**, **Cyprus**, **Israel**, **Egypt**, **Syria**, **Saudi Arabia**, **Iraq**, **Azerbaijan**, **Turkmenistan**, **Tajikistan**, **Pakistan** and **India** (records of vagrancy from up to 13 countries, and indeed in some of those above its status has dwindled towards that of vagrant only); although the total population may currently be stable at around 18,000–19,000 birds, a serious decline, attributable to extensive drainage, pollution, water management schemes and hunting, has been in progress until recently (e.g. 50,000 birds wintering in the Caspian Sea in the 1930s, no more than 1,000 since the 1960s), and hybridization with the escaped, invasive Ruddy Duck *O. jamaicensis*, which is already affecting the outpost Spanish population, may become irreversible within the next few years (Collar and Andrew 1988, Anstey 1989, Anstey and Moser 1990, Green and Anstey 1992, del Hoyo *et al*. 1992, Gantlett 1993, Inskipp and Collins 1993, Rose and Scott 1994, Tucker and Heath 1994, Heredia in prep.). **VULNERABLE:** A2d.

Freckled Duck *Stictonetta naevosa* ranges widely

across **Australia**, but breeding records are clustered in the south-west of Western Australia and the Murray–Darling drainage in New South Wales; it inhabits open lakes and swamps and gathers in a few refuge areas when the wetlands of the interior dry up (Blakers *et al*. 1984). A census in 1983 grossed 8,000 (Cowling and Davies 1983), though not all wetlands were visited and it was projected that the total population in eastern Australia was not more than 19,000 birds (Martindale 1986). The popula-

tion size appears to fluctuate greatly and is threatened by wetland drainage, for instance on the Perth coastal plain, from which most breeding records have been obtained (75% of suitable wetlands have been lost or significantly altered), and also by hunting (owing to misindentification) especially during inland drought when birds congregate closer to the coast (Garnett 1992; see also Norman *et al*. 1994). **VULNERABLE:** B1+3d.

Swan Goose *Anser cygnoides* breeds in wet

grasslands and reedbeds near rivers and lakes in Heilongjiang and Inner Mongolia, north-east **China**, **Mongolia**, south-east and southern **Russia** as far west as the Altai Mountains, and north-east **Kazakhstan** (Dement'ev *et al*. 1967, Cheng 1987). The main wintering area is around the lower and middle reaches of the Chang Jiang (= Yangtze) River in eastern China, with particularly large concentrations at Poyang Lake (up to 50,000 birds: Scott 1989) and the Yancheng Marshes (35,000 in January 1988: Scott 1989), and smaller numbers in winter and on passage elsewhere in China, and in **South Korea** (several hundred regularly wintering on the Han river estuary since 1990, with 1,858 present in March 1994: P. O. Won *in litt*. 1994), **Japan** (formerly regular in winter but now rare: Brazil 1991), **North Korea** (Gore and Won 1971) and **Taiwan** (Wang *et al*. 1991a). A dramatic decline attributed to habitat loss and large-scale hunting in the middle and lower Chang Jiang valley (Lu 1993a,b) has resulted in the total world population now being judged as low as 50,000 (Rose and Scott 1994), and the planned construction of the Three Gorges Dam will disrupt the flow of the Chang Jiang River and further reduce its wintering habitat (see Zhu *et al*. 1987). **VULNERABLE:** A1b,c; A2b,c.

Lesser White-fronted Goose *Anser erythropus*

breeds in lightly wooded tundra, on hills and by lakes south of the Arctic Circle in northern **Norway**, **Sweden**, **Finland** and predominantly **Russia**, wintering in or migrating through steppes and dry farmland in **Latvia**, **Albania**, former **Yugoslavia** (Serbia), **Hungary**, **Romania**, **Bulgaria**, **Greece**, **Turkey**, **Iraq**, **Iran**, **Azerbaijan**, **Turkmenistan**, **Pakistan**, **India**, **China** and **Japan** (records of vagrancy in up to 12 countries); a drastic decline throughout its range, attributed with only partial confidence to loss of feeding habitat and hunting in the winter quarters, has seen the Fennoscandian population dwindle to around 50 pairs, migrants in Hungary drop from up to 120,000 before 1950 to a few thousand by around 1980, and the Russian numbers, albeit with conflicting evidence, fall precipitously (Collar and Andrew 1988, del Hoyo *et al*. 1992, Inskipp and Collins

1993, Rose and Scott 1994, Tucker and Heath 1994, Heredia in prep.). **VULNERABLE:** A1a,b,c.

Nene *Branta sandvicensis* inhabits rocky, sparsely vegetated, high volcanic slopes in the Volcanoes National Park and surrounding areas on Hawaii and in the Haleakala National Park on Maui (Pratt *et al.* 1987), and also occurs in lowland grass pastures on Kauai (a feral flock established from 12 founders in 1982) in the Hawaiian Islands (**U.S.A.**), numbering some 555 birds in 1989–1990 (339, 184 and 32 birds respectively); it declined from an estimated 25,000 at the end of last century to a low of perhaps 30 in 1951, mainly through excessive hunting, and only the release of over 2,100 birds on Hawaii and Maui in the period 1960–1990 has maintained it in the wild (Black *et al.* 1991). Potential problems today include inbreeding depression, loss of adaptive skills, disease, poaching, road kills, dietary deficiencies and predation from introduced mammals (see Marshall and Black 1992; also Banko 1992). In a 'status quo' computer simulation the flock on (mongoose-free) Kauai was the only one to survive whilst in an 'optimal management' simulation (where predation was reduced and feeding opportunities enhanced) the two flocks on Hawaii and Maui quickly flourished to self-sustaining levels and approached carrying capacity at 2,000 individuals (Black and Banko 1994). **VULNERABLE:** D1.

Red-breasted Goose *Branta ruficollis* breeds on tundra in the Taymyr, Gydan and Yamal regions of **Russia** (although there is an anomalous breeding record from Erçek Gölü in Turkey), with a total population now known to be as high as 75,000, but with almost all of these birds wintering at lagoons and lakes (and feeding in adjacent cereal fields) along the northern and western shores of the Black Sea in **Ukraine**, **Romania** and **Bulgaria** (some also irregularly in Hungary, Greece, Turkey, Iran, Turkmenistan and Kazakhstan, with records of vagrancy from up to 22 countries), and concentrating at 3–4 apparently fixed roosts; these flocks at present remain highly vulnerable to illegal hunting and changes in land use (either through intensification or, paradoxically, abandonment), while breeding areas continue to be fragmented and disrupted by oil and gas exploration (Collar and Andrew 1988, Grimmett and Jones 1989, Vinokurov 1990, Vangeluwe and Stassin 1991, del Hoyo *et al.* 1992, Inskipp and Collins 1993, Sutherland and Crockford 1993, Rose and Scott 1994, Tucker and Heath 1994, Heredia in prep., J. M. Black verbally 1994). **VULNERABLE:** A2b,c; B1+2c,d.

Crested Shelduck *Tadorna cristata* is known by three specimens and a number of sight records from eastern **Russia**, **North Korea**, **South Korea** and **Japan** (details and hypothetical distribution map in Nowak 1984), the most recent confirmed sightings being of at least three on islands south-west of Vladivostok, Russia in May–June 1964, six on the north-east coast of North Korea in March 1971 and two in eastern Russia in March 1985 (J. G. Walmsley *in litt.* 1992). A project to distribute large numbers of leaflets (in four languages in all four known range states plus China) depicting the species and requesting information has resulted in a number of reports by hunters and fishermen in north-east China (Zhao *et al.* 1990, Zhao 1993) and in speculation that the species may breed in the mountains on the border between China and North Korea (E. Nowak verbally 1988). **CRITICAL:** D1.

White-winged Duck *Cairina scutulata* has a large range, extending from north-east **India** to Sumatra and Java, **Indonesia**, with recent records from India (five districts in Assam and three in Arunachal Pradesh), **Bangladesh** (Chittagong Hill Tracts), **Myanmar** (close to the border with Thailand), **Laos** (one unconfirmed sighting in Xe Piane protected area in 1992, and three seen in the Nakai Plateau/Nam Theun protected area in 1994: Duckworth *et al.* 1993a, T. D. Evans and R. J. Timmins verbally 1994), **Cambodia** (not observed during surveys in 1994, but reported to occur at Tonle Sap by local people: T. Mundkur *in litt.* 1994), **Vietnam** (Nam Cat Tien National Park and Ho Ke Go: J. C. Eames *in litt.* 1994), **Thailand** (south-west, north-east, peninsular and south-east: see Parr *et al.* 1994), peninsular **Malaysia** (possible record in Johore, but no confirmed records this century) and Indonesia (six of the eight provinces on Sumatra, with a population of 30 individuals in Way Kambas National Park: Rudyanto in press), although large parts of its range have recently been inaccessible to ornithologists, notably in Myanmar (Green 1992, 1993b). It occurs in areas with moist tropical forest (essential for nesting and roosting) holding or providing access to stagnant or slow-moving wetlands (essential for feeding), usually below 200 m but locally up to 900 m or higher. There has clearly been a major decline in numbers during this century (and it may be extinct in Malaysia and Java), and the known population is only 336 individuals (although this is very much a minimum figure), the main cause of decline being deforestation of lowlands, reducing the total area of habitat and fragmenting populations, but other threats include inappropriate forest management, drainage of wetlands, hunting, human disturbance, probably pesticides and pollution (Green

1992, 1993b), and possibly the spread of disease from escaped captive birds (R. H. Raza *in litt.* 1994). **ENDANGERED:** A1b,c,d; **C1**; **C2a**; D1.

Blue Duck *Hymenolaimus malacorhynchus* was formerly widespread in North Island and most of South Island, **New Zealand**, but since European settlement its range and numbers have decreased, and it is now largely confined to turbulent water-courses (where caddisfly larvae, an important food, thrive) in the forested mountain ranges of the west of South Island and central North Island, with a total population estimated at 2,000–4,000 birds; it has disappeared from lowland rivers because grazing and clearance of waterside vegetation has resulted in siltation and a consequent rise in nutrient levels and de-oxygenation of water (Marchant and Higgins 1990). There is anecdotal evidence of recent local population increases in North Island and local contractions in South Island, so the current overall population trend is unclear (D. Cunningham *per* J. Molloy *in litt.* 1994). **VULNERABLE:** C2a.

Salvadori's Teal *Salvadorina waigiuensis* is widely distributed on alpine lakes and fast-flowing rocky streams, usually between 500 and 3,700 m, in the Vogelkop, Central Ranges and Huon mountains of New Guinea (Irian Jaya, **Indonesia**, and **Papua New Guinea**) (Coates 1985, Beehler *et al.* 1986). Although large areas of suitable habitat remain, human disturbance in the watersheds (for example the recent establishment of copper and gold mining in central New Guinea: K. D. Bishop *in litt.* 1994) may increasingly pose a threat as will hunting (local extinctions have already occurred), while trout and other insectivorous fish, which have been introduced to various river systems, may also affect it adversely; the total population seems likely to be in the range 2,500–10,000 individuals, stable or slowly declining (Callaghan and Green 1993). **VULNERABLE:** C2a.

Hawaiian Duck *Anas wyvilliana*, once an inhabitant of all the main Hawaiian Islands (**U.S.A.**), but now restricted to (mongoose-free) Kauai and re-introduced on Oahu and Hawaii, has suffered from loss of its wetland habitat—to a tiny area (c.2 km^2) which continues to be under threat (S. L. Pimm verbally 1994)—and predation by mongooses, rats, cats and dogs (King 1978–1979, Pratt *et al.* 1987). Its population is thought to be stable at c.2,500 (2,000 on Kauai, 300 on Oahu and 200 on Hawaii) and hybridization with Mallard *A. platyrhynchos* is not the problem it was once thought likely to become (Callaghan and Green 1993, Engilis and Pratt 1993). **VULNERABLE:** D2.

Laysan Duck *Anas laysanensis* is endemic to Laysan Island (3.7 km^2) in the Northwestern Hawaiian Islands (**U.S.A.**), where it feeds on brine flies and shrimps in the central lagoon and nests in the surrounding dense stands of shrubs and grasses. It was near extinction in the late nineteenth and early twentieth centuries, partly owing to shooting for sport and food by guano-miners and feather-hunters, and partly to the denudation of vegetation by introduced rabbits (eliminated in 1923) (Marshall 1992). In 1987 numbers were estimated at 500, which probably represents the carrying capacity of the habitat, and although extreme fluctuations in the population have been noted since the 1950s, these may reflect different census methods (Marshall 1992). Control is currently under way to eradicate an aggressive alien plant *Cenchrus echinatus* which may threaten the nesting habitat (K. McDermond *in litt.* 1993), and in 1993 there was a complete breeding failure, possibly owing to drought and food shortage (USFWS *in litt.* 1994). **VULNERABLE:** D1; D2.

Madagascar Teal *Anas bernieri* is a little-known and possibly (at least formerly) much persecuted duck of shallow, open water (fresh or saline, perhaps most often brackish), endemic to **Madagascar**, apparently confined to a few sites (only one area, Analabe, is protected, but privately, and habitat there may be little: A. F. A. Hawkins *in litt.* 1994, O. Langrand *in litt.* 1994) along the west coast with a low total population, owing to extensive habitat loss and disturbance (Collar and Stuart 1985, R. J. Safford *in litt.* 1994; also Dee 1986, Nicoll and Langrand 1989, O. Langrand *in litt.* 1994). In July–August 1993 75–95 were seen and 100–500 were estimated present between Antsalova and Morondava (Safford 1993b), and at the same time four birds were captured to start a captive breeding programme (Young *et al.* 1993); a previously known site (Lake Kinkony) held no birds but a flock of 11 was seen on mudflats in the Betsiboka estuary, October 1993 (A. F. A. Hawkins *in litt.* 1994). **ENDANGERED:** C2b; D1.

Brown Teal *Anas aucklandica* is endemic to **New Zealand** and has suffered from wetland drainage (the main threat along with the deterioration of stream headwaters, which are key habitats: B. D. Bell *in litt.* 1994), introduction of predators, excessive shooting and possibly poultry disease: *A. a. chlorotis* is distributed widely but only in small relict populations, often remote from humans, and has a population of fewer than 2,100, with c.1,400 on Great Barrier Island and up to 500 in Northland, the only remaining viable strongholds; nominate *aucklandica* is flightless and occurs on the larger Auckland Islands not inhabited by cats or rats, and has a total population

thought on the basis of fieldwork in 1991–1992 to be 1,500 (Williams 1994); and *A. a. nesiotis*, also flightless, is confined to Dent Island, an offshore islet of Campbell Island, and numbers 60–100 birds (King 1978–1979, M. J. Williams *in litt*, 1994; also Marchant and Higgins 1990, the latter treating all three subspecies as full species). **VULNERABLE:** B1+2b,c,d,e.

Baikal Teal *Anas formosa* breeds in river valleys and basins within the forest zone of north and northeast Siberia, **Russia**, and winters in **South Korea**, **North Korea**, **Japan**, east and south-east **China** and **Taiwan**, with vagrant records from several other Asian and European countries (Cramp and Simmons 1977, Wang *et al.* 1991a, Inskipp and Collins 1993). A dramatic decline has occurred this century, so that in Japan it has decreased from common or abundant in winter to very uncommon within the past 50 years (Brazil 1991), and on passage at Beidaihe in eastern China very small numbers have been recorded since 1985, in contrast to large numbers in the early part of the century (Williams *et al.* 1992). The only large concentrations recorded recently are in South Korea, where counts in February 1993 at two localities (Chunan Reservoirs and Sapkyo Lake) totalled c.20,000 and 30,000–35,000 birds respectively (Mundkur and Taylor 1993, P. O. Won verbally 1994). The main cause of the decline is believed to be hunting on passage and in winter, as the birds' habit of gathering in large, dense flocks and making predictable daily movements to feeding grounds renders them unusually susceptible to shooting or netting in large numbers (there is a record of c.50,000 birds being caught in the course of 20 days by three hunters in Japan in 1947) and killing by spreading poisoned grain in feeding areas (Poole in prep.). **VULNERABLE:** A1a,c,d; D2.

Marbled Teal *Marmaronetta angustirostris* breeds on shallow eutrophic lakes with fringing cover in **Spain**, **Senegal**, **Morocco**, **Algeria**, **Tunisia**, **Egypt**, **Israel**, **Turkey**, **Iraq**, **Iran**, **Armenia**, **Azerbaijan**, **Georgia**, **Russia**, **Kazakhstan**, **Uzbekistan**, **Turkmenistan**, **Afghanistan**, **Pakistan**, **Tajikistan** and **China** (Kekamkyi Lake), with wintering areas poorly understood but extending from the countries above to include **Mali**, **Chad** and **India**, preferred habitat then being recently flooded seasonal wetlands. Hunting, pollution and above all drainage are blamed for the extreme fragmentation of range and massive decline in numbers this century (total population currently put at 33,000 birds), the most serious current threat being the conversion of the southern Iraq marshes where many thousands of pairs may breed (Collar and Andrew 1988, Scott 1989, del Hoyo *et*

al. 1992, Green 1993a, Inskipp and Collins 1993, Rose and Scott 1994, Tucker and Heath 1994, Heredia in prep.). **VULNERABLE:** A2b.

Pink-headed Duck *Rhodonessa caryophyllacea* was formerly a local species found on wet ground and pools in the forests and grass jungles of northeast **India** (Ripley 1982) and northern **Myanmar** (Smythies 1986), recorded in central **Nepal** last century, and last sighted at Bihar, India, in June 1935 (Ali and Ripley 1987, Inskipp and Inskipp 1991). It was regarded as extinct by King (1978–1979), but there are reports of sightings by hunters in northern Myanmar (e.g. U Tun Yin *in litt.* to W. B. King 1979) and its extinction cannot be confirmed until this part of its former range has been surveyed. The reasons for its decline are not fully understood, but the conversion of its habitat to agricultural land and hunting are likely causes (Ali 1978). **CRITICAL: D1.**

Ferruginous Duck *Aythya nyroca* breeds in shallow pools and marshes with abundant emergent and shoreline vegetation in **Morocco**, **Spain**, **Germany**, **Austria**, **Italy**, **Albania**, **Slovenia**, **Croatia**, former **Yugoslavia** (Serbia, Montenegro), **Bosnia-Herzegovina**, **Macedonia**, **Czech Republic**, **Slovakia**, **Hungary**, **Bulgaria**, **Romania**, **Greece**, **Moldova**, **Poland**, **Lithuania**, **Latvia**, **Belarus**, **Russia**, **Ukraine**, **Georgia**, **Azerbaijan**, **Armenia**, **Turkey**, **Israel**, **Saudi Arabia**, **Iran**, **Turkmenistan**, **Uzbekistan**, **Kazakhstan**, **Tajikistan**, **Afghanistan**, **India**, **Mongolia** and **China**, migrating through or wintering (often on larger lakes and lagoons and coastal marshes) in **France**, **Belgium**, **Netherlands**, **Switzerland**, **Malta**, **Libya**, **Tunisia**, **Algeria**, **Senegal**, **Mali**, **Niger**, **Nigeria**, **Chad**, **Cameroon**, **Central African Republic**, **Sudan**, **Ethiopia**, **Egypt**, **Cyprus**, **Lebanon**, **Jordan**, **Yemen**, **Oman**, **United Arab Emirates**, **Iraq**, **Pakistan**, **Nepal**, **Bhutan**, **Bangladesh**, **Myanmar**, **Thailand** and **Vietnam** (records of vagrancy from at least 23 countries). The various populations have apparently undergone massive declines (e.g. from 140,000 pairs in the former U.S.S.R. in 1970 to 5,200 pairs in 1984), attributed to wetland drainage compounded by high hunting pressure, so that the global total is now put at 75,000 birds (del Hoyo *et al.* 1992, Inskipp and Collins 1993, Rose and Scott 1994, Tucker and Heath 1994). **VULNERABLE:** A1a,b,c.

Madagascar Pochard *Aythya innotata* is a freshwater diving duck, endemic to **Madagascar**, apparently confined to lakes and pools (most importantly Lake Alaotra) in the northern central plateau, where—for reasons unknown—it has become increasingly rare this century, with the last certain record at Lake

Alaotra in 1960 and one reported sighting near Antananarivo in 1970 (Collar and Stuart 1985, Young and Smith 1989) until the capture alive of a single male in August 1991 (Wilmé 1993), although this bird is now dead (R. J. Safford *in litt.* 1994). Intensive searches at Alaotra in 1989–1990 and 1993 (the latter by M. Pidgeon) failed to discover more birds (Wilmé 1994, R. J. Safford *in litt.* 1994). **CRITICAL:** A1a; **D1**.

Baer's Pochard *Aythya baeri* breeds in marshes and lakes with emergent vegetation in eastern **Russia** (for details of distribution see Nechaev and Gluschenko 1993), north-east **China** (Cheng 1987) and probably North Korea (Inskipp and Collins 1993), and occurs on passage or winters in wetlands in **North Korea**, **South Korea**, **Japan** (Brazil 1991), eastern China, **Taiwan** (Wang *et al.* 1991a), **Hong Kong (to U.K.)** (Chalmers 1986), north-east **India** (Ali and Ripley 1987), **Nepal** (Inskipp and Inskipp 1991), **Bangladesh** (a total of 1,712 counted at four localities in early 1993: Thompson *et al.* 1993), **Myanmar**, **Thailand** (uncommon: Boonsong and Round 1991) and northern **Vietnam** (J. C. Eames *in litt.* 1994; see Scott 1989), with a total world population of possibly below 10,000 birds (Rose and Scott 1994). Historical records of passage migrants from Beidaihe in eastern China suggest that a substantial decline may have taken place early this century, as it was described as 'extremely abundant' between 1910 and 1917, but has only been recorded in small numbers since (Williams *et al.* 1992), there has been a sharp decline in Russia in recent years linked with drainage for rice cultivation, increased disturbance and illegal hunting (Kolosov 1983, Nechaev and Gluschenko 1993), and a locality known regularly to support large wintering concentrations, Lake Boraphet in Thailand (maximum count of 426), is currently threatened (*Oriental Bird Club Bull.* 1992, 16: 11). **VULNERABLE:** A1a,b; C1.

Spectacled Eider *Somateria fischeri* breeds on small lakes, pools, bogs and streams of the tundra along the coasts of Alaska, **U.S.A.**, and along the Arctic Ocean coast of north-east **Russia**, presumably wintering in the Bering Sea, with a total population of 200,000 breeding birds and perhaps 400,000 individuals in the mid-1970s (del Hoyo *et al.* 1992). However, a massive decline of over 90% has occurred since that time, for reasons that remain unknown, although guesses include overhunting, habitat deterioration and global warming (Alison 1993a,b). **VULNERABLE:** A1a.

Steller's Eider *Polysticta stelleri* breeds on pools, lakes, rivers and tundra bogs along the Arctic coast from the Taymyr peninsula, **Russia**, eastwards into northern Alaska, **U.S.A.**, wintering on rocky coasts, in bays and on estuaries in the Bering Sea from southern Alaska across the Aleutian Islands to the Kamchatka peninsula and the Kuril Islands, with non-breeding summer populations in western Novaya Zemlya and in northern **Norway** and adjacent Russian waters (Murmansk to the White Sea, including two breeding records), and (presumably these birds) wintering in Norwegian/Russian waters and the Baltic Sea (**Sweden**, **Finland**, **Estonia**, **Latvia**, **Lithuania**, **Poland**, **Denmark**); although locally abundant into the early 1970s, with a total population of 500,000 (80% of these wintering in the Aleutians), it has suffered a steep decline (blamed, perhaps implausibly, on excessive hunting) such that the Aleutian population is now one quarter of its recent size (del Hoyo *et al.* 1992, Alison 1993a,b, Tucker and Heath 1994). **VULNERABLE:** A1a.

Brazilian Merganser *Mergus octosetaceus* is critically endangered by the perturbation and pollution (largely as direct and indirect consequences of deforestation) of the shallow, fast-flowing rivers that are this duck's habitat in south-central **Brazil** (Goiás, Minas Gerais; formerly Mato Grosso do Sul, São Paulo, Paraná and Santa Catarina), eastern **Paraguay** and northern **Argentina** (Misiones), so that it now occurs in extremely low numbers (no more than a few pairs, and usually only one) at extremely few, highly disjunct localities (Collar *et al.* 1992). A survey of 400 km of seemingly suitable rivers in Misiones, July–September 1993, resulted in the observation of a single bird, and the speculation that the species' survival in Argentina is unlikely in the long term (Benstead 1994, Hearn 1994). In Paraguay there are now few if any suitable rivers and it is almost certainly extinct there (Brooks *et al.* 1993). **CRITICAL:** A2b,d; B1+2a,b,c,d,e; **C2a**; **D1**.

Scaly-sided Merganser *Mergus squamatus* breeds in mountainous areas of the Khabarovsk and Primorye regions of eastern **Russia**, and in **North Korea** and north-east **China**, in valleys with broadleaf and mixed broadleaf and coniferous forests, feeding along rivers and on lakes (Bocharnikov 1990). In winter it disperses to central and southern China (Cheng 1987) and in small numbers to **Japan** (Brazil 1991) and **South Korea** (10–20 in 1994: P. O. Won verbally 1994), with presumed vagrant records from northern Vietnam, Taiwan, Myanmar and Thailand, but the bulk of the population apparently stays within the breeding range (Dement'ev *et al.* 1967). The world population is currently estimated to total c.4,000 individuals and to be declining (Rose and Scott 1994), the main threats being logging and other forms of deforestation within the breeding range, hunting, disturbance from river traffic and water pollution and silting of river shallows by industrial installations (Bocharnikov 1990, Hughes 1991, Hughes and Bocharnikov 1992, Lu 1993b). **VULNERABLE:** C1; C2a.

Family CATHARTIDAE
NEW WORLD VULTURES

California Condor *Gymnogyps californianus*, confined since 1937 to California, **U.S.A.**, declined rapidly throughout the twentieth century, owing to direct persecution and accidental lead ingestion from carcasses in its rocky, open-country scrubland terrain, and in the mid-1980s the remaining eight wild birds were captured to join other zoo-held stock in a captive breeding recovery programme that aims to release birds into more secure parts of the former range (Collar *et al.* 1992). The total population now (July 1994) stands at 89 birds, 85 of which are distributed between three captive breeding facilities, but since 1992 13 birds have been released back into the wild (in Los Padres National Forest), where they are fed on clean carcasses to sidestep the lead-poisoning issue; however, four were recaptured owing to behavioural difficulties, one died from ethylene glycol ingestion, three died in collisions with powerlines (not previously a problem with the species, so perhaps caused by the familiarity of captive-bred birds with man-made structures), and one was killed by a car (W. D. Toone *in litt.* 1994). Proposals have been made to release wild-caught stock as guides, but there are doubts over the wisdom of risking birds with such critically important traditional knowledge while the problem of lead contamination within the range of the species (see Janssen *et al.* 1986, Pattee *et al.* 1990) remains unaddressed (W. D. Toone *in litt.* 1994). **CRITICAL: D1.**

Family ACCIPITRIDAE
HAWKS, EAGLES, HARRIERS, OLD WORLD VULTURES

Square-tailed Kite *Lophoictinia isura*, a specialized canopy-dwelling predator, occurs throughout **Australia**, primarily in coastal and subcoastal areas, in eucalypt forests and woodlands, along wooded watercourses and mallee, sometimes hunting over adjacent heaths and scrubby areas. There are no overall population estimates although it has always been considered uncommon and, because of a low recruitment rate, recovery is slow from any losses, such as those which result from habitat destruction, the depletion of food through forestry and pastoralism, illegal egg-collecting and shooting (Garnett 1992). **VULNERABLE:** C2b.

Sanford's Fish-eagle *Haliaeetus sanfordi* is endemic to Bougainville and Buka islands, **Papua New Guinea**, and to the **Solomon Islands**, where it frequents forest and coastal areas from sea-level to 1,500 m (Mayr 1945, Coates 1985). It requires a large territory and appears to have become uncommon (e.g. on Santa Isabel: Webb 1992), although it remains fairly common on Kolombangara (M. B. Iles *in litt.* 1993), Choiseul (D. Gibbs *in litt.* 1994) and Malaita (P. Scofield *in litt.* 1994); as coastal forests are rapidly disappearing or being degraded (K. D. Bishop *in litt.* 1987 and 1994), this long-lived, low-density species is likely to be at risk. Hunting is also a threat, e.g. on Makira, despite the protection of the tabu law, and could increase as

human populations grow (Buckingham *et al.* in prep.).
VULNERABLE: C1; C2a.

Madagascar Fish-eagle *Haliaeetus vociferoides*
survives in extremely low numbers on the lakes,
rivers, rocky shorelines and mangroves (including
offshore islands) on the west coast of **Madagascar**
north of Morondava, direct persecution and habitat
alteration (loss of both nesting and foraging habitat)
being identified as the likely problems (Collar and
Stuart 1985, Langrand 1990). These threats were
confirmed in fieldwork, 1982–1986, during which
48 occupied sites were recorded, populated by 96
birds including 40 pairs and 10 adults (Langrand
1987, Langrand and Meyburg 1989). Work is now
under way in the Antsalova region, focused on the
lakes Befotaka, Soamalipo and Ankerika, to protect
and enhance the prospects of the best remaining
subpopulation, now judged to consist of some 20–25
pairs, through productivity manipulation (Watson *et
al.* 1993, Thomsett 1994, R. J. Safford *in litt.* 1994).
CRITICAL: A2b; C1; **C2b**; D1.

Pallas's Sea-eagle *Haliaeetus leucoryphus* occurs from **Kazakhstan**, **Tajikistan** and **Uzbekistan**
east through **Mongolia** to **China**, south to northern
India, **Afghanistan** (non-breeding visitor), **Pakistan**, **Nepal** (possibly breeds, chiefly a winter visitor: Inskipp and Inskipp 1991), **Bhutan**, **Bangladesh**
and **Myanmar** (Inskipp and Collins 1993), where it
breeds in open semi-arid areas, both in the plains and
uplands, usually near river valleys or lakes
(Dement'ev *et al.* 1966). It has occurred as a vagrant
in several countries in Europe, the Middle East and
south-east Asia. There is little recent published information on its status in much of its range, but it
appears to be thinly distributed and there is evidence
for a decline in numbers in some range states (Collar
and Andrew 1988), although it remains locally common in parts of Bangladesh (S. M. A. Rashid *in litt.*
1994) and north-east India (M. Jäderblad *in litt.* 1994).
It is presumably vulnerable to wetland destruction
and human disturbance, and pollution is believed to
be the main reason for its decline in parts of India
(A. R. Rahmani *in litt.* 1994). **VULNERABLE:** C1; C2b.

Steller's Sea-eagle *Haliaeetus pelagicus* breeds
only in eastern **Russia**, along the coast of the Bering
Sea and Okhotsk Sea, including Sakhalin Island,
where it nests in tall trees along the lower reaches of
rivers and on rocky coasts (Dement'ev *et al.* 1966).
It winters south to **Japan**, **South Korea** and **North
Korea** (Gore and Won 1971, Waliczky 1991), and
has occurred as a vagrant in China and Alaska and
the Hawaiian Islands, U.S.A. (Inskipp and Collins
1993). The breeding population is estimated to be

2,200 pairs (Lobkov and Neufeldt 1986), and a survey in winter 1985/1986 indicated c.4,000 birds on
the Kamchatka peninsula (the main and almost only
Russian wintering area) and just over 2,000 in Japan
(mainly concentrated on the Shiretoko peninsula,
Hokkaido: Nakagawa *et al.* 1987), giving a total
population estimate of 6,000–7,000 (Fujimaki 1987,
Shibaev 1987). It is vulnerable to coastal development in its restricted breeding and wintering ranges,
such as the hydrological scheme which threatens the
wintering population at Lake Utonai on Hokkaido,
Japan (*World Birdwatch* 1993, 15,1: 6). **VULNER-
ABLE:** C1; C2b.

Cape Griffon *Gyps coprotheres* breeds on cliffs
in open country, foraging over scrub, grassland and
desert in **Botswana** (400 pairs, stable: Borello and
Borello 1993), **Lesotho** (estimated 552 pairs but
with a continuing decline at some colonies: Donnay
1990), **Mozambique** (no post-1985 information,
when 200 pairs guessed, save for a colony of 10–15
pairs within 5 km of the Swaziland border: D. G.
Allan *in litt.* 1994), **Namibia** (massive decline to 10
pairs; no post-1985 information), **South Africa**
(2,850 pairs estimated in the early 1980s, revised
upwards with assessments of c.3,000 pairs in Transvaal and at least 1,325 birds in the Natal Drakensberg
during this period: Brown and Piper 1988, Benson *et
al.* 1990), **Swaziland** (50 pairs guessed in 1985, but
now no longer breeds: Parker in press) and formerly
Zimbabwe, with a world population estimated in
1983 at 10,000 birds (possibly as many as 12,000 at
the start of the 1990s owing to more complete data),
steadily declining in the face of a multitude of threats
including accidental poisoning, organochlorine contamination, electrocution, disturbance at colonies,
food-stress during chick-rearing, and persecution
(Brooke 1984, Collar and Stuart 1985, Robertson
and Boshoff 1986, Boshoff and de Kock 1988, Mundy
et al. 1992, Komen and Brown 1993). **VULNERABLE:**
A1a,c,d; A2c,d; C1; C2b.

Madagascar Serpent-eagle *Eutriorchis astur*
is a very rare inhabitant of undisturbed primary rainforest in eastern **Madagascar** where, apart from
unconfirmed reports of its presence in Marojejy Reserve in the 1960s and 1970s and despite considerable search-effort within its habitat, it was not
recorded between 1930 and 1988 (Collar and Stuart
1985, Collar and Andrew 1988, Langrand 1990).
Two recent records in reserves at Marojejy, September 1988 (Sheldon and Duckworth 1990), and
Ambatovaky, February 1990 (Raxworthy and Colston
1992; see also Evans *et al.* 1992a, Thompson and
Evans 1992), and two more from the Masoala peninsula (in an area targeted as a major new national

park), 1993–1994 (Peregrine Fund press release, April 1994), confirm its survival, and local reports from the Maroantsetra region indicate the existence there of a raptor fitting its description (Langrand 1989), but although it may yet be found in any large surviving areas of low- to mid-altitude rainforest (A. F. A. Hawkins *in litt.* 1994, R. J. Safford *in litt.* 1994), it appears to be a low-density, subcanopy-dwelling denizen of lowland forest, so numbers must be very low and certainly declining with extensive habitat clearance and disturbance, and probably human persecution (Langrand 1989; also Collar and Stuart 1985). **CRITICAL: A1b,c; A2b; C1; C2a; D1.**

Imitator Sparrowhawk *Accipiter imitator* is a very rare and little-known species found only in forested areas on south Bougainville Island, **Papua New Guinea**, and Choiseul and Santa Isabel, **Solomon Islands** (Hadden 1981, Coates 1985), where it is likely to require large tracts of undisturbed forest and to be threatened as a result of logging (M. B. Iles *in litt.* 1994, H. P. Webb *in litt.* 1994). No observations of the species were made during 11 visits to Bougainville, 1980–1986 (K. D. Bishop *in litt.* 1987), or during a visit to Choiseul in 1990 (Lees 1991) or in 1994 (M. B. Iles *in litt.* 1994), but it was sighted twice on Santa Isabel, 1986–1988, in inland forest in lower valleys to c.1,000 m (Webb 1992), although difficulties in identification require all records to be scrutinized very carefully (K. D. Bishop *in litt.* 1994, D. Gibbs *in litt.* 1994). Buckingham *et al.* (in prep.) recorded birds with the plumage of this species on Makira (= San Cristobal) but classify the record as unconfirmed in view of the range extension and identification difficulties. **ENDANGERED: C2a; D1.**

New Britain Sparrowhawk *Accipiter brachyurus* is found on New Britain, **Papua New Guinea**, where it occurs at very low density in forest and forest edge at altitudes of up to 1,000 m (Schodde 1978). It is likely to be threatened as a result of forest clearance, and records are extremely sparse: Diamond (1971) collected one in 1969, one was observed on the north coast of western New Britain in 1980 (K. D. Bishop *in litt.* 1987) and another, also in western New Britain, in 1991 (I. Burrows *in litt.* 1994). It has recently been recorded from New Ireland where it was found to be the commonest (though not very common) raptor in upland forest (B. M. Beehler *in litt.* 1994). **VULNERABLE: C1.**

Gundlach's Hawk *Accipiter gundlachii*, although still spread throughout **Cuba**, has become ever rarer and more local with the loss and disturbance of wooded habitats and particularly in response to human persecution (it specializes on birds and is known to take poultry); five main population centres are known to remain, three for nominate *gundlachii* in west and central Cuba (two of which are known to hold three and 20 pairs respectively), two for race *wileyi* in the east of the island (Collar *et al.* 1992). **ENDANGERED: C2a; D1.**

Red Goshawk *Erythrotriorchis radiatus* is still known from much of its historical range in northern and eastern **Australia**, from Kimberley in Western Australia to northern New South Wales, but is sparsely distributed (Blakers *et al.* 1984). It inhabits coastal and subcoastal, tall, open forests and woodlands, tropical savannas traversed by wooded or forested rivers, and the edges of rainforest, but its breeding habitat is much more specific, with nests restricted to trees taller than 20 m within 1 km of a watercourse or wetland, and thus a substantial proportion of the range is not used for breeding; the total population is estimated to be only c.350 pairs, and is threatened by deforestation, egg-collecting and the use of agricultural chemicals (Garnett 1992). **ENDANGERED: C2b; D1.**

White-necked Hawk *Leucopternis lacernulata* occupies patches of primary lowland Atlantic forest in eastern **Brazil** (Alagoas, Bahia, Minas Gerais, Espírito Santo, Rio de Janeiro, São Paulo, Paraná, Santa Catarina), and must be at risk owing to its low density and the highly fragmented range within which it occurs; habitat loss continues in Minas Gerais (and elsewhere) and needless persecution remains a problem in São Paulo (Collar *et al.* 1992). **VULNERABLE: C1; C2a; D1.**

Grey-backed Hawk *Leucopternis occidentalis* is confined to deciduous and evergreen forests in western **Ecuador** (Esmeraldas, Manabí, Pichincha, Los Ríos, Azuay, El Oro, Loja) and immediately adjacent north-west **Peru** (Tumbes), where it is threatened by rampant habitat destruction, and where records generally only refer to one or two pairs at any one site. If these fragmented outposts represent 'stranded' birds rather than dispersive resilience, viable populations may survive at only a few sites, notably Machalilla National Park in Ecuador, which has many settlers within its boundaries, and Tumbes National Park (now the North-east Peru Biosphere Reserve) in Peru, which is currently secure only because of its remoteness (Collar *et al.* 1992, Best *et al.* 1993). **ENDANGERED: C2a; D1.**

Crowned Eagle *Harpyhaliaetus coronatus* extends over a very large area of open grassland and scrub in central and southern South America, in **Brazil** from Maranhão and Bahia south through Mato

Grosso and Mato Grosso do Sul, Goiás, Distrito Federal, Minas Gerais, Rio de Janeiro, São Paulo, Paraná and Santa Catarina into Rio Grande do Sul, **Bolivia** in Beni and Santa Cruz, **Uruguay** (a few records, formerly), **Paraguay** in Chaco and Región Oriental, and **Argentina** from Jujuy south to southern Buenos Aires and Neuquén; yet it occurs at densities too low to be certain that any decline has occurred, but large areas within its range have suffered conversion of habitat, and hunting has certainly affected it in Brazil (Collar *et al.* 1992, de Lucca 1993; see also Brooks *et al.* 1993). **VULNERABLE:** C2b.

Hispaniolan Hawk *Buteo ridgwayi* has declined steeply throughout its range on Hispaniola (**Haiti** and the **Dominican Republic**) as a result of large-scale loss of its lowland forest habitat coupled with direct persecution, so that its current stronghold appears to be a poorly protected national park (Los Haitises) in the north-east of the island (Collar *et al.* 1992). **ENDANGERED: C2a**; D1.

Galápagos Hawk *Buteo galapagoensis* was apparently once common in open rocky scrub country on most of the main islands of the Galápagos, **Ecuador**, but, probably owing to human persecution (though possibly to food competition from introduced predators), it is now extinct on five islands and greatly reduced on Santa Cruz, though still quite common on Santiago, Española, Isabela, Fernandina, Pinta, Marchena and Santa Fe. Being cooperatively polyandrous, the population is difficult to quantify except by breeding territories, of which about 130 are known (Collar *et al.* 1992). **VULNERABLE:** D1.

New Guinea Harpy Eagle *Harpyopsis novaeguineae* is widely distributed (but little-known: see, e.g., Beehler *et al.* 1992) at low density on mainland New Guinea (Irian Jaya, **Indonesia**, and **Papua New Guinea**), largely in undisturbed forest from the lowlands to 3,200 m (but commonest in mid-montane and montane forests where most New Guineans live). It is hunted for its tail and flight feathers, and this pressure on a naturally small population, combined with habitat destruction, is thought to be a threat, particularly in Papua New Guinea where firearms are prevalent and where it is now very rare or absent in many places (Beehler 1985, Coates 1985, K. D. Bishop *in litt.* 1987 and 1994, J. M. Diamond *in litt.* 1987, G. R. Kula *in litt.* 1988, K. M. Kisokau *in litt.* 1994). **VULNERABLE:** C1; C2b.

Philippine Eagle *Pithecophaga jefferyi* has been reduced by primary forest clearance, hunting and trapping to a guessed world total of only around 200

birds in the mid-1980s, shared unevenly (and with little likelihood of genetic interchange by natural means) between Luzon, Samar, Leyte, and Mindanao in the **Philippines** (Collar and Andrew 1988). There seems to be no information about its status on Samar and Leyte, but from the map in Collins *et al.* (1991) forest on Leyte is little and fragmented (but reported to be extensive in the mountains: Curio 1994) and on Samar extensive but degraded; on Luzon there were a few sight records in the Sierra Madre in 1991 and 1992, but without urgent action the island's estimated population of around 50 pairs will be extinct there in a few decades (Danielsen *et al.* 1992, 1994, Poulsen in press), while on Mindanao very few birds survive in the wild and deforestation is closing in on them (Lambert 1993b). **CRITICAL:** A1b,c; A2b,c; **C1**; C2a; D1.

Greater Spotted Eagle *Aquila clanga* occupies a massive but highly fragmented breeding range extending through lowland primary forests (always near water) from **Finland**, **Latvia**, Lithuania (extinct), **Poland**, **Belarus**, **Moldova** and **Romania** into **Russia**, **Ukraine**, **Iran**, **Pakistan**, **India**, **Kazakhstan**, **China** and **Mongolia**, with passage or wintering birds occurring regularly (but among many of the following in tiny numbers) in **Morocco** (not simply a vagrant: M. Dakki *per* G. A. Allport), **France**, **Italy**, **Germany**, **Sweden**, **Czech Republic**, **Slovakia**, **Hungary**, **Bulgaria**, **Greece**, **Turkey**, **Lebanon**, **Israel**, **Jordan**, **Egypt**, **Sudan**, **Ethiopia**, **Kenya**, **Yemen**, **Oman**, **United Arab Emirates**, **Saudi Arabia**, **Kuwait**, **Iraq**, **Afghanistan**, **Nepal**, **Bangladesh**, **Myanmar**, **Thailand**, **Cambodia**, **Laos**, **Vietnam**, peninsular **Malaysia**, **Singapore** and **Hong Kong (to U.K.)** (records of vagrancy in over 20 countries). It occurs at extremely low densities (maximum population in Europe west of the Urals is 900 pairs), and is declining at least in the western half of its range in response to disturbance and destruction of habitat (Glutz *et al.* 1971, Inskipp and Collins 1993, Tucker and Heath 1994). However, trends are generally difficult to judge because of past and continuing problems with field identification. **VULNERABLE:** C2a.

Spanish Imperial Eagle *Aquila adalberti*, having become extinct (at least as a breeding species) in north-east Algeria and northern Morocco (although two in the latter in January 1991 were behaving as if paired: Fouarge 1992), is now endemic to the Iberian peninsula, where it is confined almost entirely to central, west and, chiefly, south-west **Spain** (some 150–160 pairs), barely surviving in **Portugal** (15–20 pairs prior to 1974–1975 but no records of breeding since 1977); it inhabits coastal dunes, plains, hills and high mountain slopes, nests in trees, and faces threats from shooting, poisoning, trapping, electrocution on pylons, breeding failure caused by agricultural chemicals, and disturbance when nesting, although it is currently the subject of a major recovery programme (Collar and Andrew 1988, Negro and Hiraldo 1994, Tucker and Heath 1994, Heredia in prep.). **VULNERABLE:** D1.

Imperial Eagle *Aquila heliaca* occupies a massive but highly fragmented breeding range extending through the wooded steppes of **Slovakia**, **Croatia**, former **Yugoslavia** (Serbia), **Macedonia**, **Hungary**, **Bulgaria**, **Romania**, **Greece**, **Cyprus**, **Turkey**, **Iran**, **Moldova**, **Ukraine**, **Russia**, **Georgia**, **Azerbaijan**, **Turkmenistan**, **Uzbekistan**, **Kazakhstan** and **China**, with passage or wintering birds from the eastern populations occurring regularly in **Syria**, **Lebanon**, **Israel**, **Jordan**, **Egypt**, **Sudan**, **Ethiopia**, **Djibouti**, **Yemen**, **Oman**, **United Arab Emirates**, **Saudi Arabia**, **Kuwait**, **Iraq**, **Afghanistan**, **Pakistan**, **India**, **Bangladesh**, **Laos**, **Vietnam** and **Hong Kong (to U.K.)** (records of vagrancy from up to 23 countries). There has been a rapid decline in Europe since 1950 (where the current total lies between 320 and 570 pairs) and the world population is now down to a few thousand pairs, as a result of persecution (e.g. in Syria), disturbance while breeding, poisoning (targeted at canids), zoo collecting, habitat loss (and the attendant loss of prey species), agricultural pesticides, felling of nest trees, and collision with or electrocution by power-lines (Glutz *et al.* 1971, Inskipp and Collins 1993, Tucker and Heath 1994, del Hoyo in press). **VULNERABLE:** C2a.

Javan Hawk-eagle *Spizaetus bartelsi* is endemic to Java, **Indonesia**, where it is found in forest from the lowlands to 3,000 m (MacKinnon and Phillipps 1993), but favours the lower slopes between 200 and 1,200 m (Kuroda 1933–1936). The total population was estimated to be as low as 50–60 pairs (Meyburg *et al.* 1989), but it has since been recorded at more localities and found to be still widespread in very small numbers in the larger and less degraded patches of forest and their surroundings (van Balen 1991, van Balen and Meyburg 1994). Extensive lowland deforestation has greatly reduced its habitat (see

RePPProT 1990), it is threatened by further encroachment on slope forests (P. Jepson *in litt.* 1994), and there is some illegal hunting and trade in wild birds, particularly of dispersing immature birds which wander close to population centres (Meyburg *et al.* 1989, van Balen 1991). **ENDANGERED:** **C1**; **C2b**; D1.

Philippine Hawk-eagle *Spizaetus philippensis* has been recorded from lowland and mid-mountain forest on 10 islands (on many of which there are no recent reports either because of its rarity and possible extinction there or because there have been no visits) in the **Philippines** (Dickinson *et al.* 1991), and appears now to be weakly represented everywhere owing to habitat loss and perhaps hunting: Luzon (uncommon in Sierra Madre, rare in lowlands owing to habitat loss: Danielsen *et al.* 1994, Poulsen in press), Mindoro (where clearly threatened by deforestation: Dutson *et al.* 1992), Sibuyan (a new locality: Timmins in prep.), Samar, Biliran, Leyte, Negros (where clearly threatened by deforestation: Brooks *et al.* 1992), Siquijor (no records since 1891: Evans *et al.* 1993b), Mindanao (a few recent sightings: Timmins in prep.), Basilan and Palawan (apparently rare: F. R. Lambert verbally 1993). **VULNERABLE:** A1b; A2b; C1; C2a.

Wallace's Hawk-eagle *Spizaetus nanus* occurs in southern Tenasserim, **Myanmar**, peninsular **Thailand**, peninsular and East **Malaysia**, Kalimantan and Sumatra, **Indonesia** and **Brunei**, where it has been recorded in lowland rainforest up to 1,000 m (King *et al.* 1975, MacKinnon and Phillipps 1993), although Wells (1985) regarded it as an extreme lowland forest specialist. It is widespread but uncommon on Borneo and Sumatra (MacKinnon and Phillipps 1993, S. van Balen *in litt.* 1994), uncommon or rare in Thailand (Boonsong and Round 1991), and is threatened by the extensive habitat destruction within its range (see Collins *et al.* 1991), which is reducing, fragmenting and degrading the available lowland forest; however, it may be tolerant of some habitat degradation, as it has been recorded in heavily logged forest (S. van Balen *in litt.* 1994), although it requires tall trees for nesting (D. R. Wells *in litt.* 1994). **VULNERABLE:** A1b; A2b; C1; C2a.

Family FALCONIDAE

FALCONS, CARACARAS

Plumbeous Forest-falcon *Micrastur plumbeus*, a small and (because of the similarities and unobtrusiveness of members of its genus) poorly known raptor of the interior of undisturbed closed-canopy lowland and foothill forest (up to 1,400 m), is restricted to the Pacific slope of the Andes in south-west **Colombia** (Chocó, Valle, Cauca, Nariño, with the first records since 1959 being of three individuals mist-netted in the Río Ñambi Nature Reserve and nearby Patio in 1992, plus one in Los Farallones National Park in 1993) and north-west **Ecuador** (Esmeraldas; three specimens from two sites since 1959). These areas are extensive but nonetheless under very considerable threat from clearance; moreover, this bird may be restricted to the 'narrow, linear wet forest refugia along the Andean foothills' (Collar *et al.* 1992, Salaman and Gandy 1994, D. Gandy verbally 1994). **ENDANGERED: A2b; C1; C2a.**

Lesser Kestrel *Falco naumanni* breeds colonially in buildings, earth cliffs, quarries, tree holes, rock piles in (wooded) grassland areas of the southern Palearctic in **Morocco**, **Algeria**, **Tunisia**, **Libya**, **Portugal**, **Spain**, **Gibraltar (to U.K.)**, **France**, **Italy**, **Slovenia**, **Croatia**, former **Yugoslavia** (Serbia), **Macedonia**, **Albania**, **Bulgaria**, **Romania**, **Greece**, **Turkey**, **Syria**, **Israel**, **Jordan**, **Saudi Arabia**, **Iran**, **Armenia**, **Azerbaijan**, **Georgia**, **Russia**, **Moldova**, **Ukraine**, **Afghanistan**, **Turkmenistan**, **Uzbekistan**, **Tajikistan**, **Kyrgyzstan**, **Kazakhstan**, **China** and **Mongolia**. Passage birds occur also in **Malta**, **Cyprus**, **Egypt**, **Lebanon**, **Iraq**, **Kuwait**, **Qatar**, **United Arab Emirates**, **Oman** and **Yemen** (far-eastern birds may fly across the Indian Ocean in autumn, overland in spring), and spend the non-breeding period in the savannas, thornbush and open plains and farmland of Africa in **Mauritania**, **Senegal**, **Gambia**, **Guinea**, **Sierra Leone**, **Liberia**, **Mali**, **Ivory Coast**, **Benin**, **Burkina**, **Niger**, **Nigeria**, **Chad**, **Central African Republic**, **Sudan**, **Ethiopia**, **Eritrea**, **Djibouti**, **Somalia**, **Kenya**, **Tanzania**, **Uganda**, **Rwanda**, **Burundi**, **Zaïre**, **Gabon**, **Congo**, **Angola**, **Zambia**, **Malawi**, **Mozambique**, **Zimbabwe**, **Botswana**, **Namibia**, **South Africa** and **Lesotho**, and in similar habitat in Asia in **Pakistan**, **India**, **Maldives**, **Nepal**, **Bangladesh**, **Myanmar** and **Laos**; there are records of vagrancy, in some cases possibly representing inadequately documented regular occurrence, from up to 20 countries (Cramp and Simmons 1980, Dowsett and Forbes-Watson 1993, Inskipp and Collins 1993). Serious declines have been observed throughout its European range (and reflected in South Africa), with (e.g.) 100,000 pairs in Spain in 1950 falling to less than 5,000 in 1990, a trend attributed to agricultural intensification (including use of pesticides) and urbanization in Europe, and a decline in pastoral farming in both Europe and Africa (Auburn 1988, Fanshawe 1989, Biber 1990, Aspinall 1993, Colahan 1993, Negro and Hiraldo 1993, Nuttall 1993, Parr and Yarar 1993, Tucker and Heath 1994, Heredia in prep.). **VULNERABLE: A1a,b,d.**

Mauritius Kestrel *Falco punctatus* has continued its spectacular recovery in the rocky forests and adjacent scrubby areas of its native **Mauritius**, where in 1974—for a wide variety of speculated reasons, including organochlorine pesticide applications in the 1960s—its known population had been only six birds (of which two were captive and never bred), although a decade later six pairs were estimated present and 10 additional birds were in captivity (Collar and Stuart 1985; see also Jones 1987). Release of captive-bred birds and management (through supplementary feeding) of wild pairs bolstered the population to 35 pairs in 1992, distributed in the south-western forests, the Bambous Mountains and the Moka Mountains (Jones *et al.* 1991, in press, MWAF 1992), and by early 1993 there were probably over 50 pairs present, with releases still continuing, and the total post-breeding population was over 200 (Cade and Jones 1993). In early 1994 the total wild population was 56–68 pairs, with a post-breeding estimate, including independent young, of 229–286 birds; at that stage a total of 331 birds had been released into the wild, 109 having been captive-bred and 222 reared from wild-laid eggs, but this part of the programme has been terminated (the provision of nest-boxes being considered the most important achievement) as the wild population is expected to continue to rise to 500–600 birds (C. G. Jones *in litt.* 1994). **ENDANGERED: D1.**

Seychelles Kestrel *Falco araea* is distributed throughout upland evergreen forests and lowland plantations on three granitic islands of the **Seychelles**, with 370 pairs on Mahé (not the 50–300 pairs suggested in Skerrett and Bullock 1992), 10 pairs (minimum, possibly 20) on Praslin (to which it was reintroduced in 1977), and 30–40 pairs on Silhouette, these numbers being largely stable and threats only seeming to stem from lowered breeding success in some areas owing to human persecution, introduced predators and competitors, and possibly also displacement by introduced Barn Owls *Tyto alba* (Watson 1981, 1989, Collar and Stuart 1985, J. Watson *in litt.* 1994). **VULNERABLE:** D1.

Grey Falcon *Falco hypoleucos* is widely but very sparsely distributed in acacia scrub, spinifex and tussock grassland across **Australia**, where breeding records indicate that its range has shrunk in recent years and is now largely confined to areas within the 250 mm annual rainfall zone, such that outside its main inland range reports are incidental and years apart (Blakers *et al.* 1984, Olsen and Olsen 1986; also Cade 1982). It is threatened by the agricultural development of timbered plains (Hermes 1980) as well as by overgrazing of arid-zone rangelands, pesticide use, the taking of eggs by egg-collectors, and of eggs or young for falconry, and has a population estimated at less than 5,000 individuals (Garnett 1992). **VULNERABLE:** C2b.

Taita Falcon *Falco fasciinucha* is uncommon to rare throughout its wide but discontinuous African range, from southern **Ethiopia** (rare, with no proven breeding) through **Kenya** (including the border with Sudan; again infrequent, with no proven breeding) to north-eastern **Tanzania** (two specimens, but evidence now of a population on the Mkata Plain: Baker and Baker in press), then **Zambia** (known with certainty from only a few sites, one being the Victoria Falls Gorges), **Malawi** (probably widespread in very small numbers, but few records), **Mozambique** (no proven breeding), **Zimbabwe** (number of breeding sites conservatively estimated at 50) and **South Africa** (where first breeding recently proven and the pair is still present, but very few other possible sites exist: D. G. Allan *in litt.* 1994). Its habitat is gorges and escarpments in semi-arid country at moderate to high altitudes often overlooking river valleys (hunting over dry deciduous woodland), but, while the species' supposed rarity has been attributed simply to such habitat being in inaccessible regions within the Rift system (and a theory that deforestation has caused its retreat remains questionable), it may suffer from nest-site competition with Peregrines *F. peregrinus* and Lanners *F. biarmicus* in certain areas, and there are fears that organochlorine pesticide spraying in northern Zimbabwe may have a fatal impact on the important population there (Benson *et al.* 1971, Urban and Brown 1971, Benson and Benson 1977, Dowsett 1977, Britton 1980, Irwin 1981, Brown *et al.* 1982, Hustler 1989, Lewis and Pomeroy 1989, Möller 1989, Hartley and Mundy 1990, Jenkins *et al.* 1991, Dowsett and Forbes-Watson 1993, M. P. S. Irwin *in litt.* 1994). **VULNERABLE:** C1; D1.

Family MEGAPODIIDAE
MEGAPODES

Bruijn's Brush-turkey *Aepypodius bruijnii* is an apparently rare inhabitant of Waigeo (and Batanta) islands, Irian Jaya, **Indonesia**, where it inhabits rainforest on very rugged limestone karst. It is known with certainty only from specimens obtained by local collectors during the nineteenth century and by one specimen collected in 1939 (Rand and Gilliard 1967). It has been reported by local people on Waigeo and was probably sighted on Batanta in 1986 (K. D. Bishop *in litt.* 1987, J. M. Diamond *in litt.* 1987), and the only other record is a report of two nest-mounds on an unnamed islet in 1973 (Mountfort 1988). It was not found in 1993 during an 11-day survey in the forests (up to 500 m) of the south-easternmost part of Waigeo, possibly because it may be restricted to higher altitudes by the Dusky Scrubfowl *Megapodius freycinet*, or because the large forest fires of 1982 have resulted in a dense undergrowth and secondary vegetation which may not be suitable for recolonization (Dekker and Argeloo 1993). **VULNERABLE:** D1.

Maleo *Macrocephalon maleo* is endemic to Sulawesi and its satellite islands, **Indonesia**, where it is found in lowland and hill forest at up to 1,200 m, and lays communally in traditional nesting grounds in volcanic soil and coastal beaches (White and Bruce 1986, Dekker 1990). It is still widespread, and the total number of known nesting grounds is now 85 (48 coastal, 37 inland), of which 22 are abandoned (19 coastal, three inland), 12 of unknown status, and one or two severely threatened; the remaining population is still quite large, given that sites may support populations of 150–200 pairs (see Dekker and Wattel 1987), and that new nesting localities are still being discovered, but there are threats to nesting sites from agricultural development, human disturbance, invasive secondary vegetation, the over-harvesting of eggs (especially near transmigration settlement areas) and from road construction, which isolates nesting sites from non-breeding habitat (BirdLife IP; see Holmes 1989, Andrew and Holmes 1990, Dekker 1990). **VULNERABLE:** C1; C2a.

Nicobar Scrubfowl *Megapodius nicobariensis*
is now apparently restricted to the Nicobar Islands, **India**, where it is found in forest and secondary growth on all of the islands apart from Car Nicobar, although there is evidence that it occurred early this century on Little Andaman (India) and probably also Coco Island (Myanmar) in the Andaman Islands (R. W. R. J. Dekker *in litt.* 1993). In 1992, the population on Great Nicobar was estimated to exceed 2,000 birds (Dekker 1992), and a survey of eight islands in 1992–1993 (which did not cover the interiors of the islands and several small islands where it is reported to occur) estimated a minimum population of 6,946 individuals, including 3,422 on Great Nicobar; the species was found to be extinct on one small island, and to have declined in the Nancowry group as a result of the conversion of forest to coconut plantations, and evidence was found for further encroachment into forests, and localized hunting for food and egg collection, although introduced predators were not judged to be a problem (Sankaran 1993b). The forests on Great Nicobar are still almost pristine, but there are threats there from a proposed refuelling base for international shipping and road developments (Sankaran 1993a). **VULNERABLE:** C1.

Vanuatu Scrubfowl *Megapodius layardi* inhabits lowland forest (but can also be found at moderate altitudes) on virtually all islands in central and northern **Vanuatu**; although still common, its nesting sites (in the vicinity of craters of active volcanoes or, more usually, in coastal forest) and forest habitat are being destroyed by encroaching agriculture and other development and, whilst eggs have been collected (from the more accessible sites) as food by village people for centuries with little detrimental effect, an increase in the human population and their mobility may result in over-harvesting (Bregulla 1992). It is also hunted, and killed by feral dogs (S. Maturin *in litt.* 1994). **VULNERABLE:** A2b,c.

Micronesian Scrubfowl *Megapodius laperouse*
is restricted to limestone forest and dense coconut groves (using beaches and thermal volcanic soil for egg-laying) in **Palau (to U.S.A.)** and the **Northern Marianas Islands (to U.S.A.)**, having become extirpated from Guam (to U.S.A.), although still locally common on the limestone and outlying islands, e.g. Kayangel, but it is rare on the larger volcanic islands, e.g. Babeldaob (the total population estimate, excluding Kayangel, was 497 birds in 1991) (Engbring and Pratt 1985, Engbring 1992). In the Marianas it is restricted to the remote volcanic islands north of Saipan (Sarigan and Guguan, which support a few hundred and up to 2,000 birds respectively, the remaining islands having small numbers), except for a small remnant population on Aguijan and a reintroduced population on Saipan itself, threats including habitat destruction, poaching of eggs, predation by feral animals (including brown tree snake *Boiga irregularis* which has been introduced to Saipan: S. L. Pimm *in litt.* 1994, H. D. Pratt *in litt.* 1994), and increasing tourist use of beaches (Stinson and Glass 1992). **VULNERABLE:** C1.

Niuafoou Megapode *Megapodius pritchardii*,
with a population of less than 1,000 birds (200 territorial pairs), is endemic to the remote island of Niuafoou, **Tonga** (55 km²), where it uses hot volcanic ash to incubate its eggs, a habit which confines its nesting sites to areas of loose soil close to vents, either in forest or in open ash (total area of occupancy less than 10 km²) (Todd 1983). The major threats are from predation by feral cats, egg harvesting (as, although it is protected by law, there is no enforcement and more than 100 eggs can be collected at each breeding site in one year), development plans, and volcanic eruption (Rinke 1986). In 1991, 1992 and 1993 chicks and eggs were released on the predator-free islands of Late and Fonualei (both of which are rarely visited by man) with further transfers planned for the near future (Rinke 1991, 1993). **ENDANGERED:** B1+2e; C2a; D1; D2.

Moluccan Scrubfowl *Megapodius wallacei* is known from the islands of Buru, Seram, Ambon, Haruku, Bacan, Halmahera and Ternate in the Moluccas, and Misool Island (single record of dubious provenance: K. D. Bishop *in litt.* 1993) off Irian Jaya, **Indonesia**, where it is found in forest, usually between 700 and 1,950 m, and nests on coastal beaches (Beehler *et al.* 1986, White and Bruce 1986). Recent records include a communal nesting ground on Haruku where an estimated 4,000–5,000 pairs (including birds which fly over from nearby Seram) breed, their eggs being harvested by local people in a traditional and apparently sustainable way (Dekker 1991), three nesting sites with an estimated total of 700–900 pairs found on Halmahera in 1993 (BirdLife IP), only one bird positively identified during a two-

month survey in Manusela National Park on Seram in 1987 (Bowler and Taylor 1989), a single bird on Bacan in 1991 (Lambert in prep.) and unconfirmed sightings on Buru in 1989 (Jepson 1993); it is believed unlikely to survive on Ternate and Ambon (Holmes 1989). As a species which nests colonially on beaches, and appears to be restricted as a breeding bird to a limited number of traditional breeding grounds, it is vulnerable to egg-harvesting (it is possible for one egg collector to exterminate an entire colony in a single season: Holmes 1989), habitat destruction and hunting (K. D. Bishop *in litt.* 1994). **VULNERABLE:** A2b,c; C1.

Malleefowl *Leipoa ocellata* was formerly a widespread bird in the mallee and eucalypt woodland in **Australia** from Western Australia through South Australia, south-west Northern Territory, to north-west Victoria and western New South Wales (Blakers *et al.* 1984), but has disappeared from or is now rare through 80% of its range, it continues to decline in New South Wales (750 pairs) and is probably extinct in Northern Territory (Garnett 1992). Except in Western Australia (no population data but likely to be more birds here than in any other state), South Australia (locally common) and Victoria (less than 1,000 pairs), reserve pockets of suitable habitat are proving too small to support viable populations, and the species is vulnerable to bushfires, starvation of chicks (as livestock and kangaroos graze the same food plants), and predation of chicks by feral foxes and cats and by native raptors (Garnett 1992). **VULNERABLE:** A1b,d; A2b,d; C1; C2a.

Family CRACIDAE

CURASSOWS, GUANS, CHACHALACAS

Rufous-headed Chachalaca *Ortalis erythroptera* is confined to western **Ecuador** (Esmeraldas, Manabí, Guayas, Los Ríos, Chimborazo, El Oro, Loja) and extreme north-west **Peru** (Tumbes, Cajamarca), but has substantially declined owing to hunting pressure and, in particular, the extensive clearance of its forest habitat (ranging from deciduous woodland through to lower montane cloud-forest), and may now number in the low thousands (Best and Krabbe 1994; also Parker and Carr 1992, Best *et al.* 1993). **VULNERABLE:** C1; C2a.

Bearded Guan *Penelope barbata* possesses a fairly restricted range in humid montane and cloud-forest (occurring at roughly one pair per km²) in southern **Ecuador** (Azuay, El Oro, Loja) and northern **Peru** (Piura, Lambayeque, Cajamarca), and is probably declining (population in Ecuador put at 1,500 individuals) owing to widespread destruction and fragmentation of habitat, compounded by hunting in many key areas; even so important a site for it as Podocarpus National Park is almost completely conceded to logging and mining (Collar *et al.* 1992, Best *et al.* 1993). **VULNERABLE:** A2b,c; C1; C2a.

Baudó Guan *Penelope ortoni* formerly ranged throughout the Pacific lowlands and foothills of western **Colombia** (newly recorded in Nariño) and all but the southern quarter of **Ecuador**, in humid and wet forest in the tropical and lower subtropical zones, 0–1,500 m. The clearance and fragmentation of Chocó forests has been and continues to be extensive, and the species is heavily hunted throughout its range, so that it now appears to be very rare everywhere (Vaurie 1968, Blake 1977, Hilty and Brown 1986, Gandy and Salaman 1994, Salaman and Gandy 1994). **VULNERABLE:** A1b,c; A2b,c; C1; C2a.

Cauca Guan *Penelope perspicax* has suffered from the almost total loss of its humid forest habitat in the middle and upper Cauca valley (900–2,150 m) and Patia valley, **Colombia** (Risaralda, Quindío, Valle, Cauca), to which it is almost wholly confined; however, it survives in three protected areas (notably Ucumari Regional Park, i.e. the Risaralda section of Los Nevados National Park, where it was observed commonly in 1993 in native forest as well as in plantations of exotic broadleaf trees), although poaching is prevalent in two of them (Collar *et al.* 1992, Negret 1992, Salaman and Gandy 1993, D. Gandy verbally 1994). **ENDANGERED:** C2a; D2.

White-winged Guan *Penelope albipennis*, having been 'lost' for a hundred years after its discovery in north-westernmost **Peru** (Tumbes) in 1876, survives in a small number of dry wooded valleys in foothills chiefly in Lambayeque, where it numbers possibly less than a hundred individuals and is seriously endangered by forest clearance (Collar *et al.* 1992). **CRITICAL:** A2b; B1+2c; C1; **C2a**; D1.

Chestnut-bellied Guan *Penelope ochrogaster* occupies a broad but poorly defined area of central **Brazil** (Tocantins currently, Goiás before 1933 and again in 1979–1985 on Ilha Bananal, Mato Grosso currently, Mato Grosso do Sul in 1909, and Minas Gerais in 1912–1913), where it inhabits patches and galleries of semi-deciduous forest in drier areas; it is only known to be moderately common at a single site (though it may be secure in Araguaia National Park on Ilha Bananal), and presumably suffers from hunting pressure and habitat loss to agricultural development (Collar *et al.* 1992, R. S. Ridgely *in litt.* 1994). **VULNERABLE:** C2a.

Trinidad Piping-guan *Pipile pipile* has been reduced by hunting and habitat destruction on its native Trinidad (**Trinidad and Tobago**) to two small populations in the primary forests of the island's Northern and Southern Ranges (some 250 km² of habitat remained in the early 1970s, but around 1980 the total population was put at only 100 birds, with hunting continuing): key-site conservation and more public awareness are both urgently needed (Collar *et al.* 1992). **CRITICAL:** A2b,c; B1+2c; C1; **C2a**; D1; D2.

Black-fronted Piping-guan *Pipile jacutinga* used to be abundant in the Atlantic Forest formations of eastern **Brazil** (Bahia, Espírito Santo, Minas Gerais, Rio de Janeiro, São Paulo, Paraná, Santa Catarina and Rio Grande do Sul), eastern **Paraguay** and north-eastern **Argentina**, but the combination of enormous hunting pressure (50,000 killed in a few weeks in 1866) and the widespread (long-term and continuing) destruction of its habitat, in particular the forest palms on which it chiefly depends (and whose fruiting was and remains the apparent cause of important vertical and local movements of populations), has rendered it now very rare except in a few protected areas (Collar *et al.* 1992). Fourteen previously undocumented sites in São Paulo are now known, but the species is still greatly threatened there by uncontrolled hunting (P. Martuscelli verbally 1994). Fieldwork in 1992 found it in four forest areas in eastern Paraguay (Brooks *et al.* 1993), and in 1993 at least 43 birds were recorded at seven or more sites in Argentina (Benstead *et al.* 1994). **VULNERABLE:** C2a.

Horned Guan *Oreophasis derbianus* inhabits high cloud-forest in the Sierra Madre del Sur of southernmost **Mexico** (Chiapas and Oaxaca) and the volcanic ranges of adjacent western **Guatemala** (and the Sierra de las Minas in the east of the country), and although there is evidence that populations on remoter mountains are relatively strong and secure, the risks from habitat destruction and hunting within its limited range remain high (Collar *et al.* 1992). Confirmation of the existence of the species in Oaxaca, based on live specimens collected at Chimalapas, has been provided by J. Estudillo López (verbally 1994). **VULNERABLE:** C2a.

Alagoas Curassow *Mitu mitu*, a large ground-dwelling frugivore, known in recent decades only from a few coastal lowland forest patches in Alagoas, north-east **Brazil**, is now probably extinct in the wild owing to chronic, ineluctable habitat loss and hunting, and its only chance of survival lies in a private captive population that numbered 11 in 1984 (Collar *et al.* 1992). **EXTINCT IN THE WILD.**

Northern Helmeted Curassow *Pauxi pauxi* was formerly common (nominate *pauxi*) in dense subtropical cloud-forest in the northern mountains (500–2,000 m, but mostly 1,000–1,500 m) of central **Venezuela**, but deforestation and hunting have much reduced it there, although its status in the Andes of Mérida and the adjacent departments of **Colombia** is unknown; the race *gilliardi* from the Sierra de Perijá on the Colombia–Venezuela border is also believed to be under great pressure (Collar *et al.* 1992). A proposal to support a captive breeding and reintroduction programme in Venezuela has been elaborated (Waugh and Diaz de Waugh 1993); over 300 birds, mostly captive bred, are in the facility in Mexico belonging to J. Estudillo López (verbally 1994). **ENDANGERED:** A2b,c; C1; **C2a**.

Southern Helmeted Curassow *Pauxi unicornis* is an exceptionally poorly known species which has been found in lower montane forest (450–1,200 m) in rugged terrain at three localities in **Bolivia** (most notably Amboró National Park, Cochabamba) and two in **Peru** (Huánuco, Puno), and appears to be genuinely localized and rare, and vulnerable to hunting (Collar *et al.* 1992, Cox *et al.* in press). **ENDANGERED:** C2a.

Blue-billed Curassow *Crax alberti* occupies a restricted range in northern **Colombia** (La Guajira, Magdalena, Bolívar, Sucre, Córdoba, Antioquia, Tolima) in humid forest of the lowlands and foothills (up to 1,200 m, but less common above 600 m), where it has suffered serious (and continuing) decline and widespread local extinction owing to deforestation and hunting, such that the sites of any populations are unknown although survival in the wild is confirmed by specimens in trade in 1987 (Collar *et al.* 1992). Its persistence (owing to the presence of drug-growers, who prevent access for logging) near Alto Sinú, specifically La Terretera, has been reported by J. Estudillo López (verbally 1994). **CRITICAL: A2b; C1; C2a; D1.**

Wattled Curassow *Crax globulosa*, although seemingly very widespread in lowland humid forest (to 300 m) in the Amazon basin across western **Brazil** (Amazonas), southern **Colombia** (Caquetá), eastern **Ecuador** (Napo) and **Peru** (Loreto, Madre de Dios), and northern **Bolivia** (Beni), appears to be almost wholly unknown (often even to local people, except old hunters) despite extensive inquiries by researchers throughout its range, and is strongly suspected of suffering seriously as a consequence of loss of riverine (especially várzea) habitat as man has colonized the Amazon, with concomitant hunting pressure (Collar *et al.* 1992). However, there is a recent report that the species is 'uncommon' in Rio

Jaú National Park, Amazonas, Brazil (J. F. Pacheco *per* B. M. Whitney *in litt.* 1994), and it has been reported fairly common around Chiribiquete and Araracuate in Colombia, with live birds being collected on the Apaporis river in Caquetá (J. Estudillo López verbally 1994). **VULNERABLE: A1b,c; A2b,c; C1; C2a.**

Red-billed Curassow *Crax blumenbachii*, formerly widespread in the lowland Atlantic forest of south-east **Brazil** from Bahia and Minas Gerais south through Espírito Santo to Rio de Janeiro (where it is now extinct), has become restricted to five protected forest patches: Una and Monte Pascoal in Bahia (although several unprotected sites have recently been found in the state), Rio Doce (Minas Gerais), Sooretama and adjacent Linhares (Espírito Santo). Several of these are under threat (and are poached), and the total population (despite good numbers reproducing well in captivity) must be very small (Collar *et al.* 1992). **CRITICAL: B1+2c,e; C2a; D1.**

Family PHASIANIDAE

FRANCOLINS, QUAILS, PHEASANTS

Swamp Francolin *Francolinus gularis* is confined to the Ganges and Brahmaputra river basins in western **Nepal**, **Bangladesh**, Uttar Pradesh, northern Bihar, West Bengal, Assam and Arunachal Pradesh in north-east **India**, where it occupies tall, wet grasslands and swamps in the lowlands below 200 m (Ali and Ripley 1987, Javed and Rahmani 1991, Singh in press). Its habitat is now highly fragmented, with recent reports from only 12 protected areas in northern India (ranging from 11 to 614 km²) and three in Nepal; it is locally common in these areas, and apparently commoner in a mosaic of slightly grazed grassland, marshland and sugarcane fields than in pure, dense wet grassland (A. R. Rahmani *in litt.* 1994), but not necessarily secure in all of them as management currently concentrates on protecting habitat for ungulates, and it is declining outside protected areas owing to habitat destruction and perhaps also the effects of pesticide run-off (McGowan *et al.* in press). **VULNERABLE: A1b.**

Harwood's Francolin *Francolinus harwoodi* has recently been found to be restricted to less than 10,000 km² in the highlands of **Ethiopia** (notably

the Jemma or Jemmu valley) where, despite being reputedly common, its *Typha* habitat (used for cover) continues to be reduced and it is hunted for food (Ash and Gullick 1989). **VULNERABLE: B1+2c; C2a.**

Grey-striped Francolin *Francolinus griseostriatus* is restricted to the escarpment zone of western **Angola**, occurring in two populations (probably racially distinct) separated by 400 km, in Cuanza Sul and southern Benguela provinces; it lives in secondary and gallery forest, and penetrates thickets and weed-covered areas in the north of its range, and in general is (or was in 1983) relatively common (Collar and Stuart 1985). Review of the situation in 1992 suggested that Angola scarp forest (1,300–2,000 km²) was slowly but steadily decreasing and, more worryingly, that this bird would certainly be 'very heavily hunted' (A. F. A. Hawkins *in litt.* 1994). **VULNERABLE: B1+2b,c; C2a.**

Djibouti Francolin *Francolinus ochropectus*, a ground-dwelling gamebird endemic to **Djibouti**, faces extinction as its juniper forest habitat (records lie between 700 and 1,500 m) in its single main (and probably only viable) site, the 14 km² Forêt du Day National Park, is destroyed by overgrazing, clearance, firewood-gathering, army manoeuvres and other developments (Collar and Stuart 1985, 1988, Welch and Welch 1988). The population is claimed to have fallen from 5,600 birds in 1978 to 1,500 in 1985, 200 of which had that year been located in a second (relict) forest at Mablas (Blot 1985), or else the species may have had a lower but relatively stable population all along (Welch and Welch 1985, Welch *et al.* 1986; see also Urban *et al.* 1986); but a steep decline is now certain, since at the end of 1993 the Forêt du Day was being used for cover by one side in a civil conflict (G. R. Welch and H. J. Welch verbally 1994). **CRITICAL: A1a,b**; A2b; B1+2a,c,e; C1; C2a; D1; D2.

Mount Cameroon Francolin *Francolinus camerunensis* inhabits dense forest undergrowth and clearings above 850 m on Mount Cameroon, **Cameroon**, where clearance high on the east side of the mountain could become more serious, with hunting posing a relatively insignificant (but continuing) threat; a conservation programme is under way that should secure most of its range (Collar and Stuart 1985, Stuart and Jensen 1986, Urban *et al.* 1986, Holyoak and Seddon 1990, Tye 1991, C. G. R. Bowden *in litt.* 1994). **VULNERABLE: D2.**

Swierstra's Francolin *Francolinus swierstrai* has been found in forest and forest edge in a few montane areas in western **Angola**, principally in the Bailundu Highlands where hunting may represent a serious problem (Collar and Stuart 1985) and where even in the early 1970s the patches of surviving forest were already only a few hectares each (Collar and Stuart 1988). **VULNERABLE: B1+2a,b,c; C2a.**

Udzungwa Forest-partridge *Xenoperdix udzungwensis*, a newly discovered (June/July 1991) and distinctive species with no close relatives in Africa, is (not having been found in adjacent forest areas) restricted to the Ndundulu (240 km²) and Nyumbanitu (55 km²) mountains in the Iringa district of the Udzungwa Mountains, **Tanzania**, being locally common within this range, although only found so far at 1,350–1,900 m (Ndundulu) and 1,500–1,700 m (Nyumbanitu) (Dinesen *et al.* 1993, 1994, Lehmberg and Dinesen 1994). In January 1994 a survey of Nyumbanitu including at least two of the species' discoverers failed to confirm its presence but instead found evidence of recently started snaring of ground-haunting birds and mammals, which may have affected the population, although some seasonal influence (causing less conspicuous behaviour, or movement elsewhere in the area) may have

been at work (L. A. Hansen and J. O. Svendsen *in litt.* 1994); moreover, there is now evidence that many foreign visitors have recently been to the area, possibly in connexion with obtaining specimens of the bird (J. Komen *per* J. Fjeldså verbally 1994). **ENDANGERED: B1+2e; C1; C2b.**

Manipur Bush-quail *Perdicula manipurensis* is found in wet, tall grassland and scrub, and sometimes swamps, in foothills to c.1,000 m in north-east **India**, where it is recorded from northern West Bengal, Assam, Nagaland, Manipur and Meghalaya, and **Bangladesh**; although formerly described as local but not very rare, there appear to be no recent published records (BirdLife BPD) and this species may have become much scarcer as a result of drainage and destruction of its habitat, and perhaps hunting (Ali and Ripley 1987, McGowan *et al.* in press). **VULNERABLE: C1; C2a.**

Chestnut-breasted Partridge *Arborophila mandellii* is known from the eastern Himalayas, in **Bhutan**, Sikkim and Arunachal Pradesh, **India**, and south-east Tibet, **China**, where it has been found in evergreen forest from 350 m to 2,450 m, and possibly higher (Ali and Ripley 1987, Cheng 1987). There appear to be only a few, widely scattered historical records (BirdLife BPD), and the only recent reports are from two localities (and possibly a third: M. Katti *in litt.* 1993) in Arunachal Pradesh (Singh in press, R. Kaul verbally 1994, R. H. Raza *in litt.* 1994) and possible records from Bhutan (T. P. Inskipp and C. Inskipp *in litt.* 1993). It is believed to be threatened by forest destruction and degradation, and hunting (McGowan *et al.* in press, A. R. Rahmani *in litt.* 1994). **VULNERABLE: C1; C2a.**

Sichuan Partridge *Arborophila rufipectus* occurs in broadleaf evergreen forest between 1,000 and 2,000 m in south-central Sichuan, **China** (Cheng 1987, King 1989a). It is currently known from five localities within an area of less than 100 km² (and is locally quite common), none of which have official protection, and it is threatened by habitat loss and degradation, particularly the replacement of natural forest with monoculture plantations (King 1989a, McGowan *et al.* in press). **CRITICAL: B1+2c; C1; C2a; D1.**

White-necklaced Partridge *Arborophila gingica* is endemic to south-east **China**, where it is recorded from southern Zhejiang, Fujian, southern Jiangxi, northern Guangdong and Guangxi, in broadleaf and mixed broadleaf and coniferous forest from 500 to 1,700 m (Cheng 1987, Li *et al.* 1990). It is recorded from several protected areas, and is lo-

cally common, but natural forest cover has already been much reduced and fragmented in this densely populated region and it is threatened by further habitat destruction (G. M. Zheng *in litt.* 1994, McGowan *et al.* in press). **VULNERABLE:** C1; C2a.

Orange-necked Partridge *Arborophila davidi*
is known only from Cochinchina, southern **Vietnam**, where two specimens were collected at c.250 m in densely wooded country with rolling hills at Bu Kroai (= Bu Croi), Song Be province, in 1927, and up to four individuals were observed in non-thorny bamboo forest on small hills at 140–200 m in Nam Cat Tien National Park between 1991 and 1994 (*Oriental Bird Club Bull.* 1993, 18: 67–70, C. R. Robson *in litt.* 1994). It has probably suffered a range contraction owing to loss of habitat, as there has been extensive deforestation within its range, and if it is an extreme lowland specialist it must be critically threatened (Eames *et al.* 1992, Robson *et al.* 1993b, J. C. Eames *in litt.* 1994; see Collins *et al.* 1991). **CRITICAL:** A1b; **B1+2c; C1**; C2a; D1; D2.

Chestnut-headed Partridge *Arborophila cambodiana*
is known from evergreen forest above 700 m in the mountains of south-east **Thailand** (race *diversa*, which is possibly specifically distinct), where it is only definitely recorded from Khao Sabap within the Namtok Phliu National Park and Khao Soi Dao Wildlife Sanctuary, and the Cardamomes and Elephant mountains of south-west **Cambodia** (nominate *cambodiana*). There are only a few specimens, and several recent records from Khao Soi Dao (e.g. *Bird Conserv. Soc. Thailand Bull.* 1994, 11,6: 13), where it is probably common (Collar and Andrew 1988), and, although most of its habitat in Thailand is enclosed in protected areas, it is believed to be threatened there (and possibly also in Cambodia) by over-exploitation for food and deforestation (Round 1988, Boonsong and Round 1991, McGowan *et al.* in press). **VULNERABLE:** B1+2c; C1; C2a.

Hainan Partridge *Arborophila ardens*
is known from Hainan Island, south-east **China**, where it is found in evergreen forest between 750 and 1,200 m, although it may also occur in southern Guangxi; on Hainan, it is known from five areas (and possibly occurs at two more), including Bawangling (where it is common) and Wuzhishan Nature Reserves, and is threatened by habitat loss and degradation owing to timber extraction and conversion to agricultural land, and by hunting (McGowan *et al.* in press; see King and Liao 1989). Its former range on Hainan must have been severely reduced and fragmented by deforestation, as forest cover there is estimated to have declined from 8,630 km² (25.7% of the island) in 1949 to about 2,420 km² (7.2%) in 1991 (Collins *et al.* 1991). **ENDANGERED:** A1b,c; B1+2c; **C1**; C2a.

Annam Partridge *Arborophila merlini*
is endemic to central Annam, **Vietnam** (Delacour and Jabouille 1931), where it is believed to be confined to lowland forest below 600 m and therefore threatened by the extensive deforestation within its range. It was found to be common in Bach Ma National Park in 1990, but elsewhere has not been recorded for many years (Robson *et al.* 1993a). **ENDANGERED:** A1b; **B1+2c**; C1.

Chestnut-necklaced Partridge *Arborophila charltonii*
(for whose taxonomy see Davison 1982) is recorded from peninsular **Thailand**, peninsular and East (in Sabah, Borneo) **Malaysia** and Sumatra (and possibly north-east Kalimantan: S. van Balen *in litt.* 1994), **Indonesia**, with an isolated population (race *tonkinensis*) in northern **Vietnam**, where it is found in forest, forest edge and secondary growth in the lowlands to about 300 m (Davison 1982, MacKinnon and Phillipps 1993). In Thailand, it is only known from a single fragment (c.1 km²) of lowland forest in Khlong Phraya National Park and is believed to be on the verge of extinction (McGowan *et al.* in press), in peninsular Malaysia it is very local (Davison and Scriven 1983), in Sabah it is only known from the Danum Valley Research Centre, where it is common (D. Yong *in litt.* 1987, D. R. Wells *in litt.* 1994), in Sumatra it is known by old records from the far north and far south of the island from areas now largely converted to cultivation (van Marle and Voous 1988, D. A. Holmes *in litt.* 1993), and in Vietnam it is locally fairly common and recorded from at least three protected areas (C. R. Robson *in litt.* 1994). It is threatened throughout its range by the clearance of lowland forest and forest degradation (McGowan *et al.* in press; see Collins *et al.* 1991). **VULNERABLE:** A1b.

Himalayan Quail *Ophrysia superciliosa*
is known only from the western Himalayas in northern Uttar Pradesh, **India**, by a handful of specimens collected near Mussooree and Naini Tal in the nineteenth century, from long grass and scrub on steep hillsides between 1,650 and 2,100 m, and is presumed extinct (King 1978–1979, Ali and Ripley 1987), although there is a report of a more recent sighting (Savage 1988). Its known habitat requirements are similar to those of a more widespread western Himalayan endemic, the Cheer Pheasant *Catreus wallichii*, and the historical records of the Himalayan Quail perhaps merely reflect the presence of hill stations, so searches should be carried out over a wider area (Sankaran 1990a, Kaul 1992). **CRITICAL:** D1; D2.

Western Tragopan *Tragopan melanocephalus* is endemic to the western Himalayas, in northern **Pakistan** and north-west **India**, where it breeds in the dense undergrowth of undisturbed temperate zone coniferous and oak forest between 2,400 and 3,600 m, descending in winter to c.2,000 m (Ali and Ripley 1987). Habitat degradation resulting from excessive livestock grazing and the collection of fodder and firewood, together with timber harvesting and the subsequent conversion of land for agriculture, continues to reduce and fragment its range (Garson and McGowan in press). Populations are still present in the Neelum valley of India and Pakistan (see Islam and Crawford 1985, 1986), the Chenab valley east through the Ravi and Beas catchments to the eastern side of the Sutlej valley, India, and the valleys adjoining the Indus River in north-west Pakistan, and the species occurs in at least seven protected areas (Collar and Andrew 1988, Garson and McGowan in press; see Chaudhry 1993). The largest concentration (currently estimated at 325 pairs: Bean *et al.* 1994) in the Palas valley, Pakistan, is the focus of the BirdLife Himalayan Jungle Project (Duke 1994). **VULNERABLE:** C1; C2a.

Blyth's Tragopan *Tragopan blythii* is known from the eastern Himalayas, in eastern **Bhutan**, Arunachal Pradesh, **India**, northern **Myanmar**, and south-east Tibet and north-west Yunnan in **China**, and from the Naga and Chin Hills in Nagaland and Manipur, India, and western Myanmar, where it is found in the undergrowth (especially bamboo) of dense evergreen forest between 1,800 and 3,300 m (Ali and Ripley 1987). The only recent records are of small numbers in Yunnan (Peng *et al.* 1980, Zheng and Zhang 1993) and in eastern Arunachal Pradesh (R. Kaul *in litt.* 1994), but this paucity of information is probably largely a reflection of the inaccessibility of much of its range, and it is reported to be present by Forestry Department officials in Nagaland (in good numbers: R. Kaul *in litt.* 1994) and by local hunters in Manipur (Beaman 1991). It was, at least formerly, locally common in Myanmar (King 1978–1979), but habitat destruction and fragmentation and hunting are considered likely to be reducing its range and numbers (Garson and McGowan in press). **VULNERABLE:** C1; C2a.

Cabot's Tragopan *Tragopan caboti* is endemic to south-east **China**, where it is known from Zhejiang, Jiangxi, Guangdong, Fujian, Hunan and Guangxi, inhabiting mixed evergreen broadleaf and coniferous forests between 800 and 1,400 m (Young *et al.* 1991, Garson and McGowan in press). There are recent records from a number of localities (but it appears to be extinct at several sites), including at least three protected areas, but forest destruction and degradation by timber harvesting and the conversion of land for agriculture in this densely populated region continue to reduce and fragment suitable habitat, and it is hunted for food outside the protected areas (King 1978–1979, Zheng and Zhang 1993, Z. W. Zhang *in litt.* 1993, Garson and McGowan in press). **VULNERABLE:** C1; C2a.

Sclater's Monal *Lophophorus sclateri* is found in the eastern Himalayas, in Arunachal Pradesh, **India**, northern **Myanmar** and south-east Tibet and western Yunnan, **China**, where it inhabits coniferous forest with bamboo understorey, subalpine rhododendron scrub and rocky, precipitous slopes at 3,000–4,000 m (down to 2,500 m in winter) (Meyer de Schauensee 1984, Ali and Ripley 1987, Cheng 1987, Garson and McGowan in press). There are recent records from several sites in Yunnan and Tibet, and from one locality in Arunachal Pradesh (but none from Myanmar), including the large Gaoligong Shan Nature Reserve in Yunnan, and it is locally common; in the Chinese part of its range localized forest loss and hunting are threats, and hunting for food and feathers (to make ornaments) also takes place in India (F. Q. He verbally 1993, Garson and McGowan in press, R. Kaul verbally 1994, R. H. Raza *in litt.* 1994). **VULNERABLE:** C1; C2a.

Chinese Monal *Lophophorus lhuysii* is known from western Sichuan, south-east Qinghai and southern Gansu, and possibly also north-west Yunnan and north-east Tibet, **China** (Cheng 1987, He and Lu 1991, F. Q. He *in litt.* 1993, L. X. Han *in litt.* 1994), occurring at the upper limit of coniferous forest, in rhododendron, alpine meadows and rocky areas from 3,000 to 4,900 m, and down to 2,800 m in winter (Meyer de Schauensee 1984, C. R. Robson *in litt.* 1992). It has recently been recorded in at least 25 localities, including at least seven protected areas, but there are apparently no recent records from Qinghai; its population is believed to be declining slightly, as a result of habitat degradation by overgrazing and hunting (F. Q. He *in litt.* 1993, Garson and McGowan in press). **VULNERABLE:** C2a.

Imperial Pheasant *Lophura imperialis* is known from north and central Annam, **Vietnam** (a record from Laos, based on a description by local hunters, is probably unreliable), where the only records are of a pair captured alive in 1923, apparently on the border of the old Donghoi and Quangtri provinces, and of a live immature male trapped in secondary lowland forest at 50–200 m near Cat Bin in the Cam Ky Forestry Enterprise in 1990; authorized logging ceased in the latter area in 1978, but it is under great pressure from wood-cutters (Robson *et al.* 1991, 1993a; see Delacour and Jabouille 1931), and the species is threatened by continuing deforestation and by hunting (J. C. Eames *in litt.* 1994). **CRITICAL:** A1b,c; A2b,c; B1+2c; **C1**; **C2b**; D1; D2.

Edwards's Pheasant *Lophura edwardsi* (if Vietnamese Pheasant *L. hatinhensis* is not conspecific: see that species, below) is historically known from at least eight sites in central Annam, **Vietnam**, and is said to inhabit very wet forest with an understorey of brush and lianas from sea-level to 600 m (Delacour and Jabouille 1931, Delacour 1977), but the altitude of the collecting localities and the failure to find it in recent surveys (1988–1991) suggest that it occupied level lowland forest rather than hill slopes (Eames *et al.* 1992). The historical range is now almost completely deforested, the only protected area within this range being Bach Ma National Park, where all suitable habitat has probably been completely destroyed; the bird may, therefore, be extinct in the wild (a report in 1988 by a hunter near 'Pass 41', A Sau A Luoi, of birds possibly this species should be treated with caution), although further surveys for suitable forest are needed in southern Thua Thien and Quang Tri provinces (Eames *et al.* 1992). There are well over 500 birds in captivity (P. J. Garson *in litt.* 1994). **CRITICAL: B1+2c**; **C1**; **C2a**; **D1**; D2.

Vietnamese Pheasant *Lophura hatinhensis* (if not a subspecies of Edwards's Pheasant *L. edwardsi*: Vuilleumier *et al.* 1992) is endemic to **Vietnam**, where it is known by single specimens collected in 1964 and 1974 in north Annam, four live birds obtained in 1990 (said to have originated near the border between north and central Annam), at least 11 males and two females reported to have been trapped (some feathers and other remains examined) in 1990 near Cat Bin in the Cam Ky Forestry Enterprise, north Annam (where it is probably distributed throughout c.50 km² of secondary and logged evergreen forest from 50 to 200 m), and at least nine individuals seen in 1994 during a one week survey of an extensive area of primary forest in Quang Binh province (indicating that a major population is present, but the area is scheduled for logging); it is threatened by the combination of continuing deforestation and hunting (Robson *et al.* 1991, 1993a, Rozendaal *et al.* 1991, J. C. Eames *in litt.* 1994, F. R. Lambert verbally 1994). **ENDANGERED:** A1b; A2b,c; **B1+2c**; **C1**; C2a; D1; D2.

Sumatran Pheasant *Lophura hoogerwerfi*, possibly a subspecies of Salvadori's Pheasant *L. inornata*, is endemic to northern Sumatra, **Indonesia**, where it is known from the Gayo Highlands by two female specimens and several sightings of family parties probably of this species, in forest with little undergrowth between 600 and 2,000 m. It has been recorded in Gunung Leuser National Park (van Marle and Voous 1988), but there is some agricultural encroachment into its forest habitat within its known range (BirdLife IP). **VULNERABLE:** B1+2c; C1; C2a.

Salvadori's Pheasant *Lophura inornata* (possibly conspecific with Sumatran Pheasant *L. hoogerwerfi*) is endemic to Sumatra, **Indonesia**, where it is known from the central and southern Barisan range, in montane forest from 1,000 to 1,800 m, and locally up to 2,200 m (van Marle and Voous 1988). There are recent records of small numbers from only two localities, Gunung Kaba (Holmes 1989) and Kerinci-Seblat National Park, where much of the forest within the lower part of its altitudinal range has already been cleared, and it is vulnerable to further illegal agricultural encroachment (Lambert and Howes 1989). **VULNERABLE:** C1; C2a.

Crestless Fireback *Lophura erythrophthalma* occurs in peninsular and East **Malaysia**, Sumatra and Kalimantan, **Indonesia**, and **Brunei**, where it is an extreme lowland specialist (Wells 1985), found in rainforest up to 300 m (Davison and Scriven 1983, MacKinnon and Phillipps 1993). In peninsular Malaysia, it is the commonest *Lophura* pheasant (found at densities up to six birds per km²), occurring in both logged and unlogged forest (Davison and Scriven 1983), but it is scarce on Sumatra, with recent records from only one locality, and on Borneo it is confined to the south and the west, with few recent records (Holmes 1989, MacKinnon and Phillipps 1993, S. van Balen *in litt.* 1994). The main threat is lowland deforestation, which has much reduced and fragmented its habitat throughout its range (Holmes 1989, Garson and McGowan in press, BirdLife IP; see Collins *et al.* 1991). **VULNERABLE:** A1b; A2b.

Crested Fireback *Lophura ignita* is recorded from extreme southern Tenasserim, **Myanmar** (no recent information, but formerly scarce: Smythies 1986), peninsular **Thailand** (rare: Boonsong and Round 1991), peninsular and East **Malaysia** (historically throughout the lowlands of the peninsula, but current distribution poorly known, although there are recent records from several protected areas, and it is still locally common in Sabah: Holmes 1989, Yatim 1993), Kalimantan, Sumatra and Bangka, **Indonesia** (still locally common in Kalimantan and Sumatra, occurring in several protected areas, but probably close to extinction on Bangka: Holmes 1989, van Balen and Holmes 1993) and **Brunei**

(Mann 1987). It is considered to be an extreme low-land forest specialist (Wells 1985), which frequents river terraces along large rivers and streams (Yatim 1993), and although it occurs in logged and dis-turbed forest it is threatened by the extensive low-land deforestation within its range, and locally by hunting (Collar and Andrew 1988, Holmes 1989, Boonsong and Round 1991, van Balen and Holmes 1993, S. van Balen *in litt.* 1994, D. R. Wells *in litt.* 1994; see Collins *et al.* 1991). **VULNERABLE:** A1b,c; A2b,c.

Siamese Fireback *Lophura diardi* is found in northern and eastern **Thailand**, **Laos**, **Cambodia** and central and southern **Vietnam** (King *et al.* 1975), where it occurs in evergreen, semi-evergreen and bamboo forest, chiefly in the plains and foothills but occasionally up to 800 m (Boonsong and Round 1991, Eames *et al.* 1992), often near roads and tracks through the forest (Robson *et al.* 1993b). There are recent records from Thailand (where it is considered rare, although a recent estimate of 5,000 individuals has been made, and it occurs in several protected areas: Boonsong and Round 1991, P. D. Round *in litt.* 1993), Vietnam (recorded at several localities by recent surveys, including several protected areas: Eames *et al.* 1992, J. C. Eames *in litt.* 1994) and Laos (locally common in two protected areas, and present in a third: Duckworth *et al.* 1993a,b, Evans and Timmins 1994). It seems able to tolerate some degradation of its forest habitat (Duckworth *et al.* 1993a), but it is threatened by the continuing exten-sive lowland forest destruction within its range, and hunting (Boonsong and Round 1991, J. C. Eames *in litt.* 1994, Garson and McGowan in press; see Collins *et al.* 1991). **VULNERABLE:** A1b,c; A2b,c.

Bulwer's Pheasant *Lophura bulweri* is endemic to Borneo, in Sabah and Sarawak, East **Malaysia**, Kalimantan, **Indonesia** and **Brunei**, where it is found in primary hill and lower montane forest up to 1,600 m (Smythies 1981, Mann 1987, MacKinnon and Phillipps 1993). It is local and patchy in distribu-tion, but is (or was) very common in undisturbed parts of the interior (Smythies 1986). There are sev-eral recent records from Sabah, but very few from Kalimantan (van Balen and Holmes in press), and it is estimated that the total population lies between 1,000 and 10,000 birds (Garson and McGowan in press). Potential threats are deforestation and per-haps hunting, although extensive areas of apparently suitable habitat remain in Kalimantan (BirdLife IP). It occurs in at least three protected areas (Garson and McGowan in press) and it has been stated that there is no reason to believe that it is threatened (Holmes 1989). **VULNERABLE:** C2a.

Tibetan Eared-pheasant *Crossoptilon harmani* has been recorded in south-east Tibet, **China**, and possibly extreme northern Arunachal Pradesh, India (the records there being disputed: Ludlow 1944), where it occurs in tall dense scrub in dry river val-leys, the borders of mixed broadleaf and coniferous forest, coniferous forest, and grassy hill slopes, from 3,000 to 5,000 m (and rarely down to 2,400 m); it is locally common, and adaptable to disturbed habitats (Ali and Ripley 1987, C. R. Robson *in litt.* 1991), but deforestation and hunting may be significant threats (Garson and McGowan in press). **VULNERABLE:** C2a.

White Eared-pheasant *Crossoptilon crosso-ptilon* (from which the Tibetan Eared-pheasant *C. harmani* is now treated as specifically distinct) is endemic to **China**, where it is known from Qinghai, Sichuan, Yunnan and Tibet, and occurs in conifer-ous and mixed forests near the treeline, plus subalpine birch and rhododendron scrub, at 3,000 to 4,300 m (Meyer de Schauensee 1984, Cheng 1987). There are recent records from approximately 20 localities (Z. W. Zhang *in litt.* 1993), including several pro-tected areas, but it is believed to be declining in numbers because of deforestation and hunting (Garson and McGowan in press). **VULNERABLE:** C2a.

Brown Eared-pheasant *Crossoptilon mantchur-icum* is endemic to north-east **China**, where it occurs in Shanxi, Hebei and Beijing municipality (and for-merly Inner Mongolia: Johnsgard 1986), in broadleaf and mixed coniferous forest (including logged and secondary forest) and adjacent scrub and grassland in mountainous regions above 1,300 m, and histori-cally suffered a major decline because of the exten-sive deforestation of the mountains within its range. It is now known from four protected areas, Luyiashan (2,790 estimated present in 1989, significantly more than in the early 1980s: AOSNR 1990) and Wulushan Nature Reserves and Pangquangou (1,230 estimated present in 1989, significantly more than in the early 1980s: AOSNR 1990) National Nature Reserve in Shanxi, and Xiaowutaishan Nature Reserve in Hebei, plus at least two unprotected localities, but pop-ulations outside protected areas are threatened by habitat destruction and egg collecting for food (Cheng 1987, AOSNR 1990, Garson and McGowan in press; see *Oriental Bird Club Bull.* 1990, 12: 11, Li 1993). **VULNERABLE:** B1+2c.

Cheer Pheasant *Catreus wallichi* ranges through the western Himalayas from northern **Pakistan** and north-west **India** to central **Nepal**, where it occurs between 1,200 and 3,250 m in patchy hill grasslands dissected by scrub and wooded ravines, and locally in recently cleared areas with secondary growth, apparently having a strong affinity for early successional habitats, and is generally found as small populations within isolated pockets of suitable habitat; in India, it has been found at numerous sites in Himachal Pradesh, but appears to be rarer in Uttar Pradesh, and has populations in several protected areas (Garson *et al.* 1992). There are recent records from only a few localities in western Nepal, including two protected areas, and very few from Pakistan where it may be close to extinction (see Roberts 1991, *Oriental Bird Club Bull.* 1992, 16: 14–15, Chaudhry 1993). The main threats are hunting, habitat degradation and the conversion of land for agriculture; a reintroduction programme instigated in 1978 in the Margalla Hills, Pakistan, has so far failed to re-establish the species (Garson *et al.* 1992, Garson and McGowan in press). **VULNERABLE:** C2a.

Elliot's Pheasant *Syrmaticus ellioti* breeds in

coniferous and mixed broadleaf-coniferous forest in foothills at 500–1,000 m, moving seasonally into scrub down to 300 m and montane forest at up to 1,500 m (Ding and Zhuge 1990), in Jiangxi, Anhui, Zhejiang, Fujian, Guangdong, Hunan, Guizhou and Guangxi, southern and eastern **China**, the records from the last three regions greatly extending its known range westwards and suggesting that it is not as seriously at risk as once thought (Cheng 1987, He and Lu 1991, F. Q. He verbally 1993). There are recent records from several protected areas, but deforestation and agricultural encroachment have already rendered much of its range uninhabitable and fragmented its population, and hunting for food is also believed to be a serious problem (Garson and McGowan in press). **VULNERABLE:** C1; C2a.

Hume's Pheasant *Syrmaticus humiae* is known

from Mizoram, Manipur, Nagaland and eastern Arunachal Pradesh, **India**, **Myanmar**, north-west **Thailand** and Guangxi and Yunnan, **China**, where it occurs in broadleaf evergreen forest and mixed broadleaf and pine forest, and in adjacent clearings with grass and bracken, between 740 and 2,000 m (Ali and Ripley 1987, Garson and McGowan in press). Recent records have come from over 20 sites in China and two in Thailand (including records within protected areas in both countries), but there is no current information from the core of the range in Myanmar, and the only recent report from India is rumoured presence in two protected areas in Mizoram (R. K. Ramunujam *per* R. Kaul *in litt.* 1993). Numbers have greatly diminished in China (and presumably elsewhere) because of habitat destruction and hunting (Liu *et al.* 1990, Zheng and Zhang 1993, P. J. Garson *in litt.* 1994). **VULNERABLE:** C1; C2a.

Reeves's Pheasant *Syrmaticus reevesii* is en-

demic to **China**, where it is known from Hebei, Shanxi, Shaanxi, Gansu, Sichuan, Henan, Anhui, Hubei, Hunan, Guizhou and Yunnan, and is found in broadleaf forests dominated by oaks, and coniferous forest and scrub, from 400 to 2,600 m (Cheng 1987, Xu *et al.* 1990). It is believed to have become extinct in Hebei, Shanxi and Shaanxi within the past 10–20 years, and is known to persist at only a few sites in the southern half of its former range, including four protected areas, with a population estimated at less than 5,000 individuals; continuing deforestation within its range is reducing and fragmenting its habitat, and hunting is also believed to be a threat (Garson and McGowan in press). It has been introduced to Hawaii (U.S.A.) and various parts of Europe (Cramp and Simmons 1980, Lever 1987), and a feral population is firmly established at least in the Czech Republic (Pokorny and Pikula 1987). **VULNERABLE:** A1b; C1; C2a.

Mountain Peacock-pheasant *Polyplectron*

inopinatum is endemic to peninsular **Malaysia**, where it is found throughout the Main Range, on Gunung Hijau in the Larut Range, and on Gunungs Benom and Tahan (Medway and Wells 1976, D. R. Wells *in litt.* 1994), in unlogged upper dipterocarp, lower montane and upper montane forest at 900–2,000 m, with recent records from several localities, including four protected areas, and the population is believed to be either stable or declining slightly because of habitat conversion for agriculture and possibly urban development; however, a current plan to build a road linking the hill stations of Genting Highlands, Fraser's Hill and Cameron Highlands could greatly increase disturbance and habitat destruction and degradation within its range (G. W. H. Davison *in litt.* 1993, Garson and McGowan in press). **VULNERABLE:** B1+2c; C1; C2a.

Germain's Peacock-pheasant *Polyplectron*

germaini is known from evergreen forest, including logged, secondary and bamboo forest, in the lowlands and mountains up to 1,500 m, in (southern) central and south Annam, and Cochinchina, **Vietnam**, the inclusion of Cambodia and southern Thailand in its range by Delacour and Jabouille (1931) being apparently erroneous. There are recent records from several localities, including Nam Cat Tien National Park and Cat Loc Nature Reserve, where it is fairly common, and from the lower slopes of the Da Lat (= Langbian) and Di Linh plateaus in south Annam, but it is threatened by deforestation throughout its range and is subject to hunting (Morris 1987, Eames *et al.* 1992, Robson *et al.* 1993a,b, J. C. Eames *in litt.* 1994). **VULNERABLE:** B1+2c; C1; C2a.

Malayan Peacock-pheasant *Polyplectron malacense* is an extreme lowland specialist (Wells 1985), found in rainforest below 300 m in peninsular **Malaysia** and southern peninsular **Thailand** (on the verge of extinction with just one possible site); the evidence for its historical occurrence in southern Tenasserim, Myanmar (Smythies 1986, D. R. Wells *in litt.* 1994), is believed to be flawed and the result of confusion with the Grey Peacock-pheasant *P. bicalcaratum*. Its range has been considerably reduced by the widespread destruction and degradation of lowland forest (see Collins *et al.* 1991), and continuing loss of this habitat because of conversion of land for agriculture could eventually mean that it will be virtually confined to the five protected areas (three of which are small) which are known to support populations (Boonsong and Round 1991, Garson and McGowan in press; see Yatim 1993). **VULNERABLE:** A1b; A2b; C1; C2a.

Bornean Peacock-pheasant *Polyplectron schleiermacheri* is endemic to Borneo, in Sabah and Sarawak, East **Malaysia**, and Kalimantan, **Indonesia**, where it is found in lowland forest (Smythies 1981). It is apparently very rare, known historically from few localities, and the only recent records are from Kalimantan, namely an unconfirmed voice record in 1981 at Nangtayap in alluvial forest (since cleared) (Holmes 1989), a specimen collected at Palangkaraya in 1979 (van Balen and Holmes 1993) and a population recently discovered at another site (D. Bruning *in litt.* 1994). Deforestation in the lowlands is believed to be the bird's main threat (BirdLife IP), and it may have been affected by several forest fires which have destroyed huge areas of lowland forest on Borneo since 1982 (see Collins *et al.* 1991). **CRITICAL: A1b**; A2b; **C1**; C2a; D1.

Palawan Peacock-pheasant *Polyplectron emphanum* is endemic to Palawan in the **Philippines**, where it occurs in lowland and hill forest, with highest densities being in primary and edge habitat, lower in logged forest, but in any case in stark regression as a consequence of deforestation and hunting (Collar and Andrew 1988, McGowan *et al.* 1989). It is present in St Paul Subterranean National Park (being judged secure there in 1993: J. Hornbuckle *in litt.* 1994), and was found in the south of the island and as far north as Danlig, so may occur in the still reasonably forested Pagdanan Range (Lambert 1993b, Timmins in prep.). **ENDANGERED:** A1b,c; A2b,c; B1+2c; C1; **C2a**.

Crested Argus *Rheinardia ocellata* is found in two widely disjunct areas, nominate *ocellata* in central and southern **Vietnam** and neighbouring areas

of **Laos**, and the race *nigrescens* in central peninsular **Malaysia** (Collar and Andrew 1988). In Vietnam, it is found in primary, logged and secondary forest, in the lowlands and mountains to 1,900 m, and although its range has been much reduced and fragmented by deforestation it is still widespread and locally common (and occurs further south and at higher altitudes than previously known, in the Da Lat plateau region of south Annam) with populations in several protected areas (Robson *et al.* 1993a,b), but is threatened by further deforestation resulting from logging and clearance for agriculture and is widely hunted for food (Eames *et al.* 1992). It is historically known from several localities in the Annamite Mountains in Laos, and has recently been found still locally common at one of these sites (Evans and Timmins 1994). In Malaysia, it is locally distributed in the mountains of north Pahang and south Kelatan, where it is found in the foothills from 700 to 1,200 m, and its range is largely contained within Taman Negara National Park (Yatim 1993, G. W. H. Davison *in litt.* 1993). **VULNERABLE:** A1b,c.

Congo Peafowl *Afropavo congensis* is a shy, ground-haunting pheasant (the only species native to Africa) known from a wide area of equatorial rainforest in eastern **Zaïre**, where it appears to be uncommon but secure (Collar and Stuart 1985; see also Urban *et al.* 1986). Local people know it in the lowland Kahuzi-Biega National Park Extension, and report a recent sighting south-west of Nkuba in the north of the extension (Wilson and Catsis 1990). There is also a recent sighting, with other evidence of its existence, including dust baths with identifiable feathers and a general awareness of it among local people, suggesting it is not rare in the area (but is trapped for food), near the Loya River in September 1993 (Fanshawe 1994); there are about 10 known or probable locations for the species in this area (Maiko Park and vicinity), but outside this and Kahuzi-Biega the situation appears very poor (J. Hart *in litt.* 1994). In June 1991 there were 62 captive males and 26 females registered with the international zoo studbook (R. van Bocxstaele *in litt.* 1991). **VULNERABLE:** C2b.

Green Peafowl *Pavo muticus* has a large range, extending from the hills south of the Brahmaputra River in north-east India to peninsular Malaysia, where it is usually found in lowland forest and forest edge near rivers or marshes (and locally in scrub and open country up to 1,000 m), with a disjunct population on Java, **Indonesia**, where it occurs in open woodland, teak plantations and forest edge from sea-level to 3,000 m and in montane grassland (King *et al.* 1975, Robson *et al.* 1993a,b, van Balen and

Holmes 1993). It was formerly common in many parts of this range, but is believed to be extinct in India, Bangladesh, peninsular Thailand and peninsular Malaysia (as a result of hunting: D. R. Wells *in litt.* 1994; see Yatim 1993), and appears to have declined virtually everywhere else, leaving relatively small, fragmented populations, with recent records from **Myanmar** (locally common: Salter 1983), south-central Yunnan, **China** (range contracted and population declined, and now known from about 10 sites: Zheng and Zhang 1993), **Laos** (recorded in at least five protected areas since 1989, but mainly in small, rapidly declining populations, and extinct in most of its former range as a result of hunting for food and the feather trade: T. D. Evans and R. J. Timmins verbally 1994), **Cambodia** (not recorded during surveys in 1994, but reported to be present at one locality by local people, who hunt them: T. Mundkur *in litt.* 1994), **Vietnam** (recently recorded at several sites, including in or near three or more protected areas, but much reduced as a result of continuing habitat loss and hunting: Eames *et al.* 1992, Robson *et al.* 1993a,b, J. C. Eames *in litt.* 1994), **Thailand** (recently reported from four sites, but only confirmed in Hwai Kha Kaeng Wildlife Sanctuary where 300 are estimated: Garson and McGowan in press) and Java (recently found at c.20 localities, including several protected areas, but threatened by habitat loss and hunting: van Balen and Holmes 1993). **VULNERABLE:** A1b,c; A2b,c.

Bearded Wood-partridge *Dendrortyx barbatus* is confined to the dwindling and highly fragmented cloud-forests (humid evergreen montane forest, mostly 1,220–2,135 m) on the Sierra Madre Oriental of eastern **Mexico** (San Luis Potosí, Hidalgo, Puebla, Veracruz), where it is extinct locally and severely threatened elsewhere (only two sites with confirmed records in the past 20 years, in 1977 and 1986), largely as a result of habitat destruction on a major scale, probably compounded by hunting (Collar *et al.* 1992). **CRITICAL:** A1b,c; **A2b,c**; B1+2c; C1; C2a; D1.

Gorgeted Wood-quail *Odontophorus strophium* is endemic to severely threatened subtropical- and temperate-zone forests (dominated by oak and laurel) encompassing a small area of the western slope of the eastern Andes of **Colombia** (at uncertain altitudes: possibly 1,500–2,500 m, but the species is recorded only from 1,750 to 2,050 m; until 1923 it was known only from Cundinamarca (whence no reports since), but recent records have come from one of the only remaining areas of suitable habitat, around Virolín in Santander department, where however habitat destruction and hunting of game are still prevalent (Collar *et al.* 1992). In November 1993 100 km² of forest at Virolín was gazetted as a reserve (Andrade and Repizzo 1994). **ENDANGERED:** A1b,c; A2b,c; **B1+2c**; C1; C2a.

Family NUMIDIDAE
GUINEAFOWL

White-breasted Guineafowl *Agelastes meleagrides*, endemic to the rapidly receding Upper Guinea rainforest block of West Africa, requires primary or mature secondary forest and freedom from persecution to survive, and is consequently becoming isolated and depleted in the ever-diminishing pockets of such habitat in **Ghana** (where approaching extinction), **Ivory Coast** (notably Taï National Park), **Liberia** and **Sierra Leone** (Gola forest region only) (Collar and Stuart 1985, Thiollay 1985, Urban *et al.* 1986, Gatter *et al.* 1988, Allport 1991), although its population levels in Taï (30,000–40,000 birds: Francis *et al.* 1992) and Gola (7,100 birds: Allport *et al.* 1989, Wood 1993) indicate that it is less immediately threatened than previously judged. **VULNERABLE:** A1b,c; A2b,c.

Family MESITORNITHIDAE

MESITES

White-breasted Mesite *Mesitornis variegata* is an inconspicuous, rail-like ground-dweller of deciduous forest at a small number of sites (some protected areas) in north and west **Madagascar**, with one anomalous record from the eastern rainforest within the range of the threatened Brown Mesite *M. unicolor* (Appert 1985, Collar and Stuart 1985, Nicoll and Langrand 1989, Hawkins *et al.* 1990, Langrand 1990, Thompson and Evans 1992). Recent fieldwork shows that minima of 2,000 birds occur at one site (Menabe) and 6,000 at another (Ankarafantsika), the other locations perhaps being relicts (Hawkins in press). It prefers foraging sites with dense overhead cover, deep leaf-litter and a herb-layer clear of dead sticks, and while it occurs in reasonable numbers at some of these sites at least, its absence from intervening areas is genuine and all sites are under threat from slash-and-burn agriculture and uncontrolled bush fires (Hawkins 1993a, in press, A. F. A. Hawkins *in litt.* 1994). **VULNERABLE:** A2b; B1+2a,c.

Brown Mesite *Mesitornis unicolor* is a cryptic and retiring rail-like ground-dweller (preferring herb-free areas of thick leaf-litter) of the rainforest belt in eastern **Madagascar**, known for certain from as far north as Marojejy and the Masoala peninsula and extending almost as far south as Tôlaenaro (Fort Dauphin), and being recorded from at least five protected areas and as high as 1,100 m (Collar and Stuart 1985, Nicoll and Langrand 1989, Langrand 1990, Evans *et al.* 1992a, Thompson and Evans 1992, O. Langrand *in litt.* 1994); all of this tends to suggest a far stronger conservation status than was believed 15 years ago (see King 1978–1979), but it still seems to be patchy in range and to prefer lower-lying habitat, which is being depleted very fast (A. F. A. Hawkins *in litt.* 1994). **VULNERABLE:** A2b; C1; C2a.

Subdesert Mesite *Monias benschi* is an apparently group-territorial ground-dweller of subdesert scrub in south-western **Madagascar**, where with the threatened Long-tailed Ground-roller *Uratelornis chimaera* it is restricted to a 70-km wide coastal strip between the Mangoky and Fiherenana rivers and is subject to predation by dogs and trappers and to habitat destruction (Collar and Stuart 1985, 1988). It occurs in no protected area, tree removal for charcoal production is increasing, and rats *Rattus rattus* are also believed to be a threat (O. Langrand *in litt.* 1987, Langrand 1990). **VULNERABLE:** A2b; B1+2c,e; C1; C2b.

Family TURNICIDAE

BUTTONQUAILS

Black-breasted Buttonquail *Turnix melanogaster* has declined drastically this century and is now largely restricted to remnant patches of dry, closed forest in south-eastern Queensland and northeast New South Wales, **Australia**; although observations in older hoop pine *Araucaria cunninghamii* plantations with a well developed understorey of introduced *Lantana* indicate that it may be adapting to a modified environment, in the last 15 years it has been recorded from fewer than 50 sites (with less than 10 birds at each) and must be vulnerable to introduced predators (Garnett 1992). **ENDANGERED:** B1+2e; **C2a**; D1.

Chestnut-backed Buttonquail *Turnix castanota* is locally distributed and locally common in grassy eucalypt woodland in the Top End of the Northern Territory and the Kimberley region of northern Western Australia, **Australia**, where it is hard to find and identify, so the frequency with which it is recorded may not reflect its abundance (Garnett 1992). In Stage III of the Kakadu National Park it had a maximum density of 4 birds/km^2 but was recorded from too few quadrats to derive a satisfactory overall population estimate; near the McArthur River, however, where it was common in 1913, there have been no recent records, suggesting that large-scale changes in habitat, such as grazing by introduced herbivores or changes in the fire regime, may affect it (Garnett 1992). **VULNERABLE: C2a.**

Buff-breasted Buttonquail *Turnix olivii* inhabits grass clearings in forest and woodland on Cape York peninsula, possibly occurring as far south as Mareeba in north-east Queensland, **Australia** (Blakers *et al.* 1984). It was reasonably common during the early 1920s near Coen in the centre of Cape York peninsula, but was not recorded at all during five years of field observations, 1977–1981, and records during the 1980s were only of individuals or pairs (although it is assumed to be underrecorded); fire is probably the main threat, particularly when burning occurs during the late dry season while birds are nesting (Garnett 1992, Marchant and Higgins 1993). **ENDANGERED: C2b**; D1.

Worcester's Buttonquail *Turnix worcesteri* is an enigmatic species known only from Luzon in the **Philippines**, where it was described from specimens found in a Manila market and subsequently found at three localities, two (Parañaque and Benguet) without further data and one (Dalton Pass) perhaps being an intra-island migration point; it is possibly restricted to highland grasslands, and must be rare (Dickinson *et al.* 1991). **VULNERABLE: D1.**

Sumba Buttonquail *Turnix everetti* is known from Sumba, **Indonesia**, by three specimens (White and Bruce 1986) and sightings in 1989 and 1992 of up to 17 birds at Watumbaka, in sparse grassland with occasional bushes on a flat plateau of coral limestone directly behind the mangrove belt, and one in grassland at Manupeu (unidentified birds recorded at several other localities could have been Red-backed Button-quail *T. maculosa*). Its ecology remains poorly understood, but it is possible that the repeated burning of vegetation to provide land for grazing and cultivation has actually increased the area of suitable grassland habitat (Marsden and Peters 1992, Jones *et al.* in prep.). **VULNERABLE: C1; C2a; D1.**

Family PEDIONOMIDAE
PLAINS-WANDERER

Plains-wanderer *Pedionomus torquatus* was formerly widespread in short, sparse grassland in inland New South Wales, southern Queensland, western Victoria and eastern South Australia, **Australia**, but its range has shrunk markedly this century, particularly from the coast where the main threat comes from cultivation. The total population may sometimes exceed 10,000 individuals but this can be halved during drought years (Garnett 1992, Baker-Gabb 1993). **VULNERABLE: B2c+3d.**

Family GRUIDAE
CRANES

Siberian Crane *Grus leucogeranus* breeds in two (or perhaps three) discrete areas in Siberia, **Russia**, in extensive wetlands with many lakes in the tundra zone, each pair apparently requiring access to very long sections of lakeshore with floating turf to rear young successfully (Sorokin and Kotyukov 1987, Potapov 1992). Birds breeding in western Siberia winter in wetlands in **Iran**, where numbers have remained relatively stable at 10–11 since the discovery of this population 14 years ago, and at Bharatpur, **India** (arriving via **Afghanistan** and **Pakistan**), where they declined from 125 in the 1960s to just six in winter 1991/1992, with no birds being reported present in 1993/1994 (Lall and Raman 1994; but see

Birding World 1994, 7: 212), perhaps because of hunting in Afghanistan (where this species has been found for sale as food in the past), although the feeding habitat at Bharatpur has recently been degraded by an invasion of aggressive grasses and some birds may have shifted their wintering area (two were located elsewhere in 1991); efforts are being made to establish captive breeding flocks with the aim of reintroduction into this population and to use satellite tracking to study migration routes (Archibald and Landfried 1993). The much larger eastern population winters in the Chang Jiang (= Yangtze) valley, **China** (with vagrant records in Japan and Mongolia), the majority at Poyang Lake Nature Reserve (2,877 in 1993), where seasonal fluctuations in flood level produce ideal feeding conditions, and small numbers at East Dongling Lake Nature Reserve (38 in 1993) (Archibald and Landfried 1993, *ICF Bugle* 1994, 20,2: 6; see also eight papers in Archibald and Pasquier 1987), but the construction of the Three Gorges Dam threatens to disrupt the flow of the Chang Jiang River and reduce the quality of this habitat (Zhu *et al.* 1987) and there is evidence of some hunting (Lu 1993b). **ENDANGERED: A2b,c; C1; D2.**

White-naped Crane *Grus vipio* breeds in wetlands with large expanses of shallow water in north-east **China** and adjacent regions of **Mongolia** and south-east **Russia**, and winters in wetlands and agricultural land in China, **North Korea**, **South Korea** and **Japan** (vagrant in Taiwan: Wang *et al.* 1991a) (King 1978–1979, Ostapenko and Zewenmjadag 1983, Archibald 1987). The majority of the population nests in China, in at least six localities (see Scott 1989), several hundred birds breed in Mongolia (Archibald 1987), and a maximum of 18 pairs is known in three areas in Russia (Potapov and Flint 1987). The total world population is estimated to be 5,000–5,700 (Rose and Scott 1994), and important wintering concentrations are found at Arasaki, Japan, the only regular site in the country where more than 1,500 wintered in 1992 (Brazil 1994), having increased as a result of artificial feeding (Ohsako 1987), Poyang Lake (maximum recent count of 2,000: Scott 1989) and two other wetlands in the Chang Jiang (= Yangtze) valley, China, and three or four localities in South Korea (see Scott 1989). Threats include habitat destruction on the breeding grounds (Archibald 1987) and at passage and wintering sites (Higuchi *et al.* 1992), the proposed Three Gorges Dam Project, which would alter seasonal water levels of the Chang Jiang River and would put the wintering habitat at Poyang Lake at risk (Zhu *et al.* 1987), and hunting at wintering sites in China (Lu 1993b). **VULNERABLE: C1.**

Blue Crane *Grus paradiseus* occupies grasslands, grassy karoo and agricultural areas from sea-level up to c.2,000 m in **South Africa** (chiefly), northern **Namibia** (an isolated population of c.80 birds at Etosha with occasional occurrence in Bushmanland), extreme south-west **Botswana** (1–5 pairs), lowland Lesotho (now only a vagrant) and (mainly western) **Swaziland** (a small breeding population of c.12 birds: Parker in press), where the total population has fallen by half (to some 20,800 individuals, 60–70% of which are non-breeding) since the 1970s, largely as a result of accidental poisoning when foraging on growing crops (treated against other species), afforestation, open-cast mining and urbanization (Urban *et al.* 1986, D. G. Allan *in litt.* 1994, *contra* data given in Allan 1993). **VULNERABLE: A1a,b; A2b; C1; C2a.**

Wattled Crane *Grus carunculatus*, a large, shy, mainly vegetarian crane requiring very large territories and achieving very low reproductive success, occurs in marshes and floodplains in (estimated or guessed-at numbers after each country are from the mid-1980s unless otherwise referenced) **Angola** (500, perhaps declining from war), **Botswana** (numbers unknown and variable with season, but perhaps only a few hundred in the Okavango delta), **Ethiopia** (several hundred, but probably now seriously declining: P. O. Syvertsen *in litt.* 1994), **Malawi** (only known population fewer than 10 pairs: Nhlane 1993), **Mozambique** (250 or less), **Namibia** (numbers very small), **South Africa** (c.300, but declining rapidly), **Tanzania** (mid-1980s guessed-at total of 'a few hundred' bolstered by an estimated 200 in the Moyowosi-Kigosi wetlands, 1990: Borner 1990), **Zaïre** (several hundred), **Zambia** (c.5,500, with 2,700 of them on the Kafue Flats) and **Zimbabwe** (possibly only 250), declines being in response to habitat loss, disturbance, and nest loss (Collar and Stuart 1985; also Urban *et al.* 1986, Malambo and Chabwela 1992). Although surveys in the major stronghold of the Kafue Flats, Zambia, have suggested no population change in the period 1982–1987 (Howard 1989), the populations in the Zambian wetlands are reportedly under pressure from pastoral farmers and hunters (W. R. Tarboton *in litt.* 1994). **VULNERABLE: A2b,c; C1.**

Whooping Crane *Grus americana*, a victim of overhunting, habitat conversion and general human disturbance during the nineteenth century, possesses a single self-sustaining wild population of 140 birds that breeds in the wet prairies of Wood Buffalo National Park, Mackenzie and Alberta, **Canada**, and winters at and near Aransas Wildlife Refuge, Texas, **U.S.A.**, where there are risks from oil and chemical pollution (Collar *et al.* 1992). There are another 140 individuals existing in the U.S.A., divided up between an artificially created and, to date, non-reproductive population cross-fostered by Sandhill Cranes *G. canadensis* in Idaho (six birds), wintering south to New Mexico, a flock in Florida (numbering 15), and three captive flocks in Maryland (58 birds, at Patuxent), Texas (four, at San Antonio) and Alberta, Canada (18, at Calgary) (G. Archibald *in litt.* 1994). **ENDANGERED: D1**.

Black-necked Crane *Grus nigricollis* breeds in peat-bogs, sedge marshes, lakes and marshy grasslands on the Qinghai-Tibetan plateau at approximately 3,400–4,300 m, in Qinghai, Sichuan, Gansu, Xinjiang and Tibet, **China**, and Ladakh, **India** (in small numbers: Narayan *et al.* 1986), and winters in similar habitats at about 1,950–3,900 m, in Tibet, Yunnan and Guizhou (China), **Bhutan** and Arunachal Pradesh, north-east India (Gole 1993), and at least formerly in northern **Myanmar** and northern **Vietnam** (wandering to Nepal: Inskipp and Inskipp 1991); knowledge of its breeding and wintering ranges has improved dramatically during the past five years, and annual winter counts have increased rapidly as new sites are discovered, and in winter 1991/1992 a total of 5,554 were found (King 1978–1979, Meyer de Schauensee 1984, Bishop 1993, Scott 1993, Wu *et al.* 1993). Surveys in 1991 found that an important breeding area on the Hongyuan-Ruoergai plateau in Sichuan is threatened by the drainage of peat-bogs and sedge marshes for pastureland (Scott 1993), and the bird's tendency to winter in traditional areas makes it vulnerable to habitat changes and human disturbance (Bishop 1993); for example, Cao Hai, Guizhou (where c.215 winter), is seriously threat-

ened by uncontrolled building and conversion to farmland (*Oriental Bird Club Bull.* 1992, 16: 13). **VULNERABLE: C1**.

Red-crowned Crane *Grus japonensis* has a resident population in Hokkaido, **Japan**, and a migratory population which breeds in extensive wetlands with reedbeds and grassland in north-east **China**, eastern **Russia** and **Mongolia** and winters in wetlands and agricultural land in eastern China, **North Korea** and **South Korea** (with vagrants recorded from Taiwan) (King 1978–1979, Inskipp and Collins 1993). In Japan, it probably once bred on all four main islands, but declined as a result of hunting and habitat destruction, until by the 1890s it was confined to Hokkaido, where the population was only 20 individuals in the 1920s, but has increased as a result of protection and artificial feeding to c.600 (Rose and Scott 1994), although some breeding habitat continues to be lost (Brazil 1991). The continental population is estimated to total 1,050–1,200 birds (Rose and Scott 1994), with known breeding populations of 620 (located by aerial surveys) in China (Collar and Andrew 1988; see Ma and Jin 1987) and 150–200, including 30–45 breeding pairs, in Russia (Potapov and Flint 1987), and important wintering areas in Jiangsu, China (845 in 1994: T. Mundkur *in litt.* 1994), North Korea (290 in 1982: Collar and Andrew 1988) and the Cholwon Basin, South Korea (275 in 1993: P. O. Won *in litt.* 1994), with up to 630 (in 1989) recorded on autumn passage at Beidaihe in eastern China (Williams *et al.* 1992). The main threats to the continental population are believed to be habitat loss, pesticides and fire (Archibald and Meine in prep.). **VULNERABLE: C1; C2a**.

Family RALLIDAE

RAILS, CRAKES, COOTS

White-winged Flufftail *Sarothrura ayresi*, a tiny, enigmatic rail, probably nomadic in pursuit of suitable marshland conditions (wet areas but without standing water, which drainage is likely to have greatly diminished), occurs in **South Africa**, where records are from 1877 to 1901 and from 1955 down to the present (of non-breeders in summer in four areas, Dullstroom and Wakkerstroom in Transvaal, and Franklin and Penny Park in Natal, with breeding

elsewhere inside the country considered possible), **Ethiopia**, where records are from 1905 to 1957, and **Zambia** (two unconfirmed records) and **Zimbabwe** (three records); in South Africa the wetlands it favours are under severe threat from drainage, fire, over-grazing and damming (Collar and Stuart 1985; also Hopkinson and Masterson 1984, Clancey 1985, Urban *et al.* 1986, Taylor 1994, W. R. Tarboton *in litt.* 1994). A single bird in flight was seen at Sululta, an established site for the species in Ethiopia, in August 1984 (Massoli-Novelli 1988), but calls thought to be this species heard from a marsh inside Nyungwe forest, Rwanda, during December 1989 to February 1990 (Dowsett-Lemaire 1990) remain open to question (Taylor 1994). **ENDANGERED: B1+2a,b,c+ 3a,b,c**; C2a.

Slender-billed Flufftail *Sarothrura watersi*, a tiny marsh-dwelling rail, has been reliably recorded from only four well-separated areas in eastern **Madagascar** (Wilmé and Langrand 1990). If 1970–1971 records from the Antananarivo district are discounted as erroneous, the remaining sites ('south-east Betsileo' in 1875, Analamazaotra in 1928, Andapa in 1930 and Ranomafana, now a national park, since 1987) suggest a distribution coincident with that of the much-pressurized eastern rainforest, the particular micro-habitat—presumably itself increasingly rare—being elevated wetlands (at 950–1,800 m) with adjacent dense grassy terrain near rainforest (Collar and Stuart 1985, Langrand 1990). **ENDANGERED: B1+2c; C2b**; D1.

Swinhoe's Rail *Coturnicops exquisitus* breeds in wet meadows and short grass marshes in Transbaykalia and the extreme south-east of **Russia** and north-east **China**, occurring on passage and in winter in **North Korea**, **South Korea**, **Japan** (including the Nansei Shoto) and southern and eastern China (Sonobe 1982, Flint *et al.* 1984, Cheng 1987). It is known from only a handful of breeding localities, recently recorded at Zhalong Nature Reserve, Heilongjiang, China (Scott 1989) and Khanka Lake, Russia (J. Y. Park verbally 1992), and is seldom recorded on passage or in winter, recent records being of small numbers on autumn passage at Beidaihe, eastern China (Williams *et al.* 1992), and one at Poyang Lake, southern China in 1989 (*Oriental Bird Club Bull.* 1990, 11: 40–48). It is presumably threatened by the destruction and modification of wetlands, which are taking place in both its breeding and wintering ranges (M.J.C.). **VULNERABLE: C1; C2a.**

Andaman Crake *Rallina canningi* is endemic to the Andaman Islands, **India**, where the details of its range are not clear, but it has been recorded from at least North Andaman and South Andaman Islands (and could possibly occur on Great Coco or Little Coco Islands, Myanmar), formerly being described as common in marshland in forest (Ali and Ripley 1987). There only appear to be two recent records of single birds, one of which was seen in a large, open area of marshland, and the other in a small marsh on the edge of secondary forest (I. Gardner *in litt.* 1994, N. J. Redman *in litt.* 1994). Although forest cover

remains extensive on the Andamans, it is suffering slow but continuing loss (Pande *et al.* 1991), and introduced predators may also be a threat (J. C. Eames *in litt.* 1993). **VULNERABLE: C1.**

Rusty-flanked Crake *Laterallus levraudi* is confined to wetlands (lakesides, lagoons, swamps, flooded pastures, grassland) in the lowlands and the lower Caribbean slope (up to 600 m) of north-west **Venezuela** (Lara, Yaracuy, Carabobo, Falcón, Aragua, Distrito Federal, Miranda), where recent (post-1946) records are confined to three areas, two of them man-made, in Yacambú National Park (Lara), Morrocoy National Park (Falcón) and Embalse de Taguaiguai (Aragua). A continuing decline is likely, given the general degradation of wetlands caused by industrial waste, pesticides and the lowering of water-levels within the species' range (Collar *et al.* 1992; Falcón record from Lentino and Goodwin 1991 and apparently made by C. Parrish: A. Luy *in litt.* 1994). **VULNERABLE: A1b; A2b; B1+2c; C1; C2a.**

Junín Rail *Laterallus tuerosi* is a secretive waterbird inhabiting the rushy vegetation of the wide marsh habitats fringing Lago de Junín, Junín department, at 4,080 m in the Andean highlands of central **Peru**, where it may be fairly common (there are 150 km^2 of marshland around the lake, although to date the bird has been found at only two sites on the south-west shore), but is at risk from pollution and water-level changes which have been afflicting the lake since at least 1955 (Collar *et al.* 1992). **ENDANGERED: B1+2c; C2b;** D2.

Rufous-faced Crake *Laterallus xenopterus* is a highly secretive waterbird known from two areas of **Paraguay** (Concepción in 1933 and Canindeyú in 1976–1979) and one, over 1,200 km to the northeast, in central **Brazil** (IBGE Ecological Reserve and adjacent Brasília National Park, where judged 'relatively frequent', with a record from Brasília Zoo, all in Distrito Federal); records have been from stands of coarse grass or bunch-grass in shallow water or moist places, and it is possible that the wholesale loss of Brazil's wet campo habitats through drainage and plantation may have serious affects on populations yet to be discovered (Collar *et al.* 1992). **VULNERABLE: A1b; A2b.**

Woodford's Rail *Nesoclopeus woodfordi* is known from Bougainville Island, **Papua New Guinea**, Santa Isabel and Guadalcanal, and possibly Choiseul, **Solomon Islands** (and see also below): it was last collected in 1936, occurred in lowland forest (at least formerly) occasionally to 1,000 m (Collar and Andrew 1988) and is likely to have been a victim of introduced predators, as cats have wiped out most terrestrial mammals on Guadalcanal (T. Flannery *per* K. D. Bishop *in litt.* 1994). One observation in south Bougainville (lowland swamp forest, now logged) in 1985 suggested that it is probably flightless (Kaestner 1987), while three observations on Santa Isabel in 1987 and 1988 indicated that the species prefers riparian habitats, including abandoned gardens, at altitudes of up to 300 m, occasionally forming a part of the local diet when caught by dogs or in traps set for the Pacific Black Duck *Anas superciliosa* (Webb 1992, H. P. Webb *in litt.* 1993). It has also been reported from New Georgia (Sibley 1951, Blaber 1990), Kolombangara (Finch 1985)—but these may refer to Roviana Rail *Gallirallus rovianae* (D. Gibbs *in litt.* 1994; see Diamond 1991)—and Malaita (R. H. Loyn and D. M. Tully *per* P. Scofield *in litt.* 1994). **ENDANGERED: C2a**.

New Caledonian Rail *Gallirallus lafresnayanus*, known from **New Caledonia (to France)**, was treated as extinct by King (1978–1979), not having been recorded by ornithologists this century (last collected in 1890), but local reports suggest that it survives in small numbers, probably restricted to humid forest where it is likely to be threatened by introduced species such as cats, rats, deer, dogs and especially pigs (Stokes 1979). There was an unsubstantiated sighting in the north of the island in 1984 (Hannecart 1988). **CRITICAL: C2a; D1**.

Lord Howe Rail *Gallirallus sylvestris* is endemic to Lord Howe Island (**Australia**) where it was formerly an abundant bird and distributed throughout, but is now restricted to the remnant forest on the summits of Mount Lidgbird and Mount Gower and to some palm forest sites in the lowlands (where it has been reintroduced recently) with a total population estimated at 170–200 individuals; the original cause of its disappearance from the lowlands was predation by pigs, dogs, cats and people, together with disturbance to the habitat from pigs and goats, but the major threat today is from the introduced Masked Owl *Tyto novaehollandiae* (Garnett 1992). **ENDANGERED: D1; D2**.

Okinawa Rail *Gallirallus okinawae* is a flightless species, endemic to the island of Okinawa in the Nansei Shoto, southern **Japan**, where it is found near water in broadleaf evergreen forest from sea-level to the highest hilltops in the mountainous northern quarter of the island (called Yambaru), having been discovered as recently as 1978 (Yamashina and Mano 1981), and its population is estimated at approximately 1,800 birds (Yanagisawa *et al.* 1993 in Rose and Scott 1994). It is threatened by continuing

deforestation within its tiny range (Yamashina and Mano 1981, Miyagi 1989, *World Birdwatch* 1989, 11,2: 4). **ENDANGERED: B1+2c; C1; C2b; D1; D2**.

Guam Rail *Gallirallus owstoni* is flightless and endemic to **Guam (to U.S.A.)**, where it was widely distributed in forest, scrub and agricultural areas until 1968 when, along with most other indigenous species, it entered a decade or so of decline owing to the spread through the island of the accidentally introduced brown tree snake *Boiga irregularis* (Witteman *et al.* 1990). In 1981 the population was put at c.2,000, in 1983 it was reckoned to number fewer than 100, and by 1987 it was extirpated from the wild, and currently only survives in captive breeding facilities in Guam and in 16 zoos in the U.S.A. (c.180 birds in total), efforts being under way to establish a self-sustaining, experimental population on the nearby snake-free island of Rota in the Northern Mariana Islands (to U.S.A.) (Engbring and Pratt 1985, Witteman *et al.* 1990, Haig *et al.* 1993). **EXTINCT IN THE WILD**.

Plain-flanked Rail *Rallus wetmorei* is now an extremely rare and poorly known waterbird, restricted to brackish lagoons along a small stretch of the northern coast of **Venezuela** (Falcón, Carabobo, Aragua), with very few recent records (three since 1951); it is severely threatened by loss and deterioration of its wetland habitat to house and road construction (the leisure industry being important in the region) and associated pollution (Collar *et al.* 1992). **ENDANGERED: A1b; A2b; B1+2c; C1; C2a; D1**.

Bogotá Rail *Rallus semiplumbeus* is restricted to the savanna and páramo marshes (typically with dense tall fringing reeds and vegetation-rich shallows) of the temperate zone (2,100–4,000 m) of Cundinamarca and Boyacá departments in the East Andes of **Colombia**, retaining healthy populations in just a few remaining areas (notably Laguna de Tota, with perhaps 400 birds, Laguna de la Herrera, with an estimated 50 territories, and Parque La Florida, with 54 pairs), all of which are threatened by drainage, habitat loss, encroachment and the effects of agrochemicals (Collar *et al.* 1992, Lozano 1993, M. G. Kelsey verbally 1994). **ENDANGERED: A2b; B1+2c; C1; C2a; D1**.

Austral Rail *Rallus antarcticus*, known from up to 19 marshland localities (wet fields, rushy lake shores and reedbeds, mostly adjacent to coasts) in **Argentina** (Entre Ríos possibly, Buenos Aires, Río Negro, Chubut, Santa Cruz, Tierra del Fuego) and **Chile** (Valparaiso, Santiago, Colchagua, Llanquihué, Magallanes) south of 33°S, has disappeared in the course of the last hundred years (no certain records since 1959), for reasons that remain unclear, although the overgrazing and conversion of practically all tall-grass habitat in Patagonia has been suggested (Collar *et al*. 1992). It is, however, reported as occasionally seen near El Bolsón (Río Negro, Argentina), and it may yet be that when its voice has been determined it will be found with some regularity (R. S. Ridgely *in litt*. 1994). **CRITICAL: D1**.

Brown-banded Rail *Lewinia mirificus* is an enigmatic species known only from Luzon in the **Philippines**, where 191 birds were trapped at Dalton Pass in 1965–1970, apparently while undertaking intra-island migration; however, the fact that it has only been recorded at five other localities (all in foothills), most recently in 1979, suggests that it is (increasingly) rare, and very possibly (since its habitat remains unknown) with strict ecological requirements (Dickinson *et al*. 1991, Danielsen *et al*. 1994, Poulsen in press). **ENDANGERED: C2b**.

Auckland Islands Rail *Lewinia muelleri*, once thought to be extinct, persists on Adams Island (100 km^2) and Disappointment Island (4 km^2) (both part of the Auckland Islands Nature Reserve), **New Zealand**, and is only safe if introduced mammals, especially pigs and cats (present on Auckland Island) and rats, fail to reach these islands (B. D. Bell verbally 1994). Suitable habitat (coastal and cliff herbfields, *Carex* grassland, tussock-herbfields, scrubby forest) probably occupies as much as 10% of Adams Island, which is likely to hold several hundred individuals (Elliott *et al*. 1991) whilst Disappointment Island is estimated to have more than 500 (K. Walker *per* A. J. Tennyson *in litt*. 1994). **VULNERABLE: D2**.

Corncrake *Crex crex* breeds in open, wet or dry long-grass areas, including alpine meadows, marsh fringes and unimproved fields, in **Spain**, **France**, **United Kingdom**, **Ireland**, **Belgium**, **Netherlands**, **Luxembourg**, **Switzerland**, **Liechtenstein**, **Italy**, **Austria**, **Croatia**, **Bosnia-Herzegovina**, former **Yugoslavia** (Serbia, Montenegro), **Macedonia**, **Bulgaria**, **Romania**, **Hungary**, **Slovakia**, **Czech Republic**, **Germany**, **Denmark**, **Norway**, **Sweden**, **Finland**, **Estonia**, **Latvia**, **Lithuania**, **Poland**, **Belarus**, **Ukraine**, **Moldova**, **Russia**, **Georgia**, **Turkey**, **Iran**, **Afghanistan**, **Tajikistan**, **Kyrgyzstan**, **Kazakhstan** and **China**, with passage birds in many of these countries plus **Uzbekistan**, **Turkmenistan**, **Armenia**, **Azerbaijan**, **Syria**, **Iraq**, **Saudi Arabia**, **Yemen**, **Israel**, **Egypt**, **Sudan**, **Ethiopia**, **Tunisia**, **Algeria**, **Mauritania**, **Morocco** and **Portugal** en route to or from sub-Saharan African wintering

grounds in dry grasslands from sea-level to 3,000 m in (or beyond) **Kenya**, **Tanzania**, **Uganda**, **Zaïre**, **Congo**, **Zambia**, **Malawi**, **Mozambique**, **Zimbabwe** and **South Africa** (records of vagrancy from up to 15 countries) (Stowe and Becker 1992, Dowsett and Forbes-Watson 1993, Inskipp and Collins 1993). Despite still being common and widespread in parts of its range, there is clear evidence of a long-term and very steep overall decline in the order of 50% over 20 years (detected in Europe, Russia and Africa) owing to drainage of sites, agricultural intensification and changes in grassland management on the breeding grounds, compounded by the trapping of birds on migration in Egypt, where an estimated 4,600 were caught during autumn of 1991 (Ginn *et al*. 1989, Grimmett and Jones 1989, Schneider-Jacoby 1991, Stowe and Becker 1992, Baha El Din 1993, Stowe *et al*. 1993, Broyer 1994, Tucker and Heath 1994, Heredia in prep.). **VULNERABLE: A1a,b**.

Snoring Rail *Aramidopsis plateni* is a flightless endemic of Sulawesi, **Indonesia**, where it is known from 11 specimens collected in dense liana and bamboo secondary growth on the edge of lowland and montane forest (White and Bruce 1986), and from sightings in Lore Lindu National Park in 1983, in lightly disturbed hill forest bordering dense secondary growth (Andrew and Holmes 1990), in 1987 in (probably old secondary) forest with a dense understorey dominated by rattans (Lambert 1989) and in 1992 in hill or lower montane forest (K. D. Bishop *in litt*. 1994). Its elusive habits account to some extent for the paucity of records, but it appears to be genuinely rare and may be vulnerable to deforestation, which is already quite widespread in parts of Sulawesi (see RePPProT 1990), and introduced or feral predators. **VULNERABLE: C1; C2a**.

Inaccessible Rail *Atlantisia rogersi*, the smallest flightless bird in the world, is confined to Inaccessible Island (13 km^2) in the **Tristan da Cunha group (to U.K.)**, South Atlantic Ocean: an estimated 8,400 birds live at high density (probably at carrying capacity) amidst the dense grassy vegetation of the island, but there is a permanent risk that the island will be colonized by mammalian predators, particularly rats (Collar and Stuart 1985, Fraser 1989, Fraser *et al*. 1992). **VULNERABLE: D2**.

Brown Wood-rail *Aramides wolfi* occupies a narrow range in south-west **Colombia**, western **Ecuador** and north-west **Peru**, and it appears to have become extremely rare at least in Ecuador, owing to extensive destruction of mangroves (though it also occurs in riverine marsh and forest up to 900 m), and has been unreported for years from the other countries, such that any record (e.g. in February 1994 in Ecuador: Clay *et al.* 1994) represents welcome evidence of its global survival (R. S. Ridgely *in litt.* 1994; see also Graves 1982, Hilty and Brown 1986). **VULNERABLE:** A1b.

Bald-faced Rail *Gymnocrex rosenbergii* is known from north and central Sulawesi and by three specimens from Peleng, **Indonesia**, where it appears to be a rare bird of primary forest (White and Bruce 1986), but is almost certainly greatly under-recorded (K. D. Bishop *in litt.* 1994). There are recent records from (probably old secondary) forest in Lore Lindu National Park (Lambert 1989) and primary forest in Dumoga-Bone National Park (Rozendaal and Dekker 1989). It is presumably vulnerable to forest destruction and degradation, which is already quite widespread in parts of Sulawesi (see RePPProT 1990). **VULNERABLE:** C1; C2a.

Sakalava Rail *Amaurornis olivieri* is a marsh-dwelling rail known from just three widely separated areas in the Sakalava country of lowland western **Madagascar**, and is rare and localized, with extremely few records (Collar and Stuart 1985). It has possibly suffered, like the threatened Madagascar Little Grebe *Tachybaptus pelzelni*, from loss of lilypad habitat owing to rice cultivation and the impact of introduced fish, but searches since the mid-1980s even where such habitat survives have proved fruitless (O. Langrand *in litt.* 1987, A. F. A. Hawkins *in litt.* 1994, R. J. Safford *in litt.* 1994). **CRITICAL:** B1+2c; **C2a**; D1.

Dot-winged Crake *Porzana spiloptera* has been recorded from various types of wetland (temporary and tidal marshes, swamps, wet meadows, grassland, riparian scrub) in southern **Uruguay** and northern **Argentina** (La Rioja, San Juan, San Luis, Córdoba, Santa Fe, Buenos Aires), with most records having come from Buenos Aires province in Argentina; the reclamation and burning of marsh areas, and particularly the intrusion and overgrazing of cattle, may lie behind an apparent continuing decline in at least some places, the species generally being judged rare (Collar *et al.* 1992). **VULNERABLE:** A2b; C1; C2a.

Henderson Crake *Porzana atra* is endemic to Henderson Island in the **Pitcairn Islands (to U.K.)**, a small (37 km²) uninhabited raised-reef island in the south-central Pacific Ocean whose vulnerability to human impact was exposed in 1982–1983 when a millionaire sought to make it his home (Bourne and David 1983, Fosberg *et al.* 1983, Serpell *et al.* 1983). It is flightless, omnivorous and occurs in the plateau

forest and surrounding scrub, with numbers put at c.3,240 birds in 1987 (Graves 1992) and, using a different technique, at c.6,000 in 1992—the latter figure likely to be the carrying capacity for the island as most territories have more than two adults (these helpers provide extra parental care such as defending eggs and chicks from crabs and rats) (Schubel *et al.* in press). Based on a small sample, annual adult survival was at least 57%, reproductive success was high (2.45 chicks surviving six months or so per pair per year); recruitment to the population is not known, but it probably compensates easily for annual losses, such that the population is stable (Schubel *et al.* in press). **VULNERABLE:** D2.

Zapata Rail *Cyanolimnas cerverai* is an apparently flightless marsh-dwelling waterbird known from only two sites roughly 65 km apart within the Zapata Swamp, **Cuba**; despite its likely occurrence throughout or in many areas of the swamp, the very small number of records over recent decades is probably attributable to the impact of dry-season burning of habitat and perhaps also, very importantly, of introduced predators (Collar *et al.* 1992). **CRITICAL:** B1+2c; **C2b**; D1.

Invisible Rail *Habroptila wallacii* is a flightless endemic of Halmahera, **Indonesia**, where it is found in dense, impenetrable, swampy thickets, particularly areas of heavy sago swamp (White and Bruce 1986). A report by de Haan (1950) that it is locally common in 'alang-alang' *Imperata cylindrica* grassland is believed to have resulted from confusion with the Common Bush-hen *Amaurornis olivacea* (K. D. Bishop *in litt.* 1994). Invisible Rail is probably a scarce bird, as the only recent records appear to be of specimens collected in the early 1980s (White and Bruce 1986) and in the early 1990s (P. M. Taylor *per* F. R. Lambert verbally 1993), and sago swamps on Halmahera have been extensively destroyed (K. D. Bishop *in litt.* 1994). It is also likely to be vulnerable to the attentions of introduced or feral predators, which have caused the extinction of several other flightless, single-island, endemic rails (see Johnson and Stattersfield 1990). **VULNERABLE:** C1.

Takahe *Porphyrio mantelli* is flightless and in 1948 when 'rediscovered' was confined to the alpine tussock grasslands of the Murchison Mountains of South Island, **New Zealand**, having declined owing to competition from deer for food and predation by introduced mammals (King 1978–1979, Williams and Given 1981, Lavers and Mills 1984), compounded by the spread of forest in the post-glacial Holocene (Mills *et al.* 1984). It is more likely, however, that the species was once widespread in both forest and grass ecosystems, and that its modern restricted distribution is in suboptimal habitat because of the low hunting pressure there (Clout and Craig in press). Deer management has resulted in a recovery of vegetation and, with the trapping of stoats, egg manipulation, captive breeding and releases, the population in Fiordland (Murchison and Stuart mountains) numbered 150+ individuals in 1994, though trends were uncertain because of fluctuations in the main Murchison population; there are additional translocated or introduced populations on four island sanctuaries—Kapiti, Mana, Tiritiri Matangi and Maud (c.40 birds in total and plans to boost these and/or other island populations further) (A. J. Tennyson *in litt.* 1994, Clout and Craig in press). **ENDANGERED: D1**; D2.

Samoan Moorhen *Gallinula pacifica* from Savaii, **Western Samoa**, was last recorded in 1873 (and consequently is often listed as extinct); cats and rats have no doubt contributed to its disappearance as it is almost flightless (Ripley 1977; see also Mees 1977). In 1987 there were two possible sightings in upland forest west of Mount Elietoga (Bellingham and Davis 1988) and it may yet survive (B. D. Bell *in litt.* 1993). **CRITICAL: D1**.

San Cristobal Moorhen *Gallinula silvestris* is known from the type-specimen, collected in 1929 at 600 m by a local hunter in the central ranges of Makira (= San Cristobal), **Solomon Islands**, where it is reportedly hunted with dogs and flies little, if at all (Ripley 1977). It inhabits dense forest on precipitous terrain but, despite repeated attempts to secure further specimens, the only subsequent observation is of one in 1953 (King 1978–1979). It was reported by local people in 1974 (J. M. Diamond *in litt.* 1987) but does not appear to have been seen for many years (Lees 1991), although the forests where it was originally found have not been visited by ornithologists since the 1950s (Buckingham *et al.* in prep.). It is likely to have been affected by introduced mammalian predators, e.g. cats, which have wiped out most native terrestrial mammals on Guadalcanal (T. Flannery *per* K. D. Bishop *in litt.* 1994). **CRITICAL: C2b**; D1.

Gough Moorhen *Gallinula nesiotis*, a flightless relative of the Common Moorhen *G. chloropus*, survives in the race *comeri* in the dense grassy vegetation of Gough Island, having also been introduced in 1956 to Tristan da Cunha (from which nominate *nesiotis* was extirpated probably by 1900), **Tristan da Cunha group (to U.K.)**, South Atlantic Ocean (Collar and Stuart 1985). There may be up to 3,000 pairs on Gough and around 250 pairs on Tristan, but there is a permanent risk of mammalian predators becoming established on the islands (Watkins and Furness 1986), although the chances of this happening have been minimized (Cooper and Ryan 1994). There is captive stock in the zoos of Amsterdam, Stuttgart, Basel (P. Bennett *in litt.* 1988 and Paignton (N.J.C.). **VULNERABLE: D2**.

Hawaiian Coot *Fulica alai* is endemic to the Hawaiian Islands (**U.S.A.**), where it is found throughout except Lanai, with stragglers reaching as far west as Kure in the Northwestern Hawaiian Islands. It inhabits fresh and saltwater ponds, estuaries and marshes (it can be expected on virtually any body of water, but these are scattered and very limited in area) and has suffered from wetland destruction as well as being vulnerable when nesting to such introduced predators as dogs, cats and especially mongooses (Pratt *et al.* 1987, Pratt 1993, H. D. Pratt *in litt.* 1994). The current population probably fluctuates between 2,000 and 4,000 birds, with Kauai, Oahu and Maui supporting 80% of these birds (Engilis and Pratt 1993). **VULNERABLE: D2**.

Horned Coot *Fulica cornuta* lives at low densities in high Andean lakes (3,000–5,200 m), both fresh and brackish, in **Bolivia** (Oruro in 1903, Potosí), **Chile** (Tarapacá, Antofagasta, Atacama) and **Argentina** (Jujuy, Salta, Catamarca in 1918, Tucumán), with numbers not known to exceed 5,000. The lakes, although very remote, remain vulnerable to contamination and trampling by cattle and some are used to pipe water to lower levels, so the species seems very likely to be in decline (Collar *et al.* 1992). **VULNERABLE: C2a**.

Family HELIORNITHIDAE

FINFOOTS, SUN-GREBES

Masked Finfoot *Heliopais personata* is found on streams, slow-flowing rivers, creeks, ponds and lake edges in lowland forest and mangroves in **Bangladesh**, eastern Assam and probably north-east Manipur, north-east **India**, **Myanmar**, **Laos**, **Cambodia**, central and southern **Vietnam**, **Thailand**, peninsular **Malaysia** and Sumatra and Java, **Indonesia** (King *et al.* 1975, Ali and Ripley 1987, Boonsong and Round 1991, Andrew 1992, MacKinnon and Phillipps 1993; see Robson *et al.* 1989, Duckworth *et al.* 1993a). In the southern part of this range it is believed to be mainly a non-breeding visitor, but it almost certainly nests in peninsular Thailand (*Oriental Bird Club Bull.* 1992, 16: 50–52; 1993, 18: 13–14) and perhaps Malaysia (D. R. Wells *in litt.* 1994). It is local and generally uncommon (although perhaps often overlooked: T. Mundkur *in litt.* 1994) with a world population estimated to be below 10,000 (Rose and Scott 1994), and is threatened by the destruction of lowland forest and mangroves throughout its range (J. C. Eames *in litt.* 1994; see Collins *et al.* 1991), increased traffic and development along river courses (BirdLife IP) and perhaps the fouling of forest waterways from logging (D. R. Wells *in litt.* 1994). **VULNERABLE:** C1; C2a.

Family RHYNOCHETIDAE

KAGU

Kagu *Rhynochetos jubatus* is endemic to **New Caledonia (to France)** where it is found in a variety of habitats, from closed-canopy scrub to wet forest, and at 100 to 1,400 m, with the greatest concentrations in isolated areas free from forestry activities (e.g. around Mounts Do and Nakada: 135 birds) (King 1978–1979, Hunt 1992). A survey of calling birds in 1991–1992 (excluding the Rivière Bleue Territorial Park) found 491 adults, of which 403 were in the Southern and 88 were in the Northern Province, with most regions known to have held Kagus in the past still doing so, but with over half the subpopulations being small (1–4 birds) (Hunt 1992). The population in the Rivière Bleue Territorial Park was estimated at 200 in 1992 and growing (M. Boulet, F. Hannecart, Y. Létocart and S. Sirgouant *in litt.* 1993). Birds are caught by dogs and other introduced predators, and pigs probably take eggs or compete for food (Hay 1986), but dogs have been branded the chief threat (Bregulla 1987, Hannecart 1988) and in April–May 1993 there were 14 known fatal attacks in the Pic Ningua population (24 birds in total prior to the deaths) (Hunt 1993). **ENDANGERED:** A2d; B1+2c,d,e; C1; **C2a**; D1.

Family OTIDIDAE

BUSTARDS

Great Bustard *Otis tarda* is declining throughout its broad but increasingly disjunct Palearctic range as a consequence of agricultural intensification (including pesticide applications, irrigation and rotation regimes, power-lines to farms, various manifestations of mechanization) and in some places hunting on its farmland and steppe habitats, birds now remaining in the following countries (population in brackets): **Morocco** (100), **Portugal** (500–700), **Spain** (an estimated 13,500–14,000), **Austria** (15), **Germany** (150), **Czech Republic** (7–13), **Slovakia** (25–40), **Hungary** (1,000–1,200), former **Yugoslavia** (Serbia) (30–40), **Romania** (10–15), **Moldova** (2–3), **Turkey** (several hundred, though a speculated 4,000 now seems increasingly improbable), **Syria** (probably extinct), **Iraq** (few if any), **Iran** (100–200), the former Soviet Union territories of **Russia, Ukraine, Kazakhstan, Kyrgyzstan, Tajikistan, Uzbekistan** (2,980–4,000 in late 1980s, but Russia now judged to hold 10,000–11,000, with Ukraine holding 320–480), **Mongolia** (at least 1,000), **China** (probably at least 1,500); without the impending but as yet unfunded European Commission zonal programmes in Spain, which will allow traditional farming to continue in important bustard areas, the indications remain that the centuries-long decline will only accelerate, while information from Russia eastwards remains too uncertain for any confidence (Collar and Andrew 1988, Kollar 1988, Kasparek 1989, Alonso and Alonso 1990, Hidalgo and Carranza 1990, Hellmich 1991, 1992, Goriup 1992, Block *et al.* 1993, Faragó 1993, Litzbarski 1993, Tucker and Heath 1994, Heredia in prep.). **VULNERABLE:** A2b.

Great Indian Bustard *Ardeotis nigriceps* has declined in range and density since 1830, owing to habitat loss and disturbance (which still apply as threats), the early impact of hunting for food and sport, and the taking of eggs for food, so that it is now confined to grassland patches (mostly in protected areas) in the western half of **India** (King 1978–1979, Goriup 1983, Rahmani and Manakadam 1985, 1990), with the most important populations surviving in Rajasthan (500–1,000 out of an estimated total of 1,500–2,000 birds), smaller numbers in Gujarat, Madhya Pradesh, Maharashtra, Karnataka and Andhra Pradesh, and populations in other states extinct or virtually so (Rahmani 1987, 1989, Johnsgard 1991). **ENDANGERED:** C1; **C2b.**

Bengal Florican *Houbaropsis bengalensis* has suffered from chronic loss of its wet grassland (notably the relatively short *Imperata*) habitat so that it now survives almost exclusively in very small, fragmented populations (totalling as few as 300–400 birds) in protected areas on the border of **Nepal** and **India** and in north-eastern India (Inskipp and Inskipp 1983, 1985, Narayan 1990, Narayan and Rosalind 1990, Rahmani *et al.* 1990, 1991, Weaver 1990). A subspecifically distinct but virtually unknown population (*blandini*) exists in southern **Cambodia** (collected in a presumed wintering area in 1928) and adjacent north-west 'Cochinchina', southern **Vietnam**, whence there have been recent (1990–1994) records involving four or fewer birds from Dong Thap province, in very restricted and diminishing grass areas in and near Tram Chim Nature Reserve (Inskipp and Collar 1984, Johnsgard 1991, J. C. Eames *in litt.* 1994). **ENDANGERED:** C1; **C2a.**

Lesser Florican *Sypheotides indica* has been in decline since at least the 1870s, owing to the steady conversion of its primary grassland habitat coupled with the early influence of hunting and the recent effects of drought, such that it is now restricted as a breeding bird (May–October) to tiny patches of habitat in western **India** (though recorded at this time in **Nepal**), dispersing mostly south-eastwards to south-central India for the non-breeding period (November–April). Its population is judged to have plummeted by 80% from 1982 (4,374 birds) to 1989 (750), with little optimism for its long-term survival (Goriup and Karpowicz 1985, Magrath *et al.* 1985, Lachungpa and Rahmani 1990, Sankaran 1990b, Sankaran and Rahmani 1990, Sankaran *et al.* 1990, 1992, Johnsgard 1991). **CRITICAL:** A1a; C1; C2b; D1.

Family HAEMATOPODIDAE

OYSTERCATCHERS

Chatham Islands Oystercatcher *Haematopus chathamensis*, treated as a separate species by Turbott (1990) but not by Sibley and Monroe (1990, 1993) who regard it as a subspecies of Variable Oystercatcher *H. unicolor*, occurs on rocky shorelines on Chatham, Pitt, South East (= Rangatira) and Mangere islands in the Chatham Islands, **New Zealand**, where introduced predators (cats, rats and Weka *Gallirallus* *australis*) and browsing mammals are a threat to its survival with only South East and Mangere Islands being predator-free (King 1978–1979, Williams and Given 1981), whilst Brown Skua *Catharacta lonnbergi* (present in high numbers) may also be a contributory factor (B. D. Bell *in litt.* 1994). On the main island some pairs nest on sandy beaches but are pushed down by (introduced) marram grass to the tideline, where nests are more vulnerable to very high tides and storms, but nest manipulation (i.e. moving them back up the beach, started in 1992) and artificial incubation of eggs (which are returned when due to hatch and which therefore reduces egg predation) may increase breeding success (B. D. Bell *in litt.* 1994, S. Sawyer *per* G. A. Taylor *in litt.* 1994). The current population is c.100 individuals (A. Davis *per* G. A. Taylor *in litt.* 1994). **ENDANGERED: D1**; D2.

Family CHARADRIIDAE

PLOVERS

New Zealand Dotterel *Charadrius obscurus* breeds on exposed mountain tops at 500–900 m on Stewart Island (c.60 birds and declining: Dowding and Murphy 1993), among sand-dunes in the northern part of North Island (c.1,350 birds) and formerly on mountain slopes, foothills and plains of eastern South Island, **New Zealand**. Introduced predators are a threat (cats and rats on Stewart Island; cats, rats, stoats, possums and hedgehogs on North Island) as well as disturbance by people (and their dogs) especially on the breeding beaches of North Island, whilst Kelp Gull *Larus dominicanus*, Silver Gull *L. novaehollandiae* and Swamp Harrier *Circus approximans* are all native predators (Dowding 1993). **ENDANGERED: C2a**.

Madagascar Plover *Charadrius thoracicus* occurs on sandy beaches, mudflats, saltflats and coastal grassy areas from Soalala south to Lake Tsimanampetsotsa in western **Madagascar**. It is generally rare, and greatly outnumbered (and perhaps outcompeted) by Kittlitz's Plover *C. pecuarius* and/or White-fronted Plover *C. marginatus*, although it is found in three protected areas (Collar and Stuart 1985, Nicoll and Langrand 1989, Langrand 1990, A. F. A. Hawkins *in litt.* 1994). **VULNERABLE: B1+2e; C2b**.

St Helena Plover *Charadrius sanctaehelenae* occurs only in the northern, flatter parts of the interior of **St Helena (to U.K.)**, southern Atlantic Ocean, where in the mid-1980s several hundred pairs were considered to survive (Collar and Stuart 1985). Intensive study, 1988–1989, showed that some 450 birds were then present, at highest densities in relatively dry, flat pastures, and that, apart from possible (but undocumented) predation by or competition from certain introduced species, the only threat would appear to lie in potential land-use changes (McCulloch 1991, 1992). Censuses in 1991, 1992 and 1993 have suggested a steady decline from c.375 (1991) to c.315 (1993), with numbers on Deadwood Plain, a key area, halved since the late 1980s (Chief Agriculture and Forestry Officer for St Helena *in litt.* 1993). **ENDANGERED: C1; C2b; D1; D2**.

Piping Plover *Charadrius melodus* inhabits open beaches, alkali flats and sandflats, breeding primarily along the Atlantic coast from North Carolina, **U.S.A.**, to southern **Canada**, along rivers and wetlands of the northern Great Plains from Nebraska to the southern prairie provinces and the Great Lakes, wintering on coasts from the Carolinas to Quintana Roo and the Pacific Coast, **Mexico**, with some birds scattering to the **Bahamas, Barbados, Bermuda (to U.K.), Cuba, Jamaica, Puerto Rico (to U.S.A.), Virgin Islands (to U.K.)** and **Virgin Islands (to U.S.A.)** (Collar *et al.* 1992). Fewer than 2,500 pairs were recorded throughout the breeding range in 1991, and numbers are declining in reaction to drought and inappropriate water management, disturbance on beaches and increased predation in some areas (Haig 1992, Howell 1993). **VULNERABLE: C2a**.

Mountain Plover *Charadrius montanus* nests (or until recently nested) in the shortgrass prairie (disturbed prairie or semi-desert) mainly east of the Rocky Mountains in Montana, Wyoming, Colorado, extreme north-east New Mexico, extreme western Oklahoma and extreme northern Texas, **U.S.A** (and formerly Canada), wintering in flocks in semi-desert or dry agricultural country in California, Texas and northern **Mexico**, where, having once (pre-1900) been an abundant and important gamebird, numbers had fallen to 200,000–300,000 individuals by c.1970; there was a 63% decline in these numbers between 1966 and 1991 related to loss and disturbance of its habitat (Graul and Webster 1976, Hayman *et al.* 1986, Knopf and Miller 1994). **VULNERABLE: A1b.**

Hooded Plover *Charadrius rubricollis*, whose population is thought to be at least 5,000 individuals, has a contracting range on the coast and around salt-lakes in southern Western Australia, **Australia**, and on coastal beaches and dune systems in Victoria, South Australia, New South Wales and Tasmania (Garnett 1992). The small population in Western Australia is probably secure but the species is easily disturbed, and in eastern Australia the increasing human use of beaches has probably contributed to its decline, as well as, in some areas, predation by foxes and Silver Gull *Larus novaehollandiae* and the trampling of nests by stock (Garnett 1992). **VULNERABLE: C2a.**

Shore Plover *Thinornis novaeseelandiae* is now confined to rock wave-platforms and salt meadows on South East Island (= Rangatira, c.2 km^2) in the Chatham Islands, **New Zealand**; reintroduction to Mangere Island was unsuccessful owing to the birds' strong homing instinct (King 1978–1979). The population was estimated at c.130 birds in the autumn of 1993 (106 adults), and, as it is generally assumed that cats, mustelids and rats *Rattus norvegicus* were responsible for its decline elsewhere in the Chathams, the accidental or deliberate introduction of cats, rats or even Weka *Gallirallus australis* could easily result in its rapid extinction (Dowding and Kennedy 1993). **ENDANGERED: D1; D2.**

Wrybill *Anarhynchus frontalis* breeds on the river-beds of Canterbury and Otago (26 riverbeds in total but only numerous on ten), South Island, and winters mainly north of 38°S, North Island, **New Zealand**; it

numbers just over 5,000 birds and is suffering from habitat deterioration (the encroachment of weeds) as hydroelectric schemes reduce the seasonal flushing of riverbeds, and from predation by stoats and cats (O'Donnell and Moore 1983, Robertson *et al.* 1983, Turbott 1990, B. D. Bell verbally 1993 and *in litt.* 1994). **VULNERABLE: C2a.**

Sociable Lapwing *Vanellus gregarius* breeds semi-colonially, chiefly in transition zones between *Stipa* and *Artemisia* steppes, in **Russia** and **Kazakh-stan** (apparently also once in Ukraine), dispersing through **Kyrgyzstan**, **Tajikistan**, **Uzbekistan**, **Turkmenistan**, **Iran**, **Turkey** and **Israel** to and from wintering grounds on dry plains, sandy wastes and shortgrass areas, often adjacent to water, including: the western Indian subcontinent in **Pakistan** (now very rare: last record in 1980) and north-west **India**, the Mesopotamian region of **Iraq** (widespread in small numbers), **Sri Lanka** (at least occasionally), **Oman** (scarce), and north-east Africa in **Eritrea** (scarce), **Sudan** (no records since 1950) and **Egypt** (few recent reports) (also records of casual occurrence in up to 25 countries) (Nikolaus and Hamed 1984, Urban *et al.* 1986, Nikolaus 1987, Paz 1987, Roberts 1991, Kasparek 1992, Inskipp and Collins 1993). There has been a rapid decline and range contraction owing to intensifying cultivation (including pesticide spraying) of and increased pastoralism (heavy grazing, trampling of nests) on virgin steppe areas (plus the expansion into them of the Rook *Corvus frugilegus*, a serious nest predator), such that in northern Kazakhstan a dramatic decline between 1930 and 1960 was compounded by a further halving of numbers between 1960 and 1987, and, with only 1,000–2,100 pairs in Russia west of the Urals, it is not clear that more than 10,000 mature individuals now survive (Cramp and Simmons 1980, Tucker and Heath 1994; also M. D. Gallagher *in litt.* 1990, V. V. Khrokov *in litt.* 1993, S. Ericsson *in litt.* 1994). **VULNERABLE: A1a,b; C1; C2a.**

Family SCOLOPACIDAE
WOODCOCKS, SNIPES, SANDPIPERS

Amami Woodcock *Scolopax mira* is known from Amami, Tokunoshima, Okinawa and the Tokashiki Islands in the Nansei Shoto, southern **Japan**, where it is found in broadleaf evergreen

forest, being locally common on Amami, but less numerous on the other islands (Brazil 1991), and its total population is estimated at less than 10,000 individuals (Yanagisawa *et al.* 1993 in Rose and Scott

1994). It is threatened by deforestation in some parts of its range (e.g. Miyagi 1989), but predation by mongooses (introduced to Amami and Okinawa to control poisonous snakes) may prove to be a more serious threat, and already appears to have caused a population decline in part of Amami (N. Ichida *in litt.* 1994). **VULNERABLE:** A2d; B1+2c,e; C1.

Moluccan Woodcock *Scolopax rochussenii* is known by eight specimens (the most recent collected in 1980) from Obi and Bacan, in the north Moluccas, **Indonesia**, where it is believed to occur in hill forest (White and Bruce 1986, Collar and Andrew 1988). It was not observed during surveys of Bacan and Obi in 1991 and 1992, but a guide resident on Obi reported that birds probably of this species were occasionally flushed during dry periods from forest on ridgetops above 500 m (Lambert in prep.). The area of hill forest on Bacan and Obi is naturally small, but has protected status (RePPProT 1990, BirdLife IP). **VULNERABLE:** D1; D2.

Wood Snipe *Gallinago nemoricola* is known as a breeding bird from the Himalayas in north-west and north-east **India**, **Nepal** and **Bhutan** (and possibly Pakistan: Roberts 1991), and in central Sichuan, **China**, where it has been found to nest in alpine meadows with scattered bushes and a few streams, and dwarf scrub in barren, boulder-strewn areas, between 3,000 and 5,000 m (Meyer de Schauensee 1984, Buckton and Morris 1993). Outside the breeding season it occurs at lower altitudes in the Himalayas and is dispersed sparingly through small wetlands in the hill ranges of most of India (Ali and Ripley 1987), and is also recorded from **Bangladesh** (Thompson *et al.* 1993), **Myanmar**, **Laos**, northern **Vietnam** and **Thailand** (King *et al.* 1975) (and as a vagrant to Singapore and Sri Lanka: Medway and Wells 1976, Ali and Ripley 1987). Recent records indicate that it is sparsely distributed throughout its range, and there is evidence that it has declined in Nepal (at least locally), and, as its breeding habitat would seem to be secure, loss of habitat in the wintering range is likely to be an important factor in this decline (Buckton and Morris 1993). **VULNERABLE:** C2a.

Chatham Islands Snipe *Coenocorypha pusilla* is confined to forest and grasslands on two small predator-free islands in the Chatham Islands, **New Zealand**, with a total population of c.1,000 pairs (700–800 pairs on South East Island or Rangatira; 200–250 on Mangere where reintroduced), having become extirpated from the main Chatham and Pitt islands owing to (introduced) predators, especially cats, rats, pigs and Weka *Gallirallus australis*

(Marchant and Higgins 1993, C. M. Miskelly *in litt.* 1994). **VULNERABLE:** D2.

Eskimo Curlew *Numenius borealis* formerly bred on tundra in a narrow band across the Northwest Territories, **Canada** (where rumour hints at sightings of breeding birds even yet), migrating in huge flocks south along the Atlantic coast of the **U.S.A.** (occasional records persist), across the Caribbean to winter in **Uruguay**, **Argentina** (recent unconfirmed reports at one site, a few years apart) and **Chile**, returning via Central America and the central prairies of North America (now almost entirely and perhaps not coincidentally vanished, like the bird's pampas winter quarters); although hunting, especially in spring on the prairies, is blamed for its decline to near-extinction, the fact that no recovery has taken place since hunting was outlawed and abandoned suggests some major ecological factor militating against the species (Collar *et al.* 1992). **CRITICAL: D1**.

Bristle-thighed Curlew *Numenius tahitiensis* inhabits montane tundra during the breeding season in western Alaska (**U.S.A.**), and tidal mudflats, beaches and grassy fields in its wintering range in the Northwestern Hawaiian Islands (U.S.A.), **Marshall Islands**, **Kiribati**, **Tuvalu**, **Tokelau (to New Zealand)**, **Fiji**, **Tonga**, **Niue (to New Zealand)**, **Western Samoa**, **American Samoa**, **Cook Islands (to New Zealand)**, Society Islands, Marquesas Islands and Tuamotu archipelago (all **French Polynesia**) (AOU 1983, Pratt *et al.* 1987), also reaching as far as the Kermadec Islands (**New Zealand**), **Norfolk Island (to Australia)** (Turbott 1990) and the **Pitcairn Islands (to U.K.)** (Brooke in press), with the possibility that small numbers breed at least intermittently on the Chukotka peninsula in Russia (Konyukhov and McCaffery 1993). The breeding population has recently been estimated at c.7,000 birds, although, including subadults oversummering in the Pacific, the total population may be as high as 10,000, and it is not known if it is declining (Collar *et al.* 1992). However, on the breeding grounds it is potentially threatened by off-road hunting and activities associated with gold-mining (as well as predation by several species of bird of prey, Arctic Skua *Stercorarius parasiticus*, Common Raven *Corvus corax* and foxes: McCaffery and Gill 1992), whilst during the autumn (when adults undergo a flightless moult) it is highly vulnerable to predation by introduced cats and dogs (and possibly pigs), and throughout the Tuamotus it has been traditionally trapped for food (Collar *et al.* 1992); following the decline of this subsistence hunting since the French government imposed sanctions on the possession and use of firearms, the greatest threat is from predators, so that on Rangiroa Atoll (250–350 birds and possibly declining) the species' distribution is in inverse relation to that of humans and their commensal animals (Gill and Redmond 1992; see also Marks and Redmond in press), although the relationship between the presence of humans and curlews in Polynesia is largely unclear (J.-C. Thibault *in litt.* 1994). **VULNERABLE: C2b.**

Slender-billed Curlew *Numenius tenuirostris*, considered common in the nineteenth century, has been recorded breeding (in peat bogs) only in **Russia** (possibly in the northern part of the forest–steppe region, near the southern taiga between the Urals and the Ob valley) and not with certainty for the last 70 years, during which time it has undergone a dramatic decline to the point where only 50–270 birds are judged likely to survive (although the only known wintering birds numbered as few as six in early 1994), based on a sifting of evidence from the main countries in the western Palearctic to or through which it migrates: **Ukraine**, **Turkey**, **Romania**, **Bulgaria**, **Greece**, **Hungary**, former **Yugoslavia** (Serbia), **Italy**, **Tunisia** and **Morocco**, this last holding the key wintering areas (Gretton 1991, A. Gretton verbally 1994). If it was in fact a steppe species, its loss could be attributed to massive conversion of this habitat (V. Belik, G. Boere *per* A. Gretton verbally 1994), otherwise the chief cause of decline appears to be hunting, particularly on passage, coupled with isolation and fragmentation of passage habitat owing to drainage (the birds utilize margins of brackish lagoons and similar short-grass areas adjacent to water throughout the non-breeding period) and possibly a breakdown in social behaviour patterns (Gretton 1991, Tucker and Heath 1994, Heredia in prep.). **CRITICAL: C2b**; **D1.**

Nordmann's Greenshank *Tringa guttifer* breeds on Sakhalin Island, probably along the coast of the Sea of Okhotsk, and possibly on the Kamchatka peninsula and in the lower reaches of the Novy Semyachik River (close to the Kronotsk Reserve), in eastern **Russia**, where it nests in lowland swamps, and swamped and thinned coniferous forest, adjacent to shallow bays; studies in 1985–1988 indicate that the total population on Sakhalin is about 30–40 pairs, that some breeding areas have already been destroyed by urbanization, and that other threats include increased crow predation and human disturbance because of new settlements near to breeding areas, and increased hunting pressure (Nechaev 1989). It has been recorded widely as a migrant and winter visitor, in **China**, **Japan**, **North Korea**, **South Korea** (98–135 individuals estimated at west coast

locations in May 1988: Long *et al.* 1988), **Taiwan**, **Hong Kong (to U.K.)** (regular in spring, maximum count 58 in 1993: D. S. Melville *in litt.* 1994), the **Philippines**, **Vietnam**, **Thailand** (up to 11 on Ko Libong Island), peninsular and East **Malaysia** (regular on passage in the peninsula, but numbers have recently declined: D. R. Wells *in litt.* 1994), **Singapore**, **Indonesia** (up to 21 in south-east Sumatra), **Myanmar**, **Bangladesh** (an exceptional count of c.300 reported in winter 1988/1989) and **India**, but is known by few records (generally involving small numbers) in many of these countries and in some is probably only a vagrant (King 1978–1979, Kennerley and Bakewell 1987, Inskipp and Collins 1993). The total world population is estimated to be c.1,000 (Rose and Scott 1994). **ENDANGERED: C1**; **C2b**; **D1.**

Tuamotu Sandpiper *Prosobonia cancellata* is extinct on Kiritimati (= Christmas Island), Kiribati, where the type-specimen was collected, but survives in the Tuamotu archipelago, **French Polynesia** (King 1978–1979). It was formerly widespread in the archipelago, occurring at least as far north-west as Kauehi, but the introduction of rats and cats has probably eliminated it from all but the most infrequently visited islands (Hay 1986). There are recent records from Nukutavake (date unknown), Marutea Sud (1965), Matureivavao (1970), Fakarava (reports from fishermen for the 1980s), Raevski Group (Hiti, Tuanake, perhaps Tepoto: reports from fishermen for 1984), Tenararo (1986), Tahanea (1989: 12–15 birds), Anuanuraro (1990: 30–40), Morane (1990: 150–200) and there are a further four localities where it has not been found in recent searches (Pukapuka, Raraka, Pinaki and the Gambier Islands), six atolls identified before 1925 as holding birds that have not subsequently been visited, and about 20 atolls, some apparently suitable, which have never been ornithologically surveyed for birds (Thibault 1988, Lovegrove *et al.* undated, Seitre and Seitre 1991; details in Holyoak and Thibault 1984; see also Hay 1984). **ENDANGERED: B1+2d,e**; **C2a**; **D1.**

Spoon-billed Sandpiper *Eurynorhynchus pygmeus* breeds only in north-east **Russia**, on the Chukotski (= Chukchi) peninsula and southwards up the isthmus of the Kamchatka peninsula, where it nests on sea coasts with sparsely vegetated sandy ridges near lakes and marshes, a habitat which is patchily distributed along the narrow coastal zone, especially near to the mouths of some rivers and lagoons and sandy spits; its total population has been estimated to be 2,000–2,800 pairs (Tomkovich 1991). It has been recorded on passage or in winter in **China**, **North Korea**, **South Korea**, **Japan**, **Taiwan**, **Hong Kong (to U.K.)**, **Vietnam**, **Thailand**, peninsular **Malaysia**, **Singapore**, **Myanmar**, **Bangladesh**, the east coast of **India** and **Sri Lanka** (and as a vagrant to Canada and U.S.A.) (Inskipp and Collins 1993, J. C. Eames verbally 1994), but is known by few records in most of these countries and in some is perhaps only a vagrant. The largest known wintering concentration is on islands in the Bay of Bengal in Bangladesh, where 257 were counted in 1989 (Thompson *et al.* 1993). It only breeds suc-cessfully in years when lemming *Dicrostonyx groenlandicus* populations are moderate or high, as predators destroy most nests when lemmings are not available; this, in combination with its low numbers, limited distribution and specialized habitat requirements, makes it a vulnerable species, although a new protected area on the Chukotski peninsula is under discussion (Tomkovich 1991). **VULNERABLE:** C1; C2b.

Family RECURVIROSTRIDAE

AVOCETS, STILTS

Black Stilt *Himantopus novaezelandiae*, whose population is estimated at only c.60 birds (B. D. Bell verbally 1993), is restricted during its breeding season to the upper Waitaki valley (c.7,000 km^2) on South Island, **New Zealand**, where hybridization with the Pied Stilt *H. himantopus* occurs (King 1978–1979). Nesting areas have been destroyed by drainage and by hydroelectric development (and by weed growth, tree planting and flood control pro-grammes: B. D. Bell *in litt.* 1994) and it suffers from heavy predation (Williams and Given 1981) which is sharply increased by its nesting preference for dry banks, the favoured hunting habitat of cats and ferrets (Pierce 1986), so that predator-trapping and artificial incubation of eggs are necessary to keep the population from declining (B. D. Bell verbally 1993). **CRITICAL: D1**.

Family GLAREOLIDAE

COURSERS, PRATINCOLES

Jerdon's Courser *Rhinoptilus bitorquatus* is a nocturnal bird known historically from a handful of records in the Penner and Godaveri valleys in Andhra Pradesh, east-central **India**, which had been assumed extinct (King 1978–1979) until its rediscovery in January 1986. It is found in thin thorny and non-thorny scrub on rocky and undulating ground, including disturbed areas where regeneration is affected by grazing and the collection of fuelwood (Bhushan 1986a,b, Ali and Ripley 1987). There are recent records from six sites in the vicinity of the Lankamalai ranges (near the Penner valley), southern Andhra Pradesh, where its known from two valleys in an area of c.2,000 km^2 (Bhushan 1992). A planned irrigation scheme which would have affected its two valleys has been diverted in response to lobbying, and two protected areas, Sri Lankamalleswara Wildlife Sanctuary and Sri Venkateswara National Park, have recently been gazetted there, and a third is planned in a nearby area where this species has been reported (Bhushan 1992). **ENDANGERED: B1+2c; C1; C2a; D1**.

Family LARIDAE

GULLS, TERNS

Olrog's Gull *Larus atlanticus* is a crab-eating and apparently scavenging seabird of the coast of **Argentina** (where it breeds), **Uruguay** (where some birds winter) and southernmost **Brazil** (two winter records from Rio Grande do Sul), occurring in low overall numbers (less than 1,400 pairs), with its few known colonies vulnerable to both deliberate and accidental disturbance and destruction, egg-collecting for food being a known threat (Collar *et al.* 1992). **VULNERABLE:** A2b,c; C1; C2b.

White-eyed Gull *Larus leucophthalmus* breeds in the Gulf of Aden and the Red Sea: **Egypt** (islands at the mouth of the Gulf of Suez, up to 2,000 pairs, 1973–1978; up to seven other localities, none with more than 50 pairs), **Sudan** (Mukawar, Taila and Mayetib islands), **Eritrea** (Dahlak archipelago, 1,400 adults and 200+ young spread over 10 islands, 1962), **Saudi Arabia** (at least nine colonies, none holding more than 60 pairs, in at least six sites in early 1980s) and **Yemen** (Hanish group, possibly bred 1961; islands near Hodeida, 200 adults in 1979; with birds fairly widespread throughout the year) (Clapham 1964, Cooper *et al.* 1984, Gallagher *et al.* 1984, Nikolaus 1987, Brooks *et al.* 1987, Goodman *et al.* 1989). Many wintering birds move down the Red Sea, extending south to the Kenya coast between October and April, although not in recent years (Bednall and Williams 1989; also Cramp and Simmons 1983). A claim of 'thousands' breeding on Aibat and Saad Din islands off Zeyla (Saylac), **Somalia** (Urban *et al.* 1986), and of common residency along the country's north coast (Ash and Miskell 1983), all seems to be based on information, now in need of confirmation, in Archer and Godman (1937). The species is permanently at risk from floating and beached oil (Jennings *et al.* 1985), and the important islands at the mouth of the Gulf of Suez are under increasing human pressure involving egg- and chick-collecting, disturbance by tourists (and related building) and oil exploration (S. Baha El Din verbally 1994). **VULNERABLE:** C1.

Saunders's Gull *Larus saundersi* breeds in coastal eastern **China** and winters in **South Korea**, southern **Japan**, eastern China, **Taiwan**, **Hong Kong (to U.K.)** and northern **Vietnam**, with the largest known wintering concentrations in southern Japan (where records have recently increased, perhaps as a result of birds being displaced from elsewhere), Hong Kong (where numbers have also increased in recent years) and northern Vietnam, and the total world population is estimated at 3,000 (Wong 1993, J. C. Eames *in litt.* 1994, Rose and Scott 1994). It is specialized to breed on salt marshes and tidal mudflats built up by silt deposition from the great rivers of eastern China, and is currently known to breed at a few coastal/estuarine sites in Jiangsu, Shandong, Hebei and Liaoning, the vast majority of suitable breeding habitat in China having already been reclaimed, and the surviving breeding sites (as well as some wintering sites) being threatened by coastal degradation, reclamation, development and pollution, plus disturbance by humans and hunting at some localities (Wong and Liang 1992, Brazil and Moores 1993, Takeshita *et al.* 1993, Hsu and Melville 1994). **ENDANGERED:** A1b,c,d; **A2b,c,d**; C1; C2a.

Lava Gull *Larus fuliginosus* breeds only in the Galápagos Islands, **Ecuador**, where probably less than 300–400 pairs nest solitarily in sheltered places (at low density) near coastal lagoons, spread widely around the rocky coasts of the many islands (concentrating locally to scavenge). No threat is known save in the level of its population (Snow and Snow 1969, Cepeda and Cruz 1994). **VULNERABLE:** D1.

Red-legged Kittiwake *Rissa brevirostris* was as recently as 1976 estimated to have c.240,000 individuals, with colonies at only four locations in the Bering Sea: on St George and St Paul islands in the Pribilof group, **U.S.A.** (the colony on St George accounting for 75% of the total population); small colonies on the Bogoslof Islands and Buldir Island in the Aleutian chain; and colonies on three of the Commander Islands, **Russia** (Lensink 1984, Byrd and Williams 1993, Harrison 1993). Although colonies on Buldir and the Commanders have increased during the last 20 years (to 6,600 and c.34,000 birds respectively), these do not counteract the poor reproductive success and resultant 50% decline in the Pribilof population, which has been attributed to unexplained food shortages (Byrd and Williams 1993, Hatch *et al.* 1993). **VULNERABLE:** A1a.

Chinese Crested Tern *Sterna bernsteini* is believed to breed on the eastern coast of **China**, where there are several historical records, including 21 collected on islands off Shandong in 1937 (Mees 1975, King 1978–1979), but the only recent records in

China are sightings of three in Hebei in 1978 (Boswell 1987) and three birds probably of this species at the mouth of the Yellow River, Shandong, in September 1991, where local ornithologists believe it may breed (Wang *et al.* 1991b). There are records outside the breeding season from Fujian and Guangdong, China (Cheng 1987), Halmahera, **Indonesia**, Sarawak, East **Malaysia**, **Thailand** (King 1978–1979) and the **Philippines** (Dickinson *et al.* 1991), but the only recent report is of 10 seen in Thailand in 1980 (Humphrey and Bain 1990). The habitat requirements and threats to this species remain unknown. **CRITICAL: D1**.

Kerguelen Tern *Sterna virgata* breeds in the southern Indian Ocean on Prince Edward Islands (**South Africa**) (50 pairs), Crozet Islands (**French Southern Territories**) (over 148 pairs in 1980–1982; later written as 150–200 pairs) and Kerguelen Islands (to French Southern Territories) (1,000–2,000 pairs in 1982–1985). Introduction of salmonid fish into rivers on Kerguelen has provided a new food source, but the large numbers of feral cats remain a major threat and will cause a decline once they have depleted the petrels which they currently target for food (Jouventin *et al.* 1984, 1988, Williams 1984, Jouventin 1994a). **VULNERABLE: A2d; C1**.

Fairy Tern *Sterna nereis* occurs on the coasts of Victoria, Tasmania, South Australia, Western Australia, **Australia**, **New Caledonia (to France)** and **New Zealand**, and although there are records (pre-1971) of one flock of 15,000 in Western Australia, the Australian population has been estimated at 2,000 pairs (Garnett 1992). In Victoria many long-standing colonies have disappeared because estuarine and offshore islands used as nesting sites are easily disturbed as they become more accessible to people (Garnett 1992). In New Zealand it breeds only on the coasts of Northland, where it is rare (Turbott 1990), with 10 pairs in the 1993/1994 breeding season (A. J.

Tennyson *in litt.* 1994), disturbance on beaches and predation by cats and rats being the main threats (B. D. Bell *in litt.* 1994). In New Caledonia its status is not known. **VULNERABLE**: C2a.

Black-bellied Tern *Sterna acuticauda* is known from most of **India**, **Pakistan**, **Nepal**, **Bangladesh**, **Myanmar**, Yunnan, southern **China**, northern **Thailand**, **Laos**, **Cambodia** and southern **Vietnam**, where it is found on large rivers and marshes in the plains (not on the coast) up to 730 m (Ali and Ripley 1987, Inskipp and Inskipp 1991). There is evidence of a decline in Thailand (very rare, possibly now extinct: Boonsong and Round 1991), Laos and Cambodia (not recorded by recent surveys: T. Mundkur *in litt.* 1994), and in Gujarat, India (Mundkur 1988), and the world population is believed to be below 10,000 individuals and falling (Rose and Scott 1994). Threats include destruction of breeding habitat (islands and sandspits in larger rivers are used for watermelon cultivation), the collection of eggs for food, and natural flooding of nests (T. Mundkur *in litt.* 1994, A. R. Rahmani *in litt.* 1994). **VULNERABLE**: C1.

Black-fronted Tern *Chlidonias albostriatus* is confined to South Island, **New Zealand**, where it breeds along dry river-beds and lake shores. The population has been estimated at 1,000–5,000 pairs (also 10,000 pairs, but all estimates are largely speculative), with introduced predators a major threat, alongside hydroelectric development, weed growth and tree-planting on river and lake margins (Robertson and Bell 1984, B. D. Bell *in litt.* 1994, C. O'Donnell *in litt.* 1994), although breeding sites found in the tundra zone may have been established following the loss of lower riverbed habitat (Child 1986). It can also breed on gravel islands and could possibly therefore increase in numbers, although flood control programmes which concentrate flow into a single channel reduce this habitat (B. D. Bell verbally 1993 and *in litt.* 1994). **VULNERABLE**: C2a.

Family RYNCHOPIDAE

SKIMMERS

Indian Skimmer *Rynchops albicollis* ranges throughout northern **India** (not recorded south of c.16°N, locally fairly common, nomadic and locally migratory depending on water conditions: Ali and

Ripley 1987), **Pakistan** (rare, declining markedly in the past 50 or 60 years: Roberts 1991), **Nepal** (irregular and uncommon, having possibly bred: Inskipp and Inskipp 1991), **Bangladesh** (winter visitor, a total of 3,263 counted in 1988/1989: Harvey 1990, *Oriental Bird Club Bull.* 1989, 9: 38–44), **Myanmar** (formerly locally common, but not recorded during recent surveys: Smythies 1986, T. Mundkur *in litt.* 1994), southern **Laos** (not observed recently: Salter 1993) and **Cambodia** (not recorded during recent surveys of prime habitats, but reported by local people to breed at one site: T. Mundkur *in litt.* 1994) (and a vagrant in south-east China, Thailand and Vietnam: Vo Quy 1975, Cheng 1987, Boonsong and Round 1991), where it is found on placid, expansive reaches of large rivers with sandbanks (Ali and Ripley 1987). The world population is estimated at c.10,000 (Rose and Scott 1994). It is believed to have declined in Pakistan because irrigation barrages have allowed the gradual encroachment of temporary cultivation into the river beds and river island tracts (Roberts 1991), and the destruction of breeding habitat, and possibly pesticides and the collection of eggs, are considered the main threats (T. Mundkur *in litt.* 1994, A. R. Rahmani *in litt.* 1994). **VULNERABLE:** C1; C2a.

Family ALCIDAE

AUKS, MURRES, PUFFINS

Japanese Murrelet *Synthliboramphus wumizusume* breeds in southern **Japan** (estimated 4,000–5,000 birds, nesting mainly on small offshore islands/stacks: Hasegawa 1984, N. Ichida *in litt.* 1994), **South Korea** (less than 10 pairs: P. O. Won verbally 1994) and possibly south-east Russia (Litvinenko and Shibaev 1991). It disperses at sea as far north as Sakhalin Island, **Russia**, and presumably to North Korea (Dement'ev and Gladkov 1968), and as far south as Taiwan (vagrant: Wang *et al.* 1991a). Increased sport-fishing activities are a threat in Japan, as fishermen landing at breeding sites sometimes destroy nesting habitat and disturb breeding activities (Hasegawa 1984), and other threats include introduced predators (Takeishi 1987) and incidental capture in driftnets (Piatt and Gould in press). **VULNERABLE:** C1.

Family COLUMBIDAE

PIGEONS, DOVES

Somali Pigeon *Columba oliviae* is an extremely poorly known ground-feeding, rock-dwelling species endemic to the arid coastal regions of north-east **Somalia**, not known to be declining but in need of survey to establish its status and requirements (Collar and Stuart 1985; see also Urban *et al.* 1986). The chronic and continuing political crisis in Somalia may be causing as yet undocumented loss of habitats for this and other species endemic to the country. **VULNERABLE:** C2a.

Pale-backed Pigeon *Columba eversmanni* migrates from its breeding grounds (where it uses holes in trees, buildings, cliffs and earth banks) in the deserts and settled regions of **Uzbekistan, Turkmen-** istan, **Tajikistan, Kyrgyzstan**, southern **Kazakhstan** and **Afghanistan** (one record from Tibet, **China**) into riverine plains and fields in western **Pakistan** and northern **India**; it was formerly to be found in substantial flocks at regular sites each winter (Vaurie 1972, Ali and Ripley 1987, Flint *et al.* 1984, Roberts 1991; also Vittery 1994). For unknown reasons it has dramatically decreased in central Asia in recent years, and is now widely regarded as very rare there (S. C. Madge *in litt.* 1993). **VULNERABLE:** A1a.

Dark-tailed Laurel Pigeon *Columba bollii* is confined to tracts of lower montane laurel forest on Tenerife (at least 350–400 birds), La Palma (250–300), La Gomera (over 1,000) and El Hierro (small numbers; at least 10–15) in the Canary Islands, **Spain**, where inappropriate forestry management and small-scale clearance, both inside and outside existing protected areas, coupled with the unknown but feared effects of illegal hunting and introduced predators, continue to pose threats to the long-term security of the species (Collar and Stuart 1985, Tucker and Heath 1994, Heredia in prep.). **VULNERABLE:** C2a.

White-tailed Laurel Pigeon *Columba junoniae* is confined to tracts of lower montane laurel forest on Tenerife (80–120 birds), La Palma (1,000–1,200) and La Gomera (120–160) in the Canary Islands, **Spain**, where considerable illegal hunting pressure and habitat loss throughout La Palma (where much of the remaining forest is privately owned) combine with the effects of introduced predators to pose threats to the long-term security of the species (Collar and Stuart 1985, Tucker and Heath 1994, Heredia in prep.). **VULNERABLE:** C2a.

Maroon Pigeon *Columba thomensis* occurs in primary rainforest on São Tomé, **São Tomé e Príncipe**, where its population appears (from various items of evidence) to have dwindled beyond viability at lower levels owing to habitat loss and continuing intensive hunting (Collar and Stuart 1985, Urban *et al.* 1986, Jones and Tye 1988, in press, Jones *et al.* 1992, P. Christy *in litt.* 1994), so that it is now reasonably common only within the very restricted part of the island that lies above c.1,600 m (Atkinson *et al.* 1991, Nadler 1993). **VULNERABLE:** D1.

Sri Lanka Wood-pigeon *Columba torringtoni* is endemic to **Sri Lanka**, where it breeds in montane forest above 1,000 m (Henry 1955) in the hill zone in the centre of the island, although it regularly moves to lower areas, down to c.300 m (S. W. Kotagama *in litt.* 1992). It is believed to be declining, probably as a result of continuing loss of habitat, as natural forests are replaced by monoculture plantations which do not support the species (Hoffmann 1984), but there is recent evidence that it has at least partially adapted to man-made environments, as there are recent records from wooded village areas and gardens (T. W. Hoffmann *in litt.* 1993). **VULNERABLE:** B1+2c; C1; C2a.

Pale-capped Pigeon *Columba punicea* has been recorded in north-east **India**, **Bangladesh**, **Myanmar**, **Thailand**, southern **China** (Tibet and Hainan Island), southern **Laos** and central and southern **Vietnam**, where it is found in evergreen forest, mangroves, scrub and cultivated areas in the lowlands to c.1,600 m (King *et al.* 1975, Ali and Ripley 1987,

Cheng 1987, Boonsong and Round 1991). It is extremely local in distribution, and its breeding range and migratory movements are poorly understood (Collar and Andrew 1988). Recent records are from India, where one was seen in the Dibru Saikhowa Wildlife Sanctuary, Assam, in 1993, in an area of secondary forest under considerable human pressure (A. R. Rahmani *in litt.* 1994, R. H. Raza *in litt.* 1994), Bangladesh, where two or three were recorded at Bhanugach Forest Reserve in 1988 and 1989 (Thompson *et al.* 1993), Thailand, where it is uncommon or rare (Boonsong and Round 1991) and south Annam, Vietnam, where flocks of 14 and 41 were seen in 1991 and 1992, plus a report from the Thuong Da Nhim Nature Reserve, the species being threatened by deforestation and recorded in trade (Eames *et al.* 1992, *Oriental Bird Club Bull.* 1992, 15: 43–47, J. C. Eames *in litt.* 1994). **VULNERABLE:** C1; C2a.

Silvery Wood-pigeon *Columba argentina* is principally an island species, recorded from the Mentawai Islands and Simeulue off western Sumatra, and the Riau and Lingga archipelagos, **Indonesia**, and Burong Island, **Malaysia**, dispersing between islands according to food supply, although it has been recorded from the mainland of Sumatra and Borneo; it was formerly locally common, but there are very few recent records (Smythies 1986, van Marle and Voous 1988, D. R. Wells *in litt.* 1994). However, birds suspected (but not confirmed) to be this species were widespread and seen in large numbers in South Sumatra Province, especially along the Sembilang River in March 1989, in mangroves and swamp forests (Verheugt *et al.* 1993). Threats may include deforestation and disturbance in a region of Indonesia subject to increasing industrial and other development (BirdLife IP) and hunting (D. R. Wells *in litt.* 1994). **VULNERABLE:** C1; C2a.

Yellow-legged Pigeon *Columba pallidiceps* is a very rare forest bird of the Bismarck archipelago, **Papua New Guinea**, and the **Solomon Islands** (Coates 1985, Diamond 1987), although, like some congeners, it is probably highly elusive (B. J. Coates *in litt.* 1994). It appeared uncommon on New Britain in 1959 (Gilliard and LeCroy 1967). There were no records from West New Britain during the period 1978–1988 (and including three years of intensive fieldwork, 1978–1980), and none from Bougainville during 1979–1988 (K. D. Bishop *in litt.* 1989). One was seen on New Ireland in 1984 (Finch and McKean 1987) but it was not recorded there in a recent search (B. M. Beehler *in litt.* 1994). The first records from the Solomon Islands since 1928 include one record from Guadalcanal in 1987 and five sightings on Makira in 1990, these indicating that it is dependent on primary forest at a wide range of altitudes (1,300 m on Guadalcanal, 0–600 m on Makira) but still vulnerable to logging, with hunting a possible threat near population centres on the coast (Buckingham *et al.* in prep.). **CRITICAL: C2a**; D1.

Ring-tailed Pigeon *Columba caribaea*, endemic to the montane forests of **Jamaica** (notably Cockpit Country, Blue Mountains and John Crow Mountains, ranging from as little as 150 m in winter up to 2,000 m), has been greatly reduced in numbers and range over the past 150 years by illegal hunting (making this bird a particular target) and extensive habitat loss (compounded by a recent hurricane), and this trend continues with unabating pressure from both hunting and forest clearance (Collar *et al.* 1992). **CRITICAL: A1b,c; A2b,c; B1+2c,e; C1; C2a; D1.**

Peruvian Pigeon *Columba oenops* occupies a restricted range (chiefly the upper Marañón valley, at 850–2,400 m) in northern **Peru** (Cajamarca and Amazonas, with one record from Piura and two from La Libertad) and, within it, a restricted habitat (chiefly riparian woodland and adjacent dry forest on steep valley slopes); it is a generally uncommon to scarce, seems likely to suffer some hunting pressure, and is certainly declining with the gradual degradation and loss of its habitat (Collar *et al.* 1992). There is now evidence of its occurrence in extreme south-east **Ecuador** (P. Coopmans *per*/and R. S. Ridgely *in litt.* 1994). **VULNERABLE:** B1+2b,c; C2a.

Plain Pigeon *Columba inornata*, once abundant and widespread in forest, scrub, open savanna and cultivation on **Cuba**, **Jamaica**, **Haiti**, **Dominican Republic** and **Puerto Rico (to U.S.A.)**, has declined through hunting and habitat loss and is now threatened everywhere and gravely at risk in Cuba (highest known population c.100 pairs), Puerto Rico (apparently under 300 birds) and Jamaica (situation perhaps worse than on Puerto Rico). A recent decline has occurred in the Dominican Republic (a 3,500-km drive in search of the species in 1986 failed to record a single bird but found sites cleared where it was present 10 years before), and only in Haiti, where firearms and ammunition are too expensive, have there been reports of birds in some numbers (Collar *et al.* 1992). **ENDANGERED:** A1b; **C2a.**

Pink Pigeon *Columba mayeri*, having experienced almost total loss of habitat compounded (in particular) by nest predation by introduced rats and monkeys (also cyclones), survives in very low numbers (c.20) in the upland areas of native forest in southwest **Mauritius**, where all breeding takes place in a single small (now known to be 6 ha) grove of exotic

Cryptomeria trees (Collar and Stuart 1985, Jones 1987; also Seal and Bruford 1991, R. J. Safford *in litt.* 1994). Between July 1987 and October 1992 51 captive-bred birds were released into appropriate-seeming habitat at Brise Fer, and the combination of supplementary feeding and rat control both there and at the *Cryptomeria* grove (which is now inside the Black River National Park) caused dramatic improvements in survival and breeding success respectively of the two populations (Jones *et al.* 1992), so that by September 1993 the introduced population stood at 28, with 12 pairs and four juveniles (Swinnerton *et al.* 1993), and by May 1994 this population was 52, half of which were born in the wild, with the original wild population at c.25 (C. G. Jones *in litt.* 1994). The release programme is being extended to the 25 ha predator-free Ile aux Aigrettes and to a lowland site at Bel Ombre during 1994, with the hope of establishing a free-living population of at least 200 birds (C. G. Jones *in litt.* 1994). **CRITICAL:** B1+2c; **D1**; D2.

Black Cuckoo-dove *Turacoena modesta* is endemic to Timor and Wetar, **Indonesia**, where it is found in monsoon forest in the lowlands to 1,100 m (White and Bruce 1986), a habitat which is much reduced and fragmented in west Timor but apparently more widespread in east Timor (see RePPProT 1990). Recent observers have found it scarce or failed to record it on Timor (S. van Balen *in litt.* 1994), and it was seen at only two localities during a nine-week survey of the remnant lowland forests of west Timor in 1993, where some hunting occurs (Noske and Saleh 1993). However, it was seen on a short visit to Wetar in 1990, the first by ornithologists to this island since 1911, where extensive forest remains (K. D. Bishop *in litt.* 1990). **VULNERABLE:** A1b; C1; C2a.

Socorro Dove *Zenaida graysoni* was formerly a common ground-dwelling frugivore in forests especially above 500 m on Socorro in the Revillagigedo Islands, **Mexico**, but was last seen there in January 1958 (although it may possibly survive in small numbers in the remote, unsurveyed north of the island), its decline being attributed to predation by cats, which became established in the 1950s, and perhaps to sheep, which have grazed out the understorey; however, over 200 birds are held captive in the U.S.A. and Europe, and eradications and reintroduction are being planned (Collar *et al.* 1992, Walter 1993). **EXTINCT IN THE WILD.**

Blue-eyed Ground-dove *Columbina cyanopis*, although recorded from a very wide area of interior **Brazil** (Mato Grosso in 1823–1825 and again in the

1980s near Cuiabá and at the Serra das Araras Ecological Station, Goiás in 1940–1941 and São Paulo in 1904), has always been extremely rare, possibly through natural factors, although probably (at least now) also owing to massive habitat loss, assuming that it depends to some extent on grasslands, which are under intense pressure from agricultural development (Collar *et al.* 1992). **CRITICAL: C2a**; D1.

Purple-winged Ground-dove *Claravis godefrida*, probably a bamboo specialist and apparently with a preference for edge habitats in rather hilly, broken terrain (records ranging from near sea-level to 2,300 m), has become extremely rare in the evergreen forests of south-east **Brazil** (records originally stemming from Bahia, Espírito Santo, Minas Gerais, Rio de Janeiro, São Paulo, Paraná and Santa Catarina), eastern **Paraguay** (two nineteenth century records) and northern **Argentina** (Misiones: three records of four birds, 1957–1977); while there are records of flocks of up to 100 at the start of the century, the few post-1980 records are of single birds or pairs, and the species has doubtless suffered from the clearance and fragmentation of its habitat and the increasing physical and temporal distance between bamboo flowerings (Collar *et al.* 1992). **CRITICAL: B1+2c; C2b**; D1.

Grenada Dove *Leptotila wellsi* is confined to lowland (up to 150 m) dry-scrub woods of **Grenada**, West Indies, where a much reduced population of c.100 individuals (almost entirely now on the south-west peninsula, on the Mount Hartman Estate, but with a small population at Halifax Harbour plus a few probably doomed birds at Beausejour) is greatly threatened by chronic and continuing habitat alteration and destruction (plantations and construction developments), possibly compounded by predation of fledglings by introduced mongooses (Collar *et al.* 1992). A reconsideration of data from various surveys, including one in 1992, indicates that the total population in 1992 was c.75 birds (B. L. Rusk and S. A. Temple *in litt.* 1994). In April 1994 there was increased habitat degradation (many new clearings for agriculture) at Mount Hartman, with significant increase in disturbance (squatters and a rum distillery) at Halifax Harbour (B. L. Rusk verbally 1994). **CRITICAL: A1b; A2b,d; B1+2c,e; C1; C2b**; D1; D2.

Ochre-bellied Dove *Leptotila ochraceiventris* inhabits undergrowth of deciduous and evergreen moist forests in the tropical and subtropical zones of western **Ecuador** (Manabí, Los Ríos, Guayas, Chimborazo, El Oro, Loja) and north-west **Peru** (Tumbes, Piura), but has occurred in lower montane cloud-forests (altitude mainly 500–1,800 m, although

originally down to sea-level and occasionally up to 2,625 m); all types of forest within its range have greatly diminished and (without urgent intervention) face near-total destruction, the population is small and fragmented, and the situation is compounded by its apparent seasonal displacements between habitats (Collar *et al.* 1992, Best *et al.* 1993, Best 1994). **VULNERABLE:** A1b; A2b; B1+2c,d; C1; C2a.

Tolima Dove *Leptotila conoveri* is endemic to the eastern slope (1,600–2,225 m) of the Central Andes of **Colombia** (Tolima and Huila), where it has been recorded (chiefly in humid forest and bushy forest borders, but recently in coffee groves and second growth, possibly indicating a degree of adaptability) at only a few localities (three in the 1990s) in one of the most disturbed montane forest areas of this region, much original habitat having been cleared in the past half-century (Collar *et al.* 1992). **ENDANGERED:** A1b; B1+2c; C1; **C2a**.

Veracruz Quail-dove *Geotrygon carrikeri* (split from Purplish-backed Quail-dove *G. lawrencii* since Sibley and Monroe 1990) remains known only from two mountains in the Los Tuxtlas region of southeast Veracruz, **Mexico**, where it is rare at 1,300–2,100 m, and clearance of its unprotected cloud-forest habitat is rampant in both known areas, Volcán de San Martín (84% of the original forest area had been lost by 1986) and the Sierra de Santa Marta (Edwards 1989, Dirzo and García 1992, Peterson 1993). **ENDANGERED:** A1b; **A2b; C1; C2a**.

Blue-headed Quail-dove *Starnoenas cyanocephala* was once common and widespread in the undergrowth of lowland and occasionally highland forest on its native **Cuba** (Pinar del Río across to Guantánamo), but through the combined and chronic effects of excessive hunting and the destruction of its habitat it has become extremely rare almost everywhere (and extinct on the Isle of Pines), with reasonable numbers being reported in the late 1980s from only a single locality (Collar *et al.* 1992). **ENDANGERED: C2a**; D1.

Mindoro Bleeding-heart *Gallicolumba platenae* is restricted to lowland forest on Mindoro in the **Philippines**, where it was of local occurrence several decades ago and is now extremely rare, being recorded in 1991 from a single locality (Sablayan, the largest remaining tract of lowland forest on the island) and reported by local people from two other places, none of them secure from clearance or from the trapping of ground-dwelling animals for food (Dutson *et al.* 1992). **CRITICAL:** A1b,c; A2b,c; **B1+2c**; C1; **C2a**; D1.

Negros Bleeding-heart *Gallicolumba keayi* is restricted to Negros in the **Philippines**, where it was historically uncommon (in primary and secondary forest, feeding on the forest floor: Dickinson *et al.* 1991) and had not been seen since 1927, but after a probable sighting at c.1,200 m on Mount Canlaon in January 1990 (Lambert 1993b) a single bird was observed in the same area at 900 m in 1991 (Brooks *et al.* 1992) and good views of a perched bird were obtained there at 1,000 m in March 1994 (C. R. Robson *in litt.* 1994); all records have been from lower-lying forest, now mostly cleared or being cleared, and this fact plus considerable local hunting pressure must account for the species' current extreme rarity (Brooks *et al.* 1992). **CRITICAL:** A1b; A2b; **B1+2c,e**; C1; **C2a**; D1.

Mindanao Bleeding-heart *Gallicolumba criniger* is a ground-feeding inhabitant of primary and secondary forest in the **Philippines**, with race *leytensis* on Samar (no information), Leyte (no information) and Bohol (many recent records in Rajah Sikatuna National Park, presumably this race), *criniger* on Dinagat (no information) and Mindanao (apparently very rare: seen by few recent observers), and *bartletti* on Basilan (no information) (Dickinson *et al.* 1991, N. J. Redman verbally 1993, N. Bostock *in litt.* 1994, C. R. Robson *in litt.* 1994); although it is possible that it survives in reasonable numbers on islands from which there are no new data information, its rarity on Mindanao and the general level of habitat loss (see Collins *et al.* 1991) in the islands strongly suggests a low and declining population. **VULNERABLE:** C2a.

Sulu Bleeding-heart *Gallicolumba menagei* is restricted to Tawitawi in the **Philippines** (a sight record from Jolo was never confirmed and the island is now devoid of forest), a rare inhabitant of primary and secondary forest, feeding on the forest floor; uncontrolled hunting is a problem in the Sulu archipelago and there have been no recent records (Dickinson *et al.* 1991, Lambert 1993b). In August 1994 the last forests on Tawitawi were being rapidly cleared (T. M. Brooks and G. C. L. Dutson *in litt.* 1994). **ENDANGERED:** B1+2c,e; C1; **C2b**; D1.

Caroline Islands Ground-dove *Gallicolumba kubaryi* is endemic to **Micronesia**, occurring on the islands of Pohnpei (brushy ravines, lowland forests and, less commonly, interior forest; total population estimated at 841 birds in 1983–1984) and Chuuk (= Truk) (atoll strand, agricultural and native forest at all elevations; 294 in 1983–1984); it is inconspicuous, may be commoner than is indicated by the survey results, and populations should remain rela-

tively stable, especially if protective legislation and education minimize losses from hunting (Engbring *et al.* 1990). However, in recent visits it appeared scarce on Pohnpei (mostly recorded in mangroves) and may have suffered a severe decline on Chuuk since the 1970s (only one individual on Tol Island and none on Weno) (H. D. Pratt *in litt.* 1994). **EN-DANGERED:** B1+2e; **C2a**; D1.

Polynesian Ground-dove *Gallicolumba erythroptera* was formerly distributed on Tahiti and Moorea in the Society Islands and throughout the Tuamotu archipelago, **French Polynesia**; its ground-dwelling habits having apparently resulted in its extirpation by rats and cats over much of its range (King 1978–1979, Hay 1986). Two races are at stake, nominate *erythroptera*, known from eight islands (extinct on three, four unvisited since 1922–1923, and Matureivavao where seen in 1968), and race *pectoralis*, also known from eight islands (extinct on six, two unvisited since 1923, although, in 1989, not recognized by local people who visit these islands), but c.20 atolls in the Tuamotus, some apparently suitable, have never been surveyed for birds (Holyoak and Thibault 1984, Thibault 1988, Lovegrove *et al.* undated). In 1990–1991 a previously unknown population (perhaps a separate subspecies or colour morph of *pectoralis*) of 12–20 birds was discovered on two forested islets in Rangiroa Atoll (Monnet *et al.* in press). **CRITICAL:** B1+2d,e; **C2a**; D1.

Santa Cruz Ground-dove *Gallicolumba sanctaecrucis* is known from Tinakula and Utupua (may be extinct on latter: D. Gibbs *in litt.* 1994) in Temotu province (= Santa Cruz Islands), **Solomon Islands**, and Espiritu Santo, **Vanuatu**; on Vanuatu it is rarely seen, inhabiting mid-mountain forest to c.1,000 m, and likely to be threatened by habitat destruction, as the greatest pressures on native birds are from human expansion and development (Bregulla 1992), there being a lack of effective controls on logging (R. Hills verbally 1994). It is also hunted, and killed by feral dogs (S. Maturin *in litt.* 1994). There may have been a race (or population, now extinct) on Tanna as the 'Tanna Ground-dove *G. ferruginea*', supposedly collected there in 1774, is generally assumed to be an error and could be attributed to this species (Diamond and Marshall 1976). **VULNERABLE:** A2b; C1.

Thick-billed Ground-dove *Gallicolumba salamonis* has been recorded from Makira (= San Cristobal) and Ramos, **Solomon Islands** (Mayr 1945). It was collected in lowland forest to an altitude of 300 m but has not been recorded since 1927 (Diamond 1987), suggesting that any surviving population is likely to be very small; moreover, most of the remaining accessible forest on Makira has been committed for logging concessions (Lees 1991). It is likely to have suffered from introduced predators, for example cats which have wiped out all native terrestrial mammals on Guadalcanal (T. Flannery *per* K. D. Bishop *in litt*. 1994). However, the lack of recent observations may be partly due to a very retiring nature (like its congeners), to identification problems (it is difficult to separate from the more abundant Bronze Ground-dove *G. beccarii*) or because it may inhabit a different habitat (than expected), such as (unexplored) swamps (Buckingham *et al*. in prep.). **CRITICAL: A2b; C2a; D1**.

Marquesan Ground-dove *Gallicolumba rubescens* is restricted to shrubby vegetation on two uninhabited and cat-free islets, Hatuta'a (18 km²) and Fatu Huku (1 km²) in the Marquesas Islands, **French Polynesia**, where the population on Hatuta'a, estimated at c.225 birds in 1975, remained stable in 1987 (Thibault 1988). It probably formerly occurred on Nuku Hiva, where the type-specimen is reputed to have been collected, and subfossils are known from a further three islets, suggesting that it was originally distributed throughout the entire group and that predation by cats has caused its disappearance (King 1978–1979, Holyoak and Thibault 1984, Pratt *et al*. 1987, Steadman 1989, Seitre and Seitre 1991). **ENDANGERED: D1**; D2.

Wetar Ground-dove *Gallicolumba hoedtii* is known from Timor and Wetar, **Indonesia**, and is clearly rare (though possibly under-recorded) on Timor, where there have been only three records, including a single sighting near Soe during a nine-week forest bird survey in 1993 (White and Bruce 1986, Noske and Saleh 1993), and its forest habitat there has been much reduced and fragmented (see RePPProT 1990). Its status on Wetar is unknown, none being seen on a brief visit in 1990, the first by ornithologists to this island since 1911; however, extensive forest was found to cover much of the north-west corner of the island (K. D. Bishop *in litt*. 1990). **VULNERABLE: C1; C2a**.

Dark-eared Brown-dove *Phapitreron cinereiceps* inhabits forest from 1,000 sometimes up to 2,000 m on Mindanao and Basilan (race *brunneiceps*) and Tawitawi (nominate *cinereiceps*) in the **Philippines**; although much forest remains on Tawitawi, uncontrolled hunting is a problem in the Sulu archipelago and presumably elsewhere, while on Mindanao habitat loss is a major concern (see Collins *et al*. 1991), and the failure of most observers to find the species (one was seen and several other possibles

glimpsed at 1,100 m in mid-mountain forest at Lake Sebu, South Cotabato province, in 1992) indicates its extreme rarity (Dickinson *et al*. 1991, Evans *et al*. 1993a, R. J. Timmins *in litt*. 1994). **VULNERABLE: A2b,c; C1**.

Timor Green-pigeon *Treron psittacea* is endemic to Timor and its satellite islands of Roti and Semau, **Indonesia**, where it is found in monsoon forest in the lowlands (White and Bruce 1986), a habitat which is much reduced and fragmented in west Timor but apparently more widespread in east Timor (see RePPProT 1990). None was recorded on a nine-week survey of the remnant lowland forests of west Timor in 1993 (Noske and Saleh 1993), and the few recent records there include a flock of c.60 near Bipolo in 1989 (K. D. Bishop *in litt*. 1994) and small numbers seen in 1993 (N. Bostock verbally 1993), but it has been reported in the past to be more common in east Timor (J. McKean *in litt*. 1987). **VULNERABLE: A1b; C1; C2a**.

Red-naped Fruit-dove *Ptilinopus dohertyi* is endemic to Sumba, **Indonesia**, where surveys during 1992 estimated a total population of 7,452 birds (based upon a density of 6.9 per km² ± 1.2 s.e.) and found it widespread, but with higher densities tending to occur in primary forest at higher altitudes; monsoon forest on Sumba has been cleared rapidly in the last 50 years to provide grazing and agricultural land, and it has presumably suffered greatly as a result, but the montane rainforest which it favours has not been as seriously affected (Jones *et al*. in prep., BirdLife IP). **VULNERABLE: B1+2c; C1**.

Flame-breasted Fruit-dove *Ptilinopus marchei* is a rare and local resident of primary forest from 500 to 2,500 m on Luzon in the **Philippines** (Dickinson *et al*. 1991), recent fieldwork showing it to be uncommon or rare in the Sierra Madre (except perhaps at Los Dos Cuernos, where fairly common: T. H. Fisher *per* C. R. Robson *in litt*. 1994), only above 850 m and indeed only in primary forest; habitat loss and hunting combine as threats (Danielsen *et al*. 1994, Poulsen in press). **VULNERABLE: A2b,c; B1+2c,e; C1; C2a**.

Rapa Fruit-dove *Ptilinopus huttoni* is endemic to Rapa in the Tubuai Islands, **French Polynesia**, where it is confined to less than 3 km² of remaining (fragmented) forest between 40 and 450 m, and was estimated to number 274 individuals in 1989–1990 (with no serious decline since 1974); the main threat is regression of habitat, although hunting and predation by cats and/or rats may also have an effect (Thibault and Varney 1991). **VULNERABLE: D1; D2**.

Makatea Fruit-dove *Ptilinopus chalcurus* is endemic to Makatea (28 km²) in the Tuamotu archipelago, **French Polynesia**, where, despite the destruction of half the forest cover as a result of phospate mining during the period 1917–1964, it was found to be common in all remaining wooded habitats in 1972 and 1986–1987 (Thibault and Guyot 1987) and is likely to extend its range as the vegetation recovers (R. Seitre *in litt*. 1993). The population is estimated at less than 1,000 (Toone *et al*. 1993). **VULNERABLE: D1; D2.**

Henderson Fruit-dove *Ptilinopus insularis* is confined to the interior forest of Henderson Island in the **Pitcairn Islands (to U.K.)**, a small (37 km²) uninhabited raised-reef island in the south-central Pacific Ocean whose vulnerability to human impact was exposed in 1982–1983 when a millionaire sought to make it his home (Bourne and David 1983, Fosberg *et al*. 1983, Serpell *et al*. 1983). It is a specialist frugivore (possibly territorial so that it can exploit fruits as they become available), with numbers put at c.3,420 in 1987 and, using a different technique, at c.4,000 birds in 1992 (Graves 1992, Brooke and Jones in press). **VULNERABLE: D2.**

Carunculated Fruit-dove *Ptilinopus granulifrons* is endemic to Obi, in the north Moluccas, **Indonesia**, where it is found in forest, including secondary forest, forest edge and agricultural land, but is probably confined to the lowlands below 550 m (White and Bruce 1986, Lambert in prep.). Nine were collected in a short period of time in 1982 (F. G. Rozendaal *in litt*. 1987), and in a 1992 survey it was found to be widely distributed but apparently scarce (Lambert in prep.). The single proposed protected area on Obi, Pulau Obi, only includes land at 500 m and above (FAO 1981), and the island's lowland forests are under selective logging concessions (BirdLife IP). **VULNERABLE: A2b; B1+2c; C1; C2b.**

Negros Fruit-dove *Ptilinopus arcanus*, if not based on a runt specimen of Yellow-breasted Fruit-dove *P. occipitalis*, is restricted to Negros in the **Philippines**, where it remains known from a single female collected (and a sighting of another bird) at 1,250 m on Mount Canlaon in 1953; no trace of it was found during fieldwork in 1991 (including nine days at the type-locality), and intensive (and continuing) hunting and habitat destruction may have eliminated it, especially if its usual altitude was lower, since all forest below 750 m has been cleared (Brooks *et al*. 1992). **CRITICAL: B1+2c,e; C2b; D1; D2.**

Cloven-feathered Dove *Drepanoptila holosericea* is locally distributed on **New Caledonia (to France)**, and is hunted and trapped as areas are opened up by logging or nickel-mining (King 1978–1979). The population was considered in excess of 1,000 birds in 1974 (Stokes 1980, Hannecart 1988), recently revised to more than 5,000 and declining (Toone *et al*. 1993). It inhabits dense forest, but has been found nesting in more open wooded areas and niaouli savanna (dominated by the myrtle *Melaleuca quinquenervia*), and is still common in the north, sparse in the south (c.30 individuals in the Rivière Bleue Territorial Park), with a small population on Ile des Pins (M. Boulet, F. Hannecart, Y. Létocart and S. Sirgouant *in litt*. 1993). **VULNERABLE: C2b.**

Mindoro Imperial-pigeon *Ducula mindorensis* is restricted to Mindoro in the **Philippines**, where observations in 1991 suggested that, although records stem from only two areas (Mount Halcon or Ilong in the north and Mount Hinungunang in the south), it is probably distributed throughout the island's mountains where sufficient forest remains in its altitudinal range (700–2,000 m, but apparently mostly in the lowest portions); however, it is a large, low-density species, one of a genus targeted by hunters, and logging continues to erode its habitat (Dutson *et al*. 1992). **ENDANGERED: A2b,c; B1+2c; C1; C2a; D1.**

Spotted Imperial-pigeon *Ducula carola* is endemic to the **Philippines**, where it occurs in forest and forest edge from lowlands to 2,000 m, nominate *carola* on Luzon (a flock of 23 near Angat Dam in January 1990 but nevertheless rare where once fairly common in the Sierra Madre), Mindoro (a recent report from one locality, but not found in a 1991 survey) and Sibuyan (status unknown), *nigrorum* on Negros (not found in 1991) and Siquijor (record based on a single 40-year-old specimen; not found in 1991), and *mindanensis* on Mindanao (apparently rare); habitat destruction and hunting, both continuing, are blamed for its clearly serious diminution in numbers and contraction in range (Dickinson *et al*. 1991, Brooks *et al*. 1992, Dutson *et al*. 1992, Evans *et al*. 1993b, Lambert 1993b, Danielsen *et al*. 1994, Poulsen in press; also N. J. Redman verbally 1993). **VULNERABLE: A2b,c; C1; C2a.**

Polynesian Imperial-pigeon *Ducula aurorae* is known from Tahiti (only 10 birds estimated in 1972) in the Society Islands and Makatea (c.500 in 1972) in the Tuamotu archipelago, **French Polynesia** (King 1978–1979). It remains rare on Tahiti, being restricted to Papeno'o and Hitia'a valleys in 1986–1990 (Monnet *et al*. 1993), whilst on Makatea the population appears stable, but is now judged to lie between 100–500 birds (Thibault and Guyot 1987). It apparently once inhabited Moorea and possibly certain other islands where its extinction may have been the consequence of the spread through Polynesia of the Swamp Harrier *Circus approximans* (Holyoak and Thibault 1984, Thibault 1988), although hunting and forest destruction or deterioration are also factors in its demise (Seitre and Seitre 1992). **VULNERABLE:** D1; D2.

Marquesan Imperial-pigeon *Ducula galeata*
is endemic to Nuku Hiva in the Marquesas Islands, **French Polynesia** (although there is subfossil evidence that it was once widespread in the Pacific, occurring in the Society, Cook and Pitcairn islands: Steadman 1989). It is now restricted to valleys at the western end of the island, where the population was estimated at 75–105 in 1972 (Holyoak 1975), 200–400 in 1975 (Holyoak and Thibault 1984) and 150–300 in 1993 (W. T. Everett, T. Burr and A. Varney *per* A. Lieberman verbally 1994). The grazing of cattle, pigs and goats has degraded the habitat, but the major threat is from illegal hunting (King 1978–1979, Thibault 1988, Seitre and Seitre 1991). **CRITICAL:** A2c; **B1+2e**; C1; **C2b**; D1; D2.

Christmas Island Imperial-pigeon *Ducula whartoni*
is endemic to **Christmas Island (to Australia)** (135 km²), in the Indian Ocean, where in 1887 it was considered abundant, in 1940 it was hunted to near extinction, in 1977 it was widespread and increasingly common (King 1978–1979) and today it continues to be widespread and common (R. Hill *in litt.* 1994). It inhabits forest and to some extent secondary growth dominated by the introduced cherry *Muntingia calabura* which is a good food plant, and although it has suffered from forest clearance (25% of the island for phosphate mining), most of its habitat is now included in the Christmas Island National Park (Garnett 1992). No population estimate has been made but it is unlikely to be less than 1,000 individuals, and although illegal hunting is probably the main current threat, it does not appear to be causing a decline in numbers (H. Rumpff *per* R. Hill *in litt.* 1994). **VULNERABLE:** D2.

Grey Imperial-pigeon *Ducula pickeringii*
is known from lowland forest on small islands off the coast of northern Borneo (and also recorded in coastal Borneo), in Sabah, East **Malaysia** and Kalimantan, **Indonesia**, in the Sulu archipelago and Ursula Island (off southern Palawan) in the **Philippines**, and on Miangas and Talaud, which lie to the north of Sulawesi in Indonesia; it used to be seasonally common on some islands, but the few recent records generally involve small numbers (Smythies 1981,

White and Bruce 1986, Dickinson *et al.* 1991, N. Bostock verbally 1993, Lambert 1993b; see Bishop 1992). It is threatened by loss of habitat and hunting (Toone *et al.* 1993, BirdLife IP, D. R. Wells *in litt.* 1994). **VULNERABLE:** B1+2c,d,e; C1; C2a.

Chestnut-bellied Imperial-pigeon *Ducula brenchleyi*
occurs in the forests (200–700 m: G. C. L. Dutson *in litt.* 1992) of Guadalcanal, Malaita and Makira (= San Cristobal), **Solomon Islands** (Mayr 1945). There is no estimate of population numbers although it appears rare and is shot by villagers (Lees 1991, K. D. Bishop *in litt.* 1993, D. Gibbs *in litt.* 1994, Buckingham *et al.* in prep.) and will almost certainly be affected by intense logging which has destroyed most of the lowland and some foothill forest on Guadalcanal (K. D. Bishop *in litt.* 1994); moreover, most of the remaining accessible forest on Makira has been committed for logging concessions, and the timber industry is an important part of the local economy on Malaita (Lees 1991). **ENDANGERED:** A2b; C1; C2a.

Vanuatu Imperial-pigeon *Ducula bakeri*
occurs in highland forest above 600 m on the larger islands of northern and central **Vanuatu**: Ureparapara, Vanua Lava and Santa Maria (Banks group), Espiritu Santo, Maewo, Ambae, Pentecost and Ambrym, where it is rather uncommon (Bregulla 1992) with a population estimated at less than 10,000 and declining (Toone *et al.* 1993). It is hunted (Bregulla 1992) and may suffer from loss of habitat. **VULNERABLE:** C2a.

New Caledonian Imperial-pigeon *Ducula goliath*
is restricted to the forested mountains of **New Caledonia (to France)**, where it is likely to be declining as a result of hunting (Hannecart 1988). There is a small population on the Ile des Pins and it is common in the Rivière Bleue Territorial Park; highest densities have been observed in riverine forest (M. Boulet, F. Hannecart, Y. Létocart and S. Sirgouant *in litt.* 1993). **VULNERABLE:** C2b.

Timor Imperial-pigeon *Ducula cineracea*
is endemic to Timor and Wetar, **Indonesia**, where it is found in montane forest between 1,000 and 2,200 m (White and Bruce 1986). The area of montane forest remaining on Timor is small (White and Bruce 1986), and there are records from only four localities there (BirdLife BPD), although it has recently been found to be locally common, particularly in *Eucalyptus euryphila* forest (P. Andrew *in litt.* 1987); its current status on Wetar is unknown. It is believed to be vulnerable to loss of habitat (Toone *et al.* 1993). **VULNERABLE:** B1+2c; C1; C2a.

Western Crowned-pigeon *Goura cristata* occurs on the West Papuan Islands of Misool, Waigeo, Salawati and Batanta (although islanders from this latter say that it has disappeared: D. Gibbs *in litt.* 1994), and on the Vogelkop and Onin peninsulas in north-east Irian Jaya, **Indonesia** (Beehler *et al.* 1986), and has been reported from Seram, also in Indonesia (Kitchener *et al.* 1993), where it was probably introduced (K. D. Bishop *in litt.* 1994). The three members of the New Guinea genus *Goura* are all hunted for food and plumes, although pressure is less on *cristata* as shotguns are not so readily available in Irian Jaya (Beehler 1985, J. M. Diamond *in litt.* 1987); however, it has been identified as the subject of 'significant' levels of trade (King and Nijboer 1994) and is also threatened locally by forest clearance, for example on Salawati where a new road will improve access (K. D. Bishop *in litt.* 1994, P. Gregory *in litt.* 1994). **VULNERABLE:** A1a,b,c; A2b,c; C1; C2a.

Victoria Crowned-pigeon *Goura victoria* is found in swamp forest, as well as drier forest, mainly in the lowlands but sometimes to 600 m, on Biak and Yapen islands, and in northern New Guinea (e.g. along the Rouffaer River where it is moderately common: K. D. Bishop *in litt.* 1994) from Geelvink Bay, Irian Jaya, **Indonesia**, to Milne Bay in easternmost **Papua New Guinea** (Coates 1985, Beehler *et al.* 1986). These lowland forests are high on the list for timber extraction (King and Nijboer 1994). Prized by hunters and threatened in areas accessible to man (Rand and Gilliard 1967), it is now absent from large areas of forest (Coates 1985) whilst capture for trade may also be 'significant' in its decline (King and Nijboer 1994). **VULNERABLE:** A1a,b,c; A2b,c; C1; C2a.

Southern Crowned-pigeon *Goura scheepmakeri* inhabits undisturbed alluvial forest in the lowlands to 500 m in southern Irian Jaya, **Indo**-nesia, from Etna Bay to Milne Bay in easternmost **Papua New Guinea** (Coates 1985, Beehler *et al.* 1986), these forests being high on the list for timber extraction and not protected in Papua New Guinea (King and Nijboer 1994). As a prized, large and easy target for hunters (Rand and Gilliard 1967), it has already been hunted to extinction throughout much of its range in the south-east (Schodde 1978, G. R. Kula *in litt.* 1988) and is absent from much, if not all, of southern Trans-Fly (N. Stronach *in litt.* 1994) but was observed on the lower reaches of the Fly River in 1993 (Simpson in press), whilst capture for trade may also be 'significant' throughout its range (King and Nijboer 1994). It is still locally common in the extensive lowland forests of southern Irian Jaya and along tributaries of the Fly River north of Kiunga (K. D. Bishop *in litt.* 1994) and occurs in the sparsely populated forests of Gulf Province but these latter areas are under threat from logging activities (I. Burrows *in litt.* 1994, P. Gregory *in litt.* 1994). **VULNERABLE:** A1a,b,c; A2b,c.

Tooth-billed Pigeon *Didunculus strigirostris* is restricted to Savaii and Upolu, **Western Samoa**, where it is locally distributed in forest between 300–1,400 m, but is apparently unable to adapt to areas that have been logged or replanted with exotic species (King 1978–1979, Beichle 1987; also 1982). It was avidly hunted in the past but is now fully protected, although some may still be taken in the seasonal harvest of unprotected pigeon species (D. J. Butler *in litt.* 1993). Today it is threatened by deforestation, particularly combined with the severe effects of cyclones, e.g. in 1990 and 1991, when canopy cover was reduced from 100% to 27% (Elmqvist 1993; see also Elmqvist *et al.* in press). **VULNERABLE:** C1.

Family PSITTACIDAE

PARROTS, COCKATOOS, LORIES, MACAWS

Red-and-blue Lory *Eos histrio* is known from Miangas and the Talaud and Sangihe islands, north of Sulawesi, **Indonesia** (White and Bruce 1986). Since 1978, when it was present on Sangihe, it has apparently been recorded in the wild only on Karakelong in the Talaud Islands, where it is found in small numbers in open country but more commonly in forest (F. G. Rozendaal *in litt.* 1987). The population on Karakelong has recently been estimated at less than 2,000 birds, but several hundred birds, perhaps as many as 700, were found being illegally traded in 1992 and early 1993, a level of exploitation which could soon lead to extinction in the wild (Nash 1993). It is possibly already extinct on Sangihe, where virtually all of the island has been converted to coconut and nutmeg plantations (Whitten *et al.* 1987a,b), and the other islands where is has been recorded are small and largely deforested, and could not support more than small populations (Bishop 1992, Nash 1993). **ENDANGERED: A1b,c; A2b,c; B1+2c,d,e; C1**.

Black-winged Lory *Eos cyanogenia* is known from Biak-Supiori, Numfor, Manim and Meos Num islands in Geelvink Bay, Irian Jaya, **Indonesia** (Beehler *et al.* 1986). On Biak it is generally uncommon (but sometimes in flocks of 40–60), feeding in inland forest (to 460 m) and roosting in coconut plantations and nearby coastal forest; on adjacent Supiori it was common in 1982 along the coast and inland to c.200 m, but less common at higher altitudes (Bishop 1982). Like many lories it is highly nomadic and so it is difficult to assess true numbers, but it is threatened by continuing trapping for trade and the destruction of large areas of primary lowland forest on Biak (K. D. Bishop *in litt.* 1994; see also Arndt 1992). **VULNERABLE: A1b,c; B1+2c; C1**.

Mindanao Lorikeet *Trichoglossus johnstoniae* is restricted to montane forest and forest edge (but including logged and degraded areas) above 800 m on Mindanao in the **Philippines**, where it occurs in two races, *johnstoniae* on five mountains, *pistra* on one (Dickinson *et al.* 1991); recent field observations suggest that it is very uncommon (notably on Mount Katanglad) and that forest destruction is eating into its very limited range (A. Lewis *in litt.* 1993, N. J. Redman verbally 1993, N. Bostock *in litt.* 1994, C. R. Robson *in litt.* 1994). **VULNERABLE: C1; C2a**.

Iris Lorikeet *Psitteuteles iris* is endemic to Timor and Wetar, **Indonesia**, in monsoon forest from lowlands to 1,500 m (White and Bruce 1986), apparently mainly at higher elevations (K. D. Bishop *in litt.* 1994), a habitat much reduced and fragmented in west Timor but apparently more widespread in east Timor (see RePPProT 1990). Formerly common, probably moving a good deal in search of flowering trees, it appears to have declined, as recent observers have found it scarce: it was seen at only two localities during a nine-week survey of west Timor's remnant lowland forest in 1993 (Noske and Saleh 1993), and it was not recorded on a short visit to Wetar in 1990, although extensive forest remains there (K. D. Bishop *in litt.* 1990). **VULNERABLE: C1; C2a**.

Chattering Lory *Lorius garrulus* is endemic to the north Moluccas, **Indonesia**, where it is known from Halmahera, Widi, Morotai, Rau, Bacan, Obi

and possibly Ternate (White and Bruce 1986). It is found in forest, including logged forest, but not normally in agricultural land, from the lowlands to 1,300 m; survey work carried out in 1991 and 1992 resulted in a population estimate of 46,360–295,540 birds, and it is believed that the levels of legal and illegal trade in this species at that time (a minimum of 9,600–9,927 are estimated to have been captured in 1991) were not sustainable, particularly when combined with current levels of habitat loss and degradation (Lambert 1993a). However, PHPA has recently revised its (legal) quota to the level recommended by Lambert (1993) (P. Jepson *in litt.* 1994). **VULNERABLE: A2b,c**.

Purple-naped Lory *Lorius domicella* is endemic to Seram and Ambon in the Moluccas, **Indonesia** (White and Bruce 1986), where it is uncommon in hill forest within a narrow altitudinal range from 400 to 900 m, suggesting a low overall population. It is a popular cagebird on the island and any external trade in this species would pose a serious threat to its survival (Bowler and Taylor 1989, 1993, Bishop 1992). **VULNERABLE: B1+2e; C1**.

Kuhl's Lorikeet *Vini kuhlii* is restricted to Rimatara and possibly Tubuai in the Tubuai Islands, **French Polynesia**, and to Teraina (= Washington), Tabuaeran (= Fanning) and Kiritimati (= Christmas Island), all in **Kiribati**, to which it appears to have been introduced, and formerly it may have occurred in the southern Cook Islands (Forshaw 1989, Holyoak and Thibault 1984). On Rimatara (estimated at c.905 birds) the favoured habitat is mixed horticultural woodlands, and preliminary trapping indicated an absence of rats *Rattus rattus* (McCormack and Künzle 1993), whilst on Teraina (1,000 individuals minimum) and Tabuaeran (50, perhaps less, on a single islet in the atoll), it is effectively confined to coconut plantations and is especially vulnerable to nest predation by rats and, in particular, to *Rattus rattus* which is present on Tabuaeran (Watling in press). Only a couple of individuals survive on Kiritimati (K. Teeb'ai, T. Beai and J. Bryden *per* D. Watling *in litt.* 1993). **ENDANGERED: B1+2e; C2a; D2**.

Henderson Lorikeet *Vini stepheni* is restricted to the forest on Henderson Island in the **Pitcairn Islands (to U.K.)**, a uninhabited raised-reef island (37 km[2]) in the south-central Pacific whose vulnerability to human impact was exposed in 1982–1983 when a millionaire sought to make it his home (Bourne and David 1983, Fosberg *et al.* 1983, Serpell *et al.* 1983). It is a generalist feeder utilizing a wide variety of sources including nectar, pollen, arthropod larvae and fruits, and in 1987 the total population was estimated at between 720 and 1,820 individuals, whilst in 1992 the population was estimated at c.1,200 pairs (but difficult to assess because of their mobility and patchy distribution) (Graves 1992, Trevelyan in press). **VULNERABLE: D2.**

Blue Lorikeet *Vini peruviana* is widespread but unevenly distributed (recorded from 23 islands but now extinct on many of these, most likely owing to predation by rats *Rattus rattus* and cats) in lowland coconut plantations and gardens in south-east Polynesia, including the Society Islands (**French Polynesia**: formerly all, now Motu One and Manuae only, possibly up to 250 and 300–400 pairs respectively), the northern atolls of the Tuamotu archipelago (French Polynesia: Rangiroa, Arutua and Tikehau, the latter holding 30 pairs) and Aitutaki, **Cook Islands (to New Zealand)** (where it was probably introduced, with under 500 pairs, but no evidence of a decline in the last decade, and extensive trapping in March 1994 indicating the absence of rats *Rattus rattus*: Wilson 1993, G. McCormack *in litt*. 1994), with two further atolls (Apataki and Kaukura, Tuamotu archipelago) unvisited since 1923 and several other suitable islands that remain unsurveyed (Holyoak and Thibault 1984, Pratt *et al.* 1987, Thibault 1988, Seitre and Seitre 1992). A survey of Tiamanu motu (in Apataki atoll) in 1989 revealed a minimum population of at least 300 individuals (Lovegrove *et al.* undated) and in 1993 36 birds were observed on two different locations on Rangiroa, with the possiblity that several hundred birds live there; although trade is illegal birds are still captured and sold by local people (P. Raust *in litt*. 1994). **VULNERABLE: B1+2d; C2a.**

Ultramarine Lorikeet *Vini ultramarina* occurs in all habitats with trees on Ua Pou, Nuku Hiva and Ua Huka in the Marquesas Islands, **French Polynesia**, although subfossil remains indicate it formerly had a wider distribution (Steadman 1989); on Ua Pou, although the population was estimated to be 250–300 pairs in 1975, it suffered an unexplained 60% decline in 15 years so that in 1990 it was rare from 0 to 800 m; on Nuku Hiva an estimated 70 birds were restricted to high valleys and ridges, 700–1,000 m, at the north-western end of the island in 1972–1975 although by 1990 it was possibly extinct; it was (re)introduced to Ua Huka in the 1940s (apparently involving a single captive pair: A. Lieberman verbally 1994) and the population had risen to around 200–250 pairs in the early 1970s, was still strong in 1987, with birds abundant in 1990 up to 500 m and numbering some 1,000–1,500 birds in 1991 (Holyoak and Thibault 1984, Thibault 1988, Seitre and Seitre 1991, Kuehler and Lieberman 1993).

It is likely that rats *Rattus rattus* are responsible for its decline, being present on Nuku Hiva since the beginning of the century, on Ua Pou (probably) since 1980 and introduced to a motu a few hundred metres from Ua Huka a couple of years ago, although it is not clear if they have become established on the main island too (Seitre and Seitre 1991). In 1992 and 1993 seven lories were translocated (each year) to Fatu Hiva and at least five have survived from the first group; further translocations to the island are planned (Kuehler and Lieberman 1993, A. Lieberman verbally 1994). **ENDANGERED: B1+2b,d; D2.**

Blue-fronted Lorikeet *Charmosyna toxopei* is endemic to Buru, **Indonesia**, where it is known from seven specimens collected on the west side of Lake Rana between 850 and 1,000 m in the 1920s (Siebers 1930, White and Bruce 1986). Smiet (1985) described it as quite common in plantations, secondary and primary forest around Teluk Bara in 1980, and Jepson (1993) briefly saw four small lorikeets in the same area, but Smiet's observations have been attributed to the more widespread Red-flanked Lorikeet *C. placentis* by Forshaw (1989), who believed it to occur on Buru, although this is probably erroneous (Jepson 1993; see van Bemmel 1948). The paucity of historical records suggests that *C. toxopei* is rare, nomadic or is restricted to a specific habitat, and, if it proves to be confined to lowland forest, it could be seriously threatened by deforestation (Jepson 1993). **VULNERABLE: B1+2c; C1; C2b; D1.**

New Caledonian Lorikeet *Charmosyna diadema* was described from two specimens, both females, collected in 1859, and an observation in 1913 on **New Caledonia (to France)** (Forshaw 1989). It was treated as extinct by King (1978–1979) but in 1976 islanders reported that it might still exist, and two birds were reported by an experienced bushman in forest west of Mount Panié (Stokes 1980). It might survive in the cloud-forest of Mount Panié, Mount Humboldt and the Massif of Kouakoué (Bregulla 1993). **ENDANGERED: D1.**

Red-throated Lorikeet *Charmosyna amabilis* is a rare endemic of the mature forests (usually above 500 m) on the islands of Viti Levu, Vanua Levu, Taveuni and Ovalau, **Fiji** (Watling 1982, Clunie 1984). There are no confirmed records this century except from Viti Levu where recent observations are all of small flocks (two to six birds); the cause of this apparent rarity is unknown but is possibly predation by rats *Rattus rattus* (D. Watling *in litt*. 1994). **VULNERABLE: C2a; D1.**

White-tailed Black-cockatoo *Calyptorhynchus baudinii* occurs in the temperate forests of the south-west of Western Australia, **Australia**, requiring hollows in mature eucalypts for breeding, and having a population estimated at 5,000–25,000 in 1977 (Garnett 1992). There has been no estimate since or indication of trend, but its presumed longevity may be masking insufficient recruitment, as in the past it was shot when visiting orchards and sometimes still is (as licences for shooting remain available) and it is also threatened by clear-felling, with regenerating forest providing food but no nest-sites (Garnett 1992). **VULNERABLE:** C2a.

Slender-billed Black-cockatoo *Calyptorhynchus latirostris* occurs in woodland in south-west Western Australia, **Australia**, where it nests in hollow eucalypts and often has to travel between nesting and feeding sites along corridors of native vegetation, the total population being estimated at 9,000–35,000 individuals in 1977; since then there has been a decline that is likely to continue for some decades, the main threats being clearance and fragmentation of habitat, insufficient regeneration to supply suitable nesting trees owing to introduced grazers, agriculture (which favours the Galah *Cacatua roseicapilla*), and nest-robbing for trade (Garnett 1992). **VULNERABLE:** C2a.

Glossy Black-cockatoo *Calyptorhynchus lathami* is thinly and patchily distributed in eucalypt woodland and forest with casuarinas in Queensland, New South Wales and Victoria (nominate *lathami*) and also occurs on Kangaroo Island (race *halmaturinus*, c.100 individuals), **Australia**. It has suffered from habitat loss since European settlement (further loss of habitat may occur as a result of fire or grazing by rabbits), and, although much of the remaining habitat is now conserved in a large number of national parks, the effect of habitat loss on population levels may not yet be fully evident because of the presumed longevity of the species (Garnett 1992). A third subspecies, *erebus*, has been recognized, localized on outcropping ranges and adjacent lowlands in the Dawson–Mackenzie–Isaac basin in east-central coastal Queensland (Schodde *et al.* 1993). **VULNERABLE:** C2a.

Yellow-crested Cockatoo *Cacatua sulphurea* is endemic to **Indonesia** (and introduced to Singapore and Hong Kong), where it occurs virtually throughout the Lesser Sundas, on Sulawesi and its satellite islands, and on Nusa Penida (off Bali) and the Masalembu islands (in the Java Sea), and is found in forested habitat in the lowlands to 500 m on Sulawesi and to 800 m, sometimes 1,200 m, in the Lesser Sundas (White and Bruce 1986, MacKinnon and Phillipps 1993, Jones *et al.* in prep.). It was formerly locally common throughout much of its range, but there is evidence for substantial population declines on Sulawesi, where it may already be beyond recovery (Andrew and Holmes 1990, Cahyadin and Arif 1994, D. A. Holmes *in litt.* 1994), the Lesser Sundas, where it is believed close to extinction on Sumbawa and Flores, but remains fairly common in the Komodo National Park (Butchart *et al.* 1993, D. A. Holmes *in litt.* 1994), on Sumba, where the endemic subspecies *citrinocristata* was estimated to number 2,376 birds in 1992 (based upon a density of 2.2 per km^2 ± 1.1 s.e.) and is considered to be seriously threatened (Jones *et al.* in prep.), on the Masalembu islands, where only 8–10 of the endemic subspecies *abbotti* were located in 1993 (Cahyadin and Arif 1994), and on Nusa Penida, where it was last recorded in 1986 (S. van Helvoort *per* S. van Balen 1994). The reason for this continuing decline is believed to be a combination of habitat destruction and unsustainable levels of trapping for the bird trade (Jones *et al.* in prep., BirdLife IP). **ENDANGERED:** A1b,c; A2b,c.

Salmon-crested Cockatoo *Cacatua moluccensis* is endemic to Seram and its satellite islands (Saparua, Haruku and Ambon), in the Moluccas, **Indonesia** (White and Bruce 1986). It is found in lowland forest to 1,000 m, and surveys in 1989 found that it occurs at highest densities in primary (9.1 per km^2) and disturbed primary forest (9.8 per km^2), rather lower in secondary forest (6.4 per km^2) and much lower in recently logged forest (1.9 per km^2), suggesting that large-scale logging could considerably reduce its total population, but it is unclear whether these figures reflect its specialized habitat requirements or the patterns and volume of bird capture; evidence that trade levels in this species were not sustainable and that its population was declining led to a complete ban on trade being imposed by CITES in 1989 (Marsden 1992; see Inskipp *et al.* 1988, Bowler and Taylor 1989) and the species being given protected status in Indonesia (P. Jepson *in litt.* 1994), but illegal trade could still be a threat (BirdLife IP). **VULNERABLE:** A1b,c; A2b,c; B1+2c,e.

White Cockatoo *Cacatua alba* is endemic to Halmahera, Bacan, Kasiruta and Mandiole in the north Moluccas, **Indonesia** (specimens from Bisa and Obi seem most likely to derive from captive birds, or a feral population on Bisa, now extinct), where it is found in primary and logged forest, visiting tall trees within recently cleared areas, in the lowlands to 600 m; survey work carried out in 1991 and 1992 resulted in a population estimate of

49,765–212,430 birds, and it is believed that the levels of legal and illegal trade in this species at that time (a minimum of 5,120–7,500 are estimated to have been captured in 1991) were not sustainable, particularly when combined with current levels of habitat loss and degradation (Lambert 1993a). However, PHPA has recently revised its quota to the (legal) level recommended by Lambert (1993a) (P. Jepson *in litt.* 1994). **VULNERABLE: A2b,c.**

Philippine Cockatoo *Cacatua haematuropygia* formerly occurred on all major and many minor islands (up to 45) of the **Philippines**, but visits to roughly half of these in past five years has shown that intensive trapping ('the young of every known accessible nest are taken for the pet trade': Dickinson *et al.* 1991) combined with destruction of its lowland forest habitat (amongst which mangrove may be critically important) have left very reduced and often possibly unviable numbers on as few as 10, chief among them being Palawan and its satellites, plus Tawitawi (a six-week survey in August–September 1991 yielded a population estimate for Palawan of 800–3,000 birds, of which Pandanas, Bugsuk and Bancalan probably support 100–300 and Dumaran 150–250, with Tawitawi possibly holding several hundred more: Lambert 1993b); a single pair survives on Siquijor (Evans *et al.* 1993b), a few were at Mount Isarog, Luzon, in 1988 (Goodman and Gonzales 1990), a few pairs reputedly hang on in Mindoro, chiefly at Malpalon (Dutson *et al.* 1992), birds were seen on Masbate in 1993 (Curio 1994), up to 12 survive on Bohol (T. H. Fisher *per* A. Jensen *in litt.* 1994), while a number of smaller islands, plus those such as Samar and Leyte that have been difficult to visit in recent years, may yet prove (or have been reported) to hold birds, so that the total population may lie between 1,000 and 4,000 (Lambert 1992, Tabaranza 1992). **CRITICAL: A1b,c;** C1; C2a.

New Zealand Kaka *Nestor meridionalis* occurs on North Island (race *septentrionalis*) and South and Stewart islands (nominate *meridionalis*) and on some offshore islands, **New Zealand** (Turbott 1990). Its distribution follows the larger remaining areas of low and mid-altitude native forest and its future on the mainland, and in particular on North Island, is threatened by introduced mammalian predators (e.g. stoats and rats), introduced wasps which compete for 'honey dew' (an important food source in beech *Nothofagus* forest), introduced possums which also compete for food, and by the destruction of much of its habitat; numbers are only high on islands such as Little Barrier, Codfish and Kapiti where the only introduced mammals are rats (O'Donnell and Rasch 1991). **VULNERABLE: C2a.**

Salvadori's Fig-parrot *Psittaculirostris salvadorii* occurs in northern Irian Jaya, **Indonesia**, from the Cyclops Mountains to the eastern shore of Geelvink Bay, where it affects evergreen forest from the lowlands to 400 m (Rand and Gilliard 1967, Beehler *et al.* 1986). It is locally common (Diamond 1985, K. D. Bishop *in litt.* 1994), for example in the flat lowlands west of Jayapura (D. Gibbs *in litt.* 1994), but large numbers are being trapped for the cagebird trade (K. D. Bishop *in litt.* 1987, 1994) and it is also likely to decline locally owing to extensive logging and land clearance for the increasing human population (the result of transmigration policy) (R. Burrows *in litt.* 1994), although much of its range is remote and inaccessible (P. Gregory *in litt.* 1994). **VULNERABLE: A2b,c.**

Luzon Racquet-tail *Prioniturus montanus* is restricted to Luzon in the **Philippines**, where it is still common in the Cordillera Central and Sierra Madre in primary forest above 700 m (but population estimated at below 10,000: Lambert *et al.* 1993), and the combination of habitat destruction, hunting and trapping for the cagebird trade will soon cause a major decline in numbers (Danielsen *et al.* 1994, Poulsen in press). **VULNERABLE: A2b,c; C1; C2a.**

Mindanao Racquet-tail *Prioniturus waterstradti* is restricted to forest above 1,000 m (but apparently making rapid daily vertical migrations) on Mindanao in the **Philippines**, where nominate *waterstradti* is known from four mountains and race *malindangensis* from (apparently) three; it is certainly local and uncommon, apparently occurring at lower density than some of its congeners, and must be suffering from habitat destruction (Dickinson *et al.* 1991, N. J. Redman verbally 1993, N. Bostock *in litt.* 1994, F. R. Lambert verbally 1994, C. R. Robson *in litt.* 1994). **VULNERABLE: C2a.**

Blue-headed Racquet-tail *Prioniturus platenae* occurs in lowland forest and adjacent cultivation in the Calamian Islands, Palawan and Balabac in the **Philippines** (Dickinson *et al.* 1991), where it is uncommon and declining with the rapid and extensive clearance of its habitat (N. Bostock *in litt.* 1994; also Danielsen *et al.* 1994, Poulsen in press). It is uncommon but regularly recorded in St Paul Subterranean National Park (C. R. Robson *in litt.* 1994). **VULNERABLE:** C1; C2a.

Green Racquet-tail *Prioniturus luconensis* inhabits forest edge and cultivated areas of the lowlands and foothills of Luzon and Marinduque in the **Philippines**, where as a consequence of habitat loss and trapping for the cagebird trade it has become uncommon and local (Collar and Andrew 1988, Dickinson *et al.* 1991); while there is no news on its status on Marinduque (though it must be in very low numbers), evidence from Luzon since 1988 suggests that (other than in Subic Bay Naval Forest Reserve: A. Jensen *in litt.* 1994) it is now very rare throughout, with all records in the Sierra Madre coming from 300–700 m, and none near habitation (Danielsen *et al.* 1994, Poulsen in press; also N. Bostock *in litt.* 1994). **ENDANGERED: A1b,c**; A2b,c; C1; **C2a**.

Blue-winged Racquet-tail *Prioniturus verticalis*

is endemic to the islands of Tawitawi, Bongao, Manuk Manka, Tumindao, Sanga Sanga and Sibutu in the **Philippines**, and was reportedly abundant in mangroves on Tawitawi a century ago (Dickinson *et al.* 1991). In September 1991 the species could be found only near undisturbed forest and in small numbers, habitat clearance and human use for target practice being blamed for this serious reversal (Lambert 1993b). In August 1994 Tawitawi was being rapidly cleared of its last forests, and only six racquet-tails were seen (T. M. Brooks and G. C. L. Dutson *in litt.* 1994). **ENDANGERED: A1b,c; C1; C2a**.

Blue-naped Parrot *Tanygnathus lucionensis*

formerly occurred in lowland forest up to 1,000 m throughout the **Philippines** (in the races *lucionensis* on Luzon and Mindoro, *hybridus* on Polillo, and *salvadorii* in the rest of its range, including 45 Philippine islands), the Talaud Islands, **Indonesia**, and islands off the north and east of Borneo, **Malaysia** (Dickinson *et al.* 1991). Following failure to find it on Negros and Siquijor (Evans *et al.* 1993b) and the confirmation of its extreme rarity on Mindoro (Dutson *et al.* 1992), Luzon (M. K. Poulsen verbally 1994) and elsewhere (F. R. Lambert verbally 1994, N. Bostock *in litt.* 1994) (in every case as a result of habitat loss and heavy trapping)—although it was noted on Ticao in 1993 (Curio 1994)—it may be that Palawan is its last Philippine stronghold, though even there it is uncommon and heavily targeted for the pet trade (Lambert 1993b). It was common on Salebabu, Talaud, in 1978 (White and Bruce 1986). **ENDANGERED: A1b,c**; A2b,c; C1; C2a.

Black-lored Parrot *Tanygnathus gramineus*

is endemic to Buru in the Moluccas, **Indonesia**, where it is known from forest above c.600 m but has rarely been collected, being at least partly nocturnal (like most species of *Tanygnathus*: K. D. Bishop *in litt.* 1994) and not uncommonly heard in montane forest at night, although there is only one recent record, of two birds perched in treetops in daytime in 1980 (Smiet 1985, White and Bruce 1986). It was not found during a one-month survey in 1989, perhaps

because suitable habitat was not visited at night (Jepson 1993), so its current status remains unknown, although montane forests on Buru are likely to be relatively secure (BirdLife IP). **VULNERABLE: D2**.

Pesquet's Parrot *Psittrichas fulgidus*

is patchily distributed in primary and secondary forest, mostly at 600–1,200 m, in New Guinea (Irian Jaya, **Indonesia**, and **Papua New Guinea**), needing to forage widely for fruits; it is absent from many areas owing to hunting for feathers and food, especially in Papua New Guinea (Coates 1985, Beehler *et al.* 1986, J. M. Diamond *in litt.* 1987) where skins are clearly very much in demand, being used as 'bride' price in the highlands (Schmid 1993) and being even more valuable than those of birds-of-paradise (K. D. Bishop *in litt.* 1994). It is also threatened by logging (R. Burrows *in litt.* 1994, P. Gregory *in litt.* 1994) and to a lesser degree by trapping for the bird trade (K. D. Bishop *in litt.* 1994). **VULNERABLE: A1c; A2b,c**.

Superb Parrot *Polytelis swainsonii*

occurs in loose colonies in riparian woodland in New South Wales and northern Victoria, **Australia**, and has a breeding population (apparently confined to the southern part of its range) of under 5,000 pairs. Threats include a dearth of nest-sites (hollows in the largest available trees), degradation or clearance of foraging habitat and flight paths to foraging sites, and (probably heavy) trapping (Garnett 1992). **VULNERABLE: C2b**.

Alexandra's Parrot *Polytelis alexandrae*

is a rare inhabitant of Western Australia, Northern Territory and north-western South Australia, **Australia**, where it formerly bred colonially, some evidence of a decline this century being provided by the low number of recent breeding records involving more than one pair (Blakers *et al.* 1984). The preferred habitat appears to be the sandy deserts characterized by large areas of hummock grassland, and changes to this habitat may have brought about the decline, for example, on pastoral lands where increased water availability may have favoured more water-dependent parrot taxa to its detriment (Garnett 1992). Examination of recent and historical records suggests that it may be irruptive rather than nomadic and that the core population may be resident in the area surrounding Lake Tobin, in the eastern region of Western Australia's Great Sandy Desert (Carter 1993). **VULNERABLE: B2c+3d; C2a**.

Golden-shouldered Parrot *Psephotus chrysopterygius*

was formerly found in the southern and central Cape York region, Queensland, **Australia**, but now only occupies a 120 × 225 km strip in the centre of its original range (Garnett 1992), affecting eucalypt and paperbark woodland with a grass understorey and nesting in termite mounds in water-logged drainage depressions (Blakers *et al.* 1984). It was heavily trapped in the 1950s and 1960s (Wheeler 1975) and trapping may still continue on a small scale, with other possible threats including the destruction of seeding grasses during breeding as result of grazing and burning, predation by feral cats and disturbance of nests by tourists; there are no population estimates, but it is only found in small numbers (Garnett 1992; see also *Antbird* nos. 1,2,3). **ENDANGERED: B1+2e; C2b.**

Antipodes Parakeet *Cyanoramphus unicolor* is
endemic to the uninhabited and protected islands of the Antipodes, **New Zealand**, where in 1978 it was common on the main island (20 km²) and Bollons Island (50 ha) and occurred in smaller numbers on Leeward (10 ha), Inner Windward (8 ha) and Archway (6 ha) islets, with an estimated total of 2,000–3,000 birds (Williams and Given 1981). It nests in burrows among tall dense tussocks or sedges (Taylor 1985), and is threatened by accidental introductions which once seemed unlikely because of its isolated location, but are now a possibility owing to increased fishing in the Southern Ocean (B. D. Bell *in litt.* 1987). **VULNERABLE: D2.**

Norfolk Island Parakeet *Cyanoramphus cookii*
is endemic to **Norfolk Island (to Australia)** where it lives in forest and visits nearby orchards, having suffered from hunting in the past and from habitat destruction, although the main modern threat comes from predation by introduced black rats *Rattus rattus* and from competition for nest-sites by introduced Crimson Rosellas *Platycercus elegans*, European Starlings *Sturnus vulgaris* and feral honey bees *Apis mellifera*. In 1991 the species numbered 40 individuals and was showing some signs of recovery after many years of active management (Garnett 1992). **CRITICAL: D1; D2.**

Horned Parakeet *Eunymphicus cornutus* is en-
demic to the forests of **New Caledonia (to France)**, with two races, nominate *cornutus* on the mainland, and *uvaeensis* confined to Uvea (15–25 km² of habitat remaining: Bregulla 1993) in the Loyalty Islands (Forshaw 1989). It has suffered from habitat destruction and capture for the cagebird trade, with *cornutus* declining since 1882, when it was reported from all forested areas, to fairly common in more inaccessible areas above 470 m in the 1940s, to relatively frequent in suitable habitat in the 1960s and 1970s (Bregulla 1993), with a population estimated at 2,000–10,000 (possibly stable) (Lambert *et al.* 1993; also M. Boulet, F. Hannecart, Y. Létocart and

S. Sirgouant *in litt.* 1993). Numbers of *uvaeensis* were estimated at 70–90 birds and declining (Hahn 1993), but a survey in December 1993 indicated a much larger population, in both the north (the stronghold) and the south where the species was thought to have disappeared; earlier attempts to release wild-caught stock on nearby Lifu island (to establish a second population) have failed (O. Robinet *in litt.* 1994, Robinet *et al.* in press). **VULNERABLE: C1.**

Orange-bellied Parrot *Neophema chrysogaster*
breeds in tree hollows in the forested margins of the coastal plains and feeds on sedgelands in the World Heritage Area of south-western Tasmania, **Australia**, and migrates across the islands in the west of the Bass Strait to the southern coast of the Australian mainland in the winter, mostly to the shores of Port Philip Bay in Victoria, where it feeds on saltmarshes and coastal dunes. In the nineteenth century there were supposedly flocks of thousands, but in 1981 the population was estimated at 150 individuals with no evidence of a marked decrease in numbers in the wintering range in the period 1978–1990, continuing threats including loss of favoured feeding habitat in Port Philip Bay, competition from introduced herbivores, and lack of safety in numbers for a small bird attractive to avian predators (Garnett 1992). **ENDANGERED: D1.**

Scarlet-chested Parrot *Neophema splendida*
occurs in mallee and acacia shrublands of southern semi-arid inland **Australia**, where under suitable conditions it apparently breeds rapidly and becomes common (a flock of 240+ was recorded recently in the Great Victoria Desert: Andrew and Palliser 1993), only to disperse and decline until the next favourable season (Blakers *et al.* 1984). There are no data to show a continuing decline, although some threatening process may be having an effect (K. Fitzherbert *in litt.* 1994), such as altered fire regimes and increased availablility of water in pastoral lands (which may have favoured competitors); however, trapping is now unlikely to be a major problem as the species is kept in large numbers and breeds readily (Garnett 1992). **VULNERABLE: B2c+3d.**

Swift Parrot *Lathamus discolor* breeds in north-
ern and eastern Tasmania (where it inhabits eucalypt forests, especially those with blue gum *Eucalyptus globulus*, breeding in mature and senescent trees) and winters in south-east mainland **Australia** (where it occurs in remnant forest patches within agricultural land and suburbs). A survey in 1988/1989 estimated a population of 1,320 breeding pairs with an end-of-breeding-season population in excess of 5,000 individuals, but eucalypt forest has been extensively

cleared for agriculture and timber throughout its range and some birds continue to be trapped for trade (Garnett 1992). **VULNERABLE:** B1+2c; C2b.

Night Parrot *Geopsittacus occidentalis*, thought to be nomadic, may feed almost exclusively on spinifex within samphire flats and associated lake systems in arid central **Australia** from central Western Australia to south-west Queensland, western New South Wales and north-west Victoria. It was presumably more abundant in the 1870s, when 16 specimens were collected in the Lake Eyre region, compared to a total of six reliable records between 1935 and 1984 in the whole of Australia (Blakers *et al.* 1984). During the last decade there have been 15 sight records though none has been authenticated (and a corpse was found in 1990: Boles *et al.* 1994); habitat degradation (as a result of altered fire regimes and grazing by domestic stock and feral animals), predation by cats and foxes, and reduction of available water by introduced camels may all be causes of decline (Garnett 1992). Several independent reports in an area of c.200 km^2 near Cloncurry suggest that it may indeed be nocturnal, relying principally on seed (Garnett *et al.* 1993). **CRITICAL: C2a**; D1.

Kakapo *Strigops habroptilus*, the largest parrot in the world (weighing up to 3.6 kg), formerly occurred at all altitudes throughout forest and scrubland of North, South and Stewart Islands, **New Zealand**, but its range had shrunk considerably before European settlement, although it remained abundant in the south and west of South Island until c.1900 (Robertson 1985). Thereafter the remaining populations in Fiordland and Stewart Island suffered further decline, and it became extinct on South Island by 1989 (Clout and Craig in press). From 1987 to 1992 all 37 Kakapo known to remain on Stewart Island were translocated to the predator-free islands of Codfish, Maud and Mana (the translocation subsequently failed on Mana), some birds having already been transferred to Little Barrier Island, and it is thus extinct throughout its natural range (D. V. Merton *in litt.* 1994). This flightless, lekking, nocturnal parrot is especially vulnerable to predation by mammalian carnivores, particularly during breeding, and has a slow and often erratic reproductive rate (Merton *et al.* 1984), e.g. twice in 10 years on Stewart Island after prolific autumn mast-fruiting of podocarps; supplementary feeding has induced breeding in four out of five years on Little Barrier Island with the first successfully reared chicks in a decade in 1991, so that in March 1994 the total population was 47 birds (but nine missing birds) including 17 females, only eight of which are proven breeders (D. V. Merton *in litt.* 1994, Clout and Craig in press; see also Lloyd

and Powlesland 1994, Powlesland and Lloyd 1994). **EXTINCT IN THE WILD.**

Black-cheeked Lovebird *Agapornis nigrigenis* seems never to have recovered from heavy exploitation for the cagebird trade in the 1920s. It occupies a range of c.6,000 km^2 (not merely 10 km^2, contra Them 1989) in *Colophospermum mopane* and adjacent *Baikiaea plurijuga* woodland in southern **Zambia** (extending in tiny numbers into the Kafue National Park on the northern fringe of its range: D. R. Aspinwall *in litt.* 1994), having once also occurred in northern Zimbabwe (perhaps only as a vagrant: M. P. S. Irwin *in litt.* 1994) and Namibia's Caprivi Strip (Collar and Stuart 1985, D. Rockingham-Gill *in litt.* 1987). Possible modern threats are agricultural encroachment and illegal hunting (Them 1989), perhaps also disease transmissible from captive birds (see Kock 1989). **ENDANGERED:** B1+2c; **C2b**; D1.

Sangihe Hanging-parrot *Loriculus catamene* is only known from Sangihe Island, north of Sulawesi, **Indonesia** (White and Bruce 1986), where the original vegetation has been almost completely replaced by coconut and nutmeg plantations, and the secondary vegetation of abandoned gardens (Whitten *et al.* 1987a,b). In the mid-1980s, it was found to be not uncommon outside forest and was regularly observed in coconut groves (F. G. Rozendaal *in litt.* 1987), and at least two pairs were observed on steep, tree-cropped, volcanic slopes in 1986, but further investigation is required to determine whether is can survive in purely secondary habitats (Bishop 1992). **ENDANGERED:** B1+2c; **C1**; **C2b**; D1; D2.

Wallace's Hanging-parrot *Loriculus flosculus* is endemic to Flores in the Lesser Sundas, **Indonesia** (White and Bruce 1986), where it was historically known from just one documented locality (Schmutz 1977, Forshaw 1989). Surveys in 1993 found it to be locally common in primary semi-evergreen rainforest between 450 and 1,000 m (most sightings in fruiting fig trees between 850 and 1,000 m) in the Tanjung Kerita Mese proposed protected area, near Paku, west Flores, and it was also seen at 1,000 m on Gunung Egon in east Flores in 1987; little evergreen forest below 1,000 m is included within the gazetted protected areas on Flores (BirdLife IP), so this species is vulnerable to habitat destruction (Butchart *et al.* 1993). **VULNERABLE:** B1+2c; **C1**; C2a.

Mauritius Parakeet *Psittacula eques*, having long since become extinct in the nominate form on Réunion (to France), and having experienced massive habitat loss compounded by several likely but unproven pressures (competition from introduced birds, nest predation by monkeys, hunting, cyclones), survives in the race *echo* in very low numbers in the forested upland regions of south-west **Mauritius**, where from the 1970s to the mid-1980s the 10 or so known birds appeared to suffer almost total breeding failure (Collar and Stuart 1985, Jones 1987). However, breeding subsequently began to be successful (see Young 1987), and 16–22 birds (including five pairs, three of which bred but without success) were present, 1993–1994, and an additional pair in captivity produced one young in 1993 (Jones and Duffy 1993, C. G. Jones *in litt.* 1994, R. J. Safford *in litt.* 1994). **CRITICAL: D1.**

Intermediate Parakeet *Psittacula intermedia* is known by seven skins of unknown origin (Ali and Ripley 1987) and small numbers of live specimens, reputed to have come from the plains of Uttar Pradesh, which have recently appeared in bird markets in **India** (Sane *et al.* 1986). It has been suggested that it may be of hybrid origin (Husain 1959), but this is disputed (Walters 1985). Its habitat requirements, status and any threats are unknown, although it is presumably rare. **VULNERABLE: D1.**

Hyacinth Macaw *Anodorhynchus hyacinthinus*, with a naturally very low reproductive rate and long generation time, has been seriously reduced by massive, illegal trade to an estimated 3,000 birds divided unequally between three main areas of **Brazil** (although the western boundary of its distribution is still poorly understood, with recent records from as far west as Alta Floresta in Mato Grosso, and with the possibility of populations near Manaus and in Amapá): (1) east Amazon (only reliably or recently in Pará), where it lives in várzeas and savannas adjacent to tropical forest, (2) the 'Gerais' of the north-east (Maranhão, Piauí, Bahia, Tocantins, Goiás, Mato Grosso, Minas Gerais), where it is a bird of cerrado and palm stands, and (3) the pantanals of Mato Grosso and Mato Grosso do Sul (and marginally western **Bolivia** in Santa Cruz, and north-east **Paraguay**) (Collar *et al.* 1992). In all areas it exploits hard palm fruits, and nests in tree-holes or, in the Gerais, cliffs, but the destruction of nest-trees during clearance for pastures, general habitat loss in eastern Amazonia, and local hunting for food and feathers, compound the impact of trapping (Collar *et al.* 1992; also D. B. Trent and A. Whittaker *in litt.* 1993). **VULNERABLE:** A1b,c; A2b,c.

Lear's Macaw *Anodorhynchus leari* (having been known to science for a century and a half without any clear idea of where it lived) numbered only some 60 birds (not all mature) in the wild by the time it was finally traced in 1978 to two cliff-nesting

colonies (with very low rates of productivity) in the Raso da Catarina in north-eastern Bahia, **Brazil**, an area of some 8,000 km² in which, without considerable intervention, it faces extinction in the fairly near term from the destruction and disturbance of its feeding habitat (licuri palm stands), compounded by hunting for food and for trade (Collar *et al.* 1992). In the early 1990s two more tiny populations (14 and three birds respectively) were discovered in adjacent parts of Bahia (M. Da-Ré verbally 1993), and since 1991 an environmental education programme has started to address the problems of illegal shooting and clearance of licuri palms (C. A. R. Carvalho verbally 1994). **CRITICAL:** A2b; B1+2c; C1; C2b; **D1.**

Spix's Macaw *Cyanopsitta spixii*, known for over a century and a half from small numbers of traded birds from somewhere in the interior of **Brazil**, was traced in the 1980s to some remnant caraiba gallery woodland adjoining the Rio São Francisco in northern Bahia, when, however, only three birds remained and these were all believed captured for illegal trade in 1987 and 1988, although a single bird, now well publicized and guarded, was discovered at the site in July 1990 (Collar *et al.* 1992). The species might be heavily dependent on caraiba woodland for nest-sites, so that its long-term rarity could be attributed to the long-since loss of most such habitat, although the illegal bird trade since around 1970 is certainly responsible for its current proximity to extinction (Collar *et al.* 1992). The total of publicly acknowledged birds in captivity (now under the overall control of the Brazilian government's Permanent Committee for the Recovery of Spix's Macaw) was 31 in September 1994, although at least 21 of these are captive-bred and the degree of relatedness between all the birds is unknown. The single wild bird was still present in September 1994 and the release of a captive bird to partner it is planned for late 1994 (M. I. Bampi verbally 1994). **CRITICAL: D1**; D2.

Blue-throated Macaw *Ara glaucogularis* is currently known only from a small mosaic area of seasonally inundated savanna, palm groves and low-stature forest in Beni, northern **Bolivia**, where it is exploited for the cage-bird trade. It appears to be rare (possibly less than 1,000 birds in total) within its range (two other sites have, however, been reported) and seems to require the presence of the (locally abundant) palm *Attalea phalerata* (Collar *et al.* 1992, Jordan and Munn 1993, Munn and Munn 1993). **ENDANGERED:** C2b; D1.

Military Macaw *Ara militaris* occupies a massive but now extremely fragmented range extending from **Mexico** south through eastern **Honduras**, **Nicara-**

gua, **Costa Rica**, **Panama**, north-west and possibly south-west **Colombia**, western and eastern **Ecuador**, northern **Venezuela**, north-west and eastern **Peru**, northern and south-east **Bolivia** and north-west **Argentina**, in humid lowland forest and adjacent cleared areas, wooded foothills, slopes and canyons to 1,500 m, its nomadic habits apparently associated with the fruiting of *Dipteryx* (Ridgely 1981, Forshaw 1989). It has become very local, with many and perhaps the great majority of its populations under threat of extinction in the near future, owing to habitat loss and trade (R. S. Ridgely *in litt.* 1994, R. Wirth verbally 1994). **VULNERABLE:** A1b; C2a.

Red-fronted Macaw *Ara rubrogenys* inhabits

fairly arid scrubby intermontane valleys (narrow gorges and wide floodplains, generally at 1,100–2,500 m) in south-central **Bolivia** (Santa Cruz, Cochabamba, Chuquisaca), where it numbers only a few thousand individuals (possibly only a thousand) and has suffered from capture for the cagebird trade, from persecution as a pest in peanut and maize fields, and from loss of trees within its habitat, these two latter factors continuing to affect the species (Collar *et al.* 1992). **ENDANGERED: C2a**; D1.

Blue-winged Macaw *Ara maracana* formerly

occupied a huge range in central-eastern South America, in **Brazil** (Pernambuco, Piauí, Maranhão, Pará, Tocantins, Goiás, Mato Grosso, Mato Grosso do Sul, Minas Gerais, Bahia, Espírito Santo, Rio de Janeiro, São Paulo, Paraná, Santa Catarina, Rio Grande do Sul), eastern **Paraguay** and northern **Argentina** (Misiones), inhabiting gallery forest and forest edge, but has undergone an exceptionally steep decline, only partly explicable through loss of habitat (Ridgely 1981, Forshaw 1989, Olmos 1993). It is recolonizing one area in Rio de Janeiro state, and may be commoner there than anywhere else in its range (J. F. Pacheco *per* B. M. Whitney *in litt.* 1994) other than in its last strongholds, the Serra Negra in Pernambuco and the Serra do Cachimbo in southern Pará (C. Yamashita verbally 1994). **VULNERABLE:** A1a,b; C1; C2a.

Golden Parakeet *Guaruba guarouba*, a highly

distinctive parrot endemic to the Amazon basin of **Brazil**, occurs in northern Maranhão (five localities, four of them close to or within the Gurupi Biological Reserve) and Pará (many localities all north of 5°S), with a single recent record from Rondônia, and suffers from both the destruction of its (almost exclusively terra firme) rainforest habitat and the depredations of trappers (being a much desired aviary bird, both internationally and nationally) and hunters; ts conservation is rendered problematic by its apparent nomadism, birds seeming to wander widely and not predictably found in one area at any given season (Collar *et al.* 1992). **ENDANGERED:** A2b,c; C1; **C2b**.

Socorro Parakeet *Aratinga brevipes* occupies

forest chiefly above 500 m on Socorro in the Revillagigedo Islands, **Mexico**, where in 1991 its population was estimated to be 400–500 birds; although numbers appear to be stable, the range may have contracted over the past 30 years and there may be some risk from erosion of habitat through sheep grazing, and the possibility of predation by cats (Collar *et al.* 1992). **VULNERABLE:** D1.

Cuban Parakeet *Aratinga euops* has become a

rare bird throughout **Cuba** (and extinct on the Isle of Pines, where it was once abundant) owing to excessive trapping and the loss of its semi-deciduous woodland and palm savanna habitat, such that it now appears to survive in only a few more remote regions of the country, notably the Península de Zapata and the Cuchillas del Toa (Collar *et al.* 1992). **VULNERABLE:** A1b,c; B1+2c; C1; C2a.

Hispaniolan Parakeet *Aratinga chloroptera* is

endemic to the forests of Hispaniola (**Haiti** and the **Dominican Republic**), with an extinct race *maugei* from Isla Mona, Puerto Rico (to U.S.A.) (Forshaw 1989). It is generally rare throughout its range with populations very small except for one area, the Sierra de Baoruco in the Dominican Republic, where it remains reasonably common, having elsewhere suffered a serious decline from habitat loss, persecution as a crop pest, use as a house pet, and even for international trade (Forshaw 1989, F. J. Vilella verbally 1994). **VULNERABLE:** C2a.

Golden-capped Parakeet *Aratinga auricapilla*

occupies a wide range in central-eastern **Brazil** (Bahia, Goiás, Minas Gerais, Espírito Santo, Rio de Janeiro, São Paulo, Paraná), with one citation from adjacent Paraguay, and depends on semi-deciduous forest although it is capable of foraging in adjacent more open areas. It has become extinct in many regions and extremely local in others, owing to the extensive clearance and fragmentation of its habitat and, perhaps, the impact of national trade levels (Collar *et al.* 1992). **VULNERABLE:** A1a,b; C1; C2a.

Golden-plumed Parakeet *Leptosittaca*

branickii is found very locally (but with records from many areas) in temperate Andean forests and orchards (2,400–3,400 m) in **Colombia** (Nevado del Ruiz–Nevado del Tolima region in Tolima, Risaralda, Quindío and Caldas; Volcán Puracé region in Cauca;

also Nariño), **Ecuador** (Imbabura, Azuay, El Oro, Morona-Santiago, Loja) and **Peru** (Cajamarca, Amazonas, San Martín, La Libertad, Huánuco, Pasco, Junín, Cuzco), in the first two of which it has suffered from very considerable habitat loss. Its nomadism, which may be related to a heavy dependence on *Podocarpus* cones, renders it highly problematic to conserve, and make the assessment of population levels very difficult, total numbers being possibly in the thousands (Collar *et al.* 1992, Salaman and Gandy 1993). **VULNERABLE:** A1b; A2b; C1; C2a.

Yellow-eared Parrot *Ognorhynchus icterotis*, although formerly found at scattered localities in all three ranges of **Colombia** (Norte de Santander, Antioquia, Caldas, Cundinamarca, Tolima, Cauca, Huila, Nariño) and in north-west **Ecuador** (Imbabura, Pichincha, Cotopaxi, possibly Carchi), when it was in places common or even abundant, is now so rare as to be on the point of extinction owing to the widespread loss of its wax palm *Ceroxylon* habitat (1,200–3,400 m, but mostly 2,000–3,000 m), with recent records from only a few localities in the southern half of the West Andes, the Central Andes of Tolima, and at the head of the Magdalena valley in Colombia and in Cotopaxi in Ecuador (Collar *et al.* 1992). Reports of several large flocks in Los Nevados National Park, Colombia (Salaman and Gandy 1994), refer to Rufous-fronted Parakeet *Bolborhynchus ferrugineifrons* (D. Gandy verbally 1994); however, there is a reliable report of a tiny colony elsewhere which could be at great risk from trappers (M. G. Kelsey verbally 1994). **CRITICAL:** A1b; C1; **C2a**; D1.

Thick-billed Parrot *Rhynchopsitta pachyrhyncha* formerly ranged into and probably bred in the **U.S.A.**, and has done so recently owing to a major and ingenious reintroduction project, but is basically endemic to the pine forests of the Sierra Madre Occidental in **Mexico** (chiefly north-east Sonora, western Chihuahua and south and west Durango, 1,200–3,600 m, but mostly 2,000–3,000 m), where extensive deforestation has occurred throughout its range (affecting not only its foraging options but also, through the selective clearance of old trees, nest-site availability); because it is nomadic in response to variations in cone abundance (which makes numbers very hard to assess), it requires the preservation of substantial areas of pine in different but adjacent parts of its range if it is to be secure (Collar *et al.* 1992). Fieldwork in 1994 in southern Chihuahua discovered extensive penetration and degradation of habitat by drug-growers, logging operations and huge numbers of cattle, with only two birds seen (N. F. R. Snyder verbally 1994). **ENDANGERED:** A1b; **A2b**; **C1**; **C2a**.

Maroon-fronted Parrot *Rhynchopsitta terrisi*, with a population not known with certainty to exceed 2,000, a range of 18,000 km^2 and habitat within it (mature pine forest generally between 2,000 and 3,500 m) covering no more than 7,000 km^2, risks gradual decline through forest destruction (although it nests colonially in cliffs) in both the north and south of its limited range (seasonal migrations or else relatively predictable nomadic movements between the two occur) in the Sierra Madre Oriental in Nuevo León, Coahuila and Tamaulipas, **Mexico** (Collar *et al.* 1992). **VULNERABLE:** B1+2c; C2a.

Blue-chested Parakeet *Pyrrhura cruentata* survives in scattered Atlantic Forest fragments in southern Bahia, Minas Gerais, Espírito Santo and Rio de Janeiro, **Brazil**, and, although sometimes fairly common where it occurs, its ability to move between these fragments (often hundreds of kilometres apart) is probably negligible. It thus faces extinction both from the continuing clearance of its lowland habitat and from less obvious factors that may impinge on populations confined to particular sites (Collar *et al.* 1992, N.J.C.). **VULNERABLE:** A1b; B1+2c; C2a.

Santa Marta Parakeet *Pyrrhura viridicata* is endemic to the Sierra Nevada de Santa Marta, **Colombia**, where it was recently judged relatively common and, because within a protected area, relatively secure (Ridgely 1981, Hilty and Brown 1986, Forshaw 1989). However, it is now clear that destruction of its humid montane forest habitat has been extensive (for marijuana growth, then by herbicides targeting the marijuana), so that only some 15% of the mountain's original habitat remains, mostly on the northern slopes (though being cleared even there) (L. M. Renjifo *in litt.* 1993, L. G. Olarte *in litt.* 1993). The species' altitudinal range, including seasonal movements, lies between 1,800 and 2,800 m, within which only some 200 km^2 of habitat remains, and certainly no more than 5,000 birds can now survive (T. Arndt *in litt.* 1993). **VULNERABLE:** C1; C2b.

El Oro Parakeet *Pyrrhura orcesi* is restricted to very humid upper tropical forest on the west slope of the Andes in Azuay and El Oro provinces, southwest **Ecuador**, where it occurs at altitudes between 300 and 1,300 m, with a population estimated roughly at 2,000–20,000 birds. It is threatened by continuing habitat clearance for cattle production (Collar *et al.* 1992, Best *et al.* 1993). **VULNERABLE:** B1+2c; C2a.

White-necked Parakeet *Pyrrhura albipectus* is confined to upper tropical rainforest in three small areas of south-eastern **Ecuador** (Podocarpus National Park, Cordillera de Cutucú and Cordillera del Condor, from 900 to 2,000 m), where its numbers appear to be fairly low (total population possibly a few thousand individuals) and where habitat destruction (in all three areas) is either beginning to have an effect or is predicted soon to occur (Collar *et al.* 1992, Toyne *et al.* 1992, Krabbe and Sornoza 1994). There are recent records from as far south as Panguri in Zamora-Chinchipe, and it now appears likely to be found in adjacent Peru, so this species may yet prove reasonably secure (R. S. Ridgely *in litt.* 1994). **VULNERABLE: C2a.**

Flame-winged Parakeet *Pyrrhura calliptera* occupies upper subtropical and temperate forest (1,850–3,000 m), elfin woodland and second growth (3,000–3,400 m) and adjacent areas of páramo and subpáramo in the East Andes of **Colombia**, where it is confined to the east slope in both Boyacá and Cundinamarca, having at least formerly also occurred in the latter on the west slope; forest destruction has been extensive within its restricted range and, although still locally numerous, it continues to decline rapidly and now survives in highly fragmented populations (Collar *et al.* 1992). **VULNERABLE: A1b; A2b; C1; C2a.**

Rufous-fronted Parakeet *Bolborhynchus ferrugineifrons* is restricted to the Central Andes of **Colombia**, being recorded from only two areas (Nevado del Ruiz–Nevado del Tolima region in Tolima, Risaralda, Quindío and Caldas; Volcán Puracé region in Cauca), but is probably present at low density in the intervening areas, occurring at 3,200–4,000 m in shrublands and agricultural areas of the temperate forest–páramo ecotone. The total population has been put at 1,000–2,000 individuals, although continuing habitat degradation (caused by firewood-gathering, grazing, burning and potato cultivation) is such that the true figure may be lower (Collar *et al.* 1992). In September 1993 the species was found to be common (over 100 birds seen in eight hours) at El Bosque (Laguna de Otún) in Los Nevados National Park, its last stronghold (Salaman and Gandy 1993). **ENDANGERED: B1+2c; C2a; D1.**

Yellow-faced Parrotlet *Forpus xanthops* occurs in the arid woodland, riparian thickets and desert scrub of the upper Marañón valley at 600–1,700 m in three departments (southern Amazonas, Cajamarca and extreme eastern La Libertad) in north-central **Peru**, where it has recently declined seriously owing to trapping for trade within the country and the apparent deterioration of its habitat in response to cultivation and the impact of goats (Collar *et al.* 1992). **VULNERABLE: A1a,c; B1+2c,e; C1; C2a.**

Brown-backed Parrotlet *Touit melanonota* is very poorly known (but small and inconspicuous), recorded this century from Rio de Janeiro state and three sites in São Paulo, **Brazil** (last century also Bahia). It inhabits humid forest, chiefly in hills (500–1,000 m), but descends to lower levels (perhaps seasonally), and appears to be a victim of widespread habitat loss and fragmentation, many recent records coming from protected areas (Collar *et al.* 1992). **ENDANGERED: C2a; D1.**

Golden-tailed Parrotlet *Touit surda* has been recorded from four states in north-eastern **Brazil** (Ceará, Paraíba, Pernambuco and Alagoas) and from four in the south-east, Bahia, Espírito Santo, Rio de Janeiro and São Paulo, the majority of records being from humid lowland forest areas (some up to 800 m in foothills). It appears to be migratory in some degree, and has evidently suffered from the massive habitat destruction that has occurred over centuries (and continues) within its range, many recent records being from protected areas (Collar *et al.* 1992). **ENDANGERED: C2a.**

Spot-winged Parrotlet *Touit stictoptera* has been found in six general areas extending through **Colombia** (Cundinamarca, Meta, Cauca), **Ecuador** (Napo, Morona-Santiago, Zamora-Chinchipe) and northern **Peru** (Cajamarca, San Martín). It may be partly overlooked and more widespread, but as an inhabitant of the upper tropical and lower subtropical zone (using tall humid montane forest at 500–2,300 m, though mostly 1,050–1,700 m) it is threatened by deforestation, at present mostly so in Colombia (Collar *et al.* 1992). **VULNERABLE: C2a.**

Rusty-faced Parrot *Hapalopsittaca amazonina* occurs in three races in the Andes of **Venezuela** (Mérida, Táchira) and **Colombia** (Norte de Santander, Santander, Cundinamarca, Caldas, and possibly Cauca and Huila); all races occupy humid upper montane forest and scrub at 2,200 to 3,000 m, appear to be very local throughout their ranges (having declined seriously and being very rare at most localities), and are threatened by continuing and projected habitat destruction (Collar *et al.* 1992). **ENDANGERED: A1b; A2b; B1+2c,d; C1.**

Fuertes's Parrot *Hapalopsittaca fuertesi* is known only from humid temperate forest on the west slope of the Central Andes of **Colombia** near the border of Quindío, Risaralda and Tolima departments, where it is now extremely rare, following the destruction of most of its habitat over the course of this and previous centuries. The only definite records since its discovery in 1911 are at Alto Quindío (where there are no immediate threats) from 1989 to the present (2,610–3,490 m, though mostly 2,900–3,150 m), the largest group observed consisting of 25 birds and the total population being very small (Collar *et al.* 1992). **CRITICAL: D1**; D2.

Red-faced Parrot *Hapalopsittaca pyrrhops* is confined to very wet upper montane cloud-forest and low, open forest and shrubbier growth near the páramos on the east Andean slopes at 2,500–3,500 m in the southern half of **Ecuador** (Morona-Santiago, Azuay, Loja) and immediately adjacent **Peru** (Piura). It is local and uncommon (all but two observations consisting of five birds or fewer), has declined seriously in response to habitat destruction, and faces further losses as forest is cleared in Ecuador's Chilla Mountains, where the species has been found most numerous (Collar *et al.* 1992; also Toyne *et al.* in prep.). **ENDANGERED: A1b; A2b; B1+2c; C1; C2a; D1**.

Black-billed Amazon *Amazona agilis* is endemic to **Jamaica**, being confined to wet mid-level limestone forests, including the John Crow Mountains, where it suffers from clearance of (and sometimes hurricane damage to) its habitat, poaching for food and trapping for local trade (Downer and Sutton 1990, Varty 1991). **VULNERABLE: C2a**.

Puerto Rican Amazon *Amazona vittata*, endemic to **Puerto Rico (to U.S.A.)**, suffered from the almost total loss of its forest habitat and the crippling effects of being taken for pets and food, so that by the 1930s its population of c.2,000 was confined to rainforest in the Luquillo Mountains, where it endured a long decline only halted through major intervention beginning in 1968 and involving experiments with artificial nest-sites, control of nest predators and competitors, and captive breeding; recovery since the all-time low of 13 birds in 1975 has been steady except for the impact of Hurricane Hugo in September 1989, and by the beginning of 1992 there were a minimum 22–23 in the wild and 58 in captivity, with a record fledging success in July 1992 taking the wild total up to 39–40 (Collar *et al.* 1992). By September 1993 the wild population stood at 41 birds and the captive stock was achieving new levels of nesting success (Vilella and Arnizaut 1994), although future hurricanes may adversely affect nest-site availability (Meyers 1994). By June 1994 10 birds had fledged and four were about to do so, indicating another successful year (F. J. Vilella verbally 1994). **CRITICAL: D1**; D2.

Red-spectacled Amazon *Amazona pretrei* has a small range in south-east **Brazil**, virtually endemic to Rio Grande do Sul, the more southerly birds (which

breed in lowland riverine forests among hills) migrating to the north of the state, with tiny numbers once occurring in neighbouring Misiones province, north-east **Argentina**, and recent confirmation (one bird, probably a vagrant, in the private Itabó Reserve, August 1992: Brooks *et al.* 1993) for eastern Paraguay; formerly abundant, it is partially dependent on *Araucaria* forest as a food source and roosting cover for much of the year, and its decline (although its apparent nomadism prevents a clear assessment of its status) is related to the destruction and fragmentation of these and other forests, compounded by trade at the national level (Collar *et al.* 1992). Recent counts at roosting sites estimate the wild population to number 7,500–8,500 birds (Varty *et al.* 1994). **ENDANGERED: A1b,c; A2b,c; C1**.

Green-cheeked Amazon *Amazona viridigenalis* is confined to tropical evergreen gallery forest, deciduous woodland on slopes and in canyons, partially cleared areas with woodlots, and dry open pine–oak ridges up to 1,200 m in north-east **Mexico** (Nuevo León, Tamaulipas, San Luis Potosí, Veracruz), where it has been vastly overexploited for trade and suffered from extensive habitat loss (both factors continuing), so that it has gone from being a common and widespread species a few decades ago to a generally rare bird today (Collar *et al.* 1992). The current wild population is judged to be 3,000–6,500 birds, and illegal trade continues, with no adequate protection of its habitat (E. C. Enkerlin *in litt.* 1994). **ENDANGERED: A1a,b,c; A2b,c; C1; C2a**.

Red-browed Amazon *Amazona rhodocorytha* is now rare and local in isolated patches of primary Atlantic forest (primarily humid lowlands but also interior highlands to 1,000 m) in eastern **Brazil** (Alagoas, Bahia, Minas Gerais, Espírito Santo and Rio de Janeiro, with a recently discovered resident population of around eight pairs at Pisinguaba State Park, São Paulo: P. Martuscelli verbally 1994) owing to chronic but continuing habitat destruction compounded by exploitation for trade and, possibly, by the species' apparent seasonal displacements, which (if confirmed) would multiply the problems of habitat loss. Its presence in eight protected areas (a further addition is Bocaina National Park in Rio de Janeiro: C. Yamashita verbally 1994) is only partial mitigation of these pressures (Collar *et al.* 1992). **ENDANGERED: B1+2c,e; C2a; D1**.

Red-tailed Amazon *Amazona brasiliensis* survives in a very small area of coastal São Paulo and adjacent Paraná states, **Brazil** (the habitat area now known to be only 2,000 km², not 6,000 km²), moving daily between Atlantic forest feeding areas and mangrove and littoral forest roosting and breeding areas; despite some formal protection within reserves, the remaining populations (totalling around 3,500–4,500 birds) are declining precipitously as a result of trapping, hunting, loss of nest-trees, and land development (Collar *et al.* 1992, Waugh 1994). The 1,250–1,500 birds in São Paulo are divided up into 14 populations, of which as few as three are at relatively secure sites, the rest being under pressure from trappers (P. Martuscelli verbally 1994; also Waugh 1994). **ENDANGERED:** A1b,c; **A2b,c**; B1+2c,e; C1; C2a.

Yellow-faced Amazon *Amazona xanthops* occupies the formerly very extensive cerrado (dry woodland) of interior eastern **Brazil** (Maranhão, Piauí, Tocantins, Goiás, Mato Grosso, Mato Grosso do Sul, Bahia, Minas Gerais, São Paulo), eastern **Bolivia** and northern **Paraguay** (Ridgely 1981, Forshaw 1989), but 60–70% of this habitat has been converted to croplands in the past 20 years and the species has become extremely scarce in many areas; moreover, since it moves semi-nomadically, ranging over huge areas, no protected area can permanently hold a population (A. Whittaker *in litt.* 1993, C. Yamashita verbally 1994). **VULNERABLE:** A1b.

Yellow-shouldered Amazon *Amazona barbadensis* is a bird of xerophytic vegetation, ranging disjunctly along the northern coastal region of **Venezuela** (Falcón, Lara; Anzoátegui, Sucre) onto Margarita, La Blanquilla and Bonaire (this last in the **Netherlands Antilles**), having become extinct on the Dutch island of Aruba; numbers on the mainland generally seem low, while those on the islands (650–800 on Margarita, 100 on Blanquilla, 400 on Bonaire) appear to fluctuate (though all show declines), the species is widely exploited for trade (which at least in Venezuela serves a strong internal pet market), and tourist and associated developments on Margarita are a serious threat (Collar *et al.* 1992). **VULNERABLE:** C2a.

Yellow-headed Amazon *Amazona oratrix*, the most popular and sought-after amazon in trade, is known from four discrete areas, three in **Mexico** (Atlantic lowland race '*magna*' in Tamaulipas, San Luis Potosí, Veracruz, Chiapas and Tabasco; Pacific lowland race *oratrix* in Jalisco, Colima, Michoacán, Guerrero, Oaxaca and—a new record—Campeche; and the Islas Marías race *tresmariae*) and one in **Belize** (race *belizensis*; see below for record from Guatemala), inhabiting dense thorn forest, savanna, tall deciduous forest and humid riverine woodland in the tropical lowlands (below 500 m) (Collar *et al.* 1992). It has suffered enormously from trade pres-

sures and habitat loss throughout its Mexican range (both factors continuing), and is also now under pressure in Belize, so that it has undergone one of the most dramatic population declines of any bird in the Americas (Collar *et al.* 1992), judged to be 90% in the past 20 years, with less than 7,000 now remaining (E. C. Enkerlin *in litt.* 1994). The previously unpublished evidence for Campeche concerns a population of c.200 on a private reserve near Laguna de Terminos (E. C. Enkerlin *in litt.* 1994). A party of five birds (at least two of them young), race *belizensis*, was observed near Flores, central Petén, **Guatemala**, in September 1993 (R. P. Clay *in litt.* 1994). **ENDANGERED:** A1a,b,c; A2b,c; C1; C2a.

Vinaceous Amazon *Amazona vinacea* was formerly abundant and widespread from Bahia and Minas Gerais south through Espírito Santo, Rio de Janeiro, São Paulo, Paraná, Santa Catarina and Rio Grande do Sul, **Brazil**, the eastern half of **Paraguay** (now chiefly Canindeyú and Alto Paraná) and northern **Argentina** (Misiones), but has declined very dramatically in numbers as its populations have retreated into isolated pockets of forest, mostly in the south of its range (where it occurs in lowland areas, being found further north in foothills up to around 1,500 m): although perhaps still secure in places, the reasons for its long-term decline and the basic details of its ecological needs remain obscure, although a link between the species and *Araucaria* trees, and between the widespread destruction of these trees and the parrot's decline, appears strong in the south of its range (Collar *et al.* 1992, Brooks *et al.* 1993). One of the species' best populations is at Jacupiranga, on the São Paulo/Paraná border (C. Yamashita verbally 1994). **ENDANGERED:** A1a,b,c; A2b,c; C1; C2a.

St Lucia Amazon *Amazona versicolor*, endemic to moist forest on the central-southern mountains of **St Lucia**, has experienced depletion of numbers owing to habitat loss (295 km^2 of habitat available in 1950, 65–70 km^2 since the mid-1970s), hurricanes, hunting and trade, but recent action by government and non-government agencies has reversed the situation, with some 300–350 individuals extant and the nation sensitized to the importance of the species (Collar *et al.* 1992). **VULNERABLE:** D1; D2.

Red-necked Amazon *Amazona arausiaca* is confined to **Dominica**, where it occurs chiefly in the canopy of rainforests around Morne Diablotin (and chiefly at 300–800 m) but, having suffered from a combination of habitat loss at lower levels, hunting, trade and hurricanes, in recent years (post-1980) it has benefited from joint government and non-government efforts to protect its habitat and sensitize local citizens to its needs, and its numbers have risen from possibly as few as 150 in 1980 to possibly more than 500 in 1992 and 1993 (Collar *et al.* 1992, Evans 1994). **VULNERABLE:** D1; D2.

St Vincent Amazon *Amazona guildingii*, endemic to moist forest (125–1,000 m, but preferring mature growth at lower levels where trees large enough to nest in remain) on the upper west and east ridges of **St Vincent**, has declined owing to habitat loss, hunting, hurricanes and trade, but following recent action by government and non-government agencies is now relatively secure, with some 440–500 individuals extant (Collar *et al.* 1992). Indeed, census work coordinated by F. Springer in 1992 and 1994 suggests an increase to around 800 birds (Greenwood 1994). **VULNERABLE:** D1; D2.

Imperial Amazon *Amazona imperialis* is highly endangered on its native **Dominica**, where it occurs now only in the rainforests of Morne Diablotin (primarily occurring at 600–1,300 m), and, having suffered from a combination of habitat loss, hunting,

trade and hurricanes, in 1992 numbered only c.80 individuals (80–100 in 1993: Evans 1994), although in recent years it has benefited from joint government and non-government efforts to protect its habitat and sensitize local citizens to its needs (Collar *et al.* 1992). Observations in early 1994 suggested higher numbers than previously (N. F. R. Snyder verbally 1994). **VULNERABLE:** D1; D2.

Blue-bellied Parrot *Triclaria malachitacea* is restricted to the Atlantic forest region of south-east **Brazil** (Bahia, Minas Gerais, Espírito Santo, Rio de Janeiro, São Paulo, Paraná, Santa Catarina and Rio Grande do Sul), with two records from **Argentina**, living in low numbers in the shade of moister valleys (300–1,000 m) although venturing out seasonally to lower areas. Its rarity (apparent low density and/or patchy distribution) appears to be related to this habitat preference, but also to overall habitat loss and to competition with man (who destroys the plant in the process) for fruits of the palm *Euterpe edulis*, a main food resource (Collar *et al.* 1992). **ENDANGERED: C2a.**

Family MUSOPHAGIDAE
TURACOS

Bannerman's Turaco *Turaco bannermani*, an arboreal forest frugivore, is restricted to the Bamenda-Banso Highlands of western **Cameroon**, where it is under very serious threat from forest clearance (habitat reduced by half in the period 1965–1985) and is only likely to survive if forest (which only covers c.100 km²) on Mount Oku (= Kilum) is preserved (Collar and Stuart 1985, 1988, Stuart and Jensen 1986, Macleod and Parrott 1991, Fotso 1993b). Intensive work has been directed towards the conservation of its habitat by BirdLife's Kilum Mountain Forest Project (e.g. Macleod 1987, Wilson 1987, Green 1991, Macleod and Parrott 1992, Alpert 1993, Edwards 1993). **VULNERABLE:** A1b; B1+2b; C2b.

Prince Ruspoli's Turaco *Turaco ruspolii*, an arboreal frugivore, has a very small range in the south of **Ethiopia** where it has been found in juniper

forest, mixed broadleaf woodland and acacia woodland along streams between 1,275 and 1,800 m, and may be as much at risk from competition with the White-cheeked Turaco *T. leucotis* as from any loss of its habitat (Collar and Stuart 1985). However, a survey in 1989 revealed the loss or decline in quality of certain sites (Ash and Gullick 1989), and although in 1990 the species was rediscovered in reasonable numbers around Arero, human pressure on habitat there is intensifying (Dellelegn 1991, Syvertsen and Dellelegn 1991) such that by February 1994 the Arero site was thought possibly to have been lost (J. A. Wolstencroft verbally 1994), with fires being reported in neighbouring forest areas in March 1994 (P. O. Syvertsen *in litt.* 1994). **ENDANGERED:** A2b; B1+2a,c; C1; **C2a**; D1.

Family CUCULIDAE

CUCKOOS, COUCALS

Red-faced Malkoha *Phaenicophaeus pyrrhocephalus* is known from **Sri Lanka**, with unconfirmed records from southern Kerala and western Tamil Nadu, India, being found in dense forest, chiefly evergreen, from the lowlands to 1,700 m (Ali and Ripley 1987). In the dry zone of northern and eastern Sri Lanka it is confined mostly to riverine forest (S. W. Kotagama *in litt*. 1992), and occurs in scattered colonies, and in the wet zone of south-west Sri Lanka suitable habitat is much reduced and fragmented (see Collins *et al.* 1991). It is now scarce and declining because of loss of habitat and hunting (Hoffmann 1984). **VULNERABLE:** A1b; C1; C2a.

Sunda Ground-cuckoo *Carpococcyx radiceus* is known from Sumatra and Kalimantan, **Indonesia**, Sabah and Sarawak, East **Malaysia** and **Brunei**, recorded in dry, level forest in Sarawak (Davison 1981), and hill forest in Brunei (Holmes and Burton 1987) and Sumatra (though no recent records), where it has been found as high as 1,700 m (van Marle and Voous 1988). A call attributed to this species by local people (who trapped one individual) was commonly heard in Brunei in 1968 (Holmes and Burton 1987), but otherwise it appears to be rare and patchily distributed throughout its range, perhaps because of specialized habitat requirements (specimens collected in Sabah in 1980 were probably in primary forest on limestone soils: F. H. Sheldon *in litt*. 1993), so it may be particularly vulnerable to the forest destruction and degradation which is widespread within its range (see Collins *et al.* 1991). **VULNERABLE:** C2a.

Black-hooded Coucal *Centropus steerii* stands at the brink of extinction on its native Mindoro, **Philippines**, being a bird of primary lowland forest (to 750 m), a habitat now extremely scarce, greatly fragmented, and likely to be entirely cleared in the next 10–20 years; in 1991 two birds were found at Malpalon and two at Sablayan, but in other forests only Philippine Coucal *C. viridis*, which replaces *C. steerii* in degraded habitat, was recorded (Dutson *et al.* 1992). Up to four were noted at Sablayan in 1994 (Custodio *et al.* 1994). **CRITICAL:** A1b; A2b; B1+2c; C1; **C2a; D1**.

Sunda Coucal *Centropus nigrorufus* is known from Java and possibly Sumatra (one old specimen of doubtful origin, and recent unconfirmed sight records: Andrew 1990, P. Jepson *in litt*. 1994), **Indonesia**, where it is found in mangroves and associated swamp vegetation in the coastal lowlands, habitats which on Java have largely been converted to fishponds and agricultural land (S. van Balen *in litt*. 1994). There are recent records from several remnant coastal wetlands, where it is locally common (Andrew 1990), but an old record from teak forest well inland and recent sightings in scrub away from the coastal wetlands, together with substantial numbers in the local bird trade, suggest that it may be less specific in its habitat requirements, and hence less threatened by habitat destruction and degradation, than was previously thought (S. van Balen *in litt*. 1994). **VULNERABLE:** A1b; C1; C2a.

Green-billed Coucal *Centropus chlororhynchus* is endemic to **Sri Lanka**, where it is found in high humid forest with a dense undergrowth, particularly of bamboo and rattan in disturbed areas, below 800 m in the wet zone in the south-west of the island (Ali and Ripley 1987, S. W. Kotagama *in litt*. 1992). It is rare, local and severely threatened by loss of habitat (Hoffmann 1984), as forest cover in this part of the island is much reduced and fragmented, the largest remaining area being Sinharaja National Heritage Wilderness Area (Collins *et al.* 1991). **ENDANGERED:** A1b; **B1+2c**; C1; C2a.

Cocos Cuckoo *Coccyzus ferrugineus* frequents second-growth forest, *Hibiscus* thickets and streamside tangles on the 47 km² Cocos Island (which is a national park), **Costa Rica**, and is widespread but probably under-recorded in the interior forests, although there are rats and cats present, and overgrazing by introduced deer, pigs and goats is occurring (Slud 1967, Stiles and Skutch 1989; T. W. Sherry *in litt*. 1985). **VULNERABLE:** D2.

Rufous-breasted Cuckoo *Hyetornis rufigularis* appears to have undergone a strong decline in both range and numbers during the twentieth century in response to deforestation, hunting (for its supposed medicinal value) and possibly also the use of agrochemicals, in **Haiti** and the **Dominican Republic**, although its choice of habitat is catholic and unspecialized, ranging from arid lowlands through patchy broadleaf woodland to mountain rainforest. While there is little hope for it in Haiti (where it is thought extremely rare and seems to have gone already from Gonave Island), it occurs in four protected areas in the Dominican Republic, although elsewhere it is for the most part increasingly rare (Collar *et al.* 1992). **VULNERABLE:** A1a,b,c; C1; C2a.

Banded Ground-cuckoo *Neomorphus radiolosus* inhabits wet foothill forests (450–1,525 m) on the Pacific slope of the West Andes of south-west **Colombia** (Valle, Cauca, Nariño) and north-west **Ecuador** (Esmeraldas, Imbabura, Pichincha), where it is known from few localities (six in each country) and is threatened by widespread forest destruction, with only three records (in 1988 and 1989) of single birds in Colombia since 1956, and just one (in 1992) in Ecuador since 1936, suggesting that the bird is genuinely local (Collar *et al.* 1992). Local hunters in Nariño in the 1990s reported it as fairly common at two localities (its extreme shyness being blamed for the paucity of records), but its very localized distribution and the threat from loss of habitat was recently confirmed (Salaman and Gandy 1993, 1994). **ENDANGERED:** A1b; A2b; C1; **C2a**.

Family TYTONIDAE

BARN OWLS

Taliabu Masked-owl *Tyto nigrobrunnea* is known from Taliabu in the Sula Islands, **Indonesia**, and is clearly scarce, as the only records are a single specimen collected in 1938 (White and Bruce 1986) and a bird seen in selectively logged lowland forest during a seven-week survey in 1991; most of the island's forest below 800 m is designated for commercial logging, but the effects of the consequent habitat degradation on this species are unknown (Davidson *et al.* 1993). **VULNERABLE:** C2b; D1.

Manus Masked-owl *Tyto manusi* is endemic to Manus Island in the Admiralty Islands, **Papua New Guinea** (Coates 1985), where it presumably occurs in forest. It has not been recorded recently, perhaps because of its unobtrusiveness (Dutson and Newman 1991) but no islanders appear familiar with it (D. Gibbs *in litt.* 1994) and thus it is likely to be very rare. **VULNERABLE:** D1.

Bismarck Masked-owl *Tyto aurantia* occurs in forest to 1,800 m on New Britain, **Papua New Guinea** (Schodde 1978). It is rare, recorded in 1978 and 1984 in lowland forest edge (K. D. Bishop *in litt.* 1987), there are few other field records (J. M. Diamond *in litt.* 1987) and it is probably affected by ongoing forest destruction. **VULNERABLE:** C2b.

Madagascar Red Owl *Tyto soumagnei* is known with certainty only from a circumscribed region of humid forest (elevations of recorded sites being 900–1,200 m: Langrand 1990) in eastern-central **Madagascar**, where, with habitat loss continuing, it has been seen only once (in 1973) in the wild since 1934 (Collar and Stuart 1985), although a captive live specimen was discovered in August 1993 at Andapa, in Anjanaharibe Sud Special Reserve, some 300 km to the north of its known range (Scott 1994, O. Langrand *in litt.* 1994, Halleux and Goodman in press). **ENDANGERED: C2a**; D1.

Congo Bay-owl *Phodilus prigoginei* must be a rare species, having defied many attempts to relocate it since the type-specimen was collected in 1951 in a grass clearing in montane forest at Muusi, 2,430 m, in the Itombwe Mountains, **Zaïre**, although almost certainly one was observed on a tea estate in Burundi in the mid-1970s; habitat loss is the most likely threat, although recent evidence suggests that habitat in Itombwe is at present reasonably intact (Collar and Stuart 1985, 1988, Wilson and Catsis 1990). Calls of an unidentified owl, structurally similar to that of the only congener, Asian Bay Owl *P. badius*, were heard in Nyungwe forest, Rwanda, in January–February 1990; this forest is at serious (but remediable) risk (Dowsett-Lemaire 1990; also Dowsett-Lemaire and Dowsett 1990a, Gibson 1992). **VULNERABLE:** B1+2a,c; C2a.

Family STRIGIDAE

OWLS

White-fronted Scops-owl *Otus sagittatus* is known from Tenasserim, **Myanmar** (rare: Smythies 1986), peninsular **Thailand** (rare: Boonsong and Round 1991), peninsular **Malaysia** (apparently local but may prove locally common: Medway and Wells 1976) and northern Sumatra, **Indonesia** (one record: van Marle and Voous 1988). It is found in evergreen forest (and in quite degraded swampy forest), and suspected (but not proved) to be an extreme lowland specialist, although it has been recorded to 600 m (Medway and Wells 1976, van Marle and Voous 1988, D. R. Wells *in litt.* 1994). It is threatened by the extensive lowland deforestation which is taking place within its range (Boonsong and Round 1991, D. R. Wells *in litt.* 1994; see Collins *et al.* 1991). **VULNERABLE:** A1b; A2b; C1; C2a.

Sokoke Scops-owl *Otus ireneae* was until recently believed endemic to the 372 km² Arabuko–Sokoke forest in coastal **Kenya**, where the population, estimated at 1,000 pairs in 1984 (Collar and Stuart 1985, 1988), has recently been confirmed at around this level by fieldwork showing c.787 pairs in red-soil *Cynometra–Manilkara* forest (111 km²), 111 pairs in *Cynometra* thicket (131 km²) and 24 pairs in white-soil *Afzelia–Cynometra* forest (11 km²) (M. Z. A. Virani *in litt.* 1994); however, the endeavours of a major integrated forest conservation programme at the site (Fanshawe 1991, 1993) are now jeopardized by sudden withdrawal of long-term funding (J. H. Fanshawe *in litt.* 1994). In mid-1992 an individual largely resembling *O. ireneae* (tape-recorded calls sounding identical: J. H. Fanshawe verbally 1994) was trapped in the lowland Kambai Forest Reserve (2 km²) in the East Usambara Mountains, **Tanzania**, and significant numbers may yet be found in the area (Watson and Perkin undated, Hipkiss *et al.* 1994), increasing the importance of the forest conservation projects there (see Usambara Eagle Owl *Bubo vosseleri*, next page). **VULNERABLE:** D2.

Javan Scops-owl *Otus angelinae* has a highly restricted range, being known from two localities, Gunung Gede Pangrango National Park and Gunung Tangkubanprahu, in West Java, **Indonesia**, where it has been recorded in montane forest between 1,400 and 2,000 m. The most recent published record is of two seen on the northern slope of Gunung Pangrango in 1985, but its calls are not documented (and it may be an unusually silent species), so that its status (and

any threats) remain unclear (Andrew and Milton 1988). **VULNERABLE:** D1; D2.

Luzon Scops-owl *Otus longicornis* is restricted to forest above 350 m on Luzon in the **Philippines**, where it was recently found in Quezon National Park (J. Hornbuckle *in litt.* 1994), and on Mounts Cetaceo and Dipalayag (Sierra Madre) in lower montane forest, 700–1,500 m, having probably become rare as a result of habitat loss (Danielsen *et al.* 1994, Poulsen in press; also N. Bostock *in litt.* 1994). **VULNERABLE:** C2a.

Mindoro Scops-owl *Otus mindorensis* remains common in the little remaining montane forest on Mindoro in the **Philippines**, but this is now all above 870 m and progressively decreasing in size owing to habitat clearance (Dickinson *et al.* 1991, Dutson *et al.* 1992). **VULNERABLE:** A1b; B1+2c; C1; C2a.

Mindanao Scops-owl *Otus mirus* is known from rainforest on two mountains (Hilong-Hilong and Apo) on Mindanao in the **Philippines** (Dickinson *et al.* 1991), and recently from Mount Katanglad (N. Bostock *in litt.* 1994, C. R. Robson *in litt.* 1994), but it appears to be rare and must be assumed to be increasingly at risk from steady destruction of its habitat at these sites. **VULNERABLE:** B1+2c; C1; C2a.

Seychelles Scops-owl *Otus insularis* (retained here as a species separate from Moluccan Scops-owl *O. magicus*, contra Sibley and Monroe 1990) is endemic to upland, often mist-shrouded forest (virtually all records are in secondary forest at 250–600 m) on Mahé in the **Seychelles**, where total numbers may be only 80 pairs yet where some logging is inevitable despite much habitat falling within the Morne Seychellois National Park (Collar and Stuart 1985). Fieldwork in 1992–1993 showed a population still of c.80 pairs (though reports from elsewhere suggest this may be a minimum), with extreme site-fidelity (J. Watson *in litt.* 1994). Birds need clefts in hills with water where their treefrog prey occurs; forestry may not be a problem but there is habitat encroachment from real estate development (J. Stevenson verbally 1994). **CRITICAL:** B1+2a,c; **C2b**; D1.

Anjouan Scops-owl *Otus capnodes* (treated under Madagascar Scops-owl *O. rutilus* in Sibley and Monroe 1990) was rediscovered in fragments of upland forest in the centre of Anjouan (= Ndzuani) in the **Comoro Islands** in June 1992 after an absence of records dating back to 1886, voice and plumage analysis showing it to be a good species; at least several tens of pairs, probably 100–200, survive, but accelerating habitat clearance and capture for food render the species highly threatened (Safford 1993a). **CRITICAL:** A2b; B1+2c; C1; **C2a**; D1.

Grand Comoro Scops-owl *Otus pauliani* is limited to the highest forests of Mount Karthala on Grand Comoro (= Ngazidja), **Comoro Islands**, where its habitat is vulnerable (Collar and Stuart 1985). In November 1989 studies located it at 1,000–1,900 m on the north, west and south flanks of the volcano, on which c.100 km² of suitable habitat exists, and the population may prove to be over 1,000 pairs; but habitat fragmentation (fires and logging) and the spread of the introduced Common Myna *Acridotheres tristis* render the species 'very much threatened' (Herremans *et al.* 1991, Louette and Stevens 1992). **CRITICAL:** A2d; **B1+2a,b,c**; C1; C2b; D2.

Palawan Scops-owl *Otus fuliginosus* is restricted to lowland forest and trees in mixed cultivation on Palawan, **Philippines**, where, despite recent records from at least three localities (St Paul Subterranean National Park, Iwahig, Balsahan) it is likely to be genuinely and increasingly rare, since there is very substantial lowland clearance on the island (Dickinson *et al.* 1991, N. Bostock *in litt.* 1994, P. Morris *in litt.* 1994). **VULNERABLE:** A1b; A2b; C1; C2a.

Lesser Eagle-owl *Mimizuku gurneyi* is a naturally low-density species recorded on Dinagat, Siargao and Mindanao in the **Philippines**, chiefly in lowland forest although recent records have included Mount Apo and Mount Katanglad; it is rare, and must be suffering from the extensive habitat clearance taking place within its range (Dickinson *et al.* 1991, A. Lewis *in litt.* 1993, N. J. Redman verbally 1993, N. Bostock *in litt.* 1994, C. R. Robson *in litt.* 1994). **ENDANGERED:** A1b; C1; **C2a**.

Usambara Eagle-owl *Bubo vosseleri* is endemic to the Usambara Mountains in north-east **Tanzania**, where until recently it was believed to be montane, all records coming from 900–1,500 m, and numbers being thought to lie between 200 and 1,000 birds (Collar and Stuart 1985; also Turner *et al.* 1991). Records from three lowland patches suggest that the species may be commoner in such habitat, although this is extremely limited in extent and even more at risk of destruction than the montane forest (Watson and Perkin undated; also Evans and Anderson 1992, 1993, Hipkiss *et al.* 1994); possibly, however, these

birds were cold-season altitudinal migrants (N. E. Baker *in litt.* 1994). Two current projects aimed at reconciling conservation and development in the East Usambaras, one by IUCN, the other by Finnida and the Tanzanian Forest Division, aim to increase the amount of forest, including all lowland remnants, in protected areas (see Hamilton and Bensted-Smith 1989, Tye 1993; A. Tye *in litt.* 1994), with lowland forest conservation at Kambai being supported by the Tanzania Forest Conservation Group (N. E. Baker *in litt.* 1994). **VULNERABLE:** B1+2a,c; C2b.

Philippine Eagle-owl *Bubo philippensis* occurs in lower elevation forest, often near water, in Luzon and Catanduanes (nominate race), Samar, Leyte and Mindanao (*mindanensis*) in the **Philippines** (Dickinson *et al.* 1991); apart from a range extension to Bohol in January 1994 (J. Hornbuckle *in litt.* 1994), the very few recent records have all been from Luzon, and it is evident that the species is rare and threatened at least partly as a result of extensive lowland habitat destruction, possibly also hunting (A. Lewis *in litt.* 1993, Danielsen *et al.* 1994, Poulsen in press). **ENDANGERED:** A1b; A2b; C1; **C2a**.

Blakiston's Fish-owl *Ketupa blakistoni* is found in south-east **Russia**, including Sakhalin and the southern Kuril Islands (total population estimated at 300–400 pairs: Borodin 1984), Heilongjiang and Inner Mongolia, north-east **China** (rare and local: Cheng 1987) and Hokkaido, **Japan** (total population estimated to be 80–100 birds, with 20 breeding pairs: Brazil 1991), where it occurs in broadleaf or mixed broadleaf and coniferous forest along rivers, favouring areas near the confluence of tributaries and the main river where there are channels with still, clear water; along the Bikin River in Russia nesting pairs were typically found to have territories extending 6–12 km or more (Pukinskiy 1973), although the provision of nest boxes has been successfully used to increase breeding densities in the Kunashir State Reserve (Berezan 1993). The main threats are continuing deforestation and riverside development, and in Japan the depletion of fish stocks by fishermen (Brazil 1991, Environment Agency 1992, N. Ichida *in litt.* 1994). **ENDANGERED:** C1; **C2a**.

Rufous Fishing-owl *Scotopelia ussheri*, endemic to the rapidly receding Upper Guinea rainforest in West Africa where its riverine forest (also mangrove) habitat is at risk from clearance and pollution, occurs or occurred in **Ghana** (three records up to 1941, two more recently), **Guinea** (one record, 1951), **Ivory Coast** (very few records, owing partly to uncertainty over voice), **Liberia** (fairly widely distributed and 'rare to uncommon', but no recent published

records) and **Sierra Leone** (four records up to 1969, but in 1992 found moderately commonly on Mount Loma) (Collar and Stuart 1985, Gatter 1988, Allport 1991, Demey and Fishpool 1991, Atkinson *et al.* 1994). **ENDANGERED:** A1b; A2b; B1+2b; C1; **C2a.**

Sichuan Wood-owl *Strix davidi* (sometimes considered an isolated subspecies of Ural Owl *S. uralensis*) is endemic to **China**, known from central and western Sichuan and south-east Qinghai, where it is found in open coniferous and mixed forest from c.2,700 to 4,200 m; it appears to be rare, and extensive deforestation is taking place within its range (Meyer de Schauensee 1984, Cheng 1987, P. Alström *in litt.* 1993, M.J.C.). **VULNERABLE:** C1; C2a.

Albertine Owlet *Glaucidium albertinum* is known from just five specimens, all collected in montane forest, in the Itombwe Mountains (two), forest west of Lake Edward (two), plus a recent sight record from the Kahuzi-Biega National Park west of Lake Kivu (Catterall 1992), **Zaïre**, and the Nyungwe forest (one, with a recent sound record that suggests the species is no more than a race of African Barred Owlet *G. capense*: Dowsett-Lemaire 1990), **Rwanda**; habitat loss is the most likely threat, and although recent evidence suggests that habitat in Itombwe is at present reasonably intact, Nyungwe is at serious (but remediable) risk (Collar and Stuart 1985, 1988, Dowsett-Lemaire and Dowsett 1990a, Wilson and Catsis 1990, Gibson 1992). **VULNERABLE:** B1+2a,c,d.

Forest Owlet *Athene blewitti* ranges (or formerly ranged) along the length of the Satpura mountains in south-east Gujarat, southern Madhya Pradesh, northern Maharashtra and north-west Orissa, **India**, and has been recorded in moist deciduous forest and wild mango groves, usually near to streams. It is known historically from less than 12 specimens, the

last collected in 1914, and the only recent record is of an individual attributed to this species (but not conclusively identified) which was photographed near Nagpur, Madhya Pradesh, in 1968 (Ripley 1976, Ali and Ripley 1987; see photograph in Burton 1984). If it survives at all, it is presumably threatened by habitat destruction. **CRITICAL: D1.**

Powerful Owl *Ninox strenua* occurs in wet and dry eucalypt forest of south-east **Australia**, being uncommon in Queensland, and population estimates in Victoria (fewer than 500 pairs) and New South Wales (1,000–10,000 individuals) need verification; the main threat is the loss of old-growth forest (nesting sites) and intensive forestry, which reduces prey density (Garnett 1992). **VULNERABLE:** C2b.

Sumba Boobook *Ninox rudolfi* is endemic to Sumba, **Indonesia** (White and Bruce 1986), where surveys in 1989 and 1992 recorded small numbers at only five localities, in monsoon forest and rainforest, both primary and secondary; it has presumably been affected by the extensive reduction in closed-canopy forest which now covers less than 11% of the island (Jones *et al.* in prep.). **VULNERABLE:** B1+2c; C1.

Fearful Owl *Nesasio solomonensis* occurs in lowland primary and tall secondary forest on Bougainville Island, **Papua New Guinea**, Choiseul and Santa Isabel, **Solomon Islands**, being little known and apparently rare (Coates 1985). It reportedly feeds on phalangers *Phalanger orientalis*, and in 1986–1988 was found (generally rare and local) in forest over a range of altitudes (mostly in lowlands and hills to c.500 m) on Santa Isabel, where large numbers of this prey occurred (Webb 1992). Although Solomon Islanders eat phalangers it is likely to be more threatened by forest destruction (M. B. Iles *in litt.* 1994, H. P. Webb *in litt.* 1994). **VULNERABLE:** C2a.

Family AEGOTHELIDAE

OWLET-NIGHTJARS

New Caledonian Owlet-nightjar *Aegotheles savesi*, treated as extinct by King (1978–1979), is known from one specimen collected in 1880 near to Nouméa, **New Caledonia (to France)**, and from one

individual killed by a hunter in the region of Païta in 1960 (Hannecart 1988). If it persists, numbers are likely to be small. **ENDANGERED: D1.**

Family CAPRIMULGIDAE
NIGHTJARS

Satanic Eared-nightjar *Eurostopodus diabolicus* is endemic to Sulawesi, **Indonesia**, and only definitely known from the type, collected at 250 m in forest on the Minahassa peninsula, although a number of unidentified calls elsewhere on the island have been attributed to this species (Holmes and Wood 1980, White and Bruce 1986), and there was a probable sighting at c.1,700 m in Lore Lindu National Park, central Sulawesi, in 1993 (King 1994). It appears to be genuinely rare, and it is perhaps threatened by deforestation, which is already quite extensive in the lowlands of the Minahassa peninsula (see RePPProT 1990). **VULNERABLE: D1.**

Jamaican Pauraque *Siphonorhis americanus* is known from very few records on its native **Jamaica**, the last of which was in 1863, although there have been some recent unconfirmed reports of caprimulgids that do not fit other known species on the island; so little of the bird is known that it is still uncertain whether it inhabited tall forest or arid scrub, but its disappearance seems as likely to be linked to the impact of introduced rats and mongooses as to any habitat loss (Collar *et al.* 1992, C. Levy *in litt.* 1994). **CRITICAL: D1.**

Puerto Rican Nightjar *Caprimulgus noctitherus* is believed originally to have occupied the various dry and moist lowland forests that once fringed **Puerto Rico (to U.S.A.)**, but is now restricted to three separate areas of dry limestone forest in the south-west of the island, where the total population is in the order of 670–800 pairs distributed over 100 km² of habitat (Vilella in press). Despite protected area status for much of the relevant land, piecemeal forest destruction (caused by adjacent residential, industrial and recreational expansion) remains a serious threat, and the concomitant increase in disturbance, fire risk and the numbers of rats, dogs and cats could be serious (Collar *et al.* 1992, Vilella in press). **CRITICAL: B1+2c; C2b; D2.**

White-winged Nightjar *Caprimulgus candicans* is a distinctive nightbird of which only two old specimens from open grasslands in Mato Grosso and São Paulo in central **Brazil** are known, with even older evidence from Paraguay. The only known population (number unknown but conceivably in the hundreds) exists in the grasslands and open cerrado of the 1,320 km² Emas National Park in Goiás, Brazil, although if it is migratory then the wholesale conversion of such habitat elsewhere in central South America may compromise its chances of survival, and even within the park the effects of burning are not known (Collar *et al.* 1992). In September 1987 a male was captured at the Beni Biological Station, Beni department, Yucuma province, **Bolivia**, causing speculation whether a viable population exists in the area (Davis and Flores 1994). **CRITICAL: A1b; A2b; B1+2b,c; C1; C2b; D1.**

Vaurie's Nightjar *Caprimulgus centralasicus*, perhaps of questionable taxonomic status (N. Cleere verbally 1994), is known from a single female collected at Guma on the edge of the Taklimakan Desert (in the Tarim Basin), western Xinjiang, western **China** (Vaurie 1960), a report of specimens collected at a second locality (*World Birdwatch* 1993, 15,2: 2) being found to refer to Eurasian Nightjar *C. europaeus* (*World Birdwatch* 1993, 15,4: 3). It is unknown in life, but is probably a bird of the sandy foothills and plains of the Tarim Basin and adjacent mountains (Meyer de Schauensee 1984). A recent survey found that the habitats at Guma have changed very considerably since the type was collected, and did not locate the species (Dissing *et al.* 1990). Degradation of desert habitats by intensive grazing of goats and camels, extraction of fuelwood and conversion of huge areas to irrigated land is widespread in this region (Grimmett 1991). **VULNERABLE: D1.**

Itombwe Nightjar *Caprimulgus prigoginei*, only recently described to science, remains known from a single female collected in August 1955 at Malenge, 1,280 m, in the Itombwe Mountains of eastern **Zaïre**, where forest clearance may pose a significant threat, especially if the species is restricted to the transitional (between lowland and montane) forest in which the type was found (Louette 1990, Catterall 1992). **VULNERABLE:** B1+2a,c.

117

Family APODIDAE

SWIFTS

White-chested Swift *Cypseloides lemosi* is known from open bushy grassland and pastures in the southern end of the Cauca valley, south-west **Colombia** (Valle and Cauca), with a recent record (and some subsequent sightings: R. S. Ridgely *in litt.* 1994) from Napo province in **Ecuador** suggesting that it may be found elsewhere or range much more widely; but it has apparently only been recorded five times at two sites in Colombia since 1966 (for 15 years before which it was recorded moderately often in flocks of 20–25), and may have suffered a decline as a result (e.g.) of agrochemical applications (Collar *et al.* 1992, A. J. Negret *in litt.* 1994). **VULNERABLE:** C2b.

Seychelles Swiftlet *Collocalia elaphra*, which feeds over a variety of habitats including forest and wetlands, is endemic to **Seychelles** (the islands of Mahé, Praslin and La Digue, over which it ranges widely), has a low total population (under 1,000 birds), and its few nest-caves (only some half-dozen are known) remain vulnerable to disturbance or vandalism (Collar and Stuart 1985). A colony on Félicité has disappeared, possibly having combined with one on La Digue, which appears to have increased (J. Stevenson verbally 1994), although this may have been due to increased breeding success after the restriction of outflow from water on the island's 'plateau' led to more extensive marsh there (J. Watson *in litt.* 1994). **VULNERABLE:** D1.

Volcano Swiftlet *Collocalia vulcanorum* is endemic to West Java, **Indonesia**, where it nests in rock crevices in volcanic craters and feeds around the open peaks and ridges of the highest mountains; it is known from three peaks, but the only recent records are from the crater of Gunung Gede in Gunung Gede Pangrango National Park, and as all known breeding localities are active volcanoes, colonies may be susceptible to periodic extinction (MacKinnon and Phillipps 1993, S. van Balen *in litt.* 1994). **VULNERABLE:** D1; D2.

Whitehead's Swiftlet *Collocalia whiteheadi* is a rare aerial feeder over forested mountains that remains known from two sites in the **Philippines**, Mount Data in the Cordillera Central in northern Luzon (nominate *whiteheadi*, taken in 1895) and Mount Apo in southern Mindanao (race *origenis*, taken at 1,200 m in 1904) (Dickinson *et al.* 1991);

despite great difficulties in identification, it may be as restricted as the records show, and it may therefore also be at risk from habitat loss. **VULNERABLE:** B1+2c; C2a.

Atiu Swiftlet *Collocalia sawtelli* was collected in 1973 from the Anatakitaki Cave on Atiu in the **Cook Islands (to New Zealand)**: the cave contained about 60 nests and the local inhabitants reported that there were a few smaller colonies elsewhere on the island (Holyoak 1974). A detailed survey in 1987–1988 recorded 190 active nests in two caves and identified the major causes of chick mortality as starvation after falling out of the nest and predation by coconut crabs *Burgus latro* and land crabs *Cardisoma longipes* (Tarburton 1990). The species feeds over fernlands and mixed horticultural areas and there is no reason to believe that it is declining in numbers, although disturbance by tourists could be a problem in the future (G. McCormack *in litt.* and verbally 1994). **VULNERABLE:** D1; D2.

Tahiti Swiftlet *Collocalia leucophaeus* is now known to breed only on Tahiti in the Society Islands, **French Polynesia**, where it was recorded in six valleys (out of 39 visited) during 1986–1991, foraging along rivers and over tree-tops, but only estimated to number 200–500 birds in 1984, apparently never having been abundant this century, perhaps because of the introduction of the Common Myna *Acridotheres tristis*, a possible predator of eggs or young; it was formerly encountered on Huahine and (possibly) Bora Bora, while records from Moorea in 1973 may have referred to vagrants from Tahiti (Holyoak and Thibault 1984, M. K. Poulsen *in litt.* 1985, Pratt *et al.* 1987, Thibault 1988, Monnet *et al.* 1993). **VULNERABLE:** D1.

Schouteden's Swift *Schoutedenapus schoutedeni* is known from only five records at low and intermediate altitudes to the east and north-east of the Itombwe Mountains in eastern **Zaïre**; habitat loss is the most likely threat, although recent evidence suggests that habitat in Itombwe is at present reasonably intact (Collar and Stuart 1985, 1988, Wilson and Catsis 1990). **VULNERABLE:** B1+2a,c; C2b.

Dark-rumped Swift *Apus acuticauda* is known to breed only in **India**, around rocky cliffs and deep gorges at two localities in the Khasi Hills, Meghalaya

(Ali and Ripley 1987), and is presumed to breed in Mizoram (Brooke 1969); however, the type-specimen may be from Nepal (Inskipp and Inskipp 1991), there is an old record from the Andaman Islands, India, in July (Ali and Ripley 1987), it possibly

occurs in Myanmar (Smythies 1986) and it is a vagrant to north-west Thailand (Boonsong and Round 1991), so its true status, and any threats, are unknown. **VULNERABLE:** D2.

Family TROCHILIDAE

HUMMINGBIRDS

Hook-billed Hermit *Glaucis dohrnii* is a rare and seldom-seen hummingbird of humid evergreen forest interior (notably along streambeds, particularly where *Heliconia* plants grow) which has been reduced by massive habitat loss to a few widely scattered localities in Bahia (possibly only the CVRD Porto Seguro Reserve and Pau Brasil Ecological Station) and Espírito Santo (possibly only the CVRD Linhares Reserve, but reported there by only one observer among many in recent years), **Brazil**, and is possibly not present year-round in any of them; its status remains obscure and it may be unable to survive even in the short term in what little habitat remains (Collar *et al.* 1992, Y. Oniki *in litt.* 1994). **CRITICAL:** B1+2c,e; **C2a**; D1.

White-tailed Sabrewing *Campylopterus ensipennis* is endemic to the lower and upper montane forests of the coastal Cordillera de Caripe (760–1,830 m) and Paria peninsula (460–1,200 m), north-east **Venezuela** (Anzoátegui, Monagas, Sucre), plus the island of Tobago (**Trinidad and Tobago**) (Collar *et al.* 1992). On the mainland, despite being relatively common within its restricted range, it is threatened by widespread habitat destruction on both the cordillera and peninsula, and on Tobago (where it is the subject of a project by the Tobago Society for the Prevention of Cruelty to Animals and RARE Center: A. Blade *in litt.* 1994) it is only just starting to recover from a hurricane that destroyed much forest in 1963 (Collar *et al.* 1992). However, observations on Cerro Negro in February 1993 suggested that the species may be able to survive well (or at least seasonally) in very degraded forest (J. Curson *in litt.* 1993). **VULNERABLE:** A2b.

Short-crested Coquette *Lophornis brachylopha* is still only known from (though relatively common at least seasonally along) a 40 km stretch of the Atoyac de Alvarez–Chilpancingo road (north-west

of Acapulco) through rapidly decreasing semi-deciduous tropical forest and evergreen subtropical (cloud-)forest (900–1,800 m) on the slopes of the Sierra Madre del Sur of Guerrero, **Mexico** (Collar *et al.* 1992). **ENDANGERED: A2b**; **B1+2c**; C1; C2b.

Mexican Woodnymph *Thalurania ridgwayi* is patchily distributed within humid forested canyons and foothills in western **Mexico** (Nayarit, Jalisco, Colima), and although locally common it may well prove to be threatened by habitat destruction when its range and the causes of its patchiness are better understood (Collar *et al.* 1992). **VULNERABLE:** B1+2c.

Sapphire-bellied Hummingbird *Lepidopyga lilliae* (which requires taxonomic validation) is confined to mangroves along the north coast of **Colombia** (Atlántico, Magdalena and La Guajira), where it is so rare as to be impossible to locate consistently; alteration of salinity levels caused by a new road across Isla de Salamanca National Park has led to the death of large areas of mangrove there and in the adjacent Ciénaga Grande, two key areas for the species, and urbanization and pollution add to the pressure on mangroves within its range (Collar *et al.* 1992). **CRITICAL:** A1b; A2b; B1+2c; C1; **C2b**; **D1**; D2.

Honduran Emerald *Amazilia luciae* is endemic to the arid interior valleys of **Honduras** (six sites traced, one at 1,220 m, the rest below 410 m), where it is common in thorn-forest and scrub which, however, has a restricted range within the country, and these same areas are under severe pressure from agricultural development including livestock grazing and pineapple plantations (Collar *et al.* 1992). **CRITICAL: A2b**; B1+2c; C1; C2a.

Táchira Emerald *Amazilia distans* is only known from foothill evergreen or semi-deciduous forest (300–800 m) of the Andes in westernmost **Venezuela**

(Táchira, Apure), an area undergoing rampant deforestation. Since its discovery in 1954 there have been just five (apparent) observations, so no population estimates are yet possible and the bird remains almost completely unknown (Collar *et al.* 1992). **ENDANGERED:** A2b; B1+2c; C1; C2a.

Mangrove Hummingbird *Amazilia boucardi* is endemic to and locally common along the Pacific coast of **Costa Rica** from the head of Golfo de Nicoya to Golfo Dulce, in areas with a predominance of the Pacific mangrove *Pelliciera rhizophorae*: it is the destruction of this mangrove habitat to make way for salinas and shrimp ponds that has been the cause of the bird's decline (Collar *et al.* 1992). **VULNERABLE:** B1+2c; C2b.

Chestnut-bellied Hummingbird *Amazilia castaneiventris* inhabits lower montane humid forest (850–2,045 m) in the Serranía de San Lucas and on the western slope of the East Andes, **Colombia** (Bolívar, one record in 1947; Santander, two sites with records in 1962 and 1963; Boyacá, two sites with records in 1949–1953 and 1977 respectively), and although it has been found common on occasion its range is part of an area now extensively deforested and there has been only one record in the past 30 years (Collar *et al.* 1992). **ENDANGERED:** A1b.

White-tailed Hummingbird *Eupherusa poliocerca* is endemic to the Pacific slope of the Sierra Madre del Sur in Guerrero and western Oaxaca, south-western **Mexico**, where it is a locally common inhabitant of cloud-forest, evergreen subtropical and semi-humid forest and forest edge (possibly making altitudinal migrations, since records range from 915 to 2,440 m); all such habitat is rapidly being destroyed for its timber, coffee plantations and other uses (Collar *et al.* 1992). **ENDANGERED:** A1b; **A2b**; B1+2c.

Oaxaca Hummingbird *Eupherusa cyanophrys* is permanently resident on just one mountain range (Sierra Miahuatlán, where to date it has been recorded in two general areas 70 km apart) in southernmost Oaxaca, **Mexico**, and although it is locally common in cloud-forest (1,300–1,950 m) this is a habitat that is unprotected and has been and continues to be rapidly destroyed for corn cultivation (Collar *et al.* 1992). **ENDANGERED:** A1b; **A2b**; **B1+2c**; C1; C2a.

Scissor-tailed Hummingbird *Hylonympha macrocerca* is endemic to the cloud-forests (lower and upper montane rainforest) of the Paria peninsula, north-eastern **Venezuela** (recorded from 800 to 1,200 m on Cerro Humo, proportionately lower fur-

ther east, where mountains themselves only reach 920 m); although locally common within this restricted range, and despite the entire range falling within the Paria Peninsula National Park, its habitat is under great threat from agricultural encroachment (possibly as little as 15 km² remaining on Cerro Humo) and other developments (Collar *et al.* 1992). In February 1993 only three birds were seen in three days on Cerro Humo (J. Curson *in litt.* 1993), although up to six per day were seen there in April 1994 (P. Boesman *in litt.* 1994). **CRITICAL:** A1b; A2b; **B1+2c**; C1; C2a; D2.

Purple-backed Sunbeam *Aglaeactis aliciae* is a rare montane hummingbird confined to a tiny area (all records within 20 km of each other) of montane shrubbery at just over (and possibly just below) 3,000 m in the upper Marañón drainage of western **Peru**, where it is poorly known and in need of investigation (Collar *et al.* 1992). **VULNERABLE:** D2.

Black Inca *Coeligena prunellei* occurs in humid montane forest (especially oak *Quercus humboldti* and *Trigonobalanus excelsa* forest) on the western slope of the East Andes (Santander, Boyacá, Cundinamarca) and the western slope of the Central Andes (Quindío) of **Colombia** (observed between 1,675 and 2,500 m, although probably ranging both higher and lower). It is locally common, most so in relatively extensive patches of habitat, so the serious depletion and fragmentation of forest (especially oak-dominated forest) within its range must be causing considerable loss of populations (Collar *et al.* 1992). In November 1993, 100 km² of forest at Virolín, a key site in Santander, was gazetted as a reserve (Andrade and Repizzo 1994). **VULNERABLE:** A1b; A2b; C1; C2a.

Juan Fernández Firecrown *Sephanoides fernandensis* survives in 11 km² of forest on Robinson Crusoe (= Más á Tierra) in the Juan Fernández Islands, **Chile**, the race *leyboldi* having last been seen on its native Alejandro Selkirk in 1908. Numbers have recently been estimated at up to 800 birds in summer, falling to 440 or so in winter, but there is also a long-term decline related to loss and degradation of natural vegetation (caused by human clearance and the effects of animal browsing and rootling), increased interspecific competition from the congeneric Green-backed Firecrown *S. sephaniodes* as a result of the latter's greater use of invasive exotic plants, and predation by introduced animals such as rats (Collar *et al.* 1992). **CRITICAL:** B1+2c; C1; C2b; D1; D2.

Royal Sunangel *Heliangelus regalis* is known from two localities (above San José de Lourdes in the Cordillera del Condor, 1,800–2,200 m, Cajamarca; and north-east of Jirillo, 1,450 m, San Martín; but presumably also between them) in northern **Peru**, where it inhabits subtropical forest-edge shrubbery on very poor soils; at the one locality where it is common (San José de Lourdes), its habitat borders cultivated areas (Collar *et al.* 1992). **VULNERABLE:** A2b; B1+2c; C1; C2a.

Bogotá Sunangel *Heliangelus zusii* (described after Sibley and Monroe 1990, 1993) is known from a single specimen purchased in 1909 in Bogotá and speculated to have been collected on the East Andes or possibly the Central Andes of **Colombia** within a few hundred kilometres of the capital; because no other specimen is known, it is assumed to be (or have been) a relict species of restricted range, and because it is a sunangel, it is judged to occur (or have occurred) in cloud-forest and shrubbery between 1,200 and 3,400 m, the range 1,400–2,200 m being proposed as the height at which searches in appropriate habitat—if any remains—on both slopes of the East Andes should now be made (Graves 1993). **CRITICAL: D1**; D2.

Black-breasted Puffleg *Eriocnemis nigrivestis* is restricted to two adjacent volcanoes (Pichincha and Atacazo) in north-west **Ecuador** (Pichincha province), where it seems to be confined to temperate-zone ridge-top elfin forest, though ranging from 2,745–3,050 m in April–June to 3,100–4,570 m in November–February. Over 100 museum skins exist, yet recent records have been extremely few (three were seen at Loma Gramalote on Pichincha in February–March 1993), suggesting a decline related to the (continuing) destruction of some of these ridge-top forests for cultivation, and without remedial action the species could conceivably become extinct in the near future (Collar *et al.* 1992, Krabbe *et al.* 1994a). **CRITICAL: A1b; A2b; B1+2c**; C1; C2b; D1; D2.

Turquoise-throated Puffleg *Eriocnemis godini* is possibly extinct, being known from just one locality (Guaillabamba, 2,100–2,300 m in ravines of the Río Guaillabamba south of Perucho, Pichincha) in northern **Ecuador**, in an area that has now been largely cleared of natural (presumably arid) vegetation and where it has not been certainly recorded this century. There are possible or speculated records from Pasto in Nariño, Colombia, and from near Quito, and it has been suggested the bird is or was an inhabitant of temperate zones (Collar *et al.* 1992). **CRITICAL: B1+2c; C2b; D1**; D2.

Colourful Puffleg *Eriocnemis mirabilis* remains known only from subtropical wet forest and its borders in the vicinity of the type-locality, Charguayaco, north of Cerro Munchique (but within Munchique National Park) on the Pacific slope of the West Andes in Cauca, south-west **Colombia**; records of the species, ranging from 2,195 to 2,440 m, suggest that it is extremely local, although large tracts of forest remain unexplored in the area (Collar *et al.* 1992). **VULNERABLE: D1**; D2.

Violet-throated Metaltail *Metallura baroni* is confined to the edge of the páramo zone in elfin forest and treeline shrubbery at 3,150–3,700 m above both slopes of the interandean plateau west of Cuenca, Azuay province, southern **Ecuador**. Numbers may reach 2,000 birds, and have presumably been declining with steady habitat destruction (observed in the 1970s), but may now be stabilizing as conservation is implemented in one key area, Mazán (Collar *et al.* 1992). **VULNERABLE: B1+2c**; C2a.

Grey-bellied Comet *Taphrolesbia griseiventris* inhabits semi-arid country (rocky inaccessible places, deep canyons) in north-central **Peru**, where it is known from four localities (one on the Pacific slope in Cajamarca and three in the Río Marañón drainage in Cajamarca and Huánuco) between 2,750 and 3,170 m, and is everywhere rare, with apparently only three records this century, in 1922, 1975 and 1983 (Collar *et al.* 1992), the last of these three being by T. S. Schulenberg (*in litt.* 1994) at Nuevas Flores (= Cullcui). **VULNERABLE: D1**; D2.

Marvellous Spatuletail *Loddigesia mirabilis* appears to be confined to the right bank of the Río Utcubamba (an affluent on the right bank of the Río Marañón), Bongara and Chachapoyas provinces, northern **Peru**, occurring in forest edge, second growth, montane scrub and, especially, thorny impenetrable *Rubus* thickets admixed with *Alnus* trees, at 2,100–2,900 m. Its extent of occurrence is put at 2,000–3,000 km^2 and it is uncommon within it, the extent of habitat destruction being unknown (Collar *et al.* 1992). **VULNERABLE: B1+2c**; C2b.

Chilean Woodstar *Eulidia yarrellii* appears to be confined to but common in two adjacent, heavily cultivated valleys (generally from sea-level to 750 m) in the desert of Arica department, extreme northern **Chile**, straggling north into immediately adjacent **Peru** (Tacna), and south to northern Antofagasta province. The indigenous plants it favours may be severely threatened since the valleys are heavily cultivated, although birds appear to fare well in gardens (Collar *et al.* 1992). **VULNERABLE: B1+2c**; C2b.

Little Woodstar *Acestrura bombus* has historically been recorded from west-central **Ecuador** (fourteen provinces) to central **Peru** (seven departments) at elevations ranging from sea-level to 3,050 m, in humid evergreen forest and, more commonly, in the transitional zone between dry and wet forests. Thus it may occur primarily in moist forest (or at least rely on it for part of the annual cycle), a seriously threatened habitat in western South America, and this may perhaps explain the paucity of modern records (Collar *et al.* 1992). **ENDANGERED:** A1b; A2b; C1; **C2b**.

Esmeraldas Woodstar *Acestrura berlepschi* is apparently restricted to and very rare and localized within lowland evergreen moist forest in a small area of western **Ecuador** (Esmeraldas, Manabí, Guayas), this being one of the most threatened forest types in the Neotropics, with only a very few patches of any size remaining and all (even Machalilla National Park) under intense pressure (Collar *et al.* 1992).

Small numbers occur in semi-humid forest south of the Río Ayampe in extreme north-western Guayas in the period January–March, when they appear to be breeding, but are absent at other times; a female was seen in forest south of Súa, Esmeraldas, in January 1993 (R. S. Ridgely *in litt.* 1994; also M. K. Poulsen *in litt.* 1994). **ENDANGERED:** A1b; A2b; B1+2c; C1; **C2b**; D1.

Glow-throated Hummingbird *Selasphorus ardens* is restricted to shrubby growth in clearings and forest borders of western and central **Panama** in the Serranía de Tabasará (eastern Chiriquí and Veraguas at cerros Flores and Tute) above 750 m, and (found in 1994) south-west Azuero peninsula (on Cerro Hoya, Los Santos). In this small range it remains relatively unprotected (although Cerro Hoya is within a national park) and poorly known but seemingly uncommon and difficult to locate (Collar *et al.* 1992, Engleman 1994). **VULNERABLE:** D1; D2.

Family TROGONIDAE

QUETZALS, TROGONS

Eared Quetzal *Euptilotis neoxenus*, although found almost throughout the mountains of western **Mexico** (Sonora, Chihuahua, Sinaloa, Durango, Nayarit, Zacatecas, Jalisco, Michoacán) and even sporadically within Arizona and New Mexico, **U.S.A.**, is very locally distributed in montane pine and pine–oak forests, very uncommon and poorly known ecologically, and threatened by the widespread destruction (or modification) of its habitat (particularly the removal of potential nest-trees), a problem compounded by uncertainty over its seasonal movements and requirements (Collar *et al.* 1992). **ENDANGERED:** A1b; A2b; C1; **C2b**.

Ward's Trogon *Harpactes wardi* is known from the eastern Himalayas, in **Bhutan** (uncommon, with only eight individuals collected in surveys between 1966 and 1973, and two recorded in 1993: Ali *et al.* in prep., K. D. Bishop *in litt.* 1994), Arunachal Pradesh, **India** (small numbers have been seen recently at three localities: Singh in press), northern **Myanmar** (where formerly locally common, but no recent records: Smythies 1986), north-west Yunnan, **China** (three collected in 1973: Peng *et al.* 1980), and in the mountains of north-west Tonkin, northern **Vietnam** (no recent records), where it is found in tall broadleaf evergreen forest at altitudes between 1,500 and 3,000 m (Ali and Ripley 1987). It is threatened by clearance and degradation of its forest habitat over much of its range (see Collins *et al.* 1991). **VULNERABLE:** C1; C2a.

Family ALCEDINIDAE

KINGFISHERS

Blyth's Kingfisher *Alcedo hercules* ranges from eastern **Nepal**, **Bhutan**, north-east **India**, **Bangladesh**, **Myanmar**, **China** (southern Yunnan and Hainan Island), north-west **Thailand** (very rare visitor: Boonsong and Round 1991), northern and central **Laos** and **Vietnam** (King *et al*. 1975), where it is found along streams in evergreen forest in hills up to 1,200 m (Ali and Ripley 1987), mainly at 625–1,000 m (Fry and Fry 1992). Recent records are of single birds from Nepal (Inskipp and Inskipp 1991), Bhutan (Clements 1992), Bangladesh (Thompson *et al*. 1993), China (seen in 1989 in Mengyang Nature Reserve, Yunnan: L. X. Han *in litt*. 1994), Laos (eight sightings in Nakai Plateau/Nam Theun protected area in 1994: T. D. Evans and R. J. Timmins verbally 1994) and Vietnam (at several localities since 1990: Eames *et al*. 1992, Robson *et al*. 1993a,b, J. C. Eames *in litt*. 1994), indicating that it is still widespread at low densities within its historical range (much of which has not been visited by ornithologists in recent years), although deforestation is reducing and fragmenting its habitat (see Collins *et al*. 1991) and human disturbance and river pollution are possibly also threats (Eames *et al*. 1992). **VULNERABLE:** A1b; A2b; C1; C2a.

Silvery Kingfisher *Alcedo argentata* inhabits streamside banks and pools in forest on Samar, Leyte and Bohol (race *flumenicola*), and Dinagat, Siargao, Mindanao and Basilan (nominate *argentatus*) in the **Philippines** (Dickinson *et al*. 1991). It has been recorded in small numbers at a few sites on Mindanao in recent years (although not during a search of Dinagat), but appears to be rare and may prefer lowland habitat, now extensively destroyed (N. J. Redman verbally 1993, N. Bostock *in litt*. 1994, R. J. Timmins *in litt*. 1994). **ENDANGERED:** A1b; C1; C2a.

Philippine Kingfisher *Ceyx melanurus* occupies primary forest (often near small streams: C. R. Robson *in litt*. 1994 *contra* Dickinson *et al*. 1991) on Luzon, Polillo, Alabat and Catanduanes (nominate *melanurus*), Samar and Leyte (race *samarensis*), Mindanao and Basilan (race *mindanensis*) in the **Philippines** (Dickinson *et al*. 1991), where it seems to be extremely rare, probably because of habitat loss, particularly if it is a lowland species. There appear to be no recent records from Mindanao, despite relatively good observer coverage, or elsewhere

in its range except Luzon, in Quezon National Park, Angat and two sites in the Sierra Madre (Danielsen *et al*. 1994, Poulsen in press; also F. R. Lambert verbally 1993, N. Bostock *in litt*. 1994, J. Hornbuckle *in litt*. 1994). **VULNERABLE:** A1b; A2b; C1; C2a.

Rufous-lored Kingfisher *Todirhamphus winchelli* appears to be an extreme lowland forest specialist (with a penchant for small islands) in the **Philippines**, being recorded from Tablas, Romblon, Sibuyan (several seen recently: Timmins in prep.) and Sicogon (race *nesydrionetes*), Samar, Calicoan, Biliran, Leyte, Bohol (Rajah Sikatuna National Park apparently being a stronghold: N. Bostock *in litt*. 1994, J. Hornbuckle *in litt*. 1994), Cebu (Tabunan, April 1994: P. Davidson *per* C. R. Robson *in litt*. 1994), Negros (very possibly now extinct: Brooks *et al*. 1992) and Siquijor (population now tiny: Evans *et al*. 1993b) (race *nigrorum*), Mindanao (race *mindanensis*), Basilan (nominate race), Jolo, Tawi-tawi (seen recently, and possibly a stronghold: N. Bostock *in litt*. 1994), Bongao and Papahag (race *alfredi*); it may now be highly threatened following habitat destruction (Dickinson *et al*. 1991; see Collins *et al*. 1991). **ENDANGERED:** A1b; A2b; C1; C2a.

Lazuli Kingfisher *Todirhamphus lazuli* is endemic to Seram, Ambon and Haruku in the Moluccas, **Indonesia**, where it is found in forested areas in the lowlands, including mangroves, on the forest edge, and in areas partially cleared for agriculture (White and Bruce 1986, Bowler and Taylor 1989). It is locally quite common (Bishop 1992), but was recently found to be absent or rare in several areas of apparently suitable habitat (J. Bowler *in litt*. 1993, C. J. Heij *in litt*. 1993). Although it appears tolerant of disturbed habitats, it may require dead forest trees for nesting and perching and be threatened by their removal from plantations (Bowler and Taylor 1989). **VULNERABLE:** B1+2c; C1; C2a.

Chestnut-bellied Kingfisher *Todirhamphus farquhari* is found only in the central **Vanuatu** islands of Espiritu Santo (the stronghold), Malo and Malakula, where it is strictly a bird of the dark, undisturbed (or little disturbed) forests, in both lowlands and hills but seeming to prefer the former; all accessible forest on Espiritu Santo is scheduled to be logged in the next five years (Bregulla 1992, S. Maturin *in litt*. 1994). **VULNERABLE:** A2b; C1; C2a.

Mangaia Kingfisher *Todirhamphus ruficollaris* is endemic to Mangaia (52 km²), **Cook Islands (to New Zealand)**, where it inhabits forest growing on the makatea (an encircling coral limestone platform) and disturbed inland forest (G. McCormack *in litt.* 1993). It was fairly common in 1973 although possibly reduced since the introduction of Common Myna *Acridotheres tristis* (Holyoak and Thibault 1984, Pratt *et al.* 1987). In the 1992–1993 breeding season the population was estimated at 300–500 birds, spread through most of the makatea and in lowland secondary forest immediately adjacent; *A. tristis* was seen interfering with nesting in open secondary forest but not in the dense *Barringtonia* forest on the makatea (Rowe *et al.* 1993). **VULNERABLE:** D1; D2.

Marquesan Kingfisher *Todirhamphus godeffroyi* is endemic to forest on two of the Marquesas Islands, **French Polynesia**, with under 50 pairs on Hiva Oa (exceedingly rare in 1990), where it may have suffered through introduction of the Great Horned Owl *Bubo virginianus* and Common Myna *Acridotheres tristis* (although its decline is recent, while the myna was introduced at the beginning of this century: J.-C. Thibault *in litt.* 1993), and 300–500 pairs on Tahuata (possibly declining); records from Fatu Hiva, Mohotani and Ua Pou are apparently erroneous (Holyoak and Thibault 1984, Thibault 1988, Seitre and Seitre 1991). **ENDANGERED: B1+2e**; C2a; D1; D2.

Tuamotu Kingfisher *Todirhamphus gambieri* is widespread in the gardens and coconut groves of Niau in the Tuamotu archipelago, **French Polynesia**, where the race *gertrudae* was represented by 400–600 birds in 1974 and reported as common in 1990,

the nominate *gambieri* having become extinct on Mangareva, Gambier Islands, probably before 1922 (Holyoak and Thibault 1984, Pratt *et al.* 1987, Seitre and Seitre 1991). **VULNERABLE:** D1; D2.

Moustached Kingfisher *Actenoides bougainvillei* is found on Bougainville, **Papua New Guinea**, and Guadalcanal, **Solomon Islands**, and had not been reliably reported since 1953 (Diamond 1987) until it was seen on Guadalcanal in 1990 (A. Lees *in litt.* 1993, but record unconfirmed) and again in 1994, when observations and reports indicate that it only occurs in good primary forest above 900 m up to (at least) 1,325 m, most habitat at these elevations being secondary and subject to man-made clearance, natural landslides and cyclone damage (D. Gibbs *in litt.* 1994). It behaves like the two *Actenoides* species on Sulawesi, which are very unobtrusive and generally only call for 10 minutes just prior to dawn and after dusk; calls very similar to those described were heard in 1986 on the edge of lowland/swamp forest near Arawe on the north coast of Bougainville (K. D. Bishop *in litt.* 1987). **VULNERABLE:** C2a.

Blue-capped Kingfisher *Actenoides hombroni* occurs in primary montane forest on Mindanao in the **Philippines**, but appears very rare, with recent records from only a few sites (Mount Katanglad several times; Lake Sebu, South Cotabato province, several times, once as low as 800 m; Mount Apo, 1980); it is probably suffering from extensive habitat destruction (Collar and Andrew 1988, Dickinson *et al.* 1991, Evans *et al.* 1993a, N. J. Redman verbally 1993, N. Bostock *in litt.* 1994, R. J. Timmins *in litt.* 1994). **VULNERABLE:** A2b; B1+2c; C1; C2a.

Family CORACIIDAE

ROLLERS, GROUND-ROLLERS

Short-legged Ground-roller *Brachypteracias leptosomus* has been recorded throughout the rainforest belt of eastern **Madagascar**, but it is generally rare (at Marojejy only common in the least disturbed areas of primary forest, and with a preference for lower altitudes) and threatened by habitat destruction (Collar and Stuart 1985, Langrand 1990, Evans *et al.* 1992a), although recorded now from seven protected areas, the five in Nicoll and Langrand (1989) plus Mantady National Park, October 1993

(A. F. A. Hawkins *in litt.* 1994), and Ambatovaky Special Reserve, where it was considered to occupy large home ranges and to prefer gentle ridge slopes with a relatively dense growth of saplings (Thompson and Evans 1991). **VULNERABLE:** A2b; C1; C2a.

Scaly Ground-roller *Brachypteracias squamiger* has been recorded chiefly from the centre and northeast (but also much less commonly in the south-east) of the rainforest belt of eastern **Madagascar** (apparently preferring low-altitude areas of undisturbed primary habitat with damp soils and tangled undergrowth), but almost everywhere it is rare and localized, and threatened by habitat destruction, possible predation by village dogs and exploitation by man for food; it has been found in six protected areas (Collar and Stuart 1985, Nicoll and Langrand 1989, Langrand 1990, Evans *et al.* 1992a, Thompson and Evans 1992, J. C. Durbin *per*/and A. F. A. Hawkins *in litt.* 1994). **VULNERABLE:** A2b; C1; C2a.

Rufous-headed Ground-roller *Atelornis crossleyi* has been recorded in undisturbed habitat in the centre (south to Vondrozo) and north-east of the humid forest belt of **Madagascar**, where it is rare (the rarest of its family) and threatened by forest destruction (Collar and Stuart 1985, Dee 1986). While

there are records from four protected areas (Nicoll and Langrand 1989) and from sea-level to 1,500 m (Langrand 1990), it may be patchily distributed within and chiefly restricted to montane forest (Evans *et al.* 1992a). **VULNERABLE:** C2a.

Long-tailed Ground-roller *Uratelornis chimaera* is a largely terrestrial bird of subdesert scrub in south-west **Madagascar** where, like the Subdesert Mesite *Monias benschi*, it is confined to the coastal hinterland between the Mangoky and Fiherenana rivers and is subject to hunting, trapping and habitat destruction (Collar and Stuart 1985, 1988). It occurs in no protected area, tree removal for charcoal production is increasing, and introduced rats *Rattus rattus* are also believed to be a threat (O. Langrand *in litt.* 1987, Langrand 1990). **VULNERABLE:** B1+2c,e; C2b.

Family BUCEROTIDAE

HORNBILLS

Sulu Hornbill *Anthracoceros montani* occupies hill forest on the islands of Jolo, Tawitawi and Sanga Sanga in the Sulu archipelago, **Philippines** (Dickinson *et al.* 1991), and in 1971 was described as fairly common on Tawitawi; Jolo is now virtually deforested, and in September 1991 two adults and an immature were all that could be found on Tawitawi, apparently because the species is very heavily shot for food by local people and well-armed militias (Lambert 1993b). In 1994 Tawitawi was being rapidly cleared of its last forests, and only two hornbills were seen (T. M. Brooks and G. C. L. Dutson *in litt.* 1994). **CRITICAL: A1b,c**; A2b,c; B1+2c,e; **C1**; C2a; D1.

Mindoro Hornbill *Penelopides mindorensis* is restricted to Mindoro in the **Philippines**, where it was formerly fairly common at least in the lowlands (records extend up to 1,070 m) but where it has now been greatly reduced by forest loss, with records in 1991 coming from only west Mindoro; although it can occur in tiny patches of forest and edge habitats, it may well depend on larger closed-canopy tracts for food resources and breeding sites, such habitat is rapidly being cleared, and its overall density is low (Dutson *et al.* 1992, J. Hornbuckle *in litt.* 1994). **ENDANGERED: A1b**; A2b; **B1+2c**; **C1**; **C2a**.

Visayan Hornbill *Penelopides panini* is known to survive only (and only just) on Negros in the **Philippines**, being extinct or probably (or nearly) so on Guimaras, Masbate, Panay (apparently hunted out of all areas surveyed in 1990; one seen on Mt Madja-as in August 1994: T. M. Brooks and G. C. L. Dutson *in litt.* 1994), Sicogon (almost certainly now hunted out), Pan de Azucar and Ticao (endemic race *ticaensis*) (distribution from Dickinson *et al.* 1991). In 1991 it was found at three sites on Negros and reported from a fourth, appearing to require tall forest below 1,050 m (the sites where it was recorded being virtually the only ones found to contain such habitat, fast diminishing), and seeming to occur only at low density (Brooks *et al.* 1992). **CRITICAL: A1b,c**; **A2b,c**; **B1+2c,e**; **C1**; **C2a**.

Rufous-necked Hornbill *Aceros nipalensis* is known from Nepal (probably extinct: Inskipp and Inskipp 1991), **Bhutan**, north-east **India**, **Bangladesh**, **China** (southern Yunnan and south-east Tibet: Cheng 1987), **Myanmar**, western **Thailand**, northern and central **Laos** and **Vietnam**, occurring in tall evergreen forest at c.600–2,100 m (King *et al.* 1975, Ali and Ripley 1987, Boonsong and Round 1991, Ali *et al.* in prep.). It has recently been recorded, generally in small numbers, in Bhutan (Clements 1992, Inskipp and Inskipp 1993a,b, K. D. Bishop *in*

litt. 1994), India (M. Jäderblad *in litt.* 1994, R. Kaul verbally 1994, R. H. Raza *in litt.* 1994, Singh in press), Myanmar (K. D. Bishop *in litt.* 1993), Laos (common in Nakai Plateau/Nam Theun protected area: T. D. Evans and R. J. Timmins verbally 1994) and Vietnam (J. C. Eames *in litt.* 1994), and it occurs in at least two nature reserves in south-west Thailand, although it is probably close to extinction in the north of the country (Round 1988, Poonswad 1993) and it is reportedly declining in India because of the clearance of primary forest (Ali and Ripley 1987). Deforestation is reducing and fragmenting suitable habitat in much of its range (see Collins *et al.* 1991), which overlaps closely with that of shifting cultivators in the uplands of north-west Thailand (and elsewhere), so that hunting is also likely to be a problem (Round 1988). **VULNERABLE:** A1b,c; C1; C2a.

Wrinkled Hornbill *Aceros corrugatus* occurs in peninsular **Thailand** (either extinct or on the verge of extinction: Boonsong and Round 1991), peninsular (local and threatened: Medway and Wells 1976, D. R. Wells *in litt.* 1994) and East **Malaysia**, Kalimantan and Sumatra, **Indonesia** (still widespread, generally in small numbers, but locally common on Sumatra: S. van Balen *in litt.* 1994) and **Brunei**, where it is found in (e.g.) swamp forest and selectively logged forest up to 1,000 m (MacKinnon and Phillipps 1993), although it is principally an extreme lowland specialist, ranging higher only to feed (Wells 1985, D. R. Wells *in litt.* 1994). It is threatened by widespread clear-felling and logging of lowland forest and reclamation of swamp forest (BirdLife IP, D. R. Wells *in litt.* 1994; see Collins *et al.* 1991). **VULNERABLE:** A1b; A2b; C1; C2a.

Writhed-billed Hornbill *Aceros waldeni*, endemic to the **Philippines** on the islands of Panay (recent visits have produced no records and it may have been hunted out, though reportedly still present: *per* T. M. Brooks *in litt.* 1994), Guimaras (presumed extinct, given the near-total forest clearance) and Negros (recorded in 1991 for the first time anywhere in 80 years, but only at a single locality—at 950 m in mid-level forest—and only on one day, although it is speculated that it may be found elsewhere in the southern highlands); it must be extremely threatened because of extensive and continuing deforestation (Brooks *et al.* 1992, Timmins in prep.), and the one pair at the one site is the total known population and may conceivably prove to be all that remains of the species on the island (C. R. Robson *in litt.* 1994). **CRITICAL:** A1b; A2b; B1+2c,e; C1; C2a; D1.

Writhed Hornbill *Aceros leucocephalus* occurs in forests (in trees in clearings) above 800 m on Camiguin Sur, Dinagat and Mindanao in the **Philippines** (Dickinson *et al.* 1991). Despite being described as fairly common on Mindanao (Gonzales and Rees 1988) it seems to have been recorded very little in recent years (although at least at two localities) and may in fact be very rare now, presumably as a result of the combined effects of habitat loss and hunting (F. R. Lambert verbally 1994, Timmins in prep.). **ENDANGERED:** A1b,c; A2b,c; C1; C2a.

Narcondam Hornbill *Aceros narcondami* is endemic to Narcondam, a tiny island of 6.82 km² in the north-east Andaman Islands, **India**, where it is found in evergreen forest. The population was estimated to be c.400 in 1982 (and in 1993: V. Prakesh *per* R. Sankaran 1994), and not immediately threatened because the island is uninhabited, but it remains vulnerable to any future habitat destruction or introduction of alien predators or competitors (Hussain 1984). **VULNERABLE:** D1; D2.

Sumba Hornbill *Aceros everetti* is endemic to Sumba, **Indonesia** (White and Bruce 1986). During surveys in 1989 and 1992, it was recorded in a variety of forested habitats, and occasionally on the forest edge and in isolated trees in cultivated areas, but with a strong preference for primary forest and old secondary forest at low altitudes, its total population being estimated at 6,156 birds (based upon a density of 5.7 per km² ± 1.6 s.e.) (Jones *et al.* in prep.). It is threatened by deforestation, as forests on Sumba have been cleared rapidly in the last 50 years to provide grazing and agricultural land, and perhaps also by hunting (BirdLife IP; see RePPProT 1990). **VULNERABLE:** B1+2c; C1.

Plain-pouched Hornbill *Aceros subruficollis* is known from Tenasserim, **Myanmar**, south-west and peninsular **Thailand** and Sumatra, **Indonesia**, where it is recorded from evergreen and mixed deciduous forest in the lowlands and lower hills (Boonsong and Round 1991, MacKinnon and Phillipps 1993), but it is no longer believed that peninsular Malaysia is part of its range (D. R. Wells *in litt.* 1994). Its status remains essentially unknown, largely because field characters separating it from the widespread Wreathed Hornbill *A. undulatus* have only recently been defined (Kemp 1988), but it is presumably threatened by the extensive deforestation within its known range (see Collins *et al.* 1991). **VULNERABLE:** C1; C2a.

Family GALBULIDAE

JACAMARS

Three-toed Jacamar *Jacamaralcyon tridactyla*, although capable of surviving in badly degraded small woodlots (probably only if there are streams with mud banks in which to nest, and with adjacent sites to which to disperse), has undergone a major decline in overall abundance and a contraction of range in south-east **Brazil** (having once been recorded widely from eastern Minas Gerais, Espírito Santo, Rio de Janeiro, São Paulo and Paraná), occurring now chiefly in very small numbers at very few sites in the Rio Paraíba valley in Rio de Janeiro state, and in the dry regions of eastern Minas Gerais; habitat clearance must be chiefly responsible for this situation (Collar *et al.* 1992, Tobias *et al.* 1993, B. M. Whitney *in litt.* 1994). **ENDANGERED:** A1b; A2b; C1; **C2a**; D1.

Coppery-chested Jacamar *Galbula pastazae* is known from one site in **Colombia** (Nariño) at 1,525 m in 1970, and a small number of localities along the eastern slope of the Andes in **Ecuador** (Napo, Tungurahua, Morona-Santiago, Zamora-Chinchipe, Loja), chiefly occurring in humid lower montane forest between 900 and 1,300 m, with extremes of 600 and 1,700 m (Collar *et al.* 1992). This is the range within which clearance for agriculture is taking place, and the species appears to be notably scarce and local (Poulsen and Wege 1994). **VULNERABLE:** C2a.

Family CAPITONIDAE

BARBETS

White-chested Tinkerbird *Pogoniulus makawai* is judged to be a rare relict (if it is not an aberrant Yellow-rumped Tinkerbird *P. bilineatus*: Dowsett and Dowsett-Lemaire 1993) which remains known only from the type-specimen, collected in dense evergreen *Cryptosepalum* thicket in north-west **Zambia**, despite repeated attempts to relocate it (Collar and Stuart 1985; also Fry *et al.* 1988, D. R. Aspinwall *in litt.* 1994). **VULNERABLE:** D1.

White-mantled Barbet *Capito hypoleucus*, a polytypic lower montane forest species endemic to the northern Central Andes and western slope of the East Andes in **Colombia** (Bolívar, Antioquia, Caldas, Cundinamarca, Tolima), has retreated before widespread deforestation in the lower Cauca and middle Magdalena drainages, and since the early 1950s all records have come from southernmost Antioquia

and northern Caldas, where it can be locally fairly common but remains nevertheless at continuing risk from further clearance of habitat (Collar *et al.* 1992). **ENDANGERED:** B1+2c; **C2a**.

Five-coloured Barbet *Capito quinticolor* occupies wet forest in the Pacific coast lowlands of **Colombia**, localities including Quibdó, Tadó and El Tambo (Chocó), Malaguita, Buenaventura and adjacent Estero Pailón (Valle), El Papayo somewhere on the Río Saija (Cauca) and Barbacoas and Laguna del Trueno (Nariño); it is apparently local and appears to require closed-canopy forest, which is under increasing pressure within its altitudinal range, most records being below 180 m, although two skins are labelled '500 m' (Hilty and Brown 1986, Salaman and Gandy 1993, 1994, specimens in AMNH, CM, FMNH). **VULNERABLE:** A1b; A2b; C1; C2a.

Family INDICATORIDAE

HONEYGUIDES

Yellow-footed Honeyguide *Melignomon eisentrauti* has been collected from the mid-strata and canopy of primary and secondary evergreen lowland forest (including lower slopes of mountains) in **Cameroon** (two records), **Liberia** (near Mount Nimba and in the Wonegizi Mountains) and **Sierra Leone** (one sight record from Gola forest), with suspected sightings in Ghana (Kakum Forest Reserve) and Ivory Coast (Taï forest), although it probably occurs more widely in West Africa's much pressurized primary forests (Collar and Stuart 1985, Thiollay 1985, Colston and Curry-Lindahl 1986, Fry *et al.* 1988, Allport 1991). **VULNERABLE: A2b.**

Family PICIDAE

WRYNECKS, WOODPECKERS

Tawny Piculet *Picumnus fulvescens* is known from caatinga and humid woodland at 150–900 m in Pernambuco and Alagoas in north-east **Brazil** (Short 1982, Sick 1985). Within this restricted range it is a scarce bird (at least in Pedra Talhada Biological Reserve where it has recently been recorded) and there is considerable clearance of its habitat taking place (Forrester 1993, B. M. Whitney *in litt.* 1994). **VULNERABLE: B1+2c.**

Ochraceous Piculet *Picumnus limae* is known from six caatinga localities in interior Ceará and western Paraíba, north-eastern **Brazil** (Short 1982, Sick 1985), a restricted range within which considerable clearance of habitat is taking place (B. M. Whitney *in litt.* 1994). **VULNERABLE: B1+2c.**

Red-cockaded Woodpecker *Picoides borealis* was originally distributed throughout south-east **U.S.A.** in the region dominated by shortleaf *Pinus echinata*, slash *P. elliotti*, longleaf *P. palustris* and loblolly *P. taeda* pines, but is now limited to c.30 isolated populations (the largest being in South Carolina and Florida) containing c.2,000 groups or 'clans' made up of c.7,400 birds; each clan requires at least 80 ha of fire-sustained open pine forest with old-growth trees (75–100 years old) in which to nest; long-term clearance of such habitat, its economic management (which suppresses the necessary characteristics), and the impact of hurricanes have reduced the viability of any population (Collar *et al.* 1992). **VULNERABLE: A1b; A2b; B1+2b,c,d; C1; C2a.**

Cuban Flicker *Colaptes fernandinae* was once common and widespread on **Cuba**, but, for reasons unclear though probably related to the loss of its savanna habitat, it has become very rare and localized, known from only three separate areas, two of which hold very small populations while the third and largest persists in the Zapata Swamp, and total numbers are estimated at only 300 pairs (Collar *et al.* 1992). **ENDANGERED: A1a; C2a; D1.**

Helmeted Woodpecker *Dryocopus galeatus* is confined to primary Atlantic forest in southern south-east **Brazil** (São Paulo, Paraná, Santa Catarina, Rio Grande do Sul), eastern **Paraguay** (Amambay, Canindeyú, Caaguazú, Alto Paraná, Paraguarí, Itapúa) and northernmost **Argentina** (Misiones), where despite many records in very recent years its status remains unclear, still regarded by some as extremely rare and at risk from the widespread deforestation in the region (Collar *et al.* 1992). It was recorded at three localities (minimum 12 birds) in eastern Paraguay in 1992, apparently being able to persist at least in the short term in relatively small and degraded forest patches (Brooks *et al.* 1993), although possibly subject to competitive exclusion by Lineated Woodpecker *D. lineatus* and Robust Woodpecker *Campephilus robustus* in these areas (Tobias *et al.* 1993, R. P. Clay verbally 1994). **ENDANGERED: C2a.**

Imperial Woodpecker *Campephilus imperialis*, the largest woodpecker in the world, was originally distributed throughout the Sierra Madre Occidental between 1,920 and 3,050 m in **Mexico** (Sonora, Chihuahua, Durango, Nayarit, possibly Zacatecas, Jalisco, Michoacán). It has suffered from persistent exploitation for food by local Indians and by lumbermen, coupled with the widespread destruction of its specialized open pine-forest habitat, and especially the removal of trees large enough to nest, and although previously not uncommon, it has not been recorded with certainty since 1958 (Collar *et al.* 1992). There have been recent claims of sightings from three different areas (*per* A. J. Long verbally 1994). **CRITICAL: D1**.

Red-collared Woodpecker *Picus rabieri* is known from **Vietnam**, where it has recently been recorded in small numbers at five localities, including three protected areas (and its known range extended to southern Annam), **Laos**, where it has recently been found to be locally common in four large protected areas, and south-east Yunnan, **China** (where it is known by one old record: Cheng 1987), and is found in evergreen and semi-evergreen forest in the lowlands and locally in tall mixed deciduous forest (Robson *et al.* 1989, 1993a, Duckworth *et al.* 1993a,b, Timmins *et al.* 1993). It is usually scarce or absent from selectively logged and disturbed forest (although sometimes found in small and degraded remnants provided that some large trees remain), and is threatened by the widespread destruction and degradation of lowland forest which is taking place within its range (J. C. Eames *in litt.* 1994, T. D. Evans and R. J. Timmins verbally 1994; see Collins *et al.* 1991). **VULNERABLE: A1b**.

Okinawa Woodpecker *Sapheopipo noguchii* is endemic to Okinawa in the Nansei Shoto, southern **Japan**, where it is found in broadleaf evergreen forest in the mountainous northern part of the island (Yambaru). Population estimates since 1950 have ranged from 40 to 200 birds, the most recent being c.100, and it is believed to be gradually declining as a result of the continuing deforestation within its tiny range which is no more than 15 km^2 (Short 1973, 1982, King 1978–1979, Miyagi 1989, Brazil 1991). **CRITICAL: B1+2c**; C1; **C2b**; D1; D2.

Family EURYLAIMIDAE

BROADBILLS

African Green Broadbill *Pseudocalyptomena graueri* is known from only two areas in eastern **Zaïre**, the Itombwe Mountains and mountains west of Lake Kivu, and one in south-west **Uganda**, Bwindi (Impenetrable) forest, inhabiting primary rainforest (middle strata and canopy in Itombwe, upper portions of undergrowth in Bwindi) at 1,760–2,480 m; habitat loss is the most likely threat, although recent evidence suggests that habitat in Itombwe is at present reasonably intact and the Kahuzi-Biega National Park embraces much habitat west of Lake Kivu (Collar and Stuart 1985, 1988, Wilson and Catsis 1990, Ash *et al.* 1991, Keith *et al.* 1992). **VULNERABLE:** B1+2a,c.

Wattled Broadbill *Eurylaimus steerii* occupies the understorey of forest below 1,000 m on Samar, Leyte and Bohol (race *samarensis*), Dinagat, Siargao and Mindanao (race *mayri*) and Basilan (nominate *steerii*), **Philippines**, where it is uncommon and local (Dickinson *et al.* 1991). There are recent records from Bohol and Mindanao, but the consensus of fieldworkers is that it is now a rare bird, and it must have suffered from the extensive and continuing lowland deforestation to which these islands have been subjected (N. J. Redman verbally 1993, F. R. Lambert verbally 1994). **VULNERABLE:** A1b; A2b; C1; C2a.

Family DENDROCOLAPTIDAE
WOODCREEPERS

Moustached Woodcreeper *Xiphocolaptes falcirostris* (including Snethlage's Woodcreeper as a subspecies, *X. f. franciscanus*) occupies a wide range in semi-deciduous woodland, riverine forest and wooded caatinga in the interior of north-east **Brazil** (Maranhão, Piauí, Ceará, Paraíba, Pernambuco, Bahia, Minas Gerais, Goiás), but has become extremely local and uncommon through the widespread and continuing clearance of its habitat and the ever-increasing isolation of its populations (Collar *et al*. 1992). **VULNERABLE:** B1+2c; C2a.

Family FURNARIIDAE
OVENBIRDS

Royal Cinclodes *Cinclodes aricomae* has a very small global population (less than 50 pairs known with certainty) divided between a series of tiny humid patches of *Polylepis* woodland in the Andes of south-east **Peru** (Cuzco, Apurímac, Puno) and, at least previously, adjacent **Bolivia** (La Paz); its habitat is extremely scarce and has suffered extensive (recent) clearance for firewood and lack of regeneration through burning (Collar *et al*. 1992). **CRITICAL:** B1+2c; **C2a**; D1.

White-bellied Cinclodes *Cinclodes palliatus* occupies only a small part of a putative 10,000 km² range above 4,400 m in **Peru** (Huancavelica, Junín and immediately adjacent Lima), and appears to have very specific habitat requirements, being found on only a few (perhaps those that are mineral-rich) of the many bogs in this region, so that its total population is extremely small; while perhaps in the process of becoming extinct for natural reasons, its chances of survival would greatly diminish should mining commence in these areas (Collar *et al*. 1992). **VULNERABLE:** D1.

Más Afuera Rayadito *Aphrastura masafuerae* occupies chiefly *Dicksonia externa* fern forest, most often along streams, at altitudes of 600–1,300 m on Alejandro Selkirk (= Más Afuera) in the Juan Fernández Islands, **Chile**, with a total population of c.500 individuals; goat trampling of ferns may be causing the opening up and fragmentation of this habitat (Collar *et al*. 1992). **VULNERABLE:** D1; D2.

White-browed Tit-spinetail *Leptasthenura xenothorax* is restricted to a few small and often widely scattered patches of humid *Polylepis* woodland at 3,700–4,550 m in Cuzco and Apurímac, south-central **Peru**; these woods, not known to hold more than 20 families (70 birds) each (most hold one or two pairs), are being steadily cleared for firewood (Collar *et al*. 1992). **CRITICAL:** B1+2c; **C2a**; D1.

Apurímac Spinetail *Synallaxis courseni* is known from two patches of woodland (much of it *Podocarpus*) on the north and south slopes of a single mountain massif (Nevada Ampay, north of Abancay) in Apurímac department, **Peru**, where it is a common inhabitant of tangled understorey and adjacent shrubbery at 2,450–3,500 m, although the total population is estimated at 300–400 pairs (Collar *et al*. 1992). **VULNERABLE:** D1; D2.

Plain Spinetail *Synallaxis infuscata* is an inhabitant of tangled undergrowth of lowland Atlantic forest, confined by massive habitat destruction to just a few very small reserves in Pernambuco (UFPE Ecological Reserve, 4.5 km², Saltinho Biological Reserve, 5 km²) and Alagoas (Pedra Talhada Biological Reserve, 45 km²), in north-east **Brazil**, although a population exists at Murici (Alagoas) and a new race may prove to exist in Maranhão (Collar *et al*. 1992). **ENDANGERED:** A1b; A2b; **B1+2c**; **C1**; C2a; D1.

Blackish-headed Spinetail *Synallaxis tithys* is an uncommon inhabitant of dense undergrowth of evergreen and deciduous forest (sea-level to 1,100 m) in south-west **Ecuador** (Manabí, Guayas, El Oro, Loja) and immediately adjacent north-west **Peru** (Tumbes), where it is threatened both by forest clearance and by the grazing and trampling of roaming cattle in the patches that remain (Collar *et al.* 1992, Best *et al.* 1993). In Ecuador in September 1992 small numbers were found in woodlands south of the Bahía de Caráquez in Manabí, and in January 1993 more were found in woodland north of Puerto de Cayo (R. S. Ridgely *in litt.* 1994). **VULNERABLE:** A1b; A2b; B1+2c; C1; C2a.

Russet-bellied Spinetail *Synallaxis zimmeri* is confined to and patchily common in scrub and dense undergrowth in a very small area in the Andes of west-central **Peru** (five localities are known on the Pacific slope of Cordillera Negra in Ancash at 1,800–2,900 m), where it is threatened by habitat destruction by cattle-grazing and farm expansion (Collar *et al.* 1992). **ENDANGERED: B1+2c; C2b.**

Hoary-throated Spinetail *Synallaxis kollari* is known from just six specimens and one observation along four different rivers in northern Roraima, **Brazil**, where, until two birds were seen (in seasonally flooded riverine forest with an understorey of dense thickets and vines) by the Rio Tacutu in August 1992, the last known record had been in 1956 (Collar *et al.* 1992). In January 1993 it was found on the Rio Tacutu just inside **Guyana**, very close to where previously recorded inside Brazil (D. Finch *per* B. C. Forrester *in litt.* 1993). **VULNERABLE: D2.**

Red-shouldered Spinetail *Gyalophylax hellmayri* is known from 14 localities in northern Bahia and western Pernambuco, plus one in north-east Piauí, **Brazil**, inhabiting dense woody caatinga characterized by tangled small trees, some cacti and abundant terrestrial bromeliads (Whitney and Pacheco 1994). It has undoubtedly declined significantly in response to intense human pressure on this habitat for agricultural land and firewood, with little or no regeneration owing to heavy grazing by livestock (B. M. Whitney *in litt.* 1994). **VULNERABLE: C2a.**

Maquis Canastero *Asthenes heterura* is restricted to arid, scrubby, *Polylepis*-dominated slopes (3,000–4,150 m) in central Cochabamba and a small area of La Paz, **Bolivia** (Fjeldså and Krabbe 1990). Its status has been obscured by confusion with Rusty-fronted Canastero *A. ottonis* and Canyon Canastero *A. pudibunda*, but throughout its range its habitat has been highly disturbed through the collection of firewood, clearance for agriculture and overgrazing by livestock (B. M. Whitney *in litt.* 1994). **VULNERABLE:** A1b; C1; C2a.

Cipó Canastero *Asthenes luizae* was only recently discovered and as yet is known to inhabit isolated rocky outcrops and associated dry vegetation between 1,100 and 1,500 m only in a tiny area north-east of Jaboticatubas within the Serra do Cipó, Minas Gerais, **Brazil**, where it faces possible threats from cattle-grazing, fires and brood-parasitism by the increasingly abundant Shiny Cowbird *Molothrus bonariensis* (Collar *et al.* 1992). **ENDANGERED:** A2b,d; **C1**; **C2b**; D1; D2.

Pale-tailed Canastero *Asthenes huancavelicae* (whose taxonomic status requires further study) exists as four very local forms in arid intermontane valleys with scattered thorny bushes and cacti at 1,830–3,700 m in central **Peru** (Ancash, Huánuco, Huancavelica, Ayacucho, Apurímac), where at least three of them are rare and possibly threatened indirectly by habitat destruction, the only reasonably abundant one (nominate *huancavelicae*) still known from a highly circumscribed area around the towns of Yauli and Ayacucho (Collar *et al.* 1992). **VULNERABLE:** C1.

Berlepsch's Canastero *Asthenes berlepschi* is known from the vicinity of Nevado Illampu in the upper Maripi valley, an extremely small area in the semi-arid mountains of La Paz, north-west **Bolivia**, where it is reliant on the continued survival of small amounts of natural and man-managed habitat (open rocky and grassy terrain, including fields, with scrub, hedges or woodland) at 2,600–3,700 m (Collar *et al.* 1992). **VULNERABLE:** D1; D2.

Chestnut Canastero *Asthenes steinbachi* inhabits well developed, semi-arid temperate hillside scrub at 2,000–3,000 m (down to 800 m in winter) in Salta, Catamarca, Tucumán, La Rioja, San Luis and Mendoza, north-west **Argentina** (Fjeldså and Krabbe 1990), but it appears largely to have been extirpated by habitat loss, remaining common only in a few scattered and unprotected localities in the southern part of its range (B. M. Whitney *in litt.* 1994; also M. Pearman *in litt.* 1994). **VULNERABLE:** A1b; C2a.

Austral Canastero *Asthenes anthoides* is widely but now very locally distributed in Patagonian **Argentina** and adjacent **Chile**, showing some seasonal movements northwards in winter. It inhabits diverse hillside shrubbery interspersed with mature grassland from sea-level to 1,500 m, a habitat that has been drastically altered for over a century by grazing sheep, so that its total population must have declined steeply over many decades and is still decreasing, though very locally the bird may be judged common (Collar *et al.* 1992). **VULNERABLE:** C2a.

Orinoco Softtail *Thripophaga cherriei* is known from just six specimens taken in 1899 and 1970 along a single low-lying (100 m) affluent (Río Capuana) of the upper Río Orinoco, **Venezuela**, where it has been found in bushes and brush along streams and river banks. The area does not appear to be under immediate threat from habitat destruction, but a nearby trade and tourist centre development requires monitoring (Collar *et al*. 1992). **VULNER-ABLE:** D2.

Striated Softtail *Thripophaga macroura* occurs very patchily up to 1,000 m within a small range in lowland Atlantic Forest in south-east **Brazil** (Bahia, Minas Gerais, Espírito Santo, Rio de Janeiro), where it appears closely associated with lower canopy vine tangles and has suffered from much (continuing) habitat destruction (Collar *et al*. 1992). **VULNER-ABLE:** C1; C2a.

White-throated Barbtail *Margarornis tatei* is restricted to the undergrowth of montane forest in the coastal Cordillera de Caripe and Paria peninsula of north-east **Venezuela** (Anzoátegui, Sucre, Monagas), where it is threatened by habitat loss, with all recent records coming from the Paria peninsula, which has national park status but is critically compromised by agricultural development (Collar *et al*. 1992). In February 1993 only two birds were found in three days within its habitat on the peninsula's Cerro Humo (J. Curson *in litt*. 1993). **ENDANGERED: B1+2c; C2a.**

Rufous-necked Foliage-gleaner *Syndactyla ruficollis* is generally common within evergreen, semi-deciduous and deciduous forests from 400 to 2,900 m (commonest above 1,600 m) on the foothills and slopes of the western Andes in south-west **Ecuador** (El Oro, Loja) and north-west **Peru** (Tumbes, Piura, Lambayeque, Cajamarca), and is threatened by extensive and continuing habitat destruction and disturbance, including the trampling and grazing by cattle of the undergrowth in which it lives (Collar *et al*. 1992, Best *et al*. 1993). **VULNER-ABLE:** A1b; A2b; C1; C2a.

Alagoas Foliage-gleaner *Philydor novaesi* has only ever been known from Pedra (sometimes Serra) Branca, near Murici, on the south-east escarpment of the Borborema plateau in Alagoas, north-east **Brazil**, and appears now to be confined to an unprotected and rapidly diminishing tract of upland forest (550 m), only 15 km² in extent, near the type-locality; even within its tiny historical range it has been thought rare (Collar *et al*. 1992). **CRITICAL:** A1b; A2b; **B1+2c;** C1; C2b; D1; D2.

Bolivian Recurvebill *Simoxenops striatus* is known from only four specimens and a few sight records from four localities in lower montane forest in the departments of La Paz, Cochabamba (two localities, one previously unpublished—west of Villa Tunari at 1,000–1,100 m in 1992: B. M. Whitney *in litt*. 1994), and Santa Cruz, **Bolivia**, being apparently scarce and confined to a very narrow elevational zone (670–800 m, apart from the new site above), and may be severely threatened owing to rapid deforestation within its small range (Collar *et al*. 1992). **VULNERABLE:** A2b; B1+2b,c; C1; C2a.

Henna-hooded Foliage-gleaner *Hylocryptus erythrocephalus* remains moderately common (but possibly seasonal) in the understorey of deciduous, semi-deciduous and moist evergreen forest (generally from 400 to 1,350 m, though up to 1,800 m has been recorded) in a restricted area of south-west **Ecuador** (Manabí, El Oro, Loja) and north-west **Peru** (Tumbes, Piura, Lambayeque), and is threatened by extensive and continuing habitat destruction and disturbance (Collar *et al*. 1992, Best *et al*. 1993). **VULNERABLE:** A1b; A2b; C1; C2a.

Great Xenops *Megaxenops parnaguae* is a mid-storey bark-gleaner occurring in dry woodland in the heavily populated interior of north-east **Brazil** (Ceará, Piauí, Pernambuco, Bahia, Minas Gerais, Distrito Federal), but is apparently very local and is presumably suffering from extensive and continuing land clearance (Collar *et al*. 1992); although fairly common in Serra da Capivara National Park, Piauí, it may need arboreal vegetation (Olmos 1993), and indeed birds appear to prefer fairly dense woodland up to 12 m tall where abundant vines make for a generally dense tangled understorey and mid-storey (Whitney and Pacheco 1994). **VULNERABLE:** A1b; A2b; C1; C2a.

Family FORMICARIIDAE

ANTBIRDS

White-bearded Antshrike *Biatas nigropectus*, a naturally rare, bamboo-haunting bird, has been reduced in both range and numbers by the destruction of lowland and montane (to 1,300 m) Atlantic forest in **Brazil** (Minas Gerais, Rio de Janeiro, São Paulo, Paraná, Santa Catarina) and **Argentina** (Misiones), and it now seems to depend on four or five protected areas (notably Itatiaia and Iguaçu National Parks, Brazil) for its security (Collar *et al.* 1992). **VULNERABLE:** C2a.

Recurve-billed Bushbird *Clytoctantes alixii* has been recorded from few localities (and not at all since 1965) in the lowland and foothill forests (185–1,200 m) of westernmost **Venezuela** (Sierra de Perijá in Zulia) and northern **Colombia** (northern reaches of the West, Central and East Andes, in various departments); deforestation of this region has been (and continues to be) extensive, although the bird may be able to survive in dense secondary growth (Collar *et al.* 1992). **ENDANGERED:** A1b; A2b; **C1**; **C2a**.

Speckled Antshrike *Xenornis setifrons* inhabits steep slopes and damp ravine bottoms in humid lowland and foothill forest (150–600 m) in eastern **Panama** (Panamá, western and eastern San Blas, eastern Darién) and north-west **Colombia** (Chocó), where it has been recorded infrequently from very few localities (once in Colombia in 1940) and appears to be local and facing some loss of habitat in the near future (Collar *et al.* 1992). Its habitat in Nusagandi, San Blas, receives protection from the Kuna Indians, and in Darién (where most destruction is occurring) part of its range falls within the large Darién National Park (R. S. Ridgely *in litt.* 1994); however, habitat degradation in the west of its range and the possible development of the Darién highway continue to threaten the species (W. Adsett verbally 1994). **VULNERABLE:** C2a.

Plumbeous Antvireo *Dysithamnus plumbeus* haunts tangles in the lower stratum of tall, primary Atlantic Forest in south-east **Brazil** (Bahia once in 1928, Minas Gerais, Espírito Santo, extreme northwest Rio de Janeiro), where it has suffered from extensive and continuing habitat loss and seems to depend on a handful of protected areas (notably Sooretama) for its security (Collar *et al.* 1992). **VULNERABLE:** A1b; A2b; B1+2c; C1; C2a.

Bicoloured Antvireo *Dysithamnus occidentalis* has been recorded from patches of regrowth in natural forest clearings at probably no lower than 1,500 m (and up to 2,200 m) in three general areas of the subtropical Andes of **Colombia** (Valle, Cauca) and **Ecuador** (Napo, in the race *punctitectus*), and has suffered substantial habitat loss at least in Ecuador, with agriculture soon to penetrate into other areas there (Collar *et al.* 1992). **VULNERABLE:** C1; C2a.

Alagoas Antwren *Myrmotherula snowi* has only ever been known from Pedra (sometimes Serra) Branca, near Murici, on the south-eastern escarpment of the Borborema plateau in Alagoas, north-eastern **Brazil**, and appears now to be confined to an unprotected and rapidly diminishing tract of upland forest (550 m), only 15 km^2 in extent, near the type-locality (Collar *et al.* 1992, Whitney and Pacheco in press). **CRITICAL:** A1b; A2b; **B1+2c**; C1; C2b; D1; D2.

Rio de Janeiro Antwren *Myrmotherula fluminensis* is based on a single individual netted in July 1982 in a partially isolated and highly degraded woodlot near Santo Aleixo, Majé, in the middle of Rio de Janeiro state, **Brazil**, possibly having straggled from the Serra dos Órgãos and presumably representing one or more very small populations at risk from forest clearance (Collar *et al.* 1992). **VULNERABLE:** A1b; A2b; B1+2c; C1; C2a.

Salvadori's Antwren *Myrmotherula minor* is endemic to the lowland forests of south-east **Brazil** (Minas Gerais, Espírito Santo, Rio de Janeiro, São Paulo, Santa Catarina), where it inhabits the interior of undisturbed and old second-growth forest in humid regions, apparently almost always near water, and generally below 300 m (though it has been recorded at up to 780 m); it occurs in only five protected areas, some of which are themselves threatened, and is under continuing pressure from the loss of lowland forest habitat elsewhere (Whitney and Pacheco in press). **VULNERABLE:** B1+2c; C2a.

Ashy Antwren *Myrmotherula grisea* has been recorded in the middle storey and lower canopy of lower cloud-forest at seven localities (see below) in La Paz, Cochabamba and Santa Cruz, north-west **Bolivia**, its small geographic and elevational range (c.500–1,650 m) placing it seriously at risk owing to the current high degree and rate of deforestation in the yungas (Collar *et al*. 1992). The seventh site for the species was discovered in 1992 west of Villa Tunari, Cochabamba, at 1,000–1,100 m (B. M. Whitney *in litt*. 1994). **VULNERABLE:** A1b; A2b; C1; C2a.

Unicoloured Antwren *Myrmotherula unicolor* is restricted to the lower slopes and coastal plain seaward of the Serra do Mar in **Brazil** (Rio de Janeiro, São Paulo, Paraná, Santa Catarina, Rio Grande do Sul), inhabiting undisturbed and secondary humid forest (in São Paulo also restinga), always at altitudes of less than 500 m and chiefly below 200 m; the species occurs within only six protected areas, some of which are themselves threatened, and it is under continuing pressure from the loss of lowland forest habitat elsewhere (Whitney and Pacheco in press). **VULNERABLE:** B1+2c; C2a.

Band-tailed Antwren *Myrmotherula urosticta* occupies primary or moderately disturbed Atlantic Forest in eastern **Brazil** (Bahia, Espírito Santo, Rio de Janeiro). It occurs in only six protected areas, some of which are themselves threatened, and is under continuing pressure from the loss of lowland forest habitat elsewhere (Tobias *et al*. 1993, Whitney and Pacheco in press). **VULNERABLE:** B1+2c; C2a.

Ash-throated Antwren *Herpsilochmus parkeri* has been found to be fairly common in humid montane forest at the type-locality on a low isolated mountain ridge at 1,350 m in San Martín department, northern **Peru**, but its minute geographic range (only one other site is known, though possibly identical to or otherwise adjacent to the type-locality), coupled with rampant deforestation of the adjacent lowlands in the Río Huallaga drainage, renders it highly vulnerable (Collar *et al*. 1992). **VULNERABLE:** D2.

Pectoral Antwren *Herpsilochmus pectoralis* possesses an unusual and highly fragmented range in north-east **Brazil** (Maranhão, Rio Grande do Norte, Sergipe, Bahia), where it survives as a very local (though sometimes common) inhabitant of unprotected caatinga woodland, secondary woodlots and gallery forest, all of which are under pressure from man (Collar *et al*. 1992). **VULNERABLE:** A2b; B1+2c; C1; C2a.

Narrow-billed Antwren *Formicivora iheringi* inhabits the lower mid-levels of dry forest (rich in vine-tangles and terrestrial bromeliads) in a limited area of interior eastern **Brazil** (Bahia, Minas Gerais), living at reasonably high density but under great threat from continuing loss of its entirely unpro-

tected habitat (Collar *et al*. 1992, Tobias *et al*. 1993). **VULNERABLE:** B1+2c; C1; C2a.

Black-hooded Antwren *Formicivora erythronotos*, although known from about 20 nineteenth century skins, was rediscovered as recently as 1987, when it was found to be an inhabitant of the undergrowth of highly vulnerable patches of secondary forest at sea-level in a single area (Angra dos Reis) of southern coastal Rio de Janeiro state, **Brazil** (Collar *et al*. 1992). The main known site, although kept confidential, is being invaded by people taking holidays in the area, with cars being parked, habitat burnt and huts built exactly where the bird is found (Tobias *et al*. 1993, G. Sangster *in litt*. 1994). **CRITICAL:** A2b; B1+2c; **C1**; **C2a**; **D1**; D2.

Restinga Antwren *Formicivora littoralis* occupies a highly restricted range consisting of beach-scrub habitat in Rio de Janeiro state, **Brazil**, and, despite being seemingly abundant, faces extirpation through the development of the area for holiday-making (Collar *et al*. 1992) and through the increasing presence of squatters (B. M. Whitney *in litt*. 1994). The type-locality itself, near Arraial do Cabo, is a strip of dunes some 30 km long and up to 400 m wide, greatly threatened by the salt industry and beachfront housing (G. Sangster *in litt*. 1994). **ENDANGERED:** A2b; **B1+2b,c**; **C1**; **C2a**; D1; D2.

Orange-bellied Antwren *Terenura sicki* is fairly common in, but is restricted to, three localities (including 'Murici' on the south-east escarpment of the Borborema plateau in Alagoas, and to one site on this coastal range in adjacent Pernambuco, north-east **Brazil**, where it occupies the canopy of the middle storey of evergreen forest between 300 and 700 m; clearance and heavy degradation of this habitat are widespread in the region (Collar *et al*. 1992). **VULNERABLE:** A1b; A2b; B1+2c; C1; C2a.

Yellow-rumped Antwren *Terenura sharpei* has been found at a few sites between 1,100 and 1,650 m in the yungas of **Bolivia** (La Paz, Cochabamba) and immediately adjacent **Peru** (Puno), where it forages 10–20 m above ground within 1 m of the outer edge of the canopy, probably always in small to moderate numbers, in entirely unprotected upper tropical humid forest that is rapidly being cleared for cultivation, mainly of coca and coffee (Collar *et al*. 1992). **VULNERABLE:** A1b; A2b; C1; C2a.

Rio Branco Antbird *Cercomacra carbonaria* is endemic to gallery forest on the Rio Branco and some of its tributaries in northern Roraima, northernmost **Brazil**, where despite being relatively common its minute range within a very limited habitat renders it highly vulnerable to even small changes in forest use (Collar *et al.* 1992). In January 1993 it was found on the Rio Tacutu just inside **Guyana**, very close to where previously recorded inside Brazil (D. Finch *per* B. C. Forrester *in litt.* 1993). **VULNERABLE:** D2.

Fringe-backed Fire-eye *Pyriglena atra*, an undergrowth-haunting ant-follower, remains known only from west of the town of Santo Amaro, in the vicinity of Salvador, Bahia, **Brazil**; loss of habitat there—even the second growth in which it appears to be most abundant—has been substantial and the remaining tracts are likely to become ever smaller and more isolated (Collar *et al.* 1992). **ENDANGERED: A1b**; **A2b**; **B1+2c**; **C1**; **C2b**; **D1**.

Slender Antbird *Rhopornis ardesiaca* occupies a small range at c.800–900 m from Ipaoté south to Boa Nova in south-central Bahia, **Brazil**, where its dry liana-forest habitat (within which it is fairly common) is very rapidly being cleared, with already only small woodlots remaining (Collar *et al.* 1992). **ENDANGERED: A1b**; **A2b**; **B1+2c**; **C1**; **C2a**.

Black-tailed Antbird *Myrmoborus melanurus*, although described in 1866, remains known only from north-east **Peru** in eastern Loreto between the rivers Ucayali and Javari (Sibley and Monroe 1990), and seems to be genuinely rare in an area which is not immune from habitat conversion (R. S. Ridgely *in litt.* 1994). **VULNERABLE:** C2b.

Scalloped Antbird *Myrmeciza ruficauda* has been marooned by extensive and continuing clearance of Atlantic Forest in a few sites in north-east and south-east **Brazil** (Paraíba, Pernambuco, Alagoas, Bahia, Minas Gerais, Espírito Santo). In the south-east (nominate *ruficauda*) it is uncommon where it occurs, while in the north-east (race *soror*) the areas involved are extremely small, and virtually no site in either region is adequately protected (Collar *et al.* 1992). **VULNERABLE:** A1b; A2b; B1+2c; C1; C2a.

Grey-headed Antbird *Myrmeciza griseiceps* is confined to patches of *Chusquea* bamboo and dense undergrowth in semi-deciduous moist forest and cloud-forest in the Pacific-slope foothills of the Andes (600–2,900 m) in south-west **Ecuador** (El Oro, Loja) and north-west **Peru** (Tumbes, Piura), where its total numbers must be very small and it is threatened by rampant habitat destruction and degradation caused by cattle (Collar *et al.* 1992, Best *et al.* 1993). **ENDANGERED:** A1b; **A2b**; B1+2c; C1; C2a.

Rufous-fronted Antthrush *Formicarius rufifrons* is a rare and rather unpredictable inhabitant of riverine floodplain thickets (where tall forest with shaded understorey lies adjacent to second-growth vegetation with a dense understorey) in a restricted area of lowland south-east **Peru** (Madre de Dios), having been recorded only along rivers that drain into the Río Madre de Dios, and is consequently at some risk from actual and impending agricultural development (Collar *et al.* 1992). The global population is put at 700–3,500 pairs, of which 20% are within currently protected areas (Kratter in press). **VULNERABLE:** A2b; C1; C2b.

Giant Antpitta *Grallaria gigantea* was thought restricted to swampy areas in humid cloud-forest in south-west **Colombia** (race *lehmanni*, in Cauca and Huila at 3,000 m; last recorded in the 1940s) and **Ecuador** (race *gigantea* in Carchi, Tungurahua, Napo, at 2,200–2,600 m or more; and race *hylodroma* in Pichincha at 1,200–2,000 m), known from few localities outside of the Pichincha area and with a lack of recent records possibly related to the extent of deforestation continuing within its range (Collar *et al.* 1992). More recent observations of *hylodroma* on Pichincha and *gigantea* on Sierra Azul in Napo suggest that the habitat is the understorey of wet mossy forest and that a main food may be giant earthworms *Rhynodrylus*; if the species prefers flat areas it may be particularly at risk, since these are the easiest to clear for pastures (Krabbe *et al.* 1994b). The 1959 specimen record in Collar *et al.* (1992) from the West Andes of Colombia is an Undulated Antpitta *G. squamigera* (Krabbe *et al.* 1994b; also R. S. Ridgely *in litt.* 1994). **VULNERABLE:** A1b; A2b; C1; C2a.

Moustached Antpitta *Grallaria alleni* is a species of the cloud-forest understorey known from just two specimens (representing two subspecies, both collected at around 2,100 m) from the western slopes of the Central Andes (Quindío in 1911, nominate *alleni*) and East Andes (Huila in 1971, race *andaquiensis*), **Colombia**, where it has undoubtedly suffered from the widespread deforestation, and is obviously extremely rare (Collar *et al.* 1992). **ENDANGERED:** B1+2c; C2a; D1.

Táchira Antpitta *Grallaria chthonia* (which requires taxonomic validation) is known only from the type-locality, 1,800–2,100 m, apparently in high, dense cloud-forest, in El Tamá National Park in the Andes of western **Venezuela** (Táchira), where it has been recorded just twice (during the mid-1950s); although habitat at the site remains undisturbed at present above 1,600 m, deforestation in the area has been proceeding rapidly (Collar *et al.* 1992, S. L. Hilty *in litt.* 1994). **VULNERABLE:** D1; D2.

Cundinamarca Antpitta *Grallaria kaestneri* is a recently discovered terrestrial bird of the understorey of primary and secondary cloud-forest at upper subtropical elevations (1,800–2,300 m) on the eastern slope of the East Andes of **Colombia**, currently known only from near Monterredondo, Cundinamarca, 50 km south-east of Bogotá. It occurs at reasonably high densities in this area, and may prove to extend along the eastern face of the East Andes, much forest remaining at the cool, very wet middle elevations it prefers (though most forest immediately below has been cleared) (Stiles 1992). **VULNERABLE:** D2.

Bicoloured Antpitta *Grallaria rufocinerea* is localized and rare in cloud-forest and dense, humid montane forest, and old secondary growth near the tree-line at 2,200–3,150 m in the Central Andes of **Colombia**, where it has been recorded from very few localities over a wide area (embracing Antioquia, Caldas, Risaralda, Quindío and Tolima in the race *rufocinerea*, Cauca and possibly Putumayo in the race *romeroana*) that has been affected by widespread deforestation (Collar *et al.* 1992, Salaman and Gandy 1993). **ENDANGERED:** B1+2c; C1; **C2a.**

Brown-banded Antpitta *Grallaria milleri* is endemic to the west slope of the Central Andes, **Colombia** (Caldas and Quindío), where it is known from two cloud-forest areas at 2,745–3,140 m in which 10 specimens were taken, the last of them in 1942 and, as most of the original habitat within its range has now been destroyed (the exact habitat type was never recorded), it must be considered severely threatened (Collar *et al.* 1992). A specimen was, however, netted at 2,300 m in old secondary growth forest within Ucumarí Regional Park in Risaralda in May 1994, an area with much surrounding deforestation (G. Kattan *in litt.* 1994). **ENDANGERED:** B1+2c; D1; D2.

Hooded Antpitta *Grallaricula cucullata* is known from the more open parts of dense cloud-forest between 1,500 and 2,700 m (chiefly 1,800–2,135 m) at very few localities (most recently in two national parks) in the West, Central and East Andes of **Colombia** (Antioquia, Valle and Huila in the race *cucullata*), and one area in south-westernmost **Venezuela** (Táchira and Apure in the race *venezuelana*), where suitable habitat has been severely affected by continuing agricultural encroachment and deforestation of the region (Collar *et al.* 1992). **VULNERABLE:** A1b; A2b; C1; C2a.

Family RHINOCRYPTIDAE

TAPACULOS

Stresemann's Bristlefront *Merulaxis stresemanni* is an almost totally unknown bird that is presumed to live in the undergrowth of the few rapidly diminishing forests (now reduced to mere fragments) in coastal Bahia, **Brazil**, where it was recorded once during the twentieth century, near Ilhéus in 1945, and once in the previous century, near Salvador in the 1830s (Collar *et al.* 1992). **CRITICAL:** A1b; A2b; B1+2c; C1; **C2a;** D1; D2.

Brasília Tapaculo *Scytalopus novacapitalis* is a small undergrowth-haunting bird that survives locally in gallery forest and dense streamside vegetation in central **Brazil** (Goiás, Distrito Federal, Minas Gerais),

and despite its occurrence in several protected areas it faces loss of habitat around Brasília itself and from fire elsewhere (Collar *et al.* 1992). **VULNERABLE:** A1b; A2b.

Bahia Tapaculo *Scytalopus psychopompus* is known from three specimens obtained in flooded areas of thick vegetation at two small, unprotected, lowland (45 m) forest sites in coastal Bahia, **Brazil**, in 1944 at Ilhéus and in 1983 at Valença. It must be at great risk from the very extensive and continuing habitat destruction in the region, which has reduced forest there to small fragments (Collar *et al.* 1992). **ENDANGERED:** A1b; A2b; **B1+2c;** C1; **C2a;** D1; D2.

Family COTINGIDAE
COTINGAS

Shrike-like Cotinga *Laniisoma elegans* is endemic to the Atlantic Forest (occurring in both the canopy and understorey) of south-east **Brazil** (possibly Bahia, Espírito Santo, Minas Gerais, Rio de Janeiro, São Paulo, Paraná), where it seemingly undertakes migratory movements and is mostly found at a few primary forest sites on the Serra do Mar slopes, chiefly around 900 m although sometimes lower (notably in winter), and in the interior. It is everywhere rare and must have suffered from the extensive and continuing deforestation within its range (Collar *et al.* 1992). **VULNERABLE:** A1b; A2b; C1; C2a.

Grey-winged Cotinga *Tijuca condita* is restricted to two small montane areas in the region of Rio de Janeiro city, **Brazil**, where it occurs at low density in patches of extremely humid elfin cloud-forest mostly at 1,800–2,000 m; although threats are largely speculative (disturbance and fires started by hikers), the population involved is likely to be very low (Collar *et al.* 1992, Scott and Brooke 1993). In September 1993 a major forest fire was noted in or adjacent to Serra dos Órgãos National Park, indicating the real danger to the species from this source (G. Sangster *in litt.* 1994). **VULNERABLE:** D1; D2.

Black-headed Berryeater *Carpornis melanocephalus* is a frugivore of primary lowland Atlantic Forest in eastern **Brazil** (Alagoas, Bahia, Espírito Santo, Rio de Janeiro, São Paulo, Paraná), occurring generally at low density. It has suffered from the region's extensive and continuing deforestation and depends for survival on a few protected areas, notably Sooretama, Ilha do Cardoso and those owned by CVRD (Collar *et al.* 1992). **VULNERABLE:** C1; C2a.

Chestnut-bellied Cotinga *Doliornis remseni* (described since Sibley and Monroe 1990, 1993) was first recorded in 1989 and is now known from four localities, on the west slope of the Central Andes of **Colombia**, the Eastern Cordillera of the Andes of **Ecuador** and the Cordillera de Lagunillas in extreme southern **Peru**, where it is confined to dense thickets on the páramo–forest ecotone at 3,100 to 3,650 m; it is found at low densities, and its habitat is much reduced by uncontrolled burning of the páramo (and adjacent forest) (Renjifo 1994, Robbins *et al.* 1994; see Masked Mountain-tanager *Buthraupis wetmorei*). **VULNERABLE:** A1b; A2b; C1; C2a.

White-cheeked Cotinga *Zaratornis stresemanni* has a population speculated to comprise c.3,000 birds (1,500–6,000) confined to western **Peru** (La Libertad, Ancash, Lima, Ayacucho), at elevations ranging from 3,400 to 4,250 m, where it is a mistletoe specialist inhabiting *Polylepis* woodland. These patchily distributed woods are generally small in extent and thus vulnerable, and in places they have diminished owing to cutting by locals, although two areas where the species is common appear to be safe (Collar *et al.* 1992). **VULNERABLE:** B1+2c; C2a.

Buff-throated Purpletuft *Iodopleura pipra*, a tiny canopy-dwelling frugivore, has only in very recent years proved to be surviving in certain areas of north-east and south-east **Brazil** (Paraíba, Pernambuco, Alagoas; Bahia, Espírito Santo, Rio de Janeiro, São Paulo), but loss of its Atlantic Forest habitat clearly threatens it in both areas, and it requires more detailed study and some rapid intervention to secure key sites, notably around Ubatuba in São Paulo and Pedra Branca (Murici) in Alagoas (Collar *et al.* 1992, B. M. Whitney *in litt.* 1994). **VULNERABLE:** A1b; A2b; C1; C2a.

Kinglet Cotinga *Calyptura cristata*, a tiny frugivore, appears to have declined to total or near extinction as a result of deforestation within a range apparently restricted to foothills to the north of Rio de Janeiro city, **Brazil**, having not been recorded this century, although from the evidence of skins and one nineteenth-century record it was not uncommon even in secondary habitat 150 years ago (Collar *et al.* 1992). **CRITICAL: C2a; D1; D2.**

Cinnamon-vented Piha *Lipaugus lanioides*, whose range may have been misunderstood owing to identification problems even with museum specimens, seems to occupy foothill and lower montane forest (500–1,000 m) in south-east **Brazil** (Bahia, Espírito Santo, Minas Gerais, Rio de Janeiro, São Paulo, Paraná in 1946, Santa Catarina in 1918 and 1929), where it depends heavily on certain palm fruits that are also targeted by man for exploitation; it has become rare, and the extensive and continuing deforestation within its range has greatly isolated its populations (Collar *et al.* 1992). Its occurrence in Bahia has recently been confirmed: at Ouricana, near Boa Nova (B. M. Whitney *in litt.* 1994). **VULNERABLE:** A1b; A2b; C1; C2a.

Turquoise Cotinga *Cotinga ridgwayi* inhabits the canopy and borders of humid forest at up to 1,830 m on the Pacific slope of central and western **Costa Rica** and westernmost **Panama** (western Chiriquí), where it is generally rare; the widespread deforestation in Panama has now very much reduced its overall range and numbers, and it is presumably also affected by large-scale destruction in Costa Rica, where it appears to be inadequately protected (Ridgely and Gwynne 1989, Stiles and Skutch 1989; F. G. Stiles *in litt*. 1986). **VULNERABLE:** C2b.

Banded Cotinga *Cotinga maculata* is a frugivore of primary lowland Atlantic Forest in south-east **Brazil** (Bahia, Minas Gerais in 1930 and 1940, Espírito Santo, Rio de Janeiro in the last century), so inevitably has suffered from the extensive and continuing deforestation within its range, which has led to its isolation in a few key protected areas on which it now depends for its survival, notably Sooretama and those owned by CVRD (Collar *et al*. 1992). **ENDANGERED:** A1b; **B1+2c**; **C1**; C2a; D1; D2.

White-winged Cotinga *Xipholena atropurpurea* is a frugivore of primary lowland and adjacent foothill Atlantic Forest in eastern **Brazil** (Paraíba, Pernambuco, Alagoas, Sergipe, Bahia, Espírito Santo, Rio de Janeiro), and as such has suffered from the extensive and continuing deforestation within its range, which has led to its virtual confinement to a few key protected areas on which it now largely depends for its survival, notably Una, Sooretama, Desengano and those owned by CVRD (Collar *et al*. 1992, Souza 1992). **VULNERABLE:** A1b; A2b; B1+2c; C1; C2a.

Yellow-billed Cotinga *Carpodectes antoniae* is endemic to and now local and uncommon on the Pacific slope of north-west to south-east **Costa Rica** and westernmost **Panama**, where it relies on extensive areas of mangrove and to a lesser extent (and seasonally) adjacent foothill forests up to 760 m, all

habitat which has been much reduced and is under increasing pressure (Collar *et al*. 1992). **VULNERABLE:** A1b; A2b; C1; C2a.

Bare-necked Umbrellabird *Cephalopterus glabricollis* is endemic to **Costa Rica** (sparsely distributed in the Cordilleras Guanacaste, Tilarán, Central and the Dota Mountains) and western **Panama** (in Bocas del Toro, Chiriquí and Veraguas), where it breeds in adequately protected highland forests, but winters in severely threatened lowland forest, and probably as a consequence is now judged to be rare throughout its range (Collar *et al*. 1992). **VULNERABLE:** A1b; A2b; C1; C2a.

Long-wattled Umbrellabird *Cephalopterus penduliger* is rare and local in humid and wet forest (500–1,800 m) on the Pacific slope of south-west **Colombia** (Chocó—specimen in UV, Valle, Cauca, Nariño) and western **Ecuador** (Esmeraldas—where a new population was recently found in the Jatun Sacha Bilsa Biological Reserve, Pichincha, Manabí, Guayas/Los Ríos, Chimborazo, El Oro), where it is suffering from habitat destruction, to which it is particularly sensitive owing to altitudinal migration, and possibly also the effects of trapping for trade and, much more significantly, hunting for food (Chapman 1926, King 1978–1979, Hilty and Brown 1986, Collar and Andrew 1988, Clay *et al*. 1994, Salaman and Gandy 1994, R. P. Clay verbally 1994, R. S. Ridgely *in litt*. 1994). **VULNERABLE:** C2a.

Three-wattled Bellbird *Procnias tricarunculata* breeds in the foothills and highlands of **Honduras**, **Nicaragua**, **Costa Rica** and **Panama**, but has recently been shown to undertake complex migrations to various lowland areas in the non-breeding season, which strongly compounds the risks it runs from the past and continuing destruction of its tropical forest habitat, and indeed in recent years it has become much scarcer than formerly (Ridgely and Gwynne 1989, Stiles and Skutch 1989, Powell and Bjork 1993). **VULNERABLE:** A1b; A2b.

Family PIPRIDAE

MANAKINS

Golden-crowned Manakin *Pipra vilasboasi* is a small forest frugivore that remains known only from one primary rainforest locality (headwaters of

the Rio Cururu, a right-bank tributary of the Tapajós, in the Serra do Cachimbo) in south-west Pará, **Brazil**, an area in which the level of deforestation remains unknown (but is possibly high), although the species probably ranges between the rios Tapajós and Xingu and may be safe in one forest reserve (Collar *et al.* 1992). **VULNERABLE:** C2b.

Black-capped Manakin *Piprites pileatus*, a largely montane Atlantic Forest species of mixed broadleaf growth with *Araucaria* and conifers, is, for reasons unclear (though loss of its habitat must contribute), very sparsely distributed in south-east **Brazil** (Minas Gerais, Rio de Janeiro, São Paulo, Paraná, Santa Catarina, Rio Grande do Sul) and **Argentina** (Misiones: one record), with only a few current localities known, notably Itatiaia and Serra da Bocaina National Parks (Collar *et al.* 1992). **VULNERABLE:** B1+2c; C1; C2a.

Family TYRANNIDAE

TYRANT-FLYCATCHERS

Buff-breasted Tody-tyrant *Hemitriccus mirandae* is known from just five areas in three states of north-east **Brazil** (Ceará, Pernambuco, Alagoas), occurring as an apparently uncommon bird of vine tangles, old light gaps and secondary vegetation in seasonally dry semi-deciduous woodland on isolated hills at 700–1,000 m; deforestation is probably the single but very considerable threat (Collar *et al.* 1992). **VULNERABLE:** A1b; A2b; B1+2c; C1.

Kaempfer's Tody-tyrant *Hemitriccus kaempferi* remains known only by three records at two localities (Salto do Piraí near Vila Nova in 1929 and 1991, and Brusque in 1950) in humid lowland Atlantic Forest in Santa Catarina, **Brazil**, where deforestation poses at least a long-term threat to what appears to be a very rare species (Collar *et al.* 1992). **ENDANGERED:** A1b; A2b; B1+2c; **C1**.

Fork-tailed Pygmy-tyrant *Hemitriccus furcatus* is endemic to (and normally common in) a particular type of bamboo in south-east **Brazil** (Bahia—a recent range extension, Minas Gerais, Rio de Janeiro, São Paulo) where, however, it is currently known from only five localities and faces an uncertain future with continuing deforestation in the region (Collar *et al.* 1992, F. R. Lambert verbally 1993, Tobias *et al.* 1993, C. S. Balchin *in litt.* 1994). **VULNERABLE:** C2a.

Cocos Flycatcher *Nesotriccus ridgwayi* occurs commonly throughout the forests and other habitats (*Hibiscus* scrub, *Annona* swamp, wooded ravines) of the 47 km² Cocos Island, **Costa Rica** (which is a national park), although there are rats and cats present, and overgrazing by introduced deer, pigs and goats is occurring (Slud 1967, Sherry 1985, Stiles and Skutch 1989; T. W. Sherry *in litt.* 1985). **VULNERABLE:** D2.

Ash-breasted Tit-tyrant *Anairetes alpinus* is confined to isolated, semi-humid, mixed *Polylepis–Gynoxys* woods at 3,700–4,500 m in two widely disjunct but numerically tiny populations, one (nominate *alpinus*) in Cordillera Blanca, Ancash department, west-central **Peru** (many less than 300 birds), and one (race *bolivianus*) in southern Peru (Apurímac, Cuzco) and adjacent **Bolivia** (La Paz) (several hundred birds); these woodlands suffer from cutting for firewood and lack of regeneration caused by widespread burning (Collar *et al.* 1992). **ENDANGERED:** A1b; A2b; **B1+2c**; C1; **C2a**; D1.

Dinelli's Doradito *Pseudocolopteryx dinellianus* occurs in low numbers in a restricted range in the marshes of northern **Argentina** (Salta apparently, Tucumán, Santiago del Estero, Santa Fe, Córdoba), with probably wintering records from adjacent **Bolivia** (one record in 1926) and **Paraguay** (six records: in July 1945, in 1960, May and June 1990, and twice in July 1992, these last in Caaguazú). It inhabits periodically flooded rushy and grassy marsh vegetation and shrubbery near watercourses, and although no certain threats have been identified it appears likely that wetland modification could affect the species (Collar *et al.* 1992, Brooks *et al.* 1993, Hayes *et al.* 1994). **VULNERABLE:** C1; C2a.

Rufous-sided Pygmy-tyrant *Euscarthmus rufomarginatus* is known from a small number of widely scattered localities in pristine, shrubby grasslands of central **Brazil** (Maranhão in 1924, Piauí in 1903, Pará in 1955, Distrito Federal in 1989, Mato Grosso in 1946 twice, 1987, 1988, Mato Grosso do Sul in

1930, 1991 and in a year unknown, São Paulo in 1823; see also below), in the Serranía de Huanchaca in extreme north-east Santa Cruz, **Bolivia**, and at Zanja Morotí, Concepción, **Paraguay**, in December 1944 (for which see Olrog 1979), with an outlying population (race *savannophilus*) in the Sipaliwini savanna of southern **Surinam**; but it remains very severely threatened by the extensive and continuing conversion of its habitat to farmland (Collar *et al.* 1992). In October 1989 a bird was seen in Parque das Mangabeiras outside Belo Horizonte, Minas Gerais, apparently the first state record and the only encounter with the species in eight months of observations at the site (A. Whittaker *in litt.* 1993). **VULNERABLE:** A1b; A2b.

Antioquia Bristle-tyrant *Phylloscartes lanyoni*

has been found in semi-deciduous forest, tall second growth and clearings in just three localities (El Pescado and Río Claro Natural Reserve in Antioquia, and La Victoria in Caldas) in foothills (450–750 m or somewhat higher) at the northern end of the Central Andes, **Colombia**, in an area that has been subjected to widespread, intensive and continuing deforestation; the Río Claro reserve, less than 1 km², is in an area of heavy logging activity (Collar *et al.* 1992, B. M. Whitney *in litt.* 1994). **ENDANGERED:** **A1b**; **A2b**; B1+2c; C1; C2a.

Minas Gerais Tyrannulet *Phylloscartes roquettei*

is known from only a very small area (near Januária, now Brejo de Amparo, on the left bank of the Rio São Francisco) of northern Minas Gerais in east-central **Brazil**, where the type- and only specimen was collected in July 1926 and where birds were seen again in 1977 (but searches in 1985, 1986 and 1987 drew a blank, indicating its rarity); it must be suffering from the rapid loss of its unprotected semi-deciduous woodland habitat, already fragmented into woodlots (Collar *et al.* 1992). **ENDANGERED:** A2b; **B1+2c**; C1; C2b.

São Paulo Tyrannulet *Phylloscartes paulistus*

has been isolated, by the destruction of its lowland forest habitat, in a relatively small number of localities which are spread over a relatively large area of south-east **Brazil** (Espírito Santo in 1929 and 1942, Rio de Janeiro, São Paulo, Mato Grosso do Sul in 1930, Paraná, Santa Catarina), eastern **Paraguay** (Canindeyú, Caaguazú, Alto Paraná) and northern **Argentina** (Misiones); it is generally a very local and uncommon bird, and only in the Iguaçu/Iguazu region does there appear to be a reasonable population, possibly in the low thousands (Collar *et al.* 1992; also Brooks *et al.* 1993). **VULNERABLE:** A1b; A2b; C1; C2a.

Alagoas Tyrannulet *Phylloscartes ceciliae*

is fairly common in but restricted to two localities (Pedra or Serra Branca, near Murici, only 15 km² in extent; and Pedra Talhada Biological Reserve) on the south-eastern escarpment of the Borborema plateau in Alagoas, north-east **Brazil**, where it occupies the canopy of the middle storey of evergreen forest, 300–700 m; clearance and heavy degradation of this habitat are widespread in the region (Collar *et al.* 1992). **ENDANGERED:** A1b; A2b; **B1+2c**; **C1**; C2a; D2.

Restinga Tyrannulet *Phylloscartes kronei*,

a recently described species, occupies woodland edge, second growth and scrub woods in the sandy coastal restingas of São Paulo state, **Brazil**, where it faces threats from the rapid clearance of its habitat for beachfront dwellings, notably on Ilha Comprida (Willis and Oniki 1992). Recent fieldwork indicates that it is distributed throughout sandplain forest in southern São Paulo and Paraná, but that future pressure on this habitat is likely to be great (P. Martuscelli verbally 1994). **VULNERABLE:** A1b; A2b; C1; C2a.

Russet-winged Spadebill *Platyrinchus leucoryphus*

occurs at low densities in the Atlantic Forest belt of south-east **Brazil** (Espírito Santo, Rio de Janeiro, São Paulo, Paraná, Rio Grande do Sul), eastern **Paraguay** (1904, 1930, 1978—three specimens in UMMZ—1992) and northern **Argentina** (Misiones), occupying isolated territories in the understorey of primary and old secondary forest in lowlands, mountains and interior tablelands (Collar *et al.* 1992). Continuing deforestation within its range remains a significant threat (Brooks *et al.* 1993, R. S. Ridgely *in litt.* 1994). It is present at the confidential (but rapidly disappearing) site for Black-hooded Antwren *Formicivora erythronotos* at Angra dos Reis, Rio de Janeiro (G. Sangster *in litt.* 1994). **VULNERABLE:** A1b; A2b; B1+2c; C1; C2a.

Pacific Royal Flycatcher *Onychorhynchus occidentalis*

(whose taxonomic status requires clarification: here split from Royal Flycatcher *O. coronatus*) is confined to humid, low-lying forest in western **Ecuador** (Esmeraldas, Manabí, Guayas, Los Ríos, Cañar, Azuay, El Oro) and immediately adjacent north-west **Peru** (Tumbes); it occurs at low density and now has little habitat left (Collar *et al.* 1992, Berg 1994, Whittingham 1994). **VULNERABLE:** C2a.

Atlantic Royal Flycatcher *Onychorhynchus swainsoni*

(whose taxonomic status requires clarification: here split from Royal Flycatcher *O. coronatus*) is confined to the dwindling forests of eastern **Brazil** (Bahia, Minas Gerais, Rio de Janeiro, São Paulo, Paraná, possibly Goiás), where it is almost wholly unknown, being lamented as very rare over a century ago and with few modern records (Cory and Hellmayr 1927, Sick 1985, L. P. Gonzaga verbally 1991, Tobias *et al.* 1993, B. M. Whitney *in litt.* 1994), including southern Bahia, Itatiaia National Park and the Serra do Mar (Forrester 1993). **ENDANGERED: C2a.**

Grey-breasted Flycatcher *Lathrotriccus griseipectus* is confined to the viney understorey of tropical deciduous, semi-deciduous and moist forest from sea-level to 1,750 m in south-west **Ecuador** (Esmeraldas, Pichincha, Manabí, Los Ríos, Guayas, Cañar, Azuay, El Oro, Loja) and northern **Peru** (Tumbes, Piura, Lambayeque, Cajamarca); although reported to be common at two localities, it is otherwise uncommon or rare, and is threatened by widespread, chronic and continuing habitat destruction (Collar *et al.* 1992). **VULNERABLE: A1b; A2b; B1+2c; C1; C2a.**

Santa Marta Bush-tyrant *Myiotheretes pernix* is endemic to the Sierra Nevada de Santa Marta, **Colombia**, where it is uncommon in shrubby forest and second-growth borders, along road cuts, and on overgrown hillsides at 2,100–2,900 m (Hilty and Brown 1986); recent evidence of the extensive loss of habitat on the massif (see under Santa Marta Parakeet *Pyrrhura viridicata*) implies problems for an already uncommon endemic with a relatively restricted altitudinal range. **VULNERABLE: C2b.**

Black-and-white Monjita *Heteroxolmis dominicana* occurs in open scrubby grasslands close to marshes, rolling hilly pastures and boggy swales, cerrado and farmland, over a wide area of **Brazil** (Minas Gerais, São Paulo, Paraná, Santa Catarina and Rio Grande do Sul), **Uruguay** (recorded from at least 11 departments), **Paraguay** (four departments) and **Argentina** (at least seven provinces) (Madroño Nieto 1992). The conversion of its habitat to increasingly intensive agriculture has caused a catastrophic decline over the past 150 years, and it is now very rare throughout its range, with only a few reports that it survives locally in reasonable numbers, e.g. near Arcos in Minas Gerais (A. Studer verbally 1991), in parts of Paraná (F. C. Straube *in litt.* 1991), and in the north-east and south-east of Rio Grande do Sul (Belton 1984–1985), but the overall prognosis is of further habitat loss and further declines in numbers (T. A. Parker verbally 1992, M. Pearman *in litt.* 1994, R. S. Ridgely *in litt.* 1994). **VULNERABLE: A1b; A2b.**

White-tailed Shrike-tyrant *Agriornis andicola* lives high above the treeline (usually above 3,500 m) in the páramo and puna zones of **Ecuador** (Imbabura,

Pichincha, Napo, Chimborazo, Cañar, Zamora-Chinchipe, Loja; two records since the 1920s, in 1965 and 1992), **Peru** (Cajamarca, La Libertad, Huánuco, Ancash, Pasco, Cuzco, Arequipa; five records since 1952), **Bolivia** (La Paz in 1941, Oruro in 1967 and 1991, Potosí in 1967), northern **Chile** (Tarapacá and Antofagasta, the only recent records being from Lauca National Park) and north-west **Argentina** (Tucumán, Catamarca; no records since 1952) (Collar *et al.* 1992). Throughout its range (nominate *andicola* in Ecuador, race *albicauda* elsewhere) it appears to have declined dramatically, for reasons unknown, although it possibly depends on *Polylepis* and *Puya*, now themselves greatly reduced and fragmented, or else is being outcompeted by the very closely related Black-billed Shrike-tyrant *A. montana* (Krabbe 1994). **VULNERABLE: A1a; C2a.**

Strange-tailed Tyrant *Alectrurus risora* has experienced a catastrophic loss of range in **Brazil** (no certain record since 1914), **Paraguay**, **Uruguay** (one recent record) and **Argentina** (Formosa, Chaco, Misiones, Corrientes, Santa Fe; extinct in Santiago del Estero, Entre Ríos, Córdoba, San Luis, Buenos Aires), apparently as a result of the conversion of its natural low-lying humid grassland habitat to agriculture and cattle-raising land; it remains at all common only in northern Argentina (notably in the eastern borders of the Esteros de Ibera) and adjacent Paraguay, but it is not clear if even these populations are stable (Collar *et al.* 1992, Pearman and Abadie in press). **VULNERABLE: A1a,b; A2b; C1; C2a.**

Ochraceous Attila *Attila torridus* occurs at low numbers in fragments and edges of humid and semi-humid forest and plantations in the lowlands and foothills (sea-level to 1,000 m) of south-western **Colombia** (Nariño in 1958), western **Ecuador** (Esmeraldas, Pichincha, Manabí, Los Ríos, Guayas, Cañar, El Oro, Loja) and north-west **Peru** (Tumbes in 1988); it is rare almost everywhere and suffers from the extensive and continuing deforestation of the region (Collar *et al.* 1992, R. S. Ridgely *in litt.* 1994). **VULNERABLE: A1b; A2b; B1+2c; C1; C2a.**

Giant Kingbird *Tyrannus cubensis* is a naturally low-density tyrant-flycatcher that has become much rarer still throughout its native **Cuba** (there are old records from the southern Bahamas and the Turks and Caicos Islands) for reasons unknown, although the most likely culprit is clearance of its woodland and notably pine-forest habitat (Collar *et al.* 1992). **ENDANGERED: A1a,b; C2a; D1.**

Family PHYTOTOMIDAE

PLANTCUTTERS

Peruvian Plantcutter *Phytotoma raimondii* inhabits the coastal region (sea-level to 550 m) of northern **Peru** (Tumbes, Piura, Lambayeque, La Libertad, Ancash, Lima), where it may require a specific habitat (the desert scrub and riparian thicket in which it is found is much widerspread than the bird itself) that is now threatened by the almost complete cultivation of the coastal river valleys (Collar *et al.* 1992). **CRITICAL: A1b; A2b**; B1+2c; C1; C2a.

Family PITTIDAE

PITTAS

Schneider's Pitta *Pitta schneideri* is endemic to the mountains of Sumatra, **Indonesia**, where it is found in montane forest between 900 and 2,400 m and known historically from only about five localities, although it was described as very common in the Gunung Kerinci area in 1914 (van Marle and Voous 1988). It was rediscovered on Gunung Kerinci in 1988, after a gap in documented records of over 70 years, when two birds were seen at 2,375 m (Hurrell 1989), and small numbers have been seen there subsequently by several observers, and at Dolok Sibual Bual Nature Reserve (A. Adhikerana *per* P. Jepson 1994) with birds heard at Berestagi (N. Bostock verbally 1993), but it remains threatened by forest loss and degradation as lower montane forest is cleared for agricultural use, including illegal encroachment in protected areas (BirdLife IP; see Thorsell 1985). **VULNERABLE: C1; C2a.**

Gurney's Pitta *Pitta gurneyi* is endemic to peninsular **Thailand** and adjacent southern Tenasserim, **Myanmar**, where it is found in level lowland semi-evergreen rainforest below 150 m. It is close to extinction in Thailand, owing to the almost total destruction of level lowland forest within its range, and there have been no records in Myanmar since 1914 where it is feared that lowland forests are also rapidly being cleared and degraded (Collar *et al.* 1986, Round and Treesucon 1986). Recent intensive survey work in Thailand located birds at four localities, but the only possibly viable population is at Khao Nor Chuchi in Krabi province, where 24–34 pairs are estimated; a BirdLife International/Center for Conservation Biology (Mahidol University, Bangkok) project has operated here since 1990 to try to halt the deforestation, but the area of suitable habitat continues to decline gradually and territories are being lost (Gretton *et al.* 1993). **CRITICAL: A1b; B1+2c; C1; C2a; D1; D2.**

Superb Pitta *Pitta superba* is known from forest on Manus in the Admiralty Islands, **Papua New Guinea**, where, although a 1990 study extrapolated to an approximate total population of 1,000 calling birds (but based only on three birds in 3.5 km²), it may have a habitat preference (e.g. for more open, hilltop forest near a reasonably large river, where stones, which are used as anvils to break mollusc shells, are more commonly found), and thus overall numbers may be much lower; any forest loss could be a serious threat (but there is local opposition to further logging, and clearance for subsistence agriculture is currently limited to the coast), as could the brown tree snake *Boiga irregularis*, which has been responsible for the elimination of forest birds on Guam where it was introduced (Dutson and Newman 1991), although as this species is apparently native to Manus there is presumably some kind of equilibrium between predator and prey (R. E. Beck *in litt.* 1992). Observation (of two pairs) and reports (of one pair) in 1994 indicate that it may survive in secondary growth and overgrown gardens and that bamboo could be an important feature of its habitat requirements (D. Gibbs *in litt.* 1994). A proposal to build a space station on Manus (P. Gregory *in litt.* 1994) is currently shelved (I. Burrows *in litt.* 1994). **VULNERABLE: D1.**

Azure-breasted Pitta *Pitta steerii* is found in primary forest on limestone from near sea-level to 750 m on Samar, Leyte and Bohol (race *coelestis*) and the Zamboango peninsula of Mindanao (nominate *steerii*) in the **Philippines**. It is common in one area of Bohol, but recent records have otherwise been very sparse, and the extensive and continuing clearance of lowland forest remains a cause for concern (Collar and Andrew 1988, Lambert 1993b, Redman 1993). **VULNERABLE:** A1b; A2b; C1; C2a.

Whiskered Pitta *Pitta kochi* is restricted to montane forest (usually above 1,000 m) on Luzon in the **Philippines** (Dickinson *et al.* 1991), where it was observed on Mount Isarog in March 1988 (Goodman and Gonzales 1990) and found to be locally fairly common at higher altitudes in the Sierra Madre in 1991–1992, but hunted with snares and affected by habitat loss (Danielsen *et al.* 1994, Poulsen in press). **VULNERABLE:** B1+2c,e; C1; C2a.

Fairy Pitta *Pitta nympha* breeds in eastern **China** (Anhui, Henan, Fujian, Guangdong and Guangxi, with records on passage in Hebei and Jiangsu: Cheng 1987), **Taiwan** (uncommon, and has perhaps declined recently: Severinghaus *et al.* 1991), southern **Japan** (mainly on Shikoku and Kyushu, uncommon or rare: Brazil 1991) and islands off **South Korea** (probably less than 20 pairs: P. O. Won verbally 1994), in moist deciduous and evergreen forest with dense undergrowth on hill slopes below 500 m, but occasionally up to 1,200 m (Brazil 1991). The population in Guangdong and Guangxi in China is believed to be resident (Meyer de Schauensee 1984), but the northern populations winter in East **Malaysia**, **Brunei** and Kalimantan, **Indonesia** (Mann 1987, MacKinnon and Phillipps 1993), occurring on passage in eastern China, Taiwan and northern **Vietnam**, and as a vagrant to Hong Kong (to U.K.) (Inskipp and Collins 1993). The population in eastern China is presumably much reduced and fragmented by the extensive lowland deforestation which has taken place in this densely populated region (see Collins *et al.* 1991), and there is evidence that large-scale trapping in spring on Taiwan for sale as specimens may have depleted the local breeding (and perhaps also the passage migrant) population (Severinghaus *et al.* 1991). **VULNERABLE:** C1; C2a.

Black-faced Pitta *Pitta anerythra* is known from lowland and hill forest on southern Bougainville Island, **Papua New Guinea**, and Choiseul and Santa Isabel, **Solomon Islands** (Coates 1990), being formerly described as common, with 18 being collected in the first decade of this century, but had not been recorded since 1936 (Diamond 1987) until recently: in 1994 it was found to be common in south-east Santa Isabel, inhabiting a variety of habitats from 400–600 m, from cyclone-damaged primary forest, secondary forest, old gardens where regrowth is well advanced, and secondary scrub, but searches in northwest Choiseul (where locals denied its existence) failed to locate it (D. Gibbs *in litt.* 1994). One was also reported from Kolombangara in 1990 (Buckingham *et al.* in prep.), perhaps a vagrant/dispersing bird, as it has not been seen or heard during more recent searches and local people appear to have no knowledge of it (M. B. Iles *in litt.* 1994). It may have declined owing to introduced mammalian predators, e.g. cats, which have wiped out most native terrestrial mammals on Guadalcanal (T. Flannery *per* K. D. Bishop *in litt.* 1994). **VULNERABLE:** C2a.

Family PHILEPITTIDAE
ASITIES

Yellow-bellied Asity *Neodrepanis hypoxanthus*, endemic to the central part of the humid forest belt of eastern **Madagascar** but difficult to distinguish from its only congener, is known from 13 specimens collected before 1933 and recent sightings from the higher parts of the Central Floristic Domain (Marojejy, Ranomafana and Andringitra), these latter suggesting a localized distribution in montane forest relicts (under serious threat from clearance) near the top of the eastern escarpment and outlying massifs rising from the eastern lowlands (Hawkins *et al.* in prep.; also Collar and Stuart 1985, Dee 1986, Langrand 1990, Evans *et al.* 1992a). **ENDANGERED:** A2b; B1+2b,c; C1; **C2a**.

Family ATRICHORNITHIDAE

SCRUB-BIRDS

Rufous Scrub-bird *Atrichornis rufescens* occurs in isolated populations in the highlands (mostly above 600 m) of the Great Dividing Range in north-east New South Wales and south-east Queensland, **Australia**, where it affects dense undergrowth in rainforest and eucalypt forest. In the early nineteenth century the population size was probably c.12,000 pairs, but a census in 1979–1983 estimated c.2,500 pairs, the decline being attributed to the removal of lowland rainforest, with inappropriate burning and forest management practices continuing to be a threat (Garnett 1992). **VULNERABLE:** B1+2c; C2a.

Noisy Scrub-bird *Atrichornis clamosus* is a small, semi-flightless inhabitant of dense scrub and low forest on the south coast of Western Australia, **Aus-**

tralia (King 1978–1979); between 1961, when it was rediscovered, and 1976, it was largely confined to the Mount Gardner area of the Two Peoples Bay Nature Reserve 40 km east of Albany but, as a result of habitat management (fire exclusion) and translocation of birds to new sites, the range is now spread over c.30 km of coastal and near coastal land (Danks and Calver 1993), including populations at Mount Manypeaks and on one offshore island (Garnett 1992, A. Danks verbally 1993). In 1993 the population of singing males was estimated at 400 individuals (A. Danks verbally 1993) but the species remains vulnerable to a single large wildfire (Garnett 1992). **VULNERABLE:** D1; D2.

Family ALAUDIDAE

LARKS

Ash's Lark *Mirafra ashi* remains known only from a very small area of arid coastal grassy plains just north of Uarsciek in southern **Somalia**, where it may be at risk from drought and the loss of grazing livestock (Collar and Stuart 1985). The chronic and continuing political crisis in Somalia may result in an as yet undocumented loss of habitats for this and other species endemic to the country. **ENDANGERED:** B1+2a,c; C2b; D1.

Degodi Lark *Mirafra degodiensis* was known from only two specimens which were collected together in November 1971 in light bush (low acacias on bare soil) at 350 m near Bogol Manya in the Degodi region of southern **Ethiopia** (Collar and Stuart 1985), until four birds judged to be this species were observed at the type-locality in February 1989 (Ash and Gullick 1990b). The surrounding area appears to be occupied by Gillett's Lark *M. gilletti*, which may confine *M. degodiensis* to a range of a few square kilometres; increased grazing pressure is a possible future threat (Ash and Gullick 1990b). **VULNERABLE:** D1; D2.

Archer's Lark *Heteromirafra archeri* is a secretive grassland species known only from an exceptionally restricted area west of Hargeisa and Buramo in north-west **Somalia** along the Ethiopian frontier, and has been seen only once, in 1955, since 1922; its habitat may have been seriously disrupted by cultivation and settlement (Collar and Stuart 1985). The chronic and continuing political crisis in Somalia may be causing as yet undocumented loss of habitats for this and other species endemic to the country. **ENDANGERED:** B1+2a,c; C2a; D1.

Sidamo Lark *Heteromirafra sidamoensis* is known only from two specimens, collected at adjacent sites in open savanna at 1,450 m near Neghelli in Sidamo province, southern **Ethiopia**, in May 1968 and April 1974 (Collar and Stuart 1985; also Ash and Olson 1985). In early 1989 both localities were found to be affected by man—one under cultivation, the other a military training area—and no birds were seen (Ash and Gullick 1989), but adjacent areas still seem to possess suitable habitat (P. O. Syvertsen *in litt.* 1994). **ENDANGERED:** B1+2a,c; C2b; D1.

Rudd's Lark *Heteromirafra ruddi* is highly localized within short, dense, high-altitude (1,400–2,200 m) level grassland plateaus (avoiding dissected areas with steep slopes: hence very patchy) in higher rainfall areas (above 750 mm) in eastern **South Africa** (eastern Transvaal, eastern Orange Free State, northern Natal and East Griqualand in Transkei), and has deserted much of the southern part of its range in response to habitat degradation (Brooke 1984, Collar and Stuart 1985; also Hockey 1992, W. R. Tarboton *in litt*. 1994), with evidence of local population reduction as a result of land-use changes in natural grasslands involving commercial afforestation, crop farming, mining, new fire regimes and grazing practices, and dense human settlement, such that the species may not survive at all in another 20 years (Hockey *et al*. 1988, D. G. Allan *in litt*. 1994). The views that it may occur in high west Swaziland (Clancey 1985) and is conceivably commoner than current evidence suggests (Ginn *et al*. 1989) have been judged incorrect (V. Parker *per* D. G. Allan *in litt*. 1994, and D. G. Allan *in litt*. 1994 respectively), and an unsubstantiated sight record for Lesotho, accepted by Bonde (1993), is also regarded as erroneous, as no suitable (undissected) habitat exists there (D. G. Allan *in litt*. 1994, W. R. Tarboton *in litt*. 1994). **CRITICAL: A2b**; B1+2c; C1; C2a.

Red Lark *Certhilauda burra* is highly nomadic in response to localized rainfall in the red sand (semidesert) country of north-west Cape Province, east to near Prieska, **South Africa**; all records but one (from Kleinkaras, **Namibia**) are from south of the Orange River (Brooke 1984, Collar and Stuart 1985). It occurs on well vegetated sand-dunes or flats with perennial tussock-grasses, of which only 1,400 km², supporting c.9,400 birds, remains and which is under continuing heavy grazing pressure from domestic livestock (Dean *et al*. 1991). **VULNERABLE:** B1+2c; C2b.

Botha's Lark *Spizocorys fringillaris* occupies short, dense, high-altitude grasslands (apparently where coincident with black clay soils) in northern Orange Free State and south-east Transvaal, **South Africa**, where it is rare but locally common (minimum population 1,000, maximum 20,000) and permanently exposed to danger from agricultural development (Brooke 1984, Clancey 1985, Collar and Stuart 1985, Herholdt and Grobler 1987, Tarboton *et al*. 1987, Ginn *et al*. 1989). **VULNERABLE:** A2b; C1; C2b.

Raso Lark *Alauda razae* is only found on part of the very small, arid island of Raso in the **Cape Verde Islands**, where its population fluctuates in response to climate, reaching a low of only c.20 pairs in the early 1980s (Collar and Stuart 1985). In early 1985, however, a survey showed at least 150 birds to be present (M. A. S. Beaman verbally 1985), 75–100 pairs were judged present during day visits in March 1986 and January 1988 (Hazevoet 1989), 200 birds were estimated (140 different birds seen) over two days in January 1989 (K. Morgan *in litt*. 1989), and c.250 birds were estimated present in October 1988, March 1990 and March 1992 (Hazevoet in press). **ENDANGERED: D1**; D2.

Family HIRUNDINIDAE

SWALLOWS, MARTINS

White-eyed River-martin *Pseudochelidon sirintarae* is known only as a winter visitor to Lake Boraphet, central **Thailand** (King 1978–1979). It has not been reliably reported since 1980 (Sophasan and Dobias 1984), although one was reputedly trapped by a local in 1986 (Ogle 1986), and the concentrations of roosting Barn Swallows *Hirundo rustica* with which it formerly associated have been greatly reduced as a result of the harvesting of reeds and disturbance caused by illegal bird-trapping (Round 1988). **CRITICAL: D1**.

Blue Swallow *Hirundo atrocaerulea* occupies upland grasslands, breeding along streams in potholes and old antbear burrows, in **South Africa** (Natal and eastern Transvaal), **Swaziland** (D. G. Allan verbally 1994), **Zimbabwe** (eastern highlands), **Malawi**, the minute part of the Nyika plateau inside **Zambia** (where still present: D. R. Aspinwall *in litt*. 1994), south-western **Tanzania** and apparently **Mozambique**, birds from the south of this range wintering north to eastern **Zaïre**, **Uganda** and **Kenya** (Brooke 1984, Collar and Stuart 1985, Earlé 1987, Finch 1989, Keith *et al*. 1992). A major decline has occurred as parts of its range in South Africa, Zimbabwe and the Zomba plateau in Malawi have undergone afforestation, while high rural human density in Swaziland has rendered all its former habitat unsuitable (W. R. Tarboton *in litt.* 1994), and now even in Malawi (see Earlé 1987) and Tanzania its grasslands (e.g. the Kitulo plateau) are disappearing in the face of pyrethrum and potato cultivation or the planting of exotic softwoods (D. C. Moyer *in litt.* 1994). **VULNERABLE:** A1b; A2b; C1; C2a.

White-tailed Swallow *Hirundo megaensis* occupies an area of roughly 10,000 km² in open country around Mega and Yavello in southern **Ethiopia**, where it remains putatively at risk from any development of its habitat (Collar and Stuart 1985). No population estimate has been made, but while one survey in 1989 suggested densities had remained constant through the 1980s (although clearance of bush and increase in grazing pressure were apparent: Ash and Gullick 1989), another established slightly larger geographical and altitudinal ranges but recorded lower numbers (Syvertsen and Dellelegn 1991). The 2,537 km² (2,496 km² in Hillman 1993)

Yavello Sanctuary was 'set up' for this and the Ethiopian Bush-crow *Zavattariornis stresemanni* in 1985 (Hundessa 1991), but has never been gazetted and involves no active management (P. O. Syvertsen *in litt.* 1994). **VULNERABLE:** B1+2a,b,c; C2b.

Red Sea Swallow *Hirundo perdita* is known from the type-specimen which was found dead in May 1984 at Sanganeb lighthouse, to the north-east of Port Sudan, **Sudan** (Fry and Smith 1985). The species is judged most likely to be found in the Red Sea hills of Sudan or Eritrea (Fry and Smith 1985) or possibly (because two pale-rumped swallows were seen flying out over the Red Sea towards Jedda, just before the discovery of the type) in the coastal hills of western Saudi Arabia north of Jedda (Madge and Redman 1989). Unidentified cliff swallows possibly of this species have been seen at Lake Langano (about 20 birds) and in Awash National Park (3–8 birds) in Ethiopia (Turner and Rose 1989), plus three more recent sites, although they probably represent an undescribed taxon (Madge and Redman 1989, Harvey and Atkins in press, J. S. Ash *in litt.* 1994). **VULNERABLE:** D1.

Family MOTACILLIDAE
WAGTAILS, PIPITS

Yellow-breasted Pipit *Anthus chloris* is generally local and rare to uncommon within a restricted area of flat and lightly sloping dense wiry grasslands, usually at high altitudes (above 2,000 m, although it breeds between 1,400 or more usually 1,800 and 2,400 m with some birds descending lower in winter) in eastern **South Africa** (eastern Transvaal) and **Lesotho** (up to several hundred birds present in Sehlabathebe National Park, but not elsewhere: P. Osborne *per* D. G. Allan *in litt.* 1994), where burning, grazing and afforestation continue to diminish its habitat (Brooke 1984, Clancey 1985, Tarboton *et al.* 1987, Ginn *et al.* 1989, Keith *et al.* 1992). **VULNERABLE:** B1+2c.

Sokoke Pipit *Anthus sokokensis* has been recorded from seven coastal forest sites (some at risk from localized clearance and degradation), the Arabuko–Sokoke forest and Mkongani in the Shimba Hills in **Kenya**, the former the target of a now stalled conservation project (see Sokoke Scops-owl *Otus ireneae*),

and where it can survive at low densities in thickets within degraded forest (Fanshawe 1991, J. H. Fanshawe verbally 1994), the Pugu Hills (not found recently in the Forest Reserve, the record in question thought likely to stem from what is now the unsurveyed Ruvu South Forest Reserve: N. E. Baker *in litt.* 1994), a site near Moa (Kilulu Hill, now only 2 km² and with no recent records despite a survey in 1992: Mlingwa and Burgess in press), Kiono Forest Reserve (where very rare), Vikindu Forest Reserve (where also very rare), and Dondwe (near Vikindu and Dar es Salaam) (S. Davies *per* N. E. Baker *in litt.* 1994 and N. D. Burgess *in litt.* 1994), in **Tanzania** (Collar and Stuart 1985, Burgess *et al.* 1991a,b, 1992, Mlingwa 1991, 1993, Bennun and Waiyaki 1992); Kiono and Vikindu are targets of current conservation efforts (N. E. Baker *in litt.* 1994). **VULNERABLE:** B1+2a,b,c; C2a.

Ochre-breasted Pipit *Anthus nattereri* is a ground-haunting grassland-dwelling semi-nomadic insectivore that has become extremely scarce and local in south-east **Brazil** (Minas Gerais, São Paulo, Paraná, Santa Catarina, Rio Grande do Sul), **Paraguay** and northern **Argentina** (Corrientes in the 1960s, and rediscovered at the same locality, now called San Juan Bautista, in January 1993, this possibly being a stronghold of the species, since it remains very hard to find elsewhere), probably owing to overgrazing and other forms of habitat modification, as the bird requires dry natural grassland (Collar *et al.* 1992, Pearman and Abadie in press). **ENDANGERED:** A1b; A2b; C1; **C2a**.

Family CAMPEPHAGIDAE
CUCKOO-SHRIKES

Buru Cuckoo-shrike *Coracina fortis* is endemic to Buru, **Indonesia**, recorded from coast to mountains (White and Bruce 1986). It is historically known from about seven localities (BirdLife BPD), but the only recent record is of two seen in selectively logged forest during a one-month survey in 1989, so it is apparently rare, but may be adaptable to disturbed habitats (Jepson 1993). Some deforestation has occurred in Buru's coastal lowlands, and large areas have been disturbed and selectively logged (Jepson 1993). **VULNERABLE:** B1+2c; C1; C2b.

Mauritius Cuckoo-shrike *Coracina typica* is an insectivorous, forest-dwelling species, endemic to **Mauritius**, that continues to suffer from habitat degradation and heavy predation of its nests by introduced animals (Collar and Stuart 1985; see also Cheke 1987a). However, the species has increased its range (most of which is inside a new national park) and population slightly since 1975 (C. G. Jones *in litt.* 1994), with over 200 pairs estimated in 1993 (Safford in prep.). **VULNERABLE:** D1.

Réunion Cuckoo-shrike *Coracina newtoni* is an insectivorous, forest-dwelling species, endemic to **Réunion (to France)** and restricted to two connected, very small and unprotected areas (Plaine d'Affouches and Plaine des Chicots) in the northwest, where an estimated world total of 120 pairs are at some risk from poachers and their habitat is being degraded by inappropriate forestry and introduced deer (Collar and Stuart 1985, 1988, Cheke 1987b, Barré 1988). Survey work in 1991 suggested that little change in numbers had occurred since 1974 (C. Attié *in litt.* 1994). **ENDANGERED: D1**; D2.

Black-bibbed Cicadabird *Coracina mindanensis* is endemic to the **Philippines** on Luzon (race *lecroyae*), Mindoro (race *elusa*), Samar, Leyte, Bohol and Biliran (race *ripleyi*), Mindanao and Basilan (nominate *mindanensis*), and Jolo, Lapac, Tawitawi and Bongao (race *everetti*), occurring in forests and second growth, but everywhere uncommon (Dickinson *et al.* 1991). Habitat loss in parts of its range is extensive and continuing, and there appear to be no recent records of *lecroyae* or *everetti*, while *elusa* is extremely rare (Dutson *et al.* 1992, R. J. Timmins *in litt.* 1994), *ripleyi* has recently been seen on Bohol and Biliran (Dickinson *et al.* 1991, N. Bostock *in litt.* 1994) and *mindanensis* has recently been recorded from possibly only one or two areas (T. H. Fisher *per* R. J. Timmins *in litt.* 1994, P. Morris *in litt.* 1994). **VULNERABLE:** C1; C2a.

McGregor's Cuckoo-shrike *Coracina mcgregori* is restricted to Mindanao in the **Philippines**, where it has only ever been reported from four sites (three in Dickinson *et al.* 1991), and has recently been reported at only two: on Mount Katanglad, where in 1989–1990 it was observed in the canopy and subcanopy of undisturbed forest in deep valleys at 1,300–1,500 m, an altitude at which forest is now very seriously threatened (Lambert 1993b, J. Hornbuckle *in litt.* 1994); and Sitio Siete, Lake Sebu (South Cotabato province), where it is common above 1,500 m in moss forest (C. R. Robson *in litt.* 1994). **VULNERABLE:** B1+2c; C1; C2a.

White-winged Cuckoo-shrike *Coracina ostenta* is endemic to Panay (status unknown but guessed to be similar to that on Negros), Guimaras (where it is probably extinct given the almost total clearance of forest) and Negros (where it is relatively common, sometimes in mixed-species flocks, from forest edge at 700 up to 1,200 m on Mount Canlaon, extrapolation suggesting a population of approximately 10,000 birds), in the **Philippines**; despite such numbers, clearance of forest within its altitudinal range represents a serious threat (Brooks *et al.* 1992, Lambert 1993b). **VULNERABLE:** A2b; B1+2c.

Western Wattled Cuckoo-shrike *Campephaga lobata* is endemic to and generally rare in the rapidly receding Upper Guinea lowland rainforest of West Africa, where it is known from **Ghana** (two twentieth-century records), **Ivory Coast** (Taï and Marahoué National Parks, plus Mopri and Mount Nimba),

Liberia (Lofa, Nimba, Grand Gedeh County; found near rivers), **Guinea** (one recent record) and **Sierra Leone** (Gola forest) (Collar and Stuart 1985, Colston and Curry-Lindahl 1986, Gartshore 1989, 1991, Allport 1991, Demey and Fishpool 1991, Keith *et al.* 1992; see also Wood 1993). A sight record from Nigeria, listed and mapped without question in Keith *et al.* (1992), was tentative only, and is much more likely to concern Oriole Cuckoo-shrike *C. oriolina* (see Ash *et al.* 1989). **VULNERABLE:** A1b; A2b.

Family PYCNONOTIDAE

BULBULS

Straw-headed Bulbul *Pycnonotus zeylanicus* occurs in Tenasserim, southern **Myanmar**, peninsular **Thailand**, peninsular and East **Malaysia**, **Brunei** and Sumatra, Kalimantan and west Java, **Indonesia**, where it is found on the edge of lowland and hill forest, including secondary forest, often near rivers or in marshy areas, at up to 1,100 m, and locally to 1,600 m (Smythies 1981, Mann 1987, van Marle and Voous 1988, MacKinnon and Phillipps 1993, D. R. Wells *in litt.* 1994). It was formerly common or even abundant in parts of its range (e.g. on Borneo: Smythies 1981), and remains widespread and quite common in peninsular Malaysia (D. R. Wells *in litt.* 1994), but as a popular (and easily trapped) cagebird in the Greater Sundas it has declined in or been extirpated from all but the remotest parts of its range by a combination of excessive trapping and habitat destruction (van Marle and Voous 1988, Boonsong and Round 1991, MacKinnon and Phillipps 1993, BirdLife IP; see Collins *et al.* 1991). **VULNERABLE:** A1b,c.

Spot-necked Bulbul *Pycnonotus tympanistrigus* is endemic to the Barisan range of Sumatra, **Indonesia**, where it is found in hill and lower montane forest, including secondary forest and forest edge, from 600 to 900 m, but locally up to 1,400 m. It is known by few records and appears to be very local (van Marle and Voous 1988, BirdLife BPD), and is probably threatened by deforestation in the lower part of its narrow altitudinal range (BirdLife IP). **VULNERABLE:** C1; C2a.

Prigogine's Greenbul *Chlorocichla prigoginei* occurs in patches of forest at intermediate elevations (1,300–1,500 m in one account, but 1,350–1,800 m in another) to the north-west of Lake Edward and on the Lendu plateau in eastern **Zaïre**, and is under threat from forest destruction (Collar and Stuart 1985, Keith *et al.* 1992). In February 1994 the first observation since 1981 was made by T. Pedersen, M. Languy and L. Essen, who found a single bird with a group of Joyful Greenbuls *C. laetissima* at 1,700 m in Djuga forest (a known locality) on the Lendu plateau (*per* G. A. Allport). **VULNERABLE:** B1+2a,b, c,d,e; C2a.

Liberian Greenbul *Phyllastrephus leucolepis* is a newly described and obviously very rare species known only from Upper Guinea rainforest (transition zone between evergreen and semi-deciduous forest, where it follows mixed-species flocks and forages on branches near trunks 4–8 m above ground) north-west of Zwedru, Grand Gedeh County, south-east **Liberia** (Gatter 1985, Keith *et al.* 1992). Despite much rainforest fieldwork in recent years in Liberia itself (see Gola Malimbe *Malimbus ball-manni*, p. 202) and in adjacent countries (e.g. Gartshore 1989, Allport 1991, Demey and Fishpool 1991), there have been no further records, and forest in the region of the type-locality is being cleared (see Gatter and Gardner 1993). **CRITICAL:** A2b; B1+2a; **C1**; **C2b**; D1.

Appert's Greenbul *Phyllastrephus apperti* is known with certainty from only two unprotected localities (Zombitse and Vohibasia forests) in south-west **Madagascar**, where it fossicks about in the

underbrush of undisturbed deciduous forest and is at ever-increasing risk of habitat destruction by fire and from clearance for mainly maize and some charcoal production (Collar and Stuart 1985, 1988, Langrand 1990, O. Langrand *in litt*. 1987, 1994), although the two forests are currently the subject of a NORAD-funded WWF project to establish them as a national park in 1994 or 1995 (A. F. A. Hawkins *in litt*. 1994, O. Langrand *in litt*. 1994). **VULNERABLE:** B1+2a,b,c,d; C1; C2a; D1.

Dusky Greenbul *Phyllastrephus tenebrosus* is a mysterious (virtually unknown) bulbul of the lower storey of (ever decreasing areas of) undisturbed rainforest, known from eight skins and two adjacent mid-elevation localities (Analamazaotra and 'Sihanaka forest') in eastern-central **Madagascar** (Collar and Stuart 1985), with two more (lowland) areas recently determined further to the north: Maroantsetra (Langrand 1990) and a site on the western Masoala peninsula (J. C. Sinclair *per*/and F. R. Lambert verbally 1993), although there is some uncertainty whether these sites are the same (T. S. Schulenberg *in litt*. 1994). **ENDANGERED:** C1; **C2a**.

Grey-crowned Greenbul *Phyllastrephus cinereiceps*, having been encountered only twice between the early 1930s and the mid-1980s, appears on recent evidence to be confined to montane forest (900 m upwards) in the humid forest belt of eastern **Madagascar**, being threatened by habitat loss but occurring in six protected areas, at Tsaratanana (one record, presumably within the boundaries: Collar and Stuart 1985, 1988), Marojejy (locally common, but in a very narrow altitudinal band, 1,300–1,500 m: Evans *et al*. 1992a), Pic d'Ivohibe (listed by Nicoll and Langrand 1989), Ambatovaky (rare: Thompson and Evans 1992), Mantady (A. F. A. Hawkins *in litt*. 1994) and Ranomafana (locally common: Langrand 1990), plus recently in Maromiza forest near Périnet (O. Langrand *in litt*. 1994) and at Andringitra in fall 1993 (S. M. Goodman *per* T. S. Schulenberg *in litt*. 1994). **VULNERABLE:** B1+2c; C2a.

Green-tailed Bristlebill *Bleda eximia* inhabits the Upper Guinea rainforest belt from southern **Ghana**, **Ivory Coast**, **Liberia**, south-east **Guinea** to **Sierra Leone** (Keith *et al*. 1992), and although in places it may be common (e.g. in Liberia: Gatter 1988) it is generally uncommon to rare and seems to be tied to closed-canopy lowland forest (G. A. Allport and L. D. C. Fishpool verbally 1994; also Fishpool *et al*. 1994), which is everywhere very rapidly diminishing (see Collar and Stuart 1988). **VULNERABLE:** A1b; A2b.

Yellow-throated Olive Greenbul *Criniger olivaceus* is rare in the rapidly receding Upper Guinea rainforest block of West Africa where it is known from **Ghana** (in the 1870s, rediscovered in the far south-west in the 1980s), **Guinea** (one record, 1930, several in 1980s), **Ivory Coast** (recorded from Taï National Park, Yapo forest and Mopri), **Liberia** (at least five localities in recent decades, and categorized as 'rare to common'), **Senegal** (one nineteenth-century record) and **Sierra Leone** (two localities, including Gola forest, where the population is estimated to lie between 750 and 1,600 birds) (Collar and Stuart 1985, Colston and Curry-Lindahl 1986, Gatter 1988, Allport 1991, Demey and Fishpool 1991, Gartshore 1991, Wood 1993). It appears to be restricted to high forest and absent from gallery and degraded secondary forest, but anomalous records from south-west **Mali** (Lamarche 1980–1981) suggest it can occur in less humid growth (Fishpool *et al*. 1994). **VULNERABLE:** A1b; A2b.

Streak-breasted Bulbul *Ixos siquijorensis* is endemic to the **Philippines** on the small islands of Tablas and Romblon (race *cinereiceps*, sufficiently distinct to warrant consideration as a separate species) and Siquijor (nominate *siquijorensis*), but apparently extinct (race *monticola*) on Cebu. The two surviving races are common (with possibly several thousand birds on Siquijor), but are restricted to very (and increasingly) small patches of already degraded forest (Dutson *et al*. 1993, Evans *et al*. 1993b, Timmins in prep.). **ENDANGERED:** A1b; A2b; **B1+2c**; C1; C2a.

Mauritius Bulbul *Hypsipetes olivaceus* (here retained as a species separated from Olivaceous Bulbul *H. borbonicus*, contra Sibley and Monroe 1990), a frugivorous and insectivorous forest-dweller, endemic to **Mauritius**, was judged to have been reduced to c.200 pairs in the mid-1970s and possibly to have declined further since, with nest predation and competition from introduced birds the major threats (Collar and Stuart 1985; see also Cheke 1987a). Recent fieldwork, however, has revealed it to be widespread and probably stable at very low density in the island's degraded forest remnants, with over 200 pairs estimated in 1993 (Safford in prep.), although it may be slowly declining as the native forest degrades (C. G. Jones *in litt*. 1994). **VULNERABLE:** D1.

Nicobar Bulbul *Hypsipetes nicobariensis* is endemic to the small islands (total area 467 km^2: Sankaran 1993b) of the Nancourie group (Camorta, Trinkut, Nancowry and Katchall) in the central Nicobar Islands (and recorded on Pilu Milu, an islet off Little Nicobar), **India**, where it was formerly a common bird in forest and gardens (Abdulali 1967,

1978, Ali and Ripley 1987), but it appears to have declined within this small range (although still common on Katchall where a loose flock of over 100 birds was seen in 1994: R. Sankaran *in litt.* 1994), possibly through displacement by the introduced Red-whiskered Bulbul *Pycnonotus jocosus* (Sankaran 1993a). **VULNERABLE:** A1d; B1+2e; C1; C2a.

Family IRENIDAE

LEAFBIRDS, FAIRY-BLUEBIRDS

Philippine Leafbird *Chloropsis flavipennis* occurs in forest and forest edge up to at least 1,500 m on Leyte and Mindanao in the **Philippines**, having apparently become extinct on Cebu (Dickinson *et al.* 1991, Dutson *et al.* 1993). It seems to be rare, pre-sumably owing to widespread and continuing habitat destruction within its range, with very few recent records (F. R. Lambert verbally 1993, Timmins in prep.). **ENDANGERED:** A1b; A2b; C1; C2a.

Family LANIIDAE

SHRIKES

São Tomé Fiscal Shrike *Lanius newtoni*, previously encountered by only two fieldworkers, in 1888 and 1928, always in the southern (lowland and mid-altitude: to 1,000 m) rainforests of São Tomé, **São Tomé e Príncipe** (Collar and Stuart 1985), was rediscovered in July 1990 when a single bird was netted while foraging among boulders by a stream near the source of the Rio Xufexufe (Atkinson *et al.* 1991), with another individual being seen in a flat ridge on successive days in August 1991 (T. M. Gullick *in litt.* 1994; also Sargeant 1994), and another (a male) at 200 m on the right bank of the Xufexufe in early 1994 (P. Christy *in litt.* 1994). The species' extreme rarity remains baffling (Collar and Stuart 1985, Atkinson *et al.* 1991), but it may prefer ridge areas, a habitat that remains little explored (T. M. Gullick *in litt.* 1994). Meanwhile, the future of the island's forests remains uncertain (Jones *et al.* 1992). **CRITICAL: D1.**

Orange-breasted Bush-shrike *Laniarius brauni* remains known only from secondary and gallery forest at two sites in Cuanza Norte, in the northern part of the scarp of **Angola** (Hall 1960, Traylor 1963), with no recent information on its status, although deforestation on the escarpment has proceeded steadily in recent decades (A. F. A. Hawkins *in litt.* 1994). **ENDANGERED: B1+2c; C2a; D1.**

Gabela Bush-shrike *Laniarius amboimensis* remains known only from evergreen forest in a restricted area around Gabela on the scarp of **Angola**, where it is clearly uncommon, last seen in 1960 (Hall 1960, Pinto 1962, Collar and Stuart 1985) until single pairs were found twice in three days in September 1992, near Gabela, in mixed-species flocks, by when as much as 30% of forest in the Gabela region had been cleared for subsistence agriculture before resumption of the civil war in that month (A. F. A. Hawkins *in litt.* 1994). **ENDANGERED: B1+2c; C1; C2a; D1.**

Bulo Burti Bush-shrike *Laniarius liberatus* was described on the basis of blood and feather samples from a single live individual first observed in August 1988 in acacia scrub in the grounds of a hospital at Bulo Burti (Buulobarde), 140 km inland and at 140 m on the Shabeelle River in central **Somalia**. The bird was netted there in January 1989 and, after 14 months in captivity and because judged belonging to a probably highly threatened species, it was released into acacia scrub (a rapidly diminishing habitat in the region) as near as possible to its site of capture, in March 1990 (Smith *et al.* 1991; also Scott 1991). Searches in the Bulo Burti area in 1989 and 1990 were unsuccessful (J. E. Miskell *per* J. S. Ash *in litt.* 1990), and the validity of the species has been questioned (Ash 1993, Dowsett and Dowsett-Lemaire 1993). **CRITICAL: D1**.

Mount Kupe Bush-shrike *Telophorus kupeensis*, discovered in 1949 and found again in 1951 in primary forest on Mount Kupe, western **Cameroon**, where the area of habitat covers a mere 21 km² (Collar and Stuart 1985), was rediscovered there on a steep ridge in July 1989 at 1,220 and 1,310 m (D. McNiven *in litt.* 1989) and subsequently by other observers, revealing it to be scarce between 930 and 1,450 m. The forest on Kupe is now the subject of a major conservation programme (Bowden 1993, Bowden and Bowden 1993, Bowden and Andrews 1994). **CRITICAL: D1**; D2.

Green-breasted Bush-shrike *Malaconotus gladiator*, a very low-density inhabitant of montane forest canopy, occurs at a few localities in western **Cameroon** (Mount Cameroon, 950–1,500 m; Rumpi Hills, 1,300–1,520 m; Mount Kupe, 1,100–1,950 m; Mount Nlonako, 1,400–1,600 m; Mount Oku (= Kilum), 2,200–2,300 m; Bakossi Mountains in 1994; and three further localities in the Bamenda-Banso Highlands) and eastern **Nigeria** (Obudu plateau, 1,500 m) (Collar and Stuart 1985, 1988, C. G. R. Bowden *in litt.* 1994). The species is rare on Kilum (Stuart and Jensen 1986), such that it could not be found in four weeks of fieldwork in 1985 (Wilson 1987) or 10 months in 1990–1991 (R. C. Fotso *in litt.* 1994), and there is considerable loss of habitat elsewhere in the Bamenda-Banso Highlands and on the Obudu plateau (Collar and Stuart 1985, Ash 1987b); however, conservation of Kilum proceeds for other reasons (see Macleod 1987, Green 1991, Alpert 1993, Edwards 1993), as it does at Kupe, where the species is uncommon and, *contra* the above, found at 1,400–2,000 m (Bowden 1993, Bowden and Bowden 1993, Bowden and Andrews 1994). **VULNERABLE:** C2a.

Monteiro's Bush-shrike *Malaconotus monteiri* is known only from a few sites (either in gallery or evergreen forest) on the scarp of **Angola** (no record since 1954) and a nineteenth-century specimen from Mount Cameroon (distinguished as race *perspicillatus*: Prigogine 1984), **Cameroon**, the low number of records (seven in total) suggesting that it is very rare wherever it occurs, with habitat destruction the most likely current threat (Collar and Stuart 1985, 1988). It was not found during surveys of the Angolan scarp in September 1992, when considerable forest loss was noted (Hawkins 1993b, A. F. A. Hawkins *in litt.* 1994), but a single bird was found on 21 September 1992 on Mount Kupe, Cameroon (Andrews 1994), for which a major conservation programme now exists (Bowden 1993, Bowden and Bowden 1993). **ENDANGERED: C2a**; D1.

Uluguru Bush-shrike *Malaconotus alius* is an elusive, low-density inhabitant of the canopy of montane forest (records are from 1,300 m upwards) in the Uluguru Mountains, **Tanzania**, where forest covers only about 120 km² and a dense human population is steadily clearing the lower slopes (Collar and Stuart 1985, 1988). During two months' fieldwork in 1993 only three or four territories were certainly recorded, all on the eastern slopes of the Uluguru North Forest Reserve (where precipitation is highest and forest of best quality), which still holds a good area of flat forest between 1,200 and 1,500 m, although virtually all other subtropical forest, which may be its core habitat, has now been cleared (L. A. Hansen and J. O. Svendsen *in litt.* 1994; also J. Fjeldså verbally 1994). **CRITICAL:** B1+2c; **C2b**; D1.

Grey-crested Helmet-shrike *Prionops poliolophus* occurs at 1,200–2,200 m in open woodland, wooded grassland and bushland, typically in *Acacia drepanolobium* or *Tarchonanthus*, in a restricted area of south-west **Kenya** and north-west **Tanzania** (Britton 1980, Schmidl 1982, Lewis and Pomeroy 1989, Short *et al.* 1990). Despite evidence that it is recolonizing the Rift Valley, it is generally considered uncommon (very rare and virtually unknown in Tanzania: N. E. Baker *in litt.* 1994), and, being peripheral to most protected areas such as the Masai Mara Game Reserve and the Serengeti National Park, it appears to have suffered a decline owing to habitat destruction (N. Stronach *in litt.* 1993, J. H. Fanshawe verbally 1994). **VULNERABLE:** C2b.

Yellow-crested Helmet-shrike *Prionops alberti* is known from four mountain ranges (west of Lake Edward, west of Lake Kivu, Itombwe and Mount Kabobo) in **Zaïre**; a record from Bwindi (Impenetrable) forest in Uganda is rejected (Britton 1980) although repeated in Sibley and Monroe (1990). It dwells in forest above 1,400 m (Chapin 1954, Prigogine 1985), but, perhaps as a result of continuing habitat loss (see Collar and Stuart 1988), is now apparently extremely difficult to find, with few if any recent records (T. Stevenson *in litt.* 1992). **VULNERABLE:** C1; C2a.

Gabela Helmet-shrike *Prionops gabela* remains known only from a small area of forest (underplanted with coffee) and thicket near Gabela on the scarp of **Angola** (Collar and Stuart 1985, 1988). There appear to have been no recent (post mid-1970s) records and, although it probably occurs throughout the scarp (area roughly 1,300–2,000 km²), as much as 30% of forest in the Gabela region had been cleared for subsistence agriculture before resumption of the civil war in September 1992, with forest elsewhere on the scarp being cleared probably at a slower rate (Hawkins 1993b, A. F. A. Hawkins *in litt*. 1994). **ENDANGERED: B1+2b,c,d**; C1; **C2a**; D1.

Family VANGIDAE
VANGAS

Van Dam's Vanga *Xenopirostris damii*, an insectivorous bird of low-elevation (150 m) primary deciduous forest in north-west **Madagascar** (a habitat under great pressure), is known this century from only two sites (Ankarafantsika and Analamera), which are, however, protected areas (Collar and Stuart 1985, 1988, Nicoll and Langrand 1989, Langrand 1990, Hawkins *et al*. 1990). **VULNERABLE: D2.**

Pollen's Vanga *Xenopirostris polleni* has been recorded throughout the rainforest belt (0–1,000 m) of eastern **Madagascar** (Collar and Stuart 1985, Langrand 1990), where habitat loss, though extensive, is not enough to explain its very patchy distribution and abundance: it is absent or very rare in many places and only fairly common at Ranomafana (see, e.g., Razafimahaimodison and Andrianantenaina 1993) and Andohahela (Parcel One), two of five protected areas in which it has been recorded (the others being Andasibe, Marojejy and Mantady) (A. F. A. Hawkins *in litt*. 1994, O. Langrand *in litt*. 1994; also Nicoll and Langrand 1989). **VULNERABLE:** C2a.

Bernier's Vanga *Oriolia bernieri* is seemingly restricted to undisturbed tracts of the northern rainforest belt in eastern **Madagascar** (although recorded, anomalously, as far south as Vondrozo: Dee 1986). The species is described as rare, at least in parts of the Masoala peninsula (R. J. Safford *in litt*. 1994), and as 'certainly the rarest vanga in the Eastern Forest' (O. Langrand *in litt*. 1994), and this, together with the bird's restricted range and the general assault on primary forest in the country, makes it at risk (Langrand 1990, Evans *et al*. 1992a, Thompson and Evans 1992). **VULNERABLE:** C2a.

Family CINCLIDAE
DIPPERS

Rufous-throated Dipper *Cinclus schulzi* is confined to rivers and streams on the slope of the Andes in southernmost **Bolivia** (Tarija) and north-west **Argentina** (Jujuy, Salta, Tucumán, Catamarca), where it breeds in the alder zone at elevations ranging from 1,500 to 2,500 m. Its small range and general lack of formal conservation render it potentially vulnerable to modern developmental changes (Collar *et al*. 1992). In southern Tarija, Bolivia, the species appears to be relatively secure at present (S. Mayer *in litt*. 1993), but the population in Argentina (unlikely to be higher than 1,000 pairs) is threatened by habitat loss, pollution and hydro-scheme/dam developments (Tyler 1994). **VULNERABLE:** C2a.

Family TROGLODYTIDAE

WRENS

Sumichrast's Wren *Hylorchilus sumichrasti*, here split from Nava's Wren *H. navai* (see below), is confined to limestone outcrops in the shade of closed-canopy lowland evergreen forest in west-central Veracruz and northernmost Oaxaca, southern **Mexico**, where a key site (Amatlán) is threatened by encroaching limestone quarrying and coffee plantations (Collar *et al.* 1992, Atkinson *et al.* 1993). **VULNERABLE:** A1b; A2b; B1+2c; C1; C2a.

Nava's Wren *Hylorchilus navai*, here split from Sumichrast's Wren *H. sumichrasti* (see above), occurs at a very crudely calculated density of 20 birds per km^2 on limestone outcrops in the shade of primary lowland evergreen forest in easternmost Veracruz (the 'Uxpanapa' region, at the mid-point of the Isthmus of Tehuantepec) and western Chiapas, southern **Mexico**, where it is threatened by deforestation (Collar *et al.* 1992, Atkinson *et al.* 1993). **VULNERABLE:** A1b; A2b; B1+2c; C1; C2a.

Apolinar's Wren *Cistothorus apolinari* is confined to tall reedbeds fringing the dwindling marshes and lakes of the East Andes of **Colombia** (Boyacá, Cundinamarca), which are threatened by drainage and the influences of agriculture. Although considered locally still fairly common, its numbers have fallen at several formerly important sites and there appears to be no single locality at which more than 50 pairs are present, and in total possibly as few as 10 current localities exist (Collar *et al.* 1992). **ENDANGERED:** A1b; A2b; B1+2c; **C1**; **C2a**; D1.

Zapata Wren *Ferminia cerverai* is known only from within a 20 km radius of Santo Tomás in the Zapata Swamp, **Cuba**, where, having been reported common at the time of its discovery in 1926, it appears to have suffered particularly from the dry-season burning of its savanna-like habitat and perhaps from predation by introduced mongooses and rats (Collar *et al.* 1992). **CRITICAL:** B1+2e; **C2b**; D1.

Nicéforo's Wren *Thryothorus nicefori* is known only from the type-locality (San Gil on the Río Fonce south of Bucaramanga) in the East Andes of Santander department, **Colombia**, where it was originally collected in 1945 and rediscovered there in 1989 when two birds were found in a remnant patch of acacia, the habitat being heavily disturbed (Collar *et al.* 1992). **CRITICAL:** A1b; A2b; **B1+2c**; C1; C2b; D1; D2.

Cobb's Wren *Troglodytes cobbi* (split from House Wren *T. aedon* since Sibley and Monroe 1990) is resident in the **Falkland Islands (to U.K.)**, where it has been recorded only on 17 tiny offshore islands (and found absent on a further 12), showing a strong preference for areas with mature tussock grass. Its distribution is inversely related to the presence of introduced predators, whose impact may have increased with the long-term destruction of its habitat (Woods 1993). **VULNERABLE:** D2.

Clarión Wren *Troglodytes tanneri* is common on Isla Clarión (c.30 km^2), in the Revillagigedo Islands, **Mexico**, ranging from rocks on the beach to shrubbery at the highest elevations, but the total population has been put at 170–180 pairs, and the introduction of an exotic predator remains a serious possibility (Everett 1988, Howell and Webb 1989, Santaella and Sada 1991). **VULNERABLE:** D1; D2.

Family MIMIDAE

THRASHERS, MOCKINGBIRDS

Floreana Mockingbird *Nesomimus trifasciatus* survives in low numbers on Champion (200–300 birds) and Gardner (c.50) in the Galápagos Islands, **Ecuador**, having succumbed to non-native rats on Floreana within 20 years of 1868, at which time it had been judged common there. It inhabits *Opuntia* scrub and other stands of vegetation, often feeding on the ground (Collar *et al.* 1992). In wet (El Niño) years avian pox causes the populations to crash (R. L. Curry verbally 1994). **ENDANGERED: D1**; D2.

Socorro Mockingbird *Mimodes graysoni* was the most abundant and widespread landbird on Socorro, in the Revillagigedo Islands, **Mexico**, in 1925, particularly favouring wooded canyons, but by the mid-1980s it had been reduced to possibly 100–150 birds (50–60 pairs), probably as a result of predation by feral cats, compounded by the overgrazing of undergrowth by sheep (Collar *et al.* 1992, Castellanos and Rodríguez-Estrella 1993). Work between June 1993 and June 1994 resulted in 215 birds being banded and the total population being put at 300; five nests were found in trees within groves, which sheep are destroying, but where sheep are absent the species exists from the coast to the mountain top, in figs and *Ilex* in ravines, etc. (J. E. Martínez Gómez verbally 1994). **ENDANGERED: A1b,d; B1+2e; C1; C2b; D1**.

White-breasted Thrasher *Ramphocinclus brachyurus* has been reduced by habitat destruction and introduced predators to near-extinction in two dry forest areas on the islands of **Martinique (to France)**—nominate *brachyurus*, total population 15–40 pairs—on the Caravelle peninsula, where its habitat falls within a well protected nature reserve (P. Feldman and P. Villard *in litt.* 1994) and **St Lucia**—race *sanctaeluciae*, total population c.50 pairs—between Petite Anse and Dennery Knob, declining at over 4% per year (Collar *et al.* 1992). **ENDANGERED: A1a,b,d; A2b,d; B1+2e; C1; C2a; D1; D2**.

Subfamily TURDINAE

THRUSHES, ROBINS, CHATS

Benson's Rock-thrush *Monticola bensoni* is only known from arid rocky country and associated vegetation between the Mangoky and Onilahy rivers in south-west **Madagascar**, chiefly in and around the Isalo Massif (where it breeds at 700–1,000 m, dispersing into the western lowlands in winter), and, although no threats are known, the national park (Isalo) in which it occurs is burnt regularly and total numbers of the species may prove small (Collar and Stuart 1985, Collar and Tattersall 1987, Langrand 1990, A. F. A. Hawkins *in litt.* 1994). **VULNERABLE: D1**.

Sri Lanka Whistling-thrush *Myiophonus blighi* is endemic to the Hill Zone of central **Sri Lanka**, where it is found along mountain streams running through dense, damp montane forest, in fern-clad ravines and gorges above 900 m (Legge 1880, Ali and Ripley 1987), although it is now probably confined to the Hortons Plains National Park within an altitudinal range of 1,300–2,300 m (S. W. Kotagama *in litt.* 1992, Kotagama in prep.). It is rare and declining, probably as a result of the replacement of natural forest with monoculture plantations, which are largely devoid of undergrowth and hence unsuitable habitat (Hoffmann 1984). **ENDANGERED: B1+2c; C1; D1**.

Ashy Thrush *Zoothera cinerea* occurs on or near the ground in primary and selectively logged forest at 400–1,000 m on Luzon (where its habitat is still moderately extensive) and Mindoro (three records, 1891–1991) in the **Philippines**; on both islands its relatively low-lying habitat remains highly threatened, and on Luzon, where the ringing of 130 birds over seven years (before 1972) indicates that it was perhaps not uncommon and certainly undertakes some intra-island dispersal, it is also at risk from hunting with snares (Dickinson *et al.* 1991, Dutson *et al.* 1992, Danielsen *et al.* 1994, Poulsen in press). **VULNERABLE: A2b; C1; C2a**.

Spotted Ground-thrush *Zoothera guttata* (=*Turdus fischeri*), a remarkably elusive thrush of the forest floor, requiring deep shade and deep leaf-litter, has an extraordinary distribution within which it is threatened by habitat destruction: there are two migratory coastal subspecies, *fischeri* probably breeding in northern Mozambique and with recent good evidence of breeding on the 18 km^2 Rondo plateau in southern **Tanzania** (with new records also from the 5 km^2 Litipo forest near Lindi), migrating north through coastal Tanzania (e.g. Pugu Hills) to winter in a very few, very small sites in **Kenya**, such as Gede National Monument, the adjacent, much larger (but where occurrence is at much lower density) Arabuko–Sokoke forest (the target of a now stalled conservation project: see Sokoke Scops-owl *Otus ireneae*, p. 114), and Shimba Hills (Bennun and Waiyaki 1992); nominate *guttata* (= *T. f. natalicus*) in **South Africa** mostly breeding along the Transkei coast and wintering to the north-east along the Natal coast from the Transkei border to Lake St Lucia in the north, with small isolated populations (sedentary or partially migrant) breeding at Dlinza (c.50 pairs), Ennumeni and Ngoye forests in northern Natal and at Oribi Gorge in southern Natal, one resident race (*belcheri*, restricted to four small mountains— 1,200–1,700 m, down to 700 m on Mount Mulanje in August—in south-east **Malawi** and numbering 30–40 pairs in all), and two races known from single specimens, *maxis* from the Imatong Mountains in **Sudan** and *lippensi* from the Upemba National Park, **Zaïre** (Collar and Stuart 1985; also Prigogine and Louette 1984, Clancey 1985, Bennun 1987, 1992a, Bagger *et al.* 1989, Dowsett-Lemaire 1989, Fanshawe 1991, Holsten *et al.* 1991, Baker and Baker 1992, Burgess *et al.* 1992, Bhatia 1993, Harebottle 1994, D. G. Allan *in litt.* 1994, A. Berruti *in litt.* 1994). **ENDANGERED:** B1+2c; **C2a**.

Amami Thrush *Zoothera major* (formerly treated as a race of White's Thrush *Z. dauma*, but its status has been clarified: King 1978–1979, Ishihara 1986) is endemic to Amami in the Nansei Shoto, southern **Japan**, where it is found at low densities between 100 and 400 m in primary forest and old selectively logged forest (logged more than 60 years ago), with a total population estimated to be below 100 individuals; large areas of mature forest have been clear-felled on Amami in the last few decades and replaced by young secondary forests unsuitable for this species, which is vulnerable to further deforestation (Higuchi and Hanawa 1985, Sugimura 1988, K. Sugimura *in litt.* 1993). **CRITICAL:** A1b; B1+2c; C1; **C2b**; D1.

Kamao *Myadestes myadestinus* is endemic to Kauai in the Hawaiian Islands (**U.S.A.**) where it was the commonest of the forest birds in 1891, but by 1928 had disappeared from the lower altitudes (probably as a result of introduced disease-carrying mosquitoes) and is today restricted to the very highest reaches of the Alakai Wilderness Preserve (likely to be fewer than 20 individuals in the period 1976–1983) (Scott *et al.* 1986, Pratt 1993, H. D. Pratt *in litt.* 1994; see also Pratt 1994). It was last seen in 1989, although there is an unconfirmed sighting from 1993 (R. Pyle verbally 1994). **CRITICAL:** A1a; **B1+2e**; **C2b**; D1; D2.

Olomao *Myadestes lanaiensis*, a shy and retiring bird of the forest canopy from the central Hawaiian Islands (**U.S.A.**), is known from Lanai (last seen 1933), Maui (extirpated by historic times) and Molokai (Pratt *et al.* 1987), where it is known only from the Kamakou Preserve with sightings few and far between (last seen in the late 1980s: R. Pyle verbally 1994) and a population estimated at less than 20 individuals in the period 1976–1983 (Pratt 1993). It has probably suffered from introduced disease-carrying mosquitoes in the lowlands and from habitat destruction, and it is likely that Molokai is not high enough to provide a sufficiently large disease-free upland refuge (Pratt 1993, 1994). **CRITICAL:** A1a; **B1+2e**; **C2b**; **D1**; D2.

Puaiohi *Myadestes palmeri* is a very rare bird of the high elevation ohia forests on Kauai in the Hawaiian Islands (**U.S.A.**), occurring today only in the Alakai Wilderness Preserve with a population estimated at c.20 individuals in the period 1976–1983 (Scott *et al.* 1986). It has apparently always been rare historically but the population declined tenfold during the 1970s, perhaps because it cannot tolerate many changes in the environment or owing to introduced disease-carrying mosquitoes in the lowlands (Berger 1972, H. D. Pratt *in litt.* 1994; see also Pratt 1994). Since Hurricane Iniki in 1992 it has been regularly seen and, in early 1994, 18 separate encounters were recorded (R. Pyle verbally 1994). **CRITICAL:** A1a; **B1+2c,e**; **C2a**; **D1**; D2.

Somali Thrush *Turdus ludoviciae* (here split from Olive Thrush *T. olivaceus*) is locally very common within a few small juniper forests (most notably Daloh Forest Reserve) in northern **Somalia** (Ash and Miskell 1981, 1983, Collar and Stuart 1985). The Daloh Forest Reserve is a key site for bird conservation in Africa, but there are reports of plans to exploit and replant it (Collar and Stuart 1988). The chronic and continuing political crisis in Somalia may be leading to an as yet undocumented loss of habitats for this and other species endemic to the country. **ENDANGERED:** B1+2a,b,c; **C2a**.

Taita Thrush *Turdus helleri* (which does not respond to tapes of Olive Thrush *T. olivaceus* with which it is often lumped: T. Stevenson *in litt.* 1994) is apparently confined to the forest between 1,200 (or more usually 1,500) and 1,725 m on the Taita Hills and Mount Kasigau in south-east **Kenya**, available habitat in the former covering less than 3 km² and being under serious threat (Collar and Stuart 1985, 1988), available habitat on the latter certain to be similarly restricted (L. A. Bennun *in litt.* 1994). In Ngaongao forest (one of the two relatively intact patches remaining on the Taita Hills) a total of 90–190 birds was estimated in 1985 (McGuigan 1987). **CRITICAL: B1+2a,b,c**; C2b; D1; D2.

Yemen Thrush *Turdus menachensis* occurs at apparently low densities only in montane patches of remnant, dense 'natural' tree and scrub cover of (e.g.) *Acacia, Olea, Rosa* and adjacent grassy or cultivated areas at 1,200–2,900 m (but chiefly 1,800–2,000 m) in valley bottoms and on steep, rocky hillsides in western **Yemen** (the paucity of records indicating a sparse population) and south-west **Saudi Arabia** as far as 21°N (the juniper woodlands of the Asir highlands, where the birds are 'numerous' but disappear from August to February), and is at risk from the loss of this habitat to firewood collection (Cornwallis and Porter 1982, Phillips 1982, Stagg 1984, Bowden 1987). **VULNERABLE: B1+2b,c**; C2a.

Grey-sided Thrush *Turdus feae* is known to breed only in north-east **China**, where it has been recorded in Hebei, Shanxi and Beijing municipality, in broadleaf forest in the mountains (Cheng 1987, King 1987). It winters in north-east **India** (probably no recent records: T. P. Inskipp *in litt.* 1994), **Myanmar** and north-west **Thailand** (uncommon: Boonsong and Round 1991) in evergreen forest above 1,000 m (King *et al.* 1975, Ali and Ripley 1987, Boonsong and Round 1991). It is only recorded from about five localities in northern China, including Pangquanguo Nature Reserve (BirdLife BPD), and its breeding habitat must have been much reduced and fragmented by deforestation in this densely populated region of China (M.J.C.; see Collins *et al.* 1991). **VULNERABLE: B1+2c**; C1; C2a.

Izu Thrush *Turdus celaenops* is endemic to several small islands off southern **Japan**, breeding on the Izu Islands, where it was formerly common to abundant (reaching its highest densities on Miyake-jima), and Nakanoshima in the Tokara Islands in the northern Nansei Shoto (where 4–6 pairs were discovered in 1988: Kawaji *et al.* 1989), in deciduous and mixed forest, open secondary growth, orchards and gardens (Brazil 1991). However, weasels *Mustela sibirica* were introduced to Miyake-jima in the late 1970s and 1982 to control rats, and are causing a rapid decline in the thrush population on this island by predation (Takagi and Higuchi 1992). **VULNERABLE: B1+2e**; C1.

La Selle Thrush *Turdus swalesi*, despite being relatively common where it occurs (and this includes several national parks), is isolated in poorly protected pockets of habitat in the mountains of Hispaniola, nominate *swalesi* in the Massif de la Selle, **Haiti**, and Sierra de Baoruco, **Dominican Republic**, race *dodae* in the latter's Sierra de Neiba and Cordillera Central. It inhabits the dense understorey of subtropical wet forest and pine forests generally above 1,300 m, which are disappearing rapidly (Collar *et al.* 1992). **VULNERABLE: B1+2c**; C1; C2a.

Rusty-bellied Shortwing *Brachypteryx hyperythra* occurs in the eastern Himalayas in Sikkim, Assam and Arunachal Pradesh, **India** and north-west Yunnan, **China**, and the Naga Hills in Nagaland, India, where it is found in broadleaf evergreen forest and bamboo from around 1,800–3,000 m in the breeding season (Peng *et al.* 1980, Heath 1988), and forest, scrub and bamboo from the plains to 2,900 m in winter (Ali and Ripley 1987). Historical data suggest that it is a very scarce and local bird (Heath 1988), and the only recent records are of two collected at Maku in Yunnan in 1973 (Peng *et al.* 1980), three collected in and near Namdapha National Park, Arunachal Pradesh, in 1987 and 1988 (Ripley *et al.* 1991) and one seen in Kamleng Wildlife Sanctuary, Arunachal Pradesh, in 1994 (R. H. Raza *in litt.* 1994). It is presumably threatened by deforestation, particularly at the lower altitudes where it winters (M. Katti *in litt.* 1993). **VULNERABLE: C1**; C2a.

Thyolo Alethe *Alethe choloensis* is a ground-haunting, ant-following bird known from 15 small patches of submontane evergreen forest (1,200–1,900 m, but down to 700 m on Mulanje in March–October), 13 of them in south-eastern **Malawi** and two in adjacent **Mozambique**, with the bulk of Malawi's estimated 1,500 pairs being on Mount Mulanje (1,000 pairs) and Mount Thyolo (200 pairs) where, as at most other sites, deforestation is intensive (Collar and Stuart 1985, 1988, Dowsett-Lemaire 1987, 1989). **VULNERABLE: B1+2c**.

Swynnerton's Robin *Swynnertonia swynnertoni* haunts cover-free ground in middle-altitude and montane wet forests (850–1,750 m, but in the Usambaras also in the much exploited lowland forest at 200–400 m), restricted to Chirinda and a few other tiny forest patches in eastern **Zimbabwe** (nominate *swynnertoni*), Mount Gorongosa in **Mozambique** (race *umbratica*), then (1,100 km to the north) the Udzungwa Mountains (Mwanihana forest, where rare, Chita forest, where common, and the Ndundulu Mountains, where locally common; density in secondary forest as much as 25 pairs per km²) (race *rodgersi*) and (400 km north again) lowland patches within the East Usambara Mountains (apparently undescribed race; fairly common) in **Tanzania** (Collar and Stuart 1985, Stuart *et al.* 1987, Manson 1990, Evans and Anderson 1992, 1993, Jensen and Brøgger-

Jensen 1992, Keith *et al.* 1992, Dinesen *et al.* 1993, Moyer 1993, Hipkiss *et al.* 1994, Watson and Perkin undated, Moyer and Lovett in press, T. D. Evans *in litt.* 1994, A. Tye *in litt.* 1994). For current conservation in the East Usambaras see Usambara Eagle Owl *Bubo vosseleri*. (p. 115) **VULNERABLE: B1+2b,c.**

East Coast Akalat *Sheppardia gunningi* is a ground-haunting, often ant-following bird of mostly small, mostly coastal lowland forests in eastern Africa (seeming to need rather well shaded, undisturbed forest, within which it can still be extremely patchy: L. A. Bennun *in litt.* 1994), with populations around Beira in **Mozambique** (nominate *gunningi*), in the lower Tana River forests, the Arabuko–Sokoke forest (the target of a now stalled conservation project: see Sokoke Scops-owl *Otus ireneae*, p. 114), the Shimba Hills and a few other patches in **Kenya**, small lowland patches inside the Usambara Mountains (where common), the Pugu Hills (including Kazimzumbwe forest), Rondo plateau (18 km²; common there), Dondwe forest in Dar es Salaam (S. Davies and J. Kiure *per* N. E. Baker *in litt.* 1994), Chitoa and Litipo Forest Reserves (Bagger *et al.* 1989, Faldborg *et al.* 1991, T. Lehmberg *per* J. O. Svendsen *in litt.* 1994) and even, recently, Jozani forest on Zanzibar (Archer *et al.* 1991) in **Tanzania** (race *sokokensis*), and seven mountains (500–1,400 m) in northern **Malawi** (race *bensoni*) where its total population may be over 3,000 pairs (Collar and Stuart 1985, Dowsett-Lemaire 1989, Holsten *et al.* 1991, Bennun and Waiyaki 1992, Burgess *et al.* 1992, Keith *et al.* 1992, Mlingwa *et al.* 1993, Bhatia 1993, Hipkiss *et al.* 1994, Watson and Perkin undated). For current conservation in the East Usambaras see Usambara Eagle Owl *Bubo vosseleri* (p. 115). **VULNERABLE: B1+2b,c.**

Gabela Akalat *Sheppardia gabela* is known only from the dense understorey of a few primary and secondary forest patches near (within 40 km of) Gabela on the scarp of **Angola**, where there is good evidence that its habitat has largely been removed (Collar and Stuart 1985, 1988, Keith *et al.* 1992). Indeed, although it may prove to occur throughout the Angolan scarp (area roughly 1,300–2,000 km²), as much as 30% of forest in the Gabela region had been cleared for subsistence agriculture before resumption of the civil war in September 1992 (when the species was seen twice in three days in scrubby edges of managed coffee forest near the town— identification was made subsequently from examination of skins, and these records are thus not in Hawkins 1993b), with forest elsewhere on the scarp being cleared probably at a slower rate (A. F. A. Hawkins *in litt.* 1994). **ENDANGERED: B1+2a,c; C2a.**

Usambara Akalat *Sheppardia montana*, although numerically strong (the total population is conservatively estimated to be 28,000), occurs as a largely ground-dwelling ant-follower of montane forest only above 1,600(–2,200) m in the West Usambaras mountains, **Tanzania**, where its habitat covers a mere 140 km², was for some time being converted to softwood plantations (probably no longer), and presumably suffers encroachment for subsistence agriculture (Collar and Stuart 1985, 1988, Keith *et al.* 1992, S. N. Stuart *in litt.* 1994). **VULNERABLE: B1+2a,c.**

Iringa Akalat *Sheppardia lowei* is a largely ground-dwelling occasional ant-follower known from only a few areas of mainly dry (though some wet) montane forest (1,350–2,450 m) in the Southern Highlands, the Udzungwa Mountains (as many as 15 pairs per km²) and, recently, the Ukaguru Mountains (an apparently new subspecies: Stuart *et al.* 1993) of **Tanzania**. Although fairly common in places, and tolerating some habitat disturbance, it needs improved habitat protection to be secure (Collar and Stuart 1985, Evans and Anderson 1992, 1993, Jensen and Brøgger-Jensen 1992, Keith *et al.* 1992, Dinesen *et al.* 1993, Moyer 1993, Moyer and Lovett in press, D. C. Moyer *in litt.* 1994). **VULNERABLE: B1+2b,c.**

Rufous-headed Robin *Luscinia ruficeps* is known by breeding season records from four localities (including three protected areas) in southern Shaanxi and north-central Sichuan, **China**, where it has been recorded in bamboo in mixed coniferous forest, birches and dry streambeds at about 2,400 to 3,500 m (Cheng 1987, Collar and Andrew 1988, C. R. Robson *in litt.* 1992, BirdLife BPD), and a migrant trapped and ringed in the mountains of peninsular **Malaysia** (Medway and Wells 1976). Populations outside protected areas are likely to be threatened by the widespread logging of primary forests which is taking place in that part of China (P. Alström *in litt.* 1993, M.J.C.; see Collins *et al.* 1991). **VULNERABLE: C1; C2a.**

Black-throated Blue Robin *Luscinia obscura* is known by breeding season records from southeast Gansu, southern Shaanxi and north-central Sichuan, and as a migrant from Yunnan, **China** (Cheng 1987, Collar and Andrew 1988) and northern **Thailand** (Boonsong and Round 1991). It has been recorded in bamboo thickets in conifer forest at 3,050–3,400 m in the breeding season (Meyer de Schauensee 1984), but its habitat needs remain poorly understood. It has been recorded in at least four protected areas (BirdLife BPD), but populations elsewhere are probably threatened by the widespread logging of primary forest which is occurring in part of China (P. Alström *in litt.* 1993, M.J.C.; see Collins *et al.* 1991). **VULNERABLE:** C1; C2a.

White-headed Robin-chat *Cossypha heinrichi* is known from dense undergrowth of gallery forest and immediately adjacent savanna (when pursuing driver ants) at one site in northern **Angola** ('1,250 m' on labels in YPM), and from a few thick (not gallery) forest patches 500 km to the north in western **Zaïre** (with a sight record 550 km still further north), but remains very poorly known and seemingly in danger from clearance of habitat (Collar and Stuart 1985). **VULNERABLE:** B1+2a,c.

Seychelles Magpie-robin *Copsychus sechellarum*, a ground-foraging insectivore preferring open areas under tree cover or in vegetable gardens, survives only on Frégate (210 ha) in the **Seychelles**, from whose other islands its populations are assumed to have been exterminated by feral cats; however, although cats were entirely eradicated from Frégate in 1981, the bird's declining population merely levelled out (as a result of habitat degradation) rather than increasing (Collar and Stuart 1985; see also Watson *et al.* 1992, McCulloch in press). In early 1985 25 birds were counted, in early 1987 20, and later that year 23, including six immatures (Collar and Andrew 1988). Since 1988 the species has been the target of an intensive ICBP/BirdLife programme of research and management: nesting success has been boosted by habitat creation, supplementary feeding, nest defence, provision of nest boxes, and reduction of Common Mynas *Acridotheres tristis* (Gretton 1993, Komdeur in prep.). The current aim of the project is to establish a population of 80–100 birds on two or more islands in 10–15 years (Gretton 1993). In April 1994 there were 46 birds on Frégate, with an additional two (male and female) translocated to Aride (M. N. McCulloch verbally 1994). **CRITICAL: D1**; D2.

Black Shama *Copsychus cebuensis* survives in small numbers in scrub with second-growth forest, plantations and bamboo thickets throughout Cebu, **Philippines**, but the best sites (e.g. the forest patch at Tabunan critical for the Cebu Flowerpecker *Dicaeum quadricolor*, and a 1 km² area of scrub near Casili known to hold 50 birds) are under pressure from clearance and development (Dutson *et al.* 1993). **ENDANGERED:** B1+2c; C1; **C2a**; D1.

Luzon Water-redstart *Rhyacornis bicolor* is restricted to boulders and thickets along clear mountain streams and rivers above 300 m in northern Luzon in the **Philippines**, where although still lo-

cally common (e.g. in Mount Pulog National Park in the Cordillera Central) it has been recorded very little in the Sierra Madre and is threatened by increases in pollution and siltation caused by mining and logging activities, also by hunting (Collar and Andrew 1988, Dickinson *et al.* 1991, Jensen *et al.* 1991, Andersen *et al.* 1992, Danielsen *et al.* 1994, Poulsen in press). **ENDANGERED:** B1+2c,e; C1; **C2a**.

Sumatran Cochoa *Cochoa beccarii* is endemic to the Barisan range of Sumatra, **Indonesia**, where it is known from four specimens, collected at three localities in lower montane forest between 1,200 and 1,700 m, and sight records from northern Sumatra in 1982 (van Marle and Voous 1988, D. A. Holmes *in litt.* 1994) and at 1,000 m in Kerinci Seblat National Park in 1993 (W. Rodenburg *per* J. Wind *in litt.* 1994). It is threatened by forest degradation in the lower part of its altitudinal range (BirdLife IP). **VULNERABLE:** C1; C2a.

Javan Cochoa *Cochoa azurea* is endemic to West Java, **Indonesia**, where it is found in montane forest between 900 and 3,000 m (Kuroda 1933–1936). It is known from fewer than ten localities (BirdLife BPD), and is apparently found at low densities, although it is difficult to locate and may as a result be rather under-recorded. Localized deforestation for holiday resorts and other developments may become a threat, and small numbers have been recorded in the domestic bird trade (BirdLife IP). **VULNERABLE:** B1+2c.

White-browed Bushchat *Saxicola macrorhyncha* occupies open, waterless areas with scrub in the semi-deserts of **Pakistan** and north-west **India** in Rajasthan, Gujarat, Haryana, and western Uttar Pradesh, and there are also two old records from **Afghanistan** (Ali and Ripley 1987, Rahmani 1993). It has not been seen recently in Pakistan, and is possibly extinct there (Roberts 1992), while in India most recent records are from Desert National Park and other localities in Rajastan, where a survey in 1994 located a total of 75 individuals, including 24 in one day over a distance of 30 km (A. R. Rahmani *in litt.* 1994). One of the main reasons for its apparent range contraction could be loss of suitable habitat, as improved irrigation facilities have converted vast tracts of semi-arid scrubland into cropland (Rahmani 1993). **VULNERABLE:** A1a,b; C1; C2a.

White-throated Bushchat *Saxicola insignis* breeds very locally in alpine or subalpine meadows with scrub in the mountains of **Mongolia** and adjacent parts of **Kazakhstan** (Stresemann and Portenko 1982), has been recorded on passage in Inner Mongolia, Qinghai, Sichuan and Yunnan, **China** (Meyer de Schauensee 1984, Cheng 1987, BirdLife BPD), and in winter in the Gangetic plains of Uttar Pradesh and Bihar, the Sikkim foothills and northern West Bengal, **India**, and the terai of **Nepal**, where it is found in grassland, reedbeds and tamarisks near rivers (Ali and Ripley 1987, Inskipp and Inskipp 1991). The only wintering locality where it has regularly been recorded in recent years is Kosi Barrage in Nepal, where up to 10 occur annually (Inskipp and Inskipp 1991), suggesting that it may have declined, possibly as a result of the destruction and modification of grassland and wetland habitats in its wintering range (Majumdar and Brahmachari 1986, Rahmani 1986). **VULNERABLE: C1; C2a.**

Dappled Mountain-robin *Modulatrix orostruthus*, likely to be threatened by habitat destruction, lives at mid-elevations (1,300–1,700 m) near the floor of wet montane forest (prefeErentially areas, usually closed-canopy, with a dense growth of Zingiberaceae in the ground stratum, between which it moves through corridors of thick growth growing around light gaps and along streams: D. C. Moyer *in litt.* 1994 *contra* earlier reports): on Mount Namuli in **Mozambique** (nominate *orostruthus*; a site not re-visited since the species' discovery in 1932, but population bound to be small), in the East Usambaras (race *amani*; population between several hundred and several thousand, possibly nearer the former: see, e.g., Newmark 1991) and (in the race *sanjei*) on the Udzungwa escarpment in the Udzungwa National Park and the Uzungwa (*sic*) Scarp Forest Reserve (fairly common) and the Ndundulu and Nyumbanitu mountains (uncommon to fairly common), with density at a fifth site (Uhafiwa, near Chita) being as high as 31 pairs per km², in **Tanzania** (Collar and Stuart 1985, Stuart *et al.* 1987, Jensen and Brøgger-Jensen 1992, Keith *et al.* 1992, Dinesen *et al.* 1993, Moyer 1993, Moyer and Lovett in press, D. C. Moyer *in litt.* 1994). Current conservation in the East Usambaras is noted under Usambara Eagle Owl *Bubo vosseleri*. **VULNERABLE: B1+2b,c.**

Subfamily ORTHONYCHINAE
LOGRUNNERS

Western Whipbird *Psophodes nigrogularis* occurs in heath and mallee in four isolated populations in south-west and southern **Australia**: nominate *nigrogularis* (restricted to a small area east of Albany) has a total population estimated at c.500 individuals; race *oberon* (scattered localities in southern Western Australia) is relatively common in places but its population is thought to be composed of fewer than 4,000 individuals; race *lashmari* (Kangaroo Island) has no measures of abundance, and race *leucogaster* (a small number of widely scattered localities in southern South Australia and north-west Victoria) is generally rare. The species has declined as a result of habitat clearance (for agriculture) and fragmentation; fire remains a threat, and there is some evidence of nest predation by introduced predators (Garnett 1992). **VULNERABLE: B1+2c; C2a.**

Subfamily TIMALIINAE
BABBLERS

Ashy-headed Laughingthrush *Garrulax cinereifrons* is endemic to **Sri Lanka**, where it is found in the interior of dense wet forest and bamboo thickets from the lowlands of the wet zone (in the south-west of the island) to 1,200 m in the adjacent foothills in the Hill Zone (Legge 1880, Ali and Ripley 1987, T. W. Hoffmann *in litt.* 1993). It is apparently confined to undisturbed forest, and is declining because of forest destruction and the disturbance caused by (e.g.) logging and firewood collection (Hoffmann 1984). **VULNERABLE:** B1+2c; C1; C2a.

Black-hooded Laughingthrush *Garrulax milleti* is confined to the Da Lat (= Langbian) and Di Linh plateaus in south Annam, **Vietnam**, where it has been recorded at several localities by surveys since 1991, including two protected areas; it is found in the undergrowth of broadleaf evergreen forest at 900 to 1,500 m, relatively low altitudes where habitat destruction by agricultural encroachment makes it particularly vulnerable (Eames *et al.* 1992, J. C. Eames *in litt.* 1994; see Delacour and Jabouille 1931, *Oriental Bird Club Bull.* 1992, 15: 46). **VULNERABLE:** A2b; B1+2c; C1; C2a.

Snowy-cheeked Laughingthrush *Garrulax sukatschewi* is endemic to south-west Gansu and northern Sichuan, **China**, where it is found in coniferous and mixed broadleaf and coniferous (including secondary) forest, and bamboo and scrub, in mountains from about 2,000 to 3,500 m (Meyer de Schauensee 1984, BirdLife BPD). There are recent records from at least two protected areas, Xiaozhaizigou (= Jiuzhaigou) and Wanglang Nature Reserves (Collar and Andrew 1988), but outside protected areas its forest habitat is being reduced by extensive clear-felling and selective logging (P. Alström *in litt.* 1993, M.J.C.; see Collins *et al.* 1991). **VULNERABLE:** C1; C2a.

White-speckled Laughingthrush *Garrulax bieti* is known from only four areas in the mountains of north-west Yunnan and south-west Sichuan, **China**, where it is locally common in bamboo thickets in coniferous forest, including secondary forest and patches of primary forest, from 3,000 to 3,600 m; large-scale logging is taking place in at least part of its range (King 1989c, BirdLife BPD). **VULNERABLE:** B1+2c; C1; C2a.

Collared Laughingthrush *Garrulax yersini* is restricted to the Da Lat (= Langbian) plateau, south Annam, **Vietnam**, where small numbers have recently been recorded at several localities, including two protected areas, in dense undergrowth in primary and logged evergreen forest at 1,500–2,100 m; it is threatened by deforestation and habitat modification within this limited range (Eames *et al.* 1992, Robson *et al.* 1993a,b, J. C. Eames *in litt.* 1993, 1994). **VULNERABLE:** B1+2c; C1; C2a.

Omei Shan Liocichla *Liocichla omeiensis* is known only from a few mountains in **China**, including Omei Shan and Erllang Shan, in central Sichuan

(Cheng 1987, Collar and Andrew 1988), where it is found in the undergrowth of broadleaf (including secondary) forest from 1,000 to 2,400 m (C. R. Robson *in litt.* 1992, BirdLife BPD). It is locally fairly common on Omei Shan, which is protected by its status as one of China's five 'sacred' mountains (Robson 1989), although some habitat destruction is taking place there (M.J.C.), but the status of this species and its habitat at other localities is not known. Trapping may also be a threat, as this species has recently appeared in the wildlife trade in the U.K. (D. F. Jeggo *in litt.* 1994). **VULNERABLE:** B1+2c; C1.

Bagobo Babbler *Trichastoma woodi* is restricted to montane forest above 1,000 m on Mindanao in the **Philippines**, where it is known from only six localities (five in Dickinson *et al.* 1991) and is rare within them, with habitat destruction being likely to make it rarer still; there are recent records from Mount Apo, Mount Katanglad and Sitio Siete by Lake Sebu, South Cotabato province, where it is not uncommon (Collar and Andrew 1988, N. J. Redman verbally 1993, P. C. Gonzales *per* A. Jensen *in litt.* 1994, P. Morris *in litt.* 1994, C. R. Robson *in litt.* 1994). **VULNERABLE:** C1; C2a.

Vanderbilt's Babbler *Malacocincla vanderbilti* (formerly regarded as conspecific with the Black-browed Babbler *M. perspicillata* or Horsfield's Babbler *M. sepiarium*: Hoogerwerf 1966, Smythies 1981; also, tentatively, van Marle and Voous 1988) is known only by the type-specimen, collected in 1939 at Keungke in the Alas valley, northern Sumatra, **Indonesia**, on a steep slope in primary forest at 900 m (van Marle and Voous 1988), and is possibly threatened by forest degradation in this region (BirdLife IP). **VULNERABLE:** C1; D1.

Black-browed Babbler *Malacocincla perspicillata* (formerly regarded as conspecific with Vanderbilt's Babbler *M. vanderbilti* or Horsfield's Babbler *M. sepiarium*: Hoogerwerf 1966, Smythies 1981) is known only by the type-specimen, which was collected somewhere in southern Kalimantan, **Indonesia**, in the mid-nineteenth century (Smythies 1981). It is probably found in forest, and could be threatened by lowland deforestation (BirdLife IP). **VULNERABLE:** C1; D1.

Marsh Babbler *Pellorneum palustre* occurs in the plains (and adjacent foothills) of the Brahmaputra River in north-east **India**, and in northern **Bangladesh**, where it is found in reedbeds, coarse high grass alongside swamps and rivers, and elephant grass and scrub on marshy ground, from the plains to 800 m; it was formerly locally common (Ali and

Ripley 1987), but the only recent published record appears to be from Bangladesh in 1989 (Thompson *et al.* 1993), and it must be threatened by the destruction and modification of its grassland and wetland habitat (Majumdar and Brahmachari 1986, Rahmani 1986). **VULNERABLE:** A1b; C1; C2a.

Melodious Babbler *Malacopteron palawanense* is endemic to Palawan and Balabac in the **Philippines**, being confined to forest and forest edge (Dickinson *et al.* 1991), but, owing to the paucity of recent records away from Iwahag Penal Colony, it is believed to be an extreme lowland specialist and therefore at great risk from widespread habitat destruction (C. R. Robson verbally 1994). **ENDANGERED:** A1b; A2b: B1+2c; C1; **C2a.**

Short-tailed Scimitar-babbler *Jabouilleia danjoui* is known from north, central and south Annam, **Vietnam**, where small numbers have been recorded at several localities since 1988, including five protected areas (and its known range extended into north Annam), and central **Laos**, where two birds were seen in the Nakai Plateau/Nam Theun protected area in 1994 (Evans and Timmins 1994). In south Annam, the subspecies *danjoui* is found in montane evergreen forest between 1,700 and 2,000 m, but the northern subspecies *parvirostris* is mainly found in lowland forest below 900 m (although the type was collected at 1,500 m), and it is threatened by deforestation throughout its range (Robson *et al.* 1989, 1993a,b, Eames *et al.* 1992, J. C. Eames *in litt.* 1994). **VULNERABLE:** A1b; A2b; C1; C2a.

Falcated Wren-babbler *Ptilocichla falcata*, an extremely skulking denizen of the understorey of forest up to at least 800 m, is restricted to Palawan and Balabac in the **Philippines** (Dickinson *et al.* 1991), where observations in 1991 (two records from primary forest, including one in St Paul Subterranean National Park, and none from many logged or secondary forest sites) suggested that it may be unable to survive in disturbed habitat and thus would be highly threatened by the continuing clearance of lowland areas (Lambert 1993b, Timmins in prep.). **ENDANGERED:** A1b; A2b; B1+2c; C1; **C2a.**

Rabor's Wren-babbler *Napothera rabori* forages on the floor of primary forest at a number of sites in Luzon (nominate *rabori* in the north, race *mesoluzonica* in the centre and race *sorsogonensis* in south) in the **Philippines** (Goodman and Gonzales 1990, Dickinson *et al.* 1991, Lambert 1993b). Its need for such habitat, which has suffered extensive and continuing clearance, suggests a likely decline in what is already a rare (albeit highly secretive)

species (Danielsen *et al.* 1994, Poulsen in press), although there is some evidence that it can persist in secondary growth (Dickinson *et al.* 1991, N. Bostock *in litt.* 1994, C. R. Robson *in litt.* 1994). **VULNERABLE:** C1; C2a.

Rufous-throated Wren-babbler *Spelaeornis caudatus* occurs in eastern **Nepal**, **Bhutan**, and Sikkim, northern West Bengal (Darjiling) and eastern Arunachal Pradesh, **India**, where it is a scarce bird of the undergrowth of dense evergreen forest at 1,600 to 3,100 m (Ali and Ripley 1987, Inskipp and Inskipp 1991, 1993b). Within this small range, it is threatened by the destruction and fragmentation of its habitat (Inskipp 1989; see Collins *et al.* 1991). **VULNERABLE:** B1+2c; C1; C2a.

Rusty-throated Wren-babbler *Spelaeornis badeigularis* is known only from the type-specimen, collected in January 1947 in the Mishmi Hills, eastern Arunachal Pradesh, north-east **India**, in subtropical wet forest at 1,600 m (Ali and Ripley 1987). Deforestation and forest degradation are likely to be the main threats (see Collins *et al.* 1991). **VULNERABLE:** B1+2c; D1.

Tawny-breasted Wren-babbler *Spelaeornis longicaudatus* is endemic to north-east **India**, known from the Khasi Hills of Meghalaya, the Cachar Hills of Assam, and Manipur, where it is found in evergreen forest with dense undergrowth, ravines and steep, rocky hillsides with mossy outcrops, at 1,000 to 2,000 m; it is described as scarce, although more abundant in the Khasi Hills (Ali and Ripley 1987), and the only recent record appears to be of two at Shillong peak, Meghalaya, in 1979 (Grimmett 1979). It is threatened by the destruction and fragmentation of its habitat (see Collins *et al.* 1991). **VULNERABLE:** B1+2c; C1; C2a.

Deignan's Babbler *Stachyris rodolphei* is known only from Doi Chiang Dao (now designated as a wildlife sanctuary) in north-west **Thailand**, where it has been recorded in bamboo forest between 1,000 and 1,700 m. It is difficult to distinguish in the field from the Rufous-fronted Babbler *S. rufifrons* (with which it may be conspecific: C. R. Robson *in litt.* 1994), which complicates any assessment of its status (Round 1988, Boonsong and Round 1991). **VULNERABLE:** D2.

Flame-templed Babbler *Stachyris speciosa*, a bird of dense forest understorey and more open growth up to 8 m, endemic to Panay (very few records) and Negros in the **Philippines**, was judged uncommon in bird parties from the forest edge at

800 m up to 1,100 m on Mount Canlaon (Negros) in January 1990, and at considerable risk from continuing habitat clearance, although it can survive in some degraded forest (Brooks *et al.* 1992, Lambert 1993b). It was also found recently in a very limited area of habitat in southern Negros (J. Hornbuckle *in litt.* 1994), at 600 m on Cuernos de Negros (D. Allen *in litt.* 1994). **ENDANGERED:** A1b; A2b; **B1+2c**; C1; **C2a**.

Luzon Striped-babbler *Stachyris striata* is restricted to forest (including bamboo) and secondary growth on Luzon in the **Philippines** (Dickinson *et al.* 1991), where it seems patchily but unpredictably common (Poulsen in press). It has been found up to 850 m, but may undertake altitudinal movements to the lowlands for the non-breeding period (only seen at Angat in the wet season), and would thus be particularly threatened by habitat loss (T. H. Fisher *per* N. Bostock *in litt.* 1994; also Danielsen *et al.* 1994). **VULNERABLE:** A1b; A2b; C1; C2a.

Panay Striped-babbler *Stachyris latistriata* was recently described from Panay in the **Philippines**, where it occurs commonly in montane forests on Mount Baloy, chiefly from 1,400 m to the peak at 1,900 m and in an area of less than 738 km^2 (Gonzales and Kennedy 1990). Some clearance of the foothill forest may be occurring (see Collins *et al.* 1991). **VULNERABLE:** B1+2c.

Negros Striped-babbler *Stachyris nigrorum* remains known with certainty (if an unrepeated record from Mount Canlaon is discounted) only from the Cuernos de Negros massif in southern Negros, **Philippines**, where it is common in montane forest above 1,050 m but where agriculture and logging have reached as high as 1,250 m, so that available habitat is contracting (Brooks *et al.* 1992) and the species is seriously threatened (J. Hornbuckle *in litt.* 1994). **ENDANGERED:** A2b; B1+2c; C1; **C2b**.

Palawan Striped-babbler *Stachyris hypogrammica* is highly restricted in range, being known from montane forest above 1,000 m (and generally perhaps higher still) on Mount Mantalingajan and Mount Borangbato in the Mantalingajan Range, Palawan, **Philippines**, where it is common (Timmins in prep., N. Bostock *in litt.* 1994, C. R. Robson *in litt.* 1994). **VULNERABLE:** D2.

White-breasted Babbler *Stachyris grammiceps* is endemic to Java, **Indonesia**, where it is found in lowland and hill forest up to c.1,000 m (MacKinnon and Phillipps 1993), but occasionally up to 1,400 m (S. van Balen *in litt.* 1994). The area of suitable habitat must have been much reduced and fragmented

by the extensive lowland deforestation which has taken place in Java (see RePPProT 1990), but it has recently been recorded in at least seven localities, including several protected areas (S. van Balen *in litt.* 1994), and seems to be tolerant of some habitat degradation and able to persist in tiny patches of forest (BirdLife IP). **VULNERABLE:** B1+2c,d; C1; C2a.

Sooty Babbler *Stachyris herberti* was historically known from only two lowland localities in central **Laos**, where it was collected in 1920 (Delacour and Greenway 1940), but in 1994 was found to be not uncommon in primary forest on limestone at a single locality in central Annam, **Vietnam** (J. C. Eames *in litt.* 1994, F. R. Lambert verbally 1994). It is presumably threatened by lowland deforestation (see Collins *et al.* 1991). **VULNERABLE:** C1; C2a.

Snowy-throated Babbler *Stachyris oglei* is known only from the Patkai and Mishmi Hills in eastern Arunachal Pradesh, north-east **India**, where it has been recorded in moist, dense scrub in rocky ravines, with a nest found at c.1,800 m or higher (Ali and Ripley 1987). There are several recent records from Namdapha National Park (all outside the breeding season, and at relatively low altitude), where seven were collected along the middle Noa Dihang River at c.800 m in March 1979 (Ripley *et al.* 1991), flocks of 10–15 seen in February 1994, usually in bamboo (M. Jäderblad *in litt.* 1994), and birds seen along the Deban-Hornbill trek at 450 m in primary evergreen forest in February 1994 (Singh in press). It is presumably threatened by the destruction and fragmentation of habitat within its small range (see Collins *et al.* 1991). **VULNERABLE:** B1+2c; C1; C2a.

Miniature Tit-babbler *Micromacronus leytensis* occupies forest and forest edge up to 1,300 m on Samar (one record) and Leyte (nominate *leytensis*; apparently only one record) and Mindanao (race *sordidus*, with specimens from three localities and a record presumed to be from a fourth) in the **Philippines** (Dickinson *et al.* 1991). It is regarded as extremely rare and is likely to be suffering from the extensive habitat clearance that has long been occurring within its range (F. R. Lambert verbally 1993, N. J. Redman verbally 1994; see Collins *et al.* 1991). **VULNERABLE:** A1b; A2b; C1; C2a.

Jerdon's Babbler *Chrysomma altirostre* is a bird of reedbeds and seasonally inundated grasslands near rivers, known from the plains of the Indus River in **Pakistan** (rare and extremely local, with some recent records: Roberts 1992), central **Nepal** (small numbers recently recorded in Royal Chitwan National Park: Inskipp and Inskipp 1991), the plains of the

Brahmaputra River in northern West Bengal and Assam in north-east **India** (locally common: Ali and Ripley 1987, T. P. Inskipp *in litt*. 1994) and on the plains of the Irrawaddy River in north-east and south-central **Myanmar** (formerly locally common but no recent records: Smythies 1986). It appears to require extensive areas of dense vegetation and there is evidence that habitat destruction has caused substantial declines in Pakistan and Myanmar (Smythies 1986, Roberts 1991), and it is presumably threatened in India by the widespread destruction and modification of grassland and wetland habitats (see Rahmani 1986). **VULNERABLE:** A1b.

Hinde's Pied-babbler *Turdoides hindei* occurs
in a small area (originally 17,500 km², but since 1971 chiefly only 1,050 km²) of **Kenya** south and east of Mount Kenya at 1,070 to 1,700 m (chiefly 1,300–1,500 m), where although it feeds in coffee and maize plantations it requires thickets for cover and hence depends on secondary (*Lantana*) vegetation and open woodland on steep-sided valleys and in gullies in which water flows at least seasonally (i.e. it avoids permanently dry sites), and with intensive local farming even the *Lantana* patches are being cleared rapidly (Collar and Stuart 1985). There is evidence for a considerable contraction of range this century, and the population may only be in thousands, though in one study in 1978 as few as 200 could be accounted for (Lewis and Pomeroy 1989, L. A. Bennun *in litt*. 1994, P. Njoroge *in litt*. 1994). **ENDANGERED:** A1b,c; A2b,c; **B1+2a,c**; **C2a**; D1.

Gold-fronted Fulvetta *Alcippe variegaticeps* is
endemic to **China**, known from two disjunct areas, south-central Sichuan (recorded from three localities, Omei Shan, Dafengding Panda Reserve and Laba He, with recent records from the latter two: C. R. Robson *in litt*. 1994) and Guangxi (apparently not recorded at Yao Shan, also known as Dayao Shan, since the 1930s), where it is found in bamboo in broadleaf and mixed (including secondary) forest, from about 700 to 1,900 m (Cheng 1987, King 1989b, BirdLife BPD). Most subtropical zone forest within its range has been cleared or degraded (see Collins *et al*. 1991), but there are several protected areas in Sichuan and Guangxi, and perhaps also Guizhou and Guangdong (Li and Zhao 1989), where this species could occur. **VULNERABLE:** B1+2c; C1; C2a.

White-throated Mountain-babbler *Kupeornis gilberti*
appears to be dependent on primary montane forest and is restricted to a few localities (whose total forested area does not appear to exceed 2,000 km²) in western **Cameroon** (Rumpi Hills, 1,100–1,700 m; Mount Kupe, 950–2,130 m; Mount Nlonako, 1,600–1,800 m; Foto near Dschang, 1,670 m; Bakossi Mountains in 1994) and eastern **Nigeria** (Obudu plateau, 1,520 m) (Collar and Stuart 1985, 1988, Stuart and Jensen 1986, C. G. R. Bowden *in litt*. 1994). Habitat loss on the Obudu plateau, where the species was 'quite common' in 1987, is proceeding steadily (Ash 1987b). A major conservation programme now exists at Kupe, where the species is common above 1,400 m (Bowden 1993, Bowden and Bowden 1993, Bowden and Andrews 1994). **VULNERABLE:** B1+2b,c.

Grey-crowned Crocias *Crocias langbianis* is
endemic to the Da Lat (= Langbian) plateau, south Annam, **Vietnam**, where it is known by three specimens collected at 'Da Lat' in 1938, and two birds seen in January 1994 in a mixed flock in evergreen forest at 1,010 m in Chu Yang Sin Nature Reserve in the northern part of the Da Lat plateau. The paucity of records during recent surveys indicates that it is a low-density species, and it is threatened by deforestation (Eames *et al*. 1992, J. C. Eames *in litt*. 1994). **CRITICAL:** B1+2c; C1; C2b; D1; D2.

Madagascar Yellowbrow *Crossleyia xanthophrys*,
a distinctive babbler in its own genus that was seen only twice between 1930 and the mid-1980s (Collar and Stuart 1985), is now known to be a fairly rare (though locally common) ground-haunting resident of mainly montane forest (600–2,300 m, although much more narrowly at 1,200–1,400 m in Marojejy) at a small number of sites (many under pressure from habitat clearance) throughout eastern **Madagascar**, being recorded from protected areas at Tsaratanana, Marojejy, Andasibe (= Périnet), Mantady, Ranomafana and Andohahela (Nicoll and Langrand 1989, Langrand 1990, Evans *et al*. 1992a, J. C. Durbin *per*/and A. F. A. Hawkins *in litt*. 1994). **VULNERABLE:** C2a.

Subfamily PANURINAE

PARROTBILLS

Black-breasted Parrotbill *Paradoxornis flavirostris* occurs in the plains and adjacent foothills of the Brahmaputra River in north-east **India** and **Nepal** (no records during the twentieth century: Inskipp and Inskipp 1991), in northern **Bangladesh** and on Mount Victoria in western **Myanmar**, where it is found among reed thickets, elephant grass, wild cardamom and mixed grasses along the banks of rivers in the plains, and mixed grass and bamboo and elephant grass (ekra) at altitudes of up to 1,900 m in the hills (King *et al.* 1975, Ali and Ripley 1987). It was formerly a locally common species in the plains, but its current status is poorly known as the only recent records appear to be from Kaziranga National Park (C. R. Robson *in litt.* 1994), and it must now be threatened by the destruction and modification of its grassland and wetland habitats (see Majumdar and Brahmachari 1986, Rahmani 1986). **VULNERABLE:** A1a,b; C1; C2a.

Grey-hooded Parrotbill *Paradoxornis zappeyi* is known from south-central Sichuan and extreme western Guizhou, **China**, where it is found in bamboo and scrub in coniferous and rhododendron forest from 2,500 to 3,200 m (Cheng 1987, C. R. Robson *in litt.* 1992). It is quite common on the summit of Omei Shan, which is protected by its status as one of China's sacred mountains (Robson 1989), and it has recently been recorded at Dafengding Panda Reserve (King 1989b), but it is known from a total of fewer than ten localities (BirdLife BPD), and is likely to have been affected by the extensive deforestation which is taking place in this region of China (P. Alström *in litt.* 1993, M.J.C.; see Collins *et al.* 1991). **VULNERABLE:** B1+2c; C1; C2a.

Rusty-throated Parrotbill *Paradoxornis przewalskii* is endemic to south-west Gansu and northern Sichuan, **China**, where it is found in open coniferous forest with bamboo thickets and tussocks of grass from 2,440 to 3,050 m (Meyer de Schauensee 1984, C. R. Robson *in litt.* 1992), and is known from as few as three localities, the only recent records being from Xiaozhaizigou (= Jiuzhaigou) Nature Reserve, where it is scarce (Collar and Andrew 1988). It is threatened by the extensive deforestation which is taking place in this region of China (P. Alström *in litt.* 1993, M.J.C.; see Collins *et al.* 1991), and periodic bamboo flowering and die-off in combination with habitat fragmentation may affect the population of this and other species which inhabit bamboo (see MacKinnon *et al.* 1989). **VULNERABLE:** B1+2c; C1; C2a.

Short-tailed Parrotbill *Paradoxornis davidianus* has been recorded from widely scattered localities in Zhejiang and Fujian, south-east **China**, eastern **Myanmar**, northern **Thailand**, northern **Laos** and northern **Vietnam** (King *et al.* 1975, Cheng 1987), where it frequents bamboo thickets in the lowlands to 1,800 m (Meyer de Schauensee 1984). The only recent records appear to be of small numbers seen at Wuyi Scenic District, Fujian, China (Viney 1986, M.J.C.) and Tam Dao, Ho Ke Go and (probably) Vu Quang Nature Reserves, Vietnam (J. C. Eames *in litt.* 1994). As a bamboo specialist, it may have to make nomadic movements in response to changes in the availability of food, and could be especially vulnerable to the widespread destruction and fragmentation of its habitat (see Collins *et al.* 1991). **VULNERABLE:** A1b; C1; C2a.

Subfamily PICATHARTINAE

ROCKFOWL

White-necked Rockfowl *Picathartes gymnocephalus* breeds colonially in caves and on rockfaces in the rapidly receding Upper Guinea rainforest block of West Africa from **Ghana** (many records into the 1960s), **Ivory Coast** (three breeding sites now known, though one recently reported destroyed by clearance for banana cultivation: Borrow 1994), **Liberia** (large numbers claimed at one site and reported from other regions) and **Guinea** (colonies recently confirmed) into **Sierra Leone** (Gola forest, Freetown peninsula, Loma Mountains, Kambui Hills, Kangari Hills and Dodo Hills, though very small and pressurized numbers in these last four), and is threatened by forest clearance, hunting and (up to c.1990) zoo-collecting (Collar and Stuart 1985, Colston and Curry-Lindahl 1986, Morel and Morel 1988, Gartshore 1989, Allport 1991, Demey and Fishpool 1991, Thompson 1993; see also Wood 1993, H. S. S. Thompson *in litt*. 1994). Records from Togo are in error, although apparently suitable habitat exists (Cheke 1986). **VULNERABLE: A1b; A2b.**

Grey-necked Rockfowl *Picathartes oreas*, an interior rainforest ground-dweller, breeds (usually colonially) in caves and on rock faces (and remains within 300 m of these nest-sites all year round) in southern **Cameroon** (including Mount Kupe, Mount Cameroon and Korup, for which there are now major conservation programmes, the Dja Game Reserve, and the Bakossi Mountains), north and central **Gabon** (Woleu-Ntem and Ogooué-Ivindo provinces), continental **Equatorial Guinea** (occurrence proven: Ash 1991), south-west Bioko (Equatorial Guinea), possibly north-west Congo (but not yet proven), and south-east **Nigeria**, where no fewer than 91 breeding sites were located in September and October 1987, but, despite evidence that it is more numerous than was thought, it remains threatened by forest clearance and hunting, although there is currently no habitat loss and little hunting on Bioko or in Gabon (Collar and Stuart 1985, Brosset and Erard 1986, Ash 1987b, 1991, Tye 1987, Butynski and Koster 1989, Bowden 1993, Bowden and Bowden 1993, Fotso 1993a, Bowden and Andrews 1994, A. J. Cruikshank *per* P. Alexander-Marrack *in litt*. 1994, C. G. R. Bowden *in litt*. 1994, P. Christy *in litt*. 1994, R. C. Fotso *in litt*. 1994). **VULNERABLE: C2a.**

Subfamily SYLVIINAE

OLD WORLD WARBLERS

Socotra Cisticola *Cisticola haesitatus* is confined to the island of Socotra, **Yemen**, where in 1964 it was not common and found only in two localities, 2.5 km west of Habidu just below the 'Ras Hebak' foothills, and near 'Adho Dimellus' at 850 m. It inhabits light scrub and scattered bushes in grassland (Ripley and Bond 1966). In spring 1993 40 birds were found at five sites, all at sea-level; the species persists in pockets of lowland scrub and probably numbers under 1,000 individuals (R. F. Porter *in litt*. 1994). **VULNERABLE: D1.**

Rufous-vented Prinia *Prinia burnesii* has two disjunct populations, in the plains of the Indus in **Pakistan** and adjacent north-west **India**, and the plains of the Brahmaputra River, Assam and western Bihar in north-east India and adjacent northern **Bangladesh**, where it is found in long grasslands, sometimes where mixed with acacias and tamarisks, mainly in the vicinity of large rivers and their tributaries and in swamps (Ali and Ripley 1987). The population in Pakistan is locally common or abundant in its restricted habitat in the Punjab and northern Sind, much less so in southern Sind (Roberts 1992), and the eastern population was also formerly locally common (Ali and Ripley 1987), but with few recent published records (BirdLife BPD). It must be threatened by the destruction and modification of its grassland and wetland habitat (see Majumdar and Brahmachari 1986, Rahmani 1986, Roberts 1991). **VULNERABLE: A1b.**

White-eyed Prinia *Prinia leontica* occurs in north-east **Sierra Leone**, **Guinea**, **Liberia** and western **Ivory Coast**, in thickets bordering streams and in mountain gallery forests (apparently being commonest in mountain ravines), occurring on Mount Nimba at the upper forest edge, which may have increased with mining (Collar and Stuart 1985); recent fieldwork, however, has revealed it to be extremely local (it was recently found on Mount Loma in Sierra Leone: P. Atkinson *per*/and P. Wood verbally 1994), suggesting (possibly increasing) rarity of habitat (P. V. Hayman *per* G. A. Allport verbally 1994). **VULNERABLE: C2a.**

Taita Apalis *Apalis fuscigularis* (which does not respond to tape-recordings of the Bar-throated Apalis *A. thoracica*, with which it is commonly lumped: T. Stevenson *in litt*. 1994) is restricted to the tiny areas of forest (less than 3 km² in total) remaining on the Taita Hills, **Kenya**, where it does not appear to be numerically strong and is at risk from further degradation of its habitat (Collar and Stuart 1985, 1988, McGuigan 1987). **CRITICAL: B1+2b,c**; C2b; D1; D2.

Namuli Apalis *Apalis lynesi* (here split from Bar-throated Apalis *A. thoracica*) remains known only from primary forest between 1,400 and 2,000 m on Mount Namuli, **Mozambique**, where it was common in 1932 but has not subsequently been monitored (Vincent 1933–1935, Collar and Stuart 1985, 1988). **VULNERABLE: D2.**

White-winged Apalis *Apalis chariessa*, a leaf- and twig-gleaning insectivore of the forest canopy and edge (preferring *Albizia* spp., and most frequent in tall, wet, luxuriant growth), is known only from the lower Tana River in coastal **Kenya** (nominate *chariessa*, now possibly extinct (though suspected still to survive in remaining patches of vegetation: R. J. Dowsett *in litt.* 1989), the Uluguru and Udzungwa Mountains (1,000–2,000 m, being 'not uncommon' in the Ndundulu Mountains, and with a density of 17 pairs per km² at another site, and relatively common in the Nyumbanitu Mountains in January 1994) in **Tanzania**, Mount Chiperone in **Mozambique** and nine small mountain forests (500–1,500 m) in south-eastern **Malawi** (where the national total is about 100 pairs and under severe threat), all in the race *macphersoni* (Stuart *et al.* 1987, Collar and Andrew 1988, Dowsett-Lemaire 1989, Jensen and Brøgger-Jensen 1992, Dinesen *et al.* 1993, Moyer 1993, Moyer and Lovett in press, L. A. Hansen and J. O. Svendsen *in litt.* 1994). **VULNERABLE: B1+2b,c.**

Kungwe Apalis *Apalis argentea* appears to be in danger from clearance of its montane (above 1,300 m) forest habitat (it prefers the less humid areas) in parts of its fragmented range, nominate *argentea* being confined to the currently secure Mount Mahale (= Kungwe) and environs (inside Mahali National Park: N. E. Baker *in litt.* 1994) in western **Tanzania**, and the race *eidos* occurring on Idjwi Island in Lake Kivu, eastern **Zaïre**, Nyungwe forest (where commoner and more widespread than previously thought, ranging up to 2,350 m: Dowsett-Lemaire 1990, Dowsett-Lemaire and Dowsett 1990b), **Rwanda**, and the tiny Bururi forest and west of Rwegura in Kibira National Park in **Burundi** (Collar and Stuart 1985, T. Stevenson *in litt.* 1994). Forest on Idjwi is under considerable pressure and receding (J. R. Wilson *in litt.* 1988), and Nyungwe is also at serious (although remediable) risk (Dowsett-Lemaire and Dowsett 1990a, Gibson 1992). **VULNERABLE: B1+2a,c,e.**

Bamenda Apalis *Apalis bamendae* has been found at middle altitudes at two sites in central and two in western **Cameroon**, and seems to be a gallery forest specialist; although this habitat is relatively secure (some destruction is assumed), the number of records of the species is too few to assume its security (Collar and Stuart 1985, Morel and Chappuis 1992, I. S. Robertson *in litt.* 1993). **VULNERABLE: B1+2a,c,d.**

Karamoja Apalis *Apalis karamojae* is a very poorly known warbler largely associated with riverine acacia in lowland north-east **Uganda** (nominate *karamojae*; four known sites) and northern **Tanzania** (race *stronachi*; five known sites), this latter at least being at risk from habitat loss as the local human population is greatly expanding (Collar and Stuart 1985, Stuart and Collar 1986). However, it was found still to be common during a survey of Fischer's Lovebird *Agapornis fischeri* in 1993, but was restricted to stands of whistling thorn *Acacia drepanolobium*, in the southern Serengeti National Park, Maswa Game Reserve and around the Wembere Steppe, almost invariably in mixed-species flocks (D. C. Moyer *in litt.* 1994). The area between the Maswa Game Reserve and the Wembere Steppe is now under great pressure from pastoralists and farmers (N. E. Baker *in litt.* 1994). **VULNERABLE: A2b; B1+2c.**

Grauer's Swamp-warbler *Bradypterus graueri* is common within but restricted to a few highland swamps (records are from 1,950–2,600 m) inside forest in eastern **Zaïre**, south-west **Uganda**, **Rwanda** and northern **Burundi**, and remains in danger from swamp drainage (Collar and Stuart 1985; see also Bennun 1986, Ash *et al.* 1991), although recent protection of the important Kamiranzovu marsh (9 km², with a population of c.3,000 birds), which had been at great risk from gold-mining, has considerably improved the situation (Dowsett-Lemaire 1990). **VULNERABLE: B1+2a,c.**

Long-billed Bush-warbler *Bradypterus major* occurs in the western Himalayas, in northern **Pakistan** (few recent records and the distribution is imperfectly known, probably partly because of the species' extremely secretive habits: Roberts 1992) and north-west **India** (fairly common, but extremely local: Ali and Ripley 1987, Collar and Andrew 1988), Xinjiang, western **China** (very rare: Cheng 1987) and the eastern Pamir mountains in Tajikistan (perhaps only a vagrant: Inskipp and Collins 1993), where it is found from 2,400 to 3,600 m on open slopes near the forest edge and in terraced cultivation, in low thorny scrub and rank grass and bracken (Ali and Ripley 1987, Roberts 1992). It is thought that its range is contracting in Kashmir, possibly owing to changes in agricultural practices (Collar and Andrew 1988). **VULNERABLE:** C2a.

Black-capped Rufous Warbler *Bathmocercus cerviniventris* has been recorded in **Sierra Leone** (fairly common in gallery and streamside vegetation), **Guinea** (once), **Liberia** (uncommon), **Ivory Coast** (five localities) and **Ghana** (once) (Collar and Stuart 1985, Thiollay 1985, Gatter 1988); recent fieldwork has revealed it to be extremely local, suggesting (possibly increasing) rarity of habitat (G. A. Allport verbally 1994). **VULNERABLE:** C2a.

Mrs Moreau's Warbler *Bathmocercus winifredae* inhabits dense undergrowth in small light gaps, sometimes near streams, in three montane forests in eastern **Tanzania**, the Ulugurus (1,350–2,350 m), Ukagurus (1,500–1,850 m) and Udzungwas (Udzungwa National Park only, at 1,300–1,700 m), all of which require major conservation attention (Collar and Stuart 1985, 1988, Stuart *et al.* 1987, Jensen and Brøgger-Jensen 1992, Evans and Anderson 1992, 1993, L. A. Hansen and J. O. Svendsen *in litt.* 1994). Birds were recently discovered at high densities in the Ukwiwa Forest Reserve in the Rubeho mountains between the Udzungwas and Ukagurus; the reserve is highly disturbed by elephant and buffalo, which creates light gaps favoured by the species, whereas in the Ulugurus the densities are low (J. Fjeldså verbally 1994). **VULNERABLE:** B1+2b,c.

Aquatic Warbler *Acrocephalus paludicola* breeds polygynously and promiscuously in open but dense grassy marshes with scattered sedge *Carex*, in (estimated or known numbers of singing males in brackets) **Germany** (30–100), **Hungary** (150–200), **Poland** (2,500–7,500), **Lithuania** (50–200), **Latvia** (10–50), **Belarus** (possibly extinct; maximum 50), **Russia** (minimum 3,000, of which 1,000 in European Russia) and **Ukraine** (1–10) (so the total minimum number of singing males is 5,741, predicating c.11,000 mature individuals), with birds occurring on passage in western Europe (regularly in **Bulgaria**, **Czech Republic**, **Germany**, **Netherlands**, **Belgium**, **United Kingdom**, **France**, **Switzerland**, **Spain** and **Portugal**) and **Morocco**, and in winter somewhere in sub-Saharan West Africa (records to date are from **Mauritania**, **Senegal** and **Mali**) (Glutz and Bauer 1991, Cramp 1992, Inskipp and Collins 1993). The range has contracted sharply eastwards since the turn of the century with a corresponding diminution of numbers, attributed to drainage and altered management of breeding habitat, plus (possibly) drought in wintering areas, and since the species' habitat depends on traditional agriculture a

further decline in the near future is expected (Schulze-Hagen 1989, de By 1990, Morel and Morel 1990, Nankinov 1992, Dyrcz and Zdunek 1993, Tucker and Heath 1994, Heredia in prep.) **VULNERABLE:** A2b.

Streaked Reed-warbler *Acrocephalus sorghophilus* is known by records on migration in Liaoning, Hebei, Hubei, Jiangsu, Fujian and Beijing municipality in eastern **China**, with speculation that it breeds in Liaoning and Hebei, and it is an extremely local and uncommon winter visitor to reedbeds and grasslands, often near water, in the **Philippines** (Cheng 1987, Collar and Andrew 1988, Dickinson *et al.* 1991). It is threatened by habitat destruction within its limited wintering range (see Lambert 1993b), and perhaps also on the breeding grounds (see Scott 1989). **VULNERABLE:** B1+2c; C1; C2a.

Nightingale Reed-warbler *Acrocephalus luscinia* occurs in wetlands, grasslands and forest on Guam (to U.S.A.), extinct c.1970, and the **Northern Mariana Islands (to U.S.A.)**, with tiny numbers on Aguijan, 3,000–4,000 on Saipan (no detectable decline since the 1970s: H. D. Pratt *in litt.* 1994), 350–1,000 pairs on Alamagan, probably extinct on Pagan; forest clearance, overgrazing by feral ungulates, wetland disturbance, dry-season marsh fires, pesticide use, predation by the introduced brown tree snake *Boiga irregularis* (on Guam, but a potential threat on other islands, and recently found on Saipan) and volcanic eruptions (on Pagan) may have all contributed to its extirpation and decline (Reichel *et al.* 1992). **VULNERABLE:** A2d; B1+2c,d,e; C1.

Nauru Reed-warbler *Acrocephalus rehsei* is endemic to **Nauru** (21 km²), in the western Pacific, where in 1983 local people reported that it was still present in the remaining bushy areas (Pratt *et al.* 1987), despite nearly 80 years of phosphate mining which has caused devastating environmental damage (Anderson 1992). There is no recent information on its status. **VULNERABLE:** D2.

Millerbird *Acrocephalus familiaris* is endemic to the Northwestern Hawaiian Islands (**U.S.A.**) of Laysan and Nihoa. The nominate race was extirpated from Laysan between 1912 and 1923 following the destruction of the indigenous vegetation (and associated insects) by introduced rabbits, whilst the race *kingi* on Nihoa (64 ha) survives on brushy hillsides (King 1978–1979, Pratt *et al.* 1987) and fluctuates between 100 and 700 individuals with a population estimated to be 710±321 (95%CI) in 1993 (USFWS *in litt.* 1994). **VULNERABLE:** D1; D2.

Tahiti Reed-warbler *Acrocephalus caffer* is found in bamboo thickets and second-growth forests in river valleys and hillsides to 1,700 m on Tahiti in the Society Islands, **French Polynesia**, having probably formerly occupied all the high islands in the group including Huahine, Moorea and Raiatea (Thibault 1988). It has been rare and local throughout the twentieth century, being recorded in six valleys during the period 1920–1923 (out of 14 visited) and 12 during 1986–1991 (out of 39) and estimated to number a few hundred individuals (Monnet *et al.* 1993). The introduction of many bird species, notably the Common Myna *Acridotheres tristis*, may account for its rarity (Thibault 1988, Seitre and Seitre 1991) and nesting sites in the Papenoo valley are threatened by possible dam construction (P. Raust *in litt.* 1994). **VULNERABLE: D1.**

Pitcairn Reed-warbler *Acrocephalus vaughani* is endemic to the **Pitcairn Islands (to U.K.)** and Rimatara in the Tubuai Islands, **French Polynesia**, occurring as three races: *taiti*, *vaughani* and *rimatarae* on Henderson, Pitcairn and Rimatara islands (37, 5 and 8 km² respectively); on uninhabited Henderson (where the population was estimated at c.10,800 birds in 1987) it is found throughout the forest, foraging in all substrates and at all levels, whilst on Pitcairn it is rarely found at ground level perhaps because of the presence of cats and humans (Pratt *et al.* 1987, Graves 1992). On Henderson about one-third of nesting groups comprise three (not two) unrelated adults, whilst on Pitcairn it seems only to breed in pairs, and, although the output of young per adult is slightly (but not significantly) higher in pairs than trios, there could be a compensating advantage for members of trios in that on Henderson (a stable but limited habitat) young birds may be more readily able to secure a nesting territory when belonging to a trio than when in a pair (Brooke and Hartley in press). **VULNERABLE: D2.**

Cape Verde Warbler *Acrocephalus brevipennis* is now believed to be confined to and 'only locally distributed' on Santiago, **Cape Verde Islands**, with not more than 500 pairs found in 11 of the island's 50 25 km² grid squares, having apparently died out (perhaps as a result of drought and associated habitat loss) on São Nicolau (where it was formerly numerous) and Brava (where formerly scarce), favouring well-vegetated valleys (especially with patches of reeds), up to 500 m (mostly lower, and certainly not up to 1,400 m as in Cramp and Perrins 1994), but also occurring in sugarcane and banana plantations and gardens, notably near running water (Hazevoet 1991, 1993, in press). **VULNERABLE: A1a,b; B1+2b,c; C2b; D1.**

Rodrigues Warbler *Acrocephalus rodericanus*, having once been very common on its native Rodrigues, **Mauritius**, declined steadily with the clearance and disturbance of its dense thicket habitat and was (judged to be) reduced to eight pairs and a singleton after a cyclone in February 1979, recovering to an estimated 58–96 (21 birds counted) in April 1983, but during this period the black rat *Rattus rattus* was believed to have colonized the island (Collar and Stuart 1985, Cheke 1987c). Habitat conservation and creation have helped mitigate the impact of recent cyclones and the population stood at 45–65 birds in 1991 (MWAF 1992, C. G. Jones *per* R. J. Safford *in litt.* 1994), remaining stable since then (C. G. Jones *in litt.* 1994). **CRITICAL: D1; D2.**

Seychelles Warbler *Acrocephalus sechellensis* was confined to the tiny (29 ha) island of Cousin, **Seychelles**, where, following ICBP/BirdLife management as a nature reserve and the associated recovery of the *Pisonia* woodland, its population recovered from an estimated 50 in 1965 to reach 250–300 in 1981 (Collar and Stuart 1985). Subsequent monitoring and the re-examination of earlier data suggested that saturation level on Cousin had been reached at c.300 birds (on 115 territories) since the early 1980s, so 29 birds were translocated to Aride (68 ha), an RSNC nature reserve, in September 1988, resulting in immediate colonization of the island and expansion of numbers there to 229 by January 1993 (Komdeur 1991, 1992, 1994, Komdeur *et al.* 1991, Mumme 1992, Taylor 1993a). A second translocation to the privately owned Cousine (26 ha), again of 29 birds, in June/July 1990, resulted in successful colonization and breeding (Komdeur 1994), and by March 1994 the population there had risen to around 80 birds (J. Neville *per* M. N. McCulloch verbally 1994). **VULNERABLE: D1; D2.**

Papyrus Yellow Warbler *Chloropeta gracilirostris* occupies a very fragmented range mainly in papyrus swamps, but occasionally other marshy habitats, mostly in areas of high rainfall at high altitudes (1,000–2,400 m are extremes, but most sites and higher densities are above 1,750 m) in **Burundi** (just extending down the Ruvubu River into **Tanzania**: Vande weghe 1992), **Kenya**, **Rwanda**, **Uganda**, **Zaïre** and **Zambia**, and is at risk in some areas from schemes to drain or otherwise exploit papyrus swamps (Collar and Stuart 1985). **VULNERABLE: B1+2a,b,c,d.**

Long-billed Tailorbird *Orthotomus moreaui* (moved here from its earlier placement in *Apalis*) is a low-density species known from two widely separated montane forests, the East Usambaras in **Tan-**

zania (nominate *moreaui*) and the Njesi Plateau in northern **Mozambique** (race *sousae*), a site not visited since 1945; although chiefly a bird of forest clearings and edges, it remains vulnerable to forest destruction (Collar and Stuart 1985), having not been found in recent fieldwork in the Usambaras by Evans and Anderson (1992, 1993), Watson and Perkin (undated)—although apparently the right habitat was not investigated—or in two years by A. Tye (*in litt.* 1994). However, one male was found at Jaramjee Tea Estate in January 1992 (B. W. Finch *in litt.* 1994), and current conservation in the East Usambaras is noted under Usambara Eagle Owl *Bubo vosseleri* (p. 115). **CRITICAL: B1+2c; C2a.**

Turner's Eremomela *Eremomela turneri* has a patchy distribution and is very poorly known in lowland and mid-altitude forest (470–1,700 m) in the canopy of large trees but also along streams, at forest edge and in clearings, in western **Kenya** (nominate *turneri* in Kakamega and South Nandi forests) and eastern **Zaïre** in the south-east corner of the equatorial forest belt, with one record from south-westernmost **Uganda** (race *kalindei*). None of these areas is believed to be well conserved and the two Kenyan forests give grave cause for concern (Collar and Stuart 1985, L. A. Bennun *in litt.* 1994). **VULNERABLE: B1+2a,c.**

Pulitzer's Longbill *Macrosphenus pulitzeri* is known only from two general forest areas (300–1,030 m) on the scarp of **Angola** (although it is thought likely to occur in other relict patches), with no recent information on its status (Collar and Stuart 1985, 1988), being considered 'probably the rarest and least known bird species in Angola' (Dean *et al.* 1988). The full extent of Angola scarp forests, virtually all given over to coffee production, is only 1,300–2,000 km², and their destruction was judged to have been slow but steady up to September 1992, when the civil war resumed (Hawkins 1993b, A. F. A. Hawkins *in litt.* 1994). **ENDANGERED: B1+2b,c; C2a.**

São Tomé Short-tail *Amaurocichla bocagii* is a remarkable rainforest passerine of puzzling affinities—speculated as having both tree-creeping and ground-haunting habits (de Naurois 1982)—confined to southern São Tomé, **São Tomé e Príncipe**, where until recently it had been encountered only once this century, in 1928 (Collar and Stuart 1985). In July and August 1990 two populations were discovered along the rios Xufexufe and Ana Chaves (4.1–6.3 pairs and 5.6 pairs per kilometre of river, respectively) and the species was found to be restricted to riparian habitat under primary forest, where it forages rather like a Grey Wagtail *Motacilla cinerea*

(Atkinson *et al.* 1991; also Nadler 1993), thus discounting a 1987 report (Eccles 1988). Up to 10 pairs were met with in the same localities in 1991 (T. M. Gullick *in litt.* 1991), but in early 1994 it was also found to inhabit forested ridges if rocks and boulders are present on them (P. Christy *in litt.* 1994). The future of the island's forests remains uncertain (Jones *et al.* 1992). **VULNERABLE: D1.**

Ijima's Leaf-warbler *Phylloscopus ijimae* breeds mainly at low altitudes in deciduous and mixed forest, including subtropical evergreen forest and scrub, on the Izu Islands, off southern **Japan** (Brazil 1991), and has recently been found to breed on Nakanoshima in the Tokara Islands in the northern Nansei Shoto (Higuchi and Kawaji 1989), but in winter it is known only from Luzon in the **Philippines**, where it is rare in forest and forest edge (Dickinson *et al.* 1991). It was common or even locally abundant on the Izu Islands, but has become uncommon on Oshima where much of the natural forest has now been destroyed (Brazil 1991), and it has recently declined steadily on Miyake-jima, despite its breeding habitat being fully protected, perhaps because of threats (notably deforestation) acting in the wintering areas (N. Ichida *in litt.* 1994). **VULNERABLE: C1; C2a.**

Hainan Leaf-warbler *Phylloscopus hainanus* is a recently described species known only from Hainan Island, south-east **China**, where it has been recorded in evergreen forest and secondary growth on the edge of mature forest above 600 m, and is common at Jianfengling Nature Reserve and recorded from Bawangling Nature Reserve and one other locality (Olsson *et al.* 1993, P. Alström *in litt.* 1993). Its range must have been severely reduced and fragmented by deforestation, as forest cover on Hainan is estimated to have declined from 8,630 km² (25.7% of the island) in 1949 to c.2,420 km² (7.2%) in 1991 (Collins *et al.* 1991). **VULNERABLE: A1b; B1+2c.**

Sombre Leaf-warbler *Phylloscopus amoenus* is endemic to Kolombangara, **Solomon Islands**, with the only recent sightings in 1974 (J. M. Diamond *in litt.* 1987), 1975, 1990 (Buckingham *et al.* in prep.) and 1994 (D. Gibbs *in litt.* 1994, M. B. Iles *in litt.* 1994). It is confined to moss forest above c.1,200 m and is clearly scarce, with first estimates of the population varying between 930 and 2,100 individuals; although the stunted forest which it inhabits is under no threat from forestry, it is often damaged by landslides and wind so that the (small) population can be expected to fluctuate with habitat availability, and feral pigs could also be a threat both to habitat and to nests (Buckingham *et al.* in prep.). **VULNERABLE: D1; D2.**

169

Marsh Grassbird *Megalurus pryeri* breeds in marshes with reedbeds and coastal grasslands in three areas of northern and central Honshu, **Japan** (locally common, total population estimated at 750–850 in 1975: Y. Yamashina *in litt.* 1982, Brazil 1991), and has been recorded breeding or on passage in **China**, in eastern Liaoning and north-east Hebei (very rare: Cheng 1987), Zhalong Marshes in Heilongjiang (locally fairly common: P. Alström *in litt.* 1987) and Shanghai municipality (at least 10 singing at Wusi coast, and seen carrying nest-material in April 1988: *Oriental Bird Club Bull.* 1988, 8: 32–36, Scott 1989). In winter it moves to the Pacific coast of Japan (Brazil 1991) and to the wetlands of the Chang Jiang (= Yangtze) valley in China (Cheng 1987), where at least seven were recorded in one area at Poyang Lake in January 1986 (Scott 1989). There is evidence that it has declined locally in Japan as a result of the drying out of reedbeds (Nishide 1993), and it is presumably threatened by the destruction and modification of wetlands which are taking place in eastern China (see Scott 1989). **VULNERABLE:** C1; C2a.

Fly River Grassbird *Megalurus albolimbatus* is known from two localities in extreme south-western **Papua New Guinea**, from Lake Daviumbu on the middle Fly River and from the Bensbach River (although much potential habitat is unsurveyed and it could therefore occur much more widely, e.g. upper Bonader Creek, Morehead River: K. D. Bishop *in litt.* 1994, N. Bostock *in litt.* 1994, P. Gregory *in litt.* 1994, N. Stronach *in litt.* 1994), where it is apparently highly specialized in its habitat requirements, affecting stands of reeds, sedge, lotus lilies and floating rice grass; generally it is rare, being fairly numerous only in tiny scattered areas owing to overgrazing by introduced rusa deer *Cervus timorensis* (Coates 1990, N. Stronach *in litt.* 1994), which are quickly expanding their range (P. Gregory *in litt.* 1994), and it was not found in Merauke National Park almost certainly as a result of this (K. D. Bishop *in litt.* 1994). **VULNERABLE:** C2a; D2.

Long-legged Thicketbird *Trichocichla rufa* is endemic to **Fiji**, where it is known from Viti Levu by four specimens collected between 1890 and 1894, observations from 1967, 1973 and 1991 (two birds west of Laselevu: S. Ericsson *in litt.* 1994), and from Vanua Levu by a specimen taken in 1974, all from dense scrub associated with mountain forest; predation by introduced mongooses and possibly cats and rats has probably caused its decline (King 1978–1979), although the reasons for its extreme rarity are unclear (Watling and Chape 1992). **CRITICAL: B1+2e; C2a; D1.**

Bristled Grass-warbler *Chaetornis striatus* has been found in **Pakistan** (only two definite records, one in 1976, possibly only a vagrant: Roberts 1992), **Nepal** (small numbers recently found nesting in Royal Chitwan National Park: Inskipp and Inskipp 1991), **Bangladesh** (no recent records, but could still occur locally: Harvey 1990) and throughout much of **India** (very locally, though described as fairly common in Gujarat, Andhra Pradesh and southern West Bengal), being found in mixed grassland and scrub, swampy grassland and also rice fields (Ali and Ripley 1987), but there appear to be very few recent published records. It may be threatened by the widespread destruction and modification of grassland and wetland habitats within its range (see Majumdar and Brahmachari 1986, Rahmani 1986). **VULNERABLE: A1b; C1; C2a.**

Yemen Warbler *Sylvia (Parisoma) buryi* is patchily resident in small numbers between 1,700 and 2,800 m in the highlands of western **Yemen** and the adjoining Asir mountains of south-west **Saudi Arabia** as far as 19°30′N, in dense, often tall (i.e. trunk-forming) acacias and other bushes and low trees, including stands of juniper. Heavy grazing pressure minimizes regeneration of this habitat, which is diminishing as it is lopped and cleared for fuelwood (Cornwallis and Porter 1982, Stagg 1984, Brooks 1987b). **VULNERABLE: B1+2b,c; C2a.**

Subfamily MALURINAE

AUSTRALIAN WARBLERS

Carpentarian Grasswren *Amytornis dorotheae* occurs patchily (eight isolated localities are known) in a strip of sandstone country inland from the south-

ern coastline of the Gulf of Carpentaria, Northern Territory, **Australia**, where it skulks in mature, unburnt tussock grassland (its numbers are therefore difficult to assess). It has probably been adversely affected by changes in the fire regime since the arrival of Europeans, and frequent burning continues to be a threat (Garnett 1992). **VULNERABLE:** B1+2c; C2a.

Thick-billed Grasswren *Amytornis textilis* inhabits chenopod shrublands in **Australia** and has declined in areas where grazing by livestock and rabbits has prevented young plants from maturing into suitably thick old bushes. In Western Australia nominate *textilis* once ranged across much of the southern interior, but relict populations are now known only from Shark Bay, where it is common but patchy; in South Australia a similar decline has occurred in the race *modestus*, which is now largely confined to the Lake Eyre, Lake Torrens and Lake Frome basins, while the race *myall* is thinly and patchily distributed around the Gawler Ranges of western South Australia (Garnett 1992). **VULNERABLE:** C2a.

Western Bristlebird *Dasyornis longirostris* was formerly found in coastal south-west Western Australia, **Australia**, from Perth to Esperance, but is now restricted to four localities within the Fitzgerald River National Park and to an area just east of Albany where it prefers low, dense heaths, the total population being unlikely to exceed 1,000 individuals. Fire is the main threat, with fires at intervals of less than 5–10 years leading to its local extinction (Garnett 1992). **ENDANGERED: B1+2c,d; C2a;** D1.

Eastern Bristlebird *Dasyornis brachypterus* occurs in isolated and scattered populations (recent reports from about 20 locations) in the adjacent coastal regions of eastern Victoria, New South Wales and southern Queensland, **Australia**, where it lives in heath or tussock grass usually on the boundary of woodland or forest. There is no overall population estimate (although 1,000–2,000 individuals have been estimated in three reserves in New South Wales), but it has suffered from changes in fire regime, either too frequent with elimination of tussocks, or too infrequent leading to dense shrubberies unsuitable for nesting, as well as grazing, introduced exotic plants and animals, land clearance, and some recreational activities (Garnett 1992). **VULNERABLE:** B1+2c; C2a.

Rufous Bristlebird *Dasyornis broadbenti* occurs in coastal scrub and thickets in several disjunct populations in **Australia**, in south-western Victoria, mainly along the coast (nominate *broadbenti*, population size unknown), discontinuously in south-east South Australia (race *whitei*, probably at least 1,000 individuals), and extinct in Western Australia (race

litoralis). It is threatened by wildfires, habitat destruction and fragmentation as result of residential development, plus predation by foxes and cats, and concern has also been expressed about levels of infertility of the race *whitei* (Garnett 1992). **VULNERABLE:** B1+2c; C2a.

Slender-billed Thornbill *Acanthiza iredalei* is sparsely distributed in three races across southern **Australia** from the Western Australia coast to Spencer Gulf in South Australia (nominate *iredalei*, no population estimates but reports of a decline), around the Gulf of St Vincent in South Australia (race *rosinae*, common in five main strongholds), with a fragmented distribution in north-west Victoria and south-east South Australia (race *hedleyi*, no information on status). It occurs in low, treeless, chenopod shrubland, samphire shrublands, saline flats around salt lakes, and low heathland dominated by casuarinas and banksias, and has suffered from habitat degradation (owing to grazing by sheep and rabbits), fire, reclamation of saltflats, and clearance for agriculture (Garnett 1992). **VULNERABLE:** C2a.

Biak Gerygone *Gerygone hypoxantha*, split here from Large-billed Gerygone *G. magnirostris* (contra Sibley and Monroe 1990, 1993 and Beehler *et al.* 1986) on the basis of morphology (P. Gregory *in litt.* 1994), is endemic to Biak-Supiori in Geelvink Bay, Irian Jaya, **Indonesia**, where it is very rare (not recorded in three visits in the 1980s: K. D. Bishop *in litt.* 1987) and has suffered from massive habitat loss on Biak (I. Burrows *in litt.* 1994, R. Burrows *in litt.* 1994, P. Gregory *in litt.* 1994). **ENDANGERED:** A1b; **B1+2c; C2b;** D1.

Norfolk Island Gerygone *Gerygone modesta* is an abundant and widespread resident endemic on **Norfolk Island (to Australia)** (less than 35 km^2), found wherever there is some tree or shrub growth. It has coped well with the clearing of much of the island during settlement and is maintaining a viable population (Schodde *et al.* 1983). **VULNERABLE:** D2.

Chestnut-breasted Whiteface *Aphelocephala pectoralis* is widely but locally distributed (recorded at fewer than 40 localities) in north-central South Australia, **Australia**, where it occurs in stony, generally open terrain, often with a patchy cover of chenopod shrubs, particularly bluebush. This habitat is not currently threatened, but grazing by livestock and rabbits could prevent recruitment of shrubs in the longer term, opal mining is a threat in some places, the population is unlikely to exceed 6,000 individuals and there is some evidence of a decline (Garnett 1992). **VULNERABLE:** C2a.

Yellowhead *Mohoua ochrocephala* is endemic to **New Zealand** and was formerly a widespread bird in the forests of South and Stewart Islands, but it is now extinct on Stewart Island and over much of the South Island with the remaining stronghold being in Fiordland and Mount Aspiring National Parks. Periodic crashes occur in response to the stoat irruptions that follow major beech mast production, and in populations with low productivity the period between crashes is probably insufficient for the birds to recover fully, and consequently declines are occurring and the range is contracting, with several populations having become extinct over the last 10 years (O'Donnell 1993). Birds in the northern South Island have disappeared from some of the best habitat, perhaps owing to introduced wasps which compete for 'honey dew' (an important food source in *Nothofagus* forest), so that birds are restricted to a single brood and are then unable to cope with upsurges in stoat numbers (Elliott 1992). **VULNERABLE:** B2b,d,e+3c; C2a.

Silktail *Lamprolia victoriae* is endemic to mature wet rainforest on two islands in **Fiji**, being common in the remaining forest on Taveuni (nominate *victoriae*) but very rare on Vanua Levu (race *kleinschmidti*, one-third smaller than *victoriae*), where it is restricted to the Natewa peninsula which is already extensively logged and unprotected; a study of stratification of passerines in Fijian forests showed that *kleinschmidti* occupies similar feeding zones (inner and middle) to those of Fiji Shrikebill *Clytorhynchus vitiensis* (both feeding by gleaning), this overlap resulting in the larger Shrikebill displacing the smaller Silktail and perhaps contributing to its rarity, whilst nominate *victoriae* mainly occupies the undergrowth, thus reducing competition with the Shrikebill (Heather 1977, Langham 1989, A. Lees *in litt.* 1993, A.J.S.). **VULNERABLE:** B1+2c.

Subfamily MUSCICAPINAE

OLD WORLD FLYCATCHERS

Chatham Islands Robin *Petroica traversi* was formerly widespread in the Chatham Islands, **New Zealand**, but it retreated rapidly following European colonization and the introduction of predators (rats and cats) last century, and in the late 1880s it became restricted to Little Mangere Island; following deterioration of its scrub-forest habitat in the 1970s, the entire remnant population of seven birds was transferred to Mangere, and when by 1980 numbers fell to just five birds, including only one viable pair, an egg-manipulating, cross-fostering programme was instigated and resulted in 100 birds in 1988, distributed between Mangere and South East (= Rangatira) islands, and in 1991–1992 the population numbered 120–130 (Butler and Merton 1992), rising to 155 in 1994 (D. V. Merton *in litt.* 1994). **ENDANGERED: D1**; D2.

Nimba Flycatcher *Melaenornis annamarulae* is endemic to and rare in the rapidly receding Upper Guinea rainforest block in West Africa, being found from Taï National Park (where it occurs at an estimated four birds per km[2]; there is also a record from degraded land at the edge of the park) in **Ivory Coast** westwards through northern **Liberia** (few records) and adjacent **Guinea** (one record) into Gola forest (475–690 birds estimated), **Sierra Leone** (Collar and Stuart 1985, Colston and Curry-Lindahl 1986, Gartshore 1989, Balchin 1990, Allport 1991, Demey and Fishpool 1991; see also Wood 1993). **VULNERABLE:** A1b; A2b.

Streaky-breasted Jungle-flycatcher *Rhinomyias addita* is endemic to Buru in the Moluccas, **Indonesia**, where it has been found in forest and forest edge from 900 to 1,500 m in the higher mountains of the western half of the island, with no documented records since the 1920s, owing to the lack of ornithological coverage of the island (White and Bruce 1986, BirdLife BPD). A one-month survey in 1989 did not visit montane forests (Jepson 1993), but it is believed that these habitats are likely to remain secure (BirdLife IP). **VULNERABLE:** D2.

Brown-chested Jungle-flycatcher *Rhinomyias brunneata* breeds in south-east **China**, in Jiangsu, Zhejiang, Fujian, Jiangxi, Guangdong and Guangxi, in forest and bamboo thickets in the lowlands to 1,100 m (Meyer de Schauensee 1984, Cheng 1987). Outside the breeding season, it is recorded from **Thailand** (rare passage migrant: Boonsong and Round 1991), peninsular **Malaysia** (winter visitor and passage migrant: Medway and Wells 1976), **Singapore** (rare passage migrant and winter visitor: Briffett and Supari 1993), the Andaman and Nicobar Islands, **India** (status unclear, may be resident and represent another species: Collar and Andrew 1988; see Ali and Ripley 1987, *Oriental Bird Club Bull.* 1990, 11: 40–48) and **Brunei** (one record: Mann 1987). In peninsular Malaysia it winters in mature (and not secondary) forest and is an extreme lowland forest specialist (D. R. Wells *in litt.* 1994). It is locally common in China (e.g. Kennerley 1987b), and ringing records of nocturnal passage migrants from Fraser's Hill in the mountains of peninsular Malaysia (probably near the centre of its non-breeding range) indicate that it is not rare (12 trapped in spring and 640 in autumn between 1965 and 1973: Wells 1992), but it must have been affected by the extensive deforestation which has taken place in both its breeding and wintering ranges (Collar and Andrew 1988, D. R. Wells *in litt.* 1994; see Collins *et al.* 1991). **VULNERABLE: A1b; A2b.**

White-browed Jungle-flycatcher *Rhinomyias insignis* is restricted to the understorey of mid-mountain and mossy forest (possibly in a narrow altitudinal band) in northern Luzon (Cordillera Central and, recently, a single, first record from the Sierra Madre) in the **Philippines**; it is a rare and local bird, and must be at risk from the extensive and continuing deforestation occurring on the island (Dickinson *et al.* 1991, Danielsen *et al.* 1994, Poulsen in press). **ENDANGERED: A2b; C1; C2a.**

White-throated Jungle-flycatcher *Rhinomyias albigularis* is known from tall, deeply shaded forest below 900 m on Guimaras and Negros in the **Philippines**: no such forest now exists on Guimaras, while on Negros the only recent records have been from two sites (Mambucal and Ban-ban) at the lower forest margins, with local extinction already feared at Mambucal and forest at Ban-ban unlikely to last more than a few years without immediate intervention (Brooks *et al.* 1992). There is apparently a recent report from Panay (*per* T. M. Brooks *in litt.* 1994). **CRITICAL: A1b; A2b; B1+2c; C1; C2a; D1.**

Slaty-backed Jungle-flycatcher *Rhinomyias goodfellowi* inhabits the understorey of forest above 1,000 m on Mindanao in the **Philippines**, but is only known from four historical sites (Dickinson *et al.* 1991), at one of which (Mount Apo) it was relocated in May 1994 (C. R. Robson *in litt.* 1994), and one

recent one (Sitio Siete, near Lake Sebu, South Cotabato province: N. Bostock *in litt.* 1994). Habitat destruction on the island extends into the altitudinal range of the species (see Cryptic Flycatcher *Ficedula crypta*, next page). **VULNERABLE: A2b; B1+2c; C1; C2a.**

Ashy-breasted Flycatcher *Muscicapa randi* is a lowland forest species, all records being from below 1,200 m, endemic to Luzon (three recent records: at Angat Dam and two sites in the Sierra Madre) and Negros (where it is possibly extinct, having gone unrecorded since 1877) in the **Philippines**; it must be at risk from the extensive and continuing habitat destruction occurring on the islands (Brooks *et al.* 1992, Danielsen *et al.* 1994, Poulsen in press). **ENDANGERED: A1b; A2b; B1+2c; C1; C2a.**

Chapin's Flycatcher *Muscicapa lendu* is known with certainty from a narrow band of montane forest between 1,470 and 1,820 m in the Itombwe Mountains (race *itombwensis*) and (nominate *lendu*) on the Lendu Plateau (now largely deforested) in eastern **Zaïre**, in the Bwindi (= Impenetrable) forest in **Uganda**, and Kakamega and North Nandi forests in **Kenya** (with a record from Nyungwe forest, Rwanda, which requires confirmation: Dowsett-Lemaire 1990), and is rare throughout this fragmented range; habitat loss is the most likely threat, although recent evidence suggests that habitat in Itombwe is at present reasonably intact (Collar and Stuart 1985, 1988, Lewis and Pomeroy 1989, Wilson and Catsis 1990, Catterall 1992). **VULNERABLE: B1+2a,c; C2a.**

Grand Comoro Flycatcher *Humblotia flavirostris*, a distinctive flycatcher in its own genus, occurs only in forest and heath on the slopes of Mount Karthala (preferring the higher altitudes), Grand Comoro (= Ngazidja), **Comoro Islands** (Collar and Stuart 1985). Despite evidence that its status (several thousand pairs) is better than had once been believed and is stable, its habitat remains somewhat vulnerable and insufficiently protected (Louette *et al.* 1988, Louette and Stevens 1992, Stevens *et al.* 1992). **VULNERABLE: B1+2c; C2b.**

Kashmir Flycatcher *Ficedula subrubra* breeds in mixed broadleaf forest between 1,800 and 2,700 m in Kashmir and the Pir Panjal range in north-west **India** and northern **Pakistan**, and winters in gardens, tea estates and forest edge above 750 m in **Sri Lanka** and the southern Western Ghats, south-west peninsular India (Ali and Ripley 1987, Harrap and Redman 1989), occurring as a scarce migrant in **Nepal** (Inskipp and Inskipp 1991). It was formerly common within its breeding range (Ali and Ripley

1987), but appears to have declined (A. J. Gaston *in litt.* 1993), and it is vulnerable to continuing forest destruction and degradation there (C. R. Robson *in litt.* 1993). **VULNERABLE:** B1+2c.

Little Slaty Flycatcher *Ficedula basilanica* occupies the understorey of lowland forest and second growth up to 1,150 m on Samar and Leyte (race *samarensis*), Dinagat, Mindanao and Basilan (nominate *basilanica*) in the **Philippines**, the only (and very few) recent records coming from Mindanao, where (as on all other islands) the species must be suffering from extensive and continuing habitat destruction (Evans *et al.* 1993a, N. J. Redman verbally 1993, N. Bostock *in litt.* 1994, R. J. Timmins *in litt.* 1994). **VULNERABLE:** A1b; A2b; C1; C2a.

Damar Flycatcher *Ficedula henrici* is endemic to the island of Damar (c.170 km^2) in the southern Moluccas, **Indonesia**, and is probably known only from a series of nine specimens collected in 1899 (White and Bruce 1986), presumably in forest. Its status and any threats are thus unknown, but there is a recent report that extensive forests remain on the island (S. van Balen *in litt.* 1994). **VULNERABLE:** D2.

Palawan Flycatcher *Ficedula platenae* is restricted to the undergrowth of forest below 1,000 m on Palawan and Balabac in the **Philippines** (Dickinson *et al.* 1991), where records since 1991 (none from the many logged or secondary forest sites surveyed) suggest that it is now very rare and may be unable to survive in what is everywhere increasingly disturbed habitat (Lambert 1993b, N. Bostock *in litt.* 1994, J. Hornbuckle *in litt.* 1994). **ENDANGERED:** A1b; A2b; B1+2c; C1; **C2a.**

Cryptic Flycatcher *Ficedula crypta* (here treated separately from Furtive Flycatcher *F. disposita*: see below and Dutson 1993) skulks in the understorey of mossy or mid-mountain forest and second growth up to 1,500 m on Mindanao in the **Philippines**, where the five localities from which specimens have been obtained (Dickinson *et al.* 1991) were recently supplemented by several observations at Sitio Siete near Lake Sebu (South Cotabato province) in 1992 and 1994; habitat destruction on the island extends into its altitudinal range (Evans *et al.* 1993a, C. R. Robson *in litt.* 1994, R. J. Timmins *in litt.* 1994). **VULNERABLE:** A2b; B1+2c; C1; C2a.

Furtive Flycatcher *Ficedula disposita* (here treated separately from Cryptic Flycatcher *F. crypta*: see above) is known by the type-specimen from the Zambales Mountains at 760 m in 1966 (plus a recent specimen which validates *disposita* as a good spe-

cies: R. S. Kennedy *in litt.* 1994), two birds seen at 500 m at Angat in 1991, and four birds netted at 250–300 m in the Sierra Madre in 1991–1992, all on Luzon in the **Philippines**; it is clearly extremely rare, and as an apparent inhabitant of lowland forest it must be at very serious risk from the extensive and continuing habitat destruction which is taking place on the island (Dutson 1993, Evans *et al.* 1993a, Poulsen in press). **ENDANGERED:** A1b; A2b; B1+2c; C1; **C2a**; D1.

Lompobattang Flycatcher *Ficedula bonthaina* is known only from Gunung Lompobattang near the tip of the south-west peninsula of Sulawesi, **Indonesia**, where it has been recorded in montane forest at 1,100 m and above, and was evidently common, as a long series of specimens was obtained in 1931 (White and Bruce 1986). However, there have apparently been no subsequent records, and the surrounding lowlands have been cleared to 1,000 m and represent one of the more densely populated areas of Sulawesi (Whitten *et al.* 1987b), so it seems very likely to be threatened by habitat loss (BirdLife IP). **ENDANGERED: B1+2c;** C1; C2b.

Matinan Flycatcher *Cyornis sanfordi* is endemic to northern Sulawesi, **Indonesia**, where it is known from the mountains on the Minahassa peninsula, in montane forest at 1,400 m and above (White and Bruce 1986). The only documented records are nine specimens collected in the Matinan mountains (Stresemann 1940), and singles on Gunung Kabila, in Dumoga-Bone National Park, in 1981 and Gunung Muajat in 1985 (Rozendaal and Dekker 1989). It therefore has a very restricted range, but its habitat in the mountains is presumably secure (BirdLife IP). **VULNERABLE:** D2.

Rueck's Blue-flycatcher *Cyornis ruckii* is known from northern Sumatra, **Indonesia**, by two specimens collected in 1917 and 1918 in exploited forest in the lowlands at 150 m and 200 m (van Marle and Voous 1988), in an area now occupied by settlements (P. Jepson *in litt.* 1994), and doubtfully from peninsular Malaysia by two trade skins (Medway and Wells 1976). It may have been affected by the extensive lowland deforestation which has taken place in Sumatra (see RePPProT 1990), but its status, habitat requirements and range remain essentially unknown, and its taxonomic status has been questioned (van Marle and Voous 1988). **VULNERABLE:** C1; D1.

Red-tailed Newtonia *Newtonia fanovanae* remained known only from the type-specimen, collected in December 1931 in Fanovana forest (now cleared) in east-central **Madagascar** (Collar and Stuart 1985), until its almost simultaneous rediscovery as a very patchily distributed inhabitant of middle and upper sections of the canopy of humid forest at 300–1,300 m in the reserves at Andohahela in October 1989 (Goodman and Schulenberg 1991)

and Ambatovaky (where there is habitat destruction) in February 1990 (Evans 1991), with a site on the western Masoala peninsula being added subsequently (J. C. Sinclair *per*/and F. R. Lambert verbally 1993). **VULNERABLE:** B1+2c; C2a.

Subfamily PLATYSTEIRINAE

PUFFBACK-FLYCATCHERS, WATTLE-EYES

Banded Wattle-eye *Platysteira laticincta* is restricted to the Bamenda-Banso Highlands of western **Cameroon**, where it is under very serious threat from forest clearance (habitat reduced by half in the period 1965–1985) and is only likely to survive if forest (only covering c.100 km²) on Mount Oku (Kilum) is preserved (Collar and Stuart 1985, 1988,

Stuart and Jensen 1986, Fotso 1993b). Intensive work has been directed towards the conservation of Mount Kilum, and is continuing (e.g. Macleod 1987, Wilson 1987, Green 1991, Macleod and Parrott 1992, Alpert 1993, Edwards 1993). **VULNERABLE:** A1b; B1+2b,c; C1; C2b.

Subfamily MONARCHINAE

MONARCHS, PARADISE-FLYCATCHERS

Celestial Monarch *Hypothymis coelestis* inhabits the canopy and middle storey of forest, forest edge and second growth below 1,000 m on Negros (where it may be extinct, being last recorded in 1959) and Sibuyan (race *rabori*), Luzon (one old and three recent sites), Samar, Dinagat (not found in a 1972 survey, but not uncommon there in 1991: P. Gonzales *per* A. Jensen *in litt.* 1994), Mindanao (one recent area) and Basilan (nominate *coelestis*) in the **Philippines** (Dickinson *et al.* 1991). It may be a lowland riverine specialist (T. H. Fisher *per* G. C. L. Dutson verbally 1992), which may help explain its noted and puzzling rarity, and it must be suffering from the extensive and continuing habitat destruction occurring within its range (Brooks *et al.* 1992, Lambert 1993b, Danielsen *et al.* 1994, Poulsen in press, C. R. Robson *in litt.* 1994). In August two birds, probably this species, were seen on the now largely deforested island of Tawitawi (G. C. L. Dutson verbally 1994). **ENDANGERED:** A1b; A2b; C1; **C2a**.

Cerulean Paradise-flycatcher *Eutrichomyias rowleyi* is endemic to Sangihe Island, north of Sulawesi, **Indonesia**, and is known only by the type and a single bird seen in 1978 on the forested slopes of Gunung Awu at the northern end of the island (White and Bruce 1986). The original vegetation of Sangihe has been almost completely replaced by coconut and nutmeg plantations and the secondary vegetation of abandoned gardens; recent surveys to locate this species have been unsuccessful and it is feared extinct (Whitten *et al.* 1987a,b). **CRITICAL:** A1b; **B1+2c,e**; C1; **C2b**; **D1**; D2.

Annobon Paradise-flycatcher *Terpsiphone smithii* (here split from Black-headed Paradise-flycatcher *T. rufiventer*) is endemic to the very small (17 km²) Gulf of Guinea island of Annobon (**Equatorial Guinea**), where during this century it has remained common and widespread in cultivated areas, secondary forest and higher moist forest (Harrison 1990). **VULNERABLE:** D1; D2.

Seychelles Paradise-flycatcher *Terpsiphone corvina* inhabits mature stands (covering only 64 ha) of indigenous *Calophyllum* and *Terminalia* trees, especially near marshy areas chiefly on the coastal 'plateau' (160 ha) of western La Digue (16 km^2), **Seychelles**, where its population numbered c.60 in the late 1970s; very small, probably unviable populations occur (c.10 birds combined; last noted in the 1970s) on Praslin and Felicité (Collar and Stuart 1985). A census on La Digue in February 1988 found 72–75 birds (Collar and Andrew 1988), although some double-counting may have then occurred as 61 were present on the plateau in July that year and in general little change to woodland cover since 1978 was noted (Watson 1991); but a recent study, which states that in 1978 there were 53 (not 64) ha of woodland, reported 51 ha in 1988 but only 41 ha in 1992, an extremely alarming loss of habitat and hence presumably decline in flycatcher numbers (Anon. 1992). There are now no birds on Praslin and Felicité, while on La Digue, which is under greatest development pressure with much tree-felling and woodland fragmentation for tourism and private housing, the birds appear to be spreading (or are being forced) into marginal areas without increasing in numbers (J. Stevenson verbally 1994). **CRITICAL: B1+2a,b,c,e; C2b; D1; D2.**

Rarotonga Monarch *Pomarea dimidiata* is restricted to the forested interior of Rarotonga (with the entire population limited, since 1987, to the headwaters of the Totokoitu, Turoa and western Avana valleys, total area c.150 ha), **Cook Islands (to New Zealand)**. It has probably been rare for most of the twentieth century and a survey in 1983 located only 21 birds and two nests (the first ever recorded). A recovery programme identified rats (especially *Rattus rattus*) as the main obstacle to successful nesting, and rat control has resulted in an increase in its numbers: 38 in 1990, 48 in 1991, 56 in 1992 and 60 in 1993 (Hay 1986, McCormack and Künzle 1990, G. McCormack *in litt.* 1994). **CRITICAL: D1; D2.**

Tahiti Monarch *Pomarea nigra* is endemic to but approaching extinction on Tahiti in the Society Islands, **French Polynesia**, the single specimen collected in 1823 on Maupiti in the same group now being recognized as a full (extinct) species *P. pomarea* (Holyoak and Thibault 1984; also King 1978–1979). It has apparently been rare throughout this century and during the period 1986–1991 it was noted in only four valleys (several pairs at each locality) out of 39 visited (Monnet *et al.* 1993). Its recent decline on Mount Mara'u might be related to the replacing of the high, dense forest by shrubs of the botanical pest *Miconia calvescens*, introduced in

1937, whose progression has been partly facilitated by the 1983 hurricane (J.-C. Thibault *in litt.* 1993). **CRITICAL: B1+2c; C2b; D1; D2.**

Iphis Monarch *Pomarea iphis* is endemic to Ua Huka in the Marquesas Islands, **French Polynesia**, where it forages in dense brush along coastal cliffs and where several hundred pairs were present in 1975 (Holyoak and Thibault 1984). The race *fluxa*, reported as probably surviving (King 1978–1979) and 'much reduced but still present on Eiao' (Pratt *et al.* 1987), was found to be extinct in July 1987 for reasons which seem unclear: cats were introduced well before this date, favourable habitat remains (despite the loss of some once-occupied woodland), and in 1987 only Polynesian rats *Rattus exulans* (which would have been present on the island for many centuries and thus unlikely to have caused the recent demise) were collected in 130 night/traps; however, the introduction of Chestnut-breasted Munia *Lonchura castaneothorax* coincides with the extinction, implying that an avian disease may have been transmitted to this population (Thibault 1989, J.-C. Thibault *in litt.* 1994). **VULNERABLE: D2.**

Marquesan Monarch *Pomarea mendozae* was formerly widespread in the central Marquesas Islands, **French Polynesia**, occurring in four subspecies, all but one (race *motanensis*) considered threatened by the late 1970s (King 1978–1979). It is still common on Mohotani (race *motanensis*, at all altitudes in degraded forest, there being no rats on this island), where the population was estimated at 250–350 pairs, and on Ua Pou (race *mira*, above 550 m perhaps because of rat predation) with a population of 150–200 pairs, but possibly extinct (nominate *mendozae*) on Hiva Oa (one seen 1975), Tahuata (also *mendozae*) and Nuku Hiva (race *nukuhivae*), though reported on the latter by locals in 1987 (Holyoak and Thibault 1984, Thibault 1988, Seitre and Seitre 1991, 1992). **ENDANGERED: B1+2d; C2a; D1.**

Fatuhiva Monarch *Pomarea whitneyi* is endemic to Fatu Hiva (100 km^2) in the Marquesas Islands, **French Polynesia**, where it inhabits forests and wooded thickets at all elevations and where several hundred pairs were present in 1975 (Holyoak and Thibault 1984, Pratt *et al.* 1987), still persisting and common in 1977 (Montgomery *et al.* 1980), in the early 1980s (M. Fowler *in litt.* to M. K. Poulsen 1985) and in 1990 (Seitre and Seitre 1991). **VULNERABLE: D2.**

Ogea Monarch *Mayrornis versicolor* is endemic to Ogea in the southern Lau Group, **Fiji**, occurring on the two principal islands, Ogealevu and Ogeadriki

(13 and 5 km² respectively, 2 km apart), and on the smaller island of Dakuiyanuya (adjacent to Ogea-levu), where, on all three, it is restricted to forest (possibly preferring the more limited successional and edge habitats), and was estimated to have a total population of c.2,000 in 1986. There were no indications that it (or the forests) had been greatly affected by the cyclones of 1973, 1975, 1979 or 1985, but it will always remain vulnerable to chance catastrophes (Watling 1988). **VULNERABLE:** D2.

Truk Monarch *Metabolus rugensis* is sparsely distributed on all, or nearly all, of the high lagoon islands (highest densities on Tol South) as well as some of the outer reef islets of Chuuk (= Truk), **Micronesia**, where it occurs in small patches of upland native forest, well-developed stands of mangrove, atoll strand and (rarely) agroforest. It has probably never been abundant in historic times, is likely to have declined dramatically by 1945 owing to extensive agricultural development during the Japanese administration, and may still be gradually declining (most likely owing to a rapidly expanding human population), with numbers estimated at 2,168 in 1984 (Engbring *et al.* 1990). It appears to have become very rare recently (none found in a visit in 1991 and only 3–4 birds on Tol in 1993) and may have been extirpated from Weno, as a major fire recently destroyed the patch of forest where it was uncommon in the 1970s (H. D. Pratt *in litt.* 1994). **ENDANGERED: A1a**; B1+2a,c,d; C2a; D2.

Flores Monarch *Monarcha sacerdotum* is only known from Tanjung Kerita Mese (a proposed protected area: FAO 1982), near Paku, south-west Flores, in the Lesser Sundas, **Indonesia** (Schmutz 1977, White and Bruce 1986), where it is found in primary semi-evergreen rainforest between 350 and 1,000 m, and not in degraded forest or drier forest types; a survey in 1993 found it uncommon at this site, and judged it threatened by forest degradation (Butchart *et al.* 1993). **ENDANGERED:** B1+2c; C1; **C2b**.

White-tipped Monarch *Monarcha everetti* is a species restricted to Tanahjampea (c.150 km²), in the Flores Sea south of Sulawesi, **Indonesia** (White and Bruce 1986), where in 1993 it was found to be quite common in forest, but less so in scrub and mangroves; evergreen forest (which has been extensively logged) was estimated to cover about half the island. The species would be threatened by any large-scale increase in logging, which is currently carried out to provide timber for local house- and boat-

building industries (Dutson in prep.). **VULNERABLE:** C2b; D2.

Black-chinned Monarch *Monarcha boanensis* is endemic to the island of Boano (c.125 km²), off western Seram in the Moluccas, **Indonesia**; until recently, it was only known by the holotype (White and Bruce 1986), but in 1991 one adult and two juveniles were seen (and one juvenile examined in the hand) in disturbed forest in the foothills at 200 m, and it is believed that the population, probably small, is restricted to the higher parts of the island at 200–700 m (Heij and Moeliker in prep.). **ENDANGERED: B1+2c**; C1; C2b; **D1**.

Biak Monarch *Monarcha brehmii* is confined to Biak-Supiori in Geelvink Bay, Irian Jaya, **Indonesia**, where it inhabits lowland and hill forest to an altitude of 600 m (Schodde 1978) preferring forest with a fairly dense middle layer (i.e. intact habitat) and clearly very rare (e.g. taking three days to find) as a result of widespread clearance for subsistence farms (Bishop 1992, K. D. Bishop *in litt.* 1994, I. Burrows *in litt.* 1994, R. Burrows *in litt.* 1994, D. Gibbs *in litt.* 1994, P. Gregory *in litt.* 1994). **ENDANGERED:** A1b; **B1+2c**; **C2b**; D1.

Tinian Monarch *Monarcha takatsukasae* is endemic to Tinian (<100 km²) in the **Northern Mariana Islands (to U.S.A.)**, where it lives in all types of shrubby vegetation including thickets of introduced *Leucaena*. In 1945 it was reported as abundant and in 1983 was estimated to have a population numbering c.40,000 individuals (Engbring and Pratt 1985), but remains secure only so long as the brown tree snake *Boiga irregularis* is not introduced from Guam (D. W. Stinson *in litt.* 1994) or from nearby Saipan. **VULNERABLE:** D2.

Samoan Flycatcher *Myiagra albiventris* is found mostly in native forest and forest edge at all elevations (but predominantly in lowlands) on Savaii and Upolu, **Western Samoa**, where it was considered common (Pratt *et al.* 1987). However, in three days of intensive birdwatching in 1992 in appropriate habitat (which held populations of all other formerly common Samoan birds) only one individual was located and, despite being an insectivore, the species may have been affected by the severe effects of cyclones in 1990 and 1991, when canopy cover was reduced from 100% to 27% (Elmqvist 1993, H. D. Pratt *in litt.* 1994; see also Elmqvist *et al.* in press). **VULNERABLE:** A1a,b.

Subfamily RHIPIDURINAE

FANTAILS

Malaita Fantail *Rhipidura malaitae* had not been recorded since its discovery in 1930, in mountain forest on Malaita, **Solomon Islands** (Diamond 1987), until 1990 when a single bird was seen at 750 m on the slopes of Mount Ire (= Kolovrat) near the village of Raihora (P. Scofield *in litt.* 1992, 1994) and again in 1994 when a single bird was seen at 1,100 m. It probably has a very small population, but threats to its habitat are more likely to come from cyclones rather than from man in the foreseeable future (D. Gibbs *in litt.* 1994). **VULNERABLE:** D1.

Manus Fantail *Rhipidura semirubra* is endemic to the Admiralty Islands of Manus, San Miguel and Tong, **Papua New Guinea** (Coates 1990), and was also seen on Anobat (San Miguel Islands) and Sivisa Island (Fedarb Islands) in 1991 (Tolhurst 1993), as well as being recorded from nearby Pak and Rambutyo (K. M. Kisokau *in litt.* 1994). Despite visits by experienced birdwatchers, it has not been seen on Manus since 1934 when it was described as 'common everywhere in true forest and secondary bush'. Its decline may be related to the presence of the brown tree snake *Boiga irregularis*, which has been responsible for the elimination of forest birds on Guam (Dutson and Newman 1991), although as the snake is apparently native to Manus there is presumably some kind of equilibrium between predator and prey (R. E. Beck *in litt.* 1992). On Tong it was reported to be 'very friendly' (see Coates 1990), and 10 were seen in c.90 minutes in scrub and isolated trees amongst coconut palms in 1994; islanders say that it survives there because of the absence of the White-naped Friarbird *Philemon albitorques*, which may have undergone a population explosion associated with human colonization and clearance on Manus (D. Gibbs *in litt.* 1994), these latter factors being the likely threats to the species on the smaller islands too (K. M. Kisokau *in litt.* 1994). **VULNERABLE:** D1; D2.

Family PARIDAE

TITS

White-naped Tit *Parus nuchalis* is endemic to **India**, with a widely disjunct distribution in the western and southern parts of the country. In western India, it is recorded from northern Gujarat (including Kutch) and central and south-central Rajastan, where a comparison of recent with historical records indicates that it has declined drastically, and in southern India it is only known by three old records from southern Karnataka and southern Andhra Pradesh, and recent records from Wynaad, Kerala, where it is rare (Zacharias and Gaston 1993). It is confined to thorny scrub-forest dominated by *Acacia* spp., and its decline is linked to the rapid loss of dry forest cover because of the cutting of tree branches to feed livestock, and agricultural encroachment (Hussain *et al.* 1992), which perhaps leads to a lack of suitable nest holes as old trees are removed (A. R. Rahmani *in litt.* 1994). **VULNERABLE:** A1b; C1; C2a.

Family SITTIDAE

NUTHATCHES

White-browed Nuthatch *Sitta victoriae* is known only from alpine forest (not pines) at 2,300–2,800 m on Mount Victoria in the Chin Hills, **Myanmar** (King *et al.* 1975). There have apparently been no documented records since 1938, so current status and any threats are unknown. **VULNERABLE: D2.**

Algerian Nuthatch *Sitta ledanti* maintains a population of c.80 pairs in summit forest (c.2,000 m, where optimum habitat covers only 2.5 km²) on Mont Babor, **Algeria**, where it is threatened by habitat loss, although the site has national park status (Collar and Stuart 1985). A population of c.350 birds exists nearby in oak forest at 350–1,120 m within the Taza National Park on the Guerrouch massif (Chalabi 1989, Bellatreche and Chalabi 1990), and two further adjacent (uncounted, but evidently not larger) populations survive in poorly regenerating oak forest at Tamentout and Djimla (900–1,400 m), though searches elsewhere in the region have drawn a blank (Bellatreche 1991; see also Harrap 1992) and deforestation throughout it is rife (Zaimeche 1994). **ENDANGERED:** B1+2c; **C2a**; D1; D2.

Yunnan Nuthatch *Sitta yunnanensis* is known from south-east Tibet, southern Sichuan and northern Yunnan (Cheng 1987), and the western extreme of Guizhou (Wu *et al.* 1986), **China**, where it affects open mature pine forest (avoiding other types of coniferous forest) with little undergrowth or scrub, mainly from 2,400 to 3,400 m (Dolan 1938, C. R. Robson *in litt.* 1990). It is locally common (e.g. in relict pine forests at Lijiang, north-west Yunnan), but is believed to be dependent on mature pines, which are being cleared within its range (Collar and Andrew 1988). **VULNERABLE:** A1b; C1; C2a.

Yellow-billed Nuthatch *Sitta solangiae* is known from three or four widely disjunct areas: the Fansipan mountains in north-east Tonkin, Da Lat (= Langbian) plateau in southern Annam, and possibly a site in northern Annam, **Vietnam**, and the island of Hainan, south-east **China** (where birds formerly regarded as a race of Velvet-fronted Nuthatch *S. frontalis* have recently been transferred to *S. solangiae*). Recent records are from Bawangling Nature Reserve on Hainan, where up to seven birds were seen at 1,100 m in primary forest, and several localities, including two protected areas, on the Da Lat plateau, where surveys since 1990 have recorded small numbers in primary and logged evergreen forest at 1,450–2,100 m, and a report from Vu Quang Nature Reserve in northern Annam, which would be a remarkable range extension (King and Liao 1989, Eames *et al.* 1992, Robson *et al.* 1993a,b, J. C. Eames *in litt.* 1994). The major threat throughout is deforestation, e.g. forest cover on Hainan fell from an estimated 8,630 km² (25.7%) in 1949 to c.2,420 km² (7.2%) in 1991 (Collins *et al.* 1991). **VULNERABLE:** C1; C2a.

Giant Nuthatch *Sitta magna* is known from east-central **Myanmar** (formerly not uncommon locally, no recent records: Smythies 1986), north-west **Thailand** (very scarce and local, but present in at least three protected areas: Round 1988) and Yunnan and south-west Guizhou, south-west **China** (rare, only a few recent records: Cheng 1987; see, e.g., Goodwin 1987, Zheng 1988). It inhabits open evergreen hill forest where pines are frequent at 1,200–2,500 m or more (Meyer de Schauensee 1984, Round 1988). Much of its range has been deforested by shifting cultivation in Thailand and presumably elsewhere; forest degradation by firewood collection is also a threat (Round 1988). **VULNERABLE:** A1b; C1; C2a.

Beautiful Nuthatch *Sitta formosa* inhabits mountains of north-east **India** (recent records of small numbers in Arunachal Pradesh and North Cachar: Grimmett 1979, M. Jäderblad *in litt.* 1994, R. H. Raza *in litt.* 1994, Singh in press), **Bhutan** (one recent record: K. D. Bishop *in litt.* 1994), **Myanmar** (no recent information), south-east Yunnan, **China** (very rare: Cheng 1987), northern and central **Laos** (several seen in Nakai Plateau/Nam Theun protected area in 1994: T. D. Evans and R. J. Timmins verbally 1994), north-west **Thailand** (one record in 1986: *Oriental Bird Club Bull.* 1986, 3: 33–36), northern **Vietnam** (no recent records: J. C. Eames *in litt.* 1994) and possibly Bangladesh (Harvey 1990, Thompson *et al.* 1993). It occupies evergreen forest at 1,500–2,100 m, though lower in winter (King *et al.* 1975, Ali and Ripley 1987). It is extremely local within its extensive range, suggesting that it may have specialized habitat needs, and it is presumably vulnerable to habitat destruction and degradation (see Collins *et al.* 1991). **VULNERABLE:** C1; C2a.

Family DICAEIDAE

FLOWERPECKERS

Forty-spotted Pardalote *Pardalotus quadragintus*, endemic to Tasmania, **Australia**, was formerly widespread and locally common from sea-level up to 1,000 m in the eastern half of the island, and also on King and Flinders islands, but is now restricted to the coastal south-east where seven populations totalling fewer than 3,400 birds (but two colonies with more than 1,000 birds each: D. Rounsevell *in litt.* 1994) survive on islands and coastal peninsulas in the vicinity of Hobart. It affects open forest or woodland, particularly that dominated by white gum *Eucalyptus viminalis*, and its decline has been linked to habitat destruction, unsuitable fire regimes and competition from the Noisy Miner *Manorina melanocephala* (Garnett 1992). **VULNERABLE:** B1+2c.

Whiskered Flowerpecker *Dicaeum proprium* is restricted to forest, forest edge and second growth above 900 m on Mindanao in the **Philippines**, where it is uncommon (being a low-density species) and known from only seven sites, with recent records (very few) from only two (Mount Apo and Sitio Siete near Lake Sebu, South Cotabato province) (Dickinson *et al.* 1991, N. Bostock *in litt.* 1994, C. R. Robson *in litt.* 1994); habitat destruction on the island extends into its altitudinal range (see Cryptic Flycatcher *Ficedula crypta*, p. 174). **VULNERABLE:** A2b; B1+2c; C1; C2a.

Cebu Flowerpecker *Dicaeum quadricolor*, considered extinct on its native Cebu in the **Philippines** since 1906, was rediscovered in 1992 in a very small (less than 2 km²) patch of largely degraded forest (but with roughly 10 ha of closed-canopy habitat, in which the species was found) near the village of Tabunan; no other patch of closed-canopy forest appears to exist on the island, and if current levels of exploitation by local villagers continue, the patch and the flowerpecker, although within the Central Cebu National Park, will be gone in less than a decade (Dutson *et al.* 1993). However, observations in 1994 showed that the species also utilizes open-canopy forest and that competition from the very common Red-striped Flowerpecker *D. australe* was a significant problem (C. R. Robson *in litt.* 1994). **CRITICAL:** A1b; **A2b**; **B1+2c**; **C1**; **C2b**; **D1**; D2.

Visayan Flowerpecker *Dicaeum haematostictum* (a full species: Brooks *et al.* 1992) is restricted to Panay (where it was recorded at a few lowland sites in 1992), Guimaras (where it is probably extinct given the almost total clearance of forest there) and Negros (where, given that it was common in the 1950s, surprisingly few birds were found in 1991) in the **Philippines**, and it seems likely to be at risk from the continuing clearance of its forest and scrub habitats within its altitudinal range (400–1,250 m) (Brooks *et al.* 1992). **ENDANGERED: A1b**; A2b; **B1+2c**; C1; **C2a**.

Scarlet-collared Flowerpecker *Dicaeum retrocinctum* occurs on Mindoro in the **Philippines** (with a recent report from Negros: Curio 1994), where it remains common in lower altitude closed-canopy forest areas (up to 1,000 m; rare above this level) throughout the island, but is poorly tolerant of degraded forest; since deforestation will soon extend throughout its altitudinal range it is likely to suffer a very serious population decline (Dutson *et al.* 1992). **CRITICAL:** A1b; **A2b**; **B1+2c**; C1; C2a.

Family NECTARINIIDAE

SUNBIRDS

Amani Sunbird *Anthreptes pallidigaster* is largely confined to the 67 km² of coastal *Brachystegia* woodland within the Arabuko–Sokoke forest in **Kenya** (the target of a now stalled conservation project: see Sokoke Scops-owl *Otus ireneae*, p. 114), a region at up to 950 m in the East Usambara Mountains (where suitable habitat covers only 130 km² and where densities are much lower than in Arabuko–Sokoke) and in the Ndundulu mountains (240 km², at 1,500–1,550 m) and Nyumbanitu mountains (55 km², at 1,350–1,400 m), in **Tanzania** (the Udzungwa birds possibly represent a new subspecies, which is likely to be present in the nearby lowland Matundu forest) (Collar and Stuart 1985, Dinesen *et al.* 1993, Hipkiss *et al.* 1994, Watson and Perkin undated). It is a canopy specialist preferring primary forest (though it sometimes enters gardens in Amani), and forest clearance is its principal threat (J. H. Fanshawe verbally 1994, L. A. Hansen and J. O. Svendsen *in litt.* 1994, A. Tye *in litt.* 1994). Current conservation in the East Usambaras is noted under Usambara Eagle Owl *Bubo vosseleri* (see p. 115). **VULNERABLE:** B1+2b,c.

Banded Sunbird *Anthreptes rubritorques* is generally a middle-altitude species of the canopy and edge, also entering gardens (750–1,500 m, with a recent record from 200 m in the Usambaras), in four forest areas—the Usambara, Nguru, Uluguru and Udzungwa mountains (the latter now including the Ndundulu Mountains)—in eastern **Tanzania**, but is only common in the first of these where, however, it is at risk from forest destruction (Collar and Stuart 1985, Stuart *et al.* 1987, Evans and Anderson 1992, 1993, Dinesen *et al.* 1993, Hipkiss *et al.* 1994, Watson and Perkin undated, A. Tye *in litt.* 1994), although current conservation in the East Usambaras is noted under Usambara Eagle Owl *Bubo vosseleri*, p. 115. **VULNERABLE:** B1+2b,c.

Giant Sunbird *Nectarinia thomensis* is restricted to rainforest on São Tomé, **São Tomé e Príncipe**, and was originally regarded as Near-threatened (Collar and Stuart 1985). After further expressions of concern over its status (Jones and Tye 1988), it was found in 1990 to be patchily common within primary habitat (both montane and lowland), but apparently very susceptible to forest disturbance, and possibly also operating a polygynous mating system (Atkinson *et al.* 1991; also Jones *et al.* 1992, Nadler 1993, P. Christy *in litt.* 1994). **VULNERABLE:** D1.

Rockefeller's Sunbird *Nectarinia rockefelleri* occupies as little as 250 km² of high montane forest and afroalpine moorland at 2,050–3,300 m on the Itombwe Mountains, mountains west of Lake Kivu, and Mount Karisimbi (in the Virunga Mountains north of Lake Kivu, where the population must be 'vanishingly small': J. R. Wilson *in litt.* 1988), eastern **Zaïre**; a record from the Burundi side of Nyungwe forest requires confirmation, while a male in this forest on the Rwanda side in 1986 may simply have been a wanderer, as searches in appropriate habitat drew a blank in 1990 (Collar and Stuart 1985, Dowsett-Lemaire 1990). **VULNERABLE:** D1.

Rufous-winged Sunbird *Nectarinia rufipennis* is now known to be locally fairly common in the interior of wet forest, usually at light gaps, at 1,000–1,700 m (commonest at 1,500–1,700 m, although recorded as low as 600 m) in the Mwanihana forest, at 1,350–1,600 m in the Ndundulu Mountains, and at 1,100–1,500 m in the Nyumbanitu Mountains (notably commonest in a small area called Ukami forest), all in the Udzungwa Mountains (Mwanihana being in the Udzungwa National Park) of eastern **Tanzania** (Collar and Stuart 1985, Stuart *et al.* 1987, Jensen and Brøgger-Jensen 1992, Dinesen *et al.* 1993, L. A. Hansen and J. O. Svendsen *in litt.* 1994). **VULNERABLE:** D2.

Elegant Sunbird *Aethopyga duyvenbodei* is known from the Sangihe Islands (Sangihe and Siau), to the north of Sulawesi, **Indonesia** (White and Bruce 1986). On Sangihe, the original vegetation has been almost completely replaced by coconut and nutmeg plantations and by the secondary vegetation of abandoned gardens (Whitten *et al.* 1987a,b), and little or no forest habitat exists on the volcanically very active island of Siau (Bishop 1992). The only recent published records are from Sangihe, of five in a dense bamboo thicket in secondary woodland on Gunung Awu (Bishop 1992) and reports of it being rather common in forest edge on Gunung Sahendaruman (Collar and Andrew 1988). **ENDANGERED:** A1b; **B1+2c**; C1; C2a; D2.

Family ZOSTEROPIDAE

WHITE-EYES

Mount Cameroon Speirops *Speirops melano-cephalus* is restricted to Mount Cameroon, **Cameroon**, where it is common between 1,820 and 3,000 m in the canopy and mid-strata of the more open parts of the forest, avoiding the denser closed-canopy areas. At its lower altitudinal limits it is found only in clearings and is very noticeable at the upper forest–grassland boundary, above this occurring in patches of bush and thicket (Stuart and Jensen 1986). **VULNERABLE: D2.**

Fernando Po Speirops *Speirops brunneus* is known only from the higher slopes of Pico de Santa Isabel, at 1,900 m and above, on Bioko (**Equatorial Guinea**), where it inhabits lichen-forest and montane heathland (Collar and Stuart 1985); surveys in the late 1980s indicated that the species continues to occur in small groups and that its habitat remains largely intact, although the main threat might be fire, of which evidence was discovered (Koster and Butynski undated). **VULNERABLE: D2.**

Príncipe Speirops *Speirops leucophaeus* is endemic to Príncipe, **São Tomé e Príncipe**, in the Gulf of Guinea, where a 1987 survey found evidence of local persecution and of a possible decline (perhaps owing to plantation development and pesticide use) since the early 1970s, when it was described as abundant, although it may still be found in groups of up to 15 birds in forest regrowth and cocoa plantations (Jones and Tye 1988, Atkinson *et al.* 1991). **VULNERABLE: C2b.**

Kulal White-eye *Zosterops kulalensis* (here split from Broad-ringed White-eye *Z. poliogaster*) is confined to but abundant in forest on Mount Kulal, **Kenya**, where by 1980 only 40 km² remained under trees, all of this being heavily penetrated and degraded by herds of cattle (Diamond and Keith 1980, Collar and Stuart 1985). **CRITICAL: B1+2b,c**; C2b: D1; D2.

South Pare White-eye *Zosterops winifredae* (whose distinctiveness as a species from Broad-ringed White-eye *Z. poliogaster* is supported by J. Fjeldså *in litt.* 1994) is confined to the South Pare Mountains, **Tanzania** (Collar and Stuart 1985), where it was fairly common, with perhaps several thousand birds being present overall, in the Chomme Catchment Forest Reserve (143 km² at 2,000–2,465 m),

mainly in *Erica* vegetation at the forest edge and in interior light-gaps, but also in low (1 m) *Erica* heath (although perhaps then still dependent on adjacent forest edge), with a small population in Mwala forest (14 km²) and apparently also in Kwizu forest and Chambogo Catchment Forest Reserve (total for the two: 80 km²), in October–November 1992 (J. Fjeldså *in litt.* 1994). These forests are under human pressure (N. E. Baker *in litt.* 1994, J. Fjeldså *in litt.* 1994). **VULNERABLE: B1+2c; C2a.**

Taita White-eye *Zosterops silvanus* (whose distinctiveness as a species from Broad-ringed White-eye *Z. poliogaster* is supported by J. Fjeldså *in litt.* 1994) occurs in and adjacent to the tiny areas of forest (less than 3 km² in total) remaining on the Taita Hills and the similarly small forest on nearby Mount Kasigau, **Kenya**, where, despite being one of the most numerous birds of the Taitas (flock-sizes up to 30) and capable of foraging far from the forested areas, it almost certainly remains at risk from further degradation and removal of trees from the core of its small range (Collar and Stuart 1985, 1988, McGuigan 1987, Lewis and Pomeroy 1989). **CRITICAL: B1+2b,c**; C2b; D1; D2.

Mount Karthala White-eye *Zosterops mouroniensis* is restricted to although common in the single small area of *Philippia* heath woodland ringing the upper reaches of the actively volcanic Mount Karthala (1,750–2,600 m), Grand Comoro (= Ngazidja), **Comoro Islands**, where it is permanently vulnerable to and in fact 'very much threatened by' habitat degradation, particularly in the light of plans to build a road to the crater rim and in the absence of a proposed nature reserve (Collar and Stuart 1985, Louette *et al.* 1988, Louette and Stevens 1992, Safford and Evans 1992, Stevens *et al.* 1992). **CRITICAL: B1+ 2b,c**; C2b; D2.

São Tomé White-eye *Zosterops ficedulinus* is confined to forest on São Tomé and Príncipe, **São Tomé e Príncipe**, and was reported to have declined seriously on the latter, worryingly on the former (Collar and Stuart 1985). For reasons unknown, nominate *ficedulinus*, confined to Príncipe, has been rare this century, the only records being two or three collected in the 1920s and one seen in the 1970s (Jones and Tye in prep.; also Atkinson *et al.* 1991). On São Tomé the race *feae* shows fluctuations in either numbers or detectability, recent surveys concluding that it is uncommon, localized and at risk from clearance of high-altitude rainforest (Atkinson *et al*. 1991, Nadler 1993). **VULNERABLE: C2a.**

Annobon White-eye *Zosterops griseovirescens* is endemic to the very small (17 km²) Gulf of Guinea island of Annobon (**Equatorial Guinea**), where it is universally reported as abundant and occurring wherever bush- or tree-cover exists (see Collar and Stuart 1985), and its population may even be growing as vegetation is disturbed (Harrison 1990). **VULNERABLE: D2.**

Mauritius Olive White-eye *Zosterops chloronothos*, restricted to **Mauritius**, has long suffered from the destruction and (continuing) degradation of its habitat, and from nest predation by introduced mammals, so that, after 350 pairs were estimated in the mid-1970s, by the mid-1980s there were probably only some 275 pairs remaining, restricted to the wettest native upland forests in the south-west and centre of the island (Collar and Stuart 1985, Cheke 1987a). That population figure may have been over-optimistic (C. G. Jones *in litt*. 1987), and certainly by the start of the 1990s intensive fieldwork showed that only some 150 pairs survive, one-third of them in the 5 km² forested area between Piton Savanne, Montagne Cocotte and Bassin Blanc, now in the process of being acquired for inclusion within the Black River National Park (Safford 1991, R. J. Safford *in litt*. 1994). **CRITICAL: A1a; B1+2c; C2b; D1; D2.**

Seychelles White-eye *Zosterops modestus* occurs in three tiny areas, each less than 5 km² in extent, of mixed secondary forest between 300 and 600 m in central Mahé, **Seychelles**, where since the mid-1970s, when a population of c.100 was guessed, it appears to have been declining inexorably towards extinction for reasons unknown, although forestry and commercial tea-growing have been considered incompatible with the species' needs (Collar and Stuart 1985). There have been few more recent observations, all of which tend to suggest that the population is now only perhaps 20 pairs (Skerrett and Bullock 1992), apparently all located around the La Misère road and to the south (J. Watson *in litt*. 1994). Predation by an introduced species (rats are very common in these forests) needs very urgent consideration as a cause of decline (J. Stevenson verbally 1994). **CRITICAL: A1a; C1; C2b; D1; D2.**

Rota White-eye *Zosterops rotensis*, considered here as a full species on the basis of unpublished differences in plumage, vocalizations and behaviour (H. D. Pratt *in litt*. 1994), is endemic to the island of Rota (83 km²), northern **Mariana Islands (to U.S.A.)**, where it is restricted to native forest on the Sabana plateau region at c.400–490 m. It was considered uncommon by the 1960s, but was estimated to have a total population of 10,763 in 1982, with a possible 26% decline by 1987 and a further 87% decline by 1991, when the population estimate was 300–1,500 individuals; the introduced Black Drongo *Dicrurus macrocercus* is implicated in its decline (Craig and Taisacan 1994). **CRITICAL: A1a; A2d; B1+2d,e; C1; C2a; D1; D2.**

Ghizo White-eye *Zosterops luteirostris* is confined to Ghizo (37 km²), **Solomon Islands**, where it is still reasonably common in remaining forest in gullies and older secondary growth, although this latter is limited by the demand for agricultural land on this densely populated island (M. B. Iles *in litt*. 1993, Buckingham *et al*. in prep.). **VULNERABLE: D2.**

Lord Howe White-eye *Zosterops tephropleurus* is endemic to Lord Howe Island (17 km²) (**Australia**), where it occurs in all wooded habitats (Garnett 1992). It is widespread but, although it has adapted to the presence of black rats *Rattus rattus*, it could be threatened as a result of genetic swamping by the Silvereye *Z. lateralis* (with which it is sometimes regarded as conspecific), should the latter colonize the island (Garnett 1992) as it has Norfolk Island (see next species). **VULNERABLE: D2.**

Slender-billed White-eye *Zosterops tenuirostris* is endemic to **Norfolk Island (to Australia)**, less than 35 km², where it is moderately abundant occurring primarily in forests, forest remnants and tall secondary growth, and is thus dependent for its survival on the preservation of this habitat, which is centred today in the Norfolk Island National Park (Schodde *et al*. 1983). It interbred with the Silvereye *Z. lateralis* for the first ten years or so after the latter colonized the island, but this has now stopped and the two species are maintaining their own populations (Hermes 1985). **VULNERABLE: D2.**

White-chested White-eye *Zosterops albogularis* is confined to the remoter forests of the Norfolk Island National Park, **Norfolk Island (to Australia)**, where the last confirmed sighting dates from 1980, although residents on the island consistently report small numbers of birds fitting its description. The cause of its decline is predation by introduced black rats *Rattus rattus*, this threat being compounded by the clearing of the natural vegetation and invasion by exotic weeds, predation by cats and competition from the Silvereye *Z. lateralis* which colonized the island at the beginning of the twentieth century (Garnett 1992). **CRITICAL: D1**; D2.

Samoan White-eye *Zosterops samoensis* is endemic to Savaii, **Western Samoa**, where it occurs in the highlands above 900 m (Reed 1980) but has been recorded as low as 780 m (S. Ericsson *in litt.* 1994), and in 1987 was found to be not uncommon in flocks of 15–20 birds in the canopy of prime upland forests (Bellingham and Davis 1988) and again in 1991 after cyclone 'Ofa', when it was recorded in open scrub-like habitat (S. Ericsson *in litt.* 1994). It may have been affected by the early introduction of predators (B. D. Bell *in litt.* 1993) and could be threatened by the possible introduction (or colonization) of other white-eyes, e.g. Japanese White-eye *Z. japonicus* and Silvereye *Z. lateralis*, which have become established elsewhere on Pacific islands (Evans *et al.* 1992b), although given that *Z. japonicus* is only on Hawaii (i.e. a great distance away) and that *Z. lateralis* coexists (without problems) with Layard's White-eye *Z. explorator* (to which it is more closely related than *Z. samoensis*, both being native to Fiji), this seems unlikely (S. Ericsson *in litt.* 1994). **VULNERABLE: C2a; D2.**

Yap Olive White-eye *Zosterops oleagineus* is endemic to the islands of Yap (<100 km^2), **Micronesia**, where it is widely distributed in all types of forest and woody vegetation, including mangroves, and in 1991 was estimated to have a total population of 19,619 individuals and expected to remain common (Engbring *et al.* 1990). However, it could be declining as in the 1970s it could be readily found in any forest area, whilst more recently it appears to have become scarcer (H. D. Pratt *in litt.* 1994). **VULNERABLE: D2.**

Faichuk White-eye *Rukia ruki* has only been recorded from four islands in the Faichuk Group of the Chuuk (= Truk) lagoon, **Micronesia** (numbers in brackets after each island indicate birds seen in 1984): Tol South (382), Onei (19), Pata (32) and Polle (93), being confined mostly to old-growth stands of native forest, particularly the rich and well-developed forest above 400 m on Mount Winipot (Tol South), where the endemic poison tree *Semecarpus kraemeri* may play an important ecological role in its survival. The tree and, as a result, the white-eye may be under threat from the expanding human population (Engbring *et al.* 1990). **ENDANGERED: B1+2c; C2a; D1; D2.**

Golden White-eye *Cleptornis marchei* is endemic to Saipan (122 km^2), where it is abundant, and the even smaller Aguijan, where it is estimated to number 2,000, in the **Northern Mariana Islands (to U.S.A.)**, occurring in most habitats including urban areas (Pratt *et al.* 1987, D. W. Stinson *in litt.* 1994). It is very likely to be threatened by the brown tree snake *Boiga irregularis*, which has been recently introduced to Saipan (H. D. Pratt *in litt.* 1994). **VULNERABLE: A2d; D2.**

Rufous-throated White-eye *Madanga ruficollis* is endemic to Buru in the Moluccas, **Indonesia**, where it is known from four specimens which were collected between 850 and 1,550 m in the higher mountains of the western half of the island (White and Bruce 1986). There have been no documented records since the 1920s, owing to the lack of ornithological coverage of the island (BirdLife BPD). A one-month survey in 1989 did not visit the montane forests (Jepson 1993), but it is believed that these habitats are likely to remain secure (BirdLife IP). **VULNERABLE: D2.**

Family MELIPHAGIDAE
HONEYEATERS

Rotuma Myzomela *Myzomela chermesina*, endemic to Rotuma (50 km^2), **Fiji**, occupies forest edge and plantations (Pratt *et al.* 1987). **VULNERABLE: D2.**

Bonin Honeyeater *Apalopteron familiare* survives only on the tiny island of Haha-jima (race *hahasima*), and possibly its offshore islands, having

become extinct (nominate *familiare*) on Chichijima (although there were reports in 1987 that it may still exist there, or have been reintroduced) and apparently also on Muko-jima in the Ogasawara-shoto (= Bonin Islands), **Japan**; most primary forest has been cleared on Haha-jima, but the species has colonized low secondary forest, scrub, plantations and gardens, and is common (King 1978–1979, Sonobe 1982, Brazil 1991). **VULNERABLE: D2.**

Stitchbird *Notiomystis cincta* is a forest-dwelling species from **New Zealand** and is thought to have been exterminated from North Island as a result of predation, disease and collecting, surviving today only on small off-shore islands, including Hen, Kapiti and Cuvier (small numbers but may not persist because of the large variety of food sources required) and Little Barrier Island (4,000–5,000 individuals, the only self-sustaining population) (King 1978–1979, Williams and Given 1981, Angehr 1985, S. Clegg *in litt.* 1994). **VULNERABLE: D2.**

Long-bearded Melidectes *Melidectes princeps* occurs in the highlands of **Papua New Guinea** (Mount Giluwe, Mount Hagen, the Kubor Range, Mount Wilhelm and Mount Michael only), being recorded from mossy forest and copses near the treeline mostly between 3,000–3,800 m. It is fairly common (Beehler *et al.* 1986, Coates 1990), but thinly distributed and suffers disturbance to its limited habitat (J. M. Diamond *in litt.* 1987) which is patchy and dissected (B. M. Beehler *in litt.* 1994). **VULNERABLE: B1+2c,e; C2a.**

Mao *Gymnomyza samoensis* occurs in to the forests of Savaii and Upolu, **Western Samoa**, and Tutuila (last seen in 1977), American Samoa (Pratt *et al.* 1987). Good populations were recorded in 1987 (Bellingham and Davis 1988) but in 1991 it appeared to have become rarer on Savaii (S. Ericsson *in litt.* 1994) and it was not found during a three-day visit to Upolu in 1992 (H. D. Pratt *in litt.* 1994). It is likely to have suffered following the cyclones in 1990 and 1991, when canopy cover was reduced from 100% to 27% (Elmqvist 1993; see also Elmqvist *et al.* in press). **VULNERABLE: A1b; C2a.**

Crow Honeyeater *Gymnomyza aubryana* is endemic to dense forest and forest edge in **New Caledonia (to France)** where there are sparse, small populations in the south, mainly in the Rivière Bleue and Mount Humboldt regions (common in the Rivière Bleue Territorial Park); there are no data from the north, although it was formerly found in most hill and mountain forest (M. Boulet, F. Hannecart, Y. Létocart and S. Sirgouant *in litt.* 1993, H. Bregulla *in litt.* 1993). It is likely to be threatened by forest destruction for nickel mining (see Hannecart 1988). **VULNERABLE: B1+2c; C2b.**

Kauai Oo *Moho braccatus* is endemic to Kauai in the Hawaiian Islands (**U.S.A.**), where it was common in the 1890s in forests from sea-level to the highest elevations, declining drastically shortly after 1900 and confined to the Alakai Wilderness Preserve by the 1970s, declining further such that in 1985 only a few individuals were known to survive; habitat destruction and introduced disease-carrying mosquitoes in the lowlands are the probable causes of its demise (Scott *et al.* 1986, Pratt *et al.* 1987, Pratt 1993; see also Pratt 1994). **CRITICAL: A1a; B1+2c,e; C2b; D1; D2.**

Bishop's Oo *Moho bishopi*, from the Hawaiian Islands (**U.S.A.**), is known from Molokai, where it was last recorded in 1904 (treated as extinct by King 1978–1979), and Maui, where a single bird was observed in 1981 at 1,600–2,000 m in ohia forest on the north-eastern slope of Haleakala (Scott *et al.* 1986, Pratt *et al.* 1987). Habitat destruction and introduced disease-carrying mosquitoes in the lowlands are likely to have caused its decline (Pratt 1993; see also Pratt 1994). There have been subsequent reports from the 1980s but these are unconfirmed (R. Pyle verbally 1994). **CRITICAL: B1+2c,e; C2a; D1; D2.**

Painted Honeyeater *Grantiella picta*, a specialist feeder on the fruits of mistletoes growing on woodland eucalypts and acacias, is widespread but sparse (numbers fluctuate), distributed along inland slopes of the Great Dividing Range mainly from Victoria to northern Queensland, **Australia**. It may be gradually losing ground to the Mistletoebird *Dicaeum hirundinaceum*, with habitat clearance and lack of regeneration (as a result of grazing by rabbits and sheep) also contributing to its decline (Garnett 1992). **VULNERABLE: C2a.**

Regent Honeyeater *Xanthomyza phrygia* occurs in south-eastern **Australia** in temperate woodland and open forest, including forest edge, wooded farmland and urban areas with mature eucalypts; numbers probably started to decline in the 1920s and today the total population may be fewer than 1,000 birds (Garnett 1992). It is dependent on a rich nectar source and differs in this respect from the other large honeyeaters (Red Wattlebirds *Anthochaera carunculata* and Noisy Friarbirds *Philemon corniculatus*), which feed their young almost entirely on insects or manna (honey dew, secreted by insects). Loss and fragmentation of habitat may have blurred honeyeater niches, forcing several species into remaining fragments, and especially affecting the Regent Honeyeater (which is most dependent on habitat on the richest soils), so that today it cannot reach sufficient numbers in nesting aggregations to share the effort of excluding other birds from nectar sources (Ford *et al.* 1993). **ENDANGERED: C2a; D1.**

Black-eared Miner *Manorina melanotis* occurred in mature mallee woodland in north-western Victoria, south-eastern South Australia, and some parts of south-western New South Wales, **Australia**, but is now restricted to seven sites in north-western Victoria, where it is being genetically swamped by the Yellow-throated Miner *M. flavigula* (and is included with this species by Sibley and Monroe 1990, 1993) as its habitat is lost through clearance and wildfires; at the start of the 1990s there were probably less than 20 pure individuals (Garnett 1992). **CRITICAL:** B1+2e; **C2a**; **D1**.

Subfamily EMBERIZINAE

BUNTINGS

Rufous-backed Bunting *Emberiza jankowskii* breeds in low hills and valleys with sparse vegetation in Jilin and Heilongjiang, north-east **China**, southern Ussuriland, extreme south-east **Russia** and northern **North Korea**, with non-breeding records to the south in south-east Inner Mongolia, Liaoning and Hebei, eastern China (Meyer de Schauensee 1984, Cheng 1987). It was formerly locally not uncommon in Russia (Dement'ev and Gladkov 1970), but surveys of its historical range have failed to locate any (Knystautas 1993), in China there are recent records from only a few localities (BirdLife BPD), and there is no information on its current status in North Korea. The reasons for its apparent decline in Russia are unknown. **VULNERABLE:** C1; C2a.

Socotra Bunting *Emberiza socotrana* is restricted to the island of Socotra, **Yemen**, where it has been recorded from lowland plains, upland thickets and the bleak Hajhir peaks at 1,200–1,500 m, preferring thicket and scrub but also occurring on narrow rock-face ledges and open slopes, non-breeding flocks descending to forage at low altitudes (Ripley and Bond 1966); however, in 1993 it proved the rarest of the endemic birds of the island, with only two individuals being observed (Martins *et al.* 1993, R. F. Porter *in litt.* 1994), possibly in part as a consequence of being confined by competition with the Cinnamon-breasted Bunting *E. tahapisi* to slightly moister areas (Ripley and Bond 1966). **VULNERABLE:** D1.

Yellow Bunting *Emberiza sulphurata* is an uncommon and very local breeding visitor to northern and central Honshu, and possibly Kyushu, **Japan**, where it occurs in deciduous and mixed deciduous and coniferous forests in the lower mountains from about 600 to 1,500 m (WBSJ 1978, Sonobe 1982, H. Higuchi *in litt.* 1989, Brazil 1991). It has occurred on passage and in winter in **North Korea**, **South Korea**, eastern **China** (Jiangsu, Fujian and Guangdong: Cheng 1987), **Hong Kong (to U.K.)**, **Taiwan** and the **Philippines** (uncommon in winter in scrub, pine forest and cultivated areas: Dickinson *et al.* 1991) (Inskipp and Collins 1993). There is evidence that it has declined significantly over the past hundred years in Japan (Brazil 1991), but the causes are unknown. **VULNERABLE:** C1; C2a.

Guadalupe Junco *Junco insularis* was once amongst the most abundant birds on Guadalupe Island, 280 km west of Baja California, **Mexico**, but is now scattered along the northern half of the island wherever vegetation occurs, and the total population may only be 100 birds; chronic overgrazing of vegetation has been a major threat, recently solved by the removal of 20,000 goats from the island, but feral cats remain and represent a likely source of mortality (Collar *et al.* 1992). **CRITICAL: B1+2e; C2b; D1; D2.**

Sierra Madre Sparrow *Xenospiza baileyi*, originally known from three disjunct mountainous bunchgrass (zacatón) areas (roughly 2,400–3,000 m) in Durango, Jalisco and around the Distrito Federal, **Mexico**, now appears to be confined in very small numbers to the dwindling expanse of this specialized habitat near México City which, although afforded some official protection, is still subjected to widespread burning and cattle-grazing (Collar *et al.* 1992). **ENDANGERED:** A1a; **B1+2c; C1; C2a; D1**.

Worthen's Sparrow *Spizella wortheni*, although first described from New Mexico, U.S.A., in the last century, has subsequently only ever been reported from **Mexico**, in eight states in the north-east, with records in the last 30 years only from Coahuila and Nuevo León, and in the last 10 years from only two small areas (maximum wintering flock sizes 120 and 40 respectively, both in late 1986). It appears to have contracted its range in response to widespread and continuing conversion of its shrubby (mesquite or yucca–juniper) grassland habitat (Wege *et al.* 1993). **ENDANGERED:** B1+2c; **C2a**; D1.

Cuban Sparrow *Torreornis inexpectata* occurs

as three racially distinct populations in **Cuba**, in a small area of the Zapata Swamp (nominate *inexpectata*, somewhat more than 250 birds in areas of scrub grassland), on Cayo Coco in the Camagüey archipelago (race *varonai*, numerous within its very restricted range, in semi-deciduous forest, coastal xerophytic thorn-scrub and mangrove) and on a small stretch of the south-east coast in Guantánamo (race *sigmani*, 110–200 breeding birds, in hot dry scrub); each population faces a different threat, with the Zapata Swamp exposed to drainage and burning, Cayo Coco being developed as a tourist centre, and the Guantánamo coast vulnerable to burning and consequent grass invasion, and being fenced for sheep-rearing (Collar *et al.* 1992). **ENDANGERED:** A2b; **B1+2c**; **C1**; **C2a**; D1; D2.

Yellow-headed Brush-finch *Atlapetes flaviceps*

is endemic to the Central Andes of **Colombia** (Tolima and Huila), where it is known from four specimens taken in 1911 and 1942, a bird mist-netted in 1967, and a population discovered in 1989 (total number of localities three, spanning 1,300–2,255 m); clearance of most of the natural vegetation within its limited range seems likely to have caused a population decline, although at the only modern locality known it seems to survive well in thick secondary vegetation, especially when vines and remnant forest trees remain (Collar *et al.* 1992). **ENDANGERED:** B1+2a,c; C1; **C2a**.

Pale-headed Brush-finch *Atlapetes pallidiceps*

has been found at oases in the arid intermontane valleys at elevations ranging from 1,500 to 2,100 m in southern **Ecuador** (Azuay, Loja), but there have been no records since 1969, despite repeated and often intensive searches. The human pressure on areas with water in this region is great, and if the species is not extinct it can survive only in small patches of shrubbery bordering streams and irrigated farmland (Collar *et al.* 1992). **CRITICAL:** A1b; **B1+2c**; **C2b**; D1; D2.

Yellow-green Finch *Pselliophorus luteoviridis*

occupies a very restricted range in the highland cloud-forest, borders and clearings (1,200–1,800 m) of eastern Chiriquí (Cerro Flores and Cerro Colorado) and Veraguas (Santa Fe and Chitra), **Panama**, where it is

scarce and poorly known (Ridgely and Gwynne 1989, R. S. Ridgely *in litt.* 1994). **VULNERABLE:** D2.

Yellow Cardinal *Gubernatrix cristata* was for-

merly very widespread and common in open woodland, scrub and shrubby steppes throughout much of **Argentina** (Salta, Formosa, Chaco, Misiones, Tucumán, Santiago del Estero, Corrientes, Santa Fe, Entre Ríos, La Rioja, San Juan, Córdoba, San Luis, Buenos Aires, La Pampa, Río Negro) and **Uruguay**, with outlying populations in **Paraguay** (possibly now extinct) and southernmost **Brazil** (Rio Grande do Sul), but has been trapped intensively as a cagebird for over a century (possibly also suffering from conversion of habitat to cattle pasture), and is now rare everywhere except very locally in the southern parts of its range, and without urgent intervention total numbers could become extremely low in the near future (Collar *et al.* 1992, Pearman and Abadie in press). **ENDANGERED:** A1a,c; A2c; C1; C2a.

Tanager-finch *Oreothraupis arremonops* lives at

low density in the thick undergrowth of primary humid forest (mostly dense wet mossy cloud-forest) at 1,200–2,600 m in a patchy distribution through the West Andes of **Colombia** (Antioquia, Valle, Cauca, Nariño) into north-west **Ecuador** (Imbabura, Pichincha); much deforestation has occurred, but other reasons for its apparent rarity remain unknown (Collar *et al.* 1992). However, recent observations in primary forest on the western slopes in Cauca have suggested the species can be fairly frequent, generally at 2,300–2,500 m (A. J. Negret *in litt.* 1994). **VULNERABLE:** C2a.

Black-masked Finch *Coryphaspiza melanotis*

has been recorded in tall grasslands extending from south-east **Peru** east across northern **Bolivia** into central and south-east **Brazil** (Mato Grosso do Sul, Mato Grosso, Goiás, Minas Gerais, São Paulo) south through eastern **Paraguay** into northern **Argentina**; extensive conversion of its habitat has caused it to become extremely local and rare (Ridgely and Tudor 1989, D. F. Stotz *in litt.* 1994), and for example in extensive fieldwork in Corrientes, Argentina, during the early 1990s, when many other very rare grassland species were encountered and studied, this bird could not be found even in good habitat at former sites (Pearman and Abadie in press). **VULNERABLE:** A1b.

Gough Bunting *Rowettia goughensis* is endemic

to Gough Island in the **Tristan da Cunha group (to U.K.)**, South Atlantic Ocean, where its 200 pairs are permanently at risk from the introduction of mammalian predators (Collar and Stuart 1985). However, a report of a rat on the island is now judged to have been a large mouse, and precautions at the station remain very stringent (Cooper and Ryan 1994, J. Cooper *in litt.* 1991). **VULNERABLE:** D1; D2.

Tristan Bunting *Nesospiza acunhae* occurs widely on Inaccessible (13 km²) and Nightingale (3 km²) plus the smaller Middle and Stoltenhoff Islands in the **Tristan da Cunha group (to U.K.)**, South Atlantic Ocean, where its populations (although totalling several thousands) remain at risk from the introduction of mammalian predators, having become extinct on Tristan itself (Collar and Stuart 1985). Analysis of work done in 1983 indicates some 5,000 birds (nominate *acunhae*) on Inaccessible, divided into two (upland and lowland) forms (Fraser and Briggs 1992). Numbers of race *questi* on Nightingale are unknown, but must be smaller (see Collar and Stuart 1985). **VULNERABLE:** D2.

Grosbeak Bunting *Nesospiza wilkinsi* is restricted to *Phylica* woodland on Inaccessible (13 km²) and Nightingale (3 km²) Islands in the **Tristan da Cunha group (to U.K.)**, South Atlantic Ocean, with a total population in the low hundreds permanently at risk from the introduction of mammalian predators (also seed-predators) and the loss of its habitat (Collar and Stuart 1985). Analysis of work done in 1983 indicates some 500 birds (race *dunnei*) on Inaccessible, fewer (nominate *wilkinsi*) on Nightingale (Fraser and Briggs 1992). **VULNERABLE:** D1; D2.

Slender-billed Finch *Xenospingus concolor* is confined to and generally rare (common at a few sites) in (at least) 12 scattered river valleys and coastal lagoons in the desert on the Pacific slope from central **Peru** (Lima, Ica, Arequipa, Moquagua) to northern **Chile** (Tarapacá, Antofagasta), where it inhabits riparian shrubbery, mainly at low elevations, but locally up to nearly 2,300 m; any change in land use in these almost completely (and already very intensively) cultivated valleys (e.g. clearance of the few remaining humid willow thickets) could severely affect the species (Collar *et al.* 1992). **VULNERABLE:** A2b; B1+2c; C1; C2a.

Plain-tailed Warbling-finch *Poospiza alticola* occupies shrubby forest and mixed *Polylepis–Gynoxys* woodland at 3,200–4,300 m in western **Peru** (Cajamarca, La Libertad, Ancash), and at least in some areas it appears to be a *Gynoxys* (Compositae) specialist, feeding on sugary secretions and insects beneath its leaves. It appears naturally scarce with a very small total population, which must be declining as its woodland habitat is steadily destroyed (Collar *et al.* 1992). **ENDANGERED:** B1+2c; C1; **C2a**; D1.

Rufous-breasted Warbling-finch *Poospiza rubecula* has been found at a few scattered localities at elevations ranging from 2,500 to 3,700 m in western **Peru** (Cajamarca, La Libertad, Ancash, Lima), where it occurs at very low density (the total population is very small) in composite scrub, woodland and dry scrub-forest adjacent to *Polylepis* woodland, and is at risk from the steady loss of these habitats (Collar *et al.* 1992). The tiny Bosque de Zárate in Lima may be an important breeding site (Barrio 1994). **ENDANGERED:** B1+2c; C1; **C2a**; D1.

Cochabamba Mountain-finch *Poospiza garleppi* is restricted to the mountain slopes surrounding Cochabamba city, Cochabamba, **Bolivia**, where it inhabits a variety of dense, often thorny bushes and thickets, chiefly between 3,000 and 3,800 m, but the burning of slopes to stimulate the regrowth of grass has confined most such vegetation to watered ravines, and the cutting of *Polylepis* may be a further threat (Collar *et al.* 1992). **ENDANGERED: B1+2c**; C1; **C2b**; D1.

Tucumán Mountain-finch *Poospiza baeri* is confined to dense scrub in semi-humid steep-sided ravines at 2,000–3,000 m in a small area of mountain slopes in north-western **Argentina** (Jujuy, Salta, Tucumán, Catamarca, La Rioja), where it is known from relatively few localities; some of these localities are relatively accessible (with a consequent danger of burning or even trapping), and the total population may be extremely small (Collar *et al.* 1992). **VULNERABLE:** D1.

Buffy-fronted Seedeater *Sporophila frontalis* has become very patchily distributed and much reduced from its former numbers as a result of the widespread and continuing clearance of Atlantic Forest (perhaps combined with trade) in south-east **Brazil**, where records exist for Espírito Santo, Minas Gerais, Rio de Janeiro (whence the majority of modern records), São Paulo, reputedly Paraná and Santa Catarina and formerly Rio Grande do Sul, formerly **Paraguay** and very rarely **Argentina**; as a bamboo specialist it is nomadic, and appears to suffer even with moderate deforestation (Collar *et al.* 1992). **ENDANGERED: A1b**; A2b; **C1**; **C2b**.

Temminck's Seedeater *Sporophila falcirostris* is a bamboo specialist within the Atlantic Forest belt of south-east **Brazil** (Bahia, Espírito Santo, Minas Gerais, Rio de Janeiro, São Paulo, Paraná), eastern **Paraguay** and northern **Argentina** (Misiones), and as a consequence is nomadic, difficult to find (and to protect in any one area) and probably genuinely rare, suffering from trapping for the cagebird trade as well as from the loss of its habitat (Collar *et al.* 1992). **ENDANGERED: A1b**; A2b; **C1**; **C2b**.

Hooded Seedeater *Sporophila melanops* is known from a single specimen taken at a lake 15 km north of Registro do Araguaia, on the east bank of the Rio Araguaia in extreme central-western Goiás, **Brazil**, in October 1823 (Collar *et al.* 1992). **VULNERABLE: D1**.

Black-and-tawny Seedeater *Sporophila nigrorufa* appears to be certainly known as yet from only five areas in extreme eastern **Bolivia** (Santa Cruz) and adjacent west-central **Brazil** (Mato Grosso, Mato Grosso do Sul), being at risk (heightened by its possible nomadism) from extensive and continuing conversion of its campo grassland habitat to agriculture (Collar *et al.* 1992). **ENDANGERED: A1b**; A2b.

Marsh Seedeater *Sporophila palustris* appears to be extremely local despite its vast range in the marshes, reedbeds and grasslands of **Brazil** (Minas Gerais, Goiás, Mato Grosso, Mato Grosso do Sul, Rio Grande do Sul), **Paraguay**, **Uruguay** and **Argentina** (Misiones, Corrientes, Entre Ríos, Buenos Aires); high trade pressure and the extensive and continuing conversion (or at least encroachment by cattle) of its wet grassland habitat lie behind its decline (Collar *et al.* 1992, Pearman and Abadie in press). **ENDANGERED: A1b,c**; A2b,c; C1; C2a.

Entre Ríos Seedeater *Sporophila zelichi* is restricted as a breeding bird to a small part of Entre Ríos province, **Argentina**, wintering in areas unknown, and may be at considerable risk from bird-

trappers (to whom it is well known in Entre Ríos, being highly prized locally) as well as from the burning of its summer habitat (grasslands and reedbeds); only tiny numbers—a few mostly isolated pairs—have ever been found in the wild (Collar *et al.* 1992, Pearman and Abadie in press). **CRITICAL: A2b,c**; B1+2c,e; **C1**; **C2b**; D1.

Tumaco Seedeater *Sporophila insulata* is known solely from four birds collected in 1912, probably in open, grassy and shrubby areas, on the low-lying inshore island of Tumaco, south-west **Colombia**, a site now so heavily developed that it seems doubtful whether it still survives there (Collar *et al.* 1992). **CRITICAL: D1**.

Mangrove Finch *Camarhynchus heliobates* is restricted to dense mangrove swamps on eastern Fernandina, and at Cartago Bay and between Punta Tortuga and Punta Moreno on Isabela, in the Galápagos Islands, **Ecuador**; potential suitable habitat on the two islands totals a mere 0.5 km², and total numbers have been estimated at 100–200 birds, but neither habitat nor population is believed to be declining (Collar *et al.* 1992). **ENDANGERED: D1**; D2.

Cocos Finch *Pinaroloxias inornata* occupies every available habitat on the 47 km² Cocos Island, **Costa Rica**; it is abundant in *Hibiscus* thickets along coasts, sparser in wet highland forests (Stiles and Skutch 1989). The island is a national park, although there are rats and cats present, and overgrazing by introduced deer, pigs and goats is occurring (Slud 1967, Smith and Sweatman 1976; T. W. Sherry *in litt.* 1985). **VULNERABLE: D2**.

Subfamily CARDINALINAE
CARDINAL-GROSBEAKS

Rufous-bellied Saltator *Saltator rufiventris* is confined to the temperate zone of central **Bolivia** (La Paz, Cochabamba, Chuquisaca; common at a few sites, scarce at most), and in north-west **Argentina** (Jujuy, Salta; very few records, status unknown), perhaps feeding predominantly on mistletoe berries

in *Polylepis* and *Alnus* woodlands, which are now highly fragmented within most of its range (Collar *et al.* 1992). However, recent fieldwork in Bolivia suggests that the species occurs in many localities, and may be missed owing to its unusually unobtrusive habits (S. Mayer *in litt.* 1994). **VULNERABLE: C2a**.

Subfamily THRAUPINAE

TANAGERS

Cone-billed Tanager *Conothraupis mesoleuca* remains known only from a single specimen collected in 1938 in dry forest (transitional to Amazonian rainforest) apparently about 400 km north-west of Cuiabá, Mato Grosso, **Brazil**. It must at best be rare and local, although no threats can be identified (Collar *et al*. 1992). **VULNERABLE: D1.**

Yellow-green Bush-tanager *Chlorospingus flavovirens* is known from only two areas in northwest **Ecuador** (Pichincha, Esmeraldas) and three in south-west **Colombia** (two in Valle, one in Nariño), where it occurs in humid moss-forest at 500–1,100 m; at one of the sites in Valle it is common, but at the site in Nariño it is uncommon and local (but probably overlooked), and generally it is threatened by habitat destruction on the Pacific slope of the Andes (Collar *et al*. 1992, Salaman and Gandy 1993, 1994). **VULNERABLE: C2a; D2.**

Slaty-backed Hemispingus *Hemispingus goeringi* is a locally common cloud-forest specialist of the south-western half of the Cordillera de Mérida, western **Venezuela** (Táchira, Mérida), where it has been recorded from just four discrete areas between 2,600 and 3,200 m; although habitat destruction has mainly been concentrated in areas too low for the bird, montane forests have been adversely affected (Collar *et al*. 1992). **VULNERABLE: B1+2c; C1; C2a.**

Cherry-throated Tanager *Nemosia rourei* is known from the nineteenth-century type-specimen from south-eastern Minas Gerais, **Brazil**, and a 1941 sighting from adjacent Espírito Santo, and could now be extinct given the deforestation and the high level of ornithological coverage (which has repeatedly drawn a blank) at the forested sites in the region (Collar *et al*. 1992). **CRITICAL: D1.**

Chat-tanager *Calyptophilus frugivorus*, a largely terrestrial feeder, chiefly eating invertebrates (despite its name), occurs in four races in Hispaniola (**Haiti** and the **Dominican Republic**). It is everywhere at risk from the clearance of its (commonly broadleaf) forest habitat, most notably the races *abbotti* from Gonave Island (Haiti) and nominate *frugivorus* from lowland north-east Dominican Republic. The two mainland montane races (*tertius* in southern Haiti and south-west Dominican Republic, and *neiba* in the latter's Cordillera Central) retain some security in certain protected areas (but these need support and others need establishment) (Collar *et al*. 1992). **VULNERABLE: A1b; C1; C2a.**

Black-cheeked Ant-tanager *Habia atrimaxillaris* is restricted to a small area of south-west **Costa Rica**, on the Osa peninsula and around the Golfo Dulce (Puntarenas), inhabiting the understorey of dense lowland forest, advanced secondary growth, streamside woodland and occasionally selectively logged forest (Slud 1964, Isler and Isler 1987). It is locally common, but is becoming increasingly scarce as its habitat is reduced, and it may well become confined to the Corcovado National Park (on the Osa peninsula) in a short period (Stiles and Skutch 1989). **VULNERABLE: B1+2c; C1; C2b.**

Black-and-gold Tanager *Bangsia melanochlamys* occurs at 1,000–2,285 m in subtropical humid cloud-forest in two disjunct areas of western **Colombia**, namely on the north and west slopes of the Central Andes in Antioquia, where it has not been recorded since 1948, and on the western slopes of the West Andes in Chocó, Risaralda and Valle, where it survives (showing what are apparently seasonal fluctuations in abundance, from rare to common) in and around Cerro Tatamá and Mistrató, including Alto de Pisones; birds have been recorded foraging in secondary habitats, but probably cannot persist without primary forest, which is diminishing in parts of its range and almost everywhere below 1,500 m (Collar *et al*. 1992). **ENDANGERED: B1+2c; C1; C2a.**

Gold-ringed Tanager *Bangsia aureocincta* was until recently known from just four specimens collected in or before 1946 in humid, mossy cloud-forest on Cerro Tatamá (at 2,040–2,195 m), on the Pacific slope of the West Andes, **Colombia** (boundary of Risaralda, Chocó and Valle), where it appears to be at best rare and at risk from continuing habitat loss; but in 1992 a healthy population was discovered at Alto de Pisones (at 1,600–1,800 m), some 40 km north of this area in Risaralda, although the area is isolated by deforestation at lower altitudes (Collar *et al*. 1992). **VULNERABLE: B1+2c; C1.**

Golden-backed Mountain-tanager *Buthraupis aureodorsalis* inhabits (and is apparently very uncommon within) three areas of currently undisturbed and remote elfin forest at 3,050–3,500 m in the departments of San Martín, La Libertad and Huánuco, north-central **Peru** (Collar *et al.* 1992). VULNERABLE: D2.

Masked Mountain-tanager *Buthraupis wetmorei* inhabits very humid páramo–forest ecotones (2,900–3,550 m, though possibly higher before the treeline was lowered by human activities) in the Andes of eastern **Ecuador** (Carchi, Azuay, Morona-Santiago, Loja, Zamora-Chinchipe) and immediately adjacent **Peru** (Piura) and **Colombia** (Cauca), but it is generally rare and declining as the ubiquitous tradition of burning páramo grassland has almost completely destroyed its habitat (Collar *et al.* 1992). VULNERABLE: A1b; A2b; B1+2c; C1; C2a.

Orange-throated Tanager *Wetmorethraupis sterrhopteron* is only known from one locality in Zamora-Chinchipe province, **Ecuador**, and northern Amazonas department, **Peru**, inhabiting (and moderately common within) mature humid forest in the upper tropical zone, at elevations (600–1,000 m) where the forested slopes are not steep or wet, and are therefore ideal for cultivation by settlers following current road construction programmes (Collar *et al.* 1992). ENDANGERED: A2b; C1; C2b.

Multicoloured Tanager *Chlorochrysa nitidissima*, formerly common but now relatively unusual to find, occurs chiefly between 1,300 and 2,195 m in the West but also to a lesser extent (two records since 1951, in 1991 and 1993, both in Ucumarí Regional Park) in the Central Andes of **Colombia** (Antioquia, Caldas, Risaralda, Quindío, Valle and Cauca), where it is threatened in places by the fragmentation of its humid, mossy, montane forest habitat in the subtropical zone (Collar *et al.* 1992, Salaman and Gandy 1993, A. J. Negret *in litt.* 1994). VULNERABLE: C1.

Azure-rumped Tanager *Tangara cabanisi* is endemic to and rare in the Sierra Madre de Chiapas, **Mexico**, and neighbouring areas of **Guatemala**, where it is restricted to humid evergreen forest in a narrow elevational band (chiefly 1,250–1,650 m) primarily on the Pacific slope, in the very habitat and at the preferred height for coffee cultivation. In Mexico, suitable remaining forest covers less than 1,300 km^2, while in Guatemala there may be only one area for the species (Collar *et al.* 1992). ENDANGERED: A2b; B1+2c; C1; C2a; D1.

Seven-coloured Tanager *Tangara fastuosa* remains reasonably numerous at a few localities in north-east **Brazil** (Paraíba, Pernambuco, Alagoas),

but is exposed to the twin threats of habitat loss (although it seems to prefer tall second growth, there is great regional pressure to clear land completely for agriculture) and heavy exploitation for trade (it commands high prices owing to its exceptional plumage); a considerable decline has occurred this century (Collar *et al.* 1992). ENDANGERED: A1b,c; **A2b,c**; B1+2c; C1; C2a.

Black-backed Tanager *Tangara peruviana*, although moderately common in some localities, faces serious difficulties from the rapid and widespread loss (largely to beachfront housing) of its coastal sandplain forest (restinga) habitat in south-east **Brazil** (Rio de Janeiro as a winter visitor from April to September, São Paulo, Paraná, Santa Catarina up to the 1930s) (Collar *et al.* 1992). Some birds appear to be resident in São Paulo, although there are fewer from November to February. The habitat in both Rio and Paraná is largely destroyed now, so that São Paulo is now its stronghold (P. Martuscelli verbally 1994). ENDANGERED: A1b; **A2b**; B1+2c; C1; C2b.

Green-capped Tanager *Tangara meyerdeschauenseei* is known from three sites in the arid region at the headwaters of Río Inambari in Puno, south-east **Peru**, where it inhabits forest edge, riverine scrub and gardens in the subtropical zone (records so far are between 1,750 and 2,180 m, but the species probably ranges beyond both these limits) (Collar *et al.* 1992). Sightings in 1990 along the Río Machariapo to the north of Apolo, north-west Bolivia (Parker and Bailey 1991), were viewed with some doubt (T. A. Parker *per* A. Perry verbally 1994), and later searches of the area have drawn a blank (M. Pearman verbally 1994, A. Perry verbally 1994). VULNERABLE: D2.

Turquoise Dacnis *Dacnis hartlaubi* is endemic to **Colombia** (Valle, Quindío and Cundinamarca, all post-1980 records coming from this last), with a very restricted and fragmented distribution in all three Andean ranges (most records falling between 1,350 and 2,200 m), and its already sparse population may be declining further in response to the continuing clearance of its humid forest habitat (Collar *et al.* 1992). VULNERABLE: A1b; B1+2c; C1; C2a.

Black-legged Dacnis *Dacnis nigripes* has been found in primary and tall secondary lowland and montane Atlantic forest (0–1,700 m) throughout coastal south-east **Brazil** (Espírito Santo in 1942, Rio de Janeiro, São Paulo, Paraná possibly, and Santa Catarina before 1935), but always very sparsely except when occasionally concentrating at a fruiting tree (which indicates somewhat unpredictable or irregular movements, in turn indicating complex year-round requirements involving some altitudinal displacements); loss of sand-plain forest in part of São Paulo threatens its winter status there, but it is perhaps at greater risk from the (illegal) cagebird trade, which prizes it for its rarity (Collar *et al.* 1992). It is present at the confidential (but rapidly disappearing) site for Black-hooded Antwren *Formicivora erythronotos* at Angra dos Reis, Rio de Janeiro (G. Sangster *in litt.* 1994). **VULNERABLE:** C1.

Scarlet-breasted Dacnis *Dacnis berlepschi* has been judged restricted to wet lowland and foothill forest edge and tall second growth (0–1,200 m) in south-west **Colombia** (Pacific slope of south-west Nariño) and north-west **Ecuador** (Esmeraldas, Imbabura, Pichincha), where it is apparently (or perhaps nowadays) rare and localized, and (particularly if it breeds only at low elevations) must be threatened by the extensive and chronic forest destruction within its range (Collar *et al.* 1992); however, failure

to find it in primary forest within its range in 1991–1994 and reconsideration of the evidence have suggested that the species may prefer degraded and fragmented forest (Salaman and Gandy 1994; also R. P. Clay *in litt.* 1994). **VULNERABLE:** C1.

Venezuelan Flowerpiercer *Diglossa venezuelensis* is restricted to montane forests (cloud-forest, forest edge, second growth) of the coastal Cordillera de Caripe (1,525–2,450 m) and Paria peninsula (885 m) in north-east **Venezuela** (Sucre, Monagas), possibly having specialized habitat requirements (e.g. an association with the ecotone between herbaceous vegetation and *Clusia*-dominated forest) which render it even more vulnerable to the widespread degradation and loss of forest in this area (Collar *et al.* 1992). Evidence from recent records strongly suggests that it is now an extremely rare and highly restricted species (D. C. Wege verbally 1994). **CRITICAL:** A1b; **A2b**; B1+2c; C1; C2a; D1.

Family PARULIDAE

NEW WORLD WARBLERS

Bachman's Warbler *Vermivora bachmani* was recorded as a breeding bird in seasonally flooded swamp-forest, apparently showing a strong association with canebrakes of the bamboo *Arundinaria gigantea*, in Missouri, Arkansas, Kentucky, Alabama and South Carolina, **U.S.A.**, birds wintering in **Cuba** and occasionally Florida. The near-total clearance of canebrakes in the U.S.A., and the conversion of much of Cuba to sugarcane plantation, offer the best explanation for the disappearance and possible extinction of the species, whose last nest was found in 1937 and whose last (unconfirmed) sighting was in 1988 (Collar *et al.* 1992). **CRITICAL:** D1.

Golden-cheeked Warbler *Dendroica chrysoparia* breeds in ashe juniper–oak woodland in Texas, **U.S.A.**, and winters in various habitats, chiefly pine or pine–oak but also lower montane and tropical broadleaf forest, in southernmost **Mexico**, **Guatemala**, **Honduras** and **Nicaragua**; following the loss of 50% of its breeding habitat since 1950, compounded by increasing rates of brood-parasitism by the Brown-headed Cowbird *Molothrus ater*, total numbers, judged at least to be 15,000 in 1974, were

put in 1992 at 2,200–4,600 (Collar *et al.* 1992). **ENDANGERED:** A1b,d; A2d; C1; C2a.

Kirtland's Warbler *Dendroica kirtlandii* breeds in level or gently rolling homogeneous stands of jack pines *Pinus banksiana* 2–4 m tall (a condition only occurring naturally after extensive fires) in a small area of central Michigan, also in Wisconsin, **U.S.A.**, and occasionally in Ontario and Quebec, **Canada**, wintering in the **Bahamas** and the **Turks and Caicos Islands (to U.K.)**. Currently, as a result of forest management policies, there remain only 18 km² of suitable breeding habitat (a 33% decline since the 1960s), while extensive brood-parasitism by the Brown-headed Cowbird *Molothrus ater* has caused massive breeding failure and requires constant human intervention to remedy (Collar *et al.* 1992). The population in 1994 was surveyed at 633 singing males (up from 485 in 1993), all in Michigan (Weinrich 1994). **VULNERABLE:** D1; D2.

Whistling Warbler *Catharopeza bishopi* occurs in primary rainforest and palm brakes, plus elfin forest, second growth and borders, at 300–600 m on

St Vincent, West Indies, where as few as 1,500 mature individuals and as many as 5,000 may survive in the remaining habitat, now greatly reduced to c.80 km² in extent (Curson 1994). **VULNERABLE:** D2.

Belding's Yellowthroat *Geothlypis beldingi* occupies reeds, cattails and tule fringing permanent lowland freshwater marshes and rivers on the Baja California peninsula, **Mexico**, where nominate race *beldingi* survives at one small marsh (less than 10 ha) near San José and the race *goldmani* remains common at two and possibly four localities to the north, both forms having suffered from drainage and drought (Curson 1994; also P. Escalante *in litt.* 1988, verbally 1994). **VULNERABLE:** A1b; A2b; B1+2c.

Black-polled Yellowthroat *Geothlypis speciosa* is restricted to the river and lake marshes of central **Mexico** (Guanajuato, Michoacán, México), and, although common in suitable habitat (cattails and hard-stemmed bulrushes), extensive wetland drainage has resulted in a number of populations becoming extinct and others becoming endangered (Collar *et al.* 1992). **VULNERABLE:** A1b; A2b; B1+2c; C1; C2a.

Semper's Warbler *Leucopeza semperi* is an extremely rare and very possibly extinct denizen of montane forest undergrowth on **St Lucia** that has eluded almost all twentieth-century efforts to find a population, there being just a handful of records since the 1920s and none certain since 1972 (one unconfirmed sighting in 1989); its disappearance may be related to the introduction of the mongoose in 1884, although habitat loss may have played a part (Collar *et al.* 1992, Curson 1994). **CRITICAL:** D1.

Paria Whitestart *Myioborus pariae* is restricted to the cloud-forests (lower and upper montane rainforest) of the Paria peninsula in Sucre, north-eastern **Venezuela** (recorded from 800 to 1,150 m on Cerro Humo, proportionately lower further east, where mountains themselves only reach 920 m); although common within a range that falls almost entirely within the Paria Peninsula National Park, its total population must be very small and its habitat is under great threat from agricultural encroachment (possibly as little as 15 km² remaining on Cerro Humo) and other developments (Collar *et al.* 1992). In February 1993 all birds seen were on the edge of or in clearings in primary forest, or in second growth adjacent to plantations, with none in undisturbed forest, confirming that the habitat and numbers must indeed be tiny (J. Curson *in litt.* 1993). **CRITICAL:** A1b; A2b; **B1+2c**; C1; C2a; D1; D2.

Guaiquinima Whitestart *Myioborus cardonai* occupies cloud-forest between 1,200 and 1,600 m on Cerro Guaiquinima, west-central Bolívar, **Venezuela**; the mountain rises to 1,800 m, and has a talus slope area of only 110 km² (Mayr and Phelps 1967, Meyer de Schauensee and Phelps 1978, Ridgely and Tudor 1989). **VULNERABLE:** D2.

Grey-headed Warbler *Basileuterus griseiceps* occupies a small range (350 km², with records from 1,200 to 2,440 m) in the montane forests (cloud-forest, second growth) of the coastal Cordillera de Caripe in Anzoátegui, Monagas and Sucre, northeast **Venezuela**, and is currently known from just two areas (one of them Cerro Negro, and both within El Guácharo National Park). The forests in this region are, however, being extensively degraded and depleted, and the situation on Cerro Negro is critical (Collar *et al.* 1992, Curson 1994, P. Boesman *in litt.* 1994, J. Curson *in litt.* 1994). **CRITICAL:** A1b; **A2b**; B1+2c; C1; C2a; D1.

White-winged Warbler *Xenoligea montana* is endemic to the main mountainous areas (above 1,200 m, and chiefly from 1,300 to 1,800 m) of Hispaniola, being recorded from Massifs de la Hotte and de la Selle in **Haiti**, where its situation is considered critical, and the Sierras de Baoruco and de Neiba and the Cordillera Central in the **Dominican Republic**, where it can still prove to be common. It inhabits dense stands of broadleaved vegetation including low trees, open thickets and humid shrubbery, sometimes also pines, but vast amounts of montane growth have been cleared on the island (Collar *et al.* 1992). **VULNERABLE:** A1b; B1+2c; C1; C2a.

Tamarugo Conebill *Conirostrum tamarugense* is confined to and at least locally common in a small area of southern **Peru** (Arequipa, Tacna) and northern **Chile** (Tarapacá), where it appears to be an altitudinal migrant (records extend from near sea-level to 4,050 m), with breeding grounds and ecological needs as yet to be positively identified, although the widespread destruction of *Polylepis* (which it utilizes in Peru) is evidently a threat (Collar *et al.* 1992). However, fieldwork during 1993 located two populations, including one which 'clearly should be counted in thousands' in plantations of tamarugos *Prosopis tamarugo* in the 'Pampa del Tamarugal' National Reserve (C. F. Estades *in litt.* 1993). **VULNERABLE:** C1.

Family DREPANIDIDAE

HAWAIIAN HONEYCREEPERS

Nihoa Finch *Telespiza ultima* is endemic to Nihoa (64 ha) in the Northwestern Hawaiian Islands (**U.S.A.**), where it nests in cliff outcroppings and is common, numbering 1,080–2,340 (95% confidence interval) in 1992 and 1,350–3,810 (95% confidence interval) in 1993; an attempted introduction to French Frigate Shoals in 1967 failed, and its survival still depends on the maintenance of the native vegetation on Nihoa and the prevention of the introduction of rats and other mammalian predators (Berger 1972, Pratt *et al.* 1987, USFWS *in litt.* 1994). **VULNERABLE:** D2.

Laysan Finch *Telespiza cantans* is confined to Laysan (3.7 km²) in the Northwestern Hawaiian Islands (**U.S.A.**), where it nests in grass tussocks, with small numbers persisting on Hermes and Pearl Atoll from an introduction in 1967 (though not on Midway Island, where an introduced population succumbed to rats during the Second World War). It is said to have survived the defoliation of Laysan caused by introduced rabbits (and resulting in the elimination of the Millerbird *Acrocephalus familiaris*) by feeding on seabird eggs (Pratt *et al.* 1987), recovering rapidly after the rabbits were exterminated in 1923 and numbering 1,000 in 1928, 5,000 in 1951 (Berger 1972) and fluctuating between 5,000 and 20,000 between 1968 and 1990. These apparent fluctuations may be due to unpredictable weather, which has a major influence on breeding success every year, but census results may also have been influenced by vegetation types, the stage of the breeding cycle, and variability among individual fieldworkers (Morin 1992, Morin and Conant 1994). Work is currently under way to eradicate an aggressive alien plant *Cenchrus echinatus* which may threaten the nesting habitat (K. McDermond *in litt.* 1993). **VULNERABLE:** D2.

Ou *Psittirostra psittacea* was originally widespread in the forests of Kauai, Oahu, Molokai, Lanai, Maui and Hawaii in the Hawaiian Islands (**U.S.A.**) but is likely to have suffered from habitat loss and modification, and from introduced mosquito-borne diseases. It survived in the Alakai Wilderness Preserve on Kauai into the mid-1970s, but only two were found in a survey in 1989 and none has been seen since Hurricane Iniki in 1992, whilst on Hawaii several populations were still present in the early 1980s (c.400 birds estimated in total in the period 1976–1983), but a lava flow from Mauna Loa in 1984 passed through the heart of its range (Scott *et al.* 1986, Pratt 1993; see also Pratt 1994). **CRITICAL: A1a,b; B1+2a,b,c,d,e; C2a; D1**; D2.

Palila *Loxioides bailleui* is restricted to Hawaii in the Hawaiian Islands (**U.S.A.**) where it was abundant though locally distributed until the turn of the century, but is now confined (with population estimates ranging from 1,371–5,354 during the period 1986–1993) to the upper slopes, at 2,000–2,850 m, on Mauna Kea (a total area of 139 km²), favouring mamane and mamane-naio forest (a distinctive forest type found in dry areas usually at high elevations), these forests having been overbrowsed by feral ungulates. The recent removal of goats and sheep from Mauna Kea has allowed regeneration, but it appears that strong site-tenacity might prevent the population of favourable habitats in the former range (Scott *et al.* 1986, Fancy *et al.* 1993). In addition, hatching failure (perhaps as a result of inbreeding and/or inadequate food supply) and predation (by cats and rats) limit breeding success (Pletschet and Kelly 1990). **ENDANGERED: B1+2e; C2a.**

Maui Parrotbill *Pseudonestor xanthophrys* is endemic to montane forest on Maui in the Hawaiian Islands (**U.S.A.**), where it is found on the eastern slopes of Haleakala between 1,200–2,150 m and where it numbered c.500 individuals in the period 1976–1983. It was considered rare even in the 1890s and it is likely (as subfossils suggest that it occupied a wider range of habitats in the past) that its range had long since contracted to remote forests because of habitat modification and introduced disease-carrying mosquitoes in the lowlands (Scott *et al.* 1986). There is no evidence of a current decline (S. L. Pimm *in litt.* 1994, H. D. Pratt *in litt.* 1994; see also Pratt 1994). **VULNERABLE:** D1; D2.

Kauai Amakihi *Viridonia stejnegeri* is endemic to Kauai in the Hawaiian Islands (**U.S.A.**) where it is common in upland forests above c.800 m and estimated to have a population of c.11,000 in the 1980s; however, this area was devastated by Hurricane Iniki in 1992 and all bird populations were drastically reduced (Scott *et al.* 1986, Pratt 1993, H. D. Pratt *in litt.* 1994; see also Pratt 1994). **VULNERABLE:** A1a,b,c; D2.

Anianiau *Viridonia parva* inhabits the ohia forests of Kauai in the Hawaiian Islands (**U.S.A.**) where it was extremely numerous over the whole island in the nineteenth century and estimated to have a population of c.24,000 in the 1980s, largely restricted to the upper elevations; however, this area was devastated by Hurricane Iniki in 1992 and all bird populations were drastically reduced (Scott *et al.* 1986, Pratt 1993, H. D. Pratt *in litt.* 1994; see also Pratt 1994). **VULNERABLE:** A1a,b,c; D2.

Nukupuu *Hemignathus lucidus* is endemic to the forests of the Hawaiian Islands (**U.S.A.**), where it is extinct on Oahu, very rare on Kauai (largely confined to the Alakai Wilderness Preserve, last sightings in the mid-1980s) and on Maui (north-east slope of Haleakala at high elevations only, with fewer than 30 birds present in 1976–1983, last sightings in the late 1980s), and may have occurred on Hawaii (one nineteenth century specimen and a questionable 1971 record) (Scott *et al.* 1986). It appears to have been uncommon since the 1890s, and habitat destruction and introduced disease-carrying mosquitoes in the lowlands have probably caused its virtual extinction (Pratt *et al.* 1987, Pratt 1993, S. L. Pimm *in litt.* 1994; see also Pratt 1994, R. Pyle verbally 1994). **CRITICAL: A1a**; **B1+2c,e**; **C1**; **C2a**; **D1**; D2.

Akiapolaau *Hemignathus wilsoni* is endemic to Hawaii in the Hawaiian Islands (**U.S.A.**), where it was formerly widespread throughout the mesic and dry forests, but goat, cattle and sheep activity, plus sandalwood harvesting in the nineteenth century, have destroyed or fragmented this habitat, and it was found only in four disjunct populations totalling c.1,500 birds in the period 1976–1983 (900 birds in Hamakua; 500 in Kau; 50 on Mauna Kea; and 20 in central Kona), with annual surveys showing significant fluctuations between years in the Mauna Kea population (Scott *et al.* 1986), which continues to decline (H. D. Pratt *in litt.* 1994; see also Pratt 1994). **ENDANGERED: B1+2c,e**; **C2a**.

Akikiki *Oreomystis bairdi*, common and widely distributed in the 1890s in forest at all altitudes on Kauai in the Hawaiian Islands (**U.S.A.**), is today restricted to the high-elevation forest of the Alakai Wilderness Preserve and in the Kokee region, with a total (declining) population estimated at c.6,800 birds in the period 1976–1983 (Scott *et al.* 1986). It is likely that habitat destruction and introduced disease-carrying mosquitoes in the lowlands have caused its demise, and it continues to retreat into the heart of its historic range, having survived Hurricane Iniki in 1992, but now disappearing from localities that had regularly produced post-hurricane sightings (D. Kuhn

verbally to H. D. Pratt *in litt.* 1994; see also Pratt 1993, 1994). **ENDANGERED:** A1a,b; **B1+2a,b,c,d,e**; C2a; D2.

Hawaii Creeper *Oreomystis mana* is endemic to Hawaii in the Hawaiian Islands (**U.S.A.**), where it occurs mainly in koa-ohia forest at 500–2,300 m in four disjunct populations totalling c.12,500 birds (2,100 on Kau, 10,000 on Hamakua, 200 on northern Hualalai—but see below—and 75 on central Kona) and may have declined owing to competition from Japanese White-eye *Zosterops japonicus* or the spread of avian disease (Scott *et al.* 1986). Since 1983 the Hualalai population has disappeared (H. D. Pratt *in litt.* 1994; see also Pratt 1994). **ENDANGERED: B1+2a,b,c,d,e**.

Oahu Alauahio *Paroreomyza maculata* is endemic to forest on Oahu in the Hawaiian Islands (**U.S.A.**), where only a few sightings have been confirmed in the past two decades, with several of these from the area around north Halawa valley which is being destroyed by freeway construction (Pratt 1993). Recent searches specifically for this species have failed to find it (H. D. Pratt *in litt.* 1994; see also Pratt 1994), and the last confirmed sighting was in late 1985 (R. Pyle verbally 1994). **CRITICAL: A1a**; **B1+2c,e**; **C2a**; **D1**; D2.

Akekee *Loxops caeruleirostris* is found in the upper forests of Kauai in the Hawaiian Islands (**U.S.A.**), where it is uncommon (c.5,000 individuals, 1976–1983) but easily seen around Kokee and on the fringes of the Alakai, having suffered from habitat destruction and introduced disease-carrying mosquitoes in the lowlands (Scott *et al.* 1986, Pratt *et al.* 1987, Pratt 1993, S. L. Pimm *in litt.* 1994). It appears to have declined (perhaps temporarily), along with all Kauai forest birds, following Hurricane Iniki in 1992 (H. D. Pratt *in litt.* 1994; see also Pratt 1994). **EN-DANGERED: B1+2c,e**; C2a; D2.

Akepa *Loxops coccineus* is known from the forests of Oahu (race *wolstenholmei*, considered extinct by King 1978–1979), Maui (race *ochraceus*, rare and patchily distributed above 1,100 m on Haleakala, c.230 birds) and Hawaii (nominate *coccineus*, locally common at 1,100–2,100 m, in three separate populations totalling c.14,000) in the Hawaiian Islands (**U.S.A.**) (Scott *et al.* 1986). Habitat destruction and introduced disease-carrying mosquitoes in the lowlands have probably caused its decline, and in the past decade several peripheral populations have virtually disappeared, most notably that on Hualalai Volcano in Kona (H. D. Pratt *in litt.* 1994; see also Pratt 1993, 1994). **ENDANGERED: B1+2a,b,c,d,e**.

Akohekohe *Palmeria dolei* is known from the forests of Maui and Molokai (last confirmed observations in 1907) in the Hawaiian Islands (**U.S.A.**); habitat destruction and introduced disease-carrying mosquitoes in the lowlands have caused its decline, but it remains moderately common above 1,500 m on the eastern slopes of Haleakala where the population was estimated at c.3,800 birds in the period 1976–1983, and where it appears to be more secure than previously thought (Scott *et al.* 1986, Pratt 1993; see also Pratt 1994) with no obvious signs of decline (S. L. Pimm *in litt.* 1994). **VULNERABLE:** D2.

Poo-uli *Melamprosops phaeosoma* was discovered in 1973 in the Koolau Forest Reserve on the north-eastern flanks of Haleakala on Maui in the Hawaiian Islands (**U.S.A.**), but is extremely rare (total population estimated at c.140 birds in the period 1976–1983) in remote ohia forest at 1,400–2,100 m and, being a bird of the undergrowth, appears particularly sensitive to disturbance by feral pigs; other major limiting factors include predation (rats, cats and mongooses), introduced mosquito-borne avian diseases (at lower elevations), interspecific competition from the introduced garlic snail *Oxychilus alliarius* (which predates the native snails that are an important food for the Poo-uli) and possibly gene-pool impoverishment (King 1978–1979, Scott *et al.* 1986, Pratt *et al.* 1987, Mountainspring *et al.* 1990, Pratt 1993). It appears to have undergone a recent drastic decline and no longer occurs at the type-locality, which has been degraded by pigs (H. D. Pratt *in litt.* 1994), but there were two observations from nearby in September 1993 (Pratt *et al.* 1993). **CRITICAL:** A1a,b,d; B1+2a,b,c,d,e; C2a; D1; D2.

Family VIREONIDAE

VIREOS

Chocó Vireo *Vireo* sp. (description forthcoming: Salaman and Stiles in prep.) appears to be restricted to (ever-retreating) primary subtropical pluvial forests at 1,400–1,800 m on the Pacific slope of the West Andes of **Colombia**, and is currently known from two sites, Río Ñambi in Nariño and Alto de Pisones in Risaralda, 11 birds being observed at the former locality and eight at the latter during 1992 (Salaman and Gandy 1994). **VULNERABLE:** D2.

Black-capped Vireo *Vireo atricapillus* once bred from Kansas through central Oklahoma and central Texas, **U.S.A.**, into central Coahuila, **Mexico**, with birds wintering primarily in Durango, Sinaloa, Nayarit and Jalisco (Mexico), nesting in shrubby deciduous growth (early successional stages) in the forest–grassland ecotone, but a substantial contraction of its U.S. breeding range (to a few key sites in Oklahoma and Texas) has been accompanied by a dramatic fall in numbers to less than 2,000 mature birds, although breeding numbers in Coahuila remain disputed (Collar *et al.* 1992). Near-total nest-parasitism by the Brown-headed Cowbird *Molothrus ater*, whose expansion in the vireo's range has been facilitated by habitat conversion (which has also directly affected the vireo), is the major threat (Grzybowski *et al.* 1994). **ENDANGERED:** A1b,c; A2c; C1.

San Andrés Vireo *Vireo caribaeus* inhabits brushy pastures and inland mangroves on the densely populated tourist island of San Andrés (**Colombia**) in the western Caribbean, where it is apparently now restricted to an area of 17 km² (although breeding territories are only 0.5 ha) and is threatened by encroaching urbanization, agriculture and coconut palm cultivation (Collar *et al.* 1992). **CRITICAL:** B1+2b,c; C1; C2b; D2.

Noronha Vireo *Vireo gracilirostris* is restricted to the 18.4 km² island of Fernando de Noronha (**Brazil**) in the central Atlantic Ocean, being generally common wherever there is forest, gardens or scrub (with greatest numbers around Morro do Pico and in the western quarter), being absent only from cleared areas (Nacinovic and Teixeira 1989, Olson 1994). **VULNERABLE:** D2.

Family ICTERIDAE
NEW WORLD ORIOLES

Baudó Oropendola *Psarocolius cassini* is known from just three localities in humid lowland forest and forest edge (100–365 m) along rivers in the vicinity of the isolated Serranías de los Saltos and de Baudó, Chocó department, north-western **Colombia**, where four specimens were taken in 1858, 1940 and 1945. There have been no further observations of this seemingly very rare bird, and the Serranía de Baudó faces serious deforestation as a result of road-building programmes and logging activities (Collar *et al.* 1992). **ENDANGERED: A2b**; B1+2c; C1; C2a.

Selva Cacique *Cacicus koepckeae* is known only from the type-locality, Balta in Loreto (although probably also Manu National Park in Madre de Dios), in the humid forested lowlands of **Peru**, may be genuinely rare and, if a species of riverine habitats, possibly at some risk from actual and impending agricultural development (Collar *et al.* 1992). **VULNERABLE: A2b**; C1; C2b.

Martinique Oriole *Icterus bonana* is endemic to **Martinique (to France)** where, although present in most habitat types below 700 m throughout the island, it has suffered severe levels of brood-parasitism from the recently established Shiny Cowbird *Molothrus bonariensis*, and the population has declined dramatically (Collar *et al.* 1992). However, there may have been a recent recovery in numbers with an apparent decline in the cowbird (P. Bulens and A. Ledru *per* P. Feldmann and P. Villard *in litt.* 1994). **ENDANGERED: A1d**; A2d; **B1+2e**; **C1**; **C2b**; D1.

Saffron-cowled Blackbird *Xanthopsar flavus* has declined steeply and sharply contracted its range in response to the many different uses and abuses (stock-raising, agriculture, pesticides, burning, pine plantation, drainage, settlement) of the open country (grasslands, dry bushland, pasture and boggy swales) in which it lives in southern **Brazil** (Santa Catarina, Rio Grande do Sul), eastern **Paraguay**, **Uruguay** and north-east **Argentina** (Formosa, Chaco, Misiones, Corrientes, Santa Fe, Entre Ríos, Buenos Aires). It is now very rare throughout its range, albeit with conflicting evidence from Rio Grande do Sul, where, however, brood-parasitism by the Shiny Cowbird *Molothrus bonariensis* may now be significant (Collar *et al.* 1992, Pearman and Abadie in press). **ENDANGERED: A1a,b**; **A2b,d**; C1; C2a.

Yellow-shouldered Blackbird *Agelaius xanthomus* was formerly widespread in various habitats (mangroves, pastures, coconut and palm stands, cactus scrub and coastal cliffs) on **Puerto Rico (to U.S.A.)** and is still so on adjacent Mona and Monito islands, but it has declined steeply and has retreated into two areas on Puerto Rico, in the south-west and the east, having now almost vanished in the latter. The total population of 770–1,210 birds (which was twice that level in 1975) is under pressure from a range of threats, most notably brood-parasitism by Shiny Cowbird *Molothrus bonariensis*, loss of mangroves, and predation by introduced carnivores (Collar *et al.* 1992). **ENDANGERED: A1a,b,d**; **A2b,d**; **B1+2c,d**; **C1**; **C2a**; D1.

Pampas Meadowlark *Sturnella militaris*, although always rare in southern **Brazil** (Paraná once, Santa Catarina once, Rio Grande do Sul twice, these all probably being winter visitors) and **Uruguay** (last dated record 1958), was once common and widespread in central-eastern **Argentina** (Corrientes, Santa Fe, Entre Ríos, Córdoba, Buenos Aires, San Luis, Pampa) where, however, cultivation (notably of sunflowers) and overgrazing of its natural grassland habitat have contributed to a steep and apparently continuing decline, with almost no recent records outside (and relatively few inside) the province of Buenos Aires (Collar *et al.* 1992). **ENDANGERED: A1b**; A2b; C1; C2a.

Red-bellied Grackle *Hypopyrrhus pyrohypogaster* is now very rare and localized in the West and Central Andes and southern East Andes of **Colombia** (Antioquia, Risaralda, Caldas, Quindío, Tolima, Huila, Caquetá), having suffered a massive decline with the near-total clearance of its subtropical forest habitat (records fall between 800 and 2,400 m) and continuing human pressure on the last remnants; since 1980 records have been from only five areas in four departments, with small numbers present in each (Collar *et al.* 1992). **ENDANGERED: A1b**; A2b; B1+2c; **C1**; **C2a**; D1.

Forbes's Blackbird *Curaeus forbesi* is known with certainty now from only two areas of forest and adjacent farmland 1,400 km apart in eastern **Brazil**: the Rio Doce State Park in Minas Gerais, where the highest number reported to date is c.40 individuals, and three sites in Alagoas, where the only breeding population of c.150 birds suffered 100% brood-parasitism by the Shiny Cowbird *Molothrus bonariensis* in 1987, and has declined in numbers since, its problems there being compounded by a loss of habitat and by trapping for the cagebird trade (Collar *et al.* 1992). **CRITICAL:** A1a,b,c,d; **A2b,c,d**; B1+2c; **C1**; **C2a**; D1; D2.

Family FRINGILLIDAE

FINCHES

Yellow-throated Serin *Serinus flavigula* was known until recently only from three century-old specimens (the most recent dating from 1886) taken in a single small area (only 30 km²) of Shoa province in eastern **Ethiopia** (Collar and Stuart 1985). It was rediscovered within this range in March 1989, when at least seven birds were found (and the species was judged uncommon) in arid vegetation (scattered trees interspersed with thick patches of scrub) on rocky hillsides along the valley of a small stream at 1,400–1,500 m (Ash and Gullick 1990a). Groups of birds possibly of this species were observed c.70 km south of this site in 1993 and 1994 (J. Atkins *in litt.* 1994). **ENDANGERED: D1**; D2.

Salvadori's Serin *Serinus xantholaema* (treated here as split from Abyssinian Yellow-rumped Seed-eater *S. xanthopygius* in accordance with Erard 1974) is known from central Harar, northern Bale and central Sidamo provinces of **Ethiopia**, although it is expected to be found elsewhere (Erard 1974, Collar and Stuart 1985). It was relocated in the scrubby vegetation of a remote gorge at a known site (Sof Omar) in March 1989, but the area was under intense pressure from resettled people and their livestock (Ash and Gullick 1989), so it must be in decline. **VULNERABLE:** C2b.

Ankober Serin *Serinus ankoberensis* is a small, cliff-frequenting, montane finch, known from a small area (less than 5 km²) at 2,900–3,100 m near Ankober, Shoa province, eastern **Ethiopia** (Collar and Stuart 1985), where 60 were seen in March 1989 (Ash and Gullick 1989), from a second site some 15 km to the north, inside the top of a ravine south of Debre Sina at 3,250 m, where 20–40 were seen on lichen-covered rocks, earth and grass in October 1991 (Atkins 1992a,b), and from a third area between the two previous ones, at Goshmeda, in autumn 1993, with up to 40 birds seen (M. Gunther *per* J. S. Ash *in litt.* 1994), some still present in January 1994 (P. O. Syvertsen *in litt.* 1994). Habitat in the Ankober area is under pressure from increased grazing and cultivation, and from eucalyptus planting (Atkins 1992b). **ENDANGERED: B1+2c**.

São Tomé Grosbeak *Neospiza concolor*, a remarkable bird of uncertain affinities (now judged to be cardueline: de Naurois 1988), is known only from three nineteenth-century specimens from rainforest in southern São Tomé, **São Tomé e Príncipe** (Collar and Stuart 1985). Even the original collector described it as 'very rare', and absence of records this century led to the assumption that it was extinct (de Naurois 1988). However, two birds were observed on two successive days in August 1991 in a small bare tree at a tree-fall on a ridge within closed-canopy forest at 230 m above the Rio Xufexufe, observations suggesting that the species normally lives in the canopy (Sargeant *et al.* 1992, Sargeant 1994); however, a possible sighting in 1992 at another locality was of a bird on the ground (Clement *et al.* 1993). The future of the island's forests is uncertain (Jones *et al.* 1992). **CRITICAL: D1**.

Yellow-faced Siskin *Carduelis yarrellii* has been recorded in south-eastern Carabobo, **Venezuela** (no recent or clear information; it has been suggested that birds here were escapees), and is present in caatinga, forest edge, second growth and croplands in north-east **Brazil** (Ceará, Paraíba, Pernambuco, Alagoas, Bahia and, recently, Piauí: Olmos 1993), where, however, it is subject to illegal but high volume trade feeding both national and international demand (Collar *et al.* 1992). **VULNERABLE:** A1c; A2c.

Red Siskin *Carduelis cucullata* is subject to enormous, long-term (but, since the 1940s, illegal) pressure from trappers because of its capacity to hybridize with canaries, and has consequently (with the aid of clear-felling and intensive agriculture) become extremely rare (total numbers either in the high hundreds or low thousands) and locally extinct throughout its range in the foothills in northern **Venezuela** (15 states), where it moves semi-nomadically and altitudinally (seasonally and partly also daily) between 280 and 1,300 m and from moist evergreen forest, dry deciduous woodland and associated edge habitats to shrubby grassland and pastures. It has disappeared from Trinidad, a tiny population exists in Norte de Santander, **Colombia**, and another, derived from escaped cagebirds, is in Puerto Rico (to U.S.A.) (Collar *et al.* 1992). **ENDANGERED:** A1c; A2c; C1; **C2a**; D1.

Saffron Siskin *Carduelis siemiradzkii* is confined to south-west **Ecuador** (Manabí, Guayas, Loja) and adjacent north-west **Peru** (Tumbes), where it inhabits semi-arid scrub and dry forest up to 750 m; however, only two areas are known where it appears even fairly common, and if it proves to depend on deciduous forest for part of its life-cycle it is likely to be seriously threatened by deforestation (Collar *et al.* 1992). **VULNERABLE:** B1+2c; C1; C2a.

Warsangli Linnet *Carduelis johannis*, recorded from five sites (numerous only in one: Daloh Forest Reserve, Erigavo) in two small areas of the northern **Somalia** highlands, occurs in both open country and juniper forest, but its long-term security depends on fuller knowledge of its needs (Collar and Stuart 1985). The Daloh Forest Reserve is a key site for bird conservation in Africa, yet there are reports of plans to exploit and replant it (Collar and Stuart 1988). The chronic and continuing political crisis in Somalia may be causing as yet undocumented loss of habitats for this and other species endemic to the country. **ENDANGERED: B1+2a,b,c**; C2a; D1.

Family ESTRILDIDAE

WAXBILLS

Shelley's Crimson-wing *Cryptospiza shelleyi* is known from many of the mountain ranges (inhabiting closed, moist forest understorey as well as low second growth at edges, in *Sericostachys* clearings, mixed *Impatiens/Urtica* glades, in bamboo thickets and within the upper forest/moorland ecotone) along the Albertine Rift at 1,550–2,600 m, namely the Itombwe Mountains (including Kahuzi-Biega National Park) and mountains west of Lake Kivu, **Zaïre**, the Virunga Mountains (2,200–3,000 m), Nyungwe, Gishwati and Makwa forests, **Rwanda**, Bururi forest and elsewhere, **Burundi**, Mount Rwenzori and Impenetrable (= Bwindi) forest, **Uganda** (Britton 1980, Collar and Stuart 1985, Dowsett-Lemaire 1990). However, it is generally rare (only common in a few threatened forests; but it shows curious fluctuations in abundance, suggesting seasonal movements) and appears to have suffered a dramatic decline since the 1970s for reasons unknown (Catterall 1992, M. C. Catsis *in litt.* 1994, T. Stevenson *in litt.* 1994). **VULNERABLE:** A1a; C1; C2a.

Anambra Waxbill *Estrilda poliopareia* occurs in long grass and herbage along rivers and on lagoon sandbanks in southern **Nigeria**, where it remains known with certainty from only four localities, though reportedly common in one of them (Onitsha) in 1954 (Collar and Stuart 1985). A sighting of 2(–5) birds at Onitsha in January 1987 (Ash 1987b, 1990) is the only record since at least 1980 despite considerable search effort, which has led to concerns that this species may be under pressure from habitat degradation (Ash and Sharland 1986), with possibly under a thousand remaining (J. S. Ash *in litt.* 1994). **VULNERABLE:** B1+2b,c; D1.

Black-lored Waxbill *Estrilda nigriloris* is restricted to an area judged less than 2,600 km² in level grassy plains around the Lualaba River and Lake Upemba in southern **Zaïre**, where its status requires elucidation, as there have been no records since 1950, and its habitat might well be undergoing conversion (Collar and Stuart 1985; also Clement *et al.* 1993). **VULNERABLE:** B1+2a,c.

Green Avadavat *Amandava formosa* is endemic to central **India**, where it is very locally and unevenly distributed, and generally scarce, from southern Rajastan and northern Madhya Pradesh south to southern Maharashtra and northern Andhra Pradesh (other than a few isolated records further north, including in Delhi Union Territory, probably of escaped cagebirds: Gaston and Macrell 1980, T. P. Inskipp *in litt.* 1994). It is found in tall grassland, scrub and sometimes in agricultural land (Ali and Ripley 1987). A small breeding colony which was formerly present in Lahore, Pakistan, is believed to have resulted from escaped cagebirds (Roberts 1992). There has been widespread habitat destruction and disturbance within its range (Gaston 1984), but the main threat may be trapping, as it is still regularly seen in bird markets (A. R. Rahmani *in litt.* 1994). **VULNERABLE: C1; C2a.**

Star Finch *Neochmia ruficauda* occurs from north-east New South Wales to north-east Queensland in **Australia** (nominate *ruficauda*, which favours grassy woodland near water and is extremely rare, with few reports during the last 50 years that cannot be attributed to aviary escapes), and throughout northern Australia (race *clarescens*, which favours dense grass and rushes beside fresh water and is often patchily abundant, but whose overall population may not be very large). It has declined owing to the degradation of its habitat by the activities of livestock and feral animals, the spread of the exotic rubber vine *Cryptostegia grandiflora* (which smothers riverside vegetation) and large-scale trapping in the past (Garnett 1992). **VULNERABLE: C2a.**

Green-faced Parrotfinch *Erythrura viridifacies* appears to be closely allied to flowering bamboo and hence is highly erratic in its occurrence on Luzon (only two recent records despite searches in known areas) and Negros (only one record, from Siaton, where recent maps indicate a patch of forest still survives) in the **Philippines**; despite usually keeping above 1,000 m, it occasionally irrupts into the lowlands, and as a nomadic species it is very likely to be suffering from the extensive and continuing habitat destruction taking place throughout Luzon (Dickinson *et al.* 1991, Brooks *et al.* 1992, Danielsen *et al.* 1994, Poulsen in press, D. Allen *in litt.* 1994). **ENDANGERED: A1b; A2b; C1; C2a.**

Red-eared Parrotfinch *Erythrura coloria* inhabits forest understorey and edge, second growth and grassy areas at altitudes over 1,000 m on Mount Katanglad and Mount Apo on Mindanao in the **Philippines**, where it is a moderately common bird but likely to be under increasing pressure from the loss of forest which is extending into its altitudinal and geographically restricted range (Dickinson *et al.* 1991, Lambert 1993b, Timmins in prep.). **VULNERABLE: B1+2c; C2a.**

Royal Parrotfinch *Erythrura regia* is endemic to **Vanuatu** where it is generally confined to the highlands (possibly extinct) on Anatom, uncommon on Efate, more numerous in suitable habitats on most of the northern islands, and fairly common on Tongoa and Emae. The present relatively high number of individuals on the smaller islands may be due to an increase in food supply from the considerable number of different species of fig trees that have become established in the many partly cleared areas and thinned-out forests, but the number of birds could decrease in coming decades if the natural forest cover further diminishes (and with this the number of fig trees) as the land is taken over for various developments (this is especially likely on Tongoa with its high human population) (Bregulla 1992). **VULNERABLE: A2b.**

Pink-billed Parrotfinch *Erythrura kleinschmidti* is endemic to the wet forests of Viti Levu, **Fiji**, where it has always been considered rare (King 1978–1979), although there are records from secondary scrub (Watling 1982) and plantations (Hay 1986). The reasons for its apparent rarity (e.g. recently only found in one out of 56 randomly selected forest plots throughout the island) are unknown (Watling and Chape 1992, D. Watling *in litt.* 1994). **ENDANGERED: B1+2e; C2a; D1.**

Gouldian Finch *Chloebia gouldiae*, having been abundant early in the twentieth century, is now only patchily distributed in open woodland with a grassy understorey across northern **Australia** in north-western Queensland, the northern Northern Territory and the Kimberley region of northern Western Australia, with breeding confirmed at just a small number of sites. The main problem appears to be an introduced parasitic mite which is found in 60% of individuals in Northern Territory and which may prevent the return of the population to its former numbers. Other possibly exacerbating factors are fires which destroy trees with suitable nest hollows, trapping for the cagebird trade, grazing by cattle, and mining at one of the major breeding sites at Yinberrie Hills, Northern Territory (Garnett 1992). **ENDANGERED: A1d; B1+2d,e; C1; C2a.**

Grey-banded Munia *Lonchura vana* is a shy inhabitant of mid-mountain grasslands (a scarce habitat: N. Bostock *in litt.* 1993) at Anggi Lakes and in the Tamrau and Arfak mountains of the Vogelkop, Irian Jaya, **Indonesia** (Beehler *et al.* 1986), and could be very rare (D. Gibbs *in litt.* 1994) as there are few records. **VULNERABLE: B1+2c.**

Java Sparrow *Padda oryzivora* is endemic to Java, Bali and Kangean, **Indonesia** (although widely introduced elsewhere: see Lever 1987), where it used to be one of the commonest birds in towns, villages, gardens and cultivated areas up to 1,500 m, sometimes occurring in huge flocks; a major population decline has taken place, apparently entirely as a result of massive capture for the cagebird trade, and it is now very scarce, although still widespread (MacKinnon and Phillipps 1993, S. van Balen *in litt.* 1994). **VULNERABLE:** A1c.

Subfamily PLOCEINAE
WEAVERS

Bannerman's Weaver *Ploceus bannermani*, while relatively common, occupies ever-receding forest-edge habitat in a few montane areas (1,100–2,850 m) of western **Cameroon**, chiefly in the Bamenda Highlands and notably at Mount Oku (Kilum) (but with a recent range extension to Mount Tchabal Mbabo: Smith and McNiven 1993), and of eastern **Nigeria**, on the Obudu and Mambilla Plateaus, where 12–40 were seen per day in April 1988 (Collar and Stuart 1985, 1988; also Stuart and Jensen 1986, Ash *et al.* 1989, Ash 1990, Tye 1991). Kilum is now the focus of a major conservation programme (Macleod 1987, Green 1991, Alpert 1993, Edwards 1993). **VULNERABLE:** B1+2a,b,c; C2a.

Bates's Weaver *Ploceus batesi* is a rarely re-corded species from lowland rainforest in southern **Cameroon**, where it remains known from only a few localities including Mount Kupe (two records at 900 m in 1990, but none since, despite intensive searches) (Collar and Stuart 1985, 1988). Although it is likely to occur in the Dja Game Reserve which has been proposed as a national park, and although Kupe is now the subject of a major conservation programme, habitat loss in the region is extensive and the species must be suffering accordingly (Bowden 1993, Bowden and Bowden 1993, Bowden and Andrews 1994, C. G. R. Bowden verbally 1994). **VULNERABLE:** C2a.

Black-chinned Weaver *Ploceus nigrimentum* occurs very sparsely above 1,500 m in the Bailundu Highlands of western **Angola** (one post-1927 observation or set of observations), on the Bateke Plateaus (750 m) in **Congo** (one record in November 1951) (Collar and Stuart 1985), and with repeated records since 1989 of birds near Lekoni (500–700 m), eastern **Gabon**, and on the Gabon side of the Bateke Plateaus (only 4,500 km², and only patchily within this area), the evidence suggesting that the species genuinely occurs at low density (but semi-coloni-ally) and in rather specific and presumably in places

vulnerable habitat, namely open savannas gener-ously dotted with medium height (2–6 m) bushes and trees (e.g. *Albizia, Dialium*), preferably adjacent to gallery forest (P. Christy *in litt.* 1994, T. M. Gullick *in litt.* 1994, D. E. Sargeant *in litt.* 1994). **VULNER-ABLE:** C2a.

Loango Weaver *Ploceus subpersonatus* is known only from the coastal strip from **Gabon** and **Zaïre** (no records yet from Congo, and it may not occur owing to lack of appropriate habitat: Dowsett-Lemaire *et al.* 1993) into Cabinda (**Angola**), and remains little known (Collar and Stuart 1985). It is uncommon at Cap Lopez, Gabon, where it appears to be thinly spread in suitable habitat (swamp-forest, landward mangrove edge, savanna) within 2.5 km of the coast (total area probably below 3,000 km²), and a recent economic downturn has forced many local people around Port Gentil, Cap Lopez and Libreville to convert coastal bush into allotments (P. D. Alex-ander-Marrack *in litt.* 1989, 1993, 1994); further south in the country it appears to be confined to beach scrub only (D. E. Sargeant *in litt.* 1994), but nests are generally placed in *Phoenix reclinata* or *Caesalpina bonduc* (P. Christy *in litt.* 1994). **VUL-NERABLE:** B1+2c; C2a.

Kilombero Weaver *Ploceus burnieri* is known only from the type-locality in the immediate vicinity of Kivukoni Ferry at Ifakara on the Kilombero river in south-central **Tanzania**, where it is reasonably common—in January 1991 several hundred were breeding (T. Stevenson *per* N. E. Baker *in litt.* 1994), and birds were common, sitting on roads, in July 1993 (A. Tye *in litt.* 1994)—in an extensive river-side swamp fringed with tall *Phragmites mauritianus* (used in nest construction) and where recent road works have destroyed several colony sites. The area to the east of the ferry holds only African Golden Weaver *P. subaureus*, so although the species may extend south-west along the extensive Kilombero flood-plain, the valley is geographically isolated and the home of two putative new cisticoline warblers (Baker and Baker 1990, N. E. Baker *in litt.* 1994). **VULNERABLE:** B1+2c; C2b; D1.

Lake Lufira Weaver *Ploceus ruweti*, the type-specimen of which was collected in 1960 but only recognized as representing a new species c.20 years later, is restricted to (and in 1960 was common in) the swamps bordering Lake Lufira in southern **Zaïre**, but there has been no recent information on its status (Collar and Stuart 1985), a situation which still applies. **VULNERABLE:** D2.

Clarke's Weaver *Ploceus golandi* is known only from the Arabuko–Sokoke forest in south-east **Kenya**, the target of a now stalled conservation project (see Sokoke Scops-owl *Otus ireneae*, p. 114); speculation that the species might breed elsewhere, because most records had been from the period August–September, seems mistaken, as it has recently been found present in almost all months (Collar and Stuart 1985, 1988, Fanshawe 1991, J. H. Fanshawe verbally 1994). **VULNERABLE:** D1; D2.

Golden-naped Weaver *Ploceus aureonucha* has been found only in a small part of the Ituri forest, north of Beni in eastern **Zaïre**, where it had not been seen since 1926 (Collar and Stuart 1985), until encountered several times during 1986, once in a flock of up to 60 birds, in forest edge at Epulu (M. C. Catsis *in litt.* 1989, 1994), in an area in danger from forest clearance but now being established for conservation (Blom 1990, S. N. Stuart *in litt.* 1994). A pair feeding two young was observed at the same locality in June 1994 (M. Languy *in litt.* 1994). **VULNERABLE:** C2b; D1.

Yellow Weaver *Ploceus megarhynchus* is only known from **India**, in the plains and foothills of northern Uttar Pradesh, southern and eastern West Bengal, western Assam (Ali and Ripley 1987) and near Delhi (up to 35 nests since 1979 at Hastinapur, near Meerut, and several near nests at Okhla in 1993: Rai 1986, *Oriental Bird Club Bull.* 1993, 18: 67–70), where it is found in grasslands with scrub and trees, particularly seasonally inundated grassland and marshes dotted with isolated trees (Ali and Ripley 1987). It appears to be extremely local, and is threatened by the widespread destruction and modification of grasslands and wetlands within its range (see Majumdar and Brahmachari 1986, Rahmani 1986). **VULNERABLE:** C1; C2a.

Tanzanian Mountain Weaver *Ploceus nicolli*, a low-density montane forest species, inhabits the East and West Usambara Mountains (nominate *nicolli*, 900–2,200 m) and the Uluguru and Udzungwa Mountains, including the Nyumbanitu Mountains, where it was found in 1993–1994 (race *anderseni*, 1,100–2,150 m), **Tanzania**, and is under some threat from forest destruction (Collar and Stuart 1985, Stuart *et al.* 1987, Jensen and Brøgger-Jensen 1992, Dinesen *et al.* 1993, L. A. Hansen and J. O. Svendsen *in litt.* 1994). Current conservation in the East Usambaras is noted under Usambara Eagle Owl *Bubo vosseleri* (p. 115), but the weaver had not been seen there since 1932 (Evans and Anderson 1992, Tye 1993) until August 1994 when it was observed twice in degraded montane habitat at 1,250 m on the previously unsurveyed Mount Nilo (N. J. Cordeiro *in litt.* 1994). **VULNERABLE:** B1+2b,c; C2a; D1.

Yellow-legged Weaver *Ploceus flavipes* is known only from the Ituri forest (in danger from forest clearance) in eastern **Zaïre**, where it appears to be rare and up to the mid-1980s had not been seen since 1953 (Collar and Stuart 1985), but it has since been recorded, albeit only twice, in what is now the Okapi Faunal Reserve (Blom 1990, J. Hart *in litt.* 1994). A specimen from Lima, taken in 1959, has recently come to light and represents a new locality for the species in Ituri (Louette 1988a). **VULNERABLE:** C2a; D1.

Gola Malimbe *Malimbus ballmanni* is confined to the rapidly receding Upper Guinea rainforest block of West Africa in **Ivory Coast** (first found near but not in Taï National Park), **Liberia** and **Sierra Leone** (Gola forest) (Collar and Stuart 1985). Recent fieldwork failed to relocate the species in Gola (Allport 1991; see also Wood 1993) or in Taï (Gartshore 1989), but has shown that it survives in two populations, one in western Liberia in an area of 200–300 km^2 (numbers unclear), one in eastern Liberia and western Ivory Coast in an area of 18,000 km^2 (between 20,000 and 50,000 birds), though both are seriously at risk from clearance of habitat (Gatter and Gardner 1993). **ENDANGERED:** A1b; **A2b**; B1+2a,b,c.

Ibadan Malimbe *Malimbus ibadanensis* must be seriously threatened by the massive habitat destruction that has occurred within its small range focused on lands around (up to 110 km from) Ibadan in southwestern **Nigeria**, the most recent records being from forest patches near Ibadan itself (Collar and Stuart 1985). In November 1987 four birds, including a male feeding a juvenile, were observed in secondary woodland in Ibadan, but this was the only record in 10 days' intensive searching, suggesting that the species has indeed become very rare (Ash 1987b, 1991, Elgood 1988), an impression which the discovery of a nest in highly degraded farmland (Ash *et al.* 1989, Ash 1991) cannot dispel. Nevertheless, it may occur more widely, with possible records from Owerri, east of the Niger river in Nigeria, and from Ghana (Elgood 1992, Morel and Chappuis 1992). **CRITICAL:** B1+2a,e; **C2a**; D1.

Mauritius Fody *Foudia rubra* suffered catastrophically from the clearance of its upland forest habitat in south-west **Mauritius** during the 1970s, declining from around 250 pairs in 1975 to what at one stage was judged to be as few as 20–40 pairs during the course of the decade (though the observer now thinks that this was a considerable underestimate: C. G. Jones *in litt.* 1994), and sustaining heavy losses at the nest from introduced predators (Collar and Stuart 1985, Cheke 1987a). However, despite what proved to be almost total breeding failure from this cause over most of the range (currently being remedied by birds nesting in dense exotic *Cryptomeria* trees and by a rat control programme), 81–102 pairs were estimated to be present in 1990 (Safford 1991), and the species is calculated to have undergone a 60% decline in both population and range since 1975 (Safford in prep.). **CRITICAL:** A1a,b; **B1+2a,b,c,e**; **C2b**; D1; D2.

Seychelles Fody *Foudia sechellarum* survives in woodland and plantations on three rat-free islands, Cousin (27 ha), Cousine (c.50 ha) and Frégate (210 ha), in the **Seychelles**, but may still face competition and predation from introduced birds (Collar and Stuart 1985). The population on Cousin was c.1,300 birds in the late 1970s (Brooke 1985). **VULNERABLE:** D2.

Rodrigues Fody *Foudia flavicans*, having once been abundant on its native Rodrigues, **Mauritius**, declined drastically owing to habitat loss, competition from an introduced congener, and cyclone impact (by which it was reduced to less than 10 pairs in 1968), recovering by April 1983 to c.110 birds in a small area of patchy mixed evergreen forest on the island's northern slopes, but was still facing possible annihilation by a cyclone and several new threats from introduced predators and competitors (Collar and Stuart 1985, Cheke 1987c). However, habitat is now more extensive and better developed, giving fuller protection and greater range area, and numbers have risen accordingly, with 190–230 birds in July 1989 (C. G. Jones *in litt.* 1994), c.150 pairs in April 1991 (Safford 1992), and 350–450 birds in August 1991 (MWAF 1992). **VULNERABLE:** D1; D2.

Family STURNIDAE
STARLINGS

Mountain Starling *Aplonis santovestris* is restricted to cloud-forest on the highest peaks of Espiritu Santo, **Vanuatu**, with records from Mount Watiamasan at c.1,200 m in 1934, Mount Tabwemasana in 1961 (c.17 separate encounters of birds, above the village of Nokovula, where local people said that they found this species in the Mount Kotamtam and Tawuloaba area), and Peak Santo at 1,700 m in 1991 (10 encounters) (Reside 1991, Bregulla 1992). Thus numbers appear to be small, although the Man Hill people at Matantas Big Bay say that they see it commonly in the mountains of south Espiritu Santo and regularly eat it (S. Maturin *in litt.* 1994). **VULNERABLE:** D2.

Pohnpei Mountain Starling *Aplonis pelzelni* is endemic to forest on Pohnpei, **Micronesia**, where it was once widespread but has declined drastically (although upland forest remains largely unchanged)

since 1930, when 59 specimens were collected (King 1978–1979). The last specimen was taken in 1956 and, although there have been several recent reports (at least one seen in 1975:), it was not located in a survey conducted in 1983, indicating that it may be extinct, possibly owing to predation by rats (Engbring *et al.* 1990). **CRITICAL:** A1a; **B1+2b,e**; **C2b**; **D1**; D2.

Rarotonga Starling *Aplonis cinerascens* is widespread in Rarotonga in the **Cook Islands (to New Zealand)**, where it occurs in montane native forest and fringing disturbed forest (Hay 1986). It was regarded as abundant early this century and still not uncommon in 1973, but conservative estimates made in 1984 put the population at 100, more recently revised to a few hundred; the reasons for its current rarity are unknown (Hay 1986, G. McCormack *in litt.* 1993, 1994). **VULNERABLE:** D1; D2.

White-eyed Starling *Aplonis brunneicapilla* is a very rare species confined to Bougainville Island, **Papua New Guinea**, Choiseul, Guadalcanal and Rendova, **Solomon Islands**, breeding in colonies of up to 40 pairs in both lowland swamp and hill forest and favouring isolated trees (Cain and Galbraith 1956, Finch 1986, Kaestner 1987, Coates 1990, D. Gibbs *in litt.* 1994, Buckingham *et al.* in prep.). The species appears to be nomadic, as colonies disappear and birds then become very scarce (K. D. Bishop *in litt.* 1987), and this fact, suggesting dependence on an unidentified temporally patchy resource (it feeds on fruits and berries: Hadden 1981), plus the evidence that local people cut trees to eat nestlings wherever they find a colony (Cain and Galbraith 1956), indicates a high level of vulnerability. Furthermore, large areas of lowland forest on Bougainville and Guadalcanal have been cleared and replanted with oil palms and/or 'selectively' logged, these latter areas being invariably hunted out and then cleared by bush-squatters (K. D. Bishop *in litt.* 1994). **ENDANGERED:** B1+2c+3c; **C2a.**

Socotra Starling *Onychognathus frater* is restricted to the island of Socotra, **Yemen**, its habitat in 1964 being given as (below 60 m) towns, lagoons, pools and plains, (60–1,200 m) foothills, valleys, slopes, thickets and grassy uplands, and (1,200–1,500 m) the bleak Hajhir peaks. Unlike the commoner, non-endemic Somali Starling *O. blythii*, it seems not to forage on the ground in the open or near livestock, but acts more like a thrush and obtains insects more within than on bushes (Ripley and Bond 1966). In 1993 it was found to be considerably rarer than *O. blythii*, 36 birds being recorded at five sites as against 478 at 14 sites for *O. blythii*, and it probably numbers under 1,000 individuals (Martins *et al.* 1993, R. F. Porter *in litt.* 1994), but there was no evidence that it is confined through competition with *O. blythii* to slightly moister areas as has been suggested by Ripley and Bond (1966). **VULNERABLE:** D1.

Abbott's Starling *Cinnyricinclus femoralis* is an extremely local and little-known inhabitant of highland forest canopy (1,800–2,600 m), occurring at a few localities in **Kenya**, including Mount Kenya National Park, and **Tanzania**, including Arusha National Park and Mount Kilimanjaro National Park, although the Arusha population may be only seasonal in occurrence and those in the other two parks may be subject to decline from habitat destruction (Collar and Stuart 1985; see also Lewis and Pomeroy 1989), with the population on Kilimanjaro now evidently being very sparse indeed (N. J. Cordeiro *in litt.* 1994). The species is, however, common (occurring in flocks of up to 40 birds) in the Kikuyu escarpment forest (southern Aberdares) of Kenya, apparently present there throughout the year, albeit with seasonal fluctuations (Taylor and Taylor 1988), and a flock of 20–25 was seen at 1,600 m in the North Pare Mountains in July 1993 (Cordeiro 1994). **VULNERABLE:** B1+2c; C2a.

Bali Starling *Leucopsar rothschildi* is endemic to Bali, **Indonesia**, where it formerly ranged across the western third of the island, but as a result of deforestation is now confined to a small area of monsoon forest and acacia savanna on the island's extreme north-west tip (King 1978–1979). Within this much reduced range, which lies inside the Bali Barat National Park, illegal poaching for the cagebird trade has reduced its numbers to a critically low level, and in 1990 the wild population was estimated to be as low as 13 individuals (van Balen and Gepak 1994), although the world's captive population was then estimated at c.700 (van Helvoort 1990). The Bali Starling Project, lauched in 1987 by ICBP/BirdLife in cooperation with the Indonesian government and American and British zoos, has helped to improve guarding of the park and has bolstered the wild population by release of a small number of captive-bred birds, which has brought the number of wild-living stock back to between 35 and 55 (S. van Balen *in litt.* 1994). However, despite excellent breeding success (36 young fledged in 1992/1993), the post-breeding census in 1993 estimated only 42–48 birds (a zero net growth over the year, the result of continuing illegal poaching) (van Balen and Jepson 1992, van Balen and Dirgayusa 1993), and only 36–40 in 1994 (P. Jepson *in litt.* 1994). **CRITICAL:** A1a,b,c; **B1+2e; C1; C2b; D1; D2.**

Family ORIOLIDAE

ORIOLES

Isabela Oriole *Oriolus isabellae* is restricted to Luzon in the **Philippines**, where it has been found in the canopy of forests (especially bamboo) and forest edge in only two areas—one in Bataan province in the west and the other in the Sierra Madre in Isabela province at c.600 m in the east—though there have been no records since 1961 (Dickinson *et al.* 1991). There is virtually no forest left at the site from which it was recorded in the Sierra Madre, and it may be close to extinction (Danielsen *et al.* 1994, Poulsen in press). **CRITICAL:** A1b; B1+2c; C1; **C2a**; **D1**.

São Tomé Oriole *Oriolus crassirostris*, though evidently far more abundant 50–100 years ago than now, has proved to be a low-density species of the canopy (4–8 pairs per km²) in remote and undisturbed areas of rainforest (over whose future some doubts remain) on São Tomé, **São Tomé e Príncipe**, failing to recolonize plantations after the application of pesticides (Eccles 1988, Jones and Tye 1988,

Atkinson *et al.* 1991, Jones *et al.* 1992, Nadler 1993). **VULNERABLE:** C2b.

Silver Oriole *Oriolus mellianus* breeds in **China**, where it is known from eight widely spread localities in central Sichuan, southern Guizhou, northern Guangdong and Guangxi, in broadleaf forest, perhaps only primary forest, from as low as 300 to c.1,450 m (Crosby 1991, Z. K. Wu *in litt.* 1994). It winters in **Cambodia** (King *et al.* 1975) and southern **Thailand**, where it is rare, in evergreen forest up to at least 800 m (Boonsong and Round 1991), and has been recorded as a non-breeding visitor to Hainan, China (Crosby 1991). There are recent records from at least three breeding localities, all unprotected and two scheduled for logging (Collar and Andrew 1988), but there are a number of protected areas containing subtropical broadleaf forest within its range (Li and Zhao 1989) where it could occur. **VULNERABLE:** B1+2c; C1; C2a.

Family DICRURIDAE

DRONGOS

Grand Comoro Drongo *Dicrurus fuscipennis* has a highly localized distribution within the 500–900 m altitudinal zone around Mount Karthala, Grand Comoro (= Ngazidja), **Comoro Islands**, and is everywhere rare (Collar and Stuart 1985). In 1985 it was judged that few more than 100 birds existed, but because they appear to prefer forest edge they are probably at no immediate risk, although locally so from habitat degradation (Louette *et al.* 1988, Louette and Stevens 1992). In 1989 three pairs were found displaying in coconut plantations on the southwest coast (Stevens *et al.* 1992). **CRITICAL:** B1+2c; **C2a**; D1.

Mayotte Drongo *Dicrurus waldenii* occurs sparsely and locally at the margins of evergreen forest, thickets and plantations (its distribution being linked to that of large trees above the 200 m contour) on **Mayotte (to France)** in the Comoro group. Its habitat, historically once more extensive, continues to decline in the face of local exploitation for domestic needs and burning for cultivation, and the entire population may not exceed a few dozen pairs (Collar and Stuart 1985, Louette 1988b, Safford and Evans 1992). **CRITICAL:** B1+2c; **C2b**; **D1**.

Family CALLAEIDAE

NEW ZEALAND WATTLEBIRDS

Kokako *Callaeas cinerea* from **New Zealand** has suffered from predation by introduced mammals, competition for food from exotic herbivores, and the destruction of forests (King 1978–1979, Williams and Given 1981, Hay *et al*. 1985). There is recent evidence that the South Island race *cinerea*, for long now considered extinct, still exists on Stewart Island, but its numbers are not known (B. D. Bell verbally 1993). The North Island race *wilsoni* has a fragmented and declining range, and was considered vulnerable to habitat destruction and deterioration (O'Donnell 1984). Birds have been transferred to Little Barrier and Kapiti islands, making 29 discrete populations altogether, with an estimated total of 1,500–2,000 individuals (R. Hay *per* A. J. Tennyson *in litt*. 1994). The Kokako's forests have been largely saved today, but it continues to decline on the mainland, and the influence of predators and browsers on this decline is not fully understood (Rasch 1992; see also Meenken *et al*. 1994), although recent research indicates that predators (including possums, rats and stoats) are the major threats (J. Innes *per* B. D. Bell *in litt*. 1994). **ENDANGERED: C2a**.

Family PTILONORHYNCHIDAE

BOWERBIRDS

Archbold's Bowerbird *Archboldia papuensis* is very patchily distributed in the Central Ranges of New Guinea, from the Weyland Mountains of Irian Jaya, **Indonesia**, to the highland provinces of **Papua New Guinea** (with westen and eastern populations, *A. p. papuensis* and *A. p. sanfordi*, appearing to be widely isolated). It is generally rare but locally moderately common, inhabiting mixed beech forest, mixed coniferous forest and frost-disturbed high mountain forest between 2,300 and 2,900 m, rarely as low as 1,800 m (Beehler *et al*. 1986, Coates 1990) and is locally threatened by timber operations (Beehler 1985, Collar 1986). Active nests appear to be built mostly adjacent to older nests, but it is considered unlikely that these 'traditional' nesting places reflect a sparcity of sites, rather proximity to long-established bowers (Frith and Frith 1994). Recent information on the bowers (the same unique 'mat' construction is built by both western and eastern males) and on plumage (all adult males have full yellow crests) indicates that there is no justification for treating the different populations as any more than relatively poorly defined subspecies of a single species (Frith *et al*. in press). **VULNERABLE: C1**.

Fire-maned Bowerbird *Sericulus bakeri* inhabits hill forest in the Adelbert Mountains in northwest **Papua New Guinea** (Coates 1990), where it is fairly common within its very restricted range (roughly 1,200 km²) (R. D. Mackay *in litt*. 1986), occupying a narrow altitudinal band at 900–1,400 m and being replaced at higher altitudes by the widespread Macgregor's Bowerbird *Amblyornis macgregoriae* (Beehler *et al*. 1986). Although the range is not heavily populated, villagers rely substantially on hunting for food (R. D. Mackay *in litt*. 1986) and it occurs at the optimum altitudes for indigenous agriculture and settlement (Schodde 1978) and thus the species could be declining. **VULNERABLE: C2b**.

Family PARADISAEIDAE

BIRDS OF PARADISE

Macgregor's Bird-of-paradise *Macgregoria pulchra* is distributed in small remnant populations in the highest areas of the Central Ranges of New Guinea, namely the Snow and Star mountains of Irian Jaya, **Indonesia**, and the Wharton and Owen Stanley ranges of **Papua New Guinea**, where it is largely restricted to subalpine woodland dominated by its major food plant, the conifer *Dacrycarpus compactus* (Beehler *et al.* 1986, Coates 1990), having vanished from great swathes of likely former range in the central highlands perhaps owing to habitat changes and hunting pressures in historic times (P. Gregory *in litt.* 1994). It is a popular gamebird, being unwary and site-faithful, and therefore easy to kill (Beehler 1985), and is threatened owing to its small fragmented populations (B. M. Beehler *in litt.* 1994). It remains common and tame above 3,000 m in the Star Mountains, where the Ketenban people consider that it harbours the spirits of their ancestors and consequently protect it (K. D. Bishop *in litt.* 1994). **VULNERABLE:** B1+2e; C2a.

Black Sicklebill *Epimachus fastuosus* is patchily distributed in the mountains of western and central New Guinea, from the Tamrau and Arfak Mountains in Vogelkop, Irian Jaya, **Indonesia**, to the Kubor and Kratke ranges and a few localities in the Torricelli and Bewani mountains in **Papua New Guinea** (Rand and Gilliard 1967, B. M. Beehler *in litt.* 1987). It occurs in mid-montane forest at 1,280–2,550 m (mainly 1,800–2,150 m), but is only locally common and generally scarce to rare or locally absent (Coates 1990). It is the largest-plumed member of its family and is much hunted both for its tail feathers and for food (Beehler 1985), and also suffers extensively from habitat destruction (Coates 1990). Skins are becoming increasingly valuable and hunting pressure will increase with the spread of shotguns (P. Gregory *in litt.* 1994). **VULNERABLE:** A2b,c; C2a.

Wahnes's Parotia *Parotia wahnesi* is known from the mountains of the Huon peninsula and the Adelbert Mountains, **Papua New Guinea** (Beehler *et al.* 1986, Coates 1990), where it is rarely hunted but is found primarily between 1,200 and 1,800 m, which are the optimum altitudes for indigenous agriculture and settlement (Schodde 1978) and thus it is possibly threatened by habitat destruction as the human population expands (I. Burrows *in litt.* 1994). **VULNERABLE:** C1.

Ribbon-tailed Astrapia *Astrapia mayeri* occupies montane forest between 2,400 and 3,400 m in the Central Ranges of **Papua New Guinea**, from Mount Hagen and Mount Giluwe to approximately 130 km further west, although its western limits are unclear and in the east hybridization occurs with Stephanie's Astrapia *A. stephaniae* (Beehler *et al.* 1986, Coates 1990). Observations by helicopter pilots c.40 km west of Tari (an unnamed peak in the Karius Range) represents a significant westward extension of the known range and indicates that it also occurs on the Muller Range (Frith and Frith 1993). It is generally common, occurring singly or in twos or threes at fruiting trees (Coates 1990), but is threatened in some areas owing to hunting for tail plumes which feature in local costumes (P. Gregory *in litt.* 1994). Potentially greater threats are forest destruction and modification because, although the birds are able to utilize disturbed forest growth for foraging and nesting, larger trees and their associated epiphytic growth may provide significant food resources and the only suitable dead limbs for male display (Frith and Frith 1993). **VULNERABLE:** B1+2c,e.

Goldie's Bird-of-paradise *Paradisaea decora* is restricted to Fergusson and Normanby in the East Papuan Islands, **Papua New Guinea**, where it is found in forest and at forest edge on ridges and is apparently limited to an altitudinal range of between 300 and at least 700 m (Beehler *et al.* 1986, G. R. Kula *in litt.* 1988). It is fairly common (Coates 1990) but is not known to visit native gardens, even those abandoned and overgrown, so that the preservation of undisturbed forest is essential to its survival (LeCroy *et al.* 1984). **VULNERABLE:** B1+2c.

Blue Bird-of-paradise *Paradisaea rudolphi* occurs in the eastern portions of the Central Ranges of New Guinea, **Papua New Guinea**, west to Mount Hagen and the Tari area, in primary lower montane oak forest, mainly between 1,400 and 1,800 m (the elevations most preferred by humans), also foraging at the forest edge and in nearby disturbed areas (Beehler *et al.* 1986, Coates 1990). It is a fairly common to common species in undisturbed forest (and in heavily gardened habitat, e.g. at Tari: I. Burrows *in litt.* 1994), but is rare or absent in certain areas mostly because of loss of habitat (a direct cause of competition with the more adaptable Raggiana Bird-of-paradise *P. raggiana* in marginal habitats: Schodde 1978), though also (and more importantly) because of hunting (Coates 1990). A hunting moratorium may allow it to colonize secondary

growth near villages, although these populations are likely to have difficulty fledging young owing to disturbance (Mack 1992). **VULNERABLE:** C1; C2a.

Family CORVIDAE

CROWS

Dwarf Jay *Cyanolyca nana* has been recorded only in humid temperate zone (pine–oak–fir) forests at roughly 2,000–3,000 m in Veracruz and Oaxaca, **Mexico**, and is currently to be found in just one area of Oaxaca, where it is still very common, having apparently been extirpated from much of its historical range by the extensive and continuing destruction and fragmentation of habitat (Collar *et al.* 1992). **ENDANGERED: A1b; A2b; B1+2c; C1; C2b.**

White-throated Jay *Cyanolyca mirabilis* is locally common in undisturbed tracts of the upper cloud- and pine–oak forests of Guerrero (records from 1,525–3,500 m) and Oaxaca (2,000–2,600 m), south-west **Mexico**, but this habitat is rapidly being cleared, grazed and burnt out of existence (Collar *et al.* 1992). **ENDANGERED: A1b; A2b; B1+2c; C1; C2a.**

Lidth's Jay *Garrulus lidthi* is endemic to Amami (although it is said also to have occurred on Tokunoshima where it is presumed to be extinct, unless records there were mistaken) in the Nansei Shoto, southern **Japan**, occupying broadleaf evergreen forest, coniferous forest and woodland around cultivation and human habitation (Brazil 1991). It is quite common, and a survey in 1974 estimated the total population to be c.5,800 birds (Y. Yamashina *in litt.* 1982). However, large areas of mature forest have been clear-felled on Amami in the last few decades and largely replaced by young secondary forests, but while it has been found to be as common in the secondary forest as in the older forests, it is very rare in logged forest (Sugimura 1988), so its population has presumably been reduced by forestry activities, and it remains vulnerable to further deforestation. **VULNERABLE:** C1; C2b.

Sichuan Jay *Perisoreus internigrans* is endemic to **China**, known from south-east Qinghai, south-west Gansu, western Sichuan and eastern Tibet, where it is found in dense, relatively dry coniferous forest with a poorly developed understorey, from 3,050 to 4,300 m (Meyer de Schauensee 1984, Cheng 1987, C. R. Robson *in litt.* 1992). There are recent records from at least one protected area, Xiaozhaizigou Nature Reserve, but the amount of suitable habitat within protected areas is probably small, and unprotected forest in this region is rapidly being clear-felled or selectively logged (P. Alström *in litt.* 1993, M.J.C.; see Collins *et al.* 1991). **VULNERABLE:** C1; C2a.

Sri Lanka Magpie *Urocissa ornata* is endemic to **Sri Lanka**, where it is found in dense evergreen forest up to 2,100 m in the south-west aspects of the Hill Zone and the adjacent parts of the wet zone down to 50 m (Ali and Ripley 1987, T. W. Hoffmann *in litt.* 1993). It appears to be confined to primary forest, and is declining because of forest loss and disturbance, particularly as natural forests are replaced by monoculture plantations (Hoffmann 1984), and because of the spread of Asian Koel *Eudynamys scolopacea*, which parasitizes the magpie along forest edges (S. W. Kotagama *in litt.* 1994). **VULNERABLE:** B1+2a,c; C1; C2a.

Hooded Treepie *Crypsirina cucullata* is endemic to the dry zone of central **Myanmar**, on the plains of the Irrawaddy and Sittang Rivers, where it is found in dry dipterocarp forest, dry scrub and secondary growth on the edge of agricultural land in the lowlands to 1,000 m (King *et al.* 1975, Smythies 1986). It was formerly common (Smythies 1986), but there are few recent records (K. D. Bishop *in litt.* 1993) and the forests of the Irrawaddy plains are now almost entirely cleared for agriculture (Collins *et al.* 1991). **VULNERABLE:** A1b; C1; C2a.

Ethiopian Bush-crow *Zavattariornis stresemanni*, remarkable both for its habits (possibly a cooperative breeder) and for its uncertain affinities (probably a crow, possibly a starling), is confined to c.6,000 km² of park-like thorn-bush and short-grass savanna around Yavello and Mega, southern **Ethiopia**, and could easily suffer from habitat alteration

(Collar and Stuart 1985). No population estimate has been made, but brief surveys in 1989 (Ash and Gullick 1989), 1989/1990 (Hundessa 1991) and 1990 (Syvertsen and Dellelegn 1991, Dellelegn 1993) suggested densities had remained constant through the 1980s but that threats remain from general habitat destruction, cattle-ranching, settlement of the area, and fire; a 2,537 km² (2,496 km² in Hillman 1993) Yavello Sanctuary was 'set up' for this and the White-tailed Swallow *Hirundo megaensis* in 1985 (Hundessa 1991), but has never been gazetted and involves no active management (P. O. Syvertsen *in litt.* 1994). **VULNERABLE:** B1+2a,b,c; C2b.

Xinjiang Ground-jay *Podoces biddulphi* is known from Xinjiang, western **China**, where it is found in sandy desert, scrub and desert poplar along the edge of the Taklimakan Desert in the Tarim Basin (and there is a recent sight record well to the east of this area, near Golmud in Qinghai: Turton and Speight 1986). It was described as being common in 1929–1930, but was scarce and difficult to locate in the same areas in 1988, and may be threatened by the degradation of desert habitats through the intensive grazing of goats and camels, extraction of fuelwood and the conversion of huge areas to irrigated land (Grimmett 1991; see Ludlow and Kinnear 1933–1934, Meyer de Schauensee 1984, Grimmett and Taylor 1992). **VULNERABLE:** C1; C2a.

Banggai Crow *Corvus unicolor* is known by two specimens, believed to have been collected on the island of Banggai, to the east of Sulawesi, **Indonesia** (White and Bruce 1986), although the origin of these specimens is questionable (K. D. Bishop *in litt.* 1994). Unidentified crows have recently been seen on Banggai (White and Bruce 1986), where rapid development is believed to be taking place (BirdLife IP). It is presumably rare, but its status remains unclear. **VULNERABLE:** D1.

Flores Crow *Corvus florensis* is endemic to Flores, **Indonesia**, where it is probably confined to the low-lands in the western half of the island (Verhoeye in prep.). A survey in 1993 recorded it in moist and semi-deciduous forest (including degraded forest), especially along watercourses, from sea-level to 950 m, and found it to be uncommon at two sites, including the Tanjung Kerita Mese proposed protected area. It is a large, low-density, forest-dependent species, threatened by lowland clearance, but it appears tolerant of some forest degradation (Butchart *et al.* 1993). **VULNERABLE:** B1+2c; C1; C2a.

Marianas Crow *Corvus kubaryi* inhabits forest on the islands of **Guam (to U.S.A.)** and Rota in the **Northern Marianas Islands (to U.S.A.)**, where an estimated 350 birds on Guam in 1981 declined to less than 50 in 1993 (with very few or no young in recent years), most likely owing to predation by the brown tree snake *Boiga irregularis*. The Rota population was thought to have remained stable since 1945 and estimated at 1,300 birds in 1982, although Jenkins (1983) suggested it may be declining there too (a more recent estimate of 500 supports this) and there is concern that the snake may colonize Rota and that development will be a threat (Engbring and Pratt 1985, Grout 1993, S. L. Pimm *in litt.* 1994). **CRITICAL:** A1a; **B1+2c,d,e**; C1; C2a; D1.

White-necked Crow *Corvus leucognaphalus* is now confined to the island of Hispaniola (**Haiti** and the **Dominican Republic**), having become extinct around 1963 on Puerto Rico (to U.S.A.), where it was once abundant, owing to habitat loss and hunting for food (Raffaele 1989); on Hispaniola even into the 1980s it was considered locally common (M. A. McDonald *in litt.* 1986, C. A. Woods *in litt.* 1986), but more recently a substantial drop in numbers (certainly less than 10,000) and loss of range have been recognized (again, from habitat loss and hunting), with good populations now restricted in the Dominican Republic to Los Haitises and Jaragua National Parks plus the Sierra de Baoruco (F. J. Vilella verbally 1994; also T. A. Parker verbally 1992). **VULNERABLE:** A1b; C1; C2a.

Hawaiian Crow *Corvus hawaiiensis*, an omnivorous but primarily fruit-eating, forest-inhabiting corvid, is endemic to Hawaii in the Hawaiian Islands (**U.S.A.**), where it is now found only in a relatively small area (c.260 km² of not necessarily prime habitat) in central Kona, having been exterminated from all but this one ranch as a result of habitat destruction and, in the later stages, illegal hunting (National Research Council 1992, S. L. Pimm *in litt.* 1994). In 1993 seven chicks were raised in captivity from eggs removed from wild nests, and five of these were subsequently released to join the remaining three wild pairs, increasing the total number in existence (both wild and captive flocks) to 31. In July 1994 there were nine captive-reared chicks (to be hacked back), three wild reproductive pairs (out of a total adult population estimated at 8–12 birds) and three captive reproductive pairs (out of 10) bringing the latest total to 31–36 birds (Maxfield 1993, A. Lieberman verbally 1994). **CRITICAL:** D1; D2.

EXTINCT SPECIES

THE DECISION to regard a species as extinct (see p. 15 for definition) is usually very difficult to take, and is occasionally overturned by later events. It has been the policy in BirdLife Red Data Books since 1980 to allow species the benefit of any doubt, even where the chances of survival appear to be paper-thin, while species judged undoubtedly extinct have simply not been listed. However, the new IUCN criteria (p. 14) make it rather less satisfactory to retain within the threatened categories those species that are probably extinct (and it would be inappropriate to list them as Data Deficient, since they cannot be non-threatened), so we list here those birds where the balance of the evidence strongly indicates extinction. In all of the following cases there does remain a remote chance that one or two birds survive, and if they do they would almost inevitably be listed as Critical. In order to indicate this potential priority, we have listed all 'Extinct' species by country in Appendix 1.

Two species absent from this list, which might be expected to be here, are Guadalupe Storm-petrel *Oceanodroma macrodactyla* (p. 37) and Pink-headed Duck *Rhodonessa caryophyllacea* (p. 50). Although widely assumed to be extinct, searches at the right season for the storm-petrel, and in the right area for the duck, have still not been conducted, so we prefer for the moment to list them among the living.

Species classified as Extinct in the Wild form a separate category (defined on p. 15) and are included in the listing of globally threatened species: Alagoas Curassow *Mitu mitu* (p. 61), Guam Rail *Rallus owstoni* (p. 76), Socorro Dove *Zenaida graysoni* (p. 91) and Kakapo *Strigops habroptilus* (p. 104).

Atitlán Grebe *Podilymbus gigas* was endemic to Lake Atitlán, **Guatemala**, where its long-term decline was variously attributed to breeding habitat (reedbed) clearance, habitat disturbance by boat traffic, drowning in gill-nets, competition for food from introduced bass, water-level variation caused by an earthquake and competition and hybridization with the colonizing Pied-billed Grebe *P. podiceps* (King 1978–1979, LaBastille 1983, 1984, Forbes 1985). It is now regarded as extinct (Hunter 1988, LaBastille 1990).

Colombian Grebe *Podiceps andinus* was originally restricted to a few lakes throughout the Bogotá-Ubate plateaus of the East Andes of **Colombia**, and was apparently last seen in 1977; habitat loss caused by drainage, and habitat alteration caused by falling water levels, soil erosion, chemical run-off from surrounding farmland and introduced fish species, compounded by hunting, are to blame for the species' now almost certain extinction (Collar *et al.* 1992, Fjeldså 1993).

Barred-wing Rail *Nesoclopeus poecilopterus* is known from 12 specimens collected on the islands of Viti Levu and Ovalau, **Fiji**, in the last century and, despite a recent (1973) but unconfirmed record from north of Waisa, near Vunindawa, on Viti Levu, it is likely to be extinct; a number of other ground-dwelling species, including two (non-endemic) rails, the Banded Rail *Rallus philippensis* and the Purple Gallinule *Porphyrio porphyrio*, have disappeared from Viti Levu as a result of predation by introduced mongooses and feral cats (King 1978–1979, Hay 1986, D. Watling *in litt.* 1993).

Canary Islands Oystercatcher *Haematopus meadewaldoi* cannot realistically now be expected still to survive, having always been uncommon and known with certainty only from the eastern Canary Islands (**Spain**); repeated recent searches have drawn a blank, although there have been four apparently genuine records of black oystercatchers in the region since 1968 (two on Tenerife, two on the West African coast), and it is just conceivable that a population remains undetected in the western Canaries

(Collar and Stuart 1985). Surveys of the eastern islands in 1985 and 1986 drew a blank but gathered evidence that the species' disappearance is related to competition from man for the intertidal invertebrates on which both depended (Hockey 1986, 1987, Piersma 1986).

Javanese Lapwing *Vanellus macropterus* was known from Java, and doubtfully from Sumatra and Timor, **Indonesia** (King 1978–1979). It was regularly reported from the marshes of north-west Java until 1930 and survived in the river deltas on the south coast of east Java until at least 1940 (Kooiman 1940), but recent visits to several former localities have failed to locate it, and it is almost certainly extinct (S. van Balen *in litt.* 1994). The reason for its decline is believed to be the conversion of its habitat, grassland adjacent to coastal swamps, for aquaculture and agricultural land (Collar and Andrew 1988).

Choiseul Pigeon *Microgoura meeki* is known from Choiseul, **Solomon Islands**, where it was discovered and last reliably recorded in 1904 (Diamond 1987). Suitable habitat is not lacking but it is likely to have been preyed on by dogs and feral cats (Schodde 1978), and has long been listed as extinct (King 1978–1979). Information from local villagers on Choiseul tends to confirm this (J. M. Diamond *in litt.* 1987) and rumours of its continued existence probably refer to Crested Cuckoo-dove *Reinwardtoena crassirostris* (D. Gibbs *in litt.* 1994).

Red-moustached Fruit-dove *Ptilinopus mercierii* is almost certainly extinct, as listed by King (1978–1979). It is known from Hiva Oa and Nuku Hiva in the Marquesas Islands, **French Polynesia**, and was apparently extinct on Nuku Hiva by 1922 (Holyoak and Thibault 1984). It was reported on Hiva Oa in 1980 (Hay 1986), but not in 1985 (Pratt *et al.* 1987), and there is some doubt over the 1980 record given the observers' failure to record the common White-capped Fruit-dove *P. dupetithouarsii* and previous observers' failure to find the species in the 1970s, when the cause of its extinction was speculated to be the introduction of the Great Horned Owl *Bubo virginianus* (Holyoak and Thibault 1984, Thibault 1988)—although predation by rats and cats (prior to the introduction of the owl) seems a more likely cause (Seitre and Seitre 1991).

Paradise Parrot *Psephotus pulcherrimus*, from **Australia**, was last reliably recorded in 1927 and is presumed extinct by King (1978–1979) and Garnett (1992). It formerly occurred in south-east Queensland and north-east New South Wales, in savanna woodlands with a grass ground-cover, feeding on

seeds (Garnett 1992). Its extinction has been attributed to the practice of firing seeding grass to provide green growth for cattle (Blakers *et al.* 1984) and a reduction in the availability of food as a result of drought, overgrazing and the spread of prickly pears; disease, trapping and egg-collecting may have also contributed (Garnett 1992). No evidence is forthcoming to suggest that this species is still extant as rumours and reports of the birds, sometimes dating back to the 1950s and sometimes more recent (e.g. Schmidt 1986), are usually unsubstantiated and often shrouded in secrecy (Joseph 1988).

Glaucous Macaw *Anodorhynchus glaucus* was formerly fairly widespread but clearly very local in south-central South America in northern **Argentina**, southern **Paraguay**, north-east **Uruguay** and **Brazil** from Paraná state southwards, being mostly found along major rivers where it nested in cliffs. The species is now usually considered extinct. Claims that the cause of its decline must have been natural are made in ignorance of the impact of human colonization of the river systems where it occurred, since it is clear that gallery forest destruction, disturbance at breeding colonies, direct human exploitation and, perhaps most importantly, agricultural development of palm savannas (leading to the elimination of its key food plants, probably *Butia yatay*), were likely to have been major influences (Collar *et al.* 1992, Yamashita and Valle 1993).

Snail-eating Coua *Coua delalandei*, a large terrestrial cuckoo endemic to **Madagascar** and only certainly recorded from the offshore island of Nosy Boraha (Ile Sainte Marie), has not been recorded since 1834 but was thought conceivably to survive in one poorly explored rainforest region, the hinterland of Pointe-à-Larrée (Collar and Stuart 1985); however, fieldwork and inquiries in the nearby Ambatovaky Reserve in 1990 drew a blank (Thompson and Evans 1992). Despite reports that all forest on Nosy Boraha had been cleared (Collar and Stuart 1985), a search was made in 1991 which concluded that the species was extinct there; and investigations and interviews with local people on the adjacent mainland and elsewhere, combined with reconsideration of the historical evidence, have failed to indicate that the species ever occurred anywhere other than on Nosy Boraha (Goodman 1993).

Ivory-billed Woodpecker *Campephilus principalis* is very probably extinct in the **U.S.A.**, and the most recent evidence suggests that there is almost as little hope for the form on **Cuba**, which was last reported in 1987 or 1988 (with glimpses in 1991), despite much intensive searching in the Sierra de

Moa, the area to which it finally retreated in the course of this century (Lammertink and Estrada in press). Destruction of its virgin forest habitat, of which each pair evidently needed very large amounts, is chiefly to blame for the loss of the species (Collar *et al.* 1992).

Bush Wren *Xenicus longipes*, endemic to **New Zealand**, declined rapidly following the introduction of predatory mammals, the North Island race *stokesi* last being recorded in 1949, the Stewart Island race *variabilis* in 1965, and the South Island race *longipes* in 1972 (King 1978–1979, Williams and Given 1981, Turbott 1990). On the main islands it was found mostly in dense mountain forest, whilst on smaller islands it was found in coastal forest or scrub (Robertson 1985).

Aldabra Warbler *Nesillas aldabrana* is only known from a 10-ha strip of coastal vegetation on Aldabra, **Seychelles**, where no more than five birds were ever seen and, since 1977, only two, both males. Rat predation on nests is perhaps the main cause of the species' plight (Collar and Stuart 1985; see also Hambler *et al.* 1985). Searches from July to November 1986 produced no records and it is feared extinct (Roberts 1987).

Guam Flycatcher *Myiagra freycineti* is endemic to **Guam (to U.S.A.)**, where it was once widespread in wooded areas, but the population has crashed over the last decade or so, most likely owing to depredation by the introduced brown tree snake *Boiga irregularis*, and it is now judged to be extinct (Engbring and Pratt 1985, D. W. Stinson *in litt.* 1994).

Akialoa *Hemignathus obscurus* was known from the forests of all of the larger Hawaiian Islands (**U.S.A.**) except Maui. It had been extirpated on most islands by early in the twentieth century (perhaps owing to habitat destruction and introduced disease-carrying mosquitoes in the lowlands), the Kauai race surviving into the 1960s in the Alakai Wilderness Preserve, but now probably extinct (King 1978–1979, Pratt *et al.* 1987, Pratt 1993). The last convincing sighting was by P. Bruner in 1969 (H. D. Pratt *in litt.* 1994; see also Pratt 1994).

Kakawahie *Paroreomyza flammea* was endemic to Molokai in the Hawaiian Islands (**U.S.A.**), where it was common and widespread in the 1890s, but suffered a catastrophic drop in numbers during the following century (presumably as a result of habitat destruction and introduced disease-carrying mosquitoes in the lowlands), and was last seen in 1963 in the Kamakou Preserve, with exhaustive searches proving unproductive (King 1978–1979, Scott *et al.* 1986, Pratt *et al.* 1987, Pratt 1993; see also Pratt 1994).

CONSERVATION DEPENDENT SPECIES

THE DEFINITION of and rationale for the Conservation Dependent category have been given on pp. 15 and 18. The category is not a threatened one, but the species it contains require the continuation of existing management in order to prevent them from falling into such a category. These species remain, therefore, a priority.

Hooded Crane *Grus monacha* is known to breed in wetlands on wooded steppes in two areas of central Siberia in **Russia** (Potapov and Flint 1987), and small numbers have been found nesting since 1991 in Heilongjiang, **China** (*Oriental Bird Club Bull.* 1993, 18: 18). It winters at a few localities in **Japan**, **North Korea**, **South Korea** and eastern China (wandering to Taiwan, India and Mongolia: Ali and Ripley 1987, Cheng 1987, Inskipp and Collins 1993), in wetlands and agricultural land, especially rice fields (King 1978–1979). The total world population is estimated at c.11,800 birds (Rose and Scott 1994), a high (and increasing because of artificial feeding: Ohsako 1987, Higuchi 1991) proportion of which winter at Izumi (= Arasaki), on Kyushu, Japan (nearly 9,000 in 1992: Brazil 1994) and other important areas include Yashiro, on Honshu, Japan (about 100: Brazil 1994), near Taegu, South Korea (200–300: Cho and Won 1990) and the Chang Jiang (= Yangtze) valley in China (c.800: Rose and Scott 1994). The wintering population in South Korea is threatened by the reduction in feeding area as farmland is urbanized (P. O. Won verbally 1994), and the large concentration at Izumi may be susceptible to disease, causes damage on nearby agricultural land, and requires improved management, possibly including dispersal to other areas (Higuchi 1991).

Audouin's Gull *Larus audouinii* is confined as a breeding species to the Mediterranean, the great majority of the population nesting at various sites in or administered by **Spain** (chiefly the Chafarinas Islands and the Ebro delta, but also the Islas Columbretes and Balearic Islands), with other important colonies in Corsica (**France**) and Sardinia and the Tuscan archipelago (**Italy**), and further, smaller colonies in **Cyprus**, **Greece**, **Turkey**, **Tunisia** and **Algeria**, many birds then wintering along the African coast from **Libya** west to **Morocco** into the Atlantic and down the West African coast (Western Sahara almost certainly, **Mauritania** and **Senegal**); the total Spanish population alone was 12,631 pairs in 1992 out of a global total of under 14,000, a doubling of known numbers in under a decade (apparently as a result of greatly improved breeding success as birds increasingly exploit discarded material from local fishing fleets: see, e.g., Paterson *et al.* 1992), but human disturbance and interference from the Mediterranean Herring Gull *L. cachinnans*, which could cause total failure or even abandonment at these Spanish sites, are only prevented by continuing conservation measures (Hoogendoorn and Mackrill 1987, de Juana *et al.* 1987, Grimmett and Jones 1989, del Nevo *et al.* 1994, Tucker and Heath 1994, Heredia in prep.).

Madeira Laurel Pigeon *Columba trocaz* is confined to tracts of laurel forest on Madeira, **Portugal**, a habitat now reduced to 13.5% of the island's land area, and in which its numbers are estimated to lie between 2,000 and 5,000 birds, an improvement on previous figures that may in part reflect a genuine recovery; habitat loss has recently been curtailed by the creation of the Parque Natural da Madeira, and the hunting of birds, often previously practised when they invaded crops following food shortages in the forests, is prohibited under the European Union Wild Birds Directive, with park officials providing farmers with bird-scarers instead (Collar and Stuart 1985, Zino and Zino 1986a, Jones 1990, Tucker and Heath 1994, Heredia in prep., F. Zino *in litt.* 1994).

Mallee Emuwren *Stipiturus mallee* has a patchy distribution (no estimates of population size) in the Victorian and South Australian mallee regions of **Australia**, south and east of the Murray River, where it has been affected by the clearance and fragmentation of its heathland and mallee shrubland habitat, particularly as its ability to recolonize may be limited, but an extensive reserve system incorporates most of its remaining range including Hattah-Kulkyne and Wyperfeld National Parks, Murray-Sunset National Park and the Big Desert Wilderness in Victoria and Ngarkat Conservation Park in South Australia; grazing by stock and wildfires remain threats (Garnett 1992) and the population may fluctuate owing to fire patterns, but it responds well to management practices which provide medium-aged (c.10–20 years) mallee (D. Franklin *in litt.* to K. Fitzherbert 1994).

Atherton Scrubwren *Sericornis keri* seems scarce in the upland rainforests of the Atherton region in north-eastern Queensland, **Australia**, where it apparently has a disjunct distribution between mountain tops (Garnett 1992) and there is evidence of hybridization with the widespread White-browed Scrubwren *S. frontalis* (Joseph and Moritz 1993). Its area of occupancy is estimated at 1,500 km^2 and, as there are still areas of forest which are in private freehold and which are likely to be cleared for agriculture and housing development (G. N. Harrington *in litt.* 1993), its long-term future is likely to depend on the integrity of the Wet Tropics Heritage Site which covers the majority of its range.

Mountain Thornbill *Acanthiza katherina* is confined to rainforest above 450 m in the Atherton region of **Australia** where its population size is unknown (Blakers *et al.* 1984). Its area of occupancy is estimated to be 1,700 km^2 and, as there are still areas of forest which are in private freehold and which are likely to be cleared for agriculture and housing development (G. N. Harrington *in litt.* 1993), its long-term future is likely to depend on the integrity of the Wet Tropics Heritage Site which covers the majority of its range.

Red-lored Whistler *Pachycephala rufogularis* is restricted to eastern South Australia and adjacent north-west Victoria, with outlying populations in New South Wales, **Australia**, with much of the overall population (no estimate of size) in reserves and found only where mallee eucalypts form an open canopy over a moderately dense but patchy shrub layer (the species being sensitive to the clearing and burning of the ground vegetation and preferring vegetation 10–30 years after fire). It is replaced by Gilbert's Whistler *P. inornata* in some places, probably as a result of changes in habitat (Garnett 1992). The extensive wildfires of the 1970s and 1980s may

have increased the amount of available habitat now or in the near future and thus, apart from the small and peripheral population in New South Wales, no decline is likely and the core populations (e.g. in the Big Desert Wilderness and Sunset Country) are intact (D. Franklin *in litt.* to K. Fitzherbert 1994).

Eungella Honeyeater *Lichenostomus hindwoodi* occurs only in the rainforests of the Clarke Range in central-eastern Queensland, **Australia**, where most of its small range is included in some form of conservation reserve and where there appear to be substantial populations (Garnett 1992).

Blue Chaffinch *Fringilla teydea* is confined to tracts of pine forest on Tenerife (nominate *teydea*, roughly 1,000 pairs) and Gran Canaria (race *polatzeki*, 180–260 individuals) in the Canary Islands, **Spain**, but although the latter population remains at high risk of extinction the species as a whole, and its habitat on Tenerife, now enjoys protection under national and regional laws, in accordance with the European Union Wild Birds Directive (Collar and Stuart 1985, Tucker and Heath 1994, Heredia in prep.).

Saddleback *Philesturnus carunculatus* inhabits coastal scrub forest and understorey vegetation in **New Zealand**; after the introduction of predators, the range of the North Island race *rufusater* contracted to Hen Island, and that of the South Island race *carunculatus* to three islets off Stewart Island; reintroductions to other islands have proved successful (King 1978–1979) and resulted in an increase in population to c.2,000 *rufusater* and 650 *carunculatus* on some 10 islands (Rasch and McClelland 1993, S. Clegg *in litt.* 1994), including (recently) Moutuara in the Marlborough Sounds (B. D. Bell *in litt.* 1994).

Golden Bowerbird *Prionodura newtoniana* is widely if patchily distributed in the remaining rainforests above 700 m of the Atherton region in north-eastern Queensland, **Australia**, including rainforests that have been selectively logged and others isolated by forest clearance (Garnett 1992). Its area of occupancy is estimated to be 1,500 km^2 and, as there are still areas of forest which are in private freehold and which are likely to be cleared for agriculture and housing development (G. N. Harrington *in litt.* 1993), its long-term future is likely to depend on the integrity of the Wet Tropics Heritage Site which covers the majority of its range.

DATA DEFICIENT SPECIES

THE DEFINITION of and rationale for the Data Deficient category have been given on pp. 15 and 18. This is neither a threatened nor a non-threatened category; it acknowledges that the species it contains are potentially either. The guidelines for the new criteria stress the importance of precaution in listing species, so that if the evidence most tends to suggest threatened status, then the species should be treated accordingly. Those that remain intractable clearly have some right to be considered priorities for fuller investigation, but given the possibility that their status will prove to be secure they remain less significant than those in threatened categories, perhaps more closely parallel to Near-threatened species (p. 222).

■

Black Tinamou *Tinamus osgoodi* is an uncommon gamebird known from two disjunct areas of humid forest separated by almost 2,000 km, the northern subspecies *hershkovitzi* in the eastern Andes of **Colombia** chiefly at 1,400–1,500 m (status unknown), the nominate form only on the east Andean slope in Cuzco department, south-east **Peru**, at 600–1,400 m (where a sizeable population may be safe within Manu National Park) (Collar *et al.* 1992).

White-vented Storm-petrel *Oceanites gracilis* occupies tropical waters of the eastern Pacific Ocean, where it is numerous, but only a single nest has ever been found, on Isla Chungungo, **Chile** (where rats and fire may have caused an assumed decline), while a breeding population (subspecies *galapagoensis*) of several thousands is suspected for the Galápagos, **Ecuador** (del Hoyo *et al.* 1992).

Markham's Storm-petrel *Oceanodroma markhami* occurs in tropical waters of the eastern Pacific Ocean, with breeding confirmed on the Paracas peninsula, **Peru**, and other colonies likely on islands along the coast of Peru and Chile, but data on overall numbers, trends and threats are lacking (Collar and Andrew 1988, del Hoyo *et al.* 1992).

Matsudaira's Storm-petrel *Oceanodroma matsudairae* ranges through tropical waters from the western Pacific into the Indian Ocean, although the only breeding reports are from Kita-io-jima and Minami-io-jima in the Kazan-retto (Volcano Islands), **Japan**, the former remaining unvisited for many years and data on numbers, trends and threats being absent (del Hoyo *et al.* 1992).

Ringed Storm-petrel *Oceanodroma hornbyi* occurs in waters of the eastern Pacific Ocean south of the Equator, along the coast of **Peru** and **Chile**, but although observed in thousands its nesting grounds have never been found, so that data on overall numbers, trends and threats are lacking (Collar and Andrew 1988, del Hoyo *et al.* 1992).

Kenyon's Shag *Phalacrocorax kenyoni* is known only from 800-year-old midden bones plus three specimens collected in the late 1950s (but preserved only as skeletons) from Amchitka Island in the central Aleutian archipelago, **U.S.A.**, where it is assumed to survive although it may be a non-breeding visitor from islands belonging to Russia (Siegel-Causey 1991, Siegel-Causey *et al.* 1991; see also Kenyon 1961, Bourne 1993, DeBenedictis 1993).

Mountain Serpent-eagle *Spilornis kinabaluensis* is known only from montane forest above 1,600 m (occasionally down to 1,000 m) on Gunong Kinabalu and Gunong Trus Madi in Sabah, and Gunong Mulu and Gunong Murad in Sarawak, East **Malaysia** (Smythies 1981), and Bukit Tudal, **Brunei** (Mann 1987). A large raptor with such a localized distribution must have a small population and be sensitive to minor degradation of its habitat (Collar and Andrew 1988).

Chestnut-shouldered Goshawk *Erythrotriorchis buergersi* is a rare and little-known species (having been recorded only a few times), apparently restricted to hill forest at 450–1,580 m, in eastern New Guinea including the mountains of the Central Ranges, Huon peninsula, North Coastal Range and from near Port Moresby, **Papua New Guinea**, with a single record from the Foya Mountains, Irian Jaya, **Indonesia** (Coates 1985, Beehler *et al.* 1986). Only a small part of its range is threatened by deforestation and hunting should not be a problem (B. J. Coates *in litt.* 1994, B. W. Finch *in litt.* 1994). An observation of a soaring bird at a site in Veimauri Central Province in 1991 (now extensively logged) may indicate that this is not an inconspicuous species, the paucity of records being perhaps a true reflection of its rarity (I. Burrows *in litt.* 1994).

Nahan's Francolin *Francolinus nahani* is known only from a few localities in lowland forest in eastern **Zaïre** and central and western **Uganda**, where the overall paucity of records and lack of recent contact have rendered its status obscure (Collar and Stuart 1985; see also Urban *et al.* 1986). It is now known to be uncommon in the still extensive Ituri forest, Zaïre (J. Hart *in litt.* 1994; also P. A. Dejaifve *in litt.* 1994, D. A. Turner *in litt.* 1994), but there is only intermittent evidence of its survival in Uganda since 1970, at one site: three birds in Budongo forest in September 1992 (I. S. Robertson *in litt.* 1993) and up to six reportedly present in early 1993 (T. Stevenson *in litt.* 1994).

Speckled Crake *Coturnicops notatus* has been recorded in **Colombia** (Meta, once in 1959), **Venezuela** (twice, in 1914 or 1916 in Mérida and 1954 or 1960 in Portuguesa), **Guyana** (once in 1907), **Brazil** (São Paulo at three sites, of which one, Taubaté, has recent and repeated sightings; Rio Grande do Sul in 1928), **Paraguay** (thrice, in Presidente Hayes, Concepción and Alto Paraná, all before 1945), **Uruguay** (five records, from Durazno in 1915 and 1918, Colonia in 1985 when breeding was confirmed, Montevideo in 1985, and at sea off Rocha in 1875) and **Argentina** (at least 10 records, from the type-specimen on the *Beagle* in 1831 to two in the 1980s and two in the 1990s). Its habitat is variable, generally involving wetland vegetation but with records from crops and stubble, and it seems likely that it is in some way irruptive in pursuit of temporary wetland conditions (Collar *et al.* 1992).

White-striped Forest-rail *Rallina leucospila* inhabits montane forest from 1,450 to 1,600 m in the Tamrau, Arfak and Wandammen Mountains of the Vogelkop region of Irian Jaya, **Indonesia** (Beehler *et al.* 1986). There is no recent information on its status but no reason to expect it to be threatened (J. M. Diamond *in litt.* 1987) as its habitat is likely to be secure (BirdLife Indonesian Programme), although local hunting with dogs occurs throughout the Vogelkop (N. Bostock *in litt.* 1993).

Mayr's Forest-rail *Rallina mayri* occurs in forest between 1,000 and 2,200 m in the isolated mountain ranges of Cyclops, Bewani and Torricelli on the central north coast of Irian Jaya, **Indonesia**, and **Papua New Guinea** (Coates 1985, Beehler *et al.* 1986), where it is common in secure habitat (J. M. Diamond *in litt.* 1987), although it was not found more recently on a visit to the Cyclops (K. D. Bishop *in litt.* 1994).

New Guinea Flightless Rail *Megacrex inepta* inhabits wet thickets, swamp forest and mangroves in the lowlands of the north and south of New Guinea (Idenburg River, Humboldt Bay and Sepik River in the north; and Setekwa, Noord, Digul and Fly rivers in the south) (Irian Jaya, **Indonesia**, and **Papua New Guinea**) (Coates 1985, Beehler *et al.* 1986). It is very rarely seen (although not uncommon near Kiunga according to local people) and there are no obvious threats except perhaps from feral pigs (P. Gregory *in litt.* 1994) and possibly casual hunting by local people whilst collecting sago (K. D. Bishop *in litt.* 1994).

Moluccan Cuckoo *Cacomantis heinrichi* is known from Bacan and Halmahera in the north Moluccas, **Indonesia**, by five specimens collected in 1931 in forest between 1,000 and 1,500 m (White and Bruce 1986). There are no subsequent records (K. D. Bishop *in litt.* 1994), so its current status and any threats are unknown.

Green-cheeked Bronze-cuckoo *Chrysococcyx rufomerus* is known from Romang, Kisar, Leti, Moa, Sermata and Damar, small, low islands east of Timor, **Indonesia**, where it is believed to parasitize the Rufous-sided Gerygone *Gerygone dorsalis*. Its status and any threats are unknown, and its taxonomic relationship to the Pied Bronze-cuckoo *C. crassirostris* is poorly understood (White and Bruce 1986).

Minahassa Masked-owl *Tyto inexspectata* is endemic to Sulawesi, **Indonesia**, where it is known by eleven specimens collected on the Minahassa

peninsula and in the north-central part of the island, in lowland and hill forest between 100 and 1,500 m, and a recent sight record from Dumoga-Bone National Park (M. Aurivillius *per* K. D. Bishop *in litt.* 1994). It appears to be rare, but it is probably shy and easily overlooked like other forest dwelling members of the genus *Tyto*, so its status and the effects of the extensive forest clearance and degradation which have taken place within its known range remain unclear (Bishop 1989, K. D. Bishop *in litt.* 1994).

Lesser Masked-owl *Tyto sororcula* is known from Buru and Tanimbar in the Moluccas, **Indonesia**, where it is presumed to occur in lowland forest, but it is known from few specimens (White and Bruce 1986) and by a recent photograph of a bird almost certainly this species taken on Seram (K. D. Bishop *in litt.* 1994). It is probably scarce, as it was not recorded during surveys of Buru in 1989 or Tanimbar in 1993. There has been some deforestation in the coastal lowlands of Buru (although Tanimbar remains almost entirely forested), but it is unclear whether this represents a threat (Jepson 1993, N. Brickle and Y. Cahyadin verbally 1993).

Papuan Hawk-owl *Uroglaux dimorpha* is sparsely distributed in forest in the New Guinean lowlands, rarely to 1,500 m (Irian Jaya, **Indonesia**, and **Papua New Guinea**), so far being recorded only from the north-west (Vogelkop, Geelvink Bay, Weyland Mountains and Yapen Island) and the southeast (Collingwood Bay, Milne Bay, Port Moresby region and Mount Victoria), but probably occurring throughout (Coates 1985). One was reported near Vanimo in 1991, but there are no other recent records (I. Burrows *in litt.* 1994).

Large Frogmouth *Batrachostomus auritus* is a nocturnal species found in lowland (including secondary) forest in peninsular **Thailand**, peninsular and East **Malaysia**, Sumatra and Kalimantan, **Indonesia** and **Brunei** (Mann 1987). It is rarely seen in the Greater Sundas (MacKinnon and Phillipps 1993), very rare in Thailand (Boonsong and Round 1991), and there are recent records from only a small number of localities, despite its vocalizations being relatively well known (F. R. Lambert verbally 1994). It is not known how seriously it is threatened by the extensive lowland forest clearance and degradation which has taken place within its range (see Collins *et al.* 1991).

Dulit Frogmouth *Batrachostomus harterti* is known from only seven specimens collected in forest between 300 and 1,500 m in Sarawak, East **Malaysia** and Kalimantan, **Indonesia** (Smythies 1981).

As a nocturnal species in a region which has been relatively poorly worked by ornithologists it is undoubtably greatly under-recorded, and is probably fairly widespread on the central mountain spine of Borneo (Collar and Andrew 1988). Forest within its known altitudinal range is probably not particularly threatened (BirdLife IP).

Short-tailed Frogmouth *Batrachostomus poliolophus* is endemic to Sumatra, **Indonesia**, where it is known from a small number of records from the Barisan range, in forest between 660 and 1,400 m, but is presumably greatly under-recorded because it is nocturnal (van Marle and Voous 1988). Deforestation in the lower part of its altitudinal range could be a threat (BirdLife IP).

Bornean Frogmouth *Batrachostomus mixtus* is known from a few specimens collected in hill and lower montane forest in East **Malaysia** and Kalimantan, **Indonesia** (Smythies 1981). As a nocturnal species in a region which has been relatively poorly worked by ornithologists it is undoubtably greatly under-recorded, and forest within its known altitudinal range is probably not particularly threatened (BirdLife IP).

Cayenne Nightjar *Caprimulgus maculosus* is known with certainty from just one specimen taken in **French Guiana** during 1917, but remains unknown in life (Collar *et al.* 1992). A re-examination of the type appears to confirm its status as a good species (N. Cleere *in litt.* 1994).

Salvadori's Nightjar *Caprimulgus pulchellus* is a poorly known montane forest species of Sumatra and Java, **Indonesia**, although there is also a possible record from the lowlands of Sumatra (Kuroda 1936, van Marle and Voous 1988). Recent records are of a bird taped at 2,000 m (Marshall 1978) and up to five individuals regularly seen feeding about a cliff face at 1,400 m, on Gunung Pangrango, West Java (Andrew 1985), and of an incubating bird in Aceh, Sumatra (van Marle and Voous 1988), but in all three cases identification is best treated as tentative (Collar and Andrew 1988); there are further unconfirmed records of calling birds from two localities in East Java (S. van Balen *in litt.* 1994). Montane habitats on Sumatra and Java are relatively well represented in protected areas (see IUCN 1992), so habitat destruction is presumably not a major threat (see RePPProT 1990).

White-fronted Swift *Cypseloides storeri* is known from five specimens taken in Guerrero (Sierra de Atoyac at 2,500 m), Michoacán (Tacámbaro at

1,500 m) and Jalisco (Sierra de Manantlán at 1,800 m), **Mexico**, and although it remains unknown in life the evidence suggests that it occurs over montane pine-oak forest with high waterfalls and deep canyons (Navarro *et al.* 1992, 1993).

Mayr's Swiftlet *Collocalia orientalis* inhabits open country and forest, breeding in caves, in New Ireland, Bougainville (**Papua New Guinea**) and Guadalcanal (**Solomon Islands**) (Sibley and Monroe 1990). It is very difficult to identify in the field, although apparently rare (D. Gibbs *in litt.* 1994).

Fernando Po Swift *Apus sladeniae* is known from only 10 specimens from Bioko (**Equatorial Guinea**), **Cameroon**, **Nigeria** and **Angola**, and its true status (including its taxonomic position) remains uncertain (Collar and Stuart 1985, Fry *et al.* 1988).

Coppery Thorntail *Popelairia letitiae* (if a good species) is known from perhaps three nineteenth-century skins from **Bolivia**, and may prove to inhabit the Amazonian lowlands in the north-east of the country (Collar *et al.* 1992).

Shovel-billed Kookaburra *Clytoceyx rex* is uncommon and patchily distributed through nearly all forested habitats (including forest edge and fringes of gardens) to 2,400 m in New Guinea (Irian Jaya, **Indonesia** and **Papua New Guinea**) (Coates 1985, Beehler *et al.* 1986). The recent lack of records suggests that it has declined since the beginning of the century (D. Gibbs *in litt.* 1994).

Little Paradise-kingfisher *Tanysiptera hydrocharis* is found only in lowland and swamp forest on the Aru Islands and the southern Trans-Fly region of New Guinea (Irian Jaya, **Indonesia**, and **Papua New Guinea**), including the area bordered by the Digul River in the west, the Oriomo River in the east and the Fly River in the north (Coates 1985, Beehler *et al.* 1986), and has been recorded as far north as Kiunga in 1988, 1992 and 1994 (P. Gregory *in litt.* 1994). It appears rare with few recent documented records from the Trans-Fly (N. Bostock *in litt.* 1994) and was not recorded during a recent month-long expedition to the Aru Islands (K. D. Bishop *in litt.* 1994).

Rondônia Bushbird *Clytoctantes atrogularis* is known from a single female specimen and from two sightings of males at the type-locality along the Rio Ji-paraná (100 m) in Rondônia, **Brazil**, in 1986, where its habitat is mature terra firme forest dominated by dense vine tangles; although its range almost certainly includes adjacent parts of Amazonas

and Mato Grosso, deforestation and hydroelectric projects in this part of Brazil must be cause for concern (Collar *et al.* 1992).

White-masked Antbird *Pithys castanea* is known from a single specimen collected in September 1937 in the Amazonian forest lowlands at Andoas on the lower Río Pastaza in what is now **Peru** (Collar *et al.* 1992).

Sinaloa Martin *Progne sinaloae* breeds locally in pine–oak forest in mountains of **Mexico** (Sonora, Jalisco, Michoacán; nine locality records in all), wintering on Pacific coast in Nayarit, Jalisco and Chiapas, with casual records from **Guatemala**. Its status and trends remain unknown (Phillips 1986).

Blue-wattled Bulbul *Pycnonotus nieuwenhuisii* is known from north-east Kalimantan (one specimen collected at 600 m in 1900: Smythies 1981) and Sumatra (one specimen collected in secondary scrub in pasture land at 700 m in 1937: van Marle and Voous 1988), **Indonesia**, and **Brunei**, where single birds were seen on five occasions in 1992 in Batu Apoi National Park, in lowland dipterocarp forest at c.60 m. It is unusual for a species of bulbul to be widespread but to occur at such low densities, so this form may represent an extremely rare morph of another species or else hybrids, although its apparent rarity could also be because of the difficulty in locating and identifying it amongst other bulbuls (Williams in prep.).

Moluccan Thrush *Zoothera dumasi* is endemic to Buru and Seram in the Moluccas, **Indonesia**, where it is found in montane forest from 800 to 1,500 m (White and Bruce 1986). It was formerly not uncommon in the mountains of Buru (Hartert 1924), which have not been visited by ornithologists since the 1920s (Jepson 1993), and the only recent record is of three birds seen in Manusela National Park (during a two-month survey) in 1987, where it appears to be rare (Bowler and Taylor 1989). Its montane habitat is not very extensive, but is believed to be relatively secure (BirdLife IP).

Papuan Whipbird *Androphobus viridis* occurs in mountain forest at 1,400–2,700 m in Irian Jaya, **Indonesia**, having been collected in three areas only: Mount Goliath, the Lake Habbema/Ibele River region and the Weyland Mountains (Beehler *et al.* 1986). However, there are at least four sight records since 1990 in the Ambua area, near Tari, **Papua New Guinea**, and, as the intervening range between Tari and the Snow Mountains is little visited, it may be found more widely in time (P. Gregory *in litt.*

1994). A distinctive and unknown song recorded in the Star Mountains in 1992 may have been this species (K. D. Bishop *in litt.* 1994).

Brown-capped Laughingthrush *Garrulax austeni* occurs in the mountains of north-east **India** to the south of the Brahmaputra River, in Meghalaya, Assam, Nagaland and Manipur, and the Chin Hills in western **Myanmar**, where it is found in oak and rhododendron forest, including secondary growth, and bamboo thickets on the forest edge, from 1,500 to 2,700 m, rarely down to 1,200 m (Ali and Ripley 1987). It is a scarce bird, although locally common on Mount Victoria in Myanmar (Smythies 1986). There appear to be no recent records and it may be threatened by forest clearance and degradation (see Collins *et al.* 1991).

Tana River Cisticola *Cisticola restrictus* is known from a small number of specimens, all collected in the lower Tana basin in eastern **Kenya**, though it may also be found in Somalia; recent attempts to locate the species in the field have been unsuccessful (Collar and Stuart 1985). Speculation over the validity of the taxon (e.g. Lewis and Pomeroy 1989) has shifted into rejection (D. A. Turner *in litt.* 1993), but further examination of the type-material is desirable for a final conclusion.

River Prinia *Prinia fluviatilis* has been found in only a few localities in riverine vegetation in **Senegal**, **Niger** (along the Niger into **Mali**), **Chad** and northern **Cameroon**, where it may be under pressure from habitat loss, but it is likely to prove to be spread throughout the contact area between the Sahelian and Sudanese biogeographic zones, from Senegal to Ethiopia (Collar and Stuart 1985, Giraudoux *et al.* 1988, Chappuis *et al.* 1989, 1992, Morel and Chappuis 1992).

Kabobo Apalis *Apalis kaboboensis* is known only from montane forest on Mount Kabobo, west of Lake Tanganyika, in eastern **Zaïre**, where records stem from between 1,600 and 2,480 m and where habitat (entirely unprotected) covers no more than 2,000 km^2, with no recent (post-1957) information on the status of the species or its habitat (Collar and Stuart 1985, 1988).

Dja River Warbler *Bradypterus grandis* is an apparently rare bird of dense undergrowth (though not in primary forest), known only from a few localities in southern **Cameroon** and **Gabon** (Collar and Stuart 1985, D. E. Sargeant *in litt.* 1992), although recently discovered in the La Lopé-Okanda Reserve, central Gabon, where it was found in a *Rhynchospora*

corymbosa marsh and has proved to be a bird of contact zones between forest and open areas such as savannas and river borders (the published site Makokou being in error) (P. Christy *in litt.* 1994).

Bismarck Thicketbird *Megalurulus grosvenori* is known from montane forest above 1,580 m in the Whiteman Mountains, New Britain, **Papua New Guinea**. It is little known, generally considered rare, but shy, secretive and easily missed and may perhaps be expected to occur on New Ireland (Coates 1990). It was not recorded in the Whiteman Mountains recently (J. Clay *in litt.* 1994, D. Gibbs *in litt.* 1994).

Bougainville Thicketbird *Megalurulus llaneae* occurs in mist-forest at c.1,500 m in the Crown Prince Range, Bougainville, **Papua New Guinea**, where it was first recorded in 1979 (Hadden 1981), and is little known, perhaps occurring more widely on the island.

Campbell's Fairywren *Malurus campbelli* (whose taxonomic status is in doubt: Vuilleumier *et al.* 1992) is only known from Mount Bosavi, Kiunga and probably the Nomad River, **Papua New Guinea**, where it is found in swampy secondary and primary hill forest with sago palm, probably extending westwards along the southern slopes of the Central Ranges into Irian Jaya, Indonesia, and perhaps east to the Purari River (Schodde and Weatherly 1983, Coates 1990). It was recorded at Kiunga in 1988 (I. Burrows *in litt.* 1994, P. Gregory *in litt.* 1994) and again in 1992 (Simpson in press).

Snow Mountain Robin *Petroica archboldi* is known only from the highest peaks of the Snow Mountains (Mounts Wilhelmina and Carstensz), Irian Jaya, **Indonesia** (Beehler *et al.* 1986), from where there are no recent records (K. D. Bishop *in litt.* 1994).

Olive-yellow Robin *Poecilodryas placens* is very patchily distributed in Irian Jaya, **Indonesia**, and **Papua New Guinea**, through lower hill forest to 1,100 m, being recorded from Batanta Island and from six mainland areas: near Port Moresby (= Veimauri, being logged: P. Gregory *in litt.* 1994), Madang, Karimui, Lake Kutubu, Bosavi and the Weyland Mountains (Beehler *et al.* 1986). Although its distribution is perhaps continuous along the south side of the eastern Central Ranges from Mount Bosavi east to the Goldie River, there is little doubt that it is absent from many locations, presumably owing to interspecific competition (Coates 1990). It has also been recorded from the Fakfak Mountains (Gibbs

1994) and a 1994 report from Kiunga is very likely to be correct (P. Gregory *in litt.* 1994).

Sumba Brown Flycatcher *Muscicapa segregata* (considered conspecific with Asian Brown Flycatcher *M. dauurica* by Andrew 1992, but a full species by Sibley and Monroe 1990) is endemic to Sumba, **Indonesia**, where it has been recorded in primary forest and secondary forest edge, with a nest found on the border between cultivation and secondary forest, but it appears to be scarce, and was very rarely recorded during surveys in 1989 and 1992; until its habitat requirements are better understood, it is not possible to judge the likely impact of the extensive deforestation which has taken place on Sumba (Jones *et al.* in prep.).

Gabon Batis *Batis minima* is endemic to **Gabon** where it was recently reported to be common and tolerant of forest disturbance (Collar and Stuart 1985), but more recently still the same informants have described it as rare, localized and known only from the Makokou region (Brosset and Erard 1986), but with a record from the western Monts de Cristal (P. Christy *in litt.* 1994). It is now also known to occur in the lowland Dja area of **Cameroon**, being described as an uncommon bird of old second growth, not primary forest (Erard and Colston 1988).

White-breasted Monarch *Monarcha menckei* is endemic to the forests of Mussau Island (400 km²) in the St Matthias Islands, **Papua New Guinea**. It is little known but apparently not uncommon (Coates 1990), although large-scale logging could have a devastating effect (B. J. Coates *in litt.* 1994).

Matthias Fantail *Rhipidura matthiae* is endemic to forest on Mussau Island (400 km²) in the St Matthias Group, **Papua New Guinea**, where its status is unknown although it is probably not rare (Coates 1990). However, large-scale logging could have a devastating effect (B. J. Coates *in litt.* 1994).

Obscure Berrypecker *Melanocharis arfakiana* is known from only two specimens, one collected in 1867 from the Arfak Mountains, Irian Jaya, **Indonesia**, and a second collected in 1933 from the upper Angabunga River, **Papua New Guinea**, while several claimed sight records may have involved juveniles of other species. Its apparent extreme rarity and patchy distribution suggest either that it may be disappearing, compressed into a narrow altitudinal belt between ecologically similar congeners (Black Berrypecker *M. nigra* of the lowlands and either Lemon-breasted Berrypecker *M. longicauda* or Fantailed Berrypecker *M. versteri* of the mountains), or

that it could be an overlooked canopy-haunting species (Coates 1990). Sightings have been reported from near Tabubil in the late 1980s (Murray 1988), an unidentified berrypecker north of the town may be this bird or an undescribed species (Gregory 1993), and similar birds have also been recorded on the southern Huon peninsula (P. Gregory *in litt.* 1994).

White-throated White-eye *Zosterops meeki* is confined to Tagula (Sudest) Island (c.700 km²) in the Louisiade archipelago, **Papua New Guinea**, where it inhabits lowland forest and forest edge to an altitude of 300 m (Schodde 1978). There are no modern records (K. D. Bishop *in litt.* 1994); none was seen during a 10-day trek from the north coast up to Mount Riu in 1992 (I. Burrows *in litt.* 1994). Large-scale logging could have a devastating effect (B. J. Coates *in litt.* 1994).

White-chinned Myzomela *Myzomela albigula* is a little-known species from the smaller islands of the Louisiade archipelago (Bonvouloir Islands, Conflict Group, Deboyne Islands, Misima, Rossel), **Papua New Guinea**. Its habitat preference and status are unknown, but it is possibly fairly common locally (Coates 1990).

Crimson-hooded Myzomela *Myzomela kuehni* is endemic to the island of Wetar, **Indonesia** (White and Bruce 1986). It was found to be quite common in secondary forest and gardens during a brief visit in 1990, the first by ornithologists to this island since 1911, and extensive forest remains in the north-west corner of the island (K. D. Bishop *in litt.* 1990), but elsewhere forest is being cleared and degraded by illegal logging (F. R. Lambert verbally 1994).

Black-chested Honeyeater *Lichmera notabilis* is endemic to the island of Wetar, **Indonesia** (White and Bruce 1986). Small numbers were seen in secondary forest during a brief visit in 1990, the first by ornithologists to this island since 1911, and extensive forest remains in the north-west corner of the island (K. D. Bishop *in litt.* 1990), but elsewhere forest is being cleared and degraded by illegal logging (F. R. Lambert verbally 1994).

Tagula Honeyeater *Meliphaga vicina* is endemic to Tagula (Sudest) Island (c.700 km²) in the Louisiade archipelago, **Papua New Guinea**, where it inhabits forest and forest edge in the lowlands to 800 m (Schodde 1978) and is little known. Two were seen during a 10-day trek from the north coast up to Mount Riu in 1992 (I. Burrows *in litt.* 1994). Large-scale logging could have a devastating effect (B. J. Coates *in litt.* 1994).

Grey Friarbird *Philemon kisserensis* is known from the islands of Kisar, Leti and Moa, to the east of Timor, **Indonesia** (White and Bruce 1986), where its habitat requirements, status and any threats are unknown. It is treated as a full species by Sibley and Monroe (1990), but as a subspecies of Little Friarbird *P. citreogularis* by White and Bruce (1986) and Andrew (1992).

Brass's Friarbird *Philemon brassi* is known from a small area of flooded canegrass and dense secondary forest around a lagoon on the Idenburg River, a tributary of the Mamberamo River in north-east Irian Jaya, **Indonesia**, where it was discovered in 1939 (Beehler 1985, J. M. Diamond *in litt.* 1987), and from the lower Mamberamo River (B. M. Beehler *in litt.* 1990).

Dusky Friarbird *Philemon fuscicapillus* is known from Halmahera, Bacan and Morotai, in the north Moluccas, **Indonesia** (White and Bruce 1986). It is an enigmatic species, reasonably well represented in museum collections but now rarely reported by field ornithologists (Collar and Andrew 1988). However, it has recently been regularly seen at one locality on Halmahera, sometimes in heavily logged forest, and is probably under-recorded elsewhere (BirdLife IP).

Sillem's Mountain-finch *Leucosticte sillemi* was recently described from two specimens collected in 1929, at c.5,125 m on the barren plateau between the upper Kara Kash and the upper Yarkand River, in southern Xinjiang, **China** (in an area under Chinese administration but claimed by India) (Roselaar 1992). Its status, habitat requirements and any threats are unknown.

Tibetan Rosefinch *Carpodacus roborowskii* is endemic to central Qinghai, **China**, where it is found in barren, rocky steppes between 4,700 and 5,100 m, in the vicinity of the headwaters of the Huang He and Chang Jiang (Yangtze) rivers (Meyer de Schauensee 1984, Cheng 1987). It was formerly not uncommon (Dolan 1938), but there appear to be no recent records (P. Alström *in litt.* 1993), so its current status and any threats are unknown.

Scottish Crossbill *Loxia scotica* is believed to be confined to native stands of Scots pine *Pinus sylvestris* in Scotland, **U.K.**, with core areas to the north-west of the Great Glen and in Strathspey and Deeside, a habitat which has declined from 15,000 km² a few centuries ago to a still locally diminishing 120 km² today. The population is currently estimated at 300–1,250 pairs, though it fluctuates with the pine crop, and a true understanding of the species' numbers and distribution is hindered by the extreme difficulty in identification, which causes continuing doubt over its validity as distinct from Common Crossbill *L. curvirostra* (Tucker and Heath 1994).

Entebbe Weaver *Ploceus victoriae* is known only from Entebbe, **Uganda**, where it is 'undoubtedly rare' and encountered on only a few occasions during fieldwork between February 1983 and January 1984 (Ash 1986), although the validity of the form remains open to question (Ash 1987a, Louette 1987, Vuilleumier *et al.* 1992).

Wetar Figbird *Sphecotheres hypoleucus* is endemic to the island of Wetar, **Indonesia** (White and Bruce 1986). Small numbers were seen in secondary forest during a brief visit in 1990, the first by ornithologists to this island since 1911, and extensive forest remains in the north-west corner of the island (K. D. Bishop *in litt.* 1990), but elsewhere forest is being cleared and degraded by illegal logging (F. R. Lambert verbally 1994).

Tagula Butcherbird *Cracticus louisiadensis* is a little known species (habits and ecology undescribed) endemic to Tagula (Sudest) Island (c.700 km²) in the Louisiade archipelago, **Papua New Guinea** (Coates 1990). Ten were seen during a 10-day trek from the north coast up to Mount Riu in 1992 (I. Burrows *in litt.* 1994). Large-scale logging could have a devastating effect (B. J. Coates *in litt.* 1994).

Yellow-breasted Bird-of-paradise *Loboparadisea sericea* occurs in montane forest, from 625 to 2,000 m, along the length of the Central Ranges of New Guinea (Irian Jaya, **Indonesia**, and **Papua New Guinea**), where it is often uncommon or absent from seemingly appropriate habitats for reasons unknown but possibly related to the presence or absence of important food plants (Beehler *et al.* 1986, Coates 1990). It may be overlooked because it is unobtrusive and inhabits very rugged, rarely visited terrain (K. D. Bishop *in litt.* 1994), but it is likely to be threatened by habitat destruction in some areas, e.g. the possible future extension of the Ok Tedi mine could threaten this particular locality and the traditional site at Jimi Ridge is in a 'fighting zone' (P. Gregory *in litt.* 1994).

NEAR-THREATENED SPECIES

THE CONCEPT of 'near-threatened' has been espoused by BirdLife since the publication of *Threatened birds of Africa and related islands* in 1985. We accept here, as all previous such listings have done (see commentaries in Collar and Stuart 1985, p. 708; Collar and Andrew 1988, pp. xi–xii; Collar *et al.* 1992, p. 1047), that the application of this category is relatively subjective and necessarily based on reduced levels of research (deadlines for all these books have required that, once sufficient evidence of a species' non-threatened status is gathered, research on it terminates). The list below cannot pretend to total comprehensiveness or consistency, and the boundary between near-threatened and non-threatened remains vague.

Nevertheless, this category has proved of enormous practical value in stimulating and directing ornithologists towards species of concern beyond those that are 'officially' designated as threatened, particularly in countries and areas with no or few fully threatened species. It has also led to the accumulation of information that allows reassessments to be made with relative ease (particularly important for species that fall just outside the threat criteria but which require monitoring for early evidence of deteriorating status). We thus regard near-threatened listing as an essential component of any responsible programme of threatened species evaluation.

Although the term remains outside the formal proposals in the new IUCN criteria, the concept itself occurs in them, since there is allowance for distinguishing species that come very close to qualifying as threatened, for example by meeting parts of the criteria (see definition of Low Risk, p. 15). In practice the grouping of such species in separate lists is likely to follow, and a name will be needed. If, as we hope, the term 'near-threatened' is eventually adopted more widely, the only important point will be to ensure that the abbreviation 'NT' is not misinterpreted as 'non-threatened' ('near-threatened' is, it should be remembered, a subdivision of 'non-threatened').

In the following list, each species is followed by its range states. We have attempted to be as complete as possible, but have excluded countries in which a species is judged to be of no more than vagrant status. Countries which are known or believed to harbour only non-breeding populations are indicated by [N], although for (saltwater) seabirds just the breeding range states are listed.

■ Rheidae
Greater Rhea *Rhea americana*
 Argentina, Bolivia, Brazil, Paraguay, Uruguay.
Lesser Rhea *Rhea pennata*
 Argentina, Bolivia, Chile, Peru.

■ Casuariidae
Dwarf Cassowary *Casuarius bennetti*
 Indonesia, Papua New Guinea.

■ Tinamidae
Solitary Tinamou *Tinamus solitarius*
 Argentina, Brazil, Paraguay.
Hooded Tinamou *Nothocercus nigrocapillus*
 Bolivia, Peru.
Pale-browed Tinamou *Crypturellus transfasciatus*
 Ecuador, Peru.

Colombian Tinamou *Crypturellus columbianus*
 Argentina, Bolivia, Brazil, Paraguay, Peru.
Yellow-legged Tinamou *Crypturellus noctivagus*
 Brazil.

■ Spheniscidae
Jackass Penguin *Spheniscus demersus*
 Namibia, South Africa.
Humboldt Penguin *Spheniscus humboldti*
 Chile, Peru.

■ Podicipedidae
Hooded Grebe *Podiceps gallardoi*
 Argentina.

Diomedeidae

Royal Albatross *Diomedea epomophora*
New Zealand.
Waved Albatross *Diomedea irrorata*
Ecuador.
Grey-headed Albatross *Diomedea chrysostoma*
Australia, French Southern Territories, New
Zealand, South Africa, South Georgia (to U.K.).
Buller's Albatross *Diomedea bulleri*
New Zealand.
Sooty Albatross *Phoebetria fusca*
French Southern Territories, South Africa,
Tristan da Cunha group (to U.K.).

Procellariidae

Northern Giant-petrel *Macronectes halli*
Australia, French Southern Territories, New
Zealand, South Africa.
Buller's Shearwater *Puffinus bulleri*
New Zealand.

Hydrobatidae

Wedge-rumped Storm-petrel *Oceanodroma tethys*
Ecuador, Peru.
Swinhoe's Storm-petrel *Oceanodroma monorhis*
Japan, South Korea, Taiwan.
Tristram's Storm-petrel *Oceanodroma tristrami*
Japan, U.S.A.
Ashy Storm-petrel *Oceanodroma homochroa*
Mexico, U.S.A.

Sulidae

Cape Gannet *Morus capensis*
Namibia, South Africa.

Phalacrocoracidae

Crowned Cormorant *Phalacrocorax coronatus*
Angola, Namibia, South Africa.
Pygmy Cormorant *Phalacrocorax pygmeus*
Afghanistan[N], Albania, Austria[N], Azerbaijan,
Bulgaria, Georgia[N], Greece, Hungary, Iran, Iraq,
Israel[N], Italy, Kazakhstan, Moldova, Romania,
Russia, Tajikistan, Turkey, Turkmenistan,
Uzbekistan, former Yugoslavia.
Bank Cormorant *Phalacrocorax neglectus*
Namibia, South Africa.
Socotra Cormorant *Phalacrocorax nigrogularis*
Yemen.
Red-legged Cormorant *Phalacrocorax gaimardi*
Argentina, Chile, Peru.

Anhingidae

Oriental Darter *Anhinga melanogaster*
Bangladesh, Brunei, Cambodia, India, Indonesia,
Laos, Malaysia, Myanmar, Nepal, Pakistan,
Philippines, Sri Lanka, Vietnam.

Ardeidae

Great-billed Heron *Ardea sumatrana*
Australia, Brunei, India, Indonesia, Malaysia,
Myanmar, Papua New Guinea, Philippines,
Thailand, Vietnam.
Madagascar Pond-heron *Ardeola idae*
Burundi[N], Comoros[N], Kenya[N], Madagascar,
Malawi[N], Rwanda[N], Seychelles, Tanzania[N],
Uganda[N], Zaïre[N], Zimbabwe[N].
Agami Heron *Agamia agami*
Argentina, Bolivia, Brazil, Colombia, Costa Rica,
Ecuador, French Guiana, Guatemala, Guyana,
Honduras, Mexico, Nicaragua, Panama,
Suriname, Trinidad and Tobago, Venezuela.
Fasciated Tiger-heron *Tigrisoma fasciatum*
Bolivia, Brazil, Colombia, Costa Rica, Ecuador,
Panama, Peru, Venezuela.
Forest Bittern *Zonerodius heliosylus*
Indonesia, Papua New Guinea.
Zigzag Heron *Zebrilus undulatus*
Bolivia, Brazil, Colombia, Ecuador, French
Guiana, Guyana, Peru, Suriname, Venezuela.
Schrenck's Bittern *Ixobrychus eurhythmus*
Brunei[N], China, Indonesia[N], Japan, Laos[N],
Malaysia[N], Myanmar[N], North Korea, Philippines[N],
Russia, South Korea, Taiwan[N], Thailand[N],
Vietnam[N].

Balaenicipitidae

Shoebill *Balaeniceps rex*
Central African Republic[N], Ethiopia, Malawi,
Rwanda, Sudan, Tanzania, Uganda, Zambia,
Zaïre.

Ciconiidae

Painted Stork *Mycteria leucocephala*
Bangladesh, Cambodia, China, India, Laos,
Myanmar, Nepal, Pakistan, Sri Lanka, Thailand,
Vietnam.
Asian Openbill *Anastomus oscitans*
Bangladesh, Cambodia, India, Myanmar, Nepal,
Pakistan, Sri Lanka, Thailand, Vietnam.

Threskiornithidae

Madagascar Crested Ibis *Lophotibis cristata*
Madagascar.
Black-headed Ibis *Threskiornis melanocephalus*
Bangladesh, Cambodia, China, Hong Kong (to
U.K.)[N], India, Indonesia, Japan[N], Laos[N],
Malaysia[N], Myanmar[N], Nepal, Pakistan, Sri
Lanka, Taiwan, Thailand[N], Vietnam.
Red-naped Ibis *Pseudibis papillosa*
Bangladesh, India, Nepal, Pakistan.

■ **Phoenicopteridae**

Lesser Flamingo *Phoenicopterus minor*
Angola[N], Botswana, Burundi[N], Cameroon[N],
Djibouti, Eritrea[N], Ethiopia[N], Gabon[N], Gambia[N],
Guinea[N], Guinea-Bissau[N], India[N], Kenya,
Madagascar[N], Malawi[N], Mauritania, Mozam-
bique[N], Namibia, Pakistan[N], Senegal[N], Sierra
Leone[N], South Africa, Tanzania[N], Uganda[N],
Yemen[N], Zambia, Zaïre, Zimbabwe[N].

■ **Anhimidae**

Northern Screamer *Chauna chavaria*
Colombia, Venezuela.

■ **Anatidae**

Black-headed Duck *Heteronetta atricapilla*
Argentina, Bolivia, Brazil, Chile, Paraguay,
Uruguay.

Trumpeter Swan *Cygnus buccinator*
Canada, U.S.A.

Ruddy-headed Goose *Chloephaga rubidiceps*
Argentina, Chile, Falkland Islands (to U.K.).

Orinoco Goose *Neochen jubata*
Argentina, Bolivia, Brazil, Colombia, French
Guiana, Guyana, Paraguay, Peru, Suriname,
Venezuela.

Chubut Steamerduck *Tachyeres leucocephalus*
Argentina.

Mandarin Duck *Aix galericulata*
China, Japan, North Korea, Russia, South Korea,
Taiwan[N].

Spectacled Duck *Anas specularis*
Argentina, Chile.

Philippine Duck *Anas luzonica*
Philippines.

Meller's Duck *Anas melleri*
Madagascar.

■ **Accipitridae**

Jerdon's Baza *Aviceda jerdoni*
Brunei, China, India, Indonesia, Laos, Malaysia,
Myanmar, Philippines, Thailand.

Black Honey-buzzard *Henicopernis infuscatus*
Papua New Guinea.

White-tailed Eagle *Haliaeetus albicilla*
Afghanistan[N], Armenia, Austria, Azerbaijan,
Belarus, Bulgaria, China, Czech Republic,
Estonia, Faroe Islands[N], Finland, France[N], Georgia,
Germany, Greece, Greenland, Hungary, Iceland,
India[N], Iran, Israel, Japan, Kazakhstan, Latvia,
Lithuania, Moldova, Mongolia, Nepal, North
Korea[N], Norway, Pakistan[N], Poland, Romania,
Russia, South Korea[N], Sweden, Taiwan[N],
Tajikistan[N], Turkey, Turkmenistan, Ukraine,
United Kingdom, Uzbekistan[N], former Yugosla-
via.

Lesser Fish-eagle *Ichthyophaga humilis*
China, India, Indonesia, Laos, Malaysia,
Myanmar, Nepal, Thailand, Vietnam.

Grey-headed Fish-eagle *Ichthyophaga ichthyaetus*
Bangladesh, Brunei, Cambodia, India, Indonesia,
Laos, Malaysia, Myanmar, Nepal, Philippines,
Singapore, Thailand, Vietnam.

White-rumped Vulture *Gyps bengalensis*
Bangladesh, Cambodia, China, India, Laos,
Malaysia, Myanmar, Nepal, Pakistan, Thailand,
Vietnam.

Long-billed Vulture *Gyps indicus*
Bangladesh, Cambodia, India, Laos, Malaysia,
Myanmar, Nepal, Thailand, Vietnam.

Cinereous Vulture *Aegypius monachus*
Afghanistan, Armenia, Azerbaijan, Bangladesh[N],
China, Egypt[N], Georgia, Greece, Hong Kong (to
U.K.)[N], India[N], Iran, Italy[N], Kazakhstan,
Kyrgyzstan, Mongolia, Morocco[N], Myanmar[N],
Nepal[N], North Korea[N], Oman[N], Pakistan,
Portugal, Russia, Saudi Arabia[N], South Korea[N],
Spain, Tajikistan, Thailand[N], Turkey,
Turkmenistan, Uzbekistan.

Red-headed Vulture *Sarcogyps calvus*
Bangladesh, Bhutan, Cambodia, China, India,
Laos, Malaysia, Myanmar, Pakistan, Thailand,
Vietnam.

Southern Banded Snake-eagle *Circaetus fasciolatus*
Kenya, Mozambique, Somalia, South Africa,
Tanzania, Zimbabwe.

Nicobar Serpent-eagle *Spilornis minimus*
India.

Andaman Serpent-eagle *Spilornis elgini*
India.

Madagascar Harrier *Circus maillardi*
Comoros, Madagascar, Réunion (to France).

Black Harrier *Circus maurus*
Lesotho, Namibia, South Africa.

Pallid Harrier *Circus macrourus*
Afghanistan[N], Albania[N], Algeria[N], Angola[N],
Bangladesh[N], Benin[N], Botswana[N], Burundi[N],
Cameroon[N], Central African Republic[N], Chad[N],
China, Cyprus[N], Djibouti[N], Egypt[N], Eritrea[N],
Ethiopia[N], Gambia[N], Ghana[N], Greece[N], India[N],
Iran[N], Iraq[N], Israel[N], Ivory Coast[N], Jordan[N],
Kenya[N], Lebanon[N], Liberia[N], Libya[N], Malawi[N],
Mali[N], Mauritania[N], Moldova, Mozambique[N],
Myanmar[N], Namibia[N], Nepal[N], Niger[N], Nigeria[N],
Oman[N], Pakistan[N], Russia, Rwanda[N], Saudi
Arabia[N], Senegal[N], Sierra Leone[N], Somalia[N],
South Africa[N], Sri Lanka[N], Sudan[N], Syria[N],
Tanzania[N], Togo[N], Tunisia[N], Turkey[N], Uganda[N],
Ukraine, Yemen[N], Zambia[N], Zimbabwe[N].

Grey-bellied Goshawk *Accipiter poliogaster*
Argentina, Bolivia, Brazil, Colombia, Ecuador,
Guyana, Paraguay, Peru, Suriname, Venezuela.

Nicobar Sparrowhawk *Accipiter butleri*
India.

Slaty-mantled Sparrowhawk *Accipiter luteoschistaceus*
Papua New Guinea.

New Britain Goshawk *Accipiter princeps*
Papua New Guinea.

Semicollared Hawk *Accipiter collaris*
Colombia, Ecuador, Peru, Venezuela.

Small Sparrowhawk *Accipiter nanus*
Indonesia.

Madagascar Sparrowhawk *Accipiter madagascariensis*
Madagascar.

Henst's Goshawk *Accipiter henstii*
Madagascar.

Doria's Goshawk *Megatriorchis doriae*
Indonesia, Papua New Guinea.

Rufous-winged Buzzard *Butastur liventer*
Cambodia, China, Indonesia, Laos, Myanmar, Thailand, Vietnam.

Plumbeous Hawk *Leucopternis plumbea*
Colombia, Ecuador, Panama, Peru.

Semiplumbeous Hawk *Leucopternis semiplumbea*
Colombia, Costa Rica, Ecuador, Honduras, Panama.

Mantled Hawk *Leucopternis polionota*
Argentina, Brazil, Paraguay.

Solitary Eagle *Harpyhaliaetus solitarius*
Argentina, Bolivia, Brazil, Colombia, Costa Rica, Ecuador, French Guiana, Guatemala, Guyana, Honduras, Mexico, Nicaragua, Panama, Paraguay, Peru, Suriname, Venezuela.

Hawaiian Hawk *Buteo solitarius*
U.S.A.

Rufous-tailed Hawk *Buteo ventralis*
Argentina, Chile.

Crested Eagle *Morphnus guianensis*
Argentina, Bolivia, Brazil, Colombia, Costa Rica, Ecuador, French Guiana, Guatemala, Guyana, Honduras, Panama, Paraguay, Peru, Suriname, Venezuela.

Harpy Eagle *Harpia harpyja*
Argentina, Belize, Bolivia, Brazil, Colombia, Costa Rica, Ecuador, French Guiana, Guatemala, Guyana, Honduras, Mexico, Nicaragua, Panama, Paraguay, Peru, Suriname.

Gurney's Eagle *Aquila gurneyi*
Indonesia, Papua New Guinea.

Black-and-white Hawk-eagle *Spizastur melanoleucus*
Argentina, Bolivia, Colombia, Costa Rica, French Guiana, Guatemala, Guyana, Honduras, Mexico, Nicaragua, Panama, Peru, Suriname, Venezuela.

Sulawesi Hawk-eagle *Spizaetus lanceolatus*
Indonesia.

Black-and-chestnut Eagle *Oroaetus isidori*
Argentina, Bolivia, Colombia, Ecuador, Peru, Venezuela.

■ Falconidae

Striated Caracara *Phalcoboenus australis*
Argentina, Chile, Falkland Islands (to U.K.).

White-rumped Falcon *Polihierax insignis*
Cambodia, Laos, Myanmar, Thailand, Vietnam.

White-fronted Falconet *Microhierax latifrons*
Malaysia.

Pied Falconet *Microhierax melanoleucus*
Bangladesh, China, India, Laos, Vietnam.

Red-necked Falcon *Falco chicquera*
Bangladesh, India, Nepal, Pakistan.

New Zealand Falcon *Falco novaeseelandiae*
New Zealand.

Orange-breasted Falcon *Falco deiroleucus*
Argentina, Bolivia, Brazil, Colombia, Costa Rica, Ecuador, Guatemala, Guyana, Honduras, Mexico, Nicaragua, Panama, Paraguay, Peru, Suriname, Trinidad and Tobago, Venezuela.

■ Megapodiidae

Tabon Scrubfowl *Megapodius cumingii*
Indonesia, Malaysia, Philippines.

Sula Scrubfowl *Megapodius bernsteinii*
Indonesia.

■ Cracidae

White-crested Guan *Penelope pileata*
Brazil.

White-browed Guan *Penelope jacucaca*
Brazil.

Wattled Guan *Aburria aburri*
Colombia, Ecuador, Peru, Venezuela.

Black Guan *Chamaepetes unicolor*
Costa Rica, Panama.

■ Tetraonidae

Siberian Grouse *Dendragapus falcipennis*
China, Russia.

Caucasian Black Grouse *Tetrao mlokosiewiczi*
Armenia, Azerbaijan, Georgia, Iran, Turkey.

Chinese Grouse *Bonasa sewerzowi*
China.

■ Phasianidae

Chestnut-throated Partridge *Tetraophasis obscurus*
China.

Buff-throated Partridge *Tetraophasis szechenyii*
China, India.

Rusty-necklaced Partridge *Alectoris magna*
China.

Black Partridge *Melanoperdix nigra*
Indonesia, Malaysia.

Snow Mountain Quail *Anurophasis monorthonyx*
Indonesia.

White-cheeked Partridge *Arborophila atrogularis*
Bangladesh, China, India, Myanmar.

Taiwan Partridge *Arborophila crudigularis*
Taiwan.

Satyr Tragopan *Tragopan satyra*
Bhutan, China, India, Nepal.

Temminck's Tragopan *Tragopan temminckii*
China, India, Myanmar, Vietnam.

Grey Junglefowl *Gallus sonneratii*
India.

Swinhoe's Pheasant *Lophura swinhoii*
Taiwan.

Blue Eared-pheasant *Crossoptilon auritum*
China.

Mikado Pheasant *Syrmaticus mikado*
Taiwan.

Copper Pheasant *Syrmaticus soemmerringii*
Japan.

Golden Pheasant *Chrysolophus pictus*
China.

Lady Amherst's Pheasant *Chrysolophus amherstiae*
China, Myanmar.

Bronze-tailed Peacock-pheasant *Polyplectron chalcurum*
Indonesia.

Long-tailed Wood-partridge *Dendrortyx macroura*
Mexico.

Black-fronted Wood-quail *Odontophorus atrifrons*
Colombia, Venezuela.

Chestnut Wood-quail *Odontophorus hyperythrus*
Colombia.

Dark-backed Wood-quail *Odontophorus melanonotus*
Colombia, Ecuador.

Tacarcuna Wood-quail *Odontophorus dialeucos*
Panama.

Venezuelan Wood-quail *Odontophorus columbianus*
Venezuela.

Black-breasted Wood-quail *Odontophorus leucolaemus*
Costa Rica, Panama.

Ocellated Quail *Cyrtonyx ocellatus*
Guatemala, Honduras, Mexico, Nicaragua.

■ Meleagrididae

Ocellated Turkey *Agriocharis ocellata*
Belize, Guatemala, Mexico.

■ Turnicidae

Spotted Buttonquail *Turnix ocellata*
Philippines.

■ Gruidae

Sarus Crane *Grus antigone*
Australia, Bangladesh, Cambodia, India, Laos, Nepal, Myanmar, Vietnam.

■ Rallidae

Ocellated Crake *Micropygia schomburgkii*
Bolivia, Brazil, Colombia, French Guiana, Guyana, Peru, Suriname, Venezuela.

Galápagos Rail *Laterallus spilonotus*
Ecuador.

Weka *Gallirallus australis*
New Zealand.

Roviana Rail *Gallirallus rovianae*
Solomon Islands.

Rouget's Rail *Rougetius rougetii*
Eritrea, Ethiopia.

Band-bellied Crake *Porzana paykullii*
China, Indonesia[N], Malaysia[N], Philippines[N], Russia, South Korea[N], Thailand[N], Vietnam[N].

Colombian Crake *Neocrex colombianus*
Colombia, Ecuador, Panama.

■ Otididae

Little Bustard *Tetrax tetrax*
Algeria, Azerbaijan[N], China, Egypt[N], France, Georgia[N], Iran, Israel[N], Italy, Kazakhstan, Kyrgyzstan, Libya[N], Morocco, Pakistan[N], Portugal, Romania[N], Russia, Spain, Tajikistan[N], Tunisia[N], Turkey, Turkmenistan[N], Ukraine.

Nubian Bustard *Neotis nuba*
Chad, Mali, Mauritania, Niger, Sudan.

Little Brown Bustard *Eupodotis humilis*
Ethiopia, Somalia.

Blue Bustard *Eupodotis caerulescens*
Lesotho, South Africa.

■ Haematopodidae

African Oystercatcher *Haematopus moquini*
Namibia, South Africa.

■ Charadriidae

Magellanic Plover *Pluvianellus socialis*
Argentina, Chile.

Long-billed Plover *Charadrius placidus*
China, India[N], Japan, Laos[N], Malaysia[N], Myanmar[N], North Korea, Russia, South Korea[N].

Malaysian Plover *Charadrius peronii*
Brunei, Indonesia, Malaysia, Philippines, Thailand, Vietnam.

Javan Plover *Charadrius javanicus*
Indonesia.

Diademed Sandpiper-plover *Phegornis mitchellii*
Argentina, Bolivia, Chile, Peru.

Grey-headed Lapwing *Vanellus cinereus*
Bangladesh[N], Cambodia[N], China, India[N], Japan,

Laos[N], Mongolia, Myanmar[N], Nepal[N], Philippines[N], Taiwan[N], Thailand[N], Vietnam[N].

■ Scolopacidae

Sulawesi Woodcock *Scolopax celebensis*
Indonesia.

Latham's Snipe *Gallinago hardwickii*
Australia[N], China[N], Indonesia[N], Japan, Papua
New Guinea[N], Taiwan[N].

Great Snipe *Gallinago media*
Angola[N], Belarus, Burkina Faso[N], Burundi[N],
Cameroon[N], Chad[N], Congo[N], Cyprus[N], Egypt[N],
Estonia, Ethiopia[N], Finland, Gabon[N], Ghana[N],
India[N], Iran[N], Ivory Coast[N], Kenya[N], Latvia,
Liberia[N], Lithuania, Malawi[N], Mali[N],
Mauritania[N], Mozambique[N], Namibia[N], Nigeria[N],
Norway, Poland, Russia, Rwanda[N], Saudi
Arabia[N], Sierra Leone[N], South Africa[N], Sudan[N],
Sweden, Tanzania[N], Togo[N], Turkey[N], Uganda[N],
Ukraine, Yemen[N], Zambia[N], Zaïre[N], Zimbabwe[N].

Fuegian Snipe *Gallinago stricklandii*
Argentina, Chile, Falkland Islands (to U.K.).

Imperial Snipe *Gallinago imperialis*
Colombia, Ecuador, Peru.

New Zealand Snipe *Coenocorypha aucklandica*
New Zealand.

Hudsonian Godwit *Limosa haemastica*
Argentina[N], Barbados[N], Bolivia[N], Brazil[N],
Canada, Chile[N], Falkland Islands (to U.K.)[N],
Mexico[N], Paraguay[N], Peru[N], Uruguay[N], U.S.A.,
Venezuela[N].

Far Eastern Curlew *Numenius madagascariensis*
Australia[N], Brunei[N], China, Hong Kong (to
U.K.)[N], Indonesia[N], Japan[N], Malaysia[N],
Mongolia, New Zealand[N], North Korea[N], Papua
New Guinea[N], Philippines[N], Russia, South
Korea[N], Taiwan[N], Thailand[N].

Asian Dowitcher *Limnodromus semipalmatus*
Australia[N], Bangladesh[N], Brunei[N], China, Hong
Kong (to U.K.)[N], India[N], Indonesia[N], Japan[N],
Malaysia[N], Mongolia, Myanmar[N], Philippines[N],
Russia, Singapore[N], Thailand[N], Vietnam[N].

■ Glareolidae

Black-winged Pratincole *Glareola nordmanni*
Angola[N], Armenia, Belarus, Botswana[N],
Burundi[N], Cameroon[N], Chad[N], Cyprus[N], Egypt[N],
Ethiopia[N], Hungary, Iran[N], Iraq, Israel[N],
Kazakhstan, Mali[N], Mauritania[N], Moldova,
Namibia[N], Nigeria[N], Romania, Russia, Rwanda[N],
Saudi Arabia[N], South Africa[N], Sudan[N], Syria,
Turkey[N], Uganda[N], Ukraine, Zambia[N], Zaïre[N].

■ Laridae

Pacific Gull *Larus pacificus*
Australia.

Heermann's Gull *Larus heermanni*
Mexico, U.S.A.

Relict Gull *Larus relictus*
China, Mongolia, Russia, South Korea[N], Vietnam[N].

Elegant Tern *Sterna elegans*
Mexico, U.S.A.

Damara Tern *Sterna balaenarum*
Namibia, South Africa.

■ Alcidae

Marbled Murrelet *Brachyramphus marmoratus*
Canada, Russia, U.S.A.

Xantus's Murrelet *Synthliboramphus hypoleucus*
Canada, Mexico, U.S.A.

Craveri's Murrelet *Synthliboramphus craveri*
Mexico, U.S.A.

■ Columbidae

Comoro Olive-pigeon *Columba pollenii*
Comoros.

White-naped Pigeon *Columba albinucha*
Cameroon, Sudan, Uganda, Zaïre.

Nilgiri Wood-pigeon *Columba elphinstonii*
India.

Andaman Wood-pigeon *Columba palumboides*
India.

Japanese Wood-pigeon *Columba janthina*
Japan, South Korea, Taiwan.

Chilean Pigeon *Columba araucana*
Argentina, Chile.

White-winged Collared-dove *Streptopelia
reichenowi*
Ethiopia, Kenya, Somalia.

Andaman Cuckoo-dove *Macropygia rufipennis*
India.

New Guinea Bronzewing *Henicophaps albifrons*
Indonesia, Papua New Guinea.

New Britain Bronzewing *Henicophaps foersteri*
Papua New Guinea.

Flock Bronzewing *Phaps histrionica*
Australia.

Partridge Pigeon *Geophaps smithii*
Australia.

Brown-backed Dove *Leptotila battyi*
Panama.

Grey-headed Quail-dove *Geotrygon caniceps*
Cuba, Dominican Republic, Haiti.

Crested Quail-dove *Geotrygon versicolor*
Jamaica.

Russet-crowned Quail-dove *Geotrygon goldmani*
Colombia, Panama.

Bridled Quail-dove *Geotrygon mystacea*
Anguilla (to U.K.), Antigua and Barbuda,
Bahamas, Dominica, Guadeloupe (to France),
Martinique (to France), Montserrat (to U.K.),
Netherlands Antilles, Puerto Rico (to U.S.A.),

St Kitts and Nevis, St Lucia, Virgin Islands (to U.K.), Virgin Islands (to U.S.A.).

Nicobar Pigeon *Caloenas nicobarica*
Cambodia, India, Indonesia, Malaysia, Myanmar, Palau (to U.S.A.), Papua New Guinea, Philippines, Solomon Islands, Thailand, Vietnam.

Luzon Bleeding-heart *Gallicolumba luzonica*
Philippines.

White-throated Ground-dove *Gallicolumba xanthonura*
Micronesia, Northern Mariana Islands (to U.S.A.).

Shy Ground-dove *Gallicolumba stairi*
American Samoa, Fiji, Tonga, Wallis and Futuna Islands (to France), Western Samoa.

Palau Ground-dove *Gallicolumba canifrons*
Palau (to U.S.A.).

Thick-billed Ground-pigeon *Trugon terrestris*
Indonesia, Papua New Guinea.

Cinnamon-headed Green-pigeon *Treron fulvicollis*
Brunei, Indonesia, Malaysia, Myanmar, Thailand.

Flores Green-pigeon *Treron floris*
Indonesia.

Sumba Green-pigeon *Treron teysmannii*
Indonesia.

Large Green-pigeon *Treron capellei*
Brunei, Indonesia, Malaysia, Myanmar, Thailand.

Pemba Green-pigeon *Treron pembaensis*
Tanzania.

Sumatran Green-pigeon *Treron oxyura*
Indonesia.

Yellow-vented Green-pigeon *Treron seimundi*
Laos, Malaysia, Thailand, Vietnam.

White-bellied Green-pigeon *Treron sieboldii*
China, Japan, Laos, Taiwan, Thailand, Vietnam.

Whistling Green-pigeon *Treron formosae*
Japan, Philippines, Taiwan.

Black-banded Fruit-dove *Ptilinopus alligator*
Australia.

Cream-bellied Fruit-dove *Ptilinopus merrilli*
Philippines.

Tanna Fruit-dove *Ptilinopus tannensis*
Vanuatu.

Blue-capped Fruit-dove *Ptilinopus monacha*
Indonesia.

Mariana Fruit-dove *Ptilinopus roseicapilla*
Northern Mariana Islands (to U.S.A.).

Cook Islands Fruit-dove *Ptilinopus rarotongensis*
Cook Islands (to New Zealand).

Atoll Fruit-dove *Ptilinopus coralensis*
French Polynesia.

White-headed Fruit-dove *Ptilinopus eugeniae*
Solomon Islands.

Whistling Dove *Ptilinopus layardi*
Fiji.

Finsch's Imperial-pigeon *Ducula finschii*
Papua New Guinea.

Bismarck Imperial-pigeon *Ducula melanochroa*
Papua New Guinea.

Sombre Pigeon *Cryptophaps poecilorrhoa*
Indonesia.

Long-tailed Mountain-pigeon *Gymnophaps mada*
Indonesia.

■ Psittacidae

Blue-streaked Lory *Eos reticulata*
Indonesia.

Blue-eared Lory *Eos semilarvata*
Indonesia.

White-naped Lory *Lorius albidinuchus*
Papua New Guinea.

Palm Lorikeet *Charmosyna palmarum*
Solomon Islands, Vanuatu.

Striated Lorikeet *Charmosyna multistriata*
Indonesia, Papua New Guinea.

Duchess Lorikeet *Charmosyna margarethae*
Papua New Guinea, Solomon Islands.

Palm Cockatoo *Probosciger aterrimus*
Australia, Indonesia, Papua New Guinea.

Pink Cockatoo *Cacatua leadbeateri*
Australia.

Tanimbar Cockatoo *Cacatua goffini*
Indonesia.

Western Corella *Cacatua pastinator*
Australia.

Kea *Nestor notabilis*
New Zealand.

Geelvink Pygmy-parrot *Micropsitta geelvinkiana*
Indonesia.

Blue-rumped Parrot *Psittinus cyanurus*
Brunei, Indonesia, Malaysia, Myanmar, Thailand.

Blue-crowned Racquet-tail *Prioniturus discurus*
Philippines.

Yellowish-breasted Racquet-tail *Prioniturus flavicans*
Indonesia.

Buru Racquet-tail *Prioniturus mada*
Indonesia.

Crimson Shining-parrot *Prosopeia splendens*
Fiji.

Masked Shining-parrot *Prosopeia personata*
Fiji.

Moluccan King-parrot *Alisterus amboinensis*
Indonesia.

Olive-shouldered Parrot *Aprosmictus jonquillaceus*
Indonesia.

Hooded Parrot *Psephotus dissimilis*
Australia.

Yellow-fronted Parakeet *Cyanoramphus auriceps*
New Zealand.

Turquoise Parrot *Neophema pulchella*
Australia.

Fischer's Lovebird *Agapornis fischeri*
Tanzania.

Green-fronted Hanging-parrot *Loriculus tener*
Papua New Guinea.

Yellow-throated Hanging-parrot *Loriculus pusillus*
Indonesia.

Derbyan Parakeet *Psittacula derbiana*
China, India.

Nicobar Parakeet *Psittacula caniceps*
India.

Red-masked Parakeet *Aratinga erythrogenys*
Ecuador, Peru.

Rose-headed Parakeet *Pyrrhura rhodocephala*
Venezuela.

Slender-billed Parakeet *Enicognathus leptorhynchus*
Chile.

Grey-cheeked Parakeet *Brotogeris pyrrhopterus*
Ecuador, Peru.

Amazonian Parrotlet *Nannopsittaca dachilleae*
Peru.

Red-fronted Parrotlet *Touit costaricensis*
Costa Rica, Panama.

Pileated Parrot *Pionopsitta pileata*
Argentina, Brazil, Paraguay.

Cuban Parrot *Amazona leucocephala*
Bahamas, Cayman Islands (to U.K.), Cuba.

Yellow-billed Parrot *Amazona collaria*
Jamaica.

Hispaniolan Parrot *Amazona ventralis*
Dominican Republic, Haiti.

Lilac-crowned Parrot *Amazona finschi*
Mexico.

Blue-cheeked Parrot *Amazona dufresniana*
French Guiana, Guyana, Suriname, Venezuela.

■ Musophagidae

Fischer's Turaco *Tauraco fischeri*
Kenya, Somalia, Tanzania.

■ Cuculidae

Coral-billed Ground-cuckoo *Carpococcyx renauldi*
Cambodia, Laos, Thailand, Vietnam.

Verreaux's Coua *Coua verreauxi*
Madagascar.

Kai Coucal *Centropus spilopterus*
Indonesia.

Biak Coucal *Centropus chalybeus*
Indonesia.

Short-toed Coucal *Centropus rectunguis*
Brunei, Indonesia, Malaysia.

Brown Coucal *Centropus andamanensis*
India, Myanmar.

Rufous Coucal *Centropus unirufus*
Philippines.

Scaled Ground-cuckoo *Neomorphus squamiger*
Brazil.

■ Tytonidae

Lesser Sooty-owl *Tyto multipunctata*
Australia.

■ Strigidae

Andaman Scops-owl *Otus balli*
India.

São Tomé Scops-owl *Otus hartlaubi*
São Tomé e Príncipe.

Pemba Scops-owl *Otus pembaensis*
Tanzania.

Wallace's Scops-owl *Otus silvicola*
Indonesia.

Santa Barbara Screech-owl *Otus barbarus*
Guatemala, Mexico.

Colombian Screech-owl *Otus colombianus*
Colombia, Ecuador.

Spot-bellied Eagle-owl *Bubo nipalensis*
Bangladesh, Bhutan, Cambodia, China, India,
Laos, Myanmar, Nepal, Sri Lanka, Thailand,
Vietnam.

Tawny Fish-owl *Ketupa flavipes*
Bangladesh, Bhutan, China, India, Laos,
Myanmar, Nepal, Taiwan, Vietnam.

Spotted Owl *Strix occidentalis*
Canada, Mexico, U.S.A.

Chestnut-backed Owlet *Glaucidium castanonotum*
Sri Lanka.

Long-whiskered Owlet *Xenoglaux loweryi*
Peru.

Unspotted Saw-whet Owl *Aegolius ridgwayi*
Costa Rica, El Salvador, Guatemala, Mexico.

Buff-fronted Owl *Aegolius harrisii*
Argentina, Bolivia, Brazil, Colombia, Ecuador,
Paraguay, Peru, Venezuela.

Andaman Hawk-owl *Ninox affinis*
India.

■ Podargidae

Sri Lanka Frogmouth *Batrachostomus moniliger*
India, Sri Lanka.

Javan Frogmouth *Batrachostomus javensis*
Indonesia.

■ Caprimulgidae

Least Poorwill *Siphonorhis brewsteri*
Dominican Republic, Haiti.

Chocó Poorwill *Nyctiphrynus rosenbergi*
Colombia, Ecuador.

Eared Poorwill *Otophanes mcleodii*
Mexico.

Roraiman Nightjar *Caprimulgus whitelyi*
Venezuela.

Pygmy Nightjar *Caprimulgus hirundinaceus*
Brazil.

Bonaparte's Nightjar *Caprimulgus concretus*
Brunei, Indonesia, Malaysia.

Long-trained Nightjar *Macropsalis creagra*
Argentina, Brazil.

Sickle-winged Nightjar *Eleothreptus anomalus*
Argentina, Brazil, Paraguay, Uruguay.

■ Apodidae

Rothschild's Swift *Cypseloides rothschildi*
Argentina, Bolivia, Peru.

Waterfall Swift *Hydrochrous gigas*
Indonesia, Malaysia.

Mascarene Swiftlet *Collocalia francica*
Réunion (to France).

■ Trochilidae

Koepcke's Hermit *Phaethornis koepckeae*
Peru.

Saw-billed Hermit *Ramphodon naevius*
Brazil.

Long-tailed Sabrewing *Campylopterus excellens*
Mexico.

Santa Marta Sabrewing *Campylopterus phainopeplus*
Colombia.

Napo Sabrewing *Campylopterus villaviscensio*
Ecuador, Peru.

Fiery-tailed Awlbill *Avocettula recurvirostris*
Brazil, Colombia, Ecuador, French Guiana,
Guyana, Suriname, Venezuela.

Spangled Coquette *Lophornis stictolophus*
Argentina, Bolivia, Brazil, Colombia, Ecuador,
Peru, Venezuela.

Rufous-cheeked Hummingbird *Goethalsia bella*
Colombia, Panama.

Blossomcrown *Anthocephala floriceps*
Colombia.

Ecuadorian Piedtail *Phlogophilus hemileucurus*
Colombia, Ecuador, Peru.

Peruvian Piedtail *Phlogophilus harterti*
Peru.

Pink-throated Brilliant *Heliodoxa gularis*
Colombia, Ecuador, Peru.

Wedge-tailed Hillstar *Oreotrochilus adela*
Bolivia.

Black-thighed Puffleg *Eriocnemis derbyi*
Colombia, Ecuador.

Hoary Puffleg *Haplophaedia lugens*
Colombia, Ecuador.

Bronze-tailed Comet *Polyonymus caroli*
Argentina, Brazil, Paraguay.

Neblina Metaltail *Metallura odomae*
Ecuador, Peru.

Perijá Metaltail *Metallura iracunda*
Colombia, Venezuela.

Hooded Visorbearer *Augastes lumachellus*
Brazil.

Hyacinth Visorbearer *Augastes scutatus*
Brazil.

Magenta-throated Woodstar *Philodice bryantae*
Costa Rica, Panama.

Bee Hummingbird *Calypte helenae*
Cuba.

■ Trogonidae

Resplendent Quetzal *Pharomachrus mocinno*
Costa Rica, El Salvador, Guatemala, Honduras,
Mexico, Nicaragua, Panama.

Hispaniolan Trogon *Priotelus roseigaster*
Dominican Republic, Haiti.

Baird's Trogon *Trogon bairdii*
Costa Rica, Panama.

■ Alcedinidae

Indigo-banded Kingfisher *Alcedo cyanopecta*
Philippines.

Brown-winged Kingfisher *Pelargopsis amauropterus*
Bangladesh, India, Malaysia, Myanmar, Thailand.

Blue-black Kingfisher *Todirhamphus nigrocyaneus*
Indonesia, Papua New Guinea.

Sombre Kingfisher *Todirhamphus funebris*
Indonesia.

Talaud Kingfisher *Todirhamphus enigma*
Indonesia.

Cinnamon-banded Kingfisher *Todirhamphus australasia*
Indonesia.

Spotted Kingfisher *Actenoides lindsayi*
Philippines.

Biak Paradise-kingfisher *Tanysiptera riedelii*
Indonesia.

■ Todidae

Narrow-billed Tody *Todus angustirostris*
Dominican Republic, Haiti.

■ Momotidae

Keel-billed Motmot *Electron carinatum*
Belize, Costa Rica, Guatemala, Honduras,
Mexico, Nicaragua.

■ Coraciidae

Pitta-like Ground-roller *Atelornis pittoides*
Madagascar.

■ Bucerotidae

Malabar Grey-hornbill *Ocyceros griseus*
India.

Malabar Pied-hornbill *Anthracoceros coronatus*
India, Sri Lanka.

Black Hornbill *Anthracoceros malayanus*
Brunei, Indonesia, Malaysia, Thailand.
Rufous Hornbill *Buceros hydrocorax*
Philippines.
Helmeted Hornbill *Buceros vigil*
Brunei, Indonesia, Malaysia, Myanmar, Thailand.
Brown Hornbill *Anorrhinus tickelli*
China, India, Laos, Myanmar, Thailand, Vietnam.
Luzon Hornbill *Penelopides manillae*
Philippines.
Samar Hornbill *Penelopides samarensis*
Philippines.
Mindanao Hornbill *Penelopides affinis*
Philippines.
Brown-cheeked Hornbill *Ceratogymna cylindricus*
Benin, Ghana, Guinea, Ivory Coast, Liberia,
Nigeria, Sierra Leone.
Yellow-casqued Hornbill *Ceratogymna elata*
Cameroon, Ghana, Guinea, Guinea-Bissau, Ivory
Coast, Liberia, Mali, Nigeria, Senegal, Sierra
Leone, Togo.

◼ Bucconidae
Sooty-capped Puffbird *Bucco noanamae*
Colombia.
Lanceolated Monklet *Micromonacha lanceolata*
Brazil, Colombia, Costa Rica, Ecuador, Panama,
Peru.
Chestnut-headed Nunlet *Nonnula amaurocephala*
Brazil.

◼ Capitonidae
Brown-throated Barbet *Megalaima corvina*
Indonesia.
Red-crowned Barbet *Megalaima rafflesii*
Brunei, Indonesia, Malaysia, Myanmar, Thailand.
Black-banded Barbet *Megalaima javensis*
Indonesia.
Chaplin's Barbet *Lybius chaplini*
Zambia.
Red-faced Barbet *Lybius rubrifacies*
Rwanda, Tanzania, Uganda.
Orange-fronted Barbet *Capito squamatus*
Colombia, Ecuador.
Scarlet-hooded Barbet *Eubucco tucinkae*
Peru.
Toucan Barbet *Semnornis ramphastinus*
Colombia, Ecuador.

◼ Indicatoridae
Malaysian Honeyguide *Indicator archipelagicus*
Brunei, Indonesia, Malaysia, Thailand.
Dwarf Honeyguide *Indicator pumilio*
Rwanda, Uganda, Zaïre.
Yellow-rumped Honeyguide *Indicator xanthonotus*
Bhutan, India, Myanmar, Nepal, Pakistan.

◼ Ramphastidae
Yellow-browed Toucanet *Aulacorhynchus huallagae*
Peru.
Saffron Toucanet *Baillonius bailloni*
Brazil.
Plate-billed Mountain-toucan *Andigena laminirostris*
Colombia, Ecuador.
Grey-breasted Mountain-toucan *Andigena hypoglauca*
Colombia, Ecuador, Peru.
Hooded Mountain-toucan *Andigena cucullata*
Bolivia, Peru.
Black-billed Mountain-toucan *Andigena nigrirostris*
Colombia, Ecuador, Venezuela.

◼ Picidae
Speckle-chested Piculet *Picumnus steindachneri*
Peru.
Mottled Piculet *Picumnus nebulosus*
Argentina, Brazil, Uruguay.
Fine-barred Piculet *Picumnus subtilis*
Peru.
Antillean Piculet *Nesoctites micromegas*
Dominican Republic, Haiti.
Guadeloupe Woodpecker *Melanerpes herminieri*
Guadeloupe (to France).
Knysna Woodpecker *Campethera notata*
South Africa.
Ground Woodpecker *Geocolaptes olivaceus*
Lesotho, South Africa.
Stierling's Woodpecker *Dendropicos stierlingi*
Malawi, Mozambique, Tanzania.
Arabian Woodpecker *Dendrocopos dorae*
Saudi Arabia, Yemen.
White-winged Woodpecker *Dendrocopos leucopterus*
Afghanistan, China, Kazakhstan, Kyrgyzstan,
Tajikistan, Turkmenistan, Uzbekistan.
Chocó Woodpecker *Veniliornis chocoensis*
Colombia, Ecuador.
Yellow-browed Woodpecker *Piculus aurulentus*
Brazil.
Black-bodied Woodpecker *Dryocopus schulzi*
Argentina, Bolivia, Paraguay.
Andaman Woodpecker *Dryocopus hodgei*
India.

◼ Dendrocolaptidae
Greater Scythebill *Campylorhamphus pucherani*
Colombia, Ecuador, Peru.

◼ Furnariidae
Bolivian Earthcreeper *Upucerthia harterti*
Bolivia.

Tawny Tit-spinetail *Leptasthenura yanacensis*
Bolivia, Peru.

Araucaria Tit-spinetail *Leptasthenura setaria*
Argentina, Brazil.

Perijá Thistletail *Schizoeaca perijana*
Colombia, Venezuela.

Chestnut-throated Spinetail *Synallaxis cherriei*
Brazil, Colombia, Ecuador, Peru.

Rusty-headed Spinetail *Synallaxis fuscorufa*
Colombia.

Coiba Spinetail *Cranioleuca dissita*
Panama.

Cactus Canastero *Asthenes cactorum*
Peru.

Line-fronted Canastero *Asthenes urubambensis*
Bolivia, Peru.

Russet-mantled Softtail *Thripophaga berlepschi*
Peru.

Great Spinetail *Siptornopsis hypochondriacus*
Peru.

Chestnut-backed Thornbird *Phacellodomus dorsalis*
Peru.

Canebrake Groundcreeper *Clibanornis
   dendrocolaptoides*
Argentina, Brazil, Paraguay.

Bay-capped Wren-spinetail *Spartonoica maluroides*
Argentina, Brazil, Uruguay.

Straight-billed Reedhaunter *Limnornis rectirostris*
Argentina, Brazil, Uruguay.

Equatorial Greytail *Xenerpestes singularis*
Ecuador, Peru.

Beautiful Treerunner *Margarornis bellulus*
Panama.

Russet-mantled Foliage-gleaner *Philydor dimidiatus*
Brazil, Paraguay.

White-browed Foliage-gleaner *Philydor amaurotis*
Argentina, Brazil.

Peruvian Recurvebill *Simoxenops ucayalae*
Bolivia, Brazil, Peru.

Chestnut-capped Foliage-gleaner *Hylocryptus
   rectirostris*
Brazil.

■ Formicariidae

Cocha Antshrike *Thamnophilus praecox*
Ecuador.

Spot-breasted Antvireo *Dysithamnus stictothorax*
Argentina, Brazil.

Klages's Antwren *Myrmotherula klagesi*
Brazil.

Black-capped Antwren *Herpsilochmus pileatus*
Brazil.

Serra Antwren *Formicivora serrana*
Brazil.

Rufous-tailed Antbird *Drymophila genei*
Brazil.

Ochre-rumped Antbird *Drymophila ochropyga*
Brazil.

Rio de Janeiro Antbird *Cercomacra brasiliana*
Brazil.

White-breasted Antbird *Rhegmatorhina hoffmannsi*
Brazil.

Santarem Antbird *Rhegmatorhina gymnops*
Brazil.

Great Antpitta *Grallaria excelsa*
Venezuela.

Elusive Antpitta *Grallaria eludens*
Peru.

Santa Marta Antpitta *Grallaria bangsi*
Colombia.

Chestnut Antpitta *Grallaria blakei*
Peru.

White-browed Antpitta *Hylopezus ochroleucus*
Brazil.

Scallop-breasted Antpitta *Grallaricula loricata*
Venezuela.

Peruvian Antpitta *Grallaricula peruviana*
Ecuador, Peru.

Ochre-fronted Antpitta *Grallaricula ochraceifrons*
Peru.

Crescent-faced Antpitta *Grallaricula lineifrons*
Colombia, Ecuador.

■ Conopophagidae

Hooded Gnateater *Conopophaga roberti*
Brazil.

■ Rhinocryptidae

Marañón Crescent-chest *Melanopareia maranonica*
Peru.

Spotted Bamboowren *Psilorhamphus guttatus*
Argentina, Brazil.

Slaty Bristlefront *Merulaxis ater*
Brazil.

■ Cotingidae

Slaty Becard *Pachyramphus spodiurus*
Ecuador, Peru.

Swallow-tailed Cotinga *Phibalura flavirostris*
Argentina, Bolivia, Brazil.

Black-and-gold Cotinga *Tijuca atra*
Brazil.

Hooded Berryeater *Carpornis cucullatus*
Brazil.

Black-chested Fruiteater *Pipreola lubomirskii*
Colombia, Ecuador, Peru.

Fiery-throated Fruiteater *Pipreola chlorolepidota*
Colombia, Ecuador, Peru.

Scarlet-breasted Fruiteater *Pipreola frontalis*
Bolivia, Colombia, Ecuador, Peru.

Scaled Fruiteater *Ampelioides tschudii*
Bolivia, Colombia, Ecuador, Peru, Venezuela.

Purple-throated Cotinga *Porphyrolaema porphyrolaema*
Brazil, Colombia, Ecuador, Peru.
Black-tipped Cotinga *Carpodectes hopkei*
Colombia, Ecuador, Panama.
Black-faced Cotinga *Conioptilon mcilhennyi*
Peru.
Bare-throated Bellbird *Procnias nudicollis*
Argentina, Brazil, Paraguay.

■ Pipridae
Yellow-headed Manakin *Chloropipo flavicapilla*
Colombia.
Grey-headed Piprites *Piprites griseiceps*
Costa Rica, Guatemala, Honduras, Nicaragua.
Opal-crowned Manakin *Pipra iris*
Brazil.

■ Tyrannidae
White-cheeked Tody-tyrant *Poecilotriccus albifacies*
Peru.
Boat-billed Tody-tyrant *Hemitriccus josephinae*
Guyana, Suriname, Brazil.
Zimmer's Tody-tyrant *Hemitriccus aenigma*
Brazil.
Eye-ringed Tody-tyrant *Hemitriccus orbitatus*
Brazil.
Hangnest Tody-tyrant *Hemitriccus nidipendulus*
Brazil.
Buff-throated Tody-tyrant *Hemitriccus rufigularis*
Bolivia, Peru.
Cinnamon-breasted Tody-tyrant *Hemitriccus cinnamomeipectus*
Peru.
Maracaibo Tody-flycatcher *Todirostrum viridanum*
Venezuela.
Reiser's Tyrannulet *Phyllomyias reiseri*
Brazil, Paraguay.
Grey-capped Tyrannulet *Phyllomyias griseocapilla*
Brazil.
Sharp-tailed Grass-tyrant *Culicivora caudacuta*
Argentina, Bolivia, Brazil, Paraguay.
Bearded Tachuri *Polystictus pectoralis*
Argentina, Bolivia, Brazil, Colombia, Guyana, Paraguay, Suriname, Uruguay, Venezuela.
Grey-backed Tachuri *Polystictus superciliaris*
Brazil.
Venezuelan Bristle-tyrant *Phylloscartes venezuelanus*
Venezuela.
Southern Bristle-tyrant *Phylloscartes eximius*
Argentina, Brazil, Paraguay.
Oustalet's Tyrannulet *Phylloscartes oustaleti*
Brazil.

Serra do Mar Tyrannulet *Phylloscartes difficilis*
Brazil.
Bay-ringed Tyrannulet *Phylloscartes sylviolus*
Argentina, Brazil, Paraguay.
White-bellied Pygmy-tyrant *Myiornis albiventris*
Bolivia, Peru.
Orange-banded Flycatcher *Myiophobus lintoni*
Ecuador, Peru.
Tawny-chested Flycatcher *Aphanotriccus capitalis*
Costa Rica, Nicaragua.
Black-billed Flycatcher *Aphanotriccus audax*
Colombia, Panama.
Belted Flycatcher *Xenotriccus callizonus*
Guatemala, Mexico.
Pileated Flycatcher *Xenotriccus mexicanus*
Mexico.
Ochraceous Pewee *Contopus ochraceus*
Costa Rica, Panama.
Piura Chat-tyrant *Ochthoeca piurae*
Peru.
Tumbes Tyrant *Ochthoeca salvini*
Peru.
Rufous-bellied Bush-tyrant *Myiotheretes fuscorufus*
Bolivia, Peru.
Salinas Monjita *Xolmis salinarum*
Argentina.
Hudson's Black-tyrant *Knipolegus hudsoni*
Argentina, Bolivia, Paraguay.
Cock-tailed Tyrant *Alectrurus tricolor*
Argentina, Bolivia, Brazil, Paraguay.
Shear-tailed Grey Tyrant *Muscipipra vetula*
Argentina, Brazil, Paraguay.

■ Pittidae
Blue-naped Pitta *Pitta nipalensis*
Bangladesh, Bhutan, China, India, Laos, Myanmar, Nepal, Vietnam.
Blue-rumped Pitta *Pitta soror*
Cambodia, China, Laos, Thailand, Vietnam.
Giant Pitta *Pitta caerulea*
Indonesia, Malaysia, Myanmar, Thailand.
Bar-bellied Pitta *Pitta elliotii*
Cambodia, Laos, Vietnam.
Blue-headed Pitta *Pitta baudii*
Brunei, Indonesia, Malaysia.
Sula Pitta *Pitta dohertyi*
Indonesia.
Mangrove Pitta *Pitta megarhyncha*
Bangladesh, Indonesia, Malaysia, Myanmar, Thailand.

■ Acanthisittidae
South Island Rock Wren *Xenicus gilviventris*
New Zealand.

■ **Philepittidae**

Schlegel's Asity *Philepitta schlegeli*
Madagascar.

■ **Menuridae**

Albert's Lyrebird *Menura alberti*
Australia.

■ **Alaudidae**

Williams's Lark *Mirafra williamsi*
Kenya.

Friedmann's Lark *Mirafra pulpa*
Ethiopia, Kenya.

Short-clawed Lark *Certhilauda chuana*
Botswana, South Africa.

Sclater's Lark *Spizocorys sclateri*
Namibia, South Africa.

Obbia Lark *Spizocorys obbiensis*
Somalia.

■ **Hirundinidae**

Bahama Swallow *Tachycineta cyaneoviridis*
Bahamas, Cuba, U.S.A.

Golden Swallow *Tachycineta euchrysea*
Dominican Republic, Haiti, Jamaica.

Mountain Sawwing *Psalidoprocne fuliginosa*
Cameroon, Equatorial Guinea, Nigeria.

■ **Motacillidae**

Abyssinian Longclaw *Macronyx flavicollis*
Ethiopia.

Grimwood's Longclaw *Macronyx grimwoodi*
Angola, Zambia, Zaïre.

Sharpe's Pipit *Macronyx sharpei*
Kenya.

Mountain Pipit *Anthus hoeschi*
Lesotho, South Africa.

Malindi Pipit *Anthus melindae*
Kenya, Somalia.

Chaco Pipit *Anthus chacoensis*
Argentina, Paraguay.

■ **Campephagidae**

Pied Cuckoo-shrike *Coracina bicolor*
Indonesia.

Grauer's Cuckoo-shrike *Coracina graueri*
Uganda, Zaïre.

Blackish Cuckoo-shrike *Coracina coerulescens*
Philippines.

Sumba Cicadabird *Coracina dohertyi*
Indonesia.

Kai Cicadabird *Coracina dispar*
Indonesia.

Samoan Triller *Lalage sharpei*
Western Samoa.

Brown-rumped Minivet *Pericrocotus cantonensis*
China.

White-bellied Minivet *Pericrocotus erythropygius*
India, Myanmar.

■ **Pycnonotidae**

Grey-headed Bulbul *Pycnonotus priocephalus*
India.

Styan's Bulbul *Pycnonotus taivanus*
Taiwan.

Yellow-throated Bulbul *Pycnonotus xantholaemus*
India.

Yellow-eared Bulbul *Pycnonotus penicillatus*
Sri Lanka.

Cameroon Greenbul *Andropadus montanus*
Cameroon, Nigeria.

Baumann's Greenbul *Phyllastrephus baumanni*
Ghana, Ivory Coast, Liberia, Nigeria, Sierra
Leone, Togo.

Sassi's Greenbul *Phyllastrephus lorenzi*
Uganda, Zaïre.

Grey-headed Greenbul *Phyllastrephus
poliocephalus*
Cameroon, Nigeria.

Hook-billed Bulbul *Setornis criniger*
Brunei, Indonesia, Malaysia.

Yellowish Bulbul *Ixos everetti*
Philippines.

■ **Irenidae**

Blue-masked Leafbird *Chloropsis venusta*
Indonesia.

■ **Laniidae**

Mountain Shrike *Lanius validirostris*
Philippines.

Bornean Bristlehead *Pityriasis gymnocephala*
Brunei, Indonesia, Malaysia.

Turati's Boubou *Laniarius turatii*
Guinea, Guinea-Bissau, Sierra Leone.

Papyrus Gonolek *Laniarius mufumbiri*
Burundi, Kenya, Rwanda, Uganda, Zaïre.

Lagden's Bush-shrike *Malaconotus lagdeni*
Ivory Coast, Liberia, Rwanda, Sierra Leone,
Uganda, Zaïre.

■ **Vangidae**

Helmet Vanga *Euryceros prevostii*
Madagascar.

■ **Bombycillidae**

Japanese Waxwing *Bombycilla japonica*
China[N], Japan[N], North Korea[N], Russia, South
Korea[N], Taiwan[N].

■ Troglodytidae
Socorro Wren *Thryomanes sissonii*
Mexico.
Bar-winged Wood-wren *Henicorhina leucoptera*
Peru.

■ Mimidae
Black Catbird *Melanoptila glabrirostris*
Belize, Guatemala, Honduras, Mexico.
Cozumel Thrasher *Toxostoma guttatum*
Mexico.

■ Prunellidae
Yemen Accentor *Prunella fagani*
Saudi Arabia, Yemen.

■ Turdinae
Rufous Rockjumper *Chaetops frenatus*
South Africa.
Orange-breasted Rockjumper *Chaetops aurantius*
Lesotho, South Africa.
Forest Rock-thrush *Monticola sharpei*
Madagascar.
Malayan Whistling-thrush *Myiophonus robinsoni*
Malaysia.
Geomalia *Geomalia heinrichi*
Indonesia.
Slaty-backed Thrush *Zoothera schistacea*
Indonesia.
Red-backed Thrush *Zoothera erythronota*
Indonesia.
Pied Thrush *Zoothera wardii*
Bhutan, India, Nepal, Sri Lanka[N].
Orange-banded Thrush *Zoothera peronii*
Indonesia.
Everett's Thrush *Zoothera everetti*
Malaysia.
Kivu Ground-thrush *Zoothera tanganjicae*
Uganda, Zaïre.
Crossley's Ground-thrush *Zoothera crossleyi*
Cameroon, Nigeria.
Forest Ground-thrush *Zoothera oberlaenderi*
Uganda, Zaïre.
Spot-winged Thrush *Zoothera spiloptera*
Sri Lanka.
Fawn-breasted Thrush *Zoothera machiki*
Indonesia.
New Britain Thrush *Zoothera talaseae*
Papua New Guinea.
San Cristobal Thrush *Zoothera margaretae*
Solomon Islands.
Long-billed Thrush *Zoothera monticola*
Bangladesh, Bhutan, India, Myanmar, Nepal, Vietnam.
Tristan Thrush *Nesocichla eremita*
Tristan da Cunha group (to U.K.).

Forest Thrush *Cichlherminia lherminieri*
Dominica, Guadeloupe (to France), Montserrat (to U.K.), St Lucia.
Cuban Solitaire *Myadestes elisabeth*
Cuba.
Rufous-brown Solitaire *Myadestes leucogenys*
Brazil, Guyana, Venezuela.
São Tomé Thrush *Turdus olivaceofuscus*
São Tomé e Príncipe.
Black-breasted Thrush *Turdus dissimilis*
Bangladesh[N], China, India, Myanmar, Thailand[N], Vietnam.
Chinese Thrush *Turdus mupinensis*
China.
Unicoloured Thrush *Turdus haplochrous*
Bolivia.
Grayson's Thrush *Turdus graysoni*
Mexico.
Gould's Shortwing *Brachypteryx stellata*
Bhutan, China, India, Myanmar, Nepal, Vietnam.
White-bellied Shortwing *Brachypteryx major*
India.
Ryukyu Robin *Erithacus komadori*
Japan.
Firethroat *Luscinia pectardens*
Bangladesh[N], China, India[N].
Rufous-breasted Bush-robin *Tarsiger hyperythrus*
Bhutan, China, India, Myanmar[N], Nepal.
Angola Cave-chat *Xenocopsychus ansorgei*
Angola.
Herero Chat *Namibornis herero*
Angola, Namibia.
Ala Shan Redstart *Phoenicurus alaschanicus*
China.
Blue-fronted Robin *Cinclidium frontale*
Bhutan, China, India, Laos, Thailand, Vietnam.
Purple Cochoa *Cochoa purpurea*
Bhutan, China, India, Laos, Myanmar, Nepal, Thailand, Vietnam.
Green Cochoa *Cochoa viridis*
China, India, Laos, Myanmar, Nepal, Thailand, Vietnam.
Fuerteventura Chat *Saxicola dacotiae*
Spain.
Jerdon's Bushchat *Saxicola jerdoni*
Bangladesh, China, India, Laos, Myanmar, Thailand, Vietnam.
White-bellied Bushchat *Saxicola gutturalis*
Indonesia.
Buff-streaked Chat *Saxicola bifasciata*
South Africa.
Sombre Chat *Cercomela dubia*
Ethiopia, Somalia.

■ Timaliinae

Rufous-fronted Laughingthrush *Garrulax rufifrons*
Indonesia.

Grey Laughingthrush *Garrulax maesi*
China, Laos, Vietnam.

Chestnut-backed Laughingthrush *Garrulax nuchalis*
India, Myanmar.

Yellow-throated Laughingthrush *Garrulax galbanus*
Bangladesh, China, India, Myanmar.

Wynaad Laughingthrush *Garrulax delesserti*
India.

Barred Laughingthrush *Garrulax lunulatus*
China.

Spot-breasted Laughingthrush *Garrulax merulinus*
China, Laos, Myanmar, Nepal, Thailand, Vietnam.

Rufous-breasted Laughingthrush *Garrulax cachinnans*
India.

Grey-breasted Laughingthrush *Garrulax jerdoni*
India.

Striped Laughingthrush *Garrulax virgatus*
India, Myanmar.

Red-winged Laughingthrush *Garrulax formosus*
China, Vietnam.

Red-tailed Laughingthrush *Garrulax milnei*
China, Laos, Myanmar, Thailand, Vietnam.

White-chested Babbler *Trichastoma rostratum*
Brunei, Indonesia, Malaysia, Myanmar, Thailand.

Ferruginous Babbler *Trichastoma bicolor*
Brunei, Indonesia, Malaysia, Myanmar, Thailand.

Grey-breasted Babbler *Malacopteron albogulare*
Brunei, Indonesia, Malaysia.

Rufous-winged Illadopsis *Illadopsis rufescens*
Ghana, Ivory Coast, Liberia, Senegal, Sierra Leone, Togo.

Slender-billed Scimitar-babbler *Xiphirhynchus superciliaris*
Bangladesh, Bhutan, China, India, Myanmar, Nepal, Vietnam.

Long-billed Wren-babbler *Rimator malacoptilus*
Bhutan, India, Indonesia, Myanmar, Vietnam.

Bornean Wren-babbler *Ptilocichla leucogrammica*
Brunei, Indonesia, Malaysia.

Striated Wren-babbler *Ptilocichla mindanensis*
Philippines.

Large Wren-babbler *Napothera macrodactyla*
Indonesia, Malaysia, Thailand.

Marbled Wren-babbler *Napothera marmorata*
Indonesia, Malaysia.

Nepal Wren-babbler *Pnoepyga immaculata*
Nepal.

Spotted Wren-babbler *Spelaeornis formosus*
Bangladesh, Bhutan, China, India, Myanmar.

Wedge-billed Wren-babbler *Sphenocichla humei*
China, India, Myanmar.

Wedge-tailed Jery *Hartertula flavoviridis*
Madagascar.

Pygmy Babbler *Stachyris plateni*
Philippines.

Golden-crowned Babbler *Stachyris dennistouni*
Philippines.

Rusty-crowned Babbler *Stachyris capitalis*
Philippines.

Chestnut-faced Babbler *Stachyris whiteheadi*
Philippines.

Grey-faced Tit-babbler *Macronous kelleyi*
Laos, Vietnam.

Rufous-tailed Babbler *Chrysomma poecilotis*
China.

Iraq Babbler *Turdoides altirostris*
Iran, Iraq.

Slender-billed Babbler *Turdoides longirostris*
India, Myanmar, Nepal.

Giant Babax *Babax waddelli*
China, India.

Tibetan Babax *Babax koslowi*
China.

Black-headed Shrike-babbler *Pteruthius rufiventer*
Bhutan, China, India, Myanmar, Nepal, Vietnam.

Streaked Barwing *Actinodura souliei*
China, Vietnam.

Yellow-throated Fulvetta *Alcippe cinerea*
Bangladesh, Bhutan, China, India, Laos, Myanmar.

Spectacled Fulvetta *Alcippe ruficapilla*
China, Laos.

Rufous-throated Fulvetta *Alcippe rufogularis*
Bangladesh, Bhutan, Cambodia, China, India, Laos, Myanmar, Thailand, Vietnam.

Bush Blackcap *Lioptilus nigricapillus*
South Africa.

Red-collared Mountain-babbler *Kupeornis rufocinctus*
Rwanda, Uganda, Zaïre.

Chapin's Mountain-babbler *Kupeornis chapini*
Zaïre.

Spotted Crocias *Crocias albonotatus*
Indonesia.

Grey Sibia *Heterophasia gracilis*
China, India, Myanmar.

Burmese Yuhina *Yuhina humilis*
Myanmar, Thailand.

■ Panurinae

Spectacled Parrotbill *Paradoxornis conspicillatus*
China.

Brown-winged Parrotbill *Paradoxornis brunneus*
China, Myanmar.

Black-browed Parrotbill *Paradoxornis atrosuperciliaris*
Bangladesh, China, India, Laos, Myanmar, Thailand.

Rufous-headed Parrotbill *Paradoxornis ruficeps*
Bangladesh, Bhutan, China, India, Laos, Myanmar, Vietnam.
Reed Parrotbill *Paradoxornis heudei*
China, Russia.

■ Polioptilinae
Cuban Gnatcatcher *Polioptila lembeyei*
Cuba.
Creamy-bellied Gnatcatcher *Polioptila lactea*
Argentina, Brazil, Paraguay.

■ Sylviinae
Churring Cisticola *Cisticola njombe*
Malawi, Tanzania, Zambia.
Grey-crowned Prinia *Prinia cinereocapilla*
Bhutan, India, Nepal.
Timor Stubtail *Urosphena subulata*
Indonesia.
Shade Warbler *Cettia parens*
Solomon Islands.
Tanimbar Bush-warbler *Cettia carolinae*
Indonesia.
Cameroon Bracken-warbler *Bradypterus bangwaensis*
Cameroon.
Sri Lanka Bush-warbler *Bradypterus palliseri*
Sri Lanka.
Long-tailed Bush-warbler *Bradypterus caudatus*
Philippines.
Brown Emu-tail *Dromaeocercus brunneus*
Madagascar.
Moheli Brush-warbler *Nesillas mariae*
Comoros.
Basra Reed-warbler *Acrocephalus griseldis*
Ethiopia[N], Iraq, Kenya[N], Malawi[N], Mozambique[N], Saudi Arabia[N], Somalia[N], Sudan[N], Tanzania[N].
Yellow-breasted Tailorbird *Orthotomus samarensis*
Philippines.
Black-headed Tailorbird *Orthotomus nigriceps*
Philippines.
Rand's Warbler *Randia pseudozosterops*
Madagascar.
Short-billed Crombec *Sylvietta philippae*
Ethiopia, Somalia.
Crested Tit-warbler *Leptopoecile elegans*
China.
Tytler's Leaf-warbler *Phylloscopus tytleri*
Afghanistan, India, Nepal, Pakistan.
Yellow-vented Warbler *Phylloscopus cantator*
Bangladesh, Bhutan, China[N], India, Laos[N], Myanmar[N], Nepal[N], Thailand[N].
San Cristobal Leaf-warbler *Phylloscopus makirensis*
Solomon Islands.
Broad-billed Warbler *Tickellia hodgsoni*
China, India, Laos, Myanmar, Nepal, Vietnam.

Buff-banded Grassbird *Buettikoferella bivittata*
Indonesia.
Guadalcanal Thicketbird *Megalurulus whitneyi*
Solomon Islands, Vanuatu.
Broad-tailed Grassbird *Schoenicola platyura*
India.

■ Malurinae
Broad-billed Fairywren *Malurus grayi*
Indonesia, Papua New Guinea.
Purple-crowned Fairywren *Malurus coronatus*
Australia.
Grey Grasswren *Amytornis barbatus*
Australia.
White-throated Grasswren *Amytornis woodwardi*
Australia.
Black Grasswren *Amytornis housei*
Australia.
Yellow Chat *Epthianura crocea*
Australia.
Origma *Origma solitaria*
Australia.
Fernwren *Oreoscopus gutturalis*
Australia.
Chatham Islands Warbler *Gerygone albofrontata*
New Zealand.

■ Muscicapinae
Golden-bellied Flyrobin *Microeca hemixantha*
Indonesia.
Grey-headed Robin *Heteromyias cinereifrons*
Australia.
Russet-backed Jungle-flycatcher *Rhinomyias oscillans*
Indonesia.
Henna-tailed Jungle-flycatcher *Rhinomyias colonus*
Indonesia.
Brown-breasted Flycatcher *Muscicapa muttui*
China, India, Myanmar[N], Sri Lanka[N], Thailand[N].
Rufous-throated Flycatcher *Ficedula rufigula*
Indonesia.
Sumba Flycatcher *Ficedula harterti*
Indonesia.
Black-and-rufous Flycatcher *Ficedula nigrorufa*
India.
Black-banded Flycatcher *Ficedula timorensis*
Indonesia.
Dull-blue Flycatcher *Eumyias sordida*
Sri Lanka.
Nilgiri Flycatcher *Eumyias albicaudata*
India.
Fujian Niltava *Niltava davidi*
China, Hong Kong (to U.K.)[N], Laos, Thailand[N], Vietnam.
Blue-breasted Flycatcher *Cyornis herioti*
Philippines.

White-bellied Blue-flycatcher *Cyornis pallipes*
India.

Large-billed Blue-flycatcher *Cyornis caerulatus*
Brunei, Indonesia, Malaysia.

Malaysian Blue-flycatcher *Cyornis turcosus*
Brunei, Indonesia, Malaysia.

■ Platysteirinae

Ward's Flycatcher *Pseudobias wardi*
Madagascar.

White-fronted Wattle-eye *Platysteira albifrons*
Angola.

■ Monarchinae

Short-crested Monarch *Hypothymis helenae*
Philippines.

Bedford's Paradise-flycatcher *Terpsiphone bedfordi*
Zaïre.

Japanese Paradise-flycatcher *Terpsiphone atrocaudata*
China[N], Indonesia[N], Japan, Laos[N], Malaysia[N], North Korea, Philippines, South Korea, Taiwan[N], Thailand[N], Vietnam[N].

Rufous Paradise-flycatcher *Terpsiphone cinnamomea*
Philippines.

Blue Paradise-flycatcher *Terpsiphone cyanescens*
Philippines.

Vanikoro Monarch *Mayrornis schistaceus*
Solomon Islands.

Black-throated Shrikebill *Clytorhynchus nigrogularis*
Fiji, Solomon Islands.

Rennell Shrikebill *Clytorhynchus hamlini*
Solomon Islands.

Loetoe Monarch *Monarcha castus*
Indonesia.

Black-bibbed Monarch *Monarcha mundus*
Indonesia.

Black-tipped Monarch *Monarcha loricatus*
Indonesia.

White-tailed Monarch *Monarcha leucurus*
Indonesia.

Manus Monarch *Monarcha infelix*
Papua New Guinea.

Kolombangara Monarch *Monarcha browni*
Solomon Islands.

Yap Monarch *Monarcha godeffroyi*
Micronesia.

Biak Flycatcher *Myiagra atra*
Indonesia.

Ochre-tailed Flycatcher *Myiagra cervinicauda*
Solomon Islands.

■ Rhipidurinae

White-bellied Fantail *Rhipidura euryura*
Indonesia.

Cinnamon-tailed Fantail *Rhipidura fuscorufa*
Indonesia.

Dusky Fantail *Rhipidura tenebrosa*
Solomon Islands.

Kadavu Fantail *Rhipidura personata*
Fiji.

Tawny-backed Fantail *Rhipidura superflua*
Indonesia.

Long-tailed Fantail *Rhipidura opistherythra*
Indonesia.

■ Pachycephalinae

Vogelkop Whistler *Pachycephala meyeri*
Indonesia.

Fawn-breasted Whistler *Pachycephala orpheus*
Indonesia.

Tongan Whistler *Pachycephala jacquinoti*
Tonga.

Hooded Whistler *Pachycephala implicata*
Papua New Guinea, Solomon Islands.

Bower's Shrike-thrush *Colluricincla boweri*
Australia.

■ Aegithalidae

White-throated Tit *Aegithalos niveogularis*
India, Nepal, Pakistan.

White-necklaced Tit *Aegithalos fuliginosus*
China.

■ Paridae

Red-throated Tit *Parus fringillinus*
Kenya, Tanzania.

Yellow Tit *Parus holsti*
Taiwan.

White-fronted Tit *Parus semilarvatus*
Philippines.

■ Sittidae

Corsican Nuthatch *Sitta whiteheadi*
France.

Snowy-browed Nuthatch *Sitta villosa*
China.

■ Rhabdornithidae

Long-billed Rhabdornis *Rhabdornis grandis*
Philippines.

■ Dicaeidae

Brown-backed Flowerpecker *Dicaeum everetti*
Indonesia, Malaysia.

White-throated Flowerpecker *Dicaeum vincens*
Sri Lanka.

Flame-crowned Flowerpecker *Dicaeum anthonyi*
Philippines.

■ Nectariniidae

Plain-backed Sunbird *Anthreptes reichenowi*
Kenya, Mozambique, South Africa, Tanzania,
Zimbabwe.

Ursula's Sunbird *Nectarinia ursulae*
Cameroon, Equatorial Guinea.

Neergaard's Sunbird *Nectarinia neergaardi*
Mozambique, South Africa.

Loveridge's Sunbird *Nectarinia loveridgei*
Tanzania.

Moreau's Sunbird *Nectarinia moreaui*
Tanzania.

Pemba Sunbird *Nectarinia pembae*
Tanzania.

Apo Sunbird *Aethopyga boltoni*
Philippines.

Naked-faced Spiderhunter *Arachnothera clarae*
Philippines.

■ Zosteropidae

Pemba White-eye *Zosterops vaughani*
Tanzania.

Saipan Bridled White-eye *Zosterops saypani*
Northern Mariana Islands (to U.S.A.).

Plain White-eye *Zosterops hypolais*
Micronesia.

Christmas Island White-eye *Zosterops natalis*
Christmas Island (to Australia).

Javan White-eye *Zosterops flavus*
Indonesia, Malaysia.

Pearl-bellied White-eye *Zosterops grayi*
Indonesia.

Golden-bellied White-eye *Zosterops uropygialis*
Indonesia.

Pale-bellied White-eye *Zosterops consobrinorum*
Indonesia.

Lemon-throated White-eye *Zosterops anomalus*
Indonesia.

Biak White-eye *Zosterops mysorensis*
Indonesia.

Ambon Yellow White-eye *Zosterops kuehni*
Indonesia.

Rennell White-eye *Zosterops rennellianus*
Solomon Islands.

Long-billed White-eye *Rukia longirostra*
Micronesia.

Crested White-eye *Lophozosterops dohertyi*
Indonesia.

Spot-breasted White-eye *Heleia muelleri*
Indonesia.

Sanford's White-eye *Woodfordia lacertosa*
Solomon Islands.

Giant White-eye *Megazosterops palauensis*
Palau (to U.S.A.).

■ Meliphagidae

Red-rumped Myzomela *Myzomela vulnerata*
Indonesia.

Buru Honeyeater *Lichmera deningeri*
Indonesia.

Streaky-breasted Honeyeater *Meliphaga reticulata*
Indonesia.

Bridled Honeyeater *Lichenostomus frenatus*
Australia.

Kadavu Honeyeater *Xanthotis provocator*
Fiji.

Plain Friarbird *Philemon inornatus*
Indonesia.

Vogelkop Melidectes *Melidectes leucostephes*
Indonesia.

■ Emberizinae

Slaty Bunting *Latoucheornis siemsseni*
China.

Tibetan Bunting *Emberiza koslowi*
China.

Cinereous Bunting *Emberiza cineracea*
Bahrain[N], Egypt[N], Eritrea[N], Ethiopia[N], Greece,
Iran, Israel[N], Jordan[N], Kuwait[N], Lebanon[N], Saudi
Arabia[N], Sudan[N], Syria[N], Turkey, United Arab
Emirates[N], Yemen[N].

Ochre-rumped Bunting *Emberiza yessoensis*
China, Japan, North Korea[N], Russia, South
Korea[N].

Henslow's Sparrow *Ammodramus henslowii*
Canada, U.S.A.

Cinnamon-tailed Sparrow *Aimophila sumichrasti*
Mexico.

Oaxaca Sparrow *Aimophila notosticta*
Mexico.

White-rimmed Brush-finch *Atlapetes leucopis*
Colombia, Ecuador.

Dusky-headed Brush-finch *Atlapetes fuscoolivaceus*
Colombia.

Rufous-eared Brush-finch *Atlapetes rufigenis*
Peru.

Coal-crested Finch *Charitospiza eucosma*
Argentina, Brazil.

Canary-winged Finch *Melanodera melanodera*
Argentina, Chile, Falkland Islands (to U.K.).

Peg-billed Finch *Acanthidops bairdii*
Costa Rica, Panama.

Grey-winged Inca-finch *Incaspiza ortizi*
Peru.

Little Inca-finch *Incaspiza watkinsi*
Peru.

Cinereous Warbling-finch *Poospiza cinerea*
Brazil.

Citron-headed Yellow-finch *Sicalis luteocephala*
Bolivia.

Grey-cheeked Grass-finch *Emberizoides*
ypiranganus
Argentina, Bolivia, Paraguay.

Pale-throated Pampa-finch *Embernagra longicauda*
Brazil.

Dark-throated Seedeater *Sporophila ruficollis*
Argentina, Bolivia, Brazil, Paraguay, Uruguay.

Grey-and-chestnut Seedeater *Sporophila*
hypochroma
Argentina, Bolivia, Brazil.

Chestnut Seedeater *Sporophila cinnamomea*
Argentina, Brazil, Paraguay.

Black-bellied Seedeater *Sporophila melanogaster*
Brazil.

Large-billed Seed-finch *Oryzoborus crassirostris*
Brazil, Colombia, Ecuador, French Guiana,
Guyana, Peru, Suriname, Trinidad and Tobago,
Venezuela.

Great-billed Seed-finch *Oryzoborus maximiliani*
Brazil, French Guiana, Trinidad and Tobago,
Venezuela.

Slate-blue Seedeater *Amaurospiza relicta*
Mexico.

Blackish-blue Seedeater *Amaurospiza moesta*
Argentina, Brazil, Paraguay.

Santa Marta Seedeater *Catamenia oreophila*
Colombia.

St Lucia Black Finch *Melanospiza richardsoni*
St Lucia.

Medium Tree-finch *Camarhynchus pauper*
Ecuador.

■ Cardinalinae

Thick-billed Saltator *Saltator maxillosus*
Argentina, Brazil, Paraguay.

Masked Saltator *Saltator cinctus*
Ecuador, Peru.

Rose-bellied Bunting *Passerina rositae*
Mexico.

Yellow-billed Blue Finch *Porphyrospiza*
caerulescens
Bolivia, Brazil.

■ Thraupinae

Giant Conebill *Oreomanes fraseri*
Bolivia, Colombia, Ecuador, Peru.

Brown Tanager *Orchesticus abeillei*
Brazil.

White-banded Tanager *Neothraupis fasciata*
Bolivia, Brazil, Paraguay.

White-rumped Tanager *Cypsnagra hirundinacea*
Bolivia, Brazil, Paraguay.

Black-and-white Tanager *Conothraupis speculigera*
Ecuador, Peru.

Rufous-browed Hemispingus *Hemispingus*
rufosuperciliaris
Ecuador, Peru.

Sooty Ant-tanager *Habia gutturalis*
Colombia.

Azure-shouldered Tanager *Thraupis cyanoptera*
Brazil.

Blue-and-gold Tanager *Bangsia arcaei*
Costa Rica, Panama.

Purplish-mantled Tanager *Iridosornis*
porphyrocephala
Colombia, Ecuador.

Green-chinned Euphonia *Euphonia chalybea*
Argentina, Brazil, Paraguay.

Blue-whiskered Tanager *Tangara johannae*
Colombia, Ecuador.

Dotted Tanager *Tangara varia*
Brazil, French Guiana, Suriname, Venezuela.

Green-naped Tanager *Tangara fucosa*
Panama.

Sira Tanager *Tangara phillipsi*
Peru.

White-bellied Dacnis *Dacnis albiventris*
Brazil, Colombia, Ecuador, Peru, Venezuela.

Viridian Dacnis *Dacnis viguieri*
Colombia, Panama.

Tit-like Dacnis *Xenodacnis parina*
Ecuador, Peru.

Chestnut-bellied Flowerpiercer *Diglossa*
gloriosissima
Colombia.

■ Parulidae

Colima Warbler *Vermivora crissalis*
Mexico, U.S.A.

Vitelline Warbler *Dendroica vitellina*
Cayman Islands (to U.K.), Honduras.

Elfin-woods Warbler *Dendroica angelae*
Puerto Rico (to U.S.A.).

Altamira Yellowthroat *Geothlypis flavovelata*
Mexico.

Pink-headed Warbler *Ergaticus versicolor*
Guatemala, Mexico.

White-faced Whitestart *Myioborus albifacies*
Venezuela.

Santa Marta Warbler *Basileuterus basilicus*
Colombia.

Grey-throated Warbler *Basileuterus cinereicollis*
Colombia, Venezuela.

White-lored Warbler *Basileuterus conspicillatus*
Colombia.

Pirre Warbler *Basileuterus ignotus*
Colombia, Panama.

Pearly-breasted Conebill *Conirostrum margaritae*
Brazil, Peru.

■ Drepanididae

Maui Alauahio *Paroreomyza montana*
U.S.A.

■ Vireonidae

Chestnut-sided Shrike-vireo *Vireolanius melitophrys*
Guatemala, Mexico.

Slaty Vireo *Vireo brevipennis*
Mexico.

Dwarf Vireo *Vireo nelsoni*
Mexico.

Blue Mountain Vireo *Vireo osburni*
Jamaica.

■ Icteridae

Montserrat Oriole *Icterus oberi*
Montserrat (to U.K.).

St Lucia Oriole *Icterus laudabilis*
St Lucia.

Jamaican Blackbird *Nesopsar nigerrimus*
Jamaica.

Mountain Grackle *Macroagelaius subalaris*
Colombia.

Nicaraguan Grackle *Quiscalus nicaraguensis*
Costa Rica, Nicaragua.

■ Fringillidae

Kipengere Seedeater *Serinus melanochrous*
Tanzania.

Protea Canary *Serinus leucopterus*
South Africa.

Drakensberg Siskin *Serinus symonsi*
Lesotho, South Africa.

Cape Siskin *Serinus totta*
South Africa.

Vietnam Greenfinch *Carduelis monguilloti*
Vietnam.

Black-capped Siskin *Carduelis atriceps*
Guatemala, Mexico.

White-cheeked Bullfinch *Pyrrhula leucogenis*
Philippines.

Orange Bullfinch *Pyrrhula aurantiaca*
India, Pakistan.

■ Estrildidae

Mali Firefinch *Lagonosticta virata*
Mali.

Cinderella Waxbill *Estrilda thomensis*
Angola, Namibia.

Red-eared Firetail *Stagonopleura oculata*
Australia.

Grey-crowned Munia *Lonchura nevermanni*
Indonesia, Papua New Guinea.

Yellow-rumped Munia *Lonchura flaviprymna*
Australia.

Black Munia *Lonchura stygia*
Indonesia, Papua New Guinea.

Pictorella Munia *Heteromunia pectoralis*
Australia.

Timor Sparrow *Padda fuscata*
Indonesia.

■ Ploceinae

Fox's Weaver *Ploceus spekeoides*
Uganda.

Asian Golden Weaver *Ploceus hypoxanthus*
Cambodia, Indonesia, Laos, Myanmar, Thailand, Vietnam.

Golden-backed Bishop *Euplectes aureus*
Angola.

Jackson's Widowbird *Euplectes jacksoni*
Kenya, Tanzania.

■ Sturnidae

Rusty-winged Starling *Aplonis zelandica*
Solomon Islands, Vanuatu.

Tanimbar Starling *Aplonis crassa*
Indonesia.

Rennell Starling *Aplonis insularis*
Solomon Islands.

Yellow-eyed Starling *Aplonis mystacea*
Indonesia, Papua New Guinea.

Copper-tailed Glossy-starling *Lamprotornis cupreocauda*
Ghana, Guinea, Ivory Coast, Liberia, Sierra Leone.

Spot-winged Starling *Saroglossa spiloptera*
Bangladesh[N], India, Myanmar[N], Nepal, Thailand[N].

White-faced Starling *Sturnus senex*
Sri Lanka.

White-headed Starling *Sturnus erythropygius*
India.

Red-billed Starling *Sturnus sericeus*
China, Hong Kong (to U.K.)[N], Vietnam[N].

Chestnut-cheeked Starling *Sturnus philippensis*
China[N], Indonesia[N], Japan, Philippines[N], Russia, Taiwan[N].

Black-winged Starling *Sturnus melanopterus*
Indonesia.

Collared Myna *Acridotheres albocinctus*
China, India, Myanmar.

Helmeted Myna *Basilornis galeatus*
Indonesia.

Apo Myna *Basilornis miranda*
Philippines.

Bare-eyed Myna *Streptocitta albertinae*
Indonesia.

■ Oriolidae

Black Oriole *Oriolus hosii*
Malaysia.

◼ Dicruridae

Príncipe Drongo *Dicrurus modestus*
 São Tomé e Príncipe.
Aldabra Drongo *Dicrurus aldabranus*
 Seychelles.
Sumatran Drongo *Dicrurus sumatranus*
 Indonesia.
Andaman Drongo *Dicrurus andamanensis*
 India, Myanmar.

◼ Ptilonorhynchidae

Tooth-billed Catbird *Ailuroedus dentirostris*
 Australia.
Golden-fronted Bowerbird *Amblyornis flavifrons*
 Indonesia.

◼ Paradisaeidae

Standardwing *Semioptera wallacii*
 Indonesia.
Long-tailed Paradigalla *Paradigalla carunculata*
 Indonesia.
Pale-billed Sicklebill *Epimachus bruijnii*
 Indonesia, Papua New Guinea.
Paradise Riflebird *Ptiloris paradiseus*
 Australia.
Wilson's Bird-of-paradise *Cicinnurus respublica*
 Indonesia.
Arfak Astrapia *Astrapia nigra*
 Indonesia.
Red Bird-of-paradise *Paradisaea rubra*
 Indonesia.

Emperor Bird-of-paradise *Paradisaea guilielmi*
 Papua New Guinea.

◼ Corvidae

Black Magpie *Platysmurus leucopterus*
 Brunei, Indonesia, Malaysia, Myanmar, Thailand.
Beautiful Jay *Cyanolyca pulchra*
 Colombia, Ecuador.
Azure Jay *Cyanocorax caeruleus*
 Argentina, Brazil.
Tufted Jay *Cyanocorax dickeyi*
 Mexico.
White-winged Magpie *Urocissa whiteheadi*
 China, Laos, Vietnam.
Yellow-breasted Magpie *Cissa hypoleuca*
 China, Laos, Thailand, Vietnam.
Short-tailed Magpie *Cissa thalassina*
 Indonesia, Malaysia.
White-bellied Treepie *Dendrocitta leucogastra*
 India.
Andaman Treepie *Dendrocitta bayleyi*
 India.
Bougainville Crow *Corvus meeki*
 Papua New Guinea, Solomon Islands.
White-billed Crow *Corvus woodfordi*
 Solomon Islands.
Brown-headed Crow *Corvus fuscicapillus*
 Indonesia.
Palm Crow *Corvus palmarum*
 Cuba, Dominican Republic, Haiti.

◼

EACH COUNTRY or other relevant geopolitical unit is here given a coded summary of key items of information on all the important species in its custody. The total number of species in each of the categories included in this book (Extinct, Extinct in the Wild, Critical, Endangered, Vulnerable, Conservation Dependent, Data Deficient and Near-threatened) is given for each geopolitical unit, and the species are listed by category (note that species are only listed for units where they are believed to occur regularly). For all species entries, tabular information is given on status in the range state under con-

sideration (B = breeding, N = non-breeding) and on the total numbers of breeding and non-breeding range states; thus '4' indicates that a species occurs and breeds in four range states, and '3/7' indicates that a species occurs in a total of 10 range states, in three of which it breeds and in an additional seven where it is only a non-breeding visitor. For threatened species (placed within a tinted block) additional columns give the codings for habitat and threat (see below) which were used in the analyses that generated Figures 5 and 6 on p. 25); the IUCN threat status criteria codings (see pp. 16–18) are also added.

Habitat codes		Threat codes	
F	All forest and woodland types	0	Unknown
S	Scrub	1	Loss or alteration of habitat
V	Savanna	2	Hunting, persecution (including accidental
G	Grassland		trapping), egg-collecting (subsistence)
W	Wetlands, including littoral habitats	3	Disturbance (by humans, stock)
D	Desert	4	Fisheries
R	Rocky areas, including cliffs	5	Pollution, pesticides, poisoning (accidental)
A	Agricultural areas	6	Introduced species (predators, competitors,
X	Introduced/exotic vegetation, e.g. plantations		herbivores, diseases)
U	Urban areas	7	Trade, egg-collecting (commercial)
M	Marine environment	8	Natural causes (exacerbated by other influences)
Z	Unknown	9	Small range or population

AFGHANISTAN

Species totals   Endangered 1   Near-threatened 6
Vulnerable 11

	Status (breeding/ non-br.)	Breeding/ non-br. countries	Habitat codes	Threat codes	IUCN threat status codes (pp. 16–18)
Endangered					
Siberian Crane *Grus leucogeranus*	N	1/5	W	129	**A2b,c**; C1; D2
Vulnerable					
Dalmatian Pelican *Pelecanus crispus*	N	16/9	W	1235	C2a
White-headed Duck *Oxyura leucocephala*	B	12/16	W	1256	A2d
Marbled Teal *Marmaronetta angustirostris*	B	21/3	W	125	A2b
Ferruginous Duck *Aythya nyroca*	B	38/32	W	12	A1a,b,c
Pallas's Sea-eagle *Haliaeetus leucoryphus*	N	11/1	GW	135	C1; C2b
Greater Spotted Eagle *Aquila clanga*	N	14/35	FW	13	C2a
Imperial Eagle *Aquila heliaca*	N	24/21	FG	12357	C2a
Lesser Kestrel *Falco naumanni*	B	37/52	FSVGA	15	A1a,b,d
Corncrake *Crex crex*	B	40/31	GWA	12	A1a,b
Pale-backed Pigeon *Columba eversmanni*	B	7/2	GDA	0	A1a
White-browed Bushchat *Saxicola macrorhyncha*	B	3	SD	1	A1a,b; C1; C2a

Near-threatened				
Pygmy Cormorant *Phalacrocorax pygmeus*	N 17/4	Pallid Harrier *Circus macrourus*		N 4/57
White-tailed Eagle *Haliaeetus albicilla*	N 34/10	White-winged Woodpecker *Dendrocopos leucopterus*		B 7
Cinereous Vulture *Aegypius monachus*	B 18/13	Tytler's Leaf-warbler *Phylloscopus tytleri*		B 4

ALBANIA

Species totals	Vulnerable	5
	Near-threatened	2

Vulnerable	Status (breeding/ non-br.)	Breeding/ non-br. countries	Habitat codes (p. 243)	Threat codes (p. 243)	IUCN threat status codes (pp. 16–18)
Dalmatian Pelican *Pelecanus crispus*	B	16/9	W	1235	C2a
White-headed Duck *Oxyura leucocephala*	N	12/16	W	1256	A2d
Ferruginous Duck *Aythya nyroca*	B	38/32	W	12	A1a,b,c
Lesser Kestrel *Falco naumanni*	B	37/52	FSVGA	15	A1a,b,d
Corncrake *Crex crex*	N	40/31	GWA	12	A1a,b

Near-threatened
Pygmy Cormorant *Phalacrocorax pygmeus*   B   17/4   Pallid Harrier *Circus macrourus*   N   4/57

ALGERIA

Species totals	Critical	1	Conservation	
	Endangered	1	Dependent	1
	Vulnerable	5	Near-threatened	2

Critical	Status (breeding/ non-br.)	Breeding/ non-br. countries	Habitat codes (p. 243)	Threat codes (p. 243)	IUCN threat status codes (pp. 16–18)
Northern Bald Ibis *Geronticus eremita*	B	4	GW	012589	A1a; C1; **C2a**; D1
Endangered					
Algerian Nuthatch *Sitta ledanti*	B	1	F	19	B1+2c; **C2a**; D1; D2
Vulnerable					
White-headed Duck *Oxyura leucocephala*	B	12/16	W	1256	A2d
Marbled Teal *Marmaronetta angustirostris*	B	21/3	W	125	A2b
Ferruginous Duck *Aythya nyroca*	N	38/32	W	12	A1a,b,c
Lesser Kestrel *Falco naumanni*	B	37/52	FSVGA	15	A1a,b,d
Corncrake *Crex crex*	N	40/31	GWA	12	A1a,b

Conservation Dependent   **Near-threatened**
Audouin's Gull *Larus audouinii*   B   8/7   Pallid Harrier *Circus macrourus*   N   4/57
                                                      Little Bustard *Tetrax tetrax*   B   13/10

AMERICAN SAMOA (to U.S.A.)

Species totals	Vulnerable	1
	Near-threatened	1

Vulnerable	Status (breeding/ non-br.)	Breeding/ non-br. countries	Habitat codes (p. 243)	Threat codes (p. 243)	IUCN threat status codes (pp. 16–18)
Bristle-thighed Curlew *Numenius tahitiensis*	N	1/14	GW	1268	C2b

Near-threatened
Shy Ground-dove *Gallicolumba stairi*   B   5

ANGOLA

Species totals	Endangered	6	Data Deficient	1
	Vulnerable	7	Near-threatened	11

Endangered	Status (breeding/ non-br.)	Breeding/ non-br. countries	Habitat codes (p. 243)	Threat codes (p. 243)	IUCN threat status codes (pp. 16–18)
Orange-breasted Bush-shrike *Laniarius brauni*	B	1	F	19	**B1+2c**; C2a; D1
Gabela Bush-shrike *Laniarius amboimensis*	B	1	F	19	**B1+2c**; **C1**; C2a; D1
Monteiro's Bush-shrike *Malaconotus monteiri*	B	2	F	19	**C2a**; D1
Gabela Helmet-shrike *Prionops gabela*	B	1	F	19	**B1+2b,c,d**; **C1**; **C2a**; D1
Gabela Akalat *Sheppardia gabela*	B	1	F	19	**B1+2a,c**; **C2a**
Pulitzer's Longbill *Macrosphenus pulitzeri*	B	1	F	1	**B1+2b,c**; **C2a**
Vulnerable					
Lesser Kestrel *Falco naumanni*	N	37/52	FSVGA	15	A1a,b,d
Grey-striped Francolin *Francolinus griseostriatus*	B	1	FS	12	B1+2b,c; **C2a**

cont.

Angola (cont.)

Swierstra's Francolin *Francolinus swierstrai*	B	1	F	12	B1+2a,b,c; C2a
Wattled Crane *Grus carunculatus*	B	11	W	123	A2b,c; C1
White-headed Robin-chat *Cossypha heinrichi*	B	2	F	1	B1+2a,c
Black-chinned Weaver *Ploceus nigrimentum*	B	3	V	1	C2a
Loango Weaver *Ploceus subpersonatus*	B	3	FSV	1	B1+2c; C2a

Data Deficient

Fernando Po Swift *Apus sladeniae*	B	4			

Near-threatened

Crowned Cormorant *Phalacrocorax coronatus*	B	3			
Lesser Flamingo *Phoenicopterus minor*	N	8/20			
Pallid Harrier *Circus macrourus*	N	4/57			
Great Snipe *Gallinago media*	N	10/35			

Black-winged Pratincole *Glareola nordmanni*	N	10/22
Grimwood's Longclaw *Macronyx grimwoodi*	B	3
Angola Cave-chat *Xenocopsychus ansorgei*	B	1
Herero Chat *Namibornis herero*	B	2
White-fronted Wattle-eye *Platysteira albifrons*	B	1
Cinderella Waxbill *Estrilda thomensis*	B	2
Golden-backed Bishop *Euplectes aureus*	B	1

ANGUILLA (to U.K.)

Species totals	Near-threatened	1

Near-threatened

Bridled Quail-dove *Geotrygon mystacea*	B	13

ANTIGUA AND BARBUDA

Species totals	Vulnerable	1
	Near-threatened	1

	Status (breeding/ non-br.)	Breeding/ non-br. countries	Habitat codes (p. 243)	Threat codes (p. 243)	IUCN threat status codes (pp. 16–18)
Vulnerable					
West Indian Whistling-duck *Dendrocygna arborea*	B	12	W	12	C2a
Near-threatened					
Bridled Quail-dove *Geotrygon mystacea*	B	13			

ARGENTINA

Species totals	Critical	5	Extinct	1
	Endangered	11	Data Deficient	1
	Vulnerable	24	Near-threatened	65

	Status (breeding/ non-br.)	Breeding/ non-br. countries	Habitat codes (p. 243)	Threat codes (p. 243)	IUCN threat status codes (pp. 16–18)
Critical					
Brazilian Merganser *Mergus octosetaceus*	B	3	W	159	**A2b,d**; B1+2a,b,c,d,e; **C2a**; **D1**
Austral Rail *Rallus antarcticus*	B	2	W	019	**D1**
Eskimo Curlew *Numenius borealis*	N	2/3	GW	0129	**D1**
Purple-winged Ground-dove *Claravis godefrida*	B	3	F	19	B1+2c; **C2b**; D1
Entre Ríos Seedeater *Sporophila zelichi*	B	1	GW	179	**A2b,c**; B1+2c,e; **C1**; **C2b**; D1
Endangered					
Red-spectacled Amazon *Amazona pretrei*	B	2	F	17	A1b,c; **A2b,c**; **C1**
Vinaceous Amazon *Amazona vinacea*	B	3	F	1	**A1a,b,c**; A2b,c; C1; C2a
Blue-bellied Parrot *Triclaria malachitacea*	B	2	F	1	**C2a**
Helmeted Woodpecker *Dryocopus galeatus*	B	3	F	1	**C2a**
Ochre-breasted Pipit *Anthus nattereri*	B	3	G	1	A1b; A2b; C1; **C2a**
Yellow Cardinal *Gubernatrix cristata*	B	4	FSG	17	**A1a,c**; **A2c**; C1; C2a
Buffy-fronted Seedeater *Sporophila frontalis*	B	3	F	17	**A1b**; A2b; **C1**; **C2b**
Temminck's Seedeater *Sporophila falcirostris*	B	3	F	17	**A1b**; A2b; **C1**; **C2b**
Marsh Seedeater *Sporophila palustris*	B	4	GW	17	**A1b,c**; **A2b,c**; C1; C2a
Saffron-cowled Blackbird *Xanthopsar flavus*	B	4	SGWA	158	**A1a,b**; **A2b,d**; C1; C2a
Pampas Meadowlark *Sturnella militaris*	B	3	G	1	**A1b**; A2b; C1; C2a
Vulnerable					
Dwarf Tinamou *Taoniscus nanus*	B	2	VG	1	A1b; C2a
Andean Flamingo *Phoenicopterus andinus*	B	4	W	123	A2b,c
Puna Flamingo *Phoenicopterus jamesi*	B	4	W	23	A2b,c
Crowned Eagle *Harpyhaliaetus coronatus*	B	4	SG	12	C2b
Black-fronted Piping-guan *Pipile jacutinga*	B	3	F	12	C2a

cont.

Argentina (cont.)

Dot-winged Crake *Porzana spiloptera*	B	2	SGW	1	A2b; C1; C2a
Horned Coot *Fulica cornuta*	B	3	W	1	C2a
Olrog's Gull *Larus atlanticus*	B	1/3	WM	123	A2b,c; C1; C2b
Military Macaw *Ara militaris*	B	11	F	17	A1b; C2a
Blue-winged Macaw *Ara maracana*	B	3	F	01	A1a,b; C1; C2a
Chestnut Canastero *Asthenes steinbachi*	B	1	S	1	A1b; C2a
Austral Canastero *Asthenes anthoides*	B	2	SG	1	C2a
White-bearded Antshrike *Biatas nigropectus*	B	2	F	1	C2a
Black-capped Manakin *Piprites pileatus*	B	2	F	1	B1+2c; C1; C2a
Dinelli's Doradito *Pseudocolopteryx dinellianus*	B	1/2	SW	1	C1; C2a
São Paulo Tyrannulet *Phylloscartes paulistus*	B	3	F	1	A1b; A2b; C1; C2a
Russet-winged Spadebill *Platyrinchus leucoryphus*	B	3	F	1	A1b; A2b; B1+2c; C1; C2a
Black-and-white Monjita *Heteroxolmis dominicana*	B	4	GWA	1	A1b; A2b
White-tailed Shrike-tyrant *Agriornis andicola*	B	5	GZ	18	A1a; C2a
Strange-tailed Tyrant *Alectrurus risora*	B	4	G	1	A1a,b; A2b; C1; C2a
Rufous-throated Dipper *Cinclus schulzi*	B	2	W	15	C2a
Black-masked Finch *Coryphaspiza melanotis*	B	5	G	1	A1b
Tucumán Mountain-finch *Poospiza baeri*	B	1	S	19	D1
Rufous-bellied Saltator *Saltator rufiventris*	B	2	F	1	C2a

Extinct

Glaucous Macaw *Anodorhynchus glaucus* — B 4

Data Deficient

Speckled Crake *Coturnicops notatus* — B 7

Near-threatened

Greater Rhea *Rhea americana* — B 5
Lesser Rhea *Rhea pennata* — B 4
Solitary Tinamou *Tinamus solitarius* — B 3
Colombian Tinamou *Crypturellus columbianus* — B 5
Hooded Grebe *Podiceps gallardoi* — B 1
Red-legged Cormorant *Phalacrocorax gaimardi* — B 3
Agami Heron *Agamia agami* — B 16
Black-headed Duck *Heteronetta atricapilla* — B 6
Ruddy-headed Goose *Chloephaga rubidiceps* — B 3
Orinoco Goose *Neochen jubata* — B 10
Chubut Steamerduck *Tachyeres leucocephalus* — B 1
Spectacled Duck *Anas specularis* — B 2
Grey-bellied Goshawk *Accipiter poliogaster* — B 10
Mantled Hawk *Leucopternis polionota* — B 3
Solitary Eagle *Harpyhaliaetus solitarius* — B 17
Rufous-tailed Hawk *Buteo ventralis* — B 2
Crested Eagle *Morphnus guianensis* — B 15
Harpy Eagle *Harpia harpyja* — B 17
Black-and-white Hawk-eagle *Spizastur melanoleucus* — B 14
Black-and-chestnut Eagle *Oroaetus isidori* — B 6
Striated Caracara *Phalcoboenus australis* — B 3
Orange-breasted Falcon *Falco deiroleucus* — B 17
Magellanic Plover *Pluvianellus socialis* — B 2
Diademed Sandpiper-plover *Phegornis mitchellii* — B 4
Hudsonian Godwit *Limosa haemastica* — N 2/11
Fuegian Snipe *Gallinago stricklandii* — B 3
Chilean Pigeon *Columba araucana* — B 2
Pileated Parrot *Pionopsitta pileata* — B 3
Buff-fronted Owl *Aegolius harrisii* — B 8
Long-trained Nightjar *Macropsalis creagra* — B 2
Sickle-winged Nightjar *Eleothreptus anomalus* — B 4

Rothschild's Swift *Cypseloides rothschildi* — B 3
Spangled Coquette *Lophornis stictolophus* — B 7
Bronze-tailed Comet *Polyonymus caroli* — B 3
Mottled Piculet *Picumnus nebulosus* — B 3
Black-bodied Woodpecker *Dryocopus schulzi* — B 3
Araucaria Tit-spinetail *Leptasthenura setaria* — B 2
Canebrake Groundcreeper
  Clibanornis dendrocolaptoides — B 3
Bay-capped Wren-spinetail *Spartonoica maluroides* — B 3
Straight-billed Reedhaunter *Limnornis rectirostris* — B 3
White-browed Foliage-gleaner *Philydor amaurotis* — B 2
Spot-breasted Antvireo *Dysithamnus stictothorax* — B 2
Spotted Bamboowren *Psilorhamphus guttatus* — B 2
Swallow-tailed Cotinga *Phibalura flavirostris* — B 3
Bare-throated Bellbird *Procnias nudicollis* — B 3
Sharp-tailed Grass-tyrant *Culicivora caudacuta* — B 4
Bearded Tachuri *Polystictus pectoralis* — B 9
Southern Bristle-tyrant *Phylloscartes eximius* — B 3
Bay-ringed Tyrannulet *Phylloscartes sylviolus* — B 3
Salinas Monjita *Xolmis salinarum* — B 1
Hudson's Black-tyrant *Knipolegus hudsoni* — B 3
Cock-tailed Tyrant *Alectrurus tricolor* — B 4
Shear-tailed Grey Tyrant *Muscipipra vetula* — B 3
Chaco Pipit *Anthus chacoensis* — B 2
Creamy-bellied Gnatcatcher *Polioptila lactea* — B 3
Coal-crested Finch *Charitospiza eucosma* — B 2
Canary-winged Finch *Melanodera melanodera* — B 3
Grey-cheeked Grass-finch *Emberizoides ypiranganus* — B 3
Dark-throated Seedeater *Sporophila ruficollis* — B 5
Grey-and-chestnut Seedeater *Sporophila hypochroma* — B 3
Chestnut Seedeater *Sporophila cinnamomea* — B 3
Blackish-blue Seedeater *Amaurospiza moesta* — B 3
Thick-billed Saltator *Saltator maxillosus* — B 3
Green-chinned Euphonia *Euphonia chalybea* — B 3
Azure Jay *Cyanocorax caeruleus* — B 2

ARMENIA

| | | | Species totals | Vulnerable | 5 |
| | | | | Near-threatened | 4 |

Vulnerable	Status (breeding/ non-br.)	Breeding/ non-br. countries	Habitat codes (p. 243)	Threat codes (p. 243)	IUCN threat status codes (pp. 16–18)
Dalmatian Pelican *Pelecanus crispus*	B	16/9	W	1235	C2a
Marbled Teal *Marmaronetta angustirostris*	B	21/3	W	125	A2b
Ferruginous Duck *Aythya nyroca*	B	38/32	W	12	A1a,b,c
Lesser Kestrel *Falco naumanni*	B	37/52	FSVGA	15	A1a,b,d
Corncrake *Crex crex*	N	40/31	GWA	12	A1a,b

Near-threatened

White-tailed Eagle *Haliaeetus albicilla*	B	34/10	Caucasian Black Grouse *Tetrao mlokosiewiczi*	B	5
Cinereous Vulture *Aegypius monachus*	B	18/13	Black-winged Pratincole *Glareola nordmanni*	B	10/22

ASCENSION ISLAND (to U.K.)

| | | | Species totals | Critical | 1 |

Critical	Status (breeding/ non-br.)	Breeding/ non-br. countries	Habitat codes (p. 243)	Threat codes (p. 243)	IUCN threat status codes (pp. 16–18)
Ascension Frigatebird *Fregata aquila*	B	1	RM	369	A1a; **B1+2e**; C2b; D2

AUSTRALIA

Species totals	Critical	2	Conservation	
	Endangered	10	Dependent	6
	Vulnerable	32	Near-threatened	33
	Extinct	1		

See also: Christmas Islands (p. 263), Cocos (Keeling) Islands (p. 263), Norfolk Island (p. 306).

Critical	Status (breeding/ non-br.)	Breeding/ non-br. countries	Habitat codes (p. 243)	Threat codes (p. 243)	IUCN threat status codes (pp. 16–18)
Night Parrot *Geopsittacus occidentalis*	B	1	S	169	**C2a**; D1
Black-eared Miner *Manorina melanotis*	B	1	F	189	B1+2e; **C2a**; **D1**
Endangered					
Australasian Bittern *Botaurus poiciloptilus*	B	3	W	12	**C2a**
Red Goshawk *Erythrotriorchis radiatus*	B	1	FVW	1579	**C2b**; D1
Black-breasted Buttonquail *Turnix melanogaster*	B	1	FX	169	B1+2e; **C2a**; D1
Buff-breasted Buttonquail *Turnix olivii*	B	1	FG	19	**C2b**; D1
Lord Howe Rail *Gallirallus sylvestris*	B	1	F	69	**D1**; D2
Golden-shouldered Parrot *Psephotus chrysopterygius*	B	1	FS	1367	B1+2e; **C2b**
Orange-bellied Parrot *Neophema chrysogaster*	B	1	FSW	1689	**D1**
Western Bristlebird *Dasyornis longirostris*	B	1	S	19	**B1+2c,d**; **C2a**; D1
Regent Honeyeater *Xanthomyza phrygia*	B	1	F	189	**C2a**; D1
Gouldian Finch *Chloebia gouldiae*	B	1	F	167	A1d; **B1+2d,e**; C1; C2a
Vulnerable					
Southern Cassowary *Casuarius casuarius*	B	3	F	126	A1a,b,c,d; A2b,c,d
Wandering Albatross *Diomedea exulans*	B	6	MG	4	A1a,c; A2c
Providence Petrel *Pterodroma solandri*	B	1	FRM	9	D2
Freckled Duck *Stictonetta naevosa*	B	1	W	12	B1+3d
Square-tailed Kite *Lophoictinia isura*	B	1	FS	127	C2b
Grey Falcon *Falco hypoleucos*	B	1	SG	157	C2b
Malleefowl *Leipoa ocellata*	B	1	FS	168	A1b,d; A2b,d; C1; C2a
Chestnut-backed Buttonquail *Turnix castanota*	B	1	FG	16	C2a
Plains-wanderer *Pedionomus torquatus*	B	1	G	1	B2c+3d
Hooded Plover *Charadrius rubricollis*	B	1	W	368	C2a
Fairy Tern *Sterna nereis*	B	3	WM	36	C2a
White-tailed Black-cockatoo *Calyptorhynchus baudinii*	B	1	F	12	C2a
Slender-billed Black-cockatoo *Calyptorhynchus latirostris*	B	1	F	17	C2a
Glossy Black-cockatoo *Calyptorhynchus lathami*	B	1	F	16	C2a
Superb Parrot *Polytelis swainsonii*	B	1	F	17	C2b

cont.

Australia (cont.)

Alexandra's Parrot *Polytelis alexandrae*	B	1	GD	18	B2c+3d; C2a
Scarlet-chested Parrot *Neophema splendida*	B	1	S	18	B2c+3d
Swift Parrot *Lathamus discolor*	B	1	F	17	B1+2c; C2b
Powerful Owl *Ninox strenua*	B	1	F	1	C2b
Rufous Scrub-bird *Atrichornis rufescens*	B	1	F	1	B1+2c; C2a
Noisy Scrub-bird *Atrichornis clamosus*	B	1	FS	9	D1; D2
Western Whipbird *Psophodes nigrogularis*	B	1	S	16	B1+2c; C2a
Carpentarian Grasswren *Amytornis dorotheae*	B	1	G	1	B1+2c; C2a
Thick-billed Grasswren *Amytornis textilis*	B	1	S	16	C2a
Eastern Bristlebird *Dasyornis brachypterus*	B	1	SG	136	B1+2c; C2a
Rufous Bristlebird *Dasyornis broadbenti*	B	1	S	168	B1+2c; C2a
Slender-billed Thornbill *Acanthiza iredalei*	B	1	SW	16	C2a
Chestnut-breasted Whiteface *Aphelocephala pectoralis*	B	1	SD	16	C2a
Forty-spotted Pardalote *Pardalotus quadragintus*	B	1	F	18	B1+2c
Lord Howe White-eye *Zosterops tephropleurus*	B	1	F	9	D2
Painted Honeyeater *Grantiella picta*	B	1	F	168	C2a
Star Finch *Neochmia ruficauda*	B	1	FGW	16	C2a

Extinct

Paradise Parrot *Psephotus pulcherrimus* — B 1

Conservation Dependent

Mallee Emuwren *Stipiturus mallee* — B 1
Atherton Scrubwren *Sericornis keri* — B 1
Mountain Thornbill *Acanthiza katherina* — B 1
Red-lored Whistler *Pachycephala rufogularis* — B 1
Eungella Honeyeater *Lichenostomus hindwoodi* — B 1
Golden Bowerbird *Prionodura newtoniana* — B 1

Near-threatened

Northern Giant-petrel *Macronectes halli* — B 4
Grey-headed Albatross *Diomedea chrysostoma* — B 5
Great-billed Heron *Ardea sumatrana* — B 10
Sarus Crane *Grus antigone* — B 8
Latham's Snipe *Gallinago hardwickii* — N 1/5
Far Eastern Curlew *Numenius madagascariensis* — N 3/14
Asian Dowitcher *Limnodromus semipalmatus* — N 3/14
Pacific Gull *Larus pacificus* — B 1
Flock Bronzewing *Phaps histrionica* — B 1
Partridge Pigeon *Geophaps smithii* — B 1
Black-banded Fruit-dove *Ptilinopus alligator* — B 1
Palm Cockatoo *Probosciger aterrimus* — B 3

Pink Cockatoo *Cacatua leadbeateri* — B 1
Western Corella *Cacatua pastinator* — B 1
Hooded Parrot *Psephotus dissimilis* — B 1
Turquoise Parrot *Neophema pulchella* — B 1
Lesser Sooty-owl *Tyto multipunctata* — B 1
Albert's Lyrebird *Menura alberti* — B 1
Purple-crowned Fairywren *Malurus coronatus* — B 1
Grey Grasswren *Amytornis barbatus* — B 1
White-throated Grasswren *Amytornis woodwardi* — B 1
Black Grasswren *Amytornis housei* — B 1
Yellow Chat *Epthianura crocea* — B 1
Origma *Origma solitaria* — B 1
Fernwren *Oreoscopus gutturalis* — B 1
Grey-headed Robin *Heteromyias cinereifrons* — B 1
Bower's Shrike-thrush *Colluricincla boweri* — B 1
Bridled Honeyeater *Lichenostomus frenatus* — B 1
Red-eared Firetail *Stagonopleura oculata* — B 1
Yellow-rumped Munia *Lonchura flaviprymna* — B 1
Pictorella Munia *Heteromunia pectoralis* — B 1
Tooth-billed Catbird *Ailuroedus dentirostris* — B 1
Paradise Riflebird *Ptiloris paradiseus* — B 1

AUSTRIA	**Species totals**	Vulnerable	3
		Near-threatened	2

Vulnerable	Status (breeding/ non-br.)	Breeding/ non-br. countries	Habitat codes (p. 243)	Threat codes (p. 243)	IUCN threat status codes (pp. 16–18)
Ferruginous Duck *Aythya nyroca*	B	38/32	W	12	A1a,b,c
Corncrake *Crex crex*	B	40/31	GWA	12	A1a,b
Great Bustard *Otis tarda*	B	23	GA	125	A2b

Near-threatened

Pygmy Cormorant *Phalacrocorax pygmeus* — N 17/4   White-tailed Eagle *Haliaeetus albicilla* — B 34/10

AZERBAIJAN

| | | | | | **Species totals** | Vulnerable 6 |
| | | | | | | Near-threatened 5 |

Vulnerable	Status (breeding/ non-br.)	Breeding/ non-br. countries	Habitat codes (p. 243)	Threat codes (p. 243)	IUCN threat status codes (pp. 16–18)
Dalmatian Pelican *Pelecanus crispus*	B	16/9	W	1235	C2a
White-headed Duck *Oxyura leucocephala*	N	12/16	W	1256	A2d
Marbled Teal *Marmaronetta angustirostris*	B	21/3	W	125	A2b
Ferruginous Duck *Aythya nyroca*	B	38/32	W	12	A1a,b,c
Imperial Eagle *Aquila heliaca*	B	24/21	FG	12357	C2a
Lesser Kestrel *Falco naumanni*	B	37/52	FSVGA	15	A1a,b,d

Near-threatened

Pygmy Cormorant *Phalacrocorax pygmeus*	B	17/4	Caucasian Black Grouse *Tetrao mlokosiewiczi*	B	5
White-tailed Eagle *Haliaeetus albicilla*	B	34/10	Little Bustard *Tetrax tetrax*	N	13/10
Cinereous Vulture *Aegypius monachus*	B	18/13			

BAHAMAS

| | | | | | **Species totals** | Vulnerable 3 |
| | | | | | | Near-threatened 3 |

Vulnerable	Status (breeding/ non-br.)	Breeding/ non-br. countries	Habitat codes (p. 243)	Threat codes (p. 243)	IUCN threat status codes (pp. 16–18)
West Indian Whistling-duck *Dendrocygna arborea*	B	12	W	12	C2a
Piping Plover *Charadrius melodus*	N	2/9	W	138	C2a
Kirtland's Warbler *Dendroica kirtlandii*	N	2/2	S	9	D1; D2

Near-threatened

Bridled Quail-dove *Geotrygon mystacea*	B	13	Bahama Swallow *Tachycineta cyaneoviridis*	B 2
Cuban Parrot *Amazona leucocephala*	B	3		

BAHRAIN

| | | **Species totals** | Near-threatened 1 |

Near-threatened

Cinereous Bunting *Emberiza cineracea*   N 3/13

BANGLADESH

| | | | | | **Species totals** | Endangered 5   Near-threatened 35 |
| | | | | | | Vulnerable 23 |

Endangered	Status (breeding/ non-br.)	Breeding/ non-br. countries	Habitat codes (p. 243)	Threat codes (p. 243)	IUCN threat status codes (pp. 16–18)
White-bellied Heron *Ardea insignis*	B	4	FW	1	A1a,b; **C1; C2a**
Oriental Stork *Ciconia boyciana*	N	2/9	W	1235	A2b; **C1**
Greater Adjutant *Leptoptilos dubius*	B	8	FWU	129	A1b,c; **C1**; C2a; D1
White-winged Duck *Cairina scutulata*	B	9	FW	1239	A1b,c,d; **C1**; **C2a**; D1
Nordmann's Greenshank *Tringa guttifer*	N	1/15	FW	12389	**C1**; C2b; D1
Vulnerable					
Dalmatian Pelican *Pelecanus crispus*	N	16/9	W	1235	C2a
Spot-billed Pelican *Pelecanus philippensis*	N	3/8	W	1235	A1a,b,c,d; C1
Lesser Adjutant *Leptoptilos javanicus*	B	12/1	FW	123	C1
Ferruginous Duck *Aythya nyroca*	N	38/32	W	12	A1a,b,c
Baer's Pochard *Aythya baeri*	N	2/12	W	123	A1a,b; C1
Pallas's Sea-eagle *Haliaeetus leucoryphus*	B	11/1	GW	135	C1; C2b
Greater Spotted Eagle *Aquila clanga*	N	14/35	FW	13	C2a
Imperial Eagle *Aquila heliaca*	N	24/21	FG	12357	C2a
Lesser Kestrel *Falco naumanni*	N	37/52	FSVGA	15	A1a,b,d
Swamp Francolin *Francolinus gularis*	B	3	GWA	15	A1b
Manipur Bush-quail *Perdicula manipurensis*	B	2	SGW	12	C1; C2a
Masked Finfoot *Heliopais personata*	B	9	FW	13	C1; C2a

cont.

Bangladesh (cont.)

Wood Snipe *Gallinago nemoricola*	N	4/6	SGW	1	C2a
Spoon-billed Sandpiper *Eurynorhynchus pygmeus*	N	1/14	W	18	C1; C2b
Black-bellied Tern *Sterna acuticauda*	B	9	W	128	C1
Indian Skimmer *Rynchops albicollis*	B	7	W	1	C1; C2a
Pale-capped Pigeon *Columba punicea*	B	7	FSA	1	C1; C2a
Blyth's Kingfisher *Alcedo hercules*	B	9	F	1	A1b; A2b; C1; C2a
Rufous-necked Hornbill *Aceros nipalensis*	B	8	F	12	A1b,c; C1; C2a
Marsh Babbler *Pellorneum palustre*	B	2	GW	1	A1b; C1; C2a
Black-breasted Parrotbill *Paradoxornis flavirostris*	B	4	SGW	1	A1a,b; C1; C2a
Rufous-vented Prinia *Prinia burnesii*	B	3	SGW	1	A1b
Bristled Grass-warbler *Chaetornis striatus*	B	4	SGWA	1	A1b; C1; C2a

Near-threatened

Oriental Darter *Anhinga melanogaster*	B	13	Brown-winged Kingfisher *Pelargopsis amauropterus*	B	5
Painted Stork *Mycteria leucocephala*	B	11	Blue-naped Pitta *Pitta nipalensis*	B	8
Asian Openbill *Anastomus oscitans*	B	9	Mangrove Pitta *Pitta megarhyncha*	B	5
Black-headed Ibis *Threskiornis melanocephalus*	B	10/8	Long-billed Thrush *Zoothera monticola*	B	6
Red-naped Ibis *Pseudibis papillosa*	B	4	Black-breasted Thrush *Turdus dissimilis*	N	4/2
Grey-headed Fish-eagle *Ichthyophaga ichthyaetus*	B	13	Firethroat *Luscinia pectardens*	N	1/2
White-rumped Vulture *Gyps bengalensis*	B	11	Jerdon's Bushchat *Saxicola jerdoni*	B	7
Long-billed Vulture *Gyps indicus*	B	9	Yellow-throated Laughingthrush *Garrulax galbanus*	B	4
Cinereous Vulture *Aegypius monachus*	N	18/13	Slender-billed Scimitar-babbler		
Red-headed Vulture *Sarcogyps calvus*	B	11	*Xiphirhynchus superciliaris*	B	7
Pallid Harrier *Circus macrourus*	N	4/57	Spotted Wren-babbler *Spelaeornis formosus*	B	5
Pied Falconet *Microhierax melanoleucus*	B	5	Yellow-throated Fulvetta *Alcippe cinerea*	B	6
Red-necked Falcon *Falco chicquera*	B	4	Rufous-throated Fulvetta *Alcippe rufogularis*	B	9
White-cheeked Partridge *Arborophila atrogularis*	B	4	Black-browed Parrotbill		
Sarus Crane *Grus antigone*	B	8	*Paradoxornis atrosuperciliaris*	B	6
Grey-headed Lapwing *Vanellus cinereus*	N	3/11	Rufous-headed Parrotbill *Paradoxornis ruficeps*	B	7
Asian Dowitcher *Limnodromus semipalmatus*	N	3/14	Yellow-vented Warbler *Phylloscopus cantator*	B	3/6
Spot-bellied Eagle-owl *Bubo nipalensis*	B	11	Spot-winged Starling *Saroglossa spiloptera*	N	2/5
Tawny Fish-owl *Ketupa flavipes*	B	9			

BARBADOS

Species totals	Vulnerable	1
	Near-threatened	1

Vulnerable	Status (breeding/ non-br.)	Breeding/ non-br. countries	Habitat codes (p. 243)	Threat codes (p. 243)	IUCN threat status codes (pp. 16–18)
Piping Plover *Charadrius melodus*	N	2/9	W	138	C2a

Near-threatened

Hudsonian Godwit *Limosa haemastica*	N	2/11

BELARUS

Species totals	Vulnerable	4
	Near-threatened	3

Vulnerable	Status (breeding/ non-br.)	Breeding/ non-br. countries	Habitat codes (p. 243)	Threat codes (p. 243)	IUCN threat status codes (pp. 16–18)
Ferruginous Duck *Aythya nyroca*	B	38/32	W	12	A1a,b,c
Greater Spotted Eagle *Aquila clanga*	B	14/35	FW	13	C2a
Corncrake *Crex crex*	B	40/31	GWA	12	A1a,b
Aquatic Warbler *Acrocephalus paludicola*	B	8/13	W	18	A2b

Near-threatened

White-tailed Eagle *Haliaeetus albicilla*	B	34/10	Black-winged Pratincole *Glareola nordmanni*	B	10/22
Great Snipe *Gallinago media*	B	10/35			

BELGIUM

Species totals Vulnerable 3

Vulnerable	Status (breeding/ non-br.)	Breeding/ non-br. countries	Habitat codes (p. 243)	Threat codes (p. 243)	IUCN threat status codes (pp. 16–18)
Ferruginous Duck *Aythya nyroca*	N	38/32	W	12	A1a,b,c
Corncrake *Crex crex*	B	40/31	GWA	12	A1a,b
Aquatic Warbler *Acrocephalus paludicola*	N	8/13	W	18	A2b

BELIZE

Species totals Endangered 1
Near-threatened 4

Endangered	Status (breeding/ non-br.)	Breeding/ non-br. countries	Habitat codes (p. 243)	Threat codes (p. 243)	IUCN threat status codes (pp. 16–18)
Yellow-headed Amazon *Amazona oratrix*	B	3	FV	17	**A1a,b,c**; A2b,c; C1; C2a

Near-threatened

Harpy Eagle *Harpia harpyja*	B 17		Keel-billed Motmot *Electron carinatum*		B 6
Ocellated Turkey *Agriocharis ocellata*	B 3		Black Catbird *Melanoptila glabrirostris*		B 4

BENIN

Species totals Vulnerable 1
Near-threatened 2

Vulnerable	Status (breeding/ non-br.)	Breeding/ non-br. countries	Habitat codes (p. 243)	Threat codes (p. 243)	IUCN threat status codes (pp. 16–18)
Lesser Kestrel *Falco naumanni*	N	37/52	FSVGA	15	A1a,b,d

Near-threatened

Pallid Harrier *Circus macrourus*	N 4/57		Brown-cheeked Hornbill *Ceratogymna cylindricus*		B 7

BERMUDA (to U.K.)

Species totals Endangered 1
Vulnerable 1

	Status (breeding/ non-br.)	Breeding/ non-br. countries	Habitat codes (p. 243)	Threat codes (p. 243)	IUCN threat status codes (pp. 16–18)
Endangered					
Bermuda Petrel *Pterodroma cahow*	B	1	RM	9	**D1**; D2
Vulnerable					
Piping Plover *Charadrius melodus*	N	2/9	W	138	C2a

BHUTAN

Species totals Endangered 1   Near-threatened 21
Vulnerable 11

	Status (breeding/ non-br.)	Breeding/ non-br. countries	Habitat codes (p. 243)	Threat codes (p. 243)	IUCN threat status codes (pp. 16–18)
Endangered					
White-bellied Heron *Ardea insignis*	B	4	FW	1	A1a,b; **C1**; **C2a**
Vulnerable					
Ferruginous Duck *Aythya nyroca*	N	38/32	W	12	A1a,b,c
Pallas's Sea-eagle *Haliaeetus leucoryphus*	B	11/1	GW	135	C1; C2b
Chestnut-breasted Partridge *Arborophila mandellii*	B	3	F	12	C1; C2a
Blyth's Tragopan *Tragopan blythii*	B	4	F	12	C1; C2a
Black-necked Crane *Grus nigricollis*	N	2/5	GW	13	C1
Wood Snipe *Gallinago nemoricola*	B	4/6	SGW	1	C2a
Ward's Trogon *Harpactes wardi*	B	5	F	1	C1; C2a
Blyth's Kingfisher *Alcedo hercules*	B	9	F	1	A1b; A2b; C1; C2a

cont.

Bhutan (cont.)

Rufous-necked Hornbill *Aceros nipalensis*	B	8	F	12	A1b,c; C1; C2a
Rufous-throated Wren-babbler *Spelaeornis caudatus*	B	3	F	1	B1+2c; C1; C2a
Beautiful Nuthatch *Sitta formosa*	B	7	F	1	C1; C2a

Near-threatened

Red-headed Vulture *Sarcogyps calvus*	B	11	Purple Cochoa *Cochoa purpurea*	B	8
Satyr Tragopan *Tragopan satyra*	B	4	Slender-billed Scimitar-babbler		
Spot-bellied Eagle-owl *Bubo nipalensis*	B	11	*Xiphirhynchus superciliaris*	B	7
Tawny Fish-owl *Ketupa flavipes*	B	9	Long-billed Wren-babbler *Rimator malacoptilus*	B	5
Yellow-rumped Honeyguide *Indicator xanthonotus*	B	5	Spotted Wren-babbler *Spelaeornis formosus*	B	5
Blue-naped Pitta *Pitta nipalensis*	B	8	Black-headed Shrike-babbler *Pteruthius rufiventer*	B	6
Pied Thrush *Zoothera wardii*	B	3/2	Yellow-throated Fulvetta *Alcippe cinerea*	B	6
Long-billed Thrush *Zoothera monticola*	B	6	Rufous-throated Fulvetta *Alcippe rufogularis*	B	9
Gould's Shortwing *Brachypteryx stellata*	B	6	Rufous-headed Parrotbill *Paradoxornis ruficeps*	B	7
Rufous-breasted Bush-robin *Tarsiger hyperythrus*	B	4/1	Grey-crowned Prinia *Prinia cinereocapilla*	B	3
Blue-fronted Robin *Cinclidium frontale*	B	6	Yellow-vented Warbler *Phylloscopus cantator*	B	3/6

BOLIVIA		**Species totals**	Critical	2	Data Deficient	1
			Endangered	6	Near-threatened	48
			Vulnerable	19		

	Status (breeding/ non-br.)	Breeding/ non-br. countries	Habitat codes (p. 243)	Threat codes (p. 243)	IUCN threat status codes (pp. 16–18)
Critical					
White-winged Nightjar *Caprimulgus candicans*	B	2	G	19	A1b; A2b; B1+2b,c; C1; **C2b**; D1
Royal Cinclodes *Cinclodes aricomae*	B	2	F	19	B1+2c; **C2a**; D1
Endangered					
Southern Helmeted Curassow *Pauxi unicornis*	B	2	F	12	**C2a**
Blue-throated Macaw *Ara glaucogularis*	B	1	FV	79	**C2b**; D1
Red-fronted Macaw *Ara rubrogenys*	B	1	S	1279	**C2a**; D1
Ash-breasted Tit-tyrant *Anairetes alpinus*	B	2	F	19	A1b; A2b; **B1+2c**; C1; **C2a**; D1
Cochabamba Mountain-finch *Poospiza garleppi*	B	1	FS	19	**B1+2c**; **C1**; **C2b**; D1
Black-and-tawny Seedeater *Sporophila nigrorufa*	B	2	SG	1	**A1b**; A2b
Vulnerable					
Andean Flamingo *Phoenicopterus andinus*	B	4	W	123	A2b,c
Puna Flamingo *Phoenicopterus jamesi*	B	4	W	23	A2b,c
Crowned Eagle *Harpyhaliaetus coronatus*	B	4	SG	12	C2b
Wattled Curassow *Crax globulosa*	B	5	F	12	A1b,c; A2b,c; C1; C2a
Horned Coot *Fulica cornuta*	B	3	W	1	C2a
Hyacinth Macaw *Anodorhynchus hyacinthinus*	B	3	FV	127	A1b,c; A2b,c
Military Macaw *Ara militaris*	B	11	F	17	A1b; C2a
Yellow-faced Amazon *Amazona xanthops*	B	2	FV	1	A1b
Maquis Canastero *Asthenes heterura*	B	1	FS	1	A1b; C1; C2a
Berlepsch's Canastero *Asthenes berlepschi*	B	1	S	9	D1; D2
Bolivian Recurvebill *Simoxenops striatus*	B	1	F	1	A2b; B1+2b,c; C1; C2a
Ashy Antwren *Myrmotherula grisea*	B	1	F	1	A1b; A2b; C1; C2a
Yellow-rumped Antwren *Terenura sharpei*	B	2	F	1	A1b; A2b; C1; C2a
Dinelli's Doradito *Pseudocolopteryx dinellianus*	N	1/2	SW	1	C1; C2a
Rufous-sided Pygmy-tyrant					
Euscarthmus rufomarginatus	B	4	VSG	1	A1b; A2b
White-tailed Shrike-tyrant *Agriornis andicola*	B	5	GZ	18	A1a; C2a
Rufous-throated Dipper *Cinclus schulzi*	B	2	W	15	C2a
Black-masked Finch *Coryphaspiza melanotis*	B	5	G	1	A1b
Rufous-bellied Saltator *Saltator rufiventris*	B	2	F	1	C2a

Data Deficient			Fasciated Tiger-heron *Tigrisoma fasciatum*	B	8
Coppery Thorntail *Popelairia letitiae*	B	1	Zigzag Heron *Zebrilus undulatus*	B	9
Near-threatened			Black-headed Duck *Heteronetta atricapilla*	B	6
Greater Rhea *Rhea americana*	B	5	Orinoco Goose *Neochen jubata*	B	10
Lesser Rhea *Rhea pennata*	B	4	Grey-bellied Goshawk *Accipiter poliogaster*	B	10
Hooded Tinamou *Nothocercus nigrocapillus*	B	2	Solitary Eagle *Harpyhaliaetus solitarius*	B	17
Colombian Tinamou *Crypturellus columbianus*	B	5	Crested Eagle *Morphnus guianensis*	B	15
Agami Heron *Agamia agami*	B	16	Harpy Eagle *Harpia harpyja*	B	17

cont.

Bolivia (cont.)

Black-and-white Hawk-eagle *Spizastur melanoleucus*	B	14	Scaled Fruiteater *Ampelioides tschudii*	B	5
Black-and-chestnut Eagle *Oroaetus isidori*	B	6	Buff-throated Tody-tyrant *Hemitriccus rufigularis*	B	2
Orange-breasted Falcon *Falco deiroleucus*	B	17	Sharp-tailed Grass-tyrant *Culicivora caudacuta*	B	4
Ocellated Crake *Micropygia schomburgkii*	B	8	Bearded Tachuri *Polystictus pectoralis*	B	9
Diademed Sandpiper-plover *Phegornis mitchellii*	B	4	White-bellied Pygmy-tyrant *Myiornis albiventris*	B	2
Hudsonian Godwit *Limosa haemastica*	N	2/11	Rufous-bellied Bush-tyrant *Myiotheretes fuscorufus*	B	2
Buff-fronted Owl *Aegolius harrisii*	B	8	Hudson's Black-tyrant *Knipolegus hudsoni*	B	3
Rothschild's Swift *Cypseloides rothschildi*	B	3	Cock-tailed Tyrant *Alectrurus tricolor*	B	4
Spangled Coquette *Lophornis stictolophus*	B	7	Unicoloured Thrush *Turdus haplochrous*	B	1
Wedge-tailed Hillstar *Oreotrochilus adela*	B	1	Citron-headed Yellow-finch *Sicalis luteocephala*	B	1
Hooded Mountain-toucan *Andigena cucullata*	B	2	Grey-cheeked Grass-finch *Emberizoides ypiranganus*	B	3
Black-bodied Woodpecker *Dryocopus schulzi*	B	3	Dark-throated Seedeater *Sporophila ruficollis*	B	5
Bolivian Earthcreeper *Upucerthia harterti*	B	1	Grey-and-chestnut Seedeater *Sporophila hypochroma*	B	3
Tawny Tit-spinetail *Leptasthenura yanacensis*	B	2	Yellow-billed Blue Finch		
Line-fronted Canastero *Asthenes urubambensis*	B	2	*Porphyrospiza caerulescens*	B	2
Peruvian Recurvebill *Simoxenops ucayalae*	B	3	Giant Conebill *Oreomanes fraseri*	B	4
Swallow-tailed Cotinga *Phibalura flavirostris*	B	3	White-banded Tanager *Neothraupis fasciata*	B	3
Scarlet-breasted Fruiteater *Pipreola frontalis*	B	4	White-rumped Tanager *Cypsnagra hirundinacea*	B	3

BOSNIA AND HERZEGOVINA

Species totals   Vulnerable   2

Vulnerable	Status (breeding/ non-br.)	Breeding/ non-br. countries	Habitat codes (p. 243)	Threat codes (p. 243)	IUCN threat status codes (pp. 16–18)
Ferruginous Duck *Aythya nyroca*	B	38/32	W	12	A1a,b,c
Corncrake *Crex crex*	B	40/31	GWA	12	A1a,b

BOTSWANA

Species totals   Vulnerable   5
                       Near-threatened   4

Vulnerable	Status (breeding/ non-br.)	Breeding/ non-br. countries	Habitat codes (p. 243)	Threat codes (p. 243)	IUCN threat status codes (pp. 16–18)
Slaty Egret *Egretta vinaceigula*	B	3	W	1	C2a
Cape Griffon *Gyps coprotheres*	B	6	SGDR	235	A1a,c,d; A2c,d; C1; C2b
Lesser Kestrel *Falco naumanni*	N	37/52	FSVGA	15	A1a,b,d
Blue Crane *Grus paradisea*	B	4	GWA	15	A1a,b; A2b; C1; C2a
Wattled Crane *Grus carunculatus*	B	11	W	123	A2b,c; C1

Near-threatened

Lesser Flamingo *Phoenicopterus minor*	B	8/20	Black-winged Pratincole *Glareola nordmanni*	N	10/22
Pallid Harrier *Circus macrourus*	N	4/57	Short-clawed Lark *Certhilauda chuana*	B	2

BRAZIL

Species totals   Critical   15   Extinct in the Wild   1
                     Endangered   31   Data Deficient   2
                     Vulnerable   56   Near-threatened   103
                     Extinct   1

Critical	Status (breeding/ non-br.)	Breeding/ non-br. countries	Habitat codes (p. 243)	Threat codes (p. 243)	IUCN threat status codes (pp. 16–18)
Brazilian Merganser *Mergus octosetaceus*	B	3	W	159	**A2b,d**; B1+2a,b,c,d,e; **C2a; D1**
Red-billed Curassow *Crax blumenbachii*	B	1	F	129	B1+2c,e; **C2a**; D1
Blue-eyed Ground-dove *Columbina cyanopis*	B	1	G	19	**C2a**; D1
Purple-winged Ground-dove *Claravis godefrida*	B	3	F	19	B1+2c; **C2b**; D1
Lear's Macaw *Anodorhynchus leari*	B	1	SR	1279	A2b; B1+2c; C1; C2b; **D1**
Spix's Macaw *Cyanopsitta spixii*	B	1	F	179	**D1; D2**

cont.

Brazil (cont.)

White-winged Nightjar *Caprimulgus candicans*	B	2	G	19	A1b; A2b; B1+2b,c; C1; **C2b**; D1
Hook-billed Hermit *Glaucis dohrnii*	B	1	F	19	B1+2c,e; **C2a**; D1
Alagoas Foliage-gleaner *Philydor novaesi*	B	1	F	19	A1b; A2b; **B1+2c**; C1; C2b; D1; D2
Alagoas Antwren *Myrmotherula snowi*	B	1	F	19	A1b; A2b; **B1+2c**; C1; C2b; D1; D2
Black-hooded Antwren *Formicivora erythronotos*	B	1	F	19	**A2b**; B1+2c; **C1**; **C2a**; **D1**; D2
Stresemann's Bristlefront *Merulaxis stresemanni*	B	1	F	19	A1b; A2b; B1+2c; C1; **C2a**; D1; D2
Kinglet Calyptura *Calyptura cristata*	B	1	F	19	**C2a**; **D1**; D2
Cherry-throated Tanager *Nemosia rourei*	B	1	F	19	**D1**
Forbes's Blackbird *Curaeus forbesi*	B	1	FA	1789	A1a,b,c,d; **A2b,c,d**; B1+2c; **C1**; **C2a**; D1; D2

Endangered

Golden Parakeet *Guaruba guarouba*	B	1	F	127	A2b,c; C1; **C2b**
Brown-backed Parrotlet *Touit melanonota*	B	1	F	19	**C2a**; D1
Golden-tailed Parrotlet *Touit surda*	B	1	F	1	**C2a**
Red-spectacled Amazon *Amazona pretrei*	B	2	F	17	A1b,c; **A2b,c**; **C1**
Red-browed Amazon *Amazona rhodocorytha*	B	1	F	179	B1+2c,e; **C2a**; D1
Red-tailed Amazon *Amazona brasiliensis*	B	1	F	127	A1b,c; **A2b,c**; B1+2c,e; C1; C2a
Vinaceous Amazon *Amazona vinacea*	B	3	F	1	**A1a,b,c**; A2b,c; C1; C2a
Blue-bellied Parrot *Triclaria malachitacea*	B	2	F	1	**C2a**
Three-toed Jacamar *Jacamaralcyon tridactyla*	B	1	FW	19	A1b; A2b; C1; **C2a**; D1
Helmeted Woodpecker *Dryocopus galeatus*	B	3	F	1	**C2a**
Plain Spinetail *Synallaxis infuscata*	B	1	S	19	A1b; A2b; **B1+2c**; **C1**; C2a; D1
Cipó Canastero *Asthenes luizae*	B	1	GR	189	A2b,d; C1; **C2b**; D1; D2
Restinga Antwren *Formicivora littoralis*	B	1	S	19	**A2b**; **B1+2c**; **C1**; **C2a**; D1; D2
Fringe-backed Fire-eye *Pyriglena atra*	B	1	F	19	**A1b**; **A2b**; **B1+2c**; **C1**; **C2b**; D1
Slender Antbird *Rhopornis ardesiaca*	B	1	F	1	A1b; **A2b**; **B1+2c**; C1; C2a
Bahia Tapaculo *Scytalopus psychopompus*	B	1	F	19	A1b; A2b; **B1+2c**; **C1**; **C2a**; D1; D2
Banded Cotinga *Cotinga maculata*	B	1	F	19	A1b; **B1+2c**; **C1**; C2a; D1; D2
Kaempfer's Tody-tyrant *Hemitriccus kaempferi*	B	1	F	19	A1b; A2b; B1+2c; **C1**
Minas Gerais Tyrannulet *Phylloscartes roquettei*	B	1	F	19	A2b; **B1+2c**; C1; C2b; D2
Alagoas Tyrannulet *Phylloscartes ceciliae*	B	1	F	19	A1b; A2b; **B1+2c**; **C1**; C2a; D2
Atlantic Royal Flycatcher *Onychorhynchus swainsoni*	B	1	F	1	**C2a**
Ochre-breasted Pipit *Anthus nattereri*	B	3	G	1	A1b; A2b; C1; **C2a**
Yellow Cardinal *Gubernatrix cristata*	B	4	FSG	17	**A1a,c**; **A2c**; C1; C2a
Buffy-fronted Seedeater *Sporophila frontalis*	B	3	F	17	**A1b**; A2b; **C1**; **C2b**
Temminck's Seedeater *Sporophila falcirostris*	B	3	F	17	**A1b**; A2b; **C1**; **C2b**
Black-and-tawny Seedeater *Sporophila nigrorufa*	B	2	SG	1	**A1b**; A2b
Marsh Seedeater *Sporophila palustris*	B	4	GW	17	**A1b,c**; **A2b,c**; C1; C2a
Seven-coloured Tanager *Tangara fastuosa*	B	1	FS	17	A1b,c; **A2b,c**; B1+2c; C1; C2a
Black-backed Tanager *Tangara peruviana*	B	1	F	1	A1b; **A2b**; B1+2c; C1; C2b
Saffron-cowled Blackbird *Xanthopsar flavus*	B	4	SGWA	158	**A1a,b**; **A2b,d**; C1; C2a
Pampas Meadowlark *Sturnella militaris*	B	3	G	1	**A1b**; A2b; C1; C2a

Vulnerable

Lesser Nothura *Nothura minor*	B	1	GV	1	A1b; C2a
Dwarf Tinamou *Taoniscus nanus*	B	2	VG	1	A1b; C2a
White-necked Hawk *Leucopternis lacernulata*	B	1	F	129	C1; C2a; D1
Crowned Eagle *Harpyhaliaetus coronatus*	B	4	SG	12	C2b
Chestnut-bellied Guan *Penelope ochrogaster*	B	1	F	12	C2a
Black-fronted Piping-guan *Pipile jacutinga*	B	3	F	12	C2a
Wattled Curassow *Crax globulosa*	B	5	F	12	A1b,c; A2b,c; C1; C2a
Rufous-faced Crake *Laterallus xenopterus*	B	2	GW	1	A1b; A2b
Olrog's Gull *Larus atlanticus*	N	1/3	WM	123	A2b,c; C1; C2b
Hyacinth Macaw *Anodorhynchus hyacinthinus*	B	3	FV	127	A1b,c; A2b,c
Blue-winged Macaw *Ara maracana*	B	3	F	01	A1a,b; C1; C2a
Golden-capped Parakeet *Aratinga auricapilla*	B	1	FV	17	A1a,b; C1; C2a
Blue-chested Parakeet *Pyrrhura cruentata*	B	1	F	1	A1b; B1+2c; C2a
Yellow-faced Amazon *Amazona xanthops*	B	2	FV	1	A1b
Coppery-chested Jacamar *Galbula pastazae*	B	3	F	1	C2a
Tawny Piculet *Picumnus fulvescens*	B	1	F	1	B1+2c
Ochraceous Piculet *Picumnus limae*	B	1	F	1	B1+2c
Moustached Woodcreeper *Xiphocolaptes falcirostris*	B	1	F	1	B1+2c; C2a
Red-shouldered Spinetail *Gyalophylax hellmayri*	B	1	FS	1	C2a
Hoary-throated Spinetail *Synallaxis kollari*	B	2	F	9	D2

cont.

Brazil (cont.)

Striated Softtail *Thripophaga macroura*	B	1	F	1	C1; C2a
Great Xenops *Megaxenops parnaguae*	B	1	F	1	A1b; A2b; C1; C2a
White-bearded Antshrike *Biatas nigropectus*	B	2	F	1	C2a
Plumbeous Antvireo *Dysithamnus plumbeus*	B	1	F	1	A1b; A2b; B1+2c; C1; C2a
Rio de Janeiro Antwren *Myrmotherula fluminensis*	B	1	F	1	A1b; A2b; B1+2c; C1; C2a
Salvadori's Antwren *Myrmotherula minor*	B	1	F	1	B1+2c; C2a
Unicoloured Antwren *Myrmotherula unicolor*	B	1	F	1	B1+2c; C2a
Band-tailed Antwren *Myrmotherula urosticta*	B	1	F	1	B1+2c; C2a
Pectoral Antwren *Herpsilochmus pectoralis*	B	1	F	1	A2b; B1+2c; C1; C2a
Narrow-billed Antwren *Formicivora iheringi*	B	1	F	1	B1+2c; C1; C2a
Orange-bellied Antwren *Terenura sicki*	B	1	F	19	A1b; A2b; B1+2c; C1; C2a
Rio Branco Antbird *Cercomacra carbonaria*	B	2	F	9	D2
Scalloped Antbird *Myrmeciza ruficauda*	B	1	F	1	A1b; A2b; B1+2c; C1; C2a
Brasília Tapaculo *Scytalopus novacapitalis*	B	1	F	1	A1b; A2b
Shrike-like Cotinga *Laniisoma elegans*	B	1	F	1	A1b; A2b; C1; C2a
Grey-winged Cotinga *Tijuca condita*	B	1	F	19	D1; D2
Black-headed Berryeater *Carpornis melanocephalus*	B	1	F	1	C1; C2a
Buff-throated Purpletuft *Iodopleura pipra*	B	1	FS	1	A1b; A2b; C1; C2a
Cinnamon-vented Piha *Lipaugus lanioides*	B	1	F	1	A1b; A2b; C1; C2a
White-winged Cotinga *Xipholena atropurpurea*	B	1	F	1	A1b; A2b; B1+2c; C1; C2a
Golden-crowned Manakin *Pipra vilasboasi*	B	1	F	1	C2b
Black-capped Manakin *Piprites pileatus*	B	2	F	1	B1+2c; C1; C2a
Buff-breasted Tody-tyrant *Hemitriccus mirandae*	B	1	F	1	A1b; A2b; B1+2c; C1
Fork-tailed Pygmy-tyrant *Hemitriccus furcatus*	B	1	F	1	C2a
Rufous-sided Pygmy-tyrant *Euscarthmus rufomarginatus*	B	4	VSG	1	A1b; A2b
São Paulo Tyrannulet *Phylloscartes paulistus*	B	3	F	1	A1b; A2b; C1; C2a
Restinga Tyrannulet *Phylloscartes kronei*	B	1	FS	1	A1b; A2b; C1; C2a
Russet-winged Spadebill *Platyrinchus leucoryphus*	B	3	F	1	A1b; A2b; B1+2c; C1; C2a
Black-and-white Monjita *Heteroxolmis dominicana*	B	4	GWA	1	A1b; A2b
Strange-tailed Tyrant *Alectrurus risora*	B	4	G	1	A1a,b; A2b; C1; C2a
Black-masked Finch *Coryphaspiza melanotis*	B	5	G	1	A1b
Hooded Seedeater *Sporophila melanops*	B	1	GW	9	D1
Cone-billed Tanager *Conothraupis mesoleuca*	B	1	F	9	D1
Black-legged Dacnis *Dacnis nigripes*	B	1	F	17	C1
Noronha Vireo *Vireo gracilirostris*	B	1	FS	9	D2
Yellow-faced Siskin *Carduelis yarrellii*	B	2	FA	7	A1c; A2c

Extinct in the Wild

Alagoas Curassow *Mitu mitu*	B	1	F	129	

Extinct

Glaucous Macaw *Anodorhynchus glaucus* — B 4

Data Deficient

Speckled Crake *Coturnicops notatus* — B 7
Rondônia Bushbird *Clytoctantes atrogularis* — B 1

Near-threatened

Greater Rhea *Rhea americana* — B 5
Solitary Tinamou *Tinamus solitarius* — B 3
Colombian Tinamou *Crypturellus columbianus* — B 5
Yellow-legged Tinamou *Crypturellus noctivagus* — B 1
Agami Heron *Agamia agami* — B 16
Fasciated Tiger-heron *Tigrisoma fasciatum* — B 8
Zigzag Heron *Zebrilus undulatus* — B 9
Black-headed Duck *Heteronetta atricapilla* — B 6
Orinoco Goose *Neochen jubata* — B 10
Grey-bellied Goshawk *Accipiter poliogaster* — B 10
Mantled Hawk *Leucopternis polionota* — B 3
Solitary Eagle *Harpyhaliaetus solitarius* — B 17
Crested Eagle *Morphnus guianensis* — B 15
Harpy Eagle *Harpia harpyja* — B 17
Orange-breasted Falcon *Falco deiroleucus* — B 17
White-crested Guan *Penelope pileata* — B 1
White-browed Guan *Penelope jacucaca* — B 1
Ocellated Crake *Micropygia schomburgkii* — B 8

Hudsonian Godwit *Limosa haemastica* — N 2/11
Pileated Parrot *Pionopsitta pileata* — B 3
Scaled Ground-cuckoo *Neomorphus squamiger* — B 1
Buff-fronted Owl *Aegolius harrisii* — B 8
Pygmy Nightjar *Caprimulgus hirundinaceus* — B 1
Long-trained Nightjar *Macropsalis creagra* — B 2
Sickle-winged Nightjar *Eleothreptus anomalus* — B 4
Saw-billed Hermit *Ramphodon naevius* — B 1
Fiery-tailed Awlbill *Avocettula recurvirostris* — B 7
Spangled Coquette *Lophornis stictolophus* — B 7
Bronze-tailed Comet *Polyonymus caroli* — B 3
Hooded Visorbearer *Augastes lumachellus* — B 1
Hyacinth Visorbearer *Augastes scutatus* — B 1
Lanceolated Monklet *Micromonacha lanceolata* — B 6
Chestnut-headed Nunlet *Nonnula amaurocephala* — B 1
Saffron Toucanet *Baillonius bailloni* — B 1
Mottled Piculet *Picumnus nebulosus* — B 3
Yellow-browed Woodpecker *Piculus aurulentus* — B 1
Araucaria Tit-spinetail *Leptasthenura setaria* — B 2
Chestnut-throated Spinetail *Synallaxis cherriei* — B 4
Canebrake Groundcreeper
   Clibanornis dendrocolaptoides — B 3
Bay-capped Wren-spinetail *Spartonoica maluroides* — B 3
Straight-billed Reedhaunter *Limnornis rectirostris* — B 3

cont.

Brazil (cont.)

Russet-mantled Foliage-gleaner *Philydor dimidiatus*	B	2
White-browed Foliage-gleaner *Philydor amaurotis*	B	2
Peruvian Recurvebill *Simoxenops ucayalae*	B	3
Chestnut-capped Foliage-gleaner		
Hylocryptus rectirostris	B	1
Spot-breasted Antvireo *Dysithamnus stictothorax*	B	2
Klages's Antwren *Myrmotherula klagesi*	B	1
Black-capped Antwren *Herpsilochmus pileatus*	B	1
Serra Antwren *Formicivora serrana*	B	1
Rufous-tailed Antbird *Drymophila genei*	B	1
Ochre-rumped Antbird *Drymophila ochropyga*	B	1
Rio de Janeiro Antbird *Cercomacra brasiliana*	B	1
White-breasted Antbird *Rhegmatorhina hoffmannsi*	B	1
Santarem Antbird *Rhegmatorhina gymnops*	B	1
White-browed Antpitta *Hylopezus ochroleucus*	B	1
Hooded Gnateater *Conopophaga roberti*	B	1
Spotted Bamboowren *Psilorhamphus guttatus*	B	2
Slaty Bristlefront *Merulaxis ater*	B	1
Swallow-tailed Cotinga *Phibalura flavirostris*	B	3
Black-and-gold Cotinga *Tijuca atra*	B	1
Hooded Berryeater *Carpornis cucullatus*	B	1
Purple-throated Cotinga		
Porphyrolaema porphyrolaema	B	4
Bare-throated Bellbird *Procnias nudicollis*	B	3
Opal-crowned Manakin *Pipra iris*	B	1
Boat-billed Tody-tyrant *Hemitriccus josephinae*	B	3
Zimmer's Tody-tyrant *Hemitriccus aenigma*	B	1
Eye-ringed Tody-tyrant *Hemitriccus orbitatus*	B	1
Hangnest Tody-tyrant *Hemitriccus nidipendulus*	B	1
Buff-cheeked Tody-flycatcher *Todirostrum senex*	B	1
Reiser's Tyrannulet *Phyllomyias reiseri*	B	2
Grey-capped Tyrannulet *Phyllomyias griseocapilla*	B	1

Sharp-tailed Grass-tyrant *Culicivora caudacuta*	B	4
Bearded Tachuri *Polystictus pectoralis*	B	9
Grey-backed Tachuri *Polystictus superciliaris*	B	1
Southern Bristle-tyrant *Phylloscartes eximius*	B	3
Oustalet's Tyrannulet *Phylloscartes oustaleti*	B	1
Serra do Mar Tyrannulet *Phylloscartes difficilis*	B	1
Bay-ringed Tyrannulet *Phylloscartes sylviolus*	B	3
Cock-tailed Tyrant *Alectrurus tricolor*	B	4
Shear-tailed Grey Tyrant *Muscipipra vetula*	B	3
Rufous-brown Solitaire *Myadestes leucogenys*	B	3
Creamy-bellied Gnatcatcher *Polioptila lactea*	B	3
Coal-crested Finch *Charitospiza eucosma*	B	2
Cinereous Warbling-finch *Poospiza cinerea*	B	1
Pale-throated Pampa-finch *Embernagra longicauda*	B	1
Dark-throated Seedeater *Sporophila ruficollis*	B	5
Grey-and-chestnut Seedeater *Sporophila hypochroma*	B	3
Chestnut Seedeater *Sporophila cinnamomea*	B	3
Black-bellied Seedeater *Sporophila melanogaster*	B	1
Large-billed Seed-finch *Oryzoborus crassirostris*	B	9
Great-billed Seed-finch *Oryzoborus maximiliani*	B	4
Blackish-blue Seedeater *Amaurospiza moesta*	B	3
Thick-billed Saltator *Saltator maxillosus*	B	3
Yellow-billed Blue Finch *Porphyrospiza caerulescens*	B	2
Brown Tanager *Orchesticus abeillei*	B	1
White-banded Tanager *Neothraupis fasciata*	B	3
White-rumped Tanager *Cypsnagra hirundinacea*	B	3
Azure-shouldered Tanager *Thraupis cyanoptera*	B	1
Green-chinned Euphonia *Euphonia chalybea*	B	3
Dotted Tanager *Tangara varia*	B	4
White-bellied Dacnis *Dacnis albiventris*	B	5
Pearly-breasted Conebill *Conirostrum margaritae*	B	2
Azure Jay *Cyanocorax caeruleus*	B	2

BRUNEI

Species totals

Endangered	2	Data Deficient	3
Vulnerable	12	Near-threatened	27

	Status (breeding/ non-br.)	Breeding/ non-br. countries	Habitat codes (p. 243)	Threat codes (p. 243)	IUCN threat status codes (pp. 16–18)
Endangered					
Chinese Egret *Egretta eulophotes*	N	3/10	WR	1	**C1**; C2a
Storm's Stork *Ciconia stormi*	B	4	FW	19	A1b,c; **C1**; **C2a**; D1
Vulnerable					
Christmas Island Frigatebird *Fregata andrewsi*	N	1/9	FM	9	D2
Japanese Night-heron *Gorsachius goisagi*	N	2/10	F	1	C1; C2a
Lesser Adjutant *Leptoptilos javanicus*	B	12/1	FW	123	C1
Wallace's Hawk-eagle *Spizaetus nanus*	B	5	F	1	A1b; A2b; C1; C2a
Crestless Fireback *Lophura erythrophthalma*	B	3	F	1	A1b; A2b
Crested Fireback *Lophura ignita*	B	5	F	12	A1b,c; A2b,c
Bulwer's Pheasant *Lophura bulweri*	B	3	F	12	C2a
Sunda Ground-cuckoo *Carpococcyx radiceus*	B	3	F	1	C2a
Wrinkled Hornbill *Aceros corrugatus*	B	4	F	1	A1b; A2b; C1; C2a
Fairy Pitta *Pitta nympha*	N	4/6	F	17	C1; C2a
Straw-headed Bulbul *Pycnonotus zeylanicus*	B	5	F	17	A1b,c
Brown-chested Jungle-flycatcher *Rhinomyias brunneata*	N	1/5	F	1	A1b; A2b

Data Deficient		
Mountain Serpent-eagle *Spilornis kinabaluensis*	B	2
Large Frogmouth *Batrachostomus auritus*	B	4
Blue-wattled Bulbul *Pycnonotus nieuwenhuisii*	B	2
Near-threatened		
Oriental Darter *Anhinga melanogaster*	B	13
Great-billed Heron *Ardea sumatrana*	B	10

Schrenck's Bittern *Ixobrychus eurhythmus*	N	5/10
Jerdon's Baza *Aviceda jerdoni*	B	9
Grey-headed Fish-eagle *Ichthyophaga ichthyaetus*	B	13
Malaysian Plover *Charadrius peronii*	B	6
Far Eastern Curlew *Numenius madagascariensis*	N	3/14
Asian Dowitcher *Limnodromus semipalmatus*	N	3/14
Cinnamon-headed Green-pigeon *Treron fulvicollis*	B	5

cont.

Brunei (cont.)

Large Green-pigeon *Treron capellei*	B 5	Hook-billed Bulbul *Setornis criniger*	B 3
Blue-rumped Parrot *Psittinus cyanurus*	B 5	Bornean Bristlehead *Pityriasis gymnocephala*	B 3
Short-toed Coucal *Centropus rectunguis*	B 3	White-chested Babbler *Trichastoma rostratum*	B 5
Bonaparte's Nightjar *Caprimulgus concretus*	B 3	Ferruginous Babbler *Trichastoma bicolor*	B 5
Black Hornbill *Anthracoceros malayanus*	B 4	Grey-breasted Babbler *Malacopteron albogulare*	B 3
Helmeted Hornbill *Buceros vigil*	B 5	Bornean Wren-babbler *Ptilocichla leucogrammica*	B 3
Red-crowned Barbet *Megalaima rafflesii*	B 5	Large-billed Blue-flycatcher *Cyornis caerulatus*	B 3
Malaysian Honeyguide *Indicator archipelagicus*	B 4	Malaysian Blue-flycatcher *Cyornis turcosus*	B 3
Blue-headed Pitta *Pitta baudii*	B 3	Black Magpie *Platysmurus leucopterus*	B 5

BULGARIA

Species totals Critical 1 Near-threatened 2
Vulnerable 10

	Status (breeding/ non-br.)	Breeding/ non-br. countries	Habitat codes (p. 243)	Threat codes (p. 243)	IUCN threat status codes (pp. 16–18)
Critical					
Slender-billed Curlew *Numenius tenuirostris*	N	1/10	WG	1289	**C2b**; D1
Vulnerable					
Dalmatian Pelican *Pelecanus crispus*	B	16/9	W	1235	C2a
White-headed Duck *Oxyura leucocephala*	N	12/16	W	1256	A2d
Lesser White-fronted Goose *Anser erythropus*	N	4/11	SWA	012	A1a,b,c
Red-breasted Goose *Branta ruficollis*	N	1/4	SWA	12	A2b,c; B1+2c,d
Ferruginous Duck *Aythya nyroca*	B	38/32	W	12	A1a,b,c
Greater Spotted Eagle *Aquila clanga*	N	14/35	FW	13	C2a
Imperial Eagle *Aquila heliaca*	B	24/21	FG	12357	C2a
Lesser Kestrel *Falco naumanni*	B	37/52	FSVGA	15	A1a,b,d
Corncrake *Crex crex*	B	40/31	GWA	12	A1a,b
Aquatic Warbler *Acrocephalus paludicola*	N	8/13	W	18	A2b

Near-threatened

Pygmy Cormorant *Phalacrocorax pygmeus*	B 17/4	White-tailed Eagle *Haliaeetus albicilla*	B 34/10

BURKINA FASO

Species totals Vulnerable 1
Near-threatened 1

	Status (breeding/ non-br.)	Breeding/ non-br. countries	Habitat codes (p. 243)	Threat codes (p. 243)	IUCN threat status codes (pp. 16–18)
Vulnerable					
Lesser Kestrel *Falco naumanni*	N	37/52	FSVGA	15	A1a,b,d
Near-threatened					
Great Snipe *Gallinago media*	N 10/35				

BURUNDI

Species totals Vulnerable 5
Near-threatened 6

	Status (breeding/ non-br.)	Breeding/ non-br. countries	Habitat codes (p. 243)	Threat codes (p. 243)	IUCN threat status codes (pp. 16–18)
Vulnerable					
Lesser Kestrel *Falco naumanni*	N	37/52	FSVGA	15	A1a,b,d
Kungwe Apalis *Apalis argentea*	B	4	F	1	B1+2a,c,e
Grauer's Swamp-warbler *Bradypterus graueri*	B	4	W	1	B1+2a,c
Papyrus Yellow Warbler *Chloropeta gracilirostris*	B	7	W	1	B1+2a,b,c,d
Shelley's Crimson-wing *Cryptospiza shelleyi*	B	4	FS	0	A1a; C1; C2a

Near-threatened

Madagascar Pond-heron *Ardeola idae*	N 2/9	Great Snipe *Gallinago media*	N 10/35
Lesser Flamingo *Phoenicopterus minor*	N 8/20	Black-winged Pratincole *Glareola nordmanni*	N 10/22
Pallid Harrier *Circus macrourus*	N 4/57	Papyrus Gonolek *Laniarius mufumbiri*	B 5

CAMBODIA

Species totals	Critical	1	Vulnerable	11
	Endangered	4	Near-threatened	19

	Status (breeding/ non-br.)	Breeding/ non-br. countries	Habitat codes (p. 243)	Threat codes (p. 243)	IUCN threat status codes (pp. 16–18)
Critical					
Giant Ibis *Pseudibis gigantea*	B	4	FW	1239	A1b; A2b,c; B1+2c; **C1**; C2a; D1
Endangered					
Greater Adjutant *Leptoptilos dubius*	B	8	FWU	129	A1b,c; **C1**; C2a; D1
White-shouldered Ibis *Pseudibis davisoni*	B	8	FW	1239	A1b; A2b; **C1**; **C2a**; D1
White-winged Duck *Cairina scutulata*	B	9	FW	1239	A1b,c,d; **C1**; **C2a**; D1
Bengal Florican *Houbaropsis bengalensis*	B	4	GW	1	C1; **C2a**
Vulnerable					
Spot-billed Pelican *Pelecanus philippensis*	B	3/8	W	1235	A1a,b,c,d; C1
Milky Stork *Mycteria cinerea*	B	4	FW	123	C1
Lesser Adjutant *Leptoptilos javanicus*	B	12/1	FW	123	C1
Greater Spotted Eagle *Aquila clanga*	N	14/35	FW	13	C2a
Chestnut-headed Partridge *Arborophila cambodiana*	B	2	F	12	B1+2c; C1; C2a
Siamese Fireback *Lophura diardi*	B	4	F	12	A1b,c; A2b,c
Green Peafowl *Pavo muticus*	B	7	FSG	12	A1b,c; A2b,c
Masked Finfoot *Heliopais personata*	B	9	FW	13	C1; C2a
Black-bellied Tern *Sterna acuticauda*	B	9	W	128	C1
Indian Skimmer *Rynchops albicollis*	B	7	W	1	C1; C2a
Silver Oriole *Oriolus mellianus*	N	1/2	F	1	B1+2c; C1; C2a

Near-threatened

Oriental Darter *Anhinga melanogaster*	B	13	Sarus Crane *Grus antigone*	B	8
Painted Stork *Mycteria leucocephala*	B	11	Grey-headed Lapwing *Vanellus cinereus*	N	3/11
Asian Openbill *Anastomus oscitans*	B	9	Nicobar Pigeon *Caloenas nicobarica*	B	11
Black-headed Ibis *Threskiornis melanocephalus*	B	10/8	Coral-billed Ground-cuckoo *Carpococcyx renauldi*	B	4
Grey-headed Fish-eagle *Ichthyophaga ichthyaetus*	B	13	Spot-bellied Eagle-owl *Bubo nipalensis*	B	11
White-rumped Vulture *Gyps bengalensis*	B	11	Blue-rumped Pitta *Pitta soror*	B	5
Long-billed Vulture *Gyps indicus*	B	9	Bar-bellied Pitta *Pitta elliotii*	B	3
Red-headed Vulture *Sarcogyps calvus*	B	11	Rufous-throated Fulvetta *Alcippe rufogularis*	B	9
Rufous-winged Buzzard *Butastur liventer*	B	7	Asian Golden Weaver *Ploceus hypoxanthus*	B	6
White-rumped Falcon *Polihierax insignis*	B	5			

CAMEROON

Species totals	Critical	1	Data Deficient	4
	Endangered	1	Near-threatened	12
	Vulnerable	12		

	Status (breeding/ non-br.)	Breeding/ non-br. countries	Habitat codes (p. 243)	Threat codes (p. 243)	IUCN threat status codes (pp. 16–18)
Critical					
Mount Kupe Bush-shrike *Telophorus kupeensis*	B	1	F	9	**D1**; D2
Endangered					
Monteiro's Bush-shrike *Malaconotus monteiri*	B	2	F	19	**C2a**; D1
Vulnerable					
Ferruginous Duck *Aythya nyroca*	N	38/32	W	12	A1a,b,c
Mount Cameroon Francolin *Francolinus camerunensis*	B	1	F	129	D2
Bannerman's Turaco *Tauraco bannermani*	B	1	F	1	A1b; B1+2b; C2b
Yellow-footed Honeyguide *Melignomon eisentrauti*	B	3	F	1	A2b
Green-breasted Bush-shrike *Malaconotus gladiator*	B	2	F	1	C2a
White-throated Mountain-babbler *Kupeornis gilberti*	B	2	F	1	B1+2b,c
Grey-necked Rockfowl *Picathartes oreas*	B	4	FR	12	C2a
Bamenda Apalis *Apalis bamendae*	B	1	F	1	B1+2a,c,d
Banded Wattle-eye *Platysteira laticincta*	B	1	F	1	A1b; B1+2b,c; C1; C2b
Mount Cameroon Speirops *Speirops melanocephalus*	B	1	FS	9	D2
Bannerman's Weaver *Ploceus bannermani*	B	2	F	1	B1+2a,b,c; C2a
Bates's Weaver *Ploceus batesi*	B	1	F	1	C2a

Data Deficient

Fernando Po Swift *Apus sladeniae*	B	4	Dja River Warbler *Bradypterus grandis*	B	2
River Prinia *Prinia fluviatilis*	B	5	Gabon Batis *Batis minima*	B	2

cont.

Cameroon (cont.)

Near-threatened

Lesser Flamingo *Phoenicopterus minor*	N 8/20	Mountain Sawwing *Psalidoprocne fuliginosa* B 3
Pallid Harrier *Circus macrourus*	N 4/57	Cameroon Greenbul *Andropadus montanus* B 2
Great Snipe *Gallinago media*	N 10/35	Grey-headed Greenbul *Phyllastrephus poliocephalus* B 2
Black-winged Pratincole *Glareola nordmanni*	N 10/22	Crossley's Ground-thrush *Zoothera crossleyi* B 2
White-naped Pigeon *Columba albinucha*	B 4	Cameroon Bracken-warbler *Bradypterus bangwaensis* B 1
Yellow-casqued Hornbill *Ceratogymna elata*	B 11	Ursula's Sunbird *Nectarinia ursulae* B 2

CANADA

Species totals Critical 1 Vulnerable 2
Endangered 1 Near-threatened 6

	Status (breeding/ non-br.)	Breeding/ non-br. countries	Habitat codes (p. 243)	Threat codes (p. 243)	IUCN threat status codes (pp. 16–18)
Critical					
Eskimo Curlew *Numenius borealis*	B	2/3	GW	0129	**D1**
Endangered					
Whooping Crane *Grus americana*	B	1/1	W	59	**D1**
Vulnerable					
Piping Plover *Charadrius melodus*	B	2/9	W	138	C2a
Kirtland's Warbler *Dendroica kirtlandii*	B	2/2	S	9	D1; D2

Near-threatened

Trumpeter Swan *Cygnus buccinator*	B 2	Xantus's Murrelet *Synthliboramphus hypoleucus* B 3
Hudsonian Godwit *Limosa haemastica*	B 2/11	Spotted Owl *Strix occidentalis* B 3
Marbled Murrelet *Brachyramphus marmoratus*	B 3	Henslow's Sparrow *Ammodramus henslowii* B 2

CAPE VERDE

Species totals Endangered 1
Vulnerable 2

	Status (breeding/ non-br.)	Breeding/ non-br. countries	Habitat codes (p. 243)	Threat codes (p. 243)	IUCN threat status codes (pp. 16–18)
Endangered					
Raso Lark *Alauda razae*	B	1	D	9	**D1; D2**
Vulnerable					
Fea's Petrel *Pterodroma feae*	B	2	GRM	29	D1; D2
Cape Verde Warbler *Acrocephalus brevipennis*	B	1	SAX	189	A1a,b; B1+2b,c; C2b; D1

CAYMAN ISLANDS (to U.K.)

Species totals Vulnerable 1
Near-threatened 2

	Status (breeding/ non-br.)	Breeding/ non-br. countries	Habitat codes (p. 243)	Threat codes (p. 243)	IUCN threat status codes (pp. 16–18)
Vulnerable					
West Indian Whistling-duck *Dendrocygna arborea*	B	12	W	12	C2a

Near-threatened

Cuban Parrot *Amazona leucocephala*	B 3	Vitelline Warbler *Dendroica vitellina* B 2

CENTRAL AFRICAN REPUBLIC

Species totals Vulnerable 2
Near-threatened 2

	Status (breeding/ non-br.)	Breeding/ non-br. countries	Habitat codes (p. 243)	Threat codes (p. 243)	IUCN threat status codes (pp. 16–18)
Vulnerable					
Ferruginous Duck *Aythya nyroca*	N	38/32	W	12	A1a,b,c
Lesser Kestrel *Falco naumanni*	N	37/52	FSVGA	15	A1a,b,d

Near-threatened

Shoebill *Balaeniceps rex*	N 8/1	Pallid Harrier *Circus macrourus* N 4/57

CHAD

Species totals	Vulnerable	3	Near-threatened	4
	Data Deficient	1		

	Status (breeding/ non-br.)	Breeding/ non-br. countries	Habitat codes (p. 243)	Threat codes (p. 243)	IUCN threat status codes (pp. 16–18)
Vulnerable					
Marbled Teal *Marmaronetta angustirostris*	N	21/3	W	125	A2b
Ferruginous Duck *Aythya nyroca*	N	38/32	W	12	A1a,b,c
Lesser Kestrel *Falco naumanni*	N	37/52	FSVGA	15	A1a,b,d

Data Deficient					
River Prinia *Prinia fluviatilis*	B 5		Nubian Bustard *Neotis nuba*		B 5
Near-threatened			Great Snipe *Gallinago media*		N 10/35
Pallid Harrier *Circus macrourus*	N 4/57		Black-winged Pratincole *Glareola nordmanni*		N 10/22

CHILE

Species totals	Critical	3	Data Deficient	2
	Endangered	1	Near-threatened	15
	Vulnerable	11		

	Status (breeding/ non-br.)	Breeding/ non-br. countries	Habitat codes (p. 243)	Threat codes (p. 243)	IUCN threat status codes (pp. 16–18)
Critical					
Austral Rail *Rallus antarcticus*	B	2	W	019	**D1**
Eskimo Curlew *Numenius borealis*	N	2/3	GW	0129	**D1**
Juan Fernández Firecrown *Sephanoides fernandensis*	B	1	F	1689	**B1+2c**; C1; C2b; D1; D2
Endangered					
Peruvian Diving-petrel *Pelecanoides garnotii*	B	2	RM	1246	**A1a**; C2a
Vulnerable					
Defilippe's Petrel *Pterodroma defilippiana*	B	1	GM	69	D2
Pink-footed Shearwater *Puffinus creatopus*	B	1	GM	169	D2
Andean Flamingo *Phoenicopterus andinus*	B	4	W	123	A2b,c
Puna Flamingo *Phoenicopterus jamesi*	B	4	W	23	A2b,c
Horned Coot *Fulica cornuta*	B	3	W	1	C2a
Chilean Woodstar *Eulidia yarrellii*	B	2	DA	19	B1+2c; C2b
Más Afuera Rayadito *Aphrastura masafuerae*	B	1	F	19	D1; D2
Austral Canastero *Asthenes anthoides*	B	2	SG	1	C2a
White-tailed Shrike-tyrant *Agriornis andicola*	B	5	GZ	18	A1a; C2a
Slender-billed Finch *Xenospingus concolor*	B	2	SWD	19	A2b; B1+2c; C1; C2a
Tamarugo Conebill *Conirostrum tamarugense*	B	2	FZ	01	C1

Data Deficient					
White-vented Storm-petrel *Oceanites gracilis*	B 2		Rufous-tailed Hawk *Buteo ventralis*		B 2
Ringed Storm-petrel *Oceanodroma hornbyi*	B 2		Striated Caracara *Phalcoboenus australis*		B 3
Near-threatened			Magellanic Plover *Pluvianellus socialis*		B 2
Lesser Rhea *Rhea pennata*	B 4		Diademed Sandpiper-plover *Phegornis mitchellii*		B 4
Humboldt Penguin *Spheniscus humboldti*	B 2		Hudsonian Godwit *Limosa haemastica*		N 2/11
Red-legged Cormorant *Phalacrocorax gaimardi*	B 3		Fuegian Snipe *Gallinago stricklandii*		B 3
Black-headed Duck *Heteronetta atricapilla*	B 6		Chilean Pigeon *Columba araucana*		B 2
Ruddy-headed Goose *Chloephaga rubidiceps*	B 3		Slender-billed Parakeet *Enicognathus leptorhynchus*		B 1
Spectacled Duck *Anas specularis*	B 2		Canary-winged Finch *Melanodera melanodera*		B 3

CHINA

Species totals	Critical	5	Conservation	
	Endangered	8	Dependent	1
	Vulnerable	73	Data Deficient	2
			Near-threatened	91

	Status (breeding/ non-br.)	Breeding/ non-br. countries	Habitat codes (p. 243)	Threat codes (p. 243)	IUCN threat status codes (pp. 16–18)
Critical					
White-eared Night-heron *Gorsachius magnificus*	B	1/2	F	19	A1b; **C1**; **C2a**; D1
Crested Ibis *Nipponia nippon*	B	1/1	FWA	159	B1+2e; C1; **C2b**; **D1**; D2
Black-faced Spoonbill *Platalea minor*	N	2/8	WR	12359	**A2b**; C1; C2a; D1; D2
Sichuan Partridge *Arborophila rufipectus*	B	1	F	19	**B1+2c**; C1; C2a; D1
Chinese Crested-tern *Sterna bernsteini*	B	1/5	MZ	09	**D1**

cont.

China (cont.)

Endangered

Chinese Egret *Egretta eulophotes*	B	3/10	WR	1	**C1**; **C2a**
Oriental Stork *Ciconia boyciana*	B	2/9	W	1235	A2b; **C1**
White-shouldered Ibis *Pseudibis davisoni*	B	8	FW	1239	A1b; A2b; **C1**; **C2a**; D1
Hainan Partridge *Arborophila ardens*	B	1	F	12	**A1b,c**; B1+2c; **C1**; **C2a**
Siberian Crane *Grus leucogeranus*	N	1/5	W	129	**A2b,c**; C1; D2
Nordmann's Greenshank *Tringa guttifer*	N	1/15	FW	12389	**C1**; **C2b**; D1
Saunders's Gull *Larus saundersi*	B	1/6	W	1235	A1b,c,d; **A2b,c,d**; C1; C2a
Blakiston's Fish-owl *Ketupa blakistoni*	B	3	FW	134	**C1**; **C2a**

Vulnerable

Dalmatian Pelican *Pelecanus crispus*	B	16/9	W	1235	C2a
Spot-billed Pelican *Pelecanus philippensis*	N	3/8	W	1235	A1a,b,c,d; C1
Christmas Island Frigatebird *Fregata andrewsi*	N	1/9	FM	9	D2
Japanese Night-heron *Gorsachius goisagi*	N	2/10	F	1	C1; C2a
Lesser Adjutant *Leptoptilos javanicus*	N	12/1	FW	123	C1
White-headed Duck *Oxyura leucocephala*	B	12/16	W	1256	A2d
Swan Goose *Anser cygnoides*	B	4/5	W	12	A1b,c; A2b,c
Lesser White-fronted Goose *Anser erythropus*	N	4/11	SWA	012	A1a,b,c
Baikal Teal *Anas formosa*	N	1/5	FW	259	A1a,c,d; D2
Marbled Teal *Marmaronetta angustirostris*	B	21/3	W	125	A2b
Ferruginous Duck *Aythya nyroca*	B	38/32	W	12	A1a,b,c
Baer's Pochard *Aythya baeri*	B	2/12	W	123	A1a,b; C1
Scaly-sided Merganser *Mergus squamatus*	B	3/3	FW	1235	C1; C2a
Pallas's Sea-eagle *Haliaeetus leucoryphus*	B	11/1	GW	135	C1; C2b
Greater Spotted Eagle *Aquila clanga*	B	14/35	FW	13	C2a
Imperial Eagle *Aquila heliaca*	B	24/21	FG	12357	C2a
Lesser Kestrel *Falco naumanni*	B	37/52	FSVGA	15	A1a,b,d
Chestnut-breasted Partridge *Arborophila mandellii*	B	3	F	12	C1; C2a
White-necklaced Partridge *Arborophila gingica*	B	1	F	1	C1; C2a
Blyth's Tragopan *Tragopan blythii*	B	4	F	12	C1; C2a
Cabot's Tragopan *Tragopan caboti*	B	1	F	12	C1; C2a
Sclater's Monal *Lophophorus sclateri*	B	3	FSR	12	C1; C2a
Chinese Monal *Lophophorus lhuysii*	B	1	FSGR	12	C2a
Tibetan Eared-pheasant *Crossoptilon harmani*	B	1	FSG	12	C2a
White Eared-pheasant *Crossoptilon crossoptilon*	B	1	FS	12	C2a
Brown Eared-pheasant *Crossoptilon mantchuricum*	B	1	FSG	12	B1+2c
Elliot's Pheasant *Syrmaticus ellioti*	B	1	FS	12	C1; C2a
Hume's Pheasant *Syrmaticus humiae*	B	4	FG	12	C1; C2a
Reeves's Pheasant *Syrmaticus reevesii*	B	1	FS	12	A1b; C1; C2a
Green Peafowl *Pavo muticus*	B	7	FSG	12	A1b,c; A2b,c
White-naped Crane *Grus vipio*	B	3/4	WA	12	C1
Black-necked Crane *Grus nigricollis*	B	2/5	GW	13	C1
Red-crowned Crane *Grus japonensis*	B	4/4	GWA	15	C1; C2a
Swinhoe's Rail *Coturnicops exquisitus*	B	2/4	GW	1	C1; C2a
Corncrake *Crex crex*	B	40/31	GWA	12	A1a,b
Great Bustard *Otis tarda*	B	23	GA	125	A2b
Wood Snipe *Gallinago nemoricola*	B	4/6	SGW	1	C2a
Spoon-billed Sandpiper *Eurynorhynchus pygmeus*	N	1/14	W	18	C1; C2b
Pale-backed Pigeon *Columba eversmanni*	B	7/2	GDA	0	A1a
Pale-capped Pigeon *Columba punicea*	B	7	FSA	1	C1; C2a
Sichuan Wood-owl *Strix davidi*	B	1	F	1	C1; C2a
Vaurie's Nightjar *Caprimulgus centralasicus*	B	1	DZ	19	D1
Ward's Trogon *Harpactes wardi*	B	5	F	1	C1; C2a
Blyth's Kingfisher *Alcedo hercules*	B	9	F	1	A1b; A2b; C1; C2a
Rufous-necked Hornbill *Aceros nipalensis*	B	8	F	12	A1b,c; C1; C2a
Red-collared Woodpecker *Picus rabieri*	B	3	F	1	A1b
Fairy Pitta *Pitta nympha*	B	4/6	F	17	C1; C2a
Grey-sided Thrush *Turdus feae*	B	1/3	F	1	B1+2c; C1; C2a
Rusty-bellied Shortwing *Brachypteryx hyperythra*	B	2	FS	1	C1; C2a
Rufous-headed Robin *Luscinia ruficeps*	B	1/1	F	1	C1; C2a
Black-throated Blue Robin *Luscinia obscura*	B	1/2	F	1	C1; C2a
White-throated Bushchat *Saxicola insignis*	N	3/3	SGW	1	C1; C2a
Snowy-cheeked Laughingthrush *Garrulax sukatschewi*	B	1	FS	1	C1; C2a

cont.

China (cont.)

White-speckled Laughingthrush *Garrulax bieti*	B	1	F	1	B1+2c; C1; C2a
Omei Shan Liocichla *Liocichla omeiensis*	B	1	F	17	B1+2c; C1
Gold-fronted Fulvetta *Alcippe variegaticeps*	B	1	F	1	B1+2c; C1; C2a
Grey-hooded Parrotbill *Paradoxornis zappeyi*	B	1	FS	1	B1+2c; C1; C2a
Rusty-throated Parrotbill *Paradoxornis przewalskii*	B	1	F	1	B1+2c; C1; C2a
Short-tailed Parrotbill *Paradoxornis davidianus*	B	5	S	1	A1b; C1; C2a
Long-billed Bush-warbler *Bradypterus major*	B	3	FSA	1	C2a
Streaked Reed-warbler *Acrocephalus sorghophilus*	N	0/2	WAZ	1	B1+2c; C1; C2a
Hainan Leaf-warbler *Phylloscopus hainanus*	B	1	F	1	A1b; B1+2c
Marsh Grassbird *Megalurus pryeri*	B	2	GW	1	C1; C2a
Brown-chested Jungle-flycatcher *Rhinomyias brunneata*	B	1/5	F	1	A1b; A2b
Yunnan Nuthatch *Sitta yunnanensis*	B	1	F	1	A1b; C1; C2a
Yellow-billed Nuthatch *Sitta solangiae*	B	2	F	1	C1; C2a
Giant Nuthatch *Sitta magna*	B	3	F	1	A1b; C1; C2a
Beautiful Nuthatch *Sitta formosa*	B	7	F	1	C1; C2a
Rufous-backed Bunting *Emberiza jankowskii*	B	3	GR	0	C1; C2a
Yellow Bunting *Emberiza sulphurata*	N	1/6	FSA	0	C1; C2a
Silver Oriole *Oriolus mellianus*	B	1/2	F	1	B1+2c; C1; C2a
Sichuan Jay *Perisoreus internigrans*	B	1	F	1	C1; C2a
Xinjiang Ground-jay *Podoces biddulphi*	B	1	DS	1	C1; C2a

Conservation Dependent

Hooded Crane *Grus monacha*	B	2/4

Data Deficient

Sillem's Mountain-finch *Leucosticte sillemi*	B	1
Tibetan Rosefinch *Carpodacus roborowskii*	B	1

Near-threatened

Schrenck's Bittern *Ixobrychus eurhythmus*	B	5/10
Painted Stork *Mycteria leucocephala*	B	11
Black-headed Ibis *Threskiornis melanocephalus*	B	10/8
Mandarin Duck *Aix galericulata*	B	5/4
Jerdon's Baza *Aviceda jerdoni*	B	9
White-tailed Eagle *Haliaeetus albicilla*	B	34/10
Lesser Fish-eagle *Ichthyophaga humilis*	B	9
White-rumped Vulture *Gyps bengalensis*	B	11
Cinereous Vulture *Aegypius monachus*	B	18/13
Red-headed Vulture *Sarcogyps calvus*	B	11
Pallid Harrier *Circus macrourus*	B	4/57
Rufous-winged Buzzard *Butastur liventer*	B	7
Pied Falconet *Microhierax melanoleucus*	B	5
Siberian Grouse *Dendragapus falcipennis*	B	2
Chinese Grouse *Bonasa sewerzowi*	B	1
Chestnut-throated Partridge *Tetraophasis obscurus*	B	1
Buff-throated Partridge *Tetraophasis szechenyii*	B	2
Rusty-necklaced Partridge *Alectoris magna*	B	1
White-cheeked Partridge *Arborophila atrogularis*	B	4
Satyr Tragopan *Tragopan satyra*	B	4
Temminck's Tragopan *Tragopan temminckii*	B	4
Blue Eared-pheasant *Crossoptilon auritum*	B	1
Golden Pheasant *Chrysolophus pictus*	B	1
Lady Amherst's Pheasant *Chrysolophus amherstiae*	B	2
Band-bellied Crake *Porzana paykullii*	B	2/7
Little Bustard *Tetrax tetrax*	B	13/10
Long-billed Plover *Charadrius placidus*	B	4/8
Grey-headed Lapwing *Vanellus cinereus*	B	3/11
Latham's Snipe *Gallinago hardwickii*	N	1/5
Far Eastern Curlew *Numenius madagascariensis*	B	3/14
Asian Dowitcher *Limnodromus semipalmatus*	B	3/14
Relict Gull *Larus relictus*	B	3/3
White-bellied Green-pigeon *Treron sieboldii*	B	6
Derbyan Parakeet *Psittacula derbiana*	B	2
Spot-bellied Eagle-owl *Bubo nipalensis*	B	11
Tawny Fish-owl *Ketupa flavipes*	B	9

Brown Hornbill *Anorrhinus tickelli*	B	6
White-winged Woodpecker *Dendrocopos leucopterus*	B	7
Blue-naped Pitta *Pitta nipalensis*	B	8
Blue-rumped Pitta *Pitta soror*	B	5
Brown-rumped Minivet *Pericrocotus cantonensis*	B	1
Japanese Waxwing *Bombycilla japonica*	N	1/5
Black-breasted Thrush *Turdus dissimilis*	B	4/2
Chinese Thrush *Turdus mupinensis*	B	1
Gould's Shortwing *Brachypteryx stellata*	B	6
Firethroat *Luscinia pectardens*	B	1/2
Rufous-breasted Bush-robin *Tarsiger hyperythrus*	B	4/1
Ala Shan Redstart *Phoenicurus alaschanicus*	B	1
Blue-fronted Robin *Cinclidium frontale*	B	6
Purple Cochoa *Cochoa purpurea*	B	8
Green Cochoa *Cochoa viridis*	B	7
Jerdon's Bushchat *Saxicola jerdoni*	B	7
Grey Laughingthrush *Garrulax maesi*	B	3
Yellow-throated Laughingthrush *Garrulax galbanus*	B	4
Barred Laughingthrush *Garrulax lunulatus*	B	1
Spot-breasted Laughingthrush *Garrulax merulinus*	B	6
Red-winged Laughingthrush *Garrulax formosus*	B	2
Red-tailed Laughingthrush *Garrulax milnei*	B	5
Slender-billed Scimitar-babbler		
Xiphirhynchus superciliaris	B	7
Spotted Wren-babbler *Spelaeornis formosus*	B	5
Wedge-billed Wren-babbler *Sphenocichla humei*	B	3
Rufous-tailed Babbler *Chrysomma poecilotis*	B	1
Giant Babax *Babax waddelli*	B	2
Tibetan Babax *Babax koslowi*	B	1
Black-headed Shrike-babbler *Pteruthius rufiventer*	B	6
Streaked Barwing *Actinodura souliei*	B	2
Yellow-throated Fulvetta *Alcippe cinerea*	B	6
Spectacled Fulvetta *Alcippe ruficapilla*	B	2
Rufous-throated Fulvetta *Alcippe rufogularis*	B	9
Grey Sibia *Heterophasia gracilis*	B	3
Spectacled Parrotbill *Paradoxornis conspicillatus*	B	1
Brown-winged Parrotbill *Paradoxornis brunneus*	B	2
Black-browed Parrotbill *Paradoxornis atrosuperciliaris*	B	6
Rufous-headed Parrotbill *Paradoxornis ruficeps*	B	7
Reed Parrotbill *Paradoxornis heudei*	B	2
Crested Tit-warbler *Leptopoecile elegans*	B	1
Yellow-vented Warbler *Phylloscopus cantator*	N	3/6

cont.

China (cont.)

Broad-billed Warbler *Tickellia hodgsoni*	B	6	Tibetan Bunting *Emberiza koslowi*	B 1
Brown-breasted Flycatcher *Muscicapa muttui*	B	2/4	Ochre-rumped Bunting *Emberiza yessoensis*	B 3/3
Fujian Niltava *Niltava davidi*	B	3/2	Red-billed Starling *Sturnus sericeus*	B 1/2
Japanese Paradise-flycatcher *Terpsiphone atrocaudata*	N	4/8	Chestnut-cheeked Starling *Sturnus philippensis*	N 2/5
White-necklaced Tit *Aegithalos fuliginosus*	B	1	Collared Myna *Acridotheres albocinctus*	B 3
Snowy-browed Nuthatch *Sitta villosa*	B	1	White-winged Magpie *Urocissa whiteheadi*	B 3
Slaty Bunting *Latoucheornis siemsseni*	B	1	Yellow-breasted Magpie *Cissa hypoleuca*	B 4

CHRISTMAS ISLAND (to Australia)

Species totals   Vulnerable   3
Near-threatened   1

	Status (breeding/ non-br.)	Breeding/ non-br. countries	Habitat codes (p. 243)	Threat codes (p. 243)	IUCN threat status codes (pp. 16–18)
Vulnerable					
Abbott's Booby *Papasula abbotti*	B	1/1	FM	189	C2b; D2
Christmas Island Frigatebird *Fregata andrewsi*	B	1/9	FM	9	D2
Christmas Island Imperial-pigeon *Ducula whartoni*	B	1	F	29	D2
Near-threatened					
Christmas Island White-eye *Zosterops natalis*	B	1			

COCOS (KEELING) ISLANDS (to Australia)

Species totals   Vulnerable   1

	Status (breeding/ non-br.)	Breeding/ non-br. countries	Habitat codes (p. 243)	Threat codes (p. 243)	IUCN threat status codes (pp. 16–18)
Vulnerable					
Christmas Island Frigatebird *Fregata andrewsi*	N	1/9	FM	9	D2

COLOMBIA

Species totals   Critical   9   Extinct   1
Endangered   22   Data Deficient   2
Vulnerable   31   Near-threatened   76

	Status (breeding/ non-br.)	Breeding/ non-br. countries	Habitat codes (p. 243)	Threat codes (p. 243)	IUCN threat status codes (pp. 16–18)
Critical					
Magdalena Tinamou *Crypturellus saltuarius*	B	1	F	129	**B1+2c**; **C2b**; D1; D2
Blue-billed Curassow *Crax alberti*	B	1	F	129	A2b; C1; **C2a**; D1
Yellow-eared Parrot *Ognorhynchus icterotis*	B	2	F	179	A1b; C1; **C2a**; D1
Fuertes's Parrot *Hapalopsittaca fuertesi*	B	1	F	19	**D1**; D2
Sapphire-bellied Hummingbird *Lepidopyga lilliae*	B	1	F	159	A1b; A2b; B1+2c; C1; **C2b**; **D1**; D2
Bogotá Sunangel *Heliangelus zusii*	B	1	F	19	**D1**; D2
Niceforo's Wren *Thryothorus nicefori*	B	1	F	19	A1b; A2b; **B1+2c**; C1; C2b; D1; D2
Tumaco Seedeater *Sporophila insulata*	B	1	GS	9	**D1**
San Andrés Vireo *Vireo caribaeus*	B	1	FS	19	**B1+2b,c**; C1; C2b; D2
Endangered					
Plumbeous Forest-falcon *Micrastur plumbeus*	B	2	F	1	A2b; C1; **C2a**
Cauca Guan *Penelope perspicax*	B	1	FX	129	**C2a**; D2
Northern Helmeted Curassow *Pauxi pauxi*	B	2	F	12	A2b,c; C1; **C2a**
Gorgeted Wood-quail *Odontophorus strophium*	B	1	F	12	A1b,c; A2b,c; **B1+2c**; C1; C2a
Bogotá Rail *Rallus semiplumbeus*	B	1	W	159	A2b; **B1+2c**; C1; **C2a**; D1
Tolima Dove *Leptotila conoveri*	B	1	FX	1	A1b; B1+2c; C1; **C2a**
Rufous-fronted Parakeet *Bolborhynchus ferrugineifrons*	B	1	GS	19	B1+2c; **C2a**; D1
Rusty-faced Parrot *Hapalopsittaca amazonina*	B	3	FS	1	A1b; A2b; B1+2c,d; **C1**
Banded Ground-cuckoo *Neomorphus radiolosus*	B	2	F	1	A1b; A2b; C1; **C2a**
Chestnut-bellied Hummingbird *Amazilia castaneiventris*	B	1	F	1	**A1b**
White-mantled Barbet *Capito hypoleucus*	B	1	F	1	B1+2c; **C2a**
Recurve-billed Bushbird *Clytoctantes alixii*	B	2	F	1	A1b; A2b; **C1**; **C2a**
Moustached Antpitta *Grallaria alleni*	B	1	F	19	**B1+2c**; **C2a**; D1

cont.

Colombia (cont.)

Bicoloured Antpitta *Grallaria rufocinerea*	B	1	F	1	B1+2c; C1; **C2a**
Brown-banded Antpitta *Grallaria milleri*	B	1	F	19	**B1+2c**; D1; D2
Antioquia Bristle-tyrant *Phylloscartes lanyoni*	B	1	F	1	**A1b**; **A2b**; B1+2c; C1; C2a
Apolinar's Wren *Cistothorus apolinari*	B	1	W	19	A1b; A2b; B1+2c; **C1**; **C2a**; D1
Yellow-headed Brush-finch *Atlapetes flaviceps*	B	1	FS	1	**B1+2a,c**; C1; **C2a**
Black-and-gold Tanager *Bangsia melanochlamys*	B	1	F	1	B1+2c; **C1**; **C2a**
Baudó Oropendola *Psarocolius cassini*	B	1	F	1	**A2b**; B1+2c; C1; C2a
Red-bellied Grackle *Hypopyrrhus pyrohypogaster*	B	1	F	19	A1b; A2b; B1+2c; **C1**; **C2a**; D1
Red Siskin *Carduelis cucullata*	B	2	FSGA	179	A1c; A2c; C1; **C2a**; D1
Vulnerable					
Chocó Tinamou *Crypturellus kerriae*	B	2	F	1	B1+2c; C2a
Baudó Guan *Penelope ortoni*	B	2	F	12	A1b,c; A2b,c; C1; C2a
Wattled Curassow *Crax globulosa*	B	5	F	12	A1b,c; A2b,c; C1; C2a
Brown Wood-rail *Aramides wolfi*	B	3	FW	1	A1b
Military Macaw *Ara militaris*	B	11	F	17	A1b; C2a
Golden-plumed Parakeet *Leptosittaca branickii*	B	3	F	1	A1b; A2b; C1; C2a
Santa Marta Parakeet *Pyrrhura viridicata*	B	1	F	1	C1; C2b
Flame-winged Parakeet *Pyrrhura calliptera*	B	1	F	1	A1b; A2b; C1; C2a
Spot-winged Parrotlet *Touit stictoptera*	B	3	F	1	C2a
White-chested Swift *Cypseloides lemosi*	B	2	SG	05	C2b
Black Inca *Coeligena prunellei*	B	1	F	1	A1b; A2b; C1; C2a
Colourful Puffleg *Eriocnemis mirabilis*	B	1	F	9	D1; D2
Coppery-chested Jacamar *Galbula pastazae*	B	3	F	1	C2a
Five-coloured Barbet *Capito quinticolor*	B	1	F	1	A1b; A2b; C1; C2a
Speckled Antshrike *Xenornis setifrons*	B	2	F	1	C2a
Bicoloured Antvireo *Dysithamnus occidentalis*	B	2	F	1	C1; C2a
Giant Antpitta *Grallaria gigantea*	B	2	F	1	A1b; A2b; C1; C2a
Cundinamarca Antpitta *Grallaria kaestneri*	B	1	F	9	D2
Hooded Antpitta *Grallaricula cucullata*	B	2	F	1	A1b; A2b; C1; C2a
Chestnut-bellied Cotinga *Doliornis remseni*	B	3	F	1	A1b; A2b; B1+2c; C1; C2a
Long-wattled Umbrellabird *Cephalopterus penduliger*	B	2	F	127	C2a
Santa Marta Bush-tyrant *Myiotheretes pernix*	B	1	FS	1	C2b
Ochraceous Attila *Attila torridus*	B	3	FX	1	A1b; A2b; B1+2c; C1; C2a
Tanager-finch *Oreothraupis arremonops*	B	2	F	01	C2a
Yellow-green Bush-tanager *Chlorospingus flavovirens*	B	2	F	19	C2a; D2
Gold-ringed Tanager *Bangsia aureocincta*	B	1	F	19	B1+2c; C1
Masked Mountain-tanager *Buthraupis wetmorei*	B	3	F	1	A1b; A2b; B1+2c; C1; C2a
Multicoloured Tanager *Chlorochrysa nitidissima*	B	1	F	1	C1
Turquoise Dacnis *Dacnis hartlaubi*	B	1	F	1	A1b; B1+2c; C1; C2a
Scarlet-breasted Dacnis *Dacnis berlepschi*	B	2	F	1	C1
Chocó Vireo *Vireo* sp.	B	1	F	19	D2

Extinct
Colombian Grebe *Podiceps andinus* B 1

Data Deficient
Black Tinamou *Tinamus osgoodi* B 2
Speckled Crake *Coturnicops notatus* B 7

Near-threatened
Agami Heron *Agamia agami* B 16
Fasciated Tiger-heron *Tigrisoma fasciatum* B 8
Zigzag Heron *Zebrilus undulatus* B 9
Northern Screamer *Chauna chavaria* B 2
Orinoco Goose *Neochen jubata* B 10
Grey-bellied Goshawk *Accipiter poliogaster* B 10
Semicollared Hawk *Accipiter collaris* B 4
Plumbeous Hawk *Leucopternis plumbea* B 4
Semiplumbeous Hawk *Leucopternis semiplumbea* B 5
Solitary Eagle *Harpyhaliaetus solitarius* B 17
Crested Eagle *Morphnus guianensis* B 15
Harpy Eagle *Harpia harpyja* B 17
Black-and-white Hawk-eagle *Spizastur melanoleucus* B 14
Black-and-chestnut Eagle *Oroaetus isidori* B 6
Orange-breasted Falcon *Falco deiroleucus* B 17

Wattled Guan *Aburria aburri* B 4
Black-fronted Wood-quail *Odontophorus atrifrons* B 2
Chestnut Wood-quail *Odontophorus hyperythrus* B 1
Dark-backed Wood-quail *Odontophorus melanonotus* B 2
Ocellated Crake *Micropygia schomburgkii* B 8
Colombian Crake *Neocrex colombianus* B 3
Imperial Snipe *Gallinago imperialis* B 3
Russet-crowned Quail-dove *Geotrygon goldmani* B 2
Colombian Screech-owl *Otus colombianus* B 2
Buff-fronted Owl *Aegolius harrisii* B 8
Chocó Poorwill *Nyctiphrynus rosenbergi* B 2
Santa Marta Sabrewing *Campylopterus phainopeplus* B 1
Fiery-tailed Awlbill *Avocettula recurvirostris* B 7
Spangled Coquette *Lophornis stictolophus* B 7
Rufous-cheeked Hummingbird *Goethalsia bella* B 2
Blossomcrown *Anthocephala floriceps* B 1
Ecuadorian Piedtail *Phlogophilus hemileucurus* B 3
Pink-throated Brilliant *Heliodoxa gularis* B 3
Black-thighed Puffleg *Eriocnemis derbyi* B 2
Hoary Puffleg *Haplophaedia lugens* B 2
Perijá Metaltail *Metallura iracunda* B 2

cont.

Colombia (cont.)

Sooty-capped Puffbird *Bucco noanamae*	B	1
Lanceolated Monklet *Micromonacha lanceolata*	B	6
Orange-fronted Barbet *Capito squamatus*	B	2
Toucan Barbet *Semnornis ramphastinus*	B	2
Plate-billed Mountain-toucan *Andigena laminirostris*	B	2
Grey-breasted Mountain-toucan *Andigena hypoglauca*	B	3
Black-billed Mountain-toucan *Andigena nigrirostris*	B	3
Chocó Woodpecker *Veniliornis chocoensis*	B	2
Greater Scythebill *Campylorhamphus pucherani*	B	3
Perijá Thistletail *Schizoeaca perijana*	B	2
Chestnut-throated Spinetail *Synallaxis cherriei*	B	4
Rusty-headed Spinetail *Synallaxis fuscorufa*	B	1
Santa Marta Antpitta *Grallaria bangsi*	B	1
Crescent-faced Antpitta *Grallaricula lineifrons*	B	2
Black-chested Fruiteater *Pipreola lubomirskii*	B	3
Fiery-throated Fruiteater *Pipreola chlorolepidota*	B	3
Scarlet-breasted Fruiteater *Pipreola frontalis*	B	4
Scaled Fruiteater *Ampelioides tschudii*	B	5
Purple-throated Cotinga		
Porphyrolaema porphyrolaema	B	4
Black-tipped Cotinga *Carpodectes hopkei*	B	3

Yellow-headed Manakin *Chloropipo flavicapilla*	B	1
Bearded Tachuri *Polystictus pectoralis*	B	9
Black-billed Flycatcher *Aphanotriccus audax*	B	2
White-rimmed Brush-finch *Atlapetes leucopis*	B	2
Dusky-headed Brush-finch *Atlapetes fuscoolivaceus*	B	1
Large-billed Seed-finch *Oryzoborus crassirostris*	B	9
Santa Marta Seedeater *Catamenia oreophila*	B	1
Giant Conebill *Oreomanes fraseri*	B	4
Sooty Ant-tanager *Habia gutturalis*	B	1
Purplish-mantled Tanager *Iridosornis porphyrocephala*	B	2
Blue-whiskered Tanager *Tangara johannae*	B	2
White-bellied Dacnis *Dacnis albiventris*	B	5
Viridian Dacnis *Dacnis viguieri*	B	2
Chestnut-bellied Flower-piercer *Diglossa gloriosissima*	B	1
Santa Marta Warbler *Basileuterus basilicus*	B	1
Grey-throated Warbler *Basileuterus cinereicollis*	B	2
White-lored Warbler *Basileuterus conspicillatus*	B	1
Pirre Warbler *Basileuterus ignotus*	B	2
Mountain Grackle *Macroagelaius subalaris*	B	1
Beautiful Jay *Cyanolyca pulchra*	B	2

COMOROS

Species totals Critical 4 Near-threatened 4
Vulnerable 2

	Status (breeding/ non-br.)	Breeding/ non-br. countries	Habitat codes (p. 243)	Threat codes (p. 243)	IUCN threat status codes (pp. 16–18)
Critical					
Anjouan Scops-owl *Otus capnodes*	B	1	F	129	A2b; B1+2c; C1; **C2a**; D1
Grand Comoro Scops-owl *Otus pauliani*	B	1	F	169	A2d; **B1+2a,b,c**; C1; **C2b**; D2
Mount Karthala White-eye *Zosterops mouroniensis*	B	1	S	19	**B1+2b,c**; C2b; D2
Grand Comoro Drongo *Dicrurus fuscipennis*	B	1	F	19	B1+2c; **C2a**; D1
Vulnerable					
Madagascar Heron *Ardea humbloti*	N	1/2	W	2	C2a
Grand Comoro Flycatcher *Humblotia flavirostris*	B	1	FS	1	B1+2c; **C2b**
Near-threatened					
Madagascar Pond-heron *Ardeola idae*	N	2/9			Comoro Olive-pigeon *Columba pollenii* B 1
Madagascar Harrier *Circus maillardi*	B	3			Moheli Brush-warbler *Nesillas mariae* B 1

CONGO

Species totals Vulnerable 3
Near-threatened 1

	Status (breeding/ non-br.)	Breeding/ non-br. countries	Habitat codes (p. 243)	Threat codes (p. 243)	IUCN threat status codes (pp. 16–18)
Vulnerable					
Lesser Kestrel *Falco naumanni*	N	37/52	FSVGA	15	A1a,b,d
Corncrake *Crex crex*	N	40/31	GWA	12	A1a,b
Black-chinned Weaver *Ploceus nigrimentum*	B	3	V	1	C2a
Near-threatened					
Great Snipe *Gallinago media*	N	10/35			

COOK ISLANDS (to New Zealand)

Species totals Critical 1 Near-threatened 1
Vulnerable 5

	Status (breeding/ non-br.)	Breeding/ non-br. countries	Habitat codes (p. 243)	Threat codes (p. 243)	IUCN threat status codes (pp. 16–18)
Critical					
Rarotonga Monarch *Pomarea dimidiata*	B	1	F	69	**D1**; D2

cont.

Cook Islands (cont.)

Vulnerable

Bristle-thighed Curlew *Numenius tahitiensis*	N	1/14	GW	1268	C2b
Blue Lorikeet *Vini peruviana*	B	2	X	67	B1+2d; C2a
Atiu Swiftlet *Collocalia sawtelli*	B	1	SRA	9	D1; D2
Mangaia Kingfisher *Todirhamphus ruficollaris*	B	1	F	69	D1; D2
Rarotonga Starling *Aplonis cinerascens*	B	1	F	09	D1; D2

Near-threatened

Cook Islands Fruit-dove *Ptilinopus rarotongensis*	B	1

COSTA RICA

Species totals   Vulnerable   10
Near-threatened   23

	Status (breeding/ non-br.)	Breeding/ non-br. countries	Habitat codes (p. 243)	Threat codes (p. 243)	IUCN threat status codes (pp. 16–18)
Vulnerable					
Military Macaw *Ara militaris*	B	11	F	17	A1b; C2a
Cocos Cuckoo *Coccyzus ferrugineus*	B	1	FS	169	D2
Mangrove Hummingbird *Amazilia boucardi*	B	1	F	1	B1+2c; C2b
Turquoise Cotinga *Cotinga ridgwayi*	B	2	F	1	C2b
Yellow-billed Cotinga *Carpodectes antoniae*	B	2	F	1	A1b; A2b; C1; C2a
Bare-necked Umbrellabird *Cephalopterus glabricollis*	B	2	F	1	A1b; A2b; C1; C2a
Three-wattled Bellbird *Procnias tricarunculata*	B	4	F	1	A1b; A2b
Cocos Flycatcher *Nesotriccus ridgwayi*	B	1	FS	169	D2
Cocos Finch *Pinaroloxias inornata*	B	1	FS	169	D2
Black-cheeked Ant-tanager *Habia atrimaxillaris*	B	1	F	1	B1+2c; C1; C2b

Near-threatened

Agami Heron *Agamia agami*	B	16	Unspotted Saw-whet Owl *Aegolius ridgwayi*	B	4
Fasciated Tiger-heron *Tigrisoma fasciatum*	B	8	Magenta-throated Woodstar *Philodice bryantae*	B	2
Semiplumbeous Hawk *Leucopternis semiplumbea*	B	5	Resplendent Quetzal *Pharomachrus mocinno*	B	7
Solitary Eagle *Harpyhaliaetus solitarius*	B	17	Baird's Trogon *Trogon bairdii*	B	2
Crested Eagle *Morphnus guianensis*	B	15	Keel-billed Motmot *Electron carinatum*	B	6
Harpy Eagle *Harpia harpyja*	B	17	Lanceolated Monklet *Micromonacha lanceolata*	B	6
Black-and-white Hawk-eagle *Spizastur melanoleucus*	B	14	Grey-headed Piprites *Piprites griseiceps*	B	4
Orange-breasted Falcon *Falco deiroleucus*	B	17	Tawny-chested Flycatcher *Aphanotriccus capitalis*	B	2
Black Guan *Chamaepetes unicolor*	B	2	Ochraceous Pewee *Contopus ochraceus*	B	2
Black-breasted Wood-quail *Odontophorus leucolaemus*	B	2	Peg-billed Finch *Acanthidops bairdii*	B	2
Red-fronted Parrotlet *Touit costaricensis*	B	2	Blue-and-gold Tanager *Bangsia arcaei*	B	2
			Nicaraguan Grackle *Quiscalus nicaraguensis*	B	2

CROATIA

Species totals   Vulnerable   4

	Status (breeding/ non-br.)	Breeding/ non-br. countries	Habitat codes (p. 243)	Threat codes (p. 243)	IUCN threat status codes (pp. 16–18)
Vulnerable					
Ferruginous Duck *Aythya nyroca*	B	38/32	W	12	A1a,b,c
Imperial Eagle *Aquila heliaca*	B	24/21	FG	12357	C2a
Lesser Kestrel *Falco naumanni*	B	37/52	FSVGA	15	A1a,b,d
Corncrake *Crex crex*	B	40/31	GWA	12	A1a,b

CUBA

Species totals   Critical   3   Extinct   1
Endangered   7   Near-threatened   7
Vulnerable   3

	Status (breeding/ non-br.)	Breeding/ non-br. countries	Habitat codes (p. 243)	Threat codes (p. 243)	IUCN threat status codes (pp. 16–18)
Critical					
Zapata Rail *Cyanolimnas cerverai*	B	1	W	169	B1+2c; **C2b**; D1
Zapata Wren *Ferminia cerverai*	B	1	S	169	B1+2e; **C2b**; D1
Bachman's Warbler *Vermivora bachmanii*	B	2	F	19	**D1**

cont.

Cuba (cont.)

Endangered

Black-capped Petrel *Pterodroma hasitata*	B	3	FRM	689	C2a; D1; D2
Gundlach's Hawk *Accipiter gundlachii*	B	1	F	129	C2a; D1
Plain Pigeon *Columba inornata*	B	5	FSVA	12	A1b; **C2a**
Blue-headed Quail-dove *Starnoenas cyanocephala*	B	1	F	129	C2a; D1
Cuban Flicker *Colaptes fernandinae*	B	1	V	19	A1a; **C2a**; D1
Giant Kingbird *Tyrannus cubensis*	B	1	F	19	A1a,b; **C2a**; D1
Cuban Sparrow *Torreornis inexpectata*	B	1	FSGW	19	A2b; **B1+2c; C1; C2a**; D1; D2

Vulnerable

West Indian Whistling-duck *Dendrocygna arborea*	B	12	W	12	C2a
Piping Plover *Charadrius melodus*	N	2/9	W	138	C2a
Cuban Parakeet *Aratinga euops*	B	1	F	17	A1b,c; B1+2c; C1; C2a

Extinct

Ivory-billed Woodpecker *Campephilus principalis*   B   2

Near-threatened

Grey-headed Quail-dove *Geotrygon caniceps*   B   3
Cuban Parrot *Amazona leucocephala*   B   3

Bee Hummingbird *Calypte helenae*   B   1
Bahama Swallow *Tachycineta cyaneoviridis*   B   2
Cuban Solitaire *Myadestes elisabeth*   B   1
Cuban Gnatcatcher *Polioptila lembeyei*   B   1
Palm Crow *Corvus palmarum*   B   3

CYPRUS

Species totals	Vulnerable	4	Conservation	
	Near-threatened	3	Dependent	1

Vulnerable	Status (breeding/ non-br.)	Breeding/ non-br. countries	Habitat codes (p. 243)	Threat codes (p. 243)	IUCN threat status codes (pp. 16–18)
White-headed Duck *Oxyura leucocephala*	N	12/16	W	1256	A2d
Ferruginous Duck *Aythya nyroca*	N	38/32	W	12	A1a,b,c
Imperial Eagle *Aquila heliaca*	B	24/21	FG	12357	C2a
Lesser Kestrel *Falco naumanni*	N	37/52	FSVGA	15	A1a,b,d

Conservation Dependent

Audouin's Gull *Larus audouinii*   B   8/7

Near-threatened

Pallid Harrier *Circus macrourus*	N	4/57
Great Snipe *Gallinago media*	N	10/35
Black-winged Pratincole *Glareola nordmanni*	N	10/22

CZECH REPUBLIC

Species totals	Vulnerable	5
	Near-threatened	1

Vulnerable	Status (breeding/ non-br.)	Breeding/ non-br. countries	Habitat codes (p. 243)	Threat codes (p. 243)	IUCN threat status codes (pp. 16–18)
Ferruginous Duck *Aythya nyroca*	B	38/32	W	12	A1a,b,c
Greater Spotted Eagle *Aquila clanga*	N	14/35	FW	13	C2a
Corncrake *Crex crex*	B	40/31	GWA	12	A1a,b
Great Bustard *Otis tarda*	B	23	GA	125	A2b
Aquatic Warbler *Acrocephalus paludicola*	N	8/13	W	18	A2b

Near-threatened

White-tailed Eagle *Haliaeetus albicilla*   B   34/10

DENMARK

Species totals	Vulnerable	2

See also: Faroe Islands (p. 272), Greenland (p. 276).

Vulnerable	Status (breeding/ non-br.)	Breeding/ non-br. countries	Habitat codes (p. 243)	Threat codes (p. 243)	IUCN threat status codes (pp. 16–18)
Steller's Eider *Polysticta stelleri*	N	2/8	WM	0	A1a
Corncrake *Crex crex*	B	40/31	GWA	12	A1a,b

DJIBOUTI	Species totals	Critical	1	Near-threatened	2
		Vulnerable	2		

	Status (breeding/ non-br.)	Breeding/ non-br. countries	Habitat codes (p. 243)	Threat codes (p. 243)	IUCN threat status codes (pp. 16–18)
Critical					
Djibouti Francolin *Francolinus ochropectus*	B	1	F	139	**A1a,b**; **A2b**; B1+2a,c,e; C1; C2a; D1; D2
Vulnerable					
Imperial Eagle *Aquila heliaca*	N	24/21	FG	12357	C2a
Lesser Kestrel *Falco naumanni*	N	37/52	FSVGA	15	A1a,b,d
Near-threatened					
Lesser Flamingo *Phoenicopterus minor*	B 8/20		Pallid Harrier *Circus macrourus*		N 4/57

DOMINICA	Species totals	Vulnerable	2
		Near-threatened	2

	Status (breeding/ non-br.)	Breeding/ non-br. countries	Habitat codes (p. 243)	Threat codes (p. 243)	IUCN threat status codes (pp. 16–18)
Vulnerable					
Red-necked Amazon *Amazona arausiaca*	B	1	F	89	D1; D2
Imperial Amazon *Amazona imperialis*	B	1	F	89	D1; D2
Near-threatened					
Bridled Quail-dove *Geotrygon mystacea*	B 13		Forest Thrush *Cichlherminia lherminieri*		B 4

DOMINICAN REPUBLIC	Species totals	Endangered	3	Near-threatened	8
		Vulnerable	7		

	Status (breeding/ non-br.)	Breeding/ non-br. countries	Habitat codes (p. 243)	Threat codes (p. 243)	IUCN threat status codes (pp. 16–18)
Endangered					
Black-capped Petrel *Pterodroma hasitata*	B	3	FRM	689	**C2a**; D1; D2
Hispaniolan Hawk *Buteo ridgwayi*	B	2	F	129	**C2a**; D1
Plain Pigeon *Columba inornata*	B	5	FSVA	12	A1b; **C2a**
Vulnerable					
West Indian Whistling-duck *Dendrocygna arborea*	B	12	W	12	C2a
Hispaniolan Parakeet *Aratinga chloroptera*	B	2	F	127	C2a
Rufous-breasted Cuckoo *Hyetornis rufigularis*	B	2	FS	125	A1a,b,c; C1; C2a
La Selle Thrush *Turdus swalesi*	B	2	F	1	B1+2c; C1; C2a
Chat-tanager *Calyptophilus frugivorus*	B	2	F	1	A1b; C1; C2a
White-winged Warbler *Xenoligea montana*	B	2	FS	1	A1b; B1+2c; C1; C2a
White-necked Crow *Corvus leucognaphalus*	B	2	F	12	A1b; C1; C2a
Near-threatened					
Grey-headed Quail-dove *Geotrygon caniceps*	B 3		Narrow-billed Tody *Todus angustirostris*		B 2
Hispaniolan Parrot *Amazona ventralis*	B 2		Antillean Piculet *Nesoctites micromegas*		B 2
Least Poorwill *Siphonorhis brewsteri*	B 2		Golden Swallow *Tachycineta euchrysea*		B 3
Hispaniolan Trogon *Priotelus roseigaster*	B 2		Palm Crow *Corvus palmarum*		B 3

ECUADOR	Species totals	Critical	5	Data Deficient	1
		Endangered	11	Near-threatened	65
		Vulnerable	34		

	Status (breeding/ non-br.)	Breeding/ non-br. countries	Habitat codes (p. 243)	Threat codes (p. 243)	IUCN threat status codes (pp. 16–18)
Critical					
Galápagos Petrel *Pterodroma phaeopygia*	B	1	GM	16	**A1a,b,d**; **A2b,d**; B1+2b,c,e
Yellow-eared Parrot *Ognorhynchus icterotis*	B	2	F	179	A1b; C1; **C2a**; D1
Black-breasted Puffleg *Eriocnemis nigrivestis*	B	1	F	19	A1b; **A2b**; **B1+2c**; C1; C2b; D1; D2

cont.

Ecuador (cont.)

Turquoise-throated Puffleg *Eriocnemis godini*	B	1	F	19	**B1+2c; C2b; D1**; D2
Pale-headed Brush-finch *Atlapetes pallidiceps*	B	1	S	19	**A1b; B1+2c; C2b**; D1; D2

Endangered

Grey-backed Hawk *Leucopternis occidentalis*	B	2	F	19	C2a; D1
Plumbeous Forest-falcon *Micrastur plumbeus*	B	2	F	1	A2b; C1; **C2a**
Rusty-faced Parrot *Hapalopsittaca amazonina*	B	3	FS	1	A1b; A2b; B1+2c,d; **C1**
Red-faced Parrot *Hapalopsittaca pyrrhops*	B	2	FS	19	A1b; **A2b**; B1+2c; **C1; C2a**; D1
Banded Ground-cuckoo *Neomorphus radiolosus*	B	2	F	1	A1b; A2b; C1; **C2a**
Little Woodstar *Acestrura bombus*	B	2	F	1	A1b; A2b; C1; **C2b**
Esmeraldas Woodstar *Acestrura berlepschi*	B	1	F	19	A1b; A2b; B1+2c; C1; **C2b**; D1
Grey-headed Antbird *Myrmeciza griseiceps*	B	2	F	1	A1b; **A2b**; B1+2c; C1; C2a
Floreana Mockingbird *Nesomimus trifasciatus*	B	1	V	89	**D1**; D2
Mangrove Finch *Camarhynchus heliobates*	B	1	F	9	**D1**; D2
Orange-throated Tanager *Wetmorethraupis sterrhopteron*	B	2	F	1	**A2b**; C1; C2b

Vulnerable

Galápagos Penguin *Spheniscus mendiculus*	B	1	RM	8	A1a; C2b
Galápagos Cormorant *Phalacrocorax harrisi*	B	1	RM	389	B1+3c; D1; D2
Galápagos Hawk *Buteo galapagoensis*	B	1	SR	269	D1
Rufous-headed Chachalaca *Ortalis erythroptera*	B	2	F	12	C1; C2a
Bearded Guan *Penelope barbata*	B	2	F	12	A2b,c; C1; C2a
Baudó Guan *Penelope ortoni*	B	2	F	12	A1b,c; A2b,c; C1; C2a
Wattled Curassow *Crax globulosa*	B	5	F	12	A1b,c; A2b,c; C1; C2a
Brown Wood-rail *Aramides wolfi*	B	3	FW	1	A1b
Lava Gull *Larus fuliginosus*	B	1	RM	9	D1
Ochre-bellied Dove *Leptotila ochraceiventris*	B	2	F	1	A1b; A2b; B1+2c,d; C1; C2a
Military Macaw *Ara militaris*	B	11	F	17	A1b; C2a
Golden-plumed Parakeet *Leptosittaca branickii*	B	3	F	1	A1b; A2b; C1; C2a
El Oro Parakeet *Pyrrhura orcesi*	B	1	F	1	B1+2c; C2a
White-necked Parakeet *Pyrrhura albipectus*	B	1	F	1	C2a
Spot-winged Parrotlet *Touit stictoptera*	B	3	F	1	C2a
White-chested Swift *Cypseloides lemosi*	B	2	SG	05	C2b
Violet-throated Metaltail *Metallura baroni*	B	1	FS	1	B1+2c; C2a
Coppery-chested Jacamar *Galbula pastazae*	B	3	F	1	C2a
Blackish-headed Spinetail *Synallaxis tithys*	B	2	FS	1	A1b; A2b; B1+2c; C1; C2a
Rufous-necked Foliage-gleaner *Syndactyla ruficollis*	B	2	F	1	A1b; A2b; C1; C2a
Henna-hooded Foliage-gleaner					
Hylocryptus erythrocephalus	B	2	F	1	A1b; A2b; C1; C2a
Bicoloured Antvireo *Dysithamnus occidentalis*	B	2	F	1	C1; C2a
Giant Antpitta *Grallaria gigantea*	B	2	F	1	A1b; A2b; C1; C2a
Chestnut-bellied Cotinga *Doliornis remseni*	B	3	F	1	A1b; A2b; B1+2c; C1; C2a
Long-wattled Umbrellabird *Cephalopterus penduliger*	B	2	F	127	C2a
Pacific Royal Flycatcher *Onychorhynchus occidentalis*	B	2	F	1	C2a
Grey-breasted Flycatcher *Lathrotriccus griseipectus*	B	2	F	1	A1b; A2b; B1+2c; C1; C2a
White-tailed Shrike-tyrant *Agriornis andicola*	B	5	GZ	18	A1a; C2a
Ochraceous Attila *Attila torridus*	B	3	FX	1	A1b; A2b; B1+2c; C1; C2a
Tanager-finch *Oreothraupis arremonops*	B	2	F	01	C2a
Yellow-green Bush-tanager *Chlorospingus flavovirens*	B	2	F	19	C2a; D2
Masked Mountain-tanager *Buthraupis wetmorei*	B	3	F	1	A1b; A2b; B1+2c; C1; C2a
Scarlet-breasted Dacnis *Dacnis berlepschi*	B	2	F	1	C1
Saffron Siskin *Carduelis siemiradzkii*	B	2	FS	1	B1+2c; C1; C2a

Data Deficient

White-vented Storm-petrel *Oceanites gracilis*	B	2

Near-threatened

Pale-browed Tinamou *Crypturellus transfasciatus*	B	2
Waved Albatross *Diomedea irrorata*	B	1
Wedge-rumped Storm-petrel *Oceanodroma tethys*	B	2
Agami Heron *Agamia agami*	B	16
Fasciated Tiger-heron *Tigrisoma fasciatum*	B	8
Zigzag Heron *Zebrilus undulatus*	B	9
Grey-bellied Goshawk *Accipiter poliogaster*	B	10
Semicollared Hawk *Accipiter collaris*	B	4
Plumbeous Hawk *Leucopternis plumbea*	B	4

Semiplumbeous Hawk *Leucopternis semiplumbea*	B	5
Solitary Eagle *Harpyhaliaetus solitarius*	B	17
Crested Eagle *Morphnus guianensis*	B	15
Harpy Eagle *Harpia harpyja*	B	17
Black-and-chestnut Eagle *Oroaetus isidori*	B	6
Orange-breasted Falcon *Falco deiroleucus*	B	17
Wattled Guan *Aburria aburri*	B	4
Dark-backed Wood-quail *Odontophorus melanonotus*	B	2
Galapagos Rail *Laterallus spilonotus*	B	1
Colombian Crake *Neocrex colombianus*	B	3
Imperial Snipe *Gallinago imperialis*	B	3
Red-masked Parakeet *Aratinga erythrogenys*	B	2

cont.

Ecuador (cont.)

Grey-cheeked Parakeet *Brotogeris pyrrhopterus*	B	2	Cocha Antshrike *Thamnophilus praecox*	B	1
Colombian Screech-owl *Otus colombianus*	B	2	Peruvian Antpitta *Grallaricula peruviana*	B	2
Buff-fronted Owl *Aegolius harrisii*	B	8	Crescent-faced Antpitta *Grallaricula lineifrons*	B	2
Chocó Poorwill *Nyctiphrynus rosenbergi*	B	2	Slaty Becard *Pachyramphus spodiurus*	B	2
Napo Sabrewing *Campylopterus villaviscensio*	B	2	Black-chested Fruiteater *Pipreola lubomirskii*	B	3
Fiery-tailed Awlbill *Avocettula recurvirostris*	B	7	Fiery-throated Fruiteater *Pipreola chlorolepidota*	B	3
Spangled Coquette *Lophornis stictolophus*	B	7	Scarlet-breasted Fruiteater *Pipreola frontalis*	B	4
Ecuadorian Piedtail *Phlogophilus hemileucurus*	B	3	Scaled Fruiteater *Ampelioides tschudii*	B	5
Pink-throated Brilliant *Heliodoxa gularis*	B	3	Purple-throated Cotinga *Porphyrolaema porphyrolaema*	B	4
Black-thighed Puffleg *Eriocnemis derbyi*	B	2	Black-tipped Cotinga *Carpodectes hopkei*	B	3
Hoary Puffleg *Haplophaedia lugens*	B	2	Orange-banded Flycatcher *Myiophobus lintoni*	B	2
Neblina Metaltail *Metallura odomae*	B	2	White-rimmed Brush-finch *Atlapetes leucopis*	B	2
Lanceolated Monklet *Micromonacha lanceolata*	B	6	Large-billed Seed-finch *Oryzoborus crassirostris*	B	9
Orange-fronted Barbet *Capito squamatus*	B	2	Medium Tree-finch *Camarhynchus pauper*	B	1
Toucan Barbet *Semnornis ramphastinus*	B	2	Masked Saltator *Saltator cinctus*	B	2
Plate-billed Mountain-toucan *Andigena laminirostris*	B	2	Giant Conebill *Oreomanes fraseri*	B	4
Grey-breasted Mountain-toucan *Andigena hypoglauca*	B	3	Black-and-white Tanager *Conothraupis speculigera*	B	2
Black-billed Mountain-toucan *Andigena nigrirostris*	B	3	Purplish-mantled Tanager *Iridosornis porphyrocephala*	B	2
Chocó Woodpecker *Veniliornis chocoensis*	B	2	Blue-whiskered Tanager *Tangara johannae*	B	2
Greater Scythebill *Campylorhamphus pucherani*	B	3	White-bellied Dacnis *Dacnis albiventris*	B	5
Chestnut-throated Spinetail *Synallaxis cherriei*	B	4	Tit-like Dacnis *Xenodacnis parina*	B	2
Equatorial Greytail *Xenerpestes singularis*	B	2	Beautiful Jay *Cyanolyca pulchra*	B	2

EGYPT

Species totals	Vulnerable	10
	Near-threatened	6

Vulnerable	Status (breeding/ non-br.)	Breeding/ non-br. countries	Habitat codes (p. 243)	Threat codes (p. 243)	IUCN threat status codes (pp. 16–18)
Dalmatian Pelican *Pelecanus crispus*	N	16/9	W	1235	C2a
White-headed Duck *Oxyura leucocephala*	N	12/16	W	1256	A2d
Marbled Teal *Marmaronetta angustirostris*	B	21/3	W	125	A2b
Ferruginous Duck *Aythya nyroca*	N	38/32	W	12	A1a,b,c
Greater Spotted Eagle *Aquila clanga*	N	14/35	FW	13	C2a
Imperial Eagle *Aquila heliaca*	N	24/21	FG	12357	C2a
Lesser Kestrel *Falco naumanni*	N	37/52	FSVGA	15	A1a,b,d
Corncrake *Crex crex*	N	40/31	GWA	12	A1a,b
Sociable Lapwing *Vanellus gregarius*	N	2/15	GW	158	A1a,b; C1; C2a
White-eyed Gull *Larus leucophthalmus*	B	5/1	WM	1235	C1

Near-threatened

Cinereous Vulture *Aegypius monachus*	N	18/13	Great Snipe *Gallinago media*	N	10/35
Pallid Harrier *Circus macrourus*	N	4/57	Black-winged Pratincole *Glareola nordmanni*	N	10/22
Little Bustard *Tetrax tetrax*	N	13/10	Cinereous Bunting *Emberiza cineracea*	N	3/13

EL SALVADOR

Species totals	Near-threatened	2

Near-threatened

Unspotted Saw-whet Owl *Aegolius ridgwayi*	B	4	Resplendent Quetzal *Pharomachrus mocinno*	B	7

EQUATORIAL GUINEA

Species totals	Vulnerable	4	Near-threatened	2
	Data Deficient 1			

Vulnerable	Status (breeding/ non-br.)	Breeding/ non-br. countries	Habitat codes (p. 243)	Threat codes (p. 243)	IUCN threat status codes (pp. 16–18)
Grey-necked Rockfowl *Picathartes oreas*	B	4	FR	12	C2a
Annobon Paradise-flycatcher *Terpsiphone smithii*	B	1	FA	9	D1; D2

Equatorial Guinea (cont.)

Fernando Po Speirops *Speirops brunneus*	B	1	FS	9	D2
Annobon White-eye *Zosterops griseovirescens*	B	1	FSA	9	D2

Data Deficient			**Near-threatened**		
Fernando Po Swift *Apus sladeniae*	B 4		Mountain Sawwing *Psalidoprocne fuliginosa*	B 3	
			Ursula's Sunbird *Nectarinia ursulae*	B 2	

ERITREA

		Species totals	Vulnerable	3
			Near-threatened	4

Vulnerable	Status (breeding/ non-br.)	Breeding/ non-br. countries	Habitat codes (p. 243)	Threat codes (p. 243)	IUCN threat status codes (pp. 16–18)
Lesser Kestrel *Falco naumanni*	N	37/52	FSVGA	15	A1a,b,d
Sociable Lapwing *Vanellus gregarius*	N	2/15	GW	158	A1a,b; C1; C2a
White-eyed Gull *Larus leucophthalmus*	B	5/1	WM	1235	C1

Near-threatened					
Lesser Flamingo *Phoenicopterus minor*	N 8/20		Rouget's Rail *Rougetius rougetii*	B 2	
Pallid Harrier *Circus macrourus*	N 4/57		Cinereous Bunting *Emberiza cineracea*	N 3/13	

ESTONIA

		Species totals	Vulnerable	2
			Near-threatened	2

Vulnerable	Status (breeding/ non-br.)	Breeding/ non-br. countries	Habitat codes (p. 243)	Threat codes (p. 243)	IUCN threat status codes (pp. 16–18)
Steller's Eider *Polysticta stelleri*	N	2/8	WM	0	A1a
Corncrake *Crex crex*	B	40/31	GWA	12	A1a,b

Near-threatened					
White-tailed Eagle *Haliaeetus albicilla*	B 34/10		Great Snipe *Gallinago media*	B 10/35	

ETHIOPIA

		Species totals	Endangered	5	Near-threatened	14
			Vulnerable	12		

Endangered	Status (breeding/ non-br.)	Breeding/ non-br. countries	Habitat codes (p. 243)	Threat codes (p. 243)	IUCN threat status codes (pp. 16–18)
White-winged Flufftail *Sarothrura ayresi*	B	4	W	1	**B1+2a,b,c+3a,b,c**; C2a
Prince Ruspoli's Turaco *Tauraco ruspolii*	B	1	F	189	A2b; B1+2a,c; C1; **C2a**; D1
Sidamo Lark *Heteromirafra sidamoensis*	B	1	V	19	**B1+2a,c**; **C2b**; D1
Yellow-throated Serin *Serinus flavigula*	B	1	SR	9	**D1**; D2
Ankober Serin *Serinus ankoberensis*	B	1	GR	1	**B1+2c**
Vulnerable					
Ferruginous Duck *Aythya nyroca*	N	38/32	W	12	A1a,b,c
Greater Spotted Eagle *Aquila clanga*	N	14/35	FW	13	C2a
Imperial Eagle *Aquila heliaca*	N	24/21	FG	12357	C2a
Lesser Kestrel *Falco naumanni*	N	37/52	FSVGA	15	A1a,b,d
Taita Falcon *Falco fasciinucha*	B	8	VR	1589	C1; D1
Harwood's Francolin *Francolinus harwoodi*	B	1	W	12	B1+2c; C2a
Wattled Crane *Grus carunculatus*	B	11	W	123	A2b,c; C1
Corncrake *Crex crex*	N	40/31	GWA	12	A1a,b
Degodi Lark *Mirafra degodiensis*	B	1	S	19	D1; D2
White-tailed Swallow *Hirundo megaensis*	B	1	GS	1	B1+2a,b,c; C2b
Salvadori's Serin *Serinus xantholaema*	B	1	SR	1	C2b
Ethiopian Bush-crow *Zavattariornis stresemanni*	B	1	SV	1	B1+2a,b,c; C2b

Near-threatened					
Shoebill *Balaeniceps rex*	B 8/1		Pallid Harrier *Circus macrourus*	N 4/57	
Lesser Flamingo *Phoenicopterus minor*	N 8/20		Rouget's Rail *Rougetius rougetii*	B 2	

cont.

Ethiopia (cont.)

Little Brown Bustard *Eupodotis humilis*	B	2	Abyssinian Longclaw *Macronyx flavicollis*	B	1
Great Snipe *Gallinago media*	N	10/35	Sombre Chat *Cercomela dubia*	B	2
Black-winged Pratincole *Glareola nordmanni*	N	10/22	Basra Reed-warbler *Acrocephalus griseldis*	N	1/8
White-winged Collared-dove *Streptopelia reichenowi*	B	3	Short-billed Crombec *Sylvietta philippae*	B	2
Friedmann's Lark *Mirafra pulpa*	B	2	Cinereous Bunting *Emberiza cineracea*	N	3/13

FALKLAND ISLANDS (to U.K.)

Species totals	Vulnerable	1
	Near-threatened	5

	Status (breeding/ non-br.)	Breeding/ non-br. countries	Habitat codes (p. 243)	Threat codes (p. 243)	IUCN threat status codes (pp. 16–18)
Vulnerable					
Cobb's Wren *Troglodytes cobbi*	B	1	G	169	D2

Near-threatened

Ruddy-headed Goose *Chloephaga rubidiceps*	B	3	Fuegian Snipe *Gallinago stricklandii*	B	3
Striated Caracara *Phalcoboenus australis*	B	3	Canary-winged Finch *Melanodera melanodera*	B	3
Hudsonian Godwit *Limosa haemastica*	N	2/11			

FAROE ISLANDS (to Denmark)

Species totals	Near-threatened	1

Near-threatened

White-tailed Eagle *Haliaeetus albicilla*	N	34/10

FIJI

Species totals	Critical	2	Extinct	1
	Endangered	1	Near-threatened	7
	Vulnerable	5		

	Status (breeding/ non-br.)	Breeding/ non-br. countries	Habitat codes (p. 243)	Threat codes (p. 243)	IUCN threat status codes (pp. 16–18)
Critical					
Fiji Petrel *Pterodroma macgillivrayi*	B	1	FM	69	**C2b**; **D1**; D2
Long-legged Thicketbird *Trichocichla rufa*	B	1	F	069	**B1+2e**; **C2a**; D1
Endangered					
Pink-billed Parrotfinch *Erythrura kleinschmidti*	B	1	F	09	**B1+2e**; **C2a**; D1
Vulnerable					
Bristle-thighed Curlew *Numenius tahitiensis*	N	1/14	GW	1268	C2b
Red-throated Lorikeet *Charmosyna amabilis*	B	1	F	069	C2a; D1
Silktail *Lamprolia victoriae*	B	1	F	18	B1+2c
Ogea Monarch *Mayrornis versicolor*	B	1	F	9	D2
Rotuma Myzomela *Myzomela chermesina*	B	1	F	9	D2

Extinct			Crimson Shining-parrot *Prosopeia splendens*	B	1
Bar-winged Rail *Nesoclopeus poecilopterus*	B	1	Masked Shining-parrot *Prosopeia personata*	B	1
Near-threatened			Black-throated Shrikebill *Clytorhynchus nigrogularis*	B	2
Shy Ground-dove *Gallicolumba stairi*	B	5	Kadavu Fantail *Rhipidura personata*	B	1
Whistling Dove *Ptilinopus layardi*	B	1	Kadavu Honeyeater *Xanthotis provocator*	B	1

FINLAND

Species totals	Vulnerable	4
	Near-threatened	2

	Status (breeding/ non-br.)	Breeding/ non-br. countries	Habitat codes (p. 243)	Threat codes (p. 243)	IUCN threat status codes (pp. 16–18)
Vulnerable					
Lesser White-fronted Goose *Anser erythropus*	B	4/11	SWA	012	A1a,b,c
Steller's Eider *Polysticta stelleri*	N	2/8	WM	0	A1a
Greater Spotted Eagle *Aquila clanga*	B	14/35	FW	13	C2a
Corncrake *Crex crex*	B	40/31	GWA	12	A1a,b

cont.

Finland (cont.)

Near-threatened			
White-tailed Eagle *Haliaeetus albicilla*	B 34/10	Great Snipe *Gallinago media*	B 10/35

FRANCE

Species totals Vulnerable 5 Near-threatened 3
Conservation
Dependent 1

See also: French Guiana (below), French Polynesia (below),
French Southern Territories (p. 274), Guadeloupe (p. 276),
Martinique (p. 296), Mayotte (p. 297), New Caledonia
(p. 303), Réunion (p. 316), Wallis and Futuna Islands (p. 338).

Vulnerable	Status (breeding/ non-br.)	Breeding/ non-br. countries	Habitat codes (p. 243)	Threat codes (p. 243)	IUCN threat status codes (pp. 16–18)
Ferruginous Duck *Aythya nyroca*	N	38/32	W	12	A1a,b,c
Greater Spotted Eagle *Aquila clanga*	N	14/35	FW	13	C2a
Lesser Kestrel *Falco naumanni*	B	37/52	FSVGA	15	A1a,b,d
Corncrake *Crex crex*	B	40/31	GWA	12	A1a,b
Aquatic Warbler *Acrocephalus paludicola*	N	8/13	W	18	A2b

Conservation Dependent		**Near-threatened**	
Audouin's Gull *Larus audouinii*	B 8/7	White-tailed Eagle *Haliaeetus albicilla*	N 34/10
		Little Bustard *Tetrax tetrax*	B 13/10
		Corsican Nuthatch *Sitta whiteheadi*	B 1

FRENCH GUIANA (to France)

Species totals Data Deficient 1
Near-threatened 13

Data Deficient			
Cayenne Nightjar *Caprimulgus maculosus*	B 1	Harpy Eagle *Harpia harpyja*	B 17
Near-threatened		Black-and-white Hawk-eagle *Spizastur melanoleucus*	B 14
Agami Heron *Agamia agami*	B 16	Ocellated Crake *Micropygia schomburgkii*	B 8
Zigzag Heron *Zebrilus undulatus*	B 9	Blue-cheeked Parrot *Amazona dufresniana*	B 4
Orinoco Goose *Neochen jubata*	B 10	Fiery-tailed Awlbill *Avocettula recurvirostris*	B 7
Solitary Eagle *Harpyhaliaetus solitarius*	B 17	Large-billed Seed-finch *Oryzoborus crassirostris*	B 9
Crested Eagle *Morphnus guianensis*	B 15	Great-billed Seed-finch *Oryzoborus maximiliani*	B 4
		Dotted Tanager *Tangara varia*	B 4

FRENCH POLYNESIA (to France)

Species totals Critical 3 Extinct 1
Endangered 6 Near-threatened 1
Vulnerable 11

Critical	Status (breeding/ non-br.)	Breeding/ non-br. countries	Habitat codes (p. 243)	Threat codes (p. 243)	IUCN threat status codes (pp. 16–18)
Polynesian Ground-dove *Gallicolumba erythroptera*	B	1	F	69	B1+2d,e; **C2a**; D1
Marquesan Imperial-pigeon *Ducula galeata*	B	1	F	1269	A2c; **B1+2e**; C1; **C2b**; D1; D2
Tahiti Monarch *Pomarea nigra*	B	1	F	1689	B1+2c; **C2b**; **D1**; D2
Endangered					
Tuamotu Sandpiper *Prosobonia cancellata*	B	1	W	69	B1+2d,e; **C2a**; D1
Marquesan Ground-dove *Gallicolumba rubescens*	B	1	S	9	**D1**; D2
Kuhl's Lorikeet *Vini kuhlii*	B	2	FX	69	**B1+2e**; **C2a**; D2
Ultramarine Lorikeet *Vini ultramarina*	B	1	FX	69	**B1+2b,d**; D2
Marquesan Kingfisher *Todirhamphus godeffroyi*	B	1	F	69	**B1+2e**; C2a; D1; D2
Marquesan Monarch *Pomarea mendozae*	B	1	F	69	**B1+2d**; **C2a**; D1
Vulnerable					
Bristle-thighed Curlew *Numenius tahitiensis*	N	1/14	GW	1268	C2b
Rapa Fruit-dove *Ptilinopus huttoni*	B	1	F	1269	D1; D2
Makatea Fruit-dove *Ptilinopus chalcurus*	B	1	F	9	D1; D2
Polynesian Imperial-pigeon *Ducula aurorae*	B	1	F	129	D1; D2
Blue Lorikeet *Vini peruviana*	B	2	X	67	B1+2d; C2a
Tahiti Swiftlet *Collocalia leucophaeus*	B	1	F	69	D1
Tuamotu Kingfisher *Todirhamphus gambieri*	B	1	X	9	D1; D2

cont.

Tahiti Reed-warbler *Acrocephalus caffer*	B	1	FS	169	D1
Pitcairn Reed-warbler *Acrocephalus vaughani*	B	2	F	9	D2
Iphis Monarch *Pomarea iphis*	B	1	S	9	D2
Fatuhiva Monarch *Pomarea whitneyi*	B	1	F	9	D2

Extinct
Red-moustached Fruit-dove *Ptilinopus mercierii* B 1

Near-threatened
Atoll Fruit-dove *Ptilinopus coralensis* B 1

FRENCH SOUTHERN TERRITORIES (to France)

Species totals Critical 1 Near-threatened 3
Vulnerable 2

	Status (breeding/ non-br.)	Breeding/ non-br. countries	Habitat codes (p. 243)	Threat codes (p. 243)	IUCN threat status codes (pp. 16–18)
Critical					
Amsterdam Albatross *Diomedea amsterdamensis*	B	2	GM	1469	**D1**; D2
Vulnerable					
Wandering Albatross *Diomedea exulans*	B	6	MG	4	A1a,c; A2c
Kerguelen Tern *Sterna virgata*	B	2	WM	6	A2d; C1

Near-threatened
Grey-headed Albatross *Diomedea chrysostoma* B 5
Sooty Albatross *Phoebetria fusca* B 3

Northern Giant-petrel *Macronectes halli* B 4

GABON

Species totals Vulnerable 4 Data Deficient 2
Conservation Near-threatened 2
Dependent 1

	Status (breeding/ non-br.)	Breeding/ non-br. countries	Habitat codes (p. 243)	Threat codes (p. 243)	IUCN threat status codes (pp. 16–18)
Vulnerable					
Lesser Kestrel *Falco naumanni*	N	37/52	FSVGA	15	A1a,b,d
Grey-necked Rockfowl *Picathartes oreas*	B	4	FR	12	C2a
Black-chinned Weaver *Ploceus nigrimentum*	B	3	V	1	C2a
Loango Weaver *Ploceus subpersonatus*	B	3	FSV	1	B1+2c; C2a

Conservation Dependent
Audouin's Gull *Larus audouinii* N 8/7
Data Deficient
Dja River Warbler *Bradypterus grandis* B 2
Gabon Batis *Batis minima* B 2

Near-threatened
Lesser Flamingo *Phoenicopterus minor* N 8/20
Great Snipe *Gallinago media* N 10/35

GAMBIA

Species totals Vulnerable 1
Near-threatened 2

	Status (breeding/ non-br.)	Breeding/ non-br. countries	Habitat codes (p. 243)	Threat codes (p. 243)	IUCN threat status codes (pp. 16–18)
Vulnerable					
Lesser Kestrel *Falco naumanni*	N	37/52	FSVGA	15	A1a,b,d

Near-threatened
Lesser Flamingo *Phoenicopterus minor* N 8/20

Pallid Harrier *Circus macrourus* N 4/57

GEORGIA

| | Species totals | Vulnerable | 5 |
| | | Near-threatened | 5 |

Vulnerable	Status (breeding/ non-br.)	Breeding/ non-br. countries	Habitat codes (p. 243)	Threat codes (p. 243)	IUCN threat status codes (pp. 16–18)
Marbled Teal *Marmaronetta angustirostris*	B	21/3	W	125	A2b
Ferruginous Duck *Aythya nyroca*	B	38/32	W	12	A1a,b,c
Imperial Eagle *Aquila heliaca*	B	24/21	FG	12357	C2a
Lesser Kestrel *Falco naumanni*	B	37/52	FSVGA	15	A1a,b,d
Corncrake *Crex crex*	B	40/31	GWA	12	A1a,b

Near-threatened

Pygmy Cormorant *Phalacrocorax pygmeus*	N	17/4	Caucasian Black Grouse *Tetrao mlokosiewiczi*		B	5
White-tailed Eagle *Haliaeetus albicilla*	B	34/10	Little Bustard *Tetrax tetrax*		N	13/10
Cinereous Vulture *Aegypius monachus*	B	18/13				

GERMANY

| | Species totals | Vulnerable | 5 |
| | | Near-threatened | 1 |

Vulnerable	Status (breeding/ non-br.)	Breeding/ non-br. countries	Habitat codes (p. 243)	Threat codes (p. 243)	IUCN threat status codes (pp. 16–18)
Ferruginous Duck *Aythya nyroca*	B	38/32	W	12	A1a,b,c
Greater Spotted Eagle *Aquila clanga*	N	14/35	FW	13	C2a
Corncrake *Crex crex*	B	40/31	GWA	12	A1a,b
Great Bustard *Otis tarda*	B	23	GA	125	A2b
Aquatic Warbler *Acrocephalus paludicola*	B	8/13	W	18	A2b

Near-threatened

White-tailed Eagle *Haliaeetus albicilla*	B	34/10

GHANA

| | Species totals | Endangered | 1 | Near-threatened | 7 |
| | | Vulnerable | 6 | | |

Endangered	Status (breeding/ non-br.)	Breeding/ non-br. countries	Habitat codes (p. 243)	Threat codes (p. 243)	IUCN threat status codes (pp. 16–18)
Rufous Fishing-owl *Scotopelia ussheri*	B	5	FW	15	A1b; A2b; B1+2b; C1; **C2a**
Vulnerable					
White-breasted Guineafowl *Agelastes meleagrides*	B	5	F	12	A1b,c; A2b,c
Western Wattled Cuckoo-shrike *Campephaga lobata*	B	5	F	1	A1b; A2b
Green-tailed Bristlebill *Bleda eximia*	B	5	F	1	A1b; A2b
Yellow-throated Olive Greenbul *Criniger olivaceus*	B	7	F	1	A1b; A2b
White-necked Rockfowl *Picathartes gymnocephalus*	B	5	FR	127	A1b; A2b
Black-capped Rufous Warbler *Bathmocercus cerviniventris*	B	5	F	1	C2a

Near-threatened

Pallid Harrier *Circus macrourus*	N	4/57	Baumann's Greenbul *Phyllastrephus baumanni*		B	6
Great Snipe *Gallinago media*	N	10/35	Rufous-winged Illadopsis *Illadopsis rufescens*		B	6
Brown-cheeked Hornbill *Ceratogymna cylindricus*	B	7	Copper-tailed Glossy-starling			
Yellow-casqued Hornbill *Ceratogymna elata*	B	11	*Lamprotornis cupreocauda*		B	5

GIBRALTAR (to U.K.)

| | Species totals | Vulnerable | 1 |

Vulnerable	Status (breeding/ non-br.)	Breeding/ non-br. countries	Habitat codes (p. 243)	Threat codes (p. 243)	IUCN threat status codes (pp. 16–18)
Lesser Kestrel *Falco naumanni*	B	37/52	FSVGA	15	A1a,b,d

GREECE

Species totals	Critical	1	Conservation	
	Vulnerable	8	Dependent	1
	Near-threatened	5		

	Status (breeding/ non-br.)	Breeding/ non-br. countries	Habitat codes (p. 243)	Threat codes (p. 243)	IUCN threat status codes (pp. 16–18)
Critical					
Slender-billed Curlew *Numenius tenuirostris*	N	1/10	WG	1289	**C2b**; D1
Vulnerable					
Dalmatian Pelican *Pelecanus crispus*	B	16/9	W	1235	C2a
White-headed Duck *Oxyura leucocephala*	N	12/16	W	1256	A2d
Lesser White-fronted Goose *Anser erythropus*	N	4/11	SWA	012	A1a,b,c
Ferruginous Duck *Aythya nyroca*	B	38/32	W	12	A1a,b,c
Greater Spotted Eagle *Aquila clanga*	N	14/35	FW	13	C2a
Imperial Eagle *Aquila heliaca*	B	24/21	FG	12357	C2a
Lesser Kestrel *Falco naumanni*	B	37/52	FSVGA	15	A1a,b,d
Corncrake *Crex crex*	N	40/31	GWA	12	A1a,b

Conservation Dependent
Audouin's Gull *Larus audouinii*   B 8/7

Near-threatened
Pygmy Cormorant *Phalacrocorax pygmeus*   B 17/4

White-tailed Eagle *Haliaeetus albicilla*   B 34/10
Cinereous Vulture *Aegypius monachus*   B 18/13
Pallid Harrier *Circus macrourus*   N 4/57
Cinereous Bunting *Emberiza cinerea*   B 3/13

GREENLAND (to Denmark)

Species totals	Near-threatened	1

Near-threatened
White-tailed Eagle *Haliaeetus albicilla*   B 34/10

GUADELOUPE (to France)

Species totals	Near-threatened	3

Near-threatened
Bridled Quail-dove *Geotrygon mystacea*   B 13
Guadeloupe Woodpecker *Melanerpes herminieri*   B 1

Forest Thrush *Cichlherminia lherminieri*   B 4

GUAM (to U.S.A.)

Species totals	Critical	1	Extinct	1
	Extinct in the Wild	1		

	Status (breeding/ non-br.)	Breeding/ non-br. countries	Habitat codes (p. 243)	Threat codes (p. 243)	IUCN threat status codes (pp. 16–18)
Critical					
Mariana Crow *Corvus kubaryi*	B	2	F	169	A1a; **B1+2c,d,e**; C1; C2a; D1
Extinct in the Wild					
Guam Rail *Gallirallus owstoni*	B	1	FSA	69	
Extinct					
Guam Flycatcher *Myiagra freycineti*	B	1			

GUATEMALA

Species totals	Endangered	3	Extinct	1
	Vulnerable	1	Near-threatened	18

	Status (breeding/ non-br.)	Breeding/ non-br. countries	Habitat codes (p. 243)	Threat codes (p. 243)	IUCN threat status codes (pp. 16–18)
Endangered					
Yellow-headed Amazon *Amazona oratrix*	B	3	FV	17	**A1a,b,c**; A2b,c; C1; C2a
Azure-rumped Tanager *Tangara cabanisi*	B	2	F	19	**A2b**; B1+2c; C1; C2a; D1
Golden-cheeked Warbler *Dendroica chrysoparia*	N	1/4	FS	18	**A1b,d**; A2d; C1; C2a
Vulnerable					
Horned Guan *Oreophasis derbianus*	B	2	F	12	C2a

cont.

Guatemala (cont.)

Extinct		
Atitlán Grebe *Podilymbus gigas*	B	1

Near-threatened		
Agami Heron *Agamia agami*	B	16
Solitary Eagle *Harpyhaliaetus solitarius*	B	17
Crested Eagle *Morphnus guianensis*	B	15
Harpy Eagle *Harpia harpyja*	B	17
Black-and-white Hawk-eagle *Spizastur melanoleucus*	B	14
Orange-breasted Falcon *Falco deiroleucus*	B	17
Ocellated Quail *Cyrtonyx ocellatus*	B	4
Ocellated Turkey *Agriocharis ocellata*	B	3
Santa Barbara Screech-owl *Otus barbarus*	B	2
Unspotted Saw-whet Owl *Aegolius ridgwayi*	B	4
Resplendent Quetzal *Pharomachrus mocinno*	B	7
Keel-billed Motmot *Electron carinatum*	B	6
Grey-headed Piprites *Piprites griseiceps*	B	4
Belted Flycatcher *Xenotriccus callizonus*	B	2
Black Catbird *Melanoptila glabrirostris*	B	4
Pink-headed Warbler *Ergaticus versicolor*	B	2
Chestnut-sided Shrike-vireo *Vireolanius melitophrys*	B	2
Black-capped Siskin *Carduelis atriceps*	B	2

GUINEA

Species totals Endangered 2 Near-threatened 5 Vulnerable 9

	Status (breeding/ non-br.)	Breeding/ non-br. countries	Habitat codes (p. 243)	Threat codes (p. 243)	IUCN threat status codes (pp. 16–18)
Endangered					
Rufous Fishing-owl *Scotopelia ussheri*	B	5	FW	15	A1b; A2b; B1+2b; C1; **C2a**
Gola Malimbe *Malimbus ballmanni*	B	4	F	1	A1b; **A2b**; B1+2a,b,c
Vulnerable					
Lesser Kestrel *Falco naumanni*	N	37/52	FSVGA	15	A1a,b,d
White-breasted Guineafowl *Agelastes meleagrides*	B	5	F	12	A1b,c; A2b,c
Western Wattled Cuckoo-shrike *Campephaga lobata*	B	5	F	1	A1b; A2b
Green-tailed Bristlebill *Bleda eximia*	B	5	F	1	A1b; A2b
Yellow-throated Olive Greenbul *Criniger olivaceus*	B	7	F	1	A1b; A2b
White-necked Rockfowl *Picathartes gymnocephalus*	B	5	FR	127	A1b; A2b
White-eyed Prinia *Prinia leontica*	B	4	F	1	C2a
Black-capped Rufous Warbler *Bathmocercus cerviniventris*	B	5	F	1	C2a
Nimba Flycatcher *Melaenornis annamarulae*	B	4	F	1	A1b; A2b

Near-threatened		
Lesser Flamingo *Phoenicopterus minor*	N	8/20
Brown-cheeked Hornbill *Ceratogymna cylindricus*	B	7
Yellow-casqued Hornbill *Ceratogymna elata*	B	11
Turati's Boubou *Laniarius turatii*	B	3
Copper-tailed Glossy-starling *Lamprotornis cupreocauda*	B	5

GUINEA-BISSAU

Species totals Near-threatened 3

Near-threatened		
Lesser Flamingo *Phoenicopterus minor*	N	8/20
Yellow-casqued Hornbill *Ceratogymna elata*	B	11
Turati's Boubou *Laniarius turatii*	B	3

GUYANA

Species totals Vulnerable 2 Near-threatened 16 Data Deficient 1

	Status (breeding/ non-br.)	Breeding/ non-br. countries	Habitat codes (p. 243)	Threat codes (p. 243)	IUCN threat status codes (pp. 16–18)
Vulnerable					
Hoary-throated Spinetail *Synallaxis kollari*	B	2	F	9	D2
Rio Branco Antbird *Cercomacra carbonaria*	B	2	F	9	D2

Data Deficient		
Speckled Crake *Coturnicops notatus*	B	7

Near-threatened		
Agami Heron *Agamia agami*	B	16
Zigzag Heron *Zebrilus undulatus*	B	9
Orinoco Goose *Neochen jubata*	B	10
Grey-bellied Goshawk *Accipiter poliogaster*	B	10
Solitary Eagle *Harpyhaliaetus solitarius*	B	17
Crested Eagle *Morphnus guianensis*	B	15
Harpy Eagle *Harpia harpyja*	B	17
Black-and-white Hawk-eagle *Spizastur melanoleucus*	B	14
Orange-breasted Falcon *Falco deiroleucus*	B	17
Ocellated Crake *Micropygia schomburgkii*	B	8
Blue-cheeked Parrot *Amazona dufresniana*	B	4

cont.

Guyana (cont.)

Fiery-tailed Awlbill *Avocettula recurvirostris*	B	7	Rufous-brown Solitaire *Myadestes leucogenys*	B	3	
Bearded Tachuri *Polystictus pectoralis*	B	9	Large-billed Seed-finch *Oryzoborus crassirostris*	B	9	
Boat-billed Tody-tyrant *Hemitriccus josephinae*	B	3				

HAITI

Species totals Endangered 3 Near-threatened 8
Vulnerable 7

	Status (breeding/ non-br.)	Breeding/ non-br. countries	Habitat codes (p. 243)	Threat codes (p. 243)	IUCN threat status codes (pp. 16–18)
Endangered					
Black-capped Petrel *Pterodroma hasitata*	B	3	FRM	689	**C2a**; D1; D2
Hispaniolan Hawk *Buteo ridgwayi*	B	2	F	129	**C2a**; D1
Plain Pigeon *Columba inornata*	B	5	FSVA	12	A1b; **C2a**
Vulnerable					
West Indian Whistling-duck *Dendrocygna arborea*	B	12	W	12	C2a
Hispaniolan Parakeet *Aratinga chloroptera*	B	2	F	127	C2a
Rufous-breasted Cuckoo *Hyetornis rufigularis*	B	2	FS	125	A1a,b,c; C1; C2a
La Selle Thrush *Turdus swalesi*	B	2	F	1	B1+2c; C1; C2a
Chat-tanager *Calyptophilus frugivorus*	B	2	F	1	A1b; C1; C2a
White-winged Warbler *Xenoligea montana*	B	2	FS	1	A1b; B1+2c; C1; C2a
White-necked Crow *Corvus leucognaphalus*	B	2	F	12	A1b; C1; C2a

Near-threatened

Grey-headed Quail-dove *Geotrygon caniceps*	B	3	Narrow-billed Tody *Todus angustirostris*	B	2
Hispaniolan Parrot *Amazona ventralis*	B	2	Antillean Piculet *Nesoctites micromegas*	B	2
Least Poorwill *Siphonorhis brewsteri*	B	2	Golden Swallow *Tachycineta euchrysea*	B	3
Hispaniolan Trogon *Priotelus roseigaster*	B	2	Palm Crow *Corvus palmarum*	B	3

HONDURAS

Species totals Critical 1 Vulnerable 2
Endangered 1 Near-threatened 13

	Status (breeding/ non-br.)	Breeding/ non-br. countries	Habitat codes (p. 243)	Threat codes (p. 243)	IUCN threat status codes (pp. 16–18)
Critical					
Honduran Emerald *Amazilia luciae*	B	1	FS	1	**A2b**; B1+2c; C1; C2a
Endangered					
Golden-cheeked Warbler *Dendroica chrysoparia*	N	1/4	FS	18	**A1b,d**; A2d; C1; C2a
Vulnerable					
Military Macaw *Ara militaris*	B	11	F	17	A1b; C2a
Three-wattled Bellbird *Procnias tricarunculata*	B	4	F	1	A1b; A2b

Near-threatened

Agami Heron *Agamia agami*	B	16	Ocellated Quail *Cyrtonyx ocellatus*	B	4
Semiplumbeous Hawk *Leucopternis semiplumbea*	B	5	Resplendent Quetzal *Pharomachrus mocinno*	B	7
Solitary Eagle *Harpyhaliaetus solitarius*	B	17	Keel-billed Motmot *Electron carinatum*	B	6
Crested Eagle *Morphnus guianensis*	B	15	Grey-headed Piprites *Piprites griseiceps*	B	4
Harpy Eagle *Harpia harpyja*	B	17	Black Catbird *Melanoptila glabrirostris*	B	4
Black-and-white Hawk-eagle *Spizastur melanoleucus*	B	14	Vitelline Warbler *Dendroica vitellina*	B	2
Orange-breasted Falcon *Falco deiroleucus*	B	17			

HONG KONG (to U.K.)

Species totals Critical 1 Vulnerable 8
Endangered 4 Near-threatened 6

	Status (breeding/ non-br.)	Breeding/ non-br. countries	Habitat codes (p. 243)	Threat codes (p. 243)	IUCN threat status codes (pp. 16–18)
Critical					
Black-faced Spoonbill *Platalea minor*	N	2/8	WR	12359	**A2b**; C1; C2a; D1; D2
Endangered					
Chinese Egret *Egretta eulophotes*	N	3/10	WR	1	**C1**; C2a

cont.

Hong Kong (cont.)

Oriental Stork *Ciconia boyciana*	N	2/9	W	1235	A2b; **C1**
Nordmann's Greenshank *Tringa guttifer*	N	1/15	FW	12389	**C1**; C2b; D1
Saunders's Gull *Larus saundersi*	N	1/6	W	1235	A1b,c,d; **A2b,c,d**; C1; C2a
Vulnerable					
Dalmatian Pelican *Pelecanus crispus*	N	16/9	W	1235	C2a
Christmas Island Frigatebird *Fregata andrewsi*	N	1/9	FM	9	D2
Japanese Night-heron *Gorsachius goisagi*	N	2/10	F	1	C1; C2a
Baer's Pochard *Aythya baeri*	N	2/12	W	123	A1a,b; C1
Greater Spotted Eagle *Aquila clanga*	N	14/35	FW	13	C2a
Imperial Eagle *Aquila heliaca*	N	24/21	FG	12357	C2a
Spoon-billed Sandpiper *Eurynorhynchus pygmeus*	N	1/14	W	18	C1; C2b
Yellow Bunting *Emberiza sulphurata*	N	1/6	FSA	0	C1; C2a

Near-threatened

Black-headed Ibis *Threskiornis melanocephalus*	N 10/8	Asian Dowitcher *Limnodromus semipalmatus*	N 3/14
Cinereous Vulture *Aegypius monachus*	N 18/13	Fujian Niltava *Niltava davidi*	N 3/2
Far Eastern Curlew *Numenius madagascariensis*	N 3/14	Red-billed Starling *Sturnus sericeus*	N 1/2

HUNGARY

Species totals — Critical 1 — Near-threatened 3 — Vulnerable 6

	Status (breeding/ non-br.)	Breeding/ non-br. countries	Habitat codes (p. 243)	Threat codes (p. 243)	IUCN threat status codes (pp. 16–18)
Critical					
Slender-billed Curlew *Numenius tenuirostris*	N	1/10	WG	1289	**C2b**; D1
Vulnerable					
Ferruginous Duck *Aythya nyroca*	B	38/32	W	12	A1a,b,c
Greater Spotted Eagle *Aquila clanga*	N	14/35	FW	13	C2a
Imperial Eagle *Aquila heliaca*	B	24/21	FG	12357	C2a
Corncrake *Crex crex*	B	40/31	GWA	12	A1a,b
Great Bustard *Otis tarda*	B	23	GA	125	A2b
Aquatic Warbler *Acrocephalus paludicola*	B	8/13	W	18	A2b

Near-threatened

Pygmy Cormorant *Phalacrocorax pygmeus*	B 17/4	Black-winged Pratincole *Glareola nordmanni*	B 10/22
White-tailed Eagle *Haliaeetus albicilla*	B 34/10		

ICELAND

Species totals — Near-threatened 1

Near-threatened

White-tailed Eagle *Haliaeetus albicilla*	B 34/10

INDIA

Species totals — Critical 4 — Data Deficient 1 — Endangered 9 — Near-threatened 99 — Vulnerable 58

	Status (breeding/ non-br.)	Breeding/ non-br. countries	Habitat codes (p. 243)	Threat codes (p. 243)	IUCN threat status codes (pp. 16–18)
Critical					
Pink-headed Duck *Rhodonessa caryophyllacea*	B	3	FW	0129	**D1**
Himalayan Quail *Ophrysia superciliosa*	B	1	SG	09	**D1**; D2
Lesser Florican *Sypheotides indica*	B	2	G	189	**A1a**; C1; C2b; D1
Forest Owlet *Athene blewitti*	B	1	F	19	**D1**
Endangered					
White-bellied Heron *Ardea insignis*	B	4	FW	1	A1a,b; **C1**; **C2a**
Oriental Stork *Ciconia boyciana*	N	2/9	W	1235	A2b; **C1**
Greater Adjutant *Leptoptilos dubius*	B	8	FWU	129	A1b,c; **C1**; C2a; D1
White-winged Duck *Cairina scutulata*	B	9	FW	1239	A1b,c,d; **C1**; **C2a**; D1
Siberian Crane *Grus leucogeranus*	N	1/5	W	129	**A2b,c**; C1; D2
Great Indian Bustard *Ardeotis nigriceps*	B	1	G	13	C1; **C2b**

cont.

India (cont.)

Bengal Florican *Houbaropsis bengalensis*	B	4	GW	1	C1; **C2a**
Nordmann's Greenshank *Tringa guttifer*	N	1/15	FW	12389	**C1**; C2b; D1
Jerdon's Courser *Rhinoptilus bitorquatus*	B	1	SR	19	**B1+2c; C1; C2a; D1**
Vulnerable					
Dalmatian Pelican *Pelecanus crispus*	N	16/9	W	1235	C2a
Spot-billed Pelican *Pelecanus philippensis*	B	3/8	W	1235	A1a,b,c,d; C1
Lesser Adjutant *Leptoptilos javanicus*	B	12/1	FW	123	C1
White-headed Duck *Oxyura leucocephala*	N	12/16	W	1256	A2d
Lesser White-fronted Goose *Anser erythropus*	N	4/11	SWA	012	A1a,b,c
Marbled Teal *Marmaronetta angustirostris*	N	21/3	W	125	A2b
Ferruginous Duck *Aythya nyroca*	B	38/32	W	12	A1a,b,c
Baer's Pochard *Aythya baeri*	N	2/12	W	123	A1a,b; C1
Pallas's Sea-eagle *Haliaeetus leucoryphus*	B	11/1	GW	135	C1; C2b
Greater Spotted Eagle *Aquila clanga*	B	14/35	FW	13	C2a
Imperial Eagle *Aquila heliaca*	N	24/21	FG	12357	C2a
Lesser Kestrel *Falco naumanni*	N	37/52	FSVGA	15	A1a,b,d
Nicobar Scrubfowl *Megapodius nicobariensis*	B	1	F	12	C1
Swamp Francolin *Francolinus gularis*	B	3	GWA	15	A1b
Manipur Bush-quail *Perdicula manipurensis*	B	2	SGW	12	C1; C2a
Chestnut-breasted Partridge *Arborophila mandellii*	B	3	F	12	C1; C2a
Western Tragopan *Tragopan melanocephalus*	B	2	F	1	C1; C2a
Blyth's Tragopan *Tragopan blythii*	B	4	F	12	C1; C2a
Sclater's Monal *Lophophorus sclateri*	B	3	FSR	12	C1; C2a
Cheer Pheasant *Catreus wallichi*	B	3	FSG	12	C2a
Hume's Pheasant *Syrmaticus humiae*	B	4	FG	12	C1; C2a
Black-necked Crane *Grus nigricollis*	B	2/5	GW	13	C1
Andaman Crake *Rallina canningi*	B	1	FW	16	C1
Masked Finfoot *Heliopais personata*	B	9	FW	13	C1; C2a
Sociable Lapwing *Vanellus gregarius*	N	2/15	GW	158	A1a,b; C1; C2a
Wood Snipe *Gallinago nemoricola*	B	4/6	SGW	1	C2a
Spoon-billed Sandpiper *Eurynorhynchus pygmeus*	N	1/14	W	18	C1; C2b
Black-bellied Tern *Sterna acuticauda*	B	9	W	128	C1
Indian Skimmer *Rynchops albicollis*	B	7	W	1	C1; C2a
Pale-backed Pigeon *Columba eversmanni*	N	7/2	GDA	0	A1a
Pale-capped Pigeon *Columba punicea*	B	7	FSA	1	C1; C2a
Intermediate Parakeet *Psittacula intermedia*	B	1	Z	09	D1
Dark-rumped Swift *Apus acuticauda*	B	1	R	9	D2
Ward's Trogon *Harpactes wardi*	B	5	F	1	C1; C2a
Blyth's Kingfisher *Alcedo hercules*	B	9	F	1	A1b; A2b; C1; C2a
Rufous-necked Hornbill *Aceros nipalensis*	B	8	F	12	A1b,c; C1; C2a
Narcondam Hornbill *Aceros narcondami*	B	1	F	9	D1; D2
Nicobar Bulbul *Hypsipetes nicobariensis*	B	1	F	6	A1d; B1+2e; C1; C2a
Grey-sided Thrush *Turdus feae*	N	1/3	F	1	B1+2c; C1; C2a
Rusty-bellied Shortwing *Brachypteryx hyperythra*	B	2	FS	1	C1; C2a
White-browed Bushchat *Saxicola macrorhyncha*	B	3	SD	1	A1a,b; C1; C2a
White-throated Bushchat *Saxicola insignis*	N	3/3	SGW	1	C1; C2a
Marsh Babbler *Pellorneum palustre*	B	2	GW	1	A1b; C1; C2a
Rufous-throated Wren-babbler *Spelaeornis caudatus*	B	3	F	1	B1+2c; C1; C2a
Rusty-throated Wren-babbler *Spelaeornis badeigularis*	B	1	F	19	B1+2c; D1
Tawny-breasted Wren-babbler *Spelaeornis longicaudatus*	B	1	FR	1	B1+2c; C1; C2a
Snowy-throated Babbler *Stachyris oglei*	B	1	FSR	1	B1+2c; C1; C2a
Jerdon's Babbler *Chrysomma altirostre*	B	4	GW	1	A1b
Black-breasted Parrotbill *Paradoxornis flavirostris*	B	4	SGW	1	A1a,b; C1; C2a
Rufous-vented Prinia *Prinia burnesii*	B	3	SGW	1	A1b
Long-billed Bush-warbler *Bradypterus major*	B	3	FSA	1	C2a
Bristled Grass-warbler *Chaetornis striatus*	B	4	SGWA	1	A1b; C1; C2a
Brown-chested Jungle-flycatcher *Rhinomyias brunneata*	N	1/5	F	1	A1b; A2b
Kashmir Flycatcher *Ficedula subrubra*	N	2/3	F	1	B1+2c
White-naped Tit *Parus nuchalis*	B	1	FS	1	A1b; C1; C2a
Beautiful Nuthatch *Sitta formosa*	B	7	F	1	C1; C2a
Green Avadavat *Amandava formosa*	B	1	SGA	17	C1; C2a
Yellow Weaver *Ploceus megarhynchus*	B	1	SGW	1	C1; C2a

cont.

India (cont.)

Data Deficient		
Brown-capped Laughingthrush *Garrulax austeni*	B	2
Near-threatened		
Oriental Darter *Anhinga melanogaster*	B	13
Great-billed Heron *Ardea sumatrana*	B	10
Painted Stork *Mycteria leucocephala*	B	11
Asian Openbill *Anastomus oscitans*	B	9
Black-headed Ibis *Threskiornis melanocephalus*	B	10/8
Red-naped Ibis *Pseudibis papillosa*	B	4
Lesser Flamingo *Phoenicopterus minor*	N	8/20
Jerdon's Baza *Aviceda jerdoni*	B	9
White-tailed Eagle *Haliaeetus albicilla*	N	34/10
Lesser Fish-eagle *Ichthyophaga humilis*	B	9
Grey-headed Fish-eagle *Ichthyophaga ichthyaetus*	B	13
White-rumped Vulture *Gyps bengalensis*	B	11
Long-billed Vulture *Gyps indicus*	B	9
Cinereous Vulture *Aegypius monachus*	N	18/13
Red-headed Vulture *Sarcogyps calvus*	B	11
Nicobar Serpent-eagle *Spilornis minimus*	B	1
Andaman Serpent-eagle *Spilornis elgini*	B	1
Pallid Harrier *Circus macrourus*	N	4/57
Nicobar Sparrowhawk *Accipiter butleri*	B	1
Pied Falconet *Microhierax melanoleucus*	B	5
Red-necked Falcon *Falco chicquera*	B	4
Buff-throated Partridge *Tetraophasis szechenyii*	B	2
White-cheeked Partridge *Arborophila atrogularis*	B	4
Satyr Tragopan *Tragopan satyra*	B	4
Temminck's Tragopan *Tragopan temminckii*	B	4
Grey Junglefowl *Gallus sonneratii*	B	1
Sarus Crane *Grus antigone*	B	8
Long-billed Plover *Charadrius placidus*	N	4/8
Grey-headed Lapwing *Vanellus cinereus*	N	3/11
Great Snipe *Gallinago media*	N	10/35
Asian Dowitcher *Limnodromus semipalmatus*	N	3/14
Nilgiri Wood-pigeon *Columba elphinstonii*	B	1
Andaman Wood-pigeon *Columba palumboides*	B	1
Andaman Cuckoo-dove *Macropygia rufipennis*	B	1
Nicobar Pigeon *Caloenas nicobarica*	B	11
Derbyan Parakeet *Psittacula derbiana*	B	2
Nicobar Parakeet *Psittacula caniceps*	B	1
Brown Coucal *Centropus andamanensis*	B	2
Andaman Scops-owl *Otus balli*	B	1
Spot-bellied Eagle-owl *Bubo nipalensis*	B	11
Tawny Fish-owl *Ketupa flavipes*	B	9
Andaman Hawk-owl *Ninox affinis*	B	1
Sri Lanka Frogmouth *Batrachostomus moniliger*	B	2
Brown-winged Kingfisher *Pelargopsis amauropterus*	B	5
Malabar Grey-hornbill *Ocyceros griseus*	B	1
Malabar Pied-hornbill *Anthracoceros coronatus*	B	2
Brown Hornbill *Anorrhinus tickelli*	B	6
Yellow-rumped Honeyguide *Indicator xanthonotus*	B	5
Andaman Woodpecker *Dryocopus hodgei*	B	1

Blue-naped Pitta *Pitta nipalensis*	B	8
White-bellied Minivet *Pericrocotus erythropygius*	B	2
Grey-headed Bulbul *Pycnonotus priocephalus*	B	1
Yellow-throated Bulbul *Pycnonotus xantholaemus*	B	1
Pied Thrush *Zoothera wardii*	B	3/2
Long-billed Thrush *Zoothera monticola*	B	6
Black-breasted Thrush *Turdus dissimilis*	B	4/2
Gould's Shortwing *Brachypteryx stellata*	B	6
White-bellied Shortwing *Brachypteryx major*	B	1
Firethroat *Luscinia pectardens*	N	1/2
Rufous-breasted Bush-robin *Tarsiger hyperythrus*	B	4/1
Blue-fronted Robin *Cinclidium frontale*	B	6
Purple Cochoa *Cochoa purpurea*	B	8
Green Cochoa *Cochoa viridis*	B	7
Jerdon's Bushchat *Saxicola jerdoni*	B	7
Chestnut-backed Laughingthrush *Garrulax nuchalis*	B	2
Yellow-throated Laughingthrush *Garrulax galbanus*	B	4
Wynaad Laughingthrush *Garrulax delesserti*	B	1
Rufous-breasted Laughingthrush *Garrulax cachinnans*	B	1
Grey-breasted Laughingthrush *Garrulax jerdoni*	B	1
Striped Laughingthrush *Garrulax virgatus*	B	2
Slender-billed Scimitar-babbler		
Xiphirhynchus superciliaris	B	7
Long-billed Wren-babbler *Rimator malacoptilus*	B	5
Spotted Wren-babbler *Spelaeornis formosus*	B	5
Wedge-billed Wren-babbler *Sphenocichla humei*	B	3
Slender-billed Babbler *Turdoides longirostris*	B	3
Giant Babax *Babax waddelli*	B	2
Black-headed Shrike-babbler *Pteruthius rufiventer*	B	6
Yellow-throated Fulvetta *Alcippe cinerea*	B	6
Rufous-throated Fulvetta *Alcippe rufogularis*	B	9
Grey Sibia *Heterophasia gracilis*	B	3
Black-browed Parrotbill *Paradoxornis atrosuperciliaris*	B	6
Rufous-headed Parrotbill *Paradoxornis ruficeps*	B	7
Grey-crowned Prinia *Prinia cinereocapilla*	B	3
Tytler's Leaf-warbler *Phylloscopus tytleri*	B	4
Yellow-vented Warbler *Phylloscopus cantator*	B	3/6
Broad-billed Warbler *Tickellia hodgsoni*	B	6
Broad-tailed Grassbird *Schoenicola platyura*	B	1
Brown-breasted Flycatcher *Muscicapa muttui*	B	2/4
Black-and-rufous Flycatcher *Ficedula nigrorufa*	B	1
Nilgiri Flycatcher *Eumyias albicaudata*	B	1
White-bellied Blue-flycatcher *Cyornis pallipes*	B	1
White-throated Tit *Aegithalos niveogularis*	B	3
Orange Bullfinch *Pyrrhula aurantiaca*	B	2
Spot-winged Starling *Saroglossa spiloptera*	B	2/5
White-headed Starling *Sturnus erythropygius*	B	1
Collared Myna *Acridotheres albocinctus*	B	3
Andaman Drongo *Dicrurus andamanensis*	B	2
White-bellied Treepie *Dendrocitta leucogastra*	B	1
Andaman Treepie *Dendrocitta bayleyi*	B	1

INDONESIA		**Species totals**	Critical	4	Extinct	1
			Endangered	16	Data Deficient	30
			Vulnerable	84	Near-threatened	152

Critical	Status (breeding/ non-br.)	Breeding/ non-br. countries	Habitat codes (p. 243)	Threat codes (p. 243)	IUCN threat status codes (pp. 16–18)
Bornean Peacock-pheasant *Polyplectron schleiermacheri*	B	2	F	19	**A1b**; A2b; **C1**; C2a; D1
Chinese Crested-tern *Sterna bernsteini*	N	1/5	MZ	09	**D1**

cont.

Indonesia (cont.)

Cerulean Paradise-flycatcher *Eutrichomyias rowleyi*	B	1	F	19	A1b; **B1+2c,e**; C1; **C2b**; **D1**; D2
Bali Starling *Leucopsar rothschildi*	B	1	FV	79	A1a,b,c; **B1+2e**; **C1**; **C2b**; **D1**; D2
Endangered					
Chinese Egret *Egretta eulophotes*	N	3/10	WR	1	**C1**; C2a
Storm's Stork *Ciconia stormi*	B	4	FW	19	A1b,c; **C1**; **C2a**; D1
White-shouldered Ibis *Pseudibis davisoni*	B	8	FW	1239	A1b; A2b; **C1**; **C2a**; D1
White-winged Duck *Cairina scutulata*	B	9	FW	1239	A1b,c,d; **C1**; **C2a**; D1
Javan Hawk-eagle *Spizaetus bartelsi*	B	1	F	1279	**C1**; **C2b**; D1
Nordmann's Greenshank *Tringa guttifer*	N	1/15	FW	12389	**C1**; C2b; D1
Red-and-blue Lory *Eos histrio*	B	1 ⋅	F	17	**A1b,c**; **A2b,c**; **B1+2c,d,e**; **C1**
Yellow-crested Cockatoo *Cacatua sulphurea*	B	1	F	17	**A1b,c**; **A2b,c**
Blue-naped Parrot *Tanygnathus lucionensis*	B	3	F	17	**A1b,c**; A2b,c; C1; C2a
Sangihe Hanging-parrot *Loriculus catamene*	B	1	FX	19	**B1+2c**; **C1**; **C2b**; D1; D2
Biak Gerygone *Gerygone hypoxantha*	B	1	F	19	A1b; **B1+2c**; **C2b**; D1
Lompobattang Flycatcher *Ficedula bonthaina*	B	1	F	1	**B1+2c**; C1; C2b
Flores Monarch *Monarcha sacerdotum*	B	1	F	19	B1+2c; C1; **C2b**
Black-chinned Monarch *Monarcha boanensis*	B	1	F	19	**B1+2c**; C1; C2b; **D1**
Biak Monarch *Monarcha brehmii*	B	1	F	19	A1b; **B1+2c**; **C2b**; D1
Elegant Sunbird *Aethopyga duyvenbodei*	B	1	F	19	A1b; **B1+2c**; C1; C2a; D2
Vulnerable					
Southern Cassowary *Casuarius casuarius*	B	3	F	126	A1a,b,c,d; A2b,c,d
Northern Cassowary *Casuarius unappendiculatus*	B	2	F	12	A1a,b,c; A2b,c
Spot-billed Pelican *Pelecanus philippensis*	N	3/8	W	1235	A1a,b,c,d; C1
Abbott's Booby *Papasula abbotti*	N	1/1	FM	189	C2b; D2
Christmas Island Frigatebird *Fregata andrewsi*	N	1/9	FM	9	D2
Japanese Night-heron *Gorsachius goisagi*	N	2/10	F	1	C1; C2a
Milky Stork *Mycteria cinerea*	B	4	FW	123	C1
Lesser Adjutant *Leptoptilos javanicus*	B	12/1	FW	123	C1
Salvadori's Teal *Salvadorina waigiuensis*	B	2	W	1236	C2a
New Guinea Harpy Eagle *Harpyopsis novaeguineae*	B	2	F	12	C1; C2b
Wallace's Hawk-eagle *Spizaetus nanus*	B	5	F	1	A1b; A2b; C1; C2a
Bruijn's Brush-turkey *Aepypodius bruijnii*	B	1	F	0189	D1
Maleo *Macrocephalon maleo*	B	1	FR	1238	C1; C2a
Moluccan Scrubfowl *Megapodius wallacei*	B	1	F	127	A2b,c; C1
Chestnut-necklaced Partridge *Arborophila charltonii*	B	4	F	1	A1b
Sumatran Pheasant *Lophura hoogerwerfi*	B	1	F	1	B1+2c; C1; C2a
Salvadori's Pheasant *Lophura inornata*	B	1	F	1	C1; C2a
Crestless Fireback *Lophura erythrophthalma*	B	3	F	1	A1b; A2b
Crested Fireback *Lophura ignita*	B	5	F	12	A1b,c; A2b,c
Bulwer's Pheasant *Lophura bulweri*	B	3	F	12	C2a
Green Peafowl *Pavo muticus*	B	7	FSG	12	A1b,c; A2b,c
Sumba Buttonquail *Turnix everetti*	B	1	G	19	C1; C2a; D1
Snoring Rail *Aramidopsis plateni*	B	1	F	16	C1; C2a
Bald-faced Rail *Gymnocrex rosenbergii*	B	1	F	1	C1; C2a
Invisible Rail *Habroptila wallacii*	B	1	W	016	C1
Masked Finfoot *Heliopais personata*	B	9	FW	13	C1; C2a
Moluccan Woodcock *Scolopax rochussenii*	B	1	F	9	D1; D2
Silvery Wood-pigeon *Columba argentina*	B	2	F	123	C1; C2a
Black Cuckoo-dove *Turacoena modesta*	B	1	F	12	A1b; C1; C2a
Wetar Ground-dove *Gallicolumba hoedtii*	B	1	F	1	C1; C2a
Timor Green-pigeon *Treron psittacea*	B	1	F	1	A1b; C1; C2a
Red-naped Fruit-dove *Ptilinopus dohertyi*	B	1	F	1	B1+2c; C1
Carunculated Fruit-dove *Ptilinopus granulifrons*	B	1	FA	1	A2b; B1+2c; C1; C2b
Grey Imperial-pigeon *Ducula pickeringii*	B	3	F	12	B1+2c,d,e; C1; C2a
Timor Imperial-pigeon *Ducula cineracea*	B	1	F	1	B1+2c; C1; C2a
Western Crowned-pigeon *Goura cristata*	B	1	F	127	A1a,b,c; A2b,c; C1; C2a
Victoria Crowned-pigeon *Goura victoria*	B	2	F	127	A1a,b,c; A2b,c; C1; C2a
Southern Crowned-pigeon *Goura scheepmakeri*	B	2	F	127	A1a,b,c; A2b,c
Black-winged Lory *Eos cyanogenia*	B	1	FX	127	A1b,c; B1+2c; C1
Iris Lorikeet *Psitteuteles iris*	B	1	F	1	C1; C2a
Chattering Lory *Lorius garrulus*	B	1	F	17	A2b,c
Purple-naped Lory *Lorius domicella*	B	1	F	7	B1+2e; C1
Blue-fronted Lorikeet *Charmosyna toxopei*	B	1	F	19	B1+2c; C1; C2b; D1

cont.

Indonesia (cont.)

Salmon-crested Cockatoo *Cacatua moluccensis*	B	1	F	17	A1b,c; A2b,c; B1+2c,e
White Cockatoo *Cacatua alba*	B	1	F	17	A2b,c
Salvadori's Fig-parrot *Psittaculirostris salvadorii*	B	1	F	17	A2b,c
Black-lored Parrot *Tanygnathus gramineus*	B	1	F	9	D2
Pesquet's Parrot *Psittrichas fulgidus*	B	2	F	127	A1c; A2b,c
Wallace's Hanging-parrot *Loriculus flosculus*	B	1	F	19	B1+2c; C1; C2a
Sunda Ground-cuckoo *Carpococcyx radiceus*	B	3	F	1	C2a
Sunda Coucal *Centropus nigrorufus*	B	1	FSW	1	A1b; C1; C2a
Taliabu Masked-owl *Tyto nigrobrunnea*	B	1	F	19	C2b; D1
White-fronted Scops-owl *Otus sagittatus*	B	4	F	1	A1b; A2b; C1; C2a
Javan Scops-owl *Otus angelinae*	B	1	F	9	D1; D2
Sumba Boobook *Ninox rudolfi*	B	1	F	1	B1+2c; C1
Satanic Eared-nightjar *Eurostopodus diabolicus*	B	1	F	19	D1
Volcano Swiftlet *Collocalia vulcanorum*	B	1	R	89	D1; D2
Lazuli Kingfisher *Todirhamphus lazuli*	B	1	FA	1	B1+2c; C1; C2a
Wrinkled Hornbill *Aceros corrugatus*	B	4	F	1	A1b; A2b; C1; C2a
Sumba Hornbill *Aceros everetti*	B	1	F	1	B1+2c; C1
Plain-pouched Hornbill *Aceros subruficollis*	B	3	F	1	C1; C2a
Schneider's Pitta *Pitta schneideri*	B	1	F	1	C1; C2a
Fairy Pitta *Pitta nympha*	N	4/6	F	17	C1; C2a
Buru Cuckoo-shrike *Coracina fortis*	B	1	F	1	B1+2c; C1; C2b
Straw-headed Bulbul *Pycnonotus zeylanicus*	B	5	F	17	A1b,c
Spot-necked Bulbul *Pycnonotus tympanistrigus*	B	1	F	1	C1; C2a
Sumatran Cochoa *Cochoa beccarii*	B	1	F	1	C1; C2a
Javan Cochoa *Cochoa azurea*	B	1	F	17	B1+2c
Vanderbilt's Babbler *Malacocincla vanderbilti*	B	1	F	019	C1; D1
Black-browed Babbler *Malacocincla perspicillata*	B	1	F	019	C1; D1
White-breasted Babbler *Stachyris grammiceps*	B	1	F	1	B1+2c,d; C1; C2a
Streaky-breasted Jungle-flycatcher *Rhinomyias addita*	B	1	F	9	D2
Damar Flycatcher *Ficedula henrici*	B	1	F	9	D2
Matinan Flycatcher *Cyornis sanfordi*	B	1	F	9	D2
Rueck's Blue-flycatcher *Cyornis ruckii*	B	1	F	019	C1; D1
White-tipped Monarch *Monarcha everetti*	B	1	FS	19	C2b; D2
Rufous-throated White-eye *Madanga ruficollis*	B	1	F	9	D2
Grey-banded Munia *Lonchura vana*	B	1	G	1	B1+2c
Java Sparrow *Padda oryzivora*	B	1	AU	7	A1c
Archbold's Bowerbird *Archboldia papuensis*	B	1	F	1	C1
Macgregor's Bird-of-paradise *Macgregoria pulchra*	B	2	F	2	B1+2e; C2a
Black Sicklebill *Epimachus fastuosus*	B	2	F	12	A2b,c; C2a
Banggai Crow *Corvus unicolor*	B	1	Z	9	D1
Flores Crow *Corvus florensis*	B	1	F	1	B1+2c; C1; C2a

Extinct

Javanese Lapwing *Vanellus macropterus* B 1

Data Deficient

Chestnut-shouldered Goshawk
 Erythrotriorchis buergersi B 2
White-striped Forest-rail *Rallina leucospila* B 1
Mayr's Forest-rail *Rallina mayri* B 2
New Guinea Flightless Rail *Megacrex inepta* B 2
Moluccan Cuckoo *Cacomantis heinrichi* B 1
Green-cheeked Bronze-cuckoo *Chrysococcyx rufomerus* B 1
Minahassa Masked-owl *Tyto inexspectata* B 1
Lesser Masked-owl *Tyto sororcula* B 1
Papuan Hawk-owl *Uroglaux dimorpha* B 2
Large Frogmouth *Batrachostomus auritus* B 4
Dulit Frogmouth *Batrachostomus harterti* B 2
Short-tailed Frogmouth *Batrachostomus poliolophus* B 1
Bornean Frogmouth *Batrachostomus mixtus* B 2
Salvadori's Nightjar *Caprimulgus pulchellus* B 1
Shovel-billed Kookaburra *Clytoceyx rex* B 2
Little Paradise-kingfisher *Tanysiptera hydrocharis* B 2
Blue-wattled Bulbul *Pycnonotus nieuwenhuisii* B 2
Moluccan Thrush *Zoothera dumasi* B 1

Papuan Whipbird *Androphobus viridis* B 2
Snow Mountain Robin *Petroica archboldi* B 1
Olive-yellow Robin *Poecilodryas placens* B 2
Sumba Brown Flycatcher *Muscicapa segregata* B 1
Obscure Berrypecker *Melanocharis arfakiana* B 2
Crimson-hooded Myzomela *Myzomela kuehni* B 1
Black-chested Honeyeater *Lichmera notabilis* B 1
Grey Friarbird *Philemon kisserensis* B 1
Brass's Friarbird *Philemon brassi* B 1
Dusky Friarbird *Philemon fuscicapillus* B 1
Wetar Figbird *Sphecotheres hypoleucus* B 1
Yellow-breasted Bird-of-paradise
 Loboparadisea sericea B 2

Near-threatened

Dwarf Cassowary *Casuarius bennetti* B 2
Oriental Darter *Anhinga melanogaster* B 13
Great-billed Heron *Ardea sumatrana* B 10
Forest Bittern *Zonerodius heliosylus* B 2
Schrenck's Bittern *Ixobrychus eurhythmus* N 5/10
Black-headed Ibis *Threskiornis melanocephalus* B 10/8
Jerdon's Baza *Aviceda jerdoni* B 9
Lesser Fish-eagle *Ichthyophaga humilis* B 9

cont.

Indonesia (cont.)

Grey-headed Fish-eagle *Ichthyophaga ichthyaetus*	B	13	Mangrove Pitta *Pitta megarhyncha*	B	5
Small Sparrowhawk *Accipiter nanus*	B	1	Pied Cuckoo-shrike *Coracina bicolor*	B	1
Doria's Goshawk *Megatriorchis doriae*	B	2	Sumba Cicadabird *Coracina dohertyi*	B	1
Rufous-winged Buzzard *Butastur liventer*	B	7	Kai Cicadabird *Coracina dispar*	B	1
Gurney's Eagle *Aquila gurneyi*	B	2	Hook-billed Bulbul *Setornis criniger*	B	3
Sulawesi Hawk-eagle *Spizaetus lanceolatus*	B	1	Blue-masked Leafbird *Chloropsis venusta*	B	1
Tabon Scrubfowl *Megapodius cumingii*	B	3	Bornean Bristlehead *Pityriasis gymnocephala*	B	3
Sula Scrubfowl *Megapodius bernsteinii*	B	1	Geomalia *Geomalia heinrichi*	B	1
Black Partridge *Melanoperdix nigra*	B	2	Slaty-backed Thrush *Zoothera schistacea*	B	1
Snow Mountain Quail *Anurophasis monorthonyx*	B	1	Red-backed Thrush *Zoothera erythronota*	B	1
Bronze-tailed Peacock-pheasant			Orange-banded Thrush *Zoothera peroni*	B	1
Polyplectron chalcurum	B	1	Fawn-breasted Thrush *Zoothera machiki*	B	1
Band-bellied Crake *Porzana paykullii*	N	2/7	White-bellied Bushchat *Saxicola gutturalis*	B	1
Malaysian Plover *Charadrius peronii*	B	6	Rufous-fronted Laughingthrush *Garrulax rufifrons*	B	1
Javan Plover *Charadrius javanicus*	B	1	White-chested Babbler *Trichastoma rostratum*	B	5
Sulawesi Woodcock *Scolopax celebensis*	B	1	Ferruginous Babbler *Trichastoma bicolor*	B	5
Latham's Snipe *Gallinago hardwickii*	N	1/5	Grey-breasted Babbler *Malacopteron albogulare*	B	3
Far Eastern Curlew *Numenius madagascariensis*	N	3/14	Long-billed Wren-babbler *Rimator malacoptilus*	B	5
Asian Dowitcher *Limnodromus semipalmatus*	N	3/14	Bornean Wren-babbler *Ptilocichla leucogrammica*	B	3
New Guinea Bronzewing *Henicophaps albifrons*	B	2	Large Wren-babbler *Napothera macrodactyla*	B	3
Nicobar Pigeon *Caloenas nicobarica*	B	11	Marbled Wren-babbler *Napothera marmorata*	B	2
Thick-billed Ground-pigeon *Trugon terrestris*	B	2	Spotted Crocias *Crocias albonotatus*	B	1
Cinnamon-headed Green-pigeon *Treron fulvicollis*	B	5	Timor Stubtail *Urosphena subulata*	B	1
Flores Green-pigeon *Treron floris*	B	1	Tanimbar Bush-warbler *Cettia carolinae*	B	1
Sumba Green-pigeon *Treron teysmannii*	B	1	Buff-banded Grassbird *Buettikoferella bivittata*	B	1
Large Green-pigeon *Treron capellei*	B	5	Broad-billed Fairywren *Malurus grayi*	B	2
Sumatran Green-pigeon *Treron oxyura*	B	1	Golden-bellied Flyrobin *Microeca hemixantha*	B	1
Blue-capped Fruit-dove *Ptilinopus monacha*	B	1	Russet-backed Jungle-flycatcher *Rhinomyias oscillans*	B	1
Sombre Pigeon *Cryptophaps poecilorrhoa*	B	1	Henna-tailed Jungle-flycatcher *Rhinomyias colonus*	B	1
Long-tailed Mountain-pigeon *Gymnophaps mada*	B	1	Rufous-throated Flycatcher *Ficedula rufigula*	B	1
Blue-streaked Lory *Eos reticulata*	B	1	Sumba Flycatcher *Ficedula harterti*	B	1
Blue-eared Lory *Eos semilarvata*	B	1	Black-banded Flycatcher *Ficedula timorensis*	B	1
Striated Lorikeet *Charmosyna multistriata*	B	2	Large-billed Blue-flycatcher *Cyornis caerulatus*	B	3
Palm Cockatoo *Probosciger aterrimus*	B	3	Malaysian Blue-flycatcher *Cyornis turcosus*	B	3
Tanimbar Cockatoo *Cacatua goffini*	B	1	Japanese Paradise-flycatcher *Terpsiphone atrocaudata*	N	4/8
Geelvink Pygmy-parrot *Micropsitta geelvinkiana*	B	1	Loetoe Monarch *Monarcha castus*	B	1
Blue-rumped Parrot *Psittinus cyanurus*	B	5	Black-bibbed Monarch *Monarcha mundus*	B	1
Yellowish-breasted Racquet-tail *Prioniturus flavicans*	B	1	Black-tipped Monarch *Monarcha loricatus*	B	1
Buru Racquet-tail *Prioniturus mada*	B	1	White-tailed Monarch *Monarcha leucurus*	B	1
Moluccan King-parrot *Alisterus amboinensis*	B	1	Biak Flycatcher *Myiagra atra*	B	1
Olive-shouldered Parrot *Aprosmictus jonquillaceus*	B	1	White-bellied Fantail *Rhipidura euryura*	B	1
Yellow-throated Hanging-parrot *Loriculus pusillus*	B	1	Cinnamon-tailed Fantail *Rhipidura fuscorufa*	B	1
Kai Coucal *Centropus spilopterus*	B	1	Tawny-backed Fantail *Rhipidura superflua*	B	1
Biak Coucal *Centropus chalybeus*	B	1	Long-tailed Fantail *Rhipidura opistherythra*	B	1
Short-toed Coucal *Centropus rectunguis*	B	3	Vogelkop Whistler *Pachycephala meyeri*	B	1
Wallace's Scops-owl *Otus silvicola*	B	1	Fawn-breasted Whistler *Pachycephala orpheus*	B	1
Javan Frogmouth *Batrachostomus javensis*	B	1	Brown-backed Flowerpecker *Dicaeum everetti*	B	2
Bonaparte's Nightjar *Caprimulgus concretus*	B	3	Javan White-eye *Zosterops flavus*	B	2
Waterfall Swift *Hydrochrous gigas*	B	2	Pearl-bellied White-eye *Zosterops grayi*	B	1
Blue-black Kingfisher *Todirhamphus nigrocyaneus*	B	2	Golden-bellied White-eye *Zosterops uropygialis*	B	1
Sombre Kingfisher *Todirhamphus funebris*	B	1	Pale-bellied White-eye *Zosterops consobrinorum*	B	1
Talaud Kingfisher *Todirhamphus enigma*	B	1	Lemon-throated White-eye *Zosterops anomalus*	B	1
Cinnamon-banded Kingfisher			Biak White-eye *Zosterops mysorensis*	B	1
Todirhamphus australasia	B	1	Ambon Yellow White-eye *Zosterops kuehni*	B	1
Biak Paradise-kingfisher *Tanysiptera riedelii*	B	1	Crested White-eye *Lophozosterops dohertyi*	B	1
Black Hornbill *Anthracoceros malayanus*	B	4	Spot-breasted White-eye *Heleia muelleri*	B	1
Helmeted Hornbill *Buceros vigil*	B	5	Red-rumped Myzomela *Myzomela vulnerata*	B	1
Brown-throated Barbet *Megalaima corvina*	B	1	Buru Honeyeater *Lichmera deningeri*	B	1
Red-crowned Barbet *Megalaima rafflesii*	B	5	Streaky-breasted Honeyeater *Meliphaga reticulata*	B	1
Black-banded Barbet *Megalaima javensis*	B	1	Plain Friarbird *Philemon inornatus*	B	1
Malaysian Honeyguide *Indicator archipelagicus*	B	4	Vogelkop Melidectes *Melidectes leucostephes*	B	1
Giant Pitta *Pitta caerulea*	B	4	Grey-crowned Munia *Lonchura nevermanni*	B	2
Blue-headed Pitta *Pitta baudii*	B	3	Black Munia *Lonchura stygia*	B	2
Sula Pitta *Pitta dohertyi*	B	1	Timor Sparrow *Padda fuscata*	B	1

cont.

Indonesia (cont.)

Asian Golden Weaver *Ploceus hypoxanthus*	B	6	Standardwing *Semioptera wallacii*	B	1
Tanimbar Starling *Aplonis crassa*	B	1	Long-tailed Paradigalla *Paradigalla carunculata*	B	1
Yellow-eyed Starling *Aplonis mystacea*	B	2	Pale-billed Sicklebill *Epimachus bruijnii*	B	2
Chestnut-cheeked Starling *Sturnus philippensis*	N	2/5	Wilson's Bird-of-paradise *Cicinnurus respublica*	B	1
Black-winged Starling *Sturnus melanopterus*	B	1	Arfak Astrapia *Astrapia nigra*	B	1
Helmeted Myna *Basilornis galeatus*	B	1	Red Bird-of-paradise *Paradisaea rubra*	B	1
Bare-eyed Myna *Streptocitta albertinae*	B	1	Black Magpie *Platysmurus leucopterus*	B	5
Sumatran Drongo *Dicrurus sumatranus*	B	1	Short-tailed Magpie *Cissa thalassina*	B	2
Golden-fronted Bowerbird *Amblyornis flavifrons*	B	1	Brown-headed Crow *Corvus fuscicapillus*	B	1

IRAN

Species totals Endangered 1 Near-threatened 10
Vulnerable 11

	Status (breeding/ non-br.)	Breeding/ non-br. countries	Habitat codes (p. 243)	Threat codes (p. 243)	IUCN threat status codes (pp. 16–18)
Endangered					
Siberian Crane *Grus leucogeranus*	N	1/5	W	129	**A2b,c**; C1; D2
Vulnerable					
Dalmatian Pelican *Pelecanus crispus*	B	16/9	W	1235	C2a
White-headed Duck *Oxyura leucocephala*	B	12/16	W	1256	A2d
Lesser White-fronted Goose *Anser erythropus*	N	4/11	SWA	012	A1a,b,c
Marbled Teal *Marmaronetta angustirostris*	B	21/3	W	125	A2b
Ferruginous Duck *Aythya nyroca*	B	38/32	W	12	A1a,b,c
Greater Spotted Eagle *Aquila clanga*	B	14/35	FW	13	C2a
Imperial Eagle *Aquila heliaca*	B	24/21	FG	12357	C2a
Lesser Kestrel *Falco naumanni*	B	37/52	FSVGA	15	A1a,b,d
Corncrake *Crex crex*	B	40/31	GWA	12	A1a,b
Great Bustard *Otis tarda*	B	23	GA	125	A2b
Sociable Lapwing *Vanellus gregarius*	N	2/15	GW	158	A1a,b; C1; C2a

Near-threatened

Pygmy Cormorant *Phalacrocorax pygmeus*	B	17/4	Little Bustard *Tetrax tetrax*	B	13/10
White-tailed Eagle *Haliaeetus albicilla*	B	34/10	Great Snipe *Gallinago media*	N	10/35
Cinereous Vulture *Aegypius monachus*	B	18/13	Black-winged Pratincole *Glareola nordmanni*	N	10/22
Pallid Harrier *Circus macrourus*	N	4/57	Iraq Babbler *Turdoides altirostris*	B	2
Caucasian Black Grouse *Tetrao mlokosiewiczi*	B	5	Cinereous Bunting *Emberiza cineracea*	B	3/13

IRAQ

Species totals Vulnerable 11
Near-threatened 5

	Status (breeding/ non-br.)	Breeding/ non-br. countries	Habitat codes (p. 243)	Threat codes (p. 243)	IUCN threat status codes (pp. 16–18)
Vulnerable					
Dalmatian Pelican *Pelecanus crispus*	N	16/9	W	1235	C2a
White-headed Duck *Oxyura leucocephala*	N	12/16	W	1256	A2d
Lesser White-fronted Goose *Anser erythropus*	N	4/11	SWA	012	A1a,b,c
Marbled Teal *Marmaronetta angustirostris*	B	21/3	W	125	A2b
Ferruginous Duck *Aythya nyroca*	N	38/32	W	12	A1a,b,c
Greater Spotted Eagle *Aquila clanga*	N	14/35	FW	13	C2a
Imperial Eagle *Aquila heliaca*	N	24/21	FG	12357	C2a
Lesser Kestrel *Falco naumanni*	N	37/52	FSVGA	15	A1a,b,d
Corncrake *Crex crex*	N	40/31	GWA	12	A1a,b
Great Bustard *Otis tarda*	B	23	GA	125	A2b
Sociable Lapwing *Vanellus gregarius*	N	2/15	GW	158	A1a,b; C1; C2a

Near-threatened

Pygmy Cormorant *Phalacrocorax pygmeus*	B	17/4	Iraq Babbler *Turdoides altirostris*	B	2
Pallid Harrier *Circus macrourus*	N	4/57	Basra Reed-warbler *Acrocephalus griseldis*	B	1/8
Black-winged Pratincole *Glareola nordmanni*	B	10/22			

IRELAND

Species totals   Vulnerable   1

Vulnerable	Status (breeding/ non-br.)	Breeding/ non-br. countries	Habitat codes (p. 243)	Threat codes (p. 243)	IUCN threat status codes (pp. 16–18)
Corncrake *Crex crex*	B	40/31	GWA	12	A1a,b

ISRAEL

Species totals   Vulnerable   8
   Near-threatened   6

Vulnerable	Status (breeding/ non-br.)	Breeding/ non-br. countries	Habitat codes (p. 243)	Threat codes (p. 243)	IUCN threat status codes (pp. 16–18)
White-headed Duck *Oxyura leucocephala*	N	12/16	W	1256	A2d
Marbled Teal *Marmaronetta angustirostris*	B	21/3	W	125	A2b
Ferruginous Duck *Aythya nyroca*	B	38/32	W	12	A1a,b,c
Greater Spotted Eagle *Aquila clanga*	N	14/35	FW	13	C2a
Imperial Eagle *Aquila heliaca*	B	24/21	FG	12357	C2a
Lesser Kestrel *Falco naumanni*	B	37/52	FSVGA	15	A1a,b,d
Corncrake *Crex crex*	N	40/31	GWA	12	A1a,b
Sociable Lapwing *Vanellus gregarius*	N	2/15	GW	158	A1a,b; C1; C2a

Near-threatened

Pygmy Cormorant *Phalacrocorax pygmeus*	N 17/4	Little Bustard *Tetrax tetrax*	N 13/10
White-tailed Eagle *Haliaeetus albicilla*	B 34/10	Black-winged Pratincole *Glareola nordmanni*	N 10/22
Pallid Harrier *Circus macrourus*	N 4/57	Cinereous Bunting *Emberiza cineracea*	N 3/13

ITALY

Species totals   Critical   1   Conservation
   Vulnerable   5   Dependent   1
   Near-threatened   3

	Status (breeding/ non-br.)	Breeding/ non-br. countries	Habitat codes (p. 243)	Threat codes (p. 243)	IUCN threat status codes (pp. 16–18)
Critical					
Slender-billed Curlew *Numenius tenuirostris*	N	1/10	WG	1289	**C2b**; D1
Vulnerable					
White-headed Duck *Oxyura leucocephala*	N	12/16	W	1256	A2d
Ferruginous Duck *Aythya nyroca*	B	38/32	W	12	A1a,b,c
Greater Spotted Eagle *Aquila clanga*	N	14/35	FW	13	C2a
Lesser Kestrel *Falco naumanni*	B	37/52	FSVGA	15	A1a,b,d
Corncrake *Crex crex*	B	40/31	GWA	12	A1a,b

Conservation Dependent

Audouin's Gull *Larus audouinii*   B 8/7

Near-threatened

Pygmy Cormorant *Phalacrocorax pygmeus*	B 17/4
Cinereous Vulture *Aegypius monachus*	N 18/13
Little Bustard *Tetrax tetrax*	B 13/10

IVORY COAST

Species totals   Endangered   2   Near-threatened   8
   Vulnerable   9

Endangered	Status (breeding/ non-br.)	Breeding/ non-br. countries	Habitat codes (p. 243)	Threat codes (p. 243)	IUCN threat status codes (pp. 16–18)
Rufous Fishing-owl *Scotopelia ussheri*	B	5	FW	15	A1b; A2b; B1+2b; C1; **C2a**
Gola Malimbe *Malimbus ballmanni*	B	4	F	1	A1b; **A2b**; B1+2a,b,c
Vulnerable					
Lesser Kestrel *Falco naumanni*	N	37/52	FSVGA	15	A1a,b,d
White-breasted Guineafowl *Agelastes meleagrides*	B	5	F	12	A1b,c; A2b,c
Western Wattled Cuckoo-shrike *Campephaga lobata*	B	5	F	1	A1b; A2b
Green-tailed Bristlebill *Bleda eximia*	B	5	F	1	A1b; A2b
Yellow-throated Olive Greenbul *Criniger olivaceus*	B	7	F	1	A1b; A2b

cont.

Ivory Coast (cont.)

White-necked Rockfowl *Picathartes gymnocephalus*	B	5	FR	127	A1b; A2b
White-eyed Prinia *Prinia leontica*	B	4	F	1	C2a
Black-capped Rufous Warbler *Bathmocercus cerviniventris*	B	5	F	1	C2a
Nimba Flycatcher *Melaenornis annamarulae*	B	4	F	1	A1b; A2b

Near-threatened

Pallid Harrier *Circus macrourus*	N 4/57	Lagden's Bush-shrike *Malaconotus lagdeni*	B 6	
Great Snipe *Gallinago media*	N 10/35	Rufous-winged Illadopsis *Illadopsis rufescens*	B 6	
Brown-cheeked Hornbill *Ceratogymna cylindricus*	B 7	Copper-tailed Glossy-starling		
Yellow-casqued Hornbill *Ceratogymna elata*	B 11	*Lamprotornis cupreocauda*	B 5	
Baumann's Greenbul *Phyllastrephus baumanni*	B 6			

JAMAICA

Species totals	Critical	3	Vulnerable	3
	Endangered	1	Near-threatened	5

	Status (breeding/ non-br.)	Breeding/ non-br. countries	Habitat codes (p. 243)	Threat codes (p. 243)	IUCN threat status codes (pp. 16–18)
Critical					
Jamaica Petrel *Pterodroma caribbaea*	B	1	FM	269	**C2b**; D1; D2
Ring-tailed Pigeon *Columba caribaea*	B	1	F	1289	A1b,c; **A2b,c**; B1+2c,e; C1; C2a;D1
Jamaican Pauraque *Siphonorhis americanus*	B	1	Z	169	**D1**
Endangered					
Plain Pigeon *Columba inornata*	B	5	FSVA	12	A1b; **C2a**
Vulnerable					
West Indian Whistling-duck *Dendrocygna arborea*	B	12	W	12	C2a
Piping Plover *Charadrius melodus*	N	2/9	W	138	C2a
Black-billed Amazon *Amazona agilis*	B	1	F	1278	C2a

Near-threatened

Crested Quail-dove *Geotrygon versicolor*	B 1	Blue Mountain Vireo *Vireo osburni*	B 1	
Yellow-billed Parrot *Amazona collaria*	B 1	Jamaican Blackbird *Nesopsar nigerrimus*	B 1	
Golden Swallow *Tachycineta euchrysea*	B 3			

JAPAN

Species totals	Critical	4	Conservation	
	Endangered	7	Dependent	1
	Vulnerable	20	Near-threatened	20
	Data Deficient	1		

	Status (breeding/ non-br.)	Breeding/ non-br. countries	Habitat codes (p. 243)	Threat codes (p. 243)	IUCN threat status codes (pp. 16–18)
Critical					
Black-faced Spoonbill *Platalea minor*	N	2/8	WR	12359	**A2b**; C1; C2a; D1; D2
Crested Shelduck *Tadorna cristata*	N	0/4	W	09	**D1**
Okinawa Woodpecker *Sapheopipo noguchii*	B	1	F	19	**B1+2c**; C1; **C2b**; D1; D2
Amami Thrush *Zoothera major*	B	1	F	19	A1b; B1+2c; C1; **C2b**; D1
Endangered					
Short-tailed Albatross *Diomedea albatrus*	B	2	RM	1489	**C1**; D1; D2
Chinese Egret *Egretta eulophotes*	N	3/10	WR	1	**C1**; C2a
Oriental Stork *Ciconia boyciana*	N	2/9	W	1235	A2b; **C1**
Okinawa Rail *Gallirallus okinawae*	B	1	F	19	**B1+2c**; C1; **C2b**; D1; D2
Nordmann's Greenshank *Tringa guttifer*	N	1/15	FW	12389	**C1**; C2b; D1
Saunders's Gull *Larus saundersi*	N	1/6	W	1235	A1b,c,d; **A2b,c,d**; C1; C2a
Blakiston's Fish-owl *Ketupa blakistoni*	B	3	FW	134	**C1**; **C2a**
Vulnerable					
Japanese Night-heron *Gorsachius goisagi*	B	2/10	F	1	C1; C2a
Swan Goose *Anser cygnoides*	N	4/5	W	12	A1b,c; A2b,c
Lesser White-fronted Goose *Anser erythropus*	N	4/11	SWA	012	A1a,b,c
Baikal Teal *Anas formosa*	N	1/5	FW	259	A1a,c,d; D2
Baer's Pochard *Aythya baeri*	N	2/12	W	123	A1a,b; C1
Scaly-sided Merganser *Mergus squamatus*	N	3/3	FW	1235	C1; C2a
Steller's Sea-eagle *Haliaeetus pelagicus*	N	1/4	FWR	1	C1; C2b
White-naped Crane *Grus vipio*	N	3/4	WA	12	C1

Japan (cont.)

Red-crowned Crane *Grus japonensis*	B	4/4	GWA	15	C1; C2a
Swinhoe's Rail *Coturnicops exquisitus*	N	2/4	GW	1	C1; C2a
Amami Woodcock *Scolopax mira*	B	1	F	16	A2d; B1+2c,e; C1
Spoon-billed Sandpiper *Eurynorhynchus pygmeus*	N	1/14	W	18	C1; C2b
Japanese Murrelet *Synthliboramphus wumizusume*	B	2/3	RM	1346	C1
Fairy Pitta *Pitta nympha*	B	4/6	F	17	C1; C2a
Izu Thrush *Turdus celaenops*	B	1	F	6	B1+2e; C1
Ijima's Leaf-warbler *Phylloscopus ijimae*	B	1/1	FS	01	C1; C2a
Marsh Grassbird *Megalurus pryeri*	B	2	GW	1	C1; C2a
Bonin Honeyeater *Apalopteron familiare*	B	1	FSAX	9	D2
Yellow Bunting *Emberiza sulphurata*	B	1/6	FSA	0	C1; C2a
Lidth's Jay *Garrulus lidthi*	B	1	F	1	C1; C2b

Conservation Dependent

Hooded Crane *Grus monacha*	N 2/4		Grey-headed Lapwing *Vanellus cinereus*	B 3/11

Data Deficient

		Latham's Snipe *Gallinago hardwickii*	B 1/5
Matsudaira's Storm-petrel *Oceanodroma matsudairae* B 1		Far Eastern Curlew *Numenius madagascariensis*	N 3/14

Near-threatened

		Asian Dowitcher *Limnodromus semipalmatus*	N 3/14
		Japanese Wood-pigeon *Columba janthina*	B 3
Swinhoe's Storm-petrel *Oceanodroma monorhis*	B 3	White-bellied Green-pigeon *Treron sieboldii*	B 6
Tristram's Storm-petrel *Oceanodroma tristrami*	B 2	Whistling Green-pigeon *Treron formosae*	B 3
Schrenck's Bittern *Ixobrychus eurhythmus*	B 5/10	Japanese Waxwing *Bombycilla japonica*	N 1/5
Black-headed Ibis *Threskiornis melanocephalus*	N 10/8	Ryukyu Robin *Erithacus komadori*	B 1
Mandarin Duck *Aix galericulata*	B 5/4	Japanese Paradise-flycatcher *Terpsiphone atrocaudata* B 4/8
White-tailed Eagle *Haliaeetus albicilla*	B 34/10	Ochre-rumped Bunting *Emberiza yessoensis*	B 3/3
Copper Pheasant *Syrmaticus soemmerringii*	B 1	Chestnut-cheeked Starling *Sturnus philippensis*	B 2/5
Long-billed Plover *Charadrius placidus*	B 4/8		

JORDAN

Species totals Vulnerable 4
Near-threatened 2

	Status (breeding/ non-br.)	Breeding/ non-br. countries	Habitat codes (p. 243)	Threat codes (p. 243)	IUCN threat status codes (pp. 16–18)
Vulnerable					
Ferruginous Duck *Aythya nyroca*	N	38/32	W	12	A1a,b,c
Greater Spotted Eagle *Aquila clanga*	N	14/35	FW	13	C2a
Imperial Eagle *Aquila heliaca*	N	24/21	FG	12357	C2a
Lesser Kestrel *Falco naumanni*	B	37/52	FSVGA	15	A1a,b,d

Near-threatened

Pallid Harrier *Circus macrourus*	N 4/57	Cinereous Bunting *Emberiza cineracea*	N 3/13

KAZAKHSTAN

Species totals Vulnerable 14
Near-threatened 6

	Status (breeding/ non-br.)	Breeding/ non-br. countries	Habitat codes (p. 243)	Threat codes (p. 243)	IUCN threat status codes (pp. 16–18)
Vulnerable					
Dalmatian Pelican *Pelecanus crispus*	B	16/9	W	1235	C2a
White-headed Duck *Oxyura leucocephala*	B	12/16	W	1256	A2d
Swan Goose *Anser cygnoides*	B	4/5	W	12	A1b,c; A2b,c
Marbled Teal *Marmaronetta angustirostris*	B	21/3	W	125	A2b
Ferruginous Duck *Aythya nyroca*	B	38/32	W	12	A1a,b,c
Pallas's Sea-eagle *Haliaeetus leucoryphus*	B	11/1	GW	135	C1; C2b
Greater Spotted Eagle *Aquila clanga*	B	14/35	FW	13	C2a
Imperial Eagle *Aquila heliaca*	B	24/21	FG	12357	C2a
Lesser Kestrel *Falco naumanni*	B	37/52	FSVGA	15	A1a,b,d
Corncrake *Crex crex*	B	40/31	GWA	12	A1a,b
Great Bustard *Otis tarda*	B	23	GA	125	A2b
Sociable Lapwing *Vanellus gregarius*	B	2/15	GW	158	A1a,b; C1; C2a
Pale-backed Pigeon *Columba eversmanni*	B	7/2	GDA	0	A1a
White-throated Bushchat *Saxicola insignis*	B	3/3	SGW	1	C1; C2a

cont.

Kazakhstan (cont.)

Near-threatened			
Pygmy Cormorant *Phalacrocorax pygmeus*	B 17/4	Little Bustard *Tetrax tetrax*	B 13/10
White-tailed Eagle *Haliaeetus albicilla*	B 34/10	Black-winged Pratincole *Glareola nordmanni*	B 10/22
Cinereous Vulture *Aegypius monachus*	B 18/13	White-winged Woodpecker *Dendrocopos leucopterus* B 7	

KENYA

Species totals: Critical 4 — Data Deficient 1; Endangered 2 — Near-threatened 17; Vulnerable 16

	Status (breeding/ non-br.)	Breeding/ non-br. countries	Habitat codes (p. 243)	Threat codes (p. 243)	IUCN threat status codes (pp. 16–18)
Critical					
Taita Thrush *Turdus helleri*	B	1	F	19	**B1+2a,b,c**; C2b; D1; D2
Taita Apalis *Apalis fuscigularis*	B	1	F	19	**B1+2b,c**; C2b; D1; D2
Kulal White-eye *Zosterops kulalensis*	B	1	F	19	**B1+2b,c**; C2b; D1; D2
Taita White-eye *Zosterops silvanus*	B	1	F	19	**B1+2b,c**; C2b; D1; D2
Endangered					
Spotted Ground-thrush *Zoothera guttata*	N	5/1	F	1	B1+2c; **C2a**
Hinde's Pied-babbler *Turdoides hindei*	B	1	SA	19	A1b,c; A2b,c; **B1+2a,c**; **C2a**; D1
Vulnerable					
Greater Spotted Eagle *Aquila clanga*	N	14/35	FW	13	C2a
Lesser Kestrel *Falco naumanni*	N	37/52	FSVGA	15	A1a,b,d
Taita Falcon *Falco fasciinucha*	B	8	VR	1589	C1; D1
Corncrake *Crex crex*	N	40/31	GWA	12	A1a,b
Sokoke Scops-owl *Otus ireneae*	B	2	F	9	D2
Blue Swallow *Hirundo atrocaerulea*	N	7/3	G	1	A1b; A2b; C1; C2a
Sokoke Pipit *Anthus sokokensis*	B	2	F	1	B1+2a,b,c; C2a
Grey-crested Helmet-shrike *Prionops poliolophus*	B	2	FSV	1	C2b
East Coast Akalat *Sheppardia gunningi*	B	4	F	1	B1+2b,c
White-winged Apalis *Apalis chariessa*	B	4	F	1	B1+2b,c
Papyrus Yellow Warbler *Chloropeta gracilirostris*	B	7	W	1	B1+2a,b,c,d
Turner's Eremomela *Eremomela turneri*	B	3	F	1	B1+2a,c
Chapin's Flycatcher *Muscicapa lendu*	B	3	F	1	B1+2a,c; C2a
Amani Sunbird *Anthreptes pallidigaster*	B	2	F	1	B1+2b,c
Clarke's Weaver *Ploceus golandi*	B	1	F	19	D1; D2
Abbott's Starling *Cinnyricinclus femoralis*	B	2	F	1	B1+2c; C2a

Data Deficient
Tana River Cisticola *Cisticola restrictus* — B 1

Near-threatened
Madagascar Pond-heron *Ardeola idae* — N 2/9
Lesser Flamingo *Phoenicopterus minor* — B 8/20
Southern Banded Snake-eagle *Circaetus fasciolatus* — B 6
Pallid Harrier *Circus macrourus* — N 4/57
Great Snipe *Gallinago media* — N 10/35
White-winged Collared-dove *Streptopelia reichenowi* — B 3
Fischer's Turaco *Tauraco fischeri* — B 3

Williams's Lark *Mirafra williamsi* — B 1
Friedmann's Lark *Mirafra pulpa* — B 2
Sharpe's Pipit *Macronyx sharpei* — B 1
Sharpe's Longclaw *Macronyx sharpei* — B 1
Malindi Pipit *Anthus melindae* — B 2
Papyrus Gonolek *Laniarius mufumbiri* — B 5
Basra Reed-warbler *Acrocephalus griseldis* — N 1/8
Red-throated Tit *Parus fringillinus* — B 2
Plain-backed Sunbird *Anthreptes reichenowi* — B 5
Jackson's Widowbird *Euplectes jacksoni* — B 2

KIRIBATI

Species totals: Endangered 1; Vulnerable 1

	Status (breeding/ non-br.)	Breeding/ non-br. countries	Habitat codes (p. 243)	Threat codes (p. 243)	IUCN threat status codes (pp. 16–18)
Endangered					
Kuhl's Lorikeet *Vini kuhlii*	B	2	FX	69	**B1+2e**; **C2a**; D2
Vulnerable					
Bristle-thighed Curlew *Numenius tahitiensis*	N	1/14	GW	1268	C2b

KUWAIT

		Species totals	Vulnerable	3	
			Near-threatened	1	

Vulnerable	Status (breeding/ non-br.)	Breeding/ non-br. countries	Habitat codes (p. 243)	Threat codes (p. 243)	IUCN threat status codes (pp. 16–18)
Greater Spotted Eagle *Aquila clanga*	N	14/35	FW	13	C2a
Imperial Eagle *Aquila heliaca*	N	24/21	FG	12357	C2a
Lesser Kestrel *Falco naumanni*	N	37/52	FSVGA	15	A1a,b,d
Near-threatened					
Cinereous Bunting *Emberiza cineracea*	N 3/13				

KYRGYZSTAN

		Species totals	Vulnerable	5	
			Near-threatened	3	

Vulnerable	Status (breeding/ non-br.)	Breeding/ non-br. countries	Habitat codes (p. 243)	Threat codes (p. 243)	IUCN threat status codes (pp. 16–18)
Lesser Kestrel *Falco naumanni*	B	37/52	FSVGA	15	A1a,b,d
Corncrake *Crex crex*	B	40/31	GWA	12	A1a,b
Great Bustard *Otis tarda*	B	23	GA	125	A2b
Sociable Lapwing *Vanellus gregarius*	N	2/15	GW	158	A1a,b; C1; C2a
Pale-backed Pigeon *Columba eversmanni*	B	7/2	GDA	0	A1a
Near-threatened					
Cinereous Vulture *Aegypius monachus*	B 18/13		White-winged Woodpecker *Dendrocopos leucopterus*	B 7	
Little Bustard *Tetrax tetrax*	B 13/10				

LAOS

		Species totals	Critical	1	Vulnerable	19
			Endangered	3	Near-threatened	45

Critical	Status (breeding/ non-br.)	Breeding/ non-br. countries	Habitat codes (p. 243)	Threat codes (p. 243)	IUCN threat status codes (pp. 16–18)
Giant Ibis *Pseudibis gigantea*	B	4	FW	1239	A1b; A2b,c; B1+2c; **C1**; C2a; D1
Endangered					
Greater Adjutant *Leptoptilos dubius*	B	8	FWU	129	A1b,c; **C1**; C2a; D1
White-shouldered Ibis *Pseudibis davisoni*	B	8	FW	1239	A1b; A2b; **C1**; **C2a**; D1
White-winged Duck *Cairina scutulata*	B	9	FW	1239	A1b,c,d; **C1**; **C2a**; D1
Vulnerable					
Lesser Adjutant *Leptoptilos javanicus*	B	12/1	FW	123	C1
Greater Spotted Eagle *Aquila clanga*	N	14/35	FW	13	C2a
Imperial Eagle *Aquila heliaca*	N	24/21	FG	12357	C2a
Lesser Kestrel *Falco naumanni*	N	37/52	FSVGA	15	A1a,b,d
Siamese Fireback *Lophura diardi*	B	4	F	12	A1b,c; A2b,c
Crested Argus *Rheinardia ocellata*	B	3	F	12	A1b,c
Green Peafowl *Pavo muticus*	B	7	FSG	12	A1b,c; A2b,c
Masked Finfoot *Heliopais personata*	B	9	FW	13	C1; C2a
Wood Snipe *Gallinago nemoricola*	N	4/6	SGW	1	C2a
Black-bellied Tern *Sterna acuticauda*	B	9	W	128	C1
Indian Skimmer *Rynchops albicollis*	B	7	W	1	C1; C2a
Pale-capped Pigeon *Columba punicea*	B	7	FSA	1	C1; C2a
Blyth's Kingfisher *Alcedo hercules*	B	9	F	1	A1b; A2b; C1; C2a
Rufous-necked Hornbill *Aceros nipalensis*	B	8	F	12	A1b,c; C1; C2a
Red-collared Woodpecker *Picus rabieri*	B	3	F	1	A1b
Short-tailed Scimitar-babbler *Jabouilleia danjoui*	B	2	F	1	A1b; A2b; C1; C2a
Sooty Babbler *Stachyris herberti*	B	2	F	1	C1; C2a
Short-tailed Parrotbill *Paradoxornis davidianus*	B	5	S	1	A1b; C1; C2a
Beautiful Nuthatch *Sitta formosa*	B	7	F	1	C1; C2a
Near-threatened					
Oriental Darter *Anhinga melanogaster*	B 13		Schrenck's Bittern *Ixobrychus eurhythmus*	N 5/10	

cont.

Laos (cont.)

Painted Stork *Mycteria leucocephala*	B	11	Bar-bellied Pitta *Pitta elliotii*	B	3
Black-headed Ibis *Threskiornis melanocephalus*	N	10/8	Blue-fronted Robin *Cinclidium frontale*	B	6
Jerdon's Baza *Aviceda jerdoni*	B	9	Purple Cochoa *Cochoa purpurea*	B	8
Lesser Fish-eagle *Ichthyophaga humilis*	B	9	Green Cochoa *Cochoa viridis*	B	7
Grey-headed Fish-eagle *Ichthyophaga ichthyaetus*	B	13	Jerdon's Bushchat *Saxicola jerdoni*	B	7
White-rumped Vulture *Gyps bengalensis*	B	11	Grey Laughingthrush *Garrulax maesi*	B	3
Long-billed Vulture *Gyps indicus*	B	9	Spot-breasted Laughingthrush *Garrulax merulinus*	B	6
Red-headed Vulture *Sarcogyps calvus*	B	11	Red-tailed Laughingthrush *Garrulax milnei*	B	5
Rufous-winged Buzzard *Butastur liventer*	B	7	Grey-faced Tit-babbler *Macronous kelleyi*	B	2
White-rumped Falcon *Polihierax insignis*	B	5	Yellow-throated Fulvetta *Alcippe cinerea*	B	6
Pied Falconet *Microhierax melanoleucus*	B	5	Spectacled Fulvetta *Alcippe ruficapilla*	B	2
Sarus Crane *Grus antigone*	B	8	Rufous-throated Fulvetta *Alcippe rufogularis*	B	9
Long-billed Plover *Charadrius placidus*	N	4/8	Black-browed Parrotbill		
Grey-headed Lapwing *Vanellus cinereus*	N	3/11	*Paradoxornis atrosuperciliaris*	B	6
Yellow-vented Green-pigeon *Treron seimundi*	B	4	Rufous-headed Parrotbill *Paradoxornis ruficeps*	B	7
White-bellied Green-pigeon *Treron sieboldii*	B	6	Yellow-vented Warbler *Phylloscopus cantator*	N	3/6
Coral-billed Ground-cuckoo *Carpococcyx renauldi*	B	4	Broad-billed Warbler *Tickellia hodgsoni*	B	6
Spot-bellied Eagle-owl *Bubo nipalensis*	B	11	Fujian Niltava *Niltava davidi*	B	3/2
Tawny Fish-owl *Ketupa flavipes*	B	9	Japanese Paradise-flycatcher *Terpsiphone atrocaudata*	N	4/8
Brown Hornbill *Anorrhinus tickelli*	B	6	Asian Golden Weaver *Ploceus hypoxanthus*	B	6
Blue-naped Pitta *Pitta nipalensis*	B	8	White-winged Magpie *Urocissa whiteheadi*	B	3
Blue-rumped Pitta *Pitta soror*	B	5	Yellow-breasted Magpie *Cissa hypoleuca*	B	4

LATVIA

	Species totals	Vulnerable	5
		Near-threatened	2

Vulnerable	Status (breeding/ non-br.)	Breeding/ non-br. countries	Habitat codes (p. 243)	Threat codes (p. 243)	IUCN threat status codes (pp. 16–18)
Ferruginous Duck *Aythya nyroca*	B	38/32	W	12	A1a,b,c
Steller's Eider *Polysticta stelleri*	N	2/8	WM	0	A1a
Greater Spotted Eagle *Aquila clanga*	B	14/35	FW	13	C2a
Corncrake *Crex crex*	B	40/31	GWA	12	A1a,b
Aquatic Warbler *Acrocephalus paludicola*	B	8/13	W	18	A2b

Near-threatened

White-tailed Eagle *Haliaeetus albicilla*	B 34/10		Great Snipe *Gallinago media*		B 10/35

LEBANON

	Species totals	Vulnerable	5
		Near-threatened	2

Vulnerable	Status (breeding/ non-br.)	Breeding/ non-br. countries	Habitat codes (p. 243)	Threat codes (p. 243)	IUCN threat status codes (pp. 16–18)
Dalmatian Pelican *Pelecanus crispus*	N	16/9	W	1235	C2a
Ferruginous Duck *Aythya nyroca*	N	38/32	W	12	A1a,b,c
Greater Spotted Eagle *Aquila clanga*	N	14/35	FW	13	C2a
Imperial Eagle *Aquila heliaca*	N	24/21	FG	12357	C2a
Lesser Kestrel *Falco naumanni*	N	37/52	FSVGA	15	A1a,b,d

Near-threatened

Pallid Harrier *Circus macrourus*	N 4/57		Cinereous Bunting *Emberiza cineracea*		N 3/13

LESOTHO

	Species totals	Vulnerable	3
		Near-threatened	6

Vulnerable	Status (breeding/ non-br.)	Breeding/ non-br. countries	Habitat codes (p. 243)	Threat codes (p. 243)	IUCN threat status codes (pp. 16–18)
Southern Bald Ibis *Geronticus calvus*	B	3	GR	1	C2b

cont.

Lesotho (cont.)

Cape Griffon *Gyps coprotheres*	B	6	SGDR	235	A1a,c,d; A2c,d; C1; C2b
Yellow-breasted Pipit *Anthus chloris*	B	2	G	1	B1+2c

Near-threatened

Black Harrier *Circus maurus*	B 3	Mountain Pipit *Anthus hoeschi*	B 2
Blue Bustard *Eupodotis caerulescens*	B 2	Orange-breasted Rockjumper *Chaetops aurantius*	B 2
Ground Woodpecker *Geocolaptes olivaceus*	B 2	Drakensberg Siskin *Serinus symonsi*	B 2

LIBERIA

Species totals	Critical	1	Vulnerable	10
	Endangered	2	Near-threatened	8

	Status (breeding/ non-br.)	Breeding/ non-br. countries	Habitat codes (p. 243)	Threat codes (p. 243)	IUCN threat status codes (pp. 16–18)
Critical					
Liberian Greenbul *Phyllastrephus leucolepis*	B	1	F	19	**A2b**; B1+2a; **C1**; **C2b**; D1
Endangered					
Rufous Fishing-owl *Scotopelia ussheri*	B	5	FW	15	A1b; A2b; B1+2b; C1; **C2a**
Gola Malimbe *Malimbus ballmanni*	B	4	F	1	A1b; **A2b**; B1+2a,b,c
Vulnerable					
Lesser Kestrel *Falco naumanni*	N	37/52	FSVGA	15	A1a,b,d
White-breasted Guineafowl *Agelastes meleagrides*	B	5	F	12	A1b,c; A2b,c
Yellow-footed Honeyguide *Melignomon eisentrauti*	B	3	F	1	A2b
Western Wattled Cuckoo-shrike *Campephaga lobata*	B	5	F	1	A1b; A2b
Green-tailed Bristlebill *Bleda eximia*	B	5	F	1	A1b; A2b
Yellow-throated Olive Greenbul *Criniger olivaceus*	B	7	F	1	A1b; A2b
White-necked Rockfowl *Picathartes gymnocephalus*	B	5	FR	127	A1b; A2b
White-eyed Prinia *Prinia leontica*	B	4	F	1	C2a
Black-capped Rufous Warbler *Bathmocercus cerviniventris*	B	5	F	1	C2a
Nimba Flycatcher *Melaenornis annamarulae*	B	4	F	1	A1b; A2b

Near-threatened

Pallid Harrier *Circus macrourus*	N 4/57	Lagden's Bush-shrike *Malaconotus lagdeni*	B 6
Great Snipe *Gallinago media*	N 10/35	Rufous-winged Illadopsis *Illadopsis rufescens*	B 6
Brown-cheeked Hornbill *Ceratogymna cylindricus*	B 7	Copper-tailed Glossy-starling	
Yellow-casqued Hornbill *Ceratogymna elata*	B 11	*Lamprotornis cupreocauda*	B 5
Baumann's Greenbul *Phyllastrephus baumanni*	B 6		

LIBYA

Species totals	Vulnerable	2	Conservation	
	Near-threatened	2	Dependent	1

	Status (breeding/ non-br.)	Breeding/ non-br. countries	Habitat codes (p. 243)	Threat codes (p. 243)	IUCN threat status codes (pp. 16–18)
Vulnerable					
Ferruginous Duck *Aythya nyroca*	N	38/32	W	12	A1a,b,c
Lesser Kestrel *Falco naumanni*	B	37/52	FSVGA	15	A1a,b,d

Conservation Dependent		**Near-threatened**	
Audouin's Gull *Larus audouinii*	N 8/7	Pallid Harrier *Circus macrourus*	N 4/57
		Little Bustard *Tetrax tetrax*	N 13/10

LIECHTENSTEIN

Species totals	Vulnerable	1

	Status (breeding/ non-br.)	Breeding/ non-br. countries	Habitat codes (p. 243)	Threat codes (p. 243)	IUCN threat status codes (pp. 16–18)
Vulnerable					
Corncrake *Crex crex*	B	40/31	GWA	12	A1a,b

LITHUANIA

Species totals Vulnerable 4
Near-threatened 2

	Status (breeding/ non-br.)	Breeding/ non-br. countries	Habitat codes (p. 243)	Threat codes (p. 243)	IUCN threat status codes (pp. 16–18)
Vulnerable					
Ferruginous Duck *Aythya nyroca*	B	38/32	W	12	A1a,b,c
Steller's Eider *Polysticta stelleri*	N	2/8	WM	0	A1a
Corncrake *Crex crex*	B	40/31	GWA	12	A1a,b
Aquatic Warbler *Acrocephalus paludicola*	B	8/13	W	18	A2b

Near-threatened

White-tailed Eagle *Haliaeetus albicilla*	B 34/10	Great Snipe *Gallinago media*	B 10/35

LUXEMBOURG

Species totals Vulnerable 1

	Status (breeding/ non-br.)	Breeding/ non-br. countries	Habitat codes (p. 243)	Threat codes (p. 243)	IUCN threat status codes (pp. 16–18)
Vulnerable					
Corncrake *Crex crex*	B	40/31	GWA	12	A1a,b

MADAGASCAR

Species totals Critical 5 Extinct 1
Endangered 5 Near-threatened 16
Vulnerable 18

	Status (breeding/ non-br.)	Breeding/ non-br. countries	Habitat codes (p. 243)	Threat codes (p. 243)	IUCN threat status codes (pp. 16–18)
Critical					
Alaotra Grebe *Tachybaptus rufolavatus*	B	1	W	12689	A1d; B1+2a,b,c,d,e; C1; C2b; **D1**
Madagascar Pochard *Aythya innotata*	B	1	W	09	A1a; **D1**
Madagascar Fish-eagle *Haliaeetus vociferoides*	B	1	FW	129	A2b; C1; **C2b**; D1
Madagascar Serpent-eagle *Eutriorchis astur*	B	1	F	1239	A1b,c; A2b; **C1**; **C2a**; D1
Sakalava Rail *Amaurornis olivieri*	B	1	W	0169	B1+2c; **C2a**; D1
Endangered					
Madagascar Teal *Anas bernieri*	B	1	W	1239	**C2b**; D1
Slender-billed Flufftail *Sarothrura watersi*	B	1	FWG	019	**B1+2c**; **C2b**; D1
Madagascar Red Owl *Tyto soumagnei*	B	1	F	19	**C2a**; D1
Yellow-bellied Asity *Neodrepanis hypoxanthus*	B	1	F	1	A2b; B1+2b,c; C1; **C2a**
Dusky Greenbul *Phyllastrephus tenebrosus*	B	1	F	1	C1; **C2a**
Vulnerable					
Madagascar Grebe *Tachybaptus pelzelnii*	B	1	W	168	A1a,b,d; A2b,d; C1; C2b
Madagascar Heron *Ardea humbloti*	B	1/2	W	2	C2a
White-breasted Mesite *Mesitornis variegata*	B	1	F	18	A2b; B1+2a,c
Brown Mesite *Mesitornis unicolor*	B	1	F	1	A2b; C1; C2a
Subdesert Mesite *Monias benschi*	B	1	S	126	A2b; B1+2c,e; C1; C2b
Madagascar Plover *Charadrius thoracicus*	B	1	GW	08	B1+2e; C2b
Short-legged Ground-roller *Brachypteracias leptosomus*	B	1	F	1	A2b; C1; C2a
Scaly Ground-roller *Brachypteracias squamiger*	B	1	F	126	A2b; C1; C2a
Rufous-headed Ground-roller *Atelornis crossleyi*	B	1	F	1	C2a
Long-tailed Ground-roller *Uratelornis chimaera*	B	1	S	126	B1+2c,e; C2b
Appert's Greenbul *Phyllastrephus apperti*	B	1	F	19	B1+2a,b,c,d; C1; C2a; D1
Grey-crowned Greenbul *Phyllastrephus cinereiceps*	B	1	F	1	B1+2c; C2a
Van Dam's Vanga *Xenopirostris damii*	B	1	F	19	D2
Pollen's Vanga *Xenopirostris polleni*	B	1	F	1	C2a
Bernier's Vanga *Oriolia bernieri*	B	1	F	1	C2a
Benson's Rock-thrush *Monticola bensoni*	B	1	SR	19	D1
Madagascar Yellowbrow *Crossleyia xanthophrys*	B	1	F	1	C2a
Red-tailed Newtonia *Newtonia fanovanae*	B	1	F	1	B1+2c; C2a

Extinct

Snail-eating Coua *Coua delalandei*	B 1

Near-threatened

Madagascar Pond-heron *Ardeola idae*	B 2/9

cont.

Madagascar (cont.)

Madagascar Crested Ibis *Lophotibis cristata*	B	1	Schlegel's Asity *Philepitta schlegeli*	B	1
Lesser Flamingo *Phoenicopterus minor*	N	8/20	Helmet Vanga *Euryceros prevostii*	B	1
Meller's Duck *Anas melleri*	B	1	Forest Rock-thrush *Monticola sharpei*	B	1
Madagascar Harrier *Circus maillardi*	B	3	Wedge-tailed Jery *Hartertula flavoviridis*	B	1
Madagascar Sparrowhawk *Accipiter madagascariensis*	B	1	Brown Emu-tail *Dromaeocercus brunneus*	B	1
Henst's Goshawk *Accipiter henstii*	B	1	Rand's Warbler *Randia pseudozosterops*	B	1
Verreaux's Coua *Coua verreauxi*	B	1	Ward's Flycatcher *Pseudobias wardi*	B	1
Pitta-like Ground-roller *Atelornis pittoides*	B	1			

MALAWI

Species totals Endangered 1 Near-threatened 8
Vulnerable 8

	Status (breeding/ non-br.)	Breeding/ non-br. countries	Habitat codes (p. 243)	Threat codes (p. 243)	IUCN threat status codes (pp. 16–18)
Endangered					
Spotted Ground-thrush *Zoothera guttata*	B	5/1	F	1	B1+2c; **C2a**
Vulnerable					
Lesser Kestrel *Falco naumanni*	N	37/52	FSVGA	15	A1a,b,d
Taita Falcon *Falco fasciinucha*	B	8	VR	1589	C1; D1
Wattled Crane *Grus carunculatus*	B	11	W	123	A2b,c; C1
Corncrake *Crex crex*	N	40/31	GWA	12	A1a,b
Blue Swallow *Hirundo atrocaerulea*	B	7/3	G	1	A1b; A2b; C1; C2a
Thyolo Alethe *Alethe choloensis*	B	2	F	1	B1+2c
East Coast Akalat *Sheppardia gunningi*	B	4	F	1	B1+2b,c
White-winged Apalis *Apalis chariessa*	B	4	F	1	B1+2b,c

Near-threatened					
Madagascar Pond-heron *Ardeola idae*	N	2/9	Great Snipe *Gallinago media*	N	10/35
Shoebill *Balaeniceps rex*	B	8/1	Stierling's Woodpecker *Dendropicos stierlingi*	B	3
Lesser Flamingo *Phoenicopterus minor*	N	8/20	Churring Cisticola *Cisticola njombe*	B	3
Pallid Harrier *Circus macrourus*	N	4/57	Basra Reed-warbler *Acrocephalus griseldis*	N	1/8

MALAYSIA

Species totals Critical 2 Data Deficient 4
Endangered 6 Near-threatened 52
Vulnerable 23

	Status (breeding/ non-br.)	Breeding/ non-br. countries	Habitat codes (p. 243)	Threat codes (p. 243)	IUCN threat status codes (pp. 16–18)
Critical					
Bornean Peacock-pheasant *Polyplectron schleiermacheri*	B	2	F	19	**A1b**; A2b; **C1**; **C2a**; D1
Chinese Crested-tern *Sterna bernsteini*	N	1/5	MZ	09	**D1**
Endangered					
Chinese Egret *Egretta eulophotes*	N	3/10	WR	1	**C1**; **C2a**
Storm's Stork *Ciconia stormi*	B	4	FW	19	A1b,c; **C1**; **C2a**; D1
White-shouldered Ibis *Pseudibis davisoni*	B	8	FW	1239	A1b; A2b; **C1**; **C2a**; D1
White-winged Duck *Cairina scutulata*	B	9	FW	1239	A1b,c,d; **C1**; **C2a**; D1
Nordmann's Greenshank *Tringa guttifer*	N	1/15	FW	12389	**C1**; C2b; D1
Blue-naped Parrot *Tanygnathus lucionensis*	B	3	F	17	**A1b,c**; A2b,c; C1; C2a
Vulnerable					
Christmas Island Frigatebird *Fregata andrewsi*	N	1/9	FM	9	D2
Milky Stork *Mycteria cinerea*	B	4	FW	123	C1
Lesser Adjutant *Leptoptilos javanicus*	B	12/1	FW	123	C1
Greater Spotted Eagle *Aquila clanga*	N	14/35	FW	13	C2a
Wallace's Hawk-eagle *Spizaetus nanus*	B	5	F	1	A1b; A2b; C1; C2a
Chestnut-necklaced Partridge *Arborophila charltonii*	B	4	F	1	A1b
Crestless Fireback *Lophura erythrophthalma*	B	3	F	1	A1b; A2b
Crested Fireback *Lophura ignita*	B	5	F	12	A1b,c; A2b,c
Bulwer's Pheasant *Lophura bulweri*	B	3	F	12	C2a
Mountain Peacock-pheasant *Polyplectron inopinatum*	B	1	F	1	B1+2c; C1; C2a
Malayan Peacock-pheasant *Polyplectron malacense*	B	2	F	1	A1b; A2b; C1; C2a
Crested Argus *Rheinardia ocellata*	B	3	F	12	A1b,c

cont.

Malaysia (cont.)

Masked Finfoot *Heliopais personata*	B	9	FW	13	C1; C2a
Spoon-billed Sandpiper *Eurynorhynchus pygmeus*	N	1/14	W	18	C1; C2b
Silvery Wood-pigeon *Columba argentina*	B	2	F	123	C1; C2a
Grey Imperial-pigeon *Ducula pickeringii*	B	3	F	12	B1+2c,d,e; C1; C2a
Sunda Ground-cuckoo *Carpococcyx radiceus*	B	3	F	1	C2a
White-fronted Scops-owl *Otus sagittatus*	B	4	F	1	A1b; A2b; C1; C2a
Wrinkled Hornbill *Aceros corrugatus*	B	4	F	1	A1b; A2b; C1; C2a
Fairy Pitta *Pitta nympha*	N	4/6	F	17	C1; C2a
Straw-headed Bulbul *Pycnonotus zeylanicus*	B	5	F	17	A1b,c
Rufous-headed Robin *Luscinia ruficeps*	N	1/1	F	1	C1; C2a
Brown-chested Jungle-flycatcher *Rhinomyias brunneata*	N	1/5	F	1	A1b; A2b

Data Deficient

Mountain Serpent-eagle *Spilornis kinabaluensis*	B	2
Large Frogmouth *Batrachostomus auritus*	B	4
Dulit Frogmouth *Batrachostomus harterti*	B	2
Bornean Frogmouth *Batrachostomus mixtus*	B	2

Near-threatened

Oriental Darter *Anhinga melanogaster*	B	13
Great-billed Heron *Ardea sumatrana*	B	10
Schrenck's Bittern *Ixobrychus eurhythmus*	N	5/10
Black-headed Ibis *Threskiornis melanocephalus*	N	10/8
Jerdon's Baza *Aviceda jerdoni*	B	9
Lesser Fish-eagle *Ichthyophaga humilis*	B	9
Grey-headed Fish-eagle *Ichthyophaga ichthyaetus*	B	13
White-rumped Vulture *Gyps bengalensis*	B	11
Long-billed Vulture *Gyps indicus*	B	9
Red-headed Vulture *Sarcogyps calvus*	B	11
White-fronted Falconet *Microhierax latifrons*	B	1
Tabon Scrubfowl *Megapodius cumingii*	B	3
Black Partridge *Melanoperdix nigra*	B	2
Band-bellied Crake *Porzana paykullii*	N	2/7
Long-billed Plover *Charadrius placidus*	N	4/8
Malaysian Plover *Charadrius peronii*	B	6
Far Eastern Curlew *Numenius madagascariensis*	N	3/14
Asian Dowitcher *Limnodromus semipalmatus*	N	3/14
Nicobar Pigeon *Caloenas nicobarica*	B	11
Cinnamon-headed Green-pigeon *Treron fulvicollis*	B	5
Large Green-pigeon *Treron capellei*	B	5
Yellow-vented Green-pigeon *Treron seimundi*	B	4
Blue-rumped Parrot *Psittinus cyanurus*	B	5
Short-toed Coucal *Centropus rectunguis*	B	3
Bonaparte's Nightjar *Caprimulgus concretus*	B	3
Waterfall Swift *Hydrochrous gigas*	B	2
Brown-winged Kingfisher *Pelargopsis amauropterus*	B	5
Black Hornbill *Anthracoceros malayanus*	B	4
Helmeted Hornbill *Buceros vigil*	B	5
Red-crowned Barbet *Megalaima rafflesii*	B	5
Malaysian Honeyguide *Indicator archipelagicus*	B	4
Giant Pitta *Pitta caerulea*	B	4
Blue-headed Pitta *Pitta baudii*	B	3
Mangrove Pitta *Pitta megarhyncha*	B	5
Hook-billed Bulbul *Setornis criniger*	B	3
Bornean Bristlehead *Pityriasis gymnocephala*	B	3
Malayan Whistling-thrush *Myiophonus robinsoni*	B	1
Everett's Thrush *Zoothera everetti*	B	1
White-chested Babbler *Trichastoma rostratum*	B	5
Ferruginous Babbler *Trichastoma bicolor*	B	5
Grey-breasted Babbler *Malacopteron albogulare*	B	3
Bornean Wren-babbler *Ptilocichla leucogrammica*	B	3
Large Wren-babbler *Napothera macrodactyla*	B	3
Marbled Wren-babbler *Napothera marmorata*	B	2
Large-billed Blue-flycatcher *Cyornis caerulatus*	B	3
Malaysian Blue-flycatcher *Cyornis turcosus*	B	3
Japanese Paradise-flycatcher *Terpsiphone atrocaudata*	N	4/8
Brown-backed Flowerpecker *Dicaeum everetti*	B	2
Javan White-eye *Zosterops flavus*	B	2
Black Oriole *Oriolus hosii*	B	1
Black Magpie *Platysmurus leucopterus*	B	5
Short-tailed Magpie *Cissa thalassina*	B	2

MALDIVES

Species totals   Vulnerable   1

	Status (breeding/ non-br.)	Breeding/ non-br. countries	Habitat codes (p. 243)	Threat codes (p. 243)	IUCN threat status codes (pp. 16–18)
Vulnerable					
Lesser Kestrel *Falco naumanni*	N	37/52	FSVGA	15	A1a,b,d

MALI

Species totals   Vulnerable   5   Near-threatened   6
Data Deficient 1

	Status (breeding/ non-br.)	Breeding/ non-br. countries	Habitat codes (p. 243)	Threat codes (p. 243)	IUCN threat status codes (pp. 16–18)
Vulnerable					
Marbled Teal *Marmaronetta angustirostris*	N	21/3	W	125	A2b
Ferruginous Duck *Aythya nyroca*	N	38/32	W	12	A1a,b,c
Lesser Kestrel *Falco naumanni*	N	37/52	FSVGA	15	A1a,b,d
Yellow-throated Olive Greenbul *Criniger olivaceus*	B	7	F	1	A1b; A2b
Aquatic Warbler *Acrocephalus paludicola*	N	8/13	W	18	A2b

cont.

Mali (cont.)

Data Deficient		Great Snipe *Gallinago media*	N 10/35
River Prinia *Prinia fluviatilis*	B 5	Black-winged Pratincole *Glareola nordmanni*	N 10/22
Near-threatened		Yellow-casqued Hornbill *Ceratogymna elata*	B 11
Pallid Harrier *Circus macrourus*	N 4/57	Mali Firefinch *Lagonosticta virata*	B 1
Nubian Bustard *Neotis nuba*	B 5		

MALTA

Species totals Vulnerable 2

	Status (breeding/ non-br.)	Breeding/ non-br. countries	Habitat codes (p. 243)	Threat codes (p. 243)	IUCN threat status codes (pp. 16–18)
Vulnerable					
Ferruginous Duck *Aythya nyroca*	N	38/32	W	12	A1a,b,c
Lesser Kestrel *Falco naumanni*	N	37/52	FSVGA	15	A1a,b,d

MARSHALL ISLANDS

Species totals Vulnerable 1

	Status (breeding/ non-br.)	Breeding/ non-br. countries	Habitat codes (p. 243)	Threat codes (p. 243)	IUCN threat status codes (pp. 16–18)
Vulnerable					
Bristle-thighed Curlew *Numenius tahitiensis*	N	1/14	GW	1268	C2b

MARTINIQUE (to France)

Species totals Endangered 2
Near-threatened 1

	Status (breeding/ non-br.)	Breeding/ non-br. countries	Habitat codes (p. 243)	Threat codes (p. 243)	IUCN threat status codes (pp. 16–18)
Endangered					
White-breasted Thrasher *Ramphocinclus brachyurus*	B	2	F	169	A1a,b,d; A2b,d; **B1+2e**; **C1**; **C2a**; **D1**; D2
Martinique Oriole *Icterus bonana*	B	1	F	89	**A1d**; A2d; **B1+2e**; **C1**; **C2b**; D1
Near-threatened					
Bridled Quail-dove *Geotrygon mystacea*	B 13				

MAURITANIA

Species totals Vulnerable 3 Conservation
Near-threatened 5 Dependent 1

	Status (breeding/ non-br.)	Breeding/ non-br. countries	Habitat codes (p. 243)	Threat codes (p. 243)	IUCN threat status codes (pp. 16–18)
Vulnerable					
Lesser Kestrel *Falco naumanni*	N	37/52	FSVGA	15	A1a,b,d
Corncrake *Crex crex*	N	40/31	GWA	12	A1a,b
Aquatic Warbler *Acrocephalus paludicola*	N	8/13	W	18	A2b

Conservation Dependent		Pallid Harrier *Circus macrourus*	N 4/57
Audouin's Gull *Larus audouinii*	N 8/7	Nubian Bustard *Neotis nuba*	B 5
Near-threatened		Great Snipe *Gallinago media*	N 10/35
Lesser Flamingo *Phoenicopterus minor*	B 8/20	Black-winged Pratincole *Glareola nordmanni*	N 10/22

MAURITIUS

Species totals   Critical   5   Vulnerable   3
   Endangered   1

	Status (breeding/ non-br.)	Breeding/ non-br. countries	Habitat codes (p. 243)	Threat codes (p. 243)	IUCN threat status codes (pp. 16–18)
Critical					
Pink Pigeon *Columba mayeri*	B	1	FSX	1689	B1+2c; **D1**; D2
Mauritius Parakeet *Psittacula eques*	B	1	F	9	**D1**
Rodrigues Warbler *Acrocephalus rodericanus*	B	1	S	1689	**D1**; D2
Mauritius Olive White-eye *Zosterops chloronothos*	B	1	F	169	**A1a**; **B1+2c**; **C2b**; D1; D2
Mauritius Fody *Foudia rubra*	B	1	FX	169	A1a,b; **B1+2a,b,c,e**; **C2b**; D1; D2
Endangered					
Mauritius Kestrel *Falco punctatus*	B	1	FSR	09	**D1**
Vulnerable					
Mauritius Cuckoo-shrike *Coracina typica*	B	1	F	169	D1
Mauritius Bulbul *Hypsipetes olivaceus*	B	1	F	169	D1
Rodrigues Fody *Foudia flavicans*	B	1	F	1689	D1; D2

MAYOTTE (to France)

Species totals   Critical   1
   Vulnerable   1

	Status (breeding/ non-br.)	Breeding/ non-br. countries	Habitat codes (p. 243)	Threat codes (p. 243)	IUCN threat status codes (pp. 16–18)
Critical					
Mayotte Drongo *Dicrurus waldenii*	B	1	FSX	19	B1+2c; **C2b**; **D1**
Vulnerable					
Madagascar Heron *Ardea humbloti*	N	1/2	W	2	C2a

MEXICO

Species totals   Critical   4   Extinct in the Wild   1
   Endangered   16   Data Deficient   2
   Vulnerable   14   Near-threatened   40

	Status (breeding/ non-br.)	Breeding/ non-br. countries	Habitat codes (p. 243)	Threat codes (p. 243)	IUCN threat status codes (pp. 16–18)
Critical					
Guadalupe Storm-petrel *Oceanodroma macrodactyla*	B	1	FM	69	**D1**; D2
Bearded Wood-partridge *Dendrortyx barbatus*	B	1	F	129	A1b,c; **A2b,c**; B1+2c; C1; C2a; D1
Imperial Woodpecker *Campephilus imperialis*	B	1	F	129	**D1**
Guadalupe Junco *Junco insularis*	B	1	F	169	**B1+2e**; **C2b**; D1; D2
Endangered					
Veracruz Quail-dove *Geotrygon carrikeri*	B	1	F	1	A1b; **A2b**; **C1**; **C2a**
Thick-billed Parrot *Rhynchopsitta pachyrhyncha*	B	2	F	1	A1b; **A2b**; **C1**; **C2a**
Green-cheeked Amazon *Amazona viridigenalis*	B	1	F	17	**A1a,b,c**; A2b,c; C1; C2a
Yellow-headed Amazon *Amazona oratrix*	B	3	FV	17	**A1a,b,c**; A2b,c; C1; C2a
Short-crested Coquette *Lophornis brachylopha*	B	1	F	19	**A2b**; **B1+2c**; C1; C2b
White-tailed Hummingbird *Eupherusa poliocerca*	B	1	F	1	A1b; **A2b**; B1+2c
Oaxaca Hummingbird *Eupherusa cyanophrys*	B	1	F	19	A1b; **A2b**; **B1+2c**; C1; C2a
Eared Quetzal *Euptilotis neoxenus*	B	2	F	1	A1b; A2b; C1; **C2b**
Socorro Mockingbird *Mimodes graysoni*	B	1	FS	169	A1b,d; **B1+2e**; C1; **C2b**; D1
Sierra Madre Sparrow *Xenospiza baileyi*	B	1	G	19	A1a; **B1+2c**; **C1**; **C2a**; D1
Worthen's Sparrow *Spizella wortheni*	B	1	SG	19	B1+2c; **C2a**; D1
Azure-rumped Tanager *Tangara cabanisi*	B	2	F	19	**A2b**; B1+2c; C1; C2a; D1
Golden-cheeked Warbler *Dendroica chrysoparia*	N	1/4	FS	18	**A1b,d**; A2d; C1; C2a
Black-capped Vireo *Vireo atricapillus*	B	2	FSG	18	**A1b,c**; **A2c**; C1
Dwarf Jay *Cyanolyca nana*	B	1	F	1	A1b; **A2b**; **B1+2c**; **C1**; C2b
White-throated Jay *Cyanolyca mirabilis*	B	1	F	1	A1b; **A2b**; **B1+2c**; **C1**; **C2a**
Vulnerable					
Townsend's Shearwater *Puffinus auricularis*	B	1	RM	689	A1d; A2d; B1+2e; C1; C2b
Black-vented Shearwater *Puffinus opisthomelas*	B	1	GRM	469	D2
Horned Guan *Oreophasis derbianus*	B	2	F	12	C2a
Piping Plover *Charadrius melodus*	N	2/9	W	138	C2a
Mountain Plover *Charadrius montanus*	N	1/1	G	1	A1b

cont.

Military Macaw *Ara militaris*	B	11	F	17	A1b; C2a
Socorro Parakeet *Aratinga brevipes*	B	1	F	169	D1
Maroon-fronted Parrot *Rhynchopsitta terrisi*	B	1	FR	1	B1+2c; C2a
Mexican Woodnymph *Thalurania ridgwayi*	B	1	F	1	B1+2c
Sumichrast's Wren *Hylorchilus sumichrasti*	B	1	F	1	A1b; A2b; B1+2c; C1; C2a
Nava's Wren *Hylorchilus navai*	B	1	F	1	A1b; A2b; B1+2c; C1; C2a
Clarión Wren *Troglodytes tanneri*	B	1	SR	9	D1; D2
Belding's Yellowthroat *Geothlypis beldingi*	B	1	W	18	A1b; A2b; B1+2c
Black-polled Yellowthroat *Geothlypis speciosa*	B	1	W	1	A1b; A2b; B1+2c; C1; C2a

Extinct in the Wild

Socorro Dove *Zenaida graysoni*	B	1	FS	169	

Data Deficient

White-fronted Swift *Cypseloides storeri*	B	1	Eared Poorwill *Otophanes mcleodii*	B	1
Sinaloa Martin *Progne sinaloae*	B	1	Long-tailed Sabrewing *Campylopterus excellens*	B	1

Near-threatened

			Resplendent Quetzal *Pharomachrus mocinno*	B	7
Ashy Storm-petrel *Oceanodroma homochroa*	B	2	Keel-billed Motmot *Electron carinatum*	B	6
Agami Heron *Agamia agami*	B	16	Belted Flycatcher *Xenotriccus callizonus*	B	2
Solitary Eagle *Harpyhaliaetus solitarius*	B	17	Pileated Flycatcher *Xenotriccus mexicanus*	B	1
Harpy Eagle *Harpia harpyja*	B	17	Socorro Wren *Thryomanes sissonii*	B	1
Black-and-white Hawk-eagle *Spizastur melanoleucus*	B	14	Black Catbird *Melanoptila glabrirostris*	B	4
Orange-breasted Falcon *Falco deiroleucus*	B	17	Cozumel Thrasher *Toxostoma guttatum*	B	1
Long-tailed Wood-partridge *Dendrortyx macroura*	B	1	Grayson's Thrush *Turdus graysoni*	B	1
Ocellated Quail *Cyrtonyx ocellatus*	B	4	Cinnamon-tailed Sparrow *Aimophila sumichrasti*	B	1
Ocellated Turkey *Agriocharis ocellata*	B	3	Oaxaca Sparrow *Aimophila notosticta*	B	1
Hudsonian Godwit *Limosa haemastica*	N	2/11	Slate-blue Seedeater *Amaurospiza relicta*	B	1
Heermann's Gull *Larus heermanni*	B	2	Rose-bellied Bunting *Passerina rositae*	B	1
Elegant Tern *Sterna elegans*	B	2	Colima Warbler *Vermivora crissalis*	B	2
Xantus's Murrelet *Synthliboramphus hypoleucus*	B	3	Altamira Yellowthroat *Geothlypis flavovelata*	B	1
Craveri's Murrelet *Synthliboramphus craveri*	B	2	Pink-headed Warbler *Ergaticus versicolor*	B	2
Lilac-crowned Parrot *Amazona finschi*	B	1	Chestnut-sided Shrike-vireo *Vireolanius melitophrys*	B	2
Santa Barbara Screech-owl *Otus barbarus*	B	2	Slaty Vireo *Vireo brevipennis*	B	1
Spotted Owl *Strix occidentalis*	B	3	Dwarf Vireo *Vireo nelsoni*	B	1
Unspotted Saw-whet Owl *Aegolius ridgwayi*	B	4	Black-capped Siskin *Carduelis atriceps*	B	2
			Tufted Jay *Cyanocorax dickeyi*	B	1

MICRONESIA

Species totals Critical 1 Vulnerable 1
Endangered 3 Near-threatened 4

	Status (breeding/ non-br.)	Breeding/ non-br. countries	Habitat codes (p. 243)	Threat codes (p. 243)	IUCN threat status codes (pp. 16–18)
Critical					
Pohnpei Mountain Starling *Aplonis pelzelni*	B	1	F	69	A1a; **B1+2b,e; C2b; D1**; D2
Endangered					
Caroline Islands Ground-dove *Gallicolumba kubaryi*	B	1	FSX	29	**B1+2e; C2a**; D1
Truk Monarch *Metabolus rugensis*	B	1	F	19	A1a; **B1+2a,c,d; C2a**; D2
Faichuk White-eye *Rukia ruki*	B	1	F	19	**B1+2c; C2a**; D1; D2
Vulnerable					
Yap Olive White-eye *Zosterops oleagineus*	B	1	FS	9	D2

Near-threatened

White-throated Ground-dove *Gallicolumba xanthonura*	B	2	Plain White-eye *Zosterops hypolais*	B	1
Yap Monarch *Monarcha godeffroyi*	B	1	Long-billed White-eye *Rukia longirostra*	B	1

MOLDOVA

Species totals Vulnerable 6
Near-threatened 4

	Status (breeding/ non-br.)	Breeding/ non-br. countries	Habitat codes (p. 243)	Threat codes (p. 243)	IUCN threat status codes (pp. 16–18)
Vulnerable					
Ferruginous Duck *Aythya nyroca*	B	38/32	W	12	A1a,b,c
Greater Spotted Eagle *Aquila clanga*	B	14/35	FW	13	C2a

cont.

Moldova (cont.)

Imperial Eagle *Aquila heliaca*	B	24/21	FG	12357	C2a
Lesser Kestrel *Falco naumanni*	B	37/52	FSVGA	15	A1a,b,d
Corncrake *Crex crex*	B	40/31	GWA	12	A1a,b
Great Bustard *Otis tarda*	B	23	GA	125	A2b

Near-threatened

Pygmy Cormorant *Phalacrocorax pygmeus*	B	17/4	Pallid Harrier *Circus macrourus*	B	4/57
White-tailed Eagle *Haliaeetus albicilla*	B	34/10	Black-winged Pratincole *Glareola nordmanni*	B	10/22

MONGOLIA

Species totals   Vulnerable   11
                         Near-threatened   6

	Status (breeding/ non-br.)	Breeding/ non-br. countries	Habitat codes (p. 243)	Threat codes (p. 243)	IUCN threat status codes (pp. 16–18)
Vulnerable					
Dalmatian Pelican *Pelecanus crispus*	B	16/9	W	1235	C2a
White-headed Duck *Oxyura leucocephala*	B	12/16	W	1256	A2d
Swan Goose *Anser cygnoides*	B	4/5	W	12	A1b,c; A2b,c
Ferruginous Duck *Aythya nyroca*	B	38/32	W	12	A1a,b,c
Pallas's Sea-eagle *Haliaeetus leucoryphus*	B	11/1	GW	135	C1; C2b
Greater Spotted Eagle *Aquila clanga*	B	14/35	FW	13	C2a
Lesser Kestrel *Falco naumanni*	B	37/52	FSVGA	15	A1a,b,d
White-naped Crane *Grus vipio*	B	3/4	WA	12	C1
Red-crowned Crane *Grus japonensis*	B	4/4	GWA	15	C1; C2a
Great Bustard *Otis tarda*	B	23	GA	125	A2b
White-throated Bushchat *Saxicola insignis*	B	3/3	SGW	1	C1; C2a

Near-threatened

White-tailed Eagle *Haliaeetus albicilla*	B	34/10	Far Eastern Curlew *Numenius madagascariensis*	B	3/14
Cinereous Vulture *Aegypius monachus*	B	18/13	Asian Dowitcher *Limnodromus semipalmatus*	B	3/14
Grey-headed Lapwing *Vanellus cinereus*	B	3/11	Relict Gull *Larus relictus*	B	3/3

MONTSERRAT (to U.K.)

Species totals   Near-threatened   3

Near-threatened

Bridled Quail-dove *Geotrygon mystacea*	B	13	Montserrat Oriole *Icterus oberi*	B	1
Forest Thrush *Cichlherminia lherminieri*	B	4		

MOROCCO

Species totals   Critical   2   Conservation
                         Vulnerable   9   Dependent   1
                         Near-threatened   2

	Status (breeding/ non-br.)	Breeding/ non-br. countries	Habitat codes (p. 243)	Threat codes (p. 243)	IUCN threat status codes (pp. 16–18)
Critical					
Northern Bald Ibis *Geronticus eremita*	B	4	GW	012589	A1a; C1; **C2a**; D1
Slender-billed Curlew *Numenius tenuirostris*	N	1/10	WG	1289	**C2b**; D1
Vulnerable					
White-headed Duck *Oxyura leucocephala*	N	12/16	W	1256	A2d
Marbled Teal *Marmaronetta angustirostris*	B	21/3	W	125	A2b
Ferruginous Duck *Aythya nyroca*	B	38/32	W	12	A1a,b,c
Greater Spotted Eagle *Aquila clanga*	N	14/35	FW	13	C2a
Spanish Imperial Eagle *Aquila adalberti*	N	2/1	FG	2359	D1
Lesser Kestrel *Falco naumanni*	B	37/52	FSVGA	15	A1a,b,d
Corncrake *Crex crex*	N	40/31	GWA	12	A1a,b
Great Bustard *Otis tarda*	B	23	GA	125	A2b
Aquatic Warbler *Acrocephalus paludicola*	N	8/13	W	18	A2b

Conservation Dependent			**Near-threatened**		
Audouin's Gull *Larus audouinii*	N	8/7	Cinereous Vulture *Aegypius monachus*	N	18/13
			Little Bustard *Tetrax tetrax*	B	13/10

MOZAMBIQUE

Species totals Critical 1 Near-threatened 8
Vulnerable 12

	Status (breeding/ non-br.)	Breeding/ non-br. countries	Habitat codes (p. 243)	Threat codes (p. 243)	IUCN threat status codes (pp. 16–18)
Critical					
Long-billed Tailorbird *Orthotomus moreaui*	B	2	F	1	B1+2c; **C2a**
Vulnerable					
Cape Griffon *Gyps coprotheres*	B	6	SGDR	235	A1a,c,d; A2c,d; C1; C2b
Lesser Kestrel *Falco naumanni*	N	37/52	FSVGA	15	A1a,b,d
Taita Falcon *Falco fasciinucha*	B	8	VR	1589	C1; D1
Wattled Crane *Grus carunculatus*	B	11	W	123	A2b,c; C1
Corncrake *Crex crex*	N	40/31	GWA	12	A1a,b
Blue Swallow *Hirundo atrocaerulea*	B	7/3	G	1	A1b; A2b; C1; C2a
Thyolo Alethe *Alethe choloensis*	B	2	F	1	B1+2c
Swynnerton's Robin *Swynnertonia swynnertoni*	B	3	F	1	B1+2b,c
East Coast Akalat *Sheppardia gunningi*	B	4	F	1	B1+2b,c
Dappled Mountain-robin *Modulatrix orostruthus*	B	2	F	1	B1+2b,c
Namuli Apalis *Apalis lynesi*	B	1	F	9	D2
White-winged Apalis *Apalis chariessa*	B	4	F	1	B1+2b,c

Near-threatened

Lesser Flamingo *Phoenicopterus minor*	N 8/20		Stierling's Woodpecker *Dendropicos stierlingi*	B 3
Southern Banded Snake-eagle *Circaetus fasciolatus*	B 6		Basra Reed-warbler *Acrocephalus griseldis*	N 1/8
Pallid Harrier *Circus macrourus*	N 4/57		Plain-backed Sunbird *Anthreptes reichenowi*	B 5
Great Snipe *Gallinago media*	N 10/35		Neergaard's Sunbird *Nectarinia neergaardi*	B 2

MYANMAR

Species totals Critical 2 Data Deficient 1
Endangered 6 Near-threatened 74
Vulnerable 35

	Status (breeding/ non-br.)	Breeding/ non-br. countries	Habitat codes (p. 243)	Threat codes (p. 243)	IUCN threat status codes (pp. 16–18)
Critical					
Pink-headed Duck *Rhodonessa caryophyllacea*	B	3	FW	0129	**D1**
Gurney's Pitta *Pitta gurneyi*	B	2	F	19	**A1b**; **B1+2c**; **C1**; C2a; D1; D2
Endangered					
White-bellied Heron *Ardea insignis*	B	4	FW	1	A1a,b; **C1**; **C2a**
Oriental Stork *Ciconia boyciana*	N	2/9	W	1235	A2b; **C1**
Greater Adjutant *Leptoptilos dubius*	B	8	FWU	129	A1b,c; **C1**; C2a; D1
White-shouldered Ibis *Pseudibis davisoni*	B	8	FW	1239	A1b; A2b; **C1**; **C2a**; D1
White-winged Duck *Cairina scutulata*	B	9	FW	1239	A1b,c,d; **C1**; **C2a**; D1
Nordmann's Greenshank *Tringa guttifer*	N	1/15	FW	12389	**C1**; **C2b**; D1
Vulnerable					
Spot-billed Pelican *Pelecanus philippensis*	N	3/8	W	1235	A1a,b,c,d; C1
Christmas Island Frigatebird *Fregata andrewsi*	N	1/9	FM	9	D2
Lesser Adjutant *Leptoptilos javanicus*	B	12/1	FW	123	C1
Ferruginous Duck *Aythya nyroca*	N	38/32	W	12	A1a,b,c
Baer's Pochard *Aythya baeri*	N	2/12	W	123	A1a,b; C1
Pallas's Sea-eagle *Haliaeetus leucoryphus*	B	11/1	GW	135	C1; C2b
Greater Spotted Eagle *Aquila clanga*	N	14/35	FW	13	C2a
Wallace's Hawk-eagle *Spizaetus nanus*	B	5	F	1	A1b; A2b; C1; C2a
Lesser Kestrel *Falco naumanni*	N	37/52	FSVGA	15	A1a,b,d
Blyth's Tragopan *Tragopan blythii*	B	4	F	12	C1; C2a
Sclater's Monal *Lophophorus sclateri*	B	3	FSR	12	C1; C2a
Crested Fireback *Lophura ignita*	B	5	F	12	A1b,c; A2b,c
Hume's Pheasant *Syrmaticus humiae*	B	4	FG	12	C1; C2a
Green Peafowl *Pavo muticus*	B	7	FSG	12	A1b,c; A2b,c
Black-necked Crane *Grus nigricollis*	N	2/5	GW	13	C1
Masked Finfoot *Heliopais personata*	B	9	FW	13	C1; C2a
Wood Snipe *Gallinago nemoricola*	N	4/6	SGW	1	C2a
Spoon-billed Sandpiper *Eurynorhynchus pygmeus*	N	1/14	W	18	C1; C2b
Black-bellied Tern *Sterna acuticauda*	B	9	W	128	C1
Indian Skimmer *Rynchops albicollis*	B	7	W	1	C1; C2a

cont.

Myanmar (cont.)

Pale-capped Pigeon *Columba punicea*	B	7	FSA	1	C1; C2a
White-fronted Scops-owl *Otus sagittatus*	B	4	F	1	A1b; A2b; C1; C2a
Ward's Trogon *Harpactes wardi*	B	5	F	1	C1; C2a
Blyth's Kingfisher *Alcedo hercules*	B	9	F	1	A1b; A2b; C1; C2a
Rufous-necked Hornbill *Aceros nipalensis*	B	8	F	12	A1b,c; C1; C2a
Plain-pouched Hornbill *Aceros subruficollis*	B	3	F	1	C1; C2a
Straw-headed Bulbul *Pycnonotus zeylanicus*	B	5	F	17	A1b,c
Grey-sided Thrush *Turdus feae*	N	1/3	F	1	B1+2c; C1; C2a
Jerdon's Babbler *Chrysomma altirostre*	B	4	GW	1	A1b
Black-breasted Parrotbill *Paradoxornis flavirostris*	B	4	SGW	1	A1a,b; C1; C2a
Short-tailed Parrotbill *Paradoxornis davidianus*	B	5	S	1	A1b; C1; C2a
White-browed Nuthatch *Sitta victoriae*	B	1	F	9	D2
Giant Nuthatch *Sitta magna*	B	3	F	1	A1b; C1; C2a
Beautiful Nuthatch *Sitta formosa*	B	7	F	1	C1; C2a
Hooded Treepie *Crypsirina cucullata*	B	1	FS	1	A1b; C1; C2a

Data Deficient

Brown-capped Laughingthrush *Garrulax austeni* — B 2

Near-threatened

Oriental Darter *Anhinga melanogaster* — B 13
Great-billed Heron *Ardea sumatrana* — B 10
Schrenck's Bittern *Ixobrychus eurhythmus* — N 5/10
Painted Stork *Mycteria leucocephala* — B 11
Asian Openbill *Anastomus oscitans* — B 9
Black-headed Ibis *Threskiornis melanocephalus* — N 10/8
Jerdon's Baza *Aviceda jerdoni* — B 9
Lesser Fish-eagle *Ichthyophaga humilis* — B 9
Grey-headed Fish-eagle *Ichthyophaga ichthyaetus* — B 13
White-rumped Vulture *Gyps bengalensis* — B 11
Long-billed Vulture *Gyps indicus* — B 9
Cinereous Vulture *Aegypius monachus* — N 18/13
Red-headed Vulture *Sarcogyps calvus* — B 11
Pallid Harrier *Circus macrourus* — N 4/57
Rufous-winged Buzzard *Butastur liventer* — B 7
White-rumped Falcon *Polihierax insignis* — B 5
White-cheeked Partridge *Arborophila atrogularis* — B 4
Temminck's Tragopan *Tragopan temminckii* — B 4
Lady Amherst's Pheasant *Chrysolophus amherstiae* — B 2
Sarus Crane *Grus antigone* — B 8
Long-billed Plover *Charadrius placidus* — N 4/8
Grey-headed Lapwing *Vanellus cinereus* — N 3/11
Asian Dowitcher *Limnodromus semipalmatus* — N 3/14
Nicobar Pigeon *Caloenas nicobarica* — B 11
Cinnamon-headed Green-pigeon *Treron fulvicollis* — B 5
Large Green-pigeon *Treron capellei* — B 5
Blue-rumped Parrot *Psittinus cyanurus* — B 5
Brown Coucal *Centropus andamanensis* — B 2
Spot-bellied Eagle-owl *Bubo nipalensis* — B 11
Tawny Fish-owl *Ketupa flavipes* — B 9
Brown-winged Kingfisher *Pelargopsis amauropterus* — B 5
Helmeted Hornbill *Buceros vigil* — B 5
Brown Hornbill *Anorrhinus tickelli* — B 6
Red-crowned Barbet *Megalaima rafflesii* — B 5
Yellow-rumped Honeyguide *Indicator xanthonotus* — B 5
Blue-naped Pitta *Pitta nipalensis* — B 8
Giant Pitta *Pitta caerulea* — B 4

Mangrove Pitta *Pitta megarhyncha* — B 5
White-bellied Minivet *Pericrocotus erythropygius* — B 2
Long-billed Thrush *Zoothera monticola* — B 6
Black-breasted Thrush *Turdus dissimilis* — B 4/2
Gould's Shortwing *Brachypteryx stellata* — B 6
Rufous-breasted Bush-robin *Tarsiger hyperythrus* — N 4/1
Purple Cochoa *Cochoa purpurea* — B 8
Green Cochoa *Cochoa viridis* — B 7
Jerdon's Bushchat *Saxicola jerdoni* — B 7
Chestnut-backed Laughingthrush *Garrulax nuchalis* — B 2
Yellow-throated Laughingthrush *Garrulax galbanus* — B 4
Spot-breasted Laughingthrush *Garrulax merulinus* — B 6
Striped Laughingthrush *Garrulax virgatus* — B 2
Red-tailed Laughingthrush *Garrulax milnei* — B 5
White-chested Babbler *Trichastoma rostratum* — B 5
Ferruginous Babbler *Trichastoma bicolor* — B 5
Slender-billed Scimitar-babbler
 Xiphirhynchus superciliaris — B 7
Long-billed Wren-babbler *Rimator malacoptilus* — B 5
Spotted Wren-babbler *Spelaeornis formosus* — B 5
Wedge-billed Wren-babbler *Sphenocichla humei* — B 3
Slender-billed Babbler *Turdoides longirostris* — B 3
Black-headed Shrike-babbler *Pteruthius rufiventer* — B 6
Yellow-throated Fulvetta *Alcippe cinerea* — B 6
Rufous-throated Fulvetta *Alcippe rufogularis* — B 9
Grey Sibia *Heterophasia gracilis* — B 3
Burmese Yuhina *Yuhina humilis* — B 2
Brown-winged Parrotbill *Paradoxornis brunneus* — B 2
Black-browed Parrotbill
 Paradoxornis atrosuperciliaris — B 6
Rufous-headed Parrotbill *Paradoxornis ruficeps* — B 7
Yellow-vented Warbler *Phylloscopus cantator* — N 3/6
Broad-billed Warbler *Tickellia hodgsoni* — B 6
Brown-breasted Flycatcher *Muscicapa muttui* — N 2/4
Asian Golden Weaver *Ploceus hypoxanthus* — B 6
Spot-winged Starling *Saroglossa spiloptera* — N 2/5
Collared Myna *Acridotheres albocinctus* — B 3
Andaman Drongo *Dicrurus andamanensis* — B 2
Black Magpie *Platysmurus leucopterus* — B 5

NAMIBIA

Species totals	Vulnerable	6
	Near-threatened	14

Vulnerable	Status (breeding/ non-br.)	Breeding/ non-br. countries	Habitat codes (p. 243)	Threat codes (p. 243)	IUCN threat status codes (pp. 16–18)
Slaty Egret *Egretta vinaceigula*	B	3	W	1	C2a
Cape Griffon *Gyps coprotheres*	B	6	SGDR	235	A1a,c,d; A2c,d; C1; C2b
Lesser Kestrel *Falco naumanni*	N	37/52	FSVGA	15	A1a,b,d
Blue Crane *Grus paradisea*	B	4	GWA	15	A1a,b; A2b; C1; C2a
Wattled Crane *Grus carunculatus*	B	11	W	123	A2b,c; C1
Red Lark *Certhilauda burra*	B	2	G	1	B1+2c; C2b

Near-threatened

Jackass Penguin *Spheniscus demersus*	B 2		African Oystercatcher *Haematopus moquini*	B 2	
Cape Gannet *Morus capensis*	B 2		Great Snipe *Gallinago media*	N 10/35	
Crowned Cormorant *Phalacrocorax coronatus*	B 3		Black-winged Pratincole *Glareola nordmanni*	N 10/22	
Bank Cormorant *Phalacrocorax neglectus*	B 2		Damara Tern *Sterna balaenarum*	B 2	
Lesser Flamingo *Phoenicopterus minor*	B 8/20		Sclater's Lark *Spizocorys sclateri*	B 2	
Black Harrier *Circus maurus*	B 3		Herero Chat *Namibornis herero*	B 2	
Pallid Harrier *Circus macrourus*	N 4/57		Cinderella Waxbill *Estrilda thomensis*	B 2	

NAURU

Species totals	Vulnerable	1

Vulnerable	Status (breeding/ non-br.)	Breeding/ non-br. countries	Habitat codes (p. 243)	Threat codes (p. 243)	IUCN threat status codes (pp. 16–18)
Nauru Reed-warbler *Acrocephalus rehsei*	B	1	S	19	D2

NEPAL

Species totals	Critical	2	Vulnerable	19
	Endangered	2	Near-threatened	37

Critical	Status (breeding/ non-br.)	Breeding/ non-br. countries	Habitat codes (p. 243)	Threat codes (p. 243)	IUCN threat status codes (pp. 16–18)
Pink-headed Duck *Rhodonessa caryophyllacea*	B	3	FW	0129	**D1**
Lesser Florican *Sypheotides indica*	B	2	G	189	**A1a**; C1; C2b; D1
Endangered					
Greater Adjutant *Leptoptilos dubius*	B	8	FWU	129	A1b,c; **C1**; C2a; D1
Bengal Florican *Houbaropsis bengalensis*	B	4	GW	1	C1; **C2a**
Vulnerable					
Spot-billed Pelican *Pelecanus philippensis*	N	3/8	W	1235	A1a,b,c,d; C1
Lesser Adjutant *Leptoptilos javanicus*	B	12/1	FW	123	C1
Ferruginous Duck *Aythya nyroca*	N	38/32	W	12	A1a,b,c
Baer's Pochard *Aythya baeri*	N	2/12	W	123	A1a,b; C1
Pallas's Sea-eagle *Haliaeetus leucoryphus*	B	11/1	GW	135	C1; C2b
Greater Spotted Eagle *Aquila clanga*	N	14/35	FW	13	C2a
Lesser Kestrel *Falco naumanni*	N	37/52	FSVGA	15	A1a,b,d
Swamp Francolin *Francolinus gularis*	B	3	GWA	15	A1b
Cheer Pheasant *Catreus wallichi*	B	3	FSG	12	C2a
Wood Snipe *Gallinago nemoricola*	B	4/6	SGW	1	C2a
Black-bellied Tern *Sterna acuticauda*	B	9	W	128	C1
Indian Skimmer *Rynchops albicollis*	B	7	W	1	C1; C2a
Blyth's Kingfisher *Alcedo hercules*	B	9	F	1	A1b; A2b; C1; C2a
White-throated Bushchat *Saxicola insignis*	N	3/3	SGW	1	C1; C2a
Rufous-throated Wren-babbler *Spelaeornis caudatus*	B	3	F	1	B1+2c; C1; C2a
Jerdon's Babbler *Chrysomma altirostre*	B	4	GW	1	A1b
Black-breasted Parrotbill *Paradoxornis flavirostris*	B	4	SGW	1	A1a,b; C1; C2a
Bristled Grass-warbler *Chaetornis striatus*	B	4	SGWA	1	A1b; C1; C2a
Kashmir Flycatcher *Ficedula subrubra*	N	2/3	F	1	B1+2c

cont.

Nepal (cont.)

Near-threatened

Oriental Darter *Anhinga melanogaster*	B	13
Painted Stork *Mycteria leucocephala*	B	11
Asian Openbill *Anastomus oscitans*	B	9
Black-headed Ibis *Threskiornis melanocephalus*	B	10/8
Red-naped Ibis *Pseudibis papillosa*	B	4
White-tailed Eagle *Haliaeetus albicilla*	B	34/10
Lesser Fish-eagle *Ichthyophaga humilis*	B	9
Grey-headed Fish-eagle *Ichthyophaga ichthyaetus*	B	13
White-rumped Vulture *Gyps bengalensis*	B	11
Long-billed Vulture *Gyps indicus*	B	9
Cinereous Vulture *Aegypius monachus*	N	18/13
Pallid Harrier *Circus macrourus*	N	4/57
Red-necked Falcon *Falco chicquera*	B	4
Satyr Tragopan *Tragopan satyra*	B	4
Sarus Crane *Grus antigone*	B	8
Grey-headed Lapwing *Vanellus cinereus*	N	3/11
Spot-bellied Eagle-owl *Bubo nipalensis*	B	11
Tawny Fish-owl *Ketupa flavipes*	B	9
Yellow-rumped Honeyguide *Indicator xanthonotus*	B	5

Blue-naped Pitta *Pitta nipalensis*	B	8
Pied Thrush *Zoothera wardii*	B	3/2
Long-billed Thrush *Zoothera monticola*	B	6
Gould's Shortwing *Brachypteryx stellata*	B	6
Rufous-breasted Bush-robin *Tarsiger hyperythrus*	B	4/1
Purple Cochoa *Cochoa purpurea*	B	8
Green Cochoa *Cochoa viridis*	B	7
Spot-breasted Laughingthrush *Garrulax merulinus*	B	6
Slender-billed Scimitar-babbler		
Xiphirhynchus superciliaris	B	7
Nepal Wren-babbler *Pnoepyga immaculata*	B	1
Slender-billed Babbler *Turdoides longirostris*	B	3
Black-headed Shrike-babbler *Pteruthius rufiventer*	B	6
Grey-crowned Prinia *Prinia cinereocapilla*	B	3
Tytler's Leaf-warbler *Phylloscopus tytleri*	B	4
Yellow-vented Warbler *Phylloscopus cantator*	N	3/6
Broad-billed Warbler *Tickellia hodgsoni*	B	6
White-throated Tit *Aegithalos niveogularis*	B	3
Spot-winged Starling *Saroglossa spiloptera*	B	2/5

NETHERLANDS

Species totals Vulnerable 3

See also: Netherlands Antilles (below).

	Status (breeding/ non-br.)	Breeding/ non-br. countries	Habitat codes (p. 243)	Threat codes (p. 243)	IUCN threat status codes (pp. 16–18)
Vulnerable					
Ferruginous Duck *Aythya nyroca*	N	38/32	W	12	A1a,b,c
Corncrake *Crex crex*	B	40/31	GWA	12	A1a,b
Aquatic Warbler *Acrocephalus paludicola*	N	8/13	W	18	A2b

NETHERLAND ANTILLES (to Netherlands)

Species totals Vulnerable 1
Near-threatened 1

	Status (breeding/ non-br.)	Breeding/ non-br. countries	Habitat codes (p. 243)	Threat codes (p. 243)	IUCN threat status codes (pp. 16–18)
Vulnerable					
Yellow-shouldered Amazon *Amazona barbadensis*	B	2	S	17	C2a
Near-threatened					
Bridled Quail-dove *Geotrygon mystacea*	B	13			

NEW CALEDONIA (to France)

Species totals Critical 1   Vulnerable 5
Endangered 4

	Status (breeding/ non-br.)	Breeding/ non-br. countries	Habitat codes (p. 243)	Threat codes (p. 243)	IUCN threat status codes (pp. 16–18)
Critical					
New Caledonian Rail *Gallirallus lafresnayanus*	B	1	F	69	**C2a; D1**
Endangered					
Australasian Bittern *Botaurus poiciloptilus*	B	3	W	12	**C2a**
Kagu *Rhynochetos jubatus*	B	1	FS	169	A2d; B1+2c,d,e; C1; **C2a; D1**
New Caledonian Lorikeet *Charmosyna diadema*	B	1	F	09	**D1**
New Caledonian Owlet-nightjar *Aegotheles savesi*	B	1	F	09	**D1**
Vulnerable					
Fairy Tern *Sterna nereis*	B	3	WM	36	C2a
Cloven-feathered Dove *Drepanoptila holosericea*	B	1	FV	12	C2b
New Caledonian Imperial-pigeon *Ducula goliath*	B	1	F	2	C2b
Horned Parakeet *Eunymphicus cornutus*	B	1	F	17	C1
Crow Honeyeater *Gymnomyza aubryana*	B	1	F	1	B1+2c; C2b

NEW ZEALAND

See also: Cook Islands (p. 265), Niue (p. 306), Tokelau (p. 329).

Species totals

Critical	3	Extinct	1
Endangered	9	Conservation	
Vulnerable	32	Dependent	1
Extinct in the Wild	1	Near-threatened	13

	Status (breeding/ non-br.)	Breeding/ non-br. countries	Habitat codes (p. 243)	Threat codes (p. 243)	IUCN threat status codes (pp. 16–18)
Critical					
Chatham Islands Petrel *Pterodroma axillaris*	B	1	FM	89	**B1+2e**; C2b; D1; D2
Magenta Petrel *Pterodroma magentae*	B	1	FM	69	A1d; **B1+2e**; **C2b**; D1; D2
Black Stilt *Himantopus novaezelandiae*	B	1	W	1689	**D1**
Endangered					
New Zealand Dabchick *Poliocephalus rufopectus*	B	1	W	136	**C2a**
Hutton's Shearwater *Puffinus huttoni*	B	1	SGM	169	**B1+2b,c,e**; D2
Australasian Bittern *Botaurus poiciloptilus*	B	3	W	12	**C2a**
Takahe *Porphyrio mantelli*	B	1	G	69	**D1**; D2
Chatham Islands Oystercatcher *Haematopus chathamensis*	B	1	WR	1689	**D1**; D2
New Zealand Dotterel *Charadrius obscurus*	B	1	GW	368	**C2a**
Shore Plover *Thinornis novaeseelandiae*	B	1	RG	9	**D1**; D2
Chatham Islands Robin *Petroica traversi*	B	1	FS	9	**D1**; D2
Kokako *Callaeas cinerea*	B	1	F	6	**C2a**
Vulnerable					
Brown Kiwi *Apteryx australis*	B	1	FSAX	26	A1d
Little Spotted Kiwi *Apteryx owenii*	B	1	F	689	D2
Great Spotted Kiwi *Apteryx haastii*	B	1	F	26	B1+2e
Fiordland Penguin *Eudyptes pachyrhynchus*	B	1	FM	68	C2a
Snares Islands Penguin *Eudyptes robustus*	B	1	FSM	9	D2
Erect-crested Penguin *Eudyptes sclateri*	B	1	RM	9	D2
Yellow-eyed Penguin *Megadyptes antipodes*	B	1	FSA	136	C2a
Wandering Albatross *Diomedea exulans*	B	6	MG	4	A1a,c; A2c
White-necked Petrel *Pterodroma cervicalis*	B	2	SM	9	D2
Cook's Petrel *Pterodroma cookii*	B	1	FM	9	D2
Pycroft's Petrel *Pterodroma pycrofti*	B	1	FM	68	C2a
Black Petrel *Procellaria parkinsoni*	B	1	FM	2469	D2
Westland Petrel *Procellaria westlandica*	B	1	FM	689	D2
Campbell Island Shag *Phalacrocorax campbelli*	B	1	RM	9	D2
New Zealand King Shag *Phalacrocorax carunculatus*	B	1	RM	2389	D1; D2
Stewart Island Shag *Phalacrocorax chalconotus*	B	1	RM	34	C2a
Chatham Islands Shag *Phalacrocorax onslowi*	B	1	RM	389	B1+2d; D1
Auckland Islands Shag *Phalacrocorax colensoi*	B	1	RM	689	D2
Bounty Islands Shag *Phalacrocorax ranfurlyi*	B	1	RM	89	D2
Pitt Island Shag *Phalacrocorax featherstoni*	B	1	RM	9	D2
Blue Duck *Hymenolaimus malacorhynchus*	B	1	W	1	C2a
Brown Teal *Anas aucklandica*	B	1	W	126	B1+2b,c,d,e
Auckland Islands Rail *Lewinia muelleri*	B	1	GF	9	D2
Wrybill *Anarhynchus frontalis*	B	1	W	16	C2a
Chatham Islands Snipe *Coenocorypha pusilla*	B	1	FG	9	D2
Bristle-thighed Curlew *Numenius tahitiensis*	N	1/14	GW	1268	C2b
Fairy Tern *Sterna nereis*	B	3	WM	36	C2a
Black-fronted Tern *Chlidonias albostriatus*	B	1	W	16	C2a
New Zealand Kaka *Nestor meridionalis*	B	1	F	16	C2a
Antipodes Parakeet *Cyanoramphus unicolor*	B	1	G	9	D2
Yellowhead *Mohoua ochrocephala*	B	1	F	6	B2b,d,e+3c; C2a
Stitchbird *Notiomystis cincta*	B	1	F	9	D2
Extinct in the Wild					
Kakapo *Strigops habroptilus*	B	1	FS	69	

Extinct		Buller's Shearwater *Puffinus bulleri*	B 1
Bush Wren *Xenicus longipes*	B 1	New Zealand Falcon *Falco novaeseelandiae*	B 1
Conservation Dependent		Weka *Gallirallus australis*	B 1
Saddleback *Philesturnus carunculatus*	B 1	New Zealand Snipe *Coenocorypha aucklandica*	B 1
Near-threatened		Far Eastern Curlew *Numenius madagascariensis*	N 3/14
Royal Albatross *Diomedea epomophora*	B 1	Kea *Nestor notabilis*	B 1
Grey-headed Albatross *Diomedea chrysostoma*	B 5	Yellow-fronted Parakeet *Cyanoramphus auriceps*	B 1
Buller's Albatross *Diomedea bulleri*	B 1	South Island Rock Wren *Xenicus gilviventris*	B 1
Northern Giant-petrel *Macronectes halli*	B 4	Chatham Islands Warbler *Gerygone albofrontata*	B 1

NICARAGUA

Species totals   Endangered   1   Near-threatened   11
Vulnerable   2

	Status (breeding/ non-br.)	Breeding/ non-br. countries	Habitat codes (p. 243)	Threat codes (p. 243)	IUCN threat status codes (pp. 16–18)
Endangered					
Golden-cheeked Warbler *Dendroica chrysoparia*	N	1/4	FS	18	**A1b,d**; A2d; C1; C2a
Vulnerable					
Military Macaw *Ara militaris*	B	11	F	17	A1b; C2a
Three-wattled Bellbird *Procnias tricarunculata*	B	4	F	1	A1b; A2b

Near-threatened

Agami Heron *Agamia agami*	B	16	Resplendent Quetzal *Pharomachrus mocinno*	B 7
Solitary Eagle *Harpyhaliaetus solitarius*	B	17	Keel-billed Motmot *Electron carinatum*	B 6
Harpy Eagle *Harpia harpyja*	B	17	Grey-headed Piprites *Piprites griseiceps*	B 4
Black-and-white Hawk-eagle *Spizastur melanoleucus*	B	14	Tawny-chested Flycatcher *Aphanotriccus capitalis*	B 2
Orange-breasted Falcon *Falco deiroleucus*	B	17	Nicaraguan Grackle *Quiscalus nicaraguensis*	B 2
Ocellated Quail *Cyrtonyx ocellatus*	B	4		

NIGER

Species totals   Vulnerable   2   Near-threatened   2
Data Deficient 1

	Status (breeding/ non-br.)	Breeding/ non-br. countries	Habitat codes (p. 243)	Threat codes (p. 243)	IUCN threat status codes (pp. 16–18)
Vulnerable					
Ferruginous Duck *Aythya nyroca*	N	38/32	W	12	A1a,b,c
Lesser Kestrel *Falco naumanni*	N	37/52	FSVGA	15	A1a,b,d

Data Deficient			**Near-threatened**	
River Prinia *Prinia fluviatilis*	B	5	Pallid Harrier *Circus macrourus*	N 4/57
			Nubian Bustard *Neotis nuba*	B 5

NIGERIA

Species totals   Critical   1   Data Deficient   1
Vulnerable   7   Near-threatened   10

	Status (breeding/ non-br.)	Breeding/ non-br. countries	Habitat codes (p. 243)	Threat codes (p. 243)	IUCN threat status codes (pp. 16–18)
Critical					
Ibadan Malimbe *Malimbus ibadanensis*	B	1	F	19	B1+2a,e; **C2a**; D1
Vulnerable					
Ferruginous Duck *Aythya nyroca*	N	38/32	W	12	A1a,b,c
Lesser Kestrel *Falco naumanni*	N	37/52	FSVGA	15	A1a,b,d
Green-breasted Bush-shrike *Malaconotus gladiator*	B	2	F	1	C2a
White-throated Mountain-babbler *Kupeornis gilberti*	B	2	F	1	B1+2b,c
Grey-necked Rockfowl *Picathartes oreas*	B	4	FR	12	C2a
Anambra Waxbill *Estrilda poliopareia*	B	1	GW	19	B1+2b,c; D1
Bannerman's Weaver *Ploceus bannermani*	B	2	F	1	B1+2a,b,c; C2a

Data Deficient			Yellow-casqued Hornbill *Ceratogymna elata*	B 11
Fernando Po Swift *Apus sladeniae*	B	4	Mountain Sawwing *Psalidoprocne fuliginosa*	B 3
Near-threatened			Cameroon Greenbul *Andropadus montanus*	B 2
Pallid Harrier *Circus macrourus*	N	4/57	Baumann's Greenbul *Phyllastrephus baumanni*	B 6
Great Snipe *Gallinago media*	N	10/35	Grey-headed Greenbul *Phyllastrephus poliocephalus*	B 2
Black-winged Pratincole *Glareola nordmanni*	N	10/22	Crossley's Ground-thrush *Zoothera crossleyi*	B 2
Brown-cheeked Hornbill *Ceratogymna cylindricus*	B	7		

NIUE (to New Zealand)

Species totals   Vulnerable   1

	Status (breeding/ non-br.)	Breeding/ non-br. countries	Habitat codes (p. 243)	Threat codes (p. 243)	IUCN threat status codes (pp. 16–18)
Vulnerable					
Bristle-thighed Curlew *Numenius tahitiensis*	N	1/14	GW	1268	C2b

NORFOLK ISLAND (to Australia)

Species totals   Critical   2
Vulnerable   4

	Status (breeding/ non-br.)	Breeding/ non-br. countries	Habitat codes (p. 243)	Threat codes (p. 243)	IUCN threat status codes (pp. 16–18)
Critical					
Norfolk Island Parakeet *Cyanoramphus cookii*	B	1	FA	69	**D1**; D2
White-chested White-eye *Zosterops albogularis*	B	1	F	1689	**D1**; D2
Vulnerable					
White-necked Petrel *Pterodroma cervicalis*	B	2	SM	9	D2
Bristle-thighed Curlew *Numenius tahitiensis*	N	1/14	GW	1268	C2b
Norfolk Island Gerygone *Gerygone modesta*	B	1	FS	9	D2
Slender-billed White-eye *Zosterops tenuirostris*	B	1	F	9	D2

NORTH KOREA

Species totals   Critical   2   Conservation
Endangered   3   Dependent   1
Vulnerable   11   Near-threatened   9

	Status (breeding/ non-br.)	Breeding/ non-br. countries	Habitat codes (p. 243)	Threat codes (p. 243)	IUCN threat status codes (pp. 16–18)
Critical					
Black-faced Spoonbill *Platalea minor*	B	2/8	WR	12359	**A2b**; C1; C2a; **D1**; D2
Crested Shelduck *Tadorna cristata*	N	0/4	W	09	**D1**
Endangered					
Chinese Egret *Egretta eulophotes*	B	3/10	WR	1	**C1**; C2a
Oriental Stork *Ciconia boyciana*	N	2/9	W	1235	A2b; **C1**
Nordmann's Greenshank *Tringa guttifer*	N	1/15	FW	12389	**C1**; C2b; D1
Vulnerable					
Swan Goose *Anser cygnoides*	N	4/5	W	12	A1b,c; A2b,c
Baikal Teal *Anas formosa*	N	1/5	FW	259	A1a,c,d; D2
Baer's Pochard *Aythya baeri*	N	2/12	W	123	A1a,b; C1
Scaly-sided Merganser *Mergus squamatus*	B	3/3	FW	1235	C1; C2a
Steller's Sea-eagle *Haliaeetus pelagicus*	N	1/4	FWR	1	C1; C2b
White-naped Crane *Grus vipio*	N	3/4	WA	12	C1
Red-crowned Crane *Grus japonensis*	N	4/4	GWA	15	C1; C2a
Swinhoe's Rail *Coturnicops exquisitus*	N	2/4	GW	1	C1; C2a
Spoon-billed Sandpiper *Eurynorhynchus pygmeus*	N	1/14	W	18	C1; C2b
Rufous-backed Bunting *Emberiza jankowskii*	B	3	GR	0	C1; C2a
Yellow Bunting *Emberiza sulphurata*	N	1/6	FSA	0	C1; C2a

Conservation Dependent
Hooded Crane *Grus monacha*   N 2/4

Near-threatened
Schrenck's Bittern *Ixobrychus eurhythmus*   B 5/10
Mandarin Duck *Aix galericulata*   B 5/4
White-tailed Eagle *Haliaeetus albicilla*   N 34/10

Cinereous Vulture *Aegypius monachus*   N 18/13
Long-billed Plover *Charadrius placidus*   B 4/8
Far Eastern Curlew *Numenius madagascariensis*   N 3/14
Japanese Waxwing *Bombycilla japonica*   N 1/5
Japanese Paradise-flycatcher *Terpsiphone atrocaudata*   B 4/8
Ochre-rumped Bunting *Emberiza yessoensis*   N 3/3

NORTHERN MARIANA ISLANDS (to U.S.A.)

Species totals   Critical   2   Near-threatened   3
   Vulnerable   4

	Status (breeding/ non-br.)	Breeding/ non-br. countries	Habitat codes (p. 243)	Threat codes (p. 243)	IUCN threat status codes (pp. 16–18)
Critical					
Rota White-eye *Zosterops rotensis*	B	1	F	69	**A1a**; A2d; **B1+2d,e**; C1; C2a; D1; D2
Mariana Crow *Corvus kubaryi*	B	2	F	169	A1a; **B1+2c,d,e**; C1; C2a; D1
Vulnerable					
Micronesian Scrubfowl *Megapodius laperouse*	B	2	FX	1236	C1
Nightingale Reed-warbler *Acrocephalus luscinia*	B	1	FGW	1568	A2d; B1+2c,d,e; C1
Tinian Monarch *Monarcha takatsukasae*	B	1	FS	9	D2
Golden White-eye *Cleptornis marchei*	B	1	FSAX	69	A2d; D2

Near-threatened

White-throated Ground-dove *Gallicolumba xanthonura*	B 2		Mariana Fruit-dove *Ptilinopus roseicapilla*		B 1
			Saipan Bridled White-eye *Zosterops saypani*		B 1

NORWAY

Species totals   Vulnerable   3
   Near-threatened   2

	Status (breeding/ non-br.)	Breeding/ non-br. countries	Habitat codes (p. 243)	Threat codes (p. 243)	IUCN threat status codes (pp. 16–18)
Vulnerable					
Lesser White-fronted Goose *Anser erythropus*	B	4/11	SWA	012	A1a,b,c
Steller's Eider *Polysticta stelleri*	N	2/8	WM	0	A1a
Corncrake *Crex crex*	B	40/31	GWA	12	A1a,b

Near-threatened

White-tailed Eagle *Haliaeetus albicilla*	B 34/10	Great Snipe *Gallinago media*		B 10/35

OMAN

Species totals   Vulnerable   5
   Near-threatened   2

	Status (breeding/ non-br.)	Breeding/ non-br. countries	Habitat codes (p. 243)	Threat codes (p. 243)	IUCN threat status codes (pp. 16–18)
Vulnerable					
Ferruginous Duck *Aythya nyroca*	N	38/32	W	12	A1a,b,c
Greater Spotted Eagle *Aquila clanga*	N	14/35	FW	13	C2a
Imperial Eagle *Aquila heliaca*	N	24/21	FG	12357	C2a
Lesser Kestrel *Falco naumanni*	N	37/52	FSVGA	15	A1a,b,d
Sociable Lapwing *Vanellus gregarius*	N	2/15	GW	158	A1a,b; C1; C2a

Near-threatened

Cinereous Vulture *Aegypius monachus*	N 18/13	Pallid Harrier *Circus macrourus*		N 4/57

PAKISTAN

Species totals   Endangered   1   Near-threatened   17
   Vulnerable   21

	Status (breeding/ non-br.)	Breeding/ non-br. countries	Habitat codes (p. 243)	Threat codes (p. 243)	IUCN threat status codes (pp. 16–18)
Endangered					
Siberian Crane *Grus leucogeranus*	N	1/5	W	129	**A2b,c**; C1; D2
Vulnerable					
Dalmatian Pelican *Pelecanus crispus*	N	16/9	W	1235	C2a
White-headed Duck *Oxyura leucocephala*	N	12/16	W	1256	A2d
Lesser White-fronted Goose *Anser erythropus*	N	4/11	SWA	012	A1a,b,c
Marbled Teal *Marmaronetta angustirostris*	B	21/3	W	125	A2b
Ferruginous Duck *Aythya nyroca*	N	38/32	W	12	A1a,b,c

cont.

Pakistan (cont.)

Pallas's Sea-eagle *Haliaeetus leucoryphus*	B	11/1	GW	135	C1; C2b
Greater Spotted Eagle *Aquila clanga*	B	14/35	FW	13	C2a
Imperial Eagle *Aquila heliaca*	N	24/21	FG	12357	C2a
Lesser Kestrel *Falco naumanni*	N	37/52	FSVGA	15	A1a,b,d
Western Tragopan *Tragopan melanocephalus*	B	2	F	1	C1; C2a
Cheer Pheasant *Catreus wallichi*	B	3	FSG	12	C2a
Sociable Lapwing *Vanellus gregarius*	N	2/15	GW	158	A1a,b; C1; C2a
Black-bellied Tern *Sterna acuticauda*	B	9	W	128	C1
Indian Skimmer *Rynchops albicollis*	B	7	W	1	C1; C2a
Pale-backed Pigeon *Columba eversmanni*	N	7/2	GDA	0	A1a
White-browed Bushchat *Saxicola macrorhyncha*	B	3	SD	1	A1a,b; C1; C2a
Jerdon's Babbler *Chrysomma altirostre*	B	4	GW	1	A1b
Rufous-vented Prinia *Prinia burnesii*	B	3	SGW	1	A1b
Long-billed Bush-warbler *Bradypterus major*	B	3	FSA	1	C2a
Bristled Grass-warbler *Chaetornis striatus*	B	4	SGWA	1	A1b; C1; C2a
Kashmir Flycatcher *Ficedula subrubra*	B	2/3	F	1	B1+2c

Near-threatened

Oriental Darter *Anhinga melanogaster*	B	13	Red-headed Vulture *Sarcogyps calvus*	B	11
Painted Stork *Mycteria leucocephala*	B	11	Pallid Harrier *Circus macrourus*	N	4/57
Asian Openbill *Anastomus oscitans*	B	9	Red-necked Falcon *Falco chicquera*	B	4
Black-headed Ibis *Threskiornis melanocephalus*	B	10/8	Little Bustard *Tetrax tetrax*	N	13/10
Red-naped Ibis *Pseudibis papillosa*	B	4	Yellow-rumped Honeyguide *Indicator xanthonotus*	B	5
Lesser Flamingo *Phoenicopterus minor*	N	8/20	Tytler's Leaf-warbler *Phylloscopus tytleri*	B	4
White-tailed Eagle *Haliaeetus albicilla*	N	34/10	White-throated Tit *Aegithalos niveogularis*	B	3
White-rumped Vulture *Gyps bengalensis*	B	11	Orange Bullfinch *Pyrrhula aurantiaca*	B	2
Cinereous Vulture *Aegypius monachus*	B	18/13			

PALAU (to U.S.A.)

Species totals   Vulnerable   2
   Near-threatened   3

Vulnerable	Status (breeding/ non-br.)	Breeding/ non-br. countries	Habitat codes (p. 243)	Threat codes (p. 243)	IUCN threat status codes (pp. 16–18)
Japanese Night-heron *Gorsachius goisagi*	N	2/10	F	1	C1; C2a
Micronesian Scrubfowl *Megapodius laperouse*	B	2	FX	1236	C1

Near-threatened

Nicobar Pigeon *Caloenas nicobarica*	B	11	Giant White-eye *Megazosterops palauensis*	B	1
Palau Ground-dove *Gallicolumba canifrons*	B	1			

PANAMA

Species totals   Vulnerable   9
   Near-threatened   31

Vulnerable	Status (breeding/ non-br.)	Breeding/ non-br. countries	Habitat codes (p. 243)	Threat codes (p. 243)	IUCN threat status codes (pp. 16–18)
Chocó Tinamou *Crypturellus kerriae*	B	2	F	1	B1+2c; C2a
Military Macaw *Ara militaris*	B	11	F	17	A1b; C2a
Glow-throated Hummingbird *Selasphorus ardens*	B	1	FS	9	D1; D2
Speckled Antshrike *Xenornis setifrons*	B	2	F	1	C2a
Turquoise Cotinga *Cotinga ridgwayi*	B	2	F	1	C2b
Yellow-billed Cotinga *Carpodectes antoniae*	B	2	F	1	A1b; A2b; C1; C2a
Bare-necked Umbrellabird *Cephalopterus glabricollis*	B	2	F	1	A1b; A2b; C1; C2a
Three-wattled Bellbird *Procnias tricarunculata*	B	4	F	1	A1b; A2b
Yellow-green Finch *Pselliophorus luteoviridis*	B	1	F	9	D2

Near-threatened

Agami Heron *Agamia agami*	B	16	Solitary Eagle *Harpyhaliaetus solitarius*	B	17
Fasciated Tiger-heron *Tigrisoma fasciatum*	B	8	Crested Eagle *Morphnus guianensis*	B	15
Plumbeous Hawk *Leucopternis plumbea*	B	4	Harpy Eagle *Harpia harpyja*	B	17
Semiplumbeous Hawk *Leucopternis semiplumbea*	B	5	Black-and-white Hawk-eagle *Spizastur melanoleucus*	B	14
			Orange-breasted Falcon *Falco deiroleucus*	B	17

cont.

Panama (cont.)

Black Guan *Chamaepetes unicolor*	B	2	Lanceolated Monklet *Micromonacha lanceolata*	B	6
Tacarcuna Wood-quail *Odontophorus dialeucos*	B	1	Coiba Spinetail *Cranioleuca dissita*	B	1
Black-breasted Wood-quail *Odontophorus leucolaemus*	B	2	Beautiful Treerunner *Margarornis bellulus*	B	1
Colombian Crake *Neocrex colombianus*	B	3	Black-tipped Cotinga *Carpodectes hopkei*	B	3
Brown-backed Dove *Leptotila battyi*	B	1	Black-billed Flycatcher *Aphanotriccus audax*	B	2
Russet-crowned Quail-dove *Geotrygon goldmani*	B	2	Ochraceous Pewee *Contopus ochraceus*	B	2
Red-fronted Parrotlet *Touit costaricensis*	B	2	Peg-billed Finch *Acanthidops bairdii*	B	2
Rufous-cheeked Hummingbird *Goethalsia bella*	B	2	Blue-and-gold Tanager *Bangsia arcaei*	B	2
Magenta-throated Woodstar *Philodice bryantae*	B	2	Green-naped Tanager *Tangara fucosa*	B	1
Resplendent Quetzal *Pharomachrus mocinno*	B	7	Viridian Dacnis *Dacnis viguieri*	B	2
Baird's Trogon *Trogon bairdii*	B	2	Pirre Warbler *Basileuterus ignotus*	B	2

PAPUA NEW GUINEA

Species totals Critical 2 Data Deficient 20
Endangered 4 Near-threatened 32
Vulnerable 25

	Status (breeding/ non-br.)	Breeding/ non-br. countries	Habitat codes (p. 243)	Threat codes (p. 243)	IUCN threat status codes (pp. 16–18)
Critical					
Beck's Petrel *Pterodroma becki*	B	2	MZ	09	**D1**; D2
Yellow-legged Pigeon *Columba pallidiceps*	B	2	F	129	**C2a**; D1
Endangered					
Heinroth's Shearwater *Puffinus heinrothi*	B	2	MF	16	**C2b**
Imitator Sparrowhawk *Accipiter imitator*	B	2	F	19	**C2a**; D1
Woodford's Rail *Nesoclopeus woodfordi*	B	2	FA	26	**C2a**
White-eyed Starling *Aplonis brunneicapilla*	B	2	F	128	B1+2c+3c; **C2a**
Vulnerable					
Southern Cassowary *Casuarius casuarius*	B	3	F	126	A1a,b,c,d; A2b,c,d
Northern Cassowary *Casuarius unappendiculatus*	B	2	F	12	A1a,b,c; A2b,c
Salvadori's Teal *Salvadorina waigiuensis*	B	2	W	1236	C2a
Sanford's Fish-eagle *Haliaeetus sanfordi*	B	2	F	12	C1; C2a
New Britain Sparrowhawk *Accipiter brachyurus*	B	1	F	1	C1
New Guinea Harpy Eagle *Harpyopsis novaeguineae*	B	2	F	12	C1; C2b
Victoria Crowned-pigeon *Goura victoria*	B	2	F	127	A1a,b,c; A2b,c; C1; C2a
Southern Crowned-pigeon *Goura scheepmakeri*	B	2	F	127	A1a,b,c; A2b,c
Pesquet's Parrot *Psittrichas fulgidus*	B	2	F	127	A1c; A2b,c
Manus Masked-owl *Tyto manusi*	B	1	F	09	D1
Bismarck Masked-owl *Tyto aurantia*	B	1	F	1	C2b
Fearful Owl *Nesasio solomonensis*	B	2	F	1	C2a
Moustached Kingfisher *Actenoides bougainvillei*	B	2	F	1	C2a
Superb Pitta *Pitta superba*	B	1	F	9	D1
Black-faced Pitta *Pitta anerythra*	B	2	F	16	C2a
Fly River Grassbird *Megalurus albolimbatus*	B	1	W	69	C2a; D2
Manus Fantail *Rhipidura semirubra*	B	1	FS	09	D1; D2
Long-bearded Melidectes *Melidectes princeps*	B	1	F	1	B1+2c,e; C2a
Fire-maned Bowerbird *Sericulus bakeri*	B	1	F	12	C2b
Macgregor's Bird-of-paradise *Macgregoria pulchra*	B	2	F	2	B1+2e; C2a
Black Sicklebill *Epimachus fastuosus*	B	2	F	12	A2b,c; C2a
Wahnes's Parotia *Parotia wahnesi*	B	1	F	1	C1
Ribbon-tailed Astrapia *Astrapia mayeri*	B	1	F	12	B1+2c,e
Goldie's Bird-of-paradise *Paradisaea decora*	B	1	F	1	B1+2c
Blue Bird-of-paradise *Paradisaea rudolphi*	B	1	F	1238	C1; C2a

Data Deficient			Bismarck Thicketbird *Megalurulus grosvenori*	B	1
Chestnut-shouldered Goshawk			Bougainville Thicketbird *Megalurulus llaneae*	B	1
Erythrotriorchis buergersi	B	2	Campbell's Fairywren *Malurus campbelli*	B	1
Mayr's Forest-rail *Rallina mayri*	B	2	Olive-yellow Robin *Poecilodryas placens*	B	2
New Guinea Flightless Rail *Megacrex inepta*	B	2	White-breasted Monarch *Monarcha menckei*	B	1
Papuan Hawk-owl *Uroglaux dimorpha*	B	2	Matthias Fantail *Rhipidura matthiae*	B	1
Mayr's Swiftlet *Collocalia orientalis*	B	2	Obscure Berrypecker *Melanocharis arfakiana*	B	2
Shovel-billed Kookaburra *Clytoceyx rex*	B	2	White-throated White-eye *Zosterops meeki*	B	1
Little Paradise-kingfisher *Tanysiptera hydrocharis*	B	2	White-chinned Myzomela *Myzomela albigula*	B	1
Papuan Whipbird *Androphobus viridis*	B	2	Tagula Honeyeater *Meliphaga vicina*	B	1

cont.

Papua New Guinea (cont.)

Tagula Butcherbird *Cracticus louisiadensis*	B 1	Finsch's Imperial-pigeon *Ducula finschii*	B 1
Yellow-breasted Bird-of-paradise		Bismarck Imperial-pigeon *Ducula melanochroa*	B 1
Loboparadisea sericea	B 2	White-naped Lory *Lorius albidinuchus*	B 1
Near-threatened		Striated Lorikeet *Charmosyna multistriata*	B 2
Dwarf Cassowary *Casuarius bennetti*	B 2	Duchess Lorikeet *Charmosyna margarethae*	B 2
Great-billed Heron *Ardea sumatrana*	B 10	Palm Cockatoo *Probosciger aterrimus*	B 3
Forest Bittern *Zonerodius heliosylus*	B 2	Green-fronted Hanging-parrot *Loriculus tener*	B 1
Black Honey-buzzard *Henicopernis infuscatus*	B 1	Blue-black Kingfisher *Todirhamphus nigrocyaneus*	B 2
Slaty-mantled Sparrowhawk *Accipiter luteoschistaceus*	B 1	New Britain Thrush *Zoothera talaseae*	B 1
New Britain Goshawk *Accipiter princeps*	B 1	Broad-billed Fairywren *Malurus grayi*	B 2
Doria's Goshawk *Megatriorchis doriae*	B 2	Manus Monarch *Monarcha infelix*	B 1
Gurney's Eagle *Aquila gurneyi*	B 2	Hooded Whistler *Pachycephala implicata*	B 2
Latham's Snipe *Gallinago hardwickii*	N 1/5	Grey-crowned Munia *Lonchura nevermanni*	B 2
Far Eastern Curlew *Numenius madagascariensis*	N 3/14	Black Munia *Lonchura stygia*	B 2
New Guinea Bronzewing *Henicophaps albifrons*	B 2	Yellow-eyed Starling *Aplonis mystacea*	B 2
New Britain Bronzewing *Henicophaps foersteri*	B 1	Pale-billed Sicklebill *Epimachus bruijnii*	B 2
Nicobar Pigeon *Caloenas nicobarica*	B 11	Emperor Bird-of-paradise *Paradisaea guilielmi*	B 1
Thick-billed Ground-pigeon *Trugon terrestris*	B 2	Bougainville Crow *Corvus meeki*	B 2

PARAGUAY

Species totals			
Critical	2	Extinct	1
Endangered	8	Data Deficient	1
Vulnerable	12	Near-threatened	38

	Status (breeding/ non-br.)	Breeding/ non-br. countries	Habitat codes (p. 243)	Threat codes (p. 243)	IUCN threat status codes (pp. 16–18)
Critical					
Brazilian Merganser *Mergus octosetaceus*	B	3	W	159	**A2b,d**; B1+2a,b,c,d,e; **C2a**; **D1**
Purple-winged Ground-dove *Claravis godefrida*	B	3	F	19	B1+2c; **C2b**; D1
Endangered					
Vinaceous Amazon *Amazona vinacea*	B	3	F	1	**A1a,b,c**; A2b,c; C1; C2a
Helmeted Woodpecker *Dryocopus galeatus*	B	3	F	1	**C2a**
Ochre-breasted Pipit *Anthus nattereri*	B	3	G	1	A1b; A2b; C1; **C2a**
Yellow Cardinal *Gubernatrix cristata*	B	4	FSG	17	**A1a,c**; **A2c**; C1; C2a
Buffy-fronted Seedeater *Sporophila frontalis*	B	3	F	17	**A1b**; A2b; **C1**; **C2b**
Temminck's Seedeater *Sporophila falcirostris*	B	3	F	17	**A1b**; A2b; **C1**; **C2b**
Marsh Seedeater *Sporophila palustris*	B	4	GW	17	**A1b,c**; **A2b,c**; C1; C2a
Saffron-cowled Blackbird *Xanthopsar flavus*	B	4	SGWA	158	**A1a,b**; **A2b,d**; C1; C2a
Vulnerable					
Crowned Eagle *Harpyhaliaetus coronatus*	B	4	SG	12	C2b
Black-fronted Piping-guan *Pipile jacutinga*	B	3	F	12	C2a
Rufous-faced Crake *Laterallus xenopterus*	B	2	GW	1	A1b; A2b
Hyacinth Macaw *Anodorhynchus hyacinthinus*	B	3	FV	127	A1b,c; A2b,c
Blue-winged Macaw *Ara maracana*	B	3	F	01	A1a,b; C1; C2a
Dinelli's Doradito *Pseudocolopteryx dinellianus*	N	1/2	SW	1	C1; C2a
Rufous-sided Pygmy-tyrant *Euscarthmus rufomarginatus*	B	4	VSG	1	A1b; A2b
São Paulo Tyrannulet *Phylloscartes paulistus*	B	3	F	1	A1b; A2b; C1; C2a
Russet-winged Spadebill *Platyrinchus leucoryphus*	B	3	F	1	A1b; A2b; B1+2c; C1; C2a
Black-and-white Monjita *Heteroxolmis dominicana*	B	4	GWA	1	A1b; A2b
Strange-tailed Tyrant *Alectrurus risora*	B	4	G	1	A1a,b; A2b; C1; C2a
Black-masked Finch *Coryphaspiza melanotis*	B	5	G	1	A1b

Extinct		Mantled Hawk *Leucopternis polionota*	B 3
Glaucous Macaw *Anodorhynchus glaucus*	B 4	Solitary Eagle *Harpyhaliaetus solitarius*	B 17
Data Deficient		Crested Eagle *Morphnus guianensis*	B 15
Speckled Crake *Coturnicops notatus*	B 7	Harpy Eagle *Harpia harpyja*	B 17
Near-threatened		Orange-breasted Falcon *Falco deiroleucus*	B 17
Greater Rhea *Rhea americana*	B 5	Hudsonian Godwit *Limosa haemastica*	N 2/11
Solitary Tinamou *Tinamus solitarius*	B 3	Pileated Parrot *Pionopsitta pileata*	B 3
Colombian Tinamou *Crypturellus columbianus*	B 5	Buff-fronted Owl *Aegolius harrisii*	B 8
Black-headed Duck *Heteronetta atricapilla*	B 6	Sickle-winged Nightjar *Eleothreptus anomalus*	B 4
Orinoco Goose *Neochen jubata*	B 10	Bronze-tailed Comet *Polyonymus caroli*	B 3
Grey-bellied Goshawk *Accipiter poliogaster*	B 10	Black-bodied Woodpecker *Dryocopus schulzi*	B 3

cont.

Paraguay (cont.)

Canebrake Groundcreeper			Shear-tailed Grey Tyrant *Muscipipra vetula*	B	3
Clibanornis dendrocolaptoides	B	3	Chaco Pipit *Anthus chacoensis*	B	2
Russet-mantled Foliage-gleaner *Philydor dimidiatus*	B	2	Creamy-bellied Gnatcatcher *Polioptila lactea*	B	3
Bare-throated Bellbird *Procnias nudicollis*	B	3	Grey-cheeked Grass-finch *Emberizoides ypiranganus*	B	3
Reiser's Tyrannulet *Phyllomyias reiseri*	B	2	Dark-throated Seedeater *Sporophila ruficollis*	B	5
Sharp-tailed Grass-tyrant *Culicivora caudacuta*	B	4	Chestnut Seedeater *Sporophila cinnamomea*	B	3
Bearded Tachuri *Polystictus pectoralis*	B	9	Blackish-blue Seedeater *Amaurospiza moesta*	B	3
Southern Bristle-tyrant *Phylloscartes eximius*	B	3	Thick-billed Saltator *Saltator maxillosus*	B	3
Bay-ringed Tyrannulet *Phylloscartes sylviolus*	B	3	White-banded Tanager *Neothraupis fasciata*	B	3
Hudson's Black-tyrant *Knipolegus hudsoni*	B	3	White-rumped Tanager *Cypsnagra hirundinacea*	B	3
Cock-tailed Tyrant *Alectrurus tricolor*	B	4	Green-chinned Euphonia *Euphonia chalybea*	B	3

PERU		**Species totals**	Critical	6	Data Deficient	4
			Endangered	12	Near-threatened	87
			Vulnerable	42		

	Status (breeding/ non-br.)	Breeding/ non-br. countries	Habitat codes (p. 243)	Threat codes (p. 243)	IUCN threat status codes (pp. 16–18)
Critical					
Kalinowski's Tinamou *Nothoprocta kalinowskii*	B	1	Z	09	**D1**
Junín Grebe *Podiceps taczanowskii*	B	1	W	159	**A1a,b,d**; **A2b,d**; **B1+2c,d,e**; **C1**; **C2b**; D1; D2
White-winged Guan *Penelope albipennis*	B	1	F	19	A2b; B1+2c; C1; **C2a**; D1
Royal Cinclodes *Cinclodes aricomae*	B	2	F	19	B1+2c; **C2a**; D1
White-browed Tit-spinetail *Leptasthenura xenothorax*	B	1	F	19	B1+2c; **C2a**; D1
Peruvian Plantcutter *Phytotoma raimondii*	B	1	S	19	A1b; **A2b**; B1+2c; C1; C2a
Endangered					
Peruvian Diving-petrel *Pelecanoides garnotii*	B	2	RM	1246	**A1a**; C2a
Grey-backed Hawk *Leucopternis occidentalis*	B	2	F	19	**C2a**; D1
Southern Helmeted Curassow *Pauxi unicornis*	B	2	F	12	**C2a**
Junín Rail *Laterallus tuerosi*	B	1	W	159	**B1+2c**; C2b; D2
Red-faced Parrot *Hapalopsittaca pyrrhops*	B	2	FS	19	A1b; **A2b**; B1+2c; **C1**; **C2a**; D1
Little Woodstar *Acestrura bombus*	B	2	F	1	A1b; A2b; C1; **C2b**
Russet-bellied Spinetail *Synallaxis zimmeri*	B	1	FS	1	**B1+2c**; **C2b**
Grey-headed Antbird *Myrmeciza griseiceps*	B	2	F	1	A1b; **A2b**; B1+2c; C1; C2a
Ash-breasted Tit-tyrant *Anairetes alpinus*	B	2	F	19	A1b; A2b; **B1+2c**; C1; **C2a**; D1
Plain-tailed Warbling-finch *Poospiza alticola*	B	1	FS	19	B1+2c; C1; **C2a**; D1
Rufous-breasted Warbling-finch *Poospiza rubecula*	B	1	FS	19	B1+2c; C1; **C2a**; D1
Orange-throated Tanager *Wetmorethraupis sterrhopteron*	B	2	F	1	**A2b**; C1; C2b
Vulnerable					
Taczanowski's Tinamou *Nothoprocta taczanowskii*	B	1	SG	12	C2a
Andean Flamingo *Phoenicopterus andinus*	B	4	W	123	A2b,c
Puna Flamingo *Phoenicopterus jamesi*	B	4	W	23	A2b,c
Rufous-headed Chachalaca *Ortalis erythroptera*	B	2	F	12	C1; C2a
Bearded Guan *Penelope barbata*	B	2	F	12	A2b,c; C1; C2a
Wattled Curassow *Crax globulosa*	B	5	F	12	A1b,c; A2b,c; C1; C2a
Brown Wood-rail *Aramides wolfi*	B	3	FW	1	A1b
Peruvian Pigeon *Columba oenops*	B	1	F	12	B1+2b,c; C2a
Ochre-bellied Dove *Leptotila ochraceiventris*	B	2	F	1	A1b; A2b; B1+2c,d; C1; C2a
Military Macaw *Ara militaris*	B	11	F	17	A1b; C2a
Golden-plumed Parakeet *Leptosittaca branickii*	B	3	F	1	A1b; A2b; C1; C2a
Yellow-faced Parrotlet *Forpus xanthops*	B	1	FS	17	A1a,c; B1+2c,e; C1; C2a
Spot-winged Parrotlet *Touit stictoptera*	B	3	F	1	C2a
Purple-backed Sunbeam *Aglaeactis aliciae*	B	1	S	9	D2
Royal Sunangel *Heliangelus regalis*	B	1	S	19	A2b; B1+2c; C1; C2a
Grey-bellied Comet *Taphrolesbia griseiventris*	B	1	SR	9	D1; D2
Marvellous Spatuletail *Loddigesia mirabilis*	B	1	FS	1	B1+2c; C2b
Chilean Woodstar *Eulidia yarrellii*	B	2	DA	19	B1+2c; C2b
White-bellied Cinclodes *Cinclodes palliatus*	B	1	WS	9	D1
Apurímac Spinetail *Synallaxis courseni*	B	1	F	9	D1; D2
Blackish-headed Spinetail *Synallaxis tithys*	B	2	FS	1	A1b; A2b; B1+2c; C1; C2a
Pale-tailed Canastero *Asthenes huancavelicae*	B	1	S	1	C1
Rufous-necked Foliage-gleaner *Syndactyla ruficollis*	B	2	F	1	A1b; A2b; C1; C2a

cont.

Peru (cont.)

Henna-hooded Foliage-gleaner					
Hylocryptus erythrocephalus	B	2	F	1	A1b; A2b; C1; C2a
Ash-throated Antwren *Herpsilochmus parkeri*	B	1	F	19	D2
Yellow-rumped Antwren *Terenura sharpei*	B	2	F	1	A1b; A2b; C1; C2a
Black-tailed Antbird *Myrmoborus melanurus*	B	1	F	1	C2b
Rufous-fronted Antthrush *Formicarius rufifrons*	B	1	F	1	A2b; C1; C2b
Chestnut-bellied Cotinga *Doliornis remseni*	B	3	F	1	A1b; A2b; B1+2c; C1; C2a
White-cheeked Cotinga *Zaratornis stresemanni*	B	1	F	1	B1+2c; C2a
Pacific Royal Flycatcher *Onychorhynchus occidentalis*	B	2	F	1	C2a
Grey-breasted Flycatcher *Lathrotriccus griseipectus*	B	2	F	1	A1b; A2b; B1+2c; C1; C2a
White-tailed Shrike-tyrant *Agriornis andicola*	B	5	GZ	18	A1a; C2a
Ochraceous Attila *Attila torridus*	B	3	FX	1	A1b; A2b; B1+2c; C1; C2a
Black-masked Finch *Coryphaspiza melanotis*	B	5	G	1	A1b
Slender-billed Finch *Xenospingus concolor*	B	2	SWD	19	A2b; B1+2c; C1; C2a
Golden-backed Mountain-tanager					
Buthraupis aureodorsalis	B	1	F	9	D2
Masked Mountain-tanager *Buthraupis wetmorei*	B	3	F	1	A1b; A2b; B1+2c; C1; C2a
Green-capped Tanager *Tangara meyerdeschauenseei*	B	1	FSA	9	D2
Tamarugo Conebill *Conirostrum tamarugense*	B	2	FZ	01	C1
Selva Cacique *Cacicus koepckeae*	B	1	F	1	A2b; C1; C2b
Saffron Siskin *Carduelis siemiradzkii*	B	2	FS	1	B1+2c; C1; C2a

Data Deficient

Black Tinamou *Tinamus osgoodi* B 2
Markham's Storm-petrel *Oceanodroma markhami* B 1
Ringed Storm-petrel *Oceanodroma hornbyi* B 2
White-masked Antbird *Pithys castanea* B 1

Near-threatened

Lesser Rhea *Rhea pennata* B 4
Hooded Tinamou *Nothocercus nigrocapillus* B 2
Pale-browed Tinamou *Crypturellus transfasciatus* B 2
Colombian Tinamou *Crypturellus columbianus* B 5
Humboldt Penguin *Spheniscus humboldti* B 2
Wedge-rumped Storm-petrel *Oceanodroma tethys* B 2
Red-legged Cormorant *Phalacrocorax gaimardi* B 3
Fasciated Tiger-heron *Tigrisoma fasciatum* B 8
Zigzag Heron *Zebrilus undulatus* B 9
Orinoco Goose *Neochen jubata* B 10
Grey-bellied Goshawk *Accipiter poliogaster* B 10
Semicollared Hawk *Accipiter collaris* B 4
Plumbeous Hawk *Leucopternis plumbea* B 4
Solitary Eagle *Harpyhaliaetus solitarius* B 17
Crested Eagle *Morphnus guianensis* B 15
Harpy Eagle *Harpia harpyja* B 17
Black-and-white Hawk-eagle *Spizastur melanoleucus* B 14
Black-and-chestnut Eagle *Oroaetus isidori* B 6
Orange-breasted Falcon *Falco deiroleucus* B 17
Wattled Guan *Aburria aburri* B 4
Ocellated Crake *Micropygia schomburgkii* B 8
Diademed Sandpiper-plover *Phegornis mitchellii* B 4
Hudsonian Godwit *Limosa haemastica* N 2/11
Imperial Snipe *Gallinago imperialis* B 3
Red-masked Parakeet *Aratinga erythrogenys* B 2
Grey-cheeked Parakeet *Brotogeris pyrrhopterus* B 2
Amazonian Parrotlet *Nannopsittaca dachilleae* B 1
Long-whiskered Owlet *Xenoglaux loweryi* B 1
Buff-fronted Owl *Aegolius harrisii* B 8
Rothschild's Swift *Cypseloides rothschildi* B 3
Koepcke's Hermit *Phaethornis koepckeae* B 1
Napo Sabrewing *Campylopterus villaviscensio* B 2
Spangled Coquette *Lophornis stictolophus* B 7
Ecuadorian Piedtail *Phlogophilus hemileucurus* B 3
Peruvian Piedtail *Phlogophilus harterti* B 1
Pink-throated Brilliant *Heliodoxa gularis* B 3

Neblina Metaltail *Metallura odomae* B 2
Lanceolated Monklet *Micromonacha lanceolata* B 6
Scarlet-hooded Barbet *Eubucco tucinkae* B 1
Yellow-browed Toucanet *Aulacorhynchus huallagae* B 1
Grey-breasted Mountain-toucan *Andigena hypoglauca* B 3
Hooded Mountain-toucan *Andigena cucullata* B 2
Speckle-chested Piculet *Picumnus steindachneri* B 1
Fine-barred Piculet *Picumnus subtilis* B 1
Greater Scythebill *Campylorhamphus pucherani* B 3
Tawny Tit-spinetail *Leptasthenura yanacensis* B 2
Chestnut-throated Spinetail *Synallaxis cherriei* B 4
Cactus Canastero *Asthenes cactorum* B 1
Line-fronted Canastero *Asthenes urubambensis* B 2
Russet-mantled Softtail *Thripophaga berlepschi* B 1
Great Spinetail *Siptornopsis hypochondriacus* B 1
Chestnut-backed Thornbird *Phacellodomus dorsalis* B 1
Equatorial Greytail *Xenerpestes singularis* B 2
Peruvian Recurvebill *Simoxenops ucayalae* B 3
Elusive Antpitta *Grallaria eludens* B 1
Chestnut Antpitta *Grallaria blakei* B 1
Peruvian Antpitta *Grallaricula peruviana* B 1
Ochre-fronted Antpitta *Grallaricula ochraceifrons* B 1
Marañón Crescent-chest *Melanopareia maranonica* B 1
Slaty Becard *Pachyramphus spodiurus* B 2
Black-chested Fruiteater *Pipreola lubomirskii* B 3
Fiery-throated Fruiteater *Pipreola chlorolepidota* B 3
Scarlet-breasted Fruiteater *Pipreola frontalis* B 4
Scaled Fruiteater *Ampelioides tschudii* B 5
Purple-throated Cotinga
 Porphyrolaema porphyrolaema B 4
Black-faced Cotinga *Conioptilon mcilhennyi* B 1
White-cheeked Tody-tyrant *Poecilotriccus albifacies* B 1
Buff-throated Tody-tyrant *Hemitriccus rufigularis* B 2
Cinnamon-breasted Tody-tyrant
 Hemitriccus cinnamomeipectus B 1
White-bellied Pygmy-tyrant *Myiornis albiventris* B 2
Orange-banded Flycatcher *Myiophobus lintoni* B 2
Piura Chat-tyrant *Ochthoeca piurae* B 1
Tumbes Tyrant *Ochthoeca salvini* B 1
Rufous-bellied Bush-tyrant *Myiotheretes fuscorufus* B 2
Bar-winged Wood-wren *Henicorhina leucoptera* B 1
Rufous-eared Brush-finch *Atlapetes rufigenis* B 1

cont.

Peru (cont.)

Grey-winged Inca-finch *Incaspiza ortizi*	B	1	Rufous-browed Hemispingus			
Little Inca-finch *Incaspiza watkinsi*	B	1	*Hemispingus rufosuperciliaris*	B	1	
Large-billed Seed-finch *Oryzoborus crassirostris*	B	9	Sira Tanager *Tangara phillipsi*	B	1	
Masked Saltator *Saltator cinctus*	B	2	White-bellied Dacnis *Dacnis albiventris*	B	5	
Giant Conebill *Oreomanes fraseri*	B	4	Tit-like Dacnis *Xenodacnis parina*	B	2	
Black-and-white Tanager *Conothraupis speculigera*	B	2	Pearly-breasted Conebill *Conirostrum margaritae*	B	2	

PHILIPPINES	Species totals	Critical	16	Vulnerable	41
		Endangered	29	Near-threatened	49

	Status (breeding/ non-br.)	Breeding/ non-br. countries	Habitat codes (p. 243)	Threat codes (p. 243)	IUCN threat status codes (pp. 16–18)
Critical					
Black-faced Spoonbill *Platalea minor*	N	2/8	WR	12359	**A2b**; C1; C2a; D1; D2
Philippine Eagle *Pithecophaga jefferyi*	B	1	F	129	A1b,c; A2b,c; **C1**; C2a; D1
Chinese Crested-tern *Sterna bernsteini*	N	1/5	MZ	09	**D1**
Mindoro Bleeding-heart *Gallicolumba platenae*	B	1	F	129	A1b,c; A2b,c; **B1+2c**; C1; **C2a**; D1
Negros Bleeding-heart *Gallicolumba keayi*	B	1	F	129	A1b; A2b; **B1+2c,e**; C1; **C2a**; D1
Negros Fruit-dove *Ptilinopus arcanus*	B	1	F	129	**B1+2c,e**; **C2b**; **D1**; D2
Sulu Bleeding-heart *Gallicolumba menagei*	B	1	F	129	**B1+2c,e**; C1; **C2b**; D1
Philippine Cockatoo *Cacatua haematuropygia*	B	1	F	17	**A1b,c**; C1; C2a
Black-hooded Coucal *Centropus steerii*	B	1	F	189	**A1b**; A2b; B1+2c; **C1**; **C2a**; **D1**
Sulu Hornbill *Anthracoceros montani*	B	1	F	129	**A1b,c**; A2b,c; B1+2c,e; **C1**; C2a; D1
Visayan Hornbill *Penelopides panini*	B	1	F	12	**A1b,c**; **A2b,c**; **B1+2c,e**; **C1**; **C2a**
Writhed-billed Hornbill *Aceros waldeni*	B	1	F	129	**A1b**; **A2b**; **B1+2c,e**; **C1**; C2a; D1
White-throated Jungle-flycatcher *Rhinomyias albigularis*	B	1	F	19	**A1b**; **A2b**; **B1+2c**; **C1**; **C2a**; **D1**
Cebu Flowerpecker *Dicaeum quadricolor*	B	1	F	189	A1b; **A2b**; **B1+2c**; **C1**; **C2b**; **D1**; D2
Scarlet-collared Flowerpecker *Dicaeum retrocinctum*	B	1	F	1	A1b; **A2b**; **B1+2c**; C1; C2a
Isabela Oriole *Oriolus isabellae*	B	1	F	19	A1b; B1+2c; C1; **C2a**; **D1**
Endangered					
Chinese Egret *Egretta eulophotes*	N	3/10	WR	1	**C1**; C2a
Palawan Peacock-pheasant *Polyplectron emphanum*	B	1	F	12	A1b,c; A2b,c; B1+2c; C1; **C2a**
Brown-banded Rail *Lewinia mirificus*	B	1	Z	0	**C2b**
Nordmann's Greenshank *Tringa guttifer*	N	1/15	FW	12389	**C1**; C2b; D1
Mindoro Imperial-pigeon *Ducula mindorensis*	B	1	F	129	A2b,c; **B1+2c**; C1; **C2a**; D1
Green Racquet-tail *Prioniturus luconensis*	B	1	FA	17	**A1b,c**; A2b,c; C1; **C2a**
Blue-winged Racquet-tail *Prioniturus verticalis*	B	1	F	12	A1b,c; C1; **C2a**
Blue-naped Parrot *Tanygnathus lucionensis*	B	3	F	17	**A1b,c**; A2b,c; C1; C2a
Lesser Eagle-owl *Mimizuku gurneyi*	B	1	F	1	A1b; C1; **C2a**
Philippine Eagle-owl *Bubo philippensis*	B	1	F	12	A1b; A2b; C1; **C2a**
Silvery Kingfisher *Alcedo argentata*	B	1	F	1	A1b; C1; **C2a**
Rufous-lored Kingfisher *Todirhamphus winchelli*	B	1	F	1	**A1b**; **A2b**; C1; C2a
Mindoro Hornbill *Penelopides mindorensis*	B	1	F	1	**A1b**; A2b; **B1+2c**; **C1**; **C2a**
Writhed Hornbill *Aceros leucocephalus*	B	1	F	12	**A1b,c**; A2b,c; C1; C2a
Streak-breasted Bulbul *Ixos siquijorensis*	B	1	F	1	A1b; A2b; **B1+2c**; C1; C2a
Philippine Leafbird *Chloropsis flavipennis*	B	1	F	1	A1b; A2b; **C1**; C2a
Black Shama *Copsychus cebuensis*	B	1	FSX	19	B1+2c; C1; **C2a**; D1
Luzon Water-redstart *Rhyacornis bicolor*	B	1	SW	125	**B1+2c,e**; C1; **C2a**
Melodious Babbler *Malacopteron palawanense*	B	1	F	1	A1b; A2b; B1+2c; C1; **C2a**
Falcated Wren-babbler *Ptilocichla falcata*	B	1	F	1	A1b; A2b; B1+2c; C1; **C2a**
Flame-templed Babbler *Stachyris speciosa*	B	1	F	1	A1b; A2b; B1+2c; C1; **C2a**
Negros Striped-babbler *Stachyris nigrorum*	B	1	F	1	A2b; B1+2c; C1; **C2b**
White-browed Jungle-flycatcher *Rhinomyias insignis*	B	1	F	1	A2b; C1; **C2a**
Ashy-breasted Flycatcher *Muscicapa randi*	B	1	F	1	A1b; A2b; B1+2c; C1; **C2a**
Palawan Flycatcher *Ficedula platenae*	B	1	F	1	A1b; A2b; B1+2c; C1; **C2a**
Furtive Flycatcher *Ficedula disposita*	B	1	F	19	A1b; A2b; B1+2c; C1; **C2a**; D1
Celestial Monarch *Hypothymis coelestis*	B	1	F	1	A1b; A2b; C1; **C2a**
Visayan Flowerpecker *Dicaeum haematostictum*	B	1	FS	1	**A1b**; A2b; **B1+2c**; C1; **C2a**
Green-faced Parrotfinch *Erythrura viridifacies*	B	1	F	1	A1b; **A2b**; **C1**; **C2a**

cont.

Philippines (cont.)

Vulnerable

Species					
Spot-billed Pelican *Pelecanus philippensis*	N	3/8	W	1235	A1a,b,c,d; C1
Japanese Night-heron *Gorsachius goisagi*	N	2/10	F	1	C1; C2a
Philippine Hawk-eagle *Spizaetus philippensis*	B	1	F	12	A1b; A2b; C1; C2a
Worcester's Buttonquail *Turnix worcesteri*	B	1	Z	09	D1
Mindanao Bleeding-heart *Gallicolumba criniger*	B	1	F	1	C2a
Dark-eared Brown-dove *Phapitreron cinereiceps*	B	1	F	12	A2b,c; C1
Flame-breasted Fruit-dove *Ptilinopus marchei*	B	1	F	12	A2b,c; B1+2c,e; C1; C2a
Spotted Imperial-pigeon *Ducula carola*	B	1	F	12	A2b,c; C1; C2a
Grey Imperial-pigeon *Ducula pickeringii*	B	3	F	12	B1+2c,d,e; C1; C2a
Mindanao Lorikeet *Trichoglossus johnstoniae*	B	1	F	1	C1; C2a
Luzon Racquet-tail *Prioniturus montanus*	B	1	F	127	A2b,c; C1; C2a
Mindanao Racquet-tail *Prioniturus waterstradti*	B	1	F	1	C2a
Blue-headed Racquet-tail *Prioniturus platenae*	B	1	FA	1	C1; C2a
Luzon Scops-owl *Otus longicornis*	B	1	F	1	C2a
Mindoro Scops-owl *Otus mindorensis*	B	1	F	19	A1b; B1+2c; C1; C2a
Mindanao Scops-owl *Otus mirus*	B	1	F	1	B1+2c; C1; C2a
Palawan Scops-owl *Otus fuliginosus*	B	1	FA	1	A1b; A2b; C1; C2a
Whitehead's Swiftlet *Collocalia whiteheadi*	B	1	F	1	B1+2c; C2a
Philippine Kingfisher *Ceyx melanurus*	B	1	F	1	A1b; A2b; C1; C2a
Blue-capped Kingfisher *Actenoides hombroni*	B	1	F	19	A2b; B1+2c; C1; C2a
Wattled Broadbill *Eurylaimus steerii*	B	1	F	1	A1b; A2b; C1; C2a
Azure-breasted Pitta *Pitta steerii*	B	1	F	1	A1b; A2b; C1; C2a
Whiskered Pitta *Pitta kochi*	B	1	F	12	B1+2c,e; C1; C2a
Black-bibbed Cicadabird *Coracina mindanensis*	B	1	F	1	C1; C2a
McGregor's Cuckoo-shrike *Coracina mcgregori*	B	1	F	1	B1+2c; C1; C2a
White-winged Cuckoo-shrike *Coracina ostenta*	B	1	F	1	A2b; B1+2c
Ashy Thrush *Zoothera cinerea*	B	1	F	12	A2b; C1; C2a
Bagobo Babbler *Trichastoma woodi*	B	1	F	1	C1; C2a
Rabor's Wren-babbler *Napothera rabori*	B	1	F	1	C1; C2a
Luzon Striped-babbler *Stachyris striata*	B	1	F	1	A1b; A2b; C1; C2a
Panay Striped-babbler *Stachyris latistriata*	B	1	F	1	B1+2c
Palawan Striped-babbler *Stachyris hypogrammica*	B	1	F	9	D2
Miniature Tit-babbler *Micromacronus leytensis*	B	1	F	1	A1b; A2b; C1; C2a
Streaked Reed-warbler *Acrocephalus sorghophilus*	N	0/2	WAZ	1	B1+2c; C1; C2a
Ijima's Leaf-warbler *Phylloscopus ijimae*	N	1/1	FS	01	C1; C2a
Slaty-backed Jungle-flycatcher *Rhinomyias goodfellowi*	B	1	F	1	A2b; B1+2c; C1; C2a
Little Slaty Flycatcher *Ficedula basilanica*	B	1	F	1	A1b; A2b; C1; C2a
Cryptic Flycatcher *Ficedula crypta*	B	1	F	1	A2b; B1+2c; C1; C2a
Whiskered Flowerpecker *Dicaeum proprium*	B	1	F	1	A2b; B1+2c; C1; C2a
Yellow Bunting *Emberiza sulphurata*	N	1/6	FSA	0	C1; C2a
Red-eared Parrotfinch *Erythrura coloria*	B	1	F	1	B1+2c; C2a

Near-threatened

Oriental Darter *Anhinga melanogaster*	B	13
Great-billed Heron *Ardea sumatrana*	B	10
Schrenck's Bittern *Ixobrychus eurhythmus*	N	5/10
Philippine Duck *Anas luzonica*	B	1
Jerdon's Baza *Aviceda jerdoni*	B	9
Grey-headed Fish-eagle *Ichthyophaga ichthyaetus*	B	13
Tabon Scrubfowl *Megapodius cumingii*	B	3
Spotted Buttonquail *Turnix ocellata*	B	1
Band-bellied Crake *Porzana paykullii*	N	2/7
Malaysian Plover *Charadrius peronii*	B	6
Grey-headed Lapwing *Vanellus cinereus*	N	3/11
Far Eastern Curlew *Numenius madagascariensis*	N	3/14
Asian Dowitcher *Limnodromus semipalmatus*	N	3/14
Nicobar Pigeon *Caloenas nicobarica*	B	11
Luzon Bleeding-heart *Gallicolumba luzonica*	B	1
Whistling Green-pigeon *Treron formosae*	B	3
Cream-bellied Fruit-dove *Ptilinopus merrilli*	B	1
Blue-crowned Racquet-tail *Prioniturus discurus*	B	1
Rufous Coucal *Centropus unirufus*	B	1
Indigo-banded Kingfisher *Alcedo cyanopecta*	B	1
Spotted Kingfisher *Actenoides lindsayi*	B	1
Rufous Hornbill *Buceros hydrocorax*	B	1
Luzon Hornbill *Penelopides manillae*	B	1
Samar Hornbill *Penelopides samarensis*	B	1
Mindanao Hornbill *Penelopides affinis*	B	1
Blackish Cuckoo-shrike *Coracina coerulescens*	B	1
Yellowish Bulbul *Ixos everetti*	B	1
Mountain Shrike *Lanius validirostris*	B	1
Striated Wren-babbler *Ptilocichla mindanensis*	B	1
Pygmy Babbler *Stachyris plateni*	B	1
Golden-crowned Babbler *Stachyris dennistouni*	B	1
Rusty-crowned Babbler *Stachyris capitalis*	B	1
Chestnut-faced Babbler *Stachyris whiteheadi*	B	1
Long-tailed Bush-warbler *Bradypterus caudatus*	B	1
Yellow-breasted Tailorbird *Orthotomus samarensis*	B	1
Black-headed Tailorbird *Orthotomus nigriceps*	B	1
Blue-breasted Flycatcher *Cyornis herioti*	B	1
Short-crested Monarch *Hypothymis helenae*	B	1
Japanese Paradise-flycatcher *Terpsiphone atrocaudata*	B	4/8
Rufous Paradise-flycatcher *Terpsiphone cinnamomea*	B	1
Blue Paradise-flycatcher *Terpsiphone cyanescens*	B	1

cont.

Philippines (cont.)

White-fronted Tit *Parus semilarvatus*	B	1	Naked-faced Spiderhunter *Arachnothera clarae*	B	1
Long-billed Rhabdornis *Rhabdornis grandis*	B	1	White-cheeked Bullfinch *Pyrrhula leucogenis*	B	1
Flame-crowned Flowerpecker *Dicaeum anthonyi*	B	1	Chestnut-cheeked Starling *Sturnus philippensis*	N	2/5
Apo Sunbird *Aethopyga boltoni*	B	1	Apo Myna *Basilornis miranda*	B	1

PITCAIRN ISLANDS (to U.K.)

Species totals   Vulnerable   5

	Status (breeding/ non-br.)	Breeding/ non-br. countries	Habitat codes (p. 243)	Threat codes (p. 243)	IUCN threat status codes (pp. 16–18)
Vulnerable					
Henderson Crake *Porzana atra*	B	1	FS	9	D2
Bristle-thighed Curlew *Numenius tahitiensis*	N	1/14	GW	1268	C2b
Henderson Fruit-dove *Ptilinopus insularis*	B	1	F	9	D2
Henderson Lorikeet *Vini stepheni*	B	1	F	9	D2
Pitcairn Reed-warbler *Acrocephalus vaughani*	B	2	F	9	D2

POLAND

Species totals   Vulnerable   5
                     Near-threatened   2

	Status (breeding/ non-br.)	Breeding/ non-br. countries	Habitat codes (p. 243)	Threat codes (p. 243)	IUCN threat status codes (pp. 16–18)
Vulnerable					
Ferruginous Duck *Aythya nyroca*	B	38/32	W	12	A1a,b,c
Steller's Eider *Polysticta stelleri*	N	2/8	WM	0	A1a
Greater Spotted Eagle *Aquila clanga*	B	14/35	FW	13	C2a
Corncrake *Crex crex*	B	40/31	GWA	12	A1a,b
Aquatic Warbler *Acrocephalus paludicola*	B	8/13	W	18	A2b

Near-threatened

White-tailed Eagle *Haliaeetus albicilla*	B	34/10	Great Snipe *Gallinago media*	B	10/35

PORTUGAL

Species totals   Critical   1   Conservation
                     Vulnerable   6   Dependent   1
                     Near-threatened   2

	Status (breeding/ non-br.)	Breeding/ non-br. countries	Habitat codes (p. 243)	Threat codes (p. 243)	IUCN threat status codes (pp. 16–18)
Critical					
Zino's Petrel *Pterodroma madeira*	B	1	RM	169	**D1**; D2
Vulnerable					
Fea's Petrel *Pterodroma feae*	B	2	GRM	29	D1; D2
Spanish Imperial Eagle *Aquila adalberti*	B	2/1	FG	2359	D1
Lesser Kestrel *Falco naumanni*	B	37/52	FSVGA	15	A1a,b,d
Corncrake *Crex crex*	N	40/31	GWA	12	A1a,b
Great Bustard *Otis tarda*	B	23	GA	125	A2b
Aquatic Warbler *Acrocephalus paludicola*	N	8/13	W	18	A2b

Conservation Dependent   **Near-threatened**

Madeira Laurel Pigeon *Columba trocaz*	B	1	Cinereous Vulture *Aegypius monachus*	B	18/13
			Little Bustard *Tetrax tetrax*	B	13/10

PUERTO RICO (to U.S.A.)

Species totals   Critical   2   Vulnerable   2
                     Endangered   2   Near-threatened   2

	Status (breeding/ non-br.)	Breeding/ non-br. countries	Habitat codes (p. 243)	Threat codes (p. 243)	IUCN threat status codes (pp. 16–18)
Critical					
Puerto Rican Amazon *Amazona vittata*	B	1	F	89	**D1**; D2
Puerto Rican Nightjar *Caprimulgus noctitherus*	B	1	F	1369	**B1+2c**; C2b; D2

cont.

Puerto Rico (cont.)

	Status (breeding/non-br.)	Breeding/non-br. countries	Habitat codes (p. 243)	Threat codes (p. 243)	IUCN threat status codes (pp. 16–18)
Endangered					
Plain Pigeon *Columba inornata*	B	5	FSVA	12	A1b; **C2a**
Yellow-shouldered Blackbird *Agelaius xanthomus*	B	1	FSRAX	1689	A1a,b,d; A2b,d; **B1+2c,d; C1; C2a**; D1
Vulnerable					
West Indian Whistling-duck *Dendrocygna arborea*	B	12	W	12	C2a
Piping Plover *Charadrius melodus*	N	2/9	W	138	C2a
Near-threatened					
Bridled Quail-dove *Geotrygon mystacea*	B 13		Elfin-woods Warbler *Dendroica angelae*		B 1

| **QATAR** | | **Species totals** | Vulnerable | 1 |

	Status (breeding/non-br.)	Breeding/non-br. countries	Habitat codes (p. 243)	Threat codes (p. 243)	IUCN threat status codes (pp. 16–18)
Vulnerable					
Lesser Kestrel *Falco naumanni*	N	37/52	FSVGA	15	A1a,b,d

| **RÉUNION (to France)** | | **Species totals** | Critical | 2 | Near-threatened | 2 |
| | | | Endangered | 1 | | |

	Status (breeding/non-br.)	Breeding/non-br. countries	Habitat codes (p. 243)	Threat codes (p. 243)	IUCN threat status codes (pp. 16–18)
Critical					
Mascarene Black Petrel *Pterodroma aterrima*	B	1	ZM	029	**D1**; D2
Barau's Petrel *Pterodroma baraui*	B	1	RM	2	**A1c**; A2c; C1; C2b
Endangered					
Réunion Cuckoo-shrike *Coracina newtoni*	B	1	F	1269	**D1**; D2
Near-threatened					
Madagascar Harrier *Circus maillardi*	B 3		Mascarene Swiftlet *Collocalia francica*		B 1

| **ROMANIA** | | **Species totals** | Critical | 1 | Near-threatened | 4 |
| | | | Vulnerable | 10 | | |

	Status (breeding/non-br.)	Breeding/non-br. countries	Habitat codes (p. 243)	Threat codes (p. 243)	IUCN threat status codes (pp. 16–18)
Critical					
Slender-billed Curlew *Numenius tenuirostris*	N	1/10	WG	1289	**C2b**; D1
Vulnerable					
Dalmatian Pelican *Pelecanus crispus*	B	16/9	W	1235	C2a
White-headed Duck *Oxyura leucocephala*	B	12/16	W	1256	A2d
Lesser White-fronted Goose *Anser erythropus*	N	4/11	SWA	012	A1a,b,c
Red-breasted Goose *Branta ruficollis*	N	1/4	SWA	12	A2b,c; B1+2c,d
Ferruginous Duck *Aythya nyroca*	B	38/32	W	12	A1a,b,c
Greater Spotted Eagle *Aquila clanga*	B	14/35	FW	13	C2a
Imperial Eagle *Aquila heliaca*	B	24/21	FG	12357	C2a
Lesser Kestrel *Falco naumanni*	B	37/52	FSVGA	15	A1a,b,d
Corncrake *Crex crex*	B	40/31	GWA	12	A1a,b
Great Bustard *Otis tarda*	B	23	GA	125	A2b
Near-threatened					
Pygmy Cormorant *Phalacrocorax pygmeus*	B 17/4		Little Bustard *Tetrax tetrax*		N 13/10
White-tailed Eagle *Haliaeetus albicilla*	B 34/10		Black-winged Pratincole *Glareola nordmanni*		B 10/22

RUSSIA	Species totals	Critical	2	Conservation	
		Endangered	4	Dependent	1
		Vulnerable	29	Near-threatened	20

	Status (breeding/ non-br.)	Breeding/ non-br. countries	Habitat codes (p. 243)	Threat codes (p. 243)	IUCN threat status codes (pp. 16–18)
Critical					
Crested Shelduck *Tadorna cristata*	N	0/4	W	09	**D1**
Slender-billed Curlew *Numenius tenuirostris*	B	1/10	WG	1289	**C2b**; D1
Endangered					
Oriental Stork *Ciconia boyciana*	B	2/9	W	1235	A2b; **C1**
Siberian Crane *Grus leucogeranus*	B	1/5	W	129	**A2b,c**; C1; D2
Nordmann's Greenshank *Tringa guttifer*	B	1/15	FW	12389	**C1**; C2b; D1
Blakiston's Fish-owl *Ketupa blakistoni*	B	3	FW	134	**C1**; **C2a**
Vulnerable					
Dalmatian Pelican *Pelecanus crispus*	B	16/9	W	1235	C2a
Japanese Night-heron *Gorsachius goisagi*	N	2/10	F	1	C1; C2a
White-headed Duck *Oxyura leucocephala*	B	12/16	W	1256	A2d
Swan Goose *Anser cygnoides*	B	4/5	W	12	A1b,c; A2b,c
Lesser White-fronted Goose *Anser erythropus*	B	4/11	SWA	012	A1a,b,c
Red-breasted Goose *Branta ruficollis*	B	1/4	SWA	12	A2b,c; B1+2c,d
Baikal Teal *Anas formosa*	B	1/5	FW	259	A1a,c,d; D2
Marbled Teal *Marmaronetta angustirostris*	B	21/3	W	125	A2b
Ferruginous Duck *Aythya nyroca*	B	38/32	W	12	A1a,b,c
Baer's Pochard *Aythya baeri*	B	2/12	W	123	A1a,b; C1
Spectacled Eider *Somateria fischeri*	B	2	WM	0	A1a
Steller's Eider *Polysticta stelleri*	B	2/8	WM	0	A1a
Scaly-sided Merganser *Mergus squamatus*	B	3/3	FW	1235	C1; C2a
Steller's Sea-eagle *Haliaeetus pelagicus*	B	1/4	FWR	1	C1; C2b
Greater Spotted Eagle *Aquila clanga*	B	14/35	FW	13	C2a
Imperial Eagle *Aquila heliaca*	B	24/21	FG	12357	C2a
Lesser Kestrel *Falco naumanni*	B	37/52	FSVGA	15	A1a,b,d
White-naped Crane *Grus vipio*	B	3/4	WA	12	C1
Red-crowned Crane *Grus japonensis*	B	4/4	GWA	15	C1; C2a
Swinhoe's Rail *Coturnicops exquisitus*	B	2/4	GW	1	C1; C2a
Corncrake *Crex crex*	B	40/31	GWA	12	A1a,b
Great Bustard *Otis tarda*	B	23	GA	125	A2b
Sociable Lapwing *Vanellus gregarius*	B	2/15	GW	158	A1a,b; C1; C2a
Spoon-billed Sandpiper *Eurynorhynchus pygmeus*	B	1/14	W	18	C1; C2b
Red-legged Kittiwake *Rissa brevirostris*	B	2	RM	0	A1a
Japanese Murrelet *Synthliboramphus wumizusume*	N	2/3	RM	1346	C1
White-throated Bushchat *Saxicola insignis*	B	3/3	SGW	1	C1; C2a
Aquatic Warbler *Acrocephalus paludicola*	B	8/13	W	18	A2b
Rufous-backed Bunting *Emberiza jankowskii*	B	3	GR	0	C1; C2a

Conservation Dependent

Hooded Crane *Grus monacha*	B	2/4

Near-threatened

Pygmy Cormorant *Phalacrocorax pygmeus*	B	17/4
Schrenck's Bittern *Ixobrychus eurhythmus*	B	5/10
Mandarin Duck *Aix galericulata*	B	5/4
White-tailed Eagle *Haliaeetus albicilla*	B	34/10
Cinereous Vulture *Aegypius monachus*	B	18/13
Pallid Harrier *Circus macrourus*	B	4/57
Siberian Grouse *Dendragapus falcipennis*	B	2
Band-bellied Crake *Porzana paykullii*	B	2/7
Little Bustard *Tetrax tetrax*	B	13/10

Long-billed Plover *Charadrius placidus*	B	4/8
Great Snipe *Gallinago media*	B	10/35
Far Eastern Curlew *Numenius madagascariensis*	B	3/14
Asian Dowitcher *Limnodromus semipalmatus*	B	3/14
Black-winged Pratincole *Glareola nordmanni*	B	10/22
Relict Gull *Larus relictus*	B	3/3
Marbled Murrelet *Brachyramphus marmoratus*	B	3
Japanese Waxwing *Bombycilla japonica*	B	1/5
Reed Parrotbill *Paradoxornis heudei*	B	2
Ochre-rumped Bunting *Emberiza yessoensis*	B	3/3
Chestnut-cheeked Starling *Sturnus philippensis*	B	2/5

RWANDA

Species totals Vulnerable 6
Near-threatened 10

Vulnerable	Status (breeding/ non-br.)	Breeding/ non-br. countries	Habitat codes (p. 243)	Threat codes (p. 243)	IUCN threat status codes (pp. 16–18)
Lesser Kestrel *Falco naumanni*	N	37/52	FSVGA	15	A1a,b,d
Albertine Owlet *Glaucidium albertinum*	B	2	F	1	B1+2a,c,d
Kungwe Apalis *Apalis argentea*	B	4	F	1	B1+2a,c,e
Grauer's Swamp-warbler *Bradypterus graueri*	B	4	W	1	B1+2a,c
Papyrus Yellow Warbler *Chloropeta gracilirostris*	B	7	W	1	B1+2a,b,c,d
Shelley's Crimson-wing *Cryptospiza shelleyi*	B	4	FS	0	A1a; C1; C2a

Near-threatened

Madagascar Pond-heron *Ardeola idae*	N 2/9	Red-faced Barbet *Lybius rubrifacies*	B	3
Shoebill *Balaeniceps rex*	B 8/1	Dwarf Honeyguide *Indicator pumilio*	B	3
Pallid Harrier *Circus macrourus*	N 4/57	Papyrus Gonolek *Laniarius mufumbiri*	B	5
Great Snipe *Gallinago media*	N 10/35	Lagden's Bush-shrike *Malaconotus lagdeni*	B	6
Black-winged Pratincole *Glareola nordmanni*	N 10/22	Red-collared Mountain-babbler *Kupeornis rufocinctus*	B	3

SÃO TOMÉ E PRÍNCIPE

Species totals Critical 3 Near-threatened 3
Vulnerable 6

Critical	Status (breeding/ non-br.)	Breeding/ non-br. countries	Habitat codes (p. 243)	Threat codes (p. 243)	IUCN threat status codes (pp. 16–18)
Dwarf Olive Ibis *Bostrychia bocagei*	B	1	F	19	**D1**
São Tomé Fiscal Shrike *Lanius newtoni*	B	1	F	019	**D1**
São Tomé Grosbeak *Neospiza concolor*	B	1	F	19	**D1**
Vulnerable					
Maroon Pigeon *Columba thomensis*	B	1	F	129	D1
São Tomé Short-tail *Amaurocichla bocagii*	B	1	FR	19	D1
Giant Sunbird *Nectarinia thomensis*	B	1	F	19	D1
Príncipe Speirops *Speirops leucophaeus*	B	1	FX	125	C2b
São Tomé White-eye *Zosterops ficedulinus*	B	1	F	1	C2a
São Tomé Oriole *Oriolus crassirostris*	B	1	F	15	C2b

Near-threatened

		São Tomé Thrush *Turdus olivaceofuscus*	B	1
São Tomé Scops-owl *Otus hartlaubi*	B 1	Príncipe Drongo *Dicrurus modestus*	B	1

SAUDI ARABIA

Species totals Critical 1 Near-threatened 8
Vulnerable 9

Critical	Status (breeding/ non-br.)	Breeding/ non-br. countries	Habitat codes (p. 243)	Threat codes (p. 243)	IUCN threat status codes (pp. 16–18)
Northern Bald Ibis *Geronticus eremita*	B	4	GW	012589	A1a; C1; **C2a**; D1
Vulnerable					
White-headed Duck *Oxyura leucocephala*	N	12/16	W	1256	A2d
Ferruginous Duck *Aythya nyroca*	B	38/32	W	12	A1a,b,c
Greater Spotted Eagle *Aquila clanga*	N	14/35	FW	13	C2a
Imperial Eagle *Aquila heliaca*	N	24/21	FG	12357	C2a
Lesser Kestrel *Falco naumanni*	B	37/52	FSVGA	15	A1a,b,d
Corncrake *Crex crex*	N	40/31	GWA	12	A1a,b
White-eyed Gull *Larus leucophthalmus*	B	5/1	WM	1235	C1
Yemen Thrush *Turdus menachensis*	B	2	FSGA	1	B1+2b,c; C2a
Yemen Warbler *Sylvia buryi*	B	2	FS	1	B1+2b,c; C2a

Near-threatened

Cinereous Vulture *Aegypius monachus*	N 18/13	Arabian Woodpecker *Dendrocopos dorae*	B	2
Pallid Harrier *Circus macrourus*	N 4/57	Yemen Accentor *Prunella fagani*	B	2
Great Snipe *Gallinago media*	N 10/35	Basra Reed-warbler *Acrocephalus griseldis*	N	1/8
Black-winged Pratincole *Glareola nordmanni*	N 10/22	Cinereous Bunting *Emberiza cineracea*	N	3/13

SENEGAL

Species totals Vulnerable 5 Data Deficient 1
Conservation Near-threatened 4
Dependent 1

Vulnerable	Status (breeding/ non-br.)	Breeding/ non-br. countries	Habitat codes (p. 243)	Threat codes (p. 243)	IUCN threat status codes (pp. 16–18)
Marbled Teal *Marmaronetta angustirostris*	B	21/3	W	125	A2b
Ferruginous Duck *Aythya nyroca*	N	38/32	W	12	A1a,b,c
Lesser Kestrel *Falco naumanni*	N	37/52	FSVGA	15	A1a,b,d
Yellow-throated Olive Greenbul *Criniger olivaceus*	B	7	F	1	A1b; A2b
Aquatic Warbler *Acrocephalus paludicola*	N	8/13	W	18	A2b

Conservation Dependent
Audouin's Gull *Larus audouinii* N 8/7

Data Deficient
River Prinia *Prinia fluviatilis* B 5

Near-threatened
Lesser Flamingo *Phoenicopterus minor* N 8/20
Pallid Harrier *Circus macrourus* N 4/57
Yellow-casqued Hornbill *Ceratogymna elata* B 11
Rufous-winged Illadopsis *Illadopsis rufescens* B 6

SEYCHELLES

Species totals Critical 4 Extinct 1
Vulnerable 4 Near-threatened 2

Critical	Status (breeding/ non-br.)	Breeding/ non-br. countries	Habitat codes (p. 243)	Threat codes (p. 243)	IUCN threat status codes (pp. 16–18)
Seychelles Scops-owl *Otus insularis*	B	1	F	19	B1+2a,c; **C2b**; D1
Seychelles Magpie-robin *Copsychus sechellarum*	B	1	FSA	9	**D1**; D2
Seychelles Paradise-flycatcher *Terpsiphone corvina*	B	1	F	19	**B1**+2a,b,c,e; **C2b**; D1; D2
Seychelles White-eye *Zosterops modestus*	B	1	F	0169	A1a; C1; **C2b**; **D1**; D2
Vulnerable					
Seychelles Kestrel *Falco araea*	B	1	FX	269	D1
Seychelles Swiftlet *Collocalia elaphra*	B	1	RF	139	D1
Seychelles Warbler *Acrocephalus sechellensis*	B	1	F	9	D1; D2
Seychelles Fody *Foudia sechellarum*	B	1	FX	69	D2

Extinct
Aldabra Warbler *Nesillas aldabrana* B 1

Near-threatened
Madagascar Pond-heron *Ardeola idae* B 2/9
Aldabra Drongo *Dicrurus aldabranus* B 1

SIERRA LEONE

Species totals Endangered 2 Near-threatened 10
Vulnerable 10

Endangered	Status (breeding/ non-br.)	Breeding/ non-br. countries	Habitat codes (p. 243)	Threat codes (p. 243)	IUCN threat status codes (pp. 16–18)
Rufous Fishing-owl *Scotopelia ussheri*	B	5	FW	15	A1b; A2b; B1+2b; C1; **C2a**
Gola Malimbe *Malimbus ballmanni*	B	4	F	1	A1b; **A2b**; B1+2a,b,c
Vulnerable					
Lesser Kestrel *Falco naumanni*	N	37/52	FSVGA	15	A1a,b,d
White-breasted Guineafowl *Agelastes meleagrides*	B	5	F	12	A1b,c; A2b,c
Yellow-footed Honeyguide *Melignomon eisentrauti*	B	3	F	1	A2b
Western Wattled Cuckoo-shrike *Campephaga lobata*	B	5	F	1	A1b; A2b
Green-tailed Bristlebill *Bleda eximia*	B	5	F	1	A1b; A2b
Yellow-throated Olive Greenbul *Criniger olivaceus*	B	7	F	1	A1b; A2b
White-necked Rockfowl *Picathartes gymnocephalus*	B	5	FR	127	A1b; A2b
White-eyed Prinia *Prinia leontica*	B	4	F	1	C2a
Black-capped Rufous Warbler *Bathmocercus cerviniventris*	B	5	F	1	C2a
Nimba Flycatcher *Melaenornis annamarulae*	B	4	F	1	A1b; A2b

Near-threatened
Lesser Flamingo *Phoenicopterus minor* N 8/20 Pallid Harrier *Circus macrourus* N 4/57

cont.

Sierra Leone (cont.)

Great Snipe *Gallinago media*	N 10/35	Lagden's Bush-shrike *Malaconotus lagdeni*	B 6
Brown-cheeked Hornbill *Ceratogymna cylindricus*	B 7	Rufous-winged Illadopsis *Illadopsis rufescens*	B 6
Yellow-casqued Hornbill *Ceratogymna elata*	B 11	Copper-tailed Glossy-starling	
Baumann's Greenbul *Phyllastrephus baumanni*	B 6	*Lamprotornis cupreocauda*	B 5
Turati's Boubou *Laniarius turatii*	B 3		

SINGAPORE

Species totals   Endangered   2   Near-threatened   2
Vulnerable   4

	Status (breeding/ non-br.)	Breeding/ non-br. countries	Habitat codes (p. 243)	Threat codes (p. 243)	IUCN threat status codes (pp. 16–18)
Endangered					
Chinese Egret *Egretta eulophotes*	N	3/10	WR	1	**C1**; C2a
Nordmann's Greenshank *Tringa guttifer*	N	1/15	FW	12389	**C1**; C2b; D1
Vulnerable					
Greater Spotted Eagle *Aquila clanga*	N	14/35	FW	13	C2a
Imperial Eagle *Aquila heliaca*	B	24/21	FG	12357	C2a
Spoon-billed Sandpiper *Eurynorhynchus pygmeus*	N	1/14	W	18	C1; C2b
Brown-chested Jungle-flycatcher *Rhinomyias brunneata*	N	1/5	F	1	A1b; A2b
Near-threatened					
Grey-headed Fish-eagle *Ichthyophaga ichthyaetus*	B 13	Asian Dowitcher *Limnodromus semipalmatus*			N 3/14

SLOVAKIA

Species totals   Vulnerable   4

	Status (breeding/ non-br.)	Breeding/ non-br. countries	Habitat codes (p. 243)	Threat codes (p. 243)	IUCN threat status codes (pp. 16–18)
Vulnerable					
Greater Spotted Eagle *Aquila clanga*	N	14/35	FW	13	C2a
Imperial Eagle *Aquila heliaca*	B	24/21	FG	12357	C2a
Corncrake *Crex crex*	B	40/31	GWA	12	A1a,b
Great Bustard *Otis tarda*	B	23	GA	125	A2b

SLOVENIA

Species totals   Vulnerable   3

	Status (breeding/ non-br.)	Breeding/ non-br. countries	Habitat codes (p. 243)	Threat codes (p. 243)	IUCN threat status codes (pp. 16–18)
Vulnerable					
Ferruginous Duck *Aythya nyroca*	B	38/32	W	12	A1a,b,c
Lesser Kestrel *Falco naumanni*	B	37/52	FSVGA	15	A1a,b,d
Corncrake *Crex crex*	B	40/31	GWA	12	A1a,b

SOLOMON ISLANDS

Species totals   Critical   4   Extinct   1
Endangered   5   Data Deficient   1
Vulnerable   9   Near-threatened   22

	Status (breeding/ non-br.)	Breeding/ non-br. countries	Habitat codes (p. 243)	Threat codes (p. 243)	IUCN threat status codes (pp. 16–18)
Critical					
Beck's Petrel *Pterodroma becki*	B	2	MZ	09	**D1**; D2
San Cristobal Moorhen *Gallinula silvestris*	B	1	F	269	**C2b**; D1
Yellow-legged Pigeon *Columba pallidiceps*	B	2	F	129	**C2a**; D1
Thick-billed Ground-dove *Gallicolumba salamonis*	B	1	F	169	A2b; **C2a; D1**
Endangered					
Heinroth's Shearwater *Puffinus heinrothi*	B	2	MF	16	**C2b**
Imitator Sparrowhawk *Accipiter imitator*	B	2	F	19	**C2a**; D1
Woodford's Rail *Nesoclopeus woodfordi*	B	2	FA	26	**C2a**

cont.

Solomon Islands (cont.)

Chestnut-bellied Imperial-pigeon *Ducula brenchleyi*	B	1	F	12	**A2b**; C1; C2a
White-eyed Starling *Aplonis brunneicapilla*	B	2	F	128	B1+2c+3c; **C2a**
Vulnerable					
Christmas Island Frigatebird *Fregata andrewsi*	N	1/9	FM	9	D2
Sanford's Fish-eagle *Haliaeetus sanfordi*	B	2	F	12	C1; C2a
Santa Cruz Ground-dove *Gallicolumba sanctaecrucis*	B	2	F	126	A2b; C1
Fearful Owl *Nesasio solomonensis*	B	2	F	1	C2a
Moustached Kingfisher *Actenoides bougainvillei*	B	2	F	1	C2a
Black-faced Pitta *Pitta anerythra*	B	2	F	16	C2a
Sombre Leaf-warbler *Phylloscopus amoenus*	B	1	F	689	D1; D2
Malaita Fantail *Rhipidura malaitae*	B	1	F	89	D1
Ghizo White-eye *Zosterops luteirostris*	B	1	F	19	D2

Extinct
Choiseul Pigeon *Microgoura meeki* — B 1

Data Deficient
Mayr's Swiftlet *Collocalia orientalis* — B 2

Near-threatened
Roviana Rail *Gallirallus rovianae* — B 1
Nicobar Pigeon *Caloenas nicobarica* — B 11
White-headed Fruit-dove *Ptilinopus eugeniae* — B 1
Palm Lorikeet *Charmosyna palmarum* — B 2
Duchess Lorikeet *Charmosyna margarethae* — B 2
San Cristobal Thrush *Zoothera margaretae* — B 1
Shade Warbler *Cettia parens* — B 1
San Cristobal Leaf-warbler *Phylloscopus makirensis* — B 1
Guadalcanal Thicketbird *Megalurulus whitneyi* — B 2

Vanikoro Monarch *Mayrornis schistaceus* — B 1
Black-throated Shrikebill *Clytorhynchus nigrogularis* — B 2
Rennell Shrikebill *Clytorhynchus hamlini* — B 1
Kolombangara Monarch *Monarcha browni* — B 1
Ochre-tailed Flycatcher *Myiagra cervinicauda* — B 1
Dusky Fantail *Rhipidura tenebrosa* — B 1
Hooded Whistler *Pachycephala implicata* — B 2
Rennell White-eye *Zosterops rennellianus* — B 1
Sanford's White-eye *Woodfordia lacertosa* — B 1
Rusty-winged Starling *Aplonis zelandica* — B 2
Rennell Starling *Aplonis insularis* — B 1
Bougainville Crow *Corvus meeki* — B 2
White-billed Crow *Corvus woodfordi* — B 1

SOMALIA	**Species totals**	Critical	1	Vulnerable	3
		Endangered	4	Near-threatened	10

Critical	Status (breeding/ non-br.)	Breeding/ non-br. countries	Habitat codes (p. 243)	Threat codes (p. 243)	IUCN threat status codes (pp. 16–18)
Bulo Burti Bush-shrike *Laniarius liberatus*	B	1	S	19	**D1**
Endangered					
Ash's Lark *Mirafra ashi*	B	1	G	19	**B1+2a,c; C2b**; D1
Archer's Lark *Heteromirafra archeri*	B	1	G	19	**B1+2a,c; C2a**; D1
Somali Thrush *Turdus ludoviciae*	B	1	F	1	**B1+2a,b,c**; C2a
Warsangli Linnet *Carduelis johannis*	B	1	F	19	**B1+2a,b,c**; C2a; D1
Vulnerable					
Lesser Kestrel *Falco naumanni*	N	37/52	FSVGA	15	A1a,b,d
White-eyed Gull *Larus leucophthalmus*	N	5/1	WM	1235	C1
Somali Pigeon *Columba oliviae*	B	1	SR	01	C2a

Near-threatened
Southern Banded Snake-eagle *Circaetus fasciolatus* — B 6
Pallid Harrier *Circus macrourus* — N 4/57
Little Brown Bustard *Eupodotis humilis* — B 2
White-winged Collared-dove *Streptopelia reichenowi* — B 3
Fischer's Turaco *Tauraco fischeri* — B 3

Obbia Lark *Spizocorys obbiensis* — B 1
Malindi Pipit *Anthus melindae* — B 2
Sombre Chat *Cercomela dubia* — B 2
Basra Reed-warbler *Acrocephalus griseldis* — N 1/8
Short-billed Crombec *Sylvietta philippae* — B 2

SOUTH AFRICA	**Species totals**	Critical	1	Vulnerable	13
		Endangered	2	Near-threatened	30

Critical	Status (breeding/ non-br.)	Breeding/ non-br. countries	Habitat codes (p. 243)	Threat codes (p. 243)	IUCN threat status codes (pp. 16–18)
Rudd's Lark *Heteromirafra ruddi*	B	1	G	1	**A2b**; B1+2c; C1; C2a

cont.

South Africa (cont.)

Endangered
White-winged Flufftail *Sarothrura ayresi*	B	4	W	1	**B1+2a,b,c+3a,b,c**; C2a
Spotted Ground-thrush *Zoothera guttata*	B	5/1	F	1	B1+2c; **C2a**

Vulnerable
Wandering Albatross *Diomedea exulans*	B	6	MG	4	A1a,c; A2c
Southern Bald Ibis *Geronticus calvus*	B	3	GR	1	C2b
Cape Griffon *Gyps coprotheres*	B	6	SGDR	235	A1a,c,d; A2c,d; C1; C2b
Lesser Kestrel *Falco naumanni*	N	37/52	FSVGA	15	A1a,b,d
Taita Falcon *Falco fasciinucha*	B	8	VR	1589	C1; D1
Blue Crane *Grus paradisea*	B	4	GWA	15	A1a,b; A2b; C1; C2a
Wattled Crane *Grus carunculatus*	B	11	W	123	A2b,c; C1
Corncrake *Crex crex*	N	40/31	GWA	12	A1a,b
Kerguelen Tern *Sterna virgata*	B	2	WM	6	A2d; C1
Red Lark *Certhilauda burra*	B	2	G	1	B1+2c; C2b
Botha's Lark *Spizocorys fringillaris*	B	1	G	1	A2b; C1; C2b
Blue Swallow *Hirundo atrocaerulea*	B	7/3	G	1	A1b; A2b; C1; C2a
Yellow-breasted Pipit *Anthus chloris*	B	2	G	1	B1+2c

Near-threatened
Jackass Penguin *Spheniscus demersus*	B	2	Damara Tern *Sterna balaenarum*	B	2
Grey-headed Albatross *Diomedea chrysostoma*	B	5	Knysna Woodpecker *Campethera notata*	B	1
Sooty Albatross *Phoebetria fusca*	B	3	Ground Woodpecker *Geocolaptes olivaceus*	B	2
Northern Giant-petrel *Macronectes halli*	B	4	Short-clawed Lark *Certhilauda chuana*	B	2
Cape Gannet *Morus capensis*	B	2	Sclater's Lark *Spizocorys sclateri*	B	2
Crowned Cormorant *Phalacrocorax coronatus*	B	3	Mountain Pipit *Anthus hoeschi*	B	2
Bank Cormorant *Phalacrocorax neglectus*	B	2	Rufous Rockjumper *Chaetops frenatus*	B	1
Lesser Flamingo *Phoenicopterus minor*	B	8/20	Orange-breasted Rockjumper *Chaetops aurantius*	B	2
Southern Banded Snake-eagle *Circaetus fasciolatus*	B	6	Buff-streaked Chat *Saxicola bifasciata*	B	1
Black Harrier *Circus maurus*	B	3	Bush Blackcap *Lioptilus nigricapillus*	B	1
Pallid Harrier *Circus macrourus*	N	4/57	Plain-backed Sunbird *Anthreptes reichenowi*	B	5
Blue Bustard *Eupodotis caerulescens*	B	2	Neergaard's Sunbird *Nectarinia neergaardi*	B	2
African Oystercatcher *Haematopus moquini*	B	2	Protea Canary *Serinus leucopterus*	B	1
Great Snipe *Gallinago media*	N	10/35	Cape Siskin *Serinus totta*	B	1
Black-winged Pratincole *Glareola nordmanni*	N	10/22	Drakensberg Siskin *Serinus symonsi*	B	2

SOUTH GEORGIA (to U.K.)

Species totals   Vulnerable   1
Near-threatened   1

	Status (breeding/ non-br.)	Breeding/ non-br. countries	Habitat codes (p. 243)	Threat codes (p. 243)	IUCN threat status codes (pp. 16–18)
Vulnerable					
Wandering Albatross *Diomedea exulans*	B	6	MG	4	A1a,c; A2c
Near-threatened					
Grey-headed Albatross *Diomedea chrysostoma*	B	5			

SOUTH KOREA

Species totals   Critical   2   Conservation
Endangered   4   Dependent   1
Vulnerable   13   Near-threatened   13

	Status (breeding/ non-br.)	Breeding/ non-br. countries	Habitat codes (p. 243)	Threat codes (p. 243)	IUCN threat status codes (pp. 16–18)
Critical					
Black-faced Spoonbill *Platalea minor*	B	2/8	WR	12359	**A2b**; C1; **C2a**; D1; D2
Crested Shelduck *Tadorna cristata*	N	0/4	W	09	**D1**
Endangered					
Chinese Egret *Egretta eulophotes*	B	3/10	WR	1	**C1**; C2a
Oriental Stork *Ciconia boyciana*	N	2/9	W	1235	A2b; **C1**
Nordmann's Greenshank *Tringa guttifer*	N	1/15	FW	12389	C1; C2b; D1
Saunders's Gull *Larus saundersi*	N	1/6	W	1235	A1b,c,d; **A2b,c,d**; C1; C2a
Vulnerable					
Japanese Night-heron *Gorsachius goisagi*	N	2/10	F	1	C1; C2a

cont.

South Korea (cont.)

Swan Goose *Anser cygnoides*	N	4/5	W	12	A1b,c; A2b,c
Baikal Teal *Anas formosa*	N	1/5	FW	259	A1a,c,d; D2
Baer's Pochard *Aythya baeri*	N	2/12	W	123	A1a,b; C1
Scaly-sided Merganser *Mergus squamatus*	N	3/3	FW	1235	C1; C2a
Steller's Sea-eagle *Haliaeetus pelagicus*	N	1/4	FWR	1	C1; C2b
White-naped Crane *Grus vipio*	N	3/4	WA	12	C1
Red-crowned Crane *Grus japonensis*	N	4/4	GWA	15	C1; C2a
Swinhoe's Rail *Coturnicops exquisitus*	N	2/4	GW	1	C1; C2a
Spoon-billed Sandpiper *Eurynorhynchus pygmeus*	N	1/14	W	18	C1; C2b
Japanese Murrelet *Synthliboramphus wumizusume*	B	2/3	RM	1346	C1
Fairy Pitta *Pitta nympha*	B	4/6	F	17	C1; C2a
Yellow Bunting *Emberiza sulphurata*	N	1/6	FSA	0	C1; C2a

Conservation Dependent

Hooded Crane *Grus monacha*	N	2/4		

Band-bellied Crake *Porzana paykullii*	N	2/7
Long-billed Plover *Charadrius placidus*	N	4/8

Near-threatened

Swinhoe's Storm-petrel *Oceanodroma monorhis*	B	3		
Schrenck's Bittern *Ixobrychus eurhythmus*	B	5/10		
Mandarin Duck *Aix galericulata*	B	5/4		
White-tailed Eagle *Haliaeetus albicilla*	N	34/10		
Cinereous Vulture *Aegypius monachus*	N	18/13		

Far Eastern Curlew *Numenius madagascariensis*	N	3/14
Relict Gull *Larus relictus*	N	3/3
Japanese Wood-pigeon *Columba janthina*	B	3
Japanese Waxwing *Bombycilla japonica*	N	1/5
Japanese Paradise-flycatcher *Terpsiphone atrocaudata*	B	4/8
Ochre-rumped Bunting *Emberiza yessoensis*	N	3/3

SPAIN

Species totals Vulnerable 10 Conservation
 Extinct 1 Dependent 2
 Near-threatened 3

	Status (breeding/ non-br.)	Breeding/ non-br. countries	Habitat codes (p. 243)	Threat codes (p. 243)	IUCN threat status codes (pp. 16–18)
Vulnerable					
White-headed Duck *Oxyura leucocephala*	B	12/16	W	1256	A2d
Marbled Teal *Marmaronetta angustirostris*	B	21/3	W	125	A2b
Ferruginous Duck *Aythya nyroca*	B	38/32	W	12	A1a,b,c
Spanish Imperial Eagle *Aquila adalberti*	B	2/1	FG	2359	D1
Lesser Kestrel *Falco naumanni*	B	37/52	FSVGA	15	A1a,b,d
Corncrake *Crex crex*	B	40/31	GWA	12	A1a,b
Great Bustard *Otis tarda*	B	23	GA	125	A2b
Dark-tailed Laurel Pigeon *Columba bollii*	B	1	F	126	C2a
White-tailed Laurel Pigeon *Columba junoniae*	B	1	F	126	C2a
Aquatic Warbler *Acrocephalus paludicola*	N	8/13	W	18	A2b

Extinct

Canary Islands Oystercatcher *Haematopus meadewaldoi*	B	1

Conservation Dependent

Audouin's Gull *Larus audouinii*	B	8/7
Blue Chaffinch *Fringilla teydea*	B	1

Near-threatened

Cinereous Vulture *Aegypius monachus*	B	18/13
Little Bustard *Tetrax tetrax*	B	13/10
Fuerteventura Chat *Saxicola dacotiae*	B	1

SRI LANKA

Species totals Endangered 2 Near-threatened 17
 Vulnerable 9

	Status (breeding/ non-br.)	Breeding/ non-br. countries	Habitat codes (p. 243)	Threat codes (p. 243)	IUCN threat status codes (pp. 16–18)
Endangered					
Green-billed Coucal *Centropus chlororhynchus*	B	1	F	1	A1b; **B1+2c**; C1; C2a
Sri Lanka Whistling-thrush *Myiophonus blighi*	B	1	FR	19	**B1+2c; C1**; D1
Vulnerable					
Spot-billed Pelican *Pelecanus philippensis*	B	3/8	W	1235	A1a,b,c,d; C1
Lesser Adjutant *Leptoptilos javanicus*	B	12/1	FW	123	C1
Sociable Lapwing *Vanellus gregarius*	N	2/15	GW	158	A1a,b; C1; C2a
Spoon-billed Sandpiper *Eurynorhynchus pygmeus*	N	1/14	W	18	C1; C2b
Sri Lanka Wood-pigeon *Columba torringtoni*	B	1	F	1	B1+2c; C1; C2a
Red-faced Malkoha *Phaenicophaeus pyrrhocephalus*	B	1	F	12	A1b; C1; C2a
Ashy-headed Laughingthrush *Garrulax cinereifrons*	B	1	F	1	B1+2c; C1; C2a

cont.

Sri Lanka (cont.)

Kashmir Flycatcher *Ficedula subrubra*	N	2/3	F	1	B1+2c
Sri Lanka Magpie *Urocissa ornata*	B	1	F	18	B1+2a,c; C1; C2a

Near-threatened

Oriental Darter *Anhinga melanogaster*	B	13	Yellow-eared Bulbul *Pycnonotus penicillatus*	B	1
Painted Stork *Mycteria leucocephala*	B	11	Pied Thrush *Zoothera wardii*	N	3/2
Asian Openbill *Anastomus oscitans*	B	9	Spot-winged Thrush *Zoothera spiloptera*	B	1
Black-headed Ibis *Threskiornis melanocephalus*	B	10/8	Sri Lanka Bush-warbler *Bradypterus palliseri*	B	1
Pallid Harrier *Circus macrourus*	N	4/57	Brown-breasted Flycatcher *Muscicapa muttui*	N	2/4
Spot-bellied Eagle-owl *Bubo nipalensis*	B	11	Dull-blue Flycatcher *Eumyias sordida*	B	1
Chestnut-backed Owlet *Glaucidium castanonotum*	B	1	White-throated Flowerpecker *Dicaeum vincens*	B	1
Sri Lanka Frogmouth *Batrachostomus moniliger*	B	2	White-faced Starling *Sturnus senex*	B	1
Malabar Pied-hornbill *Anthracoceros coronatus*	B	2			

ST HELENA (to U.K.)

Species totals Endangered 1

	Status (breeding/ non-br.)	Breeding/ non-br. countries	Habitat codes (p. 243)	Threat codes (p. 243)	IUCN threat status codes (pp. 16–18)
Endangered					
St Helena Plover *Charadrius sanctaehelenae*	B	1	GA	169	**C1; C2b**; D1; D2

ST KITTS AND NEVIS

Species totals Vulnerable 1
Near-threatened 1

	Status (breeding/ non-br.)	Breeding/ non-br. countries	Habitat codes (p. 243)	Threat codes (p. 243)	IUCN threat status codes (pp. 16–18)
Vulnerable					
West Indian Whistling-duck *Dendrocygna arborea*	B	12	W	12	C2a
Near-threatened					
Bridled Quail-dove *Geotrygon mystacea*	B	13			

ST LUCIA

Species totals Critical 1 Vulnerable 1
Endangered 1 Near-threatened 4

	Status (breeding/ non-br.)	Breeding/ non-br. countries	Habitat codes (p. 243)	Threat codes (p. 243)	IUCN threat status codes (pp. 16–18)
Critical					
Semper's Warbler *Leucopeza semperi*	B	1	F	9	**D1**
Endangered					
White-breasted Thrasher *Ramphocinclus brachyurus*	B	2	F	169	A1a,b,d; A2b,d; **B1+2e; C1; C2a; D1**; D2
Vulnerable					
St Lucia Amazon *Amazona versicolor*	B	1	F	89	D1; D2

Near-threatened

Bridled Quail-dove *Geotrygon mystacea*	B	13	St Lucia Black Finch *Melanospiza richardsoni*	B	1
Forest Thrush *Cichlherminia lherminieri*	B	4	St Lucia Oriole *Icterus laudabilis*	B	1

ST VINCENT

Species totals Vulnerable 2

	Status (breeding/ non-br.)	Breeding/ non-br. countries	Habitat codes (p. 243)	Threat codes (p. 243)	IUCN threat status codes (pp. 16–18)
Vulnerable					
St Vincent Amazon *Amazona guildingii*	B	1	F	89	D1; D2
Whistling Warbler *Catharopeza bishopi*	B	1	F	9	D2

SUDAN

| | Species totals | Endangered | 1 | Near-threatened | 8 |
| | | Vulnerable | 8 | | |

	Status (breeding/ non-br.)	Breeding/ non-br. countries	Habitat codes (p. 243)	Threat codes (p. 243)	IUCN threat status codes (pp. 16–18)
Endangered					
Spotted Ground-thrush *Zoothera guttata*	B	5/1	F	1	B1+2c; **C2a**
Vulnerable					
Ferruginous Duck *Aythya nyroca*	N	38/32	W	12	A1a,b,c
Greater Spotted Eagle *Aquila clanga*	N	14/35	FW	13	C2a
Imperial Eagle *Aquila heliaca*	N	24/21	FG	12357	C2a
Lesser Kestrel *Falco naumanni*	N	37/52	FSVGA	15	A1a,b,d
Corncrake *Crex crex*	N	40/31	GWA	12	A1a,b
Sociable Lapwing *Vanellus gregarius*	N	2/15	GW	158	A1a,b; C1; C2a
White-eyed Gull *Larus leucophthalmus*	B	5/1	WM	1235	C1
Red Sea Swallow *Hirundo perdita*	B	1	Z	09	D1

Near-threatened				
Shoebill *Balaeniceps rex*	B 8/1	Black-winged Pratincole *Glareola nordmanni*	N 10/22
Pallid Harrier *Circus macrourus*	N 4/57	White-naped Pigeon *Columba albinucha*	B 4
Nubian Bustard *Neotis nuba*	B 5	Basra Reed-warbler *Acrocephalus griseldis*	N 1/8
Great Snipe *Gallinago media*	N 10/35	Cinereous Bunting *Emberiza cineracea*	N 3/13

SURINAME

| | Species totals | Vulnerable | 1 |
| | | Near-threatened | 16 |

	Status (breeding/ non-br.)	Breeding/ non-br. countries	Habitat codes (p. 243)	Threat codes (p. 243)	IUCN threat status codes (pp. 16–18)
Vulnerable					
Rufous-sided Pygmy-tyrant *Euscarthmus rufomarginatus*	B	4	VSG	1	A1b; A2b

Near-threatened				
Agami Heron *Agamia agami*	B 16	Orange-breasted Falcon *Falco deiroleucus*	B 17
Zigzag Heron *Zebrilus undulatus*	B 9	Ocellated Crake *Micropygia schomburgkii*	B 8
Orinoco Goose *Neochen jubata*	B 10	Blue-cheeked Parrot *Amazona dufresniana*	B 4
Grey-bellied Goshawk *Accipiter poliogaster*	B 10	Fiery-tailed Awlbill *Avocettula recurvirostris*	B 7
Solitary Eagle *Harpyhaliaetus solitarius*	B 17	Bearded Tachuri *Polystictus pectoralis*	B 9
Crested Eagle *Morphnus guianensis*	B 15	Boat-billed Tody-tyrant *Hemitriccus josephinae*	B 3
Harpy Eagle *Harpia harpyja*	B 17	Large-billed Seed-finch *Oryzoborus crassirostris*	B 9
Black-and-white Hawk-eagle *Spizastur melanoleucus*	B 14	Dotted Tanager *Tangara varia*	B 4

SWAZILAND

| | Species totals | Vulnerable | 4 |

	Status (breeding/ non-br.)	Breeding/ non-br. countries	Habitat codes (p. 243)	Threat codes (p. 243)	IUCN threat status codes (pp. 16–18)
Vulnerable					
Southern Bald Ibis *Geronticus calvus*	B	3	GR	1	C2b
Cape Griffon *Gyps coprotheres*	B	6	SGDR	235	A1a,c,d; A2c,d; C1; C2b
Blue Crane *Grus paradisea*	B	4	GWA	15	A1a,b; A2b; C1; C2a
Blue Swallow *Hirundo atrocaerulea*	B	7/3	G	1	A1b; A2b; C1; C2a

SWEDEN

| | Species totals | Vulnerable | 4 |
| | | Near-threatened | 2 |

	Status (breeding/ non-br.)	Breeding/ non-br. countries	Habitat codes (p. 243)	Threat codes (p. 243)	IUCN threat status codes (pp. 16–18)
Vulnerable					
Lesser White-fronted Goose *Anser erythropus*	B	4/11	SWA	012	A1a,b,c
Steller's Eider *Polysticta stelleri*	N	2/8	WM	0	A1a

cont.

Sweden (cont.)

	Status (breeding/non-br.)	Breeding/non-br. countries	Habitat codes	Threat codes	IUCN threat status codes
Greater Spotted Eagle *Aquila clanga*	N	14/35	FW	13	C2a
Corncrake *Crex crex*	B	40/31	GWA	12	A1a,b

Near-threatened
White-tailed Eagle *Haliaeetus albicilla*   B 34/10   Great Snipe *Gallinago media*   B 10/35

SWITZERLAND

Species totals Vulnerable 3

	Status (breeding/non-br.)	Breeding/non-br. countries	Habitat codes (p. 243)	Threat codes (p. 243)	IUCN threat status codes (pp. 16–18)
Vulnerable					
Ferruginous Duck *Aythya nyroca*	N	38/32	W	12	A1a,b,c
Corncrake *Crex crex*	B	40/31	GWA	12	A1a,b
Aquatic Warbler *Acrocephalus paludicola*	N	8/13	W	18	A2b

SYRIA

Species totals Vulnerable 6
Near-threatened 3

	Status (breeding/non-br.)	Breeding/non-br. countries	Habitat codes (p. 243)	Threat codes (p. 243)	IUCN threat status codes (pp. 16–18)
Vulnerable					
Dalmatian Pelican *Pelecanus crispus*	N	16/9	W	1235	C2a
White-headed Duck *Oxyura leucocephala*	N	12/16	W	1256	A2d
Imperial Eagle *Aquila heliaca*	N	24/21	FG	12357	C2a
Lesser Kestrel *Falco naumanni*	B	37/52	FSVGA	15	A1a,b,d
Corncrake *Crex crex*	N	40/31	GWA	12	A1a,b
Great Bustard *Otis tarda*	B	23	GA	125	A2b

Near-threatened
Pallid Harrier *Circus macrourus*   N 4/57   Cinereous Bunting *Emberiza cineracea*   N 3/13
Black-winged Pratincole *Glareola nordmanni*   B 10/22

TAIWAN

Species totals Critical 1   Vulnerable 7
Endangered 4   Near-threatened 20

	Status (breeding/non-br.)	Breeding/non-br. countries	Habitat codes (p. 243)	Threat codes (p. 243)	IUCN threat status codes (pp. 16–18)
Critical					
Black-faced Spoonbill *Platalea minor*	N	2/8	WR	12359	**A2b**; C1; C2a; D1; D2
Endangered					
Chinese Egret *Egretta eulophotes*	N	3/10	WR	1	**C1**; C2a
Oriental Stork *Ciconia boyciana*	N	2/9	W	1235	A2b; **C1**
Nordmann's Greenshank *Tringa guttifer*	N	1/15	FW	12389	**C1**; C2b; D1
Saunders's Gull *Larus saundersi*	N	1/6	W	1235	A1b,c,d; **A2b,c,d**; C1; C2a
Vulnerable					
Japanese Night-heron *Gorsachius goisagi*	B	2/10	F	1	C1; C2a
Swan Goose *Anser cygnoides*	N	4/5	W	12	A1b,c; A2b,c
Baikal Teal *Anas formosa*	N	1/5	FW	259	A1a,c,d; D2
Baer's Pochard *Aythya baeri*	N	2/12	W	123	A1a,b; C1
Spoon-billed Sandpiper *Eurynorhynchus pygmeus*	N	1/14	W	18	C1; C2b
Fairy Pitta *Pitta nympha*	B	4/6	F	17	C1; C2a
Yellow Bunting *Emberiza sulphurata*	N	1/6	FSA	0	C1; C2a

Near-threatened
Swinhoe's Storm-petrel *Oceanodroma monorhis*   B 3   White-tailed Eagle *Haliaeetus albicilla*   N 34/10
Schrenck's Bittern *Ixobrychus eurhythmus*   N 5/10   Taiwan Partridge *Arborophila crudigularis*   B 1
Black-headed Ibis *Threskiornis melanocephalus*   B 10/8   Swinhoe's Pheasant *Lophura swinhoii*   B 1
Mandarin Duck *Aix galericulata*   N 5/4   Mikado Pheasant *Syrmaticus mikado*   B 1

cont.

Taiwan (cont.)

Grey-headed Lapwing *Vanellus cinereus*	N	3/11	Tawny Fish-owl *Ketupa flavipes*	B	9
Latham's Snipe *Gallinago hardwickii*	N	1/5	Styan's Bulbul *Pycnonotus taivanus*	B	1
Far Eastern Curlew *Numenius madagascariensis*	N	3/14	Japanese Waxwing *Bombycilla japonica*	N	1/5
Japanese Wood-pigeon *Columba janthina*	B	3	Japanese Paradise-flycatcher *Terpsiphone atrocaudata*	N	4/8
White-bellied Green-pigeon *Treron sieboldii*	B	6	Yellow Tit *Parus holsti*	B	1
Whistling Green-pigeon *Treron formosae*	B	3	Chestnut-cheeked Starling *Sturnus philippensis*	N	2/5

TAJIKISTAN

Species totals Vulnerable 9
Near-threatened 5

	Status (breeding/ non-br.)	Breeding/ non-br. countries	Habitat codes (p. 243)	Threat codes (p. 243)	IUCN threat status codes (pp. 16–18)
Vulnerable					
White-headed Duck *Oxyura leucocephala*	N	12/16	W	1256	A2d
Marbled Teal *Marmaronetta angustirostris*	B	21/3	W	125	A2b
Ferruginous Duck *Aythya nyroca*	B	38/32	W	12	A1a,b,c
Pallas's Sea-eagle *Haliaeetus leucoryphus*	B	11/1	GW	135	C1; C2b
Lesser Kestrel *Falco naumanni*	B	37/52	FSVGA	15	A1a,b,d
Corncrake *Crex crex*	B	40/31	GWA	12	A1a,b
Great Bustard *Otis tarda*	B	23	GA	125	A2b
Sociable Lapwing *Vanellus gregarius*	N	2/15	GW	158	A1a,b; C1; C2a
Pale-backed Pigeon *Columba eversmanni*	B	7/2	GDA	0	A1a
Near-threatened					
Pygmy Cormorant *Phalacrocorax pygmeus*	B	17/4	Little Bustard *Tetrax tetrax*	N	13/10
White-tailed Eagle *Haliaeetus albicilla*	N	34/10	White-winged Woodpecker *Dendrocopos leucopterus*	B	7
Cinereous Vulture *Aegypius monachus*	B	18/13			

TANZANIA

Species totals Critical 2 Vulnerable 26
Endangered 2 Near-threatened 22

	Status (breeding/ non-br.)	Breeding/ non-br. countries	Habitat codes (p. 243)	Threat codes (p. 243)	IUCN threat status codes (pp. 16–18)
Critical					
Uluguru Bush-shrike *Malaconotus alius*	B	1	F	19	B1+2c; **C2b**; D1
Long-billed Tailorbird *Orthotomus moreaui*	B	2	F	1	B1+2c; **C2a**
Endangered					
Udzungwa Forest-partridge *Xenoperdix udzungwensis*	B	1	F	2	**B1+2e**; C1; C2b
Spotted Ground-thrush *Zoothera guttata*	B	5/1	F	1	B1+2c; **C2a**
Vulnerable					
Lesser Kestrel *Falco naumanni*	N	37/52	FSVGA	15	A1a,b,d
Taita Falcon *Falco fasciinucha*	B	8	VR	1589	C1; D1
Wattled Crane *Grus carunculatus*	B	11	W	123	A2b,c; C1
Corncrake *Crex crex*	N	40/31	GWA	12	A1a,b
Sokoke Scops-owl *Otus ireneae*	B	2	F	9	D2
Usambara Eagle-owl *Bubo vosseleri*	B	1	F	19	B1+2a,c; C2b
Blue Swallow *Hirundo atrocaerulea*	B	7/3	G	1	A1b; A2b; C1; C2a
Sokoke Pipit *Anthus sokokensis*	B	2	F	1	B1+2a,b,c; C2a
Grey-crested Helmet-shrike *Prionops poliolophus*	B	2	FSV	1	C2b
Swynnerton's Robin *Swynnertonia swynnertoni*	B	3	F	1	B1+2b,c
East Coast Akalat *Sheppardia gunningi*	B	4	F	1	B1+2b,c
Usambara Akalat *Sheppardia montana*	B	1	F	1	B1+2a,c
Iringa Akalat *Sheppardia lowei*	B	1	F	1	B1+2b,c
Dappled Mountain-robin *Modulatrix orostruthus*	B	2	F	1	B1+2b,c
White-winged Apalis *Apalis chariessa*	B	4	F	1	B1+2b,c
Kungwe Apalis *Apalis argentea*	B	4	F	1	B1+2a,c,e
Karamoja Apalis *Apalis karamojae*	B	2	S	1	A2b; B1+2c
Mrs Moreau's Warbler *Bathmocercus winifredae*	B	1	F	1	B1+2b,c
Papyrus Yellow Warbler *Chloropeta gracilirostris*	B	7	W	1	B1+2a,b,c,d
Amani Sunbird *Anthreptes pallidigaster*	B	2	F	1	B1+2b,c
Banded Sunbird *Anthreptes rubritorques*	B	1	F	1	B1+2b,c

cont.

Tanzania (cont.)

Rufous-winged Sunbird *Nectarinia rufipennis*	B	1	F	9	D2
South Pare White-eye *Zosterops winifredae*	B	1	FS	1	B1+2c; C2a
Kilombero Weaver *Ploceus burnieri*	B	1	W	19	B1+2c; C2b; D1
Tanzanian Mountain Weaver *Ploceus nicolli*	B	1	F	19	B1+2b,c; C2a; D1
Abbott's Starling *Cinnyricinclus femoralis*	B	2	F	1	B1+2c; C2a

Near-threatened

Madagascar Pond-heron *Ardeola idae*	N	2/9	Stierling's Woodpecker *Dendropicos stierlingi*	B	3
Shoebill *Balaeniceps rex*	B	8/1	Churring Cisticola *Cisticola njombe*	B	3
Lesser Flamingo *Phoenicopterus minor*	N	8/20	Basra Reed-warbler *Acrocephalus griseldis*	N	1/8
Southern Banded Snake-eagle *Circaetus fasciolatus*	B	6	Red-throated Tit *Parus fringillinus*	B	2
Pallid Harrier *Circus macrourus*	N	4/57	Plain-backed Sunbird *Anthreptes reichenowi*	B	5
Great Snipe *Gallinago media*	N	10/35	Loveridge's Sunbird *Nectarinia loveridgei*	B	1
Pemba Green-pigeon *Treron pembaensis*	B	1	Moreau's Sunbird *Nectarinia moreaui*	B	1
Fischer's Lovebird *Agapornis fischeri*	B	1	Pemba Sunbird *Nectarinia pembae*	B	1
Fischer's Turaco *Tauraco fischeri*	B	3	Pemba White-eye *Zosterops vaughani*	B	1
Pemba Scops-owl *Otus pembaensis*	B	1	Kipengere Seedeater *Serinus melanochrous*	B	1
Red-faced Barbet *Lybius rubrifacies*	B	3	Jackson's Widowbird *Euplectes jacksoni*	B	2

THAILAND

Species totals	Critical	5	Data Deficient	1
	Endangered	6	Near-threatened	57
	Vulnerable	33		

	Status (breeding/ non-br.)	Breeding/ non-br. countries	Habitat codes (p. 243)	Threat codes (p. 243)	IUCN threat status codes (pp. 16–18)
Critical					
Giant Ibis *Pseudibis gigantea*	B	4	FW	1239	A1b; A2b,c; B1+2c; **C1**; C2a; D1
Black-faced Spoonbill *Platalea minor*	N	2/8	WR	12359	**A2b**; C1; C2a; D1; D2
Chinese Crested-tern *Sterna bernsteini*	N	1/5	MZ	09	**D1**
Gurney's Pitta *Pitta gurneyi*	B	2	F	19	**A1b**; **B1+2c**; **C1**; C2a; D1; D2
White-eyed River-martin *Pseudochelidon sirintarae*	N	0/1	W	09	**D1**
Endangered					
Chinese Egret *Egretta eulophotes*	N	3/10	WR	1	**C1**; C2a
Storm's Stork *Ciconia stormi*	B	4	FW	19	A1b,c; **C1**; **C2a**; D1
Greater Adjutant *Leptoptilos dubius*	B	8	FWU	129	A1b,c; **C1**; C2a; D1
White-shouldered Ibis *Pseudibis davisoni*	B	8	FW	1239	A1b; A2b; **C1**; **C2a**; D1
White-winged Duck *Cairina scutulata*	B	9	FW	1239	A1b,c,d; **C1**; **C2a**; D1
Nordmann's Greenshank *Tringa guttifer*	N	1/15	FW	12389	**C1**; C2b; D1
Vulnerable					
Spot-billed Pelican *Pelecanus philippensis*	N	3/8	W	1235	A1a,b,c,d; C1
Christmas Island Frigatebird *Fregata andrewsi*	N	1/9	FM	9	D2
Lesser Adjutant *Leptoptilos javanicus*	B	12/1	FW	123	C1
Ferruginous Duck *Aythya nyroca*	N	38/32	W	12	A1a,b,c
Baer's Pochard *Aythya baeri*	N	2/12	W	123	A1a,b; C1
Greater Spotted Eagle *Aquila clanga*	N	14/35	FW	13	C2a
Wallace's Hawk-eagle *Spizaetus nanus*	B	5	F	1	A1b; A2b; C1; C2a
Chestnut-headed Partridge *Arborophila cambodiana*	B	2	F	12	B1+2c; C1; C2a
Chestnut-necklaced Partridge *Arborophila charltonii*	B	4	F	1	A1b
Crested Fireback *Lophura ignita*	B	5	FS	12	A1b,c; A2b,c
Siamese Fireback *Lophura diardi*	B	4	F	12	A1b,c; A2b,c
Hume's Pheasant *Syrmaticus humiae*	B	4	FG	12	C1; C2a
Malayan Peacock-pheasant *Polyplectron malacense*	B	2	F	1	A1b; A2b; C1; C2a
Green Peafowl *Pavo muticus*	B	7	FSG	12	A1b,c; A2b,c
Masked Finfoot *Heliopais personata*	B	9	FW	13	C1; C2a
Wood Snipe *Gallinago nemoricola*	N	4/6	SGW	1	C2a
Spoon-billed Sandpiper *Eurynorhynchus pygmeus*	N	1/14	W	18	C1; C2b
Black-bellied Tern *Sterna acuticauda*	B	9	W	128	C1
Pale-capped Pigeon *Columba punicea*	B	7	FSA	1	C1; C2a
White-fronted Scops-owl *Otus sagittatus*	B	4	F	1	A1b; A2b; C1; C2a
Blyth's Kingfisher *Alcedo hercules*	B	9	F	1	A1b; A2b; C1; C2a
Rufous-necked Hornbill *Aceros nipalensis*	B	8	F	12	A1b,c; C1; C2a
Wrinkled Hornbill *Aceros corrugatus*	B	4	F	1	A1b; A2b; C1; C2a
Plain-pouched Hornbill *Aceros subruficollis*	B	3	F	1	C1; C2a

cont.

Thailand (cont.)

Straw-headed Bulbul *Pycnonotus zeylanicus*	B	5	F	17	A1b,c
Grey-sided Thrush *Turdus feae*	N	1/3	F	1	B1+2c; C1; C2a
Black-throated Blue Robin *Luscinia obscura*	N	1/2	F	1	C1; C2a
Deignan's Babbler *Stachyris rodolphei*	B	1	F	9	D2
Short-tailed Parrotbill *Paradoxornis davidianus*	B	5	S	1	A1b; C1; C2a
Brown-chested Jungle-flycatcher *Rhinomyias brunneata*	N	1/5	F	1	A1b; A2b
Giant Nuthatch *Sitta magna*	B	3	F	1	A1b; C1; C2a
Beautiful Nuthatch *Sitta formosa*	B	7	F	1	C1; C2a
Silver Oriole *Oriolus mellianus*	N	1/2	F	1	B1+2c; C1; C2a

Data Deficient

Large Frogmouth *Batrachostomus auritus* — B 4

Near-threatened

Great-billed Heron *Ardea sumatrana* — B 10
Schrenck's Bittern *Ixobrychus eurhythmus* — N 5/10
Painted Stork *Mycteria leucocephala* — B 11
Asian Openbill *Anastomus oscitans* — B 9
Black-headed Ibis *Threskiornis melanocephalus* — N 10/8
Jerdon's Baza *Aviceda jerdoni* — B 9
Lesser Fish-eagle *Ichthyophaga humilis* — B 9
Grey-headed Fish-eagle *Ichthyophaga ichthyaetus* — B 13
White-rumped Vulture *Gyps bengalensis* — B 11
Long-billed Vulture *Gyps indicus* — B 9
Cinereous Vulture *Aegypius monachus* — N 18/13
Red-headed Vulture *Sarcogyps calvus* — B 11
Rufous-winged Buzzard *Butastur liventer* — B 7
White-rumped Falcon *Polihierax insignis* — B 5
Band-bellied Crake *Porzana paykullii* — N 2/7
Malaysian Plover *Charadrius peronii* — B 6
Grey-headed Lapwing *Vanellus cinereus* — N 3/11
Far Eastern Curlew *Numenius madagascariensis* — N 3/14
Asian Dowitcher *Limnodromus semipalmatus* — N 3/14
Nicobar Pigeon *Caloenas nicobarica* — B 11
Cinnamon-headed Green-pigeon *Treron fulvicollis* — B 5
Large Green-pigeon *Treron capellei* — B 5
Yellow-vented Green-pigeon *Treron seimundi* — B 4
White-bellied Green-pigeon *Treron sieboldii* — B 6
Blue-rumped Parrot *Psittinus cyanurus* — B 5
Coral-billed Ground-cuckoo *Carpococcyx renauldi* — B 4
Spot-bellied Eagle-owl *Bubo nipalensis* — B 11

Brown-winged Kingfisher *Pelargopsis amauropterus* — B 5
Black Hornbill *Anthracoceros malayanus* — B 4
Helmeted Hornbill *Buceros vigil* — B 5
Brown Hornbill *Anorrhinus tickelli* — B 6
Red-crowned Barbet *Megalaima rafflesii* — B 5
Malaysian Honeyguide *Indicator archipelagicus* — B 4
Blue-rumped Pitta *Pitta soror* — B 5
Giant Pitta *Pitta caerulea* — B 4
Mangrove Pitta *Pitta megarhyncha* — B 5
Black-breasted Thrush *Turdus dissimilis* — N 4/2
Blue-fronted Robin *Cinclidium frontale* — B 6
Purple Cochoa *Cochoa purpurea* — B 8
Green Cochoa *Cochoa viridis* — B 7
Jerdon's Bushchat *Saxicola jerdoni* — B 7
Spot-breasted Laughingthrush *Garrulax merulinus* — B 6
Red-tailed Laughingthrush *Garrulax milnei* — B 5
White-chested Babbler *Trichastoma rostratum* — B 5
Ferruginous Babbler *Trichastoma bicolor* — B 5
Large Wren-babbler *Napothera macrodactyla* — B 3
Rufous-throated Fulvetta *Alcippe rufogularis* — B 9
Burmese Yuhina *Yuhina humilis* — B 2
Black-browed Parrotbill *Paradoxornis atrosuperciliaris* — B 6
Yellow-vented Warbler *Phylloscopus cantator* — N 3/6
Brown-breasted Flycatcher *Muscicapa muttui* — N 2/4
Fujian Niltava *Niltava davidi* — N 3/2
Japanese Paradise-flycatcher *Terpsiphone atrocaudata* — N 4/8
Asian Golden Weaver *Ploceus hypoxanthus* — B 6
Spot-winged Starling *Saroglossa spiloptera* — N 2/5
Black Magpie *Platysmurus leucopterus* — B 5
Yellow-breasted Magpie *Cissa hypoleuca* — B 4

TOGO

Species totals Near-threatened 5

Near-threatened

Pallid Harrier *Circus macrourus* — N 4/57
Great Snipe *Gallinago media* — N 10/35
Yellow-casqued Hornbill *Ceratogymna elata* — B 11

Baumann's Greenbul *Phyllastrephus baumanni* — B 6
Rufous-winged Illadopsis *Illadopsis rufescens* — B 6

TOKELAU (to New Zealand)

Species totals Vulnerable 1

	Status (breeding/ non-br.)	Breeding/ non-br. countries	Habitat codes (p. 243)	Threat codes (p. 243)	IUCN threat status codes (pp. 16–18)
Vulnerable					
Bristle-thighed Curlew *Numenius tahitiensis*	N	1/14	GW	1268	C2b

TONGA

	Species totals	Endangered	1	Near-threatened	2
		Vulnerable	1		

	Status (breeding/ non-br.)	Breeding/ non-br. countries	Habitat codes (p. 243)	Threat codes (p. 243)	IUCN threat status codes (pp. 16–18)
Endangered					
Niuafoou Scrubfowl *Megapodius pritchardii*	B	1	F	12689	**B1+2e; C2a**; D1; D2
Vulnerable					
Bristle-thighed Curlew *Numenius tahitiensis*	N	1/14	GW	1268	C2b

Near-threatened

Shy Ground-dove *Gallicolumba stairi*	B 5	Tongan Whistler *Pachycephala jacquinoti*	B 1	

TRINIDAD AND TOBAGO

	Species totals	Critical	1	Near-threatened	4
		Vulnerable	1		

	Status (breeding/ non-br.)	Breeding/ non-br. countries	Habitat codes (p. 243)	Threat codes (p. 243)	IUCN threat status codes (pp. 16–18)
Critical					
Trinidad Piping-guan *Pipile pipile*	B	1	F	129	A2b,c; B1+2c; C1; **C2a**; D1; D2
Vulnerable					
White-tailed Sabrewing *Campylopterus ensipennis*	B	2	F	18	A2b

Near-threatened

Agami Heron *Agamia agami*	B 16	Large-billed Seed-finch *Oryzoborus crassirostris*	B 9	
Orange-breasted Falcon *Falco deiroleucus*	B 17	Great-billed Seed-finch *Oryzoborus maximiliani*	B 4	

TRISTAN DA CUNHA GROUP (to U.K.)

	Species totals	Vulnerable	7
		Near-threatened	2

	Status (breeding/ non-br.)	Breeding/ non-br. countries	Habitat codes (p. 243)	Threat codes (p. 243)	IUCN threat status codes (pp. 16–18)
Vulnerable					
Wandering Albatross *Diomedea exulans*	B	6	MG	4	A1a,c; A2c
Atlantic Petrel *Pterodroma incerta*	B	1	GM	69	D2
Inaccessible Rail *Atlantisia rogersi*	B	1	G	9	D2
Gough Moorhen *Gallinula nesiotis*	B	1	G	9	D2
Gough Bunting *Rowettia goughensis*	B	1	G	9	D1; D2
Tristan Bunting *Nesospiza acunhae*	B	1	G	9	D2
Grosbeak Bunting *Nesospiza wilkinsi*	B	1	S	9	D1; D2

Near-threatened

Sooty Albatross *Phoebetria fusca*	B 3	Tristan Thrush *Nesocichla eremita*	B 1	

TUNISIA

	Species totals	Critical	1	Conservation	
		Vulnerable	5	Dependent	1
		Near-threatened	2		

	Status (breeding/ non-br.)	Breeding/ non-br. countries	Habitat codes (p. 243)	Threat codes (p. 243)	IUCN threat status codes (pp. 16–18)
Critical					
Slender-billed Curlew *Numenius tenuirostris*	N	1/10	WG	1289	**C2b**; D1
Vulnerable					
White-headed Duck *Oxyura leucocephala*	B	12/16	W	1256	A2d
Marbled Teal *Marmaronetta angustirostris*	B	21/3	W	125	A2b
Ferruginous Duck *Aythya nyroca*	N	38/32	W	12	A1a,b,c
Lesser Kestrel *Falco naumanni*	B	37/52	FSVGA	15	A1a,b,d
Corncrake *Crex crex*	N	40/31	GWA	12	A1a,b

Conservation Dependent		**Near-threatened**	
Audouin's Gull *Larus audouinii*	B 8/7	Pallid Harrier *Circus macrourus*	N 4/57
		Little Bustard *Tetrax tetrax*	N 13/10

TURKEY

Species totals	Critical	1	Conservation	
	Vulnerable	12	Dependent	1
	Near-threatened	9		

	Status (breeding/ non-br.)	Breeding/ non-br. countries	Habitat codes (p. 243)	Threat codes (p. 243)	IUCN threat status codes (pp. 16–18)
Critical					
Slender-billed Curlew *Numenius tenuirostris*	N	1/10	WG	1289	**C2b**; D1
Vulnerable					
Dalmatian Pelican *Pelecanus crispus*	B	16/9	W	1235	C2a
White-headed Duck *Oxyura leucocephala*	B	12/16	W	1256	A2d
Lesser White-fronted Goose *Anser erythropus*	N	4/11	SWA	012	A1a,b,c
Red-breasted Goose *Branta ruficollis*	N	1/4	SWA	12	A2b,c; B1+2c,d
Marbled Teal *Marmaronetta angustirostris*	B	21/3	W	125	A2b
Ferruginous Duck *Aythya nyroca*	B	38/32	W	12	A1a,b,c
Greater Spotted Eagle *Aquila clanga*	N	14/35	FW	13	C2a
Imperial Eagle *Aquila heliaca*	B	24/21	FG	12357	C2a
Lesser Kestrel *Falco naumanni*	B	37/52	FSVGA	15	A1a,b,d
Corncrake *Crex crex*	B	40/31	GWA	12	A1a,b
Great Bustard *Otis tarda*	B	23	GA	125	A2b
Sociable Lapwing *Vanellus gregarius*	N	2/15	GW	158	A1a,b; C1; C2a

Conservation Dependent			Pallid Harrier *Circus macrourus*	N 4/57
Audouin's Gull *Larus audouinii*	B	8/7	Caucasian Black aGrouse *Tetrao mlokosiewiczi*	B 5
Near-threatened			Little Bustard *Tetrax tetrax*	B 13/10
Pygmy Cormorant *Phalacrocorax pygmeus*	B	17/4	Great Snipe *Gallinago media*	N 10/35
White-tailed Eagle *Haliaeetus albicilla*	B	34/10	Black-winged Pratincole *Glareola nordmanni*	N 10/22
Cinereous Vulture *Aegypius monachus*	B	18/13	Cinereous Bunting *Emberiza cineracea*	B 3/13

TURKMENISTAN

Species totals	Vulnerable	9
	Near-threatened	5

	Status (breeding/ non-br.)	Breeding/ non-br. countries	Habitat codes (p. 243)	Threat codes (p. 243)	IUCN threat status codes (pp. 16–18)
Vulnerable					
Dalmatian Pelican *Pelecanus crispus*	B	16/9	W	1235	C2a
White-headed Duck *Oxyura leucocephala*	N	12/16	W	1256	A2d
Marbled Teal *Marmaronetta angustirostris*	B	21/3	W	125	A2b
Ferruginous Duck *Aythya nyroca*	B	38/32	W	12	A1a,b,c
Imperial Eagle *Aquila heliaca*	B	24/21	FG	12357	C2a
Lesser Kestrel *Falco naumanni*	B	37/52	FSVGA	15	A1a,b,d
Corncrake *Crex crex*	N	40/31	GWA	12	A1a,b
Sociable Lapwing *Vanellus gregarius*	N	2/15	GW	158	A1a,b; C1; C2a
Pale-backed Pigeon *Columba eversmanni*	B	7/2	GDA	0	A1a

Near-threatened				
Pygmy Cormorant *Phalacrocorax pygmeus*	B	17/4	Little Bustard *Tetrax tetrax*	N 13/10
White-tailed Eagle *Haliaeetus albicilla*	B	34/10	White-winged Woodpecker *Dendrocopos leucopterus* B 7
Cinereous Vulture *Aegypius monachus*	B	18/13	

TURKS AND CAICOS ISLANDS (to U.K.)

Species totals	Vulnerable	2

	Status (breeding/ non-br.)	Breeding/ non-br. countries	Habitat codes (p. 243)	Threat codes (p. 243)	IUCN threat status codes (pp. 16–18)
Vulnerable					
West Indian Whistling-duck *Dendrocygna arborea*	B	12	W	12	C2a
Kirtland's Warbler *Dendroica kirtlandii*	N	2/2	S	9	D1; D2

TUVALU

Species totals   Vulnerable   1

	Status (breeding/ non-br.)	Breeding/ non-br. countries	Habitat codes (p. 243)	Threat codes (p. 243)	IUCN threat status codes (pp. 16–18)
Vulnerable					
Bristle-thighed Curlew *Numenius tahitiensis*	N	1/14	GW	1268	C2b

UGANDA

Species totals   Vulnerable   10   Near-threatened   17
Data Deficient 2

	Status (breeding/ non-br.)	Breeding/ non-br. countries	Habitat codes (p. 243)	Threat codes (p. 243)	IUCN threat status codes (pp. 16–18)
Vulnerable					
Lesser Kestrel *Falco naumanni*	N	37/52	FSVGA	15	A1a,b,d
Corncrake *Crex crex*	N	40/31	GWA	12	A1a,b
African Green Broadbill *Pseudocalyptomena graueri*	B	2	F	1	B1+2a,c
Blue Swallow *Hirundo atrocaerulea*	N	7/3	G	1	A1b; A2b; C1; C2a
Karamoja Apalis *Apalis karamojae*	B	2	S	1	A2b; B1+2c
Grauer's Swamp-warbler *Bradypterus graueri*	B	4	W	1	B1+2a,c
Papyrus Yellow Warbler *Chloropeta gracilirostris*	B	7	W	1	B1+2a,b,c,d
Turner's Eremomela *Eremomela turneri*	B	3	F	1	B1+2a,c
Chapin's Flycatcher *Muscicapa lendu*	B	3	F	1	B1+2a,c; C2a
Shelley's Crimson-wing *Cryptospiza shelleyi*	B	4	FS	0	A1a; C1; C2a

Data Deficient

Nahan's Francolin *Francolinus nahani*	B	2
Entebbe Weaver *Ploceus victoriae*	B	1

Near-threatened

Madagascar Pond-heron *Ardeola idae*	N	2/9
Shoebill *Balaeniceps rex*	B	8/1
Lesser Flamingo *Phoenicopterus minor*	N	8/20
Pallid Harrier *Circus macrourus*	N	4/57
Great Snipe *Gallinago media*	N	10/35
Black-winged Pratincole *Glareola nordmanni*	N	10/22
White-naped Pigeon *Columba albinucha*	B	4

Red-faced Barbet *Lybius rubrifacies*	B	3
Dwarf Honeyguide *Indicator pumilio*	B	3
Grauer's Cuckoo-shrike *Coracina graueri*	B	2
Sassi's Greenbul *Phyllastrephus lorenzi*	B	2
Papyrus Gonolek *Laniarius mufumbiri*	B	5
Lagden's Bush-shrike *Malaconotus lagdeni*	B	6
Kivu Ground-thrush *Zoothera tanganjicae*	B	2
Forest Ground-thrush *Zoothera oberlaenderi*	B	2
Red-collared Mountain-babbler *Kupeornis rufocinctus*	B	3
Fox's Weaver *Ploceus spekeoides*	B	1

UKRAINE

Species totals   Critical   1   Near-threatened   5
Vulnerable   9

	Status (breeding/ non-br.)	Breeding/ non-br. countries	Habitat codes (p. 243)	Threat codes (p. 243)	IUCN threat status codes (pp. 16–18)
Critical					
Slender-billed Curlew *Numenius tenuirostris*	N	1/10	WG	1289	**C2b; D1**
Vulnerable					
Dalmatian Pelican *Pelecanus crispus*	B	16/9	W	1235	C2a
Red-breasted Goose *Branta ruficollis*	N	1/4	SWA	12	A2b,c; B1+2c,d
Ferruginous Duck *Aythya nyroca*	B	38/32	W	12	A1a,b,c
Greater Spotted Eagle *Aquila clanga*	B	14/35	FW	13	C2a
Imperial Eagle *Aquila heliaca*	B	24/21	FG	12357	C2a
Lesser Kestrel *Falco naumanni*	B	37/52	FSVGA	15	A1a,b,d
Corncrake *Crex crex*	B	40/31	GWA	12	A1a,b
Great Bustard *Otis tarda*	B	23	GA	125	A2b
Aquatic Warbler *Acrocephalus paludicola*	B	8/13	W	18	A2b

Near-threatened

White-tailed Eagle *Haliaeetus albicilla*	B	34/10
Pallid Harrier *Circus macrourus*	B	4/57
Little Bustard *Tetrax tetrax*	B	13/10

Great Snipe *Gallinago media*	B	10/35
Black-winged Pratincole *Glareola nordmanni*	B	10/22

UNITED ARAB EMIRATES

Species totals   Vulnerable   4
Near-threatened   1

Vulnerable	Status (breeding/ non-br.)	Breeding/ non-br. countries	Habitat codes (p. 243)	Threat codes (p. 243)	IUCN threat status codes (pp. 16–18)
Ferruginous Duck *Aythya nyroca*	N	38/32	W	12	A1a,b,c
Greater Spotted Eagle *Aquila clanga*	N	14/35	FW	13	C2a
Imperial Eagle *Aquila heliaca*	N	24/21	FG	12357	C2a
Lesser Kestrel *Falco naumanni*	N	37/52	FSVGA	15	A1a,b,d

Near-threatened
Cinereous Bunting *Emberiza cineracea*   N   3/13

UNITED KINGDOM

Species totals   Vulnerable   2   Near-threatened   1
Data Deficient   1

See also: Anguilla (p. 245), Ascension Island (p. 247), Bermuda (p. 251), Cayman Islands (p. 259), Falkland Islands (p. 272), Gibraltar (p. 275), Hong Kong (p. 278), Montserrat (p. 299), Pitcairn Islands (p. 315), South Georgia (p. 322), St Helena (p. 324), Tristan da Cunha Group (p. 330), Turks and Caicos Islands (p. 331), Virgin Islands (p. 338).

Vulnerable	Status (breeding/ non-br.)	Breeding/ non-br. countries	Habitat codes (p. 243)	Threat codes (p. 243)	IUCN threat status codes (pp. 16–18)
Corncrake *Crex crex*	B	40/31	GWA	12	A1a,b
Aquatic Warbler *Acrocephalus paludicola*	N	8/13	W	18	A2b

Data Deficient
Scottish Crossbill *Loxia scotica*   B   1

Near-threatened
White-tailed Eagle *Haliaeetus albicilla*   B   34/10

UNITED STATES OF AMERICA

Species totals   Critical   13   Extinct   3
Endangered   12   Data Deficient   1
Vulnerable   21   Near-threatened   14

See also: American Samoa (p. 244), Guam (p. 276), Northern Mariana Islands (p. 307), Palau (p. 308), Puerto Rico (p. 315), Virgin Islands (p. 338).

Critical	Status (breeding/ non-br.)	Breeding/ non-br. countries	Habitat codes (p. 243)	Threat codes (p. 243)	IUCN threat status codes (pp. 16–18)
California Condor *Gymnogyps californianus*	B	1	SGR	2589	**D1**
Eskimo Curlew *Numenius borealis*	B	2/3	GW	0129	**D1**
Kamao *Myadestes myadestinus*	B	1	F	69	**A1a; B1+2e; C2b; D1**; D2
Olomao *Myadestes lanaiensis*	B	1	F	69	**A1a; B1+2e; C2b; D1**; D2
Puaiohi *Myadestes palmeri*	B	1	F	689	**A1a; B1+2c,e; C2a; D1**; D2
Kauai Oo *Moho braccatus*	B	1	F	169	**A1a; B1+2c,e; C2b; D1**; D2
Bishop's Oo *Moho bishopi*	B	1	F	169	**B1+2c,e; C2a; D1**; D2
Bachman's Warbler *Vermivora bachmanii*	B	2	F	19	**D1**
Ou *Psittirostra psittacea*	B	1	F	1689	**A1a,b; B1+2a,b,c,d,e; C2a; D1; D2**
Nukupuu *Hemignathus lucidus*	B	1	F	169	**A1a; B1+2c,e; C1; C2a; D1**; D2
Oahu Alauahio *Paroreomyza maculata*	B	1	F	19	**A1a; B1+2c,e; C2a; D1**; D2
Poo-uli *Melamprosops phaeosoma*	B	1	F	1689	**A1a,b,d; B1+2a,b,c,d,e; C2a; D1; D2**
Hawaiian Crow *Corvus hawaiiensis*	B	1	F	129	**D1; D2**
Endangered					
Short-tailed Albatross *Diomedea albatrus*	B	2	RM	1489	**C1; D1; D2**
Whooping Crane *Grus americana*	N	1/1	W	59	**D1**
Thick-billed Parrot *Rhynchopsitta pachyrhyncha*	B	2	F	1	A1b; **A2b; C1; C2a**
Eared Quetzal *Euptilotis neoxenus*	B	2	F	1	A1b; **A2b; C1; C2b**
Golden-cheeked Warbler *Dendroica chrysoparia*	B	1/4	FS	18	**A1b,d**; A2d; **C1; C2a**
Palila *Loxioides bailleui*	B	1	F	168	**B1+2e; C2a**
Akiapolaau *Hemignathus wilsoni*	B	1	F	1	**B1+2c,e; C2a**
Akikiki *Oreomystis bairdi*	B	1	F	1689	A1a,b; **B1+2a,b,c,d,e**; C2a; D2
Hawaii Creeper *Oreomystis mana*	B	1	F	6	**B1+2a,b,c,d,e**

cont.

United States of America (cont.)

	Status	Breeding/non-br.	Habitat	Threat	IUCN threat status
Akekee *Loxops caeruleirostris*	B	1	F	1689	**B1+2c,e; C2a; D2**
Akepa *Loxops coccineus*	B	1	F	16	**B1+2a,b,c,d,e**
Black-capped Vireo *Vireo atricapillus*	B	2	FSG	18	**A1b,c; A2c; C1**
Vulnerable					
Hawaiian Petrel *Pterodroma sandwichensis*	B	1	SM	269	D2
Newell's Shearwater *Puffinus newelli*	B	1	GM	1269	D2
Nene *Branta sandvicensis*	B	1	SGR	2689	D1
Hawaiian Duck *Anas wyvilliana*	B	1	W	169	D2
Laysan Duck *Anas laysanensis*	B	1	SW	9	D1; D2
Spectacled Eider *Somateria fischeri*	B	2	WM	0	A1a
Steller's Eider *Polysticta stelleri*	B	2/8	WM	0	A1a
Hawaiian Coot *Fulica alai*	B	1	W	169	D2
Piping Plover *Charadrius melodus*	B	2/9	W	138	C2a
Mountain Plover *Charadrius montanus*	B	1/1	G	1	A1b
Bristle-thighed Curlew *Numenius tahitiensis*	B	1/14	GW	1268	C2b
Red-legged Kittiwake *Rissa brevirostris*	B	2	RM	0	A1a
Red-cockaded Woodpecker *Picoides borealis*	B	1	F	18	A1b; A2b; B1+2b,c,d; C1; C2a
Millerbird *Acrocephalus familiaris*	B	1	S	9	D1; D2
Kirtland's Warbler *Dendroica kirtlandii*	B	2/2	S	9	D1; D2
Nihoa Finch *Telespiza ultima*	B	1	SR	9	D2
Laysan Finch *Telespiza cantans*	B	1	G	69	D2
Maui Parrotbill *Pseudonestor xanthophrys*	B	1	F	169	D1; D2
Kauai Amakihi *Viridonia stejnegeri*	B	1	F	189	A1a,b,c; D2
Anianiau *Viridonia parva*	B	1	F	189	A1a,b,c; D2
Akohekohe *Palmeria dolei*	B	1	F	9	D2

Extinct
Ivory-billed Woodpecker *Campephilus principalis* B 2
Akialoa *Hemignathus obscurus* B 1
Kakawahie *Paroreomyza flammea* B 1

Data Deficient
Kenyon's Shag *Phalacrocorax kenyoni* B 1

Near-threatened
Tristram's Storm-petrel *Oceanodroma tristrami* B 2
Ashy Storm-petrel *Oceanodroma homochroa* B 2
Trumpeter Swan *Cygnus buccinator* B 2
Hawaiian Hawk *Buteo solitarius* B 1

Hudsonian Godwit *Limosa haemastica* B 2/11
Heermann's Gull *Larus heermanni* B 2
Elegant Tern *Sterna elegans* B 2
Marbled Murrelet *Brachyramphus marmoratus* B 3
Xantus's Murrelet *Synthliboramphus hypoleucus* B 3
Craveri's Murrelet *Synthliboramphus craveri* B 2
Spotted Owl *Strix occidentalis* B 3
Henslow's Sparrow *Ammodramus henslowii* B 2
Colima Warbler *Vermivora crissalis* B 2
Maui Alauahio *Paroreomyza montana* B 1

URUGUAY

Species totals			
Critical	1	Extinct	1
Endangered	4	Data Deficient	1
Vulnerable	4	Near-threatened	9

	Status (breeding/non-br.)	Breeding/non-br. countries	Habitat codes (p. 243)	Threat codes (p. 243)	IUCN threat status codes (pp. 16–18)
Critical					
Eskimo Curlew *Numenius borealis*	N	2/3	GW	0129	**D1**
Endangered					
Yellow Cardinal *Gubernatrix cristata*	B	4	FSG	17	**A1a,c; A2c; C1; C2a**
Marsh Seedeater *Sporophila palustris*	B	4	GW	17	**A1b,c; A2b,c; C1; C2a**
Saffron-cowled Blackbird *Xanthopsar flavus*	B	4	SGWA	158	**A1a,b; A2b,d; C1; C2a**
Pampas Meadowlark *Sturnella militaris*	B	3	G	1	**A1b; A2b; C1; C2a**
Vulnerable					
Dot-winged Crake *Porzana spiloptera*	B	2	SGW	1	A2b; C1; C2a
Olrog's Gull *Larus atlanticus*	N	1/3	WM	123	A2b,c; C1; C2b
Black-and-white Monjita *Heteroxolmis dominicana*	B	4	GWA	1	A1b; A2b
Strange-tailed Tyrant *Alectrurus risora*	B	4	G	1	A1a,b; A2b; C1; C2a

Extinct
Glaucous Macaw *Anodorhynchus glaucus* B 4

Data Deficient
Speckled Crake *Coturnicops notatus* B 7

Near-threatened
Greater Rhea *Rhea americana* B 5
Black-headed Duck *Heteronetta atricapilla* B 6

Hudsonian Godwit *Limosa haemastica* N 2/11
Sickle-winged Nightjar *Eleothreptus anomalus* B 4
Mottled Piculet *Picumnus nebulosus* B 3
Bay-capped Wren-spinetail *Spartonoica maluroides* B 3
Straight-billed Reedhaunter *Limnornis rectirostris* B 3
Bearded Tachuri *Polystictus pectoralis* B 9
Dark-throated Seedeater *Sporophila ruficollis* B 5

UZBEKISTAN

Species totals Vulnerable 11
Near-threatened 4

Vulnerable	Status (breeding/ non-br.)	Breeding/ non-br. countries	Habitat codes (p. 243)	Threat codes (p. 243)	IUCN threat status codes (pp. 16–18)
Dalmatian Pelican *Pelecanus crispus*	B	16/9	W	1235	C2a
White-headed Duck *Oxyura leucocephala*	B	12/16	W	1256	A2d
Marbled Teal *Marmaronetta angustirostris*	B	21/3	W	125	A2b
Ferruginous Duck *Aythya nyroca*	B	38/32	W	12	A1a,b,c
Pallas's Sea-eagle *Haliaeetus leucoryphus*	B	11/1	GW	135	C1; C2b
Imperial Eagle *Aquila heliaca*	B	24/21	FG	12357	C2a
Lesser Kestrel *Falco naumanni*	B	37/52	FSVGA	15	A1a,b,d
Corncrake *Crex crex*	N	40/31	GWA	12	A1a,b
Great Bustard *Otis tarda*	B	23	GA	125	A2b
Sociable Lapwing *Vanellus gregarius*	N	2/15	GW	158	A1a,b; C1; C2a
Pale-backed Pigeon *Columba eversmanni*	B	7/2	GDA	0	A1a

Near-threatened

Pygmy Cormorant *Phalacrocorax pygmeus*	B	17/4	Cinereous Vulture *Aegypius monachus*	B	18/13
White-tailed Eagle *Haliaeetus albicilla*	N	34/10	White-winged Woodpecker *Dendrocopos leucopterus*	B	7

VANUATU

Species totals Vulnerable 6
Near-threatened 4

Vulnerable	Status (breeding/ non-br.)	Breeding/ non-br. countries	Habitat codes (p. 243)	Threat codes (p. 243)	IUCN threat status codes (pp. 16–18)
Vanuatu Scrubfowl *Megapodius layardi*	B	1	F	126	A2b,c
Santa Cruz Ground-dove *Gallicolumba sanctaecrucis*	B	2	F	126	A2b; C1
Vanuatu Imperial-pigeon *Ducula bakeri*	B	1	F	12	C2a
Chestnut-bellied Kingfisher *Todirhamphus farquhari*	B	1	F	1	A2b; C1; C2a
Royal Parrotfinch *Erythrura regia*	B	1	F	1	A2b
Mountain Starling *Aplonis santovestris*	B	1	F	29	D2

Near-threatened

Tanna Fruit-dove *Ptilinopus tannensis*	B	1	Guadalcanal Thicketbird *Megalurulus whitneyi*	B	2
Palm Lorikeet *Charmosyna palmarum*	B	2	Rusty-winged Starling *Aplonis zelandica*	B	2

VENEZUELA

Species totals Critical 4 Data Deficient 1
Endangered 7 Near-threatened 39
Vulnerable 11

Critical	Status (breeding/ non-br.)	Breeding/ non-br. countries	Habitat codes (p. 243)	Threat codes (p. 243)	IUCN threat status codes (pp. 16–18)
Scissor-tailed Hummingbird *Hylonympha macrocerca*	B	1	F	19	A1b; A2b; **B1+2c**; C1; C2a; D2
Venezuelan Flowerpiercer *Diglossa venezuelensis*	B	1	F	19	A1b; **A2b**; B1+2c; C1; C2a; D1
Paria Whitestart *Myioborus pariae*	B	1	F	19	A1b; A2b; **B1+2c**; C1; C2a; D1; D2
Grey-headed Warbler *Basileuterus griseiceps*	B	1	F	19	A1b; **A2b**; B1+2c; C1; C2a; D1
Endangered					
Northern Helmeted Curassow *Pauxi pauxi*	B	2	F	12	A2b,c; C1; **C2a**
Plain-flanked Rail *Rallus wetmorei*	B	1	W	159	A1b; **A2b**; B1+2c; C1; **C2a**; D1
Rusty-faced Parrot *Hapalopsittaca amazonina*	B	3	FS	1	A1b; A2b; B1+2c,d; **C1**
Táchira Emerald *Amazilia distans*	B	1	F	1	**A2b**; B1+2c; C1; C2a
White-throated Barbtail *Margarornis tatei*	B	1	F	1	**B1+2c**; **C2a**
Recurve-billed Bushbird *Clytoctantes alixii*	B	2	F	1	A1b; A2b; **C1**; **C2a**
Red Siskin *Carduelis cucullata*	B	2	FSGA	179	A1c; A2c; C1; **C2a**; D1
Vulnerable					
Tepuí Tinamou *Crypturellus ptaritepui*	B	1	F	19	D2
Rusty-flanked Crake *Laterallus levraudi*	B	1	W	159	A1b; A2b; B1+2c; C1; C2a
Military Macaw *Ara militaris*	B	11	F	17	A1b; C2a

cont.

Venezuela (cont.)

Yellow-shouldered Amazon *Amazona barbadensis*	B	2	S	17	C2a
White-tailed Sabrewing *Campylopterus ensipennis*	B	2	F	18	A2b
Orinoco Softtail *Thripophaga cherriei*	B	1	S	9	D2
Táchira Antpitta *Grallaria chthonia*	B	1	F	19	D1; D2
Hooded Antpitta *Grallaricula cucullata*	B	2	F	1	A1b; A2b; C1; C2a
Slaty-backed Hemispingus *Hemispingus goeringi*	B	1	F	19	B1+2c; C1; C2a
Guaiquinima Whitestart *Myioborus cardonai*	B	1	F	9	D2
Yellow-faced Siskin *Carduelis yarrellii*	B	2	FA	7	A1c; A2c

Data Deficient

Speckled Crake *Coturnicops notatus*	B	7

Near-threatened

Agami Heron *Agamia agami*	B	16
Fasciated Tiger-heron *Tigrisoma fasciatum*	B	8
Zigzag Heron *Zebrilus undulatus*	B	9
Northern Screamer *Chauna chavaria*	B	2
Orinoco Goose *Neochen jubata*	B	10
Grey-bellied Goshawk *Accipiter poliogaster*	B	10
Semicollared Hawk *Accipiter collaris*	B	4
Solitary Eagle *Harpyhaliaetus solitarius*	B	17
Crested Eagle *Morphnus guianensis*	B	15
Black-and-white Hawk-eagle *Spizastur melanoleucus*	B	14
Black-and-chestnut Eagle *Oroaetus isidori*	B	6
Orange-breasted Falcon *Falco deiroleucus*	B	17
Wattled Guan *Aburria aburri*	B	4
Black-fronted Wood-quail *Odontophorus atrifrons*	B	2
Venezuelan Wood-quail *Odontophorus columbianus*	B	1
Ocellated Crake *Micropygia schomburgkii*	B	8
Hudsonian Godwit *Limosa haemastica*	N	2/11
Rose-headed Parakeet *Pyrrhura rhodocephala*	B	1

Blue-cheeked Parrot *Amazona dufresniana*	B	4
Buff-fronted Owl *Aegolius harrisii*	B	8
Roraiman Nightjar *Caprimulgus whitelyi*	B	1
Fiery-tailed Awlbill *Avocettula recurvirostris*	B	7
Spangled Coquette *Lophornis stictolophus*	B	7
Perijá Metaltail *Metallura iracunda*	B	2
Black-billed Mountain-toucan *Andigena nigrirostris*	B	3
Perijá Thistletail *Schizoeaca perijana*	B	2
Great Antpitta *Grallaria excelsa*	B	1
Scallop-breasted Antpitta *Grallaricula loricata*	B	1
Scaled Fruiteater *Ampelioides tschudii*	B	5
Maracaibo Tody-flycatcher *Todirostrum viridanum*	B	1
Bearded Tachuri *Polystictus pectoralis*	B	9
Venezuelan Bristle-tyrant *Phylloscartes venezuelanus*	B	1
Rufous-brown Solitaire *Myadestes leucogenys*	B	3
Large-billed Seed-finch *Oryzoborus crassirostris*	B	9
Great-billed Seed-finch *Oryzoborus maximiliani*	B	4
Dotted Tanager *Tangara varia*	B	4
White-bellied Dacnis *Dacnis albiventris*	B	5
White-faced Whitestart *Myioborus albifacies*	B	1
Grey-throated Warbler *Basileuterus cinereicollis*	B	2

VIETNAM

Species totals   Critical   7   Vulnerable   30
Endangered   9   Near-threatened   57

	Status (breeding/ non-br.)	Breeding/ non-br. countries	Habitat codes (p. 243)	Threat codes (p. 243)	IUCN threat status codes (pp. 16–18)
Critical					
White-eared Night-heron *Gorsachius magnificus*	N	1/2	F	19	A1b; **C1**; **C2a**; D1
Giant Ibis *Pseudibis gigantea*	B	4	FW	1239	A1b; A2b,c; B1+2c; **C1**; C2a; D1
Black-faced Spoonbill *Platalea minor*	N	2/8	WR	12359	**A2b**; C1; C2a; D1; D2
Orange-necked Partridge *Arborophila davidi*	B	1	F	19	A1b; **B1+2c**; **C1**; C2a; D1; D2
Imperial Pheasant *Lophura imperialis*	B	1	F	129	A1b,c; A2b,c; B1+2c; **C1**; **C2b**; D1; D2
Edwards's Pheasant *Lophura edwardsi*	B	1	F	19	**B1+2c**; **C1**; **C2a**; **D1**; D2
Grey-crowned Crocias *Crocias langbianis*	B	1	F	19	**B1+2c**; C1; C2b; D1; D2
Endangered					
Chinese Egret *Egretta eulophotes*	N	3/10	WR	1	**C1**; C2a
Greater Adjutant *Leptoptilos dubius*	B	8	FWU	129	A1b,c; **C1**; **C2a**; D1
White-shouldered Ibis *Pseudibis davisoni*	B	8	FW	1239	A1b; A2b; **C1**; **C2a**; D1
White-winged Duck *Cairina scutulata*	B	9	FW	1239	A1b,c,d; **C1**; **C2a**; D1
Annam Partridge *Arborophila merlini*	B	1	F	1	A1b; **B1+2c**; **C1**
Vietnamese Pheasant *Lophura hatinhensis*	B	1	F	129	A1b; A2b,c; **B1+2c**; **C1**; C2a; D1; D2
Bengal Florican *Houbaropsis bengalensis*	B	4	GW	1	**C1**; **C2a**
Nordmann's Greenshank *Tringa guttifer*	N	1/15	FW	12389	**C1**; **C2b**; D1
Saunders's Gull *Larus saundersi*	N	1/6	W	1235	A1b,c,d; **A2b,c,d**; C1; C2a
Vulnerable					
Spot-billed Pelican *Pelecanus philippensis*	N	3/8	W	1235	A1a,b,c,d; C1
Milky Stork *Mycteria cinerea*	B	4	FW	123	C1
Lesser Adjutant *Leptoptilos javanicus*	B	12/1	FW	123	C1
Ferruginous Duck *Aythya nyroca*	N	38/32	W	12	A1a,b,c
Baer's Pochard *Aythya baeri*	N	2/12	W	123	A1a,b; C1

cont.

Vietnam (cont.)

Greater Spotted Eagle *Aquila clanga*	N	14/35	FW	13	C2a
Imperial Eagle *Aquila heliaca*	N	24/21	FG	12357	C2a
Chestnut-necklaced Partridge *Arborophila charltonii*	B	4	F	1	A1b
Siamese Fireback *Lophura diardi*	B	4	F	12	A1b,c; A2b,c
Germain's Peacock-pheasant *Polyplectron germaini*	B	1	F	12	B1+2c; C1; C2a
Crested Argus *Rheinardia ocellata*	B	3	F	12	A1b,c
Green Peafowl *Pavo muticus*	B	7	FSG	12	A1b,c; A2b,c
Black-necked Crane *Grus nigricollis*	N	2/5	GW	13	C1
Masked Finfoot *Heliopais personata*	B	9	FW	13	C1; C2a
Wood Snipe *Gallinago nemoricola*	N	4/6	SGW	1	C2a
Spoon-billed Sandpiper *Eurynorhynchus pygmeus*	N	1/14	W	18	C1; C2b
Black-bellied Tern *Sterna acuticauda*	B	9	W	128	C1
Pale-capped Pigeon *Columba punicea*	B	7	FSA	1	C1; C2a
Ward's Trogon *Harpactes wardi*	B	5	F	1	C1; C2a
Blyth's Kingfisher *Alcedo hercules*	B	9	F	1	A1b; A2b; C1; C2a
Rufous-necked Hornbill *Aceros nipalensis*	B	8	F	12	A1b,c; C1; C2a
Red-collared Woodpecker *Picus rabieri*	B	3	F	1	A1b
Fairy Pitta *Pitta nympha*	N	4/6	F	17	C1; C2a
Black-hooded Laughingthrush *Garrulax milleti*	B	1	F	1	A2b; B1+2c; C1; C2a
Collared Laughingthrush *Garrulax yersini*	B	1	F	1	B1+2c; C1; C2a
Short-tailed Scimitar-babbler *Jabouilleia danjoui*	B	2	F	1	A1b; A2b; C1; C2a
Sooty Babbler *Stachyris herberti*	B	2	F	1	C1; C2a
Short-tailed Parrotbill *Paradoxornis davidianus*	B	5	S	1	A1b; C1; C2a
Yellow-billed Nuthatch *Sitta solangiae*	B	2	F	1	C1; C2a
Beautiful Nuthatch *Sitta formosa*	B	7	F	1	C1; C2a

Near-threatened

Oriental Darter *Anhinga melanogaster*	B	13	Blue-rumped Pitta *Pitta soror*	B	5
Great-billed Heron *Ardea sumatrana*	B	10	Bar-bellied Pitta *Pitta elliotii*	B	3
Schrenck's Bittern *Ixobrychus eurhythmus*	N	5/10	Long-billed Thrush *Zoothera monticola*	B	6
Painted Stork *Mycteria leucocephala*	B	11	Black-breasted Thrush *Turdus dissimilis*	B	4/2
Asian Openbill *Anastomus oscitans*	B	9	Gould's Shortwing *Brachypteryx stellata*	B	6
Black-headed Ibis *Threskiornis melanocephalus*	B	10/8	Blue-fronted Robin *Cinclidium frontale*	B	6
Lesser Fish-eagle *Ichthyophaga humilis*	B	9	Purple Cochoa *Cochoa purpurea*	B	8
Grey-headed Fish-eagle *Ichthyophaga ichthyaetus*	B	13	Green Cochoa *Cochoa viridis*	B	7
White-rumped Vulture *Gyps bengalensis*	B	11	Jerdon's Bushchat *Saxicola jerdoni*	B	7
Long-billed Vulture *Gyps indicus*	B	9	Grey Laughingthrush *Garrulax maesi*	B	3
Red-headed Vulture *Sarcogyps calvus*	B	11	Spot-breasted Laughingthrush *Garrulax merulinus*	B	6
Rufous-winged Buzzard *Butastur liventer*	B	7	Red-winged Laughingthrush *Garrulax formosus*	B	2
White-rumped Falcon *Polihierax insignis*	B	5	Red-tailed Laughingthrush *Garrulax milnei*	B	5
Pied Falconet *Microhierax melanoleucus*	B	5	Slender-billed Scimitar-babbler		
Temminck's Tragopan *Tragopan temminckii*	B	4	*Xiphirhynchus superciliaris*	B	7
Sarus Crane *Grus antigone*	B	8	Long-billed Wren-babbler *Rimator malacoptilus*	B	5
Band-bellied Crake *Porzana paykullii*	N	2/7	Grey-faced Tit-babbler *Macronous kelleyi*	B	2
Malaysian Plover *Charadrius peronii*	B	6	Black-headed Shrike-babbler *Pteruthius rufiventer*	B	6
Grey-headed Lapwing *Vanellus cinereus*	N	3/11	Streaked Barwing *Actinodura souliei*	B	2
Asian Dowitcher *Limnodromus semipalmatus*	N	3/14	Rufous-throated Fulvetta *Alcippe rufogularis*	B	9
Relict Gull *Larus relictus*	N	3/3	Rufous-headed Parrotbill *Paradoxornis ruficeps*	B	7
Nicobar Pigeon *Caloenas nicobarica*	B	11	Broad-billed Warbler *Tickellia hodgsoni*	B	6
Yellow-vented Green-pigeon *Treron seimundi*	B	4	Fujian Niltava *Niltava davidi*	B	3/2
White-bellied Green-pigeon *Treron sieboldii*	B	6	Japanese Paradise-flycatcher *Terpsiphone atrocaudata*	N	4/8
Coral-billed Ground-cuckoo *Carpococcyx renauldi*	B	4	Vietnam Greenfinch *Carduelis monguilloti*	B	1
Spot-bellied Eagle-owl *Bubo nipalensis*	B	11	Asian Golden Weaver *Ploceus hypoxanthus*	B	6
Tawny Fish-owl *Ketupa flavipes*	B	9	Red-billed Starling *Sturnus sericeus*	N	1/2
Brown Hornbill *Anorrhinus tickelli*	B	6	White-winged Magpie *Urocissa whiteheadi*	B	3
Blue-naped Pitta *Pitta nipalensis*	B	8	Yellow-breasted Magpie *Cissa hypoleuca*	B	4

VIRGIN ISLANDS (to U.K.)

Species totals	Vulnerable	2
	Near-threatened	1

	Status (breeding/ non-br.)	Breeding/ non-br. countries	Habitat codes (p. 243)	Threat codes (p. 243)	IUCN threat status codes (pp. 16–18)
Vulnerable					
West Indian Whistling-duck *Dendrocygna arborea*	B	12	W	12	C2a
Piping Plover *Charadrius melodus*	N	2/9	W	138	C2a
Near-threatened					
Bridled Quail-dove *Geotrygon mystacea*	B	13			

VIRGIN ISLANDS (to U.S.A.)

Species totals	Vulnerable	2
	Near-threatened	1

	Status (breeding/ non-br.)	Breeding/ non-br. countries	Habitat codes (p. 243)	Threat codes (p. 243)	IUCN threat status codes (pp. 16–18)
Vulnerable					
West Indian Whistling-duck *Dendrocygna arborea*	B	12	W	12	C2a
Piping Plover *Charadrius melodus*	N	2/9	W	138	C2a
Near-threatened					
Bridled Quail-dove *Geotrygon mystacea*	B	13			

WALLIS AND FUTUNA ISLANDS (to France)

Species totals	Near-threatened	1

Near-threatened		
Shy Ground-dove *Gallicolumba stairi*	B	5

WESTERN SAHARA

Species totals	Conservation Dependent	1

Conservation Dependent		
Audouin's Gull *Larus audouinii*	N	8/7

WESTERN SAMOA

Species totals	Critical	1	Near-threatened	2
	Vulnerable	5		

	Status (breeding/ non-br.)	Breeding/ non-br. countries	Habitat codes (p. 243)	Threat codes (p. 243)	IUCN threat status codes (pp. 16–18)
Critical					
Samoan Moorhen *Gallinula pacifica*	B	1	F	69	**D1**
Vulnerable					
Bristle-thighed Curlew *Numenius tahitiensis*	N	1/14	GW	1268	C2b
Tooth-billed Pigeon *Didunculus strigirostris*	B	1	F	128	C1
Samoan Flycatcher *Myiagra albiventris*	B	1	F	18	A1a,b
Samoan White-eye *Zosterops samoensis*	B	1	FS	69	C2a; D2
Mao *Gymnomyza samoensis*	B	1	F	18	A1b; C2a
Near-threatened					
Shy Ground-dove *Gallicolumba stairi*	B	5	Samoan Triller *Lalage sharpei*		B 1

YEMEN

Species totals   Critical   1   Near-threatened   7
Vulnerable   11

	Status (breeding/ non-br.)	Breeding/ non-br. countries	Habitat codes (p. 243)	Threat codes (p. 243)	IUCN threat status codes (pp. 16–18)
Critical					
Northern Bald Ibis *Geronticus eremita*	B	4	GW	012589	A1a; C1; **C2a**; D1
Vulnerable					
Ferruginous Duck *Aythya nyroca*	N	38/32	W	12	A1a,b,c
Greater Spotted Eagle *Aquila clanga*	N	14/35	FW	13	C2a
Imperial Eagle *Aquila heliaca*	N	24/21	FG	12357	C2a
Lesser Kestrel *Falco naumanni*	N	37/52	FSVGA	15	A1a,b,d
Corncrake *Crex crex*	N	40/31	GWA	12	A1a,b
White-eyed Gull *Larus leucophthalmus*	B	5/1	WM	1235	C1
Yemen Thrush *Turdus menachensis*	B	2	FSGA	1	B1+2b,c; C2a
Socotra Cisticola *Cisticola haesitatus*	B	1	S	9	D1
Yemen Warbler *Sylvia buryi*	B	2	FS	1	B1+2b,c; C2a
Socotra Bunting *Emberiza socotrana*	B	1	SR	89	D1
Socotra Starling *Onychognathus frater*	B	1	SGU	89	D1

Near-threatened

Socotra Cormorant *Phalacrocorax nigrogularis*	B 1	Arabian Woodpecker *Dendrocopos dorae*	B 2
Lesser Flamingo *Phoenicopterus minor*	N 8/20	Yemen Accentor *Prunella fagani*	B 2
Pallid Harrier *Circus macrourus*	N 4/57	Cinereous Bunting *Emberiza cineracea*	N 3/13
Great Snipe *Gallinago media*	N 10/35		

Former YUGOSLAVIA (Serbia and Montenegro)

Species totals   Critical   1   Near-threatened   2
Vulnerable   7

	Status (breeding/ non-br.)	Breeding/ non-br. countries	Habitat codes (p. 243)	Threat codes (p. 243)	IUCN threat status codes (pp. 16–18)
Critical					
Slender-billed Curlew *Numenius tenuirostris*	N	1/10	WG	1289	**C2b**; D1
Vulnerable					
Dalmatian Pelican *Pelecanus crispus*	B	16/9	W	1235	C2a
Lesser White-fronted Goose *Anser erythropus*	N	4/11	SWA	012	A1a,b,c
Ferruginous Duck *Aythya nyroca*	B	38/32	W	12	A1a,b,c
Imperial Eagle *Aquila heliaca*	B	24/21	FG	12357	C2a
Lesser Kestrel *Falco naumanni*	B	37/52	FSVGA	15	A1a,b,d
Corncrake *Crex crex*	N	40/31	GWA	12	A1a,b
Great Bustard *Otis tarda*	B	23	GA	125	A2b

Near-threatened

Pygmy Cormorant *Phalacrocorax pygmeus*	B 17/4	White-tailed Eagle *Haliaeetus albicilla*	B 34/10

ZAÏRE

Species totals   Endangered   1   Data Deficient   2
Vulnerable   25   Near-threatened   17

	Status (breeding/ non-br.)	Breeding/ non-br. countries	Habitat codes (p. 243)	Threat codes (p. 243)	IUCN threat status codes (pp. 16–18)
Endangered					
Spotted Ground-thrush *Zoothera guttata*	B	5/1	F	1	B1+2c; **C2a**
Vulnerable					
Lesser Kestrel *Falco naumanni*	N	37/52	FSVGA	15	A1a,b,d
Congo Peafowl *Afropavo congensis*	B	1	F	2	C2b
Wattled Crane *Grus carunculatus*	B	11	W	123	A2b,c; C1
Corncrake *Crex crex*	N	40/31	GWA	12	A1a,b
Congo Bay-owl *Phodilus prigoginei*	B	1	F	1	B1+2a,c; C2a
Albertine Owlet *Glaucidium albertinum*	B	2	F	1	B1+2a,c,d
Itombwe Nightjar *Caprimulgus prigoginei*	B	1	F	1	B1+2a,c
Schouteden's Swift *Schoutedenapus schoutedeni*	B	1	F	1	B1+2a,c; C2b

cont.

Zaïre (cont.)

African Green Broadbill *Pseudocalyptomena graueri*	B	2	F	1	B1+2a,c
Blue Swallow *Hirundo atrocaerulea*	N	7/3	G	1	A1b; A2b; C1; C2a
Prigogine's Greenbul *Chlorocichla prigoginei*	B	1	F	1	B1+2a,b,c,d,e; C2a
Yellow-crested Helmet-shrike *Prionops alberti*	B	1	F	1	C1; C2a
White-headed Robin-chat *Cossypha heinrichi*	B	2	F	1	B1+2a,c
Kungwe Apalis *Apalis argentea*	B	4	F	1	B1+2a,c,e
Grauer's Swamp-warbler *Bradypterus graueri*	B	4	W	1	B1+2a,c
Papyrus Yellow Warbler *Chloropeta gracilirostris*	B	7	W	1	B1+2a,b,c,d
Turner's Eremomela *Eremomela turneri*	B	3	F	1	B1+2a,c
Chapin's Flycatcher *Muscicapa lendu*	B	3	F	1	B1+2a,c; C2a
Rockefeller's Sunbird *Nectarinia rockefelleri*	B	1	F	9	D1
Shelley's Crimson-wing *Cryptospiza shelleyi*	B	4	FS	0	A1a; C1; C2a
Black-lored Waxbill *Estrilda nigriloris*	B	1	G	1	B1+2a,c
Loango Weaver *Ploceus subpersonatus*	B	3	FSV	1	B1+2c; C2a
Lake Lufira Weaver *Ploceus ruweti*	B	1	F	9	D2
Golden-naped Weaver *Ploceus aureonucha*	B	1	F	19	C2b; D1
Yellow-legged Weaver *Ploceus flavipes*	B	1	F	19	C2a; D1

Data Deficient

Nahan's Francolin *Francolinus nahani*	B	2
Kabobo Apalis *Apalis kaboboensis*	B	1

Near-threatened

Madagascar Pond-heron *Ardeola idae*	N	2/9
Shoebill *Balaeniceps rex*	B	8/1
Lesser Flamingo *Phoenicopterus minor*	B	8/20
Great Snipe *Gallinago media*	N	10/35
Black-winged Pratincole *Glareola nordmanni*	N	10/22
White-naped Pigeon *Columba albinucha*	B	4
Dwarf Honeyguide *Indicator pumilio*	B	3

Grimwood's Longclaw *Macronyx grimwoodi*	B	3
Grauer's Cuckoo-shrike *Coracina graueri*	B	2
Sassi's Greenbul *Phyllastrephus lorenzi*	B	2
Papyrus Gonolek *Laniarius mufumbiri*	B	5
Lagden's Bush-shrike *Malaconotus lagdeni*	B	6
Kivu Ground-thrush *Zoothera tanganjicae*	B	2
Forest Ground-thrush *Zoothera oberlaenderi*	B	2
Red-collared Mountain-babbler *Kupeornis rufocinctus*	B	3
Chapin's Mountain-babbler *Kupeornis chapini*	B	1
Bedford's Paradise-flycatcher *Terpsiphone bedfordi*	B	1

ZAMBIA

Species totals   Endangered   2   Near-threatened   8

Vulnerable   8

	Status (breeding/ non-br.)	Breeding/ non-br. countries	Habitat codes (p. 243)	Threat codes (p. 243)	IUCN threat status codes (pp. 16–18)
Endangered					
White-winged Flufftail *Sarothrura ayresi*	B	4	W	1	**B1+2a,b,c+3a,b,c**; C2a
Black-cheeked Lovebird *Agapornis nigrigenis*	B	1	S	129	B1+2c; **C2b**; D1
Vulnerable					
Slaty Egret *Egretta vinaceigula*	B	3	W	1	C2a
Lesser Kestrel *Falco naumanni*	N	37/52	FSVGA	15	A1a,b,d
Taita Falcon *Falco fasciinucha*	B	8	VR	1589	C1; D1
Wattled Crane *Grus carunculatus*	B	11	W	123	A2b,c; C1
Corncrake *Crex crex*	N	40/31	GWA	12	A1a,b
White-chested Tinkerbird *Pogoniulus makawai*	B	1	V	09	D1
Blue Swallow *Hirundo atrocaerulea*	B	7/3	G	1	A1b; A2b; C1; C2a
Papyrus Yellow Warbler *Chloropeta gracilirostris*	B	7	W	1	B1+2a,b,c,d

Near-threatened

Shoebill *Balaeniceps rex*	B	8/1
Lesser Flamingo *Phoenicopterus minor*	B	8/20
Pallid Harrier *Circus macrourus*	N	4/57
Great Snipe *Gallinago media*	N	10/35

Black-winged Pratincole *Glareola nordmanni*	N	10/22
Chaplin's Barbet *Lybius chaplini*	B	1
Grimwood's Longclaw *Macronyx grimwoodi*	B	3
Churring Cisticola *Cisticola njombe*	B	3

| ZIMBABWE | | **Species totals** | | Endangered | 1 | Near-threatened | 6 |
| | | | | Vulnerable | 6 | | |

	Status (breeding/ non-br.)	Breeding/ non-br. countries	Habitat codes (p. 243)	Threat codes (p. 243)	IUCN threat status codes (pp. 16–18)
Endangered					
White-winged Flufftail *Sarothrura ayresi*	B	4	W	1	**B1+2a,b,c+3a,b,c**; C2a
Vulnerable					
Lesser Kestrel *Falco naumanni*	N	37/52	FSVGA	15	A1a,b,d
Taita Falcon *Falco fasciinucha*	B	8	VR	1589	C1; D1
Wattled Crane *Grus carunculatus*	B	11	W	123	A2b,c; C1
Corncrake *Crex crex*	N	40/31	GWA	12	A1a,b
Blue Swallow *Hirundo atrocaerulea*	B	7/3	G	1	A1b; A2b; C1; C2a
Swynnerton's Robin *Swynnertonia swynnertoni*	B	3	F	1	B1+2b,c

Near-threatened

Madagascar Pond-heron *Ardeola idae*	N	2/9	Pallid Harrier *Circus macrourus*	N	4/57
Lesser Flamingo *Phoenicopterus minor*	N	8/20	Great Snipe *Gallinago media*	N	10/35
Southern Banded Snake-eagle *Circaetus fasciolatus*	B	6	Plain-backed Sunbird *Anthreptes reichenowi*	B	5

THE FOLLOWING list includes all (211) geopolitical units holding threatened bird species—i.e. species in the categories Critical (CR, tabulated here as including also Extinct in the Wild), Endangered (EN) and Vulnerable (VU)—and ranks them according to the total number of these species. Units with equal complements of threatened species are ranked according to number of higher-ranking species (CR, EN), or else alphabetically.

The two last columns on the right indicate the rank of these units when only the more threatened species—Critical (including Extinct in the Wild) and Endangered, listed in Appendix 3 (p. 344)—are counted, and when only these more threatened species that are also endemic to the geopolitical unit are counted; the top 25 units in each of these ranking orders are given in Box 1 on p. 24. Note that ranking in the first of these two columns was terminated at geopolitical units with only two species, and that ranking in the final column inevitably involves a much smaller subset of the units.

	Total	CR	EN	VU	CR+EN	CR+EN endemic
1. Indonesia	104	4	16	84	5 =	6 =
2. Brazil	103	16	31	56	1	2
3. Philippines	86	16	29	41	2	1
4. China	86	5	8	73	11	
5. India	71	4	9	58	12 =	20 =
6. Colombia	62	9	22	31	3	3
7. Peru	60	6	12	42	7	10
8. Ecuador	50	5	11	34	9 =	13 =
9. U.S.A.	46	13	12	21	4	4
10. Vietnam	45	7	9	29	8	16 =
11. New Zealand	45	4	9	32	12 =	6 =
12. Thailand	44	5	6	33	15	
13. Australia	44	2	10	32	14	
14. Myanmar	43	2	6	35	23 =	
15. Argentina	40	5	11	24	9 =	
16. Russia	35	2	4	29	28 =	
17. Mexico	34	4	16	14	5 =	5
18. Japan	31	4	7	20	16 =	
19. Malaysia	31	2	6	23	23 =	
20. Papua New Guinea	31	2	4	25	28 =	
21. Tanzania	30	2	2	26	45 =	
22. Madagascar	28	5	5	18	18	9
23. Bangladesh	28	0	5	23	39 =	
24. Bolivia	27	2	6	19	23 =	
25. Zaïre	26	0	1	25		
26. Nepal	23	2	2	19	45 =	
27. Laos	23	1	3	19	48 =	
28. Venezuela	22	4	7	11	16 =	11 =
29. Kenya	22	4	2	16	27	16 =
30. Paraguay	22	2	8	12	20	
31. Pakistan	22	0	1	21		
32. French Polynesia	20	3	6	11	22	11 =
33. South Korea	19	2	4	13	28 =	
34. Solomon Islands	18	4	5	9	21	
35. Ethiopia	17	0	5	12	39 =	20 =
36. North Korea	16	2	3	11	32	
37. Cambodia	16	1	4	11	33 =	
38. South Africa	16	1	2	13	53 =	
39. Chile	15	3	1	11	43 =	
40. Cameroon	14	1	1	12	62 =	
41. Brunei	14	0	2	12	67 =	
42. Kazakhstan	14	0	0	14		
43. Cuba	13	3	7	3	19	13 =
44. Hong Kong	13	1	4	8	33 =	
45. Liberia	13	1	2	10	53 =	
46. Mozambique	13	1	0	12		
46. Turkey	13	1	0	12		
48. Angola	13	0	6	7	31	16 =
49. Taiwan	12	1	4	7	33 =	
50. Yemen	12	1	0	11		
51. Sierra Leone	12	0	2	10	67 =	
52. Afghanistan	12	0	1	11		
52. Bhutan	12	0	1	11		
52. Iran	12	0	1	11		
55. Morocco	11	2	0	9	58 =	
56. Bulgaria	11	1	0	10		
56. Romania	11	1	0	10		
58. Ivory Coast	11	0	2	9	67 =	
58. Guinea	11	0	2	9	67 =	
58. Sri Lanka	11	0	2	9	67 =	
61. Iraq	11	0	0	11		
62. Mongolia	11	0	0	11		
62. Uzbekistan	11	0	0	11		
64. New Caledonia	10	1	4	5	33 =	
65. Saudi Arabia	10	1	0	9		
65. Ukraine	10	1	0	9		
67. Dominican Rep.	10	0	3	7	55 =	
67. Haiti	10	0	3	7	55 =	
69. Zambia	10	0	2	8	67 =	
70. Costa Rica	10	0	0	10		
70. Egypt	10	0	0	10		
70. Spain	10	0	0	10		
70. Uganda	10	0	0	10		
74. Mauritius	9	5	1	3	26	13 =
75. São Tomé e Príncipe	9	3	0	6	50	
76. Uruguay	9	1	4	4	33 =	
77. Greece	9	1	0	8		
78. Malawi	9	0	1	8		
78. Sudan	9	0	1	8		
80. Panama	9	0	0	9		
80. Tajikistan	9	0	0	9		
82. Turkmenistan	9	0	0	9		
83. Seychelles	8	4	0	4	41 =	20 =
84. Fiji	8	2	1	5	51 =	
85. Somalia	8	1	4	3	33 =	16 =
86. Nigeria	8	1	0	7		
86. Yugoslavia (Serbia & Montenegro)	8	1	0	7		

Column headers: Number of species (Total, CR, EN, VU) — Rank with only: (CR+EN, CR+EN endemic)

Appendix 2: Geopolitical Units by Number of Threatened Species

	Number of species			Rank with only:				Number of species			Rank with only:	
	Total	CR	EN	VU	CR+EN	CR+EN endemic			Total	CR	EN	VU	CR+EN	CR+EN endemic

		Total	CR	EN	VU	CR+EN	CR+EN endemic
88.	Israel	8	0	0	8		
89.	Jamaica	7	3	1	3	43 =	
90.	Algeria	7	1	1	5	62 =	
91.	Hungary	7	1	0	6		
91.	Portugal	7	1	0	6		
93.	Ghana	7	0	1	6		
93.	Zimbabwe	7	0	1	6		
95.	Tristan da Cunha	7	0	0	7		
96.	Comoros	6	4	0	2	41 =	20 =
97.	Puerto Rico	6	2	2	2	45 =	
98.	Norfolk Island	6	2	0	4	58 =	
98.	N. Mariana I.	6	2	0	4	58 =	
100.	Cook Islands	6	1	0	5		
100.	Italy	6	1	0	5		
100.	Tunisia	6	1	0	5		
100.	Western Samoa	6	1	0	5		
104.	Singapore	6	0	2	4	67 =	
105.	Azerbaijan	6	0	0	6		
105.	Moldova	6	0	0	6		
105.	Namibia	6	0	0	6		
105.	Rwanda	6	0	0	6		
105.	Syria	6	0	0	6		
105.	Vanuatu	6	0	0	6		
111.	Micronesia	5	1	3	1	48 =	20 =
112.	Albania	5	0	0	5		
112.	Armenia	5	0	0	5		
112.	Botswana	5	0	0	5		
112.	Burundi	5	0	0	5		
112.	Czech Republic	5	0	0	5		
112.	France	5	0	0	5		
112.	Georgia	5	0	0	5		
112.	Germany	5	0	0	5		
112.	Kyrgyzstan	5	0	0	5		
112.	Latvia	5	0	0	5		
112.	Lebanon	5	0	0	5		
112.	Mali	5	0	0	5		
112.	Oman	5	0	0	5		
112.	Pitcairn Islands	5	0	0	5		
112.	Poland	5	0	0	5		
112.	Senegal	5	0	0	5		
128.	Canada	4	1	1	2	62 =	
128.	Honduras	4	1	1	2	62 =	
130.	Guatemala	4	0	3	1	55 =	
131.	Belarus	4	0	0	4		
131.	Croatia	4	0	0	4		
131.	Cyprus	4	0	0	4		
131.	Equatorial Guinea	4	0	0	4		
131.	Finland	4	0	0	4		
131.	Gabon	4	0	0	4		
131.	Jordan	4	0	0	4		
131.	Lithuania	4	0	0	4		
131.	Slovakia	4	0	0	4		
131.	Swaziland	4	0	0	4		
131.	Sweden	4	0	0	4		
131.	U.A.E.	4	0	0	4		
143.	Réunion	3	2	1	0	51 =	
144.	St Lucia	3	1	1	1	62 =	
145.	Djibouti	3	1	0	2		
146.	Cape Verde I.	3	0	1	2		
146.	Nicaragua	3	0	1	2		
148.	Austria	3	0	0	3		
148.	Bahamas	3	0	0	3		
148.	Belgium	3	0	0	3		
148.	Chad	3	0	0	3		
148.	Christmas Island	3	0	0	3		
148.	Congo	3	0	0	3		
148.	Eritrea	3	0	0	3		
148.	Kuwait	3	0	0	3		
148.	Lesotho	3	0	0	3		
148.	Mauritania	3	0	0	3		
148.	Netherlands	3	0	0	3		
148.	Norway	3	0	0	3		
148.	Slovenia	3	0	0	3		
148.	Switzerland	3	0	0	3		
162.	Guam	2	2	0	0	58 =	
163.	French Southern Territories	2	1	0	1		
163.	Mayotte	2	1	0	1		
163.	Trinidad & Tobago	2	1	0	1		
166.	Martinique	2	0	2	0	67 =	
167.	Bermuda	2	0	1	1		
167.	Kiribati	2	0	1	1		
167.	Tonga	2	0	1	1		
170.	Bosnia & Herzegovina	2	0	0	2		
170.	Cent. African Rep.	2	0	0	2		
170.	Denmark	2	0	0	2		
170.	Dominica	2	0	0	2		
170.	Estonia	2	0	0	2		
187.	Guyana	2	0	0	2		
170.	Libya	2	0	0	2		
170.	Malta	2	0	0	2		
170.	Niger	2	0	0	2		
170.	Palau	2	0	0	2		
170.	St Vincent	2	0	0	2		
170.	Turks & Caicos I.	2	0	0	2		
170.	United Kingdom	2	0	0	2		
170.	Virgin I. (U.K.)	2	0	0	2		
170.	Virgin I. (U.S.A.)	2	0	0	2		
185.	Ascension Island	1	1	0	0		
186.	Belize	1	0	1	0		
186.	St Helena	1	0	1	0		
188.	American Samoa	1	0	0	1		
188.	Antigua & Barbuda	1	0	0	1		
188.	Barbados	1	0	0	1		
188.	Benin	1	0	0	1		
188.	Burkina Faso	1	0	0	1		
188.	Cayman Islands	1	0	0	1		
188.	Cocos (Keeling) I.	1	0	0	1		
188.	Falkland Islands	1	0	0	1		
188.	Gambia	1	0	0	1		
188.	Gibraltar	1	0	0	1		
188.	Ireland	1	0	0	1		
188.	Liechtenstein	1	0	0	1		
188.	Luxembourg	1	0	0	1		
188.	Maldives	1	0	0	1		
188.	Marshall Islands	1	0	0	1		
188.	Nauru	1	0	0	1		
188.	Netherlands Antilles	1	0	0	1		
188.	Niue	1	0	0	1		
188.	Qatar	1	0	0	1		
188.	South Georgia	1	0	0	1		
188.	St Kitts & Nevis	1	0	0	1		
188.	Suriname	1	0	0	1		
188.	Tokelau	1	0	0	1		
188.	Tuvalu	1	0	0	1		

RED DATA BOOKS usually carry a complete list of species by category. However, such a list is usually much shorter than it would be here owing to the regional focus of each RDB volume. It was felt that to list here all the species treated in this review would be unnecessary: the categories Extinct, Conservation Dependent and Data Deficient each have their own sections in this book, making the species involved easy to track, while the Vulnerable category is too extensive, and perhaps of insufficient interest, to warrant the listing of its 704 species. Therefore we list here only those threatened species in the higher categories—Extinct in the Wild (4 species), Critical (168) and Endangered (235)—that are not grouped elsewhere in the book.

■ Extinct in the Wild

Alagoas Curassow *Mitu mitu*
Guam Rail *Gallirallus owstoni*
Socorro Dove *Zenaida graysoni*
Kakapo *Strigops habroptilus*

■ Critical

Magdalena Tinamou *Crypturellus saltuarius*
Kalinowski's Tinamou *Nothoprocta kalinowskii*
Alaotra Grebe *Tachybaptus rufolavatus*
Junín Grebe *Podiceps taczanowskii*
Amsterdam Albatross *Diomedea amsterdamensis*
Mascarene Black Petrel *Pterodroma aterrima*
Beck's Petrel *Pterodroma becki*
Fiji Petrel *Pterodroma macgillivrayi*
Chatham Islands Petrel *Pterodroma axillaris*
Galápagos Petrel *Pterodroma phaeopygia*
Barau's Petrel *Pterodroma baraui*
Magenta Petrel *Pterodroma magentae*
Zino's Petrel *Pterodroma madeira*
Jamaica Petrel *Pterodroma caribbaea*
Guadalupe Storm-petrel *Oceanodroma macrodactyla*
Ascension Frigatebird *Fregata aquila*
White-eared Night-heron *Gorsachius magnificus*
Dwarf Olive Ibis *Bostrychia bocagei*
Northern Bald Ibis *Geronticus eremita*
Giant Ibis *Pseudibis gigantea*
Crested Ibis *Nipponia nippon*
Black-faced Spoonbill *Platalea minor*
Crested Shelduck *Tadorna cristata*
Pink-headed Duck *Rhodonessa caryophyllacea*
Madagascar Pochard *Aythya innotata*
Brazilian Merganser *Mergus octosetaceus*
California Condor *Gymnogyps californianus*
Madagascar Fish-eagle *Haliaeetus vociferoides*
Madagascar Serpent-eagle *Eutriorchis astur*
Philippine Eagle *Pithecophaga jefferyi*
White-winged Guan *Penelope albipennis*
Trinidad Piping-guan *Pipile pipile*
Blue-billed Curassow *Crax alberti*
Red-billed Curassow *Crax blumenbachii*
Djibouti Francolin *Francolinus ochropectus*
Sichuan Partridge *Arborophila rufipectus*
Orange-necked Partridge *Arborophila davidi*
Himalayan Quail *Ophrysia superciliosa*
Imperial Pheasant *Lophura imperialis*
Edwards's Pheasant *Lophura edwardsi*
Bornean Peacock-pheasant *Polyplectron schleiermacheri*
Bearded Wood-partridge *Dendrortyx barbatus*
New Caledonian Rail *Gallirallus lafresnayanus*
Austral Rail *Rallus antarcticus*

Sakalava Rail *Amaurornis olivieri*
Zapata Rail *Cyanolimnas cerverai*
Samoan Moorhen *Gallinula pacifica*
San Cristobal Moorhen *Gallinula silvestris*
Lesser Florican *Sypheotides indica*
Eskimo Curlew *Numenius borealis*
Slender-billed Curlew *Numenius tenuirostris*
Black Stilt *Himantopus novaezelandiae*
Chinese Crested Tern *Sterna bernsteini*
Yellow-legged Pigeon *Columba pallidiceps*
Ring-tailed Pigeon *Columba caribaea*
Pink Pigeon *Columba mayeri*
Blue-eyed Ground-dove *Columbina cyanopis*
Purple-winged Ground-dove *Claravis godefrida*
Grenada Dove *Leptotila wellsi*
Mindoro Bleeding-heart *Gallicolumba platenae*
Negros Bleeding-heart *Gallicolumba keayi*
Sulu Bleeding-heart *Gallicolumba menagei*
Polynesian Ground-dove *Gallicolumba erythroptera*
Thick-billed Ground-dove *Gallicolumba salamonis*
Negros Fruit-dove *Ptilinopus arcanus*
Marquesan Imperial-pigeon *Ducula galeata*
Philippine Cockatoo *Cacatua haematuropygia*
Norfolk Island Parakeet *Cyanoramphus cookii*
Night Parrot *Geopsittacus occidentalis*
Mauritius Parakeet *Psittacula eques*
Lear's Macaw *Anodorhynchus leari*
Spix's Macaw *Cyanopsitta spixii*
Yellow-eared Parrot *Ognorhynchus icterotis*
Fuertes's Parrot *Hapalopsittaca fuertesi*
Puerto Rican Amazon *Amazona vittata*
Black-hooded Coucal *Centropus steerii*
Seychelles Scops-owl *Otus insularis*
Anjouan Scops-owl *Otus capnodes*
Grand Comoro Scops-owl *Otus pauliani*
Forest Owlet *Athene blewitti*
Jamaican Pauraque *Siphonorhis americanus*
Puerto Rican Nightjar *Caprimulgus noctitherus*
White-winged Nightjar *Caprimulgus candicans*
Hook-billed Hermit *Glaucis dohrnii*
Sapphire-bellied Hummingbird *Lepidopyga lilliae*
Honduran Emerald *Amazilia luciae*
Scissor-tailed Hummingbird *Hylonympha macrocerca*
Juan Fernández Firecrown *Sephanoides fernandensis*
Bogotá Sunangel *Heliangelus zusii*
Black-breasted Puffleg *Eriocnemis nigrivestis*
Turquoise-throated Puffleg *Eriocnemis godini*
Sulu Hornbill *Anthracoceros montani*
Visayan Hornbill *Penelopides panini*
Writhed-billed Hornbill *Aceros waldeni*
Imperial Woodpecker *Campephilus imperialis*

Okinawa Woodpecker *Sapheopipo noguchii*
Royal Cinclodes *Cinclodes aricomae*
White-browed Tit-spinetail *Leptasthenura xenothorax*
Alagoas Foliage-gleaner *Philydor novaesi*
Alagoas Antwren *Myrmotherula snowi*
Black-hooded Antwren *Formicivora erythronotos*
Stresemann's Bristlefront *Merulaxis stresemanni*
Kinglet Calyptura *Calyptura cristata*
Peruvian Plantcutter *Phytotoma raimondii*
Gurney's Pitta *Pitta gurneyi*
Rudd's Lark *Heteromirafra ruddi*
White-eyed River-martin *Pseudochelidon sirintarae*
Liberian Greenbul *Phyllastrephus leucolepis*
Sao Tomé Fiscal Shrike *Lanius newtoni*
Bulo Burti Bush-shrike *Laniarius liberatus*
Mount Kupe Bush-shrike *Telophorus kupeensis*
Uluguru Bush-shrike *Malaconotus alius*
Zapata Wren *Ferminia cerverai*
Niceforo's Wren *Thryothorus nicefori*
Amami Thrush *Zoothera major*
Kamao *Myadestes myadestinus*
Olomao *Myadestes lanaiensis*
Puaiohi *Myadestes palmeri*
Taita Thrush *Turdus helleri*
Seychelles Magpie-robin *Copsychus sechellarum*
Grey-crowned Crocias *Crocias langbianis*
Taita Apalis *Apalis fuscigularis*
Rodrigues Warbler *Acrocephalus rodericanus*
Long-billed Tailorbird *Orthotomus moreaui*
Long-legged Thicketbird *Trichocichla rufa*
White-throated Jungle-flycatcher *Rhinomyias albigularis*
Cerulean Paradise-flycatcher *Eutrichomyias rowleyi*
Seychelles Paradise-flycatcher *Terpsiphone corvina*
Rarotonga Monarch *Pomarea dimidiata*
Tahiti Monarch *Pomarea nigra*
Cebu Flowerpecker *Dicaeum quadricolor*
Scarlet-collared Flowerpecker *Dicaeum retrocinctum*
Kulal White-eye *Zosterops kulalensis*
Taita White-eye *Zosterops silvanus*
Mount Karthala White-eye *Zosterops mouroniensis*
Mauritius Olive White-eye *Zosterops chloronothos*
Seychelles White-eye *Zosterops modestus*
Rota White-eye *Zosterops rotensis*
White-chested White-eye *Zosterops albogularis*
Kauai Oo *Moho braccatus*
Bishop's Oo *Moho bishopi*
Black-eared Miner *Manorina melanotis*
Guadalupe Junco *Junco insularis*
Pale-headed Brush-finch *Atlapetes pallidiceps*
Entre Ríos Seedeater *Sporophila zelichi*
Tumaco Seedeater *Sporophila insulata*
Cherry-throated Tanager *Nemosia rourei*
Venezuelan Flowerpiercer *Diglossa venezuelensis*
Bachman's Warbler *Vermivora bachmanii*
Semper's Warbler *Leucopeza semperi*
Paria Whitestart *Myioborus pariae*
Grey-headed Warbler *Basileuterus griseiceps*
Ou *Psittirostra psittacea*
Nukupuu *Hemignathus lucidus*
Oahu Alauahio *Paroreomyza maculata*
Poo-uli *Melamprosops phaeosoma*
San Andrés Vireo *Vireo caribaeus*
Forbes's Blackbird *Curaeus forbesi*
Sao Tomé Grosbeak *Neospiza concolor*
Ibadan Malimbe *Malimbus ibadanensis*
Mauritius Fody *Foudia rubra*

Pohnpei Mountain Starling *Aplonis pelzelni*
Bali Starling *Leucopsar rothschildi*
Isabela Oriole *Oriolus isabellae*
Grand Comoro Drongo *Dicrurus fuscipennis*
Mayotte Drongo *Dicrurus waldenii*
Mariana Crow *Corvus kubaryi*
Hawaiian Crow *Corvus hawaiiensis*

■ Endangered

New Zealand Dabchick *Poliocephalus rufopectus*
Short-tailed Albatross *Diomedea albatrus*
Bermuda Petrel *Pterodroma cahow*
Black-capped Petrel *Pterodroma hasitata*
Hutton's Shearwater *Puffinus huttoni*
Heinroth's Shearwater *Puffinus heinrothi*
Peruvian Diving-petrel *Pelecanoides garnotii*
Chinese Egret *Egretta eulophotes*
White-bellied Heron *Ardea insignis*
Australasian Bittern *Botaurus poiciloptilus*
Storm's Stork *Ciconia stormi*
Oriental Stork *Ciconia boyciana*
Greater Adjutant *Leptoptilos dubius*
White-shouldered Ibis *Pseudibis davisoni*
White-winged Duck *Cairina scutulata*
Madagascar Teal *Anas bernieri*
Imitator Sparrowhawk *Accipiter imitator*
Gundlach's Hawk *Accipiter gundlachii*
Red Goshawk *Erythrotriorchis radiatus*
Grey-backed Hawk *Leucopternis occidentalis*
Hispaniolan Hawk *Buteo ridgwayi*
Javan Hawk-eagle *Spizaetus bartelsi*
Plumbeous Forest-falcon *Micrastur plumbeus*
Mauritius Kestrel *Falco punctatus*
Niaufoou Scrubfowl *Megapodius pritchardii*
Cauca Guan *Penelope perspicax*
Northern Helmeted Curassow *Pauxi pauxi*
Southern Helmeted Curassow *Pauxi unicornis*
Udzungwa Forest-partridge *Xenoperdix udzungwensis*
Hainan Partridge *Arborophila ardens*
Annam Partridge *Arborophila merlini*
Vietnamese Pheasant *Lophura hatinhensis*
Palawan Peacock-pheasant *Polyplectron emphanum*
Gorgeted Wood-quail *Odontophorus strophium*
Black-breasted Buttonquail *Turnix melanogaster*
Buff-breasted Buttonquail *Turnix olivii*
Siberian Crane *Grus leucogeranus*
Whooping Crane *Grus americana*
White-winged Flufftail *Sarothrura ayresi*
Slender-billed Flufftail *Sarothrura watersi*
Junín Rail *Laterallus tuerosi*
Woodford's Rail *Nesoclopeus woodfordi*
Lord Howe Rail *Gallirallus sylvestris*
Okinawa Rail *Gallirallus okinawae*
Plain-flanked Rail *Rallus wetmorei*
Bogotá Rail *Rallus semiplumbeus*
Brown-banded Rail *Lewinia mirificus*
Takahe *Porphyrio mantelli*
Kagu *Rhynochetos jubatus*
Great Indian Bustard *Ardeotis nigriceps*
Bengal Florican *Houbaropsis bengalensis*
Chatham Islands Oystercatcher *Haematopus chathamensis*
New Zealand Dotterel *Charadrius obscurus*
St Helena Plover *Charadrius sanctaehelenae*
Shore Plover *Thinornis novaeseelandiae*
Nordmann's Greenshank *Tringa guttifer*
Tuamotu Sandpiper *Prosobonia cancellata*

Jerdon's Courser *Rhinoptilus bitorquatus*
Saunders's Gull *Larus saundersi*
Plain Pigeon *Columba inornata*
Tolima Dove *Leptotila conoveri*
Veracruz Quail-dove *Geotrygon carrikeri*
Blue-headed Quail-dove *Starnoenas cyanocephala*
Caroline Islands Ground-dove *Gallicolumba kubaryi*
Marquesan Ground-dove *Gallicolumba rubescens*
Mindoro Imperial-pigeon *Ducula mindorensis*
Chestnut-bellied Imperial-pigeon *Ducula brenchleyi*
Red-and-blue Lory *Eos histrio*
Kuhl's Lorikeet *Vini kuhlii*
Ultramarine Lorikeet *Vini ultramarina*
New Caledonian Lorikeet *Charmosyna diadema*
Yellow-crested Cockatoo *Cacatua sulphurea*
Green Racquet-tail *Prioniturus luconensis*
Blue-winged Racquet-tail *Prioniturus verticalis*
Blue-naped Parrot *Tanygnathus lucionensis*
Golden-shouldered Parrot *Psephotus chrysopterygius*
Orange-bellied Parrot *Neophema chrysogaster*
Black-cheeked Lovebird *Agapornis nigrigenis*
Sangihe Hanging-parrot *Loriculus catamene*
Blue-throated Macaw *Ara glaucogularis*
Red-fronted Macaw *Ara rubrogenys*
Golden Parakeet *Guaruba guarouba*
Thick-billed Parrot *Rhynchopsitta pachyrhyncha*
Rufous-fronted Parakeet *Bolborhynchus ferrugineifrons*
Brown-backed Parrotlet *Touit melanonota*
Golden-tailed Parrotlet *Touit surda*
Rusty-faced Parrot *Hapalopsittaca amazonina*
Red-faced Parrot *Hapalopsittaca pyrrhops*
Red-spectacled Amazon *Amazona pretrei*
Green-cheeked Amazon *Amazona viridigenalis*
Red-browed Amazon *Amazona rhodocorytha*
Red-tailed Amazon *Amazona brasiliensis*
Yellow-headed Amazon *Amazona oratrix*
Vinaceous Amazon *Amazona vinacea*
Blue-bellied Parrot *Triclaria malachitacea*
Prince Ruspoli's Turaco *Tauraco ruspolii*
Green-billed Coucal *Centropus chlororhynchus*
Banded Ground-cuckoo *Neomorphus radiolosus*
Madagascar Red Owl *Tyto soumagnei*
Lesser Eagle-owl *Mimizuku gurneyi*
Philippine Eagle-owl *Bubo philippensis*
Blakiston's Fish-owl *Ketupa blakistoni*
Rufous Fishing-owl *Scotopelia ussheri*
New Caledonian Owlet-nightjar *Aegotheles savesi*
Short-crested Coquette *Lophornis brachylopha*
Táchira Emerald *Amazilia distans*
Chestnut-bellied Hummingbird *Amazilia castaneiventris*
White-tailed Hummingbird *Eupherusa poliocerca*
Oaxaca Hummingbird *Eupherusa cyanophrys*
Little Woodstar *Acestrura bombus*
Esmeraldas Woodstar *Acestrura berlepschi*
Eared Quetzal *Euptilotis neoxenus*
Silvery Kingfisher *Alcedo argentata*
Rufous-lored Kingfisher *Todirhamphus winchelli*
Marquesan Kingfisher *Todirhamphus godeffroyi*
Mindoro Hornbill *Penelopides mindorensis*
Writhed Hornbill *Aceros leucocephalus*
Three-toed Jacamar *Jacamaralcyon tridactyla*
White-mantled Barbet *Capito hypoleucus*
Cuban Flicker *Colaptes fernandinae*
Helmeted Woodpecker *Dryocopus galeatus*
Plain Spinetail *Synallaxis infuscata*
Russet-bellied Spinetail *Synallaxis zimmeri*

Cipó Canastero *Asthenes luizae*
White-throated Barbtail *Margarornis tatei*
Recurve-billed Bushbird *Clytoctantes alixii*
Restinga Antwren *Formicivora littoralis*
Fringe-backed Fire-eye *Pyriglena atra*
Slender Antbird *Rhopornis ardesiaca*
Grey-headed Antbird *Myrmeciza griseiceps*
Moustached Antpitta *Grallaria alleni*
Bicoloured Antpitta *Grallaria rufocinerea*
Brown-banded Antpitta *Grallaria milleri*
Bahia Tapaculo *Scytalopus psychopompus*
Banded Cotinga *Cotinga maculata*
Kaempfer's Tody-tyrant *Hemitriccus kaempferi*
Ash-breasted Tit-tyrant *Anairetes alpinus*
Antioquia Bristle-tyrant *Phylloscartes lanyoni*
Minas Gerais Tyrannulet *Phylloscartes roquettei*
Alagoas Tyrannulet *Phylloscartes ceciliae*
Atlantic Royal Flycatcher *Onychorhynchus swainsoni*
Giant Kingbird *Tyrannus cubensis*
Yellow-bellied Asity *Neodrepanis hypoxanthus*
Ash's Lark *Mirafra ashi*
Archer's Lark *Heteromirafra archeri*
Sidamo Lark *Heteromirafra sidamoensis*
Raso Lark *Alauda razae*
Ochre-breasted Pipit *Anthus nattereri*
Réunion Cuckoo-shrike *Coracina newtoni*
Dusky Greenbul *Phyllastrephus tenebrosus*
Streak-breasted Bulbul *Ixos siquijorensis*
Philippine Leafbird *Chloropsis flavipennis*
Orange-breasted Bush-shrike *Laniarius brauni*
Gabela Bush-shrike *Laniarius amboimensis*
Monteiro's Bush-shrike *Malaconotus monteiri*
Gabela Helmet-shrike *Prionops gabela*
Apolinar's Wren *Cistothorus apolinari*
Floreana Mockingbird *Nesomimus trifasciatus*
Socorro Mockingbird *Mimodes graysoni*
White-breasted Thrasher *Ramphocinclus brachyurus*
Sri Lanka Whistling-thrush *Myiophonus blighi*
Spotted Ground-thrush *Zoothera guttata*
Somali Thrush *Turdus ludoviciae*
Gabela Akalat *Sheppardia gabela*
Black Shama *Copsychus cebuensis*
Luzon Water-redstart *Rhyacornis bicolor*
Melodious Babbler *Malacopteron palawanense*
Falcated Wren-babbler *Ptilocichla falcata*
Flame-templed Babbler *Stachyris speciosa*
Negros Striped-babbler *Stachyris nigrorum*
Hinde's Pied-babbler *Turdoides hindei*
Pulitzer's Longbill *Macrosphenus pulitzeri*
Western Bristlebird *Dasyornis longirostris*
Biak Gerygone *Gerygone hypoxantha*
Chatham Islands Robin *Petroica traversi*
White-browed Jungle-flycatcher *Rhinomyias insignis*
Ashy-breasted Flycatcher *Muscicapa randi*
Palawan Flycatcher *Ficedula platenae*
Furtive Flycatcher *Ficedula disposita*
Lompobattang Flycatcher *Ficedula bonthaina*
Celestial Monarch *Hypothymis coelestis*
Marquesan Monarch *Pomarea mendozae*
Truk Monarch *Metabolus rugensis*
Flores Monarch *Monarcha sacerdotum*
Black-chinned Monarch *Monarcha boanensis*
Biak Monarch *Monarcha brehmii*
Algerian Nuthatch *Sitta ledanti*
Visayan Flowerpecker *Dicaeum haematostictum*
Elegant Sunbird *Aethopyga duyvenbodei*

Faichuk White-eye *Rukia ruki*
Regent Honeyeater *Xanthomyza phrygia*
Sierra Madre Sparrow *Xenospiza baileyi*
Worthen's Sparrow *Spizella wortheni*
Cuban Sparrow *Torreornis inexpectata*
Yellow-headed Brush-finch *Atlapetes flaviceps*
Yellow Cardinal *Gubernatrix cristata*
Plain-tailed Warbling-finch *Poospiza alticola*
Rufous-breasted Warbling-finch *Poospiza rubecula*
Cochabamba Mountain-finch *Poospiza garleppi*
Buffy-fronted Seedeater *Sporophila frontalis*
Temminck's Seedeater *Sporophila falcirostris*
Black-and-tawny Seedeater *Sporophila nigrorufa*
Marsh Seedeater *Sporophila palustris*
Mangrove Finch *Camarhynchus heliobates*
Black-and-gold Tanager *Bangsia melanochlamys*
Orange-throated Tanager *Wetmorethraupis sterrhopteron*
Azure-rumped Tanager *Tangara cabanisi*
Seven-coloured Tanager *Tangara fastuosa*
Black-backed Tanager *Tangara peruviana*
Golden-cheeked Warbler *Dendroica chrysoparia*
Palila *Loxioides bailleui*
Akiapolaau *Hemignathus wilsoni*

Akikiki *Oreomystis bairdi*
Hawaii Creeper *Oreomystis mana*
Akekee *Loxops caeruleirostris*
Akepa *Loxops coccineus*
Black-capped Vireo *Vireo atricapillus*
Baudó Oropendola *Psarocolius cassini*
Martinique Oriole *Icterus bonana*
Saffron-cowled Blackbird *Xanthopsar flavus*
Yellow-shouldered Blackbird *Agelaius xanthomus*
Pampas Meadowlark *Sturnella militaris*
Red-bellied Grackle *Hypopyrrhus pyrohypogaster*
Yellow-throated Serin *Serinus flavigula*
Ankober Serin *Serinus ankoberensis*
Red Siskin *Carduelis cucullata*
Warsangli Linnet *Carduelis johannis*
Green-faced Parrotfinch *Erythrura viridifacies*
Pink-billed Parrotfinch *Erythrura kleinschmidti*
Gouldian Finch *Chloebia gouldiae*
Gola Malimbe *Malimbus ballmanni*
White-eyed Starling *Aplonis brunneicapilla*
Kokako *Callaeas cinerea*
Dwarf Jay *Cyanolyca nana*
White-throated Jay *Cyanolyca mirabilis*

REFERENCES

ABDULALI, H. (1967) The birds of the Nicobar Islands, with notes on some Andaman birds. *J. Bombay Nat. Hist. Soc.* 64: 139–190.

ABDULALI, H. (1978) The birds of Great and Car Nicobars with some notes on wildlife conservation in the islands. *J. Bombay Nat. Hist. Soc.* 75: 744–772.

AOSNR (ADMINISTRATIVE OFFICE OF SHANXI NATURE RESERVES), PANGQUANGUO NATURE RESERVE AND LUMAO SHAN NATURE RESERVE (1990) [*Rare bird: Brown Eared-pheasant.*] Taiyuan, China: Shanxi Popular Science Publishing House. (In Chinese.)

AKÇAKAYA, H. R. (1990) Bald Ibis *Geronticus eremita* population in Turkey: an evaluation of the captive breeding project for reintroduction. *Biol. Conserv.* 51: 225–237.

ALI, S. (1978) President's letter. Mystery birds of India 4: the Pink-headed Duck *Rhodonessa caryophyllacea.* *Hornbill*: 4–7.

ALI, S. AND RIPLEY, S. D. (1987) *Compact handbook of the birds of India and Pakistan together with those of Bangladesh, Nepal, Bhutan and Sri Lanka.* Second edition. Delhi: Oxford University Press.

ALI, S., BISWAS, B. AND RIPLEY, S. D. (in prep.) The birds of Bhutan. *Rec. Zool. Surv. India Occas. Pap. no.* 136: 1–263.

ALISON, R. (1993a) Eiders: a cause for concern. *Birds of the Wild* 2: 24–28.

ALISON, R. (1993b) Eiders down: extinction looms, but why? *BBC Wildlife* 11: 16.

ALLAN, D. (1989) The Bald Ibis returns to Cape Town. *Quagga* 25: 18–20.

ALLAN, D. (1993) The status of the Blue Crane in South Africa. *WBC News* 162: 22–23.

ALLPORT, G. (1991) The status and conservation of threatened birds in the Upper Guinea Forest. *Bird Conserv. Internatn.* 1: 53–74.

ALLPORT, G. AND WILSON, S. (1986) *Results of a census of the Milky Stork in West Java.* Cambridge, U.K.: International Council for Bird Preservation (Study Report 14).

ALLPORT, G. A., AUSDEN, M., HAYMAN, P. V., ROBERTSON, P. AND WOOD, P. (1989) *The conservation of the birds of the Gola Forest, Sierra Leone.* Cambridge, U.K.: International Council for Bird Preservation (Study Report 38).

ALONSO, J. C. AND ALONSO, J. A., EDS. (1990) *Parametros demográficos, selección de habitat y distribución de la avutarda Otis tarda en tres regiones españolas.* Madrid: Instituto Nacional para la Conservación de la Naturaleza (ICONA).

ALPERT, P. (1993) Conserving biodiversity in Cameroon. *Ambio* 22: 44–49.

ANDERSEN, C. Y., POULSEN, M. K., JACOBSEN, O. F. AND HEEGARD, M. (1992) Observations on the Luzon Water Redstart *Rhyacornis bicolor* in the Mount Pulog National Park, Philippines. *Forktail* 7: 147–150.

ANDERSON, I. (1992) Can Nauru clean up after the colonists? *New Scientist* 1830: 18–19.

ANDRADE, G. I. AND REPIZZO, A. (1994) Guanentá–Alto Fonce Fauna and Flora Sanctuary: a new protected area in the Colombian East Andes. *Cotinga* 2: 42–44.

ANDREW, D. AND PALLISER, T. (1993) Observations of Scarlet-chested Parrots. *Wingspan* 10: 4–5.

ANDREW, P. (1985) An annotated checklist of the birds of Cibodas–Gunung Gede Nature Reserve. *Kukila* 2: 10–28.

ANDREW, P. (1990) The status of the Sunda Coucal *Centropus nigrorufus* Cuvier. *Kukila* 5: 56–64.

ANDREW, P. (1992) *The birds of Indonesia: a checklist (Peters' sequence).* Jakarta: Indonesian Ornithological Society.

ANDREW, P. AND HOLMES, D. A. (1990) Sulawesi bird report. *Kukila* 5: 4–26.

ANDREW, P. AND MILTON, G. R. (1988) A note on the Javan Scops-owl *Otus angelinae* Finsch. *Kukila* 3: 79.

ANDREWS, S. M. (1994) Rediscovery of the Monteiro's Bush-shrike *Malaconotus monteiri* in Cameroon. *Bull. African Bird Club* 1: 26–27.

ANGEHR, G. R. (1985) *Stitchbird.* Dunedin, New Zealand: John McIndoe and New Zealand Wildlife Service.

ANON. (1992) Flycatchers and La Veuve Special Reserve. *CNP News (Seychelles)* 1: 2.

ANON. (1993a) Little Spot moves to Mana. *Forest and Bird* 267: 3.

ANON. (1993b) International airport threatens the ecosystem at Youngjong-do. *Asian Wetland News* 6: 7.

ANSTEY, S. (1989) *The status and conservation of the White-headed duck* Oxyura leucocephala. Slimbridge, U.K.: International Waterfowl and Wetlands Research Bureau (IWRB Spec. Publ. 10).

ANSTEY, S. AND MOSER, M. E. (1990) A recovery plan for the White-headed Duck *Oxyura leucocephala.* Pp.204–206 in G. V. T. Matthews, ed. *Managing waterfowl populations.* Slimbridge, U.K.: International Waterfowl and Wetlands Research Bureau (IWRB Spec. Publ. 12).

AOU (1983) *Check-list of North American birds.* Sixth edition. American Ornithologists' Union.

APPERT, O. (1985) Zur Biologie der Mesitornithiformes (Nakas oder 'Stelzenrallen') Madagaskars und erste fotografische Dokumente von Vertretern der Ordnung. *Orn. Beob.* 82: 31–54.

ARCHER, A. L., COLLINS, S. AND BAMPTON, I. (1991) Report on a visit to Jozani Forest, Zanzibar. *EANHS Bull.* 21: 59–66.

ARCHER, G. AND GODMAN, E. M. (1937) *The birds of British Somaliland and the Gulf of Aden,* 2. London: Gurney and Jackson.

ARCHIBALD, G. W. (1987) White-naped Crane. Unpublished.

ARCHIBALD, G. (1992) A bird's eye view of Cambodia. *ICF Bugle* 18: 1–3.

ARCHIBALD, G. AND LANDFRIED, S. (1993) Conservation measures for the Siberian Crane. Pp.85–87 in M. Moser and J. van Vessem, eds. *Wetland and waterfowl conservation in south and west Asia.* Slimbridge, U.K.: International Waterfowl and Wetlands Research Bureau.

ARCHIBALD, G. AND MEINE, C. (in prep.) Cranes: status survey and conservation action plans.

ARCHIBALD, G. W. AND PASQUIER, R. F., EDS. (1987) *Proceedings of the 1983 International Crane Workshop.* Baraboo, U.S.: International Crane Foundation.

ARHZAF, Z. L. (1993) Les oiseaux en danger et leur conservation au Maroc. *Proc. 8 Pan-Afr. Orn. Congr.* [*Ann. Sci. Zool. Mus. Roy. Afrique Centr.* 286]: 271–278.

ARNDT, T. (1992) Die Papageien von Biak. *Papageien* 2: 61–65.

ASH, J. S. (1986) A *Ploceus* sp. nov. from Uganda. *Ibis* 128: 330–336.

ASH, J. S. (1987a) *Ploceus victoriae*. *Ibis* 129: 406–407.

ASH, J. S. (1987b) Nigeria: surveys of selected bird conservation areas (wetlands and forests). Cambridge, U.K.: International Council for Bird Preservation.

ASH, J. S. (1990) Additions to the avifauna of Nigeria, with notes on distributional changes and breeding. *Malimbus* 11: 104–116.

ASH, J. (1991) The Grey-necked Picarthartes *Picathartes oreas* and Ibadan Malimbe *Malimbus ibadanensis* in Nigeria. *Bird Conserv. Internatn.* 1: 93–106.

ASH, J. S. (1993) Changes to the Somalia check-list. *Scopus* 17: 26–31.

ASH, J. S. AND GULLICK, T. M. (1989) The present situation regarding the endemic breeding birds of Ethiopia. *Scopus* 13: 90–96.

ASH, J. S. AND GULLICK, T. M. (1990a) *Serinus flavigula* rediscovered. *Bull. Brit. Orn. Club* 110: 81–83.

ASH, J. S. AND GULLICK, T. M. (1990b) Field observations on the Degodi Lark *Mirafra degodiensis*. *Bull. Brit. Orn. Club* 110: 90–93.

ASH, J. S. AND MISKELL, J. E. (1981) Present abundance of the Warsangli Linnet *Acanthis johannis*. *Bull. Brit. Orn. Club* 101: 396–398.

ASH, J. S. AND MISKELL, J. E. (1983) Birds of Somalia: their habitat, status and distribution. *Scopus* (Special Supplement) 1.

ASH, J. S. AND OLSON, S. L. (1985) A second specimen of *Mirafra (Heteromirafra) sidamoensis* Erard. *Bull. Brit. Orn. Club* 105: 141–143.

ASH, J. S. AND SHARLAND, R. E. (1986) *Nigeria: assessment of bird conservation priorities*. Cambridge, U.K.: International Council for Bird Preservation (Study Report 11).

ASH, J. S., DOWSETT, R. J. AND DOWSETT-LEMAIRE, F. (1989) New ornithological distribution records from eastern Nigeria. Pp.13–27 in R. J. Dowsett, ed. *A preliminary natural history survey of Mambilla Plateau and some lowland forests of eastern Nigeria*. Ely, U.K.: Tauraco Press (Tauraco Research Report 1).

ASH, J. S., COVERDALE, M. A. C. AND GULLICK, T. M. (1991) Comments on status and distribution of birds in western Uganda. *Scopus* 15: 24–29.

ASHMOLE, N. P., ASHMOLE, N. J. AND SIMMONS, K. E. L. (1994) Seabird conservation and feral cats on Ascension Island, South Atlantic. Pp.94–121 in D. N. Nettleship, J. Burger and M. Gochfeld, eds. *Seabirds on islands: threats, case studies and action plans*. Cambridge, U.K.: BirdLife International (BirdLife Conservation Series no. 1).

ASPINALL, S. (1993) Spring migration of Lesser Kestrel *Falco naumanni*. *Emirates Bird Report* 17: 47–48.

ATKINS, J. (1992a) Ankober Serin at the viewpoint, 2–3 miles before the Mussolini Tunnel, 26 October 1991. *Ethiopia Wildl. Nat. Hist. Soc. Newsletter* 264: 5.

ATKINS, J. D. (1992b) A new location for the Ankober Serin *Serinus ankoberensis* near Debre Sina, Ethiopia. *Scopus* 16: 105–107.

ATKINSON, P., PEET, N. AND ALEXANDER, J. (1991) The status and conservation of the endemic bird species of São Tomé and Príncipe, West Africa. *Bird Conserv. Internatn.* 1: 255–282.

ATKINSON, P. W., WHITTINGHAM, M. J., GÓMEZ DE SILVA GARZA, H., KENT, A. M. AND MAIER, R. T. (1993) Notes on the ecology, conservation and taxonomic status of *Hylorchilus* wrens. *Bird Conserv. Internatn.* 3: 75–85.

ATKINSON, P. W., KOROMA, A. P., RANFT, R., ROWE, S. G. AND WILKINSON, R. (1994) The status, identification and vocalisations of African fishing owls with particular reference to the Rufous Fishing Owl *Scotopelia ussheri*. *Bull. African Bird Club* 1: 67–72.

AUBURN, J. (1988) Do some African Lesser Kestrels migrate from the Far East across the Indian Ocean? *Gabar* 3: 5–7.

BAGGER, J., HALBERG, K. AND NYITI, P. Y. (1989) Observations of birds in Rondo and Litipo forests, S.-E. Tanzania: preliminary report of the Danish-Tanzanian ICBP Expedition. Copenhagen: Institute of Population Biology/ICBP Danish Section (unpublished).

BAHA EL DIN, S. (1993) *The catching of Corncrakes* Crex crex *and other birds in northern Egypt*. Cambridge, U.K.: BirdLife International (Study Report 55).

BAILEY, S. F. (1992) Seabirds of Madang Province, Papua New Guinea, September–November 1989. *Emu* 92: 223–232.

BAKER, N. E. AND BAKER, E. M. (1990) A new species of weaver from Tanzania. *Bull. Brit. Orn. Club* 110: 51–58.

BAKER, N. E. AND BAKER, E. M. (1992) Four Afrotropical migrants on the East African coast: evidence for a common origin. *Scopus* 15: 122–124.

BAKER, N. E. AND BAKER, E. M. (in press) Further records of the Taita Falcon from Tanzania. *Scopus*.

BAKER-GABB, D. (1993) Managing native grasslands to maintain biodiversity and conserve the Plains-wanderer. *Wingspan* 10 (Suppl., RAOU Conservation Statement 8): 1–8.

BALCHIN, C. S. (1990) Further observations of birds from the Ivory Coast. *Malimbus* 12: 52–53.

VAN BALEN, S. (1991) The Java Hawk-eagle *Spizaetus bartelsi*: WWGBP project report no. 1, March 1990. *Birds of Prey Bull.* 4: 33–40.

VAN BALEN, S. AND DIRGAYUSA, I. W. A. (1993) Bali Starling Project activity report: March–October 1993. Unpublished.

VAN BALEN, S. AND GEPAK, V. H. (1994) The captive breeding and conservation programme of the Bali Starling (*Leucopsar rothschildi*). Pp.420–430 in P. J. S. Olney, G. M. Mace and A. T. C. Feistner, eds. *Creative conservation: interactive management of wild and captive animals*. London: Chapman and Hall.

VAN BALEN, S. AND HOLMES, D. A. (1993) Status and conservation of pheasants in the Greater and Lesser Sundas, Indonesia. Pp.40–49 in D. Jenkins, ed. *Pheasants in Asia 1992*. Reading, U.K.: World Pheasant Association.

VAN BALEN, S. AND JEPSON, P. (1992) Bali Starling Project: activity report, January–August 1992. ICBP Indonesia Programme, Bogor.

VAN BALEN, S. AND MEYBURG, B.-U. (1994) The Java Hawk Eagle *Spizaetus bartelsi*: results of recent research on distribution, status and ecology. Pp.89–92 in B.-U. Meyburg and R. D. Chancellor, eds. *Raptor conservation today*. Mountfield, U.K.: Pica Press.

BANKO, P. C. (1992) Constraints on wild Nene productivity. *Wildfowl* 44: 99–106.

BARRÉ, N. (1988) Une avifaune menacée: les oiseaux de la Réunion. Pp.167–196 in J.-C. Thibault and I. Guyot, eds. *Livre rouge des oiseaux menacés des régions françaises d'Outre-Mer*. Saint-Cloud: Conseil International pour la

Protection des Oiseaux (Monogr. 5).

BARRIO, J. (1994) The Rufous-breasted Warbling-finch, *Poospiza rubecula*, in Bosque Zárate of Peru. Unpublished.

BEAMAN, M. (1991) Notes on a trip to Assam, North Cachar and Manipur. Unpublished.

BEAN, N. J., BENSTEAD, P. J., SHOWLER, D. AND WHITTINGTON, P. A. (1994) Survey of the Western Tragopan *Tragopan melanocephalus* in the Palas Valley, N.W.F.P.—Spring 1994. Final report to Himalayan Jungle Project, Islamabad, Pakistan and BirdLife International, Cambridge, U.K.

BECKING, J. H. (1976) Feeding range of Abbott's Booby *Sula abbotti* at the coast of Java. *Ibis* 118: 589–590.

BEDNALL, D. K. AND WILLIAMS, J. G. (1989) Range retraction of the White-eyed Gull *Larus leucophthalmus* from the eastern coast of Africa. *Scopus* 13: 122–123.

BEEHLER, B. (1985) Conservation of New Guinea rainforest birds. Pp.233–247 in A. W. Diamond and T. E. Lovejoy, eds. *Conservation of tropical forest birds*. Cambridge, U.K.: International Council for Bird Preservation (Techn. Publ. 4).

BEEHLER, B. M., PRATT, T. K. AND ZIMMERMAN, D. A. (1986) *Birds of New Guinea*. Princeton: Princeton University Press.

BEEHLER, B. M., CRILL, W., JEFFERIES, B. AND JEFFERIES, M. (1992) New Guinea Harpy-Eagle attempts to capture a monitor lizard. *Emu* 92: 246–247.

BEICHLE, U. (1982) Untersuchungen zur Biologie und Systematik der Zahntaube *Didunculus strigirostris* (Jardine 1845). Kiel: Christian-Albrechts Universität (Doctoral dissertation).

BEICHLE, U. (1987) Lebensraum, Bestand und Nahrungsaufnahme der Zahntaube, *Didunculus strigirostris*. *J. Orn.* 128: 75–89.

BELLATRECHE, M. (1991) Deux nouvelles localisations de la Sitelle [*sic*] kabyle *Sitta ledanti* en Algérie. *Oiseau et R.F.O.* 61: 269–272.

BELLATRECHE, M. AND CHALABI, B. (1990) Données nouvelles sur l'aire de distribution de la Sittelle kabyle *Sitta ledanti*. *Alauda* 58: 95–97.

BELLINGHAM, M. AND DAVIS, A. (1988) Forest bird communities in Western Samoa. *Notornis* 35: 117–128.

BELTON, W. (1984–1985) Birds of Rio Grande do Sul, Brazil. *Bull. Amer. Mus. Nat. Hist.* 178(4) and 180(1).

VAN BEMMEL, A. C. V. (1948) A faunal list of the birds of the Moluccan Islands. *Treubia* 19: 323–402.

BENNUN, L. A. (1986) Montane birds of the Bwindi (Impenetrable) Forest. *Scopus* 10: 87–91.

BENNUN, L. A. (1987) Ringing and recapture of Spotted Ground Thrushes *Turdus fischeri fischeri* at Gede, Kenya Coast: indications of site fidelity and population size stability. *Scopus* 11: 1–5.

BENNUN, L. A. (1992) Threatened birds of Kenya, 1: Spotted Ground Thrush. *Kenya Birds* 1: 19–21.

BENNUN, L. A. AND WAIYAKI, E. M. (1992) Forest birds of the Shimba Hills and Malunganji: a survey. [Nairobi:] Research Reports of the Centre for Biodiversity, National Museums of Kenya (Ornithology 10).

BENSON, C. W. AND BENSON, F. M. (1977) *The birds of Malawi*. Limbe, Malawi: Montfort Press.

BENSON, C. W., BROOKE, R. K., DOWSETT, R. J. AND IRWIN, M. P. S. (1971) *The birds of Zambia*. London: Collins.

BENSON, P. C., TARBOTON, W. R., ALLAN, D. G. AND DOBBS, J. C. (1990) The breeding status of the Cape Vulture in the Transvaal during 1980–1985. *Ostrich* 61: 134–142.

BENSTEAD, P. (1994) Brazilian Merganser in Argentina: going, going... *Cotinga* 1: 8.

BENSTEAD, P. J., HEARN, R. D., JEFFS, C. J. S., CALLAGHAN, D. A., CALO, J., GIL, G., JOHNSON, A. E. AND STAGI NEDELCOFF, A. R. (1993) 'Pato Serrucho 93': an expedition to assess the current status of the Brazilian Merganser *Mergus octosetaceus* in north-east Argentina. Unpublished report.

BEREZAN, A. P. (1993) Blakiston's Fish Owl in the Kunashir Island. *Raptor Link* 1: 3.

BERG, K. S. (1994) New and interesting records of birds from a dry forest reserve in south-west Ecuador. *Cotinga* 2: 14–19.

BERGER, A. J. (1972) *Hawaiian birdlife*. Honolulu: University Press of Hawaii.

BEST, B. J. (1994) Focus on: Ochre-bellied Dove *Leptotila ochraceiventris*. *Cotinga* 1: 30–33.

BEST, B. J. AND KRABBE, N. (1994) A review of the status and conservation of the Rufous-headed Chachalaca. *World Pheasant Assoc. J.* 17–18: 45–56.

BEST, B. J., CLARKE, C. T., CHECKER, M., BROOM, A. L., THEWLIS, R. M., DUCKWORTH, W. AND McNAB, A. (1993) Distributional records, natural history notes, and conservation of some poorly known birds from southwestern Ecuador and northwestern Peru. *Bull. Brit. Orn. Club* 113: 108–119, 234–255.

BEZZEL, E. AND WARTMANN, B. (1990) Neue Beobachtungen des Waldrapps (*Geronticus eremita*) im Jemen. *J. Orn.* 131: 456–457.

BHATIA, Z. (1993) A preliminary assessment of coastal forest birds in south-east Tanzania. *Proc. 8 Pan-Afr. Orn. Congr.* [*Ann. Sci. Zool. Mus. Roy. Afrique Centr.* 286]: 252–257.

BHATTACHARJEE, P. C. (1993) Conservation of Greater Adjutant Stork in Assam. Unpublished project report (WWF Project No. 4630).

BHUSHAN, B. (1986a) Rediscovery of the Jerdon's or Double-banded Courser *Cursorius bitorquatus* (Blyth). *J. Bombay Nat. Hist. Soc.* 83: 1–14.

BHUSHAN, B. (1986b) Photographic record of the Jerdon's or Double-banded Courser *Cursorius bitorquatus*. *J. Bombay Nat. Hist. Soc.* 83 (Suppl.): 159–162.

BHUSHAN, B. (1992) Red Data Bird: Jerdon's Courser. *World Birdwatch* 14(4): 12.

BIBBY, C. J. (1994) Recent past and future extinctions in birds. *Phil. Trans. R. Soc. Lond.* B 344: 35–40.

BIBER, J.-P. (1990) *Action plan for the conservation of western Lesser Kestrel Falco naumanni populations*. Cambridge, U.K.: International Council for Bird Preservation (Study Report 41).

BISHOP, K. D. (1982) Endemic birds of Biak Island. International Council for Bird Preservation survey. Unpublished report.

BISHOP, K. D. (1983) Some notes on non-passerine birds of West New Britain. *Emu* 83: 235–241.

BISHOP, K. D. (1989) Little known *Tyto* owls of Wallacea. *Kukila* 4: 37–43.

BISHOP, K. D. (1992) New and interesting records of birds in Wallacea. *Kukila* 6: 8–34.

BISHOP, M. A. (1993) The Black-necked Crane winter count

1991–1992. *J. Ecol. Soc.* 6: 55–64.

BLABER, S. J. M. (1990) Checklist and notes on the current status of birds of New Georgia, Western Province, Solomon Islands. *Emu* 90: 205–214.

BLACK, J. M. AND BANKO, P. C. (1994) Is the Hawaiian Goose (*Branta sandvicensis*) saved from extinction? Pp.394–410 in P. J. S. Olney, G. M. Mace and A. T. C. Feistner, eds. *Creative conservation: interactive management of wild and captive animals.* London: Chapman and Hall.

BLACK, J. M., DUVALL, F., HOSHIDE, H., MEDEIROS, J., HODGES, C. N., SANTOS, N. AND TELFER, T. (1991) The current status of the Hawaiian Goose *Branta sandvicensis* and its recovery programme. *Wildfowl* 42: 149–154.

BLAIR, M. (1989) The RAFOS Expedition to Ascension Island, 1987. *Roy. Air Force Orn. Soc. J.* 19: 1–35.

BLAKE, E. R. (1977) *Manual of Neotropical birds*, 1. Chicago: University of Chicago Press.

BLAKERS, M., DAVIES, S. J. J. F. AND REILLY, P. N. (1984) *The atlas of Australian birds.* Victoria: Royal Australasian Ornithologists' Union.

BLOCK, B., BLOCK, P., JASCHKE, W., LITZBARSKI, B., LITZBARSKI, H. AND PETRICK, S. (1993) Komplexer Artenschutz durch extensive Landwirtschaft im Rahmen des Schutzprojektes 'Grosstrappe'. *Natur u. Landschaft* 68: 565–576.

BLOM, A. (1990) List of the birds of the (future) Okapi Reserve and National Park. Unpublished (second) draft.

BLOT, J. (1985) Contribution à la connaissance de la biologie et de l'écologie de *Francolinus ochropectus* Dorst et Jouanin. *Alauda* 53: 244–256.

BOCHARNIKOV, V. N. (1990) Current status of the Chinese Merganser *Mergus squamatus* in Russia. *Bull. Inst. Ornith. Kyung Hee Univ.* 3: 23–27.

BOLES, W. E., LONGMORE, N. W. AND THOMPSON, M. C. (1994) A recent specimen of the Night Parrot *Geopsittacus occidentalis*. *Emu* 94: 37–40.

BONDE, K. (1993) *Birds of Lesotho: a guide to distribution past and present.* Pietermaritzburg: University of Natal Press.

BOONSONG, L. AND ROUND, P. (1991) *Birds of Thailand.* Bangkok: Saha Karn Bhaet.

BORELLO, W. D. AND BORELLO, R. M. (1993) Demographic trends in Cape Griffon *Gyps coprotheres* colonies in Botswana, 1963–1992. *Proc. 8 Pan-Afr. Orn. Congr.* [*Ann. Sci. Zool. Mus. Roy. Afrique Centr.* 286]: 123–131.

BORNER, M. (1990) Tanzania wildlife conservation monitoring: wildlife census, Moyowosi-Kigosi, 1990. Unpublished.

BORODIN, A. M., ED. (1984) [*Red data book of the USSR: rare and endangered species of animals and plants, 1: animals.*] Second edition. Moscow: Promyshlennost. (In Russian.)

BORROW, N. (1994) Yellow-headed Picathartes in Côte d'Ivoire. *Bull. African Bird Club* 1: 8.

BOSHOFF, A. F. AND DE KOCK, A. C. (1988) Further evidence of organo-chlorine contamination in Cape Vultures. *Ostrich* 59: 40–41.

BOSWELL, J. (1987) [Review of Williams (1986).] *Ibis* 129: 136–137.

BOURNE, W. R. P. (1993) Kenyon's Shag. *Sea Swallow* 42: 71.

BOURNE, W. R. P. AND DAVID, A. C. F. (1983) Henderson Island, central South Pacific, and its birds. *Notornis* 30: 233–243.

BOURNE, W. R. P. AND DIXON, T. J. (1973) Observations of seabirds 1967–1969. *Sea Swallow* 22: 29–60.

BOWDEN, C. G. R. (1987) The Yemen Thrush in North Yemen. *Sandgrouse* 9: 87–89.

BOWDEN, C. G. R. AND ANDREWS, S. M. (1994) Mount Kupe and its birds. *Bull. African Bird Club* 1: 13–16.

BOWDEN, C. G. R. AND BOWDEN, E. M. (1993) The conservation of Mount Kupe, Cameroon. *Proc. 8 Pan-Afr. Orn. Congr.* [*Ann. Sci. Zool. Mus. Roy. Afrique Centr.* 286]: 231–235.

BOWDEN, L. (1993) Where spirits meet. *World Birdwatch* 15(3): 10–13.

BOWLER, J. AND TAYLOR, J. (1989) An annotated checklist of the birds of Manusela National Park, Seram (birds recorded on the Operation Raleigh Expedition). *Kukila* 4: 3–33.

BOWLER, J. AND TAYLOR, J. (1993) The avifauna of Seram. Pp.143–160 in I. D. Edwards, A. A. Macdonald and J. Proctor, eds. *Natural history of Seram.* Andover, U.K.: Intercept.

BRAZIL, M. A. (1991) *The birds of Japan.* London: Chistopher Helm.

BRAZIL, M. (1994) Arasaki: Japan's wintering crane capital. *Birding World* 7: 67–70.

BRAZIL, M. A. AND MOORES, N. (1993) The importance of Japanese wetlands as wintering grounds for the endangered Saunders's Gull *Larus saundersi*. *Forktail* 8: 113–118.

BREGULLA, H. L. (1987) Zur Biologie des Kagu, *Rhinochetus jubatus*. *Zool. Garten N.F.* 57: 349–365.

BREGULLA, H. L. (1992) *Birds of Vanuatu.* Oswestry, U.K.: Anthony Nelson.

BREGULLA, H. (1993) Die Papageien Neukaledoniens. *Gefied. Welt* 117: 310–313, 349–351, 381–384, 412–416.

BRETAGNOLLE, V. AND ATTIÉ, C. (1991) Status of Barau's Petrel (*Pterodroma baraui*): colony sites, breeding population and taxonomic affinities. *Colonial Waterbirds* 14: 25–33.

BRIFFETT, C. AND BIN SUPARI, S. (1993) *The birds of Singapore.* Oxford: Oxford University Press.

BRITTON, P. L., ED. (1980) *Birds of East Africa: their habitat, status and distribution.* Nairobi: East Africa Natural History Society.

BROOKE, M. DE L. (1985) The annual cycle of the Toc-toc *Foudia sechellarum* on Cousin Island, Seychelles. *Ibis* 127: 7–15.

BROOKE, M. DE L. (in press) The modern avifauna of the Pitcairn Islands, South Pacific. *Biol. J. Linn. Soc.*

BROOKE, M. DE L. AND HARTLEY, I. R. (in press) Nesting Henderson Reed-warblers (*Acrocephalus vaughani taiti*) studied by DNA fingerprinting: unrelated coalitions in a stable habitat? *Auk.*

BROOKE, M. DE L. AND JONES, P. J. (in press) The diet of the Henderson Fruit Dove. 1: field observations of fruit choice. *Biol. J. Linn. Soc.*

BROOKE, R. K. (1969) Taxonomic and distributional notes on *Apus acuticauda*. *Bull. Brit. Orn. Club* 89: 97–100.

BROOKE, R. K. (1984) *South African Red Data Book—birds.* Pretoria: South African National Scientific Programmes (Report 97).

BROOKS, D. J. (1987a) Feeding observations on birds in North Yemen. *Sandgrouse* 9: 115–120.

BROOKS, D. J. (1987b) The Yemen Warbler in North Yemen. *Sandgrouse* 9: 90–93.

BROOKS, D. J., EVANS, M. I., MARTINS, R. P. AND PORTER, R. F. (1987) The status of birds in North Yemen and the records of OSME Expedition in 1985. *Sandgrouse* 9: 4–66.

BROOKS, T. M., EVANS, T. D., DUTSON, G. C. L., ANDERSON, G. Q. A., ASANE, D. C., TIMMINS, R. J. AND TOLEDO, A. G. (1992) The conservation status of the birds of Negros, Philippines. *Bird Conserv. Internatn.* 2: 273–302.

BROOKS, T. M., BARNES, R., BARTRINA, L., BUTCHART, S. H. M., CLAY, R. P., ESQUIVEL, E. Z., ETCHEVERRY, N. I., LOWEN, J. C. AND VINCENT, J. (1993) *Bird surveys and conservation in the Paraguayan Atlantic Forest: Project CANOPY '92 final report.* Cambridge, U.K.: BirdLife International (Study Report 57).

BROSSET, A. AND ERARD, C. (1986) *Les oiseaux des régions forestières du nord-est du Gabon,* 1. Paris: Société Nationale de Protection de la Nature.

BROWN, C. J. AND PIPER, S. E. (1988) Status of Cape Vultures in the Natal Drakensberg and their cliff site selection. *Ostrich* 59: 126–136.

BROWN, L. H., URBAN, E. K. AND NEWMAN, K. (1982) *The birds of Africa,* 1. London: Academic Press.

BROYER, J. (1994) La régression du Râle de genêts *Crex crex* en France et la gestion des milieux prairiaux. *Alauda* 62: 1–7.

BUCHER, E. H. (1992) The causes of extinction of the Passenger Pigeon. *Current Ornithology* 9: 1–36.

BUCKINGHAM, D. L., DUTSON, G. C. L. AND NEWMAN, J. (in prep.) Birds of Manus, Kolombangara and Makira (San Cristobal) with notes on mammals and records from other Solomon Islands.

BUCKTON, S. AND MORRIS, P. (1993) Observations of Wood Snipe *Gallinago nemoricola* in Nepal. •. 17: 31–35.

BURGESS, N. D., CUTTS, C. J. AND HUXHAM, M. (1991a) New records of the Sokoke Pipit *Anthus sokokensis* from Kiono Forest Reserve, Bagamoyo District, northeastern Tanzania. *Scopus* 15: 56–57.

BURGESS, N. D., HUXHAM, M. R., MLINGWA, C. O. F., DAVIES, S. G. F. AND CUTTS, C. J. (1991b) Preliminary assessment of forest birds in Kiono, Pande, Kisiju and Kiwengoma coastal forests, Tanzania. *Scopus* 14: 97–106.

BURGESS, N. D., MWASUMBI, L. B., HAWTHORNE, W. J., DICKINSON, A. AND DOGGETT, R. A. (1992) Preliminary assessment of the distribution, status and biological importance of coastal forests in Tanzania. *Biol. Conserv.* 62: 205–218.

BURTON, J. A., ED. (1984) *Owls of the world: their evolution, structure and ecology.* Revised edition. London: Peter Lowe.

BUTCHART, S. H. M., BROOKS, T. M., DAVIES, C. W. N., DHARMAPUTRA, G., DUTSON, G. C. L., LOWEN, J. C. AND SAHU, A. (1993) Cambridge Flores/Sumbawa Conservation Project 1993. Preliminary report.

BUTLER, D. AND MCLENNAN, J. (1990) *Kiwi recovery plan.* Wellington: Threatened Species Unit, Department of Conservation (Threatened Species Recovery Plan Series no. 2).

BUTLER, D. AND MERTON, D. (1992) *The Black Robin: saving the world's most endangered bird.* Auckland: Oxford University Press.

BUTYNSKI, T. M. AND KOSTER, S. H. (1989) Grey-necked Picathartes *Picathartes oreas* found on Bioko Island (Fernando Po). *Tauraco* 1: 186–189.

DE BY, R. A. (1990) Migration of Aquatic Warbler in western Europe. *Dutch Birding* 12: 165–181.

BYRD, G. V. AND WILLIAMS, J. C. (1993) Red-legged Kittiwake *Rissa brevirostris.* No. 60 in A. Poole and F. B. Gill, eds. *The birds of North America.* Philadelphia and Washington, D.C.: Academy of Natural Sciences and American Ornithologists' Union.

CADE, T. J. (1982) *The falcons of the world.* London: Collins.

CADE, T. J. AND JONES, C. G. (1993) Progress in restoration of the Mauritius Kestrel. *Conserv. Biol.* 7: 169–175.

CAHYADIN, Y. AND ARIF, S. (1994) Status *Acatua sulphurea abbotti* di Kepulauan Masalembu. Report to BirdLife Indonesia Programme.

CAIN, A. J. AND GALBRAITH, I. C. J. (1956) Field notes on the birds of the eastern Solomon Islands. *Ibis* 98: 100–134, 262–295.

CALLAGHAN, D. A. AND GREEN, A. J. (1993) Wildfowl at risk, 1993. *Wildfowl* 44: 149–169.

CARTER, M. (1993) Alexandra's or Princess Parrot: status and 'normal range'. *Wingspan* 12: 32–35.

CASTELLANOS, A. AND RODRÍGUEZ-ESTRELLA, R. (1993) Current status of the Socorro Mockingbird. *Wilson Bull.* 105: 167–171.

CATTERALL, M. J. (1992) Conservation priorities for the Albertine Rift Endemic Bird Area. London: Wye College, University of London (MSc thesis).

CEPEDA, F. AND CRUZ, J. B. (1994) Status and management of seabirds on the Galápagos Islands, Ecuador. Pp.268–278 in D. N. Nettleship, J. Burger and M. Gochfeld, eds. *Seabirds on islands: threats, case studies and action plans.* Cambridge, U.K.: BirdLife International (BirdLife Conservation Series no. 1).

CHALABI, B. (1989) Du nouveau à propos de l'aire de distribution de la Sittelle kabyle (*Sitta ledanti*). *Aves* 26: 233–234.

CHALMERS, M. L. (1986) *Annotated checklist of the birds of Hong Kong.* Hong Kong: Hong Kong Bird Watching Society.

CHALMERS, M. L. AND KENNERLEY, P. R. (1989) Records committee report 1988. *Hong Kong Bird Rep.* 1988: 18–35.

CHAN, S. (1991) The historical and current status of the Oriental White Stork. *Hong Kong Bird Rep.* 1990: 128–148.

CHAPIN, J. P. (1954) The birds of the Belgian Congo, part 4. *Bull. Amer. Mus. Nat. Hist.* 75b.

CHAPMAN, F. M. (1926) Distribution of bird-life in Ecuador. *Bull. Amer. Mus. Nat. Hist.* 55.

CHAPPUIS, C., ERARD, C. AND MOREL, G. J. (1989) Type specimens of *Prinia subflava* (Gmelin) and *Prinia fluviatilis* Chappuis. *Bull. Brit. Orn. Club* 109: 108–110.

CHAPPUIS, C., ERARD, C. AND MOREL, G. J. (1992) Morphology, habitat, vocalisations and distribution of the River Prinia *Prinia fluviatilis* Chappuis. *Proc. 7 Pan-Afr. Orn. Congr.:* 481–488.

CHAUDHRY, A. A. (1993) Distribution and status of pheasants in Pakistan. Pp.7–14 in D. Jenkins, ed. *Pheasants in Asia 1992.* Reading, U.K.: World Pheasant Association.

CHEKE, A. S. (1987a) The ecology of the smaller land-birds of Mauritius. Pp.151–207 in A. W. Diamond, ed. *Studies in Mascarene island birds.* Cambridge, U.K.: Cambridge

CHEKE, A. S. (1987b) The ecology of the surviving native land-birds of Réunion. Pp.301–358 in A. W. Diamond, ed. *Studies in Mascarene island birds*. Cambridge, U.K.: Cambridge University Press.

CHEKE, A. S. (1987c) Observations on the surviving endemic birds of Rodrigues. Pp.364–402 in A. W. Diamond, ed. *Studies in Mascarene island birds*. Cambridge, U.K.: Cambridge University Press.

CHEKE, R. A. (1986) The supposed occurrence of the White-necked Picathartes *Picathartes gymnocephalus* in Togo. *Bull. Brit. Orn. Club* 106: 152.

CHENG, T. (1987) *A synopsis of the avifauna of China*. Beijing: Science Press.

CHILD, P. (1986) Black-fronted Tern breeding at high altitude. *Notornis* 33: 193–194.

CHO, S. R. AND WON, P. O. (1990) Wintering ecology of Hooded Crane *Grus monacha* Temminck in Korea. *Bull. Inst. Orn. Kyung Hee Univ.* 3: 1–22.

CHOUDHURY, A. (1992) Sighting of the Great Whitebellied Heron in Jamjing Reserve Forest, Assam. *Newsletter for Birdwatchers* 32: 17.

CLANCEY, P. A. (1985) *The rare birds of southern Africa*. Johannesburg: Winchester Press.

CLAPHAM, C. S. (1964) The birds of the Dahlac Archipelago. *Ibis* 106: 376–388.

CLAY, R. P., JACK, S. R. AND VINCENT, J. P. (1994) A survey of the birds and large mammals of the proposed Jatun Sacha Bilsa Biological Reserve, north-western Ecuador. Project Esmeraldas '94 preliminary report.

CLEMENT, P., HARRIS, A. AND DAVIS, J. (1993) *Finches and sparrows: an identification guide*. London: Christopher Helm.

CLEMENTS, F. A. (1992) Recent bird records from Bhutan. *Forktail* 7: 57–74.

CLOUT, M. N. AND CRAIG, J. L. (in press) The conservation of critically endangered flightless birds in New Zealand. *Ibis*.

CLUNIE, F. (1984) *Birds of the Fiji bush*. Suva: Fiji Museum.

COATES, B. J. (1985) *The birds of Papua New Guinea*, 1: *non-passerines*. Alderley, Australia: Dove.

COATES, B. J. (1990) *The birds of Papua New Guinea*, 2: *passerines*. Alderley, Australia: Dove.

COLAHAN, B. D. (1993a) Status of the Lesser Kestrel in urban and peri-urban areas in the Orange Free State, South Africa. *Mirafra* 10: 33–39.

COLAHAN, B. D. (1993b) Periodic, large gatherings of Lesser Kestrels at Wepener, Orange Free State, South Africa, January–March 1990. *Gabar* 8: 29–30.

COLBOURNE, R. (1992) Little Spotted Kiwi (*Apteryx owenii*): recruitment and behaviour of juveniles on Kapiti Island, New Zealand. *J. Roy. Soc. New Zealand* 22: 321–328.

COLLAR, N. J. (1986) Red Data Bird: the Tomba Bowerbird. *World Birdwatch* 8(1): 5.

COLLAR, N. J. (1994a) Extinction, endangerment and everything. *World Birdwatch* 16(2): 6–9.

COLLAR, N. J. (1994b) Red Data Books, Action Plans, and the need for site-specific synthesis. *Species* 21–22: 132–133.

COLLAR, N. J. AND ANDREW, P. (1988) *Birds to watch: the ICBP world check-list of threatened birds*. Cambridge, U.K.: International Council for Bird Preservation (Techn. Publ. 8).

COLLAR, N. J. AND STATTERSFIELD, A. J. (1994) Neue Kriterien zur Identifizierung weltweit bedrohter Arten. *Ber. Vogelschutz* 32: 39–47.

COLLAR, N. J. AND STUART, S. N. (1985) *Threatened birds of Africa and related islands: the ICBP/IUCN Red Data Book*. Cambridge, U.K.: International Council for Bird Preservation and International Union for Conservation of Nature and Natural Resources.

COLLAR, N. J. AND STUART, S. N. (1988) *Key forests for threatened birds in Africa*. Cambridge, U.K.: International Council for Bird Preservation (Monogr. 3).

COLLAR, N. J. AND TATTERSALL, I. (1987) J. T. Last and the type-locality of Benson's Rockthrush *Monticola bensoni*. *Bull. Brit. Orn. Club* 107: 55–59.

COLLAR, N. J., ROUND, P. D. AND WELLS, D. R. (1986) The past and future of Gurney's Pitta *Pitta gurneyi*. *Forktail* 1: 29–51.

COLLAR, N. J., GONZAGA, L. P., KRABBE, N., MADROÑO NIETO, A., NARANJO, L. G., PARKER, T. A. AND WEGE, D. C. (1992) *Threatened birds of the Americas: the ICBP/IUCN Red Data Book*. Cambridge, U.K.: International Council for Bird Preservation.

COLLAR, N. J., WEGE, D. C. AND LONG, A. J. (in press) Patterns and causes of endangerment in the New World avifauna. In J. V. Remsen, ed. [*Memorial volume for Theodore A. Parker III*.]

COLLINS, N. M., SAYER, J. A. AND WHITMORE, T. C., EDS. (1991) *The conservation atlas of tropical forests: Asia and the Pacific*. London: Macmillan.

COLSTON, P. R. AND CURRY-LINDAHL, K. (1986) *The birds of Mount Nimba, Liberia*. London: British Museum (Natural History).

COOPER, J. AND RYAN, P. G. (1994) *Management plan for the Gough Island Wildlife Reserve*. Edinburgh, Tristan da Cunha: Government of Tristan da Cunha.

COOPER, J., WILLIAMS, A. J. AND BRITTON, P. L. (1984) Distribution, population sizes and conservation of breeding seabirds in the Afrotropical region. Pp.403–419 in J. P. Croxall, P. G. H. Evans and R. W. Schreiber, eds. *Status and conservation of the world's seabirds*. Cambridge, U.K.: International Council for Bird Preservation (Techn. Publ. 2).

CORDEIRO, N. J. (1994) Final report to the Royal Society for the Protection of Birds: an investigation of the forest avifauna in the North Pare Mountains and Kahe II Forest Reserve, Tanzania. Unpublished.

CORNWALLIS, L. AND PORTER, R. F. (1982) Spring observations on the birds of North Yemen. *Sandgrouse* 4: 1–36.

CORY, C. B. AND HELLMAYR, C. E. (1927) Catalogue of birds of the Americas, Part V. *Field Mus. Nat. Hist. Zool. Ser.* 13 (Publ. 242).

COWLING, S. J. AND DAVIES, S. J. J. F. (1983) *Status of Australian birds with special reference to captive breeding*. Melbourne: Department of Conservation.

COX, G., EASTY, V. S., CLARKE, R. O. S. AND COX, J. M. (in press) Studies of Horned Curassow *Pauxi unicornis* in Bolivia. *Bird Conserv. Internatn.*

CRAIG, R. J. AND TAISACAN, E. (1994) Notes on the ecology and population decline of the Rota Bridled White-eye. *Wilson Bull.* 106: 165–168.

CRAMP, S., ED. (1992) *The birds of the western Palearctic*, 6. Oxford: Oxford University Press.

CRAMP, S. AND PERRINS, C. M., EDS. (1994) *The birds of the western Palearctic*, 9. Oxford: Oxford University Press.

CRAMP, S. AND SIMMONS, K. E. L., EDS. (1977) *The birds of the western Palearctic*, 1. Oxford: Oxford University Press.

CRAMP, S. AND SIMMONS, K. E. L., EDS. (1980) *The birds of the western Palearctic*, 2. Oxford: Oxford University Press.

CRAMP, S. AND SIMMONS, K. E. L., EDS. (1983) *The birds of the western Palearctic*, 3. Oxford: Oxford University Press.

CRIVELLI, A. J. AND SCHREIBER, R. W. (1984) Status of the Pelecanidae. *Biol. Conserv.* 30: 147–156.

CROCKETT, D. E. (1979) Rediscovery of the Chatham Island taiko solved century-old mystery. *Forest and Bird* 13(4): 8–13.

CROSBY, M. J. (1991) Little-known Oriental bird: Silver Oriole. *Bull. Oriental Bird Club* 14: 32–35.

CROSBY, M. J. (1994) Mapping the distributions of restricted-range birds to identify global conservation priorities. Pp.145–154 in R. I. Miller, ed. *Mapping the diversity of nature*. London: Chapman and Hall.

CROXALL, J. P., ROTHERY, P., PICKERING, S. P. C. AND PRINCE, P. A. (1990) Reproductive performance, recruitment and survival of Wandering Albatrosses *Diomedea exulans* at Bird Island, South Georgia. *J. Anim. Ecol.* 59: 775–796.

CURIO, E. (1994) Zum Bedrohungs-Status endemischer Vögel auf den Philippinen: eine Expedition der Ruhr-Universität Bochum (1993). *Zool. Ges. Arten- u. Populationsschutz Mitt.* 10: 5–7.

CURSON, J. (1994) *New World warblers*. London: Christopher Helm.

CUSTODIO, C. C., DIESMOS, A. AND TOMAS, E. (1994) A preliminary report on the biodiversity of the lowland forest at Sablayan, occidental Mindoro. Unpublished.

DAHMER, T. AND FELLEY, M. (in press) Black-faced Spoonbill numbers. *Hong Kong Bird Rep*.

DANIELSEN, F., JENSEN, A., MIRANDA, H. AND CALEDA, M. (1992) *A preliminary survey of the Philippine Eagle* Pithecophaga jefferyi *and the conservation of the northern Sierra Madre mountains in the Philippines*. Manila: Department of Environment and Natural Resources, and International Council for Bird Preservation.

DANIELSEN, F., BALETE, D. S., CHRISTENSEN, T. D., HEEGAARD, M., JAKOBSEN, O. F., JENSEN, A., LUND, T. AND POULSEN, M. K. (1994) *Conservation of biological diversity in the Sierra Madre Mountains of Isabela and southern Cagayan Province, The Philippines*. Manila and Copenhagen: Department of Environment and Natural Resources, BirdLife International and Danish Ornithological Society.

DANKS, A. AND CALVER, M. C. (1993) Diet of the Noisy Scrub-bird *Atrichornis clamosus* at Two Peoples Bay, south-western Western Australia. *Emu* 93: 203–205.

DAVIDSON, P. J., LUCKING, R. S., STONES, A. J., BEAN, N. J., RAHARJANINGTRAH, W. AND BANJARANSARI, H. (1993) Report on an ornithological survey of Taliabu, Indonesia. Unpublished.

DAVIS, S. E. AND FLORES, E. (1994) First record of White-winged Nightjar *Caprimulgus candicans* for Bolivia. *Bull. Brit. Orn. Club* 114: 127–128.

DAVISON, G. W. H. (1981) A survey of terrestrial birds in the Gunung Mulu National Park, Sarawak. *Sarawak Mus. J.* 27: 283–293.

DAVISON, G. W. H. (1982) Systematics within the genus *Arborophila* Hodgson. *Fed. Mus. J.* 27: 125–134.

DAVISON, G. W. H. AND SCRIVEN, K. W. (1983) Recent

pheasant surveys in peninsular Malaysia. Pp.90–101 in C. D. W. Savage and M. W. Ridley, eds. *Pheasants in Asia 1982*. Reading, U.K.: World Pheasant Association.

DEAN, W. R. J., HUNTLEY, M. A., HUNTLEY, B. J. AND VERNON, C. J. (1988) Notes on some birds of Angola. *Durban Mus. Novit.* 14(4).

DEAN, W. R. J., MILTON, S. J., WATKEYS, M. K. AND HOCKEY, P. A. R. (1991) Distribution, habitat preference and conservation status of the Red Lark *Certhilauda burra* in Cape Province, South Africa. *Biol. Conserv.* 58: 257–274.

DEBENEDICTIS, P. A. (1993) Three new species? *Birding* 25: 277–279.

DEBUS, S. (1992) A comment on the Slaty-backed Goshawk *Accipiter luteoschistaceus*. *Muruk* 5: 61.

DEE, T. J. (1986) *The endemic birds of Madagascar*. Cambridge, U.K.: International Council for Bird Preservation.

DEKKER, R. W. R. J. (1990) The distribution and status of nesting grounds of the Maleo *Macrocephalon maleo* in Sulawesi, Indonesia. *Biol. Conserv.* 51: 139–150.

DEKKER, R. W. R. J. (1991) The Moluccan Megapode *Eulipoa wallacei* 'rediscovered'. *Megapode Newsletter* 5(2/3): 9–10.

DEKKER, R. W. R. J. (1992) *Status and breeding biology of the Nicobar Megapode* Megapodius nicobariensis abbotti *on Great Nicobar, India*. Leiden, Netherlands: National Museum of Natural History.

DEKKER, R. AND ARGELOO, M. (1993) Bruijn's Brush-turkey *Aegopodius bruijnii* remains a mystery. *Megapode Newsletter* 7: 15–17.

DEKKER, R. W. R. J. AND WATTEL, J. (1987) Egg and image: new and traditional uses for the Maleo (*Macrocephalon maleo*). Pp.83–87 in A. W. Diamond and F. L. Finion, eds. *The value of birds*. Cambridge, U.K.: International Council for Bird Preservation (Techn. Publ. No. 6).

DELACOUR, J. (1977) *The pheasants of the world*. 2nd revised edition. [Place unstated]: Spur.

DELACOUR, J. AND GREENWAY, J. C. (1940) VIIe expedition ornithologique en Indochine française. *Oiseau et R.F.O.* 10: 1–24.

DELACOUR, J. AND JABOUILLE, P. (1931) *Les oiseaux de l'Indochine française*, 1–4. Paris: Exposition Coloniale Internationale.

DELLELEGN, Y. (1991) Prince Ruspoli's Turaco. *Walia* 13: 29–35.

DELLELEGN, Y. (1993) Observations on the Ethiopian Bush Crow *Zavattariornis stresemanni* in Yabello, southern Ethiopia. *Proc. 8 Pan-Afr. Orn. Congr.* [*Ann. Sci. Zool. Mus. Roy. Afrique Centr.* 286]: 469–474.

DEMENT'EV, G. P. AND GLADKOV, N. A., EDS. (1968) *Birds of the Soviet Union*, 2. Jerusalem: Israel Program for Scientific Translations.

DEMENT'EV, G. P. AND GLADKOV, N. A., EDS. (1970) *Birds of the Soviet Union*, 5. Jerusalem: Israel Program for Scientific Translations.

DEMENT'EV, G. P., GLADKOV, N. A., PTUSHENKO, E. S., SPANGENBERG, E. P. AND SUDILOVSKAYA, A. M. (1966) *Birds of the Soviet Union*, 1. Jerusalem: Israel Program for Scientific Translations.

DEMENT'EV, G. P., GLADKOV, N. A., ISAKOV, Y. A., KARTASHEV, N., KIRIKOV, S. V., MIKHEEV, A. V. AND PTUSHENKO, E. S. (1967) *Birds of the Soviet Union*, 4. Jerusalem: Israel Program for Scientific Translations.

DEMEY, R. AND FISHPOOL, L. D. C. (1991) Additions and annotations to the avifauna of Côte d'Ivoire. *Malimbus* 12: 61–86.

DIAMOND, A. W. (1994) Seabirds of the Seychelles, Indian Ocean. Pp.258–267 in D. N. Nettleship, J. Burger and M. Gochfeld, eds. *Seabirds on islands: threats, case studies and action plans*. Cambridge, U.K.: BirdLife International (BirdLife Conservation Series no. 1).

DIAMOND, A. W. AND KEITH, G. S. (1980) Avifaunas of Kenya forest islands. I—Mount Kulal. *Scopus* 4: 49–55.

DIAMOND, J. M. (1971) Bird records from West New Britain. *Condor* 73: 481–483.

DIAMOND, J. M. (1985) New distributional records and taxa from the outlying mountain ranges of New Guinea. *Emu* 85: 65–91.

DIAMOND, J. M. (1987) Extant unless proven extinct? Or, extinct unless proven extant? *Conserv. Biol.* 1: 77–79.

DIAMOND, J. (1991) A new species of rail from the Solomon Islands and convergent evolution of insular flightlessness. *Auk* 108: 461–470.

DIAMOND, J. M. AND MARSHALL, A. G. (1976) Origin of the New Hebridean avifauna. *Emu* 76: 187–200.

DICKINSON, E. C., KENNEDY, R. S. AND PARKES, K. C. (1991) *The birds of the Philippines: an annotated checklist*. Tring, U.K.: British Ornithologists' Union (Checklist 12).

DINESEN, L., LEHMBERG, T., SVENDSEN, J. O. AND HANSEN, L. A. (1993) Range extensions and other notes on some restricted-range forest birds from West Kilombero in the Udzungwa Mountains, Tanzania. *Scopus* 17: 48–59.

DINESEN, L., LEHMBERG, T., SVENDSEN, J. O., HANSEN, L. A. AND FJELDSÅ, J. (1994) A new genus and species of perdicine bird (Phasianidae, Perdicini) from Tanzania: a relict form with Indo-Malayan affinities. *Ibis* 136: 3–11.

DING, P. AND ZHUGE, Y. (1990) The ecology of Elliot's Pheasant in the wild. Pp.65–68 in D. A. Hill, P. J. Garson and D. Jenkins, eds. *Pheasants in Asia 1989*. Reading, U.K.: World Pheasant Association.

DIRZO, R. AND GARCÍA, M. C. (1992) Rates of deforestation in Los Tuxtlas, a neotropical area in southeast Mexico. *Conserv. Biol.* 6: 84–90.

DISSING, H., JORGENSEN, M. F. AND JENSEN, S. (1990) Pakistan and Xinjiang. Unpublished report to DAFIF (Danish Ornithological Society).

DOLAN, B. (1938) Zoological results of the second Dolan expedition to western China and eastern Tibet, 1934–1936. *Proc. Acad. Nat. Sci. Philadelphia* 90: 159–260.

DONNAY, T. J. (1990) Status, nesting and nest site selection of Cape Vultures in Lesotho. *Vulture News* 24: 11–24.

DOWDING, J. (1993) *New Zealand Dotterel Recovery Plan*. Wellington: Threatened Species Unit, Department of Conservation (Threatened Species Recovery Plan Series no. 10).

DOWDING, J. E. AND KENNEDY, E. S. (1993) Size, age structure and morphometrics of the Shore Plover population on South East Island. *Notornis* 40: 213–222.

DOWDING, J. E. AND MURPHY, E. C. (1993) Decline of the Stewart Island population of the New Zealand Dotterel. *Notornis* 40: 1–14.

DOWNER, A. AND SUTTON, R. (1990) *Birds of Jamaica: a photographic field guide*. Cambridge, U.K.: Cambridge University Press.

DOWSETT, R. J. (1977) The distribution of some falcons and plovers in East Africa. *Scopus* 1: 73–78.

DOWSETT, R. J. AND DOWSETT-LEMAIRE, F. (1993) Comments on the taxonomy of some Afrotropical bird species. Pp.323–389 in R. J. Dowsett and F. Dowsett-Lemaire, eds. *A contribution to the distribution and taxonomy of Afrotropical and Malagasy birds*. Liège: Tauraco Press (Tauraco Research Report 5).

DOWSETT, R. J. AND FORBES-WATSON, A. D. (1993) *Checklist of birds of the Afrotropical and Malagasy regions*. Liège: Tauraco Press.

DOWSETT-LEMAIRE, F. (1987) On the distribution, ecology and voice of two *Alethe* species in Malawi. *Scopus* 11: 25–32.

DOWSETT-LEMAIRE, F. (1989) Ecological and biogeographical aspects of forest bird communities in Malawi. *Scopus* 13: 1–80.

DOWSETT-LEMAIRE, F. (1990) Eco-ethology, distribution and status of Nyungwe Forest birds. Pp.31–85 in R. J. Dowsett, ed. *Enquête faunistique et floristique dans la Forêt de Nyungwe, Rwanda*. Ely, U.K.: Tauraco Press (Tauraco Research Report 3).

DOWSETT-LEMAIRE, F. AND DOWSETT, R. J. (1990a) Enquête faunistique et floristique dans la Forêt de Nyungwe au Rwanda: buts, statut de la forêt et recommandations. Pp.1–9 in R. J. Dowsett, ed. *Enquête faunistique et floristique dans la Forêt de Nyungwe, Rwanda*. Ely, U.K.: Tauraco Press (Tauraco Research Report 3).

DOWSETT-LEMAIRE, F. AND DOWSETT, R. J. (1990b) Zoogeography and taxonomic relationships of the forest birds of the Albertine Rift Afromontane region. Pp.87–109 in R. J. Dowsett, ed. *Enquête faunistique et floristique dans la Forêt de Nyungwe, Rwanda*. Ely, U.K.: Tauraco Press (Tauraco Research Report 3).

DOWSETT-LEMAIRE, F., DOWSETT, R. J. AND BULENS, P. (1993) Additions and corrections to the avifauna of Congo. *Malimbus* 15: 68–80.

DRAULANS, D. (1986) On the distribution and foraging behaviour of the Malagasy Heron *Ardea humbloti*. *Ostrich* 57: 249–251.

DUC, L. D., THUY, L. D. AND THANG, H. V. (1993) Black-faced Spoonbills in the north of Vietnam 1992–1993. *Storks, Ibises and Spoonbills Spec. Gp. News.* 6: 8–9.

DUCKWORTH, J. W., EVANS, T. D. AND TIMMINS, R. J. (1993a) *A wildlife and habitat survey of the Xe Piane National Biodiversity Conservation Area*. Vientiane, Laos: National Office for Nature Conservation and Watershed Management.

DUCKWORTH, J. W., TIMMINS, R. J. AND COZZA, K. (1993b) A wildlife and habitat survey of Phou Xang He proposed protected area. Vientiane, Laos: National Office for Nature Conservation and Watershed Management (unpublished report).

DUKE, G. (1994) Mountains, forests and pheasants. *World Birdwatch* 16(1): 10–13.

DUTSON, G. (1993) A sighting of *Ficedula (crypta) disposita* in Luzon, Philippines. *Forktail* 8: 144–147.

DUTSON, G. C. L. (in prep.) The birds of Salayar and the Flores Sea islands.

DUTSON, G. C. L. AND NEWMAN, J. L. (1991) Observations on the Superb Pitta *Pitta superba* and other Manus endemics. *Bird Conserv. Internatn.* 1: 215–222.

DUTSON, G. C. L., EVANS, T. D., BROOKS, T. M., ASANE, D. C., TIMMINS, R. J. AND TOLEDO, A. (1992) Conservation status of birds on Mindoro, Philippines. *Bird Conserv. Internatn.* 2: 303–325.

DUTSON, G. C. L., MAGSALAY, P. M. AND TIMMINS, R. J. (1993) The rediscovery of the Cebu Flowerpecker *Dicaeum quadricolor*, with notes on other forest birds on Cebu, Philippines. *Bird Conserv. Internatn.* 3: 235–243.

DYRCZ, A. AND ZDUNEK, W. (1993) Breeding ecology of the Aquatic Warbler *Acrocephalus paludicola* on the Biebrza marshes, northeast Poland. *Ibis* 135: 181–189.

EAMES, J. C., ROBSON, C. R., NGUYEN CU AND TRUONG VAN LA (1992) *Forest bird surveys in Vietnam 1991*. Cambridge, U.K.: International Council for Bird Preservation (Study Report 51).

EARLÉ, R. A. (1987) Measurements, moult and timing of breeding in the Blue Swallow. *Ostrich* 58: 182–185.

ECCLES, S. D. (1988) The birds of São Tomé—record of a visit, April 1987 with notes on the rediscovery of Bocage's Longbill. *Malimbus* 10: 207–217.

EDWARDS, E. P. (1989) *A field guide to the birds of Mexico*. Sweet Briar, Virginia: Ernest P. Edwards.

EDWARDS, M. (1993) Saving the bird—saving the forest. *People and the Planet* 2: 14–15.

ELGOOD, J. H. (1988) Rediscovery of *Malimbus ibadanensis* Elgood, 1958. *Bull. Brit. Orn. Club* 108: 184–185.

ELGOOD, J. H. (1992) The range of *Malimbus ibadanensis*. *Bull. Brit. Orn. Club* 112: 205–207.

ELKIN, J. A. (1993) Japanese Night-heron *Gorsachius goisagi*: a new species for Borneo. *Forktail* 8: 154.

ELLIOTT, G. P. (1992) Habitat relationships and conservation of the Yellowhead. *New Zealand J. Ecol.* 16: 83–90.

ELLIOTT, G., WALKER, K. AND BUCKINGHAM, R. (1991) The Auckland Island Rail. *Notornis* 38: 199–209.

ELMQVIST, T., ED. (1993) *The rain forest and the flying foxes: an introduction to the rain forest perserves on Savai'i, Western Samoa*. Salelologa, Western Samoa: Fa'asao Savai'i Society.

ELMQVIST, T., RAINEY, W. E., PERSON, E. AND COX, P. A. (in press) Effects of tropical cyclones 'Ofa' and 'Val' on the structure of a Samoan lowland rain forest. *Biotropica* 24.

ENGBRING, J. (1988) *Field guide to the birds of Palau*. Koror, Palau: Conservation Office and Bureau of Education.

ENGBRING, J. (1992) *A 1991 survey of the forest birds of the Republic of Palau*. Honolulu: U.S. Fish and Wildlife Service.

ENGBRING, J. AND PRATT, H. D. (1985) Endangered birds in Micronesia: their history, status and future prospects. *Bird Conserv.* 2: 71–105.

ENGBRING, J., RAMSEY, F. L. AND WILDMAN, V. J. (1990) *Micronesian forest bird surveys, the Federated States: Pohnpei, Kosrae, Chuuk, and Yap*. Honolulu: U.S. Fish and Wildlife Service.

ENGILIS, A. AND PRATT, T. K. (1993) Status and population trends of Hawaii's native waterbirds, 1977–1987. *Wilson Bull.* 105: 142–158.

ENGLEMAN, D. (1994) The field editor's report. *Toucan* 20(7): 4–5.

ENVIRONMENT AGENCY (1992) *Nature conservation in Japan*. 3rd edition. Tokyo: Planning and Coordination Division, Nature Conservation Bureau.

ERARD, C. (1974) Taxonomie des serins à gorge jaune d'Ethiopie. *Oiseau et R.F.O.* 44: 308–323.

ERARD, C. AND COLSTON, P. R. (1988) *Batis minima* (Verreaux) new for Cameroon. *Bull. Brit. Orn. Club* 108:

182–184.

EVANS, M. I. (1991) The Red-tailed Newtonia *Newtonia fanovanae* in the Ambatovaky Reserve, north-east Madagascar. *Bird Conserv. Internatn.* 1: 47–52.

EVANS, M. I. (1994) *Important bird areas in the Middle East*. Cambridge, U.K.: BirdLife International (BirdLife Conservation Series no. 2).

EVANS, M. I., DUCKWORTH, J. W., HAWKINS, A. F. A., SAFFORD, R. J., SHELDON, B. C. AND WILKINSON, R. J. (1992a) Key bird species of Marojejy Strict Nature Reserve, Madagascar. *Bird Conserv. Internatn.* 2: 201–222.

EVANS, P. G. H. (1994) Stability in Dominica. *Cotinga* 1: 9–10.

EVANS, S. M., FLETCHER, F. J. C., LOADER, P. J. AND ROOKSBY, F. G. (1992b) Habitat exploitation by landbirds in the changing Western Samoan environment. *Bird Conserv. Internatn.* 2: 123–129.

EVANS, T. D. AND ANDERSON, G. Q. A., EDS. (1992) *A wildlife survey of the East Usambara and Ukaguru Mountains, Tanzania*. Cambridge, U.K.: International Council for Bird Preservation (Study Report 53).

EVANS, T. D. AND ANDERSON, G. Q. A. (1993) Results of an ornithological survey in the Ukaguru and East Usambara mountains, Tanzania. *Scopus* 17: 40–47.

EVANS, T. D. AND TIMMINS, R. J. (1994) Interim report on wildlife survey of Nakal Plateau/Nam Theun Protected Area. Unpublished.

EVANS, T. D., DUTSON, G. C. L. AND BROOKS, T. M. (1993a) *Cambridge Philippines Rainforest Project 1991: final report*. Cambridge, U.K.: BirdLife International (Study Report 54).

EVANS, T. D., MAGSALAY, P., DUTSON, G. C. L. AND BROOKS, T. M. (1993b) The conservation status of the forest birds of Siquijor, Philippines. *Forktail* 8: 89–96.

EVERETT, W. T. (1988) Notes from Clarion Island. *Condor* 90: 512–513.

EVERETT, W. T. AND ANDERSON, D. W. (1991) Status and conservation of the breeding seabirds on offshore Pacific islands of Baja California and the Gulf of California. Pp.115–139 in J. P. Croxall, ed. *Seabird status and conservation: a supplement*. Cambridge, U.K.: International Council for Bird Preservation (Techn. Publ. 11).

FALDBORG, J., HALBERG, K., BRAMMER, F. AND ERIKSEN, T. (1991) Observations of birds and mammals in six coastal forests of Tanzania: preliminary report of the Danish-Tanzanian ICBP Expedition 1990. Copenhagen: Institute of Population Biology/ICBP Danish Section (unpublished).

FANCY, S. G., SUGIHARA, R. T., JEFFREY, J. J. AND JACOBI, J. D. (1993) Site tenacity of the endangered Palila. *Wilson Bull.* 105: 587–596.

FANSHAWE, J. H. (1989) Migrant Lesser Kestrels *Falco naumanni* associating with plains game in Serengeti National Park, Tanzania. *Scopus* 13: 115–116.

FANSHAWE, J. (1991) Saving Sokoke. *World Birdwatch* 13(3): 10–11.

FANSHAWE, J. (1993) Red data bird: Sokoke Scops Owl. *World Birdwatch* 15(1): 18–19.

FANSHAWE, J. H. (1994) Elusive Congo Peacock found by film-maker Alan Root. *Bull. African Bird Club* 1: 27.

FAO (1981) *National conservation plan for Indonesia: Maluku and Irian Jaya*, 7. Bogor, Indonesia: Food and Agriculture Organization of the United Nations (Field

Report 18).

FAO (1982) *National conservation plan for Indonesia, 4: Nusa Tenggara*. Bogor: Food and Agriculture Organization of the United Nations (Field Report 44).

FARAGÓ, S. (1993) Development of Great Bustard populations in Hungary in the period 1981–1990. *Folia Zool.* 42: 221–236.

FINCH, B. W. (1985) Noteworthy observations in Papua New Guinea and the Solomons. *PNG Bird Soc. Newsl.* 215: 6–10.

FINCH, B. W. (1986) The *Aplonis* starlings of the Solomon Islands. *Muruk* 1: 4–16.

FINCH, B. W. (1989) Blue Swallows *Hirundo atrocaerulea* near Busia: the second record for Kenya. *Scopus* 13: 125–126.

FINCH, B. W. AND MCKEAN, J. L. (1987) Some notes on the birds of the Bismarcks. *Muruk* 2: 3–28.

FISHPOOL, L. D. C., DEMEY, R., ALLPORT, G. AND HAYMAN, P. V. (1994) Notes on the field identification of the bulbuls (Pycnonotidae) of Upper Guinea, part 1: the genera *Criniger*, *Bleda* and *Andropadus*. *Bull. African Bird Club* 1: 32–38.

FJELDSÅ, J. (1993) The decline and probable extinction of the Colombian Grebe *Podiceps andinus*. *Bird Conserv. Internatn.* 3: 221–234.

FJELDSÅ, J. AND KRABBE, N. (1990) *Birds of the high Andes*. [Copenhagen and] Svendborg: Zoological Museum, University of Copenhagen and Apollo Books.

FLINT, V. E., BOEHME, R. L., KOSTIN, Y. V. AND KUZNETSOV, A. A. (1984) *A field guide to birds of the USSR*. Princeton, New Jersey: Princeton University Press.

FLORES, E. I. (1988) Estado actual de los flamencos en Bolivia. *Flamingo Specialist Group Newsletter* 4: 41–42.

FORBES, M. R. (1985) Report on the status and conservation of the Atitlán Grebe, *Podilymbus gigas*. Unpublished.

FORD, H., DAVIS, W. E., DEBUS, S., LEY, A., RECHER, H. AND WILLIAMS, B. (1993) Foraging and aggressive behaviour of the Regent Honeyeater *Xanthomyza phrygia* in northern New South Wales. *Emu* 93: 277–281.

FORRESTER, B. C. (1993) *Birding Brazil: a check-list and site guide*. Irvine, Scotland: privately published.

FORSHAW, J. M. (1989) *Parrots of the world*. Third (revised) edition. London: Blandford Press.

FOSBERG, F. R., SACHET, M.-H. AND STODDART, D. R. (1983) Henderson Island (southeastern Polynesia): summary of current knowledge. *Atoll Res. Bull.* 272.

FOTSO, R. C. (1993a) Contribution à l'étude de la biologie du Picatharte Chauve du Cameroun *Picathartes oreas*. *Proc. 8 Pan-Afr. Orn. Congr.* [*Ann. Sci. Zool. Mus. Roy. Afrique Centr.* 286]: 431–437.

FOTSO, R. C. (1993b) Breeding of Bannerman's Turaco *Tauraco bannermani* and Banded Wattle-eye *Platysteira laticincta* in Cameroon. *Proc. 8 Pan-Afr. Orn. Congr.* [*Ann. Sci. Zool. Mus. Roy. Afrique Centr.* 286]: 438.

FOUARGE, J. P. (1992) Observation de deux Aigles impériaux ibériques (*Aquila heliaca adalberti*) dans la région de Chechaouen. *Porphyrio* 4: 25–28.

FRANCIS, I. S., PENFORD, N., GARTSHORE, M. E. AND JARAMILLO, A. (1992) The White-breasted Guineafowl *Agelastes meleagrides* in Taï National Park, Côte d'Ivoire. *Bird Conserv. Internatn.* 2: 25–60.

FRASER, M. W. AND BRIGGS, D. J. (1992) New information on the *Nesospiza* buntings at Inaccessible Island, Tristan da Cunha, and notes on their conservation. *Bull. Brit. Orn. Club* 112: 191–205.

FRASER, M. W., DEAN, W. R. J. AND BEST, I. C. (1992) Observations on the Inaccessible Island Rail *Atlantisia rogersi*: the world's smallest flightless bird. *Bull. Brit. Orn. Club* 112: 12–22.

FRASER. M. (1989) The Inaccessible Island Rail: smallest flightless bird in the world. *African Wildlife* 43: 14–19.

FRITH, C. B. AND FRITH, D. W. (1993) The nesting biology of the Ribbon-tailed Astrapia *Astrapia mayeri* (Paradisaeidae). *Emu* 93: 12–22.

FRITH, C. B. AND FRITH, D. W. (1994) The nesting biology of Archbold's Bowerbird *Archboldia papuensis* and a review of that of other bowerbirds (Ptilonorhynchidae). *Ibis* 136: 153–160.

FRITH, C. B., GIBBS, D. AND TURNER, K. (in press) The systematic status of populations of Archbold's Bowerbird *Archboldia papuensis* (Ptilonorhynchidae) in New Guinea. *Bull. Brit. Orn. Club* [submitted].

FRY, C. H. AND FRY, K. (1992) *Kingfishers, bee-eaters and rollers*. London: Christopher Helm.

FRY, C. H. AND SMITH, D. A. (1985) A new swallow from the Red Sea. *Ibis* 127: 1–6.

FRY, C. H., HOSKEN, J. H. AND SKINNER, D. (1986) Further observations on the breeding of Slaty Egrets *Egretta vinaceigula* and Rufous-bellied Herons *Ardeola rufiventris*. *Ostrich* 57: 61–64.

FRY, C. H., KEITH, S. AND URBAN, E. K. (1988) *The birds of Africa*, 3. London: Academic Press.

FUJIMAKI, Y. (1987) Joint survey report of Japan and USSR on Steller's Sea-eagle: summary. Pp.49 in *The Third Japan-USSR Bird Protection Symposium, 21 November 1986*. [Tokyo:] Wild Bird Society of Japan.

GALDIKAS, M. F. AND KING, B. (1989) Lesser Adjutant nests in S. W. Kalimantan. *Kukila* 4: 151.

GALES, R. (1993) *Co-operative mechanisms for the conservation of albatross*. Hobart: Australian Nature Conservation Agency.

GALLAGHER, M. D., SCOTT, D. A., ORMOND, R. F. G., CONNOR, R. J. AND JENNINGS, M. C. (1984) The distribution and conservation of seabirds breeding on the coasts and islands of Iran and Arabia. Pp.421–456 in J. P. Croxall, P. G. H. Evans and R. W. Schreiber, eds. *Status and conservation of the world's seabirds*. Cambridge, U.K.: International Council for Bird Preservation (Techn. Publ. 2).

GANDY, D. AND SALAMAN, P. (1994) Notes on the guans of south-west Colombia. *WPA News* 44: 31–34.

GANTLETT, S. (1993) The status and separation of White-headed Duck and Ruddy Duck. *Birding World* 6: 273–281.

GARDNER, N. (1987) Some interesting observations from Bougainville and West New Britain. *Muruk* 2: 38–39.

GARNETT, S., ED. (1992) *Threatened and extinct birds of Australia*. Moonee Ponds, Victoria: Royal Australasian Ornithologists' Union and Australian National Parks and Wildlife Service (RAOU Report 82).

GARNETT, S., ED. (1993) *Threatened and extinct birds of Australia*. Second (corrected) edition. Moonee Ponds, Victoria: Royal Australasian Ornithologists' Union (Report 82).

GARNETT, S., CROWLEY, G., DUNCAN, R., BAKER, N. AND DOHERTY, P. (1993) Notes on live Night Parrot sightings in north-western Queensland. *Emu* 93: 292–296.

GARSON, P. J. AND MCGOWAN, P. J. K., EDS. (in press) *Pheasant action plan.* Cambridge, U.K.: BirdLife International and International Union for Conservation of Nature and Natural Resources.

GARSON, P. J., YOUNG, L. AND KAUL, R. (1992) Ecology and conservation of the cheer pheasant *Catreus wallichii*: studies in the wild and the progress of a reintroduction project. *BIOL. CONSERV.* 59: 23–35.

GARTSHORE, M. E. (1989) *An avifaunal survey of Taï National Park, Ivory Coast.* Cambridge, U.K.: International Council for Bird Preservation (Study Report 39).

GARTSHORE, M. E. (1991) Biodiversity evaluation of SODEFOR plantations: avifauna. Unpublished.

GASTON, A. J. (1984) Is habitat destruction in India and Pakistan beginning to affect the status of endemic passerine birds? *J. Bombay Nat. Hist. Soc.* 81: 636–641.

GASTON, A. J. AND MACRELL, J. (1980) Green Munia (*Estrilda formosa*) at Delhi, and other interesting records for 1978. *J. Bombay Nat. Hist. Soc.* 77: 144–145.

GATTER, W. (1985) Ein neuer Bulbul aus Westafrika (Aves, Pycnonotidae). *J. Orn.* 126: 155–161.

GATTER, W. (1988) The birds of Liberia: a preliminary list with status and open questions. *Verh. orn. Ges. Bayern* 24: 689–723.

GATTER, W. AND GARDNER, R. (1993) The biology of the Gola Malimbe *Malimbus ballmanni* Wolters 1974. *Bird Conserv. Internatn.* 3: 87–103.

GATTER, W., PEAL, A., STEINER, C. AND WEICK, F. (1988) Die unbekannten Jugendkleider des seltenen Weissbrustperlhuhns (*Agelastes meleagrides* Bonaparte, 1850). *Ökol. Vögel* 10: 105–111.

GIBBS, D. (1994) Undescribed taxa and new records from the Fakfak Mountains, Irian Jaya. *Bull. Brit. Orn. Club* 114: 4–12.

GIBSON, D. (1992) The Nyungwe Forest: saving its biodiversity. *Zoonooz* 65: 6–10.

GILL, J. M. AND DARBY, J. T. (1993) Deaths in Yellow-eyed Penguins (*Megadyptes antipodes*) on the Otago Peninsula during the summer of 1990. *New Zealand Vet. J.* 41: 39–42.

GILL, R. E. AND REDMOND, R. L. (1992) Distribution, numbers, and habitat of Bristle-thighed Curlews (*Numenius tahitiensis*) on Rangiroa Atoll. *Notornis* 39: 17–26.

GILLIARD, E. T. AND LECROY, M. (1967) Results of the 1958–1959 Gilliard New Britain Expedition. 4: annotated list of birds of the Whiteman Mountains, New Britain. *Bull. Amer. Mus. Nat. Hist.* 135: 173–216.

GINN, P. J., MCILLERON, W. G. AND MILSTEIN, P. LE S. (1989) *The complete book of southern African birds.* Cape Town: Struik Winchester.

GIRAUDOUX, P., DEGAUQUIER, R., JONES, P. J., WEIGEL, J. AND ISENMANN, P. (1988) Avifaune du Niger: état des connaissances en 1986. *Malimbus* 10: 1–140.

GLADE, A. A., ED. (1988) *Red list of Chilean terrestrial vertebrates: proceedings of the symposium 'Conservation Status of Chilean Terrestrial Vertebrate Fauna'.* Santiago: Impresiones Comerciales (for CONAF).

GLUTZ VON BLOTZHEIM, U. N. AND BAUER, K. M. (1991) *Handbuch der Vögel Mitteleuropas,* 12/1(3). Wiesbaden: AULA-Verlag.

GLUTZ VON BLOTZHEIM, U. N., BAUER, K. M. AND BEZZEL, E. (1971) *Handbuch der Vögel Mitteleuropas,* 4. Frankfurt am Main: Akademische Verlagsgesellschaft.

GOCHFELD, M., BURGER, J., HAYNES-SUTTON, A., VAN HALEWYN, R. AND SALIVA, J. E. (1994) Successful approaches to seabird protection in the West Indies. Pp.186–209 in D. N. Nettleship, J. Burger and M. Gochfeld, eds. *Seabirds on islands: threats, case studies and action plans.* Cambridge, U.K.: BirdLife International (BirdLife Conservation Series no. 1).

GOLE, P. (1993) On the trail of wintering Blacknecked Cranes in India. *J. Ecol. Soc.* 6: 7–22.

GON, S. M. (1988) Observations of the 'Ua'u (Hawaiian Petrel) in the Homo O Na Pali Natural Area Reserve, Island of Kauai. *'Elepaio* 48: 113.

GONZALES, P. C. AND KENNEDY, R. S. (1990) A new species of *Stachyris* babbler (Aves: Timaliidae) from the island of Panay, Philippines. *Wilson Bull.* 102: 367–379.

GONZALES, P. C. AND REES, C. P. (1988) *Birds of the Philippines.* Manila: Haribon Foundation.

GOODMAN, S. M. (1993) A reconnaissance of Ile Sainte Marie, Madagascar: the status of the forest, avifauna, lemurs and fruit bats. *Biol. Conserv.* 65: 205–212.

GOODMAN, S. M. AND GONZALES, P. C. (1989) The birds of Mt Isarog National Park, southern Luzon, Philippines, with particular reference to altitudinal distribution. *Fieldiana Zool. N.S.* no. 60 (Publ. 1415).

GOODMAN, S. M. AND SCHULENBERG, T. S. (1991) The rediscovery of the Red-tailed Newtonia *Newtonia fanovanae* in south-eastern Madagascar with notes on the natural history of the genus *Newtonia*. *Bird Conserv. Internatn.* 1: 33–45.

GOODMAN, S. M., MEININGER, P. L., BAHA EL DIN, S. M., HOBBS, J. J. AND MULLIÉ, W. C. (1989) *The birds of Egypt.* Oxford: Oxford University Press.

GOODWIN, A. (1987) Notes on a birdwatching visit to China. Unpublished report.

GORE, M. E. J. AND WON, PYONG-OH (1971) *The birds of Korea.* Seoul: Royal Asiatic Society.

GORIUP, P. D. (1983) The decline of the Great Indian Bustard (*Ardeotis nigriceps*): a literature review. Pp.20–38 in P. D. Goriup and H. Vardhan, eds. *Bustards in decline.* Jaipur: Tourism and Wildlife Society of India.

GORIUP, P. D. (1992) Bustards in Russia and neighbouring countries. *Bustard Studies* 5.

GORIUP, P. D. AND KARPOWICZ, Z. J. (1985) A review of the past and recent status of the Lesser Florican. *Bustard Studies* 3: 163–182.

GRAUL, W. D. AND WEBSTER, L. E. (1976) Breeding status of the Mountain Plover. *Condor* 78: 265–267.

GRAVES, G. R. (1982) First record of Brown Wood Rail (*Aramides wolfi*) for Peru. *Gerfaut* 72: 237–238.

GRAVES, G. R. (1992) The endemic land birds of Henderson Island, southeastern Polynesia: notes on natural history and conservation. *Wilson Bull.* 104: 32–43.

GRAVES, G. R. (1993) Relic of a lost world: a new species of sunangel (Trochilidae: *Heliangelus*) from 'Bogotá'. *Auk* 110: 1–8.

GREEN, A. J. (1992) *The status and conservation of the White-winged Wood Duck* Cairina scutulata. Slimbridge, U.K.: International Waterfowl and Wetlands Research Bureau (IWRB Spec. Publ. 17).

GREEN, A. J. (1993a) *The status and conservation of the Marbled Teal* Marmaronetta angustirostris. Slimbridge, U.K.: International Waterfowl and Wetlands Research Bureau (IWRB Spec. Publ. 23).

GREEN, A. J. (1993b) Status and habitat of the White-winged Duck *Cairina scutulata*. *Bird Conserv. Internatn.* 3: 119–144.

GREEN, A. J. AND ANSTEY, S. (1993) The status of the White-headed Duck *Oxyura leucocephala*. *Bird Conserv. Internatn.* 2: 185–200.

GREEN, G. (1991) A closer look at Kilum. *World Birdwatch* 13(4): 8–9, 15.

GREENWOOD, A. G. (1994) St Vincent Parrot Programme: report to World Parrot Trust and the St Vincent Parrot Consortium, May 1994. Unpublished.

GREGORY, P. (1993) An unidentified berrypecker *Melanocharis* sp. from the Ok Tedi area. *Muruk* 6: 1.

GRETTON, A. (1991) *The ecology and conservation of the Slender-billed Curlew (*Numenius tenuirostris). Cambridge, U.K.: International Council for Bird Preservation (Monogr. 6).

GRETTON, A. (1993) Ecology of the Seychelles Magpie Robin *Copsychus sechellarum*. *Proc. 8 Pan-Afr. Orn. Congr.* [*Ann. Sci. Zool. Mus. Roy. Afrique Centr.* 286]: 165–172.

GRETTON, A., KOHLER, M., LANSDOWN, R. V., PANKHURST, T. J., PARR, J. AND ROBSON, C. (1993) The status of Gurney's Pitta *Pitta gurneyi*, 1987–1989. *Bird Conserv. Internatn.* 3: 351–367.

GRIMMETT, R. F. A. (1979) Notes on a birdwatching visit to the Khasi Hills, North Cachar and Assam, India. Unpublished.

GRIMMETT, R. (1991) Little known Oriental bird: Biddulph's Ground Jay. *Bull. Oriental Bird Club* 13: 26–29.

GRIMMETT, R. F. A. AND JONES, T. A. (1989) *Important bird areas in Europe*. Cambridge, U.K.: International Council for Bird Preservation (Techn. Publ. 9).

GRIMMETT, R. AND TAYLOR, H. (1992) Recent bird observations from Xinjiang Autonomous Region, China, 16 June to 5 July 1988. *Forktail*: 139–146.

GROOMBRIDGE, B. (1993a) *1994 IUCN Red List of threatened animals*. Gland, Switzerland, and Cambridge, U.K.: International Union for Conservation of Nature and Natural Resources.

GROOMBRIDGE, B. (1993b) Introduction. Pp.viii–xxiii in B. Groombridge, ed. *1994 IUCN Red List of threatened animals*. Gland, Switzerland, and Cambridge, U.K.: International Union for Conservation of Nature and Natural Resources.

GROUT, D. (1993) Captive breeding program for Mariana Island birds begins. *'Elepaio* 53: 73–74.

GRZYBOWSKI, J. A., TAZIK, D. J. AND SCHNELL, G. D. (1994) Regional analysis of Black-capped Vireo breeding habitats. *Condor* 96: 512–544.

DE HAAN, G. A. L. (1950) Notes on the Invisible Flightless Rail of Halmahera (*Habroptila wallacii* Gray). *Amst. Nat.* 1: 57–60.

HADDEN, D. (1981) *Birds of the north Solomons*. Wau, Papua New Guinea: Wau Ecology Institute (Handbook 8).

HAHN, P. (1993) Anmerkungen zur Situation des Hornsittichs *Eunymphicus cornutus* auf Neukaledonien und Ouvéa. *Papageien* 6: 189–192.

HAIG, S. M. (1992) Piping Plover. In A. Poole, P. Stettenheim and F. Gill, eds. *The birds of North America*. Philadelphia: Academy of Natural Sciences of Philadelphia and Washington, D.C.: American Ornithologists' Union.

HAIG, S. M., BALLOU, J. D. AND DERRICKSON, S. R. (1993) Genetic considerations for the Guam Rail. *Re-introduction News* 7: 11–12.

HALL, B. P. (1960) The faunistic importance of the scarp of Angola. *Ibis* 102: 420–442.

HALLEUX, D. AND GOODMAN, S. M. (in press) The rediscovery of the Madagascar Red Owl *Tyto soumagnei* (Grandidier, 1878) in north-eastern Madagascar. *BIOL. CONSERV. INTERNATN.*

HAMBLER, C., HAMBLER, K. AND EWING, J. M. (1985) Some observations on *Nesillas aldabranus*, the endangered brush warbler of Aldabra Atoll, with hypotheses on its distribution. *Atoll Res. Bull.* 290.

HAMILTON, A. C. AND BENSTED-SMITH, R., EDS. (1989) *Forest conservation in the East Usambara Mountains Tanzania*. Gland, Switzerland and Cambridge, U.K.: International Union for Conservation of Nature and Natural Resources.

HANCOCK, J. AND KUSHLAN, J. (1984) *The herons handbook*. London: Croom Helm.

HANCOCK, J. A., KUSHLAN, J. A. AND KAHL, M. P. (1992) *Storks, ibises and spoonbills of the world*. London: Academic Press.

HANNECART, F. (1988) Les oiseaux menacés de la Nouvelle Calédonie et des îles proches. Pp.143–165 in J.-C. Thibault and I. Guyot, eds. *Livre rouge des oiseaux menacés des régions françaises d'outre-mer*. Saint-Cloud: Conseil International pour la Protection des Oiseaux (Monogr. 5).

HAREBOTTLE, D. (1994) The conservation biology of the Spotted Thrush *Turdus fischeri* in southern Africa. University of Natal, Pietermaritzburg (M.Sc. thesis).

HARRAP, S. (1992) Little known West Palearctic birds: Algerian Nuthatch. *Birding World* 5: 154–156.

HARRAP, S. C. AND REDMAN, N. J. (1989) Some observations of scarce birds in Kerala and Tamil Nadu. *J. Bombay Nat. Hist. Soc.* 86: 460–461.

HARRISON, C. S. (1990) *Seabirds of Hawaii: natural history and conservation*. Ithaca and London: Cornell University Press.

HARRISON, C. S., NAUGHTON, M. B. AND FEFER, S. I. (1984) The status and conservation of seabirds in the Hawaiian Archipelago and Johnston Atoll. Pp.513–526 in J. P. Croxall, P. G. H. Evans and R. W. Schreiber, eds. *Status and conservation of the world's seabirds*. Cambridge, U.K.: International Council for Bird Preservation (Techn. Publ. 2).

HARRISON, M. J. S. (1990) A recent survey of the birds of Pagalu (Annobon). *Malimbus* 11: 135–143.

HARRISON, P. (1983) *Seabirds: an identification guide*. Beckenham, U.K.: Croom Helm.

HARTERT, E. (1924) Notes on some birds from Buru. *Novit. Zool.* 31: 104–111.

HARTLEY, R. R. AND MUNDY, P. J. (1990) Taita Falcons in captivity. *Honeyguide* 36: 66–69.

HARVEY, B. AND ATKINS, J. (in press) Further sighting of unnamed cliff swallow, Kereyou Lodge, Awash National Park, Ethiopia, 18 September 1993. *Scopus*.

HARVEY, W. G. (1990) *Birds in Bangladesh*. Dhaka: University Press.

HASEGAWA, H. (1984) Status and conservation of seabirds in Japan, with special attention to the Short-tailed Albatross. Pp.487–500 in J. P. Croxall, P. G. H. Evans and R. W. Schreiber, eds. *Status and conservation of the world's seabirds*. Cambridge, U.K.: International Council for Bird Preservation (Techn. Publ. 2).

HASEGAWA, H. (1991) Red Data Bird: Short-tailed Albatross. *World Birdwatch* 13(2): 10.

HATCH, S. A., BYRD, G. V., IRONS, D. B. AND HUNT, G. L. (1993) Status and ecology of Kittiwakes (*Rissa tridactyla* and *Rissa brevirostris*) in the North Pacific. Pp.140–153 in K. Vermeer, K. T. Briggs, K. H. Morgan and D. Siegel-Causey, eds. *The status, ecology and conservation of marine birds of the North Pacific.* Ottawa: Canadian Wildlife Service.

HAWKINS, A. F. A. (in press) Conservation status and regional population estimates of the White-breasted Mesite *Mesitornis variegata*, a rare Malagasy endemic. *Bird Conserv. Internatn.*

HAWKINS, A. F. A., CHAPMAN, P., GANZHORN, J. U., BLOXAM, Q., TONGE, S. AND BARLOW, S. (1990) Vertebrate conservation in Ankarana Special Reserve, northern Madagascar. *Biol. Conserv.* 54: 83–110.

HAWKINS, A. F. A., SAFFORD, R. J., DUCKWORTH, J. W., EVANS, M. I. AND LANGRAND, O. (in prep.) Field characters and conservation status of the Yellow-bellied Sunbird-asity *Neodrepanis hypoxantha*.

HAWKINS, F. (1993a) Relationships among vegetation structure and White-breasted Mesite *Mesitornis variegata* presence and foraging site choice. *Proc. 8 Pan-Afr. Orn. Congr.* [*Ann. Sci. Zool. Mus. Roy. Afrique Centr.* 286]: 155–163.

HAWKINS, F. (1993b) An integrated biodiversity conservation project under development: the ICBP Angola Scarp Project. *Proc. 8 Pan-Afr. Orn. Congr.* [*Ann. Sci. Zool. Mus. Roy. Afrique Centr.* 286]: 279–284.

HAY, J. R., BEST, H. A. AND POWLESLAND, R. G. (1985) *Kokako.* Dunedin, New Zealand: John McIndoe and New Zealand Wildlife Service.

HAY, R. (1984) The Tuamotu Sandpiper: little known, little cared for. *Forest and Bird* 15(4): 17.

HAY, R. (1986) *Bird conservation in the Pacific Islands.* Cambridge, U.K.: International Council for Bird Preservation (Study Report 7).

HAYES, F. E., SCHARF, P. A. AND RIDGELY, R. S. (1994) Austral bird migrants in Paraguay. *Condor* 96: 83–97.

HAYMAN, P., MARCHANT, J. AND PRATER, T. (1986) *Shorebirds.* London: Croom Helm.

HAZEVOET, C. J. (1989) Notes on behaviour and breeding of the Razo Lark *Alauda razae. Bull. Brit. Orn. Club* 109: 82–86.

HAZEVOET, C. J. (1991) The atlas of breeding birds in the Cape Verde Islands: introduction and manual. Cape Verde: Instituto Nacional de Investigação Agraria.

HAZEVOET, C. J. (1993) On the history and type specimens of the Cape Verde Cane Warbler *Acrocephalus brevipennis* (Keulemans, 1866) (Aves, Sylviidae). *Bijdr. Dierkde.* 62: 249–253.

HAZEVOET, C. J. (1994) Status and conservation of seabirds in the Cape Verde Islands. Pp.279–293 in D. N. Nettleship, J. Burger and M. Gochfeld, eds. *Seabirds on islands: threats, case studies and action plans.* Cambridge, U.K.: BirdLife International (BirdLife Conservation Series no. 1).

HE, F. AND LU, T. (1991) Changes in status and distribution of Chinese pheasants. *WPA News* 31: 19–24.

HEARN, R. (1994) The current status of the Brazilian Merganser *Mergus octosetaceus* in Argentina. *IWRB Threatened Waterfowl Research Group Newsletter* 5: 14–15.

HEATH, P. J. (1988) Little-known Oriental bird: Rusty-bellied Shortwing. *Bull. Oriental Bird Club* 8: 16–19.

HEATHER, B. D. (1977) The Vanua Levu Silktail (*Lamprolia victoriae kleinschmidti*): a preliminary look at its status and habits. *Notornis* 24: 94–128.

HEIJ, C. J. AND MOELIKER, C. W. (in prep.) The rediscovery of *Monarcha boanensis.*

HELLMICH, J. (1991) La avutarda en Extremadura. *Alytes* Monogr. 2.

HELLMICH, J. (1992) Impacto del uso de pesticidas sobre las aves: el caso de la Avutarda. *Ardeola* 39: 7–22.

VAN HELVOORT, B. E. (1990) The Bali Starling *Leucopsar rothschildi* Stresemann 1912: its current status and need for conservation. Pp.115–131 in U. S. Seal, ed. *Leucopsar rothschildi: Population Viability Assessment.* Gland, Switzerland: Species Survival Commission.

HENRY, G. M. (1955) *A guide to the birds of Ceylon.* London: Oxford University Press.

HEREDIA, B. (in prep.) Action plans for globally threatened birds in Europe. Cambridge, U.K.: BirdLife International.

HERHOLDT, J. J. AND GROBLER, N. J. (1987) Field notes on the identification of the Botha's Lark, Pinkbilled Lark and Rudd's Lark in the Orange Free State, with notes on their habitat. *Mirafra* 4: 61–62.

HERMES, N. (1980) Endangered species. Pp.7–16 in C. Haigh, ed. *Endangered animals of New South Wales.* Sydney: National Parks and Wildlife Service.

HERMES, N. (1985) *Birds of Norfolk Island.* Norfolk Island: Wonderland Publications.

HERREMANS, M., LOUETTE, M. AND STEVENS, J. (1991) Conservation status and vocal and morphological description of the Grand Comoro Scops Owl *Otus pauliani* Benson 1960. *Bird Conserv. Internatn.* 1: 123–133.

HIDALGO DE TRUCIOS, S. J. AND CARRANZA ALMANSA, J. (1990) *Ecología y comportamiento de la Avutarda (Otis tarda L.).* Cáceres: Universidad de Extremadura.

HIGUCHI, H. (1991) Cooperative work on crane migration and conservation from Japan to the U.S.S.R. through Korea and China. Pp.189–202 in T. Salathé, ed. *Conserving migratory birds.* Cambridge, U.K.: International Council for Bird Preservation (Techn. Publ. 12).

HIGUCHI, H. AND KAWAJI, N. (1989) Ijima's Willow Warbler *Phylloscopus ijimae* of the Tokara Islands, a new breeding locality, in southwest Japan. *Bull. Biogeog. Soc. Japan* 44: 11–15.

HIGUCHI, H., OZAKI, K., FUJITA, G., SOMA, M., KANMURI, N. AND UETA, M. (1992) Satellite tracking of the migration routes of cranes from southern Japan. *Strix* 11: 1–20.

HIGUCHI, Y. AND HANAWA, S. (1985) Habitats of the Amami Ground Thrush in Amami Oshima. *Research Concerning the Special Wild Birds of Japan*: 35–51.

HILLMAN, J. C. (1993) *Ethiopia: compendium of wildlife conservation information, 2: information on wildlife conservation areas.* New York and Addis Ababa: Wildlife Conservation Society and the Ethiopian Wildlife Conservation Organisation.

HILTY, S. L. AND BROWN, W. L. (1986) *A guide to the birds of Colombia.* Princeton: Princeton University Press.

HINES, C. J. H. (1992) Observations on the Slaty Egret *Egretta vinaceigula* in northern Namibia. *Ostrich* 63: 118–122.

HIPKISS, A. J., WATSON, L. G. AND EVANS, T. D. (1994) The Cambridge–Tanzania Rainforest Project 1992: brief account of ornithological results and conservation proposals. *Ibis* 136: 107–108.

HOCKEY, P. A. R. (1986) The Canary Islands Expedition. *Quagga* 16: 22–23.

HOCKEY, P. A. R. (1992) Rare birds in South Africa, 1989–1990. *Birding in Southern Africa* 44: 38–44.

HOCKEY, P. A. R., ALLAN, D. G., REBELO, A. G. AND DEAN, W. R. J. (1988) The distribution, habitat requirements and conservation status of Rudd's Lark *Heteromirafra ruddi* in South Africa. *Biol. Conserv.* 45: 255–266.

HOFFMANN, T. W. (1984) *National red data list of endangered and rare birds of Sri Lanka*. Colombo: Ceylon Bird Club.

HOLMES, D. A. (1989) Status report on Indonesian Galliformes. *Kukila* 4: 133–143.

HOLMES, D. A. (1993) Birds on Flores: a synopsis of birds recorded on the island of Flores during 1993. Unpublished.

HOLMES, D. A. AND BURTON, K. (1987) Recent notes on the avifauna of Kalimantan. *Kukila* 3: 2–32.

HOLMES, P. AND WOOD, H. (1980) The report of the ornithological expedition to Sulawesi. Unpublished.

HOLSTEN, B., BRÄUNLICH, A. AND HUXHAM, M. (1991) Rondo Forest Reserve, Tanzania: an ornithological note including new records of the East Coast Akalat *Sheppardia gunningi*, the Spotted Ground Thrush *Turdus fischeri*, and the Rondo Green Barbet *Stactolaema olivacea woodwardi*. *Scopus* 14: 125–128.

HOLYOAK, D. T. (1974) Undescribed land birds from the Cook Islands, Pacific Ocean. *Bull. Brit. Orn. Club* 94: 145–150.

HOLYOAK, D. T. (1975) Les oiseaux des îles Marquises. *Oiseau et R.F.O.* 45: 207–234.

HOLYOAK, D. T. AND SEDDON, M. B. (1990) Notes on some birds of western Cameroon. *Malimbus* 11: 123–127.

HOLYOAK, D. T. AND THIBAULT, J.-C. (1984) Contribution à l'étude des oiseaux de Polynésie orientale. *Mém. Mus. Natn. Hist. Nat. Ser. A, Zool.* 127: 1–209.

HOOGENDOORN, W. AND MACKRILL, E. J. (1987) Audouin's Gull in south-western Palearctic. *Dutch Birding* 9: 99–107.

HOOGERWERF, A. (1966) Some notes on the genus *Trichastoma* especially on the validity of *T. sepiarium minus* from east Java and about the status of *T. vanderbilti* and *T. liberale* from northern Sumatra. *Yamashina's Institute for Ornithology and Zoology* 4: 294–300.

HOPKINSON, G. AND MASTERSON, A. (1984) The occurrence and ecological preferences of certain Rallidae near Salisbury, Zimbabwe. Pp.425–440 in J. Ledger, ed. *Proc. Fifth Pan Afr. Orn. Congr.* Johannesburg: Southern African Ornithological Society.

HOWARD, G. W. (1989) Recent counts of Wattled Cranes *Bugeranus carunculatus* on the Kafue Flats, Zambia—November 1987. *Scopus* 12: 69–72.

HOWELL, S. N. G. (1993) Status of the Piping Plover in Mexico. *Euphonia* 2: 51–54.

HOWELL, S. N. G. AND WEBB, S. (1989) Additional notes from Isla Clarión, Mexico. *Condor* 91: 1007–1008.

DEL HOYO, J. (1989) *Ibis eremita*. *Quercus* 43: 28–33.

DEL HOYO, J., ELLIOTT, A. AND SARGATAL, J. (1992) *Handbook of the birds of the world*, 1. Barcelona: Lynx Edicions.

DEL HOYO, J., ELLIOTT, A. AND SARGATAL, J. (in press) *Handbook of the birds of the world*, 2. Barcelona: Lynx Edicions.

HSU, W. AND MELVILLE, D. S. (1994) Seabirds of China and adjacent seas: status and conservation. Pp.210–218 in D. N. Nettleship, J. Burger and M. Gochfeld, eds. *Seabirds on islands: threats, case studies and action plans*. Cambridge, U.K.: BirdLife International (BirdLife Conservation Series no. 1).

HUGHES, B. (1991) The Wildfowl and Wetlands Trust expedition to the Soviet Far East (20 June–19 August 1991).

HUGHES, B. AND BOCHARNIKOV, V. N. (1992) Status of the Scaly-sided Merganser *Mergus squamatus* in the far east of Russia. *Wildfowl* 43: 193–199.

HUMPHREY, S. R. AND BAIN, J. B. (1990) *Endangered animals of Thailand*. Gainsville, Florida: Sandhill Crane Press.

HUNDESSA, T. (1991) Survival status review of the Ethiopian Bushcrow (*Zavattariornis stresemanni* Moltoni, 1938) in the Borana area, Ethiopia. *Walia* 13: 9–13.

HUNT, G. (1992) Census of Kagus (*Rhynochetos jubatus*) on the main island of New Caledonia during 1991/1992. Unpublished report.

HUNT, G. (1993) Preliminary report on the Kagu deaths at Pic Nigua. Unpublished report to BirdLife International.

HUNTER, L. A. (1988) Status of the endemic Atitlán Grebe of Guatemala: is it extinct? *Condor* 90: 906–912.

HURLBERT, S. H. AND KEITH, J. O. (1979) Distribution and spatial patterning of flamingos in the Andean altiplano. *Auk* 96: 328–342.

HURRELL, P. (1989) Schneider's Pitta rediscovered in Sumatra. *Kukila* 4: 53–56.

HUSAIN, K. Z. (1959) Is *Psittacula intermedia* a valid species? *Bull. Brit. Orn. Club* 79: 89–92.

HUSSAIN, S. A. (1984) Some aspects of the biology and ecology of Narcondam Hornbill *Rhyticeros narcondami*. *J. Bombay Nat. Hist. Soc.* 81: 1–18.

HUSSAIN, S. A., AKHTAR, S. A. AND TIWARI, J. K. (1992) Status and distribution of White-winged Black Tit *Parus nuchalis* in Kachchh, Gujarat, India. *Bird Conserv. Internatn.* 2: 115–122.

HUSTLER, K. (1989) The ecological relationship of Taita and Peregrine Falcons. *Honeyguide* 35: 158–160.

ICBP (1992) *Putting biodiversity on the map: priority areas for global conservation*. Cambridge, U.K.: International Council for Bird Preservation.

IMBODEN, CH. (1994) Birds as indicators of unsustainability. Pp.61–68 in G. Bennett, ed. *Conserving Europe's natural heritage: towards a European ecological network*. London: Graham and Trotman.

INSKIPP, C. (1989) *Nepal's forest birds: their status and conservation*. Cambridge, U.K.: International Council for Bird Preservation (Monogr. 4).

INSKIPP, C. AND COLLAR, N. J. (1984) The Bengal Florican: its conservation in Nepal. *Oryx* 18: 30–35.

INSKIPP, C. AND INSKIPP, T. (1983) *Results of a preliminary survey of Bengal Floricans Houbaropsis bengalensis in Nepal and India, 1982*. Cambridge, U.K.: International Council for Bird Preservation (Study Report 2).

INSKIPP, C. AND INSKIPP, T. (1985) A survey of Bengal Floricans in Nepal and India, 1982. *Bustard Studies* 3: 141–160.

INSKIPP, C. AND INSKIPP, T. (1991) *Birds of Nepal*. Second edition. London: Christopher Helm.

INSKIPP, C. AND INSKIPP, T. P. (1993a) Birds recorded in a

visit to Bhutan in autumn 1991. *Forktail* 8: 97–112.

INSKIPP, C. AND INSKIPP, T. P. (1993b) Birds recorded during a visit to Bhutan in spring 1993. *Forktail* 9: 121–142.

INSKIPP, T. AND COLLINS, L. (1993) *World checklist of threatened birds*. Peterborough, U.K.: Joint Nature Conservation Committee.

INSKIPP, T., BROAD, S. AND LUXMOORE, R. (1988) *Significant trade in wildlife: a review of selected species in CITES Appendix 2, 3: birds*. Cambridge, U.K.: Convention on International Trade in Endangered Species of Wild Fauna and Flora and International Union for Conservation of Nature and Natural Resources.

IRWIN, M. P. S. (1981) *The birds of Zimbabwe*. Salisbury: Quest Publishing.

ISHIHARA, T. (1986) The Amami Ground Thrush distinct from the White's Ground Thrush. *Strix* 5: 60–61.

ISLAM, K. AND CRAWFORD, J. A. (1985) Brood habitat and roost sites of Western Tragopans in northeastern Pakistan. *World Pheasant Assoc. J.* 10: 7–14.

ISLAM, K. AND CRAWFORD, J. A. (1986) Summary of Western Tragopan Project in Pakistan with recommendation for conservation of the species. Unpaginated, in M. Ridley, ed. *Pheasants in Asia 1986*. Basildon, U.K.: World Pheasant Association.

ISLER, M. L. AND ISLER, P. R. (1987) *The tanagers: natural history, distribution, and identification*. Washington, D.C.: Smithsonian Institution Press.

JANSSEN, D. L., OOSTERHUIS, J. E., ALLEN, J. L., ANDERSON, M. P., KELTS, D. G. AND WIEMEYER, S. N. (1986) Lead poisoning in free-ranging California Condors. *J. Amer. Vet. Med. Assoc.* 189: 1115–1117.

JAVED, S. AND RAHMANI, A. (1991) Swamp Francolin in the north Indian terai. *WPA News* 34: 15–18.

JENKINS, A. R., WAGNER, S. T. AND HOFFMAN, I. (1991) First breeding record of the Taita Falcon in South Africa. *Ostrich* 62: 78.

JENKINS, J. M. (1983) *The native forest birds of Guam*. Washington, D.C.: American Ornithologists' Union (Orn. Monogr. 31).

JENNINGS, M. C., HEATHCOTE, P. C., PARR, D. AND BAHA EL DIN, S. (1985) Ornithological survey of the Ras Dib area and the islands at the mouth of the Gulf of Suez, Egypt. Unpublished.

JENSEN, A., POULSEN, M. K., JAKOBSEN, O. F. AND ANDERSEN, C. Y. (1991) Bird preservation and integrated conservation of Mount Pulog National Park, the Philippines. Manila: Department of Environment and Natural Resources, and International Council for Bird Preservation (unpublished draft report).

JENSEN, F. P. AND BRØGGER-JENSEN, S. (1992) The forest avifauna of the Uzungwa Mountains, Tanzania. *Scopus* 15: 65–83.

JEPSON, P. (1993) Recent ornithological observations from Buru. *Kukila* 6: 85–109.

JOHNSGARD, P. (1986) *Pheasants of the world*. Oxford: Oxford University Press.

JOHNSGARD, P. A. (1991) *Bustards, hemipodes, and sandgrouse birds of dry places*. Oxford: Oxford University Press.

JOHNSON, A. W. (1965) *The birds of Chile and adjacent regions of Argentina, Bolivia and Peru*, 1. Buenos Aires: Platt Establecimientos Gráficos.

JOHNSON, J. M., PERENNOU, C. AND CRIVELLI, A. J. (1993)

Towards the extinction of the Spot-billed Pelican *Pelecanus philippensis*. Pp.92–93 in M. Moser and J. van Vessem, eds. *Wetland and waterfowl conservation in south and west Asia*. Slimbridge, U.K.: International Waterfowl and Wetlands Research Bureau (IWRB Spec. Publ. 25).

JOHNSON, T. H. AND STATTERSFIELD, A. J. (1990) A global review of island endemic birds. *Ibis* 132: 167–180.

JOHNSTONE, R. E., VAN BALEN, S. AND DEKKER, R. W. R. J. (1993) New bird records for the island of Lombok. *Kukila* 6: 124–127.

JOLLY, J. N. (1989) A field study of the breeding biology of the Little Spotted Kiwi (*Apteryx owenii*) with emphasis on the causes of nest failures. *J. Roy. Soc. New Zealand* 19: 433–448.

JONES, C. G. (1987) The larger land-birds of Mauritius. Pp.208–300 in A. W. Diamond, ed. *Studies of Mascarene Island birds*. Cambridge, U.K.: Cambridge University Press.

JONES, C. G. AND DUFFY, K. (1993) Conservation management of the Echo Parakeet *Psittacula eques echo*. *Dodo* 29: 126–148.

JONES, C. G., HECK, W., LEWIS, R. E., MUNGROO, Y. AND CADE, T. J. (1991) A summary of the conservation management of the Mauritius Kestrel 1973–1991. *Dodo* 27: 81–99.

JONES, C. G., HECK, W., LEWIS, R. E., MUNGROO, Y., SLADE, G. AND CADE, T. J. (in press) The restoration of the Mauritius Kestrel population. *Ibis*.

JONES, M. J. (1990) A survey of the distribution, density and habitat preferences of the Long-toed Pigeon. *Bol. Mus. Mun. Funchal* 42: 71–86.

JONES, M. J., LINSLEY, M. A. AND MARSDEN, S. J. (in press) Population sizes, status and habitat associations of the restricted-range bird species of Sumba Island, Indonesia. *Bird Conserv. Internatn.*

JONES, P. J. AND TYE, A. (1988) *A survey of the avifauna of São Tomé and Príncipe*. Cambridge, U.K.: International Council for Bird Preservation (Study Report 24).

JONES, P. J. AND TYE, A. (in press) *The birds of São Tomé and Príncipe*. Tring, U.K.: British Ornithologists' Union.

JONES, P. J., BURLISON, J. P. AND TYE, A. (1992) The status of endemic birds and their habitats in São Tomé and Príncipe. *Proc. 7 Pan-Afr. Orn. Congr.*: 453–459.

JORDAN, O. C. AND MUNN, C. A. (1993) First observations of the Blue-throated Macaw in Bolivia. *Wilson Bull.* 105: 694–695.

JOSEPH, L. (1988) A review of the conservation status of Australian parrots in 1987. *Biol. Conserv.* 46: 261–280.

JOSEPH, L. AND MORITZ, C. (1993) Hybridisation between the White-browed and Atherton Scrubwrens: detection with mitochondrial DNA. *Emu* 93: 93–99.

JOUANIN, C. AND MOUGIN, J.-L. (1979) Order Procellariiformes. Pp.48–118 in E. Mayr and G. W. Cottrell, eds. *Check-list of birds of the world*, 1. Cambridge, Mass.: Museum of Comparative Zoology.

JOUVENTIN, P. (1994a) Les populations d'oiseaux marins des T.A.A.F.: résumé de 20 années de recherche. *Alauda* 62: 44–47.

JOUVENTIN, P. (1994b) Past, present and future of Amsterdam Island, Indian Ocean. Pp.122–132 in D. N. Nettleship, J. Burger and M. Gochfeld, eds. *Seabirds on islands: threats, case studies and action plans*. Cambridge, U.K.:

BirdLife International (BirdLife Conservation Series no. 1).

JOUVENTIN, P., STAHL, J.-C., WEIMERSKIRCH, H. AND MOUGIN, J.-L. (1984) The seabirds of the French subantarctic islands and Adélie Land, their status and conservation. Pp.609–625 in J. P. Croxall, P. G. H. Evans and R. W. Schreiber, eds. *Status and conservation of the world's seabirds*. Cambridge, U.K.: International Council for Bird Preservation (Techn. Publ. 2).

JOUVENTIN, P., STAHL, J.-C. AND WEIMERSKIRCH, H. (1988) La conservation des oiseaux des Terres Australes et Antarctiques Françaises. Pp.225–251 in J.-C. Thibault and I. Guyot, eds. *Livre rouge des oiseaux menacés des régions françaises d'Outre-Mer*. Saint-Cloud: Conseil International pour la Protection des Oiseaux (Monogr. 5).

JOUVENTIN, P., MARTINEZ, J. AND ROUX, J.-P. (1989) Breeding biology and current status of the Amsterdam Island Albatross. *Ibis* 131: 171–189.

DE JUANA, E., BRADLEY, P. M., VARELA, J. M. AND WITT, H.-H. (1987) Sobre los movimientos migratorios de la gaviota de Audouin (*Larus audouinii*). *Ardeola* 34: 15–24.

KAESTNER, P. (1987) Some observations from lowland swamp forest in south Bougainville. *Muruk* 2: 34–38.

KASPAREK, M. (1989) Status and distribution of the Great Bustard and the Little Bustard in Turkey. *Bustard Studies* 4: 80–113.

KASPAREK, M. (1992) *Die Vögel der Turkei: eine Übersicht*. Heidelberg: Max Kasparek Verlag.

KAUL, R. (1992) Indian Mountain Quail. *WPA News* 38: 18–19.

KAWAJI, N., HIGUCHI, H. AND HORI, H. (1989) A new breeding record of the Izu Island Thrush *Turdus celaenops* from the Takara Islands, southwest Japan. *Bull. Brit. Orn. Club* 109: 93–95.

KEITH, S., URBAN, E. K. AND FRY, C. H. (1992) *The birds of Africa*, 4. London: Academic Press.

KEMP, A. C. (1988) The systematics and zoogeography of Oriental and Australasian hornbills (Aves: Bucerotidae). *Bonn. Zool. Beitr.* 39: 315–345.

KENNERLEY, P. R. (1987a) A survey of the birds of the Poyang Lake Nature Reserve, Jiangxi Province, China, 29 December 1985–4 January 1986. *Hong Kong Bird Rep.* 1984/1985: 97–111.

KENNERLEY, P. R. (1987b) Visit to Ba Bao Shan Nature Reserve 7–11 July 1987. Unpublished report.

KENNERLEY, P. R. (1990) A review of the status and distribution of the Black-faced Spoonbill. *Hong Kong Bird Rep.* 1989: 116–125.

KENNERLEY, P. R. AND BAKEWELL, D. N. (1987) Nordmann's Greenshank in Hong Kong: a review of the identification and status. *Hong Kong Bird Rep.* 1986: 83–100.

KENYON, K. W. (1961) Birds of Amchitka Island, Alaska. *Auk* 78: 305–326.

KING, B. (1987) Some bird observations at Pangquanguo Reserve in west central Shanxi Province in NE China. *Hong Kong Bird Rep.* 1984–1985: 112–114.

KING, B. (1989a) Birds observed at Huang Nian Shan, Mabian County, southern Sichuan, China. *Forktail* 4: 63–68.

KING, B. (1989b) Birds observed at Dafengding Panda Reserve, Mabian County, southern Sichuan, China. *Forktail* 4: 69–76.

KING, B. (1989c) Some bird observations at Kangwu Liangsi, southwest Sichuan province, China. *Hong Kong Bird Rep.* 1988: 102–110.

KING, B. (1994) A possible sighting of Diabolical Eared-nightjar *Eurostopodus diabolicus* in Sulawesi. *Bull. Oriental Bird Club* 19: 56–57.

KING, B. AND LIAO, W. (1989) Hainan Island bird notes. *Hong Kong Bird Rep.* 1988: 88–101.

KING, B. F., DICKINSON, E. C. AND WOODCOCK, M. W. (1975) *A Field guide to the birds of South-east Asia*. London: Collins.

KING, C. E. AND NIJBOER, J. (1994) Conservation considerations for crowned pigeons, genus *Goura*. *Oryx* 28: 22–30.

KING, W. B. (1978) Endangered birds of the world and current efforts towards managing them. Pp.9–17 in S. A. Temple, ed. *Endangered birds: management techniques for preserving threatened species*. Madison, Wisconsin: University of Wisconsin Press.

KING, W. B. (1978–1979) *Red Data Book, 2: Aves*. Second edition. Morges, Switzerland: International Union for Conservation of Nature and Natural Resources.

KING, W. B. (1985) Island birds: will the future repeat the past? Pp.3–15 in P. J. Moors, ed. *Conservation of island birds*. Cambridge, U.K.: International Council for Bird Preservation (Techn. Publ. 3).

KITCHENER, A. C., MACDONALD, A. A. AND HOWARD, A. (1993) First record of the Blue Crowned Pigeon *Goura cristata* on Seram. *Bull. Brit. Orn. Club* 113: 42–43.

KNOPF, F. L. AND MILLER, B. J. (1994) *Charadrius montanus*—montane, grassland, or bare-ground plover? *Auk* 111: 504–506.

KNYSTAUTAS, A. (1993) *Birds of Russia*. London: Harper Collins.

KOCK, N. D. (1989) An outbreak of beak and feather disease in lovebirds (*Agapornis* sp.) in Zimbabwe. *Zimbabwe Vet. J.* 20: 97–101.

KOLLAR, H. P. (1988) *Arten- und Biotopschutz am Beispiel der Grosstrappe (Otis tarda L.)*. Vienna: Verein für Ökologie und Umweltforschung (Umwelt 11).

KOLOSOV, A. M., ED. (1983) [*Red data book of the RSFSR: animals.*] Moscow: Rossel 'khozizdat. (In Russian.)

KOMDEUR, J. (1991) Influence of territory quality and habitat saturation on dispersal options in the Seychelles Warbler: an experimental test of the habitat saturation hypothesis for cooperative breeding. Pp.1325–1332 in *Acta XX Congressus Internationalis Ornithologici*. Wellington, New Zealand: New Zealand Ornithological Congress Trust Board.

KOMDEUR, J. (1992) Importance of habitat saturation and territory quality for evolution of cooperative breeding in the Seychelles Warbler. *Nature* 358: 493–495.

KOMDEUR, J. (1994) Conserving the Seychelles Warbler *Acrocephalus sechellensis* by translocation from Cousin Island to the islands of Aride and Cousine. *Biol. Conserv.* 67: 143–152.

KOMDEUR, J. (in prep.) Ecology and conservation of the Seychelles Magpie Robin *Copsychus sechellarum*.

KOMDEUR, J., BULLOCK, I. D. AND RANDS, M. R. W. (1991) Conserving the Seychelles Warbler *Acrocephalus sechellensis* by translocation: a transfer from Cousin Island to Aride Island. *Bird Conserv. Internatn.* 1: 177–185.

KOMEN, J. AND BROWN, C. J. (1993) Food requirements and the timing of breeding of a Cape Vulture colony. *Ostrich*

64: 86–92.

KONYUKHOV, N. B. AND MCCAFFERY, B. J. (1993) Second record of a Bristle-thighed Curlew from Asia and first record for the former Soviet Union. *Wader Study Group Bull.* 70: 22–23.

KOOIMAN, J. G. (1940) Mededeelingen over het voorkomen in Oostjava voor dit gewest nog niet in de literatuur genoemde vogels. *Ardea* 29: 98–108.

KOSTER, S. H. AND BUTYNSKI, T. M. (undated) Status of avifauna on Bioko Island (Fernando Poo), Equatorial Guinea. Unpublished.

KOTAGAMA, S. W. (in prep.) The threatened birds of Sri Lanka.

KRABBE, N. (1994) Focus on: the White-tailed Shrike-tyrant, an extinction prone species? *Cotinga* 1: 33–34.

KRABBE, N. AND SORNOZA, M. F. (1994) Avifaunistic results of a subtropical camp in the Cordillera del Condor, southeastern Ecuador. *Bull. Brit. Orn. Club* 114: 55–61.

KRABBE, N., BRAUN, M. J., JÁCOME, M., ROBBINS, M. B., SCHJØRRING, S. AND SORNOZA M., F. (1994a) Black-legged Puffleg found: extant but seriously threatened. *Cotinga* 1: 8–9.

KRABBE, N., DESMET, G., GREENFIELD, P., JÁCOME, M., MATHEUS, J. C. AND SORNOZA, M. F. (1994b) Focus on: Giant Antpitta *Grallaria gigantea*. *Cotinga* 2: 31–33.

KRATTER, A. W. (in press) Status, habitat and conservation of the Rufous-fronted Antthrush *Formicarius rufifrons*. *Bird Conserv. Internatn.*

KUEHLER, C. AND LIEBERMAN, A. (1993) Ultramarine Lory update. *Re-introduction News* 7: 12.

KURODA, N. (1933–1936) *Birds of the island of Java*. Tokyo.

LABASTILLE, A. (1983) Goodbye, giant grebe? *Natural History* 92: 64–72.

LABASTILLE, A. (1984) Drastic decline in Guatemala's Giant Pied-billed Grebe population. *Envir. Conserv.* 11: 346–348.

LABASTILLE, A. (1990) And now they are gone. *Internatn. Wildlife* 20(4): 18–23.

LACHUNGPA, U. G. AND RAHMANI, A. R. (1990) Former distribution of the Lesser Florican. Pp.95–100 in *Status and ecology of the Lesser and Bengal Floricans with reports on Jerdon's Courser and Mountain Quail: final report*. Bombay: Bombay Natural History Society.

LALL, S. AND RAMAN, L. (1994) The Siberian Cranes' last Indian winter. *WWF Features* April 1994: 6–8.

LAMARCHE, B. (1980–1981) Liste commentée des oiseaux du Mali. *Malimbus* 2: 121–158; 3: 73–102.

LAMBERT, F. R. (1989) Some field observations of the endemic Sulawesi rails. *Kukila* 4: 34–36.

LAMBERT, F. R. (1992) The status of the Philippine Cockatoo *Cactua haematuropygia* in Palawan and the Sulu Islands, Philippines. Unpublished.

LAMBERT, F. R. (1993a) Trade, status and management of three parrots in the North Moluccas, Indonesia: White Cockatoo *Cacatua alba*, Chaterring Lory *Lorius garrulus* and Violet-eared Lory *Eos squamata*. *Bird Conserv. Internatn.* 3: 145–168.

LAMBERT, F. R. (1993b) Some key sites and significant records of birds in the Philippines and Sabah. *Bird Conserv. Internatn.* 3: 281–297.

LAMBERT, F. R. (in prep.) Notes on the avifauna of Bacan, Kasiruta and Obi, north Moluccas.

LAMBERT, F. R. AND HOWES, J. R. (1989) A recent sighting of Salvadori's Pheasant. *Kukila* 4: 56–58.

LAMBERT, F., WIRTH, R., SEAL, U. S., THOMSEN, J. B. AND ELLIS-JOSEPH, S. (1993) Parrots: an action plan for their conservation 1993–1998. Cambridge, U.K.: BirdLife International and International Union for Conservation of Nature and Natural Resources (draft 2).

LAMMERTINK, M. AND ESTRADA, A. R. (in press) Status of the Ivory-billed Woodpecker *Campephilus principalis* in Cuba: almost certainly extinct. *Bird Conserv. Internatn.*

LANGHAM, N. P. (1989) The stratification of passerines in Fijian forests. *Notornis* 36: 267–279.

LANGRAND, O. (1987) Distribution, status and conservation of the Madagascar Fish-eagle *Haliaeetus vociferoides* Desmurs, 1845. *Biol. Conserv.* 42: 73–77.

LANGRAND, O. (1989) Search for the Madagascar Serpent Eagle. *Newsletter World Work. Grp. Birds of Prey* no.10: 5–7.

LANGRAND, O. (1990) *Guide to the birds of Madagascar*. New Haven: Yale University Press.

LANGRAND, O. AND MEYBURG, B.-U. (1989) Range, status and biology of the Madagascar Sea Eagle *Haliaeetus vociferoides*. Pp.269–278 in B.-U. Meyburg and R. D. Chancellor, eds. *Raptors in the modern world*. Berlin: World Working Group on Birds of Prey and Owls.

LANSDOWN, R. (1990) Little-known Oriental bird: Chinese Egret. *Bull. Oriental Bird Club* 11: 27–30.

LAVERS, R. AND MILLS, J. (1984) *Takahe*. Dunedin: John McIndoe and New Zealand Wildlife Service.

LECROY, M., PECKOVER, W. S., KULUPI, A. AND MANSEIMA, J. (1984) *Bird observations on Normanby and Fergusson, D'Entrecasteaux Islands, Papua New Guinea*. Boroko, Papua New Guinea: Division of Wildlife (Wildlife in Papua New Guinea 83/1).

LEES, A. (1991) *A protected forests system for the Solomon Islands*. Nelson, New Zealand: Maruia Society.

LEGGE, W. V. (1880) *A history of the birds of Ceylon*. London: Taylor and Francis.

LEHMBERG, T. AND DINESEN, L. (1994) The bright sides of stumbling over a new bird species. *Bull. African Bird Club* 1: 24–25.

LENSINK, C. J. (1984) The status and conservation of seabirds in Alaska. Pp.13–27 in J. P. Croxall, P. G. H. Evans and R. W. Schreiber, eds. *Status and conservation of the world's seabirds*. Cambridge, U.K.: International Council for Bird Preservation (Techn. Publ. 2).

LENTINO, M. AND GOODWIN, M. L. (1991) *Parque Nacional Morrocoy, Refugio de Fauna de Cuare, Estado Falcón—Venezuela: lista de las aves*. Caracas: Sociedad Conservacionista Audubon de Venezuela.

LEVER, C. (1987) *Naturalized birds of the world*. Harlow, U.K.: Longman Scientific and Technical.

LEWIS, A. AND POMEROY, D. (1989) *A bird atlas of Kenya*. Rotterdam: A. A. Balkema.

LI, F. (1991) World's first captive breeding of the Japanese Crested Ibis *Nipponia nippon*. *J. Yamashina Inst. Orn.* 22: 70–76.

LI, W. AND ZHAO, X. (1989) *China's nature reserves*. Beijing: Foreign Languages Press.

LI, X. T. (1993) Surveys of the Brown Eared-pheasant in Dongling Mountain, Beijing. Pp.139–140 in D. Jenkins, ed. *Pheasants in Asia 1992*. Reading, U.K.: World Pheasant Association.

LI, X., TAN, H., CHENG, C. AND ZHANG, A. (1990) Ecological studies on the White-browed Hill Partridge. Pp.84 in D. A. Hill, P. J. Garson and D. Jenkins, eds. *Pheasants in Asia 1989*. Reading, U.K.: World Pheasant Association.

LITVINENKO, N. AND SHIBAEV, Y. (1991) Status and conservation of the seabirds nesting in southeast U.S.S.R. Pp.175–204 in J. P. Croxall, ed. *Seabird status and conservation: a supplement*. Cambridge, U.K.: International Council for Bird Preservation (Techn. Publ. 11).

LITZBARSKI, H. (1993) Das Schutzprojekt 'Grosstrappe' in Brandenburg. *Ber. Vogelschutz* 31: 61–66.

LIU, X., ZHOU, F., PAN, G., LAI, Y., ZHENG, Y., LIU, Z. AND AO, D. (1990) Preliminary studies on breeding behavior of the Black-necked Bar-tailed Pheasant. Pp.79 in D. A. Hill, P. J. Garson and D. Jenkins, eds. *Pheasants in Asia 1989*. Reading, U.K.: World Pheasant Association.

LLOYD, B. D. AND POWLESLAND, R. G. (1994) The decline of Kakapo *Strigops habroptilus* and attempts at conservation by translocation. *Biol. Conserv.* 69: 75–85.

LOBKOV, E. G. AND NEUFELDT, I. A. (1986) Distribution and biology of the Steller's Sea Eagle—*Haliaeetus pelagicus pelagicus* (Pallas). *Proc. Zool. Inst. Acad. Sci. USSR*. 150: 107–146.

LONG, A., POOLE, C., ELDRIDGE, M., WON, P. AND LEE, K. S. (1988) *A survey of coastal wetlands and shorebirds in South Korea*. Kuala Lumpur: Asian Wetland Bureau.

LOUETTE, M. (1987) A new weaver from Uganda? *Ibis* 129: 405–406.

LOUETTE, M. (1988a) Additions and corrections to the avifauna of Zaire (2). *Bull. Brit. Orn. Club* 108: 43–50.

LOUETTE, M. (1988b) La conservation des oiseaux de Mayotte (Maore). Pp.197–207 in J.-C. Thibault and I. Guyot, eds. *Livre rouge des oiseaux menacés des régions françaises d'Outre Mer*. Saint-Cloud: Conseil International pour la Protection des Oiseaux (Monogr. 5).

LOUETTE, M. (1990) A new species of nightjar from Zaïre. *Ibis* 132: 349–353.

LOUETTE, M. AND STEVENS, J. (1992) Conserving the endemic birds on the Comoro Islands, I: general considerations on survival prospects. *Bird Conserv. Internatn.* 2: 61–80.

LOUETTE, M., STEVENS, J., BIJNENS, L. AND JANSSENS, L. (1988) *Survey of the endemic avifauna of the Comoro Islands*. Cambridge, U.K.: International Council for Bird Preservation (Study Report 3).

LOVEGROVE, R., MANN, I., MORGAN, G. AND WILLIAMS, I. (undated) Tuamotu Islands expedition March–April 1989: report of an expedition to ascertain the status of Red Data Book species in the Tuamotu Archipelago (French Polynesia). Unpublished.

LOZANO, I. E. (1993) Observaciones sobre la ecología y el comportamiento de *Rallus semiplumbeus* en el Humedal de la Florida, Sabana de Bogotá. Unpublished.

LU, J. (1993a) Distribution and bioenergetics of Swan Goose. *Asian Wetland News* 6: 18.

LU, J. (1993b) The utilisation of migratory wildfowl in China. Pp.90–92 in M. Moser, R. C. Prentice and J. van Vessem, eds. *Waterfowl and wetland conservation in the 1990s—a global perspective*. Slimbridge, U.K.: International Waterfowl and Wetlands Research Bureau (IWRB Special Publication 26).

DE LUCCA, E. R. (1993) El Aguila Coronada. *Nuestras Aves* 11(29): 14–17.

LUDLOW, F. (1944) The birds of southeastern Tibet. *Ibis* 86: 43–86, 176–208, 348–389.

LUDLOW, F. AND KINNEAR, N. B. (1933–1934) A contribution to the ornithology of Chinese Turkestan. *Ibis* 13: 240–259, 440–473, 658–694.

LUTHIN, C. S. (1987) Status and conservation priorities for the world's stork species. *Colonial Waterbirds* 10: 181–202.

MA, J. AND JIN, L. (1987) The numerical distribution of the Red-crowned Crane in Sanjiang Plain area of Heilongjiang province. *Acta Zool. Sin.* 33: 82–87.

MACCALLUM, R. B. (1990) Slaty Egrets at Darwendale Dam. *Honeyguide* 36: 142.

MACE, G. M. AND COLLAR, N. J. (in press) Extinction risk assessment for birds via quantitative criteria. *Ibis*.

MACE, G. M. AND LANDE, R. (1991) Assessing extinction threats: toward a reevaluation of IUCN threatened species categories. *Conserv. Biol.* 5: 148–157.

MACE, G. AND STUART, S. (1994) Draft IUCN Red List categories. *Species* 21–22: 13–24.

MACE, G., COLLAR, N., COOKE, J., GASTON, K., GINSBERG, J., LEADER-WILLIAMS, N., MAUNDER, M. AND MILNER-GULLAND, E. J. (1992) The development of new criteria for listing species on the IUCN Red List. *Species* 19: 16–22.

MACK, A. L. (1992) The nest, egg and incubating behaviour of a Blue Bird of Paradise *Paradisaea rudolphi*. *Emu* 92: 244–246.

MACKEAN, J. L. (1987) A first record of Christmas Frigatebird *Fregata andrewsi* on Timor. *Kukila* 3: 47.

MACKINNON, J. AND PHILLIPPS, K. (1993) *A field guide to the birds of Borneo, Sumatra, Java and Bali*. Oxford: Oxford University Press.

MACKINNON, J., BI, F., QUI, M., FAN, C., WANG, H., YUAN, S., TIAN, A. AND LI, J. (1989) *National conservation management plan for the Giant Panda and its habitat*. Beijing and Gland, Switzerland: Ministry of Forestry and World Wide Fund for Nature.

MACLEOD, H. L. (1987) *The conservation of Oku Mountain Forest, Cameroon*. Cambridge, U.K.: International Council for Bird Preservation (Study Report 15).

MACLEOD, H. AND PARROTT, J. (1991) Red data bird: Bannerman's Turaco. *World Birdwatch* 13(4): 12.

MACLEOD, H. AND PARROTT, J. (1992) Conservation of the Kilum (Oku) mountain forests in the Bamenda Highlands of Cameroon. *Proc. 7 Pan-Afr. Orn. Congr.*: 447–451.

MADGE, S. C. AND REDMAN, N. J. (1989) The existence of a form of cliff swallow *Hirundo* sp. in Ethiopia. *Scopus* 13: 126–129.

MADROÑO NIETO, A. (1992) Black-and-white Monjita *Xolmis dominicana*: draft entry for Collar *et al.* (1992). Unpublished.

MAGRATH, R. D., RIDLEY, M. W. AND WOINARSKI, J. Z. (1985) Status and habitat requirements of Lesser Floricans in Kathiawar, western India. *Bustard Studies* 3: 185–193.

MAIER, R. AND KELLY, A. (1994) Laguna Colorada and Eduardo Avaroa National Reserve, Bolivia. *Cotinga* 1: 36–41.

MAJUMDAR, N. AND BRAHMACHARI, G. K. (1986) Major grassland types of India and their bird communities: a conservation perspective. Pp.205–214 in P. D. Goriup, ed. *Ecology and conservation of grassland birds*. Cambridge, U.K.: International Council for Bird Preservation (Techn. Publ. 7).

MALAMBO, C. H. AND CHABWELA, H. (1992) Preliminary observations on the distribution and abundance of Wattled Cranes in Zambian wetlands. *Proc. 7 Pan-Afr. Orn. Congr.*: 71–74.

MALONEY, R., WELLS, N., ELKINGTON, S. AND CHADDERTON, L. (1993) Survey of Fiordland Crested Penguins on Codfish Island. *Notornis* 40: 223–225.

MANN, C. F. (1987) A checklist of the birds of Brunei Darussalam. *Brunei Mus. J.* 6: 170–212.

MANRY, D. E. (1985a) Reproductive performance of the Bald Ibis *Geronticus calvus* in relation to rainfall and grass-burning. *Ibis* 127: 159–173.

MANRY, D. E. (1985b) Distribution, abundance and conservation of the Bald Ibis *Geronticus calvus* in southern Africa. *Biol. Conserv.* 33: 351–362.

MANSON, A. J. (1990) The biology of Swynnerton's Robin. *Honeyguide* 36: 5–13.

MARCHANT, S. AND HIGGINS, P. J., EDS. (1990) *Handbook of Australian, New Zealand and Antarctic birds*, 1. Melbourne: Oxford University Press.

MARCHANT, S. AND HIGGINS, P. J., EDS. (1993) *Handbook of Australian, New Zealand and Antarctic birds*, 2. Melbourne: Oxford University Press.

MARKS, J. S. AND REDMOND, R. L. (in press) Conservation problems and research needs for Bristle-thighed Curlews *Numenius tahitiensis* on their wintering grounds. *Bird Conserv. Internatn.*

VAN MARLE, J. G. AND VOOUS, K. H. (1988) *The birds of Sumatra*. London: British Ornithologists' Union (Checklist 10).

MARSDEN, S. J. (1992) The distribution, abundance and habitat preferences of the Salmon-crested Cockatoo *Cacatua moluccensis* on Seram, Indonesia. *Bird Conserv. Internatn.* 2: 7–14.

MARSDEN, S. AND PETERS, S. (1992) Little known bird: Sumba Buttonquail. *Bull. Oriental Bird Club* 15: 24–26.

MARSHALL, A. P. (1992) Censusing Laysan Ducks *Anas laysanensis*: a lesson in the pitfalls of estimating threatened species populations. *Bird Conserv. Internatn.* 2: 239–251.

MARSHALL, A. P. AND BLACK, J. M. (1992) The effect of rearing experience on subsequent behavioural traits in Hawaiian Geese *Branta sandvicensis*: implications for the recovery programme. *Bird Conserv. Internatn.* 2: 131–147.

MARTINDALE, J. (1986) *The Freckled Duck—an RAOU conservation statement*. Melbourne: Royal Australasian Ornithologists' Union (Report 22).

MARTINS, R. P., PORTER, R. F. AND STONE, F. (1993) Preliminary report of the OSME survey of southern Yemen and Socotra, spring 1993. Unpublished.

MASSOLI-NOVELLI, R. (1988) Segnalazione di Schiribilla Alibianche, *Sarothrura ayresi*, in Etiopia. *Riv. Ital. Orn.* 58: 40–42.

MAXFIELD, B. (1993) Cooperative program pays off for the endangered 'Alala. *Endangered Species Techn. Bull.* 18(3): 4–7.

MAYR, E. (1945) *Birds of the southwest Pacific: a field guide to the birds of the area between Samoa, New Caledonia and Micronesia*. New York: Macmillan.

MAYR, E. AND BOCK, W. J. (1994) Provisional classifications *v* standard avian sequences: heuristics and communication in ornithology. *Ibis* 136: 12–18.

MAYR, E. AND PHELPS, W. H. (1967) The origin of the bird fauna of the southern Venezuelan highlands. *Bull. Amer. Mus. Nat. Hist.* 136: 269–328.

MCCAFFERY, B. J. AND GILL, R. E. (1992) Antipredator strategies in breeding Bristle-thighed Curlews. *Amer. Birds* 46: 378–383.

MCCORMACK, G. AND KÜNZLE, J. (1990) Kakerori—Rarotonga's endangered flycatcher. Cook Islands Conservation Service.

MCCORMACK, G. AND KÜNZLE, J. (1993) The 'Ura or Rimatara Lorikeet (*Vini kuhlii*): its former range, its present status and conservation priorities. Paper presented at the Manu Conference, Tahiti, November 1993.

MCCULLOCH, M. N. (1991) Status, habitat and conservation of the St Helena Wirebird *Charadrius sanctaehelenae*. *Bird Conserv. Internatn.* 1: 361–392.

MCCULLOCH, N. (1992) *The status and ecology of the St Helena Wirebird*. Thetford, U.K.: British Trust for Ornithology (Research Report 97).

MCCULLOCH, N. (in press) Rescuing the Seychelles Magpie Robin. *RSPB Conservation Review*.

MCGOWAN, P. J. K., DOWELL, S. D., CARROLL, J. P. AND AEBISCHER, N. J., EDS. (in press) *Partridge, quail and francolin action plan*. Cambridge, U.K.: BirdLife International and International Union for Conservation of Nature and Natural Resources.

MCGUIGAN, C. (1987) Ornithology report. Pp.10–27 in S. L. Tetlow, ed. *Cambridge Conservation Study 1985: Taita Hills, Kenya*. Cambridge, U.K.: International Council for Bird Preservation (Study Report 19).

MCLEAN, I. G., STUDHOLME, B. J. S. AND RUSS, R. B. (1993) The Fiordland Crested Penguin survey, stage III: Breaksea Island, Chalky and Preservation Inlets. *Notornis* 40: 85–94.

MEDWAY, LORD AND WELLS, D. R. (1976) *The birds of the Malay Peninsula*, 5. London: H. F. and G. Witherby.

MEENKEN, D., FECHNEY, T. AND INNES, J. (1994) Population size and breeding success of North Island Kokako in the Waipapa ecological area, Pureora Forest Park. *Notornis* 41: 109–115.

MEES, G. F. (1975) Identiteit en status van *Sterna bernsteini* Schlegel. *Ardea* 63: 78–86.

MEES, G. F. (1977) Enige gegevens over de uitgestorven ral *Pareudiastes pacificus* Hartlaub & Finsch. *Zool. Meded. Leiden* 50: 231–242.

MERTON, D. V., MORRIS, R. B. AND ATKINSON, I. A. E. (1984) Lek behaviour in a parrot: the Kakapo *Strigops habroptilus* of New Zealand. *Ibis* 126: 277–283.

MEYBURG, B.-U., VAN BALEN, S., THIOLLAY, J.-M. AND CHANCELLOR, R. D. (1989) Observations on the Endangered Java Hawk Eagle *Spizaetus bartelsi*. Pp.279–299 in B.-U. Meyburg and R. D. Chancellor, eds. *Raptors in the Modern World*. Berlin and Paris: World Working Group on Birds of Prey and Owls.

MEYER DE SCHAUENSEE, R. (1984) *The birds of China*. Oxford: Oxford University Press.

MEYER DE SCHAUENSEE, R. M. AND PHELPS, W. H. (1978) *A guide to the birds of Venezuela*. Princeton: Princeton University Press.

MEYERS, J. M. (1994) Old growth forests and the Puerto Rican Parrot. *Endangered Species Techn. Bull.* 19: 12.

MILLS, J. A., LAVERS, R. B. AND LEE, W. G. (1984) The Takahe—a relict of the Pleistocene grassland avifauna of

New Zealand. *New Zealand J. Ecol.* 7: 57–70.

MIYAGI, K. (1989) Conservation of Okinawa Rail and Okinawa Woodpecker. Proceedings of the joint meeting of the International Council for Bird Preservation Asian Section and East Asia Bird Protection Conference, Bangkok, Thailand. April 1989. Unpublished.

MLINGWA, C. (1991) Further records of the Sokoke Pipit *Anthus sokokensis* from Tanzania. *Scopus* 15: 57–58.

MLINGWA, C. O. F. (1993) Vikindu Forest Reserve, Tanzania: a first ornithological survey including a record of the Sokoke Pipit *Anthus sokokensis*. *Scopus* 17: 8–13.

MLINGWA, C. O. F. AND BURGESS, N. D. (in press) Forest birds at Kilulu Hill (Moa) and Gendanga Forest Reserve in Muheza District, Tanga, Tanzania. *Scopus*.

MLINGWA, C. O. F., HUXHAM, M. R. AND BURGESS, N. D. (1993) The avifauna of Kazimzumbwe Forest Reserve, Tanzania: initial findings. *Scopus* 16: 81–88.

MÖLLER, P. (1989) The Taita Falcon *Falco fasciinucha*: results of a study at Mt Elgon. Pp.315–319 in B.-U. Meyburg and R. D. Chancellor, eds. *Raptors in the modern world*. Berlin: World Working Group on Birds of Prey and Owls.

MONNET, C., THIBAULT, J.-C. AND VARNEY, A. (1993) Stability and changes during the twentieth century in the breeding land-birds of Tahiti (Polynesia). *Bird Conserv. Internatn.* 3: 261–280.

MONNET, C., SANDFORD, L., SIU, P., THIBAULT, J.-C. AND VARNEY, A. (in press) Polynesian Ground Dove (*Gallicolumba eruthroptera*) discovered at Rangiroa Atoll, Tuamotu Islands (Polynesia). *Notornis*.

MONTGOMERY, S. L., GAGNÉ, W. C. AND GAGNÉ, B. H. (1980) Notes on birdlife and nature conservation in the Marquesas and Society Islands. *'Elepaio* 40: 152–155.

MOORE, P. J. (1992) Population estimates of Yellow-eyed Penguins (*Megadyptes antipodes*) on Campbell and Auckland Islands 1987–90. *Notornis* 39: 1–15.

MOREL, G. J. AND CHAPPUIS, C. (1992) Past and future taxonomic research in West Africa. *Bull. Brit. Orn. Club (Centenary Suppl.)* 112A: 217–224.

MOREL, G. J. AND MOREL, M.-Y. (1988) Liste des oiseaux de Guinée. *Malimbus* 10: 143–176.

MOREL, G. J. AND MOREL, M.-Y. (1990) *Les oiseaux de Sénégambie*. Paris: Editions de l'ORSTOM (Institut Français de Recherche Scientifique pour le Développement en Coopération).

MORIN, M. P. (1992) The breeding biology of an endangered Hawaiian honeycreeper, the Laysan Finch. *Condor* 94: 646–667.

MORIN, M. P. AND CONANT, S. (1994) Variables influencing population estimates of an endangered passerine. *Biol. Conserv.* 67: 73–84.

MORONY, J. J., BOCK, W. J. AND FARRAND, J. (1975) *Reference list of the birds of the world*. New York: American Museum of Natural History (Department of Ornithology).

MORRIS, G. E. (1987) News of Nam Cat Tien. *Garrulax* 2: 3–5.

MOUNTAINSPRING, S., CASEY, T. L. C., KEPLER, C. B. AND SCOTT, J. M. (1990) Ecology, behavior, and conservation of the Poo-uli (*Melamprosops phaeosoma*). *Wilson Bull.* 102: 109–122.

MOUNTFORT, G. (1988) *Rare birds of the world: a Collins/ICBP handbook*. London: Collins.

MOYER, D. C. (1993) A preliminary trial of territory mapping for estimating bird densities in Afromontane forest. *Proc. 8 Pan-Afr. Orn. Congr.* [*Ann. Sci. Zool. Mus. Roy. Afrique Centr.* 286]: 302–311.

MOYER, D. C. AND LOVETT, J. C. (in press) Ecology, community structure, and conservation status of montane forest birds in the southern Udzungwa Mountains, Tanzania. *Scopus*.

MUMME, R. L. (1992) Delayed dispersal and cooperative breeding in the Seychelles Warbler. *Trends Ecol. Evol.* 7: 330–331.

MUNDKUR, T. (1988) Time to pull the alarm—for the Blackbellied Tern. *Newsletter for Birdwatchers* 28: 6–7.

MUNDKUR, T. (1994) Survey of waterbirds in Cambodia (March–April 1994), with specific reference to large waterbirds. Report submitted to the IUCN by the Asian Wetland Bureau, Kuala Lumpur, Malaysia.

MUNDKUR, T. AND TAYLOR, V., EDS. (1993) *Asian waterfowl census 1993*. Kuala Lumpur, Malaysia and Slimbridge, U.K.: Asian Wetlands Bureau and International Waterfowl and Wetlands Research Bureau.

MUNDY, P., BUTCHART, D., LEDGER, J. AND PIPER, S. (1992) *The vultures of Africa*. London: Academic Press.

MUNN, C. AND MUNN, M. (1993) Die Wiederentdeckung des Blaukehlaras *Ara glaucogularis*. *Papageien*: 148–152.

MURRAY, A. (1988) A study of the birds of the Tabubil region, Western Province, Papua New Guinea. *Muruk* 3: 3.

MWAF (MAURITIAN WILDLIFE APPEAL FUND) (1992) Report 1990–1992. Unpublished.

NACINOVIC, J. B. AND TEIXEIRA, D. M. (1989) As aves de Fernando de Noronha: uma lista sistemática anotada. *Revta. Bras. Biol.* 49: 709–729.

NADLER, T. (1993) Beiträge zur Avifauna der Insel São Tomé (Golf von Guinea). *Faun. Abhandl. Staatl. Mus. Tierk. Dresden* 19: 37–58.

NAKAGAWA, H., LOBKOV, E. G. AND FUJIMAKI, Y. (1987) Winter censuses on *Haliaeetus pelagicus* in Kamchatka and northern Japan in 1985. *Strix* 6: 14–19.

NANKINOV, D. (1992) Ringing of *Acrocephalus* reed warblers in Bulgaria—a preliminary report. *The Ring* 14: 101–109.

NARAYAN, G. (1990) General ecology and behaviour of the Bengal Florican. Pp.17–34 in *Status and ecology of the Lesser and Bengal Floricans with reports on Jerdon's Courser and Mountain Quail: final report*. Bombay: Bombay Natural History Society.

NARAYAN, G. AND ROSALIND, L. (1990) An introduction to the Bengal Florican. Pp.9–16 in *Status and ecology of the Lesser and Bengal Floricans with reports on Jerdon's Courser and Mountain Quail: final report*. Bombay: Bombay Natural History Society.

NARAYAN, G., AKHTAR, A., ROSALIND, L. AND D'CUNHA, E. (1986) Black-necked Crane *Grus nigricollis* in Ladakh—1986. *J. Bombay Nat. Hist. Soc.* 83: 180–195.

NASH, S. V. (1993) Concern about trade in Red-and-blue Lories. *TRAFFIC Bull.* 13: 93–96.

NATIONAL RESEARCH COUNCIL (1992) *The scientific bases for the preservation of the Hawaiian Crow*. Washington, D.C.: National Academy Press.

DE NAUROIS, R. (1982) Une énigme ornithologique: *Amaurocichla bocagei* [*sic*] Sharpe, 1892. *Bull. IFAN* 44 (Sér. A): 13–25.

DE NAUROIS, R. (1988) *Neospiza concolor* (Bocage, 1888) endémique de l'île de São Tomé (Golfe de Guinée). *Boll. Mus. Reg. Sci. Nat. Torino* 6: 321–339.

NAVARRO S., A. G., PETERSON, A. T., ESCALANTE P., B. P. AND BENÍTEZ D., H. (1992) *Cypseloides storeri*, a new species of swift from Mexico. *Wilson Bull.* 104: 55–64.

NAVARRO S., A. G., BENÍTEZ D., H., SÁNCHEZ B., V., GARCÍA R., S. AND SANTANA C., E. (1993) The White-faced Swift in Jalisco, Mexico. *Wilson Bull.* 105: 366–367.

NECHAEV, V. A. (1989) The status of Normann's [*sic*] Greenshank *Tringa guttifer* in the USSR. *Asian Wetland News* 2: 11,14.

NECHAEV, V. A. AND GLUSCHENKO, Y. N. (1993) Baer's Pochard in the far east of Russia. *IWRB Threatened Waterfowl Res. Group Newsl.* 3: 5–7.

NEGRET, A. J. (1992) La avifauna del Valle del Patia. *Novedades Colombianas* 5: 45–65.

NEGRO, J. J. AND HIRALDO, F. (1993) Nest-site selection and breeding success in the Lesser Kestrel *Falco naumanni*. *Bird Study* 40: 115–119.

NEGRO, J. J. AND HIRALDO, F. (1994) Lack of allozyme variation in the Spanish Imperial Eagle *Aquila adalberti*. *Ibis* 136: 87–90.

NELSON, J. B. AND POWELL, D. (1986) The breeding ecology of Abbott's Booby *Sula abbotti*. *Emu* 86: 33–46.

DEL NEVO, A. J., RODWELL, S., SIM, I. M. W., SAUNDERS, C. R. AND WACHER, T. (1994) Audouin's Gulls *Larus audouinii* in Senegambia. *Seabird* 16: 57–61.

NEWMARK, W. D. (1991) Tropical forest fragmentation and the local extinction of understorey birds in the East Usambara Mountains, Tanzania. *Conserv. Biol.* 5: 67–78.

NHLANE, M. E. D. (1993) Notes on the Wattled Crane *Bugeranus carunculatus* in Nyika National Park, Malawi. *Proc. 8 Pan-Afr. Orn. Congr.* [*Ann. Sci. Zool. Mus. Roy. Afrique Centr.* 286]: 404.

NICOLL, M. E. AND LANGRAND, O. (1989) *Madagascar: revue de la conservation et des aires protégées.* Gland, Switzerland: World Wide Fund for Nature.

NIKOLAUS, G. (1987) *Distribution atlas of Sudan's birds with notes on habitat and status.* Bonn: Zoologisches-forschungs Institut und Museum Alexander Koenig (Bonner Zoologische Monographien 25).

NIKOLAUS, G. AND HAMED, D. M. (1984) Distinct status changes of certain Palaearctic migrants in the Sudan. *Scopus* 8: 36–38.

NISHIDE, T. (1993) The ecology of Japanese Marsh Warblers in Hachiro-gate reclaimed land—3. Population dynamics and the factors of the dynamics. *Strix* 12: 41–52.

NORMAN, F. I., KINGSFORD, R. T. AND BRIGGS, S. V. (1994) The Freckled Duck *Stictonetta naevosa* as a 'threatened' taxon. *IWRB Threatened Waterfowl Res. Group Newsl.* 5: 11–13.

NOSKE, R. AND SALEH, N. (1993) Report to LIPI: the status of lowland forest birds in West Timor. Unpublished.

NOWAK, E. (1984) Ueber das vermutliche Brut- und Ueberwinterungsgebiet der Schopfkasarka, *Tadorna cristata. J. Orn.* 125: 103–105.

NUTTALL, R. J. (1993) The Lesser Kestrel *Falco naumanni* in the Orange Free State and Lesotho: 1991–1993. *Mirafra* 10: 39–45.

O'DONNELL, C. F. J. (1984) The North Island Kokako (*Callaeas cinerea wilsoni*) in the Western King Country and Taranaki. *Notornis* 31: 131–144.

O'DONNELL, C. (1993) (*Mohua) Yellowhead Recovery Plan.* Wellington: Threatened Species Unit, Department of Conservation (Threatened Species Recovery Plan Series no. 6).

O'DONNELL, C. F. J. AND MOORE, S. G. M. (1983) *The wildlife and conservation of braided river systems in Canterbury.* Wellington: New Zealand Wildlife Service (Fauna Survey Unit Report 33).

O'DONNELL, C. F. J. AND RASCH, G. (1991) *Conservation of Kaka in New Zealand. A review of status, threats, priorities for research and implications for management.* Wellington: Department of Conservation (Science and Research Internal Report 101).

OGLE, D. (1986) The status and seasonality of birds in Nakhon Sawan Province, Thailand. *Nat. Hist. Bull. Siam Soc.* 34: 115–143.

OHSAKO, Y. (1987) Effects of artificial feeding on cranes wintering in Izumi and Ikune, Japan. Pp.89–98 in G. W. Archibald and R. F. Pasquier, eds. *Proceedings of the 1983 International Crane Workshop.* Baraboo, U.S.A.: International Crane Foundation.

OLMOS, F. (1993) Birds of Serra da Capivara National Park in the 'caatinga' of north-eastern Brazil. *Bird Conserv. Internatn.* 3: 21–36.

OLROG, C. C. (1979) Notas ornitológicas, XI: sobre la colección del Instituto Miguel Lillo. *Acta Zool. Lilloana* 33: 5–7.

OLSEN, P. D. AND OLSEN, J. (1986) Distribution, status, movements and breeding of the Grey Falcon *Falco hypoleucos. Emu* 86: 47–51.

OLSON, S. R. (1994) The endemic vireo of Fernando de Noronha (*Vireo gracilirostris*). *Wilson Bull.* 106: 1–17.

OLSSON, U., ALSTRÖM, P. AND COLSTON, P. R. (1993) A new species of *Phylloscopus* warbler from Hainan Island, China. *Ibis* 135: 2–7.

OSTAPENKO, W. A. AND ZEWENMJADAG, N. (1983) Über Verbreitung, Anzahl und Biologie der Kraniche im Ostteil der Mongolischen Volksrepublik. *Beitr. Vogelkunde* 29: 274–278.

PANDE, P., KOTHARI, A. AND SINGH, S. (1991) *Andaman and Nicobar Islands.* New Delhi: Indian Institute of Public Administration.

PARKER, T. A. AND BAILEY, B. (1991) *A biological assessment of the Alto Madidi region and adjacent areas of northwest Bolivia, May 18–June 15, 1990.* Washington, D.C.: Conservation International.

PARKER, T. A. AND CARR, J. L., EDS. (1992) *Status of forest remnants in the Cordillera de la Costa and adjacent areas of southwestern Ecuador (Rapid Assessment Program).* Washington, D.C.: Conservation International.

PARKER, V. (in press) *Swaziland bird atlas 1985–1991.* Mbabane: Webster's.

PARR, J. W. K., LAOTHONG, P. AND RUANGSREE, G. (1994) The status of White-winged Wood Duck *Cairina scutulata* in Thailand. *Tigerpaper* 21: 1–7.

PARR, S. AND YARAR, M. (1993) Preliminary results from a Lesser Kestrel survey of Turkey, Spring 1993. *Bull. Orn. Soc. Middle East* 31: 8–10.

PATERSON, A. M., MARTÍNEZ-VILALTA, A. AND DIES, J. I. (1992) Partial breeding failure of Audouin's Gull in two Spanish colonies in 1991. *Brit. Birds* 85: 97–100.

PATTEE, O. H., BLOOM, P. H., SCOTT, J. M. AND SMITH, M. R. (1990) Lead hazards within the range of the California Condor. *Condor* 92: 931–937.

PAZ, U. (1987) *The birds of Israel*. London: Christopher Helm.

PEARMAN, M. AND ABADIE, E. I. (in press) Mesopotamia grasslands and wetlands survey, 1991–1993: conservation of threatened birds and habitat in north-east Argentina.

PENG, Y., YANG, L., LIU, G. AND ZHENG, B. (1980) [*Report on studies of vertebrates in the Gaoligong mountain district, 2: birds*.] Beijing, China: Scientific Publishing House. (In Chinese.)

PETERSEN, S. (1991) A record of White-shouldered Ibis in East Kalimantan. *Kukila* 5: 144–145.

PETERSON, A. T. (1993) Species status of *Geotrygon carrikeri*. *Bull. Brit. Orn. Club* 113: 166–168.

PHILLIPS, A. R. (1986) *The known birds of North and Middle America*, 1. Denver, Colorado: Allan R. Phillips.

PHILLIPS, N. R. (1982) Observations on the birds of North Yemen. *Sandgrouse* 4: 37–59.

PIATT, J. F. AND GOULD, P. J. (in press) Endangered Japanese Murrelets: incidental catch in high seas driftnets and post-breeding dispersal. *Auk*.

PIERCE, R. J. (1986) Differences in susceptibility to predation during nesting between Pied and Black Stilts (*Himantopus* spp.). *Auk* 103: 273–280.

PIERSMA, T. (1986) Coastal waders on three Canary Islands in March–April 1986. *Wader Study Group Bull.* 48 (Suppl.): 19–20.

PINTO, A. A. DA R. (1962) As observações de maior destaque das expedições ornitológicas do Instituto de Investigação Científica de Angola. *Bol. Inst. Invest. Cient. Angola* 1: 21–38.

PLETSCHET, S. M. AND KELLY, J. F. (1990) Breeding biology and nesting success of Palila. *Condor* 92: 1012–1021.

POKORNY, F. AND PIKULA, J. (1987) Artificial breeding, rearing and release of Reeves Pheasant (*Syrmaticus reevesi*) (Gray 1929) in Czechoslovakia. *World Pheasant Assoc. J.* 12: 75–80.

POOLE, C. (in prep.) Status of Baikal Teal *Anas formosa*.

POONSWAD, P. (1993) Forest flagships. *World Birdwatch* 15(3): 14–17.

POTAPOV, E. (1992) Some breeding observations on the Siberian White Crane *Grus leucogeranus* in the Kolyma lowlands. *Bird Conserv. Internatn.* 2: 149–156.

POTAPOV, R. L. AND FLINT, V. E., EDS. (1987) [*Birds of the U.S.S.R.: Galliformes, Gruiformes*.] Leningrad: Nauka. (In Russian.)

POULSEN, M. K. (in press) The status and conservation of the threatened birds in the Sierra Madre mountains, northern Luzon, Philippines. *Bird Conserv. Internatn.*

POULSEN, M. K. AND WEGE, D. (1994) Coppery-chested Jacamar *Galbula pastazae*. *Cotinga* 2: 60–62.

POWELL, G. V. N. AND BJORK, R. D. (1993) Intratropical migrations of Three-wattled Bellbirds: identifying habitat linkages to protect biodiversity. Progress report, November 31 [*sic*], 1993.

POWLESLAND, R. G. AND LLOYD, B. D. (1994) Use of supplementary feeding to induce breeding in free-living Kakapo *Strigops habroptilus* in New Zealand. *Biol. Conserv.* 69: 97–106.

PRATT, H. D. (1993) *Enjoying birds in Hawaii: a birdfinding guide to the fiftieth state*. Honolulu: Mutual Publishing.

PRATT, H. D. (1994) Avifaunal change in the Hawaiian Islands, 1893–1993. *Stud. Avian Biol.* 15: 103–118.

PRATT, H. D., BRUNER, P. L. AND BERRETT, D. G. (1987) *A field guide to the birds of Hawaii and the tropical Pacific*. Princeton: Princeton University Press.

PRATT, T., GAGNÉ, B. AND CASEY, T. (1993) Poo'uli again seen at Hanawi. *Hawaii's Forest and Wildlife* 8: 1,9.

PRIGOGINE, A. (1984) Note sur deux gladiateurs (*Malaconotus*). *Gerfaut* 74: 75–81.

PRIGOGINE, A. (1985) Conservation of the avifauna of the forests of the Albertine Rift. Pp.277–295 in A. W. Diamond and T. E. Lovejoy, eds. *Conservation of tropical forest birds*. Cambridge, U.K.: International Council for Bird Preservation (Techn. Publ. 4).

PRIGOGINE, A. AND LOUETTE, M. (1984) A new race of the Spotted Ground-thrush, *Zoothera guttata*, from Upemba, Zaire. *Gerfaut* 74: 185–186.

PUKINSKIY, Y. B. (1973) [Ecology of Blakiston's Fish Owl in the Bikin river basin.] *Byull. Mosk. Obshch. Ispyt. Prir. Otd. Biol.* 78: 40–47.

RAFFAELE, H. A. (1989) *A guide to the birds of Puerto Rico and the Virgin Islands*. Revised edition. San Juan: Fondo Educativo Interamericano.

RAHMANI, A. (1986) Grassland birds of the Indian subcontinent: a review. Pp.187–204 in P. D. Goriup, ed. *Ecology and conservation of grassland birds*. Cambridge, U.K.: International Council for Bird Preservation (Techn. Publ. 7).

RAHMANI, A. R. (1987) Protection for the great Indian bustard. *Oryx* 21: 174–179.

RAHMANI, A. R. (1989) *The Great Indian Bustard: final report*. Bombay: Bombay Natural History Society.

RAHMANI, A. R. (1993) Little-known bird: White-browed Bushchat. *Bull. Oriental Bird Club* 17: 28–30.

RAHMANI, A. R. AND MANAKADAM, R. (1985) Present status of the Great Indian Bustard. *Bustard Studies* 3: 123–131.

RAHMANI, A. R. AND MANAKADAM, R. (1990) The past and present distribution of the Great Indian Bustard *Ardeotis nigriceps* (Vigors) in India. *J. Bombay Nat. Hist. Soc.* 87: 175–194.

RAHMANI, A. R., NARAYAN, G., ROSALIND, L. AND SANKARAN, R. (1990) Status of the Bengal Florican in India. Pp.55–82 in *Status and ecology of the Lesser and Bengal Floricans with reports on Jerdon's Courser and Mountain Quail: final report*. Bombay: Bombay Natural History Society.

RAHMANI, A. R., NARAYAN, G., ROSALIND, L., SANKARAN, R. AND GANGULI, U. (1991) Status of the Bengal Florican *Houbaropsis bengalensis* in India. *J. Bombay Nat. Hist. Soc.* 88: 349–375.

RAI, Y. M. (1986) The birds of Delhi and Meerut. *J. Bombay Nat. Hist. Soc.* 83: 212–214.

RAND, A. L. AND GILLIARD, E. T. (1967) *Handbook of New Guinea birds*. London: Weidenfeld and Nicolson.

RASCH, G. (1992) Kokako recovery. *Forest and Bird* 23(2): 28–32.

RASCH, G. AND MCCLELLAND, P. (1993) South Island Saddlebacks transferred to Breaksea Island. *Notornis* 40: 229–231.

RAUZON, M. J. (1991) Save our shearwaters! *Living Bird Quarterly* 10: 29–32.

RAXWORTHY, C. J. AND COLSTON, P. R. (1992) Conclusive evidence for the continuing existence of the Madagascar Serpent-eagle *Eutriorchis astur*. *Bull. Brit. Orn. Club* 112: 108–111.

RAZAFIMAHAIMODISON, J.-C. AND ANDRIANANTENAINA, R. (1993) Ecologie et comportement des groupes d'oiseaux dans une forêt dense humide de Madagascar. *Proc. 8 Pan-Afr. Orn. Congr.* [*Ann. Sci. Zool. Mus. Roy. Afrique Centr.* 286]: 197–200.

REDMAN, N. (1993) Two new species of birds for the Philippines and other notable records. *Forktail* 8: 119–124.

REED, S. (1980) Birds of Savai'i, Western Samoa. *Notornis* 27: 151–159.

REICHEL, J. D., WILES, G. J. AND GLASS, P. O. (1992) Island extinctions: the case of the endangered Nightingale Reed-warbler. *Wilson Bull.* 104: 44–54.

RENJIFO, L. M. (1994) First records of the Bay-vented Cotinga *Doliornis remseni* in Colombia. *Bull. Brit. Orn. Club* 114: 101–103.

REPPPROT (1990) *National overview of the regional physical planning programme for transmigration.* Chatham, U.K.: Overseas Development Natural Resources Institute.

RESIDE, J. (1991) Matawevi is alive and well: the search for the Santo Mountain Starling. *Wingspan* 4: 10–11.

REVILLE, B. J. AND STOKES, T. (1994) Conservation of seabirds on Christmas Island, Indian Ocean. Pp.244–257 in D. N. Nettleship, J. Burger and M. Gochfeld, eds. *Seabirds on islands: threats, case studies and action plans.* Cambridge, U.K.: BirdLife International (BirdLife Conservation Series no. 1).

RICHARDSON, S. A. (1994) Status of the Short-tailed Albatross on Midway Atoll. *'Elepaio* 54.

RIDGELY, R. S. (1981) The current distribution and status of mainland Neotropical parrots. Pp.233–384 in R. F. Pasquier, ed. *Conservation of New World Parrots.* Washington, D.C.: Smithsonian Institution Press for the International Council for Bird Preservation (Techn. Publ. 1).

RIDGELY, R. S. AND GWYNNE, J. A. (1989) *A guide to the birds of Panama with Costa Rica, Nicaragua, and Honduras.* Second edition. Princeton: Princeton University Press.

RIDGELY, R. S. AND TUDOR, G. (1989) *The birds of South America*, 1. Austin: University of Texas Press.

RINKE, D. (1986) The status of wildlife in Tonga. *Oryx* 20: 146–151.

RINKE, D. R. (1991) Birds of 'Ata and Late, and additional notes on the avifauna of Niuafo'ou, Kingdom of Tonga. *Notornis* 38: 131–151.

RINKE, D. (1993) Safe islands for the Malau. *OSNZ News* 69: 1.

RIPLEY, S. D. (1976) Reconsideration of *Athene blewitti* (Hume). *J. Bombay Nat. Hist. Soc.* 73: 1–4.

RIPLEY, S. D. (1977) *Rails of the world.* Toronto: M. F. Feheley.

RIPLEY, S. D. (1982) *A synopsis of the birds of India and Pakistan together with those of Nepal, Bhutan, Bangladesh and Sri Lanka.* Second edition. Bombay: Bombay Natural History Society.

RIPLEY, S. D. AND BOND, G. M. (1966) The birds of Socotra and Abd-el-Kuril. *Smithsonian Misc. Coll.* 151 (7).

RIPLEY, S. D., SAHA, S. S. AND BEEHLER, B. M. (1991) Notes on birds from the Upper Noa Dihang, Arunachal Pradesh, northeastern India. *Bull. Brit. Orn. Club* 111: 19–27.

ROBBINS, M. B., ROSENBERG, G. H. AND SORNOZA MOLINA, F. (1994) A new species of cotinga (Cotingidae: *Doliornis*) from the Ecuadorian Andes, with comments on plumage

sequences in *Doliornis* and *Ampelion. Auk* 111: 1–7.

ROBERTS, P. (1987) Is the Aldabra brush warbler extinct? *Oryx* 21: 209–210.

ROBERTS, T. J. (1991) *The birds of Pakistan*, 1. Karachi: Oxford University Press.

ROBERTS, T. J. (1992) *The birds of Pakistan*, 2. Karachi: Oxford University Press.

ROBERTSON, A. S. AND BOSHOFF, A. F. (1986) The feeding ecology of Cape Vultures *Gyps coprotheres* in a stock-farming area. *Biol. Conserv.* 35: 63–86.

ROBERTSON, C. J. R., ED. (1985) *Complete book of New Zealand birds.* Sydney: Reader's Digest.

ROBERTSON, C. J. R. AND BELL, B. D. (1984) Seabird status and conservation in the New Zealand region. Pp.573–586 in J. P. Croxall, P. G. H. Evans and R. W. Schreiber, eds. *Status and conservation of the world's seabirds.* Cambridge, U.K.: International Council for Bird Preservation (Techn. Publ. 2).

ROBERTSON, C. J. R. AND VAN TETS, G. F. (1982) The status of birds at the Bounty Islands. *Notornis* 29: 311–336.

ROBERTSON, C. J. R., O'DONNELL, C. F. J. AND OVERMARS, F. B. (1983) *Habitat requirements of wetland birds in the Ahuriri River catchment.* Wellington: Department of Internal Affairs (New Zealand Wildlife Service Occas. Publ. 3).

ROBERTSON, H. A., COLBOURNE, R. M. AND NIEUWLAND, F. (1993) Survival of Little Spotted Kiwi and other forest birds exposed to brodifacoum rat poison on Red Mercury Island. *Notornis* 40: 253–262.

ROBINET, O., BEUGNET, F., DULIEU, D. AND CHARDONNET, P. (in press) The Ouvea Horned Parakeet, *Eunymphicus cornutus uvaeensis*: state of knowledge and conservation status. *Oryx.*

ROBSON, C. (1989) Birdwatching areas: Omei Shan, Sichuan, China. *Bull. Oriental Bird Club* 9: 16–21.

ROBSON, C. R., EAMES, J. C., WOLSTENCROFT, J. A., NGUYEN CU AND TRUONG VAN LA (1989) Recent records of birds from Viet Nam. *Forktail* 5: 71–98.

ROBSON, C. R., EAMES, J. C., NEWMAN, M., NGUYEN CU AND TRUONG VAN LA (1991) Forest bird surveys in Vietnam 1989/90: final report. Cambridge, U.K.: International Council for Bird Preservation (unpublished report).

ROBSON, C. R., EAMES, J. C., NGUYEN CU AND TRUONG VAN LA (1993a) Further records of birds from Viet Nam. *Forktail* 8: 25–52.

ROBSON, C. R., EAMES, J. C., NGUYEN CU AND TRUONG VAN LA (1993b) Birds recorded during the third BirdLife/ Forest Birds Working Group expedition in Viet Nam. *Forktail* 9: 89–120.

ROSE, P. M. AND SCOTT, D. A. (1994) *Waterfowl population estimates.* Slimbridge, U.K.: International Waterfowl and Wetlands Research Bureau (IWRB Spec. Publ. 29).

ROSELAAR, C. S. (1992) A new species of mountain finch *Leucosticte* from western Tibet. *Bull. Brit. Orn. Club* 112: 225–231.

ROUND, P. D. (1988) *Resident forest birds in Thailand: their status and conservation.* Cambridge, U.K.: International Council for Bird Preservation (Monogr. 2).

ROUND, P. D. AND TREESUCON, U. (1986) The rediscovery of Gurney's Pitta *Pitta gurneyi. Forktail* 2: 53–66.

ROUX, J.-P., JOUVENTIN, P., MOUGIN, J.-L., STAHL, J.-C. AND WEIMERSKIRCH, H. (1983) Un nouvel albatros *Diomedea amsterdamensis* n. sp. découvert sur l'île

Amsterdam (37°50′S 77°35′E). *Oiseau et R.F.O.* 53: 1–11.

ROWE, S. AND MEMBERS OF THE TANGA'EO RESEARCH GROUP (1993) The Tanga'eo Research Group Project, Mangaia, Cook Islands (13 October to 8 December). Unpublished report to the Cook Islands Natural Heritage Project.

ROZENDAAL, F. G. AND DEKKER, R. W. R. J. (1989) Annotated checklist of the birds of the Dumoga-Bone National Park, North Sulawesi. *Kukila* 4: 85–109.

ROZENDAAL, F., NGUYEN CU, TRUONG VAN LA AND VO QUY (1991) Notes on Vietnamese pheasants, with description of female plumage of *Lophura hatinhensis*. *Dutch Birding* 13: 12–15.

RUDYANTO (in press) White-winged Wood Duck in Indonesia—the untold story. *Asian Wetland News* 7.

SAFFORD, R. J. (1991) Status and ecology of the Mauritius Fody *Foudia rubra* and Mauritius Olive White-eye *Zosterops chloronothos*: two Mauritian passerines in danger. *Dodo* 27: 113–138.

SAFFORD, R. J. (1992) Status in 1991 of the smaller native landbirds of Mauritius and Rodrigues. *Newsletter of the Working Group on Birds in the Madagascar Region* 2: 1–4.

SAFFORD, R. J. (1993a) Rediscovery, taxonomy and conservation of the Anjouan Scops Owl *Otus capnodes* (Gurney 1889). *Bird Conserv. Internatn.* 3: 57–74.

SAFFORD, R. J. (1993b) The Madagascar Teal *Anas bernieri*: a preliminary survey from Antsalova to Morondava. *Dodo* 29: 95–102.

SAFFORD, R. J. (in prep.) Populations, distribution and status of the native passerines of Mauritius.

SAFFORD, R. J. AND EVANS, M. I. (1992) Birds on the Comoro Islands, April 1991. *Scopus* 15: 93–101.

SALAMAN, P. AND GANDY, D. (1993) Colombia '93: Thunder Lake Expedition. Preliminary report.

SALAMAN, P. AND GANDY, D. (1994) Wildlife surveys: birds. Pp.26–49 in P. Salaman, ed. *Surveys and conservation of biodiversity in the Chocó, south-west Colombia*. Cambridge, U.K.: BirdLife International (Study Report 61).

SALAMAN, P. G. W. AND STILES, F. G. (in prep.) A distinctive new species of vireo (Passeriformes: Vireonidae) from the Western Andes of Colombia.

SALTER, R. E. (1983) *Summary of currently available information on internationally threatened wildlife species in Burma*. Rangoon: Food and Agricultural Organization of the United Nations (Working People's Settlement Board, Nature Conservation and National Parks Project, Burma, FAO: Buar/80/006 Field Document 7/83).

SALTER, R. E., ED. (1993) *Wildlife in Lao P.D.R.: a status report*. Vientiane, Laos: International Union for Conservation of Nature and Natural Resources.

SANE, S. R., KANNAN, P., RAJENDRAN, C. G., INGLE, S. T. AND BHAGWAT, A. M. (1986) On the taxonomic status of *Psittacula intermedia* (Rothschild). *J. Bombay Nat. Hist. Soc.* 83 (Supplement).

SANKARAN, R. (1990a) Mountain Quail: a preliminary survey. Pp.135–140 in *Status and ecology of the Lesser and Bengal Floricans with reports on Jerdon's Courser and Mountain Quail*. Bombay: Bombay Natural History Society.

SANKARAN, R. (1990b) Ecology and behaviour of the Lesser Florican. Pp.85–94 in *Status and ecology of the Lesser and Bengal Floricans with reports on Jerdon's Courser and Mountain Quail: final report*. Bombay: Bombay Natural History Society.

SANKARAN, R. (1993a) *A study of the ecology, status and conservation perspectives of certain rare endemic avifauna of the Andaman and Nicobar Islands*. Coimbatore, India: Salim Ali Centre for Ornithology and Natural History.

SANKARAN, R. (1993b) *The status and conservation of the Nicobar Scrubfowl* Megapodius nicobariensis. Coimbatore, India: Salim Ali Centre for Ornithology and Natural History.

SANKARAN, R. AND RAHMANI, A. R. (1990) Status of the Lesser Florican in western India. Pp.101–112 in *Status and ecology of the Lesser and Bengal Floricans with reports on Jerdon's Courser and Mountain Quail: final report*. Bombay: Bombay Natural History Society.

SANKARAN, R., LACHUNGPA, U. G. AND LACHUNGPA, G. (1990) Survey of some wintering habitats of Lesser Florican in southern India. Pp.113–116 in *Status and ecology of the Lesser and Bengal Floricans with reports on Jerdon's Courser and Mountain Quail: final report*. Bombay: Bombay Natural History Society.

SANKARAN, R., RAHMANI, A. R. AND GANGULI-LACHUNGPA, U. (1992) The distribution and status of the Lesser Florican *Sypheotides indica* (J. F. Miller) in the Indian subcontinent. *J. Bombay Nat. Hist. Soc.* 89: 156–179.

SANTAELLA, L. AND SADA, A. M. (1991) The avifauna of the Revillagigedo Islands, Mexico: additional data and observations. *Wilson Bull.* 103: 668–675.

SARGEANT, D. (1992) A birder's guide to Mauritius and Réunion. Unpublished.

SARGEANT, D. (1994) Recent ornithological observations from São Tomé and Príncipe Islands. *Bull. African Bird Club* 1: 96–102.

SARGEANT, D. E., GULLICK, T., TURNER, D. A. AND SINCLAIR, J. C. (1992) The rediscovery of the São Tomé Grosbeak *Neospiza concolor* in south-western São Tomé. *Bird Conserv. Internatn.* 2: 157–159.

SAVAGE, C. D. W. (1988) Recent publications (book reviews). *World Peasant Assoc. J.* 13: 69–70.

SCHMID, C. K. (1993) Birds of Nokopo. *Muruk* 6: 2.

SCHMIDL, D. (1982) *The birds of the Serengeti National Park Tanzania*. London: British Ornithologists' Union (Check-list 5).

SCHMIDT, M. (1986) Specific notes on the Paradise Parrot. *Bird Keeping in Australia* 29: 50–51.

SCHMUTZ, E. (1977) *Die Vögel der Manggarai (Flores)*. Ruteng, Flores: privately published.

SCHNEIDER-JACOBY, M. (1991) Verbreitung und Bestand des Wachtelkönigs in Jugoslawien. *Vogelwelt* 112: 48–57.

SCHODDE, R. (1978) The status of endangered Papuasian birds, and Appendix. Pp.133–145 and 185–206 respectively in M. J. Tyler, ed. *The status of endangered Australasian wildlife*. Adelaide: Royal Zoological Society of South Australia.

SCHODDE, R. AND WEATHERLY, R. G. (1983) Campbell's Fairy-wren *Malurus campbelli*, a new species from New Guinea. *Emu* 82: 308–309.

SCHODDE, R., FULLAGAR, P. AND HERMES, N. (1983) *A review of Norfolk Island birds: past and present*. Canberra: Australian National Parks and Wildlife Service (Spec. Publ. 8).

SCHODDE, R., MASON, I. J. AND WOOD, J. T. (1993) Geographical differentiation in the Glossy Black-cockatoo *Calyptorhynchus lathami* (Temminck) and its history. *Emu* 93: 156–166.

SCHUBEL, S., JOLLY, J. AND JONES, P. J. (in press) Behaviour and annual cycle of the Henderson Rail. *Biol. J. Linn. Soc.*

SCHUCKARD, R. (1994) New Zealand King Shag (*Leucocarbo carunculatus*) on Duffers Reef, Marlborough Sounds. *Notornis*: 93–108.

SCHULZ, H. AND SCHULZ, M. (1992) New records of the Bald Ibis (*Geronticus eremita*) from Saudi Arabia. *J. Orn.* 133: 165–172.

SCHULZE-HAGEN, K. (1989) Bekanntes und weniger Bekanntes vom Seggenrohrsänger *Acrocephalus paludicola*. *Limicola* 3: 229–246.

SCOFIELD, P. (1990) The status of Cook's Petrel on Great Barrier Island. *Notornis* 37: 130.

SCOTT, D. A. (1989) *A directory of Asian wetlands*. Gland, Switzerland and Cambridge, U.K.: International Union for Conservation of Nature and Natural Resources.

SCOTT, D. A. (1993) The Black-necked Cranes *Grus nigricollis* of Ruoergai Marshes, Sichuan, China. *Bird Conserv. Internatn.* 3: 245–259.

SCOTT, D. A. AND BROOKE, M. DE L. (1993) Rediscovery of the Grey-winged Cotinga *Tijuca condita* in south-eastern Brazil. *Bird Conserv. Internatn.* 3: 1–12.

SCOTT, D. A. AND CARBONELL, M. (1986) *A directory of Neotropical wetlands*. Cambridge and Slimbridge, U.K.: International Union for Conservation of Nature and Natural Resources and International Waterfowl Research Bureau.

SCOTT, J. M., MOUNTAINSPRING, S., RAMSEY, F. L. AND KEPLER, C. B. (1986) *Forest bird communities of the Hawaiian Islands: their dynamics, ecology, and conservation*. California: Cooper Ornithological Society (Studies in Avian Biology 9).

SCOTT, K. (1991) World first: bird survives baptism. *BBC Wildlife* 9: 534.

SEAL, U. S. AND BRUFORD, M. W. (1991) *Columba (Nesoenas) mayeri* Pink Pigeon: conservation viability assessment workshop report. International Union for Conservation of Nature and Natural Resource, Species Survival Commission and Captive Breeding Specialist Group. Unpublished.

SEITRE, R. AND SEITRE, J. (1991) *Causes de disparition des oiseaux terrestres de Polynésie Française*. Nouméa: South Pacific Regional Environment Programme (Occas. Pap. Series 8).

SEITRE, R. AND SEITRE, J. (1992) Causes of land-bird extinctions in French Polynesia. *Oryx* 26: 215–222.

SERPELL, J., COLLAR, N., DAVIS, S. AND WELLS, S. (1983) Submission to the Foreign and Commonwealth Office on the future conservation of Henderson Island in the Pitcairn Group. Unpublished.

SEVERINGHAUS, L. L. (1989) *Endangered birds in Taiwan. Proceedings of the Joint Meeting of International Council for Bird Preservation Asia Section and East Asia Bird Protection Conference, Bangkok, Thailand. April 1989*. Bangkok: International Council for Bird Preservation (abstract only).

SEVERINGHAUS, L. L., LIANG, C. T., SEVERINGHAUS, S. R. AND LO, L. C. (1991) The distribution, status and breeding of Fairy Pitta *Pitta nympha* in Taiwan. *Bull. Inst. Zool., Acad. Sinica* 30: 41–47.

SHELDON, B. C. AND DUCKWORTH, J. W. (1990) Rediscovery of the Madagascar Serpent-eagle *Eutriorchis astur*. *Bull. Brit. Orn. Club* 110: 126–130.

SHERRY, T. W. (1985) Adaptation to a novel environment: food, foraging, and morphology of the Cocos Island Flycatcher. Pp.908–920 in P. A. Buckley, M. S. Foster, E. S. Morton, R. S. Ridgely and F. G. Buckley, eds. *Neotropical ornithology*. Washington, D.C.: American Ornithologists' Union (Orn. Monogr. 36).

SHIBAEV, YU. A. (1987) Interim report on population survey of Steller's Sea-Eagle in winter in USSR. Pp.48 in *The Third Japan-USSR Bird Protection Symposium, 21 November 1986*. [Tokyo]: Wild Bird Society of Japan (summary).

SHORT, L. L. (1973) Habits, relationshiops and conservation of the Okinawa Woodpecker. *Wilson Bull.* 85: 5–20.

SHORT, L. L. (1982) *Woodpeckers of the world*. Greenville, Delaware: Delaware Museum of Natural History (Monogr. Ser. 4).

SHORT, L. L., HORNE, J. F. M. AND MURINGO-GICHUKI, C. (1990) Annotated check-list of the birds of East Africa. *Proc. West. Found. Vert. Zool.* 4(3).

SIBLEY, C. G. (1951) Notes on the birds of New Georgia, central Solomon Islands. *Condor* 53: 81–92.

SIBLEY, C. G. AND MONROE, B. L. (1990) *Distribution and taxonomy of birds of the world*. New Haven: Yale University Press.

SIBLEY, C. G. AND MONROE, B. L. (1993) *A supplement to distribution and taxonomy of birds of the world*. New Haven: Yale University Press.

SICK, H. (1985) *Ornitologia brasileira, uma introdução*. Brasília: Editora Universidade de Brasília.

SIEBERS, H. C. (1930) Fauna Buruana. *Aves* 5 (Suppl.): 164–303.

SIEGEL-CAUSEY, D. (1991) Systematics and biogeography of North Pacific shags, with a description of a new species. *Occas. Pap. Univ. Kansas Mus. Nat. Hist.* 140: 1–17.

SIEGEL-CAUSEY, D., LEFEVRE, C. AND SAVINETSKII, A. B. (1991) Historical diversity of cormorants and shags from Amchitka Island, Alaska. *Condor* 93: 840–852.

SILVIUS, M. J. AND VERHEUGT, W. J. M. (1989) The status of storks, ibises and spoonbills in Indonesia. *Kukila* 4: 119–132.

SIMONS, T. R. (1985) Biology and behaviour of the endangered Hawaiian Dark-rumped Petrel. *Condor* 87: 229–245.

SIMPSON, D. M. (1990) Heinroth's Shearwater off Bougainville Island January 1990. *Sea Swallow* 39: 64–65.

SIMPSON, D. M. (in press) Further notes from Papua New Guinea. *Sea Swallow* 43.

SINGH, P. (in press) Recent bird records from Arunachal Pradesh. *Forktail*.

SKERRETT, A. AND BULLOCK, I. (1992) *A birdwatchers' guide to Seychelles*. Perry, Huntingdon, U.K.: Prion.

SLUD, P. (1964) The birds of Costa Rica: distribution and ecology. *Bull. Amer. Mus. Nat. Hist.* 128.

SLUD, P. (1967) The birds of Cocos Island. *Bull. Amer. Mus. Nat. Hist.* 134: 261–296.

SMIET, A. C. (1985) Notes on the field status and trade in Moluccan parrots. *Biol. Conserv.* 34: 181–194.

SMITH, E. F. G., ARCTANDER, P., FJELDSÅ, J. AND GEDOW AMIR, O. (1991) A new species of shrike (Laniidae:

Laniarius) from Somalia, verified by DNA sequence data from the only known individual. *Ibis* 133: 227–235.

SMITH, J. N. M. AND SWEATMAN, H. P. A. (1976) Feeding habits and morphological variation in Cocos Finches. *Condor* 78: 244–248.

SMITH, T. B. AND MCNIVEN, D. (1993) Preliminary survey of the avifauna of Mt Tchabal Mbabo, west-central Cameroon. *Bird Conserv. Internatn.* 3: 13–19.

SMYTHIES, B. E. (1981) *The birds of Borneo.* Third edition. Kuala Lumpur: The Sabah Society and The Malayan Nature Society.

SMYTHIES, B. E. (1986) *The birds of Burma.* Liss, Hampshire and Pickering, Ontario: Nimrod Press and Silvio Mattacchione.

SNOW, B. K. AND SNOW, D. W. (1969) Observations on the Lava Gull *Larus fuliginosus. Ibis* 111: 30–35.

SONOBE, K. (1982) *A field guide to the birds of Japan.* Tokyo: Wild Bird Society of Japan.

SONOBE, K. AND IZAWA, N. (1987) *Endangered bird species in the Korean Peninsula.* Tokyo: Museum of Korean Nature (Korea University in Tokyo), and Wild Bird Society of Japan.

SOPHASAN, S. AND DOBIAS, R. (1984) The fate of the 'princess bird', or White-eyed River Martin (*Pseudochelidon sirintarae*). *Nat. Hist. Bull. Siam Soc.* 32: 1–10.

SOROKIN, A. G. AND KOTYUKOV, Y. V. (1987) Discovery of the nesting ground of the Ob River population of the Siberian Crane. Pp.209–212 in G. W. Archibald and R. F. Pasquier, eds. *Proceedings of the 1983 International Crane Workshop.* Baraboo, U.S.A.: International Crane Foundation.

SOUZA, D. (1992) Novas espécies na Bahia. *O Chorão* 17: 16.

STAGG, A. H. (1984)*The birds of S.W. Saudi Arabia.* Riyadh: A. H. Stagg.

STATTERSFIELD, A. J., CROSBY, M. J., LONG, A. J. AND WEGE, D. C. (in prep.) *Global directory of endemic bird areas.* Cambridge, U.K.: BirdLife International (BirdLife Conservation Series).

STAUS, N. (1994) Observations on the West Indian Whistling-duck in the Bahamas. *IWRB Threatened Waterfowl Research Group Newsletter* 5: 13–14.

STEADMAN, D. W. (1989) Extinctions of birds in Eastern Polynesia: a review of the records and comparisons with other Pacific Island Groups.*J. Archaeol. Sci.* 16: 177–205.

STEVENS, J., HERREMANS, M. AND LOUETTE, M. (1992) Conserving the endemic birds of the Comoro Islands, II: population fluctuations on Ngazidja. *Bird Conserv. Internatn.* 2: 81–91.

STILES, F. G. (1992) A new species of antpitta (Formicariidae: *Grallaria*) from the Eastern Andes of Colombia. *Wilson Bull.* 104: 389–399.

STILES, F. G. AND SKUTCH, A. F. (1989)*A guide to the birds of Costa Rica.* London: Christopher Helm.

STINSON, D. W. AND GLASS, P. O. (1992) The Micronesian Megapode *Megapodius laperouse*: conservation and research needs. *Zool. Verhandel.* 278: 53–55.

STOKES, T. (1979) On the possible existence of the New Caledonian Wood Rail*Tricholimnas lafresnayanus. Bull. Brit. Orn. Club* 99: 47–54.

STOKES, T. (1980) Notes on the landbirds of New Caledonia. *Emu* 80: 81–86.

STOKES, T. (1988) *A review of the birds of Christmas Island, Indian Ocean.* Canberra: Australian National Parks

and Wildlife Service (Occas. Pap. 16).

STOWE, T. J. AND BECKER, D. (1992) Status and conservation of Corncrakes*Crex crex* outside the breeding grounds. *Tauraco* 2: 1–23.

STOWE, T. J., NEWTON, A. V., GREEN, R. E. AND MAYES, E. (1993) The decline of the Corncrake *Crex crex* in Britain and Ireland in relation to habitat.*J. Appl. Ecol.* 30: 53–62.

STRESEMANN, E. (1940) Die Vögel von Celebes.*J. Orn.* 88: 1–135.

STRESEMANN, E. AND PORTENKO, L. A., EDS. (1982) *Atlas der Verbreitung Palaearktischer Vögel.* Berlin: Akademie-Verlag.

STUART, S. N. AND COLLAR, N. J. (1986) Subspeciation in the Karamoja Apalis *Apalis karamojae. Bull. Brit. Orn. Club* 105: 86–89.

STUART, S. N. AND JENSEN, F. P. (1986) The status and ecology of montane forest bird species in western Cameroon. Pp.38–105 in S. N. Stuart, ed. *Conservation of Cameroon montane forests.* Cambridge, U.K.: International Council for Bird Preservation.

STUART, S. N., JENSEN, F. P. AND BRØGGER-JENSEN, S. (1987) Altitudinal zonation of the avifauna in Mwanihana and Magombera forests, eastern Tanzania. *Gerfaut* 77: 165–186.

STUART, S. N., JENSEN, F. P., BRØGGER-JENSEN, S. AND MILLER, R. I. (1993) The zoogeography of the montane forest avifauna of eastern Tanzania. Pp.203–228 in J. C. Lovett and S. K. Wasser, eds. *Biogeography and ecology of the rain forests of East Africa.* Cambridge, U.K.: Cambridge University Press.

STUDHOLME, B. J. S., RUSS, R. B. AND MCLEAN, I. G. (1994) The Fiordland Crested Penguin Survey, stage IV: Stewart and offshore islands and Solander Island. *Notornis* 41: 133–143.

SUGIMURA, K. (1988) The role of government subsidies in the population decline of some unique wildlife species on Amami Oshima, Japan. *Envir. Conserv.* 15: 49–57.

SUTHERLAND, W. J. AND CROCKFORD, N. J. (1993) Factors affecting the feeding distribution of Red-breasted Geese *Branta ruficollis* wintering in Romania. *Biol. Conserv.* 63: 61–65.

SWENNEN, C. AND WON, P.-O. (1993) Study of Chinese Egrets in the Shin Islet colony, Korea, 1991. *Bull. Inst. Orn. Kyung Hee Univ.* 4: 106–111.

SWINNERTON, K., JONES, C. AND LIDDIARD, T. (1993) Pink Pigeon in Mauritius. *Re-introduction News* no.7: 12–13.

SYVERTSEN, P. O. AND DELLELEGN, Y. (1991) The status of some bird species endemic to south Ethiopia. *Scopus* 15: 30–34.

TABARANZA, B. R. (1992) The distribution and conservation status of the Philippine Cockatoo. Unpublished.

TAKAGI, M. AND HIGUCHI, H. (1992) Habitat preference of the Izu Islands Thrush *Turdus celaenops* and the effect of weasel introduction on the population of the thrush on Miyake Island. *Strix* 11: 47–57. (In Japanese.)

TAKEISHI, M. (1987) The mass mortality of Japanese Murrelet*Synthliboramphus wumizume* on the Koyashima Islet in Fukuoka. *Bull. Kitakyushu Mus. Nat. Hist.* 7: 121–131. (In Japanese.)

TAKESHITA, M., SAMOTO, K. AND HAYASHI, O. (1993) Annual and seasonal changes in the number of wintering Saunder's Gull *Larus saundersi* at the tidal mud flat of Sone in Kitakyusyu City, Fukuoka Prefecture, Japan.

Strix 12: 107–114. (In Japanese.)

TARBOTON, W. R., KEMP, M. I. AND KEMP, A. C. (1987) *Birds of the Transvaal*. Pretoria: Transvaal Museum.

TARBURTON, M. K. (1990) Breeding biology of the Atiu Swiftlet. *Emu* 90: 175–179.

TAYLOR, C. (1993a) News from Aride. *Birdwatch (Seychelles Bird Group)* no.7: 6–8.

TAYLOR, P. B. (1994) The biology, ecology and conservation of four flufftail species, *Sarothrura* (Aves: Rallidae). Pietermaritzburg: University of Natal (Ph.D. thesis).

TAYLOR, P. B. AND TAYLOR, C. A. (1988) The status, movements and breeding of some birds in the Kikuyu Escarpment Forest, central Kenya highlands. *Tauraco* 1: 72–89.

TAYLOR, R. H. (1985) Status, habits and conservation of *Cyanoramphus* parakeets in the New Zealand region. Pp.195–211 in P. J. Moors, ed. *Conservation of island birds*. Cambridge, U.K.: International Council for Bird Preservation (Techn. Publ. 3).

TAYLOR, V. (1993b) *African waterfowl census 1993*. Slimbridge, U.K.: International Waterfowl and Wetlands Research Group.

TEMPLE, S. A. (1986) The problem of avian extinctions. Pp.453–485 in R. F. Johnston, ed. *Current Ornithology* 3. New York: Plenum Press.

THALER, E., PEGORARO, K. AND STABINGER, S. (1992) Familienbindung und Auswilderung des Waldrapps *Geronticus eremita*—ein Pilotversuch. *J. Orn.* 133: 173–180.

THEM, P. H. (1989) Black-cheeked Lovebirds. *AFA Watchbird* 16(2): 13–14.

THIBAULT, J.-C. (1988) Menaces et conservation des oiseaux de Polynésie Française. Pp.87–124 in J.-C. Thibault and I. Guyot, eds. *Livre rouge des oiseaux menacés des régions françaises d'outre-mer*. Saint-Cloud: Conseil International pour la Protection des Oiseaux (Monogr. 5).

THIBAULT, J.-C. (1989) L'avifaune des îles Eiao et Hatuta'a (Polynésie, Pacifique Sud): modifications intervenues au XXᵉ siècle. *Oiseau et R.F.O.* 59(4): 305.

THIBAULT, J.-C. AND GUYOT, I. (1987) Recent changes in the avifauna of Makatea Island (Tuamotus, Central Pacific). *Atoll Res. Bull.* 300: 1–13.

THIBAULT, J.-C. AND VARNEY, A. (1991) Numbers and habitat of the Rapa Fruit-dove *Ptilinopus huttoni*. *Bird Conserv. Internatn.* 1: 75–81.

THIOLLAY, J.-M. (1985) The birds of Ivory Coast: status and distribution. *Malimbus* 7: 1–59.

THOMPSON, H. S. (1993) Status of White-necked Picathartes—another reason for the conservation of the Peninsula Forest, Sierra Leone. *Oryx* 27: 155–158.

THOMPSON, P. M. AND EVANS, M. I., EDS. (1991) *A survey of Ambatovaky Special Reserve, Madagascar*. London: Madagascar Environmental Research Group.

THOMPSON, P. M. AND EVANS, M. I. (1992) The threatened birds of Ambatovaky Special Reserve, Madagascar. *Bird Conserv. Internatn.* 2: 221–237.

THOMPSON, P. M., RAXWORTHY, C. J., QUANSAH, N., MURDOCH, D. A. AND STEPHENSON, P. J. (1987) *Zahamena Forest (Madagascar) Expedition 1985*. Cambridge, U.K.: International Council for Bird Preservation (Study Report 20).

THOMPSON, P. M., HARVEY, W. G., JOHNSON, D. L., MILLIN, D. J., RASHID, S. M. A., SCOTT, D. A., STANFIELD, C. AND WOOLNER, J. D. (1993) Recent notable bird records from Bangladesh. *Forktail* 9: 13–44.

THOMSETT, S. (1994) The rehabilitation of a Madagascar Fish Eagle. *Kenya Birds* 2: 31–33.

THORSELL, J. W., ED. (1985) *Conserving Asia's natural heritage: planning and management of protected areas in the Indomalayan Realm*. Gland, Switzerland: International Union for Conservation of Nature and Natural Resources.

TIMMINS, R. J. (in prep.) Significant bird records from the Philippines.

TIMMINS, R. J., EVANS, T. D. AND DUCKWORTH, J. W. (1993) *A wildlife and habitat survey of Dong Hua Sao proposed protected area*. Vientiane, Laos: National Office for Nature Conservation and Watershed Management.

TOBIAS, J. A., CATSIS, M. C. AND WILLIAMS, R. S. R. (1993) Notes on scarce birds observed in southern and eastern Brazil: 24 July–7 September 1993. Unpublished report.

TODD, D. (1983) Pritchard's Megapode on Niuafo'ou Island, Kingdom of Tonga. *World Pheasant Assoc. J.* 8: 69–68.

TOLHURST, L. P. (1993) Observations from Manus Province. *Muruk* 6: 15–18.

TOMKINS, R. J. (1985) Reproduction and mortality of Wandering Albatrosses on Macquarie Island. *Emu* 85: 40–42.

TOMKOVICH, P. S. (1991) Three-year study of breeding Spoon-billed Sandpiper. *Asian Wetland News* 4: 17.

TOONE, B., ELLIS JOSEPH, S., WIRTH, R. AND SEAL, U. S. (1993) Conservation assessment and management plan for pigeons and doves: report from a workshop help 10–13 March 1993, San Diego, CA. ICBP Pigeon and Dove Specialist Group and IUCN/SSC Captive Breeding Specialist Group. Participants first draft.

TOYNE, E. P., JEFFCOTE, M. T. AND FLANAGAN, J. N. M. (1992) Status, distribution and ecology of the White-breasted Parakeet *Pyrrhura albipectus* in Podocarpus National Park, southern Ecuador. *Bird Conserv. Internatn.* 2: 327–339.

TOYNE, E. P., JEFFCOTE, M. T. AND FLANAGAN, J. N. M. (in prep.) Distribution, status, biology and conservation of the endangered Red-faced Parrot *Hapalopsittaca pyrrhops*.

TRAYLOR, M. A. (1963) Check-list of Angolan birds. *Publ. Cult. Co. Diam. Angola, Lisboa* 61.

TREVELYAN, R. (in press) The feeding ecology of Stephen's Lory. *Biol. J. Linn. Soc.*

TUCKER, G. M. AND HEATH, M. F. (1994) *Birds in Europe: their conservation status*. Cambridge, U.K.: BirdLife International (BirdLife Conservation Series no. 3).

TURBOTT, E. G. (1990) *Checklist of the birds of New Zealand*. Third edition. Wellington: Ornithological Society of New Zealand.

TURNER, A. AND ROSE, C. (1989) *A handbook to the swallows and martins of the world*. London: Christopher Helm.

TURNER, D. A., PEARSON, D. J. AND ZIMMERMAN, D. A. (1991) Taxonomic notes on some East African birds. Part I—Non-passerines. *Scopus* 14: 84–91.

TURTON, M. AND SPEIGHT, G. (1986) China 1986. 12th May–1st August. Unpublished report.

TYE, A. (1993) Forest and bird conservation in the East Usambara Mountains, north-east Tanzania. *Proc. 8 Pan-Afr. Orn. Congr.* [*Ann. Sci. Zool. Mus. Roy. Afrique Centr.* 286]: 287–292.

TYE, H. (1987) Breeding biology of *Picathartes oreas*. *Gerfaut* 77: 313–332.

TYE, H. (1991) Reversal of breeding season by lowland birds at higher altitudes in western Cameroon. *Ibis* 134: 154–163.

TYLER, S. J. (1994) The Yungas of Argentina: in search of Rufous-throated Dipper *Cinclus schulzi*. *Cotinga* 2: 38–40.

URBAN, E. K. AND BROWN, L. H. (1971) *A checklist of the birds of Ethiopia*. Addis Ababa: Haile Sellassie I University Press.

URBAN, E. K., FRY, C. H. AND KEITH, S. (1986) *The birds of Africa*, 2. London: Academic Press.

VALQUI, T. (1994) The extinction of the Junín Flightless Grebe? *Cotinga* 1: 42–44.

VANDE WEGHE, J. P. (1992) New records for Uganda and Tanzania along the Rwandan and Burundian borders. *Scopus* 16: 59–60.

VANGELUWE, D. AND STASSIN, P. (1991) Hivernage de la Bernache à Cou Roux, *Branta ruficollis*, en Dobroudja septentrionale, Roumanie et revue du statut hivernal de l'espèce. *Gerfaut* 81: 65–99.

VARTY, N. (1991) The status and conservation of Jamaica's threatened and endemic forest avifauna and their habitats following Hurricane Gilbert. *Bird Conserv. Internatn.* 1: 135–151.

VARTY, N., BENCKE, G. A., BERNARDINI, L. DE M., DA CUNHA, A. S., DIAS, E. V., FONTANA, C. S., GUADAGNIN, D. L., KINDEL, A., KINDEL, E., RAYMUNDO, M. M., RICHTER, M., ROSA, A. AND TOSTES, C. S. (1994) The ecology and conservation of the Red-spectacled Parrot *Amazona pretrei* in southern Brazil. Final report to BirdLife International. Unpublished.

VAURIE, C. (1960) Systematic notes on Palearctic birds. No. 39. Caprimulgidae: A new species of *Caprimulgus*. *Amer. Mus. Novit.* 1985.

VAURIE, C. (1968) Taxonomy of the Cracidae (Aves). *Bull. Amer. Mus. Nat. Hist.* 138: 131–260.

VAURIE, C. (1972) *Tibet and its birds*. London: H. F. and G. Witherby.

VEITCH, C. R. (1985) Methods of eradicating feral cats from offshore islands in New Zealand. Pp.125–141 in P. J. Moors, ed. *Conservation of island birds*. Cambridge, U.K.: International Council for Bird Preservation (Techn. Publ. 3).

VEITCH, C. R. AND BELL, B. D. (1990) Eradication of introduced animals from the islands of New Zealand. Pp.137–146 in D. R. Towns, C. H. Daugherty and I. A. E. Atkinson, eds. *Ecological restoration of New Zealand's islands*. Wellington: Department of Conservation (Conservation Sciences Publ. 2).

VERHEUGT, W. J. M. (1987) Conservation status and action program for the Milky Stork *Mycteria cinerea*. *Colonial Waterbirds* 10: 211–220.

VERHEUGT, W. J. M., SKOV, H. AND DANIELSEN, F. (1993) Notes on the birds of the tidal lowlands and floodplains of South Sumatra province, Indonesia. *Kukila* 6: 53–84.

VERHOEYE, J. (in prep.) An annotated checklist of the birds of Flores.

VILELLA, F. J. (in press) Reproductive ecology and behaviour of the Puerto Rican Nightjar *Caprimulgus noctitherus*. *Bird Conserv. Internatn.*

VILELLA, F. J. AND ARNIZAUT, A. B. (1994) Making the best of Mother Nature: managing the Puerto Rican Parrot after Hurricane Hugo. *Endangered Species Techn. Bull.* 19: 10–11.

VINCENT, J. (1933–1935) The birds of northern Portuguese East Africa. *Ibis* (13)3: 611–652; (13)4: 126–160, 305–340, 495–527, 757–799; (13)5: 1–37, 355–397, 485–529, 707–762.

VINCENT, J. (1966–1971) *Red Data Book*, 2: *Aves*. Morges, Switzerland: International Union for Conservation of Nature and Natural Resources.

VINEY, C. (1986) WWF HK visit to north-west Fujian province, People's Republic of China. 28th May–7 June 1986. Unpublished report.

VINOKUROV, A. A. (1990) *Branta ruficollis* in the U.S.S.R. Pp.197–198 in G. V. T. Matthews, ed. *Managing waterfowl populations*. Slimbridge, U.K.: International Waterfowl and Wetlands Research Bureau (IWRB Spec. Publ. 12).

VITTERY, A. (1994) The birds of Pakistan: supplementary observations from the northern Punjab and hills. *Forktail* 9: 143–147.

VO QUY (1975) *Chim Viet Nam*, 1. Hanoi: Nha Xuat Ban Khoa Hoc Va Ky Thuat.

VO QUY (1983) [A catalogue of the birds of Vietnam.] Pp.12–43 in L. N. Medvedev, ed. [*Fauna and ecology of the animals of Vietnam.*] Moscow: Nauka.

VUILLEUMIER, F., LECROY, M. AND MAYR, E. (1992) New species of birds described from 1981 to 1990. *Bull. Brit. Orn. Club* 112A (Centenary Supplement): 267–310.

WALICZKY, Z. AND BÁLDI, A. (1991) Report on the Hungarian scientific expedition in North Korea. Hungarian Ornithological Society, Budapest. Unpublished.

WALTER, H. S. (1993) Socorro Dove in Mexico. *Re-introduction News* 7: 8.

WALTERS, M. (1985) On the status of *Psittacula intermedia* (Rothschild). *J. Bombay Nat. Hist. Soc.* 82: 197–199.

WANG, H. (1993) Spoonbills in Yancheng, Jiangsu Province, China. *Spec. Group on Storks, Ibises and Spoonbills Newsl.* 6: 9.

WANG, J., WU, C., HUANG, G., YANG, X., CAI, Z., CAI, M. AND XIAO, Q. (1991a) [*Field guide: birds of Taiwan.*] Taipei, Taiwan: Yashe Books Limited. (In Chinese.)

WANG, T., TANG, S. AND MA, J. (1991b) *Survey of shorebirds and coastal wetlands in Yellow River delta, Shangong Province, autumn 1991*. Shanghai: East China Waterbird Ecology Study Group.

WATKINS, B. P. AND FURNESS, R. W. (1986) Population status, breeding and conservation of the Gough Moorhen. *Ostrich* 57: 32–36.

WATLING, D. (1982) *The birds of Fiji, Tonga and Samoa*. Wellington, New Zealand: Millwood Press.

WATLING, D. (1986) Rediscovery of a petrel and new faunal records on Gau Island. *Oryx* 20: 31–34.

WATLING, D. (1988) Notes on the status and ecology of the Ogea Flycatcher *Mayrornis versicolor*. *Bull. Brit. Orn. Club* 108: 103–112.

WATLING, D. (in press) Notes on the status of the Scarlet-breasted Lorikeet *Vini kuhlii* in the Northern Line Islands, Republic of Kiribati. *Bird Conserv. Internatn.*

WATLING, D. AND CHAPE, S., EDS. (1992) *Environment Fiji: the National State of the Environment Report*. Gland, Switzerland: International Union for Conservation of Nature and Natural Resources.

WATLING, D. AND GILLISON, A. N. (1993) Endangered species in low elevation cloud forest on Gau Island, Fiji. Pp.217–223 in L. S. Hamilton, J. O. Juvik and F. N. Scatena, eds. *Tropical montane cloud forests: proceedings of an international symposium at San Juan, Puerto Rico 31 May-5 June 1993*. Honolulu: East-West Center.

WATLING, D. AND LEWANAVANUA, R. F. (1985) A note to record the continuing survival of the Fiji (MacGillivray's) Petrel *Pseudobulweria macgillivrayi*. *Ibis* 127: 230–233.

WATSON, J. (1981) Population ecology, food and conservation of the Seychelles Kestrel (*Falco araea*) on Mahé. Aberdeen: University of Aberdeen (Ph.D. dissertation).

WATSON, J. (1989) Successful translocation of the endemic Seychelles Kestrel *Falco araea* to Praslin. Pp.363–367 in B.-U. Meyburg and R. D. Chancellor, eds. *Raptors in the modern world*. Berlin: World Working Group on Birds of Prey.

WATSON, J. (1991) The Seychelles Paradise Flycatcher *Terpsiphone corvina* on La Digue: population size, habitat requirements and management options. *Bird Conserv. Internatn.* 1: 107–122.

WATSON, J., WARMAN, C., TODD, D. AND LABOUDALLON, V. (1992) The Seychelles magpie robin *Copsychus sechellarum*: ecology and conservation of an endangered species. *Biol. Conserv.* 61: 93–106.

WATSON, L. AND PERKIN, A. (undated) Biological survey results and conservation proposals from the foothill forests, East Usambara Mountains, Tanzania. Unpublished.

WATSON, R. T., BERKELMAN, J., LEWIS, R. AND RAZAFINDRA-MANANA, S. (1993) Conservation studies on the Madagascar Fish Eagle *Haliaeetus vociferoides*. *Proc. 8 Pan-Afr. Orn. Congr.* [*Ann. Sci. Zool. Mus. Roy. Afrique Centr.* 286]: 192–196.

WAUGH, D. R. (1994) Red-tailed Amazon *Amazona brasiliensis* field visit 14–20 May 1994. Report to the World Parrot Trust. Unpublished.

WAUGH, D. AND DIAZ DE WAUGH, M. (1993) The Northern Helmeted Curassow in Venezuela: simulation of captive populations as a conservation aid. *World Pheasant Assoc. J.* 17–18: 3–24.

WEAVER, D. (1990) Survey of Sukla Phanta for Bengal Floricans. *Bull. Oriental Bird Club* 12: 4–7.

WEBB, H. P. (1992) Field observations of the birds of Santa Isabel, Solomon Islands. *Emu* 92: 52–57.

WEGE, D. C., HOWELL, S. N. G. AND SADA, A. M. (1993) The distribution and status of Worthen's Sparrow *Spizella wortheni*: a review. *Bird Conserv. Internatn.* 3: 211–220.

WEGE, D. C. AND LONG, A. J. (in prep.) *Priority areas for threatened birds in the Neotropics*. Cambridge, U.K.: BirdLife International (BirdLife Conservation Series no. 5).

WEIMERSKIRCH, H. AND JOUVENTIN, P. (1987) Population dynamics of the Wandering Albatross, *Diomedea exulans*, of the Crozet Islands: causes and consequences of the population decline. *Oikos* 49: 315–322.

WEINRICH, J. (1994) Status of the Kirtland's Warbler, 1994. Michigan Department of Natural Resources (Wildlife Division report).

WELCH, G. AND WELCH, H. (1985) Observations on the endemic Djibouti Francolin (*Francolinus ochropectus*) with emphasis on potential threats to the population. *World Pheasant Assoc. J.* 10: 65–71.

WELCH, G. AND WELCH, H. (1988) Habitats and birds in Djibouti. *Walia* 11: 11–18.

WELCH, G. R., WELCH, H. J., COGHLAN, S. M. AND DENTON, M. L. (1986) Djibouti II: autumn '85. Unpublished.

WELLS, D. R. (1985) The forest avifauna of western Malesia and its conservation. Pp.213–232 in A. W. Diamond and T. E. Lovejoy, eds. *Conservation of tropical forest birds*. Cambridge, U.K.: International Council for Bird Preservation (Techn. Publ. 4).

WELLS, D. R. (1992) Night migration at Fraser's Hill, peninsular Malaysia. *Bull. Oriental Bird Club* 16: 21–25.

WEN, Z. Z. AND SUN, R. Y. (1993) The breeding, growth and development of homeothermy in Cattle Egret *Bubulcus ibis*. *Acta Zool. Sin.* 39: 263–271.

WHEELER, W. R. (1975) Report on rare and endangered species of birds from the Australian mainland. *Bull. Internatn. Counc. Bird Preserv.* 12: 159–264.

WHITE, C. M. N. AND BRUCE, M. D. (1986) *The birds of Wallacea (Sulawesi, the Moluccas and Lesser Sunda Islands, Indonesia): an annotated check-list*. London: British Ornithologists' Union (Check-list 7).

WHITNEY, B. M. AND PACHECO, J. F. (1994) Behavior and vocalizations of *Gyalophylax* and *Megaxenops* (Furnariidae), two little-known genera endemic to northeastern Brazil. *Condor* 96: 559–565.

WHITNEY, B. M. AND PACHECO, J. F. (in press) Distribution and conservation status of four *Myrmotherula* antwrens *Formicariidae* in the Atlantic Forest of Brazil. *Bird Conserv. Internatn.*

WHITTEN, A. J., BISHOP, K. D., NASH, S. V. AND CLAYTON, L. (1987a) One or more extinctions from Sulawesi, Indonesia? *Conserv. Biol.* 1: 42–48.

WHITTEN, A. J., MUSTAFA, M. AND HENDERSON, G. (1987b) *Ecology of Sulawesi*. Yogyakarta: Gadjah Mada University Press.

WHITTINGHAM, M. J. (1994) Observations at a nest of the Pacific Royal Flycatcher *Onychorhynchus coronatus occidentalis*. *Bull. Brit. Orn. Club* 114: 131–132.

WILD BIRD SOCIETY OF JAPAN (1978) *Breeding bird survey in Japan*. Tokyo: Wild Bird Society of Japan.

WILLIAMS, A. J. (1984) The status and conservation of seabirds on some islands in the African sector of the Southern Ocean. Pp.627–635 in J. P. Croxall, P. G. H. Evans and R. W. Schreiber, eds. *Status and conservation of the world's seabirds*. Cambridge, U.K.: International Council for Bird Preservation (Techn. Publ. 2).

WILLIAMS, G. R. AND GIVEN, D. R. (1981) *The Red Data Book of New Zealand*. Wellington: Nature Conservation Council.

WILLIAMS, M. (1994) Progress in the conservation of New Zealand's threatened waterfowl. *IWRB Threatened Waterfowl Res. Group Newsl.* 5: 3–6.

WILLIAMS, M. D., CAREY, G. J., DUFF, D. G. AND XU, W. (1992) Autumn bird migration at Beidaihe, China, 1986–1990. *Forktail* 7: 3–55.

WILLIAMS, R. S. R. (in prep.) The rediscovery and doubtful validity of the Blue-wattled Bulbul *Pycnonotus nieuwenhuisii*.

WILLIS, E. O. AND ONIKI, Y. (1992) A new *Phylloscartes* (Tyrannidae) from southeastern Brazil. *Bull. Brit. Orn. Club* 112: 158–165.

WILMÉ, L. (1993) A recent record of the Madagascar Pochard *Aythya innotata* on Lake Alaotra, Madagascar. *Bull. Brit. Orn. Club* 113: 188–189.

WILMÉ, L. (1994) Status, distribution and conservation of two Madagascar bird species endemic to Lake Alaotra: Delacour's grebe *Tachybaptus rufolavatus* and Madagascar pochard *Aythya innotata*. *Biol. Conserv.* 69: 15–21.

WILMÉ, L. AND LANGRAND, O. (1990) Rediscovery of Slender-billed Flufftail *Sarothrura watersi* (Bartlett, 1879), and notes on the genus *Sarothrura* in Madagascar. *Biol. Conserv.* 51: 211–223.

WILSON, J. D. (1987) A report on the status and conservation of the montane forest avifauna of Mount Oku, Cameroon, in 1985. International Council for Bird Preservation. Unpublished.

WILSON, J. R. AND CATSIS, M. C. (1990) A preliminary survey of the forests of the 'Itombwe' mountains and the Kahuzi-Biega National Park extension, east Zaire, July–September 1989. [London]: World Wide Fund for Nature, Institut Zaïrois pour la Conservation de la Nature, and the Fauna and Flora Preservation Society. Unpublished.

WILSON, K.-J. (1993) Observations of the Kurämoó (*Vini peruviana*) on Aitutaki Island, Cook Islands. *Notornis* 40: 71–75.

WIRTH, R., COLLAR, N. J., CROSBY, M. J. AND STATTERSFIELD, A. J. (in press) The conservation of globally threatened parrots. [*Proc. 2nd Internatn. Parrot Congress, Tenerife, Spain, September 1994.*]

WITTEMAN, G. J., BECK, R. E., PIMM, S. L. AND DERRICKSON, S. R. (1990) The decline and restoration of the Guam Rail, *Rallus owstoni*. *Endangered Species Update* 8: 36–39.

WONG, F. K. (1993) Status and distribution of Saunders's Gull *Larus saundersi*. Unpublished manuscript.

WONG, F. K. O. AND LIANG, Y. (1992) Field survey of selected areas along the coast of Bohai Sea, People's Republic of China. Gland, Switzerland: World Wide Fund for Nature (final report, WWF Project: CN0032 [4527]).

WOOD, P. (1993) The Gola Rain Forest Conservation Programme in Sierra Leone. *Proc. 8 Pan-Afr. Orn. Congr.* [*Ann. Sci. Zool. Mus. Roy. Afrique Centr.* 286]: 217–222.

WOODS, R. W. (1993) Cobb's Wren *Troglodytes (aedon) cobbi* of the Falkland Islands. *Bull. Brit. Orn. Club* 113: 195–207.

WU, Z., LIN, Q., YANG, J., LIU, J. AND WU, L. (1986) *The avifauna of Guizhou*. Guizhou, China: Guizhou People's Publishing House.

WU, Z., WANG, Y., LI, Z., JIANG, Y. AND LI, R. (1993) Distribution and abundance of the Black-necked Crane *Grus nigricollis* in China. Unpublished.

XU, W., WU, Z. AND LI, Z. (1990) Current status of the Reeves or White-crowned Long-tailed Pheasant in China. Pp.31–32 in D. A. Hill, P. J. Garson and D. Jenkins, eds. *Pheasants in Asia 1989*. Reading, U.K.: World Pheasant Association.

YAMASHINA, Y. AND MANO, T. (1981) A new species of rail from Okinawa Island. *J. Yamashina Inst. Orn.* 13: 1–6.

YAMASHITA, C. AND VALLE, M. DE P. (1993) On the linkage between *Anodorhynchus* macaws and palm nuts, and the extinction of the Glaucous Macaw. *Bull. Brit. Orn. Club* 113: 53–60.

YANAGISAWA, N., FUJIMAKI, Y. AND HIGUCHI, H. (1993) Japanese data on waterbird population sizes, summarised for IWRB. Unpublished report.

YATIM, S. H. (1993) The status and distribution of pheasants in Peninsular Malaysia. Pp.28–39 in D. Jenkins, ed. *Pheasants in Asia 1992*. Reading, U.K.: World Pheasant Association.

YORKSTON, H. D. AND GREEN, P. (1992) A survey of Abbott's Booby on Christmas Island. Report to Australian Nature Conservation Agency, Canberra.

YOUNG, G. (1987) Notes on the nesting behaviour of the Echo Parakeet *Psittacula eques echo*. *Dodo* 24: 102–111.

YOUNG, H. G. AND SMITH, J. G. (1989) The search for the Madagascar Pochard *Aythya innotata*: survey of Lac Alaotra, Madagascar, October–November 1989. *Dodo* 26: 17–33.

YOUNG, H. G., SAFFORD, R. J., GREEN, A., RAVONJIARISOA, P. AND RABARISOA, R. G. M. (1993) Survey and capture of the Madagascar Teal *Anas bernieri* at Lac Bemamba, Madagascar, July–August 1992, July 1993. *Dodo* 29: 77–94.

YOUNG, L., ZHENG, G. AND ZHANG, Z. (1991) Winter movements and habitat use by Cabot's Tragopan *Tragopan caboti* in southeastern China. *Ibis* 133: 121–126.

ZACHARIAS, V. J. AND GASTON, A. J. (1993) The birds of Wynaad, southern India. *Forktail* 8: 11–24.

ZAIMECHE, S. E. (1994) The consequences of rapid deforestation: a North African example. *Ambio* 23: 136–140.

ZHANG, Z. (1992) Protecting the gem of the Orient—Oriental Crested Ibis. *Spec. Group on Storks, Ibises and Spoonbills Newsl.* 5: 2–4.

ZHAO, Z. (1993) Is the Crested Shelduck extinct? *IWRB Threatened Waterfowl Res. Group Newsl.* 3: 5.

ZHAO, Z., HAN, X., WU, J., LIU, P. AND ZHANG, S. (1990) Preliminary report on investigation on the Crested Shelduck in China (Forestry Research Institute of Jilin Province). Unpublished.

ZHENG, B. (1988) [Discussion on survey of the birds from South Ailau mountains, Yunnan.] *Zool. Res.* 9: 255–261. (In Chinese.)

ZHENG, G. M. AND ZHANG, Z. W. (1993) The distribution and status of pheasants in China. Pp.15–19 in D. Jenkins, ed. *Pheasants in Asia 1992*. Reading, U.K.: World Pheasant Association.

ZHU, H., SHEN, G., WANG, Y., YU, Y. AND ZHENG, L. (1987) [Prediction of the impact of the Three Gorges Project on the ecological function and environment of the Poyang Lake.] Pp.319–332 in [*Essays on the studies of the effects and strategies of the three gorges project on ecology and environment.*] Beijing: Academia Sinica, Science Press. (In Chinese.)

ZINO, F. AND BISCOITO, M. (1994) Breeding seabirds in the Madeira archipelago. Pp.172–185 in D. N. Nettleship, J. Burger and M. Gochfeld, eds. *Seabirds on islands: threats, case studies, and action plans*. Cambridge, U.K.: BirdLife International (BirdLife Conservation Series no. 1).

ZINO, F. AND ZINO, P. A. (1986a) An account of the habitat, feeding habitats, density, breeding and need of protection of the Long-toed Wood Pigeon, *Columba trocaz*. *Bocagiana* 97.

ZINO, P. A. AND ZINO, F. (1986b) Contribution to the study of the petrels of the genus *Pterodroma* in the archipelago of Madeira. *Bol. Mus. Mun. Funchal* 38: 141–165.

INDEX OF SPECIES

The Appendices are not covered by this index.

DATE DUE

ILC			
MAY 0 7 2006			
GAYLORD 234			PRINTED IN U. S. A.